This resource
made possible
through the
generous
donation of...
UCC
Robert Robinson

THE MACMILLAN DICTIONARY OF THE FIRST WORLD WAR

THE MACMILLAN DICTIONARY OF THE FIRST WORLD WAR

BY

STEPHEN POPE
AND
ELIZABETH-ANNE WHEAL

CONSULTANT EDITOR:
PROFESSOR KEITH ROBBINS

WITH ORIGINAL MAPS BY:
BRENDAN EDDISON

First published 1995 by Macmillan Reference Books
a division of Macmillan Publishers Limited
London and Basingstoke

Associated companies throughout the world

ISBN 0-333-61822X

9 8 7 6 5 4 3 2 1

A CIP catalogue record for this book is available from the British Library

Typeset by Spottiswoode Ballantyne, Colchester, Essex.
Printed and bound in Great Britain by
Mackays of Chatham Plc, Chatham, Kent.

Contents

Acknowledgements

The authors would like to thank Owen Appleton for the best possible moral support and suppers, Ian Crofton for his warm and expert understanding of reference material, Brendan Eddison and Jan Haley for their well-known and happy flexibility, Ken Pope for vital contributions at vital times, Patrick Pentand for lightning research, and unfailingly helpful librarians too numerous to name in Norfolk, London, New York and Oxford. Above all we owe a great debt of gratitude to Professor Keith Robbins for his invaluable scholarship and enlightened pragmatism. All these people have been indispensable to the work that follows.

Notes on Usage

The Dictionary has been designed and written to enable ease of access and interconnection. Its widest-ranging essays cover fronts, theatres or broad generic terms, and major home fronts are treated as theatres of war intrinsic to the broad picture.

Entries for EASTERN FRONT, AERIAL WARFARE, FRANCE or TRENCH WARFARE (for instance) present a general picture and refer readers to important areas within the subject. A second level covers major offensives, political movements, tactics, forces and weapons systems, including among many the SERBIAN ARMY, BREAKTHROUGH TACTICS, SOVIETS, the EAST AFRICAN CAMPAIGN, DESTROYERS and ALCOHOL. Detail entries covering the individual actions, leaders, weapons and events of the period (SOPWITH CAMEL, ENVER PASHA, FOUR-MINUTE MEN, TRENCH FOOT) are signalled wherever they are relevant, and refer readers back up the chain to the big picture.

Apart from this simple pyramid, the dictionary and cross-reference format offers some sense of the three-dimensional nature of global affairs, making lateral connections with indirect or simultaneous influences elsewhere and allowing the reader to investigate their full spectrum at leisure.

Following the paths marked by cross-referencing, in any order, should eventually build a comprehensive and rounded picture of the First World War, but most entries are also intended to stand on their own as reference material. The exceptions are one-line or simple-definition entries, that exist to cover potential confusions of nomenclature and to provide the maximum number of access points for lay readers.

Technical data attached to entries describing aircraft, ships and TANKS is intended as a rough guide to performance. That the information is less complete or precise than similar material contained in the authors' *Dictionary of the Second World War* reflects contemporary weakness of measurement methods rather than any editorial decision.

The maps have been designed primarily to help readers find their way around the text, rather than as alternative illustrations of the action, with the emphasis on orientation above military movements. Front maps in particular are a quick reference guide to locations rather than armies. The chronology table is similarly planned to provide a global snapshot as well as a ready war diary.

Abbreviations

AA	anti-aircraft (gun)
a/c	aircraft
c	circa
C-in-C	commander in chief
ft	foot, feet
in	inch(es)
k	knots
km	kilometres
kph	kilometres per hour
lb/lbs	pound(s)
m	metres
mg	machine gun
mm	millimetres
mph	miles per hour
pdr	pounder
TT	torpedo tube

Introduction

Apart from a few well-used sepia images, varying from culture to culture but sharing a simple recognition of pointless carnage, the First World War is now largely forgotten by non-specialists, consigned to the vague area that is popular history before Hitler. Yet the outbreak of the Great War in 1914 was, if any single event can be so described, the moment at which the 20th century was born. In social, political, economic and military terms it marked the end of the confident 'Age of Progress' dominated by great European empires, and its passage introduced a new world order, familiar to the modern mind but unforeseen in almost every respect by the men who had unleashed it.

The circumstances that provoked and triggered the 'war to end wars' have excited academic debate ever since, mostly focused on the machinations of statesmen, generals and diplomats. Argument initially centred on apportioning blame among the leaders of the GREAT POWERS for seeking or starting the War, a debate that has been effectively resolved since the release of records in the 1960s.

If contribution to the breakdown of international relations constitutes blame, then all the main protagonists shared responsibility for the outbreak of war in August 1914. At a time when long-term partition of the planet's resources among the ruling elites of a few rich baron states seemed probable, and ever-increasing human prosperity appeared certain, almost everybody wanted a bigger share of the spoils.

A spirit of competitive expansionism characterized prewar (or 'old world') diplomacy. At every level, a race to expand and strengthen pending some decisive formulation of a new, stable world order was manifestly in progress throughout the early 20th century. European empires competed for economic, regional and colonial prizes; smaller independent states fought to expand at the expense of their neighbours or resisted imperial ambitions; ethnic self-consciousness was mushrooming within the great multiracial empires of eastern Europe.

The youngest and most aggressive of the European empires, GERMANY, was conventionally accused of 'militarism' by contemporaries, and has since been recognized as the state most committed in advance to a European war, but no major European power would have rejected war – given favourable circumstances – in 1914. The concept of crimes against humanity was a postwar invention, and bellicose intent was not perceived as intrinsically criminal by the prewar governing classes. If some states were more martial in character than others, this could be understood as a product of experience or paranoia. Germany had been forged by the conquests of the Prussian 'nation in arms' less than half a century earlier. By its crushing military defeat of FRANCE in 1870–71, the infant German Empire had cemented both its faith in martial culture and its fear of gang reprisals from neighbouring powers.

The German seizure of the French provinces of Alsace and Lorraine after 1871 was central to a build-up of European tensions that gathered fuel for more than forty years before exploding. Recovery of the provinces, and security against a repeat conquest, became the driving, overt obsession of French foreign policy. Prussian methods, broadly perceived as national armament backed by ferocious tactical aggression, were introduced to the FRENCH ARMY, and the nation as a whole waited ostentatiously for revenge.

The French alliance with RUSSIA from 1892 raised the stakes of the vendetta along the Rhine. The unlikely partnership of republic and autocracy promised security for Paris and St Petersburg, but raised the spectre of 'encirclement' in Berlin. Under the volatile, ambitious stewardship of Kaiser WILHELM II from 1888, Germany sought growth as an antidote to fear, in the firm belief that France and Russia were waiting for the moment to attack, and that they would eventually be powerful enough to do so.

In the early 20th century, with destruction the probable alternative to expansion, Germany engaged in a series of international skirmishes over its overseas colonial ambitions, conducted under the veiled threat of a wider war. In the most heated of these, German attempts to establish a colonial foothold in Morocco fell foul of international opposition and French obduracy in 1910. Prevented from territorial acquisition further east by Italian ambitions in Libya, by French designs on the eastern Mediterranean and by Anglo-Russian claims on the Ottoman Empire and PERSIA, German plans for expansion inevitably focused on central and eastern Europe, where hopes of economic and political hegemony seemed to depend on war sooner rather than later.

Germany's basic diplomatic counterweight to encirclement was alliance with AUSTRIA-HUNGARY. Dominated by German-speaking Austrians, and ruled from Vienna by the Habsburg Emperor FRANZ JOSEF I, Austria-Hungary was an ally firm in principle but relatively feeble in military or economic capacity.

The Habsburg Empire was also an important agent of European instability in its own right. Imperial foreign policy, driven by a combination of insecurity and ambition, juggled a dangerous array of grudges and grievances on its frontiers. In the southwest of the Empire, Habsburg withdrawal from ITALY in the 19th century left only the Trentino (South Tyrol) and Trieste regions in imperial hands, and these regions had become the Alsace-Lorraine of Italian national ambition. Hungarian possession of Transylvania also guaranteed the hostility of neighbouring ROMANIA, but Austria-Hungary's deepest trouble spots lay to the south, in the perpetually vexatious Balkans.

The multi-ethnic Balkan peninsula housed an unstable tangle of local antagonisms and Great Power politics in the early 20th century, and was generally regarded as Europe's most dangerous powder keg. At regional level the competing ambitions of GREECE, BULGARIA and SERBIA contested turbulent and fluctuating frontier zones with the Ottoman and Austro-Hungarian Empires. In a wider context, Austria-Hungary and Italy both sought control over ALBANIA; Russian foreign policy, forced westward after defeat in a war with JAPAN (1904–05), was committed to supporting south Slav independence as a buffer between Vienna and the Dardanelles Straits, which Russia hoped eventually to control; and France was also developing political and economic ambitions in the Aegean.

International tension around the Balkans had been heightened by a series of violent crises before 1914, triggered by the patent weakness of Ottoman TURKEY. With Russia still reeling from the Japanese war and the abortive 1905 revolution that followed it, Austria-Hungary was able to seize the Slav province of Bosnia-Herzegovina from Turkey in 1908, thereby extending the imperial frontier with Serbia, the increasingly belligerent hotbed of pan-Slav expansionism.

War between Turkey and Italy in 1911–12, for control of Ottoman Libya, gravely weakened both participants and gave the independent Balkan states an opportunity for expansion. An alliance of Greece, Serbia, Bulgaria and MONTENEGRO won a series of comprehensive military victories over Turkish forces in the First Balkan War of 1912–13, occupying Macedonia and Thrace to push the Ottoman frontier back to just east of Constantinople. Disappointed by the peace settlement, Bulgaria attacked Greek and Serbian forces in summer 1913, but its rapid defeat in this Second Balkan War was sealed by invasion from Romania. The subsequent peace cost Bulgaria the northeastern border region of the Dobrudja – which went to Romania – and left Serbia almost double its prewar size.

Nobody expected the region to remain peaceful for long, especially since Austria-Hungary's relatively quiet role in the Balkan Wars masked worsening relations with Serbia. Pan-Slav pressure in the Austro-Hungarian provinces of Bosnia-Herzegovina, Slovenia and Croatia seemed certain eventually to provoke hostile action from Vienna, and Russia was likely to give active support to Serbia, its last remaining ally in its only important sphere of expansion.

Entwined through central Europe and the Balkans, the knot of international rivalries stretched south to involve Italy and Turkey. Despite ingrained mutual hostility between Rome and Vienna, Italy had joined Austria-Hungary and Germany in a TRIPLE ALLIANCE from 1882. Though economically and politically fragile, Italy regarded itself as a Great Power, and saw protection by Germany as its guarantee of a share in generalized imperial expansion. Turkey had no formal allies in Europe before 1914, but was moving increasingly close to Germany in reaction to long-term territorial and economic predation by Britain, Russia and France. The Libyan and Balkan Wars left both Italy and Turkey in economic and military disarray in 1914, but each had reason to join the winning side in the event of war between stronger powers – Italy to ensure expansion, Turkey to forestall dismemberment.

The international atmosphere of instability and change before 1914 was reinforced by internal tensions within the Great Powers. A mounting tide of ethnic self-awareness, broadly comparable with that evident throughout central and eastern Europe since the late 1980s, had seen strong nationalist movements develop among Czech, Polish, Armenian, Irish and Arab peoples, to name but a few of the most developed in 1914. The Austro-Hungarian and Ottoman Empires in particular conducted their foreign policies against a backdrop of potential disintegration.

Leaders of the German and Russian Empires governed under the threat of political breakdown. Though fear of revolution had little impact on foreign policy at the blinkered Russian court, the excessively watchful elite classes of German society increasingly saw a successful war as the only way to maintain control over liberal and socialist challenges. The relatively democratic constitutions of France, Italy and GREAT BRITAIN allowed room for political expression to flourish without the need for revolution, but each experienced rising levels of social tension before 1914, particularly among the industrial working classes.

If it was clear to contemporaries that war would be conducted by European rivals fuelled by internal combustion, it was equally obvious that the conflict would have a global dimension. Colonial territories all over the world, and the trade routes they supplied, could expect to be battlefields in the event of European war. Meanwhile new empires were emerging, ready to benefit from any crisis of European predominance. The Japanese held a considerable lead over a pack of European predators gathered along the coasts of mainland CHINA. Capitalists in the UNITED STATES wanted secure channels for economic control of Latin America, and ultimately the Pacific Rim, and they wanted armed forces to guarantee them.

The big-business lobby in the traditionally ISOLATIONIST USA did not get its armies before 1914, but most other players in the 'great game' responded to intensifying geopolitical stress by arming for war in the early 20th century. Conscription of national armies to maximize available trained reserves became the norm in Europe. Nations great and small strove to possess a bigger, better-equipped army and/or navy than their local, regional or global rivals. The main protagonists in the central European power struggle – France, Germany, Austria-Hungary and Russia – had each developed detailed plans for offensive land war long before 1914 (see SCHLIEFFEN PLAN; PLAN 17; PLAN 19).

Anticipating war by rearmament was a costly business, likely to exacerbate internal economic and social tensions. The cost was multiplied by the perceived need for a large navy, upon which military and economic security seemed to depend. A battlefleet – generally accepted as the ultimate weapon of the period – was hugely expensive to build and maintain, especially after the British *DREADNOUGHT* revolutionized BATTLESHIP specifications in 1906. Nevertheless virtually every coastal state was engaged in acquiring the biggest navy it could possibly afford in the decade before 1914, with poorer countries relying on direct public subscription to finance purchase of vast floating fortresses.

Naval arms races broke out between Turkey and Greece in the Aegean, between Turkey and Russia in the BLACK SEA, among Austria-Hungary, Italy and France in the MEDITERRANEAN, even between BRAZIL and its South American neighbours, but the catalyst to the international obsession with NAVAL WARFARE was the shipbuilding contest between Germany and GREAT BRITAIN begun by Prussian navy minister TIRPITZ in 1898.

Frequently cited as a major 'cause' of the First World War, Anglo-German naval rivalry was an important element in the ultimate collapse of old world diplomacy. An attempt to break Britain's control over access to BALTIC sea lanes, the GERMAN NAVY's rapid expansion was a direct challenge to the aloof supremacy of Britain, the world's only truly global power and a gigantic wild card in everybody else's diplomatic calculations.

Great Britain stood apart from the scramble for European supremacy before 1898. Britain's economic power was on the wane, its manufacturing industries sluggish and outdated, but Britannia still ruled the waves, governing an empire that touched every continent and exercising effective control over most of the world's trade. Alone among the European powers, Britain had nothing to gain from violent upheaval, standing for gradual expansion of its own vast interests and against any perceived threat to imperial integrity.

Although the small BRITISH ARMY fought regular colonial campaigns, it was in no sense a major European land power, and the implement of British supremacy was the enormous ROYAL NAVY, far more powerful than any rival and theoretically capable of enforcing London's will anywhere in the world. British naval power was in comfortable decline by 1898, hardly threatened but victim to shrinking budgets and an excess of tradition. The ambitious warship construction programme announced by Germany, already recognized as a major economic rival, highlighted the stretched (and largely obsolete) condition of the British Empire's naval resources, and threatened security close to home for the first time in living memory. Followed as it was by further German expansion in 1900 and a graphic demonstration of the British Army's limitations during the Boer War in South Africa, the shock provoked military reform, prompted a massive shipbuilding response, and dragged Britain, almost unwittingly, into the maelstrom of European alliances and ambitions.

Anxious to strengthen its home defences, Britain set about mending its imperial fences. The 'Entente Cordiale' established with France in 1904 settled outstanding colonial arguments, laying the foundation for an informal friendship that fell short of alliance but that enabled the British to reduce their naval strength in the Mediterranean and to concentrate it in home waters, while French Channel forces were redeployed in the Mediterranean. A similar rationalization settled disputes between Britain and Russia over Persia in 1907, rounding off a European power bloc, the Triple Entente, that existed only in theory but nevertheless exerted a powerful influence on diplomatic thinking.

Would Britain protect the northern French coast from the German Navy if war came? It was a question the British studiously refused to ask themselves before 1914. No British prime minister, least of all the chronically circumspect ASQUITH, would publicly commit his government to a general European war in defence of France, the 'old enemy', and Russian autocracy was hardly more popular in Britain than German militarism. Britain wanted peace, or at least maintenance of the continental balance of power, but was not prepared to pay a diplomatic price to achieve it, a dangerously vague policy perfectly suited to the enigmatic technique of foreign minister GREY.

German planners asked themselves the same question, and kept coming up with different answers, but were reasonably confident that a swift military victory in any future war (as predicated in the Schlieffen Plan for the invasion of France and Belgium) would render British naval power irrelevant. The question dominated French military and political thinking right up to and during the JULY CRISIS in 1914, when the VIVIANI government went to extraordinary lengths to convince British opinion of French non-aggression in the hope of receiving guarantees of support.

The dominoes of old world diplomacy came tumbling down when Austria-Hungary lost patience with Serbia after the assassination of Archduke FRANZ FERDINAND in the Bosnian city of Sarajevo on 28 June 1914. As Vienna planned punitive action to end Serbian expansion once and for all, and Russia prepared to support Serbia, the German regime made a conscious decision for war by guaranteeing support for any Austrian action, and preparing a preemptive invasion of France through Belgium on the assumption that the Franco-Russian alliance would compel war on two fronts.

Once the vast conscript armies were being mobilized, the doubts and second thoughts of kings, premiers or generals were no match for the imperatives of mass logistics and RAILWAY timetables. Europe's four great continental empires put their attack plans into operation and trusted in destiny. Meanwhile Britain wavered indecisively until the German invasion of neutral BELGIUM on 4 August 1914 gave an emotional lustre to the pragmatic decision that France must not fall to Germany. By that time every other major European power had already chosen war or neutrality.

Statesmen and generals were not alone in helping to create the Great War (named before it began) by anticipating it. The coming war was written about, painted, sculpted and debated, and cultured European opinion in general rather approved of it.

A traditionally 'noble' activity, war successfully undertaken was conventionally recognized as purgative and refreshing in national terms, an outlet for popular unrest and a stimulus to social cohesion. On an individual level it was often held to be character building, and for the pragmatic magnates of capitalist heavy industry it offered the prospect of huge profits and rapid, government-sponsored expansion.

Conservative and bourgeois elements in European society – strongly represented in the arts and journalism – extolled the disciplines of war in a nationalist framework. The German 'patriotic leagues', great extraparliamentary combines dedicated to armed expansion of one form or another, provided the most obvious examples of social militarism at work, but this was also the age of the Boy Scout movement ('Be Prepared'), of organized international sport, and of Futurist artists convinced that human progress was possible only in the 'crucible of war'.

High-profile martial optimism and enthusiasm among the European ruling classes nevertheless masked a broad swell of opposition or indifference to the ethics of aggressive nationalism. Minority populations within the Ottoman, Russian, Austro-Hungarian and British Empires, and millions of WOMEN in Britain, the USA, Germany and elsewhere, had more important issues of enfranchisement and social equality to consider. Isolated literary or religious voices were raised against the encouragement of catastrophe and, above all, international socialism spoke for peace.

The organization of European labour was the great political achievement of the later 19th century. There were millions of socialists in every industrialized state in Europe by 1914, and they constituted an important political force regardless of the extent to which they were granted representation at central government level. The concept of internationalism, fundamental to socialist doctrine, specifically rejected war between capitalist states as a conspiracy that pitched oppressed workers against each other.

Socialism's supranational forum, the SECOND INTERNATIONAL, denounced war in a special session at Basle in 1912, instructing workers in countries with conscription to refuse mobilization. Dominated by the powerful French and German socialist parties, the International's unanimous voice carried enormous political weight, and European governments contemplated war in genuine fear of PACIFIST rebellion.

In fuelling that fear, international socialism if anything encouraged European regimes to the drastic resort of war, especially in Germany, but the real tragedy of the Second International lay not in its counterproductive effects on establishment attitudes but in the illusion of its solidarity.

Pacifist rhetoric at conferences barely concealed a deep rift at the heart of the organization between 'gradualists' and truly international revolutionaries. The gradualist majority, dominated by German parliamentarians, sought peaceful transition in a national context, and often sounded very much like liberal patriots. When the crunch came in 1914, they came out unreservedly for the national cause over the international brotherhood of labour. To the amazement of establishment authorities, their constituents followed suit, flocking to war in an unprecedented display of mass patriotic fervour. Symbolized by the assassination of Europe's greatest pacifist orator, the Frenchman Jaurès, the July Crisis signalled the death of the Second International.

Spontaneous enthusiasm, patriotism and xenophobia greeted the outbreak of war in Berlin, Paris, Vienna, London and St Petersburg (soon to be russified as Petrograd). Contemporary accounts speak of a sense of release from the tension of armed preparedness and diplomatic brinkmanship, of joyous common purpose in sweeping clean a corrupted world order. Conscript armies, even the polyglot AUSTRO-HUNGARIAN ARMY, mobilized with willing efficiency, and the British volunteered for service in droves.

Although shafts of Judgement Day gloom infiltrated high places as the lamps went out all over Europe, popular faith in the invincibility of military leaders like KITCHENER and JOFFRE reflected almost unanimous optimism. It was widely recognized that new weapons technology and million-strong national armies could make a war unlike any other, and that its results might be unpredictable, but few doubted that victory would go to their particular just cause, or that the Great War would be brief.

The logic behind the latter orthodoxy was superficially impeccable. The Age of Progress was run on accumulated European capital, which effectively controlled the world economy of 1914, and war on the grand scale would exercise an enormous drain on that wealth. Even if the swift victories planned by all sides failed to materialize, national economies would begin to atrophy after a few months, bringing the war to an inevitable halt. To continue fighting under those circumstances would be madness, throwing away 150 years of global supremacy. A year of fighting was almost unthinkable. The maximum duration considered possible by the German Army was nine months, and everyone in Britain knew that it would be over by Christmas . . .

The War defied all expectations. It produced no swift, decisive glories on land or sea, but evolved quickly into 'total war' between whole societies. Twentieth-century warfare was discovered to be hugely expensive, virtually unwinnable and socially divisive, yet galloping technology and rampant bureaucracy conspired to harness national resources to long-term socioeconomic overdrive. Against all prewar logic, a gigantic military stalemate lasted for more than four years, claimed some ten million battle deaths, and was eventually ended only by the exhaustion and collapse of several major belligerents.

The land war began in a flurry of invasions and massive, mobile confrontations: Germany invaded France and Belgium; France invaded Germany; Russia invaded EAST PRUSSIA and GALICIA; Austria-Hungary invaded Galicia and Serbia; Britain contributed its small expeditionary force (the BEF) to the defence of France. Dramatic advances and retreats characterized the Battles of the FRONTIERS, the MARNE, TANNENBERG and the KOLUBARA RIVER, along with numerous other apparently decisive engagements, but by late 1914 the battle lines on the BALKAN, WESTERN and EASTERN FRONTS had each achieved a peculiar form of stagnation.

A fateful advantage for defenders over attackers in land campaigns (see below) had already been established, and was reinforced over the following years. In the west, where the GERMAN ARMY had occupied most of Belgium and the northeastern corner of France, great offensives by both sides punctuated intense TRENCH WARFARE. Massed assaults in CHAMPAGNE and ARTOIS during 1915, at VERDUN and the SOMME in 1916, and at ARRAS, the AISNE and YPRES in 1917 were all ghastly exercises in futile slaughter on a steadily increasing scale, and all failed to alter the front line significantly. In the east, the Austro-German GORLICE–TARNOW and TRIPLE OFFENSIVES of 1915, and the Russian BRUSILOV OFFENSIVE in 1916 captured vast swathes of territory but never seriously threatened to deliver a 'knock-out blow' against either side.

The unexpected military impasse on the Western and Eastern Fronts, and the willingness of statesmen in previously neutral countries to gamble on war, promoted escalation. The German Army expended more ammunition during the three-day Marne battle in 1914 than its Prussian predecessor had used throughout the war of 1870–71, and military authorities in belligerent countries were demanding quantum increases in supplies of men and munitions by autumn 1914. While governments wrestled with production shortfalls, distribution problems and the sociopolitical implications of efficient central administration, their diplomats jostled for the favours of neutral states that might just tip the balance of military or economic power.

Japan joined its British ally at war in August 1914, a move with more significance to Pacific affairs than to the land war in Europe. Turkey, led by an ambitious, militarist cabal under ENVER and TALAAT, joined the CENTRAL POWERS in late October, igniting prolonged land campaigns on the CAUCASIAN, MESOPOTAMIAN and PALESTINE FRONTS, as well as a relatively brief campaign at GALLIPOLI. Italy was induced to join the ALLIES by lavish territorial promises included in the Treaty of LONDON, and opened hostilities against Austria-Hungary on the ITALIAN FRONT in June 1915.

Bulgaria abandoned watchful neutrality for predation in autumn 1915, and joined the Central Powers in a combined invasion of SERBIA. Serbia's subsequent collapse was the catalyst for a belated Allied relief operation based on the Macedonian port of SALONIKA, where a new Balkan front line languished in disease-ridden inactivity against a backdrop of Greek civil unrest. Romania remained neutral until August 1916, when it declared for the Allies and invaded Hungarian Transylvania. The short ROMANIAN CAMPAIGN that followed left Bucharest and most of the country under occupation by the Central Powers by early 1917, but never threatened to alter the strategic picture elsewhere in military terms.

Outside Europe and the Middle East, the War's impact was determined by the global nature of European empires. Able-bodied men from every continent were rushed to the service of the Allied empires. Volunteers poured in from the white British dominions of AUSTRALIA, CANADA, NEW ZEALAND and SOUTH AFRICA. The INDIAN ARMY was expanded and mobilized for overseas defence of the British Empire, and native recruits came from almost every other British, French and Russian imperial outpost.

At the same time German colonial possessions were steadily picked off by Allied invasions. Japan took Germany's Chinese coastal enclave of TSINGTAO by force in November 1914, and had already occupied those German Pacific island possessions not taken by AUSTRALIAN and NEW ZEALAND FORCES. The four German colonies in AFRICA were all invaded, but although TOGOLAND, SOUTHWEST AFRICA and CAMEROON were in Allied hands by early 1916, British imperial forces spent four years in vain pursuit of the German Army in EAST AFRICA.

The course of all land campaigns depended to some extent on the truly global battle for control of the world's sea lanes, which governed the supply of overseas armies and the maintenance of vital imports for home consumption. Prewar faith in battlefleets as the decisive agents of maritime control proved false, and four years of NAVAL WARFARE was superficially as indecisive as the struggles of land armies.

The only major battlefleet confrontation, at JUTLAND in 1916, was almost a metaphor for halfhearted, inconclusive deployment of battleships, but important battles were won and lost at sea, albeit without noticeably shortening the War. The German Navy's attempt to use surface warships as commerce raiders was effectively defeated by spring 1915, partly thanks to a somewhat fortunate British victory at the FALKLAND ISLANDS. The Allied offensive strategy of throttling the

Central Powers by long-range naval BLOCKADE of their ocean outlets operated without serious interruption throughout, but disappointed those who expected it to cripple Germany within a few months.

Nonetheless hurt by the Allied naval stranglehold, and unable to find a suitable retaliatory role for its battlefleet, the German high command made increasing use of SUBMARINES to attack Allied merchant shipping from early 1915, but their all-out deployment for *HANDELSKRIEG* ('trade warfare') from February 1917 was a desperate gamble, reflecting the new German THIRD SUPREME COMMAND's recognition that the depth of Anglo-French socioeconomic resources could outlast the diminishing strength of the Central Powers.

Triggered by Allied refusal to contemplate a simple ceasefire along existing front lines, the campaign failed to knock Britain out of the War before Allied ANTI-SUBMARINE measures (especially CONVOYS) were developed to contain the threat of U-BOATS. German expansion of SUBMARINE WARFARE meanwhile outraged neutral opinion and pushed the United States from a position as the Allies' chief trading partner into a declaration of war against Germany in April 1917.

Intervention by the USA marked the War's only really decisive escalation. Coming at a time when the strains of national war effort were at last breaking down the established social and political structures of prewar Europe, it presented the Allies with an enormous new source of economic and military power, effectively guaranteeing victory once this power was transferred to the battlefields. Though 1917 was a terrible year for the Allies in military terms, bringing hopeless attrition in France, final Russian collapse on the Eastern Front and Italian defeat at CAPORETTO, the minor rush of independent neutrals to join the Allies after spring 1917 (including Greece, Brazil and China) told its own story.

The German leadership also saw the writing on the wall. Despite the benefits of victory in the east, Germany's allies were patently all but exhausted, and the capacity of German society to wage war beyond 1918 was open to serious doubt. The great SPRING OFFENSIVES on the Western Front in 1918, which frightened the Allies but terminally exhausted the German Army, were a last attempt at victory before the odds became impossible, and their failure finally broke the military deadlock in France. The AMIENS and MEUSE-ARGONNE OFFENSIVES of the late summer – the latter strengthened by more than a million 'DOUGHBOYS' of the American Expeditionary Force (AEF) – began a drive east by the Allies that had forced the German Army back to its frontiers by November.

On other fronts the Central Powers disintegrated completely during the second half of 1918. After eleven fruitless attacks at the ISONZO, and the successful defence of the PIAVE, the ITALIAN ARMY's VITTORIO VENETO OFFENSIVE scattered the remnants of Austro-Hungarian strength on the Italian Front from September. The BULGARIAN ARMY evaporated during the Allied VARDAR OFFENSIVE from Salonika in the same month, and Turkish attempts to occupy Caucasian territories after the Russian withdrawal of 1917 hastened the Ottoman Empire's collapse elsewhere. The wars in Palestine and Mesopotamia ended with the Allies completely victorious in late October 1918, and all three of Germany's allies had surrendered by early November.

Fighting in the First World War ended on 11 November 1918, after the conclusion of an ARMISTICE agreement between Germany and the Allies in the Forest of Compiègne. Although the German Army remained a coherent force, and was never decisively beaten on any front, Germany had subsided into internal anarchy and Allied victory was effectively complete. But although the outbursts of spontaneous popular joy that signalled peace in Britain and France were even more spectacular than those that had greeted war, few could regard eventual success as a triumph of arms. Both popular and professional thinking about military affairs was already dominated by the question of what had gone wrong.

The first response by contemporaries, echoed by a generation of postwar commentators, was to blame the generals. The aura of invincibility that surrounded military leaders in 1914 had been comprehensively dispelled long before 1918, and First World War commanders were accused of stupidity, stubbornness, inflexibility and worse.

The wartime performances of (among many) Joffre, NIVELLE, FRENCH, HAIG, HAMILTON, CADORNA, CONRAD, Enver and most Russian generals suggest that the best and brightest of their generation were not to be found in prewar European staff colleges – but the generals faced unprecedented technical difficulties and have been harshly treated by posterity. Massive armies equipped with modern ARTILLERY and MACHINE GUNS were unwieldy instruments of offensive warfare. Although they had the industrial, transport and manpower capacity to deploy million-man armies equipped with efficient anti-personnel weapons, the generals lacked the technology to manoeuvre them efficiently in an attacking role.

Attacking forces everywhere discovered that neither infantry nor CAVALRY were sufficiently mobile or protected to turn local successes into strategically decisive victories. They needed fast, reliable, armoured forms of transport, capable of travelling over any terrain, along with genuinely portable RADIO equipment and infantry-support weapons, and neither were available during the period of the conflict.

Before the problems of strategic exploitation could be addressed, the generals faced enormous difficulties in achieving tactical success on the main European fronts. German armies quickly demonstrated the defensive inadequacy of FORTRESSES against modern field artillery, but well-constructed TRENCHES presented a more formidable challenge. If an entrenched army stayed still or retreated, it could use roads, railways and sophisticated field communications to rush reserves to any threatened point, but these facilities were not available once it advanced into enemy territory. The land war in Europe after 1914, especially on the Western, Gallipoli and Italian Fronts, can be characterized as a series of unsuccessful experiments intended to overcome these disadvantages.

The Western Front remained the definitive theatre throughout, embroiling the greatest concentrations of manpower and equipment, and serving as the main breeding ground for technical and tactical innovation in land warfare. The initial belief that greater concentration of force along a narrow front would smash through enemy trench lines – the basic assumption behind BREAKTHROUGH TACTICS – prompted a series of mass offensives from late 1914. Their abject failure left commanders on both sides convinced that breakthrough could still be achieved, but only given much more firepower.

Massive casualties were replenished and armies expanded, most notably the BEF, while rapid growth in artillery capacity took place on both sides. Artillery was seen as the key to destroying trench systems, but broke up the battle terrain and was hardly conducive to an outbreak of mobile warfare. Once the shock effect of increasingly enormous PRELIMINARY BOMBARDMENTS had been countered by improved trenches and DEFENCE IN DEPTH tactics, artillery concentration began to work against attacking infantry, warning defenders without disabling them. Bereft of alternative ideas, commanders continued to demand and deploy big guns on an increasing scale to the end.

The German Army's concentrated assault on the French fortresses at Verdun in February 1916 ushered in a new experiment, war of attrition. German chief of staff FALKENHAYN planned to 'bleed the French Army white' as it sought to defend a national symbol, but the ten-month battle for Verdun developed an unstoppable momentum of its own, inflicting terrible casualties on both sides without ultimately altering the front line to any significant degree.

Attrition was part of Allied calculations surrounding the British-led offensive on the Somme from July to November 1916, a campaign that followed a similarly appalling pattern. The Allied offensives of 1917 were amalgamations of breakthrough and attrition doctrine garnished with a few cosmetic tactical innovations such as the CREEPING BARRAGE.

Even when the development of more sophisticated INFILTRATION TACTICS and

PEACEFUL PENETRATION techniques made breakthrough possible in France, the problems of exploitation remained unsolved. The German Spring Offensives in 1918 were able to achieve initial success, but ran out of steam as they advanced far from their supply bases. The final Allied advances, against a demoralized army short of almost every supply requirement, were still slow, painstaking affairs rather than dramatic, long-range strikes.

Rapid developments in aerial techniques and technology remained marginal to the strategic picture throughout. Experiments in STRATEGIC BOMBING were underway by late 1914, but by 1919 neither ZEPPELINS nor specialist bomber designs had proved capable of delivering a significant payload with accuracy, or of achieving a reasonable chance of daylight survival against improving ANTI-AIRCRAFT defences. Aircraft were primarily used as reconnaissance or targeting tools for armies and navies, as ground support for attacking infantry, or in private battles among themselves, especially after the appearance of the first genuine FIGHTER aircraft over France from mid-1915. Aerial combat at least provided some diversion for civilians starved of derring-do, and air ACES (along with a few of the more dashing naval commanders) emerged as the popular heroes of the First World War during 1916.

Poison GAS was first used in quantity by German units at Ypres in April 1915, and chemical warfare became standard practice for both sides on European fronts by 1916. Gruesome weapon though it was, gas failed to solve any of the problems of strategic exploitation, and its effects were gradually reduced by the development of respirators. Like FLAMETHROWERS, GRENADES, MORTARS and other trench-fighting weapons coming into widespread use along the Western Front from 1915, gas was essentially a tactical device.

The most innovative weapon devised to overcome trench fortifications was the TANK, first introduced to the BEF in September 1916 and available in large numbers from late 1917. Often cited as a 'war-winning' invention, the tank was a successful trench weapon that contributed to the victories of 1918, but remained unreliable, dangerous for crews, slow, and incapable of sustaining long-range operations.

Away from the Western Front, troops in Gallipoli and Italy experienced even more congested conditions in terrain completely unsuited to mobility. Wherever congestion was less of a problem – on the Eastern Front, in the Caucasus and in the Middle Eastern theatres – vast distances, poor roads and lack of supplies crippled advancing forces before they could achieve strategically decisive results. Cold killed troops as they slept on the Italian and Eastern Fronts, and took an enormous toll of the retreating SERBIAN ARMY in late 1915. Heat and disease claimed thousands of victims in Salonika, Africa, Mesopotamia and Palestine.

The armies themselves, led by literally hundreds of newly created generals as their size mushroomed, were inferior to the formations described in textbooks. Raw recruits or reserve conscripts in vast numbers were hardly to be trusted with intricate field manoeuvres, and could not always be relied upon to fight at all. All the combatant armies lost the vast majority of their experienced junior officers and NCOs during the early campaigns, with consequent ill effects on training and operational standards, and many troops in multiracial armies did not understand the language of their officers.

The First World War was no golden age of generalship, but there were successes. LETTOW-VORBECK in East Africa, YUDENICH in the Caucasus, KEMAL at Gallipoli, and ALLENBY in Palestine all undertook strikingly successful campaigns in very different contexts. Even on the main, deadlocked fronts, commanders such as MACKENSEN, MONASH, PLUMER and HUTIER achieved consistent tactical results within the constraints forced upon them.

Naval leaders also received a bad press during and after a war in which the majority of surface actions were fought by DESTROYERS and CRUISERS in defence of trade routes worldwide, and by light forces defending bases or contesting crowded sea lanes. Broadly accused of overcaution, they too were victims of modern technology and faulty prewar planning.

After the fundraising and tub-thumping that had accompanied prewar naval expansion, big surface warships were rendered all but obsolete by cheap MINES and TORPEDOES. Fleet commanders faced opprobrium for apparently avoiding confrontations with enemy battleships, but risked profitless destruction by submarines, minefields or TORPEDO BOATS if they entered hostile waters in search of battle.

General preference for a no-risk policy was reinforced by the fate of old Allied PRE-DREADNOUGHTS committed to the DARDANELLES OPERATION in spring 1915, and the difficulties faced by German HIGH SEAS FLEET units in the IRBEN STRAITS later that year. Although the British GRAND FLEET in the North Sea managed brushes with German dreadnoughts at the DOGGER BANK and Jutland, the great fleets cowered in their bases for most of the War, functioning as deterrents and occasionally carrying out rapid coastal raids or protection duties for amphibious operations. Naval reputations plummeted across the board, but modern historians generally recognize that much-maligned fleet admirals such as JELLICOE, BEATTY, ABRUZZI, BOUÉ DE LAPEYRÈRE and HAUS had a great deal more to lose than to gain by bold adventure.

The political and military strategists who orchestrated the debacles on land and sea have been accused of narrow concentration on deadlocked theatres, of allowing expedient to dominate their deployment of resources, or of blind over-ambition.

Most leaders in most countries had little choice about where they concentrated national strength. The French, Belgian, Serbian, Italian, Austro-Hungarian, Turkish, Romanian and Bulgarian high commands were fighting around their frontiers, and could hardly contemplate major operations elsewhere. Germany was fully occupied fighting on two main fronts, and American authorities were never in a position to dictate Allied military strategy.

The British high command had more choices, and accusations of 'strategic drift' were at least partly justified. Commitment of major resources to the Western Front was necessary and inevitable, but Kitchener, ROBERTSON and other 'WESTERNERS' became embroiled in a long, fruitless debate with 'EASTERNERS', such as LLOYD GEORGE and CHURCHILL, who sought to divert significant strength to the flanks of the European deadlock. The consequent failure either to concentrate absolutely on the main battle, or to provide decisive reinforcements to 'SIDESHOWS' in Gallipoli, Salonika, Palestine and Mesopotamia, merely prolonged the agony on all fronts.

Combined strategic direction of the Central Powers was increasingly dominated by Germany, which was the only state among them capable of planning an offensive after 1916, and Allied leaders failed to achieve genuinely effective international cooperation for almost four years. Even on the shared Western Front, the main British and French forces remained under separate commands until 1918, and attempts to coordinate offensive strategy on various fronts were uniformly halfhearted until the crisis of the German Spring Offensives forced commanders and politicians to invest real authority in the SUPREME WAR COUNCIL at Versailles. A supreme Allied commander, the Frenchman FOCH, was in place during the year's subsequent campaigns, but his authority was always dependent to some extent on the consent of British, American and Belgian field commanders.

Charges of over-ambition can justifiably be levelled at the Turkish leadership, at Conrad's Austro-Hungarian general staff, and above all at the German Third Supreme Command under HINDENBURG and LUDENDORFF. German unwillingness to abandon expansionist aims in either eastern or western Europe, and the deployment of a large army of occupation in the east after the Russian collapse in 1917, fatally compromised the military effort on the Western Front in 1918 and acted as a permanent obstacle to international peace efforts.

A negotiated peace was never a realistic option while both sides considered ultimate victory possible, and as long as national populations were prepared to keep fighting. The Allies' initial stated aims of restoring all German-occupied territories and exacting the cost in REPARATIONS had expanded in practice to embrace the permanent reduction of German military potential by the time serious peace moves got underway in the second half of 1916.

The PEACE OFFER made by German chancellor BETHMANN HOLLWEG in December 1916, and the Reichstag PEACE RESOLUTION of July 1917, bore little relation to the policies of the Third Supreme Command, and Austro-Hungarian attempts to seek a separate peace brought only Allied rejection and the diplomatically disastrous SIXTUS AFFAIR. Neutral efforts, most notably the appeals of Pope BENEDICT XV and the US PEACE NOTE, only emphasized the lack of any real ground for negotiation while the battle lines remained undecided. President WILSON's FOURTEEN POINTS peace programme of early 1918 was never considered a viable option by either side's leaders until internal and military collapse forced the Central Powers to accept it as an alternative to more severe terms.

The military struggle was only one dimension of 'total war'. Unlike any war before it, but like every major conflict since, the First World War was conducted by whole societies in support of armed forces, effecting sweeping, irrevocable changes on the 'home fronts' within all the major belligerent nations.

War on the home fronts followed certain generalized patterns. Governments and armies quickly found that a fountain of patriotic fervour provided only one basic raw material for war, in the form of fighting manpower, and that planned production of arms and supplies was wholly inadequate. Backed by emergency wartime powers – such as the new Defence of the Realm Act (DORA) in Britain, or the 19th-century Prussian Siege Law in Germany – they reacted by attempting centralized control over munitions output and distribution, which led inevitably to greater jurisdiction over communications, labour, and all areas of resource consumption.

Enormous material expenditure in the War's opening battles brought almost immediate SHELL CRISES to the big continental armies, and governments generally followed the trend set by RATHENAU's German KRA (War Materials Department) and the munitions section of the French war ministry under Albert THOMAS. Established as central administrative bureaux during 1914, they gave industrialists practical control over price and distribution of war materials, along with enormous profits, in return for improved production output. At the same time restrictions on the movement and conscription of important labour forces were imposed, often in return for guarantees of improved wages and working conditions.

Other countries were eventually forced to introduce similar systems, and did so with varying degrees of efficiency. The highly effective British munitions ministry under Lloyd George was formed in mid-1915 after a SHELL SCANDAL had brought down the Liberal government. In the United States, where resources, manpower and infrastructural facilities were plentiful, big business used the War Industries Board from July 1917 to promote a massive industrial boom.

A sequence of military disasters on the Eastern Front in 1915 provoked the first real attempt to organize Russian industry under GUCHKOV, but lack of infrastructural support and poor industrial relations made growth unsustainable beyond 1916. Italian organization under General DALLOLIO, and later Francesco NITTI, was never able to keep pace with basic industrial weakness, and the Austro-Hungarian Empire produced several detailed rationalization plans but very little in the way of practical reform. The Ottoman Empire, its internal communications in chaos after the military seized all facilities in November 1914, had little industry to mobilize and relied on bureaucratic gangsterism to organize distribution.

Certain symptoms of economic overstimulation were common to most wartime societies. Diversion of resources to war industries, and the vagaries of maritime supply, brought civilian consumer shortages, varying in scale from the largely voluntary abstention practised in the USA to the acute food and fuel crises affecting urban areas in Russia and the Central Powers. Black markets flourished in the most beleaguered regions, where ubiquitous price rises approached hyperinflationary levels and hardship contributed to political breakdown.

The most developed states were generally able to sustain economic growth for war, and those regimes that based their policies on some degree of genuine public consent (and gave the process the misleading title of 'WAR SOCIALISM') survived the experience. Those that relied exclusively on the support of narrow interest groups – the cabal in Constantinople, the German-speaking leadership of Austro-Hungary, and the Russian court – were destroyed by the enormous strains placed on their socioeconomic constituencies.

Germany was a special case. Able to call on Europe's most dynamic industrial economy, but constricted by the Allied blockade and the relative feebleness of its military partners, the German leadership relied increasingly on the support of right-wing military and industrial interests to push the economy into a phenomenal war effort. Evidence of Allied material superiority in 1916 helped bring the radical Third Supreme Command to power in August, and over the following months it used a pliant Kaiser to impose a dictatorship over every aspect of German life under the HINDENBURG PROGRAMME. Conducted in defiance of parliamentary and worker opposition, and without any concession to constitutional reform, the Programme sent Germany screaming to economic and social breakdown by autumn 1918, without ever coming close to achieving its fantastic military production targets.

Voluntary suspension of parliamentary opposition in all the belligerent states was a feature of August 1914. Patriotic fervour and energetic PROPAGANDA also combined to give governing regimes a powerful reserve of popular support at the start of the War. Both parliamentary and popular support were gradually eroded in every country as the conflict progressed, but the pace and extent of reaction varied according to the levels of hardship, repression and general war weariness experienced.

In political terms, the War was generally a bad time for moderates. Coalitions of compromise in Britain, France and Italy all failed to sustain political unity, and were eventually replaced by more dynamic, hard-line regimes under Lloyd George, ORLANDO and CLEMENCEAU, respectively. The liberal political tradition in the USA, where wartime pressures were never sufficient to provoke serious popular opposition to government, was quickly overwhelmed by the combination of federal interference and unfettered big-business expansion after 1917, and spent the next decade in decline.

Moderate parliamentarians in Germany, Russia, Austria-Hungary and Turkey, along with those sections of the ruling elites willing to attempt reform, were increasingly squeezed out into a political wilderness by extreme conservative regimes on the one hand, and revolutionary opposition on the other. Though parliamentary cabinets took, or were given, a semblance of power when existing regimes collapsed, they inherited virtually unmanageable revolutionary situations. The PROVISIONAL GOVERNMENT in Russia, the MAX VON BADEN cabinet in Germany, the IZZET cabinet in Turkey and a succession of reforming ministers appointed by the new Habsburg Emperor KARL I from 1917 were all too late to satisfy more radical agendas from below.

Radical forces for social change found increasing opportunity for expression as disruption and war weariness mounted on the home fronts. The entry of organized labour into mainstream British government proceeded from popular disenchantment with prewar ideologies and from the wartime partnerships arranged between unions, employers and the administration. Italy and France were both riddled with strikes and anti-War demonstrations during 1917–18, and were saved from more widespread eruption by patriotic revivals during the crises of Caporetto and the Spring Offensives, respectively. Both countries provided fertile political ground for postwar extremists on the left and right.

Socialism was largely irrelevant in Muslim countries, where there was no industrial working class and ideology was dominated by religious affairs, and separatism absorbed much of the most radical opposition to the Ottoman regime. The successful ARAB REVOLT, and the regional rebellions that provoked the ARMENIAN MASSACRES seriously damaged the fragile cohesion of the Turkish war effort. Determined movements for the creation of independent nations within Austria-Hungary brought together liberal and socialist opposition to the Habsburg regime, resulting in the paralysis of major cities, the blocking of attempts at peaceful reform, and the spread of unrest through the imperial army.

Separatist movements on the fringes of the Russian Empire sprang into life following the 1917 FEBRUARY REVOLUTION (March by the modern calendar), but faced determined opposition from the most powerful wartime manifestation of radical socialism, the Russian SOVIET movement. The Bolshevik OCTOBER REVOLUTION (in November 1917) brought to power a doctrinaire cabal under LENIN, which took Russia out of the War, accepted a draconian peace settlement at BREST-LITOVSK in March 1918, and set about promoting revolution elsewhere, using its new RED ARMY to destabilize independent governments in TRANSCAUCASIA, ESTONIA, LATVIA, LITHUANIA, FINLAND and the UKRAINE.

An apparently similar left-wing movement seemed likely to seize power in Germany for a time in late 1918, but its ruthless suppression by right-wing militia ended the GERMAN REVOLUTIONS in early 1919. Moderate politicians were again left in ostensible control of Germany, but the Weimar Republic was never secure from rebellion by either political extreme.

The Bolshevik success in Russia provoked no spontaneous imitation in the major European states, and international socialism in general failed to recover from the shock of August 1914. The rump of the Second International was unable to achieve unity at ZIMMERWALD, and the failure of the STOCKHOLM CONFERENCE in 1917 illustrated the extent to which the torch of radicalism had passed exclusively to Russia. Left-wing politicians and publications were ruthlessly suppressed in the USA, where increasing prosperity worked against their popular acceptance.

Smaller European belligerents were in no position to contemplate large-scale industrial or financial mobilization for war, and all experienced severe political upheaval and socioeconomic crisis. Conquered territories in Serbia, Belgium and Romania underwent ruthless economic exploitation by the Central Powers, and suffered heavy civilian casualties. The Romanian, Bulgarian and Greek monarchs were deposed, and all three states were plagued by violent political instability in the postwar period.

The need to raise vast amounts of money was common to all belligerents, and although limited taxation of profits and incomes was attempted in Britain, the USA and elsewhere, the sale of government bonds to loyal citizens was the primary means by which the more developed states met the cost of war. This was nowhere sufficient, and European governments were forced to raise huge loans overseas. Germany was the primary banker for the Central Powers, lending cash or goods to all its allies in return for economic exploitation and strategic control; the Allied war effort was largely financed from Britain and the USA, the latter assuming an increasingly predominant role.

The old, Eurocentric order of world economic affairs was broken by the cost of total war. By the end of 1918 the Russian, Austro-Hungarian, Ottoman and German Empires had effectively disintegrated, and a mass of smaller new states had emerged within their former boundaries. France and Italy were impoverished, each facing the reconstruction of devastated former battle zones, and even the enormous wealth of Great Britain had been permanently undermined.

By contrast the rest of the world had profited from Europe's prolonged spending spree. The economies of many African, Australasian and Latin American states enjoyed export booms, and increased industrial development was stimulated in the better-established British colonies and dominions. Japan was able to secure regional trade domination, establishing its first trading links with Australia, and experienced a heavy industrial boom that was to mushroom after the War.

The United States, which enjoyed the benefit of relatively short trade routes to Europe, was far and away the greatest economic beneficiary of the War. Rapid industrial growth was underway on the back of an export boom to Allied nations before the end of 1914, and output of both raw and war materials soared during the USA's comparatively brief period of full-scale mobilization. Not threatened by exhaustion or popular disillusionment before the Armistice, the USA approached the peace as the world's most powerful creditor nation and the only likely source of capital investment in postwar reconstruction, factors that dominated the financial and economic world of the 1920s.

The great military, political and economic turmoil of the First World War cast a long shadow over the 20th century, establishing the bases for most of its future wars and shaping the modern framework of international affairs. Even so it is the human rather than the geopolitical dimension of the Great War that is most strongly imprinted on modern culture.

The first war fought by literate mass armies in an age of mass communication treated painters, writers, architects, artisans, peasants and factory workers with dispassionate violence, so that the horror of mass slaughter was transmitted to posterity through an unprecedented diversity of media. Our modern view of the soldier's war has been etched by an outpouring of contemporary memoirs, poems, songs, letters, novels and paintings, most emanating from the literate regions and classes of central Europe, western Europe and North America. Despite a wealth of jingoistic propaganda in wartime newspapers, books, leaflets, posters and FILMS, the bleak messages conveyed by the soldiers themselves have defined subsequent attitudes to war. Modern culture is chillingly familiar with the Great War serviceman's nightmares – WHIZZ-BANGS, TRENCH FEVER, SNIPING, cold, heat, and casual intimacy with death.

The exhilaration, bereavement, privation or abiding drudgery of the civilian war is engraved in our literary heritage and our political structures, but also in the ways we conduct our everyday lives. Permanent changes in the means by which people chose or opposed their rulers were matched by changes in the jobs they performed, their wages, the conditions in which they worked, and the goods (ERSATZ or otherwise) that they consumed.

Women were enfranchised in Britain, given new working or educational opportunities in all the main belligerent societies, liberated from some religious constraints in the Ottoman world, and in the vanguard of revolution in Russia. As the balance of power between men and women was shifting amid the high living, overcrowding and slightly hysterical atmosphere of wartime industrial cities, popular language, dress, behaviour and expectations were transforming in ways that postwar reaction could never reverse. Commentators everywhere noted a loosening of sexual morals and a rise in levels of ALCOHOL consumption – the latter subject to government restraints that still exist in some societies. From air raids to ration cards, newsreels to automobiles, new technology intruded on everyday life at a pace and with an intensity never seen before.

The civilian war away from cities presented a more uniformly sombre picture. Starvation or repression took uncounted lives in Armenia, CENTRAL ASIA and occupied states. Hundreds of small communities disappeared altogether, caught in the path of advancing armies or destroyed by the scorched-earth policies of retreating forces. Millions of women in rural societies bore the brunt of peasant labour in the absence of conscripted menfolk, many of whom never returned. Even in relatively fortunate Britain, small communities suffered the shock of sudden decimation, their men enlisting and dying together in local formations.

The huge efforts made by generals, politicians, soldiers and civilians during the war years inevitably generated an array of diverse, and often mutually incompatible, expectations about the peace. Public opinion, political expedient, international competition and military watchfulness all conspired to turn the actual creation of the peace into a sad circus of disputes and desperate compromises.

The 20th century has born out the contemporary impression that the Treaty of VERSAILLES, its subsidiaries and the LEAGUE OF NATIONS were unworkable mixtures of the liberal and punitive. The principal participants of the PARIS PEACE CONFERENCE were aware of their failure at the time, and few of the delegates came away satisfied that a lasting new order had been established. Millions of ordinary spectators were also disappointed. Popular opinion in the victorious nations had been led to expect revenge on the Kaiser, satisfaction of national ambitions, prosperity, and social reform. Populations within the Central Powers, having disposed of the regimes that conducted the War, imagined that Wilson's Fourteen Points guaranteed far more benevolent treatment than they received in its aftermath.

The treaties were rejected by the US and Chinese governments, and excited popular disgust in the western Allied countries (especially in Italy). They were also deeply resented in the defeated nations they penalized. Almost all the issues that they addressed or touched upon remained essentially unresolved, and the world over which they held nominal sway was hardly less volatile than the proud imperial edifice of 1914.

The USA had become the world's strongest economic power, free from European competition in its Latin American and Pacific markets, but had ostentatiously withdrawn from any global peacekeeping role by 1920. Rapid Japanese economic expansion into the Pacific Rim foreshadowed decades of aggressive regional imperialism. An embittered and volatile Germany, stripped of territory, population, resources and the right to arm itself, turned to a mythologized past for consolation and regeneration.

A scattering of fragile new states struggled for identity along the western frontiers of a diplomatically isolated Soviet Union, itself resentful of Allied intervention in the RUSSIAN CIVIL WAR. The establishment of European administrations through MANDATES brought only instability to the Middle East, where the BALFOUR DECLARATION and SYKES–PICOT AGREEMENT ran contrary to the independent ambitions of Syria, the Lebanon, TRANSJORDAN, Iraq and Palestine. The creation of a fractious YUGOSLAVIA in the untamed Balkans sowed the seeds of future civil war and helped push outraged Italian opinion into the arms of MUSSOLINI. Militant nationalism in INDIA, and militant white supremacism in South Africa, were stirring into prolonged life. Endemic civil war in Greece, the ruin of agricultural development in East Africa, anarchy in China . . . the list goes on.

Political extremism, dictatorship, racism, feminism, administrative centralization, economic globalization, mass production, air travel, artificial fertilizers, movies . . . the 20th century as we know it was fully underway by 1919, but the last acts of war and the first months of peace were dominated by a grim reminder of the past. After perhaps 20 million people had been killed by the fighting and 'collateral damage' of the War, a global influenza pandemic reached Europe from the east in 1918. By late the following year it had killed an estimated 70 million worldwide, a final epitaph to the lost Age of Progress, and to its illusion of human control over natural forces and resources.

SP
DECEMBER 1994

A

A7V Panzerkampfwagen The only TANK produced for the wartime GERMAN ARMY. It was both the heaviest and best-armed machine used by either side on the WESTERN FRONT, as well as one of the fastest, but it was also cumbersome and an easy target. The poor technical performance of early British vehicles in 1916–17 had convinced German planners that the clumsy new weapon could be defeated by careful use of ARTILLERY or MINES (see TANK FORTS). Mounting industrial shortages in Germany also argued against disruption of fragile production schedules for large-scale development of experimental weapons, and only a handful of A7Vs were built. They equipped three units, each of five vehicles, on the Western Front from late 1917, and another six units used captured British HEAVY TANKS, reconditioned at a special facility in Charleroi, BELGIUM. Primarily used as decoys against Allied infantry or in a direct anti-tank role, their battlefield impact was marginal.
BRIEF DATA Weight: 32 tons; Max speed: 13kph; Crew: 16; Max armour: 30mm; Armament: 1 × 570mm gun, 6 × mg.

Aa, Battle of the Limited Russian attack at the northern tip of the EASTERN FRONT in coastal KURLAND, begun on 7 January 1917 along the River Aa running west of Riga (see MAP 11). Apart from some indecisive skirmishing in the Bukovina region further south, and the final battles of the ROMANIAN CAMPAIGN, it was the only action of any size in the theatre during the first half of 1917. In a surprise attack, camouflaged by sand dunes and launched without a PRELIMINARY BOMBARDMENT, the Russian Twelfth Army struck along a 50km line against German forces depleted by withdrawals to other fronts. By 9 January they had taken the towns of Mitau and Tukkums, and German counterattacks from 22 January petered out at the end of the month without any major success. The operation re-emphasized the value of tactics employed during the BRUSILOV OFFENSIVE of 1916, but the RUSSIAN ARMY was never again strong enough to attempt them on a large scale. See also: Battle of RIGA.

Abdullah Ibn Hussein (1882–1951) Second son of HUSSEIN IBN ALI and one of the military leaders of the ARAB REVOLT (1916–19). Abdullah's forces were primarily engaged against Turkish troops in besieged MEDINA, using the guerrilla tactics that characterized his brother FEISAL's operations further north. As a reward for wartime services, he was recognized by the British as Emir of the eastern Palestinian territory of TRANSJORDAN in 1921. King of independent Transjordan from 1946, and of the Hashemite state of Jordan from 1949, he was assassinated in Jerusalem in 1951.

Abruzzi, Admiral Luigi, Duke of the (1873–1933) Commander-in-chief of the ITALIAN NAVY battlefleet in 1915, and a cousin of King VICTOR EMMANUEL III. Regarded in naval circles as a dashing figure ideal for command of an active battlefleet, he consistently refused to risk his biggest ships in strategically unnecessary surface engagements, and was hampered in smaller-scale operations by an acute lack of ANTI-SUBMARINE craft, particularly DESTROYERS. The fleet's inactivity, punctuated by incidental losses of major warships, gradually eroded his political reputation (see *BENEDETTO BRIN*). A hostile press campaign gathered pace from autumn 1916 and, though enduringly popular with fleet officers, he was replaced in February 1917 by Admiral REVEL. Abruzzi turned down an honorary post as Inspector General of the Navy and received no further wartime command, but was promoted full admiral in March 1918.

Aces Term used to describe the most successful FIGHTER pilots. Invented by the French press in 1915 to honour Adolphe Pégoud, the first AÉRONAUTIQUE MILITAIRE pilot to shoot down five aircraft, the title reflected intense public interest in AERIAL WARFARE common to all belligerents.

French fighter units began publishing individual 'scores' during the battle for VERDUN in 1916, and the GERMAN ARMY AIR SERVICE set a target of 8 confirmed 'kills', later raised to 16, for receipt of its highest decoration, the Pour le Mérite ('Blue Max'). The concept of individual celebrity was only ever tacitly accepted by British authorities, despite popular and professional interest, but 8 victories was set as the minimum requirement for award of the Distinguished Flying Cross in March 1918.

The popular cult of aces peaked from 1916 with the growth of specialized combat units, and legends were built around celebrity squadrons – the French CIGOGNES, for example – as a matter of PROPAGANDA. Their undoubted value as popular morale boosters was offset by resentment from less dashing (but equally dangerous) branches of the air services and from junior fighter pilots required to leave easy kills to aces.

Accumulated 'scores' were at best approximate. A confirmed victory – witnessed and with physical proof – was harder to achieve over enemy lines, favouring those forces committed to defensive tactics. 'Kills' were often subject to multiple claims from other pilots or ground forces, especially as airspace became more crowded in 1917–18, and most aces claimed scores far beyond their official tallies.

The highest scorers tended to operate on the WESTERN FRONT, where air traffic was always most intense, and figures for the EASTERN FRONT are even less reliable. Different standards set by various air forces were a further complication. The USAAS, for instance, awarded one kill to each party involved in a shared victory, while other forces divided scores into fractions. All sides regarded BALLOONS and AIRSHIPS as targets of equal value to aircraft.

Successful German SUBMARINE commanders were also treated as aces, given the same publicity and privileges as pilots. The system was less precisely developed, the term being loosely applied to skippers who sank large amounts of merchant shipping and to those few who destroyed Allied warships.

Leading official scores for air aces (survivors marked *):

GERMANY:		*FRANCE:*	
M. von RICHTHOFEN	80	R. FONCK*	75
E. UDET*	62	G. Guynemer*	54
E. Löwenhardt	53	C. Nungesser	45
BRITAIN:		*ITALY:*	
E. MANNOCK	73	F. BARACCA	34
W. Bishop	72		
J. McCudden	57		
RUSSIA:		*USA:*	
A. KAZAKOV	17	E. RICKENBACKER*	26
AUSTRIA-HUNGARY:			
G. Brunowski	40		

See also: BLACK FLIGHT; BOELCKE, O.; GARROS, R.; GÖRING, H.; IMMELMANN, M.

Achi Baba The focus of Allied attacks on the HELLES sector of the GALLIPOLI FRONT in 1915, a 200-metre hill (also known as Alchi Tepe) in the centre of Gallipoli Peninsula about 8km from its southern tip (see MAP 20). Achi Baba dominated the entire Helles sector, and was Allied C-in-C HAMILTON's first main objective following the GALLIPOLI LANDINGS on 25 April, but became the limit of his ambitions in June after defeats at KRITHIA.

Although the main Allied effort on Gallipoli was switched north to the ANZAC COVE sector, Helles commander General Hunter-Weston was permitted to launch two further attacks towards Achi Baba during June and July.

The first advance, along the Aegean coast on 28 June, gained about a kilometre near the shore but was defeated elsewhere. In the week that followed, faced with repeated counterattacks, the advance made no further progress. By 5 July the battle had waned through mutual exhaustion, Turkish forces having suffered 16,000 casualties to 4,000 Allied losses.

Hunter-Weston resorted to frontal assault tactics in a second attack launched on 12 July. Reinforced by a fresh division, it was no more successful than previous attempts and was called off after two days, bringing Allied battle casualties in Helles close to 12,000 men since early June.

British commanders have subsequently been accused, particularly by Australian commentators, of greatly overestimating Achi Baba's tactical importance, and Hunter-Weston's summer attacks are generally considered a pointless waste of lives.

Aden Tiny British possession on the south-western tip of Arabia, annexed in 1839. A trading post with the Arabian interior and EAST AFRICA, it was also a regular waystation for SUEZ CANAL traffic. Garrisoned in 1914 by an INDIAN ARMY brigade, it held off an attack by Ali Sa'id Pasha's TURKISH ARMY forces based in Yemen in November. Turkish troops occupied the nearby pro-British sultanate of Lahej the following summer, and an initial attempt to dislodge them collapsed in extreme heat, after which Ali Sa'id took the British outpost of Sheikh Othman. A second Indian Army brigade was sent to Aden under General Younghusband, and retook the outpost on 20 July. Although skirmishing continued into 1916, and occasional small raids were mounted against Aden's perimeter defences, the ARAB REVOLT of the summer reduced Turkish forces in Yemen to a largely passive role.

Adhaim River, Battle of the See: SAMARRAH OFFENSIVE.

Adler, Viktor (1852–1918) Senior Austrian socialist politician whose prewar efforts to unite Social Democrats behind a programme of gradual constitutional reform had been rejected by Czech separatist elements. A convinced pan-German, Adler supported close ties with GERMANY throughout a war of which he basically disapproved, favouring a compromise peace from an early stage. His political career survived the assassination by his son Friedrich of Austrian prime minister STÜRGKH on 21 October 1916, and he was appointed to the new Austro-German Council of State in autumn 1918, rejecting Emperor KARL I's efforts to make the Council responsible for signing an armistice. Foreign minister of a National Assembly formed on 31 October to establish a republican Austria, Adler worked towards formal union with Germany (later forbidden by the VERSAILLES and ST GERMAIN Treaties), but died on 11 November.

Adriatic Sea See: MEDITERRANEAN SEA; AUSTRO-HUNGARIAN NAVY; ITALIAN NAVY; OTRANTO BARRAGE.

AEF (American Expeditionary Force) The army sent to wartime Europe by the UNITED STATES, comprising elements of the regular Army, the National Guard and the wartime conscript 'national army' (see SELECTIVE SERVICE ACT). Commanded throughout by General PERSHING, who brought the regular 1st Division to France in mid-1917, it was built up for deployment in its own right rather than as an adjunct to Allied armies on the WESTERN FRONT. Pershing allowed individual divisions and units to be attached to Anglo-French operations from May 1918, in response to the crisis of the German SPRING OFFENSIVES, and the AEF as a whole took the field at ST MIHIEL in September. Subsequently employed to spearhead the MEUSE-ARGONNE OFFENSIVE, and to hold the line west of VERDUN, the AEF had a combat strength of 1.36 million men by November, divided into three armies, and its total active strength in Europe reached just over 2 million. See: US ARMY; DOUGHBOYS. See also: Battles of LE HAMEL, CANAL DU NORD, CANTIGNY, BELLEAU WOOD.

AEG C-Type Series of armed German biplanes. They were sturdy but slightly underpowered machines distinguished by a stubby fuselage and broad wings. A few C-II models reached field units in early 1916, but the C-IV was introduced almost immediately and became a standard GERMAN ARMY AIR SERVICE workhorse on the WESTERN and BALKAN FRONTS, flying reconnaissance, light-bombing and escort missions until the ARMIS-

TICE. A 180hp C-IVa version was also used in small numbers, but almost two-thirds of the 658 AEG C-Types manufactured are thought to have been C-IVs, which were also operated by the Turkish and Bulgarian Air Services.
BRIEF DATA (C-IV) Type: two-seater reconnaissance; Engine: 160hp Mercedes; Max speed: 158kph; Ceiling: 5,000m; Armament: 2 × 7.92mm mg, max bomb load 90kg.

AEG G-Types Series of twin-engined German bombers, in service as the G-I from early 1916. They lacked the range or lifting power of larger GOTHA or FRIEDRICHSHAFEN G-TYPES and were primarily employed for short-range tactical attacks. Defensively well armed, they were also used as FIGHTERS for a time and later models flew long-range reconnaissance missions with extra fuel in place of bombs. Slightly modified G-II and G-III versions appeared during 1916, but most of the 542 produced were G-IVs. Also very similar to the original, G-IVs saw service on the WESTERN, ITALIAN and BALKAN FRONTS, as well as during the ROMANIAN CAMPAIGN, their use reflecting a reliance on types already in production forced on the GERMAN ARMY AIR SERVICE from 1917.
BRIEF DATA (G-IV) Type: bomber/reconnaissance; Crew: 3–4; Engine: 2 × 260hp Mercedes; Max speed: 165kph; Armament: 2 × 7.92mm mg, max bomb load 500kg.

AEG J-Types Armoured two-seater biplanes developed from the AEG C-TYPE in 1917 as infantry support 'trench fighters'. Given a bigger engine, downward-firing forward armament and armour plate around its nose, the J-I was intended for interim use on the WESTERN FRONT until purpose-designed machines became available. The J-II had more armour and streamlined control surfaces but was otherwise similar. Production difficulties faced by the German aircraft industry from 1917 meant that over 600 AEG J-Types were used, far more than the superior JUNKERS J-I or ALBATROS J-I designs, and they remained in service until the ARMISTICE despite heavy losses.
BRIEF DATA Type: two-seater ground support; Engine: 200hp Benz; Max speed: 150kph; Armament: 3 × 7.92mm mg.

Aerial Warfare The military potential of BALLOONS and AIRSHIPS was well appreciated by 1914, but aircraft were still very new. The global impact of the Wright brothers' first successful flight, in 1903, was delayed by prolonged wrangling over licence agreements, and no aircraft entered military service anywhere until 1911, when the first squadrons were attached to the FRENCH ARMY.

By August 1914 the French AÉRONAUTIQUE MILITAIRE could field 132 frontline machines with as many again in reserve. Its only real rival was the GERMAN ARMY AIR SERVICE, developed in response to rapid French expansion, which had more aircraft but possessed generally inferior designs and fewer pilots. Apart from the small but well-organized British RFC, and the large but disorganized RUSSIAN AIR SERVICE, other air forces possessed at most a handful of imported aircraft.

The air fleets of all major belligerents expanded rapidly in wartime, especially on the WESTERN FRONT, which was always the biggest and most advanced aerial theatre. The aero industries of FRANCE, GERMANY and GREAT BRITAIN grew from cottage concerns into large-scale mass-producers, and each country fielded several thousand machines by 1918. Anglo-French technical assistance contributed to even faster growth after 1917 in the UNITED STATES, which had mass-produced thousands of aircraft by late 1918, and the USAAS grew from almost nothing to field an operational fleet of 750 aircraft.

Aircraft were always relatively scarce on the EASTERN FRONT, where the German service was able to rely on numerical, qualitative and tactical superiority over Russian forces to give effective support to ground offensives. The outbreak of war on the ITALIAN FRONT found the ITALIAN AIR FORCE (the Corpo Aeronautico Militare) dependent on 58 frontline aircraft and the AUSTRO-HUNGARIAN AIR SERVICE with less than 100. Both grew steadily and both countries received help from their allies to develop indigenous aircraft industries, but other small air forces relied completely on allied material and technical assistance.

Early military uses of aircraft were dictated by technical limitations and the weather, which combined to cause the majority of operational casualties. Lightly powered, skeletal machines could not lift substantial bomb loads and struggled to make any headway against strong winds. Most were too feeble to carry weapons, and ramming was the only effective combat tactic. Night flying only took place by accident and, like formation flying, was rightly considered dangerous.

Even after 1916, when more powerful machines began appearing on the Western Front, the elements remained a vital factor in air operations, which were often impossible during winter. Whole units could be wrecked on the ground by storms, and aircraft on other fronts were regularly crippled by extreme cold, desert sand or tropical heat.

Under these circumstances aircraft were restricted to reconnaissance, liaison and ARTILLERY observation duties in 1914, only occasionally dropping light bombs, darts or grenades. The main technical requirements were in-flight stability for unarmed reconnaissance or spotting work, and ease of packaging for transport with armies.

Though effective as the eyes of mobile armies in 1914, aircraft became much more important once infantry lines stabilized on the Western Front from early 1915. Air forces were then needed for long-range reconnaissance behind enemy lines, short-range PHOTO-RECONNAISSANCE, intensified artillery spotting, and bombing of rear installations. Their increased value was reflected in the development of ANTI-AIRCRAFT techniques and FIGHTER aircraft for air-to-air combat.

From 1916, aircraft also undertook direct support of infantry operations, attacking trenches and maintaining contact between advance ground units and command headquarters. 'Trench fighting' became the aeroplane's main tactical role during 1918, but was always highly dangerous and unpopular with pilots on all sides.

These tasks were all performed as adjuncts to infantry operations, and all air forces (except the Corpo Aeronautico Militare) were under direct army or navy control in 1914. Other than in Britain, where the RAF was established in 1918 as an independent service answerable to the government, they remained tied to parent services in 1919.

Aircraft went to war in general-purpose units, and only Aéronautique Militaire escadrilles comprised single aircraft types in 1914, but the need for specialist squadrons was quickly appreciated. The first (ill-equipped) French and German bombing units had been formed by late 1914. By 1916, fighter, day- and night-bomber, reconnaissance and artillery-spotting formations were well established, and specialist ground-support units were introduced to the German service that year.

Except for the British, whose squadrons in 1914 comprised 12 machines, early field units usually comprised 6 aircraft but grew progressively larger. Mass deployment of air strength had become standard practice by 1918, with fighter groups containing dozens of aircraft engaged in sprawling DOGFIGHTS, equally large bomber fleets assembling for strategic attacks, and both sides deploying air armadas of several hundred machines under one command to support ground offensives in France and Italy.

The only aspect of aerial warfare not directly controlled by ground forces was STRATEGIC BOMBING, regarded by some theorists as a potentially war-winning concept. Nothing capable of putting it into practice had been designed for military use by 1914, but the limited successes of Russian SIKORSKI and Italian CAPRONI bombers from 1915 encouraged development of bigger and better aircraft for the task (see HANDLEY PAGE 0/100; GOTHA G-TYPES; REISENFLUGZEUG; ZEPPELINS). Aware that technical development lagged some way behind theory, enthusiasts everywhere regarded efforts made in the field by 1918 as essentially experimental, and the strategic bombing debate remained unresolved in the 1920s (see OBENDORF RAID; INDEPENDENT AIR FORCE).

Technological development in general was hindered by the common expectation of a short war, encouraging emphasis on short-term production and modification of existing designs. Few entirely new designs were available anywhere before 1916, and the most important technological leap of 1915 was the development of INTERRUPTER GEAR, enabling the pilot of a TRACTOR aircraft to fire straight ahead. Subsequent wartime developments in arms and instrumentation included improved gun mountings, bomb sights, cameras and RADIO gear, incendiary or armour-piercing bullets, bigger and more efficient bombs, and experimental 20mm or 37mm cannon armament.

In common with the ground forces they served, and influenced by the prevailing westerly winds, Allied air arms on the Western Front regarded themselves as on the offensive at all times. Most activity took place over German lines throughout, but interrupter gear gave the German defenders an important fighting advantage from mid-1915. Allied fighters restored technical parity once they were given interrupter gear of their own early the next year, but German air-to-air combat superiority was re-established by a new generation of HALBERSTADT and ALBATROS D-TYPE fighters between autumn 1916 and the following summer.

Fighters apart, high-performance German reconnaissance two-seaters were capable of defending themselves from fighters or carrying out ground attacks by 1916 (see HALBERSTADT CL-TYPES), but the Allies relied on obsolete designs into 1917, produced in vast numbers to compensate for losses (see BLOODY APRIL; TRENCHARD, H.). Neither side was able to develop an efficient day bomber for short-range tactical attacks. Allied VOISIN, BREGUET, SALMSON and AIRCO bombers all performed daylight raids, but their vulnerability forced a general concentration on inaccurate night raids.

Excellent new Allied fighter, reconnaissance and ground-attack designs became available in significant numbers from mid-1917. Machines like the SPAD S-XIII, SOPWITH CAMEL and BRISTOL FIGHTER gained an advantage on all active fronts that was never again lost. First-class new German combat and reconnaissance aircraft subsequently appeared (the JUNKERS J-I armoured trench fighter for example), but economic collapse under the HINDENBURG PROGRAMME from 1917 precluded large-scale production. By late 1918 shortages of production materials, pilots and fuel had crippled the air services of the Central Powers.

Wartime naval aviation was dominated by the British RNAS, but aircraft were generally established as a valuable reconnaissance and coastal bombing adjunct to NAVAL WARFARE by the end of 1914. British experiments with AIRCRAFT CARRIERS were valuable as lessons for future wars, but had limited operational effect (see e.g. CUXHAVEN RAID; TONDERN RAID). Seaplane fighters fought long, almost private battles for control of the English Channel, Adriatic and BALTIC coasts. Naval aircraft became an important component of Allied ANTI-SUBMARINE efforts, sometimes carrying DEPTH CHARGES or MINES, and seaplanes were designed to launch TORPEDOES. Like all long-range warplanes, most naval patrol craft used CARRIER PIGEONS. See also: ACES; PARACHUTES.

Aéronautique Militaire The air arm of the FRENCH ARMY, formed by unification of experimental aircraft sections within its ARTILLERY and engineering departments, along with the BALLOON service, in October 1910. France led the world in early aircraft design, and rapid organizational development followed, despite arguments within the Army about the proper use of aircraft.

By mid-1912 five escadrilles (squadrons) were in service with field armies, each equipped with six of a single aircraft type, and a colonial squadron was stationed in Algeria. Another 400 aircraft were ordered in the first half of 1913, mostly FARMAN MF-7, FARMAN HF-20 or BLÉRIOT XI two-seaters, and 132 machines (21 escadrilles) were in service by August 1914. Use of reserves meant that 34 Aéronautique Militaire escadrilles were active by early October.

French aircraft performed adequately within the restrictions of contemporary AERIAL WARFARE in 1914, above all providing accurate reconnaissance immediately before the first MARNE battle, but stagnation on the WESTERN FRONT required rapid expansion from 1915. Aéronautique Militaire commander General Bernard, who had emphasized his faith in a short war by cancelling all orders for new aircraft and closing down flying schools, was replaced by his energetic predecessor, Hirschauer, who ordered 2,300 new machines.

Over the following months field strength was expanded to 65 escadrilles, and equipment standardized on four main designs, including VOISIN two-seaters for bomber groups (each of 3 escadrilles) formed in late 1914, and MORANE SAULNIER L monoplanes for 16 planned FIGHTER escadrilles. Official departments for aircraft armament and engines were established during 1915, standardizing on British VICKERS and LEWIS light MACHINE GUNS for use with INTERRUPTER GEAR, and supervising development of the French-built Hispano-Suiza aero engine.

Increased output by aircraft manufacturers in FRANCE (400–500 deliveries per month by late 1916) meant that a total of 1,149 machines were in frontline service at the start of the VERDUN battle in February 1916. Most were two-seaters for observation or reconnaissance, backed by only 135 serving fighters (mostly NIEUPORT 11s) and 188 bombers (mostly Voisins).

The Battles of Verdun and the SOMME forced both sides to reassess the numbers of aircraft needed and their combat roles. French fighter and bomber groups were deployed in progressively larger formations, culminating in the establishment of the first Air Division from April 1918. A formidable unit of some 600 aircraft, it could be assembled to provide air cover wherever needed and performed an important bombing role during the Second Battle of the MARNE.

Reorganization was not matched by technical superiority until late 1917, but the Aéronautique Militaire was never again short on quantity. From April 1917 effective strength was raised to 2,870 machines, comprising 60 fighter and 20 bomber squadrons (each of 15 planes), along with 100 reconnaissance, 40 observation and 8 special purpose squadrons (10 aircraft each). A total of 3,222 aircraft, along with thousands of reserve and training machines, were available by the ARMISTICE. Frontline forces comprised 64 fighter, 15 day-bombing, 14 night-bombing, 124 ground-support/reconnaissance and 24 artillery-spotter squadrons, employing a total of 127,630 officers and men, more than 12,000 of them trained aircrew.

New French and British fighters, like the SPAD S-XIII and SOPWITH CAMEL, led the way in establishing operational superiority on the Western Front by early 1918. Merger of the Army's procurement and technical departments at about the same time encouraged improved aircraft production (close to 100 per day by November) and allowed obsolete designs to be retired en masse. Aided by comparable development of the British RFC, the Aéronautique Militaire enjoyed almost absolute dominance of French airspace by the autumn, and although units fought on the ITALIAN and BALKAN FRONTS, and in French colonies, the Western Front was always its main concern. See also: ACES; CIGOGNES; LAFAYETTE.

Afghanistan Muslim buffer state between British INDIA and the Russian Empire, under constant pressure to concede dominant influence to one or the other for most of the 19th-century. Regular wars with Afghan tribesmen, the last in the early 1880s, had left the Indian government permanently concerned for security on its northwest frontier with Afghanistan and neighbouring PERSIA, and fear of an opportunistic uprising acted as a brake on INDIAN ARMY commitment to campaigns in AFRICA and on the MESOPOTAMIAN FRONT.

British agreement with the ruler, Amir Habibulla Khan, secured neutrality in return for guarantees to protect Afghanistan's postwar independence, but was threatened by internal unrest after Muslim TURKEY joined the CENTRAL POWERS in November 1914. A German–Turkish diplomatic mission reached the capital, Kabul, in September 1915, avoiding RUSSIAN ARMY units in the north of the country and encouraging dissident support for an anti-British alliance.

Habibulla prolonged negotiations with the Germans and Turks until May 1916, but demanded impossible levels of material aid, and kept Allied authorities well informed. He subsequently maintained a generally peaceful balance of factional interests, and unrest on the Indian northwest frontier was restricted to minor local uprisings. The British government honoured its agreement by publicly affirming Afghan independence in early 1919, but Habibulla's claim to representation at the PARIS PEACE CONFERENCE was refused and his murder in February, possibly by his brother, triggered a decade of civil war.

Africa, Wars in (1914–18) Most wartime military action in Africa reflected inter-European colonial rivalries, centring on Allied campaigns against the four German African colonies of TOGOLAND, CAMEROON, SOUTH-WEST AFRICA and German EAST AFRICA, the latter still underway at the ARMISTICE. Much of the continent had come under European control during the 'scramble for Africa' in the later 19th century, a period characterized by native uprising and European suppression. Many colonial administrators in the most recently acquired central African belt were still preoccupied with the threat of tribal revolt in 1914, and sought unsuccessfully to prevent European warfare in the region on conventional white supremacist grounds (see BERLIN ACT).

Although European or Turkish agents frequently worked to stir up revolt in enemy-controlled territories, the feared collapse of white authority in central Africa never took place, and tribal groups served both sides in the European conflicts (giving rise to a wealth of white fantasies about cannibalism and magic). A few minor rebellions erupted, notably in German East Africa (British-sponsored), the SUDAN (Turkish-sponsored) and the Belgian Congo, but were easily quashed.

The most serious internal dispute took place between white colonists in SOUTH AFRICA, where the BOER REVOLT took on the features of a civil war in late 1914. The biggest 'tribal' challenge to European dominance came in the more developed northeast, where German and Turkish support for Muslim SENUSSI attacks on British EGYPT, French Sahara and Italian Tripolitania kept Allied troops busy into 1917.

Operations against the Senussi distracted a portion of British strength from the early campaigns on the PALESTINE FRONT, and the global theatre of NAVAL WARFARE embraced Africa's ports, RAILWAYS and trading arrangements. Destruction of German RADIO stations, used to contact GERMAN NAVY commerce raiders, was the prime motive behind Allied invasions of the German colonies in 1914. Otherwise the continent's only impact on wider strategic issues was as a drain on Allied manpower and resources.

In the absence of other strategic needs for African conquests, every bullet and man-hour expended can be viewed as a loss to more important theatres, and this was the rationale behind German commander LETTOW-VORBECK's tactically brilliant East African defence. On the other hand three of the German colonies had been conquered by early 1916, and the impact of British commitment to East Africa probably extended no further than a marginal reduction of strength in other strategically dubious SIDESHOWS.

Begun as a battle between colonial forces and extended by the INDIAN ARMY, the East African campaign was later carried out almost exclusively by native African troops (local ASKARIS and regular British imperial forces) and white colonial volunteers. SOUTH AFRICAN and RHODESIAN forces were not prevented from contributing to the wider imperial war effort, and relatively few British soldiers took part. Black troops – generally reliable, durable and invaluable in African conditions – were correspondingly ineffective in European theatres.

The equipment used by colonial forces was generally obsolete, and the drain on first-line Allied small arms and ARTILLERY resources was negligible. Apart from immensely valuable ARMOURED CARS, modern technology was scarce in the African wars. British warships, mostly old and on station around Africa regardless of land wars, were joined by MONITORS and aircraft in the RUFUGI DELTA for a time in 1915, and an RFC squadron of fairly modern BE-2C two-seaters began operations in East Africa during early 1916. Much was expected of aircraft but they achieved very little in African conditions, proving unreliable in tropical heat and too slow for effective reconnaissance or ground-attack work over terrain thick with cover.

French, Belgian and Portuguese forces in Africa received no extensive support from their respective governments, and the Allied maritime BLOCKADE rendered German assistance to its colonies virtually impossible. A single supply ship got through to East Africa in April 1916, and a ZEPPELIN (L-59) broke the world flight endurance record in a failed 1918 attempt to reach Lettow-Vorbeck, but the most effective German supply operation remained the loss of the light CRUISER *Königsberg*, stripped of weapons and valuables by Lettow-Vorbeck's forces in 1915.

Though it made little difference to the result in Europe, the mutual impact of white or Asian troops and the African continent had an enormous effect on both, especially in East Africa, where British imperial forces had lost 341 casualties to disease for every one suffered in battle by July 1916. Indian and European personnel suffered equally, and 12,000 men were evacuated due to sickness in the period October–December 1916 alone.

Malaria was the biggest danger, affecting almost every soldier in the field to some degree and flourishing amid British shortage or misapplication of quinine. A huge variety of other diseases transmitted by insects, food or water included typhoid (against which some British troops were inoculated), guinea worm, amoebic dysentery and 'chiggers', a form of mass flea infestation that ate away the feet of its many victims. Sleeping sickness from the tsetse fly affected humans but was above all the major killer of animals. The East African campaign claimed 19,000 horses, 11,000 oxen, 10,000 mules and 2,500 donkeys in British service.

Colonial coastal medical facilities were generally as efficient as could be expected, but inland hospitals in East Africa were overwhelmed by shortages of nurses and sheer numbers of patients. German forces suffered less from sickness though losses were still heavy, with doctors and medicines in desperately short supply from late 1916. Reasons cited for their relative good health include: superior appreciation of personal sanitation (a trait also cited as protecting many older British troops); fuller use of native and invented remedies; the practice of leaving the sick to be cared for by the British; and the provision of more bearers for European and native troops than were available for British forces.

Uncounted thousands of bearers served forces in every African campaign, and most military formations were accompanied by several for each combat soldier, often along with their families. The social effects of large-scale contact with white culture are difficult to quantify, but tribes all over central Africa certainly learned a great deal about Europeans in a short time, not all of it entirely representative (see NAVAL AFRICA EXPEDITION). Economic upheaval, in the form of artificial war booms (as experienced in the Sudan, South Africa and Egypt) or the devastation of fertile East African croplands, was more obvious.

The immediate geopolitical repercussions of the African campaigns were predictable: all four German colonies were partitioned among the victorious Allies as MANDATES, although much private property returned to German ownership after being sold on by intermediaries. See MAPS 17, 18.

Ago C-Types Series of German reconnaissance biplanes, distinguished as one of the few 'PUSHER' designs used by the GERMAN ARMY AIR SERVICE and recognizable by the twin booms connecting tail unit and forward nacelle. Never used in any quantity, they were employed on the WESTERN FRONT from mid-1915 until replaced by the heavier, aerodynamically modified C-II at the end of the year. The C-II, also produced in a floatplane version for coastal defence work with the GERMAN NAVY, was joined by a few slightly streamlined C-IIIs before they were withdrawn in the summer of 1917.

BRIEF DATA (C-II) Type: two-seater reconnaissance; Engine: 220hp Benz; Max speed: 136kph; Ceiling: 4,000m; Armament: 1 × 7.92mm mg.

Ahwaz Small town in western PERSIA, close to the Ottoman border and site of a pumping station vital to the Abadan oil pipeline (see

MAP 23). Protection of Abadan, which provided most of the ROYAL NAVY's oil supplies, was the main task of Anglo-Indian forces on the MESOPOTAMIAN FRONT. In late January 1915 the pipeline was cut by saboteurs and a combined Arab–Turkish force crossed the border from Amara towards Ahwaz. Under pressure from London, the Indian Government sent 3,000 reinforcements to Mesopotamia specifically to secure the town, but pending their arrival a small force from BASRA was dispatched up the River Karun to Ahwaz in mid-February. It was ambushed by Arab–Turkish forces already occupying the hinterland around the town, and the reinforcements sent to its rescue were unable to coerce increasingly hostile local tribespeople into operating the pumping station. The British held off sporadic attacks from about 8,000 Turkish and tribal troops until early May, when the arrival of a strong relief force under General Gorringe prompted their withdrawal into Mesopotamia. Although supply shortages (especially of drinking water) forced Gorringe to cut short punitive measures against local tribes, the pumping station reopened and the bulk of his force returned east to join General NIXON's renewed offensives towards AMARA and NASIRIYEH.

Airco DH-1 British two-seat PUSHER biplane, designed to give the forward observer/gunner maximum field of fire. It joined the RFC as a FIGHTER and reconnaissance craft from mid-1915. A sturdy machine, faster and more manoeuvrable than the FE-2B, it lacked the armament or power to combat contemporary German fighters equipped with INTERRUPTER GEAR and was unsuitable for combat operations on the WESTERN FRONT. The 73 up-engined DH-1a models, built by various companies under licence, served as escort fighters in PALESTINE until mid-1917, and later with home defence units.

BRIEF DATA (DH-1a) Type: two-seater fighter/reconnaissance; Engine: 120hp Beardsmore; Max speed: 88mph (141kph); Ceiling: 4,100m; Armament: 1 × 0.303in mg.

Airco DH-2 British single-seat biplane, a smaller version of the earlier AIRCO DH-1 and similarly handicapped by its 'PUSHER' design. Designed for reconnaissance work in early 1915, before INTERRUPTER GEAR was available or the importance of air combat appreciated (see AERIAL WARFARE), the DH-2 was drafted into RFC units from February 1916 as a FIGHTER, armed with a fixed forward MACHINE GUN. Despite lack of speed and an unreliable engine, it was more manoeuvrable than German FOKKER E-TYPES on the WESTERN FRONT, and helped to establish Allied air supremacy over the SOMME in July. The organization of superior German HALBERSTADT and ALBATROS D-TYPES into combat groups (*Jagdstaffeln*) during the autumn doomed the DH-2 to obsolescence, but it remained in frontline service because nothing better was available, suffering heavy casualties during 'BLOODY APRIL', 1917. A few subsequently served in SALONIKA, in PALESTINE and with home defence units, but most surviving machines (of 300 used) were retired as trainers from mid-1917.

BRIEF DATA (DH-2) Type: single-seat fighter; Engine: 100hp Gnôme Monosoupape; Max speed: 90mph (144kph); Ceiling: 4,250m; Armament: 1 × 0.303in mg.

Airco DH-4 Versatile British day bomber delivered to RFC units on the WESTERN FRONT from March 1917. Agile, versatile, easy to fly and fast enough to operate without escort, the DH-4's most obvious weakness was the large distance between the pilot and observer cockpits, making communication almost impossible. Along with other new designs like the BRISTOL FIGHTER, it restored the viability of RFC two-seater squadrons on the Western Front in the early summer of 1917 (see 'BLOODY APRIL') and was standard equipment with the RFC and RNAS on all British fronts until the ARMISTICE.

DH-4s were also used for ARTILLERY spotting, PHOTO-RECONNAISSANCE and coastal patrol work, sometimes armed with DEPTH CHARGES. From mid-1918 they took part in long-range STRATEGIC BOMBING operations for the RAF, and a few were used by the RUSSIAN AIR SERVICE. A total of 1,449 British DH-4s were built by seven companies, using various engines up to 375hp (with a top speed of 230kph).

The DH-4a, a US-built version with a 400hp Liberty engine and standard four-gun defensive armament, was produced in even greater quantities, and 1,885 (of almost 5,000 built) served on the Western Front during autumn 1918, equipping 13 USAAS and four US NAVY bombing squadrons. Withdrawn from British service in 1919, the design remained standard US equipment well into the 1920s.

BRIEF DATA (DH-4, 1917) Type: two-seater day bomber; Engine: 250hp Rolls Royce; Max speed: 119mph (190kph); Ceiling: 4,850m; Armament: 2–3 × 0.303in mg (1 synchro), max bomb load 460lbs (210kg).

Airco DH-5 British biplane FIGHTER, developed in late 1916 as a replacement for the AIRCO DH-2. Fitted with INTERRUPTER GEAR, and with the upper wing staggered back to improve forward vision, it joined RFC squadrons on the WESTERN FRONT between May and October 1917. A tendency to crash on landing made it immediately unpopular with pilots, and inability to maintain performance at high altitudes limited its combat effectiveness. From August 1917 it was used as a ground-attack weapon, to which its rugged construction was well suited, and large numbers performed useful infantry support work during the YPRES and CAMBRAI attacks that year. About 550 were built, and later models were fitted with racks for four light bombs, but the type was withdrawn once SE-5s were available and the last had disappeared from France by January 1918.

BRIEF DATA Type: single-seat fighter/ground attack; Engine: 110hp Le Rhône; Max speed: 104mph (166kph); Ceiling: 4,850m; Armament: 1 × 0.303in mg, max bomb load 100lb.

Airco DH-9 British twin-engined bomber, a version of the AIRCO DH-4 design intended for long-range STRATEGIC BOMBING operations and ordered in response to raids on southern England by GOTHA bombers in 1917. In service with the RFC from March 1918, the type equipped nine squadrons on the WESTERN FRONT, served the RNAS as a coastal patrol craft and later flew long-range missions with the INDEPENDENT AIR FORCE. More than 3,200 were built, remaining in frontline service until the ARMISTICE, but they were not a success and suffered heavy losses. Despite installed RADIO equipment and improved cockpit layout, low operational ceiling made DH-9s vulnerable to attack, and unreliable engines caused more casualties than enemy action. A 400hp DH-9a version reached four squadrons in autumn 1918, and almost 900 had been built by December, but neither model ever fully replaced the DH-4.

BRIEF DATA (DH-9) Type: two-seater bomber; Engine: 2 × 230hp Bristol; Max speed: 112mph (179kph); Ceiling: 3,950m; Armament: 2 or 3 × 0.303in mg, max bomb load 460lbs (210kg).

Aircraft Carriers Aircraft carriers in the modern sense, navigable airbases with almost no visible superstructure, played no significant part in the First World War. Most vessels so described by contemporaries were aircraft tenders, capable of transporting and (eventually) launching aircraft but unsuitable for landings.

Use of aircraft aboard ships, pioneered in the prewar USA, was dominated by the British RNAS, which had first flown a seaplane from a moving ship in May 1912. The ROYAL NAVY's first seaplane tender, the old CRUISER *Hermes* (sunk by a TORPEDO in the English Channel in October 1914), was fitted with a downward-sloping take-off deck that proved too short for use. The converted collier *ARK ROYAL* was the first ship completed as a carrier, entering service in December 1914, but it invariably winched its seaplanes into and out of the water.

A number of fast passenger liners were converted as seaplane tenders from 1914 (see *ENGADINE*), and their participation in the CUXHAVEN RAID demonstrated the long-range potential of shipborne aircraft. Larger seaplane tenders (*CAMPANIA*, *Nairana* and *PEGASUS*) had entered British service by 1917, but their value was restricted by the poor performance of seaplanes in general, which could only take off from calm seas or very long flight decks, and were seldom able to intercept enemy aircraft or AIRSHIPS.

Deployment of wheeled aircraft aboard

ships was pioneered in the second half of 1916 using the Royal Navy's SOPWITH STRUTTER and SOPWITH PUP designs, which could take off quickly from short decks; the larger carriers were equipped with these planes from early 1917. After 1917 RNAS and RAF landplanes were carried aboard a wide variety of other ships for reconnaissance, ANTI-SUBMARINE, interception or bombing operations. They could be launched from short decks built onto the superstructures of most steamships, from the revolving turrets of large warships (enabling take-off into the wind without prior manoeuvre), or from 30-foot (9.1m) wooden platforms towed behind fast DESTROYERS.

These aircraft could not land back on their host ships and were usually forced to ditch in the sea, but British attempts to solve the problem ran into technical difficulties, and the landing deck of the twice-converted *FURIOUS* was never used operationally (see TONDERN RAID).

The first flush-decked carrier with efficient take-off and landing facilities, the former passenger liner *Argus*, had been under conversion since late 1916, but only entered British service in October 1918 and was still in trials at the ARMISTICE, by which time a new HMS *Hermes* was under construction, the first aircraft carrier purpose-designed from the keel up.

Although most major navies employed seaplane carriers (the FRENCH NAVY had five and the RUSSIAN NAVY operated six with its BLACK SEA fleet) no other aircraft carriers were under construction by the end of the War and the Royal Navy's dominance of the field was not challenged until the mid-1920s, when the USA and Japan embarked on major naval aviation programmes. See also: *WOLF*; *FOUDRE*.

Airships Powered lighter-than-air craft, as distinct from aeroplanes or BALLOONS, had been in military use since the 1880s. Pioneered in France, they were most enthusiastically developed in Germany, where large, rigid vessels were making regular military and commercial flights by 1914 (see ZEPPELINS, SCHÜTTE-LANZ). Although Germany used about 50 rigid ships for bombing and reconnaissance operations, most airships used by belligerents in wartime were of the non-rigid variety. Slow and vulnerable to attack or bad weather, they were occasionally employed on army observation duties (heavily protected by ANTI-AIRCRAFT weapons), but were primarily used by the major navies for long-range, high-altitude reconnaissance and SUBMARINE spotting. Non-rigid airships in British service were particularly successful as CONVOY escorts in 1917–18, and only one merchant ship was sunk by a U-BOAT while under their protection (see SEA SCOUT; COASTAL CLASS AIRSHIPS).

Aisne, First Battle of the A series of Allied attacks on new defensive positions established by the GERMAN ARMY's right wing on the WESTERN FRONT after the First Battle of the MARNE in September 1914. Although the heaviest fighting took place on the Aisne, continuous combat was in progress further east as TRENCH WARFARE developed between French and German armies contesting the line from Reims to the Swiss border.

Slow Allied pursuit from the Marne, a product of exhaustion and caution, gave the German First and Second Armies time to deploy along the north bank of the Aisne, a tributary of the Oise protected by the long, natural fortress of the Chemin des Dames Ridge. They were in position by 13 September, and the dangerous gap between them was filled by a new Seventh Army (von Heeringen).

The French Fifth and Sixth Armies, with the BEF between them, reached the Aisne on the same day, and attempted a frontal assault on the high ground across the river. Pontoon crossings under heavy fire won the Sixth Army a single bridgehead, and further frontal attacks the next day gained a little ground, until a German counterattack, supported by heavy ARTILLERY fire, drove the French back to the river.

Fighting along the Aisne continued until 28 September, but Allied attacks were scaled down from 18 September, by which time German pressure on the French Ninth Army to the east was becoming serious. The futility of frontal infantry assaults on good defensive positions was recognized by both sides and both attempted to manoeuvre north into areas not already occupied by armies, triggering a phase of mutual outflanking known as the 'RACE TO THE SEA'.

Aisne, Second Battle of the Main action, also called the Chemin des Dames Offensive, of the Allied NIVELLE OFFENSIVE on the WESTERN FRONT in spring 1917. A massed assault by French forces on German positions along the River Aisne between Soissons and Reims (see MAP 2), it incorporated a simultaneous secondary attack east of Reims, itself sometimes known as the Third Champagne Offensive. The battle was an almost unrelieved French disaster; it ruined the career of its instigator, French C-in-C NIVELLE, and triggered MUTINY in the FRENCH ARMY.

From its inception in December 1916, the Nivelle Offensive suffered delay and disruption, and the vital element of surprise was lost long before the attack on the Aisne began. Detailed plans of the operation, widely available to French officers, had been captured weeks earlier, confirming a threat heavily implied by the assembly of more than a million French troops, and a 10-day PRELIMINARY BOMBARDMENT.

The main attack of 16 April, by 19 divisions of the French Fifth and Sixth Armies (Generals Mazel and MANGIN) along an 80km front from Soissons to Reims, achieved only negligible gains at enormous cost. The German Seventh Army (von Boehm), heavily reinforced and occupying fortified high ground, inflicted an estimated 40,000 casualties on the first day, and knocked out 150 French TANKS. East of Reims, the French Fourth Army (ANTHOINE) attacked towards Moronvilliers on 17 April, but fared little better against General Fritz von Below's First Army. In both attacks, French supporting ARTILLERY failed to deliver an efficient CREEPING BARRAGE, Nivelle's main tactical innovation.

Full-scale French attacks continued until 20 April, with reserves bringing Nivelle's total commitment to 1.2 million men and 7,000 guns. Although limited gains were achieved, particularly by Mangin's left wing west of Soissons, they were costly and in no way matched expectations. All hope of a major breakthrough having disappeared, attacks were scaled down over the next two weeks. Slow progress continued, and a 4km stretch of Chemin des Dames Ridge, part of the HINDENBURG LINE system, had been secured by 5 May.

Political disillusion, signalled by the cautious PÉTAIN's appointment as chief of staff on 25 April, was completed by the failure of a final large-scale offensive. Halted on 9 May after four days of fruitless attacks, it brought total casualties to almost 355,000 men, of whom 187,000 were French, and Nivelle lost his job within a week. See also: Battle of ARRAS.

Aisne, Third Battle of the Third phase of the German SPRING OFFENSIVES on the WESTERN FRONT in 1918, and the last major attempt to end the War before significant US forces could mass in France, launched after the LYS OFFENSIVE in Flanders had lost momentum at the end of April. Effective German C-in-C LUDENDORFF still believed that attacks in the north offered the best hope of decisive success, and the switch south was intended to draw French reserves away from Flanders.

The first target of the attack was Chemin des Dames Ridge, won at enormous cost during the NIVELLE OFFENSIVE in 1917 and defended by the French Sixth Army (Duchêne). The advance began in the small hours of 27 May, after a 4,000-gun PRELIMINARY BOMBARDMENT, striking four weakened British divisions sent from Flanders for recuperation. Their commander, General Hamilton Gordon, expected an attack but could not persuade Army Group commander FRANCHET D'ESPERAY to adopt DEFENCE IN DEPTH tactics, and troops massed in forward positions with their backs to the Aisne were taken by surprise.

Artillery decimated overpopulated first-line TRENCHES and defending guns were disabled with GAS attacks before 17 divisions of Crown Prince WILHELM's Southern Army Group advanced through a 40km gap in the Allied line. The surviving defenders were compelled to retreat beyond the Aisne without destroying its bridges, and by evening German forces were at the River Vesle, about 15km beyond their start line.

German offensive momentum was maintained over the next week. By 30 May, the advance had taken some 50,000 prisoners and 800 guns, and by 3 June it had reached the Marne, 90km from Paris and apparently close to complete victory. Exhaustion, supply problems and Allied counterattacks made further progress impossible, and the offensive petered out completely on 6 June, with German forces established along a narrow but defensible front (see Battle of BELLEAU WOOD).

The defeat cost the FRENCH ARMY 98,000 men, as well as costing almost 29,000 BEF casualties, prompting an atmosphere of acute crisis in FRANCE and swift reaction from the CLEMENCEAU government. Duchêne lost his job. Franchet d'Esperay was transferred to SALONIKA, and the appointment of General GUILLAUMAT to command the Paris defences was an implicit threat to C-in-C PÉTAIN, whose subordination to Allied Supreme Commander FOCH was confirmed by the latter's promotion.

Despite relatively light German casualties and a pace of advance not witnessed in the theatre since 1914, the victory had only partly succeeded in drawing Allied forces away from Flanders. The long bulge forced in the Allied line, some 60km across at its start, tapered to a 15km front around Château-Thierry in the west, leaving advanced German units exposed to counterattack. Preparations were in hand by early June for the German Eighteenth Army (HUTIER) to attack north of the new SALIENT, as a means of widening it and as another preliminary to operations in Flanders (see Battle of the MATZ). See MAP 9.

Aitken, Sir W. Maxwell (1879–1964) Canadian financier resident in London and a Conservative member of Parliament since his retirement from business in 1910. Politically well connected, he served as a journalist with CANADIAN FORCES on the WESTERN FRONT from early 1915, becoming their official records officer in May and the Canadian government's representative in FRANCE from 1916. Personally close to LLOYD GEORGE, he was ennobled (as Baron Beaverbrook) in 1917 and appointed minister of information on 10 February 1918.

Beaverbrook's energetic ministry undertook the first coordinated British PROPAGANDA programme. Responsible for disseminating war information to the home front, Allied nations and neutrals, he commissioned celebrated artists for poster campaigns, and writers (including Kipling and Wells) to provide stories and slogans for newspapers and leaflets. He made extensive use of FILM on the home front, pioneering photographic posters and introducing cinema newsreels.

Close collaboration with Lord NORTHCLIFFE, Director of Propaganda in Enemy Countries, enabled millions of his leaflets to be dropped over German lines, but consequent disputes with the Foreign Office over jurisdiction provoked his resignation in October 1918. After the war he used his ownership of several newspapers to advocate British imperial unity, and returned to wartime politics in 1940, serving in a number of economic ministries under Winston CHURCHILL.

Albania Southern Balkan region governed as a loosely affiliated province of the Ottoman Empire until granted independence as a Muslim principality in July 1913, following TURKEY's defeat in the Balkan Wars. Albania's sovereign status and territorial integrity remained under pressure from expansionist GREECE to the south, SERBIA to the north and ITALY across the Adriatic (see MAP 1).

Chaotic internal politics, with three separate governments demanding recognition by early 1914, prompted an internationally sponsored attempt to impose order by placing Austro-Hungarian client Prince William of Wied on the throne. Former Turkish governor Essad Pasha, the last internationally recognized authority in the region, became war minister but made his own bid for power shortly after the new king's arrival in March 1914, establishing uncertain control in the centre of the region after William fled the country in September.

Serbian occupation of northern Albania was ended by the Austro-Hungarian autumn offensives on the BALKAN FRONT in 1915, and the CENTRAL POWERS also gained nominal control of Essad's province by the end of the year, forcing his flight to SALONIKA. The GREEK ARMY held the south until its retirement in 1916, but the ITALIAN NAVY had occupied the port of Valona in 1915 and the AUSTRO-HUNGARIAN NAVY took possession of Durazzo, the main central port, so that the coast formed a MEDITERRANEAN naval frontier until 1918 (see 'GREAT RETREAT').

Local warlords retained effective control of central Albania. Some accepted Austro-Hungarian patronage and engaged in guerrilla attacks on Italian units around Valona, but no credible overall Albanian leadership had emerged by late 1918, when the Central Powers withdrew. Italian units remained in Albania after the ARMISTICE, but were unable to suppress renewed guerrilla activity and withdrew in 1920. An attack by forces of the new YUGOSLAVIA was defeated by guerrillas in the mountains later in the year, and the appointment of a 'regency council' to govern the country in 1921 temporarily settled Albania's independent future to Italian, Greek and Yugoslav satisfaction.

Albatros B-Types German series of reconnaissance biplanes that were in service in August 1914 as B-I and B-II versions, the latter slightly smaller and adaptable to various engines. Reliable and durable but unarmed, they were the mainstays of the GERMAN ARMY AIR SERVICE in 1914. They served throughout the EASTERN and WESTERN FRONTS, and were joined in 1915 by a small number of 120hp B-IIIs, which had a redesigned tail. Replaced by armed ALBATROS C-TYPES during mid-1915, they remained in use as trainers until the ARMISTICE.

BRIEF DATA (B-II) Type: two-seater reconnaissance/general purpose; Engine: 100hp or 120hp Mercedes; Max speed: 105kph; Ceiling: 3,000m; Armament: observer's small arms.

Albatros C-I and C-III German C-Type (armed two-seater) aircraft were introduced to frontline units from spring 1915, when attacks by Allied scout planes had rendered unarmed craft obsolete. The Albatros C-I, among the first of the new type to appear, was a 160hp (or 180hp) development of the earlier ALBATROS B-II, with the observer moved to the back seat and equipped with a MACHINE GUN. Strong and reliable, it was a standard reconnaissance and ARTILLERY-spotting tool with GERMAN ARMY AIR SERVICE field units during 1915, and also performed occasional light bombing raids.

C-Is remained in service on the WESTERN FRONT until late 1916, and until 1917 on the EASTERN FRONT, but were gradually supplanted by the improved C-III from 1916. Aerodynamically improved and derived from the B-III design, it performed similar duties in greater numbers, serving on the Western, Eastern and BALKAN FRONTS into early 1917 before it too was replaced by the completely new ALBATROS C-V. Out-performed by single-seat FIGHTERS, the C-III's greatest asset was its ability to keep flying after taking heavy punishment. Dual-control versions of both types were produced as trainers from 1917.

BRIEF DATA (C-III) Type: two-seater reconnaissance; Engine: 160hp Mercedes; Max speed: 141kph; Armament: 1 × 7.92mm mg, max bomb load 200lb (90kg).

Albatros C-V to C-XII German series of armed reconnaissance biplanes designed from scratch in 1916 to replace the ALBATROS C-III. The first production C-Vs had a sleek, torpedo-like fuselage to accommodate a new 220hp Mercedes engine, giving a top speed of 170kph. Fitted with forward and rear MACHINE GUNS, its engine proved unreliable and it suffered acute handling difficulties. A modified C-V/17 version, introduced in 1917, solved some of the aerodynamic problems, but the design was dropped at the end of the year when production of the Mercedes engine was abandoned. Although 424 C-Vs were built, casualties and breakdowns kept serving numbers on the WESTERN FRONT below 70 at any given time.

A successor, the C-VII, was also in action from 1916, its fuselage modified to take a less controversial 200hp engine. It was much easier to fly, but armament and performance were similar to the C-V. One of the most common and successful German types on the

Western Front in early 1917, the C-VII was gradually supplanted by the C-X – essentially an expanded, up-engined model – during the second half of the year. More than 300 C-VII or C-X machines were in action at any given time between late 1916 and mid-1918, and both were built by several companies under licence. Generally used for reconnaissance or ARTILLERY spotting, and for occasional light bombing or ground support, they were joined by the more streamlined (but otherwise similar) C-XII during the last months of the War.

BRIEF DATA (C-X) Type: two-seat reconnaissance/general purpose; Engine: 260hp Mercedes; Max speed: 176kph; Ceiling: 5,000m; Armament: 2 × 7.92mm mg, light bombs.

Albatros D-I and D-II The first of a German FIGHTER series that set new standards for air combat when it appeared in autumn 1916, and vitally influenced the air war over the WESTERN FRONT. A beautifully streamlined biplane, it was produced as the D-I from August 1916, at which time Allied fighters had established combat superiority over available German FOKKER E-TYPES and HALBERSTADT D-TYPES. The GERMAN ARMY AIR SERVICE was being reorganized to create specialist fighter units (*Jagdstaffeln*), and the D-I flew with these from mid-September, its twin MACHINE GUNS and fast climb-rate restoring German dominance over France within a few weeks.

The D-I's only weakness was its poor upward visibility, corrected by lowering the top wing of the D-II model, which took over production at an early stage. Built in large numbers, it remained the best German fighter in France until the improved ALBATROS D-III arrived the following January. Some D-IIs were produced under licence by the LVG company in Germany, and twenty 185hp models were manufactured in Austria for the AUSTRO-HUNGARIAN AIR SERVICE.

BRIEF DATA (D-II) Type: single-seat fighter; Engine: 160hp Mercedes; Max speed: 174kph; Ceiling: 5,150m; Armament: 2 × 7.92mm mg (forward).

Albatros D-III An improved version of the ALBATROS D-II that reached German combat units in France during January 1917, before Allied designers had come up with a convincing response to its predecessor. The wings and tail were substantially modified to produce even faster climbing speed, and downward vision was assisted by using the 'V' strutting employed in Nieuport designs. Its only real failing was a weakness at the foot of the strut (previously suffered by the NIEUPORT 11) that occasionally caused the lower wing to disintegrate, but it was popular with pilots and maintained a high combat success rate until the arrival of new Allied types from May 1917. Up to 500 D-IIIs were active on the WESTERN FRONT at any time during the rest of 1917, and they were used on the BALKAN and PALESTINE FRONTS. Austrian-built versions, fitted with various Austro-Daimler engines, remained with the AUSTRO-HUNGARIAN AIR SERVICE until the ARMISTICE.

BRIEF DATA (D-III) As for D-II, except: Ceiling: 5,500m.

Albatros D-V The last Albatros FIGHTER design to see widespread service, the D-V was introduced to squadrons on the WESTERN FRONT in May 1917. Given a slightly rounder fuselage, greater streamlining and a bigger engine, the design was approaching the limits of its potential, and barely outperformed its predecessor at a time when Allied SOPWITH PUP, SOPWITH TRIPLANE, SE-5 and SPAD S-VII fighters had forced German combat units onto the defensive. Retained largely because the only viable alternative before mid-1918 (the FOKKER DR-1 triplane) was regarded as unreliable, it was used in large numbers alongside D-Va versions with modified control cables, seeing action on the Western, ITALIAN and PALESTINE FRONTS until the ARMISTICE. A total of 1,512 D-V/Va models were supplied to German forces, but total production figures for Albatros fighters are unknown. Estimates are complicated by the mass redesignation of Albatros machines in post war GERMANY, carried out to circumvent prohibition of warplanes imposed by the Treaty of VERSAILLES.

BRIEF DATA (D-V) Type: single-seat fighter; Engine: 180hp Mercedes; Max speed: 187kph; Ceiling: 6,200m; Armament: 2 × 7.92mm mg (forward).

Albatros J-Types German ground-attack biplanes, introduced to the WESTERN FRONT in late 1917 and intended to replace the stopgap AEG J-TYPE in the role. A development of earlier ALBATROS C-TYPE designs, with armour plate protecting the pilot and forward MACHINE GUNS firing down through the fuselage, the J-I was slow, cumbersome and difficult to fly, but was an effective trench-fighting weapon. Its main weakness, a lack of armour around the engine, was remedied in the 1918 J-II model, but both were difficult to build and only limited numbers joined the assorted strength of GERMAN ARMY AIR SERVICE infantry-support units.
BRIEF DATA (J-I) Type: two-seater ground support; Engine: 200hp Benz; Max speed: 139kph; Armament: 3 × 7.92mm mg.

Albatros W-4 German seaplane FIGHTER, a big-winged relative of the ALBATROS D-I that entered service in September 1916. Reliable and reasonably fast despite its bulky floats, it joined coastal units in Flanders and in the Adriatic and was in frontline service until gradually replaced by the bigger HANSA-BRANDENBURG W-XII in late 1917. Production was halted in December 1917, and 108 machines were built.
BRIEF DATA Type: single-seat floatplane fighter; Engine: 160hp Mercedes; Max speed: 160kph; Ceiling: 3,000m; Armament: 1 or 2 × 7.92mm mg (forward).

Alberich, Operation Planned German withdrawal to HINDENBURG LINE positions on the WESTERN FRONT between Arras and Soissons in spring 1917 (see MAPS 2, 3). Ordered on 9 February and begun on 21 February, it continued to 31 March and was cautiously pursued through unseasonal blizzards by Allied forces. The retirement disrupted Allied preparations for the NIVELLE OFFENSIVE, forcing a major supply and transportation operation to new forward positions, hindered by a German 'scorched earth' policy that left broken terrain devoid of resources and riddled with booby traps.

Albert I, King (1875–1934) Constitutional ruler of BELGIUM since the death of Leopold II in 1909, his military competence and sense of vocation contrasted starkly with his father's infamous corruption. Albert had no illusions about German plans to violate Belgian neutrality, but was obliged to refuse military aid from overseas until an invasion actually took place. With no direct peacetime control over internal defence, he was unable to dissuade army chiefs from grouping the small BELGIAN ARMY in the centre of the country (see LIÈGE; NAMUR).

Albert's commitment to fighting the German invasion reflected concern for Belgian national survival, as did his subsequent decision to withdraw the Army, first to ANTWERP and then west along the coast to Flanders (see Battle of YSER). The future sovereignty of Belgium was his guiding preoccupation after 1914, and he consciously played the role of injured nonaggressor from his temporary capital at Le Havre.

Distancing himself from Allied controversies over war aims, he remained hopeful of a compromise peace and avoided committing his army to Allied offensives on the WESTERN FRONT until 1918. His interest in peace with the CENTRAL POWERS hardened from late 1917, but was restrained by solid cabinet opposition and had evaporated by mid-1918.

Albert commanded the Allied Flanders Group of armies during the COURTRAI offensive of autumn 1918, and re-entered Brussels on 22 November, subsequently instigating limited reform of the Belgian constitution to equalize the civil rights of Flemish citizens. He remained generally popular throughout his kingdom and was mourned as a national hero after his death in a climbing accident. See also: HYMANS, P.; BROQUEVILLE, C. De.

Albert, First Battle of Inconclusive engagement, fought from 25 to 29 September 1914, that formed part of the 'RACE TO THE SEA' on the WESTERN FRONT. As the First Battle of the AISNE was petering out, General DE CASTLEN-

AU's French Second Army was transferred northwest from the LORRAINE sector to meet the threat of German northward moves to the Somme region. Deploying around Noyon, de Castlenau launched a frontal attack on German positions on 25 September, but was driven back by strong counterattacks and retreated beyond the town, holding off further attacks while a new Tenth Army was formed to repeat the attempt further north (See First Battle of ARRAS). See also: MAP 2.

Albert, Second Battle of Second phase of the successful Allied counteroffensive on the WESTERN FRONT begun at AMIENS in August 1918, an advance on the small town of Albert by the British Third (BYNG) and Fourth (RAWLINSON) Armies from 21 August (see MAP 2). After repeated frontal assaults against the German Second Army (MARWITZ) had failed to exploit initial Allied successes at Amiens, BEF commander HAIG planned an attempt to cut off Marwitz's well-entrenched line by attacking less heavily defended positions just to the north. Supreme Allied Commander FOCH resisted the idea until 15 August, by which time direct advance from the Amiens line had become manifestly impossible.

A small-scale German withdrawal on 14 August proved no more than a line-straightening exercise, and the THIRD SUPREME COMMAND's general orders instructed Western Front units to hold forward positions, reflecting its concern with territorial occupation as a counter in diplomatic bargaining

The British Third Army began its advance along a narrow front in heavy mist at dawn on 21 August, led by TANKS on relatively firm ground and supported by massed aircraft. Strictly limited in its original aims, the attack paused that afternoon after a short advance against determined rearguards in sweltering heat, and spent the next day repelling repeated German counterattacks while the British Fourth Army to the south was brought up to take Albert.

Byng and Rawlinson pushed forward towards Bâpaume on 23 August, taking 8,000 prisoners along a 55km front and forcing the German Second Army into full retreat. By the end of the day, extreme heat had reduced many of the attackers (especially tank crews) to exhaustion, but cooler, cloudy weather made further advance easier for the next two days. British forces reached the outskirts of Bapâume on 26 August, just as the British First Army to the north opened its supporting offensive on the SCARPE, and the battle officially ended with the town's occupation on 29 August. Further advances along the front over the next four days, known as the Battle of Bapâume, pushed British forces up to the CANAL DU NORD and ST QUENTIN CANAL sectors of the HINDENBURG LINE.

Albion, Operation The final German attempt to break through the IRBEN STRAITS into the Bay of Riga. It took the form of an amphibious attack on the BALTIC islands of Ösel and Moon, and began on 11 October 1917. One of the largest wartime joint military and naval operations, planned after the capture of RIGA in early September, it aimed to surround RUSSIAN NAVY warships in the Bay by cutting their only practical escape route, through the Moon Sound to the Gulf of Finland (see MAP 16).

About 20,000 troops, 5,000 horses and 60 ARTILLERY pieces were to land at several points on the north and west coasts of Ösel, and to cut off the northern shore of the Irben Straits. The huge supporting naval force, largely drawn from the HIGH SEAS FLEET in the North Sea, included a BATTLECRUISER, 10 modern BATTLESHIPS, 9 light cruisers, about 180 smaller warships; 6 AIRSHIPS and more than 100 GERMAN NAVY aircraft were also deployed. Once the Straits had been cleared, this force was to proceed to Moon and block the Russian escape.

In addition to a proliferation of minefieds, the Straits were protected by two old Russian battleships (*SLAVA* and *Cesarevic*), three cruisers, several dozen smaller ships, three British SUBMARINES and about 50 aircraft (including a few NIEUPORT 11s). Although the overland attack was expected, naval defences were concentrated against attempts to force the Straits themselves.

In theory more than 13,000 RUSSIAN ARMY troops were available to defend the islands, but depleted, ill-equipped units put up little serious resistance to the landings on 11 October. Several warships were damaged by MINES in the process of silencing shore batteries, but German troops rapidly occupied most of Ösel.

After several days of skirmishing around working minesweepers, German warships led by the dreadnought *KÖNIG* were able to penetrate the Straits and proceed slowly east towards southern Moon. Russian ships maintained a harrying campaign that slowed its advance to a crawl, and Russian commander Admiral Bachirev retreated successfully into the narrow Moon Sound on 17 October, scuttling the crippled *Slava* and several steamers as blockships in its entrance.

Most of the Russian troops on Moon and nearby Dagö Island were successfully evacuated over the next two days, before the whole Russian fleet, preceded by its minesweepers, steamed from Moon for its home bases on the afternoon of 19 October. The German occupation of all three islands was completed next day.

Albrecht, Duke of Württemberg (1865–1939) Unspectacular but successful German commander on the WESTERN FRONT. In keeping with the GERMAN ARMY's tradition of royal leadership, he led the Fourth Army through the ARDENNES in August 1914 and advanced to the eastern reaches of the MARNE by September. His army transferred north to Flanders during the 'RACE TO THE SEA' in October, and spearheaded the major German offensives around YPRES of 1914 and 1915 (see GAS). Promoted field marshal in August 1916, he took command of Army Group Albrecht the following February, and supervised the quiet southern stretch of the front closest to his home until just before the ARMISTICE. Deprived of his royal inheritance by the GERMAN REVOLUTIONS, he retired to his castle in 1921.

Alcohol Alcohol came under wartime attack in all belligerent states, both as a means of maintaining labour efficiency, especially among highly paid munitions workers, and in order to preserve resources for use as foodstuffs. The most sweeping measures were taken in imperial RUSSIA, where all production and sale of vodka was outlawed in August 1914. A characteristic own goal, the measure was unpopular, wiped out 30 per cent of the government's tax revenue at a stroke and stimulated an already flourishing cottage production industry into a black-market-led boom. In GREAT BRITAIN, FRANCE and ITALY, consumption was discouraged by energetic PROPAGANDA campaigns designed to improve labour output, counteract the clear growth in public excess, and increase food production. Restrictions on bar opening hours were reinforced by diversion of resources from the wine and pastis industries in France, and the use of whisky distilleries for manufacture of explosives in Britain. Although French restraints were dropped at the first opportunity, some British measures are still in force in the 1990s. Food shortages in GERMANY prompted ERSATZ beer production and a steady reduction in the alcohol content of the real thing, applied less severely in Bavaria than elsewhere, but general unavailability operated as effective interdiction from 1917. In AUSTRIA-HUNGARY attempts were made in both monarchies to curb consumption but had little practical effect on shortage in Austria or plenty in Hungary. Alcohol was already a hot sociopolitical issue in the UNITED STATES, which authorized PROHIBITION in 1918 but delayed enactment until 1920. In Muslim TURKEY, where alcohol consumption was forbidden to much of the population, non-Muslim elements doubled their consumption in the two years to 1916, and a slight fall in 1917 was due to production failure rather than government intervention.

Aleppo, Capture of The final, relatively cautious, British–Arab advance on the PALESTINE FRONT in October 1918. Aleppo, 400km north of DAMASCUS, guarded central TURKEY and RAILWAY links with the MESOPOTAMIAN FRONT. Eight Turkish divisions were nominally in position for the defence of a line west from Aleppo to the Mediterranean coast at Alexandretta, where German units were stationed for easy evacuation. Most contained only a few hundred combat troops and total strength was probably less than 20,000 men, with only about 3,000 in the Aleppo area. (See MAP 22.)

Amid rumours of an imminent Turkish armistice, and with troops weakened by malaria and INFLUENZA after contact with insanitary Turkish TRENCHES, British C-in-C ALLENBY attempted no large-scale operation. An infantry division occupied the small port of Beirut in early October, before moving north along the coast, and a reduced cavalry division was sent to the railway town of Homs, halfway to Aleppo. Joined by a similar number of Northern Arab Army troops on 16 October (see ARAB REVOLT), it received Allenby's permission to attack the town four days later and was ready by 24 October.

Before an attack could be launched, civil unrest in Aleppo and a false rumour of 20,000 Arab troops approaching the town prompted Turkish withdrawal north during the night of 25 September. The last serious engagement of the war in Palestine was fought next day, when 3,000 troops under Mustapha KEMAL held a cavalry brigade northwest of the town, and the last British advance ended 15km north of Aleppo on 29 October, with occupation of the railway to Mesopotamia.

Alexander, Crown Prince (1888–1934) Second son of King PETER of SERBIA, he became heir apparent in 1909 when his brother George renounced all claim to the throne under suspicion of murder and insanity. Briefly linked with the BLACK HAND society before 1914, Alexander was still relatively inexperienced when he was named regent in late June 1914, after the king was forced into effective abdication by the military. Allowing prime minister PAŠIĆ to dominate policy during the JULY CRISIS, he joined his troops on the BALKAN FRONT as nominal C-in-C but left active command to the experienced PUTNIK.

Maintaining a largely symbolic role before and during the GREAT RETREAT of late 1915, he began to assert himself once the government was re-established on Corfu. He toured Allied capitals to emphasize Serbia's willingness to keep fighting in spring 1916, hinting at support for a federalized South Slav state and meeting 'Yugoslav Committee' chairman TRUMBIĆ in April. He oversaw repression of the extremist BLACK HAND in December, but resisted Allied and exile pressure to force acceptance of federalization on Pašić and other nationalists seeking unification under Serbian control.

The rapid reconquest of Serbia and the collapse of AUSTRIA-HUNGARY in autumn 1918 put Alexander in an impregnable popular position, which he used to overrule Pašić and establish a quasi-federal 'Kingdom of Serbs, Croats and Slovenes' (later renamed YUGOSLAVIA) on 1 December. Remaining in power as regent, and king on his father's death in 1921, he presided over years of violent turmoil as Croat nationalists contested de facto Serb domination of the new state. He abolished parliament in 1929, ruling as a relatively benign dictator until his assassination by Croat-funded terrorists in Marseilles.

Alexandra, Tsarina (1872–1918) Anglo-German princess (and granddaughter of Queen Victoria) who married Tsar NICHOLAS II of RUSSIA in 1894 and gave birth to four daughters before her only son, heir to the throne Duke Alexis, was born in 1904. The child's haemophilia encouraged increasing devotion to Russian Orthodox religion and receptiveness to healers like RASPUTIN, who became a major influence in her life from 1905.

Her uncompromising belief in autocratic government, combined with her taste for intrigue, made her a powerful force for reaction at court. She resisted the Duma's attempt to remove Rasputin from court in 1911 and gave firm support to the repressive premiership of GOREMYKIN from 1914, guiding Nicholas by persuasion or exploitation of his indifference.

The tsar's assumption of command at STAVKA from September 1915 left her in effective control of court affairs. She advocated STÜRMER's appointment as premier in January 1916, and their policy of non-cooperation with liberal elements fuelled widespread (but unfounded) rumours that both were conspiring with GERMANY. Influential in the resignation of moderate ministers POLIVANOV and SAZONOV, Alexandra became a hate figure to Russia's educated classes (see MILIUKOV, P.). She barely recognized the political relevance of popular opinion and was surprised by the FEBRUARY REVOLUTION, after which she joined her family in impotent internal exile and eventual execution.

Alexeev, General Mikhail (1857–1918) Chief of staff to the Russian southwestern army group in GALICIA in August 1914, Alexeev worked closely with group commander IVANOV against STAVKA's attempts to coordinate its operations with those in EAST PRUSSIA. On his appointment to command the northwestern army group in March 1915, he refused to release reinforcements for Ivanov's attack in the CARPATHIANS and delayed detachment of reserves to face the GORLICE-TARNOW OFFENSIVE. Escaping blame for Ivanov's subsequent defeats, he was appointed overall chief of staff at Stavka when NICHOLAS II became C-in-C in September 1915.

A more influential figure than his predecessor, YANUSHKEVICH, Alexeev established some central control over operations on the EASTERN FRONT. Working with primitive communications and only a small staff, he personally monitored every detail of army procedure, an unwillingness to delegate that left little room for strategic coherence. His contribution to the successful BRUSILOV OFFENSIVE of 1916 was largely passive, and he refused reinforcement to ROMANIA (which he considered an encumbrance) until Russia's own borders were threatened in the later stages of the ROMANIAN CAMPAIGN.

A heart attack in November 1916 forced him into temporary retirement, but he returned to his post just before the FEBRUARY REVOLUTION to supervise the tsar's abdication, and was appointed commander in chief by the PROVISIONAL GOVERNMENT. Opposition to the KERENSKI OFFENSIVE brought dismissal in May, but he was recalled in September, resigning after 12 days. A leading figure in the formation of anti-Bolshevik forces after the OCTOBER REVOLUTION, he was their nominal commander until another heart attack killed him in October 1918 (see KORNILOV, L.).

Allenby, General Sir Edmund (1861–1936) Commander of the BEF's cavalry division during the opening British actions on the WESTERN FRONT at MONS and LE CATEAU, Allenby led his division at the first AISNE battle and an expanded Cavalry Corps at the First Battle of YPRES. He commanded an infantry corps at the Second Battle of YPRES and he took over the Third Army, stationed south of Arras, in October 1915. Allenby's relations with BEF commander HAIG were never good, and his argument for a brief, 'hurricane' bombardment and concentration on surprise was rejected before the Battle of ARRAS in April 1917. Failure of cavalry to exploit gaps in German lines during the battle edged his reputation into decline and he was transferred to command the PALESTINE FRONT in June 1917.

Allenby's tenure in Palestine was a spectacular military success. His concentration of numerical superiority against Turkish weak spots, vigorous deployment of CAVALRY for pursuit operations in favourable conditions, efficient use of mechanized forces and elaborate commitment to secrecy have been described as a precursor to blitzkrieg tactics used in 1939. After breaking through the Turkish BEERSHEBA–GAZA LINE in autumn 1917, and capturing JERUSALEM in December, he launched a diversionary move into TRANSJORDAN and developed full cooperation with the ARAB REVOLT before achieving decisive victory at MEGIDDO in September 1918. A celebrated figure in Britain and Arabia by the time his armies took DAMASCUS in early October, Allenby served as special high commissioner in EGYPT from 1919 until his retirement in 1925.

Allied Maritime Transport Council (AMTC) The first successful attempt at formal economic coordination between the Allies, established in late 1917 to organize distribution of merchant-shipping resources for the common good. Although it had no executive powers, the AMTC functioned reasonably well because the shipping crisis provoked by unrestricted SUBMARINE WARFARE rendered effective control by GREAT BRITAIN tolerable. Allied economic cooperation had earlier amounted to haggling with various British authorities for shipping space, financial credits and industrial goods. The UNITED STATES relieved Britain's economic burden as sole Allied benefactor from 1917, and encouraged further experiments in international coordination. The tendency of shipping control to shape national import programmes was recognized in the subsequent establishment of Allied agencies to oversee grain supplies, other foodstuffs, and munitions.

Allies, The The countries at war with the CENTRAL POWERS were originally referred to as the 'Entente Powers', reflecting prewar diplomatic relations between FRANCE, RUSSIA and GREAT BRITAIN, but as more states joined their alliance (finalized in September 1914) they came to be known on both sides as 'the Allies', inaccurately in the case of the UNITED STATES, which became and remained an 'Associated Power' after April 1917. For details of when individual states declared war, see the Chronology at the end of the book.

Amalfi Large Italian 'armoured' CRUISER, completed in 1909 and one of four Pisa Class ships sent to Venice under Admiral Cagni in mid-1915 to support old coastal-defence BATTLESHIPS guarding the northern Adriatic. On 7 July *Amalfi* was torpedoed and sunk by the German *UB-14*, (officially the Austrian *U-26*) while accompanied by only two screening torpedo boats. Cagni was blamed for the disaster, the ITALIAN NAVY's first major wartime loss, but criticism was also directed at chief of staff REVEL, who had ordered the cruisers to Venice despite opposition from fleet C-in-C ABRUZZI. The three survivors (*Pisa*, *San Giorgio* and *San Marco*) remained virtually inactive at Venice until April 1916, when they returned to the relative safety of the southern Adriatic.

BRIEF DATA (*Amalfi*, 1915) Displacement: 10,100 tons; Crew: 400; Speed: 22k; Armament: 4 × 10in gun, 8 × 7.56in.

Amara, Capture of Opening operation of the Anglo-Indian offensive on the MESOPOTAMIAN FRONT in mid-1915. After their defeat at SHAIBA in April, Turkish forces regrouped on the Rivers Tigris and Euphrates, blocking the only viable routes to BAGHDAD. Anglo-Indian commander NIXON planned to clear both rivers and occupy the main Turkish supply bases, beginning with Amara on the Tigris, more than 150km upriver from the British forward base at QURNA (see MAP 23).

The British government, already fighting Turkish forces at SUEZ and GALLIPOLI, had no wish to expand operations in Mesopotamia, but Nixon's argument that the town was a potential threat to BASRA was accepted by the Indian government, which retained operational control over the theatre. An advance by General TOWNSHEND's 6th Division from Qurna began on 31 May, mostly using shallow punts to cover flooded ground. Every other available river craft was adapted to mount some sort of ARTILLERY, which cleared Turkish units from the small hills just north of Qurna by noon on the first day.

The main Turkish force at Ruta opted to retreat by river to Amara. The sloops and gunboats of Townshend's ROYAL NAVY support, with the commander and his staff aboard, pursued the retreating troop convoy upriver, leaving slow infantry forces far behind. The next morning they caught up with and captured the last Turkish gunboat. Townshend continued to Amara in the gunboat *Comet*, accompanied by three motor launches (each towing a field gun barge) and about 100 troops. Assuming the imminent appearance of a larger force, Amara's 2,000-strong garrison surrendered as soon as this group arrived on 3 June, and the bluff held until Anglo-Indian infantry reached the town in strength the next day. See Battle for NASIRIYEH.

American Union Against Militarism (AUAM) The best-known of numerous pacifist, non-interventionist organizations formed in the neutral UNITED STATES from 1914. Led by a coalition of well-known liberal intellectuals, it organized urban peace rallies, lobbied politicians, published anti-War tracts and gave speeches to unions, farmers' associations and civic groups all over the eastern US.

The AUAM shared opposition to the

PREPAREDNESS MOVEMENT's well-funded PROPAGANDA campaign with associations like the Women's Peace Party, the American Fellowship of Reconciliation, and the more radical People's Council of America for Peace and Democracy, but all lacked the cash or cohesion to make a sustained public impact. By April 1917 the AUAM was a formal organization with 1,500 members, but subsequent divisions resembled those suffered by European socialists in the SECOND INTERNATIONAL, and although it remained in existence until 1921 it had ceased to exert any significant influence by 1918.

'Amiens Dispatch' A special report on the aftermath of the MONS and LE CATEAU battles that appeared in the London *Times* on Sunday, 30 August 1914. Reflecting the despondent mood of BEF commander FRENCH and his staff, it contradicted previous reports of British success on the WESTERN FRONT and punctured the generally festive public mood in GREAT BRITAIN. It also laid foundations for an enduring popular myth that British forces had borne the brunt of the German advance.

Though *The Times* was publicly rebuked by the government, the Dispatch was officially inspired as a means of encouraging recruitment. All British newspapers received war news through the official Press Bureau, initially headed by Lord Birkenhead, and passed their own stories (though not opinions) through its censors. Although theoretically voluntary, failure to conform to the procedure carried the threat of suppression or closure under the DEFENCE OF THE REALM ACT, and the system was coordinated into a general PROPAGANDA policy from February 1918, when the Press Bureau was absorbed into the new Ministry of Information.

Amiens Offensive Opening battle of the Allied counteroffensives on the WESTERN FRONT in autumn 1918. It took the form of an Anglo-French attack, beginning on 8 August, into the SOMME sector of the front from positions east of Amiens (see MAP 2).

Plans for a counteroffensive had emerged from conversations between Allied Supreme Commander FOCH and British C-in-C HAIG in May 1918, when provisional arrangements were made for a surprise attack just south of the Somme, meeting point of the French First Army (Debeney) and British Fourth Army (RAWLINSON). The BEF was in need of recuperation after the German LYS OFFENSIVE in Flanders, and was given a supporting role, but the German AISNE Offensive in late May forced the plan's indefinite postponement.

By late July, with the German advance stalled at the MARNE, Foch was ready to revive the idea, with the modification that exhausted French forces would take the supporting role. Haig was given overall control of the operation, and the process of massively reinforcing Rawlinson's Fourth Army got underway in elaborate secrecy at the end of the month. Rawlinson's existing two-corps strength was doubled, and every available TANK concentrated in the sector, before the main advance began on schedule at 04.20 on 8 August.

British infantry were supported by 2,070 ARTILLERY pieces and 800 aircraft, along with 342 Mark V HEAVY TANKS and 72 'WHIPPET' medium tanks, which persuaded Rawlinson to dispense with a PRELIMINARY BOMBARDMENT. French forces had no tanks but more than 1,000 supporting aircraft. The main front of the attack, about 22km across, was defended by six depleted divisions of the German Second Army (MARWITZ), less than 20,000 men outnumbered 6 to 1, and supported by only 365 GERMAN ARMY AIR SERVICE machines in the whole sector.

Massed behind the tanks, the central advance of the Fourth Army met little effective infantry resistance in the morning. Although tank crews were reduced to delirium in the searing heat, the Canadian and Australian Corps had advanced about 12km by early afternoon. Both sides recognized that a major breakthrough had taken place. LUDENDORFF later described 8 August as 'the black day of the German Army in the history of the War', and Allied strategists at the front sensed the prospect of imminent victory, but much also went wrong with the Allied advance.

An attack to protect the northern flank was stopped by German forces at CHILPILLY SPUR, and the French advance to the south of the Australians was very slow. Tanks again demonstrated their fragility as much as their tactical value, and attempts to combine them with CAVALRY failed completely. Coordination with the RAF broke down early in the day, with ground-support aircraft diverted to costly and ineffective attacks on the Somme bridges from mid-morning.

The original objective of the offensive, the 'Amiens Line' between Méricourt and Hangest, had already been reached, but Anglo-French advances became less efficient as supply and communications systems developed for TRENCH WARFARE failed under the strain of mobile operations. No German reinforcements had yet arrived, but Canadian forces advanced only a further 5km on 9 August, and other elements made little progress despite inflicting heavy casualties.

Over the next two days the advance gradually slowed to a halt as fatigue began to affect the attackers and 12 German reserve divisions reached the sector. By 12 August British tank strength was down to six, and the defenders were established on a line in front of Noyon, Ham and Péronne. Haig had already decided that a fresh attack elsewhere offered the best chance of exploitation, and Foch reached the same conclusion on 15 August, when he suspended attacks in order to prepare for a new offensive just to the north at ALBERT.

Amman, Battle of The opening British offensive into TRANSJORDAN of March 1918, and the first Turkish victory on the PALESTINE FRONT for almost a year. After British forces occupied Jericho in February, a special detachment of one infantry and one expanded CAVALRY division, with strong ARTILLERY and engineering support, was deployed on the west bank of the Jordan. Ordered to cooperate with the ARAB REVOLT further south and to provide a diversionary threat to the RAILWAY centre of Dera (while General ALLENBY's main offensive was prepared further west), its advance east on Amman was delayed by rain until 23 March, by which time new YILDERIM FORCE commander LIMAN VON SANDERS was concentrating all available reserves on the town.

The heights of Es Salt, 30km short of Amman, were taken by infantry without a fight that night, but rain prevented further movement until 27 March, when the ANZAC Mounted Division opened a three-pronged advance on Amman. It was halted by MACHINE GUNS in the Amman citadel, bombing by German aircraft stationed at Dera, and the outbreak of local civil war around Es Salt, which delayed infantry support.

Turkish reinforcements began a counterattack on 30 March. With the rising waters of the Jordan threatening to cut off his lines of retreat, operation commander General Shea withdrew across the river, leaving only a bridgehead defended at Ghoraniye. Although a defeat, costing almost 1,400 casualties, the attack had convinced Liman von Sanders to concentrate defences in Transjordan and to draw Turkish reserves from the simultaneous siege of MAAN by Arab forces. See MAP 22.

Ancre, Battle of the See: SOMME OFFENSIVE.

Ancre Heights, Battle of the See: SOMME OFFENSIVE.

Andrássy von Csik-Szent Király, Julius, Count (1860–1929) Andrássy became AUSTRIA-HUNGARY's last imperial foreign secretary on 24 October 1918, after a long career in the Hungarian parliament as a leading liberal opponent of Hungarian premier Count TISZA. Appointed by Emperor KARL I as a known advocate of peace, he discharged his role by formally ending the German alliance and presenting a hopeless offer of separate peace to the Allies (28 October) before resigning on 1 November. Elected to the new Hungarian parliament in 1920, he led its Christian Democratic Party from 1921.

Angerapp Line See: EAST PRUSSIA; First and Second Battles of the MASURIAN LAKES.

Ansaldo A-1 The first Italian-designed FIGHTER to enter wartime service, it was a small biplane developed in mid-1917 and known as the *Balilla* ('Hunter'). Fast and a quick climber, the A-1 was never sufficiently manoeuvrable for use with fighter units on the ITALIAN FRONT, which continued to use French designs, but some of the 150 built equipped home-defence units from early 1918.

BRIEF DATA Type: single-seat fighter; Engine: 220hp SPA; Max speed: 220kph; Ceiling: 7,850m; Armament: 2 × 0.303in mg.

Ansaldo SVA-5 Italian biplane designed as a large FIGHTER but used successfully for long-range reconnaissance. In action with the ITALIAN AIR FORCE from March 1918, SVA-5s were fast enough to outrun most opposition and could carry sufficient fuel for exceptionally long journeys, escorting reconnaissance and bombing raids deep into AUSTRIA-HUNGARY. The type eventually equipped six full squadrons and several smaller formations, and a floatplane modification – designated the SVA Idro-AM – was used by a single coastal squadron. Almost 1,250 SVA-5s and 50 floatplanes were eventually produced, and they remained active well into the 1920s.

BRIEF DATA (SVA-5) Type: single-seat reconnaissance; Engine: 220hp SPA; Max speed: 230kph; Ceiling: 6,650m; Armament: 2 × 0.303in mg.

Anthoine, General François (1860–1944) French staff officer who took field command of the French First Army on the WESTERN FRONT in 1917. His forces formed the northern flank of British attacks throughout the Third Battle of YPRES, pushing across the Yser Canal north of the town and advancing towards the Forest of Houthulst (see MAP 6). From November 1917, Anthoine served as chief of staff to French C-in-C PÉTAIN, but was removed in July 1918 after German successes on the AISNE and the MATZ.

Anti-Aircraft Artillery Ground forces habitually fired RIFLES and other small arms at hostile aircraft, with occasional success, but systematic destruction of machines in flight had been viewed as an ARTILLERY responsibility since the first regular use of aircraft in military manoeuvres. Known as 'Archie' (to the British) or 'flak', all wartime anti-aircraft (AA) guns were controlled by navies or army artillery sections except those of Germany's ground forces, which were administered by the GERMAN ARMY AIR SERVICE.

The first purpose-designed AA weapons were converted German field guns demonstrated in 1909. A few were in service by 1914, but the numbers of aircraft in existence were insufficient to warrant large-scale investment. The FRENCH ARMY had just two purpose-built anti-aircraft ARMOURED CARS, carrying the ubiquitous 'SOIXANTE-QUINZE' field gun, in August 1914, and the BRITISH ARMY possessed only a handful of motorized '3-inch 20cwt' guns on a usefully spacious mounting, both reasoning that the slow speed of early aircraft rendered cross-country pursuit a possibility.

Rapid wartime growth of air activity forced the major belligerents to improvise anti-aircraft weapons, and guns of all types were hastily fitted to upward-firing mountings while purpose-built designs were sought. Many of the early mutations remained in action throughout, but adaptations of standard medium field guns generally proved most suitable for long-term production.

German forces mainly used 75mm and 80mm weapons, the French stuck with the Soixante-Quinze, while British and US forces mostly employed 3-inch guns. Few major wartime technological advances were made in actual gun design, although some guns fired a lighter shell using their usual charge to increase altitude, and a rapid-firing 20mm cannon was developed in Germany during 1918 that eventually became the basis for Second World War light AA weaponry.

Batteries were originally grouped in small clusters in an attempt to catch the relatively few hostile aircraft wherever they appeared. At least two guns were used so that a ranging shot could be followed up before the target had moved too far, but dispersion was generally abandoned once it became clear that simple visual aim was very unlikely to hit a target capable of manoeuvring in three dimensions.

Anti-aircraft defences were subsequently grouped in large formations wherever air raids could be expected – especially around rear-area military installations, airfields, threatened industrial targets, population centres and coastal facilities (see STRATEGIC BOMB-

ING). Individual or paired guns were still mounted on warships, until by 1918 most major vessels were equipped with at least one medium weapon, but not in any great expectation of success.

Other wartime developments included 'barrage' techniques, intended to place blanket coverage over a particular sector of airspace, and telescope systems for tracking aircraft before firing at an anticipated position, as well as reasonably efficient central control systems for large formations. Increasing frequency of night operations required use of flares and searchlights, or of barrage balloons to force attackers into protected corridors.

Most AA commanders used shrapnel for ground-to-air shooting, which stood the best chance of hitting something, but some preferred high explosive (HE), which had an outside chance of obliterating something. Incendiary shells, originally designed for use against German ZEPPELINS, threw out balls of flaming thermite in the manner of shrapnel, and were used more often than HE by 1918. The altitude of explosion in all shells was determined simply by cutting fuses to the desired length.

Progress was generally outstripped by the rapidly improving performance of warplanes. Although AA concentrations were accepted as necessary and inflicted a small share of overall air casualties, mostly on the busiest WESTERN FRONT, they were widely viewed as intrinsically inadequate by 1918, and most immediate postwar air-defence development was concentrated on FIGHTERS.

Anti-Submarine Weapons Development of defensive techniques against SUBMARINES before 1914 was limited by the general concentration of naval resources on offensive weapons. Early submarine successes against warships prompted urgent revision of priorities, but the greatest impetus to anti-submarine capability was the German *HANDELSKRIEG* campaign against Allied seagoing commerce begun in early 1915.

Defence against submarines began with avoidance and protection. High-speed zigzagging to avoid slow submarines was effective and remained standard practice for any reasonably fast vessel. Slower merchant ships were generally advised to avoid busy harbour approaches in daylight or to adopt neutral flags. Light steel nets were initially hung around major warships beneath the water line to deflect incoming TORPEDOES, but were found not to work and soon removed. Protection for important ships was subsequently provided by screening vessels, usually DESTROYERS, which at first simply blocked a submarine's shot but were later able to employ a variety of offensive weapons.

Only surfaced submarines were vulnerable to direct attack in 1914, and the most obvious close-range method was ramming. A hit at speed from any larger ship was likely to destroy such a fragile craft, and ramming was responsible for many wartime sinkings, including 19 U-BOATS. Surfaced submarines could be attacked by gunfire, but at any distance only a lucky shot could hit such a small target before it dived, and once submerged the only option was to pursue it until its underwater batteries ran out.

The rules of SUBMARINE WARFARE in 1914 gave merchantmen a good chance of a shot at a surfaced boat, and several thousand were eventually fitted with naval guns. Arming proceeded very slowly because the only major source of surplus ARTILLERY, the Royal Navy, had very little before 1917, but Allied decoy ships with disguised guns (Q-SHIPS) enjoyed limited success before torpedo attack became standard U-boat practice.

In the absence of effective underwater detection devices, MINES, laid at various depths in narrow channels or along busy transit routes, were the only means of attacking submerged boats in 1914. The most successful anti-submarine weapon of the period, they sunk at least 75 boats and probably accounted for most unexplained losses. British mines had by far the largest number of targets and scored the most successes, but only 10 of their 48 credited sinkings took place before 1917, when the quality of minefields improved dramatically. Minefields were also used to blockade hostile submarine bases (see NORTHERN BARRAGE), but had the disadvantage of posing a serious threat to friendly shipping (10 U-boats were sunk by German mines).

Any more precise attack required knowledge of a submarine's underwater position. Allied navies strung INDICATOR NETS across narrow channels from 1915, supported by armed fishing craft, patrolling warships and minefields. They were generally ineffective in darkness until the use of searchlights (long thought to expose patrol craft to attack) was greatly expanded in 1918, and almost always suffered from lack of sufficient support craft (see DOVER BARRAGE; OTRANTO BARRAGE).

Wartime development of underwater microphones (hydrophones) for listening to submarine engines assisted the process of tracking an indicated submarine, but commanders on both sides soon learned that they could be neutralized by diving deep or running silent. The German Navy had begun experimenting with more sophisticated ultrasonic listening devices by 1918, pointing the way to postwar methods.

U-boats relied heavily on RADIO for contact with their bases, and British interceptions were indirectly responsible for avoidance and destruction of submarines on a large, if uncertain, scale. The Royal Navy's ROOM 40 intelligence unit used broadcasts to and from U-boats to build up pictures of regular transit routes, to discover target zones or rendezvous points, and occasionally to locate a boat's precise position. Development of long-range naval aircraft, AIRSHIPS and AIRCRAFT CARRIERS also aided daylight location.

Detection of submarines was of little offensive value without weapons for direct underwater attack. Electrically detonated charges ('sweeps') towed beneath destroyers were regularly employed by the British, but depended on very close contact and sunk only three U-boats. The more versatile and effective DEPTH CHARGE was introduced in 1915, and was in widespread use from late 1917.

Fast destroyers were the submarine's most dangerous opponents but were always in short supply, and a host of small warships or requisitioned private vessels was used to convey anti-submarine weaponry. Along with sloops, coastal gunboats, motor boats and 'subchasers', several thousand small auxiliaries – mostly armed trawlers, drifters and yachts – were taken into Allied (primarily British) service for escort, net-minding or harbour defence duties. All forms of MINELAYER, including submarines, were deployed to lay deep anti-submarine fields.

British submarines, which torpedoed a total of 18 U-boats, were sent to ambush known rendezvous points or towed behind unarmed decoy ships to surprise attacking boats. All sides also deployed boats near the others' bases, but with little success. Aircraft performance also improved sufficiently to enable attacks on submarines with bombs and depth charges, but they had scored only one confirmed 'kill' by 1919.

Combined application of new or refined techniques had little overall effect on the course of the commerce war until late 1917, when US shipbuilding capacity and belated abandonment of offensive search-and-destroy tactics by Allied naval commanders were reflected in the adoption of an efficient and widespread CONVOY system.

Antwerp, Siege of The reduction of the FORTRESSES surrounding the north Belgian port following the German invasion of BELGIUM and the Battles of the FRONTIERS on the WESTERN FRONT in 1914. King ALBERT had withdrawn the BELGIAN ARMY's 65,000 troops to Antwerp after the fall of LIÈGE on 16 August. Bypassed by the German drive into France, the Antwerp fortresses remained a potential threat to the flank of the German First Army (KLUCK) over the following weeks.

To relieve pressure on French and British forces at MONS and CHARLEROI, the Belgians ventured out of Antwerp to attack German rear columns on 24–25 August, forcing Kluck to detach four divisions from the main advance. A second sortie on 9 September, designed to prevent the detachment's transfer to France, convinced the German High Command to take control of Antwerp and the Belgian Channel ports once the front in France had stabilized after the MARNE battle. A force of five divisions and 173 guns, led by General von Boseler, was assigned the task.

Garrisoned by 80,000 reserve troops in addition to the Belgian field army, Antwerp was surrounded by outer and inner rings of fortresses. German siege ARTILLERY began firing on the outlying forts on 28 September, silencing them without much difficulty. The British government, convinced by navy minister CHURCHILL to secure the Channel ports, landed three brigades of ROYAL NAVY troops at Antwerp on 6 October, but the Belgian government left Antwerp for Ostend on the day they arrived and the city was evacuated next day. Antwerp surrendered on 9 October, and was occupied by German forces until the COURTRAI OFFENSIVE in late 1918, but most Allied troops in the city had escaped down the coast to take part in the subsequent defence of FLANDERS.

ANZAC Official acronym of the Australian and New Zealand Army Corps, also used informally to describe members of the Corps (see AUSTRALIAN FORCES; NEW ZEALAND FORCES). Anzac Day on 25 April commemorates the first day of the GALLIPOLI LANDINGS in 1915. See also: ANZAC COVE.

Anzac Cove Tiny Allied enclave on the Aegean coast of the Gallipoli Peninsula, occupied by the Australian and New Zealand Army Corps (ANZAC) during the GALLIPOLI LANDINGS on 25 April 1915 (see MAP 20). Some 8,000 troops sent to Z Beach, near Gaba Tepe, went ashore too far north and disembarked under steep cliffs, which were partially secured before strong Turkish reinforcements occupied the ANZAC heights around the Cove that afternoon. Denied permission to evacuate their precarious position, ANZAC forces dug in to defend an area less than a kilometre deep and two across. A ragged front was established by nightfall, and despite attacks by both sides the position remained essentially unaltered for over three months.

Turkish willingness to endure enormous casualties was a feature of the prolonged battle for Anzac Cove. All available reserves had been rushed to the front, regarded by Turkish commanders as the main threat to the whole peninsula, and by 4 May repeated massed assaults had cost 19th Division commander KEMAL perhaps 14,000 casualties. The sacrifice effectively ended the threat of an ANZAC breakout from the Cove, but Turkish premier ENVER PASHA ordered the invaders driven into the sea.

An estimated 40,000 men were massed at the front against 12,500 Australian, New Zealand and ROYAL NAVY troops for a major attack on the night of 18–19 May. Though supported by 50 well-positioned guns against fewer than 30 smaller and scattered British weapons, mostly EIGHTEEN-POUNDERS, a frontal infantry assault against the centre of the ANZAC line was cut down by efficient defensive fire and failed within two hours.

The action, known in Allied accounts as the 'Defence of Anzac', cost another estimated 10,000 Turkish casualties but the defenders lost only 600 men. A truce was arranged on 24 May to remove dead bodies from the congested battlefield and Kemal abandoned mass-assault tactics.

The only part of the sector not hemmed in by Turkish forces on high ground was at the northern flank of the enclave, where the terrain was considered impassable. Reinforced by an Indian Army brigade, ANZAC commander BIRDWOOD controlled 22,000 troops in the sector by late May, but a coincidental strengthening of Turkish defences forced postponement of his plan for an attack through the rocky ravines.

The main Allied offensives in Gallipoli were focused on the southern HELLES sector until the arrival of strong British reinforcements on the GALLIPOLI FRONT in July. A major attack towards the northern ANZAC ridge of SARI BAIR was launched as part of C-in-C HAMILTON's ambitious SUVLA BAY OFFENSIVE in early August, and its failure ended serious hopes of a large-scale breakout.

Anzac Cove remained embroiled in a peculiarly claustrophobic form of TRENCH WARFARE until its eventual and successful evacuation in December. Plentiful cover in a wild concertina of rocky ravines and gullies enabled trench systems to overlap and interlock, so that opposing positions were sometimes less than 5m apart and the entire area was sown with miniature strongpoints. Allied defenders endured unremitting pressure in the absence of sheltered supply lines or rest areas more than a few yards from the front, and were outgunned in trench weaponry, especially in GRENADES and MORTARS.

Apart from full-scale attacks and numerous local operations against troublesome strongpoints, the position was soon a warren of MINES, with both sides engaged in continuous SNIPING and SAPPING contests. Climate, congestion and casualties, which could seldom be moved or buried without attracting fire, combined to promote rampant disease. British medical facilities were never able to match the flow of evacuees, and many survivors suffered severe psychological trauma. Operations at Anzac Cove are particularly well-remembered in AUSTRALIA and NEW ZEALAND, where they inspired a combination of national pride and bitterness.

Aqaba Little-used port at the junction of Arabia and the Sinai Peninsula (see MAP 22), captured by Arab rebels in July 1917 after a small but celebrated action. Aqaba offered the ARAB REVOLT a direct supply link with British forces in EGYPT and PALESTINE, as well as a base for operations into northern Arabia, and its British advisor LAWRENCE regarded further advances as vital to the Revolt's fragile momentum. Aware of Aqaba's vulnerability to overland attack, he left Wejh on 9 May 1917 at the start of a 1,000km trek to secure diplomatic approval and military assistance for a raid.

His party included Auda abu Tayi, the 'Robin Hood of Arabia' and its most famed fighter, and attracted another 500 (mostly mounted) warriors during a sweep through northern Arabia, striking targets in southern Syria to confuse 3,000 Turkish troops stationed east of Aqaba at Maan. Aqaba's forward defences were taken with a dramatic camel charge, and the 300 troops in the town surrendered without a fight on 6 July. Arab forces suffered only two casualties and gained 2,000 local supporters.

Lawrence reached rapid agreement with the new Palestine C-in-C ALLENBY to transform Aqaba into the centre of British logistic support for the Revolt's northern operations. FEISAL moved the headquarters of his renamed Northern Arab Army to the town in August, and it became the base for operations on the right flank of Allenby's advance on DAMASCUS.

Aqqaqia, Battle of See: SENUSSI.

Arab Revolt Uprising by the native peoples of western, central and northern Arabia against the Ottoman Empire, which had governed the region since the 16th century (see TURKEY). Turkish control of the territories loosely described by contemporaries as Arabia, stretching north as far as modern Syria, was largely superficial in 1914. Most of the tribal population of some 6 million, divided about equally between settled and nomadic Arabs, owed allegiance to local chieftains, and most of them were in no position to initiate serious hostilities.

In the north, Syrian overlord Nuri-es-Shalaan was too close to central Turkey to risk provocative action. East of Sinai, Shammar Confederacy chief Ibn Rashid was a major supplier of camels to the TURKISH ARMY, and IBN SAUD's fanatical Wahabis in the heart of Arabia were too isolated for their hostility to affect Constantinople, as were the MARSH ARABS in the east and tribes near the southwest Red Sea coast.

An overt Arab independence movement had flourished only in the relatively fertile Hejaz region, where Sherif HUSSEIN IBN ALI controlled almost 1,000km of the Red Sea coastal zone in central Arabia, including the holy cities of Mecca and Medina. The region as a whole stretched north as far as the tip of the Sinai peninsula, and was connected to central Turkey by the Damascus–Medina RAILWAY.

Hussein's political power was substantiated by his senior position in the Muslim religious hierarchy, making him a natural focus for secret Arab independence societies founded in the wake of renewed repression by the YOUNG TURK regime before 1914. Close contacts with the important Al Fatat organization in Damascus were established in early 1915 through Hussein's third son, FEISAL, and tension mounted after mass executions of its membership in the spring.

Hussein's desire for independence had been known to the British since a visit by his second son, ABDULLAH, to Egyptian C-in-C KITCH-

ENER in early 1914. Diplomatic links were maintained throughout 1915, and British RIFLES were being shipped across the Red Sea in advance of an uprising by early 1916. The Turkish government was aware of preparations for revolt, blockading the Hejaz against military imports from May 1916 and readying troops in Damascus for a march south (ostensibly to support German operations in EAST AFRICA).

Ali (Hussein's eldest son) and Feisal proclaimed the revolt outside MEDINA on 5 June. Joined by 30,000 untrained tribesmen, it opened with a failed attack on the garrison, but a detachment cut the railway to the north. Further south Hussein led a simultaneous attack on 1,000 Turkish troops garrisoning Mecca, taking the city after three days of street fighting.

Another subsidiary attack forced the surrender of 1,500 Turkish troops at the port of Jiddah a few days later, with support from the ROYAL NAVY seaplane carrier *BEN-MY-CHREE*, and by late July the revolt had captured garrison ports further north at Rabegh and Yenbo. Apart from Medina, the last Turkish bastion in the southern Hejaz fell to the 'Sherifians' in late September, when 3,000 troops at the barracks town of At Taif, 100km south of Mecca, surrendered after British ARTILLERY from EGYPT (with Muslim crews) joined the attack.

Hussein took the title 'Sultan of the Arabs', later altered to 'King of the Hejaz', and his army was swelled by Arabs among 4,000 Turkish Army prisoners. Arab officers in Turkish service also defected in numbers, providing leadership for the core units of an 'Arab Army', with Hussein's four sons as its commanders.

In autumn 1916 the Arab Army comprised four main forces: some 9,000 men south of Medina under Ali; a similar number southeast of the city under Abdullah; a mixed force of some 1,500 irregulars and Egyptian troops sent from the Sudan; and up to 8,000 men with Feisal inland from Yenbo. Many were very young or very old, few were trained, and little artillery support was available. Their numbers and location were subject to random fluctuations.

Skilled defence by the veteran Turkish commander in Medina, Fakhri Din Pasha, forced the rebels to withdraw south and reopened the railway for reinforcements by October 1916, when a British liaison party reached Jiddah to find the Revolt losing momentum. British Arabist LAWRENCE travelled inland to meet Feisal, and returned to YENBO in early November as Feisal's official British advisor.

After participating in its successful defence, Lawrence encouraged Feisal onto the offensive, capturing the northern Hejaz port of WEJH in January 1917. Aware that British assurances of full Arab independence offered no guarantees, Lawrence and Feisal devised a strategy designed to provide maximum indirect support for British operations in PALESTINE while ensuring that the Arab Army achieved the best possible bargaining position.

Abandoning preparations for an expected attack on Medina, they used their new position north of the city as a base for raids all over northern Arabia, maximizing the Revolt's geographical impact and pinning large Turkish forces to the region. Accepted and assisted by senior British officers (now active in the theatre as advisors and technicians) the campaign drew Turkish reserves from Medina and Damascus, but they were generally powerless against guerrilla raiders supported by local populations.

During spring 1917 Feisal received the secret promise of south Syrian support once the Revolt spread north, and his next northward move was the capture of AQABA in July, masterminded and led by Lawrence. Converted as an important centre for the importation of British assistance, Aqaba became Feisal's main base. With forces under Abdullah and Ali preoccupied with containment of the Medina garrison and protection of Mecca, Feisal's 'Northern Army' was the Revolt's strike force, advancing on the right of ALLENBY's advance into Palestine and recruiting tribal support as it went.

Lawrence opened offensive operations in autumn 1917 with a series of train-wrecking missions, defeating a Turkish reprisal raid at PETRA in October. Lawrence played a major role in Northern Army strategy and tactics, deliberately cultivating legendary status (a standard tool of Arab leadership) and displaying a sympathy with the Revolt's aims untypical of British liaison efforts, which were often marred by prejudice and ignorance of guerrilla techniques.

Allenby requested diversionary assistance during his attack on the BEERSHEBA–GAZA LINE, and Lawrence raided far north in a vain effort to wreck the Yarmuk railway in Syria. Allenby again asked for close cooperation to support attacks into TRANSJORDAN in early 1918, prompting an advance beyond TAFILA up the Dead Sea shore. Plans to join up with British forces were disrupted by the Turkish victory at AMMAN in March, and Arab armies refocused on dislodging the garrison at MAAN in their rear.

By early 1918 the Revolt had prevented some 23,000 regular Turkish Army troops from participating in the Palestine campaign and been responsible for an estimated 15,000 Turkish casualties (including losses to sickness).

Bolstered by increased British air support, funding and technical assistance, especially the supply of ARMOURED CARS and camels, Feisal's army returned to guerrilla raids in the north (25 bridges were destroyed in May alone). In the south, where the Revolt was more stagnant and less in touch with wider strategies, Hussein's attitude to GREAT BRITAIN cooled slightly as Turkish PROPAGANDA spread news of the BALFOUR DECLARATION and the SYKES–PICOT AGREEMENT.

Feisal cooperated closely with Allenby's MEGIDDO Offensive in the autumn, sweeping north on a tide of popular support to take DERA and DAMASCUS, the latter in tandem with regular British forces. Strongly supported by Lawrence, he was careful to prevent de facto British administration of conquered regions, supervising the immediate installation of Arab governments wherever possible.

His suspicions of British intent were confirmed in early October, before the final joint advance on ALEPPO, but he reluctantly accepted temporary MANDATE status for the new Arab states of Syria, Transjordan and Lebanon, and argued in vain for full independence at the PARIS PEACE CONFERENCE. Organized military operations ended with the surrender of diehard Turkish outposts in 1919, but Arab nationalism remained an active political force in the region through the 1920s. See MAP 22.

Arabic Transatlantic passenger liner torpedoed without warning off southern Ireland by the German submarine *U-24* on 19 August 1915. En route for New York, and unarmed, the 15,000-ton ship sank in 10 minutes. Only 44 of its 429 passengers and crew were killed, but the incident rekindled anger in the UNITED STATES over the unrestricted U-boat campaign in British waters, in force since February (see *LUSITANIA*). New orders forbidding attacks on passenger ships were issued by Kaiser WILHELM II on 27 August, prompting High Seas Fleet commander Pohl to call off the main campaign. See also: *HANDELSKRIEG*.

Arctic Theatre The northern coasts of Russia and the White Sea were not expected to be war zones in 1914, and all Russian activity in the area was concerned with expanding harbour and railway facilities at Murmansk (Romanovo) and Archangel (Arkhangelsk) for use as major supply centres for coal and weapons from Britain.

No military operations took place in the region until June 1915, when a German auxiliary CRUISER laid 285 MINES in the entrances to Archangel harbour. They sank a British minesweeper and 12 merchant steamers before the end of the year, and prompted Allied formation of a makeshift minesweeping force, consisting of a few British armed trawlers and 18 Russian boats equipped by the Baltic Fleet. Miscellaneous ships were collected from other theatres to patrol the Arctic seas during the rest of 1915, including two second-line British cruisers, a Russian SUBMARINE and a minelayer transferred from the Far East. Two coastal batteries were also established and about 30 surplus naval guns fitted to steamers.

Although only £20.5 million of war materials reached Russia from Britain in 1916, supply traffic via the Arctic expanded well beyond the capacity of Russian ports, and half of all the year's imports were still awaiting rail transportation from Archangel early the following year. The RUSSIAN NAVY took further steps to protect traffic from possible German aggression in February 1916, establishing an Arctic Flotilla with a new ice-free base in Kola Bay. A scratch force based around the light cruiser *ASKOLD* and a handful of old DESTROYERS from the Far East was still forming when 6 German submarines sank 25 Allied ships, captured 2 more and damaged several small warships in a six-week campaign, helped by powerful surface weapons and at a cost of one U-BOAT lost to patrol craft.

Russian requests for more British ships to strengthen the Arctic Flotilla produced four icebreakers and a few auxiliary vessels to augment a minesweeper force of 32 boats by early 1917, but German submarine activity subsided and only 21 Allied ships were sunk that year before Russo-German hostilities ended in December.

Both the protective value of CONVOYS and a sharp drop in traffic were responsible for the decline, as western suppliers held back deliveries pending the outcome of upheavals in RUSSIA. The political situation in northern Russia became highly unstable after the OCTOBER REVOLUTION. Russian ships were deployed from the area against German submarines until the ARMISTICE of 1918, and a small Anglo-French force established a puppet regional government at Archangel to protect commercial interests during the RUSSIAN CIVIL WAR, remaining until October 1919.

Ardennes, Battle of the Name given to the collision of French and German invasion forces in the lower Ardennes forests between 21 and 23 August 1914. One of the crucial 'Battles of the FRONTIERS' fought simultaneously all along the WESTERN FRONT, it halted the second phase of the FRENCH ARMY's offensive scheme based on PLAN 17.

French plans assumed that German forces in the area would be relatively weak, and that their relatively light, mobile ARTILLERY – especially the rapid-firing 'SOIXANTE-QUINZE' field guns – would give them a crucial advantage in difficult, wooded terrain. By 20 August the setbacks suffered by French armies in LORRAINE seemed to confirm German concentration in that area, and C-in-C JOFFRE confidently ordered a slightly modified invasion of the Ardennes to begin the following morning.

At the southern end of the forest, General Ruffey's Third Army advanced on the iron-rich region of Briey some 50,000 men below strength, having lost three reserve divisions to the crisis in Lorraine. Further north, General DE LANGLE DE CARY's Fourth Army marched towards Neufchâteau, en route to the German fortified zone of Metz-Thionville, but its supporting Fifth Army had been redirected northward to CHARLEROI as a nod to reports of massive German strength in BELGIUM. To preserve surprise, the attacks were launched without infantry reconnaissance, and the numerically superior German Fourth and Fifth Armies, inner ring of the GERMAN ARMY's huge northern invasion force (see SCHLIEFFEN PLAN), were mistaken for small screening forces.

German troops had been advancing slowly through the woods since 19 August, establishing good defensive positions as they went. Inexperienced Fifth Army commander Crown Prince WILHELM was occupying Briey and threatening the towns of Longwy, Montmédy and Virton. Duke ALBRECHT of Württemberg's Fourth Army was heading towards Neufchâteau. On 21 August, in thick fog that made CAVALRY reconnaissance impossible, scattered elements of the opposing armies literally stumbled into each other.

After a day of sporadic skirmishing, general combat swamped the front on 22 August. Despite isolated French successes, notably by the Third Army's VI Corps at Virton, and heavy casualties on both sides, the battles generally reflected German tactical superiority. Brightly clad French troops charged to the attack, often without artillery support, to be cut down by well-entrenched MACHINE GUNS and heavy artillery.

Lacking the equipment, training or inclination to dig TRENCHES, both French armies in the Ardennes were in disorderly retreat by the evening of 23 August. The Third Army retired back to Verdun, pursued by most of Wilhelm's Fifth (a besieging force was left behind to take Longwy), and De Langle de

Cary's battered forces retreated to a line across Sedan and Stenay, leaving German forces in possession of vital iron resources and advancing into FRANCE. The extent of the defeat, and of comparable disasters elsewhere, only gradually became clear to Joffre, who blamed the performance of his armies rather than their circumstances, and concentrated planning on the earliest possible resumption of offensive action. See: MAP 4.

Arethusa The first of 34 light CRUISERS to see wartime service with the ROYAL NAVY. Small, fast and fairly well armoured, light cruisers were designed for operations with fast DESTROYER flotillas in the North Sea. Evolved from earlier SCOUT and TOWN designs, they generally proved very successful and were the biggest warships built in large numbers by the British.

The original eight Arethusa Class and six (slightly larger) Caroline Class ships built in 1914–15 were three-funnelled and fitted with only two 6-inch guns, but some of their largely irrelevant 4-inch guns were later removed in favour of more main and ANTI-AIRCRAFT armament. Later (two-funnelled) classes were less cramped, used more efficient geared turbine engines, had no secondary armament and featured staggered turret arrangements, often mounting aircraft on turret platforms.

Light cruisers were the most active British warships in the North Sea, and *Arethusa* was stationed at Harwich. It suffered heavy gunfire damage during the HELIGOLAND BIGHT operation in August 1914, and took part in the DOGGER BANK engagement, but was generally occupied with patrols against German destroyers and light forces, in which capacity it was sunk by a mine in February 1916. Although several other light cruisers suffered and survived heavy damage, the only other wartime loss took place in late 1918, when *Cassandra* was sunk by a MINE during Allied sweeping operations in the BALTIC SEA.
BRIEF DATA (*Arethusa*, 1916) Displacement: 3,750 tons; Crew: 325; Dimensions: length 446ft (135.2m), beam 41.5ft (12.6m); Speed: 30k; Armament: 3 × 6in gun, 4 × 4in, 2 × 3in AA, 8 × 21in TT.

Arges, Battle of the The ROMANIAN ARMY's last stand in defence of Wallachia in 1916, and the decisive battle of the ROMANIAN CAMPAIGN on the EASTERN FRONT (see MAP 14). After defeats on the northern and southern borders of Wallachia, surviving Romanian forces (some 150,000 troops) were brought together west of Bucharest, threatened by the German Ninth Army (FALKENHAYN) from the northwest, and MACKENSEN's multinational Danube Army from the west. New C-in-C AVERESCU, influenced by French military advisor BERTHELOT, planned to exploit a gap between the two and attack Mackensen's northern flank as his army crossed the River Arges. Launched on 1 December, the attack achieved some initial surprise, but the exhausted remnant of an essentially 19th-century army made almost no impact on Mackensen's advance. By the next day Romanian forces in the centre had retired some 30km east to the Bucharest–Pitesti railway, and defenders either side of Bucharest fell back with heavy losses on 3 December. Calling off further attacks on rearguards the following day, Mackensen consolidated his position, occupying Bucharest and the Ploesti oilfields on 7 December before slowly pursuing the remaining 70,000 Romanian troops towards Moldavia.

Argonne Offensive See: MEUSE–ARGONNE OFFENSIVE.

Arizona The most modern of nine US NAVY dreadnoughts that joined the British GRAND FLEET in December 1917, remaining as its Sixth Battle Squadron until the following December. Like its sister *Pennsylvania*, it was a stable, comfortable and reliable ship, regarded as one of the most successful contemporary designs, but its excellent reputation was not tested.
BRIEF DATA (*Arizona*, 1916) Displacement: 31,400 tons; Crew: 1,117; Dimensions: length 608ft (184.2m), beam 97ft (29.4m); Speed: 21k; Main armament: 12 × 14in gun, 22 × 5in, 4 × 3in AA.

Ark Royal The first ship completed as an AIRCRAFT CARRIER. Converted while under construction as a collier, it joined the ROYAL NAVY in December 1914 and was sent to support the DARDANELLES operation the following February. Far too slow for seaplanes, which needed a strong headwind, to take off from its 40-metre flight deck, it was anchored in MUDROS harbour once U-BOATS reached the Dardanelles in May, remaining in the eastern MEDITERRANEAN as an aircraft transport and depot ship. Renamed *Pegasus* in the mid-1930s, it performed the same role throughout the Second World War.

BRIEF DATA (1915) Displacement: 7,020 tons; Crew: 140; Dimensions: length 366ft (110.9m), beam 50.75ft (15.4m); Speed: 10.5k; Armament: 4 × 12pdr gun, 6 × a/c.

Armageddon, Battle of See: MEGIDDO OFFENSIVE.

Armed Merchant Cruisers (AMCs) Large, fast passenger liners requisitioned as auxiliary naval vessels and given CRUISER armament. All the major navies employed AMCs, but the ROYAL NAVY used by far the largest number, including the Tenth Cruiser Squadron of some 20 vessels, which patrolled shipping lanes between Britain and Iceland until late 1917. Allied AMCs were generally assigned to commerce-protection duties in 1914, but were very vulnerable to MINES and TORPEDOES. The British suffered 12 wartime AMC losses, the FRENCH NAVY 13, and from 1916 they were more often used as troopships or hospital ships. Only the GERMAN NAVY made much use of AMCs in an offensive role, sending 7 out as commerce raiders in 1914 (see NAVAL WARFARE). All were lost or interned by spring 1915 and one, the 18,700-ton *Cap Trafalgar*, was sunk in gun duel with the even larger British AMC *Carmenia* in the South Atlantic on 14 September 1914. Smaller or slower passenger liners were also used by the British as Commissioned Escort Ships or Armed Boarding Vessels, and the title Defensively Armed Merchant Ship was accorded to any non-naval vessel given anti-submarine armament. See also: Q-SHIPS; AUXILIARY COMMERCE RAIDERS.

Armée Navale See: FRENCH NAVY.

Armenian Massacres Allied term describing the Turkish government's wartime deportations of Armenians from their homelands in the northeast of the Ottoman Empire. Neutral estimates suggest that between 1 and 1.5 million Armenians were living in TURKEY in 1914, with perhaps another million inside RUSSIA. Unlike other large racial minorities within the Empire, including their traditional Kurd enemies, Ottoman Armenians had no officially recognized homeland, but most were scattered near the Russian Caucasian frontiers.

Despite these drawbacks a militant Armenian nationalist movement had blossomed since the turn of the century, armed and encouraged by the Russians, and several minor coups were repressed by the YOUNG TURK government before 1914. Denied the right to a national congress in October 1914, moderate Armenian politicians fled to BULGARIA, but extreme nationalists crossed the border to form a rebel division with Russian equipment. It invaded in December and slaughtered an estimated 120,000 non-Armenians while the TURKISH ARMY was preoccupied with mobilization and the CAUCASIAN FRONT offensive towards SARIKAMISH.

The Turks began disarming Armenian civilians under Ottoman control after a force of 2,500 rebels took Van in April 1915 and proclaimed a provisional government. An Ottoman order in June required all civilian non-Muslims to take up support duties near the battlefronts, but exemptions spared Greeks and the Catholic Armenian business community in Constantinople, effectively restricting the order to Orthodox and Protestant Armenians, who were subject to a military enforcement operation until late 1916.

Deportees were often given only hours to prepare, and left without transport or protection on long journeys to infertile, ill-supplied resettlement regions. Many died from starvation or exposure; many more were killed en route by hostile tribesmen (usually Kurds), some of whom colluded with Ottoman officials in search of a 'final solution' to the Armenian question.

Released through Armenian contacts with the Western press, especially strong in the

UNITED STATES, news of the catastrophe prompted the Turkish regime – which never openly associated itself with excesses against Armenians – to blame general supply and transport shortages for an estimated 300,000 deaths. Allied PROPAGANDA claimed more than a million had died, but modern consensus puts the figure at around 600,000.

An uneasy peace was imposed on frontier Armenians by the occupying RUSSIAN ARMY from 1916, but rebel forces resumed control in late 1917, killing perhaps another 50,000 non-Armenians. Subsequent attempts to restore Turkish administration caused sporadic fighting in early 1918, until the Treaty of Batum (26 May 1918) between an exhausted Turkey and a new Armenian Republic brought a period of recovery. Thousands more civilians then died attempting long journeys back to their liberated homes. See also: MAP 24; CENTRAL ASIAN REVOLT; TRANSCAUCASIA.

Armistice The cessation of hostilities as a prelude to peace negotiations. Wars on the EASTERN FRONT and in ROMANIA were halted in December 1917 (see Treaties of BREST-LITOVSK, BUCHAREST), and BULGARIA agreed an armistice with the Allies on 30 September 1918. The exhausted empires of TURKEY and AUSTRIA-HUNGARY ceased fighting on 30 October and 3 November, respectively. The final armistice, marking an Allied ceasefire with GERMANY, came into effect at 11.00 on 11 November 1918.

The German government of MAX VON BADEN formally asked US president WILSON for a ceasefire on 4 October. After gaining German acceptance of his FOURTEEN POINTS peace programme and establishing that Allied supremo FOCH would handle military negotiations, Wilson sought official Allied endorsement of the Points for the first time. British unwillingness to accept prohibition of BLOCKADE and French demands for REPARATIONS were accepted as qualifications before Wilson halted further dispute by threatening a separate peace with Germany. The SUPREME WAR COUNCIL's broad acceptance of the programme was communicated to Germany on 5 November.

Wilson's final precondition was met by the abdication of Kaiser WILHELM II, and on 10 November a German delegation of moderate politicians met Foch and Allied military representatives in the forest of Compiègne, about 65km northeast of Paris, near the Franco-German front line. Terms were dictated to the envoys and the Armistice signed next morning in Foch's railway carriage.

Peaceful evacuation of German-occupied territories on the WESTERN FRONT was required within 14 days, and Allied forces were to occupy the left bank of the Rhine within a month, with a neutral zone established on the right bank. All German conquests elsewhere were to be abandoned, along with economic exploitation, and peace treaties with RUSSIA and ROMANIA were annulled.

Germany surrendered 5,000 ARTILLERY pieces, 30,000 MACHINE GUNS, 3,000 MINENWERFER, 2,000 aircraft, 5,000 locomotives, 150,000 RAILWAY wagons, 5,000 lorries and all its SUBMARINES. Most of the GERMAN NAVY's surface fleets were interned, and the rest disarmed. As a guarantee of Franco-Belgian security, Allied economic blockade remained in force.

Entirely the work of military authorities, the Armistice terms inevitably influenced future decisions. Elements within all the Allied forces, particularly the relatively fresh AEF, had argued for a punitive ceasefire agreement to forestall Wilson's liberal intentions, and severity was moderated only by fear that Germany would resume hostilities or fall to a Bolshevik attack from the east.

Immediately condemned as a punitive gesture in Germany, but accepted because resumption of hostilities was no longer possible, the Armistice initially ran for 36 days. It was formally renewed on a regular basis during the PARIS PEACE CONFERENCE, always with the proviso that German deviation from the terms could bring a resumption of hostilities at 48 hours' notice. See also: Treaty of VERSAILLES.

Armoured Cars Armoured cars evolved from ordinary motor vehicles used by European forces for colonial policing of distant outposts. By 1914 Allied armies in Europe were using armour-plated, open-topped production vehicles carrying a MACHINE GUN or light ARTILLERY piece. Specialist cars were available by the end of the year, and an armoured, revolving turret was standard on later designs.

Armoured cars were first deployed by French, British and Belgian forces on the WESTERN FRONT as mobile infantry-support strongpoints, but their tactical value was limited in TRENCH WARFARE conditions and negated by their inability to handle broken terrain. Tracked TANKS were developed to overcome the latter problem, and later use of armoured cars was largely restricted to flatter, more open theatres until the resumption of mobile warfare in France during 1918.

British ground forces made the most widespread use of armoured cars, grouped from 1915 into four-vehicle Armoured Motor Batteries (AMB), using heavy Rolls Royce vehicles, or Light Armoured Car Batteries (LACB) equipped with conversions of various smaller British and US production cars. Eight-car Light Armoured Motor Batteries (LAMB) eventually became the usual formation.

The first British units in France were crewed by RNAS and ROYAL NAVY personnel, and a small naval contingent served (along with BELGIAN ARMY cars) under Russian tactical command during the later stages of the ROMANIAN CAMPAIGN. The BRITISH ARMY used armoured cars with great success in PALESTINE and on the MESOPOTAMIAN FRONT, where they were deployed in the CAVALRY roles of outflanking and pursuit. Often crewed by imperial troops, they also accompanied DUNSTERFORCE, proved an ideal mobile guerrilla weapon in support of the ARAB REVOLT, and were a valuable asset in campaigns against the SENUSSI.

Armoured Warfare See: ARMOURED CARS; TANKS.

Armstrong Whitworth FK-3 British bomber designed as a replacement for the BE-2 series but virtually obsolete by the time it entered RFC and RNAS service in September 1916. Although almost 500 were built, FK-3s saw action only as all-purpose infantry and ARTILLERY cooperation aircraft on the BALKAN FRONT.

BRIEF DATA Type: two-seater reconnaissance/light bomber; Engine: 90hp Royal Aircraft Factory; Max speed: 87mph (139kph); Ceiling: 3,600m; Armament: 1 × 0.303in mg (rear), max bomb load 220lbs (100 kg).

Armstrong Whitworth FK-8 An enlarged version of the British ARMSTRONG WHITWORTH FK-3, designed for reconnaissance and daylight bombing on the WESTERN FRONT. In RFC service from late 1916, it was a rugged and versatile aircraft that outperformed its immediate predecessor, the dangerously obsolete RE-8, but was no match for the latest German FIGHTERS. By early 1917 superior AIRCO DH-4 and BRISTOL FIGHTER two-seaters were becoming available and, although ordered in large numbers, only about 50 FK-8s served on the Western Front. A few also operated with home-defence units, in PALESTINE, and on the BALKAN FRONT.

BRIEF DATA Type: two-seat reconnaissance/light bomber; Engine: 160hp Beardsmore; Max speed: 98mph (157kph); Armament: 2 × 0.303in mg (1 forward), max bomb load 200lbs (91kg).

Arras, Battle of (1914) Attempt by General de Maud'huy's French Tenth Army to outflank German forces on the WESTERN FRONT by advancing along a line between Arras and Lens (see MAP 2). Part of the 'RACE TO THE SEA', the advance began as soon as sufficient French forces had moved north to the area on 1 October. After initial progress towards Douai, it was forced to withdraw by a counterattack from Crown Prince RUPPRECHT's German Sixth Army, itself transferred north from LORRAINE. The French retained Arras in the face of further heavy attacks, but the German Sixth Army had occupied Lens when the line stabilized on 4 October, by which time the battle zone had extended north to FLANDERS. See also: First Battle of ALBERT.

Arras, Battle of (1917) Major British attack on long-established German positions in Artois, east of Arras, and the opening phase of the Allied NIVELLE OFFENSIVE on the WESTERN FRONT in April 1917. Originally scheduled for February, and planned as the main Allied offensive of the spring, the attack had been delayed following the replacement of JOFFRE as French C-in-C in December. His successor, NIVELLE, required the British to lengthen their line and limit the attack in deference to his own plan for a massive offensive at the AISNE. British commander HAIG only fully accepted this when prime minister LLOYD GEORGE placed the BEF under temporary French control in February.

British preparations were further disrupted from mid-March by a German tactical withdrawal along the front southeast from Arras, limiting the BEF's immediate attacking options to a 20km front either side of the city, where German forward positions had not moved and preparations could continue unchanged (see Operation ALBERICH). Strategic success depended on a quick breakthrough north of Arras, where forward defences beyond the HINDENBURG LINE were backed by a partially complete fortified zone, known to the British as the Drocourt–Quéant Switch.

The attack opened at dawn on 9 April, after a five-day, 2,800-gun PRELIMINARY BOMBARDMENT that sacrificed any hope of surprise. Fourteen British divisions advanced along a line held by 6 divisions of the German Sixth Army (Falkenhausen). The Third Army (ALLENBY) attacked either side of Arras and the Scarpe, attackers north of the river advancing more than 3km on the first day. To its north the Canadian Corps (part of General HORNE's First Army) took the long-disputed stronghold of VIMY RIDGE at a cost of 14,000 casualties.

The attack was expected, and German reserves were quickly in position, but MINES extending towards German lines from caves and sewers beneath Arras were used as troop conduits, delivering infantry closer to their targets. Emerging from their tunnels into a snowstorm, advancing troops also benefited from improved ARTILLERY sighting and ammunition (particularly GAS shells), new CREEPING BARRAGE techniques and numerical (but not qualitative) superiority in aircraft (see BLOODY APRIL).

Progress was much slower against completed Hindenburg Line installations south of the river, where fighting focused on the village strongpoint of Monchy-le-Preux, and repeated attacks, in freezing conditions and against stiffening resistance, failed to achieve a significant breakthrough over the next few days.

Further small gains were made north of the Scarpe, and Monchy-le-Preux was taken on 11 April with the help of a rare and costly CAVALRY charge, but the narrow attacking front allowed the British little flexibility of manoeuvre, and supply lines through Arras rapidly became overcrowded.

In an attempt to stretch German defences, the British Fifth Army (GOUGH) launched an attack from recently occupied positions further south on 11 April. Marred by compound staff failures and the confused deployment of a few available TANKS, it failed completely against Hindenburg Line defences around Bullecourt. Forced to advance before supporting artillery had been properly redeployed, AUSTRALIAN infantry suffered its worst day's losses on the Western Front.

On 14 April, Haig halted British attacks to await news of the French AISNE offensive, begun on 16 April. Its failure prompted renewal of operations around Arras from 23 April, when attacks by the First and Third Armies gained another 1–2km in two days' heavy fighting. With no hope of strategic gain, repeated assaults by exhausted troops all along the line continued until late May, with losses particularly heavy during two weeks of continuous combat around Bullecourt from 3 May.

Though Haig's costly repetition of unsuccessful tactics was criticized at the time in GREAT BRITAIN, the battle as a whole was seen by Allied commanders as a relative success. Vimy Ridge was considered an important gain, and BEF losses of about 150,000 men, against an estimated 100,000 German casualties, represented a better ratio of attrition than usual for attackers on the Western Front. See MAP 2.

Artillery See: ARTILLERY, FIELD; ANTI-AIRCRAFT, COASTAL and RAILWAY ARTILLERY; MORTARS; BATTLESHIPS; FORTRESSES.

Artillery, Field Despite the importance of MACHINE GUNS for defensive operations, and claims made for the roles of TANKS and AERIAL WARFARE, the big gun was the dominant field weapon of the period. A surprise to European military planners, dependence on unprecedented levels of artillery support for any kind of offensive became a universal orthodoxy after 1914.

Late 19th-century developments in artillery technology had introduced breech-loaded weapons, with barrels rifled for accuracy and hydraulic recoil systems. They equipped most modern forces in 1914, but many old muzzle-loaders and smooth-bores remained in active service all over the world, especially in FORTRESSES, COASTAL ARTILLERY batteries and old BATTLESHIPS, and were frequently pressed into emergency use by the main belligerents as demand for guns mushroomed beyond expectations.

Artillery is generally described by its calibre – the diameter of its barrel bore – although many British guns were named according to the weight of their ammunition. The lightest and smallest modern guns regularly used by frontline forces in 1914 were 20mm or 37mm calibre 'mountain guns' for difficult terrain or 'horse artillery' for support of fast-moving CAVALRY units. Intended for antipersonnel use or destruction of light cover they were otherwise the preserve of minor armies or colonial forces not expecting to meet heavily armed opponents.

The main support weapon for major armies in 1914 was the long-barrelled field gun. Designed to support mobile forces in action, field guns fired a high-velocity shell at a visible target on a low trajectory. Necessarily mobile, they were restricted in range and weight of shell, but were the focus of most artillery preparation for what was expected to be a short, fast-moving war.

The 'quick-firing' (QF) field gun, with a recoil system that bounced the barrel back into firing position without use of wheels and muscle, was pioneered in the FRENCH ARMY's 75mm 'SOIXANTE-QUINZE', which was imitated but not bettered by the global armaments industry. By 1914 the GERMAN ARMY's standard Krupp 77mm gun (also used by the AUSTRO-HUNGARIAN ARMY), the British EIGHTEEN-POUNDER, the 3-inch RUSSIAN ARMY and 3-inch US ARMY field guns were all its rough equivalent in quality. Most other armies lacked the capacity to produce QF guns of their own, but had been buying from the Great Powers before 1914.

Wartime development of field guns was limited because they proved far less important than anticipated on the main European fronts. Although larger (100–105mm) field weapons were available to some armies, they were generally too cumbersome for efficient mobile use and always ill-suited to destruction of trench fortifications, a requirement that stimulated demand for howitzers, heavy artillery and MORTARS.

Howitzers fired heavier shells on a high trajectory through a short barrel. Their plunging fire was designed to attack at closer range, from cover or against hidden targets. Medium (or field) howitzers, generally of 120–160mm calibre, were intended to keep up with infantry movements for use against field fortifications.

Following the example of Japan, Germany and Austria-Hungary had developed a range of modern 120mm and 150mm field howitzers by 1914, but the TRIPLE ENTENTE powers were generally ill-equipped. Russia was just starting to manufacture licensed German 122mm howitzers in 1914, but Britain had only an obsolescent 4.5-inch (114mm) model in service, and the French Army had decided against any form of field howitzer development, preferring to economize by using a disc attachment (Malandrin Disc) to make field-gun shells fall short.

The Allies quickly realized their mistake, but development of suitable weapons took time and they were initially forced to rely on slow-firing, obsolete weapons, delivering inferior shells and too bulky for efficient deployment in WESTERN FRONT conditions. New models came into service from 1915, with the French 155mm Schneider and the British 6-inch (152mm) howitzers becoming standard, but the German Army's qualitative advantage was not overhauled until late 1916.

Concentration of artillery for massed bombardment was the principle tactical response to defensive superiority imposed by TRENCH WARFARE, and prolonged stalemate prompted army commanders to demand ever bigger guns. Heavy guns were generally for use from permanent defensive positions or warships until 1914, but their transformation into a viable field weapon eventually shaped the tactics and geography of the main entrenched fronts.

The German Army had giant, mobile Krupp 420mm 'BIG BERTHA' and Austrian 305mm SCHLANKE EMMA howitzers ready just in time to perform their allotted task in August 1914, the destruction of the Belgian fortresses at LIÈGE and NAMUR. Their success sparked a general rush to find heavy guns for both the Western and EASTERN FRONTS, and old fortress guns everywhere were stripped from fixed mountings for frontline use, but lack of mobility often made them either useless or vulnerable to counterattack (see e.g. PRZEMYSL).

Specialist mobile heavy weapons, theoretically light enough to be pulled across mud and shell-shattered ground, came to dominate bombardment warfare. Long-range heavy field guns (generally over 170mm) could eventually fire a 65–100kg shell to a range of up to 30km; heavy howitzers (200–400mm) lobbed projectiles weighing anything up to about 900kg over 9–18km. As in other areas, initial German superiority in heavy artillery was eventually overtaken by Allied production capacity.

The heaviest guns in action on the battlefield were mounted as RAILWAY ARTILLERY, widely employed close to the main European fronts. Other developments forced by wartime experience included adaptations for ANTI-AIRCRAFT use, but the greatest technological strides were made in targeting, ballistics, transportation and ammunition.

Mutual concealment and concentration against hostile artillery (counterbattery fire) made indirect targeting necessary on static fronts. It rapidly came to depend on accurate aerial reconnaissance from BALLOONS or spotter planes (see AERIAL WARFARE), and associated advances in PHOTO-RECONNAISSANCE and RADIO technology were of great importance. Consideration of ballistic factors, hitherto restricted to replacement of worn barrels and compensation for their age while aiming, was extended to prediction of wind, humidity and other variables in advance of firing.

Transportation of artillery became an enormous problem as guns in Europe got bigger and the fighting extended into remote tropical or subtropical regions elsewhere. The standard means of moving guns in 1914, on wheeled carriages pulled by pack animals (usually horses in Europe, mules or oxen elsewhere), was still entirely dominant in 1918, by which time some 'super-heavy' field pieces weighing above 30,000kg were operating in cratered landscapes of their own creation.

Mechanized transportation of artillery to the battlefield was limited by the terrain, with lorries only rarely used to haul or carry guns, although a few medium weapons were mounted on caterpillar tracks by the British in France, a refinement of the tank concept that previewed later self-propelled artillery. The inability to move heavy guns quickly prohibited rapid advance by either side on the Western Front, and remained a powerful restraining factor in late 1918.

The most immediate problems facing wartime gunners concerned supply, quality and precise application of ammunition. None of the belligerent armies had anticipated anything like the shell requirements of modern artillery warfare, and although the more efficient national economies were eventually able to meet the fantastic demand from field commanders, the strain in terms of both industrial output and distribution created SHELL SHORTAGES in many armies from autumn 1914.

The demands of static warfare also transformed the type of shell needed for frontline operations. Solid cannon balls were still in use for old smooth-bore weapons on secondary fronts, but most modern guns fired shrapnel in 1914. Its exploding fragments and thousands of metal pellets were ideal for anti-personnel use in open terrain, but had little effect on barbed wire, trench fortifications or enemy artillery.

Shells filled with high explosive (HE) were far more destructive, but they were a relatively new invention and had hardly been used prior to 1914. Part of the problem was finding a suitable, stable explosive, and although picric acid (known as Lyddite in Britain) had been in general use for some years it often failed to detonate on impact. The German Army was ahead of the Allies in development of a better substance, TNT, which equipped some batteries in August 1914, but early British HE shells were of particularly poor quality. By 1916 efficient HE supplies dominated artillery bombardment on both sides.

Two other types of shell became common in trench warfare conditions: smoke shells to conceal troop movements were filled with white phosphorus, which was released to react with the air on impact; and poison GAS was later enclosed in shells on the same principle.

Overwhelming concentration of resources on the Western Front often forced Allied armies elsewhere to rely exclusively on shrapnel.

Scraping together every available weapon of every sort, some 2,500 French guns supported infantry all along the front for the second CHAMPAGNE OFFENSIVE in autumn 1915, at the time considered a vast agglomeration of firepower. By mid-1917, the height of tactical dependence on bombardment, the British were using a similar number of far more powerful guns for a limited attack along a very narrow front at MESSINES, and expending some 3.5 million rounds in a two-week PRELIMINARY BOMBARDMENT. By 1918 Allied offensives on the Western and ITALIAN FRONTS were typically supported by 5,000–8,000 artillery pieces.

Mass bombardment was not truly successful against DEFENCE IN DEPTH or well-developed trench systems anywhere until the problems of exploiting its destructive power were addressed using all the other modern technologies available to armies in 1918 (see BREAKTHROUGH; INFILTRATION TACTICS; PEACEFUL PENETRATION).

European and North American production was geared to an expected 1919 campaign right up to the ARMISTICE, creating a huge postwar artillery surplus as military forces were dramatically scaled down. With unemployed munitions experts carrying their skills to new markets and the price of second-hand artillery plummeting, many of the standard big guns of 1918 were still in Allied service 20 years later.

Artois Offensive Allied offensive on the sector of the WESTERN FRONT stretching north from Arras towards Lille. Launched in May 1915, while the second YPRES battle was still in progress further north, it was the second of French C-in-C JOFFRE's major attempts to break through German lines by massed infantry assault (see First CHAMPAGNE OFFENSIVE).

On 9 May, after a five-day PRELIMINARY BOMBARDMENT of German positions, the French Ninth Army (d'Urbail) advanced along a 10km front between Arras and Lens. A breakthrough in the centre enabled PÉTAIN's corps to cover more than 5km in the first 90 minutes, and to approach VIMY RIDGE. French attacks elsewhere were held off, and German reserves were able to concentrate at the centre, exploiting French shortages of manpower in advanced areas and regaining much of the ground lost. Heavy fighting until 15 May brought no significant gains to either side, and a resumption of the battle from 15–19 June failed to break the deadlock.

The British First Army (HAIG) also attacked on 9 May, on a front either side of Neuve Chapelle towards the Aubers Ridge. British shell shortages restricted preliminary bombardment to 40 minutes, fleeting by contemporary standards, and a poorly supported infantry advance achieved only the loss of 11,000 men before it was called off later in the day (see 'SHELL SCANDAL'). Pressed for action by Joffre, Haig launched a second attack on his southern wing around Festubert on the night of 15 May. Preceded by a four-day bombardment, it made rapid initial progress but became bogged down, and had pushed German Sixth Army (RUPPRECHT) lines back by less than a kilometre when it was halted on 27 May.

Total German casualties of around 90,000 confirmed chief of staff FALKENHAYN's determination to remain on the defensive in the west. The Artois battles cost the FRENCH ARMY more than 100,000 men, and the BEF about 26,000, prompting a period of recuperation before Allied leaders resumed the offensive in the autumn (see MAP 2; ARTOIS–LOOS OFFENSIVE; Second CHAMPAGNE OFFENSIVE).

Artois–Loos Offensive Secondary, northern arm of the major Allied offensive on the WESTERN FRONT in autumn 1915, also known as the Second Battle of Artois. Attacks on both the north and south flanks of German-held territory in France opened on 25 September (see Second CHAMPAGNE OFFENSIVE), and the northern operation was further subdivided: the French attacking on VIMY RIDGE, near Arras, and the British advancing further north towards Loos (see MAP 2).

General DUBAIL's French Tenth Army paid heavily for slow progress against the formidable defensive positions of Crown Prince RUPPRECHT's German Sixth Army. One division managed to reach the crest of Vimy Ridge on 29 September, but constant German counterpressure prevented any lasting gains elsewhere. Although required to stretch its front to the north to compensate for British losses, the Tenth Army continued its attacks whenever the weather allowed, with similar results, until exhaustion forced a halt in early November.

The British First Army's six divisions attacked towards Loos on 25 September against the better judgement of its commander, HAIG, but enjoyed immediate success on its northern flank. Massive numerical superiority more than compensated for difficult terrain and continuing shell shortage, although the first British use of poison GAS was disrupted by the wind. By the end of the first day, British troops were beyond Loos and in the outskirts of Lens, but supply and control problems were compounded by BEF commander Sir John FRENCH, who forced Haig to halt by withholding reserves until that night. Forced back by strong counterattacks the next day, the British were unable to renew the action until 13 October, when a second advance was thrown back with heavy losses, after which bad weather brought combat to an end.

The offensives at Artois–Loos cost the BEF 50,000 casualties, and the French Army about 48,000. German casualties were less than half, reflecting increasing dominance of their defensive tactics over infantry-based Allied attacking methods (See DEFENCE IN DEPTH).

Arz von Straussenberg, General Artur, Baron (1857–1935) An Austrian corps commander with the First Army on the EASTERN FRONT from August 1914, and praised for his operations in support of the German BUG OFFENSIVE in 1915, Arz was given command of the First Army the following year, and led it during the victorious ROMANIAN CAMPAIGN. On 1 March 1917 he replaced CONRAD as AUSTRO-HUNGARIAN ARMY chief of staff, resisting Hungarian pressure to establish separate national armies. However, he functioned as Emperor KARL I's personal advisor rather than the instigator of strategy. Ennobled in February 1918, his options were restricted by German control over most senior staff posts, and he was unable to exert authority over his own field commanders. Disputes between Generals Conrad and BOROEVIC persuaded him to divide attacking forces for the PIAVE RIVER offensive of June 1918, and its failure triggered the Army's final disintegration. Without political ambition, Arz retired after the ARMISTICE.

Asiago Offensive See: TRENTINO OFFENSIVE.

Askari German term, in general use by white colonists all over AFRICA by 1914, for a native soldier in European service. All the standing colonial armies in Africa, except the German force in SOUTHWEST AFRICA, relied on Askaris for their manpower base. The number of Askaris employed in wartime is impossible to calculate – enlistment was often casual and temporary – but allowing for understandable panic when confronted with terrifying new weapons such as aircraft, Askaris were by far the most effective troops in African conditions. They sometimes repaid maltreatment or military failure by changing sides, and often marched with families, bearers and material possessions in train, but were generally loyal, resourceful, determined and, above all, able to remain healthy in the tropics. The best

European commanders in Africa learned to train and trust Askaris as they would first-class white troops, and the genuine meritocracy run by General LETTOW-VORBECK in EAST AFRICA was rewarded with extraordinary service throughout his campaign.

Askold The largest warship stationed with the RUSSIAN NAVY's Siberian Flotilla at Vladivostok in 1914. *Askold* was completed in 1902, and was typical of the elderly light CRUISERS in Russian service. Sent to the eastern MEDITERRANEAN on the outbreak of war with TURKEY in November 1914, it took part in Allied bombardments of Turkish coastal positions from December. The only Russian warship in action at GALLIPOLI, it remained in the Mediterranean until 1916, when it was transferred to the ARCTIC after a refit in France and replaced by the old battleship *PERESVIET*. Its varied career ended in 1918, when it was taken over by British forces in northern Russia and scrapped.
BRIEF DATA (1914) Displacement: 5,900 tons; Speed: 21k; Armament: 12 × 6in (152mm) gun, 2 × 47mm AA, 4 × TT.

Asquith, Herbert Henry (1852–1928) British politician, part of the Liberal Party's 'imperialist' wing during a decade of opposition before becoming chancellor of the exchequer (finance minister) in early 1906. He succeeded Campbell-Bannerman as prime minister in 1908, bringing universally admired intellectual talents and a gift for compromise to a turbulent party.

Attempts at social and political reform brought dwindling majorities during a period of constitutional upheaval in GREAT BRITAIN. His preferred means of reaching major decisions was exemplified by his handling of the JULY CRISIS in 1914, when he waited for cabinet unity to crystallize before committing the country to war.

He was shrewd enough to cement national unity by the immediate appointment of KITCHENER as war minister in August 1914, but masterly inactivity began to appear as sluggishness and strategic 'drift' as his large cabinet failed to formulate a consistent war policy. Basic disputes between 'EASTERNERS' and 'Westerners' remained unresolved into 1915, with strong figures like LLOYD GEORGE, Kitchener, CHURCHILL and FISHER apparently operating in mutual isolation. The 'SHELL SCANDAL' forced the cabinet's resignation in May 1915 and Asquith formed a coalition, including leader Bonar LAW among eight Conservatives and a single socialist (HENDERSON).

Asquith streamlined policy-making with the formation of a five-man war council in November 1915, but he was never a charismatic figure and became a political liability with the onset of public war weariness in 1916. After exhaustion of the SOMME OFFENSIVE had ended a year of military disappointments, Lloyd George conspired with Bonar Law and others to break up the coalition in early December 1916, relegating Asquith to technical leadership of the opposition after almost nine years in power.

Still Liberal leader, he was a characteristically mild wartime critic of the Lloyd George administration, continuing to stress national unity and seeking to heal deep splits in his party. He lost his parliamentary seat in the December 1918 elections, when the extent of Liberal decline was revealed, but returned to lead the shrunken parliamentary party as the 1st Earl of Oxford and Asquith from 1925.

Athens Landing The culmination of Allied coercive measures in 1916 designed to secure the benevolence of neutral Greek authorities towards operations from SALONIKA. A powerful (mostly French) naval force had been anchored threateningly in the Gulf of Athens since September (see SALAMIS OPERATION), and the prospect of civil war in GREECE prompted MEDITERRANEAN naval C-in-C DARTIGE to demand new guarantees of security in November.

An ultimatum of 22 November required the Greek government to hand over ARTILLERY, MACHINE GUNS and RIFLES, with the first instalment due on 1 December. After talks with King CONSTANTINE Dartige decided to land a small force at Athens to ensure delivery. Three battalions of French sailors, with a few British and Italian troops, got ashore unopposed on the morning of 1

December, but were attacked inland by GREEK ARMY forces. At least 90 men were killed (casualty figures vary) and the BATTLESHIP *Mirabeau* fired four heavy rounds in the vicinity of the royal palace, before Allied diplomats in Athens arranged a ceasefire and the sailors retreated to Piraeus.

The 'ambush of Athens' was seen as an act of treachery in FRANCE, and ended hopes of Allied reconciliation with the Greek monarchy. Salonika C-in-C SARRAIL took control of the Athens operation, and Dartige was replaced by Admiral GAUCHET on 12 December. A French BLOCKADE of Greece was announced and, still under threat of naval bombardment, the Greek government accepted Allied demands, withdrawing its army to the distant Peloponnese.

Audacious British battleship completed in late 1913 as the last of four KING GEORGE V Class 'super-dreadnoughts'. As part of the GRAND FLEET's Second Battle Squadron, *Audacious* struck a single MINE off the northern Irish coast on 27 October 1914, and sank when the magazine blew up during towing attempts. Witnessed by passengers of the nearby transatlantic liner *Olympic*, the loss was a considerable blow to the morale and prestige of the ROYAL NAVY, which tried unsuccessfully to keep it secret. Lack of German-style hull compartmentalization and of sufficient internal protection against 'flash' cordite explosions caused several more disasters on British ships (see *VANGUARD*).

BRIEF DATA As for *KING GEORGE V*.

Auffenberg, Field Marshal Moritz (1852–1928) Former Austro-Hungarian war minister (1911–12) who had attempted to modernize the AUSTRO-HUNGARIAN ARMY during his brief term of office. In command of the Fourth Army in GALICIA, he won a tactical victory over the Russian Fifth Army at KOMAROV in late August, but his army was almost surrounded at Rava Ruska in September. Auffenberg was dismissed during the subsequent retreat to the CARPATHIANS and held no further wartime commands.

Augagneur, Jean (1855–1931) French moderate socialist politician. He was education minister under VIVIANI, but was promoted to navy minister when the 1914 JULY CRISIS pushed the incumbent, Gauthier, into a breakdown. With little naval experience in a parliament well stocked with experts, Augagneur faced political criticism for the FRENCH NAVY's lack of strategic impact, and struggled to impose his authority on professionals. He was particularly condemned for allowing limited commitment to the DARDANELLES expedition in 1915, but his decision to remain 'in the game' while leaving major risks to the British has since been viewed as inevitable. Replaced by Admiral LACAZE when the government fell in October 1915, he served as a relatively obscure deputy until his electoral defeat in 1919.

Augustovo, Battle of See: Second Battle of the MASURIAN LAKES.

Australia Formally inaugurated as a self-governing dominion of the British Empire in 1901, the Commonwealth of Australia was a federation of the continent's state territories and offshore dependencies. Its constitution concentrated executive authority in the federal government, appointed by a British governor general from a two-tier parliament elected by adult male suffrage. The sparse population of some 5 million was mostly concentrated on the coast, but an estimated 200,000 native Australians were living in the interior.

War broke out in Europe immediately after the collapse of Joseph Cook's shortlived Liberal administration in late July 1914. Cook's predecessor, Labour Party leader Andrew FISHER, won a convincing victory in the subsequent election, but both main parties were firmly behind immediate dispatch of AUSTRALIAN FORCES to aid the British war effort. Virtually all the European inhabitants were of British descent, and early public enthusiasm was comparable with that in GREAT BRITAIN.

Public fervour and government popularity waned significantly as Australian casualties mounted on the GALLIPOLI FRONT, prompting a reduction of the physical requirements for military service from mid-1915 to revive flagging enlistment rates. The return of veterans from the theatre and news of conditions at ANZAC COVE (see MURDOCH, K.) made British C-in-C HAMILTON the most unpopular man in Australia.

Tainted by the campaign, Fisher resigned in late 1915 and was replaced by former attorney general William HUGHES, who ignored mounting popular disapproval of Allied war management to pursue a firmly pro-British policy. Lionized during a 1916 visit to London, but mistrusted by many of his constituents, Hughes faced political crisis over his promise to introduce conscription to Australia.

Compulsory service was against Labour Party policy and was narrowly rejected by the Australian electorate in two referenda during 1916. Hughes retained power by leaving the Labour Party and forming a mostly Liberal coalition, which remained in office until 1923. Hughes represented Australia at the PARIS PEACE CONFERENCE, arguing forcefully for Australian MANDATE control over New Guinea.

With a healthy budget, a well-established annual export surplus, excellent port facilities and plentiful RAILWAY links, Australia benefited from wartime economic conditions, but was not sufficiently developed in 1914 to achieve great industrial expansion. Trade in meat and metals to Europe mushroomed, but lack of shipping space limited food exports. Collapse of imports from Europe at the same time encouraged the first penetration of Australian markets by the Japanese cotton industry. Australia's overall share of world trade still rose by 25 per cent in the decade from 1913, and wartime pressure to establish its own armament and manufacturing capacity was reflected in rapid postwar industrialization.

Australia British INDEFATIGABLE Class BATTLECRUISER in Australian service. Completed in June 1913, it served as a troopship escort and trade protection vessel in the Pacific in 1914, taking part in the prolonged hunt for the *SCHARNHORST* and *GNEISENAU* (see Battle of CORONEL). In 1915, after escorting AUSTRALIAN FORCES to EGYPT, it joined the GRAND FLEET as flagship of the Second Battlecruiser Squadron, remaining in the North Sea until 1919 but missing the Battle of JUTLAND during a refit.

BRIEF DATA (1917) As for *Indefatigable* except: Armament: 8 × 12in gun, 14 × 4in, 1 × 4in AA, 1 × 3in AA, 2 × 21in TT.

Australian Forces Australian ground forces were organized solely for home defence before 1914. A tiny regular army, formed in 1901, was backed by a part-time volunteer militia (45,000 men in 1914), and all males of combat age were required by law to undertake minimal military training on a regular basis. The government's offer to GREAT BRITAIN (3 August 1914) to provide 20,000 troops for imperial defence prompted the creation of a new volunteer force for overseas service, the Australian Imperial Force (AIF), organized by regular army chief of staff Colonel Bridges (later a general, killed at ANZAC COVE).

Filled by a 'hard-sell' recruitment campaign and a wave of popular enthusiasm for war, the first AIF and New Zealand troopships left Western Australia on 7 November 1914 and a second CONVOY sailed on 31 December. Recruitment slowed from 1915, but conscription was only ever thought appropriate by extreme British nationalists. A total population of less than 5 million eventually contributed about 322,000 Australians to wartime overseas service, of whom more than 280,000 were casualties (including almost 60,000 dead), the highest rate of attrition suffered by any national army.

Overseas forces were eventually formed into five Australian divisions, grouped with NEW ZEALAND FORCES and a few British units to form two Australian and New Zealand Army Corps (ANZAC) until late 1917, after which most were deployed as a single Australian Corps. Their resolute lack of military etiquette outraged many British officers, but ANZAC commander BIRDWOOD was not among them and by 1918 Australians were generally recognized as the most formidable fighting troops on the

Allied side.

Sent first to EGYPT for intensive training with BRITISH ARMY weapons, some Australian units participated in the defence of SUEZ before mass transfer to the GALLIPOLI FRONT, where Australians transformed their perceived military value. Considered an elite force by the time they reached France in 1916, infantry troops cemented their reputation during a gruelling series of campaigns on the WESTERN FRONT in 1918. Under Australian General MONASH from May 1918, they led Allied counteroffensives in the central sector of the front from LE HAMEL in July until just before the ARMISTICE (see PEACEFUL PENETRATION). Australian CAVALRY (Light Horse) brigades, which fought dismounted in Gallipoli and France, were transferred to PALESTINE in 1917–18 and played a vital role in ALLENBY's decisive victories.

The Royal Australian Navy was a nominally independent force established by agreement with the ROYAL NAVY in 1909. The Australian government paid an annual subsidy for provision of warships on the understanding that they would be available for wartime imperial defence. They included a modern BATTLECRUISER, three TOWN CRUISERS, six DESTROYERS and two older 'protected' CRUISERS (see *AUSTRALIA*; *SYDNEY*; Battle of the RUFUGI DELTA). Two Australian SUBMARINES were lost in naval operations at the DARDANELLES, and one (*AE-2*) penetrated the Straits in April 1915 before being discovered and scuttled.

The Australian Flying Corps (AFC) was officially founded in 1914 and made a small but independent contribution to RFC campaigns in several theatres. Two Australian BE-2s operated on the MESOPOTAMIAN FRONT in 1915, and a squadron fought in Palestine from 1916, flying BE-12, RE-8 and SE-5 two-seaters. One reconnaissance and two FIGHTER squadrons lost about 60 aircraft in France from autumn 1917. A home squadron had been established by 1918, but the AFC was disbanded in 1919 and reformed as the Royal Australian Air Force in 1921.

Austria-Hungary The Austro-Hungarian Empire, or 'Dual Monarchy', was the largest European political bloc after RUSSIA, covering some 675,000 square kilometres of central and southern Europe (see MAP 1). Apart from ethnic Germans and Hungarians, its 51.3 million people (1910) included Poles, Croats, Bosnians, Serbians, Italians, Czechs, Ruthenes, Slovenes, Slovaks and Romanians, with an accompanying spread of religious groups.

Political authority rested with the Habsburg dynasty in the person of FRANZ JOSEF I, who, since partial union between Austria and Hungary was established by the *Ausgleich* ('compromise') agreement in 1867, was Emperor of Austria and King of Hungary. Foreign affairs, wars and most of the armed forces were controlled and financed through common imperial ministries, Austria paying two-thirds of the costs incurred, and the recently acquired territory of Bosnia-Herzegovina was also administered jointly.

The two states shared an imperial currency and customs union, but other state functions, including control of large home armies and minority populations, rested with the national governments. Despite Franz Josef's considerable powers, both states were technically constitutional monarchies, with appointed upper and elected lower houses of parliament, but their incompatibility was the most basic of numerous divisions that hampered the Empire's political development.

Comprising just under half the Empire's territory, and with over 10 million ethnic Germans among its 30 million inhabitants, Austria was to some extent an industrial state, dependent on imports of food and raw materials but able to produce its own arms and other heavy manufactured goods. Its parliament (Reichsrat) was a troublesome, polyglot hotbed of urban socialists, bourgeois liberals and provincial interests.

A combination of socialists and Czech nationalists was able to block most prewar Austrian government initiatives until conservative prime minister STÜRGKH suspended the Reichsrat in March 1914. Pan-Germanism was strong among the ruling conservative bureaucracy, which generally regarded alliance with GERMANY as basic to security against expanding SERBIA in the south and ITALY to the southwest.

Larger but with only some 20 million people, including about 9 million Hungarians and 2.5 million semi-autonomous Slavs in Croatia-Slovenia, Hungary was a predominantly rural, agricultural society. Its parliaments were dominated by landed interests and the lower house was elected by only about 5 per cent of the population.

Hungarian politicians regarded themselves as exploited junior partners to Austria. The government, led by Count TISZA from 1913, blocked attempts to increase imperial military strength and lobbied for high import duties to ensure Austria's continued dependence on Hungarian produce. A dispute with ROMANIA over Transylvania was Hungary's most important foreign-policy issue, and Tisza favoured peaceful accommodation with Serbia and Italy.

Imperial diplomacy was guided by a combination of internal divisions and external complications. Relations with Italy, an alliance partner until 1914, and Romania were inevitably fragile; control over Galicia overlapped Russian interests and a well-established movement for an independent POLAND; almost 7 million Czechs, inhabiting the most developed part of greater Austria, constituted the most coherent internal separatist movement.

On the Empire's southern borders the decline of TURKEY had left an enlarged Serbia, backed by Russia, encouraging Slav nationalism and contesting control of the eastern Adriatic coast. Prewar imperial policy in the Balkans was aggressive and expansionist, and Austria-Hungary risked war with Russia to annex Bosnia-Herzegovina in 1908. The increasingly militant mood of Serbs in Austrian-controlled Croatia, Slovenia and Bosnia-Herzegovina encouraged calls for decisive military action against them, and against expansionist Serbia itself.

Although it functioned in 15 languages and the loyalty of ethnic-minority contingents was dubious, the AUSTRO-HUNGARIAN ARMY was the Empire's greatest unifying force. Swearing allegiance to Franz Josef in person, as did the smaller AUSTRO-HUNGARIAN NAVY, it boasted many royal senior officers and enjoyed considerable political influence with the crown.

Pressure for pre-emptive wars against Serbia and Italy from a strong military faction, led by the ambitious CONRAD, had been resisted by imperial foreign minister Aerenthal until his death in 1912, and less firmly blocked by his successor, BERCHTOLD. Archduke FRANZ FERDINAND's assassination by the Serb nationalist PRINCIP in Sarajevo on 28 June provoked a crisis for which Conrad, as chief of the Army general staff, was ready. Plans for a surprise attack against Serbia were spoiled by Berchtold's insistence on diplomatic delay during the JULY CRISIS, but guarantees of German support and Russia's mobilization in support of Serbia signalled war on both the BALKAN and EASTERN FRONTS.

War brought the immediate suspension of internal divisions. To the amazement of conservatives and commanders, all nationalities and political groupings (Bosnians apart) displayed enthusiasm for the imperial cause and mobilized without dissent. Mobilization nevertheless brought instant chaos to the RAILWAYS, the product of poor management and changes of plan forced on Conrad by the early Russian threat to GALICIA.

Like other major belligerents, Austria-Hungary attempted to mobilize its economy for a short war in 1914. As the only one of Germany's wartime allies with a major armaments industry, military production was its main focus. The War Production Law of 1912 placed all militarily important industries under direct imperial control on the outbreak of hostilities. War-related factories and labour forces came under military law, with the war ministry commandeering output at fixed prices and paying compensation to shareholders.

From late 1914 government control was gradually extended to the distribution of vital raw materials, and central associations were formed to administer individual commodities. Cartels of industrialists concerned more with profits than efficient economic management, these central associations remained largely outside political control. Production orders, labour allocation, coal supplies and other vital raw materials were governed by military authorities and industrial interest groups, but never with the rigour displayed by their German counterparts (see KRA).

Tensions between Austria and Hungary mounted. A poor harvest in 1914 and the devastation of grain belts on the Eastern Front, together with Tisza's national approach to Hungary's agricultural resources, combined to create early food shortages in urban Austria. Tisza ended customs union in 1915 and restricted exports to occasional surpluses, creating impotent outrage in starving Vienna. In spite of mounting difficulties, exacerbated by Allied BLOCKADE and the end of overland trade with Italy, the imperial government was never sufficiently organized to impose a centralized food policy or systematic rationing.

War on three fronts and massive losses, especially during the Russian BRUSILOV OFFENSIVE of the summer, brought the Empire close to exhausting its military, economic and political resources by autumn 1916. The armed forces were suffering supply shortages across the board and became dependent on German aid and organization. In addition, the surprisingly durable loyalty of Czech and other Slav units began to crumble.

Economic breakdown was accelerated by another bad harvest in 1916 and a very cold winter, bringing industrial activity to a virtual standstill in all but direct military fields. Evident war weariness and mounting political instability were ignited by Stürgkh's assassination in October 1916, and the position of the new premier, KÖRBER, was rapidly undermined by the policies of Emperor KARL I, who succeeded Franz Josef in November.

Karl sought peace and moderate reform, but achieved neither. Diplomatic channels were alive with whispers of a negotiated settlement in early 1917, and Karl attempted personal diplomacy through Prince SIXTUS in the spring, but all efforts foundered on imperial unwillingness to deal separately from Germany on the one side and hardening Allied war aims on the other (see PEACE NOTE).

Conciliatory moves towards Hungarian political demands prompted Körber's resignation in December. Agriculture minister CLAM-MARTINIC took over, charged with forming a government of national consensus, but recall of the Reichsrat from 31 May 1917 only revealed the depth of ethnic and social discontent.

Berlin's deep suspicion of Karl's motives informed the powerful position enjoyed by pro-German imperial foreign minister CZERNIN, but the Emperor replaced Conrad with the more pliable ARZ VON STRAUSSENBERG in March 1917 and dismissed Tisza on 23 May. Following the resignations of Clam-Martinic in June 1917 and Esterházy (Tisza's successor) in August, a succession of premiers strove unsuccessfully to satisfy separatists with moderate reform proposals.

A belated attempt to rationalize the economy was also begun in 1917, but development of an elaborate bureaucratic structure achieved little in practice and arms production fell below 1914 levels in 1918. The OCTOBER REVOLUTION, and consequent release of PoWs from Russia, sent discernible shockwaves through the Empire, with strikes and food riots following a cut in the Austrian flour ration of January 1918. Victory over Russia and Romania provided few material benefits, the Treaties of BREST-LITOVSK and BUCHAREST being primarily designed to aid the German war effort.

The Army was used to restore order, but the reliability of its non-Germanic units and of the Navy, which suffered a mutiny at CATTARO in February 1918, became questionable as the Empire's military position degenerated to the point of German annexation. On 11 May 1918, at a meeting with WILHELM II in Germany, Karl was forced to accept formal German military control and economic union.

Supply levels to the Army fell dangerously below subsistence level. The collapse of its last offensive at the PIAVE in June and German failure on the WESTERN FRONT in the summer removed its last hope of ultimate military victory, and continued pressure on the ITALIAN FRONT prevented use of loyal units for internal policing in the autumn.

Strengthening Allied commitment to national independence movements had helped ensure disintegration of the Empire before its armistice with the Allies on 3 November (see

FOURTEEN POINTS; ROME CONGRESS). The new states of CZECHOSLOVAKIA and YUGOSLAVIA were popularly proclaimed in late October, along with an independent Hungarian Republic, and a Republic of Austria was established after the Emperor's formal abdication of 11 November.

Partition was broadly confirmed by the ST GERMAIN and TRIANON Treaties in 1919, with both Austria and Hungary reduced in size, but political turmoil remained endemic to the region for several years. Shrunken Austria, forbidden proposed annexation with Germany, remained a battleground for right- and left-wing paramilitary forces in the early 1920s. The independent Hungarian government of Count KAROLYI was overthrown by Béla Kun's Communist coup in March 1919, after which Hungary invaded Czechoslovakia and was attacked by Romania. Romanian occupation of Budapest in August forced Kun to flee and enabled a right-wing counterrevolution, eventually led by Admiral HORTHY, to take power from March 1920. See also: ADLER, V.; ANDRÁSSY, J.; BAUER, O.; Archduke FREDERICK; LAMMASCH, H.; KRAMÀR, K.; MASARYK, T.; STÖGER-STEINER, R.; TRUMBIĆ, A.; WEKERLE, A.

Austrian Aviatik D-I A product of the German Aviatik company's Austrian branch, the biplane D-I was the first single-seat FIGHTER designed and built in AUSTRIA-HUNGARY. Also known as the Berg Scout, after its designer, it was first flown in February 1917 and joined active units in the autumn. The first models, often armed with a single MACHINE GUN, suffered from weakness of the wing structure, but this was rectified in later versions. It was a mainstay of the AUSTRO-HUNGARIAN AIR SERVICE for the rest of the war on the ITALIAN FRONT, and was primarily used as a bomber escort. Aviatik and its subcontractors built some 700 D-Is, in about a dozen slightly different models with engines up to 225hp, giving it an eventual top speed of 185kph.

BRIEF DATA (original D-I) Type: single-seat fighter/escort; Engine: 185hp Austro-Daimler; Max speed: 181kph; Ceiling: 6,000m; Armament: 1 or 2 × 8mm mg (forward).

Austro-Hungarian Air Service Military aviation was neglected in prewar AUSTRIA-HUNGARY, and the first six (German-built) aircraft joined BALLOONS in the AUSTRO-HUNGARIAN ARMY as late as 1913. Wartime growth was made possible by close contacts between German and Austrian industry, which enabled manufacture of German designs under licence as HANSA-BRANDENBURG, LÖHNER, PHÖNIX or UFAG models. Limited use was made of Army aircraft on either the EASTERN FRONT or the BALKAN FRONT, and the Service was primarily employed on the ITALIAN FRONT from 1915.

A distinct initial advantage over the ill-equipped ITALIAN AIR FORCE had evaporated by late 1916, when the Austro-Hungarian Army possessed only about 250 frontline aircraft in 37 field units. Although 82 Army field units were operational by the ARMISTICE, along with 32 balloon companies, the Service was comprehensively overhauled by a burgeoning Italian aero industry as its own production base suffered desperate shortages of raw materials.

Austrian combat aircraft were generally inferior to the best German or Allied designs, and were shot down in large numbers over the Italian front after the arrival of Anglo-French FIGHTER units to join impressive new Italian ANSALDO machines from late 1917. Two-seaters designed for reconnaissance or ARTILLERY spotting dominated field units, and no aircraft were developed capable of the long-range STRATEGIC BOMBING raids that dominated Italian operations. Repeated attacks against northern Italian cities, RAILWAYS and airfields were only genuinely effective after German GOTHA G-TYPE bombers reached the theatre for the CAPORETTO OFFENSIVE in autumn 1917. Lack of fuel and spares virtually crippled the Air Service from mid 1918, and it played little part in the final battles of the PIAVE and VITTORIO VENETO.

The AUSTRO-HUNGARIAN NAVY developed a small but efficient seaplane service for reconnaissance, patrol, night-bombing and ANTI-SUBMARINE work in the Adriatic from 1915 to 1918. The Empire's leading air ACE, Gottfried Banfield, flew for the Navy, and its sturdy LÖHNER L seaplanes fought an almost private war against similar Italian MACCHI M5 machines. Although they more than held their own in aerial combat, and regularly disrupted the OTRANTO BARRAGE, they had little overall effect on MEDITERRANEAN strategy.

Austro-Hungarian Army The ground forces of AUSTRIA-HUNGARY consisted of three basic components. The Imperial and Royal (*Kaiserlich und Königlich*) Army, also known as the 'Common' or 'Active' Army, was the most powerful and visible symbol of imperial unity. Drawn from all parts of the Empire, and owing allegiance directly to the monarch, it had a peacetime strength of about 325,000 men and was regarded as the primary weapon for overseas operations. Both Austria and Hungary also possessed standing home-defence (*Landwehr*) forces of 40,000 and 30,000 men, respectively.

Recruits for all three were raised by conscription throughout the Empire, including in the recently annexed province of Bosnia-Herzegovina, but growth and modernization before 1914 were hindered by political disputes, as the parliament of rural Hungary consistently restrained industrial Austria's attempts to increase the Army's size. Cost-cutting and the regional draft variations, along with a complex pattern of exemptions, meant that maximum mobilized strength, including support formations, was just over 2.25 million men in August 1914, compared to the 4 million available from a much smaller French population.

Recruitment reflected the multilingual nature of the Empire, with mobilization posters printed in 15 languages during July 1914. Four out of five officers, but only some 30 per cent of other ranks, were German speakers, and language difficulties caused operational problems for Czechs, Ruthenes and other racial minorities. Mostly from middle-class backgrounds (despite the presence of royalty in numerous senior commands), officers were less prone to racial and class intolerance than the GERMAN ARMY's aristocratic officer corps, but many senior commanders doubted the loyalty of minority groups in wartime.

The Army high command, ostensibly under the Emperor's direct control as C-in-C, became an increasingly independent and powerful influence on policy making after the aggressive CONRAD became chief of staff in 1906. Expanding the authority of his office as Emperor FRANZ JOSEPH grew old, Conrad consistently advocated the solution of territorial disputes with ITALY and SERBIA by pre-emptive attack, but was restrained by politicians until the JULY CRISIS of 1914.

Conscripts of all races answered the call to mobilization with remarkable enthusiasm, but the Army's initial deployment was a shambles. Conrad had made plans for general war that, like the German SCHLIEFFEN PLAN, depended on the presumed slow pace of RUSSIAN ARMY mobilization. Unsure of whether he would be fighting Serbia or Russia, he divided the Army's 49 infantry and 11 CAVALRY divisions (6 armies), into three sections, allocating forces for each frontier and a mobile reserve (*Staffel B*) for deployment on either.

Convinced that Serbia could be beaten before Russia was ready, he ordered the reserve to the BALKAN FRONT upon mobilization in late July, but evidence of rapid Russian build-up in GALICIA prompted a last-minute change of heart. An inflexible RAILWAY system then transported the Second Army slowly to the Balkans (where it was diluted by General POTIOREK) and back to the EASTERN FRONT, where it arrived too late too prevent loss of initiative to the Russians.

After initial disasters on both fronts in 1914, Austro-Hungarian forces enjoyed a successful run until late 1916. Russian advances on the Eastern Front were held in the CARPATHIANS, and great territorial gains followed in the wake of the German GORLICE-TARNOW and TRIPLE OFFENSIVES in 1915. German and BULGARIAN forces also played a big part in the successful invasion of SERBIA in October 1915, but the defence of strong positions on the ITALIAN FRONT was a purely Austro-Hungarian achievement until 1917.

The Army was generally provided with good-quality infantry equipment, including TRENCH WARFARE weaponry not supplied to Allied armies, but failure to plan for a long war or massive weapons expenditure meant it was always short on quantity. Infantry regiments had only eight MACHINE GUNS each in 1914, and the field ARTILLERY arm was particularly ill-equipped. It used a serviceable, quick-firing 90mm field gun, and 24 giant SCHLANKE EMMA howitzers eventually saw service, but other heavy guns were mostly relics from the 19th century, often removed from obsolete FORTRESSES. New howitzers and field pieces were introduced from 1915, but supply and manpower shortages in the indigenous arms industry slowed manufacture and delivery.

Losses, running at over 40 per cent in the first year's fighting (including more than half a million prisoners) cost the Army most of its experienced officers and NCOs at an early stage. Their replacements were less able to contain nationalist resentments among increasingly weary troops, and the mass surrender of a CZECH unit to the Russians in April 1915 was recognized as symptomatic of rising discontent.

Echoed in separatist pressure on the home front, these evident weaknesses had not dampened Conrad's characteristic military ambition, but the edifice collapsed with huge losses to the BRUSILOV OFFENSIVE in June 1916. The defeat exhausted the Empire's replacement capacity, and German commanders took over most formations as Berlin established a grip over Austro-Hungarian strategic direction.

Conrad took little credit for the German-led victory in the subsequent ROMANIAN CAMPAIGN, and his personal position was weakened by the death of Franz Josef in the autumn. The new monarch, KARL I, wanted a compromise peace settlement and personal control over the Army, prompting Conrad's dismissal in March 1917 and increasing German determination to make military aid conditional on strategic compliance.

The new chief of staff, ARZ VON STRAUSSENBERG, was preoccupied with internal disputes, principally Hungarian demands for creation of separate national forces in place of the Common Army. He played little part in the Army's last great victory, at CAPORETTO in November 1917, which was arranged between German commanders and Austrian field officers, and he was powerless to dissuade Conrad and BOROEVIC from the PIAVE offensive of June 1918.

The failure of this offensive triggered the Army's disintegration. By early 1918 there were 66 infantry and 12 cavalry divisions (including 25 Landwehr units), but many were reduced to less than half their established strength of about 12,000 men. Economic failure had left combat units short of food, clothing, fuel, horses and ammunition, but the Army was eventually broken by the collapse of the state it represented.

Non-Germanic units called upon to restore internal order were subject to nationalist unrest during early 1918, and officer morale plummeted with German takeover, formalized in May 1918. Frontline units remained generally loyal to the crown until the autumn, but a steady dribble of desertions turned into a flood after a final Italian offensive at VITTORIO VENETO in September 1918.

Karl gave permission for Common Army troops to join the forces of their national groups in late October, and his abdication formalized its disappearance. Some Austrian and Hungarian Landwehr troops remained in service with the postwar republics, but the size of their armed forces was severely restricted by the Treaties of TRIANON and ST GERMAIN.

Official imperial casualty figures to September 1918 listed 1.54 million killed or missing and 1.22 million taken prisoner, out of some 7.8 million men eventually mobilized, but later studies suggest that 900,000–950,000 imperial troops were killed and perhaps 2 million wounded. See also: AUSTRO-HUNGARIAN AIR SERVICE.

Austro-Hungarian Navy Essentially a coastal-defence force until the turn of the century, the Imperial and Royal Navy of AUSTRIA-HUNGARY (the *Kaiserlich und Königlich Kriegsmarine*) was expanded under chief of staff Montecuccoli from 1904, with enthusiastic support from Archduke FRANZ FERDINAND. The main catalyst to reconstruction was Adriatic competition with ITALY, but the decline of the FRENCH NAVY and the gradual reduction of British strength in the MEDITERRANEAN raised the alternative possibility of an

Austro-Italian alliance becoming the dominant force in the theatre.

Three fairly modern RADETSKY Class PRE-DREADNOUGHTS and 3 (of 4) VIRIBUS UNITIS Class dreadnoughts were in service by August 1914, along with 9 older battleships, 5 old CRUISERS, 2 new light cruisers, 18 DESTROYERS, 5 SUBMARINES and about 90 TORPEDO BOATS. The main bulk of the fleet was based at the northern Adriatic port of Pola (Pula), effectively secure from all but the most determined Italian assault, but secondary bases along the eastern Adriatic coast, especially the important facility at CATTARO, were more vulnerable.

Only combination with the ITALIAN NAVY and the German MITTELMEERDIVISION could give the fleet nominal superiority over French Mediterranean forces, but doubts about Italian intentions were confirmed by a declaration of neutrality on 2 August 1914. With security of the Adriatic no longer assured Admiral HAUS (Montecuccoli's successor) adopted a defensive posture intended to prevent Allied incursion and to provide support for the land war on the BALKAN FRONT. Potential confrontation with Anglo-French warships was avoided, and he ignored German requests to send a force into the BLACK SEA.

Despite periodic pressure to assist the TURKISH NAVY, which alarmed Russian admirals but was never considered feasible, the surface fleet remained in the Adriatic throughout. Locked in theoretical (but untried) stalemate with the Italian Fleet at Taranto and the French Navy's battleships at Malta and Corfu, it never attempted a large-scale breach of the ineffectual OTRANTO BARRAGE across the sea's southern exits. The possibility of naval intervention in support of troops on the ITALIAN FRONT, though frequently raised, was dismissed as impracticable in MINE-infested waters.

Light cruisers, destroyers, torpedo boats, minecraft, naval aircraft and submarines were more active in the theatre. From May 1915 they conducted what was virtually a private war with Italian light forces, carrying out raids against coastal targets and Allied supply routes to SERBIA. Tactical advantage remained largely with Allied forces, which occasionally threatened to occupy Cattaro or other parts of the Dalmatian coast, and evacuated the SERBIAN ARMY from ALBANIA in late 1915 without significant interruption.

Austrian submarines were far less effective than their GERMAN NAVY counterparts, which used Cattaro as their main base, but several of the most successful German boats were officially part of the Austro-Hungarian Navy, flying its flag to cover attacks on Italian ships not officially at war with Germany.

The death of Haus in 1917 brought reinforced caution under Admiral NJEGOVAN. Although the Navy was less racially divided than the AUSTRO-HUNGARIAN ARMY, prolonged inactivity eventually bred unrest and mutiny at Cattaro in spring 1918. The subsequent appointment of HORTHY as fleet C-in-C represented an attempt to invigorate the Navy, but he found strategic arguments against risking major losses ships equally compelling. His only dreadnought raid in the Adriatic, against the Otranto Barrage of June 1918, was abandoned after the battleship *SZENT ISTVÁN* was lost.

The rest of the fleet remained substantially intact at Pola, though older battleships and cruisers were disarmed or reduced to coastal-defence work as an economy measure from early 1918. The political collapse of Austria-Hungary brought the Navy's dissolution and the destruction of most of its records at Pola, which was included in the newly proclaimed YUGOSLAVIA. The service ceased to exist when the fleet raised the Croatian flag on 31 October 1918, but *Viribus Unitis* was sunk in Pola by Italian 'HUMAN TORPEDOES' later the same night. See also: *MONARCH*; *NOVARA*; Battle of the OTRANTO STRAITS.

Auxiliary Commerce Raiders German warships disguised as unarmed merchant vessels, equivalent to Allied Q-SHIPS except that they flew neutral flags and were targeted at surface shipping. Perhaps a dozen are thought to have been used, and like other German commerce raiders they were a nuisance to Allied shipping worldwide out of all proportion to their numbers (see NAVAL WARFARE). Most were former auxiliary MINE-LAYERS converted to look like Scandinavian merchantmen, but one large sailing ship (the *Seeadler*) destroyed 10 ships in the southern oceans before it was wrecked in August 1917. The exploits of successful decoys were widely reported in the German press and several, the MÖWE and WÖLF for example, were among the best-known ships of the wartime GERMAN NAVY. See also: ARMED MERCHANT CRUISERS.

Averescu, General Alexandru (1859–1938) The ROMANIAN ARMY's most respected wartime commander, a former war minister who served as chief of staff during the Second Balkan War of 1913. Shortly after ROMANIA entered the War in August 1916 Averescu was given command of the Third Army, detailed to protect the southern frontier with BULGARIA, and he led an expanded 'Army Group South' in a failed attack across the Danube at FLAMANDA in late September. General PREZAN appointed Averescu to overall command of field operations in Wallachia in November, and he planned the abortive counteroffensive on the River ARGES. Regrouping his army (with Russian support) at the River Sereth in southern Moldavia, his defence of the line at FOSCANI in August 1917 greatly enhanced his popular reputation, and he succeeded BRATIANU as prime minister on 8 February 1918. Charged by King FERDINAND I with negotiating peace, but unable to accept German terms (see Treaty of BUCHAREST), he was replaced by the more pliable Marghiloman on 18 March. Averescu was a major political figure in the shrunken postwar Romania, serving as prime minister twice in the 1920s.

Aviatik B-Types German two-seater biplane, produced in small numbers for the GERMAN ARMY AIR SERVICE and used for reconnaissance work during the early battles on the WESTERN and EASTERN FRONTS. In service since early 1914, the B-I was superseded at the end of the year by the B-III, with a 160hp engine and structural improvements, but the machine was never extensively employed by the Germans. Austrian-built versions of both the original model (known as the B-II) and the B-III remained active with the AUSTRO-HUNGARIAN AIR SERVICE for long-range reconnaissance until 1917.

BRIEF DATA (B-I) Type: two-seat reconnaissance; Engine: 100hp Mercedes; Max speed: c 100kph; Armament: crew's small arms.

Aviatik C-Type Handsome reconnaissance biplane, first used with German forces in early 1915 and developed from the AVIATIK B-TYPE designs but more powerful and fitted with a rail-mounted MACHINE GUN. A 200hp C-II version appeared in early 1916, and a more streamlined 160hp C-III was produced later that year, carrying two machine-guns operated by an observer moved to the back seat. Both the C-I and C-III were used in large numbers on the WESTERN FRONT, performing reconnaissance and escort duties until 1917.

BRIEF DATA (C-I) Type: two-seat armed reconnaissance; Engine: 160hp Mercedes DIII; Max speed: 142kph; Ceiling: 3,500m; Armament: 1 × 7.92mm mg.

Avro 504 Multi-purpose British biplane, first produced in 1913 as a lightweight, box-framed two-seater with forward observer. Intended for light-bombing and reconnaissance missions, it was stable and easy to fly but displayed no more than average performance. Widely used by the RNAS in 1914–15, it served only briefly with the RFC on the WESTERN FRONT in the latter part of 1914. An RFC 504 was the first British aircraft to be shot down (on 22 August) and three machines based near Belfort performed the first STRATEGIC BOMBING raid on 21 November, when they attacked ZEPPELIN sheds at Friedrichshafen. The latter success encouraged development of single-seat versions, with extra fuel stored in the observer's place for anti-airship and long-range reconnaissance missions. The 504B naval trainer, with redesigned tailfin and wings, was the model for the RNAS 504C, which performed effectively in the role (about 80 being produced).

Obsolete by mid-1915, all 504s had been withdrawn from air combat zones by early the following year, but production was continued for training purposes and the plane's career revived dramatically from August 1917, when the two-seater 504J trainer was chosen as standard by the RFC. It was eventually superseded by the 504K, which could accommodate any available engine, and thousands of both were produced for use all over the world. At the start of 1918 a single-seat version of the 504K was produced specifically for home defence and took part in operations against German night bombers over London and southeast England. One of the best-known designs of the period, the 504 remained in service as an RAF trainer until 1924, and 8,340 of all types were built in wartime.

BRIEF DATA (504) Type: two-seat reconnaissance/light bomber; Engine: 80hp Gnôme; Max speed: 82mph (131kph); Ceiling: 3,000m; Armament: observer's small arms or 1 × 0.303in mg, 6 × 20lb bomb (hand-thrown).

Azerbaijan See: TRANSCAUCASIA.

B

Bachmann, Admiral Gustav (1860–1943) Experienced GERMAN NAVY staff officer who commanded the BALTIC squadrons at Kiel in August 1914 and became chief of naval staff the following February. A protégé of Admiral TIRPITZ, and viewed as a compliant, politically neutral figure, Bachmann became a committed convert to *HANDELSKRIEG* (commerce warfare) and a persistent advocate of unrestricted SUBMARINE WARFARE. He offered his resignation in June 1915, after the first unrestricted campaign was abandoned, and was returned to his Baltic command by Kaiser WILHELM II in September, remaining at Kiel until October 1918 when he was retired by SCHEER's new Naval Supreme Command.

Baden The last BATTLESHIP built in GERMANY, completed in October 1916 as a response to the British QUEEN ELIZABETH Class. Slower than their British counterparts, *Baden* and its sister *Bayern* (completed in March 1916) were designed for relatively short-range operations in the North Sea. Neither was ever tested. *Baden* served as HIGH SEAS FLEET flagship from 1917 until the ARMISTICE, and both were scuttled in Scapa Flow with the rest of the GERMAN NAVY's modern warships in 1919. Large, expensive warships became relatively unimportant to the German war effort after JUTLAND, and two more Baden Class vessels, *Sachsen* and *Württemberg*, were abandoned under construction in 1917.

BRIEF DATA (*Baden*, 1917) Displacement: 28,075 tons; Crew: 1,171; Dimensions: length 623.5ft (189m), beam 99ft (30m); Speed: 22k; Armament: 8 × 15in gun, 16 × 5.9in (150mm), 4 × 3.4in AA, 5 × 23.6in TT.

Baden, Max von See: MAX VON BADEN.

Baghdad, Fall of Capture of Ottoman TURKEY's southern capital by Anglo-Indian troops on the MESOPOTAMIAN FRONT in March 1917 (see MAP 23). After his victory at KUT in late February 1917, British commander MAUDE paused for orders from London at Aziziyeh, less than 70km from Baghdad. Turkish regional commander KHALIL wavered as to his best course of action: to retreat beyond Baghdad, to concentrate just in front of the city, or to attempt a repeat of the forward defence of CTESIPHON.

Khalil's available strength was about 10,000 men, including the Baghdad garrison and some 2,300 survivors from Kut. Another two divisions (perhaps 20,000 troops under Ali Ishan Bey) had been recalled from western PERSIA but were unable to extricate themselves quickly, and troops fighting on the CAUCASIAN FRONT were too far away to help.

After starting work on fortifications at Ctesiphon, Khalil chose to defend Baghdad itself, placing defences southeast of the city along the Diyala River and on either side of the Tigris some 35km downstream. He ignored the possibility of flooding overland approaches, and fortifications were incomplete when advanced British units reached the Diyala on 8 March.

The British immediately attempted to get across the river, 100 metres wide and in flood, but this failed, and night crossings at two well-defended points had established only a small bridgehead by the end of 9 March. Maude switched his main strength across the Tigris a few kilometres downriver for an attack upon the weaker southwestern position, beyond the hill of Tel Aswad. Informed of the threat by his new GERMAN ARMY AIR SERVICE squadrons, Khalil sent most of his troops across the Tigris to meet it.

The single depleted regiment left at the Diyala defences was overrun early on 10 March, persuading Khalil to retire from the Tel Aswad position that morning to protect the Baghdad–Berlin RAILWAY station. A violent sandstorm prevented further operations that day and Khalil, resisting pressure from German staff officers to launch a counterattack, ordered a general retreat and evacuation of Baghdad at 20.00 the same evening. British troops occupied the city the next day, noisily welcomed by a population of about 140,000.

Maude's advance seriously damaged Turkish forces in Mesopotamia, which are thought to have suffered 25,000–30,000 casualties from the start of 1917, and loss of the city effectively ended Turkish action in Persia. Turkish territory further north was threatened from both Baghdad and the Caucasus, and British security required a further advance on SAMARRAH.

Bait Aisa, Battle of See: First Battle of KUT.

Baker, Newton (1871–1937) US lawyer, and a reforming Democratic mayor of Cleveland (1911–15), who turned down the post of interior secretary in the WILSON cabinet of early 1913, but accepted appointment as secretary for war in early March 1916. He was chosen by Wilson for his known PACIFISM in contrast to his bellicose predecessor, Lindley Garrison. His first duty was to authorize a punitive expedition into MEXICO, and he supervised limited preparedness for war by the UNITED STATES over the next year, heading a new Council for National Defense from August.

After April 1917 his known pacifist background attracted determined attacks by Senator LODGE and the Republican right. He was criticized for removing WOOD from field command, a move inspired by Wilson, and blamed for administrative delays in the massive expansion of US armed forces. Baker also faced controversy within the US ARMY over general staff relations with the AEF, but gave steady political support to field commander PERSHING's estimates of requirements, promotions policy and insistence on independent frontline command. Baker returned to legal practice in Cleveland after the Republican victory of 1920.

Balfour, Arthur (1848–1930) British former prime minister (1902–06) and leader of the Conservative Party until his resignation in 1911. A leading opposition spokesman in August 1914, he joined the coalition cabinet from May 1915 as First Lord of the Admiralty. A stark contrast to CHURCHILL (his predecessor), Balfour's casual manner was often criticized as lethargy, and his stewardship of the ROYAL NAVY was not a success. In partnership with the stolid Admiral JACKSON, he made little impact on naval strategy, presiding over apparent failure at JUTLAND and the unchecked extension of German SUBMARINE WARFARE. Switched to the more appropriate role of foreign secretary in the LLOYD GEORGE government from December 1916, he headed the British political mission to the UNITED STATES in April 1917 and earned widespread contemporary praise for his pragmatic diplomacy as Britain's second plenipotentiary at the PARIS PEACE CONFERENCE. See also: BALFOUR DECLARATION.

Balfour Declaration Announcement of British support for the aims of international Zionism, formulated in a letter of 2 November 1917 from foreign secretary BALFOUR to Lord Rothschild, a senior spokesman for Jewish interests. The letter stated that the British government would endeavour to establish a 'national home' for the Jewish people in Palestine, provided the civil and political status of Arabs already settled there was not affected and that Jews in other countries retained full rights.

Zionism had become an organized international movement by the early 20th century, a response to the spread of violent anti-Semitism from RUSSIA into AUSTRIA-HUNGARY and GERMANY. Berlin was its main prewar centre, but an alternative headquarters emerged in neutral Copenhagen from 1914 and the activities of British forces in PALESTINE made London increasingly important (see WEIZMANN, C.).

The Declaration was principally motivated by the (false) belief that Germany planned to announce support for a Jewish Palestine and, along with the SYKES-PICOT AGREEMENT, contributed to suspicion of British motives among leaders of the ARAB REVOLT. It caused little controversy in Europe and was accepted by Allied governments as the basis for a British postwar MANDATE over Palestine. However, once the British mandate was in place the British failed to implement the Declaration in the face of Arab opposition, and it was finally abandoned in 1939.

Balkan Front Historically the great overland trading route between Asia and Europe, the multi-ethnic Balkans were a chronically unstable mix of local antagonisms and Great-Power politics in the early 20th century.

At a regional level the independent ambitions of GREECE, BULGARIA and SERBIA contested turbulent and fluctuating frontier zones with the Ottoman and Austro-Hungarian Empires. Areas of conflict in 1914 included the independent states of ALBANIA and MONTENEGRO, the Slav provinces of AUSTRIA-HUNGARY (Croatian Dalmatia, Bosnia-Herzegovina and Slovenia) and the parts of Thrace and Macedonia recently vacated by TURKEY (see MAP 19).

In a wider context, Austria-Hungary and ITALY both sought control over Albania, RUSSIA's foreign policy was committed to supporting Slav independence as a buffer between Vienna and the Dardanelles Straits, which it hoped to control, FRANCE was developing political ambitions in the Aegean, and ROMANIA was anxious to expand into both Hungary and Bulgaria.

Tension had been heightened by a series of local and international crises before 1914, culminating in two Balkan Wars. Greece, Serbia, Bulgaria and Montenegro had won a series of comprehensive military victories over Turkish forces in 1912, driving the Ottoman frontier east to the outskirts of Constantinople. Perceived failure to win a fair share of the spoils prompted Bulgaria to attack Greek and Serbian forces in summer 1913, but rapid defeat was sealed by invasion from Romania. The subsequent peace cost Bulgaria the northeastern border region of the Dobrudja, left Serbia double its prewar size, and gave Greece control over most of the Aegean coast.

Austria-Hungary's relatively quiet role in the Balkan Wars masked worsening relations with Serbia, which was a hotbed of pan-Slav expansionism. The assassination of Archduke FRANZ FERDINAND at Sarajevo in Bosnia on 28 June 1914, though not directly sponsored by the Serbian government, brought Vienna's irritation to a climax, and the ensuing JULY CRISIS was driven by Austro-Hungarian determination to end unrest on its Balkan frontiers by military action.

Despite Serbia's conciliatory attitude, Austria-Hungary declared war at noon on 28 July and began operations the next day with an ARTILLERY bombardment of the Serbian capital, Belgrade, just across the Danube. On the same day, elements of the AUSTRO-HUNGARIAN ARMY's southern forces opened the First World War's ground operations with the first of 18 unsuccessful attempts at a small-scale river crossing, while commanding general POTIOREK built up strength for a major invasion.

War between Serbia and Austria-Hungary, with the former supported by its close but tiny Montenegrin ally, remained a largely private affair during 1914. All Europe's major powers, though sucked into general war, were busy elsewhere, and regional forces (including Italy) remained prudently neutral.

Slow to mobilize, Potiorek's 450,000 troops began their first invasion of Serbia on 12 August, attacking the Serbian territory jutting into the Empire west of Belgrade. Defeated by Field Marshal PUTNIK's slightly smaller but more competent SERBIAN ARMY (with Montenegrin assistance) at the JADAR RIVER, the invasion had collapsed with heavy losses by 25 August.

Serbian forces switched to offensive operations, attacking north of Belgrade on 6 September, but Potiorek was quickly reinforced and launched a second invasion the next day. Decisively beaten on the DRINA RIVER and in retreat across the frontier from 15 September, Potiorek paused to plan more carefully for a third attempt. Serbian forces had suffered relatively few casualties, but were desperately short of supplies, and operations before November were restricted to small advances into Bosnia and ineffectual Montenegrin attempts to threaten the AUSTRO-HUNGARIAN NAVY base at CATTARO.

The break in military operations was filled by diplomatic activity. Once Turkey joined the CENTRAL POWERS in late October, Bulgaria and Greece formed a buffer blocking Allied aid to Serbia and Austro-German supply routes to Constantinople. Late 1914 was a period of hard diplomatic bargaining as the major powers anticipated renewal of regional conflagration with competing offers to potential allies. Political confusion in Greece was matched by Bulgarian caution, and both were wary of Romania, preventing any commitments pending frontline developments.

A third Austrian invasion of Serbia opened on 8 November. Again led by Potiorek, it was drawn some 80km east of the Drina by a Serbian retreat south of Belgrade. Although the capital was evacuated on 2 December, a counterattack along the KOLUBARA RIVER broke through Austrian lines to clear Serbia of invading forces again, inflicting 225,000 casualties on a chaotic retreat. The defeat cost Potiorek his command – he was replaced by Archduke EUGEN in December – but the Serbian Army could not hope to replace its 170,000 casualties. With the front again quietened by mutual exhaustion, Serbian leaders issued strong pleas for Allied support through early 1915.

The French VIVIANI government was discussing the possibility of intervention by the new year, and British chancellor of the exchequer LLOYD GEORGE proposed a full-scale expedition to the Balkans in mid-January. Both ideas were dismissed (along with other proposals) by military chiefs intent on amassing strength for offensives on the WESTERN FRONT.

Anglo-French 'EASTERNERS' maintained sufficient influence to revive the idea. In mid-January the British government considered sending a small force to Greek Salonika, the only non-Austrian port remotely within striking range of the Serbian front. A division was provisionally committed to the task on 9 February, and French public opinion compelled C-in-C JOFFRE to reciprocate. Russian aid was sought, but active support from the pro-Allied VENIZELOS government in Greece was considered vital. An Allied proposal for joint action, delivered just before the naval attack on the DARDANELLES in mid-February, was vetoed by King CONSTANTINE's impossible precondition of a Romanian holding operation against Bulgaria, which was still neutral.

Allied failure at GALLIPOLI, evident by the summer of 1915, help to sway Bulgaria against the Allies, and German interest in the Balkans was prompted by the need to clear RAILWAY supply routes to a Turkish economy starved by Russian control of the BLACK SEA. Chiefs of staff FALKENHAYN and CONRAD agreed in August to a joint Austro-German offensive against Serbian positions, and Bulgaria signed the PLESS CONVENTION on 6 September, agreeing to send two armies into Serbia from the east, cutting lines of retreat towards Salonika and the Aegean.

The appointment of General SARRAIL to command French forces at Gallipoli again brought up the possibility of their transfer to Salonika, but Joffre delayed positive action until the announcement of Bulgarian mobilization (22 September) triggered crisis throughout the Balkans.

Greek treaty obligations to Serbia required the commitment of 150,000 troops in the event of a Bulgarian attack, but only if the Allies could muster an equal force. Both Venizelos and Serbian premier PAŠIĆ immediately pressed the Allies to send troops to ensure fulfilment of the condition. France promised aid, but indecision and disillusionment with long-range adventures governed British reactions.

Sarrail, still in France, was eventually given four divisions and ordered to Salonika (some 450 mountainous kilometres short of Belgrade) on 28 September, but reluctant British preparations to move a division from Gallipoli were not begun until the end of the month. Belated Allied involvement was complicated by confusion in Athens: the GREEK ARMY had mobilized, but its attitude was uncertain; Venizelos resigned as the first troops landed on 5 October; and the Austro-German invasion of Serbia began next day.

Under the overall command of General MACKENSEN, the most successful exponent of BREAKTHROUGH TACTICS on the EASTERN FRONT, the invasion was a complete success. Austrian, German and Bulgarian armies had virtually surrounded the Serbians by mid-November, and only the Serbian Army's 'GREAT RETREAT' into Albania made its further military participation possible (see Conquest of SERBIA). Allied landings at Salonika had hardly influenced the campaign. Sarrail pushed troops up the railway towards Nis in early November, but they were stopped by Bulgarian forces less than 20km inside Serbia, and returned to Greece in December.

Unwilling to risk arguments between Bulgaria and Austria-Hungary or probable Greek hostility, Falkenhayn forbade invasion of Macedonia on the grounds that expelling the five Allied divisions in Salonika would release them for action elsewhere, and the Central Powers halted their advance at the Greek frontier. Apart from routine Austrian occupation of Montenegro and northern Albania in January 1916, and sporadic Italian activity around Valona, the evacuation of Serbian forces to Corfu in the new year marked the Front's permanent shift south to where French, British, Serbian, Russian and eventually Greek troops fought disease, boredom and occasionally Bulgarians until autumn 1918. See SALONIKA. See also: Battles of FLORINA, Lake PRESPA; MONASTIR OFFENSIVE; VARDAR OFFENSIVE.

Balkan Wars See: BALKAN FRONT; BULGARIA; MONTENEGRO; ROMANIA; SERBIA; TURKEY.

Balloons A common sight on static battlefronts throughout the War, hot-air and gas-filled balloons had been developed for observation purposes in the 19th century and remained a valuable ARTILLERY aid. Cheaper to run and a more stable viewing platform than aircraft, they were winched to various heights by a ground crew in groups of at least two or three, enabling cross-referenced observation readings, which were transmitted by flag signals or sometimes RADIO.

The rapid development of AERIAL WARFARE from 1914 made life extremely dangerous for crews in busy sectors, who were classic sitting ducks, but the balloons themselves were not easy to destroy. Standard bullets usually passed straight through the fabric, requiring repeated attacks, and aircraft faced the dangers of entanglement in wires or chains, along with the probable presence of concentrated ANTI-AIRCRAFT fire. Generally credited as a full 'kill' by air services, balloon destruction was a specialist combat form, and several leading ACES on both sides of the WESTERN FRONT earned their reputations as 'balloon busters'. Efforts were made to protect crews. They were the only British air personnel permitted to use PARACHUTES, and German ground crew were eventually equipped with a powered winch for rapid descent while under attack, but increased use of incendiary and explosive bullets by aircraft had further reduced their survival chances by 1917.

Baltic Sea The major sphere of operations for the RUSSIAN NAVY, which fought a continuous battle with GERMAN NAVY forces in the southern and eastern Baltic from August 1914 (see MAP 16). The main Russian strategic aim was denial of German access to the Gulf of Finland, which led to Petrograd (St Petersburg), with disruption of trade between GERMANY and the Scandinavian countries as a secondary consideration. German forces, outnumbered from the start but occasionally reinforced from the North Sea, never planned an invasion through the Gulf but were anxious to maintain absolute control over trade routes (see BLOCKADE).

Neither side believed itself capable of dominating the theatre with available warships. Abandoning the Bay of Riga and the coast of KURLAND, the Russian fleet remained inside the Gulf of Finland, protected by a field of almost 4,000 MINES, and the Germans laid their own line of defensive minefields. Despite occasional sweeps by the HIGH SEAS FLEET from the North Sea, German weakness in the theatre was soon apparent, and Russian Baltic C-in-C ESSEN adopted a more aggressive policy from early September 1914, reasserting control over the Bay of Riga by occupying its outlying islands and driving German minelaying operations south.

A successful Russian minelaying offensive in the southern Baltic began in late October, and DESTROYERS had laid 1,164 mines off the German coast by late December. Their effectiveness sharpened by German shortage of minesweepers, the fields sank a CRUISER and five merchant steamers in 1914, but British SUBMARINES (in the Baltic from mid-October) achieved nothing at all in 1914. Good weather enabled continuation of minelaying until the eastern Baltic froze for the winter, suspending operations between February and May.

Mining remained the main offensive tactic in the theatre through 1915, with both sides attempting to achieve surprise in the face of growing minesweeper fleets. The Russians laid more than 2,000 mines during the year and generally held the upper hand, blocking German efforts to interfere with trade routes to Sweden and taking a significant toll of German merchant shipping.

During the latter part of the year new GANGUT Class battleships joined Russian cruisers in support of minelaying destroyers, but surface fleets avoided confrontation in favour of support for land operations on the EASTERN FRONT in 1915. German attacks in support of coastal land operations, including a major attempt to force entry into the Bay of Riga in August, were effectively thwarted by minefields. Russian support operations consisted primarily of shelling from coastal gunships like the *SLAVA*, although a limited amphibious operation was undertaken behind German lines near PETRAGGE in October.

Neither German nor Russian submarines enjoyed much success in the Baltic, but both sides used submarines as minelayers to some effect. The British flotilla, raised to five boats by October 1915, was more dangerous, disrupting merchant traffic, forcing transfer of German light forces from the North Sea and sinking another cruiser.

By early 1916 German Navy warship losses were running at three times the Russian level, and large numbers of new destroyers and submarines were reaching the Russian fleet. Ice prevented naval activity on any scale between January and late March, when both sides resumed mining in earnest, often obstructing their own freedom of manoeuvre in the process but scoring occasional great successes.

Submarines had an even less successful year in 1916, and big Russian surface ships only occasionally ventured out in search of merchant traffic. Coastal warfare focused on an intensifying struggle for control of the IRBEN STRAITS, adjoining the current military frontline in Kurland, a battle fought primarily by minesweepers, small craft and seaplanes, which were becoming increasingly important for reconnaissance, ground support and light bombing (see AERIAL WARFARE).

A severe winter prevented operations in the eastern Baltic until May 1917, but the FEBRUARY REVOLUTION did not prevent the Russian fleet from receiving new destroyers, submarines, minesweepers and torpedo boats. The overall balance of power in the theatre remained with the Russians, and their big ships remained fairly safe in the Gulf of Finland, but internal political developments forced them onto the defensive.

The main action in 1917 took place in the Bay of Riga, a tactical struggle between light forces culminating in Operation ALBION, a major German amphibious attack on the large island of Ösel. This failed, however, in its aim of trapping Russian warships in the Bay. Despite the loss of RIGA in September, the general collapse of the RUSSIAN ARMY at its back, and mounting German air superiority, most of the Russian fleet escaped to the Gulf of Finland, where it remained secure but inactive until the war in the Baltic was ended by the Treaty of BREST-LITOVSK.

Bapâume See: Second Battle of ALBERT.

Baracca, Francesco (1888–1918) The most successful air ACE with the ITALIAN AIR FORCE, Baracca won all his 34 combat victories over the ITALIAN FRONT. He began his FIGHTER career using a NIEUPORT 11, flew a SPAD S-VII from May 1917, and had progressed to a SPAD S-XIII when killed by ground fire in June 1918.

Baranovitchi See: BRUSILOV OFFENSIVE.

Barchini Saltatori Literally 'jumping boats', the four *barchini saltatori* were the most ingenious of several innovative light craft developed by the ITALIAN NAVY for action against Austro-Hungarian bases in 1918. Armed with two TORPEDOES, they were fitted with tank-style caterpillar chains with which to scale the booms surrounding harbours. They made three overnight attempts to penetrate the main AUSTRO-HUNGARIAN NAVY base at Pola. The first suffered delays and was abandoned at dawn on 9 April. Austrian aircraft intercepted a second attempt four nights later, forcing crews to scuttle two of the boats. A single boat, *Grillo*, broke down before reaching the harbour on 6–7 May, but made a final effort the following week, overcoming some of the barriers before being discovered and sunk. See also: MAS BOATS; HUMAN TORPEDOES.

Basra, Capture of The first action on the MESOPOTAMIAN FRONT. At the outbreak of Anglo-Turkish war on 5 November 1914, the first 5,000 troops of General Barrett's INDIAN ARMY Expeditionary Force D from India were already in the Persian Gulf at the mouth of the Shatt-al-Arab, supported by the ROYAL NAVY's Gulf Division. Originally sent to dissuade neutral TURKEY from aggression, their prime directive was to guard Abadan and its pipeline to oilfields in PERSIA, but provision (not sanctioned by London) was made for an attack on Ottoman Basra, a small port on the east bank of the Shatt-al-Arab about 100km inland from the Gulf (see MAP 23).

After taking lightly defended coastal batteries at Fao on 6 November, the advance force (General Delamain) moved upriver, supported by shallow-draft sloops and an ARMED MERCHANT CRUISER. They reached Abadan the following day, dispersing token resistance and establishing a fortified camp 5km further upriver. Perimeter defences were ready in time to repel a dawn raid on 11 November by about 400 Turkish troops, and another 7,000 Force D troops (with light ARTILLERY) were established by 14 November.

Barrett decided on an immediate attack towards Basra, where a much larger Turkish force was gathering under Colonel Subhi Bey, Ottoman military commander of lower Mesopotamia. Forward Turkish positions at Saihan were taken next day, and on 19 November Barrett launched a full-scale attack against Subhi Bey's main force of 4,500 men, entrenched 15km to the northwest.

Hampered by rain, mud and mirage, but supported by naval artillery from the river, the attack met heavy resistance until British EIGHTEEN-POUNDERS dispersed defenders, most of whom escaped in difficult pursuit conditions. The defeat triggered an unsuccessful Turkish plan to close the Shatt-al-Arab by sinking blockships, but Basra was left undefended and officially occupied by Anglo-Indian forces on 23 November.

The apparent fragility of Turkish resistance encouraged a sense of opportunity in the Anglo-Indian command, and Basra became the springboard for an extension of British commitment to the theatre far beyond anything envisaged in London.

Battenberg, Prince Louis (1854–1921) German-born prince of the landlocked Grand Duchy of Hesse, related by birth or marriage to the British, German, Russian and Greek royal families. Battenberg enjoyed a long and successful career in the British ROYAL NAVY, becoming First Sea Lord in December 1912 and proving an efficient, if generally acquiescent, administrator for First Lord of the Admiralty CHURCHILL. By holding the Royal Navy at readiness at the end of annual manoeuvres in July 1914, he greatly eased its mobilization at the start of August. His wartime tenure was brief and overshadowed by the manner of his departure after a concerted press campaign against the presence of a German at the Admiralty. Demoralized by the attacks, which seem to have completely surprised him, Battenberg resigned on 28 October 1914 and was replaced by Admiral FISHER. Later promoted full admiral as a gesture of trust, he was never again given active employment by the Royal Navy. See also: HALDANE, LORD R.

Battlecruisers Hybrid warships with the speed of a CRUISER and the striking power of a BATTLESHIP, developed for the ROYAL NAVY at the insistence of prewar First Sea Lord FISHER. The first three INVINCIBLE Class ships (completed in 1908) set the pattern for future designs, resembling battleships but with one less turret, much less armour protection, more powerful engines and a longer hull. Battlecruisers could be used in fleet actions or to protect trade routes, and could in theory escape from any ship they could not destroy. The type aroused considerable controversy among naval strategists worldwide but was also adopted by the JAPANESE NAVY and the GERMAN NAVY, which ordered them primarily for short-range fleet operations, with slightly less speed and more protection.

The last of 12 British battlecruisers, *Renown* and *Repulse*, carried 15-inch guns and joined the GRAND FLEET late in 1916, by which time their combat value, apparently confirmed at the FALKLAND ISLANDS in 1914, was in serious doubt. Although they bore the brunt of operations by both main fleets in the North Sea, practical experience of MINES, SUBMARINES and other TORPEDO craft, as well as the presence of enemy battlecruisers with similar performance, emphasized their vulnerability.

The last battlecruisers planned for the Royal Navy were three 'light battlecruisers' specially designed for planned operations in shallow BALTIC waters, but all were eventually converted as AIRCRAFT CARRIERS, and only *FURIOUS* was operational during the War. See: *INVINCIBLE; INDEFATIGABLE; LION; TIGER; BLÜCHER; VON DER TANN; GOEBEN; SEYDLITZ; LUTZOW*. See also: Battles of the DOGGER BANK, JUTLAND.

Battleships The most powerful contemporary warships, regarded since the 18th century as the ultimate naval weapon. Mobile fortresses built to mount the largest naval guns, battleships had undergone their most dramatic period of transformation in the half century before 1914. The all-steel, armoured ships of the early 20th century carried breech-loading artillery mounted on revolving turrets with an effective range of over 10,000 metres, but were rendered obsolete by the British *DREADNOUGHT*, completed in late 1906. All the major naval powers invested most of their prewar shipbuilding budgets in comparable 'dreadnoughts'. By 1911 the chief European competitors, GREAT BRITAIN and GERMANY, were building even bigger 'super-dreadnoughts' (see *ORION*) and fast BATTLECRUISERS along similar lines.

As 'capital ships', dreadnoughts remained the universally accepted index of naval power in 1914, and it was generally assumed that they would meet in decisive confrontations, quickly establishing mastery of ocean theatres for one side or the other. No such confrontation occurred, partly because naval professionals on all sides were aware of the threat to large warships from MINES, TORPEDOES and SUBMARINES. Aircraft – even less expensive than submarines – exposed fleets to accurate long-range reconnaissance, and senior naval officers everywhere felt that modern battleships, representing huge investments of resources and major PROPAGANDA assets, should be looked after. The risks of offensive action were assigned to light forces, battlecruisers and expendable PRE-DREADNOUGHTS. Few battleships were built after 1916, by which time most vessels commissioned in 1914 had been completed, because all sides were concentrating on construction of light forces. See also: NAVAL WARFARE; Battle of JUTLAND; ANTI-SUBMARINE WEAPONS.

Bauer, Otto (1882–1938) The leading left-wing socialist in prewar Austria. A Marxist with pan-German and nationalist tendencies, Bauer fought on the EASTERN FRONT from August 1914 and was taken prisoner during the autumn. Freed after the OCTOBER REVOLUTION of 1917, he occupied relatively minor posts in the Austrian transitional governments of 1918 and became foreign secretary of the new Austrian Republic following the death of Viktor ADLER in November. His attempts to secure political union with the new German Republic were vetoed by the VERSAILLES Treaty and he resigned in July 1919.

Bayonets Blades issued to all wartime infantrymen for attachment to the barrels of RIFLES during close combat. Most were of the standard knife variety, but the FRENCH ARMY used a 'needle' bayonet on its Lebel rifle and GERMAN ARMY engineering (or 'pioneer') units used a saw-bladed version, often falsely described as a brutal anti-personnel refinement by Allied PROPAGANDA. European officers used to colonial warfare, in which the silent blade seldom faced well-armed defensive positions, tended to view the bayonet charge as a high expression of 'offensive spirit', and orthodox French and BRITISH ARMY doctrine placed great value on its psychological effects. Troops were sometimes ordered to advance with fixed bayonets to preserve silence during surprise attacks, and they were officially the infantryman's primary close combat weapon in TRENCH WARFARE conditions. However, experienced troops on all sides preferred to carry improvised clubs, blades or knuckledusters.

BE-2 British biplane developed in 1912 and immediately put into production by the Royal Aircraft Factory to become the standard military aircraft employed by the RFC in August 1914. Ponderous but stable, valuable qualities in its planned reconnaissance role, the design was used in five main wartime versions.

The BE-2a, with improved tail and wing design, was the RFC's reconnaissance and light-bombing mainstay on the WESTERN FRONT during 1914, but the first BE-2b models, with better cockpit protection and more refined controls, were entering service late in the year. More than 150 of these early types saw action, including a few with the RNAS around Dunkirk, but most had been withdrawn by autumn 1915.

The first BE-2c models, up-engined and modified for greater stability, reached France in January 1915, but were outclassed by German FOKKER E-TYPES despite the later addition of an observer's MACHINE GUN. The BE-2d, a long-range version with rear observer/gunner, and the slightly faster BE-2e (both introduced in the first half of 1916) were similarly disadvantaged and thoroughly disliked by British aircrew. Some BE-2e models remained on the Western Front for reconnaissance and ARTILLERY spotting until mid-1917, suffering heavy losses during 'BLOODY APRIL'.

All three later versions were more successful in 'SIDESHOW' theatres, where they remained in active service throughout, and in home defence against ZEPPELIN raids or on ANTI-SUBMARINE duties for the RNAS. They were also widely used as trainers in 1917–18, and a total of more than 3,000 had been manufactured by the end of the War. The BE-2c design was recycled in 1916 as the basis for the improvised BE-12 fighter, and its outer panels were interchangeable with those of the FE-2A.

BRIEF DATA (BE-2a) Type: two-seat reconnaissance; Engine: 70hp Renault; Max speed: 70mph (112kph); Ceiling: 3,000m; Armament: observer's pistol, rifle, or hand-thrown bombs.

BE-8 British reconnaissance biplane in RFC service from April 1914. More streamlined than the otherwise similar BE-2 design, it equipped five squadrons on the WESTERN FRONT from August, but was withdrawn from active service early the following year. About 60 were built, along with a similar number of structurally modified BE-8a versions that never reached the front.

BRIEF DATA (BE-8) Type: two-seat reconnaissance; Engine: 80hp Gnôme; Max speed: 70mph (112kph); Armament: observer's small arms or 100lb (45kg) bomb.

BE-12 British biplane FIGHTER, an improvised development of the BE-2C. Designed during early 1916 as an emergency response to German FOKKER E-TYPES on the WESTERN FRONT, it was an equally slow, stable craft and completely unsuited to DOGFIGHTS, as was a similarly direct development of the BE-2e known as the BE-12a. Re-assigned to light-bombing duties within weeks of their appearance with RFC squadrons in August 1916, BE-12s were soon withdrawn from France. A few remained on combat duty over the BALKAN and PALESTINE FRONTS well into 1917, some sporting one or two extra MACHINE GUNS firing wide of the propeller. About 450 BE-12 and BE-12a models were built, along with 150 of a 200hp home-defence version, the BE-12b, which had synchronized twin forward machine-guns and enjoyed limited success against German STRATEGIC BOMBING raids during 1917–18.

BRIEF DATA (BE-12) Type: single-seat fighter/light bomber; Engine: 150hp Royal Aircraft Factory; Max speed: 97mph (155kph); Ceiling: 3,800m; Armament: 2 × 0.303in mg, max bomb load 256lb.

Beardsmore WB-III See: SOPWITH PUP.

Beatty, Admiral Sir David (1871–1936) Britain's best-known and most popular naval officer in 1914, Beatty enjoyed a reputation for dash and aggression derived from colonial exploits in the late 19th century. Appointed in command of the GRAND FLEET's Battlecruiser Squadron in 1913, his perceived impetuousness worried some ROYAL NAVY leaders, including C-in-C JELLICOE, who feared he might be drawn into a trap. His boldness was a decisive factor in the minor victory at HELIGOLAND BIGHT in 1914, and was useful at the DOGGER BANK and JUTLAND, but his instinctive willingness to engage a superior enemy force also proved expensive at both the latter engagements.

He emerged from the anti-climax of Jutland with some credit, praised for aggression where Jellicoe was criticized for caution, and his enhanced reputation made him a natural choice as Jellicoe's successor. His promotion over the heads of eight senior admirals in late 1916 caused some internal resentment, but his policy was essentially identical to Jellicoe's. Cautious husbandry of big ships and maintenance of economic BLOCKADE remained his priorities until the ARMISTICE. Beatty took the surrender of the German HIGH SEAS FLEET at Rosyth and was First Sea Lord from 1921. See also: SCARBOROUGH RAID.

Beaumont Hamel See: SOMME OFFENSIVE.

Beaverbrook, Lord See: AITKEN, W.

Beersheba–Gaza Line, Battle of the Opening phase of the British offensive on the PALESTINE FRONT in late 1917. General ALLENBY took overall command of the theatre in late June, in the aftermath of defeat at GAZA, with instructions from premier LLOYD GEORGE to take Jerusalem by Christmas. He supervised a build-up of manpower, ARTILLERY, shells and other material intended to overwhelm the 40km Turkish line between Beersheba and the coast at Gaza (see MAP 22).

Reinforcements from SALONIKA (including French and Italian detachments) brought total Allied strength above 200,000 men, of which about 80,000 infantry and 12,000 CAVALRY comprised the frontline force under General Chetwode. Local TURKISH ARMY commander KRESSENSTEIN built new strongpoints north of Gaza and in the centre of the line at Tel es Sheria during the summer, but lacked TRENCH WARFARE materials and was reinforced only by four seriously understrength divisions. General FALKENHAYN's Germano-Turkish YILDERIM FORCE was belatedly committed to Palestine for a proposed offensive, but reorganization was only just in progress when the British operation got underway in late October.

Allenby followed Chetwode's plan for an attack on the weaker southwestern end of the line at Beersheba, an infantry advance along the line towards Gaza, and a cavalry sweep to cut off retreat to Jerusalem. About 40,000 troops were concentrated around Beersheba, with three reduced divisions and 218 supporting guns (the biggest concentration of artillery outside Europe up to that date) remaining as a diversion in front of Gaza. Surprise was essential, and water supply depended on capture of the town's wells within one day.

Elaborate secrecy measures were rendered effective by the reorganized RFC's new BRISTOL FIGHTERS, which prevented German air reconnaissance, and after a six-day PRELIMINARY BOMBARDMENT of Gaza the main attack opened west of Beersheba early on 31 October. The town was surrounded by evening, and a cavalry charge at dusk prevented planned contamination of the wells. By the end of the day Allenby was in position to 'roll up' the entire Turkish line, beginning with the central stronghold of Tel es Sheria.

Disappointing yields from the Beersheba wells delayed the Sheria attack for several days, but Turkish defences were disrupted by a diversionary operation to the east by a 70-strong camel company (transferred from operations with the ARAB REVOLT). Occupying Hebron, on the road to Jerusalem, it was mistaken for a large-scale flank attack, attracting two Turkish divisions and a entire cavalry division northeast.

Falkenhayn took command from Jerusalem on 5 November and allowed Kressenstein to withdraw north of Gaza, which was occupied by British troops next evening. The attack on Tel es Sheria was launched at dawn on 6 November and took the hill the following morning, offering Allenby the chance to cut off Turkish retreat.

Pursuit was delayed by Turkish counterattacks and a rearguard action at Huj, northeast of Gaza. An ammunition dump and the new headquarters of Kressenstein's Eighth Army, Huj was taken intact by another cavalry charge on 8 November, but most Turkish formations escaped encirclement. The retreat became disorganized, and desertions meant that only about 15,000 defenders took up new positions along a line southwest of JERUSALEM from 10 November.

Bees, Battle of the See: Battle of TANGA.

BEF (British Expeditionary Force) The British land army on the WESTERN FRONT from August 1914, incorporating attached RFC units until April 1918. Initially a small but highly professional army under Sir John FRENCH was sent to BELGIUM, comprising one CAVALRY and four infantry divisions. The BEF was massively expanded over the next three years, absorbing most of the new BRITISH ARMY divisions recruited from reserves or created by war minister KITCHENER. Seven regular infantry and three cavalry divisions were in France and Belgium by October 1914, and in December the BEF's two corps were redesignated armies. A Third Army was created in July 1915, with a Fourth and a Reserve Army added from March 1916. The Cavalry Corps was maintained as a separate unit except for the period from March to September 1916 when it was dispersed among the Armies, and the Reserve Army was renamed the Fifth, an arrangement still in force at the ARMISTICE. The BEF only underwent one wartime change of command, HAIG replacing French in December 1915.

Belgian Air Service Although an air squadron had been planned for each of the BELGIAN ARMY's field divisions, the Belgian *Compagnie des Aviateurs* in August 1914 comprised a single squadron (escadrille) equipped with at most 12 machines. They made little impact during the German invasion of BELGIUM, but in early 1915 a reorganized *Aviation Militaire* of five escadrilles was formed to support the Army on the WESTERN FRONT.

As an occupied country unable to produce its own weapons, Belgium purchased its aircraft from the Allies and was forced to rely on surplus designs, but morale and personnel quality remained high throughout. A three-squadron FIGHTER group was formed as technical parity with GERMAN ARMY AIR SERVICE units became feasible in 1917 (see AERIAL WARFARE), producing three certified 'ACES', and at the end of the War the *Aviation Militaire* had grown to 11 escadrilles, operating some 140 frontline aircraft.

Belgian Army The development of the Belgian Army prior to 1914 had been a matter of dispute between constitutional monarch ALBERT I, a trained soldier who became C-in-C only in wartime, and an administration opposed to military expansion. Some extension of BELGIUM's very limited conscription laws was enacted in 1912, and major reorganization was begun in 1913, but the one peacetime CAVALRY and six infantry divisions (some 43,000 men) were able to call on only about 115,000 reserves on mobilization in August 1914.

Concentrated in the field army, this number allowed insufficient garrison troops for Belgium's FORTRESSES, regarded as the country's main defence against invasion but overdue for renovation and stripped of heavy MACHINE GUNS to make up field shortages. The heavy ARTILLERY and cavalry arms also remained well below planned strength.

Most Belgian officers were trained in FRANCE, and FRENCH ARMY theories of offensive warfare enjoyed widespread support. In strict observance of the spirit of neutrality, the peacetime command planned to group the field army in the centre of Belgium, prepared for attack from any direction and gathered for a mass offensive of its own. Albert and some senior officers favoured a more realistic policy of well-organized defence against GERMANY, the most probable aggressor, but by the time Albert took command (3 August) it was too late to implement his proposed concentration around the frontier fortresses of LIÈGE and NAMUR.

Apart from the regular army, Belgium could call on a Gendarmerie of 3,000 well-trained cavalry and a reserve militia (*Garde Civique*) of perhaps 40,000 ill-equipped local volunteers. Some militiamen were pressed into emergency service at fortresses, but most remained disorganized and were not recognized as military personnel by invading German authorities, who usually treated those found with weapons as FRANC-TIREURS.

Overwhelmed by the August invasion, Albert chose to save the Army by an early withdrawal to fortified ANTWERP, retiring west to FLANDERS in October and eventually holding a line just inside western Belgium at the YSER in December. By mid-December 1914 losses had reduced strength to about 32,000 men, but reorganization during the winter established the Belgian divisions in occupation of the northernmost sector of the WESTERN FRONT.

A pattern of Allied supply and support was also established, with French (and some British) weapons, tools and ammunition generally replacing the Army's obsolete, mostly German, equipment. British-made khaki garments replaced garish 19th-century uniforms in early 1915, and a few Belgian hospitals were set up in GREAT BRITAIN, but most training and medical support was concentrated in France.

Strict conscription in the small part of Belgium under Allied control, and among exiles, enabled the Army to maintain its position in the line, and an average strength of about 170,000 men, to the ARMISTICE. Albert's refusal, as a neutral, to become entangled in major Allied offensives left troops in relatively good condition when the reconquest of Belgium became a viable possibility, and they played an active part in the successful COURTRAI advance of autumn 1918.

Small Belgian detachments served in other sectors along the front, on loan to Allied armies, and colonial troops were active in EAST AFRICA. An ARMOURED CAR company fought with the RUSSIAN ARMY on the EASTERN FRONT. In total some 267,000 men served in the wartime Belgian Army, of whom about 54,000 were wounded and 14,000 killed in almost four years of TRENCH WARFARE. Belgium did not possess naval forces. See also: BELGIAN AIR SERVICE.

Belgium An independent constitutional monarchy since liberation from the Netherlands in the revolution of 1830–31. The king, ALBERT I from 1909, possessed legislative powers and became personal commander of the BELGIAN ARMY in time of war, but was responsible to a cabinet drawn from a two-tier elected parliament. A complex universal male suffrage system allowed up to three votes for the propertied or well-educated among Belgium's 7.5 million people (1910), and in 1914 both chambers were dominated by Baron de BROQUEVILLE's Catholic Party.

A highly prosperous trading nation, with major Channel ports at ANTWERP and Ostend, Belgium's industrial economy was well-endowed with coalfields and iron ore (much of it obtained by special agreement with neighbouring LUXEMBOURG). Supporting infrastructure included some 9,000km of RAILWAYS and 2,000km of busy canals, but the large central African colony of the Belgian Congo provided few economic benefits beyond export of its rubber.

Belgium occupied the only wide open space between FRANCE and GERMANY, and Belgian neutrality, guaranteed by all the major European states since 1831, was a vital component of the European balance of power in 1914. Maintaining a neutral stance towards its two powerful, antagonistic neighbours was the basis of Belgian foreign policy. Anxious to ensure the support of its other guarantors, the cabinet reacted to probable German invasion during the JULY CRISIS by deploying its relatively meagre armed forces against all frontiers.

The German ultimatum to Belgium of 2 August gave King Albert and his government the choice of fighting or peacefully accepting effective conquest. Once war was declared and the German invasion underway, Albert took personal command of a hopelessly outnumbered Army and led it in retreat to the northwest corner of the country.

Albert and the government were eventually established at Le Havre in France, from where they governed the small patch of Flanders on the Allied side of the WESTERN FRONT after the German advance had been stopped at the YSER in December 1914. The rest of the country was ruled from Brussels by German occupying authorities, already internationally notorious for 'atrocities' committed during the conquest (see Invasion of BELGIUM).

After an initial frenzy of mass executions and destruction (see LOUVAIN; NAMUR), German administration of the occupied zone remained harsh but never matched the lurid depictions of Allied PROPAGANDA. Belgian industry was turned over to German war production, and the economy as a whole was ruthlessly stripped for German use, with plant, rolling stock, food and raw materials transported across the border en masse. Civilian populations were kept under martial law and any signs of resistance (real or imagined) dealt with by routine execution of hostages, but the views of pacifists and Belgian nationalists like Cardinal MERCIER received widespread coverage from neutral press observers throughout the occupation.

Belgium's two provinces of Flanders and Wallonia were separate in language and custom but shared the Roman Catholic faith. Attempts to foster a separatist Flemish movement (for absorption into a planned postwar German economic union) met with little success. Most Belgians also ignored high local unemployment to reject work in German factories, but enforced deportation of Belgian workers was begun under the HINDENBURG PROGRAMME in October 1916. Inefficient and diplomatically damaging, the policy was abandoned in February 1917.

Coordinated by neutral ambassadors in Brussels, international aid had been reaching Belgium since 1914 (see COMMISSION FOR THE RELIEF OF BELGIUM). Despite full German cooperation, it could not keep up with worsening shortages as poor harvests and a cold winter from late 1916 reduced hundreds of thousands of Belgians, mostly in towns and cities, to dependence on international charity for food and fuel. Malnutrition helped double the prewar civilian mortality rate in Brussels by 1917.

More than a million Belgian refugees had fled to the Netherlands, France or GREAT BRITAIN in 1914. Most of those in the neutral Netherlands eventually returned after German authorities guaranteed their safety, but some 300,000 exiles remained in Allied countries. Along with the population of free Belgium these exiles were subject to conscription for service in northwestern Flanders, which was almost completely devastated by four years of constant fighting.

Albert's guiding ambition was the repossession of an essentially intact Belgium. He obstructed Allied plans to include Belgian forces in offensives along the Western Front and, as civilian conditions worsened in the occupied zone during late 1917, he encouraged de Broqueville to consider a separate peace with Germany. Opposed by the rest of the cabinet, the idea lost ground after Paul HYMANS took over the foreign ministry in

January 1918. It had been abandoned completely by late autumn, when Albert led the Allied COURTRAI OFFENSIVE back into Belgium.

The King re-entered Brussels on 22 November 1918 to begin a process of rapid economic reconstruction and industrialization. Social reform was instituted to calm an immediate resumption of strife between Walloons and the slightly more numerous Flemings, with the Flemish language officially recognized for the first time in 1920.

Belgium, Invasion of The opening German offensive on the WESTERN FRONT, dictated by the prewar SCHLIEFFEN PLAN and launched on 4 August 1914. Speed was vital to its strategic success as a preliminary to a rapid conquest of FRANCE, due for completion within six weeks, and as a means of presenting the most powerful guarantor of Belgian neutrality, GREAT BRITAIN, with a fait accompli. The 6 field divisions of the BELGIAN ARMY were not expected to fight, but any resistance would face 38 divisions (more than 750,000 men) of the German First, Second and Third Armies.

The German Fourth Army (ALBRECHT of Württemberg) occupied LUXEMBOURG unopposed in the first three days of August, and the exquisitely timetabled invasion began next morning. An advance force of six brigades marched on the supposedly invincible fortresses around LIÈGE, and the defenders opened fire at the first sign of German troops. Initial infantry attacks on Liège were repelled, but the fortifications were shattered by massive new BIG BERTHA and SCHLANKE EMMA siege guns and surrendered on 16 August, having delayed German schedules by two days.

The main German northern wing, General von KLUCK's First Army, crossed the border that day and struck east towards Brussels. Its immediate objective was destruction of the Belgian Army, mustered in the centre of the country, but King ALBERT's retreat to ANTWERP of 18–20 August ensured its survival. Despite occasional flank attacks from Antwerp the First Army reached and took Brussels on 20 August, before turning south towards the heart of France. Britain had declared war on confirmation of the invasion, and its small expeditionary force (the BEF) delayed von Kluck just inside the French border at MONS on 23 August. When it retreated into France the next day, most of the First Army followed.

The German Second and Third armies, under overall command of General von BÜLOW, began their main drive on 17 August and marched down a broad front either side of the Meuse. Equipped with the new siege guns, the Second Army took the river's second major fortress at NAMUR on 23 August, and both armies combined to force supporting French forces into retreat from CHARLEROI. The southern tip of Belgium was invaded by the Fourth Army, which crossed from Luxembourg on 4 August and began moving through the ARDENNES on 19 August, forcing a French counter-invasion to retire from the sector after heavy fighting on 22–23 August.

Virtually the whole of Belgium was in German hands by 25 August, apart from Antwerp and the Channel coast to the west. The overall plan for conquering France was roughly on schedule and in position, but the BEF and the French Fifth Army (at Charleroi) could both have been prevented from escaping to fight again (see Battles of LE CATEAU, GUISE), and the Belgian Army remained a thorn in the German right flank.

Unexpected Belgian resistance prompted a deliberate German attempt to quash resistance through fear. Towns were shelled, bombed and burned during the invasion, hostages were taken and executed, all witnessed by an invited neutral press. Graphic reports of atrocities, especially the burning of LOUVAIN and the massacre at DINANT, handed the Allies a permanent PROPAGANDA advantage and ensured long-term international sympathy for the Belgian people (see BELGIUM). See also: MAP 4; Battles of the FRONTIERS; Battle of HAELEN; FRANC-TIREURS.

Belleau Wood, Battle of Counterattack by French and US forces, also known as the Battle of Château-Thierry, that halted German advances on the WESTERN FRONT in the latter stages of the AISNE Offensive in June 1918. By 3 June forward units of the German Seventh Army had reached the River Marne around

Château-Thierry and threatened to break through a thinly defended French line towards Paris. French reserves were rushed to the front and US commander PERSHING allowed two divisions of the AEF to join them in counterattacks that made progress around Château-Thierry on 3–4 June and took Belleau Wood (along the west flank of the German SALIENT) in a series of advances up to 12 June. See also: Battle of CANTIGNY.

Bellenglise, Battle of See: ST QUENTIN CANAL.

Bellicourt, Battle of See: ST QUENTIN CANAL.

Below, General Otto von (1857–1944) German officer whose varied wartime career began in command of I Reserve Corps on the EASTERN FRONT, which he led at GUMBINNEN and in the first MASURIAN LAKES battle. He took over the Eighth Army from General von FRANÇOIS in November 1914, taking part in the second Masurian Lakes action the following February, and commanded the new 'Niemen Army' from May 1915. In October 1916, von Below was transferred lead German forces on the BALKAN FRONT, improving his reputation during the MONASTIR OFFENSIVE before moving to the WESTERN FRONT in April 1917, leading the Sixth Army around Lille (where the proximity of his namesake, General Fritz von Below, caused some Allied confusion). In September he moved again, in command of a new Austro-German Fourteenth Army to the ITALIAN FRONT, where it played a vital part in the victory at CAPORETTO, but by February 1918 he was back in France, leading the Seventeenth Army against Arras during the KAISERSCHLACHT Offensive. His final wartime appointment, in October 1918, was to command the First Army's retreat from around Reims to positions for a possible final defence of German territory.

Ben-My-Chree Largest and fastest of the cross-Channel ferries converted by the ROYAL NAVY as primitive AIRCRAFT CARRIERS (see *ENGADINE*), *Ben-My-Chree* was sent to the DARDANELLES in summer 1915 as a replacement for the much slower *ARK ROYAL*. In August its SHORT 184 seaplanes launched the first successful aerial TORPEDO attacks, and it remained in the eastern MEDITERRANEAN until sunk by Turkish shore batteries in 1917.

BRIEF DATA (1915): 2,651 tons; Crew: c 250; Dimensions: length 375ft (113.6m), beam 46ft (13.9m); Speed: 24.5k; Armament: 2 × 4in gun, 1 × 6pdr AA, 7 × a/c.

Benedetto Brin The oldest and least useful PRE-DREADNOUGHT deployed with the wartime ITALIAN NAVY battlefleet, *Benedetto Brin* and its sister ship the *Regina Margherita* were completed in 1904. Never in fleet action and not risked in secondary operations, *Benedetto Brin* blew up in Brindisi harbour on the morning of 27 September 1915, a disaster ascribed initially to unstable gunpowder but later to sabotage. *Regina Margherita*, subsequently stationed with older BATTLESHIPS and CRUISERS at Valona, was mined and sunk en route for Taranto on 11 December 1916. Announcement of the sinking was delayed for over a month to protect low public morale in ITALY.

BRIEF DATA (*Benedetto Brin*, 1915) Displacement: 13,400 tons; Crew: 720; Dimensions: length 455ft (137.9m), beam 78ft (23.6m); Speed: 18k; Main armament: 4 × 12in gun, 4 × 8in, 12 × 6in, 4 × 18in TT.

Benedict XV, Pope (1854–1922) A cardinal since May 1914, Giacomo della Chiesa was elected to the papacy in haste on 3 September 1914, following the death of Pius X on 20 August, and took office with a reputation as an able diplomat. His religious status made him an obvious channel for peace proposals, but an attempt to promote a general Christmas truce in 1914 was ignored and from 1915 his influence with the Allies was undermined by political circumstances in ITALY. After Benedict acted as an intermediary in Italian negotiations with the CENTRAL POWERS in 1915, the Allies secretly agreed to ignore any Vatican peace proposals as part of the Treaty of LONDON with Italy, and his major diplomatic initiative, a Peace Note to belligerents issued on 14 August 1917, was brushed aside by both sides. Although the Vatican claimed a major role in any postwar settlement, Benedict was not invited to the PARIS PEACE CONFERENCE.

Beneš, Eduard (1884–1948) Czech nationalist, prominent in the prewar movement for independence from AUSTRIA-HUNGARY, who co-founded the Czechoslovak National Council (with Thomáš MASARYK) from voluntary exile in Paris in 1915, and was its first general secretary. The dominant political figure in the Council, Beneš worked to secure Allied support for the postwar establishment of CZECHOSLOVAKIA as an independent state, becoming foreign minister on its establishment in November 1918 and president of the republic on Masaryk's retirement in 1935.

Benson, Admiral William (1855–1932) Unspectacular but efficient US NAVY officer, he was the surprise choice of navy secretary DANIELS as chief of naval operations in May 1915. With instructions to institute strictly limited preparations for war, Benson supervised gradual reorganization of the fleets to stress Atlantic operations and established a logistic framework for future expansion. He viewed war with GERMANY in an essentially defensive light, and relations with pro-British Admiral SIMS were strained until late 1917, when a visit to London with WILSON's factfinding War Commission changed his mind. He subsequently reversed his opposition to the NORTH SEA BARRAGE, committed modern BATTLESHIPS to cooperation with the ROYAL NAVY in the North Sea, and made unavailing efforts to persuade the ITALIAN NAVY into attacks on Austro-Hungarian Adriatic bases. At the PARIS PEACE CONFERENCE as senior US naval advisor, and disappointed by the VERSAILLES Treaty's severity, he retired (still a rear admiral) in September 1919.

Berchtold, Leopold, Count von (1862–1942) Vienna-born diplomat who served as AUSTRIA-HUNGARY's ambassador to RUSSIA from 1907 until his appointment as imperial foreign minister in 1912. Berchtold never imposed a consistent foreign policy of his own, flirting with war against SERBIA in 1912–13 but pulling back and accepting a diplomatic defeat at the end of the Balkan Wars. Though persuaded into war by the assassination of Archduke FRANZ FERDINAND at Sarajevo in June 1914, he ignored chief of staff CONRAD's demands for an immediate attack, bowing to Hungarian premier TISZA's insistence on formal diplomatic procedures (see JULY CRISIS). Once war was in progress, Berchtold's main problem was ITALY's predictable demands for control over territories in southern Austria. By the end of 1914 he was informing the imperial Crown Council that the choice lay between complete concession or war, as recommended by Tisza and Conrad, respectively. Tainted at court as a 'defeatist', he retired on 13 January 1915 and was replaced by the more aggressive Count BURIAN.

Bergmann Guns The Bergmann 7.92mm MACHINE GUN was adopted by the GERMAN ARMY in 1915, and used to augment supplies of the superior MASCHINENGEWEHR 08 to both infantry and aircraft. The Bergmann Maschinenpistole 18/1 was produced from early 1918 and was the forerunner of modern submachine guns. Although its 32-round magazine caused some problems, the weapon was light enough for use by assault troops and entered mass production in mid-1918. Extensively employed on the WESTERN FRONT during the autumn, it was perforce restricted to defensive operations, but was successful enough to merit specific prohibition under the Treaty of VERSAILLES.

Berlin Act Agreement signed in 1885 by Britain, France, Belgium and Germany to create a neutral zone covering almost all of colonial central AFRICA in the event of European war. Known as the 'conventional basin of the Congo', the zone included part or all of three German colonies, and the British had made clear in 1911 that they regarded its implementation as voluntary. Anglo-French forces barely hesitated before invading German TOGOLAND and CAMEROON in August 1914, and a German appeal to the US government on 23 August received a cool reception. An initial plea from the Belgian government for African neutrality was withdrawn after German attacks sank Belgian

Congolese shipping on Lake Tanganyika, and the Belgian government's decision of 28 August to send troops into Cameroon marked the end of European diplomatic efforts to enforce a separate peace in Africa.

The Act more genuinely represented the views of Allied and German local colonial administrators in Africa, many of whom adhered to contemporary imperialist concepts of Europe's global 'civilizing' mission. Some, notably the British and German governors in EAST AFRICA, made strenuous efforts to prevent war between white men, seen as dangerous to routine economic and moral supremacy over African peoples, but all were overruled by local or imperial military authorities. See MAP 17.

Bernstorff, Johann, Count von (1862–1939) German ambassador to the UNITED STATES from 1908. A political moderate with pro-British tendencies, Bernstorff enjoyed good relations with US leaders WILSON, HOUSE and LANSING until his position was undermined by the gradual extension of SUBMARINE WARFARE (which he opposed) and suspicion of German agitation in Central America (see ZIMMERMANN NOTE). Ambassador to Constantinople from September 1917, he turned down EBERT's offer of the foreign ministry in November 1918 and retired from the diplomatic service, serving as a Reichstag deputy from 1921.

Berthelot, General Henri (1863–1931) Assistant chief of staff to the FRENCH ARMY in August 1914, and a committed devotee of PLAN 17, Berthelot was C-in-C JOFFRE's principal assistant and mouthpiece during the vital battles of the FRONTIERS and the MARNE, responsible for deflecting criticism or argument from politicians and field commanders. When Joffre was replaced in December 1916, Berthelot was sent to reorganize the defeated ROMANIAN ARMY, playing a major role in planning its last-ditch defence on the ARGES, but was recalled to the WESTERN FRONT in 1918 as commander of the Fifth Army, leading it during the Second Battle of the MARNE and until the end of October, when he returned east to arrange ROMANIA's belated resumption of hostilities.

Beseler, General Hans von (1850–1921) German staff officer, retired in 1910 as inspector-general of infantry but recalled to active service in August 1914. A corps commander with KLUCK's First Army during the invasion of BELGIUM, he supervised the capture of ANTWERP in October. After fighting at the battle of the YSER, Beseler was transferred to the EASTERN FRONT for the GORLICE-TARNOW OFFENSIVE of spring 1915, joining the Ninth Army as part of Army Group GALLWITZ.

On 24 August, after the summer TRIPLE OFFENSIVE had captured all of Russian POLAND, Beseler was appointed its military governor. His attempts to create a semi-independent 'Congress Poland', ruled by an aristocratic assembly, were later used by the THIRD SUPREME COMMAND to proclaim a Congress state explicitly designed to provide military and economic resources for the German war effort (5 November 1916). The arrest of Polish C-in-C PIŁSUDSKI in July 1917 wrecked the Congress facade, and Beseler's stance was henceforth regarded as dangerously 'pro-Polish' by the high command. He eventually left his command for GERMANY without warning on 12 November 1918, suffering scathing criticism from right-wing groups for the manner of his departure.

Bessarabian Offensive The RUSSIAN ARMY's first big attack on the EASTERN FRONT after its enormous loses of 1915, also called the Battle of the Strypa after the river in eastern Galicia that was the main focus of attacks (see MAP 10). Ordered by STAVKA in late November 1915, the offensive was designed to relieve pressure on the BALKAN FRONT and to impress nearby neutral ROMANIA.

The Seventh (SHCHERBACHEV) and Ninth (Lechitski) Armies enjoyed 2-to-1 manpower superiority over Austro-Hungarian forces along their Galician front, and were benefiting from improved industrial output in RUSSIA, but southwestern group commander IVANOV's preparations were slow and his tactics were a poor imitation of German BREAKTHROUGH methods used during the

1915 TRIPLE OFFENSIVE.

Launched on 27 December by a total of nine infantry and two cavalry corps massed along a very narrow front, the offensive was a total failure. Austro-Hungarian ARTILLERY contained initial attacks, which lacked reserve support, and two weeks of fighting cost the Russian Army 50,000 men.

The only Russian success came on the southern wing, where Shcherbachev concentrated all his army's artillery along a single kilometre. Without ready reserves and unprotected on both flanks, the attempted breakthrough soon collapsed against well-organized counterattacks by PFLANZER-BALTIN's Seventh Army. The operation was abandoned on 10 January, with most Russian commanders concluding that future success depended on massing a still heavier weight of concentrated assault. See also: BRUSILOV OFFENSIVE; Battle of Lake NAROCH.

Bethmann Hollweg, Theobald von (1856–1921) German civil servant, interior minister of Prussia from 1905 and of GERMANY from 1907, who replaced Bernhard von Bülow as imperial chancellor in 1909, a position he was to hold until 1917. Inexperienced in foreign affairs, his hopes of rapprochement abroad were wrecked by the expansionist aims of Germany's ruling interests (which he shared to some extent), expressed in naval challenge to GREAT BRITAIN and punitive trade tariffs against RUSSIA.

The economic strain of expansion and rearmament fuelled internal discontent, and though Bethmann Hollweg favoured limited constitutional reform, especially of the obsolete Prussian system, the idea was anathema to the crown he represented. After the 1912 Reichstag elections returned 110 socialist deputies he faced the task of persuading a reformist parliament to ratify right-wing legislation and budgets without forcing either side to abandon constitutional methods.

Inevitably unpopular all across the German political spectrum by 1914, Bethmann Hollweg became a deeply pessimistic figure, convinced that only a successful war could divert crisis at home and erosion of Germany's international position. He hoped for a short, limited war during the JULY CRISIS of 1914, encouraging Austro-Hungarian aggression against SERBIA with an unconditional guarantee of support on 6 July. Once it became clear that general war was imminent he changed his mind, but he lacked the personal or political authority to reverse the SCHLIEFFEN PLAN.

Bethmann Hollweg walked an uneasy tightrope between polarizing forces in wartime. Ultimately dependent on the crown and its supporters, he could only rely on vague promises of postwar constitutional reform to shore up a faltering political truce (*Burgfrieden*) as economic disruption reached hitherto unimagined levels.

Compromise informed his handling of the national debate over war aims, which he sought to leave as open to varied interpretation as possible. His statements on the subject appeared as rabid expansionism to overseas observers, but were moderate by right-wing German standards, and the advent of the THIRD SUPREME COMMAND in August 1916 finally obliterated any middle ground in which he could work.

His longstanding opposition to extension of SUBMARINE WARFARE collapsed after a last-ditch PEACE OFFER in late 1916 failed to elicit a positive response from US president WILSON (see *HANDELSKRIEG*), and his political position evaporated during 1917. Relations with WILHELM II remained good, and he obtained a royal promise in March to reform the Prussian constitution eventually, but it had no effect on the rapid collapse of *Burgfrieden* or right-wing measures imposed under the HINDENBURG PROGRAMME.

Bethmann Hollweg's indecision following the Reichstag's PEACE RESOLUTION of July upset both the high command and its opponents, prompting an improbable alliance between senior military commanders and liberal Reichstag leaders to secure his resignation and retirement on 13 July 1917.

'Big Bertha' Giant mobile siege gun, properly the Krupp 420mm heavy howitzer but universally known as 'Big Bertha' (*Dicke Berta*). Developed for the GERMAN ARMY after observation of Japanese operations against Russian FORTRESSES in the war of 1904–05, expressly designed to destroy the formidable frontier fortresses of LIÈGE and NAMUR as part of the SCHLIEFFEN PLAN.

The Krupp factory had the first two ready for transportation on 9 August 1914. With a full crew of over 1,000 men each they presented enormous difficulties on crowded roads but finally arrived in front of Liège on 12 August, followed by five almost equally fearsome Skoda SCHLANKE EMMA howitzers on loan from AUSTRIA-HUNGARY.

Bigger and heavier than any gun previously fired, capable of delivering ten 930kg shells per hour to a range of about 15km, the Big Berthas overwhelmed supposedly indestructible Belgian fortifications in a matter of days, demonstrating the potential of heavy ARTILLERY for field operations to other armies.

Birdwood, General Sir William (1865–1951) The BRITISH ARMY officer in command of the Australian and New Zealand Army Corps (ANZAC) from 1914 (see AUSTRALIAN FORCES; NEW ZEALAND FORCES). In EGYPT when the GALLIPOLI LANDINGS were being planned, he expected overall command of the operation, but instead led his forces at ANZAC COVE under General HAMILTON. Though his relations with Australian and New Zealand troops were better than those of many British commanders, and though he was one of the few senior officers to emerge from Gallipoli with an undamaged reputation, the mutual affection between Birdwood and his troops was exaggerated by British PROPAGANDA, and he has since been criticized as sharing Hamilton's lack of imagination. Promoted lieutenant-general in August 1915 and knighted later the same year, Birdwood led ANZAC on the WESTERN FRONT until the end of May 1918, when he took over the reconstituted British Fifth Army. A full general from 1917 by virtue of seniority on the Indian Army list, he guided the Fifth Army through the climactic COURTRAI OFFENSIVE in autumn 1918.

Bischofsberg, Battle of See: Battle of TANNENBERG.

Bissolati, Leonida (1857–1920) Italian socialist politician. A moderate reformer, his pessimistic view of the SECOND INTERNATIONAL's capacity to secure peace culminated in support for war with TURKEY, leading to his expulsion from the Socialist Party in 1912. From summer 1914 he supported war against AUSTRIA-HUNGARY (as a crusade against imperialism) and he enlisted for combat service as an NCO in 1915. Recalled to full-time politics as minister without portfolio in the coalition BOSELLI government from June 1916, Bissolati pressed for closer government supervision of General CADORNA's Army high command, and became Italy's leading political supporter of the FOURTEEN POINTS peace programme. A diehard opponent of foreign minister SONNINO's expansionism, he resigned in December 1918 over the ORLANDO government's attitude to the peace process.

Blackburn Kangaroo Twin-engined land bomber built by the British Blackburn seaplane company and used by one RAF coastal-patrol squadron from April 1918. Kangaroos were reasonably successful ANTI-SUBMARINE craft, sinking one U-BOAT and damaging several more, but were retired from service after 1918.

BRIEF DATA Type: coastal-patrol bomber; Engine: 2 × 250hp Rolls Royce; Max speed: 100mph (160kph); Armament: 2 × 0.303in mg, max bomb load 1,840lbs (836kg).

Black Flight The most celebrated wartime FIGHTER unit of the RNAS, officially B Flight of Naval 10 Squadron. Black Flight consisted of five SOPWITH TRIPLANES with black upper-fuselage paint, given the names *Black Prince*, *Black Death*, *Black Maria*, *Black Sheep* and *Black Roger* by their Canadian pilots. The flight was credited with shooting down 87 German aircraft without loss on the WESTERN FRONT between May and September 1917, and flight leader Collishaw (aboard *Black Maria*) destroyed 16 aircraft in less than a month at the height of the fighting around YPRES.

Black Hand Serbian secret society, properly called 'Unity or Death', formed in 1911 to promote the political unification of Serbia with South Slav minorities in TURKEY and

AUSTRIA-HUNGARY. Most of its members were junior SERBIAN ARMY officers working to increase military influence over civilian government and to establish Serbian dominance over a future 'YUGOSLAVIA'.

The society's leading military figure, Colonel Dimitrievic (known by the codename of 'Apis'), was responsible for training Gavrilo PRINCIP and his accomplice to assassinate Archduke FRANZ FERDINAND in Sarajevo on 28 June 1914, precipitating the JULY CRISIS and general war. The organization's known influence over cabinet policy provoked widespread suspicion of Serbian government collusion, but available evidence suggests none.

The Black Hand remained active within the Army until December 1916, when the government-in-exile in Corfu ordered the arrest of its leaders. Dimitrievic and two others were executed after a dubious trial the following June – a trial intended largely for international and Yugoslav federalist consumption – and the society ceased to exist.

Black Sea Theatre contested by the RUSSIAN and TURKISH NAVIES from late October 1914. The main strategic issues at stake were the supply of fuel and materials to TURKEY, support of land operations on the CAUCASIAN FRONT, and control of the Turkish Bosporus Channel, which connected the Black Sea to the DARDANELLES and the MEDITERRANEAN (see MAP 16).

The Russian Navy's assumptions of easy supremacy in the theatre had been jolted by Turkish naval expansion, especially the order of two new BATTLESHIPS from Britain. The Russians accordingly modified their war plans for the theatre, moving closer to the defensive posture envisaged for the BALTIC SEA, with the emphasis on minelaying operations at least until its own two new battleships were in service.

Turkish forces were in fact reinforced by the German MITTELMEERDIVISION in August 1914, and war in the Black Sea opened without a declaration on 29 October, when the ex-German *GOEBEN* and *BRESLAU* led surprise attacks on Russian warships in their main harbours of Sevastopol and Odessa. The attacks achieved little, leaving the Russian fleet's five PRE-DREADNOUGHTS, two CRUISERS, eight DESTROYERS and four SUBMARINES intact, and the pattern of Black Sea operations began to emerge in its aftermath.

Both sides concentrated on laying minefields and bombarding enemy coastal installations or harbours, with the Russians retaining both initiative and advantage. More than 4,000 Russian MINES had been used by the end of 1914, most targeted at the port of Zonguldak, the one entry point for vital Turkish coal imports.

Russian warships regularly sortied in support of mining and bombardment operations, but neither side sought a full-scale fleet confrontation. Outnumbered but always able to outrun heavily armed pursuers, *Goeben* was severely damaged by a mine at Christmas 1914 and underwent several months of repairs in inefficient Turkish dockyards, while the Russians were content to wait for their dreadnoughts, the first of which (*IMPERATRICA MARIA*) reached the fleet in July 1915.

Reinforced by new destroyers and submarines, Russian squadrons tightened their blockade of coal supplies during 1915, and Turkish attempts at counterattack achieved little success. The cruiser *MEDSHIDIYE* was lost in April during the year's only major attack on Russian harbours, and *Breslau* was put out of action by mine damage in July. Russian forces made no serious attempt to force a passage through the Bosporus, and tentative plans to support Allied operations in the Dardanelles were dropped as soon their lack of success became apparent in March.

Sorties by major Russian warships were suspended for several months from June 1915 after two U-BOATS reached Constantinople, and six were active in the Black Sea by mid-1916, as was a substantial force of Russian submarines. Both sides sank a number of merchant ships and took a heavy toll of busy coastal sailing traffic, but four U-boats had been destroyed by early 1917, and submarines were generally less effective than in other theatres.

Russian naval operations were extended to include large-scale support for land forces on the Caucasian Front during 1916. Troops were landed on the Turkish coast at Atina and

RIZE in the spring, and by early summer specialist fleet troop transports and landing craft were in service. Supported by a fleet of large warships sent to Batum, transport operations intensified until landing craft were transferred to assist in the new ROMANIAN CAMPAIGN from August. By mid-1917, when Russian troop movements virtually ceased, transport flotillas had delivered hundreds of thousands of men close to frontline positions.

Russian fleet commander EBERHARDT, competent but aging, was replaced in July 1916 by Admiral KOLCHAK, who launched a massive minelaying campaign around the entrance to the Bosporus that effectively bottled up the Turkish fleet, which still had few minesweepers, and halted coal supplies to Constantinople until some coastal approaches were cleared by a heavy storm in September.

The success of the Russian blockade was undiminished in the first part of 1917, when Turkish forces were still primarily occupied with clearing hundreds of mines from their waters, but supplies became increasingly scarce and work at Russian repair yards virtually ceased after the FEBRUARY REVOLUTION. Plans for large-scale amphibious operations on the Turkish coast were abandoned as transport ships were diverted to home use and the RUSSIAN ARMY lost coherence.

Kolchak was removed by a sailors' SOVIET in June, and replaced in quick succession by Admirals Lukin and Nemic, but the fleet remained operational and in comfortable control of the Black Sea until after the OCTOBER REVOLUTION, attacking Turkish ships in Igneada harbour as late as 31 October. News of the Revolution spread slowly through the fleet, but Russian military activity in the Black Sea had ended by 19 November. See also: RUSSIAN CIVIL WAR; BULGARIAN NAVY.

'Black-Yellow' Offensive Codename for the ambitious Austro-Hungarian attack from eastern Galicia begun in August 1915, a subsidiary of the summer's Austro-German TRIPLE OFFENSIVE on the EASTERN FRONT. Austro-Hungarian chief of staff CONRAD, always in favour of an attack deep into RUSSIA, planned to envelop the 25 divisions of General IVANOV's southwestern army group by advancing east into the Ukraine across their northern and southern flanks.

The northern part of the offensive, which opened on 27 August from the Gnila Lipa river, began well. The Fourth Army (Archduke JOSEF FERDINAND) took LUTSK on 31 August, but attacks further south by exhausted troops of the Second Army, Südarmee and Seventh Army made little or no impact against defenders concealed in marshy ground.

When the Fourth Army resumed its advance its exposed flank was counterattacked by General BRUSILOV's Eighth Army, which recaptured Lutsk on 22 September. Austrian reinforcements were diverted en route to the BALKAN FRONT, and German troops moved south from the BUG OFFENSIVE, forcing Brusilov to retire to a line between Lutsk and Rovno at the end of the month. Conrad had already abandoned offensive operations on 25 September, by which time the AUSTRO-HUNGARIAN ARMY had suffered 300,000 casualties in a month, the majority to sickness and surrender. See MAP 10.

Blériot XI Early French monoplane, a re-engined version of the machine in which Louis Blériot (one of the leading prewar French manufacturers) crossed the English Channel in July 1909. It was among the first aircraft ordered the following September by the AÉRONAUTIQUE MILITAIRE, which had 33 Blériots in first-line service in August 1914. Both the RFC and the ITALIAN AIR FORCE used a few for reconnaissance into 1915. Five main types were produced for wartime use, largely during the mobile phase of the fighting on the WESTERN FRONT, including two-seater and floatplane versions with more powerful engines. All offered pilots a clear, stable view of the ground, but their lack of speed, armament and endurance soon became dangerous and they were withdrawn from production in early 1915.

BRIEF DATA (XI.1) Type: single-seat reconnaissance; Engine: 50–80hp Gnôme/le Rhône rotary; Max speed: 105kph; Armament: pilot's small arms or hand-thrown 25kg bombs.

Bliss, General Tasker (1853–1930) Acting US ARMY chief of staff from May 1917, Bliss was regarded as an astute diplomat and was a trusted advisor to Secretary BAKER. He officially replaced General Scott as chief of staff in September and accompanied the HOUSE mission to London before his appointment as US delegate to the SUPREME WAR COUNCIL in November. Giving up his staff command in May 1918 to remain in Europe, he was a strong supporter of Allied command unification under General FOCH, but at the same time championed AEF commander PERSHING's insistence on independent operations. Bliss favoured moderate treatment of the defeated CENTRAL POWERS, and strongly supported US commitment to the LEAGUE OF NATIONS after the PARIS PEACE CONFERENCE, where he tried unsuccessfully to halt Japanese territorial acquisition in CHINA (see LANSING-ISHII AGREEMENT).

Blockade Before 1914 the capacity to halt flow of trade to and from a hostile country was generally regarded as a war-winning weapon, in line with the almost universal belief that the economic stress of 'general war' could not be sustained for more than a few weeks. Overland trade within a continental mass could hardly be prevented, and the only accepted means of directly disrupting trade was by blockade, the application of naval supremacy to regulate all shipping activity in a given area.

Blockades threatened the rights of neutral traders to deal normally with both sides, and 19th-century attempts to formulate international laws to protect them culminated in the Declaration of London, signed by all the world's major naval powers in 1908. Blockading of exports or of neutral waters was banned, and restrictions were placed on goods liable for seizure as contraband, freeing most industrial and agricultural raw materials from regulation.

The Declaration was never ratified by GREAT BRITAIN, its prime mover and by far the world's greatest sea power, prompting widespread assumption that it would be ignored by the ROYAL NAVY in any war. The prospect was particularly worrying for GERMANY, dependent on free passage through Britain's home waters for global trade to its only coastlines, and the prewar expansion of the GERMAN NAVY was intended to counteract any close blockade. German planning was upset by the British decision to mount a technically illegal long-range blockade, patrolling the whole North Sea.

The North Sea blockade (scrupulously described as 'economic warfare' by contemporary British officials) was the principal economic weapon employed by either side in wartime, and was always a matter of international controversy. Immediate German claims that it was illegal, and aimed primarily at causing civilian distress were echoed by some sections of neutral opinion, and the UNITED STATES delivered several protests to the British government over interference with legal trade.

German advocates of *HANDELSKRIEG* (commerce warfare) regarded adoption of unrestricted SUBMARINE WARFARE as a legitimate response to blockade. Their arguments were strengthened by ever-tighter British interpretation of contraband regulations and the exertion of mounting pressure on Germany's northern neutral trading partners. Britain was protected from serious diplomatic problems by the international furore over subsequent German submarine attacks on neutral shipping.

British blockade tactics at first kept reasonably close to the spirit of the 1908 Declaration. Almost every ship in the North Sea was inspected, and most of the world's oceans were effectively sealed by the end of 1914. Arrangements were made with specially formed business consortia in the Netherlands, Denmark and Sweden, exchanging preferential treatment for guarantees against re-export to Germany, but they at first accounted for only a small fraction of trade with those countries. No real pressure was brought to bear on Norway, ITALY or other neutrals thought likely to react by adopting a pro-German posture.

The German economy displayed no signs of immediate collapse, and the British were compelled to rethink tactics. In March 1915 the Allies jointly announced revised rules prohibiting all import and export traffic (including neutrals) from using German ports. Import quotas were imposed on northern neutrals, and a commercial offensive established their pro-Allied consortia as virtual monopolists of permitted trade by 1917.

Unrestricted blockade was expected to have a devastating effect on Germany. Although the domestic production of northern neutrals continued to supply raw materials and food (in quantities underestimated by the Allies), it appeared that all re-export had been halted by late 1916. However, the gravity of the German economic crisis, only partly induced by blockade, was not discernible on the battlefield by early 1917, and Allied strategists assumed that victory in the ROMANIAN CAMPAIGN had provided sufficient supplies to meet immediate needs.

The blockade was tightened after the USA declared war in April 1917. US NAVY warships participated fully in patrol duties and the USA led Allied demands for stricter quota controls on neutral imports. A new Allied trade agreement was reached with Switzerland in late 1917, after French intervention had watered down US demands, but the Netherlands and the Scandinavian states defied proposed new quotas.

They were placed under complete trade embargoes, punctuated by occasional goodwill shipments to alleviate hardship, until the coordinating Allied Blockade Committee, meeting for the first time in March 1918, had accepted a degree of compromise. Norway eventually came to terms in April, Sweden in May and Denmark in September, but the Netherlands signed no agreement and received only essential shipments until 1919.

The North Sea blockade was only the main component of a worldwide economic offensive. Keeping approximately to Declaration regulations throughout, Allied MEDITERRANEAN forces blockaded the Syrian coast, GREECE (during the country's pro-German phase), BULGARIA, the Straits of OTRANTO and the DARDANELLES Straits, as well guarding the entrances to the Mediterranean at Gibraltar and SUEZ. German merchant shipping all over the world was seized or chased into internment, and the Russian BLACK SEA fleet successfully used MINES to blockade Turkish shipping inside the Bosporus Straits.

Despite claims on both sides that blockade was the decisive factor in eventual Allied victory, it was only one of many elements contributing to the eventual economic ruin of the CENTRAL POWERS. Germany's prewar economy relied on only 20 per cent imports and 18 per cent exports. A drop in exports made room for necessary increases in military production, and imports from its European neighbour states rose steadily, so that overall wartime imports never fell below about 40 per cent of 1913 totals. See also: ERSATZ.

'Bloody April' British term describing the RFC's experience on the WESTERN FRONT before and during the Battle of ARRAS in spring 1917, when it was required to perform intensive army cooperation duties using large numbers of inferior aircraft. The latter stages of the SOMME battle in 1916 had demonstrated the combat superiority of new German FIGHTER units (*Jagdstaffeln*), but no new Allied aircraft capable of matching their ALBATROS D-TYPE machines had appeared by spring 1917. A 3-to-1 numerical advantage enabled obsolete BE-2 and RE-8 fighters manned by inexperienced aircrew to perform reconnaissance, PHOTO-RECONNAISSANCE and ARTILLERY-spotting work, but the RFC lost 151 aircraft and 316 aircrew (killed or missing) during April, against comparable German figures of 66 and 119. The average life expectancy of an RFC pilot during the period fell to 23 days, before the arrival of improved Allied designs began to redress the balance during May. Many German ACES racked up huge 'scores', and their success prompted development of larger fighter formations, *Jagdgeschwader*, in an attempt to extend control of frontline airspace over wider areas (see FLYING CIRCUSES).

Blücher German heavy CRUISER, completed in 1909 as an inaccurate imitation of *INVINCIBLE*, the first British BATTLECRUISER. Disinformation leaked from the British Admiralty during construction had described *Invincible* as a conventional BATTLESHIP with smaller main guns, and *Blücher* was designed as a similarly reduced WESTFALEN Class battleship, without the speed or firepower of true battlecruisers. Part of Admiral HIPPER's fast North Sea scouting group in 1914, *Blücher* took part in the SCARBOROUGH RAID and the DOGGER BANK battle, when it was outgunned and sank with only 234 survivors.

BRIEF DATA Displacement: 15,500 tons; Crew: 847; Dimensions: length 530.5ft (160.8m), beam 80.5ft (24.4m); Speed: 26k; Armament: 12 × 8.2in guns, 8 × 5.9in, 16 × 3.4in, 4 × 17.7in TT.

Boelcke, Oswald (1891–1916) German air ACE who won eight combat victories on the WESTERN FRONT (most flying FOKKER E-TYPES) by early 1916, enough to win fame at a time when aerial combat was relatively rare. His score and professional reputation mounted rapidly during the VERDUN offensive, and he was responsible for important developments in air fighting, advocating the formation of specialist FIGHTER units (*Jagdstaffeln*) and developing aggressive team tactics to make maximum use of superior ALBATROS D-TYPE machines. Commander of *Jagdstaffel 2* from July 1916, his stature was rivalled only by IMMELMANN at the time of his death in a mid-air collision on 15 October 1916. He eventually shot down 40 Allied aircraft.

Boer Revolt The Afrikaner peoples of SOUTH AFRICA had enjoyed a political renaissance since subjugation of their Transvaal and Orange Free State republics by British imperial forces in the Boer War (1899–1902). British-funded economic reconstruction of the territories was followed by free elections (1907) that returned many Afrikaner leaders to power. The most respected Boer commander, Louis BOTHA, became prime minister of South Africa when the four colonies were unified in 1910 and, along with defence minister SMUTS, worked in close harmony with British imperial authorities.

Botha's reconciliatory approach was not accepted by all Afrikaners, many of whom saw European war as an opportunity to throw off British control. Botha's public commitment of SOUTH AFRICAN FORCES to the British cause in August 1914, and subsequent agreement to an invasion of German SOUTHWEST AFRICA, pushed a sizable minority into direct opposition.

General Beyers, commander of the national Defence Force and a well-known Germanophile, and General Kemp, commandant of the national training centre, were among several senior officers who resigned on 14 August at a meeting of military commanders to arrange mobilization. Both raised anti-British militia in the Transvaal, and Christiaan de Wet, Boer War hero and potential rival to Botha, began raising rebel forces openly in the Orange River Colony (formerly the Orange Free State). Another famous Boer warrior, Jacobus de la Rey, was probably about to join Beyers but was killed on 14 September, after his car ran through a police road block set to catch wanted thieves.

Colonel Solomon Maritz, commanding regular South African Defence Force troops at Upington near the Southwest African border, was in contact with German forces from mid-August and represented the most dangerous military threat to the government. As widespread unrest matured into occasional skirmishing in the Afrikaner territories, Maritz publicly declared rebellion on 9 October, seeking an independent South Africa and war with Britain. De Wet announced his intention of joining Maritz, and on 26 October Botha led 6,000 horsemen (with a few field guns) to face him.

Refusing the potentially divisive option of British aid, and commanding a force of mostly Afrikaner troops, Botha surprised de Wet's 2,000 rebels at Mushroom Valley, about 100km northeast of Bloemfontein, on 12 November. Routed after heavy fighting, de Wet and the surviving rebels were captured on 1 December, eliminating the rebellion's prime figurehead.

Immediately after the victory Botha offered an amnesty to all rebels, twice extending the deadline into December and contributing to a reduction in tension. South Africa was declared ready to resume operations against Southwest Africa on 28 November, and government forces defeated the column under Beyers, who was drowned trying to escape on 8 December. Kemp's rebels were chased into German territory, where they linked up with

Maritz and German troops for an abortive attack on Upington in January 1915 before surrendering on 3 February. Maritz himself escaped into exile in Spain and Portugal.

Rebel forces were always greatly outnumbered, about 11,500 widely dispersed volunteers against some 30,000 centrally organized government troops. Casualties were relatively light – 540 rebels and 347 loyalists killed or wounded – and South Africans of British descent played virtually no part in what was essentially an Afrikaner civil war. Magnanimous treatment of captured rebel leaders, many of whom served only brief sentences and later returned to politics, accurately reflected a convalescent atmosphere in the Afrikaner community. Botha was able to resume mobilization of troops for imperial service, and subsequent opposition was restricted to legitimate political channels. See MAP 17.

Böhm-Ermolli, Field Marshal Eduard von (1856–1941) Austro-Hungarian nobleman who commanded the Second Army in August 1914. Most of his troops finally arrived in GALICIA during September after their initial posting to the BALKAN FRONT was reversed by Austrian chief of staff CONRAD. He led the Second Army's capture of Lvov during the GORLICE-TARNOW OFFENSIVE in spring 1915 and commanded Army Group Böhm-Ermolli (comprising the First and Second Armies) against the BRUSILOV OFFENSIVE the following summer. Like other senior AUSTRO-HUNGARIAN ARMY officers on the EASTERN FRONT, he was little more than a cipher in a German-dominated command after 1916. Promoted field marshal in January 1918, he nominally led occupying forces in the western Ukraine until relieved in May for failure to cooperate fully with German authorities.

Bolimov, Battle of Attack by the German Ninth Army (MACKENSEN) against part of the Russian Second Army (Smirnov) around the town of Bolimov in the Vistula plains west of Warsaw (see MAP 10). Launched on 31 January 1915, a preliminary to the major German offensive at the MASURIAN LAKES, it was used to test the effectiveness of poison GAS for the first time in battle.

The experiment was not a success: gas was blown back towards German lines by a contrary wind before sinking harmlessly to the ground in cold weather, and the attack was called off after its initial failure. A series of frontal counterattacks, by a huge Russian corps of 11 poorly trained divisions under General GURKO, suffered 40,000 casualties but achieved nothing. The ease with which German ARTILLERY defeated massed assault by closely packed infantry was not appreciated by senior Russian commanders, who continued to employ the tactic into 1917 (see BRUSILOV OFFENSIVE).

Bolsheviks See: RUSSIA; OCTOBER REVOLUTION; PACIFISM; LENIN, V.

Bonar Law See: LAW, ANDREW BONAR.

Bonnet Rouge, Le Small French PACIFIST journal that reached government notice in mid-1916 after a series of articles by left-wing writer 'Almeyreda' had espoused reconciliation with GERMANY. Interior minister MALVY cancelled plans to suppress the publication after it undertook to cease pacifist campaigning, but the promise was not kept. Right-wing accusations of leniency turned to suspicion of treason after the editor, Duval, was arrested carrying a German cheque across the Swiss frontier on 14 May 1917. The confiscated cheque was returned within a few days by Malvy's office, but subsequent investigations linked it to known German espionage agents. Prime minister RIBOT ordered the arrest of Duval and most of his staff in July, suspending *Le Bonnet rouge* indefinitely, and Malvy was forced to resign in late August. The loss of Malvy's Radical supporters doomed the cabinet, which fell on 7 September, and the scandal prompted a rash of accusations against senior figures with known or suspected pacifist leanings. Duval, Almeyreda and three of their colleagues on the journal were executed after the 'TREASON TRIALS' of 1918. See also: CAILLAUX, J.

Boot, Battle of the Final episode of the limited British SAMARRAH OFFENSIVE on the MESOPOTAMIAN FRONT in spring 1917. Attacks against Turkish forces on the Tigris above BAGHDAD had been threatened from the northeast by Ali Ishan Bey's Turkish XIII Corps, recalled to Mesopotamia from operations in PERSIA. Advancing to the Tigris after defeating a British force at JEBEL HAMRIN in late March, Ishan retreated into mountainous border country when surprised by another British force at SHIALA in mid-April. A few days later, leaving 2,000 men to occupy British cavalry in the foothills, Ishan reappeared 40km from the Tigris at Dahubu.

Two depleted brigades under corps commander General Marshall marched northeast up the River Adhaim to meet the threat, and were joined by another brigade from rearguards further south. Ishan had hoped to surprise the British and withdrew on their approach, taking up prepared positions in the foothills straddling the river at Band-i-Adhaim, where a boot-shaped peninsular of high ground jutted into the almost dry river bed.

Marshall launched his whole force against the position on 30 April, taking two lines of Turkish trenches and 300 prisoners in frontal attacks by 06.30, when a sandstorm halted troops approaching both Turkish flanks. The storm masked Ishan's transfer of reserves to the centre for a counterattack, which drove the British back with about 350 casualties. By the time the storm moderated in late afternoon, Ishan had retreated into the mountains and could not be pursued in the searing heat. Ishan remained to menace Anglo-Indian positions when temperatures dropped in the autumn. See MAP 23.

Borden, Sir Robert (1854–1937) Leader of the opposition Conservative Party in the Canadian House of Commons from 1901 until the 1911 elections, which returned him as prime minister on a platform of resistance to US economic influence. He remained in office until July 1920, promoting maximum Canadian commitment to the British imperial war effort and devoting his personal energies to establishing the country's international status. He visited London in July 1915 and represented CANADA on the Imperial War Cabinet from late 1917. His argument that self-governing British dominions should be treated as equal partners with GREAT BRITAIN in international affairs was effectively conceded at the PARIS PEACE CONFERENCE, where he served as Canadian representative.

Boroevic von Bojna, Field Marshal Svetozar (1856–1920) Croat infantry officer who commanded VI Corps with General DANKL's Austro-Hungarian First Army during the opening campaign in GALICIA. He subsequently led the Third Army through the Battle of KOMAROW, the relief of PRZEMYSL, the CARPATHIAN campaigns and the GORLICE-TARNOW OFFENSIVE before his transfer to the SOUTHERN FRONT in mid-1915 to command the newly formed Fifth Army, which took part in all 11 Battles of the ISONZO. An unsparing disciplinarian, his outnumbered troops successfully defended excellent positions against Italian attacks, but consistent reliance on BREAKTHROUGH TACTICS doomed his own offensives to costly failure.

Greatly assisted by German units and their INFILTRATION TACTICS, the Fifth Army won its greatest victory at CAPORETTO in October and November 1917, for which Boroevic was promoted field marshal in January 1918. Aware of his army's poor condition, he opposed the PIAVE Offensive of spring 1918 but was overruled, and was defeated when he tried to cross the river. After supervising the gradual disintegration of his forces during the second half of 1918, and failing to interest Emperor KARL I in a royalist counterrevolution during early November, he offered his services to Croat representatives in Belgrade, but was regarded as dangerously popular and required to retire.

Boselli, Paolo (1838–1932) Italian Liberal politician, a veteran of the 19th-century struggle for national unity who emerged from semi-retirement in August 1914 as a strong supporter of intervention on the side of the Allies. His seniority, along with a reputation as a political 'fixer', made him an obvious candidate for wartime leadership of ITALY after military defeat brought down the SALANDRA government in June 1916. Primarily concerned to promote national unity around the war effort, he included clerical representatives and the moderate socialist BISSOLATI in a large cabinet, but unpopular foreign minister SONNINO remained its most influential figure. Generally viewed as lacking the energy to hold a disparate government together, Boselli attracted criticism from pacifist elements for allowing Sonnino to guide strategy, and from the right for refusing to censor a critical press or suppress strikes in northern Italy. He was voted out of office on 25 October 1917 when worsening economic crisis was compounded by military disaster at CAPORETTO. He retained his parliamentary seat until 1921 and later acted as a spokesman for the MUSSOLINI regime in the upper house.

Botha, General Louis (1862–1919) Prime minister of his native Transvaal from 1907, and of the Union of South Africa from its formation in 1910, Botha had been one of the most respected Afrikaner generals of the Boer War (1899–1902). An energetic and decisive military leader, he guided SOUTH AFRICA's cooperation with British imperial interests prior to 1914.

His immediate offer to GREAT BRITAIN of military assistance in August 1914 pushed part of the Afrikaner community into rebellion, and he led Union forces against the BOER REVOLT. His public clemency towards its leaders startled British South Africans, but contributed to subsequent maintenance of public order. British admiration for his command of SOUTH AFRICAN FORCES during the conquest of German SOUTHWEST AFRICA was clouded only by bewilderment at similar leniency towards the defeated German colonists.

From July 1915 Botha passed direct military command to his close associate General SMUTS and concentrated on fostering political unity at home. Narrowly returned to office later in the year, he gave continued military support for British operations overseas and travelled to argue for reconciliation with the CENTRAL POWERS at the PARIS PEACE CONFERENCE in 1919. A signatory of the VERSAILLES Treaty, he died in August 1919.

Bothmer, General Felix, Graf von (1852–1924) Veteran Bavarian officer who commanded a division on the WESTERN FRONT from November 1914, and a corps from December. Transferred to the EASTERN FRONT the following March, he led a corps on the southern wing of the GORLICE-TARNOW OFFENSIVE in May, and replaced LINSINGEN in command of the Austro-German Südarmee on the Galician sector in July 1915. His largely German force was driven back but not scattered by the following summer's BRUSILOV OFFENSIVE, and turned the RUSSIAN ARMY's final KERENSKI OFFENSIVE into a retreat in July 1917. Returned to France when the Südarmee was broken up in February 1918, he commanded the Nineteenth Army in Lorraine, a relatively quiet sector, until 8 November, when he returned to Bavaria to organize its defence against Allied invasion.

Boué de Lapeyrère, Admiral Augustin (1852–1924) The most influential figure in the prewar FRENCH NAVY, and C-in-C of Allied naval forces in the MEDITERRANEAN from August 1914. As navy minister (1909–11) he reversed decades of French naval policy based on the development of SUBMARINES and coastal forces, ordering large numbers of BATTLESHIPS. Given command of the Mediterranean battlefleet (*Armée Navale*) on leaving office, he was an aggressive and confident leader not afraid to criticize or ignore orders from the naval staff.

Attacked in August 1914 for failing to prevent the German MITTELMEERDIVISION's escape into Turkish waters, he was denied the great naval battle for which his fleet had been prepared, struggling instead to protect thousands of kilometres of trade routes, blockade the Straits of OTRANTO, and support Allied operations at the DARDANELLES and SALONIKA. Lacking sufficient ANTI-SUBMARINE vessels, and unable to impose his nominal authority on British (and later Italian) commands, he resigned suddenly on 10 October 1915 and was replaced by Admiral GAUCHET. Ostensibly due to ill health, his departure caused considerable controversy, with navy minister AUGAGNEUR and President POINCARÉ subsequently denying that they had forced his removal.

Bouvet One of six very old PRE-DREADNOUGHTS actively employed by the wartime FRENCH NAVY in the MEDITERRANEAN. From August 1914 they formed a 'Special Squadron' escorting colonial troops from North Africa to France, and *Bouvet* was one of four sent to the DARDANELLES (along with *Suffren*, *Gaulois* and *Charlemagne*). On 18 March 1915, during the main naval attempt to force the Straits, *Bouvet* struck a minefield and blew up, killing most of the crew, *Gaulois* was beached after hitting a MINE and *Suffren* suffered severe damage. Both the latter were subsequently destroyed by SUBMARINES, but *Charlemagne* survived regular service off SALONIKA to be scrapped at the ARMISTICE. The oldest of the six, *St Louis* and *Jaureguiberry*, served as army-support gunships in the defence of SUEZ and on the PALESTINE FRONT before their retirement in 1918.

BRIEF DATA (*Bouvet*, 1914) Displacement: 12,200 tons; Crew: 698; Dimensions: length 389.5ft (118m), beam 70.5ft (21.4m); Speed: 18k; Armament: 2 × 12in (305mm) gun, 2 × 274mm, 8 × 137mm, 8 × 100mm, 2 × 450mm TT.

Brandenburg Aircraft See: HANSA-BRANDENBURG.

Bratianu, Ion (1864–1927) Liberal politician who became prime minister of ROMANIA in early 1914. By inclination pro-Allied, he maintained Romanian neutrality while seeking maximum inducement from belligerents on both sides, and was primarily responsible for the timing and circumstances of Romania's commitment to the Allies in August 1916. He remained in office until December 1917, when he resigned after concluding an armistice with the CENTRAL POWERS. Retaining the confidence of King FERDINAND, Bratianu guided policy behind the scenes, appointing and removing successive regimes while overseeing negotiations leading to the BUCHAREST Treaty. He organized Romania's return to war on 10 November 1918 and reclaimed the premiership in December to lead the Romanian delegation at the PARIS PEACE CONFERENCE, gaining approval for most of Romania's territorial demands (see Treaties of TRIANON, NEUILLY).

Brazil The United States of Brazil was the largest South American republic in 1914. Established in February 1891, 16 months after the overthrow of its monarchy, its democratic constitution had established universal adult male suffrage, four-year presidential terms, and representative assemblies at state and national level. Poverty-led social and political unrest among a rapidly expanding population (an estimated 25 million by 1917) sprang from economic dependence on fluctuating international coffee and rubber prices, but the election of President Braz in 1914 marked the beginning of a war boom.

Brazil's main trading partner in 1913 was the UNITED STATES, but GERMANY and GREAT BRITAIN also had substantial interests in the country. The collapse of trade with Germany after 1914 (see BLOCKADE) was compensated by a massive increase in trade to the Allies, with major new markets opening up for Brazilian meat, other agricultural produce and mined minerals.

Widespread popular support for the Allies, underpinned by hostility towards the GERMAN NAVY's expanding application of SUBMARINE WARFARE, eventually pushed Brazil from neutrality into war with Germany. In April 1917 the sinking of a Brazilian steamer off Cherbourg forced a break in diplomatic relations; another sinking in May provoked seizure of all German shipping in Brazil (150,000 tons); and loss of the steamer *Macao* brought a declaration of war on 26 October 1917.

Brazil's ground forces played no part in the fighting, but a few aircraft technicians and medical personnel served on the WESTERN FRONT, and the BRAZILIAN NAVY was committed to transatlantic operations – enough to secure a seat at the PARIS PEACE CONFERENCE and permanent possession of seized German assets.

Brazilian Navy South America witnessed a prewar naval arms race that mirrored those in

Europe. Chile, Peru and Argentina built up substantial fleets but the Brazilian Navy was the most powerful on the continent and the only one to play an active wartime role. When BRAZIL declared war in October 1917 the navy consisted of 2 modern British-built BATTLESHIPS, 2 old coastal-defence battleships, 4 CRUISERS (2 quite modern), 10 DESTROYERS, 4 TORPEDO BOATS and 3 SUBMARINES. The dreadnoughts *Minas Gerais* and *São Paulo* were refitted with a view to joining the British GRAND FLEET in the North Sea, and smaller warships were promised for the MEDITERRANEAN, but the US NAVY objected to their operation under British command. Brazilian light forces did reach the Mediterranean just before the ARMISTICE, but the battleships never sailed and the rest of the fleet carried out trade-protection patrols in the south Atlantic.

Breakthrough Tactics The first response of European infantry tacticians to the new challenges of massed TRENCH WARFARE. From late 1914 the static WESTERN FRONT could not be outflanked (see RACE TO THE SEA), forcing attacking commanders to break through lines in search of a decisive victory. Beginning with French C-in-C JOFFRE's first CHAMPAGNE OFFENSIVE, leaders on all fronts sought to smash through prepared positions by concentrating maximum strength at a single point and exploiting the 'hole' thus created to manoeuvre in space behind enemy lines.

Simple charges by massed infantry achieved little against established defences, suffering enormous casualties and gaining little ground. The vulnerability of advancing infantry to defensive fire made overwhelming manpower superiority necessary for any attack, but the time and effort required to bring up massed forces rendered surprise impossible, allowing defenders to bring up the fewer reinforcements they needed.

The solution generally adopted, and the basis of breakthrough tactics on all fronts from 1915, was to kill everything in a small specified zone, using concentrated ARTILLERY support on an ever-increasing scale (or some surprise element like TANKS or poison GAS) and to pour infantry or CAVALRY into the narrow gap created.

Communications, supply and transport weakness combined to make exploitation impossible, but the repeated ability to take forward positions by sheer weight of assault allowed frustrated commanders to believe that strategic victory was only a matter of greater firepower or of wearing out the enemy. The development of DEFENCE IN DEPTH rendered this sledgehammer approach regularly ineffective against well-established trenches, even in secondary theatres.

A more limited and painstaking version of breakthrough methods, known as 'phalanx tactics', was developed and used to great effect by German commanders MACKENSEN and SEECKT on the EASTERN and BALKAN FRONTS, where defences were more thinly stretched, trench systems less sophisticated, and transfer of defensive reserves more difficult. Meticulous concentration followed by limited advance, pause and repetition punched great holes in Russian, Serbian and Romanian lines, enabling ambitious advances into enemy territory. Even then, pursuit and destruction of retreating armies proved impossible, and ill-prepared Russian attempts to imitate phalanx tactics in 1916 failed disastrously (see e.g. KOVEL OFFENSIVE).

Foreshadowed by the success of the BRUSILOV OFFENSIVE, adaptations or revisions of breakthrough tactics were devised from late 1917, most notably German INFILTRATION TACTICS and Australian PEACEFUL PENETRATION, contributing (along with widespread exhaustion) to a resurrection of mobile warfare in Europe during 1918.

Breguet Bombers French 'PUSHER' biplane, produced as a prototype in early 1915 and manufactured later that year as the Breguet 2, with a 200hp Canton-Unné engine. Despite good range and lifting capacity, the aircraft proved clumsy and vulnerable, but the re-engined Breguet 4, with re-designed wings and an automatic Michelin bomb rack, enjoyed greater success. Used from mid-1916 until early 1918 by the AÉRONAUTIQUE MILITAIRE on the WESTERN FRONT and the British RNAS in France and the eastern Mediterranean, it remained vulnerable to fighter attack in daylight but performed effectively as a night bomber. About 200 were built. A Breguet 5 version was also produced as a bomber escort, armed with a 37mm cannon in place of the forward machine gun. See also: STRATEGIC BOMBING.

BRIEF DATA (Breguet 4) Type: two-seater bomber; Engine: 220hp Renault; Max speed: 133kph; Ceiling: 4,300m; Armament: 1 × 7.92mm mg, up to 40 × 35kg bomb (on wing racks).

Bremen The five Bremen Class light CRUISERS were completed by 1905 as the first of a new generation designed to serve both as scouts with the German HIGH SEAS FLEET and as long-range commerce raiders. A blueprint for British TOWN designs, the Bremens and other early classes were fitted with only deck armour, but hull protection and bigger main armament were fitted to later, larger designs (see *BRESLAU*, *EMDEN*). Generally even faster than their published top speeds, a total of 36 light cruisers (in 14 classes) had been built by the ARMISTICE, operating worldwide and taking part in all the GERMAN NAVY's major surface actions. Their frontline role inevitably entailed casualties and *Bremen*, sunk by a Russian minefield in the BALTIC on 17 December 1915, was one of 14 wartime losses. (*Bremen* was also the name of an unarmed German merchant submarine; see *DEUTSCHLAND*.)

BRIEF DATA (*Bremen*, 1914) Displacement: 3,250 tons; Crew: 320; Dimensions: length 364.5ft (110.5m), beam 43.5ft (13.2m); Speed: 23k; Armament: 10 × 4.1in, 2 x 17.7in TT.

Breslau One of four German light CRUISERS completed in 1912 as the first of their type with armoured hulls (see *BREMEN*), *Breslau* was part of the MITTELMEERDIVISION in the MEDITERRANEAN, and shared the epic escape of its partner, *GOEBEN*, in August. Based in Constantinople as a TURKISH NAVY vessel, *Breslau* operated in the BLACK SEA until sunk when the Mittelmeerdivision ran into a minefield on its return to the Mediterranean in early 1918. Of its sister ships, *Magdeburg* was sunk in 1914 by Russian DESTROYERS in the BALTIC, but *Stralsund* and *Strassburg* survived to become the French *Mulhouse* and Italian *Taranto* as part of the VERSAILLES settlement.

BRIEF DATA (*Breslau*, 1914) Displacement: 4,550 tons; Crew: 370; Dimensions: length 455ft (137.9m), beam 43.5ft (13.2m); Speed: 30k; Armament: 12 × 4.1in, 4 × 19.7in TT.

Brest-Litovsk, Treaty of Peace treaty signed between the CENTRAL POWERS and the Bolshevik government of RUSSIA on 3 March 1918. Negotiations took place at Brest-Litovsk, the battered town some 150km west of the EASTERN FRONT that served as German regional headquarters (see MAP 10).

After the OCTOBER REVOLUTION of 1917 the new Bolshevik government was neither willing nor able to defend the front, and the German THIRD SUPREME COMMAND was anxious to release troops for operations on the WESTERN FRONT. Armistice negotiations began on 3 December, a ceasefire was announced on 16 December, and peace talks began six days later.

Hosted by German eastern commanders Prince LEOPOLD and General HOFFMANN, the conference was attended by German foreign minister KÜHLMANN, his Austro-Hungarian counterpart CZERNIN, Bulgarian premier RADOSLAVOV and Turkish grand vizier TALAAT. A delegation from the UKRAINE represented its newly convened national assembly, and the Russian party, hastily assembled by a government with no trained diplomats, was led by Bolshevik scholar Adolf Ioffe.

Facing Russian demands for German military withdrawal without territorial annexations, Kühlmann was unwilling to abandon occupied territories or to risk revival of a Russian war party by accepting military demands for a swift imposed settlement. Czernin was anxious to release Ukrainian grain for Austrian towns by securing a quick agreement, but Bolshevik foreign minister TROTSKI, who took charge of the Russian delegation from 9 January, employed delaying tactics in the hope that socialist revolution in central Europe would strengthen his position.

Despite the doubts of Bolshevik leader LENIN, the party's central committee authorized continuation of Trotski's 'neither war nor peace' policy. He again halted talks on 10 February, immediately after the conclusion of a separate peace with the Ukrainian delegation (see *BROTFRIEDEN*), provoking a limited resumption of hostilities (Operation FAUSTSCHLAG) that brought formal acceptance of German terms on 19 February. Berlin replied with new terms on 23 February, accepted next day by Lenin with the reluctant mandate of the central committee and Petrograd SOVIET.

Signed on 3 March, the Treaty extended German influence over POLAND, FINLAND, LATVIA, LITHUANIA, ESTONIA, Belorussia and the Ukraine, depriving Russia of about 30 per cent of its imperial population. Turkish control over the CAUCASIAN provinces was confirmed, and the Bolshevik government undertook to cease interference in the internal affairs of all lost territories.

Predictably denounced by the Allies, the Treaty caused difficulties for the Central Powers: its overt concentration on German interests caused resentment in AUSTRIA-HUNGARY and BULGARIA; TURKEY was induced into a disastrous attempt to establish full control in TRANSCAUCASIA; occupation and economic exploitation of eastern Europe forced the retention of substantial German forces in the region (variously estimated at 1 to 1.5 million men), diluting strength for the KAISERSCHLACHT Offensive in France. Ignored at every opportunity by the Soviet government, the Treaty was formally annulled as part of the ARMISTICE agreement of 11 November 1918.

Bretagne Three Bretagne Class dreadnoughts (*Bretagne*, *Provence* and *Lorraine*) were the only new BATTLESHIPS completed by wartime French shipyards. Ordered in 1912, and very similar to the earlier COURBET Class, they were substantially complete by August 1914, but work was halted (and much of the workforce mobilized) in anticipation of a short war. *Provence* was eventually finished in mid-1915 and all three had joined the FRENCH NAVY in the MEDITERRANEAN by autumn 1916. They saw little wartime action, although *Provence* took part in operations at SALAMIS and ATHENS in 1916 as flagship to C-in-C DARTIGE. Work on five similar Normandie Class battleships was abandoned altogether in 1914, and their guns were sent to the WESTERN FRONT.

BRIEF DATA (*Bretagne*, 1914) Displacement: 23,320 tons; Crew: 1,133; Dimensions: length 548ft (166m), beam 89ft (27m); Speed: 20k; Armament: 10 × 13in (340mm) gun, 22 × 139mm, 4 × 47mm, 4 × 450mm TT.

Briand, Aristide (1862–1932) French politician, who eventually served six terms as prime minister (1909–11, 1913, 1915–17, 1921–22, 1925–26, 1929) and two as foreign minister (1915–17 and 1925–32). A committed anticleric expelled from the French Socialist Party for joining CLEMENCEAU's Radical coalition in 1906, Briand further alienated the left by conscripting rail strikers into the FRENCH ARMY (1909–10), and was a leading proponent of legislation extending compulsory military service in 1913.

Called into the VIVIANI cabinet as justice minister under the political truce (*Union Sacrée*) of August 1914, he was among the first 'EASTERNERS' in FRANCE, suggesting intervention on the BALKAN FRONT in November and pushing for SARRAIL's appointment as its commander designate. An increasingly powerful cabinet figure, his reputation for political flexibility and a longstanding alliance with President POINCARÉ helped his appointment to replace Viviani as premier (and foreign minister) in October.

Briand's coalition was never able to dominate policy, forced instead to shuttle between a strong Radical bloc in parliament and JOFFRE's autocratic high command. He tried to establish political control over the military, persuading the prestigious GALLIÉNI to become war minister, but never overcame JOFFRE's primary commitment to the WESTERN FRONT. British opposition forced him to accept abandonment of the SALONIKA expedition at CALAIS in December, but he only survived the consequent storm in parliament by reversing the decision at CHANTILLY.

The attack on VERDUN from February 1916 threatened the government with a scandal over the poor condition of its defences.

Insisting that the fortress must be held and pronouncing complete faith in Joffre, Briand deflected criticism to the high command and laid great public stress on the successes of other generals. Parliament was mollified with a promise to subordinate military authorities, given at a secret session in June.

Briand manoeuvred Joffre out of power in December 1916, and new C-in-C NIVELLE was given more limited jurisdiction, but strikes and pacifist agitation on the home front complicated the government's balancing act. Branded a 'defeatist' sympathizer by the right for refusal to risk an uprising by suppressing pacifists, Briand needed a military victory by early 1917 and gave his backing to the ambitious NIVELLE OFFENSIVE. Amid mounting opposition to the operation within the Army and cabinet, new war minister LYAUTEY's resignation over the issue finally cracked the coalition, which fell on 16 March 1917.

The target of unconvincing peace feelers from German sources during the summer, Briand held no further wartime office, but after the War was a world leader in the promotion of international pacifism through the LEAGUE OF NATIONS.

Brilliant One of twenty Apollo Class vessels built for the ROYAL NAVY in the early 1900s, and one of 11 still active in August 1914. Typical of small 'protected' CRUISER designs, *Brilliant* was one of three used for frontline patrol duties in 1914. Another, *Sappho*, served the GRAND FLEET as a utility vessel until 1917, and the other seven had been converted some years earlier as MINELAYERS. Each armed with 150 MINES and only light guns, they operated as a squadron in the North Sea until more modern ships became available in 1915. Two subsequently served in the ARCTIC THEATRE and two went to the MEDITERRANEAN, where *Lacona* laid the mines that sunk the German light cruiser *BRESLAU* in 1918. By that time all the others had been retired to secondary duties, but *Brilliant* was one of five resurrected in April 1918 to be sunk as blockships during the raids on ZEEBRUGGE and Ostend harbours.

BRIEF DATA (*Brilliant*, 1914) Displacement: 3,440 tons; Crew: 273; Dimensions: length 314ft (95.2m), beam 42.5ft (12.9m); Speed: 20k; Armament: 2 × 6in gun, 6 × 4.7in, 4 × 14in TT.

Bristol F-2 Fighter Large British fighter-reconnaissance biplane, in production from the end of 1916 but held back by the RFC until just before the Battle of ARRAS in April 1917. Its debut on 5 April was a shambles, as crews used standard two-seater tactics and maintained formation to give the observer's weapon priority. Four of the first six F-2a models were immediately shot down by von RICHTOFEN's fighters, but once pilots learned to use the new machine aggressively, dog-fighting with the forward MACHINE GUN, its strength, speed, agility and extra weaponry came fully into their own, and the Bristol Fighter became the most successful aircraft of its type on the WESTERN FRONT.

A modified F-2b version, with greater range and improved forward vision, took over production in June, and later examples were fitted with a variety of 200–275hp engines. From July 1917 all British reconnaissance units were equipped with the F-2b and both types remained in frontline service until the end of the War, also operating on the ITALIAN FRONT, in PALESTINE and with home-defence squadrons. A total of 3,101 Bristol Fighters were built during wartime, and later versions remained in RAF service until 1932.

BRIEF DATA (F-2a) Type: two-seater fighter/reconnaissance; Engine: 190hp Rolls-Royce Falcon; Max speed: 110mph (176kph); Ceiling: 4,850m; Armament: 2 or 3 × 0.303in mg

Bristol M-1 Sleek British monoplane FIGHTER, designed in 1916 and put into limited production from early 1917. Though an excellent aircraft – very fast, nimble and with a good climb rate – the production M-1C model was never used on the WESTERN FRONT. In theory its landing speed was considered dangerously high (78kph), but the decision also reflected official doubts about the viability of monoplanes in general. Of 125 M-1Cs produced, about 35 saw active service as ground-attack craft on the BALKAN and MESOPOTAMIAN FRONTS; the rest were used as trainers.

BRIEF DATA (M-1C) Type: single-seat fighter; Engine: 110hp Le Rhône; Max speed: 130mph (208kph); Ceiling: 6,060m; Armament: 1 × 0.303in mg

Bristol Scout Small British biplane, first produced as a sports racer in 1913. Only two Scout Bs went to France with the RFC in August 1914, but the machine was put into full production as the Scout C late in the year, joining squadrons in mid-1915. Though it was fast, manoeuvrable and featured an advanced airframe design, an occasional LEWIS GUN added to the top wing was ineffective in air combat against genuine FIGHTERS. The slightly faster Scout D (in use from December 1915) suffered the same disadvantage and it had largely disappeared from the WESTERN FRONT by mid-1916, but some of the 161 eventually produced remained with RFC units on the PALESTINE, BALKAN and MESOPOTAMIAN FRONTS into 1918. Others performed ZEPPELIN patrol duties for the RNAS, armed with metal darts, and on 3 November 1915 a Scout C achieved the world's first wheeled take-off from an aircraft carrier.

BRIEF DATA (Scout C, RFC) Type: single-seat escort; Engine: 80hp Gnôme or Le Rhône, or 110hp Clerget; Max speed: 94mph (150kph); Ceiling: 4,500m; Armament: pilot's small arms or 1 × 0.303in mg.

British Air Forces See: RFC; RNAS; RAF.

British Army The standing British Army of 1914 was a relatively small professional body of volunteer regulars charged with policing the British Empire and protecting the home islands against invasion. In both roles it was junior to the enormous ROYAL NAVY, which consumed most military resources.

Failings revealed during the Boer War (1899–1902) in SOUTH AFRICA had prompted drastic reforms over the next decade, spearheaded by war minister HALDANE. A new command system transferred administrative functions to the war ministry and created an Army Council (headed by the minister) to decide policy. The post of commander-in-chief was abolished and replaced by a new chief of imperial general staff (CIGS), the link between political and military authorities.

Ingrained political hostility to conscription precluded significant growth, as did the emphasis on naval expansion and the social reform priorities of prewar Liberal administrations. Haldane concentrated on modernizing and training an elite home-defence force of 6 infantry and 1 cavalry divisions, available for rapid mobilization as a British Expeditionary Force (BEF) in mainland Europe, backed by a reserve of 14 Territorial divisions, all volunteers and organized on regional lines.

By 1914 the BEF, under the command of Sir John FRENCH, was an exceptionally well-trained army, particularly expert at RIFLE operations, but the effectiveness of CAVALRY was overestimated and the lessons of recent international conflicts only partly applied. German, and to a lesser extent French, forces were being trained and equipped for TRENCH WARFARE on the assumption that they would be besieging each other's FORTRESSES, but the BEF went to war expecting mobility, and was weak in heavy ARTILLERY, MACHINE GUNS, MORTARS, GRENADES and other requirements for static operations.

By concentrating on home defence the reform process worked against the efficiency of British colonial forces. The INDIAN ARMY remained the biggest imperial drain on manpower, followed by the Mediterranean command, based in EGYPT and responsible for imperial security throughout northern AFRICA and the Middle East. Substantial British forces were in South Africa until the outbreak of war, and garrisons were stationed in all Britain's other overseas possessions except the white dominions of AUSTRALIA, NEW ZEALAND, CANADA and NEWFOUNDLAND. All were starved of men and resources, relying on obsolete equipment long after 1914.

Total British Army strength in August 1914 was 247,432 regular troops (about 120,000 in the BEF, the rest overseas), 224,223 reservists of all classes, and 268,777 Territorials. Most of the BEF was sent to BELGIUM, occupying a small northern portion of the Allied line during early battles on the WESTERN FRONT. Its professional core had been effectively wiped out by the end of the year, and escalating manpower and material requirements forced rapid construction of a new mass army and the equally urgent development of new weapons and supply systems.

War minister KITCHENER, appointed in August 1914, was almost alone in predicting a long conflict fought by mass armies. His immediate recruiting campaign for volunteer regular troops created 6 new divisions by the end of August, and was attracting 33,000 men per day in September (see PALS' BATTALIONS). Kitchener's 'New Armies' comprised 29 infantry divisions by March 1915, and total strength was brought up to 75 divisions by mobilization of Territorial divisions and recall of overseas regular units.

The flood of volunteers, far more than could be accommodated, created serious equipment and training problems, as well as draining the industrial labour force in GREAT BRITAIN. The expanded BEF (which absorbed most New Army recruits) remained short of everything from guns and ammunition to uniforms until after the SHELL SCANDAL of mid-1915. The new LLOYD GEORGE munitions ministry improved supply from 1916, especially in heavy artillery, but deployment of New Army resources in repeated BREAKTHROUGH attempts on the Western Front produced renewed manpower crises into 1918, especially after the SOMME and YPRES offensives of 1916 and 1917.

Although imperial forces contributed to the campaign in France and took a major share of fighting in other British theatres, high casualties and escalating commitments at GALLIPOLI and SALONIKA, in PALESTINE and EAST AFRICA and on the MESOPOTAMIAN FRONT added to the strain on British recruitment capacity. Despite conscription of 2.3 million men under the MILITARY SERVICE ACTS from January 1916, by which time more than 2.6 million had volunteered, manpower resources were always stretched, and only a surge of patriotic enthusiasm in response to the German SPRING OFFENSIVES of 1918 enabled the BEF to conduct its final offensives in France at full strength.

By autumn 1918 the British Army displayed fewer signs of exhaustion than any major European ground force, and its technical capacity had improved dramatically. Major offensives in France, Palestine and Salonika were able to call on plentiful heavy guns and ammunition, sophisticated targeting systems, TANKS, ARMOURED CARS, light machine guns and close support from the world's largest and best-equipped air force (the newly independent RAF). Excluding imperial forces, official British Army casualties to the ARMISTICE were approximately 662,000 killed, 140,000 missing, and 1.65 million wounded. See also: AUSTRALIAN, CANADIAN, NEW ZEALAND, RHODESIAN and SOUTH AFRICAN FORCES; WEST INDIES; CYPRUS; DUNSTERFORCE; SOUTH PERSIA RIFLES.

British Empire See: GREAT BRITAIN; AUSTRALIA; CANADA; CEYLON; INDIA; NEWFOUNDLAND; NEW ZEALAND; SOUTH AFRICA; WEST INDIES.

British Expeditionary Force See: BEF.

British Navy See: ROYAL NAVY.

Broodseinde, Battle of See: Third Battle of YPRES.

Brooke, Rupert (1887–1915) English poet whose work epitomized the idealistic and romantic view of warfare held by large sections of European society before and during 1914. A BRITISH ARMY volunteer, he extolled the joys of national service, and his verses received widespread exposure and acclaim in the jingoistic atmosphere of the War's first months. He was mourned in GREAT BRITAIN as a major literary loss following his death from blood poisoning en route for GALLIPOLI in spring 1915, but his work was subsequently overshadowed by the blacker, more cynical war poetry of embittered trench fighters such as SASSOON.

Broqueville, Charles, Baron de (1860–1940) Leader of the majority Belgian Catholic Party and prime minister since 1911, de Broqueville was at the centre of BELGIUM's preparations for a possible European war.

Aware that the country's independent survival depended on support from the guarantors of its neutrality, he sponsored limited expansion of the BELGIAN ARMY but obstructed King ALBERT I's attempts to deploy it along the German frontier in spring 1914. Instead its six divisions remained scattered around the country in a state of high-profile impartiality.

The subsequent German invasion forced government withdrawal to French Le Havre, where de Broqueville resumed his disputes with the King as premier and foreign minister. Solidly backed by his new coalition cabinet, he opposed both Albert's refusal to abandon technical neutrality and his willingness to consider separate German peace proposals. Allied military failures in 1917 changed de Broqueville's mind about peace, and his cabinet position collapsed after he approached the Central Powers in October. Forced to resign the foreign ministry in January 1918 and replaced by Liberal leader HYMANS, he lost the premiership when his own party voted against him in May. He returned to political prominence in postwar Belgium, serving as war minister from 1926 and again as prime minister from 1932 until his retirement in 1934.

'*Brotfrieden*' German term ('bread peace') used to describe the treaty signed between the CENTRAL POWERS and the independent Ukrainian republic on 9 February 1918. A subsidiary of the BREST-LITOVSK negotiations with Bolshevik RUSSIA, the settlement gave the German-sponsored Rada government in Kiev possession of the disputed Cholm province, also claimed by an independent POLAND, in return for immediate supplies of Ukrainian grain to starving Austrian and German cities. The concession, which wrecked Vienna's hopes of voluntary Polish subordination to imperial protection, reflected fear of a Bolshevik takeover in the UKRAINE and AUSTRIA-HUNGARY's desperation for food supplies.

Browning Guns The American Browning company produced a wide range of small arms, but its output was not seriously expanded to meet modern military requirements before the UNITED STATES entered the War. The Browning 0.30-inch MACHINE GUN, a reliable and useful weapon similar in appearance to the British VICKERS, was developed in 1910 but not ordered by the US ARMY until 1917. Only 57,000 were produced before the ARMISTICE, and they saw limited service on the WESTERN FRONT, where the AEF used French CHAUCHAT GUNS and other purchased substitutes until autumn 1918. A similar fate befell the 0.30-inch Browning Automatic Rifle, which fired a 20-round magazine but could also be used as a one-shot weapon. The first of some 52,000 wartime examples entered frontline service in September 1918, and although intended as an infantry assault weapon it was usually deployed in a static support role as a light machine gun. A few Colt-Browning 0.30-inch machine guns also saw action with the AEF, but most were converted for aircraft use as MARLIN GUNS. See also: PISTOLS.

Brusilov, General Alexei (1853–1926) Russian cavalry officer who fought throughout the campaigns on the EASTERN FRONT and was the RUSSIAN ARMY's most successful general of the period. An aristocrat free from prewar factional commitments, he commanded the Eighth Army on the southern sector of the front from the opening campaigns in GALICIA. Brusilov's meticulous attention to planning detail and imaginative tactical flexibility made the Eighth Army the most consistently effective Russian force in the theatre, and it emerged with some credit from the defeats of 1915 (see 'BLACK-YELLOW' OFFENSIVE).

Appointed to replace IVANOV as commander of the southwestern army group in March 1916, Brusilov's first operation was a mass attack all along his front, relying on surprise and efficiency rather than the overwhelming concentration of force associated with conventional BREAKTHROUGH TACTICS (see BRUSILOV OFFENSIVE). Among those generals who encouraged the abdication of Tsar NICHOLAS II, Brusilov was appointed Russian Army C-in-C by the PROVISIONAL GOVERNMENT in June 1917, shortly after being asked to resign by his predecessor, ALEXEEV.

He took field command of the combined

Seventh and Eleventh Armies (the first 'RED ARMY') during the KERENSKI OFFENSIVE of July (sometimes known as the Second Brusilov Offensive), but was himself replaced by KORNILOV on 1 August. Though many of his former aides in Galicia fought for the Bolsheviks in the RUSSIAN CIVIL WAR, Brusilov remained on the sidelines until taking a staff position with the Red Army in 1920.

Brusilov Offensive The Russian summer offensive of 1916, launched in early June along the whole southern sector of the EASTERN FRONT between the Pripet Marshes and the Romanian border (see MAP 13). After the failure at Lake NAROCH in March, another offensive was forced on pessimistic Russian commanders by continuing Allied crises at VERDUN and the TRENTINO (see CHANTILLY CONFERENCE).

Russian chief of staff ALEXEEV, along with most senior generals, remained committed to BREAKTHROUGH TACTICS. He sought time to build up overwhelming manpower and ARTILLERY superiority along a narrow front, but General BRUSILOV, just appointed to command the southern army group, offered to attack all along his lines with hardly any reinforcement. A nervous STAVKA authorized the plan in mid-April as a preliminary to the conventional offensive being prepared by EVERT's central army group.

Unlike those of Evert and northern group commander KUROPATKIN, Brusilov's forces barely outnumbered their opponents (about 600,000 men and 1,700 guns, against 500,000 and 1,350) but he planned separate, simultaneous attacks all along his front by the Eighth, Eleventh, Seventh and Ninth Armies. His preparations employed TRENCH WARFARE techniques learned from the WESTERN FRONT, making extensive use of reconnaissance aircraft, SAPPING towards Austro-Hungarian positions, and excavating huge dugouts ('platsdarmi') for protection of forward reserves. Secrecy was taken seriously and CAVALRY almost completely excluded.

Russian preparations were noted but not interrupted by Austro-Hungarian forces in the sector: the Fourth, First, Second and Seventh Armies, with the Austro-German Südarmee in the centre, under overall command of the German LINSINGEN. Confidence in a strong trench system was bolstered by accurate assessment of Russian manpower levels.

Stifling opposition from army commanders, Brusilov opened the offensive on 4 June. Untypically accurate PRELIMINARY BOMBARDMENTS by all four attacking armies inflicted heavy casualties on forward positions crowded against the usual concentrated assault (see DEFENCE IN DEPTH), and Austro-Hungarian reserves were dissipated in defence of multiple crisis points.

In the strongest attack, immediately south of the Pripet Marshes, the Eighth Army (Kaledin) assaulted a 30km front around LUTSK, decimating the Fourth Army (JOSEF FERDINAND) and capturing the town on 6 June. Further south the Eleventh Army (Sakharov), with no numerical superiority over the First and Second Armies (BÖHM-ERMOLLI), broke through at Sopanów and took 15,000 prisoners. The Seventh Army (SHCHERBACHEV) achieved a smaller success against BOTHMER's Südarmee at Jazlowiec.

The greatest victories came in the far south, where the Ninth Army (Lechitski) took an Austro-Hungarian SALIENT around Okna (with 11,000 prisoners) on 5 June. Virtually the whole of PFLANZER-BALTIN's Seventh Army swung south of the Dneister to meet it, and was forced to retreat when a secondary attack broke through weakened defences north of the river on 7 June.

Ordered to retire southwest to the Bukovina region on 9 June, then redirected west by the high command, the Austro-Hungarian Seventh Army was split in two as transport arrangements collapsed. By mid-June it had lost over 100,000 men, and part was retreating west while the rest held a line on the River Prut, west of Czernowitz, until Russian attacks drove them back into the Bukovina from 17 June.

The AUSTRO-HUNGARIAN ARMY in Galicia had virtually collapsed by mid-June, but lengthening supply lines and shortage of cavalry hampered effective Russian pursuit. Brusilov had captured almost 200,000 prisoners, along with more than 700 guns, and had advanced parts of his front by more than 80km, but Russian forces had themselves suffered an estimated 50,000 casualties. Starved of reinforcements, Brusilov allowed his commanders to halt. To protect his northern flank, where a German salient now separated his front from Evert's, he ordered the Eighth Army northwest towards Kovel, but when Evert failed to initiate significant supporting action it paused pending reinforcement.

Twelve divisions reached Brusilov from other commands during late June, but the CENTRAL POWERS were handicapped by internal disputes: German chief of staff FALKENHAYN was preoccupied with the expected attack on the SOMME; CONRAD was determined to maintain the TRENTINO OFFENSIVE in ITALY. By the end of June only 16 divisions, mostly exhausted from fighting on other fronts, had arrived to join the defence.

They were divided along the front, 9 joining a new Austro-German force of 12 divisions that counterattacked against the Russian Eighth Army's northeastern flank at the River Stokhod from 20 June. After two days of fighting the attack was switched to its southwestern flank, but neither approach achieved more than token territorial gains, and German commander MARWITZ had lost 40,000 men when the operation was called off at the end of the month.

Brusilov then used his own fresh troops to renew the offensive all along the line. In the south, the Ninth Army had resumed its advance in late June, taking the whole of the Bukovina and threatening the Südarmee's southern flank by mid-July. At the same time the Eleventh Army crossed the Galician border to threaten its northern flank, forcing a further Austro-German retreat in the centre.

The Russian Eighth Army, supported to the north by the Third Army (Lesh) from Evert's group, attacked Marwitz and the remnant of the Austro-Hungarian Fourth Army from the River Styr, forcing them back to the Stokhod by 6 July. This second phase, known as the Ukraine Offensive, had captured 40,000 more prisoners and 63 guns all along the front by 7 July, when Brusilov altered his tactics.

Evert's forces, led by Ragoza's Second Army, had begun a breakthrough-style attack at Baranovitchi on 2 July, in a belated attempt to extend the Russian offensive northward. Ill-prepared and cautiously executed, it collapsed in a week with 80,000 losses. All Russian plans for an offensive elsewhere were then dropped and more reinforcements moved south. Given control of both the Third Army and the new GUARD ARMY, Brusilov massed strength for a breakthrough assault on Kovel from the Stokhod, marking the end of the Offensive proper.

In an attempt to force the efficient transfer of his troops, Evert was given control of the Stokhod front. His unsuccessful KOVEL OFFENSIVE, begun on 28 July, continued until early October. The Eighth Army made progress against the weak Austro-German Fourth Army (now under Tersztyánszki) until it was stiffened by German units, and the advance into eastern Galicia took Brody on 28 July, eventually forcing the line west to the Zlota Lipa river before the front stabilized in early September. Lechitski continued his success along the Dniester, taking Halicz in late July and reaching the foothills of the Carpathians before being halted by supply problems.

The Offensive's initial successes had weakened Falkenhayn's position in GERMANY, and HINDENBURG was given command of the whole front north of the Dnieper from late July. Austro-Hungarian forces on the Eastern Front were all but absorbed by the GERMAN ARMY, and even Pflanzer-Baltin's army in the far south came under Hindenburg's effective control.

Steady concentration of reinforcements from other fronts, and Evert's perseverance at Kovel, meant that overall Russian losses of almost a million men, half of them prisoners, were about equal with those of their opponents by early autumn. Though greeted with delight and amazement in Allied countries, where Russia's ability to mount a major attack had been in doubt since late 1915, the Offensive's main strategic effect, persuading ROMANIA to join the Allies, proved valueless (see ROMANIAN CAMPAIGN).

Bucharest, Treaty of (1918) Treaty between ROMANIA and the CENTRAL POWERS, signed in the Romanian capital on 8 May 1918. The final collapse of Russian forces on the EASTERN FRONT in late 1917 persuaded the Romanian government to sign an armistice on 9 December, but negotiations for a final settlement achieved little until March, when Austro-Hungarian foreign minister CZERNIN persuaded King FERDINAND that German patience had run out.

The pro-German Marghiloman became Romanian prime minister and signed a preliminary treaty on 5 March, agreeing to the loss of the Dobrudja region and immediate demobilization, but further delays were caused by BULGARIA's demand for sole control of the Dobrudja and TURKEY's refusal to sign any treaty unless it regained western Thrace, given away as an inducement to Bulgaria to join the Central Powers in 1915.

A Turkish proposal for joint administration over part of the Dobrudja was eventually accepted, and AUSTRIA-HUNGARY was compensated for German control of Romanian oil, grain, RAILWAYS and financial systems with territory demanded by Hungarian nationalists. Romania was allowed to keep parts of Bessarabia disputed with Russia. Never publicly endorsed by Ferdinand, the Treaty was denounced by Romania when it re-entered hostilities on 10 November 1918, and formally annulled by the Allied ARMISTICE with Germany.

Bug Offensive Austro-German advance north from Galicia along a broad corridor between the Rivers Bug and Vistula. Along with attacks towards the River NAREV in northeast Poland, and in the far north towards Riga in KURLAND, it formed part of of the TRIPLE OFFENSIVE on the EASTERN FRONT in summer 1915.

The main attacking force, General MACKENSEN's 'Bug Army', began advancing north on 29 June, aiming towards Brest-Litovsk in central Poland (see MAP 10). Its overall manpower superiority was limited – 35 Bug Army divisions, plus 11 of the Austro-Hungarian First Army, against a total of 39 Russian divisions of the Third, Eighth and Thirteenth Armies – but Mackensen's carefully applied BREAKTHROUGH TACTICS were very effective.

Painstaking concentration of German troops in the centre, and overwhelming weight of ARTILLERY against crowded forward positions, inflicted massive casualties. Without the benefit of RAILWAYS or good roads, the advance was slowed by methodical resupply before each limited attack, but thoroughness paid off.

Four corps of the newly transferred Russian Thirteenth Army temporarily halted the Austro-Hungarian Fourth Army (advancing to the west of the main force) around Krasnik on 9 July, but were forced to retire as Mackensen steamrollered through defences elsewhere. He smashed a hole in Russian lines and took 15,000 prisoners at the Battle of Krasnostav on 18 July, but was transferred to the BALKAN FRONT immediately afterwards and replaced by LINSINGEN.

The defeat at Krasnostav, combined with losses on the Narev and in Kurland, prompted a general Russian retreat from Poland, ordered by STAVKA on 22 July. The Galician armies were pulled back to positions some 150km southeast of Warsaw, beyond Cholm and Lublin, which fell at the end of the month.

Linsingen maintained a slow pursuit of the continuing Russian retreat, taking Brest-Litovsk on 25 August but failing to inflict any serious check on the withdrawal. Moving east into the inhospitable Pripet Marshes in early September, against the wishes of German chief of staff FALKENHAYN, the Bug Army stumbled to a halt at the end of the month, stopped at a new Russian line some 350km east of Warsaw (See 'GREAT RETREAT').

Bulgaria A province of the Ottoman Empire from the 14th century until 1878, when Russian support for a nationalist revolution led to the creation of an autonomous principality. Revolution in TURKEY enabled Prince FERDINAND to establish a fully independent kingdom (and take the title Tsar of Bulgaria) in 1908.

Bulgaria's national parliament (*Sobranje*) was elected by manhood suffrage and exercised a veto over royal legislation. Dominated during the early 20th century by the Nationalist Party, which represented the rural landowning classes, it gave almost unqualified support to the Tsar's appointed cabinet.

Ferdinand led an expansionist foreign policy aimed at restoring medieval 'Greater Bulgaria', joining SERBIA, GREECE and MONTENEGRO to drive Turkey out of Macedonia during the First Balkan War of 1912. Dissatisfied with the peace, Bulgaria launched a surprise attack against its former allies the following summer, but was invaded by ROMANIA and defeated on both fronts in six weeks, losing Bulgarian-speaking parts of Macedonia and the BLACK SEA coastal region of the Dobrudja.

Russian support for Serbia undermined traditional close relations with Bulgaria. Appointment of the pro-Austrian RADOSLAVOV as prime minister in July 1913 and elections in March 1914 signalled diplomatic moves away from the ENTENTE, although the terms of large-scale loans from Vienna and Berlin in June 1914 provoked strong nationalist objections to overseas ownership of RAILWAYS (about 2,000km) and coal mines. Bulgaria's mostly rural, agricultural economy was otherwise largely dependent on imported manufactured goods, metals and industrial raw materials, with GERMANY and AUSTRIA-HUNGARY providing some 55 per cent of all prewar imports.

Bulgaria was courted as a potential ally by both sides after August 1914. Earning his reputation as the 'fox of the Balkans', Ferdinand balanced Anglo-French offers of Turkish territory against Austro-German inducements in Serbian Macedonia, cautiously monitoring the possible intentions of neutral Balkan states. By summer 1915 Russian defeats on the EASTERN FRONT and Anglo-French failure at the DARDANELLES seemed to favour the CENTRAL POWERS, and the PLESS CONVENTION of 6 September committed Bulgaria to their autumn invasion of Serbia.

Opposition from minority parliamentary parties, led by the pro-Russian Democrat MALINOV and Agrarian Party leader STAMBOLISKI, was ignored or repressed, and Allied diplomats left Sofia on 5 October. The Bulgarian wing of the planned invasion began on 11 October and war was declared next day.

Bulgaria had no domestic armaments industry, and Germany eventually provided war materials to an estimated value of over 1,000 million marks, in return for mineral ores, some foodstuffs, and tobacco. German planners expected a lot more food from Bulgaria in 1915, but transport difficulties, manpower shortages and generally primitive agricultural systems made wartime production increases difficult, and home consumption had outstripped production long before 1918.

Military victories on the BALKAN FRONT and in the ROMANIAN CAMPAIGN satisfied Bulgaria's basic territorial ambitions, and German influence prevented a concerted attack on SALONIKA in 1916. With the parliamentary opposition demanding peace, and the BULGARIAN ARMY reluctant to fight on other fronts, relations with Germany plummeted during 1917. An annual subsidy to Bulgaria under the 1915 agreement was withdrawn in January 1918, all military aid was suspended from March, and the Treaty of BUCHAREST in May assured Germany the lion's share of conquered Romania.

Poor economic management meanwhile contributed to mounting social unrest, as business interests capitalized on lucrative orders from Germany to make big profits at the expense of home consumption, leaving a population of about 4.5 million to face a dour struggle against starvation and deprivation, intensified by the poor harvest and cold winter of 1916–17.

By mid-1918 popular socialism and republicanism represented an evident threat to the regime. Unwilling to risk his throne by breaking completely with the Central Powers, Ferdinand appointed Malinov as prime minister in June. An attempt to restore calm by appeasement, the appointment brought improved control of food distribution, but the military blocked Malinov's plans to seek immediate peace.

By mid-September Allied strength in SALONIKA was more than the Bulgarian Army could handle, and the VARDAR OFFENSIVE brought it quickly to the point of surrender. Forced into reluctant defence by the Tsar, its collapse later in the month sparked an eruption of revolutionary activity.

Swelled by mass desertions from the Army, SOVIETS were established in several provincial towns, and Stamboliski proclaimed a republican government in Radomir on 27 September. Rebels marching on Sofia were halted by the Tsar's bodyguard and a German division (en route for the front), but negotiations for an ARMISTICE with the Allies began on 28 September and it was signed two days later.

Ferdinand abdicated in favour of his son Boris on 4 October, accepting exile in Germany as Allied forces marched through the west of the country to attack southern Austria-Hungary. Malinov remained in power until 28 November, when Romanian reoccupation of the Dobrudja forced his resignation. Bulgaria's final settlement with the Allies was delayed until the appointment of Stamboliski to head a minority government in October 1919. His peasant-based regime, which survived until a monarchist coup in 1923, was willing to accept territorial reduction, disarmament and REPARATIONS, enabling signature of the NEUILLY Treaty in November. See MAPS 1, 25.

Bulgarian Army Raised by conscription of males aged between 20 and 46, the Bulgarian Army comprised some 85,000 troops in peacetime. Although Muslims could buy exemption and although budget restrictions reduced annual intake to about 50 per cent of eligible conscripts, the Army could mobilize up to half a million trained men in the event of war.

Until the Balkan Wars (1912–13) the Army consisted of 9 infantry divisions, each inflated in wartime to include some 24,000 troops (3 brigades), 2 CAVALRY squadrons, up to 4 companies of MACHINE GUN troops, an average of 15 four-gun field ARTILLERY batteries, 8 or 12 light mountain guns, plus engineers and transport units. The 12 peacetime cavalry regiments provided divisional squadrons in wartime and formed a division of their own. Strength was increased from 1913, when a tenth division was formed, and by 1918 there were 14 divisions with an established strength of more than 850,000 men.

Originally expanded from a Russian-trained militia when BULGARIA became independent in the late 19th century, the Army was still using some old Russian breech-loading RIFLES in 1915, but most infantry were equipped with more modern MANNLICHER models. Most machine gunners were equipped with bulky, wheel-mounted 8mm Maxim weapons, and field batteries generally used French Creusot or older German Krupp 75mm guns. Most of the mountain guns were obsolete Krupp products, as was Bulgaria's heavy artillery – three howitzer and three siege batteries under independent command.

The terms of Bulgaria's agreement with the CENTRAL POWERS in September 1915 provided for considerable military aid, which in practice came almost exclusively from Germany. With no major arms industry of its own, the Army relied on supplies of shells, bullets, modern artillery and machine guns from its major ally, and received equally important support from technical troops, medical services and light RAILWAY engineers. The GERMAN ARMY AIR SERVICE provided both personnel and equipment (notably two-seater AEG C-TYPES) for a few Bulgarian reconnaissance and light-bombing units.

Dependence on German material assistance carried the penalty of subordination to Berlin's strategic priorities. Theoretically controlled by C-in-C ZHEKHOV and his staff, two of the three Bulgarian field armies (six divisions) were under General MACKENSEN's tactical command on the southeastern wing of the successful invasion of SERBIA in October 1915. The smaller Third Army (General Toshev) was deployed near the border in Thrace as a precaution against attack from GREECE.

Bulgarian troops on the BALKAN FRONT subsequently stood guard in the hills overlooking inert Allied forces at SALONIKA. Strengthened by German units and put under German overall command during 1916–17, they fought occasional limited defensive campaigns, losing MONASTIR to the most ambitious Allied attack but suffering less from malaria and other diseases than their opponents.

Bulgarian troops, using German equipment and again under Mackensen's command, were also deployed in the Dobrudja region during the ROMANIAN CAMPAIGN in late 1916, and the conquest of the region satisfied Bulgaria's immediate territorial ambitions. Further use of Bulgarian troops elsewhere in Romania was extremely unpopular with public and commanders, contributing to a breakdown in relations with Germany. Exacerbated by German determination to use the country for its own economic benefit (see Treaty of BUCHAREST), the breakdown in relations was sealed by the suspension of military aid after March 1918. Weary and ill-equipped, the Army was swept back from its Balkan strongholds by the major Allied VARDAR OFFENSIVE from September 1918, and was retreating across Bulgaria itself when armistice with the Allies was signed on 30 September.

About 1.2 million Bulgarians fought in the wartime Army, of whom an estimated 100,000 were killed (about 25 per cent of them by sickness) and some 160,000 wounded. The subsequent Treaty of NEUILLY reduced an army once regarded as the most effective in the Balkans to a scratch force of 33,000 men, suitable only for border and order work.

Bulgarian Navy Consisting entirely of patrol boats and smaller coastal or river craft, the largest of which displaced only 715 tons, the Bulgarian naval service was divided into Danube and BLACK SEA flotillas. Apart from a few river skirmishes it saw no military action before it was disarmed and reduced to four unarmed TORPEDO BOATS under the terms of the postwar Treaty of NEUILLY.

Bullard, General Robert (1861–1947) Aggressive US ARMY infantry officer, one-time protégé of General WOOD, who was posted to Europe at the head of a brigade in late 1917. Promoted by AEF commander PERSHING to lead the 1st Division from December, he planned the first US attack on the WESTERN FRONT at CANTIGNY in May 1918. As the AEF expanded Bullard was given III Corps from July, and took part in the opening stages of the MEUSE-ARGONNE OFFENSIVE before further promotion to command the new US Second Army removed him to a quiet sector of the front in October. Like other senior US officers, Bullard endured reduction in rank to remain a corps commander in the smaller postwar Army.

Bullecourt See: Battle of ARRAS.

Bülow, Field Marshal Karl von (1846–1921) Veteran Prussian soldier in command of the Second Army for the invasion of BELGIUM in August 1914. To regulate the attack's overall pace von Bülow, at the centre of the advance, was given overall command of the First, Second and Third Armies on 9 August, but disagreements between the naturally cautious von Bülow and the aggressive First Army commander, von KLUCK, led to the system's abandonment after 17 August.

The pessimism inherent in von Bülow's subsequent failure to exploit victories against retreating French forces was expressed immediately before the First Battle of the MARNE in early September. His decision to retreat unless immediately supported by the First Army, 50km to the west, provoked its exposure to French flank attack, and the subsequent general order for German retreat was inspired by von Bülow's sense of imminent disaster. He remained in command of his army on the WESTERN FRONT, and was promoted field marshal in January 1915, but left the front after a heart attack in March and retired in 1916. See also: NAMUR; Battles of CHARLEROI and GUISE.

Burian von Rajecz, Istvan, Count (1851–1922) Hungarian aristocrat, a former diplomat and Austro-Hungarian finance minister, who replaced Count BERCHTOLD as imperial foreign secretary in January 1915. A relative moderate, Burian proved strong enough to resist German pressure for territorial concessions as the price of Italian friendship. He subsequently antagonized German opinion by insisting on retention of Austro-Hungarian control on the BALKAN FRONT, opposing the extension of SUBMARINE WARFARE and demanding recognition of imperial interests in POLAND. Without the material resources to back up his claims for equality with Germany, he was replaced by CZERNIN in December

1916, which reflected the extent of German control over imperial policy. Burian returned to the finance ministry but was recalled in April 1918 to seek a compromise peace settlement, a course he had consistently advocated. Finding the Allies committed to unconditional surrender, he resigned finally on 24 October.

Byng, General Sir Julian (1862–1935) British CAVALRY officer, a successful field commander in the Boer War, who led the BEF's 3rd Cavalry Division from autumn 1914 and was promoted to command the Cavalry Corps in 1915. Sent to the GALLIPOLI FRONT in August, he successfully organized the withdrawal from SUVLA BAY, before returning to the WESTERN FRONT to lead the Canadian Corps. His CANADIAN FORCES captured VIMY RIDGE during the ARRAS battle in April 1917, and he became a full general in charge of the British Third Army in June. He planned the Battle of CAMBRAI in November, and his troops performed well during the German SPRING OFFENSIVES of 1918. His growing reputation was secured by the Third Army's unbroken run of successes at the Battles of ALBERT, EPÉHY, HAVRINCOURT and VALENCIENNES in autumn 1918. Rewarded with a peerage, he became governor general of Canada from 1921 to 1926. See also: CANAL DU NORD; HINDENBURG LINE.

C

Cadorna, General Luigi (1850–1928) Cadorna turned down the post of ITALIAN ARMY chief of staff in 1908 over the issue of political control in wartime, but accepted the job in late July 1914. After ITALY declared neutrality on 2 August, he worked to slowly increase the Army's strength on the frontier with AUSTRIA-HUNGARY, approving the SALANDRA government's early decision to withdraw from the French frontier but opposing any diversion of military resources to ALBANIA and the BALKAN FRONT.

An effective organizer, his tactical shortcomings were exposed once Italy was at war. His response to the geographical limitations imposed by the mountainous ITALIAN FRONT was a series of 11 very similar offensives on the ISONZO between June 1915 and September 1917, each halted with heavy casualties in return for trivial territorial gains. His conventional massed frontal assaults lacked ARTILLERY support by WESTERN FRONT standards, and faced Austro-Hungarian forces in excellent defensive positions. Having lost many of his best junior officers in the fighting, Cadorna dismissed scores of their senior colleagues for incompetence, authorized widespread executions of deserters to eradicate 'cowardice', and blamed apathy on the home front for supply shortages.

His relations with the administration paralleled JOFFRE's treatment of press and politicians in FRANCE – virtually no concrete news was released for public consumption, and ministers were actively discouraged from visiting the front. Without a major victory to his credit, he came under increasing pressure to resign after the Austro-Hungarian TRENTINO OFFENSIVE in May 1916, and only the cabinet's own precarious position prevented his dismissal.

His plans for a combined offensive from Italy were rejected by Allied leaders in January 1917 and, still short of heavy artillery, he maintained his imperfect application of BREAKTHROUGH TACTICS until all his wartime territorial gains were wiped out by the Austro-German CAPORETTO OFFENSIVE in October and November. He mooted the possibility of a separate peace in a pessimistic communiqué to the government of 3 November, repeated his accusations of troop cowardice, and again criticized civilian apathy, multiplying the shock of defeat and effectively sealing his dismissal. Allied leaders expressed lack of faith in Cadorna at the RAPALLO

CONFERENCE on 5 November, and he was replaced by General DIAZ two days later. After serving briefly on the SUPREME WAR COUNCIL, he retired from military service when parliament voted to hold an enquiry into the Caporetto defeat. Heavily criticized in its 1919 report, he was officially forgiven when MUSSOLINI made him a field marshal in 1924.

Caillaux, Joseph (1863–1944) Moderate republican finance minister in three prewar French cabinets, Caillaux was briefly premier in 1911, and won a reputation as a pro-German pacifist by making territorial concessions to the German colony of CAMEROON to prevent war over Morocco. Opposition to extension of conscription in 1913 again brought him close to power in alliance with socialists by early 1914.

Caillaux's career was interrupted when his wife responded to press criticism by assassinating the editor of *Le Figaro* on 14 March 1914. He was a background figure after August but remained the senior symbol of French PACIFISM. Withdrawing from active politics, he scrupulously avoided contact with emissaries of the CENTRAL POWERS but maintained close links with like-minded French politicians as pacifist agitation mounted from late 1916.

A series of espionage scandals involving known associates during 1917 tainted Caillaux as a 'defeatist' (see *Le BONNET ROUGE*; MALVY, L.), and he was arrested by the CLEMENCEAU regime in January 1918. Not charged until victory was certain in October, he was deprived of his parliamentary seat in 1919 and eventually tried in 1920. Acquitted of planning a dictatorship for peace, he was banished from Paris on a minor charge until a changed political climate brought an amnesty in 1924.

Calais Conference, 1915 Anglo-French war council of 4 December 1915. One of several summits held at the northern French port, it was attended by British war minister KITCHENER and French premier BRIAND, with ROBERTSON and JOFFRE as their respective military representatives. Disillusioned with 'SIDESHOWS' after prolonged failure at GALLIPOLI, the British called the conference in advance of a planned military summit at CHANTILLY. They insisted on a complete withdrawal of forces from SALONIKA, to which the French reluctantly agreed. Greeted by a political storm in FRANCE, the decision was rapidly overturned by Joffre at Chantilly, where he secured Italian, Russian and Serbian support for continued operations on 6 December. The British climbed down to avoid isolation and to preserve the relatively stable French government, sealing the final evacuation of Gallipoli.

Cambrai, Battle of The final Allied attack on the WESTERN FRONT in 1917, by the BEF against German HINDENBURG LINE positions in Artois, southeast of Arras. Begun on 20 November, it was the first battle in which TANKS were deployed en masse.

After its machines had failed in thick mud at YPRES, British Tank Corps theorists led by Colonel FULLER proposed a massed raid on dry ground between the Canal du Nord and the St Quentin Canal (see MAP 2). Intended to restore the new weapon's fragile reputation, the plan was accepted by local Third Army commander BYNG but vetoed by C-in-C HAIG until mid-October, when evident failure at Ypres persuaded him to attempt a 'theatrical blow' elsewhere before the end of the year.

Abandoning Fuller's concept of a raid followed by rapid withdrawal, Byng planned a full-scale BREAKTHROUGH attack for November, ignoring probable bad weather, definite lack of reserves to exploit any success, and dire warnings from appalled tank commanders. Six infantry and two CAVALRY divisions, and about 1,000 guns, were concentrated along with all 476 working tanks for the initial breakthrough attempt on the first day.

Launched at dawn on 20 November, along a 10km front held by two divisions of the German Second Army (MARWITZ), the attack went in without a PRELIMINARY BOMBARDMENT and achieved complete surprise. By late afternoon the British had made general gains of about 6km, opening a barely defended gap in the German lines leading to Cambrai. The only failure came in front of Flesquières, where a divisional commander (Harper) ordered his troops not to cooperate with tanks. Further small advances were made next day, and Flesquières was taken, but lack of reserves allowed German reinforcements to block the route to Cambrai.

The relatively spectacular success of the first day persuaded Haig to continue the attack. Heavy and fluctuating combat continued throughout the sector until 30 November, when 20 German divisions launched a counteroffensive using new INFILTRATION TACTICS. The northern wing of the attack made little progress, but British lines on the southern flank of the new SALIENT were pierced and German forces had regained almost all the ground lost by 7 December, when fighting died down.

Taken in isolation, the attack of 20 November was a startling demonstration of the tank's potential power, and provided a blueprint for the long-term future of armoured warfare, but the battle as a whole, which cost about 45,000 British and 50,000 German casualties, was viewed by the Allies as a disappointing failure to exploit a rare opportunity. Successful counterattacks also encouraged the prevailing German belief that tanks were a marginal weapon best countered by concentrated field ARTILLERY (see TANK FORTS).

Cambrai Offensive 1918 The initial advance of HAIG's Allied army group beyond the main defences of the HINDENBURG LINE on the WESTERN FRONT in October 1918. Haig had ordered field commanders to pause for painstaking resupply across broken terrain after the Line's central defences had been cleared, but the new offensive was begun on 8 October and met with more determined resistance than anticipated. Allied forces advanced some 5km but were slowed by frequent counterattacks, including a raid in which nine captured British HEAVY TANKS surprised and destroyed several BEF machines before being overwhelmed. German forces withdrew in the night, leaving only rearguards to delay Allied occupation of Cambrai (see MAP 2).

Cameroon German colony (*Kamerun*) on the west coast of AFRICA, generally regarded by contemporaries as one of the world's least healthy environments (see MAP 17). Larger than France and Germany together, only about 2,000 of its estimated 3.5 million population were Europeans.

Like TOGOLAND, Cameroon was bordered by Allied colonies (Nigeria and French Equatorial Africa). It was defended by a colonial army of 200 German and 1,500 native troops, backed by about 1,250 armed police with German officers. The majority of the 8,000-strong British West African Frontier Force (WAFF) was concentrated in Nigeria to the northwest, and French colonial troops were available on Cameroon's southern and eastern borders. None of the regional forces had trained or manoeuvred for large-scale operations.

Anglo-French high commands vacillated briefly before agreeing on 22 August to a joint attack on the principal port of Douala, to be led by WAFF commander General Dobell (in London at the time). Allied forces on the spot meanwhile launched independent invasions. French colonial forces under General Aymerich took frontier posts in northeastern Cameroon on 6 August, and 600 Senegalese infantry established themselves along the southwest coast by 21 September. A three-pronged British invasion crossed the northern frontier on 24 August, aimed at settlements all along the border, but was repulsed with proportionally heavy casualties by better-trained German units.

Dobell's large Anglo-French force reached DOUALA in late September, charged with destroying its powerful RADIO station, and took the port without serious resistance. Authorized to complete the conquest of the colony, he sent troops through thick forest and swampland in pursuit of retreating German forces. With most of their equipment intact, German troops moved inland up the Wuri River and along RAILWAYS leading northeast and southeast of the port.

In hot, humid conditions and harassed by rearguards, Allied troops met steady resistance until 26 October, when the capture of Edea, about 60km up the southeastern line, prompted most German forces to fall back 150km east to Yaounda, where they established a new capital and headquarters. An advance up the Wuri took Yabussi, about 50km upriver, after a fight on 14 October, although German forces again retreated inland, and a regiment fought its way 30km up the northeastern railway. The coastal area around Mount Cameroon to the west was cleared of German troops by mid-November, and Dobell sent a strong force under General Gorge towards the northeastern railhead of Nkongsamba in December. Its slow advance was halted 150km from Douala after a bloody engagement on 3 March 1915 had left both sides exhausted.

General Aymerich's Senegalese in southern Cameroon had advanced some 500km northeast to approach the central town of Dumie by March 1915. Despite tense inter-Allied relations and the approach of heavy seasonal rains, a three-pronged joint offensive with Dobell's force was launched in mid-May, aimed at the capture of Yaounda. By early June it had collapsed, halted by German rearguards, pouring rain and impenetrable jungle, and having suffered several hundred casualties.

A renewed British invasion of the drier northern frontier by an independent force under General Cunliffe got underway in early summer. It captured the German fort at Garua on 10 June and advanced another 150km south by the end of the month, but repeated attacks into September failed to take the isolated fort further north at Mora. The combined offensive on Yaounda was renewed as the rains subsided in October, Dobell attacking from the west, Aymerich from the east, and Cunliffe from the north. Though energetically defended, German strongholds throughout Cameroon fell during the autumn, and Yaounda was captured on 1 January 1916.

The German population and surviving ASKARIS escaped across 200km of hinterland to the Spanish coastal enclave of Rio Muni, fighting off pursuing Allied troops south of Yaounda on 8 January, and 832 German survivors were subsequently evacuated to internment in Spain. The last surviving German outpost at Mora could not be taken, and 388 survivors surrendered on generous terms before Britain and France officially partitioned the colony between them on 4 March 1916. The conquest, undertaken to knock out a radio station, involved 18,000 British and French imperial troops. Most of the 4,235 killed, along with an unknown number of German troops and bearers, were victims of disease. See also: MANDATES.

Campania Originally a record-breaking transatlantic liner, built in 1893, *Campania* was purchased by the ROYAL NAVY in September 1914 and given a sloping, 36-metre flying deck with space for 10 large seaplanes. Entering service in May 1915 as the world's biggest AIRCRAFT CARRIER, *Campania*'s deck proved too short for safe take-off by cumbersome seaplanes, and was extended to over 60 metres. Joining the GRAND FLEET in April 1916, still equipped with 10 seaplanes, it was accidentally left in port and missed the Battle of JUTLAND. Re-equipped with SOPWITH PUP landplanes from spring 1917, and later with purpose-designed FAIREY CAMPANIA amphibians, it remained largely inactive until November 1918, when it dragged anchor during a storm in the Firth of Forth and sank after a collision.

BRIEF DATA (1916) Displacement: 18,000 tons; Crew: 600; Dimensions: length 622ft (188.5m), beam 65ft (19.7m); Speed: 22k; Armament: 6 × 4.7in gun, 1 × 3in AA, 10 × a/c.

Canada British Dominion, virtually autonomous though subject to imperial veto by a governor general. The latter's role was largely honorific, as Canada displayed a general enthusiasm for Empire and mother country. A body of occasional dissent in the elected House of Commons was provided by representatives of the French-speaking residents of Quebec province, who comprised some 22 per cent of Canada's 7.2 million population (1911).

Robert BORDEN's Conservative Party took power in 1911 after 15 years of Liberal rule had been marked by increasing economic involvement with the UNITED STATES, but the parties publicly suspended rivalries in August 1914. Canada automatically entered hostilities alongside GREAT BRITAIN, making no separate declaration of war, and volunteer CANADIAN FORCES began assembling immediately. They reached the WESTERN FRONT in February 1915, and played an important role with the BEF throughout the War.

A coalition 'Union' government from October 1917 confirmed unity among English-speaking politicians. Conscription laws were passed with little English-speaking opposition in late 1917, and legislation the following March extended suffrage to WOMEN. French-Canadian Liberal leader Laurier, a major factor in appeasement of prewar Quebecois separatism, boycotted the coalition on the conscription issue, and wider French-Canadian opposition was reflected in low recruitment from Quebec during 1918.

Agricultural exports to Europe multiplied after 1914, but Allied demand for war materials stimulated even faster industrial growth. An 850 per cent increase in shipyard capacity and development of a thriving munitions industry encouraged migration to cities and aroused tensions between urban and rural communities, as well as jealousies between western and more developed eastern provinces. French separatist agitation had revived by 1919, and national unity appeared in danger throughout the 1920s.

Borden played an active role in wartime imperial politics, serving with the Imperial War Cabinet in London and working to achieve British recognition of Dominion partnership in foreign affairs. His signature on the Treaty of VERSAILLES as leader of a victorious Allied nation reflected both a fundamental shift in British imperial attitudes and Canada's increased international prestige.

Canadian Forces Regular Canadian ground forces in 1914 consisted of about 3,100 troops, mostly employed as garrisons of harbour fortifications, backed by a lightly trained 'active' militia of local volunteers. The Canadian government offered military assistance to GREAT BRITAIN during the JULY CRISIS in 1914, and began assembling volunteers on 6 August for a Canadian Expeditionary Force (CEF) to Europe. The first recruits reached Britain for training in mid-October and the 1st Canadian Division (General Alderson) took the field on the WESTERN FRONT in February 1915, playing an important defensive role during the second YPRES battle in April.

Strong volunteer response enabled rapid formation of a 2nd Division, deployed with the 1st to form the Canadian Corps when it reached France in September. Two more Divisions were active by August 1916 and a 5th existed from early 1917, but was disbanded a year later to provide replacements for other units. Almost 600,000 Canadians enlisted with the wartime army, and 418,000 served overseas with the CEF, of whom some 210,000 were casualties (56,500 dead).

Commanded by the British General BYNG from May 1916, the Canadian Corps won its most celebrated victory at the Battle of ARRAS the following April, taking the stronghold of VIMY RIDGE. General Currie, a prewar Canadian militia officer, took over from Byng in June 1917, and led the Corps through the AMIENS OFFENSIVE and subsequent British victories in late 1918.

The CEF generally used British equipment, although inferior home-produced Ross RIFLES were not replaced by British Lee-Enfields until 1916, and the original 1st Division had to use US Colt MACHINE GUNS until sufficient British weapons became available in late 1915. Initial shortage of heavy ARTILLERY also meant that the CEF used only EIGHTEEN-POUNDERS in 1915.

Another 13,000 Canadians served with the British air services, and about 7,000 in other British units. Some 14,500 British citizens resident in CANADA returned home to enlist, and 12,000 Canadians were retained for home defence. Canadians also garrisoned the West Indian island of St Lucia, and two regiments served outside the CEF: the Royal Canadian Regiment was manned from the prewar regular army; and Princess Patricia's Canadian Light Infantry was a privately raised force of former British soldiers in Canada. Both joined the CEF 3rd Division on its formation.

The Royal Canadian Navy, founded in 1910 but denied parliamentary funds for expansion, was a tiny force of two obsolete CRUISERS and two SUBMARINES in 1914.

Motor launches, ANTI-SUBMARINE vessels and minecraft were added in wartime for patrol duties on both coasts, and about 5,100 men (mostly reservists) were in Canadian naval service by the ARMISTICE. Another 3,000 enlisted with the ROYAL NAVY, but Canada's most important naval contribution was construction of more than 900 (mostly small) warships. See also: NEWFOUNDLAND.

Canal du Nord, Battle of the Attack by the British First Army (HORNE) on the northern end of the Siegfried Stellung, the strongest sector of the German HINDENBURG LINE, between 27 September and 1 October 1918 (see MAP 2). Part of an overall Allied attack all along the northern and central sectors of the WESTERN FRONT, it began the day after the MEUSE-ARGONNE OFFENSIVE to the south, a day before the COURTRAI OFFENSIVE and two days before the British Fourth Army's main attack on the Siegfried Stellung at the ST QUENTIN CANAL.

An integral feature of the Siegfried position, the Canal du Nord presented a formidable obstacle. Difficult for infantry to negotiate, and virtually impassable for TANKS, its far bank was protected by marshlands on either side of the Arras–Cambrai road and overlooked by German positions on high ground to the east.

The relatively fresh CANADIAN Corps was selected to spearhead the First Army's attack on the canal, and corps commander Currie planned a complex flank attack on its strongest defences. Two Canadian divisions, with the only 16 tanks available, were sent across a narrow strip of dry land to the south at dawn on 27 September, and then fanned out across a wider front while a third crossed to join them. Support from the bulk of the First Army's ARTILLERY got the Canadians across the canal, and they passed well beyond their objectives despite unexpectedly heavy resistance.

The rest of the First Army and the southern wing of the British Third Army (BYNG) advanced along a 20km front further north, making much slower progress at considerable cost, but came up level with the Canadians in the centre after another day's heavy fighting, an overall territorial gain of about 10km along the sector. British infantry gained another kilometre or so in repeated attacks before Horne suspended operations for recuperation on 1 October. Though a limited and costly success, its strategic effects were multiplied by Allied successes elsewhere.

Canopus British PRE-DREADNOUGHT completed in 1900–01. It was on BLOCKADE duty in the South Atlantic in August 1914, but in November was sent to join Admiral Cradock's under-equipped task force against the German raiders *GNEISENAU* and *SCHARNHORST*. Naval minister CHURCHILL regarded *Canopus* as a formidable addition to the force, but its uselessness was recognized by Cradock, who met the German force at CORONEL without the old battleship when it was delayed. Present at the FALKLAND ISLANDS action, where it was beached to guard the entrance to Port Stanley harbour, *Canopus* subsequently took part in the DARDANELLES operation, where two of its five sister ships (*Ocean* and *Goliath*) were sunk. Withdrawn from active service in 1916, it was used as a depot ship until scrapped in 1920.

BRIEF DATA Displacement: 12,950 tons; Crew: 750; Dimensions: length 430ft (130.3m), beam 74ft (22.4m); Speed: 18k; Armament: 4 × 12in gun, 12 × 6in, 12 × 12pdr, 4 × 18in TT.

Cantigny, Battle of Relatively minor action fought on the WESTERN FRONT on 28 May 1918, when a regiment of General BULLARD's US 1st Division advanced its front by about 1.5km and captured the village of Cantigny (see MAP 2). Strategically insignificant, and overshadowed by the battle in progress on the AISNE, the engagement was principally notable as the first wartime attack by AEF forces. It was followed by further US attacks around Château-Thierry (3–4 June) and BELLEAU WOOD (6–12 June).

Capelle, Admiral Eduard von (1855–1931) Politician and GERMAN NAVY officer. A trusted supporter of Prussian navy minister TIRPITZ, he drafted the expansionist Navy Laws of 1898 and 1900. He was ministerial deputy and head of administration under

Tirpitz in August 1914, but retired a year later due to ill health. Recalled to replace his former chief in March 1916, and expected to support chancellor BETHMANN HOLLWEG's campaign against extension of SUBMARINE WARFARE, he eventually acceded to chief of staff HOLTZENDORFF and army leaders, diverting resources from the surface fleet to SUBMARINE construction. His political position was undermined when he blamed unrest in the HIGH SEAS FLEET during August 1917 on a conspiracy by parliamentary socialists, but Kaiser WILHELM II, fearing the return of Tirpitz, refused to accept his resignation in October. Capelle remained in office, politically powerless, until retired by SCHEER's Naval Supreme Command in October 1918.

Capello, General Luigi (1859–1941) Unconventional ITALIAN ARMY officer, an inveterate critic of military bureaucracy, who led a division during the first ISONZO OFFENSIVE in June 1915 and was promoted to command VI Corps in September. His habit of allowing journalists and civilian authorities to inspect the front, interpreted as evidence of ambition by chief of staff CADORNA, helped boost his popular reputation, and he was lionized for his part in the GORIZIA victory of August 1916.

Transferred to the relatively low-profile TRENTINO sector, he returned to the Isonzo to lead the Second Army in spring 1917. His troops achieved limited success during the eleventh Isonzo battle in the late summer, but the Austro-German counteroffensive at CAPORETTO in October ruined his reputation. Aware that an attack was coming, he characteristically ignored Cadorna's orders to withdraw ARTILLERY safely west of the river and prepared his best units for an advance of their own.

Illness kept him from the battlefield until 24 October, by which time the front was already collapsing. Recommending an immediate 50km withdrawal to Cadorna, who ignored him in return, Capello again fell ill the next day. Though he recovered, he received no further wartime command and was blamed for the defeat, along with Cadorna, by a 1919 parliamentary inquiry. He remained in the postwar Army and joined MUSSOLINI's Fascist Party, but was expelled for his Masonic connections in 1923 and arrested in 1925. Charged with conspiracy to assassinate the premier, he remained in prison until 1936.

Caporetto Offensive Spectacular Austro-German success on the ITALIAN FRONT in October 1917. An attack into the northern ISONZO sector, it was the first German operation in the theatre, and prompted substantial Allied commitment to a campaign hitherto conducted exclusively by the ITALIAN and AUSTRO-HUNGARIAN ARMIES.

Italian commander CADORNA's repeated BREAKTHROUGH attempts at the Isonzo line had achieved little in territorial terms and suffered heavy casualties, but had steadily weakened Austro-Hungarian forces already depleted by massive losses on the EASTERN FRONT in 1916. The eleventh ISONZO OFFENSIVE, in August 1917, threatened to break Austrian defences in the centre of the front around GORIZIA, and prompted the German THIRD SUPREME COMMAND to accept chief of staff ARZ VON STRAUSSENBERG's latest proposal for a joint operation in September.

Austro-Hungarian plans to repeat the TRENTINO OFFENSIVE of 1916 were overruled by German staff officers, and a lightly defended 25km stretch in front of Caporetto, north of Gorizia and along the Isonzo, was chosen for a limited attack intended to give the Austrians a breathing space. Nine Austrian divisions and General von HUTIER's six German divisions from RIGA (all that could be spared during the British YPRES offensive) were concentrated on the front during October as the German Fourteenth Army under Otto von BELOW.

Deserters and aerial reconnaissance had informed Cadorna to expect German intervention, something he had long feared, and he suspended his own advances on the Isonzo in mid-September. Not apparently aware of the offensive's strength, or of his own troops' exhaustion, he regarded a general adoption of defensive positions as sufficient precaution. Italian numerical superiority along the whole front (41 divisions to 35) was not matched in the sector of German concentration, where Second Army commander CAPELLO ignored orders to prepare defences and massed his best troops for an attack on the southern flank of von Below's army east of Gorizia.

Aided by misty conditions and using Hutier's new INFILTRATION TACTICS, the Fourteenth Army's main assault from a small SALIENT west of the river at Tolmino achieved total surprise on 24 October, breaking through the Second Army's lines almost immediately and sprinting forward some 25km by the end of the day. Secondary attacks either side of the breakthrough were held by defenders, and the Austro-Hungarian Fifth Army (BOROEVIC) made little headway near the coast to the south, but the collapse of the centre threatened to cut off the bulk of Italian forces at the River Tagliamento.

Capello recommended withdrawal to the river as soon as his lines were broken on 24 October, but Cadorna maintained attempts to block the gap until 30 October, and most Italian forces crossed the river over the next four days. Although a German division established a bridgehead over the Tagliamento to the north on 2 November, Austro-German supply systems were incapable of mounting a serious attack before Cadorna ordered a further retreat to the fast-flowing River Piave, less than 30km north of Venice.

By the time surviving Italian Army units were across the Piave on 10 November, the defeat had sent multiple shock waves through the Allied command chain. The BOSELLI government in ITALY fell on 25 October, and new premier ORLANDO secured Allied military aid at RAPALLO on 6 November. Cadorna was dismissed next day and a new Allied SUPREME WAR COUNCIL created to coordinate Italian operations.

Six FRENCH ARMY divisions (FAYOLLE) and five (PLUMER) from the BEF, backed by considerable British and French air contingents, took up frontline positions from early December, but new commander DIAZ faced an attack by the Austro-Hungarian Tenth (KROBATIN) and Eleventh (CONRAD) Armies through the Trentino on 12 November. Short of reserves, it made little ground, and positions further east were held after five days' heavy fighting between the upper Piave and the Brenta from 13 November. Gradually diminishing Austro-German attacks on both sectors continued into late December, when winter and the steady withdrawal of German forces halted major operations.

The Italian Army had suffered some 300,000 casualties (90 per cent as prisoners) and lost most of its ARTILLERY, but the shock of invasion silenced popular pacifism in Italy and brought a major Allied reconstruction programme. Austro-Hungarian inability to follow up the victory without German assistance became clear during a final offensive on the PIAVE in June. See MAP 21.

Caproni Ca Series Multi-engined Italian biplanes and triplanes (in the case of the Ca4) developed for the ITALIAN AIR FORCE in the light of experimental bombing operations against Libyan targets during 1911–12. An advanced and unique design, the original production Ca2 was driven by a 100hp 'PUSHER' engine on a central nacelle with two 100hp 'tractor' engines on twin fuselage booms attached to a distinctive triple tailfin.

The first Ca2 squadron was in service when ITALY declared war in May 1915, and began STRATEGIC BOMBING raids against Austro-Hungarian targets in August. A total of 164 Ca2s saw service, carrying out regular day and night attacks on targets close to the ITALIAN FRONT or the Adriatic coast before they were gradually replaced by the improved Ca3 from early 1917.

Similar in appearance, reliable and armed with up to five MACHINE GUNS, the Ca3 was a stable bombing platform capable of surviving heavy combat damage. Its 150hp engines gave a top speed of 146kph, and it was a mainstay of the Italian strategic force for the rest of the War. About 280 Ca3s were produced in Italy, also serving the ITALIAN NAVY as TORPEDO bombers, and a few built in France were used by the AÉRONAUTIQUE MILITAIRE.

The ambitious Ca4, a much larger triplane development of the design, appeared in various models (including a naval floatplane) from late 1917. Capable of carrying a 1,365kg (3,000lb) bomb load, it was similarly tough and reliable, but was slow, cumbersome and vulnerable to attack from the ground. Less than 50 were built and they were mostly used for night raids.

The final wartime development, the Ca5, joined bombing units from early 1918. A reversion to biplane design, and again fitted with various engines (up to 300hp) by different sub-contracted manufacturers, it was smaller than the Ca4 and generally stripped down for performance. Effective against diminishing resistance, 255 Ca5s had been delivered by late 1918. Licence-built versions also flew with French and USAAS bomber squadrons in 1918.

BRIEF DATA (Ca5, Italian) Type: medium/heavy bomber; Crew: 2–4; Engine: 3 × 300hp Fiat; Span: 23.3m; Max speed: 160kph; Ceiling: 4,550m; Armament: 2 × 6.5mm mg, max bomb load 910kg (2,000lbs).

Carnet B The French government's peacetime list of known political agitators, spies, pacifists and other potentially disruptive people who were to be arrested in the event of war. The assassination of socialist leader Jean Jaurès on 31 July 1914, when war seemed imminent, provoked calls within the French cabinet to invoke Carnet B. The decision not to round up suspect French nationals was immediately vindicated by an overwhelmingly positive popular response to war with Germany, and 80 per cent of the 2,500 or so people on the list eventually volunteered for military service. See also: FRANCE; SECOND INTERNATIONAL.

Carol I, King (1839–1914) A relative of Kaiser WILHELM II, formerly Prince Charles of Hohenzollern-Sigmaringen, he was elected king by ROMANIA's national assembly in 1866 to guarantee German protection of recent independence. His strongly pro-German position contrasted with popular anti-German sentiment, focused on Austro-Hungarian possession of Transylvania, and though generally well loved he lacked the constitutional authority to force Romania to war in August 1914. Personally humiliated by neutrality, and increasingly isolated from mainstream pro-Allied opinion, Carol sacrificed his personal popularity in repeated attempts to promote links with the CENTRAL POWERS during September 1914, and was considering abdication before his death in October. See also: King FERDINAND I.

Caroline Class Cruisers See: ARETHUSA.

Carpathian Campaign, 1915 A series of gruelling mountain battles on the Galician sector of the EASTERN FRONT, where the autumn POLISH CAMPAIGNS left armies deadlocked along entrenched lines either side of the Carpathian Mountains (see MAP 11). Despite heavy losses, bad weather and difficult terrain, both sides planned offensives in the new year, partly in the hope of encouraging neighbouring ROMANIA to abandon its neutrality.

Competition for manpower between the RUSSIAN ARMY's Galician (IVANOV) and East Prussian (RUZSKI) commands pushed STAVKA (Russian central command) into allowing both to plan offensives for the new year. Ruzski formed a new Twelfth Army for an attack on the southern flank of German positions in East Prussia; Ivanov prepared for a drive through the northwestern Carpathians by the Third Army (Radko-Dimitriev) supported by the Eighth (BRUSILOV). Although only 29 of his 47 infantry divisions were available for the Galician sector, 3 of them besieging the fortress of PRZEMYSL, Ivanov received no reinforcements until two divisions extracted from Ruzski arrived at the end of January.

The CENTRAL POWERS also divided their forces. Apart from planning a preliminary attack in central Poland (see Battle of BOLIMOV), German commander LUDENDORFF demanded reinforcements from chief of staff FALKENHAYN for an East Prussian offensive at the MASURIAN LAKES. Austro-Hungarian C-in-C CONRAD meanwhile appealed for reinforcements to relieve Przemysl. Concerted pressure from both persuaded a reluctant Falkenhayn to release eight newly formed divisions (EICHHORN's Tenth Army) for East Prussia and to sanction support for Conrad's offensive.

His total strength up to 41 infantry divisions, Conrad concentrated German reinforcements against the Russian Third Army in the central Carpathians, as half of a new Austro-German 'Südarmee' (LINSINGEN) detailed to attack towards Przemysl. Supporting attacks were planned through the northwestern mountains by the Austro-Hungarian Third Army (BOROEVIC), and through the flatter Bukovina region to the southeast by PFLANZER-BALTIN's army group.

The Third Army's centre was quickly forced back by Ivanov's two fresh divisions when attacks opened from 20 February, leaving four depleted divisions isolated in the Uzsok Pass, but attempted Russian advances were defeated by the weather as their supply lines lengthened. The only Austro-Hungarian success came in the southeast, where the Seventh Army's advance through the scarcely defended lowlands brought it to the banks of the Dneister, threatening Brusilov's southern flank and taking Czernowitz on 17 February.

Reinforced by the Second Army (BÖHM-ERMOLLI), the Third Army resumed its northwestern attack on 17 February, but 20 divisions, most of them far below strength, suffered enormous casualties without making any significant progress before counterattacks finished off survivors. By the beginning of March Austro-Hungarian forces were completely exhausted and, with the fall of Przemysl on 22 March, the Russians prepared for their own offensive.

Stavka's attempts to bring reinforcements south were blocked by Ruzski, whose replacement by ALEXEEV failed to improve inter-front cooperation. Three divisions arrived after a month, but Ivanov was also required to send units from his armies in central Poland to the Bukovina, where they formed the nucleus of a new Ninth Army, and could only strengthen his invasion force by pulling the Third Army's right wing into the Carpathians from positions near Krakow.

Despite being no stronger on paper than opposing Austro-German forces, the offensive won some tactical success. The three depleted defending armies were forbidden to retreat from the mountains, perceived as the last line of defence before Budapest, and suffered yet more heavy losses from a series of limited Russian attacks. Supply problems and the arrival of a fresh German Alpine Corps (MARWITZ) brought the offensive to a halt from 10 April.

Russian casualties in the Carpathian offensives can only be guessed, but by mid-April the AUSTRO-HUNGARIAN ARMY had lost 800,000 men in the mountains since January, three-quarters to climate-related sickness. With the reliability of many surviving units in serious doubt, often on ethnic grounds, Conrad appealed for German intervention to stiffen AUSTRIA-HUNGARY's war effort (see GORLICE-TARNOW OFFENSIVE).

Carrier Pigeons Trained pigeons, used by all sides as a form of emergency communication, were carried by command units with ground forces, proving particularly useful once troops had advanced or retreated beyond prepared field telephone lines (see TRENCH WARFARE). They also equipped warships and long-range reconnaissance aircraft, particularly flying boats and seaplanes, originally as the sole alternative to reporting in person but later as a back-up to RADIO.

Carson, Sir Edward (1854–1935) Unionist MP for Dublin University since 1892, and a leading figure in Bonar LAW's British Conservative and Unionist Party. He campaigned against Home Rule for IRELAND, and organized the paramilitary Ulster Volunteers to defend Anglo-Irish interests in 1912. International war transformed many Volunteers into the BRITISH ARMY's 36th Division from September 1914, and Carson became attorney general in the ASQUITH coalition from May 1915. A committed 'EASTERNER', opposed to withdrawal from GALLIPOLI, he clashed with the prime minister over lenient treatment of the Irish 1916 EASTER RISING, and his resignation in October was designed in collusion with LLOYD GEORGE and Bonar Law to trigger the coalition's collapse. First Lord of the Admiralty from December 1916, he was unwilling to press his preference for CONVOYS on sceptical professionals and was replaced by the more forceful GEDDES the following July, remaining in office as a minister without portfolio until December 1918.

Casement, Sir Roger (1864–1916) British diplomat who retired with a knighthood in 1911 and moved to the UNITED STATES, where he worked to win support for the republican movement in his native IRELAND. After war broke out he continued his work in GERMANY, which had supplied arms for Irish republican forces during the troubles of early 1914 but never provided substantial wartime aid. His efforts to recruit Irish prisoners to the GERMAN ARMY met with little success, but he was transported to the southwest coast by SUBMARINE as a potential leader of the planned EASTER RISING in 1916. Landing on 20 April he was arrested within hours, taken to London and hanged for treason. Though subject to a posthumous smear campaign by British authorities, he remains an Irish nationalist hero.

Casualties Overall military fatalities in the First World War are generally put at about 9.8 million men, but some estimates exceed 12 million, and different figures for numbers of wounded start at around 20 million. Battle losses exceeded those of any conflict before or since, but the weakness or collapse of contemporary bureaucratic systems, and difficulties in establishing criteria, render precise measurement impossible.

Political collapse in GERMANY and AUSTRIA-HUNGARY reduced final figures to estimates. Records authorities in TURKEY and RUSSIA seldom knew the size or exact location of forces, and official casualty figures were probably even more inclined to optimism than those of other countries. Similar opacity surrounds losses in conquered countries like SERBIA, ROMANIA and BULGARIA.

Figures for military deaths generally only include those who died quickly, but victims of GAS attacks or tropical diseases often died slowly. Civilian casualties directly caused by military operations include at least half a million ARMENIANS, a similar number of CENTRAL ASIANS, perhaps 2 million Russians, 500,000 Romanians and 650,000 Serbians, along with losses in the ARAB, BOER and SENUSSI REVOLTS, the RUSSIAN CIVIL WAR and other colonial or internal battles fought outside the formal theatres of war.

Civilian bombing victims, merchant seamen, passengers on torpedoed ships, victims of reprisals by occupying forces and other 'collateral' deaths clearly constitute war casualties, but the number of civilians killed by disease or exposure as a direct result of war deprivation has never been accurately calculated. Approximate figures for Germany, one of the countries worst hit, suggest up to half a million deaths attributable to food shortage, but more severe famine struck eastern Europe and the Ottoman Empire. Given the general state of deprivation in Europe and the Middle East, some commentators also regard many of the subsequent INFLUENZA victims as war casualties.

Cattaro Southern Adriatic port (now called Kota), an Austro-Hungarian enclave on the coast of central Montenegro, used by the AUSTRO-HUNGARIAN NAVY's coastal-defence V Division (see MAP 16). Before ITALY entered the War in 1915, French forces in the MEDITERRANEAN had attempted to disrupt the base by landing a small ARTILLERY detachment on the overlooking hill of Lovcen, but it was forced to retire after Montenegrin forces failed to provide a supporting ground attack on the base itself. Cattaro was subsequently used as the main base for SUBMARINES operating in the Mediterranean (see *HANDELSKRIEG*). Often discussed as a possible target for the ITALIAN NAVY's battlefleet, it was never actually attacked.

Fuelled by nationalist tensions within individual ships during long periods of inactivity, Czech nationalist seamen seized control of V Division's MONARCH Class battleships on 1 February 1918, but the mutiny was suppressed within 48 hours. Only five ringleaders were executed, an indication of the Navy's political stability relative to the AUSTRO-HUNGARIAN ARMY. The mutiny nevertheless highlighted the need for more vigorous naval leadership, and triggered the replacement of C-in-C NJEGOVAN in March.

Caucasian Front The least well-known major campaign of the period, an extension of longstanding imperial rivalries between TURKEY and RUSSIA for control of the regions south and west of the Caucasus Mountains, covered by modern Georgia, Azerbaijan and Armenia (see MAP 24). Hill country cut by narrow strips of plain running east–west into Turkish Anatolia, the region represented the best opportunity for territorial expansion for either empire.

Russian foreign policy had been focused on ultimate possession of the DARDANELLES since defeat by JAPAN ended hopes of eastward expansion in 1905. Foreign minister SAZONOV was careful to avoid conflict before 1914, recognizing the RUSSIAN ARMY's inability to cope with an escalation into general war, but long-term plans were laid for an attack in the Caucasus, originally in concert with a major RUSSIAN NAVY offensive in the BLACK SEA.

Though military resources were concentrated against more dangerous potential opponents on the EASTERN FRONT (see PLAN 19), the Caucasus Army at Tbilisi had established frontier bases at Kars and Ardahan by 1914, and Russian agents were busy equipping Armenian nationalists inside eastern Turkey with a view to revolt.

The YOUNG TURK government in Constantinople presided over a growing pan-Turkish movement after 1909, reflected in its cooperation with ethnic Turkish minorities inside Russia and growing hostility towards Armenians. With the Empire in retreat in the Balkans and the Middle East, the expansionist ambitions of war minister ENVER PASHA could only realistically look to the land south of the Caucasian Mountains.

The outbreak of war in late October triggered limited action from both sides, with Turkish border guards retreating into the hills after skirmishes in early November. A major offensive was planned by the Turkish Third and Second Armies, which began slowly assembling north of Erzurum (without the benefit of a RAILWAY to the region) under Enver's direct command. General Mishlaevski's smaller Russian force, denied major reinforcement during the POLISH CAMPAIGNS, restricted offensive operations to the supply of an Armenian rebel division that crossed the border into Turkey as Enver's 'Eastern Army' began its advance. With few troops left to police the region, the rebels slaughtered an estimated 120,000 non-Armenians in a series of raids and seizures over the following months.

Enver's ambitious two-pronged invasion achieved its first purpose in drawing substantial Russian forces out to meet it, but the Turkish Second Army's approach on Ardahan became hopelessly bogged down in worsening conditions and the Third Army was routed at SARIKAMISH. Still too weak to contemplate large-scale follow-up operations, Russian forces edged into Armenia as Turkish strength was distracted by rebel activities in the rear.

About 30,000 armed Armenians gathered in the far west at Sivas in February 1915, and the rebel division took Van, southwest of the frontline, on 20 April. Its proclamation of a provisional independent government sparked a Turkish offensive against Armenian civilians all over the Empire as a Russian corps advanced in its wake to occupy positions west of Mus (see ARMENIAN MASSACRES).

Despite diversion of resources to meet Allied invasion at GALLIPOLI, Enver ordered another attack by the Eastern Army in July, but it was overwhelmed by a Russian counterattack at MALAZGIRT in early August, following a skilful tactical withdrawal by new Russian commander YUDENICH. The front stabilized from early autumn along a sparse 300km line east of Rize on the Black Sea and of Erzurum in the centre, but doglegged to pass west of Lake Van further south.

With the 'GREAT RETREAT' in progress on the Eastern Front and manpower shortages already affecting the TURKISH ARMY, fighting died down until early 1916. Yudenich detached 20,000 troops under General Baratov for an expedition into PERSIA in November, primarily to halt to German-inspired rebellion by the country's small army, but also to preempt any Turkish penetration (see KHANAQIN).

Yudenich had provided the only good military news in RUSSIA through 1915. As arms production mushroomed over the winter, and prospects on the Eastern Front remained poor (see BESSARABIAN OFFENSIVE), the Caucasus Army was re-equipped and brought up to 22 divisions (about 300,000 men) over the winter. Grand Duke NIKOLAI's transfer to overall command in Tbilisi from September 1915 left Yudenich in control of field operations, and he planned a series of limited offensives all along the Front.

Designed to prevent large-scale Turkish concentration of reinforcements freed from Gallipoli, the Russian 1916 campaign was one of the most effective offensive operations of the period. Attacking first towards Mus in the south and ERZURUM in the centre in January. Yudenich took the reputedly impregnable fortress town on 16 February. However, he made no attempt at a long-range advance, and switched operations to the coast.

Making innovative use of naval landings at RIZE, Yudenich advanced northwest from Kars to take TRABZON in mid-April. His main attack pushed west of Erzurum in the summer and had moved 150km west to take ERZINCAN by 25 July, stalling a planned Turkish offensive all along the line except in the south, where part of the Second Army (IZZET PASHA) reached Bitlis by mid-August. A Russian counterattack later in the month restored the southern sector to positions west of Mus.

Aware that he could not expect long-term support or reinforcement (see KOVEL OFFENSIVE), Yudenich had no intention of attempting a major sweep into Turkey, despite the hopes of British authorities, and Russian forces consolidated their control over Armenia through late 1916. The FEBRUARY REVOLUTION in Russia left the Caucasus Army and its Persian detachment reasonably coherent but incapable of offensive operations from spring 1917. The main Turkish effort was concentrated against British attacks on the PALESTINE and MESOPOTAMIAN FRONTS throughout the year.

Russian occupation disintegrated after the OCTOBER REVOLUTION, leaving a power vacuum filled by renewed Armenian rebel activity and nationalist unrest either side of the old imperial border. Armenian attacks on non-Armenian populations began again, killing an estimated 50,000 people (against 1 million claimed by the Turkish government). In September representatives of the Georgian, Azerbaijani and Armenian people had founded the joint republic of TRANSCAUCASIA, but the situation in the region remained extremely confused into 1918 as the different ambitions of the three Transcaucasian elements clashed.

Armenia (Erivan) sought reconciliation with Turkey, especially after the BREST-LITOVSK Treaty prompted a renewal of Turkish military operations in spring 1918. Enver sent 50,000 fresh troops, including a few German units from YILDERIM FORCE, to retake almost all the ground lost in the theatre by May, when Armenia broke up the new republic to sign a separate Treaty of Batum (26 May 1918).

Enver's offensive fatally weakened Turkish defences on other fronts and damaged his own political position. It also ran counter to German plans for economic exploitation of Transcaucasia, built around close contacts with the Georgian regime in Tbilisi. Threatened by Bolshevik units from the north and angry at the cession of Batum to Turkey (occupied on 15 April), the Georgians accepted German aid, and a GERMAN ARMY division occupied Tbilisi for a time in early 1918.

Azerbaijan suffered the loss of its main port, Baku on the Caspian Sea, to a SOVIET regime in early 1918, followed by a liberal Georgian nationalist government in June. The Brest-Litovsk Treaty had ceded it to Turkey and, despite surprise British assistance from 'DUNSTERFORCE', the port fell to 14,000 Turkish troops in mid-September, the last major action in the theatre before the ARMISTICE.

International interference with Baku, and generalized ill-treatment of its Muslim population, exacerbated frontier disputes between Georgia and Azerbaijan, mirrored in worsening Georgian relations with Armenia and Armenian–Azerbaijani communal violence. Subsequent British occupation imposed temporary calm, but border violence flared up in January 1919 over Georgian–Armenian customs rates, and the Azerbaijani government collapsed after British withdrawal in August.

Transcaucasian independence did not survive long without protection: a socialist uprising in Baku and RED ARMY invasion brought Azerbaijan into the Soviet Union from April 1920; Soviet and Turkish forces combined to partition Armenia in September; and Georgia offered only limited resistance to Soviet absorption in November.

Caudron G-III Introduced to French service in April 1914, this slow, unarmed but stable biplane remained in action well into 1917. Employed for reconnaissance and as an ARTILLERY spotter, and up-engined from 80hp in later models, it was eventually also used by the British, Belgian, Russian and Italian air forces. Though exact records are unavailable, hundreds of G-IIIs were built, many by licensed sub-contractors, and 200 surplus machines were taken by the USAAS as trainers in 1918.
BRIEF DATA (1917) Type: two-seater reconnaissance; Engine: 100hp Anzani; Max speed: 108kph; Armament: small arms.

Caudron G-IV French bomber and armed reconnaissance aircraft. A twin-engined development of the CAUDRON G-III design, it was in service with the AÉRONAUTIQUE MILITAIRE from November 1915. Reliable but relatively slow, the poor positioning of its forward MACHINE GUNS made it vulnerable to FIGHTER attack, and it was withdrawn from the WESTERN FRONT a year later, along with the few RFC machines built under licence in Britain. G-IVs were more successful as long-range bombers for the RNAS, which used 55 machines to attack German coastal installations until spring 1917. They also flew long-range Alpine reconnaissance missions for the ITALIAN AIR FORCE.
BRIEF DATA (1917 model) Type: two-seater bomber/reconnaissance; Engine: 2 × 100hp Renault; Max speed: 130kph; Ceiling: 4,250m; Armament: 1 or 2 × 8mm mg, 220lb bomb load.

Caudron R-11 French twin-engined bomber that joined AÉRONAUTIQUE MILITAIRE units from early 1918. A lighter, streamlined and more powerful development of an unsuccessful Caudron R-4 design, it was hampered by lack of lifting power, and although early models (usually fitted with 180hp engines) were used for night-bombing raids, it was eventually employed almost exclusively as an escort FIGHTER. Escort R-11s eventually equipped 8 escadrilles on the WESTERN FRONT, and their heavy defensive armament provided valuable protection for short- and medium-range day bombers during the Allied offensives of late 1918.
BRIEF DATA Type: light bomber/escort fighter; Crew: 3; Engine: 2 × 220hp Hispano-Suiza; Max speed: 182kph; Armament: 5 × 0.303in mg, max bomb load 120kg (264lbs).

Cavalry By the early 20th century mounted troops had been the acknowledged masters of offensive warfare for at least a thousand years. They were used as a fast reconnaissance tool, as a shock weapon to charge and terrorize hostile positions, and for rapid exploitation of tactical victories. No tested and effective alternative existed in August 1914.

The world's regular cavalry forces had much in common. Troops generally carried a sword, a short carbine RIFLE (or officer's PISTOL) for use when dismounted, and sometimes a lance, although its continued value was a matter of much prewar controversy. Cavalry regiments were usually equipped with one or two MACHINE GUNS, carried by a team and cart, and when grouped into divisions (rather than attached to infantry divisions) they were accompanied by engineers, infantry battalions and light ARTILLERY.

Armies expecting to fight in rough, mountainous territory (like the SERBIAN ARMY) made limited use of cavalry, but those forces planning operations in flat, open spaces counted up to a third of their strength in horsemen. The relatively large cavalry contingents of the FRENCH, GERMAN, BELGIAN and BRITISH ARMIES were all considered elite forces, officered by the most influential sections of military society, as was the huge mounted arm of the RUSSIAN ARMY, bolstered in wartime by up to a million COSSACKS. The TURKISH ARMY's wartime cavalry similarly relied on large numbers of Arab tribesmen with their own horses, and mounted SOUTH AFRICAN FORCES were usually self-equipped volunteers (see also: AUSTRALIAN, NEW ZEALAND FORCES).

The basic contemporary weaknesses of cavalry were quickly demonstrated during the early battles on the EASTERN and (above all) WESTERN FRONTS. Its reconnaissance function was rendered obsolete by AERIAL WARFARE developments and, whether in the charge or in pursuit, it was no match for even small foot detachments armed with machine guns (see HAELEN). Horses were expensive to transport and maintain (two-thirds of Russian food-supply trains to the Eastern Front carried fodder) and most cavalry units on the European fronts were quickly converted to infantry roles in TRENCH WARFARE conditions.

The prevalent belief in BREAKTHROUGH TACTICS called for rapid penetrative exploitation of any success, and mounted troops were still massed for the purpose before big offensives. The well-publicized failure of cavalry to exploit a few opportunities on the Western Front, notably at ARRAS in 1917, gave rise to heavy criticism of HAIG, CADORNA and other commanders for wasting cavalry in futile defiance of recent experience, but no viable alternative was available. Motor vehicles and ARMOURED CARS were unreliable and needed roads, and the new TANKS were very slow and even more prone to breakdown.

Though it never succeeded in direct assault against the best modern weapons and TRENCHES, cavalry was genuinely effective against less organized defences in more spacious theatres with few modern weapons. Horse and camel units were central to British success in PALESTINE and to the tactics used by ARAB REVOLT armies. General YUDENICH dominated the CAUCASIAN FRONT with imaginative use of cavalry in 1916. Cavalry was also valuable in sparsely populated sectors of the Eastern Front (like KURLAND), and later played a major role in the sprawling RUSSIAN CIVIL WAR.

The success of armoured cars and lorries in similar conditions pointed to cavalry's future redundancy even as an instrument of colonial policing, but the influence of powerful conservative elements ensured that this was imperfectly recognized in most surviving armies after 1918. Protected by sharply reduced investment in mechanized development, and widespread belief that the special circumstances of trench warfare were unrepeatable, cavalry occupied a reduced but distinct place in military thinking in 1939.

Cavell, Edith (1865–1915) English nurse, resident in Brussels since 1907, who remained in the city after its occupation in August 1914 and was arrested by German authorities a year later, charged with aiding the escape of more than 200 Allied troops into the Netherlands. Cavell confessed to the charges, and Dutch authorities admitted to repatriating some of the troops concerned. Her execution by firing squad on 12 October 1915, authorized by local officials without reference to the German high command, received heavy worldwide press coverage. Allied PROPAGANDA, always concerned to emphasize German brutality in BELGIUM, seized upon Cavell's story, encouraging dramatic embellishments that made a particular impression in the neutral UNITED STATES.

Central Asian Revolt Imperial RUSSIA had expanded deep into Central Asia (modern Kazakhstan, Kyrgyzstan, Tajikistan, Turkmenistan and Uzbekistan) during the second half of the 19th century, but had made little use of its barren, remote acquisitions before 1914. Populated by warlike, predominantly Muslim tribes and nomads, the region had been largely ignored by Russian traders and bureaucracy but provided cotton crops and a place of resettlement for landless Russian peasants, who comprised about 40 per cent of the region's population by 1911.

Longstanding tensions between colonists and natives exploded when the government issued a decree conscripting hitherto exempt native males for military labour service in summer 1916. Thousands of Russian settlers throughout the region were attacked and murdered before the RUSSIAN ARMY moved in to join colonists in reprisals. Estimates of the number killed before order was restored at the end of the year vary up to about 500,000. The slaughter was never subject to PROPAGANDA exposure and virtually unknown to contemporaries in Europe.

The revolt was an uncontrolled outburst rather than an expression of Central Asian nationalism. A regional assembly was established at Tashkent after the FEBRUARY REVOLUTION, but Central Asian demands were restricted to broad autonomy within a federalized empire until after the OCTOBER REVOLUTION, which prompted claims to autonomy by the Kazakh, Bashkir and Tatar peoples, and their participation in a shortlived, independent Azerbaijan (see CAUCASIAN FRONT). See also: ARMENIAN MASSACRES.

Central Powers Term used to describe the wartime alliance of GERMANY and AUSTRIA-HUNGARY, later extended to include their allies TURKEY and BULGARIA. See also: The ALLIES.

Ceylon Indian Ocean island, now the republic of Sri Lanka, that was a British colony in 1914 with a thriving agricultural economy and little interest in imperial defence. Despite the recruiting efforts of British administrators only about 600 native Sinhalese enlisted for active service, out of a population of more than 4.2 million. Another 1,600 Europeans from Ceylon served in volunteer formations, including a Ceylon Planters Rifle Corps that fought at ANZAC COVE, and some 1,200 Sinhalese joined civilian support services on the MESOPOTAMIAN FRONT.

Champagne Offensive, First The first major Allied offensive on the WESTERN FRONT after the general solidification of trench lines in the autumn of 1914. It was a long campaign of attrition that spread all along the northern and central sectors of the front for four months, starting in December 1914. Despite the failure of previous assaults on entrenched positions, French C-in-C JOFFRE remained certain that an Allied breakthrough was possible. The German line inside France in late 1914 formed a great SALIENT from northwest of Lille to Verdun, and another much smaller bulge extended further south around St Mihiel. Joffre's strategy was very simple: attacks on the northern and southern edges of the main salient, followed (if successful) by a drive north through the Ardennes to cut off German lines of retreat (see MAP 3).

The opening attacks on the long southern edge were launched near Perthes in eastern Champagne on 10 December. Five days of heavy fighting around Givenchy (18–22 December) and a set-piece battle at Perthes (20 December) achieved only small gains, and a separate advance towards Noyon from 22 December was quickly reduced to barely perceptible progress by the outnumbered but well-entrenched German Third Army. Supporting attacks by Allied forces from the Yser to Verdun met a similar fate, including costly assaults on German positions in Artois and at the Woevre. Almost continuous fighting until mid-February, including three more battles for Perthes itself, advanced the French no more than 2km anywhere along the front, and no further breakthrough was achieved when the offensive resumed in March after a brief pause to reorganize.

By the time attacks were finally suspended on 17 March, French casualties in the campaign approached 90,000 men. Aware that the German Army was transferring forces to the EASTERN FRONT, and still expecting their defences to crack eventually under massed infantry assault, Joffre switched the emphasiz of Allied attacks to the northern edge of the bulge (see ARTOIS–LOOS OFFENSIVE) before returning to the south in the autumn (see Second CHAMPAGNE OFFENSIVE). See also: Battle of NEUVE CHAPELLE.

Champagne Offensive, Second Main attack of the Allied autumn offensive on the WESTERN FRONT in 1915, an assault by half a million men of the French Second (PÉTAIN) and Fourth (DE LANGLE DE CARY) Armies against a 15km front in the Argonne region of Champagne (see MAP 2). Intended to force the German Third (EINEM) and Fifth (Crown Prince WILHELM) Armies back up the River Meuse towards Belgium, it was timed to coincide with simultaneous attacks further north in the ARTOIS–LOOS sector.

In repeating his unsuccessful strategy of the spring in CHAMPAGNE and ARTOIS, French C-in-C JOFFRE was counting on numerical superiority to achieve a decisive breakthrough. French and British forces had been substantially reinforced during the summer, and German strength steadily eroded by demands from the EASTERN FRONT. When the attack in Champagne opened on 25 September, after a four-day PRELIMINARY BOMBARDMENT from 2,500 French ARTILLERY pieces, defenders were outnumbered by almost 3 to 1.

Well-entrenched on high ground, and knowing the attack was coming, German forces gave ground slowly as far as their second line of TRENCHES and held the French less than 3km from their starting line. The attack was suspended on 28 September, by which time French casualties had passed 145,000 and German reinforcements had arrived from the Eastern Front. The French advance was renewed on 6 October, but gained only a few yards in five days before grinding to halt against counterattacks. Despite the capture of 25,000 prisoners (about half the total German loss) and 150 guns, no strategic gains had been made when the battle was officially ended on 6 November. The twin autumn offensives had cost more than 320,000 Allied casualties by early November, forcing a winter break for recuperation.

Champagne Offensive, Third See: Second Battle of the AISNE.

Chantilly Conference, 1915 The first major attempt to coordinate inter-Allied military operations on all fronts, meeting at Chantilly (near Paris) from 6 December 1915. Attended by French, British, Russian, Serbian and Italian leaders, it met at the end of a very bad autumn for the Allies, marked by comprehensive defeats on the EASTERN and BALKAN FRONTS, failure at GALLIPOLI, and a costly inability to break through on the ITALIAN or WESTERN FRONTS. French C-in-C JOFFRE used the conference to reverse political decisions made at CALAIS two days earlier, forcing renewed British commitment to operations at SALONIKA. Russian representative ZHILINSKI, complaining that the RUSSIAN ARMY had received no diversionary support during the summer's TRIPLE OFFENSIVE, gained agreement from all the Allies to attack whenever another was threatened. The German attack on VERDUN in February 1916 triggered the agreement, prompting failed Russian attacks at Lake NAROCH and the fifth abortive Italian ISONZO OFFENSIVE in March.

Charleroi, Battle of One of the pivotal 'Battles of the FRONTIERS' on the WESTERN FRONT in 1914, a major action fought on 21–23 August between the French Fifth Army, advancing north to the River Sambre, and the German Second and Third Armies moving southwest through BELGIUM. Charleroi, a medium-sized industrial town straddling the Sambre, was the focus of a battlefront stretching some 40km west of NAMUR, where the river forms a T-junction with the Meuse (see MAP 4).

According to the FRENCH ARMY's offensive PLAN 17, General LANREZAC's northernmost Fifth Army was to join the Fourth and Third Armies in an invasion of Germany through the ARDENNES. The assumption that Germany would not mount a full-scale invasion further north was never accepted by Lanrezac, but French C-in-C JOFFRE was almost impervious to his reports of massive German concentration in Belgium. Lanrezac was permitted to stretch his lines northwest to the Sambre on 12 August, but some of the Fifth Army's best troops were transferred to the Ardennes offensive and replaced by a corps from the Second Army in LORRAINE. Joffre eventually allowed Lanrezac to concentrate against the north on the night of 20 August, by which time advance units of General von BÜLOW's German Second Army were approaching Namur.

Joffre ordered an attack across the river, expecting Lanrezac's 15 divisions to be reinforced by 5 BEF divisions and the Belgian garrison at Namur, against a maximum of 18 German divisions in Belgium. Lanrezac, aware that Allied reinforcement was delayed and anticipating something like the actual German strength of 38 divisions, postponed his attack on the morning of 21 August and asked permission to wait for the British. German Second Army detachments attacked across the Sambre on the same morning, holding two bridgeheads against repeated counterattacks by French troops short of ARTILLERY and not equipped to dig TRENCHES.

With part of his strength distracted by the ongoing siege of Namur, von Bülow renewed the assault on 22 August, sending three corps against the French Fifth Army all along its front. Heavy and confused fighting continued throughout that day and the next: the French centre, holding the southern side of Charleroi, suffered heavily and fell back; the French corps west of Charleroi held its ground, as did General FRANCHET D'ESPEREY's corps in the far east; in the far west the retreat of General Sordet's CAVALRY exposed the right wing of the BEF, at last in position around MONS.

During the first night, the German Third Army reached and crossed the Meuse, but von Bülow passed up the opportunity to send them south across the French Fifth Army's rear and ordered an immediate frontal attack against the French right. Manning the only trenches dug by French troops throughout the battle, Franchet d'Esperay's corps kept the Fifth Army's lines of retreat open on the second night. Suffering communications difficulties, Lanzerac expected them to be closed at any moment. He was aware of a bridgehead established across the Meuse by German Third Army units to his south, but not that General MANGIN's brigade had held them off and was about to counterattack successfully. Belgian evacuation of Namur that morning, together with news of the French Fourth Army's retreat from the Ardennes, prompted him to order a general withdrawal.

The retreat saved the French Fifth Army from probable destruction and enabled the subsequent defence of northern France, but was viewed by contemporaries as a failure of 'offensive spirit'. Joffre, who had tacitly allowed the withdrawal, publicly blamed Lanrezac for the failure of Plan 17, a view echoed in British explanations for their own retreat from Mons and by an ill-informed Allied press. See also: Battle of GUISE.

Châteaurenault One of eight obsolete 'protected' CRUISERS that remained in FRENCH NAVY service in August 1914. Sharing the disadvantages of their larger contemporaries (see *LEON GAMBETTA*), they were unsuitable for fleet actions but proved fairly useful as all-purpose CONVOY escorts, patrol ships and occasional transports. They were never the equal of modern light cruisers employed by other major navies, but *Châteaurenault* was the only wartime loss, torpedoed by the Austro-Hungarian SUBMARINE *U-38* off the Atlantic coast in December 1917. All the crew were safely evacuated and the submarine was sunk by DESTROYERS.

BRIEF DATA (1914) Displacement: 8,200 tons; Crew: 734; Dimensions: length 462ft (140m), beam 59.5ft (18m); Speed: 23k; Armament: 2 × 164mm gun, 6 × 138.6mm, 12 × 47mm, 3 × 37mm.

Château-Thierry, Battle of See: Battle of BELLEAU WOOD.

Chauchat Gun French 8mm light MACHINE GUN developed in 1907 and modified in a 1915 version that became the FRENCH ARMY's standard close-support infantry weapon. Although some 250,000 Chauchats were produced in wartime, and the gun weighed less than 10kg, up to four men were needed to carry its distinctive ammunition drums in combat, and its notorious unreliability reflected low manufacturing standards. Despite their failings almost 50,000 were in French service by the ARMISTICE, and Chauchats were also used by many other Allied armies, most notably the AEF, which bought 34,000 in 1917 and adapted them as 0.30-inch. weapons for use in France pending the arrival of its BROWNING GUNS.

Chemical Warfare See: GAS; FLAMETHROWERS.

Chemin des Dames Offensive See: Second Battle of the AISNE.

Chilpilly Spur High ridge jutting out into the Somme near Amiens, at a point where the river takes a wide southward bend (see MAP 2). Overlooking the main advance of the Allied AMIENS OFFENSIVE on 8 August 1918, Chilpilly Spur was one of its main objectives, but the British 58th Division was held off by determined resistance from a German division fresh to the front, which was able to inflict serious casualties on Australian troops advancing to the south, caught in heavy ARTILLERY and MACHINE GUN crossfire. The position was not taken until an AEF regiment joined the assault on 9 August, by which time forward Allied elements were already some 15km ahead. As commanders on both sides were beginning to sense Allied victory on the WESTERN FRONT, the action illustrated both the enduring cohesion of many GERMAN ARMY units and the inefficiency with which tired Allied troops often applied overwhelming material superiority in late 1918.

China Political decay and industrial backwardness in the isolationist Chinese empire, a vast territory with an estimated population of 420 million in 1911, had been a major temptation to the 19th-century expansionist empires of Europe, RUSSIA and JAPAN.

The rise of warlord governments in the provinces, and increasing republican pressure in Peking (Beijing), rendered the imperial Manchu government powerless to resist economic penetration of the southern coastal zone by European powers. The Boxer Rising (1900) of nationalist elements in Peking had provided an excuse for increased European military presence. Sino-Japanese war in the 1890s had detached Formosa (Taiwan) and Korea from imperial control, and Russian defeat in the war of 1904–05 established firm Japanese control over most economic and political activity in Manchuria to the north.

The republican revolution of October 1911, instigated by Sun Yat-sen and his Alliance Society, forced the child emperor's abdication four months later. Sun Yat-sen held power for only a matter of days before Yuan Shih-kai took power as president of the new republic, and in 1912 the Alliance Society was organized into the Kuomintang (Guomindang) Party. In office until his death in June 1916, Yuan only ever controlled a small area around Peking, facing a rival Kuomintang government at Canton (under vice president Li Yuan-hung), a Japanese client regime in Manchuria, and effective provincial independence.

Concentration of modern industry in European hands precluded any significant economic benefit from the outbreak of war in August 1914. Cotton and opium remained the principal exports and lack of RAILWAYS (only about 13,000km by 1914) made trade expansion difficult.

Both GERMANY and GREAT BRITAIN made diplomatic efforts to secure official Chinese support, and Yuan promoted agreement with the Allies. The main immediate effect of the War on China was to distract the European powers from restraining Japanese expansionism. Japan took and kept the German concession around TSINGTAO (Qingdao) in November 1914, and its TWENTY-ONE DEMANDS forced major economic concessions from China under threat of war in January 1915.

Pro-Allied prime minister Tuan Chi-jui remained in office under Yuan's successor, Li Yuan-hung. Anxious to end reparations due since the Boxer Rising, he pursued negotiations with the Allies despite presidential and Kuomintang opposition. Tuan's cabinet cut diplomatic relations with Germany in March 1917 and voted to declare war on Germany in April, but Kuomintang forces reacted by driving him from office and suspending parliament.

Peking was subsequently occupied by the warlord Chang Hsun, who briefly held power as regent to a restored emperor before a military alliance between Tuan and vice president Feng Kuo-chang recaptured the capital in July. Feng replaced Li as president on 18 July, and war was declared on 14 August 1917.

China's military and economic contributions to the Allied war effort were minimal, with government resources and various CHINESE FORCES committed almost entirely to the continuing internal crisis. Much of Manchuria came under Japanese control, as did the northern Chinese Army units that helped drive RED ARMY troops out of the province in 1918.

The republican government, under President Hsu Shih-chang from September 1918, was represented at the PARIS PEACE CONFERENCE, but international guarantees of freedom from interference proved meaningless in practice and China remained in turmoil until the establishment of a reasonably secure

Communist government in the 1950s. See LANSING-ISHII AGREEMENT.

Chinese Forces The large Chinese Army, the product of reorganization under General (later President) Yuan Shih-kai, was almost entirely absorbed in internal strife throughout the period. Most of an estimated 1.25 million Chinese in military service by 1918 were under direct control of provincial or political warlords. They played no part in Allied operations after CHINA declared war in August 1917, and although a small Military Mission was sent to study conditions on the WESTERN FRONT in late 1917, the government was unable to raise an expeditionary force for service overseas. Most of the more efficient northern units were under Japanese control in Manchuria, and the only concerted Chinese military action of the period was against Bolshevik forces infiltrating the province. The Chinese Navy had been a strategic irrelevance since defeat by the JAPANESE NAVY in 1895, and its six CRUISERS, two gunboats, four small DESTROYERS and handful of TORPEDO BOATS played no active wartime role.

About 320,000 Chinese were recruited by the Allies for service overseas as labourers, mostly from coastal regions around Hong Kong and other British enclaves. Recruitment began in 1914 and was stepped up after August 1917, so that by the ARMISTICE more than 100,000 were serving in support of the BEF in France, the same number with the FRENCH ARMY, and a few with the AEF. Other Chinese served with British forces on the MESOPOTAMIAN FRONT and in EAST AFRICA, some with medical units but most as labourers.

Chunuk Bair See: Battle of SARI BAIR.

Churchill, Winston (1874–1965) British politician who entered parliament in 1900 as a Conservative but subsequently joined the Liberals, serving in the ASQUITH government as trade minister (1908) and home secretary (1910) before his keen military interests were gratified by appointment as First Lord of the Admiralty (navy minister) in 1911. Viewed by contemporaries as vigorous, imaginative, eloquent and confident, but dangerously impulsive, he was an effective peacetime navy minister, hastening reforms begun by Admiral FISHER.

His wartime tenure was less successful. His appointment of JELLICOE as GRAND FLEET C-in-C upset field commanders, and his interference with long-range operations contributed to early failures against the MITTELMEERDIVISION and at CORONEL. His offer in cabinet to lead surplus naval troops to ANTWERP in October was accepted by war minister KITCHENER, but Churchill's arrival with a few raw recruits achieved only a further dent in his reputation. His relationship with Fisher, recalled as First Sea Lord in late 1914, degenerated during 1915 into a clash of giant egos.

Churchill was under pressure to produce a big naval victory by early 1915, but his controversial promotion of the DARDANELLES expedition backfired. Mobilizing support for the expedition with vague promises of Turkish collapse in January, he pushed plans for a purely naval operation into action despite increasing military opposition, especially from naval professionals. The failure of the campaign eventually brought down the Asquith government in May, and Churchill lost his job to widespread popular and professional satisfaction.

Relegated to a minor post (Chancellor of the Duchy of Lancaster) until his mid-November resignation in protest at the decision to evacuate the GALLIPOLI FRONT, Churchill fought as a lieutenant colonel of infantry on the WESTERN FRONT for a time before his recall to office as munitions minister in July 1917. The appointment upset Conservatives in the LLOYD GEORGE coalition but was justified by the sheer energy of his performance. Becoming war minister in December 1918, he remained at the centre of British politics until his ultimate retirement as prime minister in 1955. See also: RNAS; TANKS.

Cigognes ('Storks') Elite FIGHTER units of the French AÉRONAUTIQUE MILITAIRE, named after the flying storks painted on the sides of their machines. The original elite escadrille was MS3 (MS for MORANE-SAULNIERS, with which it was equipped), staffed by eminent prewar pilots and serving with the French Sixth Army on the WESTERN FRONT. Joined by MS12 and MS23 in 1915, the Cigognes were allocated the best pilots and equipment, as well as the highest PROPAGANDA profile. The air battles over VERDUN in 1916 cemented their fame. Re-equipped with NIEUPORT 11 fighters, the Cigognes were expanded as Groupe de Combat XII, including escadrilles N26, N73, N103 and N167 (but not N12). Popularly associated with their most celebrated pilots, Guynemer and FONCK, N3 and N103 formed an elite within the elite. Staffed entirely by ACES, they subsequently flew the pick of French aircraft, using SPAD S-VIIs from autumn 1916 and SPAD S-XIIIs from the following summer.

Clam-Martinic, Heinrich, Count von (1863–1932) Bohemian nobleman and conservative politician. A close prewar confidant of Archduke FRANZ FERDINAND, he fought as a junior officer on both the EASTERN and ITALIAN FRONTS before his appointment as Austrian agriculture minister in October 1916. Though politically committed to maintenance of imperial AUSTRIA-HUNGARY and a German-speaker, he retained some contact with Austria's powerful Czech nationalist movement, and was charged with forming a genuinely multiracial cabinet when he succeeded Ernst von KÖRBER as Austrian premier in December 1916. His proposals for national unity were rejected by the country's German, Polish and Czech elements and he abandoned the effort in June 1917, resigning to become governor of occupied MONTENEGRO until the ARMISTICE.

Clemenceau, Georges (1841–1929) Veteran French politician, an energetic and powerful figure within the Radical Party but in semi-retirement from 1909. An influential voice for military preparedness as editor of his own magazine, *L'Homme libre*, he declined VIVIANI's offer of the justice ministry in August 1914, and instead became the most belligerent critic of successive wartime governments. Through his Senate position and his journal (renamed *L'Homme enchainé* in protest at censorship) he launched scathing attacks against the strategic dominance of JOFFRE's high command, bureaucratic inefficiency, and the spread of pacifist agitation.

By mid-1916 he was accusing interior minister MALVY of closet pacifism; a year later he led calls for suppression of internal unrest in the aftermath of the NIVELLE OFFENSIVE. By the time PAINLEVÉ's cabinet fell in mid-November, political polarization in FRANCE had made moderate coalition government impossible, and President POINCARÉ's appointment of Clemenceau as prime minister was a decision for 'war to the end'.

Playing the role of strong leader to the hilt (he enjoyed the nickname 'Tiger'), Clemenceau clamped down on dissent, suppressing pacifist literature, arresting senior 'defeatists' like Joseph CAILLAUX, and putting several prominent figures on trial for treason. Excluding potential rivals from his cabinet, he personally suppressed political divisions, and used a combination of wage rises and threats to halt strikes.

He was an equally powerful influence on military planning, working towards the appointment of FOCH as supreme Allied commander and insisting on attacks by exhausted French forces during late 1918. His unblinking aggression during the last year of war was a major factor in preserving French popular morale.

At the PARIS PEACE CONFERENCE, where he survived an assassination attempt, Clemenceau was unable to reconcile French demands for security with Allied ambitions. He clashed repeatedly with US president WILSON, and his failure to secure the German Rhineland by the VERSAILLES Treaty was criticized as leniency in France. Removed from office by a coalition of disgruntled wartime opponents in January 1920, he retired later that year after losing the presidential election.

Coastal Artillery The development of iron BATTLESHIPS in the mid-19th century prompted a worldwide upgrading of coastal defences. Concrete fortifications surrounding guns big enough to match the most powerful naval weapons had become standard by the 1890s, with the frontier FORTRESSES of continental

European powers serving as design models. By 1914 the world's strategically important harbours and coastlines were protected by heavy ARTILLERY backed by light weapons, MINES and a smattering of ANTI-SUBMARINE equipment, although fortifications were often very vulnerable from the inland side.

Protected by concrete and knocked out only by a direct hit, coastal guns were usually situated well above the trajectory for which most naval weapons were designed, a problem recognized by most naval professionals. Few coastal batteries saw action beyond replying to fleeting long-range bombardments, and the only major attack on coastal fortifications was the Allied DARDANELLES operation in 1915. Although the British in particular retained sufficient fear of invasion to keep coastal defences up to strength throughout, redundant weapons elsewhere were removed during wartime for emergency reinforcement of field artillery.

Coastal Class Airships Small but reliable non-rigid AIRSHIPS used by the RNAS to protect CONVOYS in the English Channel and Irish Sea during 1917–18. The final wartime development of the SEA SCOUT design, Coastal Class airships carried a purpose-designed gondola and could remain aloft for 24 hours, offering cheap and effective early-warning defence against SUBMARINES.

Commission for the Relief of Belgium (CRB) Most important of several international charities established as an expression of neutral sympathy for the plight of civilians following the German invasion of BELGIUM in 1914. Formed at the suggestion of US ambassador Page in London, the CRB was active in the UNITED STATES from September 1914. By December it controlled 35 ships delivering food and basic necessities worth an estimated $5 million per month to Belgium from the USA, CANADA and Argentina. Renamed the Comité Hispano-Néerlandais after the USA became a belligerent in 1917, the organization received full cooperation from German occupying authorities anxious to demonstrate benevolence, and relief vessels were never targets for SUBMARINE WARFARE. International wartime aid to Belgium eventually ran at more than 80,000 tons of goods per month, but was unable to prevent widespread famine after the cold winter of 1916–17.

Compiègne, Forest of See: ARMISTICE.

Conrad von Hötzendorf, Field Marshal Franz, Count (1852–1925) Chief of staff to the AUSTRO-HUNGARIAN ARMY from 1906, and a close associate of Archduke FRANZ FERDINAND, Conrad was the epitome of prewar militarism. His demands for surprise attacks on SERBIA and ITALY were initially restrained by the Imperial Crown Council, and plans for large-scale expansion of the Army's manpower base were blocked by Hungarian objections, but he was able to modernize its antiquated ARTILLERY arm.

A call for an attack on Italy during the Italo-Turkish War of 1911 led to his dismissal, but he was recalled in December 1912 and found new foreign minister BERCHTOLD willing to accept the challenge of war against Serbia in July 1914.

Diplomatic delays during the JULY CRISIS left Conrad's relatively small army facing war on both the BALKAN and EASTERN FRONTS in August. Although he had persuaded his German counterpart, MOLTKE, to station the German Eighth Army in EAST PRUSSIA, his own plans to deal a fatal blow to Serbia before facing RUSSIA required stronger support.

Forced to gamble on slow Russian mobilization, he committed the 12 divisions of his reserve ('B Staffel') to the Balkans, but redirected them to GALICIA when the speed of RUSSIAN ARMY preparations became apparent. The result was logistic chaos, with the troops spending weeks stranded in the RAILWAY system and making little contribution to either campaign.

Conrad's subsequent direct conduct of ground operations was characterized by optimism, imagination and boldness, seldom qualified by military realities. He shared LUDENDORFF's belief that Russia could be defeated by a single great attack, but after claiming credit for the successful GORLICE-

TARNOW OFFENSIVE in May 1915, and losing 300,000 men in the ambitious 'BLACK-YELLOW' OFFENSIVE, his attention switched to the Balkans.

Conrad helped convince FALKENHAYN to sanction the CENTRAL POWERS' invasion of Serbia in October, but his control over the operation itself was nominal, with field commander MACKENSEN taking orders directly from Berlin. Unable to elicit German aid for action on the ITALIAN FRONT the following spring, he launched an offensive of his own against Italian positions in the TRENTINO, abandoned in June after the Russian BRUSILOV OFFENSIVE had broken Austro-Hungarian defences in Galicia.

Hitherto protected by the crown's unwavering support, and promoted field marshal in early 1916, Conrad was attacked in Crown Council for the first time in late June, and his position weakened rapidly after the German THIRD SUPREME COMMAND assumed formal control over all CENTRAL POWERS fronts in Europe in September. Unable to deliver the crushing victory he was still planning, and unwilling to concede greater direct control over the Army to the new Emperor KARL, Conrad was dismissed on 1 March 1917.

He accepted command of the Army Group in the Trentino, playing a subsidiary role during the autumn CAPORETTO OFFENSIVE but lobbying for a further attack to exploit the victory in 1918. He led one wing of the disastrous PIAVE Offensive in May before his final dismissal from senior command on 15 July. After briefly commanding the Imperial Guard, he retired in December.

Conscientious Objectors See: PACIFISM.

Constantine I, King (1868–1923) Ruler of GREECE since his father's assassination in 1913, Constantine was educated in GERMANY, served for a time in the Prussian Army, and was married to Kaiser WILHELM II's sister. From August 1914 he faced a conflict between his German sympathies and the threat implied by Allied naval domination of the MEDITERRANEAN, complicated by his desire to avoid a direct rift with the pro-Allied VENIZELOS government.

Allied interest in the DARDANELLES triggered a rapid breakdown of relations with the cabinet from early 1915, and Constantine established a virtual autocracy behind a succession of puppet premiers after Venizelos was dismissed for the second time in October 1915. As civil war threatened, his vain efforts to secure substantial German guarantees of naval, military and economic aid during 1916 eventually made him a liability to Greek relations with the Allies, who finally demanded his abdication on pain of invasion (see SALAMIS OPERATION; ATHENS LANDINGS).

Constantine relinquished his crown in June 1917 and went into exile in Switzerland, where he sought unsuccessfully to disrupt the subsequent Greek war effort under Venizelos. After the death of Alexander, his son and successor, Constantine returned briefly to the throne in late 1920, but was again forced to abdicate in 1922. See also: METAXAS, J.

Conte di Cavour Class The ITALIAN NAVY's most modern BATTLESHIPS in 1915, the three Conte di Cavour Class vessels were slightly larger and better-armed than Italy's only other dreadnought, *Dante Alighieri*. The first pair, *Leonardo da Vinci* and *Guilio Cesare*, were completed in 1914, and *Conti di Cavour* entered service in April 1915. The only other Italian battleships completed in wartime were two very similar Andrea Doria Class vessels, which should have been ready by 1914 but eventually entered service in May 1915 (*Andrea Doria*) and May 1916 (*Caio Duilio*). Four 'super-dreadnoughts' with 15-inch guns, planned in 1914, were cancelled in 1918.

Italy's dreadnoughts generally adhered to its shipbuilding tradition, sacrificing armour protection for increased speed. They were deployed with great caution in the MEDITERRANEAN theatre, and all but *Leonardo da Vinci* (sunk at Taranto in 1916) and *Dante Alighieri* (scrapped in 1929) survived to fight in the Second World War.

BRIEF DATA (*Conti di Cavour*, 1915) Displacement: 24,500 tons; Crew: 957; Dimensions: length 558ft (169m), beam 92ft (27.8m); Speed: 22k; Main armament: 13 × 12in gun, 18 × 4.7in, 12 × 14pdr, 3 × 18in TT.

Convoys Gathering together merchant and transport shipping in convoys for close protection by naval forces had been practised for centuries but was only occasionally employed from 1914, mostly for Allied troop transports and other particularly precious cargoes. Extension of the GERMAN NAVY's campaign against Allied commerce (*Handelskrieg*) to include SUBMARINE attacks opened the question of the more general employment of convoys as an ANTI-SUBMARINE tactic. The decision rested with the ROYAL NAVY, which possessed the vast majority of Allied anti-submarine weaponry and was responsible for the bulk of world trade protection, but the British Admiralty found convincing reasons for rejecting convoys.

The large number of ships needed to escort merchant ships, perhaps one warship for every three cargo vessels, were simply not available, with Allied naval commanders in every theatre (especially the MEDITERRANEAN) crying out for DESTROYERS and smaller craft. Merchant crews were (wrongly) considered incapable of the concerted manoeuvres necessary to keep formation. The need for a convoy to travel at the speed of its slowest ship turned faster vessels into potential sitting targets and might dangerously reduce the pace of economic supply.

Underpinning all arguments against convoys was the belief, orthodox among British naval leaders, that the best way to defeat submarines was by offensive patrols or costly blockage of the narrow channels at DOVER and OTRANTO. Allied anti-submarine resources were dissipated in fruitless pursuit and barrage operations until early 1917, by which time their failure to noticeably hamper U-BOAT operations was viewed as potentially fatal in GREAT BRITAIN.

Pressure from younger British naval officers, and the new Ministry of Shipping established by the LLOYD GEORGE government in late 1916, brought experiment from February 1917, when the first 'controlled sailings' convoyed colliers to FRANCE. Only 9 of more than 4,000 ships using the system had been sunk by the end of May, at the height of sinkings elsewhere, and a reluctant Admiralty was virtually compelled to attempt convoys on longer routes.

The first long-range inbound convoys reached Britain in May (16 ships from Gibraltar and 12 from the UNITED STATES), and their success brought rapid expansion of the system for the main routes to Britain. Convoys were established for most inbound and outbound sailings by August, and overall Allied merchant shipping losses, running at 25 per cent of all sailings in April 1917, had fallen to 1 per cent by the end of the year. Applied more slowly and less consistently in the Mediterranean, where losses to U-boats remained high into 1918, the convoy system (combined with a big increase in merchant and anti-submarine shipbuilding) was a vital factor in limiting the effects of *Handelskrieg* to survivable levels.

Corfu Declaration Agreement announced on 27 July 1917 between exiled representatives of SERBIA, Croatia, Slovenia and MONTENEGRO that established the principle of unified Yugoslav statehood, rendered feasible by the potential wartime collapse of Austro-Hungarian influence. Negotiated with full Anglo-French support between Serbian prime minister PAŠIĆ and Croatian exile Ante TRUMBIĆ, the declaration confirmed mutual determination to create YUGOSLAVIA. Equal civil rights for all its ethnic groups were guaranteed, but the Serbian government made no clear statement on the subject of federalism, merely agreeing that all four regions would enjoy some autonomy in a constitutional monarchy ruled by Serbian King PETER.

Coronel, Battle of Naval action off the coast of central Chile on 1 November 1914 between the ROYAL NAVY's South American squadron under Admiral Cradock and Admiral SPEE's Pacific commerce-raiding force, the GERMAN NAVY's East Asiatic Squadron.

The search for Spee's two armoured and three light cruisers dominated Allied naval activity in the Pacific from August 1914, involving about 30 warships (plus units of the JAPANESE NAVY). Dependent on luck or interception of RADIO signals, it was hampered by routine Allied destruction of German wireless stations in the theatre, but a signal intercepted on 4 October 1914 revealed Spee's intention of harassing vital trade routes along the west coast of South America.

Cradock's squadron, patrolling the South American seaboards from its base in the Falkland Islands, consisted of the old armoured CRUISERS *Good Hope* and *Monmouth*, the modern light cruiser *Glasgow*, and the armed ex-liner *Otranto*, suitable only for action against similar vessels. Any hope of sinking Spee's bigger ships depended on the arrival of reinforcements, but the Admiralty sent only the armoured cruiser *Defence* and the old battleship *CANOPUS*.

Spee commanded the armoured cruisers *SCHARNHORST* and *GNEISENAU*, accompanied by the light cruiser *Nürnberg*, and was joined at Easter Island by two more light cruisers. Informed by shore agents that *Glasgow* was in the vicinity, all five German warships left Easter Island on 18 October in the hope of picking it off in isolation.

None of Cradock's reinforcements had reached him, and he chose not to wait, sailing from the Falklands towards a planned rendezvous with the *Glasgow* at the small Chilean port of Coronel. Navy minister CHURCHILL ordered him to halt on the evening of 28 October, citing the (remote) possibility of help from JAPANESE NAVY units in the Pacific, but Cradock may not have received Churchill's imprecise signal. Within minutes of its receipt by *Glasgow* he ordered his formation to attack, an apparently suicidal step encouraged by the high priority attached to disabling the commerce raiders.

News that *Leipzig*, Spee's slowest cruiser, was in the area reached Cradock on 1 November. Steaming north to cut it off, he ran into the entire German force coming the other way at 16.30. Spee kept his faster ships out of range until sunset at 19.00, when a rising moon silhouetted the British squadron, and then took advantage of his superior range to reduce *Good Hope* (Cradock's flagship) and *Monmouth* to blazing wrecks within minutes. Both sank with no survivors. *Glasgow* suffered five hits but was able to escape, and *Otranto* fled, as ordered, at the first shots. Completely undamaged, the German squadron retired north to the friendly port of Valparaiso.

First news of the defeat (from Valparaiso) was greeted with disbelief by the British Admiralty, but once Cradock's fate became clear a massive naval force, including two modern BATTLECRUISERS, was assembled and sent south to annihilate Spee's cruisers at the FALKLAND ISLANDS. See MAP 15.

Corpo Aeronautico Militare See: ITALIAN AIR FORCE.

Cossacks Large communities of warrior peasants who lived in the south and southwest of imperial RUSSIA. Traditionally free from serfdom in return for military service, they were still obliged to serve as CAVALRY in time of war. An estimated 1 million Cossacks mobilized with the RUSSIAN ARMY from August 1914, almost half from the largest group, the Don Cossacks. Excellent horsemen, known for fierceness rather than discipline, they were required to provide all their own equipment except for a RIFLE, which was issued on mobilization with half the cost charged to the Cossack community. Like other cavalry forces on the main European fronts, they were generally deployed as mounted infantry after 1914.

Costa Rica Small Central American republic, with a contemporary population of some 400,000 and the region's most tranquil political history. Costa Rica enjoyed a balanced economic relationship with the UNITED STATES and western Europe based on export of bananas and coffee, but inconclusive general elections in 1914 ushered in a period of unrest. President Alfredo Gonzales was deposed in 1917 by Frederico Tinoco, whose efforts to secure recognition from the USA led Costa Rica to break diplomatic relations with GERMANY in September and to declare war on 23 May 1918. With a standing army of 600 troops and a navy of two small gunboats, the country had no discernible military impact, and Tinoco remained under severe pressure from popular uprisings until his deposition in 1919.

Courbet Name ship of a class of four BATTLESHIPS ordered as the FRENCH NAVY's first dreadnoughts in 1910. Only *Courbet* and *Jean Bart* were in service by August 1914, the former as MEDITERRANEAN flagship, but *France* and *Paris* joined the fleet within a few weeks. Complete with modern DIRECTOR CONTROL equipment and much more heavily armed than previous French warships, they functioned as a deterrent to sorties by the Austro-Hungarian battlefleet, but were deployed with extreme caution after *Jean Bart* was damaged by an Austro-Hungarian SUBMARINE during a sweep of the Adriatic on 21 December 1914. Well-designed hull compartmentalization enabled it to survive comfortably, and the class otherwise escaped serious damage. Both *Jean Bart* and *France* formed part of a French naval force sent to aid anti-Bolshevik forces in the Crimea during the RUSSIAN CIVIL WAR.

BRIEF DATA (*Courbet*, 1914) Displacement: 23,200 tons; Crew: 922; Dimensions: length 544.5ft (165m), beam 89ft (27m); Speed: 21k; Armament: 12 × 12in (305mm) gun, 22 × 139mm, 4 × 47mm, 4 × 450mm TT.

Courtrai Offensive Successful advance in October 1918 on the northern sector of the WESTERN FRONT by King ALBERT's Allied Flanders Group of Armies against Crown Prince RUPPRECHT's German Army Group North. The northern sector had remained static while Allied offensives against the HINDENBURG LINE and in the MEUSE-ARGONNE area forced German armies elsewhere into retreat, but Albert's Group (the BELGIAN ARMY, plus the British Second and French Sixth Armies) was ready to attack by early October.

After delays caused by heavy rain Albert's Group began a steady advance along an 80km front from the coast to positions level with Lille on 14 October (see MAP 2), and was joined next day by the British Fifth Army, the northern wing of British C-in-C HAIG's adjoining Group. German forces retreated, and Allied advance was slowed as much by exhaustion as by defensive actions.

Confronted by skilled, if minor, rearguard actions, Allied supply and communications lines faced enormous strain. Food, equipment and ammunition (including several thousand tons of ARTILLERY shells per day) had to be hauled from the French Channel ports through the rain and mud across shattered battlescapes without the benefits of a recognizable road system or reliable motor vehicles.

The inability of CAVALRY to face rearguards armed with MACHINE GUNS, or of TANKS to cover ground quickly, made genuine pursuit impossible, but Rupprecht's unequivocal commitment to retreat rendered these problems academic. Army Group North was desperately short of ammunition, food, weapons, horses, artillery, officers, morale and manpower, so that field divisions often mustered only a few hundred exhausted men. Lille was abandoned without a fight, and taken intact by British Fifth Army units on 17 October, and the British Second Army took the industrial Turcoing-Roubaix area on the same day. The Belgian Army reached Ostend, finding the harbour repairable and so revolutionizing the supply situation.

On 19 October, Allied forces entered Bruges, Courtrai and Zeebrugge, and German activity, including SUBMARINE bases, was cleared from the coast of BELGIUM. With the Belgian Army resting against the northwestern Dutch border, exhaustion and further heavy rain forced a pause from 20 October, and subsequent Allied attacks were concentrated further south.

Creel, George (1876–1953) A single-minded advocate of social reform in the UNITED STATES and a leading prewar 'muckraker' journalist, specializing in exposés of corporate corruption and political machination. A vociferous supporter of Woodrow WILSON in the 1912 and 1916 elections, he was selected to head the wartime Committee on Public Information (CPI) in 1917, transforming it from a simple government news agency into a full-scale PROPAGANDA machine. Under Creel's confident control the CPI quickly expanded to include a Pictorial Publicity Division, employing celebrated American painters, sculptors and cartoonists, a Motion Picture Division, and 75,000 FOUR-MINUTE MEN. Prone to impulsive outbursts, Creel made frequent caustic attacks on political critics, especially Senate Foreign Affairs Committee chairman LODGE, contributing to their bitter opposition to Wilson during disputes over the VERSAILLES Treaty. Creel's weekly dispatches to Europe (through the Foreign Mail Press Bureau) helped popularize Wilson's FOURTEEN POINTS, and he was generally credited with fostering the popular adulation evident during the president's two visits to Europe after the ARMISTICE. See also: GOMPERS, S.

Creeping Barrage A refinement of massed PRELIMINARY BOMBARDMENT techniques that dominated ARTILLERY support for offensive operations in Europe. Normal practice had required an immediate switch of artillery fire to secondary objectives once an infantry attack began. Beginning in August 1916, during the Battle of the SOMME, British fire moved forward in stages just ahead of advancing infantry. Requiring precise planning and timing by both arms, a system of barrage advancing 50 metres per minute had been perfected by early autumn.

Artillery on both sides of the main trench lines subsequently adopted the creeping barrage as standard practice. Although it greatly assisted infantry in taking limited objectives, it was not in itself decisive, and the basic drawbacks of BREAKTHROUGH TACTICS were not overcome until sophisticated artillery support was combined with maximum use of TANKS, aircraft and other mechanized weapons in 1918. See also: PEACEFUL PENETRATION; INFILTRATION TACTICS; NIVELLE OFFENSIVE.

Cressy The six Cressy Class armoured CRUISERS were the oldest ships of their type active with frontline ROYAL NAVY forces in August 1914. Five were initially employed on patrols off the Dutch coast, crewed by reserves retained from the summer's fleet manoeuvres. They were generally regarded as extremely vulnerable, and the Dutch patrol was known as the 'live-bait squadron'. They were about to be withdrawn when the SUBMARINE *U-9* took advantage of a lull in storms too severe for screening DESTROYERS to sink *Cressy*, *Aboukir* and *Hogue* with TORPEDOES on 22 September. The disaster killed about 1,400 sailors, revealing the inadequacy of British ANTI-SUBMARINE techniques, and contributing to fear of submarine attacks on ill-protected GRAND FLEET harbours.

BRIEF DATA (*Cressy*, 1914) Displacement: 12,000 tons; Crew: 760; Dimensions: length 472ft (143m), beam 69.5ft (21.1m); Speed: 21k; Armament: 2 × 9.2in gun, 12 × 6in, 13 × 12pdr, 2 × 18in TT.

Cruisers Originally a British concept, cruisers as a type date from the 1880s. Fast ships, smaller than BATTLESHIPS but capable of ocean-going operations, their original roles were twofold: heavy 'armoured' cruisers, generally displacing over 10,000 tons, carrying powerful main armament and given strong side armour, were intended to operate as the fast scouting force alongside battleships in confrontations with other fleets; 'protected' cruisers, displacing anything from 2,000 to 14,000 tons, had deck armour but no side protection, and guarded trade routes, troopships and outposts.

The ROYAL NAVY built 42 armoured and 101 protected cruisers between 1885 and 1907; other navies built substantially fewer. However, the advent of BATTLECRUISERS rendered armoured cruisers obsolete, and subsequent development was largely concerned with fleet protection. Britain built 15 SCOUT CRUISERS for this purpose before 1913, and 21 larger TOWN Class ships for long-range operations (1909–15).

Wartime design concentrated on much faster light cruisers intended for scouting and screening operations. They were built in large numbers by the British and German fleets, playing a prominent role in all major North Sea actions, and the few operating with the MEDITERRANEAN navies were the most useful large surface warships in the theatre.

Older cruisers were kept very busy, especially in British service, acting as protection against German surface raiders in 1914 (along with passenger liners converted as ARMED MERCHANT CRUISERS) and forming the Royal Navy's main strike force in subsidiary theatres, often with doubtful support from old PRE-DREADNOUGHTS. Old British cruisers were later used as long-range CONVOY escorts, and six were expended as part of the ZEEBRUGGE RAID in 1918. Other navies used their old armoured and protected types in a similarly all-purpose role. See also: *ARETHUSA; ASKOLD; BLÜCHER; CHÂTEAURENAULT; CRESSY; EMDEN; FRAUENLOB; HIGHFLYER; LEIPZIG; LEON GAMBETTA; MEDSHIDIYE; NOVARA; SCHARNHORST.*

Ctesiphon, Battle of Major Anglo-Indian setback on the MESOPOTAMIAN FRONT, and a turning point in the campaign. A small settlement in 1915, its more prosperous past represented by a lone 25-metre arch beside the Tigris, Ctesiphon was the main Turkish position for forward defence of BAGHDAD (see MAP 23). By November 1915 two lines of well-constructed TRENCHES either side of the river were defended by some 18,000 troops (veterans of earlier battles plus reinforcements from Baghdad) commanded by Colonel Nur-Ud-Din.

After occupying Kut in October, 6th Indian Division commander TOWNSHEND wanted to consolidate along extended supply lines from BASRA, but C-in-C NIXON ordered a further advance on Baghdad. Initial British cabinet opposition, softened by the Indian government's manifest confidence, was withdrawn on 24 October and two Indian divisions from the WESTERN FRONT were promised as garrison troops for Baghdad. Instructed to call off the attack if it met serious resistance, Nixon turned down Townshend's requests for extra transport and TRENCH WARFARE weapons.

Some 11,000 troops, supported by a newly arrived MONITOR (*Firefly*) and a shallow-draft gunboat, began operations against the Ctesiphon position on 22 November. Too weak to attack on both sides of the river, Townshend repeated his partially successful tactics at ES SINN, night-marching a force into position for a surprise flank attack on the east bank.

Surprise was lost as marching columns got lost in the dark, and the attack broke down at the second line of Turkish trenches (stretching some 10km from the river at the arch) in the late afternoon. Close naval support was prevented by Turkish ARTILLERY on the banks and MINES all along the river.

Two Turkish attacks next day failed to dislodge Anglo-Indian infantry from first-line positions, but Townshend's active strength was down to less than 4,500 when Nur-Ud-Din, whose own exhausted troops had suffered about 9,600 casualties, ordered a general withdrawal that night. Once rumours of approaching British reserves had been dismissed the retreat was reversed and Townshend, informed of the change by his one MARTINSYDE S-1 aircraft, ordered a withdrawal of his own on 25 November.

Pursued by Turkish forces and harassed by hostile MARSH ARABS, the retreat was preceded by improvised hospital craft crammed with wounded, many of whom died in insanitary conditions during the 13-day journey to Basra. The 6th Division lost its warships to Turkish shore batteries in the process of escaping advanced Turkish units during the night of 27–28 November, but reached Kut on 3 December. Townshend chose to make a stand and began fortifying the town pending reinforcement from Basra. The unexpected resilience of the Turkish defence shocked British and Indian authorities into a rapid build-up of strength in Mesopotamia to assist Townshend's relief (see First Battle of KUT).

Cuba The largest Caribbean island, a Spanish possession until US military intervention secured its independence in 1902. Chronic unrest and revolutionary instability led to a three-year resumption of US control from 1906 and a further intervention in 1912. Cuba benefited economically from a wartime boom in exports of sugar (its sole major product) to Allied states previously supplied from the CENTRAL POWERS, but remained an effective protectorate of the UNITED STATES, receiving regular loans and military support for the recognized government. Further US landings on the island in early 1917 established President Menocal in sufficient security to enable a declaration of war on GERMANY on 7 April 1917, but concentration of the army (about 10,000 strong) on internal policing prevented any overseas military commitment beyond ANTI-SUBMARINE patrols by the navy's single CRUISER and seven small gunboats.

Curtiss H-4 Early biplane flying boat (with a genuine hull as distinct from floats attached to a conventional fuselage), developed from a 1912 design by pioneering US builder Glenn Curtiss. Used in small numbers by the neutral US NAVY, and in limited service with the British RNAS from November 1914, it was intended for coastal patrol and reconnaissance, but lacked power and was never entirely seaworthy. Known as 'Small America' after the larger CURTISS H-12 entered service, the H-4 provided a valuable blueprint for Allied development of wartime flying boats. See also: Battle of the RUFUGI DELTA.

BRIEF DATA (GB model) Type: reconnaissance flying boat; Crew: 4; Engine: 2 × 100hp Anzani; Max speed: 80mph (128kph); Armament: 2 × 0.303in mg.

Curtiss H-12 Heavily armed enlargement of the CURTISS H-4 flying boat. Also known as 'Large America', it served successfully as an RNAS and US NAVY maritime patrol craft from spring 1917. It initially suffered from the lack of performance associated with its predecessor, but 375hp engines were successfully fitted to later models, some of which also featured a redesigned, more genuinely seaworthy hull. Based in England at the Yarmouth and Felixstowe seaplane stations, RNAS H-12s were used on systematic 'SPIDER'S WEB' patrols over the North Sea, holding their own against German naval aircraft, destroying three U-BOATS and downing two ZEPPELINS.

BRIEF DATA Type: patrol flying boat; Crew: 4; Engine: 2 × 275hp Rolls Royce; Max speed: 85mph (136kph); Armament: 2–4 × 0.303in mg, max bomb load 450lbs (205kg).

Curtiss H-16 US-designed biplane flying boat, an enlarged, big-winged version of the CURTISS H-12, incorporating the advanced hull design of British FELIXSTOWE boats. Far superior to its predecessor, the H-16 entered service in the summer of 1918 and flew maritime patrols from the British coast for both the RNAS and the US NAVY, which used about 20 and 50, respectively.

BRIEF DATA (US Navy) Type: patrol flying boat; Crew: 4; Engine: 2 × 330hp Liberty; Max speed: 98mph (157kph); Armament: 6 × 0.303in mg, max bomb load 900lbs (410kg).

Curtiss JN 'Jenny' The most successful US-designed aircraft of the period, never combat-worthy but a valuable trainer. The RFC purchased a few JN-3 models in 1915–16, and they were used by the peacetime USAAS, along with a JN-4A version given ailerons and a new tailfin design. Mass production got underway with the JN-4D following the US declaration of war in 1917, and more than 5,500 'Jennies' were completed before the type was declared obsolete at the ARMISTICE. A JN-4H advanced trainer version and an N-9 naval floatplane trainer both remained in US service until 1927.

BRIEF DATA Type: trainer; Engine: 90hp Curtiss OX-5; Max speed: 70mph (112kph); Ceiling: 3,000m; Armament: none.

Cuxhaven Raid The world's first naval air raid, carried out by RNAS seaplanes launched from the converted cross-Channel steamers *ENGADINE*, *Empress* and *Riviera* on Christmas Day 1914. Its target, far beyond the range of land-based aircraft, was a ZEPPELIN base at Nordholtz, on the German North Sea coast south of Cuxhaven, but its underlying purpose was to provoke warships from nearby Wilhelmshaven into a naval action (See MAP 16).

The makeshift AIRCRAFT CARRIERS left Harwich on the evening of 24 December, escorted by two light CRUISERS and 10 DESTROYERS. Ten SUBMARINES had already taken up position to ambush German warships and rescue ditched aircrew. Seven aircraft, a variety of early SHORT seaplanes, managed to take off from the sea some 70km off Cuxhaven at 07.00, but none could find Nordholtz in a gathering coastal mist and they eventually dropped small bomb loads on Wilhelmshaven. Although a cruiser, a submarine and a seaplane base were attacked, no serious damage was confirmed and all the aircraft suffered hits from ground fire. Two returned to the British fleet, and the only aircrew not rescued were picked up by a

Dutch trawler and interned.

Technically a failure, the attack demonstrated the potential of naval air raids and provided valuable reconnaissance for the ROYAL NAVY. The German HIGH SEAS FLEET was not tempted into action, but the raid caused sufficient alarm to provoke rapid strengthening of coastal ANTI-AIRCRAFT defences, and the German battlecruiser *VON DER TANN* collided with a cruiser while quitting its anchorage to avoid the bombing. Reaction to the Raid may also have prompted WILHELM II's authorization of Zeppelin attacks on English targets from mid-January.

Czech Forces The vast majority of combatant Czechs fought for the AUSTRO-HUNGARIAN ARMY, but many did so with notorious reluctance, and four distinct Czech forces served with the Allies after 1914. Before formation of the practically independent 'CZECH LEGION' in Russia during late 1917, a Czech unit had fought with the RUSSIAN ARMY on the EASTERN FRONT since 1914, expanding steadily to become a regiment from December 1915 and a brigade during 1917. After the ROME CONGRESS of April 1918, a Czech Division was formed in the ITALIAN ARMY from prisoner-of-war labour units, and it took part in operations on the ITALIAN FRONT as the 'Czech Corps'. A small 'Czech Legion', recruited from exiles living in Allied countries, also fought with the FRENCH ARMY on the WESTERN FRONT in 1918. Except in details of insignia, all Czech forces used the uniforms and equipment of their host armies, but were recognized as parts of the same independent national army in 1918. See CZECHOSLOVAKIA.

'Czech Legion' Of the three 'Czech Legions' formed to fight against the CENTRAL POWERS, that created on the EASTERN FRONT in late 1917 was by far the best known to contemporaries and was influential in persuading Allied governments to recognize the national status of CZECH FORCES.

After the OCTOBER REVOLUTION in Russia, exiled nationalist MASARYK negotiated with the Bolshevik government to establish a Czech Corps, comprised largely of prisoners of war. Nominally under French command, and expanding as it attracted Czechs from other units on both sides, it served on the virtually inactive Eastern Front until the formal end of hostilities in March 1918. Considered as a possible Allied task force to protect supplies in the ARCTIC THEATRE, it was instead ordered from Paris to march to Vladivostok for evacuation.

En route through Siberia during May, mutual suspicion between the Legion (by now almost 100,000 strong) and Bolshevik forces erupted into fighting. Czech forces, led by General Diterichs, attacked RED ARMY units in the belief that they were co-operating with armed German renegades, and by June the Czechs had fought their way through to Vladivostok, where a small Japanese force (accompanied by a few British, French and US troops) had landed to protect Allied interests and cover their retreat (see GRAVES, W.). Having already seized part of the Trans-Siberian RAILWAY, the Legion cooperated with Admiral KOLCHAK's 'White' rebels based at Omsk during 1919 before completing its evacuation in spring 1920 (see RUSSIAN CIVIL WAR).

Czechoslovakia The modern central European states of the Czech Republic and Slovakia, joined as a single country between 1919 and 1993, formed part of AUSTRIA-HUNGARY in 1914; the former was within Austria, the latter in Hungary. Concentrated in the provinces of Bohemia and Moravia, some 6.5 million Czechs were among the most literate and urbanized peoples of eastern Europe, and they played an active role in imperial government and administration. In contrast, the 2 million Slovaks in Hungary, though ethnically self-aware, were largely excluded from the kingdom's political processes. About 3.5 million linguistically distinct Ruthenes in Austria, with another half a million in Hungary, were among the least developed rural elements of imperial society.

Czech nationalism was an established prewar political force in Austria, represented in the Reichsrat by the radical Young Czech Party and the more moderate Realist Party. Its most important wartime leaders, Thomáš

MASARYK and Eduard BENEŠ, were prominent figures in a vociferous campaign for full independence.

Like other ethnic groups within the Empire, Czechs faced mass conscription into the AUSTRO-HUNGARIAN ARMY from July 1914, and their loyalty was always considered doubtful by a predominantly German officer corps. Many Czechs shared the general early popular enthusiasm for the War, and officers often exaggerated their subsequent disaffection as a means of explaining failure, but desertion, mass surrender and refusal to fight became more common as conditions worsened (see CZECH FORCES; KRAMAR, K.).

The political campaign for Czech independence inevitably sought Allied support and, with parliamentary activity in the Empire suspended, was mostly conducted by exiles. Hopes that Russian military victory would aid liberation waned during 1915, with RUSSIA publicly discussing moves to annex Slovakia, and Czech nationalists subsequently concentrated on winning support from western Allied leaders through the Czechoslovak National Council in Paris, formed under Beneš in 1915.

Allied governments were initially unwilling to promote partition of the Austro-Hungarian Empire, but French prime minister BRIAND declared for an independent postwar Czechoslovakia in February 1916, and the CZECH LEGION's status as the only Allied force on the EASTERN FRONT after Russia left the War boosted credibility from late 1917. Along with publication of the FOURTEEN POINTS and broad Allied acceptance that a separate peace with Vienna was impossible, the Legion's high profile encouraged Italian recognition of the Council as a government-in-exile at the ROME CONGRESS of April 1918. A declaration of support by US secretary of state LANSING in May was followed by official recognition of the Czech state and army from GREAT BRITAIN in August and the UNITED STATES in September.

With Austro-Hungarian imperial authority crumbling, the National Council resumed activities in Prague from July, and a provisional national government was constituted on 14 October. It declared full independence for Bohemia and Moravia on 18 October, and took over active government following recognition by Austria-Hungary on 27 October. A National Assembly, convened in Prague on 14 November, established a Czech republic with Masaryk as president and Beneš as foreign minister. The Slovak and Ruthene National Councils both voted for unification with the Czechs in 1919. The Treaties of ST GERMAIN, TRIANON and VERSAILLES completed the new state, which included a substantial German minority (in the Sudetenland and elsewhere) and a Magyar minority in southern Slovakia (see MAP 25).

Czernin von und zu Chudenitz, Ottokar, Count (1872–1932) Conservative aristocrat who was part of the influential circle surrounding Archduke FRANZ FERDINAND until his appointment as AUSTRIA-HUNGARY's ambassador to ROMANIA in 1913. He remained in the post until August 1916, and was appointed to succeed Count BURIAN as imperial foreign minister on 22 December. Though receptive to large-scale German military aid, and a supporter of unrestricted SUBMARINE WARFARE, Czernin fought doggedly to preserve imperial interests and accepted Emperor KARL I's policy of compromise peace. Revelation of the 'SIXTUS AFFAIR', which took place in March 1917 but was made public by French premier CLEMENCEAU more than a year later, rendered Czernin's position untenable and he resigned on 14 April 1918. His family estates lost to postwar CZECHOSLOVAKIA, he became an Austrian parliamentary deputy in 1920.

D

Dallolio, General Alfredo (1853–1952) Italian artillery officer and logistics expert who was appointed undersecretary of state for munitions in July 1915. As such he was personally responsible for the wartime economic mobilization of ITALY, and equipping an ITALIAN ARMY already suffering desperate shortages of weapons and ammunition. Using the government's emergency powers, he brought more than 2,000 factories under military control and countered shortage of skilled industrial workers by exemptions or recalls from military service. Production levels rose along with Dallolio's reputation, but his expedients could never match demands on an Italian economy dependent on imported fuel and industrial raw materials. Given full ministerial status in June 1917, the munitions department lost influence after the military defeat at CAPORETTO in the autumn, and he was pressured into resignation in May 1918 (see NITTI, F.). At the end of a long postwar career, he performed a similar role for the MUSSOLINI regime as commissioner for war production from 1935 to 1939.

Damascus, Fall of Penultimate major action on the PALESTINE FRONT, the British and Arab pursuit of General LIMAN VON SANDERS' retreating forces after their overwhelming defeat at MEGIDDO in September 1918. The extent of his victory triggered British C-in-C ALLENBY's follow-up plan for an immediate CAVALRY strike on Damascus, the focal point of any major Turkish retreat. On 26 September, having already taken 50,000 prisoners in a week, he ordered two cavalry divisions up the direct road north of the Sea of Galilee, about 150km. Another was sent to link up with ARAB REVOLT forces at DERA and to approach Damascus by the longer eastern route.

About 40,000 Turkish and German troops were scattered along the roads, but few were fit for combat and the Galilee echelon met only rearguards until 29 September, when AUSTRALIAN cavalry routed almost 5,000 troops dug in 15km southwest of Damascus. About 2,000 Turkish troops south of the town were dispersed later that day, and only the eastern exit from Damascus remained open by the evening of 30 September. Survivors of the Turkish Fourth Army from Dera, together with several thousand Turkish refugees, were harried by about 1,500 Arab tribesmen until combined Arab regular and British cavalry forces caught up on 1 October, when its last coherent formations were destroyed 20km short of Damascus.

Turkish evacuation of Damascus was already underway, but 11,000 troops waited in their barracks to be captured, reducing the entire Germano-Turkish combat force south of Aleppo to about 4,000 men. Early on 1 October British and Arab forces were welcomed into Damascus by the Turkish commandant, a long-standing Arab agent. In anticipation of its fall, Arab commander FEISAL had prepared a shadow Damascene administration, which took control under the Arab flag from 2 October after overcoming disputes with the local (hitherto pro-Turkish) Druze tribe. Allenby officially informed Feisal of the SYKES-PICOT AGREEMENT the following day. See also: ALEPPO; MAP 22.

Daniels, Josephus (1862–1948) As political head of the US NAVY from 1912, Daniels instituted widespread administrative reforms and, though a confirmed liberal pacifist, carried out President WILSON's limited naval expansion programme from August 1915. His preparations for possible war drew strongly on the advice of Admiral BENSON (who held the newly created post of Chief of Naval Operations), and entailed the steady build-up of US strength in the Atlantic.

Along with secretary for war BAKER, Daniels bore the brunt of conservative criticisms of the administration's wartime policies (see LODGE, H.), but although none of the BATTLESHIPS ordered in the 1915 programme were launched before 1919, his willingness to back mass production of DESTROYERS and other ANTI-SUBMARINE craft made an important contribution to the defeat of German commerce warfare (*HANDELSKRIEG*). A committed advocate of freedom of the seas (see FOURTEEN POINTS), Daniels opposed abandonment of the principle by the Treaty of VERSAILLES, and relations with Wilson were strained during their last year in office.

Danilov, General Yuri (1866–1937) One of Russian war minister SUKHOMLINOV's chief assistants in the prewar period, and the principal author of PLAN 19, Danilov sought unsuccessfully to concentrate Russian strength for an initial conquest of EAST PRUSSIA in the event of war. In August 1914 he was appointed deputy chief of staff at STAVKA (Russian central command) under his main prewar adversary, Grand Duke NIKOLAI. Though nominally third in command at Stavka, Danilov was by far its most active and influential figure, attempting to coordinate offensive operations on the EASTERN FRONT despite terrible communication and transport problems. Once mobilization had been completed he was a largely impotent spectator, with little control over the defeats of 1915, and was removed from office when Tsar NICHOLAS II took personal command of Stavka from September 1915. Returned to corps command on the northern sector of the Eastern Front, he rose to lead the Fifth Army for a time in 1917, but retired from military service in the autumn and emigrated to France in 1918.

Dankl von Krasnik, General Viktor, Count (1854–1941) One of the more successful Austro-Hungarian generals of the War, he commanded the First Army on the EASTERN FRONT during the opening campaigns in GALICIA, and was transferred to the ITALIAN FRONT in 1915, taking command of the Eleventh Army in March 1916 and leading it during the TRENTINO OFFENSIVE in May. Blamed by chief of staff CONRAD for its failure, Dankl resigned his command in June and retired to an honorific post, receiving his title (August 1917) in recognition of his early Galician victories.

D'Annunzio, Gabriele (1863–1938) Colourful Italian writer, poet, nationalist, political agitator and part-time combat officer. He went to France in 1910 to escape debt, but returned to ITALY in May 1915 to use his oratorical talents in support of gathering interventionist momentum. His impassioned rallies to arms, conducted with considerable flair for publicity, helped convince opponents that continued neutrality would escalate civil unrest. D'Annunzio maintained a very high wartime profile, gaining permission to serve at various times as a CAVALRY officer, on board a TORPEDO BOAT, and as an air observer. Much-decorated and wounded in one eye, he led popular complaints against concessions by the PARIS PEACE CONFERENCE of parts of the Adriatic coastline to YUGOSLAVIA, entering the disputed port of Fiume at the head of an irregular force in September 1919 and holding it until an ITALIAN NAVY force compelled his surrender in January 1921.

Danton Class Completed in 1911, the six Danton Class vessels were the most modern of 17 French PRE-DREADNOUGHTS active in 1914, and were regarded as the FRENCH NAVY's main strike force in the MEDITERRANEAN. They formed a squadron at the heart of the main battlefleet, taking part in operations in the southern Adriatic from late 1914 and covering the SALONIKA landings in autumn 1915. Most took part in the Aegean SALAMIS and ATHENS operations the following year. On 19 March 1917, en route to base at Corfu after a refit, *Danton* was sunk by a U-BOAT off Sardinia, the most valuable French warship lost during the War.

Four of the survivors joined three older Verité Class pre-dreadnoughts to form a new Aegean Sea Squadron in 1918, designed to prevent a breakout by the German MITTELMEERDIVISION from Constantinople. *Voltaire* was slightly damaged by a U-boat in October. Two ships, *Vergniaud* and *Mirabeau*, were also part of a French fleet dispatched to the Crimea in early 1919 to provide assistance for 'White' forces during the RUSSIAN CIVIL WAR. Both conducted offshore support operations around Sevastopol, where *Mirabeau* was grounded during a snowstorm in February. Eventually refloated, it was towed to Toulon and scrapped, but surviving Dantons remained in active service until the late 1920s.

BRIEF DATA (*Danton*, 1914) Displacement: 18,400 tons; Crew: 922; Dimensions: length 484ft (146.6m), beam 85ft (25.8m); Speed: 19k; Armament: 4 × 12in (305mm) gun, 12 × 240mm, 16 × 75mm, 10 × 47mm, 10 × 37mm, 2 × 450mm TT.

Dardanelles Operation The attempt by Anglo-French warships in February and March 1915 to force a passage through the Turkish-held Dardanelles Straits, the key link between the BLACK SEA ports of RUSSIA and the MEDITERRANEAN, and a direct route to the heart of Ottoman TURKEY. The purely naval attack was instigated and dominated by the British under the influence of navy minister CHURCHILL, who won limited support from his French counterpart, AUGAGNEUR. Both Allies believed that the naval attack could be called off as a 'demonstration' at any time, and both recognized that land forces might be needed to secure any gains. See GALLIPOLI FRONT.

The Straits are some 65km long and never more than 7km wide, with only about 1,600 metres separating the shores in the 'Narrows', about 15km from the Mediterranean mouth. Infested by difficult currents and small islands, they are overlooked by high cliffs on the Gallipoli Peninsula (the northwestern shore) and the coast of Asia Minor on the other side. Turkish defences in 1914 were based around outer fortresses on either shore at Kum Kale and Sedd el Bahr, linked by a run of shore batteries and minefields to the Narrows fortresses of Chanak and Kilid Bahr (see MAP 10).

A combined amphibious attack on the defences had been deemed feasible but difficult by a British study in 1907, but a purely naval attack was ruled out on technical grounds that remained valid in 1915. Low-trajectory naval ARTILLERY was rightly considered unsuitable for attacks on high coastal guns, and even if the forts could be destroyed or passed, a fleet without control of the shoreline would lack supplies or fuel and be forced to return.

A British naval squadron under Admiral Carden, on station off the Dardanelles since the arrival of the German MITTELMEERDIVISION at Constantinople in August 1914, was ordered by Churchill into a demonstration bombardment of the outer forts on 2 November. Lucky shooting caused considerable damage, confirming the fears of Turkish commanders and raising Carden's confidence.

In early January 1915 he was asked by Churchill to suggest the best way of forcing the Straits with ships alone. His cautious reply to the carefully phrased question was eloquently sold to the British cabinet by Churchill, a diehard 'EASTERNER', and transformed into an authorized plan of action by the end of the month.

Carden planned to proceed slowly towards the narrows in three stages. The outer forts would be demolished, long-range gunfire preceding a steady advance into medium artillery range. Shore batteries and minefields protecting the approaches to the Narrows would be systematically destroyed in the second phase, leaving the way free for a repeat demolition of the inner forts. The creeping inevitability of the operation was designed to cause maximum damage to Turkish morale as well as installations.

Initial naval enthusiasm or passivity quickly turned to opposition in London as FISHER and others realized that ground forces would not be available, but political faith remained strong and Churchill was able to commit a powerful fleet to the attack. Carden's forces for the opening bombardment on 19 February included the new battleship *QUEEN ELIZABETH*, 3 BATTLECRUISERS, 12 PRE-DREADNOUGHTS, 4 CRUISERS, 18 DESTROYERS, 6 SUBMARINES, 21 trawlers (with civilian crews) for minesweeping, and the seaplane carrier *ARK ROYAL*. The smaller FRENCH NAVY contingent under Admiral Guépratte was based around 4 more pre-dreadnoughts.

Turkish defences were undermanned,

poorly deployed and ill-equipped in October. In anticipation of an Allied attack, widespread improvements were begun by Turkish officers, and hastened by attached German commanders, but delayed by difficulties in sending German supplies across the neutral parts of the Balkans. Twenty-four mobile heavy howitzers were brought in to protect extended minefield defences, which were close to completion in February and in position by mid-March. Ammunition supplies remained critically low, but the lack-lustre pace of Allied decision-making gave defenders time to organize sophisticated siting and camouflage arrangements.

The opening Allied bombardment of 19 February, by heavy guns beyond the range of fortress defences, was not a success. Poor performance of aircraft and general mistrust of their findings exacerbated gunnery observation problems, and most Turkish guns remained undamaged. Bad weather delayed further attacks until 25 February, when warships moved closer to their targets and the outer forts were quickly silenced. The forts were occupied unopposed by a small party of naval troops, but the plan fell apart at the next stage.

Allied warships were unable to knock out well-disguised mobile batteries without moving in close, which called for removal of the minefields they protected. Howitzers and searchlights frustrated day and night attempts at sweeping, and although *Queen Elizabeth*'s big guns were used to great (but unrecognized) effect on 5 March, it was withdrawn beyond effective range on retaliation from a relocated shore battery. Impasse prompted renewed preparations for a land invasion, and some 18,000 French colonial troops sailed for the Dardanelles on 10 March. Two days later British war minister KITCHENER gave General HAMILTON command of 75,000 troops for Gallipoli.

Despite another minesweeping failure on 13 March, when trawlers were given naval crews for the first time, intelligence of Turkish ammunition shortages convinced Churchill that success was imminent, and he urged a dispirited Carden to attempt a rush at the Narrows before the arrival of substantial ground forces. Carden ordered the attack on 17 March, before collapsing from nervous exhaustion and leaving control to his deputy, Admiral DE ROBECK.

British battleships steamed into the Straits at about 11.30 on 18 March, followed by the French squadron. Their guns knocked out a few shore batteries and wrecked defensive communications, but German howitzers remained undamaged and took a heavy toll. British minesweepers were again rendered useless by plunging shellfire, and the main fleet was driven onto minefields, particularly a field of drifting MINES set on 8 March and previously undetected. The French battleships *Gaulois* and *BOUVET* were sunk by mines, and *Suffren* was effectively crippled by gunfire. The British *Ocean* sank after an internal explosion, and *Irresistible* was seriously damaged by mines, as was the battlecruiser *Inflexible*. By early evening no Allied ships had approached the Narrows and de Robeck withdrew.

Possibly influenced by chief of staff KEYES, who began converting destroyers into more effective minesweepers, de Robeck assured Churchill that the attack would be renewed, but on 22 March he informed Hamilton that the navy could do no more alone. Despite agitation from Keyes no further naval attacks on the Straits were undertaken and Churchill, his political position weakening and relations with Fisher deteriorating, admitted failure to the cabinet on 23 March.

German authorities in Turkey had been seriously worried by lack of ammunition at the Dardanelles since mid-March, but astonishment turned to elation as it became clear that the Allies were not planning a repeat attempt. German commander LIMAN VON SANDERS, who took direct control of land defences from 25 March, expected an amphibious invasion of Gallipoli to follow and was depending on a few days to organize and reinforce his stretched command. As de Robeck and Hamilton each waited to hear of the other's attack plan, Allied delays were compounded by severe administrative confusion, and Liman von Sanders was granted over a month to prepare his defence.

During and after the GALLIPOLI LANDINGS

of 25 April, naval operations at the Dardanelles consisted of transport, supply and artillery support for ground troops. The losses of 18 March were replaced, but de Robeck had full Admiralty backing for his refusal to risk the fleet again. A steady submarine offensive was maintained against Turkish shipping in the Sea of Marmora, but the considerable successes of British submarines (see *E-11*) were answered by a German submarine campaign against Allied supply and transport traffic from May. Intense Allied ANTI-SUBMARINE measures and repeated mutual mining of the Narrows had effectively restricted German U-boats to Black Sea operations by September, but they had already forced the Allies to abandon close coastal support and to keep major warships behind INDICATOR NETS at Lemnos.

The final Allied naval operation of the campaign was the successful evacuation of land forces from Gallipoli in January 1916, but an Allied blockade was maintained on the Mediterranean end of the Straits until late 1918, when the collapse of Turkey enabled a large Anglo-French fleet to steam ceremonially through the Narrows to Constantinople. Despite Allied hopes and requests, the wartime RUSSIAN NAVY never made a serious attempt to break through the Bosporus Channel into the Sea of Marmora, but Anglo-French battleships were sent through the Channel in the opposite direction in 1919 to assist anti-Bolshevik forces in the RUSSIAN CIVIL WAR. See MAPS 16, 20.

Dartige du Fournet, Admiral Louis-René-Marie (1856–1940) French naval officer with a reputation for diplomacy earned in command of international forces at Constantinople during the Balkan War of 1913. Base commander at Bizerte in August 1914, he was transferred to lead the FRENCH NAVY's Syrian coastal squadron before replacing Admiral Guépratte in command of the French contingent at the DARDANELLES in September 1915. On the resignation of Admiral BOUÉ DE LAPEYRÈRE in October, Dartige became French and Allied Mediterranean C-in-C. Like his predecessor, he was unable to impose real authority on other commands in the theatre, and inter-Allied relations were characterized by a permanent scramble for use of limited ANTI-SUBMARINE craft, but his diplomatic talents ensured generally harmonious relations with Allied admirals. His dismissal on 12 December 1916, provoked by the furore surrounding naval operations at ATHENS, was widely regarded as unjustified in naval circles. Replaced by the diplomatically challenged Admiral GAUCHET, Dartige was not given another command.

De Castlenau, General Noël (1851–1944) Aristocratic French soldier, chief of staff to FRENCH ARMY commander JOFFRE from 1911 until he took field command of the Second Army in August 1914. A leading protagonist of 'offensive' doctrine, and influential in the formulation of PLAN 17, he witnessed failure of both in the invasion of LORRAINE, but retained faith in attacking principles during the inconclusive battles that followed German failure at the MARNE (see First Battle of ALBERT) and as commander of the French Central Army Group in 1915. Late in 1915 he again became Joffre's chief of staff and supervised the defence of VERDUN the following year, arguing against withdrawal from the fortifications and supporting the appointment of PÉTAIN as local commander. Retired from active service when NIVELLE replaced Joffre in December 1916, he returned to the WESTERN FRONT in 1918 to lead the French Eastern Army group back into Lorraine.

Defence in Depth Term used to describe the most consistently effective method of TRENCH WARFARE defence. After giving ground during opening phases of an attack, defenders regrouped at prepared positions, rather than cramming forward positions against the initial advance of enemy infantry. Defence in depth exploited the major weakness of contemporary attacking forces – their lack of mobility. Once the infantry had advanced beyond its ARTILLERY cover, which needed to be painstakingly re-targeted or moved, defenders could launch prepared counterattacks using their own heavy weaponry.

First perfected by the GERMAN ARMY, defence in depth was used to great effect during Allied offensives on the WESTERN FRONT in 1916–17. By 1918 German defences in France were built around multiple lines of withdrawal, a sophistication that forced long delays and heavy casualties on Allied advances until the ARMISTICE. The BEF had broadly adopted defence in depth by late 1916, but many FRENCH ARMY commanders persisted in packing forward positions whenever an attack was expected, exposing troops to heavy casualties during PRELIMINARY BOMBARDMENTS and inviting organizational chaos if withdrawal proved necessary (see e.g. VERDUN; Third Battle of the AISNE).

Although defence in depth initially saved lives otherwise lost to long-range fire, the tactic ultimately increased casualties. Once both attackers and counterattackers were being drawn into empty space, the most intense infantry fighting often took place in those areas covered by artillery of both sides. See also: INFILTRATION TACTICS; PEACEFUL PENETRATION.

Defence of the Realm Act (DORA) New legislation granting emergency wartime powers to the British government, passed through the House of Commons in five minutes on 8 August 1914. Regularly supplemented and in force throughout the conflict, DORA gave the government executive powers to commandeer economic resources for the war effort, suppress published criticism, and imprison without trial. Although at first used sparingly in a spirit of 'business as usual', and never fully exploited, the Act was increasingly employed to control civilian behaviour after 1915, with decrees regulating food and ALCOHOL consumption backed by detailed prohibition of wasteful or potentially suspicious activities, including flying kites and loitering near RAILWAYS. See also: GREAT BRITAIN; AMIENS DISPATCH.

Defensively Armed Merchant Ships (DAMS) See: ANTI-SUBMARINE WEAPONS; ARMED MERCHANT CRUISERS.

Deflector Gear A simple precursor to operational INTERRUPTER GEAR, used by French pilot Roland GARROS on a MORANE-SAULNIER L monoplane in March 1915 and subsequently fitted as standard on the MORANE-SAULNIER N fighter. Steel plates were attached to the propeller blades to avoid damage from MACHINE GUN bullets fired directly forwards, rendering attack much more accurate. Although the French had developed an interrupter device by 1914, poor ammunition quality made deflector gear the safest option until late 1915.

De Havilland DH Series See: AIRCO DH Series.

De Langle de Cary, General Ferdinand (1849–1927) Veteran French officer who retired in 1914 but was recalled to lead the Fourth Army for the invasion of the ARDENNES in August. A committed advocate of the FRENCH ARMY's 'offensive' doctrine, he was forced to retreat until the Battle of the MARNE in September, when the Fourth Army played a holding role. Promoted to command of Army Group Centre in February 1915, his responsibilities included the fortified zone of VERDUN. He was blamed for serious flaws revealed in the defences when German attacks on the sector opened a year later, and was retired the following month.

Delcassé, Théophile (1857–1923) The main architect of prewar French diplomacy during a seven-year term as foreign minister (1898–1905), Delcassé tightened French control over North African colonies against German expansion and strengthened relations with GREAT BRITAIN. An active navy minister in 1911, and ambassador to RUSSIA from February 1913, he returned to France the following January and was recalled to the VIVIANI government as foreign minister in August 1914. Like that of his equally prestigious British counterpart, GREY, Delcassé's wartime reputation foundered on Allied failure to win friends in the Balkans. Firmly against large-scale commitment of French forces away from the WESTERN FRONT, he resigned on 12 October 1915 over the SALONIKA landings and remained out of office for the duration. His last major gesture before retirement was a vote against the VERSAILLES

Treaty in 1919, in protest at its failure to secure the French eastern frontier.

Depth Charge A waterproof bomb set to explode at a chosen depth, developed in Britain from experiments with delayed-action shells, and in use by Allied warships from 1915. Few were available at first, with ANTI-SUBMARINE vessels typically carrying just one or two for throwing over the side, and only 9 U-BOATS were destroyed by depth charges to the end of 1917. Plentiful supplies, and introduction of a projector that threw charges some 40 metres from a ship, improved effectiveness during 1918, when they accounted for 22 confirmed U-boat sinkings.

Dera Important RAILWAY junction on the PALESTINE FRONT. About 100km northeast of the front line of summer 1918, it was the Turkish Fourth Army's supply base at the start of the MEGIDDO battle in September. As a prelude to the main British offensive, 5,000 Northern Arab Army troops (with British technical support and officers, including LAWRENCE) swept far to the northeast of their forward base at TAFILA, skirting the Turkish force at Amman to cut rail links all round Dera by 17 September. Swollen by strong local support, they surrounded the town until 20 September when their attack was repelled by the garrison, aided by nine aircraft. Arab withdrawal to avoid air strikes allowed temporary repair of the railways, but no news of the siege reached frontline forces, which were ordered to fall back on Dera from 22 September.

Remnants of the Turkish Seventh Army, about 2,000 men, were slaughtered by Arab forces on approaching the town from the southwest. The Fourth Army in Amman, finally abandoning forces in MAAN, lost about half its remaining 4,000 troops to hostile local action en route and evacuated almost as soon as it arrived. The last of a few hundred escapees left Dera for DAMASCUS on 27 September, just before 4,000 Arab regulars, with thousands of local supporters and RAF reinforcement, occupied the town. When British troops arrived next day Dera was under the Arab flag, which remained in place despite argument from British General Barrow, a pattern repeated elsewhere during the latter stages of the ARAB REVOLT. See MAP 22.

Derby, Edward, Lord (1865–1948) British Conservative politician. Born Edward Stanley, scion of a notable Conservative dynasty, he succeeded as Lord Derby in 1908 and used the upper House of Lords to express his political opinions. An opponent of prewar social reforms, he argued against the introduction of conscription in 1915 and his appointment as Director of Recruitment in October was an attempt by the ASQUITH coalition to find an alternative. Using a national register established in July, the 'Derby Scheme' asked all eligible males for voluntary 'assent' to service if called upon, promising that married men would be called last. After vital war workers had been subtracted, the scheme provided less than 350,000 potential troops and was abandoned in December (see MILITARY SERVICE ACTS).

A confirmed 'WESTERNER', and on good terms with the BRITISH ARMY high command, Stanley succeeded new prime minister LLOYD GEORGE as war minister in December 1916. He was largely excluded from inner councils, and was restrained from resignation only by the military. His opposition to an inter-Allied command under the SUPREME WAR COUNCIL was overruled in early 1918, and he was unable to prevent ROBERTSON's dismissal in February. Replaced by MILNER in April, when crisis on the WESTERN FRONT demanded a more independent figure, he was British ambassador to France during the PARIS PEACE CONFERENCE.

Derfflinger Class Slightly enlarged versions of the earlier *SEYDLITZ*, with bigger main guns, *Derfflinger* and *Lützow* were the GERMAN NAVY's last active BATTLECRUISERS. Completed in July 1914, *Derfflinger* joined Admiral HIPPER's fast scouting group in the North Sea shortly afterwards, taking part in the SCARBOROUGH RAID and the DOGGER BANK action before suffering heavy damage at JUTLAND in 1916. Despite immediate British claims to the contrary, the ship remained afloat and returned safely to base, saved by the excellence of its heavily compartmentalized hull design. *Lützow* entered service in late 1915 and was the only important German warship sunk at Jutland, going down after receiving an estimated 24 heavy shell hits from British battlecruisers. A final Derfflinger Class vessel, *Hindenburg*, was completed in May 1917 but saw no action, and both survivors were scuttled at Scapa Flow in June 1919.

BRIEF DATA (1914) Displacement: 26,180 tons; Crew: 1,112; Dimensions: length 689ft (208.8m), beam 95.25ft (28.9m); Speed: 28k; Armament: 8 × 12in gun, 12 × 5.9in, 4 × 3.4in AA, 4 × 19.7in TT.

De Robeck, Admiral Sir John (1862–1928) Commander of a ROYAL NAVY cruiser squadron in August 1914, he went to the MEDITERRANEAN as deputy to Admiral Carden at the DARDANELLES in early 1915. When Carden collapsed just before the attempt on the Straits, senior British admiral WEMYSS stood down to allow de Robeck control of the attack. After its failure, and despite initial statements to the contrary, de Robeck consistently blocked attempts by his chief of staff, KEYES, to gain authority for another naval assault. De Robeck's role during the evacuation of GALLIPOLI (much praised by British PROPAGANDA) improved his contemporary reputation, and he was promoted vice admiral in command of the GRAND FLEET's Second Battle Squadron in December 1916, remaining in the post until 1919.

Destroyers Small, fast warships developed in the late 19th century as defence for battlefleets against the new threat of torpedo craft. Originally designed as long-range TORPEDO BOATS, they had become steadily larger and more seaworthy in the prewar years.

Prewar development had reflected the divergent needs and theories of major navies. Most designed rugged vessels for ocean-going operations, but MEDITERRANEAN navies expected to use destroyers for short-range operations in relatively calm conditions, and designed them for speed at the expense of endurance. By 1914, modern destroyers generally displaced 500–800 tons, small enough to be built in quantity by the major powers and cheap enough to provide the backbone of many smaller navies.

Destroyers were generally deployed in flotillas (typically between 4 and 8 ships, but sometimes as many as 20). Fleet flotillas accompanied BATTLESHIPS and BATTLECRUISERS wherever they went. Usually led by a light CRUISER, or by a larger 'leader' destroyer, the destroyers were armed with TORPEDOES against big warships and sufficient surface or ANTI-AIRCRAFT armament to deter anything smaller.

Destroyers functioned as screens for fleets against torpedo attack, as strike weapons sent en masse to deflect enemy fleets, and as fast scouts. Their importance to the wartime operation of major units was such that no warship larger or slower than a light cruiser was considered safe in potentially hostile waters without a destroyer screen.

Although destroyers played an active part in most surface engagements and coastal support operations, their speed, range and surface armament also made them useful as fast-response coastal-protection craft, as fast MINELAYERS, and as lead ships for flotillas of smaller craft. Their qualities were most in demand for ANTI-SUBMARINE work, and Allied commanders, especially in the MEDITERRANEAN, were engaged in a constant internal scramble for destroyers, especially the larger modern boats suitable for long-range escort work.

Destroyers grew steadily larger, more heavily armed, stronger and more expensive, with new ships displacing over 1,100 tons by 1918, and their growing importance was reflected in large-scale wartime production. By the end of 1918 almost 450 destroyers had served with the wartime ROYAL NAVY, and more than 230 with the GERMAN NAVY. The RUSSIAN NAVY took delivery of 58 new destroyers in wartime, and even beleaguered French and Italian shipyards produced a few. The UNITED STATES (and to a lesser extent JAPAN) embarked on construction programmes from 1914 that both supplied the Allies and strengthened their own fleets, so that the postwar world (especially the US NAVY) faced a massive destroyer surplus.

Deutschland Large, unarmed German merchant SUBMARINE, completed in 1916 and immediately sent from Kiel to the UNITED STATES as a demonstration of its BLOCKADE-running capacity. Reaching Baltimore on 9 July with a cargo including precious stones, *Deutschland* took precious metals back to GERMANY in August. The PROPAGANDA value of the exercise was multiplied by failed British interception attempts in the western Atlantic, which offended both the authorities and public opinion in the USA.

A second merchant submarine, *Bremen*, left for the USA at the end of August, followed by *U-53* as a surprise for any British warships. The ROYAL NAVY sent no warships, *Bremen* disappeared en route and *U-53* sank five Europe-bound merchant ships just beyond US territorial waters. Strictly in accordance with SUBMARINE WARFARE 'prize rules', the attacks caused no casualties but provoked a warning from the US government against operations in the western Atlantic and swung public opinion back towards the Allies. See also: *U-155*.

DFW C-Types Series of armed German biplanes, in service as the C-I from 1915, derived from an unarmed B-type reconnaissance design that was used in small numbers during early campaigns on the WESTERN and EASTERN FRONTS. Strengthened to take greater weight, about 130 C-Is joined the mixed equipment of GERMAN ARMY AIR SERVICE field units, but their 150hp engines gave a top speed of only 125kph, and they were withdrawn as faster types became available in 1916.

Subsequent versions were produced in only small numbers until the up-engined C-V entered service in mid-1916. Nimble and easy to fly, it proved one of the most versatile and reliable reconnaissance, PHOTO-RECONNAISSANCE and ARTILLERY-spotting aircraft in German service. Increasingly pressed into infantry-support duties, to which it was less well-suited, it was used in large numbers throughout 1918, and though complete production figures are unknown some 600 were active on the Western Front at the ARMISTICE.

BRIEF DATA (C-V) Type: two-seat armed reconnaissance; Engine: 220hp Benz; Max speed: 155kph; Armament: 2 × 7.92mm mg.

Diaz, General Armando (1861–1928) A successful field commander in the Italo-Turkish War (1911–12), Diaz was an important figure among the ITALIAN ARMY's general staff during the period of neutrality after August 1914, and was given a divisional command in May 1915. One of the more successful generals involved in the repeated assaults along the ISONZO, and particularly praised for his part in the GORIZIA victory of 1916, he was a corps commander by mid-1917 and appointed chief of staff on 7 November after defeat at CAPORETTO brought General CADORNA's dismissal. Chosen for his organizational skills and willingness to consult with political leaders, Diaz successfully restructured Italian defences along the PIAVE under diminishing pressure from stretched Austro-German forces, and had stabilized the front (with Anglo-French reinforcement) by late December.

In regular communication with the ORLANDO government through a new joint war council, Diaz was a cautious contrast to his predecessor. Arguing that his forces were too weak to attack, or even to hold off a renewed Austro-Hungarian offensive, he fought unsuccessfully to prevent withdrawal of Allied units to meet the German SPRING OFFENSIVES on the WESTERN FRONT, and subsequently resisted the SUPREME WAR COUNCIL's repeated demands for an Italian advance to relieve pressure on Anglo-French defences.

His system of DEFENCE IN DEPTH repulsed the relatively feeble Piave offensive in the summer, but he expected fighting to continue at least into 1919. His own VITTORIO VENETO attack in September was undertaken only after foreign minister SONNINO demanded an offensive to secure ITALY's promised postwar territorial gains. Comprehensive victory over a demoralized AUSTRO-HUNGARIAN ARMY secured his long-term reputation. He was ennobled in 1921 and became MUSSOLINI's war minister the following year, retaining the post until his promotion to field marshal and retirement in 1924.

Dinant Medieval town on the River Meuse, about 50km south of NAMUR. It was in the path of General von Hausen's German Third Army during the invasion of BELGIUM in August 1914, and was the focus of heavy fighting during the Battle of CHARLEROI (see MAP 4). It was occupied on 23 August, and, in line with the GERMAN ARMY's policy of terrorizing occupied communities, 612 citizens, including women and children, were taken into the town square and shot. Dinant was looted and many buildings were destroyed before the Third Army proceeded towards the nearby French frontier. Described by German authorities as an act of reprisal for civilian interference with bridge repair and other logistic work, the massacre shocked worldwide neutral opinion and helped to establish Allied PROPAGANDA on the moral high ground at an early stage. See also: BELGIUM (Home Front); FRANC-TIREURS; LOUVAIN.

Director Control The contemporary method of coordinating aimed fire from the main guns of BATTLESHIPS, director control began to replace separate targeting by individual guns or turrets with the most modern navies in the years immediately before 1914. The fire-direction officer in a large warship took visual readings of targets from the foremast, with assistants positioned to cross-reference horizontal and vertical readings. Target data was then transmitted to individual guns through a variety of fire-control mechanisms.

The best of these was the GERMAN NAVY's Siemens and Halske system. Rapidly introduced to HIGH SEAS FLEET units from 1913, it was electrically operated and sent information quickly to a set of dials situated next to each gun. The British Dreyer Clock, installed in eight British GRAND FLEET battleships by August 1914, delivered readings mechanically to a central table. Slower and less reliable than the German system – as demonstrated in gunnery duels at the DOGGER BANK and JUTLAND – it was retained in preference to the slightly superior Pollen system (which had not been invented by a Navy man), and equipped all but two Grand Fleet capital ships by mid-1916. The French fleet and some Italian ships used similar control tables, but their effectiveness was hardly tested in wartime. Director-control systems generally improved rate of fire, but the pitch and roll of a large vessel in rough seas disrupted trajectory readings, and accuracy remained dependent on reasonably calm conditions.

Djaved Bey, Mehmed (1875–1926) Turkish civil servant and politician, the first Union and Progress Party (YOUNG TURK) member to hold cabinet rank, as finance minister from 1909 to 1911. He filled the same role in the government of 1914, but resigned in November in protest at alliance with the CENTRAL POWERS. Djaved retained effective control of national finances through his place on the UPP's executive council, and worked to secure loans from TURKEY's allies while avoiding German economic domination. He refused to grant postwar economic concessions to Germany or liquidate Anglo-French businesses in Turkey, and used the threat of non-repayment to deflect German pressure. Never a confidant of ENVER and the cabinet inner circle, he remained an indispensable bureaucrat. He resumed his cabinet post in February 1917, and was the only minister to remain in office when the government resigned in October 1918. Forced into exile in November, he returned to republican Turkey in 1922 and was eventually executed for subversion by the KEMAL regime.

Djemal Pasha, Ahmed (1872–1922) Turkish soldier and politician born in Constantinople, an early member of the YOUNG TURK movement whose career flourished through a succession of provincial governorships, marked by repression of counter-revolutionary opposition. After holding various senior commands during the Balkan Wars (1912–13), he was appointed to the cabinet as minister of marine in 1913.

One of the most powerful figures in an increasingly oppressive government, regarded by some commentators as part of an effective dictatorship with ENVER and TALAAT, his diplomatic overtures to the ENTENTE POWERS were rejected in July 1914, and he subsequently favoured friendship with the CENTRAL POWERS. Initially opposed to full alliance with GERMANY, he was persuaded in early October 1914 to authorize Admiral SOUCHON's preemptive strike in the BLACK SEA.

Djemal retained several offices in wartime, including command of the Fourth Army on the PALESTINE FRONT and the military governorship of Ottoman Syria, a vast province including all of Palestine and much of Arabia. His position in DAMASCUS precluded effective control of the TURKISH NAVY, and he largely ignored direct military command after the failure of his initial attack on the SUEZ CANAL. He ran his virtually independent fiefdom with diligent ruthlessness, stifling nascent ARAB REVOLT in Syria and blocking attempts by successive front commanders to withdraw Fourth Army units from southern Arabia.

Djemal left Syria for Constantinople after the fall of JERUSALEM in December 1917, remaining in office until the collapse of the government the following October, when he fled with other ministers aboard a German ship. He subsequently played a liaison role in talks between the Soviet Union and postwar TURKEY, and was briefly a military advisor to AFGHANISTAN, but was killed by ARMENIAN assassins at Tbilisi.

Dobrudja, Invasion of See: ROMANIAN CAMPAIGN.

Dogfights Popular contemporary term for aerial battles between large numbers of aircraft, subsequently extended to describe any prolonged combat between two or more machines. The formation of specialist FIGHTER units since 1916 had contributed to a steady increase in numbers of aircraft engaged in combat, but the first true dogfights took place over the WESTERN FRONT in 1917, when both sides had learned to concentrate unprecedented numbers of aircraft around major ground offensives.

A battle involving 94 aircraft over Flanders on 26 April 1917 is generally regarded as the first great dogfight, provoked by the presence of German reconnaissance two-seaters attempting to cross Allied lines at about 1,500m. A kilometre higher, 7 British AIRCO DH-5s were prevented from attacking them by 30 Albatros and HALBERSTADT D-TYPE fighters. Ten more ALBATROS D-TYPES were attacked by 30 SOPWITH CAMELS and SE-5s at about 3,500–4,000m, and another 10 were engaged by 7 naval SOPWITH TRIPLANES above 5,000m.

In numbers and depth of airspace covered the action set a pattern for future battles, which in theory protected the reconnaissance needs of army commanders during ground offensives but in practice developed a momentum of their own. Air-combat victories had a very high PROPAGANDA value throughout the War, and both sides quickly learned to send out two-seater patrols purely as bait for enemy fighters. See also: AERIAL WARFARE; ACES.

Dogger Bank, Battle of the Action in the North Sea between British and German BATTLECRUISERS on 24 January 1915. As a sop to public outrage following Admiral HIPPER's raid on SCARBOROUGH of December 1914, Admiral BEATTY's five British battlecruisers had been moved south from Cromarty in northern Scotland to Rosyth in the Firth of Forth. The ROYAL NAVY's secret ROOM 40 decoding unit provided advance warning on 23 January of another sortie by Hipper's force, reduced to four big ships because *VON DER TANN* had been damaged during the CUXHAVEN RAID.

Beatty's force steamed south that evening, accompanied by six fast light CRUISERS, to intercept a presumed coastal raid, and were joined by cruisers and DESTROYERS from Harwich before making contact with Hipper's screening forces at 07.20 next morning. Hipper's ships ran for home at first sight of what were thought to be relatively slow BATTLESHIPS, but Beatty had caught up to extreme firing range by 09.00, and the parallel lines of warships began a gun battle about half an hour later.

Despite signalling errors that confused targeting, British shells damaged *SEYDLITZ* and brought the older *BLÜCHER* to a virtual stop before remaining German ships concentrated very accurate fire on Beatty's flagship, *LION*, which was brought to a standstill and dropped out of the battle just before 11.00. A major British victory still appeared probable, but sudden fear of MINES and an imagined SUBMARINE sighting persuaded Beatty to turn his ships away.

Further signalling confusion translated Beatty's subsequent attempt to send his best ships after Hipper into an order for joint destruction of *Blücher*, which duly took place. The British GRAND FLEET, ordered to sea from distant Scapa Flow as an afterthought, was still over 200km to the north as the rest of the German squadron escaped.

Both sides claimed a success but reacted as if to failure. Admiral Moore, Beatty's second in command, was transferred to the Canary Islands, and HIGH SEAS FLEET commander Ingenohl, heavily criticized for not giving Hipper direct support, was replaced by Admiral Pohl in February. See MAP 16.

Doiran, Lake See: SALONIKA; Battle of Lake PRESPA; VARDAR and MONASTIR OFFENSIVES.

Douala, Capture of Douala was the main port of CAMEROON in 1914, housing a small German colonial settlement, some 30,000 tribal African residents, and a powerful RADIO station (see MAP 17). Despite regional competition for colonial influence, and mutual mistrust, a joint Anglo-French force under British General Dobell was sent to capture the town in September 1914.

Dobell's supporting naval squadron – the British armoured CRUISER *Cumberland*, three less powerful cruisers, a gunboat and small craft of the Nigerian marine – arrived to secure a safe landing place in early September and sank the only armed German steamer in the vicinity. Some 4,400 African troops (2,500 British, 1,900 French), with 650 Europeans and more than 4,000 bearers, were in position by 23 September, opposed by a single ARTILLERY battery.

After fighting off a small force sent ashore to cut communications, German colonists destroyed the radio station and surrendered under threat of naval bombardment on 27 September. Most German rolling stock, weapons and supplies were evacuated along inland RAILWAYS, encouraging Dobell to expand his invasion to the rest of the colony, but the Allies captured 31,000 tons of merchant shipping.

Douaumont, Fort See: Battle of VERDUN.

'Doughboys' Contemporary popular nickname, also adopted in official PROPAGANDA, for conscript infantrymen of the AEF. The origin of the name has been subject to debate. Some authorities trace it to the dough-like buttons of US infantry in the Civil War, but it was more probably a slang derivation of the word 'dobies', itself short for 'adobes' – a derisory description of dust-caked infantry applied by US Cavalry stationed along the Rio Grande.

Dover Barrage Prolonged British attempt to block the passage of German SUBMARINES through the English Channel at its narrowest point. Large minefields had been laid between the Belgian coast and Dover in August 1914, but the barrage proper was begun the following February, when a 25km line of INDICATOR NETS was laid between Dover and Ostend. A response to the announcement of submarine attacks against commercial shipping (see *HANDELSKRIEG*), they were attended by drifters (small fishing boats), surrounded by minefields at various depths, and supported by DESTROYER patrols from Dover. The new Barrage gained its first success on 4 March, when *U-8* was sunk after becoming snagged in the nets.

The system was far from impenetrable at first. British MINES were unreliable before late 1917, there were often gaps between nets, and support craft were not available in sufficient numbers. The Germans forbade U-boats to pass through the Channel from April 1915, a temporary British victory that reflected a mutual tendency to credit unexplained losses to the Barrage. Once U-BOATS based at ZEEBRUGGE and Ostend returned to the Channel route from April 1916, followed by larger boats from German bases in December, submarines passed through at will, usually travelling on the surface at night.

The Barrage was moved east to a line between Folkestone and Cap Gris Nez during November and December 1917, and a Barrage Committee (headed by KEYES) was established to advise local commander Admiral Bacon. Minefields were laid using the improved Mark H-2 mine and, despite Bacon's opposition, night patrols using flares and searchlights were instituted. Steadily increasing patrol support and continuous expansion of minefields increased effectiveness, and the Barrage sank at least 12 more submarines by mid-August 1918, after which no U-boat attempted the passage. See also: ANTI-SUBMARINE WARFARE; OTRANTO BARRAGE; NORTHERN BARRAGE.

Dreadnought British BATTLESHIP, completed in December 1906, that heralded a revolution in warship design and rendered every other capital ship in the world apparently obsolete (see PRE-DREADNOUGHTS). Its total concentration on heavy guns made it the most powerfully armed ship afloat, and it was the first major warship driven solely by economical and reliable steam turbines. It was also faster than any other battleship, without sacrificing armour protection. The driving enthusiasm of the First Sea Lord, FISHER, and his diversion of resources from other projects, enabled its completion in 14 months, a record for battleship construction that was never beaten.

At a time when naval strength was conventionally counted in capital units, *Dreadnought* gave the ROYAL NAVY a simple 1–0 advantage over all other powers, stimulating increased naval competition in the North Sea, the MEDITERRANEAN and even South America. Fisher attracted criticism for the effective loss of a hitherto massive advantage over all maritime rivals, but similarly armed battleships (generally referred to as dreadnoughts) had already been planned by other navies, and Britain's enormous shipbuilding industry was well placed to take advantage of a head start.

In August 1914 *Dreadnought* was flagship of the GRAND FLEET's Fourth Battle Squadron, and the highlight of its wartime career was the destruction of *U-29* in 1915. Refitted with two 3-inch and two 12-pounder ANTI-AIRCRAFT guns (in place of small surface weapons), it was reassigned as flagship of the home-defence squadron based in the Thames Estuary from 1916 until its retirement from active service in 1919. See also: *ORION*.

BRIEF DATA (1914) Displacement: 17,900 tons; Crew: 862; Dimensions: length 526ft (159.4m), beam 82ft (24.8m); Speed: 22k; Armament: 10 × 12in gun, 24 × 12pdr, 5 × 18in TT.

Drina River, Battle of the Serbian victory on the BALKAN FRONT in September 1914, ending the AUSTRO-HUNGARIAN ARMY's renewed invasion across the River Drina west of BELGRADE. Austro-Hungarian front commander POTIOREK received rapid reinforcement after losing 40,000 men in August and launched a repeat of the tactics that had failed at the JADAR RIVER, the bulk of his forces crossing the Drina River on 7 September. Emboldened by his initial victory, SERBIAN ARMY commander PUTNIK had already launched a limited attack of his own at the northeastern flank on 6 September, taking Semlin (Zemun) and crossing the Danube into Slovenia four days later. In the far west a smaller force of Serbian and Montenegrin troops attacked into Bosnia and took Visegrad on 14 September.

Serbian attacks were quickly scaled down to concentrate against the main Austro-Hungarian advance, which suffered the same fate as its predecessor. A simple frontal advance with only limited ARTILLERY support was thrown back across the Drina by tactically superior forces in good defensive positions. The invasion was suspended from 15 September and Potiorek's armies retreated across the frontier. Serbian troops pulled back from Slovenia two days later, and, although the western advance edged a little further into Bosnia, both sides settled into a brief period of consolidation – Potiorek to plan a third attempt, and Putnik to await urgent ammunition and supply replenishment. See: Battle of the KOLUBARA RIVER; MAP 19.

Dubail, General Auguste (1851–1934) Assisted by a reputation for staunchly conservative republican politics, Dubail became FRENCH ARMY chief of staff from 1911 but returned to field command the following year, leading the First Army into LORRAINE in August 1914. Remaining in command of the

Eastern Army Group around Belfort and VERDUN (see MAP 2), he described the latter's defences as adequate in July 1915. He became alarmed by German concentration in the sector late in the year, by which time much of its heavy ARTILLERY had been removed for field operations, but his fears were ignored by C-in-C JOFFRE. Dismissed in March, the highest-ranking head to roll after the opening German attacks, he served as military governor of Paris until spring 1918, and always claimed he was a scapegoat for Joffre's shortsightedness.

Dujaila, Battle of Pivotal Anglo-Indian attempt to break the siege of KUT in spring 1916. Attacks at SHEIKH SA'AD and HANNA in January 1916 had been costly without significantly weakening the Turkish position on the River Tigris, but in late January Tigris Corps commander Aylmer was instructed to try again by new MESOPOTAMIAN FRONT C-in-C General Lake.

Still facing the lines at Hanna, Aylmer planned to cross the river for a direct attack on the Dujaila Redoubt, a strong fortification at the extreme outer edge of the Turkish strongpoint at Es Sinn, occupied by at least 25,000 seasoned troops. He was anxious to await an additional division en route from GALLIPOLI, but Lake was unwilling to risk delay until after the approaching flood season, and ordered an attack by 15 March.

Aylmer left 6,500 troops and 24 guns in front of Hanna, where TRENCH WARFARE was in progress throughout February, and ordered the rest of his two divisions (about 35,000 men, 62 guns) to march some 20km overnight to storm the Redoubt in a conventional BREAKTHROUGH operation, preceded by an ARTILLERY bombardment. Kut commander TOWNSHEND was to make a secondary attack from the rear. Planned for 6 March but delayed by heavy rain, the main advance under General Kemball got underway at 10.00 on 8 March but was pinned down 700 metres short of the Redoubt by noon. Following a rigid timetable, a secondary attack under General Keary missed an opportunity to breach weakened parts of the Turkish line, and Townshend abandoned plans to intervene after the initial failure. The offensive disintegrated by late afternoon, and Anglo-Indian troops retreated to their original positions, having suffered about 3,500 casualties, against an estimated 1,200 Turkish losses. Aylmer was replaced by General Gorringe on 12 March, and the Tigris Corps spent the rest of the month consolidating as hopes of reaching Kut faded.

'Dunsterforce' Nickname of a composite force of just under 1,000 elite British, CANADIAN, AUSTRALIAN and NEW ZEALAND troops from the WESTERN and MESOPOTAMIAN FRONTS commanded by the Russian-speaking General Dunsterville. Assembled in late 1917 at Hamadan in western Persia, halfway between the Mesopotamian border and Tehran, it was supplied from Baghdad by a fleet of 750 lorries across more than 500km of difficult, famine-ravaged terrain (see KHANAQIN).

In January 1918 it marched north, supported by a detachment of ARMOURED CARS, to aid the establishment of an independent TRANSCAUCASIA and to protect INDIA from an improbable Germano-Turkish invasion through PERSIA. After a 350km journey Dunsterforce was turned back by 3,000 revolutionary Russian troops at Enzeli on the Caspian coast, and returned to Hamadan. A German division meanwhile occupied Georgian Tiblisi, and Turkish troops threatened to occupy the oil port of Baku.

Dunsterforce armoured cars moved north again with a regiment sent from Mesopotamia and a force of 3,000 Russians, which had placed itself under British command in western Persia, to take Enzeli with little difficulty in June 1918. The Russians departed in July for Baku, where a new nationalist regime was threatened by approaching Turkish forces, and Dunsterville followed them across the western Caspian Sea in response to an appeal for help.

About 1,000 British troops joined a town garrison of 10,000 local volunteers by 25 August, but withdrew on the night of 14 September as 14,000 Turkish troops prepared to attack. Most of Dunsterforce escaped back to Enzeli with large numbers of ARMENIAN refugees, and Dunsterville was ordered back to Britain after reoccupying Baku at the ARMISTICE. The expedition aroused criticism in GREAT BRITAIN as either a reckless adventure or a strategic coup let down by inadequate investment. See MAP 24.

E

E-11 One of three British SUBMARINES sent to the BALTIC in October 1914, *E-11* was forced to return to Harwich after twice being intercepted en route by German patrols. It was positioned to intercept German BATTLE-CRUISERS returning from the SCARBOROUGH RAID in December, but was let down by faulty TORPEDOES. Its luck changed with transfer to the DARDANELLES the following May, and it had sunk 27 steamers and 58 smaller vessels in three cruises into the Sea of Marmora by mid-December 1915, including the old Turkish battleship *HAIREDDIN BARBEROSSE* (8 August).

The British submarine campaign in the Dardanelles between April 1915 and January 1916 was an outstanding success. Four boats were lost attempting to pass through the Straits, but the other 9 (of which 3 were lost) sank 2 BATTLESHIPS, a destroyer, 5 gunboats, 9 transports, 35 steamers, 7 supply ships and 188 smaller vessels, disrupting Turkish supply operations to the GALLIPOLI peninsula but giving rise to criticism of the ROYAL NAVY for not assigning more boats to the theatre.

E-boats were the mainstays of British wartime submarine operations. Between 1913 and 1917, 57 were built (including 2 for Australia and 6 minelayers), and a total of 28 were lost.

BRIEF DATA (1914) Displacement: 660 tons; Crew: 30; Dimensions: length 181ft (54.8m), beam 22.5ft (6.8m); Speed: 16k (surface), 10k (submerged); Armament: 5 × 18inTT.

East Africa, Campaigns in Largest and longest of the colonial campaigns in AFRICA, centred on British attempts to conquer German East Africa. Occupying modern Rwanda, Burundi and mainland Tanzania (almost a million square kilometres) the German colony was surrounded by British, Belgian and Portuguese territories, and by British-held offshore islands (see MAP 18). In 1914 it contained an estimated 7.65 million Africans of over 100 different tribes, along with some 15,000 immigrant Asians and about 5,350 Europeans.

Led by liberal Governor Schnee, an intensive German developmental programme had completed two important RAILWAYS inland from the coast by mid-1914. The 'Usambara' Line ran from the main port of Tanga to the foothills of Kilimanjaro, and the Central Line from Dar-es-Salaam to Lake Tanganyika. Most European activity was concentrated near the northern coasts, and the main threat to German security came from its northern neighbour, British East Africa.

The German colonial army (*Schutztruppe*) in East Africa comprised 260 Europeans and 2,472 ASKARIS in mid-1914, supported by 31 obsolete light ARTILLERY pieces and an internal gendarmerie of almost 2,200 men (including 45 Europeans). It received better training and pay than the comparable King's African Rifles (KAR), an army of 2,300 Africans and 62 British officers scattered around 800,000 square kilometres of British East Africa, with only about 150 troops based on the southern capital of Nairobi.

Schnee and Governor Belfield of British East Africa argued for maintenance of African neutrality through the BERLIN ACT in August 1914, and a British CRUISER arranged a non-aggression pact with German authorities at Dar-es-Salaam and Tanga. The arrangement was denounced by the ROYAL NAVY and ignored by German East African C-in-C LETTOW-VORBECK. Arming a steamer to assure control of Lake Tanganyika (see NAVAL AFRICA EXPEDITION), he mobilized reserves and attacked the British Uganda Railway.

About 500 Askaris crossed the border towards Mombasa in late September, but were delayed by volunteer units and retreated after a KAR company joined the defence. German troops did capture Tavita, 120km south of the Uganda Railway, but in the south two German attempts to penetrate Northern Rhodesia (modern Zambia) were stopped by local troops in September and November.

Encouraged by easy success in TOGOLAND, the British government authorized the conquest of German East Africa in August 1914. As on the MESOPOTAMIAN FRONT, the invasion was entrusted to the Indian government, and about 4,000 troops of INDIAN ARMY Expeditionary Force 'C' reached Mombasa on 1 September, followed by 8,000 more (Expeditionary Force 'B') in late October.

Though most of his troops were ill-equipped reserves, overall commander General Aitken launched an immediate attack on TANGA (5 November) and a subsidiary advance on Longido, across the border west of Kilimanjaro. Both failed and British forces withdrew to Nairobi to regroup, while Schnee's pacifist position was weakened by ineffectual naval bombardments of Dar-es-Salaam in late November.

When the winter rains subsided in January, a small, hard-earned German victory at Jassin, on the northern coastal border, convinced Lettow-Vorbeck to fight a defensive campaign. Designed to draw maximum British commitment to East Africa, it reflected his dominant concern for German strategic interests, in contrast to Schnee's consistently colonial perspective on the campaign.

Strengthening his army with volunteer units, Lettow-Vorbeck divided it into Northern, Western and Southwestern groups, with their main headquarters 800km inland on the Central Line at Tabora. An injection of supplies and munitions from the German cruiser *KÖNIGSBERG*, trapped and eventually destroyed in the RUFUGI DELTA, included 10 105mm guns for division among the land armies, and by the end of 1915 German strength had grown to 3,000 Europeans and 11,300 African combat troops. Despite a British BLOCKADE of the colony, an impressive capacity for improvization and ERSATZ production (based on a chemical laboratory at Amani) kept the German population well supplied with most necessities.

New Indian Expeditionary Force commander General Wapshare, whose troops included British territorials, Askaris, white colonial volunteers and Indian Army formations, attempted no major offensive in 1915. Apparently as a means of raising morale, the small Lake Victoria port of Bukoba was taken (and looted) on 23 June, but attacks towards Tavita (July) and Longido (September) collapsed in disarray.

Mutual crossborder raiding elsewhere was dominated by local conditions (wild animals killed 30 British troops by the end of 1915) and German attacks on the Uganda Railway, which succeeded in destroying 32 trains and 9 bridges between May 1915 and March 1916.

General SMITH-DORRIEN was appointed to command British forces in East Africa in November 1915, but fell ill en route and was replaced by the South African General SMUTS. Smuts took over in February 1916, just after the failure of another limited attack near Tavita by 6,000 troops under General Malleson (since described as the least competent general in Africa). Encouraged from London to attack at the first opportunity, Smuts was reinforced by SOUTH AFRICAN and RHODESIAN formations, bringing total British strength in East Africa to 27,350 men with 71 field guns.

The main British MOROGORO OFFENSIVE of 1916, from March until September, used numerical superiority to clear northern East Africa of Germans, but failed to catch Lettow-Vorbeck's main forces before exhaustion forced its suspension. In simultaneous advances from East Africa's other frontiers, Anglo-Belgian forces converged from the northwest to capture TABORA on 19 September but then halted, and General Northey's force advancing from Northern Rhodesia was stopped by a German attack at IRINGA in late October.

Though well received in London and impressive in territorial terms, the 1916 campaign failed. Expert German defensive tactics, heavy rain and sickness slowed and depleted British forces, enabling the *Schutztruppe* to retreat almost intact into the Rufugi River region, the last fertile area under German control. They withdrew with exemplary efficiency, disabling railways and resupplying from the blockade runner *Marie von Stettin*, which reached the southern coast on 17 April.

During early 1916 an RFC squadron of fairly modern BE-2C two-seaters began operations in East Africa, but they were unreliable in the heat and too slow for effective reconnaissance or ground attack over terrain thick with cover.

Smuts spent late 1916 rebuilding captured railways and reorganizing armies. As elsewhere in Africa, disease was responsible for the vast majority of casualties, and 12,000 sick white British troops were evacuated. Most went to SOUTH AFRICA, where their starved and diseased condition caused a sensation. Their native African or West Indian replacements proved altogether more efficient in prevailing conditions.

Lettow-Vorbeck, facing acute supply problems as his columns converged in the more primitive south of the country, launched a prolonged but unsuccessful attack on the British southeastern supply base at Kibata in December, before withdrawing to dodge a British attempt to surround him with an advance south of Iringa.

Smuts was recalled to London in January 1917, where he encouraged the view that the campaign was effectively won. Expected to finish the job quickly but denied imperial reinforcements, new C-in-C Hoskins could only work to improve supply lines, troop welfare and the KAR, which was eventually expanded to 35,000 men. Hoskins was replaced by the South African Deventer in May, by which time British forces all over East Africa were being distracted by the maverick WINTGENS-NAUMANN EXPEDITION.

Restricted to small actions during the summer, Deventer built up strength for an offensive on the main southeastern front in September. Overwhelmingly strong British columns advanced south and southwest from the coastal bases of Kilwa and Lindi, but were temporarily halted at MAHIWA, 80km inland, before Lettow-Vorbeck again withdrew to avoid the pincer. He crossed the border into Portuguese MOZAMBIQUE, where his last 2,200 troops found plentiful supplies and easy targets, dodging British pursuit on a gruelling trek of almost 2,000km that brought them back into East Africa on 28 September 1918.

With strong British imperial forces blocking his passage north, Lettow-Vorbeck captured several supply bases before veering west into Northern Rhodesia. Fear of his next move kept most of Deventer's troops pinned to defensive positions in the north, and only about 750 KAR troops followed. Moving along the frontier towards the town of Fife, the *Schutztruppe* fought a final skirmish with KAR troops near the village of Kasama on 12 November.

News of the ARMISTICE reached Lettow-Vorbeck the following day, and after negotiation his forces had marched into Abercorn to surrender by 25 November. Along with Governor Schnee, survivors included 145 Europeans, 1,156 Askaris and 1,600 bearers, with one captured Portuguese field gun, 37 machine guns and 1,071 RIFLES.

The East African war is generally presented as a triumph for the *Schutztruppe*, forcing British authorities to expend precious resources for no strategic gain. As a precursor of modern guerrilla warfare, Lettow-Vorbeck's campaign was matched only by the contemporary ARAB REVOLT. In an extra-military context the campaign inflicted economic devastation on previously prosperous African regions, which suffered an immediate postwar INFLUENZA epidemic followed by serious famine. Widespread native military service wrought major social changes, but prolonged German resistance made little difference to East Africa's immediate political future: Belgium annexed the northwestern Rwanda and Burundi regions as MANDATES; Portugal was granted a small northern extension to Mozambique; and the rest became Tanganyika, administered as a LEAGUE OF NATIONS mandate by the British.

Easter Rising Irish republican uprising begun when leaders of Sinn Fein and the Irish Republican Brotherhood occupied the main Dublin post office and proclaimed a provisional independent government on 24 April 1916.

Several buildings covering roads into the city were taken by rebels after fierce street fighting with British garrison troops, but hopes of German aid had already faded with the arrest of Sir Roger CASEMENT. Rebel attempts to storm Dublin Castle and the local arsenal failed. The British government put the whole of IRELAND under martial law from 27 April, and troops under General Maxwell forced the surrender of rebel leaders on 1 May. About 300 died in the fighting, with more than 1,000 wounded or missing.

Coming amid a series of military setbacks, notably the simultaneous fall of KUT, the rebellion sharpened divisions within the British ASQUITH coalition. A relatively lenient response – only 14 rebel leaders were executed and those imprisoned were granted amnesty in June 1917 – was prompted by concern for Irish-American opinion and did little to reverse a PROPAGANDA victory for the republican movement.

Eastern Front Vast theatre of conflict between RUSSIA, AUSTRIA-HUNGARY and GERMANY, named from the German perspective. It ultimately extended from the BALTIC coast of LATVIA to the BLACK SEA Dobrudja region (see MAPS 10, 11). All three empires had anticipated conflict before 1914: Austro-Hungarian chief of staff CONRAD planned an invasion of Russian Galicia; the German SCHLIEFFEN PLAN assumed war in East Prussia to the north; and the RUSSIAN ARMY, by far the largest in the region, was committed to invasions of both sectors by its own PLAN 19.

The JULY CRISIS of 1914 triggered these plans, but the CENTRAL POWERS had relied on the presumed slowness of Russian mobilization to allow completion of operations on the BALKAN and WESTERN FRONTS before concentrating in the east. The speed with which Russian troops (if not weapons or supplies) were massed near the frontiers surprised both Conrad and his German counterpart, MOLTKE. Operations in the theatre began with a two-pronged Russian invasion of German EAST PRUSSIA in mid-August. Invasion of GALICIA from the north and east followed a few days later.

Russian forces in East Prussia had been defeated by a much smaller German force at TANNENBERG and the MASURIAN LAKES, and chased back across the frontier by mid-September, suffering serious but not irreplaceable losses (see MAP 12). The campaign's greatest strategic impact was in the west, where it caused sufficient initial panic for Moltke to subtract reinforcements from the MARNE. It also brought the German command team of HINDENBURG and LUDENDORFF to the front, where they remained more or less in control of strategy throughout the next two years.

The slow Russian invasions of Galicia were more successful against incomplete and disorganized AUSTRO-HUNGARIAN ARMY forces. Overall commander IVANOV's northern wing met a similarly large Austro-Hungarian force belatedly advancing in the opposite direction at KOMAROW, and was forced back into Russia, but ill-conceived attacks on the ZLOTA LIPA and GNILA LIPA rivers in the east left depleted Austro-Hungarian armies in full retreat beyond Lvov. Conrad ordered a general retreat into the Carpathian Mountains east of Kraków.

German pursuit beyond the Masurian Lakes and Russian progress towards the Carpathians were quickly halted by bad weather, defensive reinforcements, supply problems and difficult terrain. With deadlock in the north and south, the massive central SALIENT of Russian Poland became the focus of contention from autumn 1914.

The German Eighth and a new Ninth Army attacked south from East Prussia on 18 September, but Russian forces in Galicia and Poland were slowly gathering for an invasion of their own across the Vistula and the attack struck at empty space. A detachment under General MACKENSEN advanced on Warsaw, reaching the suburbs by mid-October, but was withdrawn to meet the Russian threat at the Vistula. At the same time Austro-Hungarian forces followed Russian transfers from the Carpathians beyond the besieged fortress of PRZEMYSL.

The Russian invasion opened unsuccessfully on 11 October, but had crossed the Vistula by 26 October, forcing Conrad to abandon Przemysl and retreat back into the mountains. By November both invasion plans had stalled, the Russian attack disintegrating as its two wings were pulled apart by commanders (Ivanov and RUZSKI) unwilling to stray too far from their respective supply bases.

Ludendorff responded quickly to Russian delays, attacking the northern flank of the Russian invasion from 11 November and taking ŁÓDŹ on 6 December. On the southern flank, Ivanov pushed Austro-Hungarian forces back onto Kraków during November, but abandoned a siege when Łódź fell and withdrew towards the River San, leaving both sides in their autumn positions. The year ended with fighting again focused on Poland's flanks, and the widespread establishment of TRENCH WARFARE.

The campaigns had inflicted very heavy casualties on the Russian Army, which had lost almost a million men but could replace them, and on the Austro-Hungarian Army, which had lost about half as many but was already suffering manpower shortages. Conrad's renewal of attacks in the CARPATHIANS early in the new year preempted Russian plans to do the same. A fruitless and gruelling offensive was matched by an equally costly Russian counteroffensive, and when fighting in the mountains petered out in mid-April Conrad had lost another 800,000 men, many of them frozen to death in blizzards.

Doubts about Austria-Hungary's ability to remain at war encouraged Ludendorff's plans for a decisive strike at the heart of Russia. Like Conrad he regarded complete military victory in the east as feasible, provided sufficient German forces were concentrated in the theatre. The eastern command had represented its autumn advances in Poland as great victories thwarted by lack of support from new chief of staff FALKENHAYN, and arguments continued into the spring.

Conrad's pleas for aid persuaded reluctant postponement of Falkenhayn's plans for a decisive German intervention in the Balkans, and a numerically superior force – strong on Western Front experience, ARTILLERY and TRENCH WARFARE weaponry – was concentrated under Mackensen at the GORLICE–TARNOW sector.

Russian dispositions along the front were less sophisticated. Manpower levels had been maintained but supply problems and the inability of central commanders at STAVKA to impose policy prohibited competent strategic movement. Slow preparations for renewed offensives in the north and south were still underway when Mackensen's attack smashed through lightly held positions in the centre.

Gorlice–Tarnow drove Russian forces out of Galicia and extended the front north into KURLAND. The summer's TRIPLE OFFENSIVE by Austro-German forces all along the front forced a chaotic 'GREAT RETREAT' from POLAND, and by September the Russian Army had suffered 2 million more losses since the spring.

Falkenhayn decided the Russians were crippled but could not be beaten, and halted the offensives in early September, transferring Mackensen's successful BREAKTHROUGH juggernaut to the autumn conquest of SERBIA. Ludendorff and Conrad pursued their hopes of total victory through subsequent attacks on VILNIUS in the north and the 'BLACK-YELLOW' Galician offensive, but long supply lines, poor communications and exhaustion left the front stable from the end of the month, an almost straight line from east of Riga to the Romanian frontier.

The year's defeats brought a political and economic shake-up in Russia, stimulating increased munitions output over the winter, and Tsar NICHOLAS II took personal control at Stavka in September. Disastrous for the monarchy, his decision invested the central command with greater authority under chief of staff ALEXEEV, but made little difference to strategic or tactical inertia. The failed BESSARABIAN OFFENSIVE in late 1915 displayed the strength of the Russian Army's recuperative powers, but also its inability to imitate German tactics.

The GERMAN ARMY was occupied elsewhere in early 1916, but its mass attack on VERDUN on the Western Front obliged

Alexeev to launch a diversionary operation in the north at Lake NAROCH in March (see CHANTILLY CONFERENCE). Russian forces outnumbered the Central Powers by about 2 to 1 all along the front, but simple mass concentration of infantry, insufficiently supported by artillery or reserves, again failed with heavy losses. Russian generals assumed the need for even more artillery and ammunition, even more densely concentrated, and acute pessimism affected slow preparations for a renewed attack.

The exception among Russian commanders, General BRUSILOV, was permitted to launch a limited attack in Galicia while EVERT's main offensive in Poland was prepared. Operating on a relative shoestring, he used surprise, careful timing and dispersal of attacks along a broad front to smash through Austro-Hungarian positions in June 1916, sweeping the line west to the Carpathians and southwest beyond the Dneister (see MAP 13).

Greeted with universal amazement, not least at Stavka, the BRUSILOV OFFENSIVE forced abandonment of Conrad's TRENTINO OFFENSIVE on the ITALIAN FRONT and effectively destroyed the Austro-Hungarian Army in the east, but it failed to extend to German positions further north or decisively break through into the Austro-Hungarian heartlands. Even its tactical success was a flash in the pan, Stavka returning to breakthrough policy at KOVEL from late July, and by the time attacks finally ended in October the Russian Army had suffered another million casualties in 1916.

Brusilov's one strategic achievement was to persuade ROMANIA that the Allies were winning, and the main bulk of the front remained quiet through autumn as attention shifted to the ROMANIAN CAMPAIGN.

The German THIRD SUPREME COMMAND, led by Hindenburg and Ludendorff, assumed effective control of all the Central Powers' armies to inflict swift defeat on Romania by multi-national forces from Transylvania and the Danube. German expansionist ambitions in eastern Europe, already evident in the economic exploitation of occupied Polish and Baltic territories, were extended to the grain and oil resources of Romania.

Further attacks by the Central Powers on the Eastern Front were suspended in early 1917 to give internal revolutionary pressures a chance to knock Russia out of the War. Although the new Russian PROVISIONAL GOVERNMENT, which came to power following the FEBRUARY REVOLUTION, pledged continued support for the Allies, internal instability and the revolutionary mood of frontline troops precluded any immediate military demonstration. The regional German command (effectively headed by HOFFMANN) colluded in the transportation of LENIN and other exiled revolutionaries from Switzerland to Petrograd (St Petersburg), and the failed Russian KERENSKI OFFENSIVE of July 1917 broke both the Army and the government.

German forces gave the toppling regime a nudge with a limited attack to take RIGA at the start of September, and the OCTOBER REVOLUTION brought Lenin's Bolshevik Party to power with a clear popular mandate for immediate peace. Fighting officially ended on the Eastern Front with an armistice on 16 December, Romania having ended its technical resistance a week earlier.

After prolonged wrangling between Soviet delegates and German authorities (and among the Central Powers) the treaties of BREST-LITOVSK (March) and BUCHAREST (May) released the Bolshevik regime to establish internal order, and the German supreme command began an ambitious economic exploitation programme that kept about a million troops in eastern Europe until the ARMISTICE.

The entire region covered by the Eastern Front remained at war into the early 1920s. Nationalist, RED ARMY, mercenary and counter-revolutionary forces (with Allied support at the ARCTIC and Black Sea extremes of the region) competed in the local struggles of FINLAND, LITHUANIA, ESTONIA, POLAND, Latvia and the UKRAINE, the latter caught up in the sprawling campaigns of the RUSSIAN CIVIL WAR.

'Easterners' British label applied to advocates of large-scale military diversion from the WESTERN FRONT on the grounds that the CENTRAL POWERS could best be attacked on their strategic flanks. British political Easterners – including LLOYD GEORGE, CHURCHILL and Bonar LAW – exerted sufficient wartime influence to stimulate and maintain operations on GALLIPOLI, at SALONIKA, in PALESTINE and on the MESOPOTAMIAN FRONT, but were unable to secure complete commitment against a powerful majority of the military high command. The senior political authorities, KITCHENER and ASQUITH, wavered uncertainly between the two policies, and after Lloyd George took power in 1916 he fought a continuous battle with 'WESTERNERS' HAIG and ROBERTSON until spring 1918.

A considerable body of French political opinion (and generals like SARRAIL and FRANCHET D'ESPERAY) also favoured large-scale diversion of resources to the BALKAN FRONT, but Italian fear of Allied interference in the region made virtually every senior figure a confirmed Westerner. A secondary strand of Easterner thinking, led by British Admiral FISHER, contemplated a northern invasion via the BALTIC SEA, but found little support outside the ROYAL NAVY.

East Prussia, Russian Invasion of The opening offensive of the war on the EASTERN FRONT, consisting of a two-pronged Russian attack from the eastern and southern borders of German East Prussia. Launched on 15 August 1914, only 16 days after Russian mobilization, the invasion was intended to divert German strength from the WESTERN FRONT (see SCHLIEFFEN PLAN). The decision to attack as soon as sufficient forces were in position, regardless of supply and reserve strength, fulfilled RUSSIA's alliance obligations to FRANCE and served to forestall concentration of German forces in the east (see PLAN 19).

Jutting into the Russian Empire along the BALTIC coast, East Prussia offered two obvious corridors for massed invasion. In the northwest and southeast of the region, fortified zones around Thorn (Torun) and Königsberg (Kaliningrad), respectively, protected the borders, and the centre was blocked by the Masurian Lakes, a 100km-wide chain of virtually impassable waterways. German defensive positions, known as the 'Angerapp-Stellung', were drawn up on either side of this obstacle, stretching north and southwest (see MAP 12).

The German Eighth Army – 1 CAVALRY and 13 infantry divisions under General von PRITTWITZ – was expected to hold East Prussia, or at least guard routes to central GERMANY at the Vistula, until the lightning campaign in the west was over. If Russia did mount invasions through both corridors, defence depended on defeating one before the other arrived.

Despite the simultaneous preparation of attacks in GALICIA, and aided by large peacetime forces already gathered on the western frontiers, about 29 RUSSIAN ARMY divisions were deployed either side of the Lakes by mid-August, under the overall command of General ZHILINSKI. The First (or Vilna) Army, comprising 150,000 troops under General RENNENKAMPF, was to lead the advance from the east, drawing German forces towards it. General SAMSONOV's larger Second (or Warsaw) Army, crossing the southern border two days later, would come up behind the defenders. Decisive numerical superiority depended on efficient coordination between the two armies, which would enter hostile territory at least a week's march apart.

Russian forces were poorly equipped, trained and led, their preparations further weakened by chronic logistic and transport inefficiency. Forward divisions were short of ammunition, food (for men and horses), infantry weapons, aircraft support, experienced officers and modern ARTILLERY. Primitive battle and command communications exacerbated operational confusion at all levels from the frontline to STAVKA (the Army's central command organization), and uncoded RADIO transmissions were gratefully received by German intelligence. An inferior RAILWAY system used a wide gauge incompatible with that across the border.

Widespread pessimism among Russian commanders appeared justified, but the First Army's advance survived a raid by German forces on 17 August at STALLUPÖNEN, just inside the border, and defeated a larger counterattack around prepared positions near GUMBINNEN on 20 August. Expecting to be pursued, Prittwitz ordered a general retreat to the Vistula and warned his high command to expect further withdrawal. He and chief of staff Waldersee were immediately replaced by HINDENBURG and LUDENDORFF, who reached the Eighth Army on 23 August.

Believing German forces beaten, Rennenkampf assumed they would retreat beyond the Vistula and towards Königsberg to the west. Beset by supply problems and disorganized after the battle, the Russian First Army paused. Leaving only a screen to delay or confuse Rennenkampf, the German Eighth Army dashed south and surrounded the Russian Second Army, winning a spectacular victory at TANNENBERG (26–30 August). Survivors of the Second Army (some 10,000 men) retreated back across the border on 31 August, ordered to retreat to Warsaw, and Ludendorff turned to attack the First Army, strung out between Königsberg and the northern tip of the Masurian Lakes.

Rennenkampf had been reinforced since Gumbinnen, and a new Russian Tenth Army was being formed in the southeast corner of East Prussia to protect its flanks. The German Eighth Army also received belated reinforcements – one cavalry and four infantry divisions detached from the Western Front on 26 August. Their transfer reduced German strength at the MARNE and is generally considered the invasion's main strategic achievement.

Rapidly deploying his enlarged force all along the Russian line, Ludendorff began his attack (First Battle of the MASURIAN LAKES) on 7 September, but despite initial losses Rennenkampf was able to execute an efficient retreat to the River Niemen, eventually counterattacking in late September and driving German forces back to the Angerapp positions.

Russian casualties in both major battles were high – particularly at Tannenberg – but were not crippling, and the campaign was not the strategic victory claimed by Ludendorff after the Russian First Army's retreat. It did transform Ludendorff and Hindenburg into German popular heroes, with ultimately profound consequences (see THIRD SUPREME COMMAND). On the Russian side, sustained factional infighting led to Zhilinski's dismissal, but the impact of Tannenberg was lessened by successes in Galicia. See also: POLISH CAMPAIGNS.

Eberhardt, Admiral Andrei (1856–1919) One of the relatively young officers to receive rapid promotion in the RUSSIAN NAVY after 1905, Eberhardt commanded the BLACK SEA fleet from 1911 and was responsible for a marked increase in discipline and efficiency before 1914. Reluctantly accepting the need for a broadly defensive strategy against an expanding TURKISH NAVY, his actions after November 1914 were further restricted by delays in construction of new warships (especially the IMPERATRICA MARIA Class BATTLESHIPS) and shortage of MINES. The arrival of new DESTROYERS and SUBMARINES strengthened the fleet during 1916, but Eberhardt was replaced in July by the younger Admiral KOLCHAK. Retired to a seat on the Council of State, he was briefly arrested by the Bolsheviks in 1918 (see RUSSIA).

Ebert, Friedrich (1871–1925) German socialist, a political organizer rather than a theoretician, who succeeded August Bebel as head of the Social Democratic Party (SDP) in 1913 and steered the Reichstag's largest party on a moderate course for gradual constitutional reform. Though seen as dangerous revolutionaries by the crown and its supporters, the SDP rejected direct action against the state, and Ebert returned to GERMANY from an extended holiday on 6 August 1914 to coordinate his party's support for a 'defensive' war.

Ebert and his chief spokesman, SCHEIDEMANN, remained firmly committed to national defence (and thus the war effort) until 1917, despite government failure to grant substantial constitutional reforms and a widening rift with Hugo HAASE's left-wing minority. Ebert subsequently moved closer to the Reichstag's centre parties, and joined them to frame the PEACE RESOLUTION of July, but a wave of munitions strikes in January 1918 prompted a move to the left to forestall revolution from below.

Called into Prince MAX VON BADEN's shortlived administration in October, Ebert was formally (if illegally) handed power by the Prince on 9 November 1918. As co-chairman (with Haase) of the provisional Council of People's Commissars, he accepted General GRÖNER's offer of military support for the new regime on the same day, and agreement with workers' representatives was reached on 10 November (see GERMAN REVOLUTIONS). Elected first chancellor of the new German republic on 11 February 1919, Ebert remained in office until his death, preoccupied with economic crisis and the threat of revolt from both political extremes.

Egypt A virtually autonomous province of the Ottoman Empire, ruled by a hereditary Khedive under the auspices of the Sultan of TURKEY, Egypt had been under effective British military occupation since the 1880s. British involvement sprang from concern for the security of the Suez Canal, and was politically justified as protection against endemic tribal conflict on Egypt's southern and western borders.

The post of British consul general in Egypt, held by KITCHENER from 1911 until his appointment as British war minister in August 1914, carried full military, economic and foreign-policy control over the Khedive's council of ministers, but British influence was resented by nationalist movements gathering strength in 1914. The semi-representative Legislative Assembly established in 1913 was distinctly anti-British, as was the devoutly pro-Turkish Khedive Abbas Hilmi.

During the late summer of 1914, Turkish neutrality prevented British authorities from expelling German and Austro-Hungarian agents and, with 70,000 Turkish nationals resident in the country, Egypt was a hotbed of international intrigue. Martial law and suspension of the Assembly were enacted as soon as Turkey entered the War in early November, and official declaration of a British Protectorate followed on 18 December. Abbas Hilmi, convalescing in Constantinople after an assassination attempt, was deposed next day.

His replacement (and uncle), Prince Hussein Kamel, was arbitrarily promoted to Sultan as a sop to Muslim opinion, and Egypt's new position within the British Empire confirmed by the appointment of a high commissioner early in 1915 – Sir Henry McMahon until December 1916, and General Wingate for the rest of the War. Egypt's political status remained essentially unchanged throughout the War and it functioned as a major British military base.

A Muslim rising planned to coincide with the unsuccessful Turkish attack on the SUEZ CANAL in February 1915 failed to materialize, and Hussein Kamel survived several assassination attempts to be peacefully succeeded by his brother Ahmad Fuad in October 1917. Pro-British prime minister Husein Rushdi Pasha remained in office throughout the War. Nationalist agitation for full independence, organized and led by the Wafd Party under Sa'ad Zaghlul Pasha, grew steadily in intensity but only threatened serious disruption in 1918, when it provoked some civil unrest. Security was also threatened by the prolonged SENUSSI revolt on Egypt's western border, but this and potentially unsettling border problems with the Sudan were effectively controlled by native EGYPTIAN FORCES.

British promises not to use Egyptian forces in overseas operations were honoured, but the country's agricultural resources were heavily exploited and a volunteer Egyptian Labour Corps provided about 120,000 men for support work on the PALESTINE and WESTERN FRONTS.

After 1918 preparations were begun for dissolution of the Protectorate, arranged by General ALLENBY in his role as postwar high commissioner. However, dissolution was delayed until 1922 by Wafd opposition to continued British control of the Canal zone. Despite nominal independence under King Fuad, Britain remained in de facto control of Egypt until 1936, and retained occupying forces on the Canal for another 20 years.

Egyptian Forces The Egyptian Army was a largely native home-defence force. In 1914 it comprised 17 battalions of infantry (8 Sudanese and 9 Egyptian), 3 companies of mounted infantry, a Camel Corps, support services and various local militia groups. Organized, expanded and equipped by the British during the prewar years, and led by British officers, its wartime role reflected EGYPT's position of nominal independence from the British Empire. Although a few field ARTILLERY units participated voluntarily in the defence of the SUEZ CANAL in early 1915, the Egyptian Army was never used overseas and was primarily employed to maintain order in the troubled SUDAN. Most of its equipment was obsolete British stock, although some modern Lee-Enfield RIFLES were available by the end of the War.

The Egyptian Labour Corps, a paramilitary organization used to build the roads, RAILWAYS and water pipes vital to a desert advance, made a considerable manpower contribution to British operations on the PALESTINE FRONT. Instituted in January 1916, when the British hired 10,000 workers to improve communications between Cairo and Suez, it had grown to a strength of 185,000 men by mid-1917, although arduous conditions allowed only a fraction of the force to be deployed at any given time. Another 28,000 men (mostly native drivers and attendants, but including a few British officers) and 33,000 animals performed a similarly important freight-carrying role with the Camel Transport Corps. See also: SENUSSI REVOLT.

Eichhorn, Field Marshal Hermann von (1848–1918) Veteran German general given command of the newly formed Tenth Army on the EASTERN FRONT in January 1915, leading it in the Second Battle of the MASURIAN LAKES and the capture of KOVNO. He remained in the post, based in the northern Polish sector of the front, throughout the war with RUSSIA, extending his responsibilities to overall control of the sector (Army Group Eichhorn) in July 1916 and being promoted field marshal in December 1917. After the BREST-LITOVSK Treaty had been concluded in March 1918 he was transferred to command occupying forces in the Crimea and the UKRAINE (the Kiev Army Group). As military dictator for the region, despite the existence of puppet governments, Eichhorn was responsible for economic exploitation, particularly of grain from the Ukraine. However, his attempts to force Ukrainian peasants to work the land met only limited success in an atmosphere of revolutionary unrest, and he was assassinated by nationalist rebels in Kiev on 30 July 1918.

Eighteen-Pounder The standard field gun of the wartime BRITISH ARMY, with an effective range of about 4.8km and a maximum sustained fire rate of about eight rounds per minute. Emphasis on production of heavy ARTILLERY meant that many units in secondary theatres suffered shortages of this reliable and reasonably mobile weapon.

Einem, General Karl von (1853–1934) A former modernizing Prussian war minister who spent the entire War on the WESTERN FRONT. He commanded VII Corps in von BÜLOW's Second Army from the invasion of BELGIUM until the battle of the MARNE in September 1914, when he took command of the Third Army. He led his army through two Allied CHAMPAGNE OFFENSIVES and three Battles of the AISNE before his last promotion, one day after the ARMISTICE, to lead Crown Prince WILHELM's former Army Group back into GERMANY for demobilization, after which he retired.

El Arish, Advance on Slow British advance across the Sinai peninsula in autumn 1916, distinguished by a major supply and logistic operation designed to enable long-range action in desert conditions (see MAP 22). After a second Turkish attack towards the SUEZ CANAL had been repulsed at ROMANI in August 1916, British PALESTINE FRONT commander MURRAY received permission to advance during the winter to El Arish, garrisoned by 1,600 troops from Colonel von KRESSENSTEIN's battered 'Desert Force'. The need to develop roads, RAILWAYS and water pipelines occupied Murray in Cairo, and the advance itself was entrusted to a newly designated 'Eastern Force' under General Dobell, veteran of the CAMEROON and SENUSSI campaigns.

Murray concentrated most of his valuable mounted units under Dobell, and initial operations by Eastern Force consisted of desert raids against Turkish outposts. By December

1916 supply lines were complete and General Chetwode's 'Desert Column' – a detachment of two infantry divisions, the ANZAC Mounted Division and a camel brigade – was sent against El Arish. Kressenstein had already ordered a retreat into Palestine, and unopposed British CAVALRY reached water supplies at the frontier just before Christmas. See First Battle of GAZA.

Emden One of the most effective GERMAN NAVY commerce raiders, the light CRUISER *Emden* was built in 1908 and formed part of Admiral von SPEE's East Asiatic squadron in August 1914. Detached to prey on Allied trade and troop transport routes in the Indian Ocean, it virtually paralysed them for three months, sinking 17 merchant ships and capturing a Russian auxiliary cruiser. Hunted by every Allied warship in the region, it sank the only major RUSSIAN NAVY unit in the Pacific, the small cruiser *Zemcug*, in Penang harbour on 28 October, but was itself surprised and destroyed by the Australian cruiser *SYDNEY* at the Cocos Islands on 9 November. See also: *BREMEN*.

BRIEF DATA (1914) Displacement: 3,650 tons; Crew: 360; Dimensions: length 388ft (117.6m), beam 43.5ft (13.2m); Speed: 24.5k; Armament: 10 × 5.9in, 2 × 17.7in TT.

Engadine One of six privately owned cross-Channel ferries taken over by the ROYAL NAVY between 1914 and 1917 for conversion as seaplane carriers. Their speed enabled them to work with major warships in fleet operations and (in theory) to fly wheeled floatplanes from their platform decks. In practice they were little more than mobile hangars, winching seaplanes into and out of the sea as needed.

Along with the similar *Empress* and *Riviera*, *Engadine* was converted in autumn 1914, and all three took part in the CUXHAVEN RAID at Christmas. *Engadine* subsequently operated with the BATTLECRUISER force in the North Sea, providing the only aerial reconnaissance at JUTLAND and towing the crippled *WARRIOR* away from the battle before it sank.

The other converted ferries were the larger *Manxman* and *BEN-MY-CHREE*, and the more comprehensively altered *Vindex*, with a 20-metre runway deck for use by BRISTOL SCOUT landplanes. The first successful take-off by a landplane at sea was by a Scout from *Vindex* in November 1915, and the ship later joined *Engadine* in several raids against coastal ZEPPELIN sheds. Most of the converted ferries subsequently moved to the MEDITERRANEAN as larger AIRCRAFT CARRIERS came into service for fleet work.

BRIEF DATA (*Engadine*, 1915) Gross tonnage: 1,676 tons; Crew: c 250; Dimensions: length 311ft (94.2m), beam 40ft (12.1m); Speed: 21.5k; Armament: 2 × 4in gun, 1 × 6pdr AA, 3 × a/c.

Entente Powers The usual collective term for GREAT BRITAIN, FRANCE and RUSSIA in 1914–15, after the diplomatic understandings that linked them in potential opposition to the TRIPLE ALLIANCE before 1914. See also: CENTRAL POWERS; ALLIES, The.

Enver Pasha (1881–1922) Young and ambitious TURKISH ARMY officer, who played a leading role in the YOUNG TURK revolution of 1908, but rejected political office to continue a promising military career. He made a spectacular return to politics in January 1913, heading a raiding party that expelled the government and installed a regime committed to continuing hostilities in the Balkans. Enver left active service in January 1914 to replace IZZET PASHA as war minister, instituting an immediate purge of senior military opposition.

The militarist triumvirate of Enver, TALAAT and DJEMAL, reliant on personal influence over Sultan Mohammed V (whose niece was married to Enver), had the active support of important elements in civil-service, business, military and political circles, but Enver's success in promoting military expansion and alliance with a major power bloc depended to some extent on secrecy and subterfuge.

In close concert with Talaat he pursued an adventurous diplomacy of his own. Most of the cabinet knew nothing of the alliance signed with GERMANY in July 1914, or of Enver's subsequent (and ignored) offer of alliance to RUSSIA. Even Talaat was unaware of Enver's probable collusion in Admiral

SOUCHON's raid on Russian BLACK SEA bases that ended TURKEY's neutrality.

Still in his early thirties, Enver was allowed to function as virtual dictator once Turkey was at war. Control of internal resources was accompanied by a clumsy attempt to modernize the Empire on the European state model, with orders unifying currency and language actually hastening administrative breakdown. Though he needed German military and economic involvement to maintain the war effort, Enver's nationalist ambitions were reflected in repression of the Empire's minority populations, but his role in the ARMENIAN MASSACRES remains unclear.

The same motives directed extravagant military strategies concentrated primarily on the CAUCASIAN FRONT, where Enver took command of the Third Army during the disastrous SARIKAMISH campaign and planned the abortive offensive of summer 1916. His contribution to the Army's greatest wartime success at GALLIPOLI consisted largely of repeated orders to launch offensives, and he reacted similarly to British advances on the MESOPOTAMIAN and PALESTINE FRONTS, where his determination to recapture BAGHDAD helped delay deployment of YILDERIM FORCE beyond usefulness in 1917.

Enver relaunched operations in the Caucasus after the FEBRUARY REVOLUTION of 1917 had weakened the RUSSIAN ARMY. Carried out despite strong opposition from the Turkish Army, Talaat and other cabinet members, these operations fatally diluted Turkish resources elsewhere and wrecked relations with Berlin by challenging German plans for economic exploitation of TRANSCAUCASIA.

By mid-1918 military failure and economic collapse had mobilized political opposition around a new Sultan, but Enver clung to office until the cabinet resigned on 7 October, concealing the extent of Allied advances to the end. He joined most of his colleagues aboard a German ship into exile, and was killed fighting with Turkish-speaking Central Asians against Soviet rule.

Epéhy, Battle of Attack of 18 September 1918 by the British Fourth Army (RAWLINSON) against forward outposts of the HINDENBURG LINE on the WESTERN FRONT. Alongside the French First Army (Debeney), Rawlinson's troops had reached the Hindenburg Line at its strongest points by early September, but his plan for an immediate attack on forward German positions was turned down in early September by C-in-C HAIG, who responded to popular sensitivity about casualty figures in GREAT BRITAIN by insisting on a pause for recuperation. Haig changed his mind on 13 September, after relatively easy victories at ST MIHIEL and HAVRINCOURT had emphasized the rapid decline of German fighting strength.

All three corps of the Fourth Army took part in the advance, along with the northernmost corps of the British Third Army (BYNG). Infantry was supported by a CREEPING BARRAGE from 1,500 guns and the concentrated fire of 300 machine guns. French support from the south failed to materialize, and the attack met only limited success on its flanks, but two divisions of the Australian Corps (MONASH) advanced about 5km in the centre. Though a relatively small success, Epéhy confirmed the view of Allied frontline commanders that immediate action could bring swift victory, and encouraged inter-Allied cooperation to that end. See MAP 2.

Erin One of two modern warships built in Britain for the TURKISH NAVY but commandeered by the ROYAL NAVY on its completion in August 1914. Originally the *Reshadieh*, it resembled contemporary IRON DUKE Class battleships and replaced *AUDACIOUS* with the Second Battle Squadron of the GRAND FLEET in late 1914, *Erin* remained in the North Sea until reduced to reserve duties in 1919.

BRIEF DATA (1914) Displacement: 25,250 tons; Crew: 1,130; Dimensions: length 560ft (187.9m), beam 92ft (27.9m); Speed: 21k; Armament: 10 × 13.5in gun, 16 × 6in, 2 × 3in AA, 4 × 21in TT.

Eritrea The small Italian colony of Eritrea in eastern AFRICA was a naval station for Allied shipping in the Red Sea, and recruits from its (estimated) half million native population formed the basis of Italian colonial forces on the continent, operating as garrison troops in

SOMALILAND and against the SENUSSI REVOLT in north Africa. Like other peaceful European colonies in north and central Africa, Eritrea benefited from a significant wartime increase in trade with Allied armies, particularly in cattle. See MAP 17.

Ersatz Contemporary German term, from the verb *ersetzen* (to substitute), invented to describe alternative products developed to replace goods, materials and services unavailable in wartime. Substitute production was necessary in other countries but most common in GERMANY, which possessed the technological base for ingenuity and was increasingly beset by consumer and industrial shortages as a result of Allied naval BLOCKADE. Ersatz development, along with conservation, recycling and use of streamlined production methods, was a basic tenet of German government anti-blockade policy and enjoyed a number of important successes, most notably the invention of artificial nitrogen-fixing methods to enable manufacture of synthetic explosives and fertilizers. Many other substitute products were of very poor quality, giving the word an enduring pejorative connotation and forcing the government to introduce a register of licensed ersatz goods in March 1918, eventually listing 11,000 products. See also: EAST AFRICA.

Erzberger, Matthias (1875–1921) A leading figure on the left wing of the German Catholic Centre Party, and a Reichstag deputy since 1903, Erzberger's career illustrated the political conundrum facing moderate, middle-class conservatives in GERMANY. A monarchist and nationalist, but opposed to colonial expansion and in favour of gradual constitutional reform, he regarded the socialist SDP as dangerous (anti-Catholic) revolutionaries. He relied instead on a policy of qualified, critical support for the chancellor to smooth the path to reform.

Erzberger placed his business and industrial connections unreservedly at the disposal of the state in August 1914, and was entrusted with the organization of overseas PROPAGANDA. In 1915 he took part in the unsuccessful German diplomatic mission to ITALY headed by former chancellor von Bülow, and he spoke in favour of large-scale annexations as a precondition to peace, primarily in BELGIUM and eastern FRANCE.

A strong opponent of unrestricted SUBMARINE WARFARE in 1916, Erzberger eventually led calls in the Reichstag for a negotiated end to hostilities. He introduced the PEACE RESOLUTION in July 1917 and simultaneously made public a confidential, pessimistic report by Austro-Hungarian foreign minister CZERNIN, an act of 'treason' for which he was never forgiven by right-wing groups.

He remained a marginal figure under the THIRD SUPREME COMMAND, but was called into MAX VON BADEN's government as minister without portfolio in October 1918, and was part of the commission that signed the ARMISTICE on 11 November. The Centre Party held its ground in the 1919 elections and Erzberger remained in the cabinet, working for acceptance of the VERSAILLES settlement until accusations of financial misdealing forced his resignation as finance minister in spring 1920. A symbol of 'defeatism', he was assassinated by right-wing extremists in Berlin.

Erzincan, Battle of The last major action on the CAUCASIAN FRONT, a collision in July 1916 between the Russian Caucasian Army (YUDENICH), advancing west of of ERZURUM, and the Turkish Third Army (Abdul Kerim), heavily reinforced for a counterattack after the loss of TRABZON in April.

War minister ENVER planned the counterattack using troops freed from GALLIPOLI, against the advice of LIMAN VON SANDERS and other senior TURKISH ARMY officers to reinforce KUT. With reinforcements still gathering it got off to a false start on 1 June, when an attempt to halt the Russian advance on the road from Erzurum ended in retreat after a three-day battle. Although Yudenich paused to recuperate, he resumed the attack on 3 July, with a subsidiary advance southwest of Mus delaying the Turkish Second Army's planned offensive.

The offensive reached the Turkish advance base of Erzincan, 150km west of Erzurum, on 23 July. Poorly fortified, Erzincan fell after two days. Surviving Third Army units retreated to Mosul and Sivas, briefly pursued by CAVALRY and a battery of Belgian ARMOURED CARS before the Second Army (IZZET PASHA) finally attacked in the south. Led by Mustapha KEMAL's corps, it retook Bitlis on 2 August, forcing Yudenich to transfer reserves and suspend operations west of Erzincan. Regrouped Russian forces had retaken Bitlis by 23 August, and recaptured Mus the next day, but demands for reinforcements on the EASTERN FRONT and Turkish exhaustion ended serious attacks along the front in the first few days of September. See MAP 24.

Erzurum Offensive First phase of the offensive campaign conducted by Russian General YUDENICH on the CAUCASIAN FRONT in 1916. Reinforced in expectation of an offensive in the spring or summer by Turkish troops released from the defence of GALLIPOLI, Yudenich concentrated for an immediate offensive towards the FORTRESS town of Erzurum, the main population centre in Turkish Armenia and headquarters of Abdul Kerim's Turkish Third Army.

Preliminary attacks all along the front began on 10 January and the main offensive broke through Turkish positions at Köprukoy a week later, inflicting 25,000 casualties but failing to surround the Third Army in time to prevent most units retreating to Erzurum. The fortress was besieged by the Russians from late January, and the first of its outer forts fell on 13 February. The garrison surrendered three days later, giving up 13,000 prisoners and some 350 guns. Further south a secondary advance took Mus on 18 February. As British commanders in PALESTINE contemplated a Russian sweep into the heart of TURKEY, Yudenich (only nominally directed by regional C-in-C Grand Duke NIKOLAI) swung the focus of his offensive north, marching on the BLACK SEA port of TRABZON from 22 February. See MAP 24.

Es Sinn, Battle of Pyrrhic Anglo-Indian victory on the MESOPOTAMIAN FRONT in September 1915. The easy capture of AMARA and NASIRIYEH during the summer prompted plans for a further advance on KUT (see MAP 23). British front commander NIXON proposed an advance on Kut as a primarily defensive measure, but regarded the capture of BAGHDAD as his ultimate goal. The British government, not for the first time, acquiesced reluctantly in a scheme that ran contrary to its defensive priorities in Mesopotamia, but refused reinforcements from ADEN.

The main Turkish forward defence of Kut was an intricate system of trenches either side of the Tigris at Es Sinn, about 15km downstream. General TOWNSHEND and some 11,000 troops, supported by 4 ROYAL NAVY gunboats, left their forward base beyond Amara on 12 September, but difficult conditions and delays to ARTILLERY reinforcements postponed an attack at Es Sinn until 28 September.

The bulk of Townshend's troops were sent to outflank the main position on the west bank of the river, and a smaller force feigned an attack on the weaker side. Turkish commander Nur-Ud-Din committed reserves to the feint, but Townshend's flanking column got lost overnight and its delayed attack met fierce resistance. The gunboats, unable to pass a river obstruction, played no part in the operation.

By the end of the day only outer portions of the Turkish line had fallen, but Nur-Ud-Din retreated unnoticed during the night, and could not be efficiently pursued by troops in urgent need of rest and water. Kut was occupied the next day, but Turkish forces remained essentially intact at prepared positions further upriver at CTESIPHON. See also: Battle of DUJAILA.

Essen, Admiral Nikolai von (1860–1915) Appointed supreme commander of the RUSSIAN NAVY's Baltic Fleet when the post was created in 1909, Essen was one of several relatively young and vigorous officers introduced to senior rank after 1905. His radical training and procedural reforms were an important factor in the fleet's generally successful wartime performance, and he consistently argued against the purely defensive strategy envisaged before 1914. He never shared the high command's fear of a large-scale German naval onslaught in the BALTIC, and moved onto the offensive once German limitations in the theatre became clear. However, he was forbidden to risk the fleet's new GANGUT Class BATTLESHIPS outside the Gulf of Finland. After Essen's death from illness in May 1915, subsequent fleet commanders (Admirals Kanin and Nepenin) pursued a less ambitious policy, remaining generally on the defensive despite growing material superiority over German naval forces.

Estonia Baltic province of imperial RUSSIA, effectively ruled in 1914 by an oligarchy of semi-feudal landowners but with a distinct regional culture dating back to classical times. Estonia was untouched by military operations on the EASTERN FRONT, but a National Council and a small Free Estonian Army were formed in July 1917 with the blessing of the Russian PROVISIONAL GOVERNMENT, and the country declared full independence in the face of an attempted Bolshevik coup in November.

Elections in January returned a moderate administration, but a more serious Bolshevik insurrection prompted landowners to appeal for German assistance. The GERMAN ARMY expelled revolutionary forces from the port of Revel (Tallinn) in February but imposed military occupation until the ARMISTICE in November, disbanding the Estonian Army in April and leaving the country virtually defenceless when it withdrew. An immediate RED ARMY invasion (officially by a force of Estonian rebels) retook part of the country, but was prevented from recapturing Revel by ROYAL NAVY warships in the BALTIC. It was driven back into RUSSIA during January by reconstituted Estonian forces, aided by 3,000 mercenaries from FINLAND under General Wetzer. Fighting inside Russia continued until late 1919, and a peace treaty recognizing Estonian independence was signed in February 1920. See MAP 25.

Eugen, Archduke (1863–1954) The only royal commander in the AUSTRO-HUNGARIAN ARMY to have received full staff-officer training, Eugen was overall commander of imperial forces on the BALKAN FRONT from December 1914 and on the ITALIAN FRONT from the following May. With strategic planning and dispositions largely controlled by Army chief of staff CONRAD, or later by attached German commanders, and tactical work performed by field officers, Eugen's role was almost entirely ceremonial. He was promoted field marshal on the accession of Emperor KARL I (his cousin) in late 1916, and remained at his post until January 1918, when it was abolished and he retired from active service. Exiled from postwar Austria by 'anti-Habsburg' laws, he was eventually allowed to return in 1934.

Evert, General Alexei (1857–1918) Veteran infantry officer who exemplified the caution, inefficiency and cabalism endemic among the older generation of RUSSIAN ARMY commanders. Evert replaced General Salza in command of the Fourth Army in GALICIA in early September 1914, leading it during the POLISH CAMPAIGN in the autumn and the 'GREAT RETREAT' of the following summer.

An ardent monarchist, he was promoted to command the Western Army Group in the central sector of the EASTERN FRONT when NICHOLAS II took personal command of the Army in September 1915, and spent much of the next 18 months slowly amassing strength for a series of BREAKTHROUGH assaults against German forces. His attack at Lake NAROCH in March 1916 was a costly, ill-planned failure, and he was unwilling to support the BRUSILOV OFFENSIVE in July. Subsequently given control of the front around KOVEL, he supervised three months of unproductive attrition. Despite widespread criticism and rumours of treason (a common problem for Russian officers with German names), Evert remained in the post until after the FEBRUARY REVOLUTION, when he was dismissed by the PROVISIONAL GOVERNMENT. The circumstances of his death remain unclear.

F

Fairey Campania British reconnaissance biplane. A floatplane with folding wings, it was the first aircraft purpose-designed for use on AIRCRAFT CARRIERS. Named after the carrier *CAMPANIA*, to which early production models (fitted with a 275hp engine) were assigned, it entered RNAS service in late 1917, and 62 had been built by the ARMISTICE. Launched from ships on a wheeled trolley, attached to the floats but jettisoned on take-off, it equipped two other converted carriers (*Nairana* and *Pegasus*) and was used by several coastal seaplane stations.

BRIEF DATA Type: two-seat naval reconnaissance; Engine: 345hp Rolls Royce; Max speed: 80mph (128kph); Armament: 1 × 0.303in mg, max bomb load 200lbs (91kg).

Falkenhayn, General Erich von (1861–1922) Minor Prussian aristocrat, and a general since 1912, who became Prussian war minister the following year and held the post in August 1914. He succeeded MOLTKE as GERMAN ARMY chief of staff in September, combining both jobs for the next six months.

Stagnation on the WESTERN FRONT persuaded Falkenhayn to seek decisive victory elsewhere in 1915. Aware that RUSSIA was unlikely to be beaten with the forces at his disposal, he planned a campaign against SERBIA, but CONRAD and LUDENDORFF manoeuvred him into sanctioning a series of major operations on the EASTERN FRONT. Despite bitter opposition from Ludendorff, he transferred strength to the BALKAN FRONT in the autumn and reduced HINDENBURG's eastern sphere of command.

Success against Serbia was overshadowed in GERMANY by the myth of an opportunity missed in Russia, and political opposition to Falkenhayn mounted in 1916. A dispassionate and essentially moderate strategist, he retained the Kaiser's confidence in an atmosphere of polarizing political extremism; but he was a natural target for beleaguered chancellor BETHMANN HOLLWEG, and for generals excusing their failure to win decisive victories.

Falkenhayn's reluctant attempt at victory through attrition at VERDUN went badly wrong after he allowed vast German forces to be drawn into costly BREAKTHROUGH attempts. A campaign for the promotion of Hindenburg to supreme command (led by Bethmann Hollweg and right-wing military/industrial interests) gathered pace in Germany as the British attack on the SOMME got underway in France. The summer successes of the Russian BRUSILOV OFFENSIVE threw divisions between Falkenhayn and Ludendorff into sharp relief and, on the defensive everywhere, he was forced to resign on 29 August 1916.

He accepted the insult of demotion to take field command of the Ninth Army for the successful ROMANIAN CAMPAIGN, and led YILDERIM FORCE in TURKEY and PALESTINE from July 1917. After a succession of defeats by ALLENBY's British forces he was replaced by LIMAN VON SANDERS in February 1918, and was given command of the Tenth Army in LITHUANIA, retiring after its return to Germany in February 1919.

Falkland Islands, Battle of the The destruction of the GERMAN NAVY's commerce-raiding force in the South Atlantic on 8 December 1914 by a far stronger ROYAL NAVY formation sent to reverse the British defeat at CORONEL (see MAP 15).

The British show of force reflected Admiral FISHER's recent return to the post of First Sea Lord. Two fast, modern BATTLECRUISERS (*Inflexible* and *INVINCIBLE*) left the GRAND FLEET for the British base at the Falkland Islands on 11 November. They were to be joined by three armoured CRUISERS (*Carnarvon*, *Cornwall* and *Kent*), two light cruisers (*Bristol* and *Glasgow*) and the old *CANOPUS*, grounded in Port Stanley harbour as an improvised fortress. A third battlecruiser (*Princess Royal*) and two more cruisers were sent to cover the West Indies.

Intelligence suggested German commander SPEE, whose force included the heavy cruisers *SCHARNHORST* and *GNEISENAU* and three light cruisers, was approaching the South Atlantic via Cape Horn. However, British task force commander STURDEE moved slowly, meeting his cruisers on 26 November off the coast of Brazil, and eventually reaching Port Stanley on the morning of 7 December.

Spee had rounded the Horn on 2 December, and decided to raid the apparently unprotected Falklands before proceeding north to refuel in the Plate Estuary. He missed RADIO signals indicating British battlecruisers in the region and, delayed by bad weather, was off Port Stanley at dawn on 8 December. Though scouting forces were fired on by *Canopus* and reported big masts in the harbour, Spee decided they belonged to JAPANESE NAVY vessels, and chose to flee from what he believed was a slower enemy.

British warships were coaling and could have been caught unprepared, but the battlecruisers eventually put to sea at 10.00, preceded by the equally fast Glasgow, and sped in pursuit. Intermittent fire from both battlecruisers failed to score any hits before Spee, recognizing opponents he could not hope to outrun, turned his big ships to face them at 13.20, ordering the light cruisers to scatter and save themselves.

Skilful manoeuvring and accurate shooting, combined with British inaccuracy, enabled *Scharnhorst* and *Gneisenau* to get within range of the battlecruisers and score a hit on *Invincible*, prompting Sturdee to take temporary refuge behind a smokescreen. When it cleared the German ships were out of range, steaming south into worsening weather.

Sturdee resumed the pursuit and was back in range 40 minutes later. As his battlecruisers turned to fire their broadsides Spee cut across their bows, closing sufficiently to attack with his numerous secondary guns, which scored many hits but had little effect. Heavy British shells struck both cruisers, quickly sinking *Scharnhorst* with no survivors, and *Gneisenau* went down soon after 18.00, following a prolonged, one-sided battle with both British battlecruisers; about 200 of its crew were rescued. Of the German light cruisers, *Nürnberg* and *Leipzig* were chased and destroyed by British cruisers, but *Dresden* (and one of several colliers accompanying the squadron) escaped to the southwest.

Though neither complete nor efficient, the British victory had a profound effect on the morale of both navies. It also freed Britain's trade and troop transport routes from the threat of surface raiders, and apparently justified Fisher's faith in his controversial battlecruisers.

Falluja Key flood-control point on the River Euphrates west of Baghdad, occupied as a consolidatory measure at the start of the Anglo-Indian SAMARRAH OFFENSIVE in March 1917 (see MAP 23). Though a minor affair, the occupation illustrated the problems facing both armies on the MESOPOTAMIAN FRONT. The small Turkish garrison at Falluja retreated up the Euphrates when a British brigade arrived on 19 March, but wrecked dams protecting floodplains to the south. British troops faced greater opposition from local MARSH ARABS, who harassed emergency dam reconstruction after their initial defence of Falluja had collapsed. Conducted in sweltering heat, and successful only because the river was unusually low, building work kept the brigade out of action for several days. See also: Battle of RAMADI.

Farman F-40 French 'PUSHER' biplane, an armed two-seater designed jointly in 1915 by the Farman brothers, Henri and Maurice. In service on the WESTERN FRONT from late 1915, its lack of rear armament was a severe operational drawback against German FIGHTERS armed with INTERRUPTER GEAR. In the absence of better types, the F-40 remained in widespread use with AÉRONAUTIQUE MILITAIRE units until early 1917, used for reconnaissance and short-range bombing missions, as well as attacks on BALLOONS. Several modified versions were produced with bigger engines or redesigned wings, including the F-41, F-56, F-60 and F-61. A few of the main production models were retained into 1917 as improvised night bombers, and they also served in small numbers with the RNAS. The BELGIAN AIR SERVICE was still using its few F-40s at the ARMISTICE.

BRIEF DATA (F-40) Type: two-seater armed reconnaissance/light bomber; Engine: 160hp Renault; Max speed: 134kph; Armament: 2–4 × 0.303in mg.

Farman F-50 Twin-engined biplane, in service during 1918, that was the only French heavy bomber of the period. Less effective in the role than contemporary British HANDLEY PAGE 0/400 or Italian CAPRONI CA5 designs, it equipped only two AÉRONAUTIQUE MILITAIRE squadrons on the WESTERN FRONT and was withdrawn from service soon after the ARMISTICE.

BRIEF DATA Type: medium/heavy bomber; Crew: 2; Engine: 2 × 275hp Lorraine Dietrich; Max speed: 145kph; Armament: 1 or 2 × in mg, max bomb load 600kg (1,320lbs).

Farman HF-20 Unarmed French 'PUSHER' biplane, in service with British and French reconnaissance units in August 1914. Three versions operated on the WESTERN FRONT (HF-20, HF-21 and HF-22) but their 70hp or 80hp engines were unable to lift any form of installed armament. Withdrawn from France at the first opportunity, they were also used by the RUSSIAN, BELGIAN and ROMANIAN air services, remaining in frontline action throughout in the less competitive airspace over the EASTERN FRONT.

Of many later developments in the series, only the armed HF-27 enjoyed a genuinely successful military career. Built around an all-steel airframe, it could lift a useful bomb load and was particularly suited to operations in hot climates. Active on the Western Front during 1915, it was used by the British air forces for operations on the MESOPOTAMIAN FRONT and in AFRICA, remaining standard equipment at many tropical bases until 1918.

BRIEF DATA (HF-27) Type: two-seater armed reconnaissance/light bomber; Engine: 160hp Canton-Unné; Max speed: 120kph; Armament: 1 × 0.303in mg, max bomb load 500lbs (227kg).

Farman MF-7 French 'PUSHER' biplane, a Maurice Farman design, that entered production in 1913, and was also manufactured under licence in Britain, where its protruding landing skids gave rise to the nickname 'Longhorn'. Difficult to handle and particularly slow, it was briefly used for reconnaissance work on the WESTERN FRONT by the French AÉRONAUTIQUE MILITAIRE (which employed 30 MF-7s in August 1914), and to a lesser extent by the RFC. It was replaced by the FARMAN MF-11 early in 1915, but manufacture for training and experimental purposes continued until the end of the year.

BRIEF DATA (MF-7, French) Type: two-seat reconnaissance; Engine: 70hp Renault; Max speed: 95kph; Ceiling: 3,000m; Armament: observer's small arms.

Farman MF-11 Armed modification of the FARMAN MF-7, called the 'Shorthorn' because of its smaller landing skids. It joined Allied units on the WESTERN FRONT from the end of 1914, serving with French and British forces as a reconnaissance and light bombing craft. In December 1914 an RNAS 'Shorthorn' carried out the first wartime night raid, against coastal installations near Ostend, and the type also fought on the EASTERN, ITALIAN and MESOPOTAMIAN FRONTS, where lack of forward armament was less important. Although later MF-11s were fitted with a variety of bigger engines, and large numbers were built in the absence of superior alternatives, they could never match the performance of 'TRACTOR' machines and were gradually withdrawn from late 1915.

BRIEF DATA Type: two-seater armed reconnaissance/light bomber; Engine: 80hp Renault; Max speed: 90kph; Ceiling: 3,000m; Armament: 1 × 0.303in (or 8mm) mg, max bomb load 130kg (288lbs).

Fatherland Party Right-wing German political pressure group, formed in autumn 1917 as a response to the Reichstag's PEACE RESOLUTION of July. Led by former Prussian navy minister TIRPITZ, it was funded by the THIRD SUPREME COMMAND and intended to provide a popular, extraparliamentary support base for its dictatorial home policies and ambitious war aims. Backed by an intensive PROPAGANDA campaign, it lobbied against internal constitutional reform and in favour of the vast annexations proposed by the Supreme Command. By 1918 the Fatherland Party boasted some 1.2 million members, drawn largely from the military and conservative agrarian communities, providing some kind of mandate for continuation of the HINDENBURG PROGRAMME.

Faustschlag, Operation Limited German offensive on the EASTERN FRONT of February 1918, primarily designed to shorten the front and destabilize the Bolshevik government. Undertaken in response to Russian delaying tactics during the BREST-LITOVSK peace negotiations, it was a compromise between the conciliatory policies of foreign minister KÜHLMANN and the territorial ambitions of LUDENDORFF, who had initially planned to take Petrograd (St Petersburg). Begun on 17 February, in deep midwinter, it advanced about 250km without meeting coherent opposition, and prompted formal acceptance of German peace terms two days later.

Fayolle, General Marie (1852–1928) French artillery officer who retired in 1914, but was recalled to command an infantry division in August. Rapid promotion followed, hastened by C-in-C JOFFRE's wholesale dismissals of failed generals, and Fayolle commanded the Sixth Army from February 1916. Though its participation in the SOMME OFFENSIVE was not a success, Fayolle remained in favour under NIVELLE, transferring to the First Army in early 1917, and took over Army Group Centre when PÉTAIN became C-in-C in May. He led French forces sent to the ITALIAN FRONT in November 1917 but returned to the WESTERN FRONT the following March as commander of the Reserve Army Group, which played a vital part in Allied resistance to the KAISERSCHLACHT and AISNE Offensives. After taking part in the second MARNE victory, Fayolle's Group (55 divisions) advanced steadily east in the centre of a general Allied advance in autumn 1918, its progress overshadowed by the major AMIENS, COURTRAI and MEUSE–ARGONNE OFFENSIVES on its flanks.

FE-2 Series First produced by the British Royal Aircraft Factory as the FE-2 in 1911, the series entered RFC service in late 1914 as the unarmed FE-2a reconnaissance type, using the same outer panels as the company's BE-2 biplane. Its 'PUSHER' engine proved inadequate and it was not a success, but a more powerful, streamlined FE-2b version reached the WESTERN FRONT in autumn 1915. Designed for armed FIGHTER and reconnaissance work, it was similar in performance and appearance to the contemporary AIRCO DH-2, and was a staple RFC weapon against German FOKKER E-TYPES by early 1916. Its single LEWIS GUN was soon augmented by a second (also fired by the observer), and the slightly faster FE-2d, in service from July 1916, could mount two more forward guns on the cowling of its 250hp engine.

Both versions helped to establish Allied air superiority over the WESTERN FRONT in mid-1916, reflected in total production figures of 1,484 FE-2b and 385 FE-2d models, but were outclassed by new German fighters introduced that autumn. Lack of suitable new designs forced the RFC to retain FE-2s in frontline service until autumn 1917, and they suffered heavily during 'BLOODY APRIL'.

FE-2bs armed with up to three 112lb bombs were also used extensively as night bombers in France from early 1917, some remaining in service until the ARMISTICE, and a few were fitted with small cannon for ground-support operations. Others were transferred to home-defence squadrons in 1917–18, but they were handicapped by a low ceiling and a slow rate of climb.

BRIEF DATA (FE-2b) Type: two-seater fighter/reconnaissance; Engine: 120 or 160hp Beardsmore; Max speed: 92mph (147kph); Ceiling: 2,700m (3,300m for 160hp); Armament: 2 × 0.303in mg.

FE-8 The last 'PUSHER' aircraft to be used in numbers as a FIGHTER by the RFC, the FE-8 was ordered into full production in early 1915 but delayed by a series of accidents to prototypes. By the time it eventually arrived on the WESTERN FRONT in August 1916, it had been rendered obsolete by the introduction of

INTERRUPTER GEAR and outclassed by new German ALBATROS D-TYPES. It was replaced with frontline units as soon as new NIEUPORT 17 or AIRCO DH-5 fighters became available, but a few of the 300 or so eventually produced remained in active service until mid-1917.

BRIEF DATA Type: single-seat fighter; Engine: 100hp Gnôme Monosoupape; Max speed: 94mph (150kph); Ceiling: 4,400m; Armament: 1 × 0.303in mg.

Fearless Last of the prewar SCOUT cruisers built for the ROYAL NAVY between 1904 and 1913, *Fearless* led the First Destroyer Flotilla at the battles of HELIGOLAND BIGHT and JUTLAND. As leader of the Twelfth Submarine Flotilla, it was one of the few Scouts still in the North Sea at the end of the War.

BRIEF DATA (*Fearless*, 1916) Displacement: 3,440 tons; Crew: 270; Dimensions: length 406ft (123m), beam 41ft (12.4m); Speed: 26k; Armament: 10 × 4in gun, 1 × 4in AA, 2 × 21in TT.

February Revolution Popular uprising in RUSSIA of March 1917 (February by the contemporary Russian calendar) that overthrew the imperial government and dynasty of Tsar NICHOLAS II. The product of long-standing social tensions, exacerbated by wartime civilian shortages and a repressive regime, it was essentially unplanned, erupting from a series of mass strikes called by socialist and workers' groups in Petrograd (St Petersburg).

A strike call for 22 January 1917 was answered by 140,000 workers and followed by the arrest of their leaders. Another 85,000 struck in the capital on 27 February, and from early March the movement developed a disorganized life of its own. Wildcat stoppages all over the city were joined by civilians protesting at rumours of bread rationing, and demonstrators concentrated in the centre of Petrograd from 8 March to demand food, peace and ultimately revolution. Troops began refusing royal orders to fire on demonstrators from 11 March, and most of the city garrison had joined the rebels by 13 March. Similar scenes put Moscow in the hands of insurgents the following day.

The imperial cabinet resigned en masse late on 12 March, and the army command's refusal of support compelled abandonment of plans for a monarchist advance on the capital. In the hope of saving the monarchy, STAVKA (army central command) supported demands for the Tsar's abdication by liberal Duma politicians, who attempted to take control of the revolution by forming a Temporary Committee on 12 March.

Nicholas abdicated on 15 March, far too late to satisfy mass opinion, and the monarchy ended next day when the crown was declined by his brother, Grand Duke Michael. The Duma Committee formed itself into a PROVISIONAL GOVERNMENT under Prince LVOV (and including KERENSKI) on 15 March, partly in response to the perceived challenge to its authority from the newly formed Petrograd SOVIET. The Army high command had little choice but to accept a new regime that might defuse unrest among the troops.

The volatile dual powers of cabinet and soviet that governed Russia from March to November 1917 were never in full control of the countryside, and successive Provisional coalitions failed to check rising urban radicalism. The Revolution galvanized socialist activists all over the world (see STOCKHOLM CONFERENCE), enabled liberal opinion in the UNITED STATES to support war against autocracy with a clear conscience, and revitalized international debates about war aims with demands for peace 'without annexations or indemnities'. However, the actual commitment of the Provisional Government to war against 'imperialist' invaders on the EASTERN FRONT – especially the effort of the summer KERENSKI OFFENSIVE – fatally weakened its internal position. Having raised mass expectations for peace and reform, but also created a precedent for violent change of government, the liberal regime was swept away by the OCTOBER REVOLUTION on 7 November.

Feisal Ibn Hussein (1885–1933) Leading military commander of ARAB REVOLT forces and third son of its leader, Sherif HUSSEIN IBN ALI. Feisal functioned as Hussein's emissary during the build-up of support for Arab independence from TURKEY in 1914–15, returning to Hussein's power base in the Hejaz after most of his Arab nationalist contacts in Damascus had been executed by Turkish authorities. From the Hejaz he led the Revolt's initial attack on MEDINA in June 1916. He took command of forces based near the western Arabian coast, where he received military aid from the British after a meeting with LAWRENCE in October. An adequate military tactician, Feisal's personal charisma and diplomatic skill sealed a series of unlikely agreements between mutually hostile Arab tribes, and his position as the Revolt's practical leader was unchallenged at the ARMISTICE. After serving as Arab delegate to the PARIS PEACE CONFERENCE, and receiving little satisfaction, he proclaimed himself King of Syria and Palestine in March 1920. Deposed by French forces in June, Feisal's nomination by the British for the throne of Mesopotamia (Iraq) was accepted by a popular referendum, and he held the throne as Feisal I from 1921.

Felixstowe F-Types Successful series of British flying boats developed from the US CURTISS H-4 design. The first production model, the F-2A, combined the wings and tail of the H-4 with a more streamlined and seaworthy hull design. In RNAS service at British coastal stations from early 1917, the F-2A was an effective long-range patrol craft. Though relatively slow, it handled well, mounted powerful defensive armament, and could fly for 10 hours with extra fuel drums. Its combat successes included the destruction of ZEPPELIN L-62 in May 1918 and a starring role in one of the few major wartime seaplane battles, when 5 F-2As and a CURTISS H-12 drove off 14 German naval FIGHTERS in a prolonged DOGFIGHT on 4 June 1918, destroying 6 for the loss of only the Curtiss. The 100 wartime F-2As were joined during 1918 by a similar number of larger (345hp) F-3 versions, which sacrificed some performance and seaworthiness in doubling the bomb load. Both remained in postwar service, and Felixstowe designs exerted a powerful influence on future flying-boat development.

BRIEF DATA (F-2A) Type: long-range patrol flying boat; Crew: 4; Engine: 2 × 245hp Rolls Royce; Max speed: 95mph (152kph); Ceiling: 3,050m; Armament: 4–7 × 0.303in mg, max bomb load 460lbs (210kg).

Ferdinand I, King (1865–1927) Successor to King CAROL I of ROMANIA in October 1914, Ferdinand shared his uncle's connections with Austro-German royalty and was a close friend of Emperor FRANZ JOSEF, but any commitment to the CENTRAL POWERS was tempered by the influence of his British wife and popular support for neutrality. Increasingly inclined towards premier BRATIANU's policy of intervention at the right time and price, he soon found himself struggling to maintain popular support after declaration of war against the Central Powers in August 1916 was followed by almost immediate defeat (see ROMANIAN CAMPAIGN).

Penned in the northeast of the country, Ferdinand was only able to maintain recruitment of new troops by promising extended postwar suffrage and limited land reform. He resigned as nominal C-in-C of the ROMANIAN ARMY just before an armistice was agreed in December 1917, and avoided signing the Treaty of BUCHAREST the following May, enabling him to reopen hostilities on 10 November 1918. Ferdinand officially re-entered Bucharest on 1 December, and accompanied Bratianu to the PARIS PEACE CONFERENCE. Crowned King of Greater Romania in 1922, he subsequently fulfilled few of his constitutional pledges.

Ferdinand I, Tsar (1861–1948) Vienna-born son of a Franco-German royal marriage, Ferdinand was a junior officer in the AUSTRO-HUNGARIAN ARMY when offered the vacant throne of BULGARIA by its national assembly in 1887. From the late 1890s he established almost complete personal control over the principality by astute rotation of patronage and cabinet appointments, earning an enduring reputation for Machiavellian manoeuvring before turning his energies to the extension of Bulgarian territory.

Frustrated by ultimate defeat in the Balkan Wars (1912–13), and anxious to end diplomatic dependence on RUSSIA, Ferdinand and pro-Austrian prime minister RADOSLAVOV were unable to secure an alliance with GERMANY or AUSTRIA-HUNGARY before August 1914. Once they were at war Ferdinand held out for maximum territorial gain, especially in Macedonia, and only joined the CENTRAL POWERS when they appeared to be winning in autumn 1915.

The commitment ultimately proved fatal to his position, as ruthless German economic exploitation and diminishing military success fuelled internal opposition to the War, barely appeased by the appointment of pro-Allied prime minister MALINOV. Remaining on the throne through revolution, military collapse and eventual surrender in September 1918, Ferdinand was forced to abdicate under combined Allied and internal pressure on 4 October and spent the rest of his life in Germany.

Festubert, Battle of See: ARTOIS OFFENSIVE.

Fiat-Revelli Gun The first MACHINE GUN mass-produced in ITALY, designed in 1908 and adopted by the ITALIAN ARMY in 1914. A water-cooled weapon with a complex 50-round magazine, it jammed more frequently than most contemporary designs, but remained standard infantry equipment throughout the War. A lighter, air-cooled version was adopted for aircraft use in 1915, but was replaced by British VICKERS and LEWIS GUNS from late 1917.

Fighter Aircraft Warplanes designed for air-to-air combat did not exist in 1914, but were found to be necessary on the WESTERN FRONT once its lines became stabilized and air forces were competing for operational freedom over small areas. The first fighters were standard reconnaissance two-seaters with a MACHINE GUN mounted in the passenger seat, deployed to prevent enemy reconnaissance or bombing craft from penetrating rear areas, and ultimately to stop opposing fighters.

To achieve maximum combat efficiency forward armament was required, and a variety of methods were used to achieve this in 1914–15. High-firing gun positions, 'PUSHER' aircraft with the engine behind the pilot, DEFLECTOR GEAR to protect the propeller from bullets, and even observer nacelles in front the airscrew were tried before INTERRUPTER GEAR finally solved the problem from late 1915 (see FOKKER E-TYPES). Synchronized forward machine guns, often in pairs, remained standard single-seater armament for the duration.

Once both sides had mastered forward armament, fighter design was dominated by streamlined, high-powered biplanes or triplanes. Key features were speed, agility, rapid rate of climb, and ease of flying. It was also important that fighters were easy to build, repair and transport, and that they could operate from improvised airfields. A succession of small single-seat designs – ALBATROS D-TYPES, SOPWITH TRIPLANE, FOKKER D-VII, SPAD S-TYPES, SOPWITH CAMEL and others – established themselves as the best of their kind in the 1916–18 period.

By 1917 the same performance criteria were being applied to larger, better-armed two-seaters, like the BRISTOL FIGHTER, which could also serve as relatively long-range escorts for bombers or as ground-attack craft. The best machines were usually reserved for daylight combat over France, and older or less efficient designs remained active as home defence interceptors and night fighters, or on the other battlefronts. Fighters (usually in floatplane versions) were also used by naval services, both as interceptors aboard warships (see AIRCRAFT CARRIERS) and in a coastal defence role.

'Trench fighters' were a breed of ground-attack aircraft, additionally armed with light bombs and GRENADES, that were used in direct support of infantry on the battlefield from late 1916 (see JUNKERS J-I, SOPWITH SALAMANDER). See also: AERIAL WARFARE; ACES; DOGFIGHTS.

Film The relatively new medium of film played a growing wartime role in both military and civilian life. In a military context the development of PHOTO-RECONNAISSANCE was an important aspect of AERIAL WARFARE, especially in the static conditions of the WESTERN and ITALIAN FRONTS. Limited use was also made of motion pictures to record 'historic' moments, with the GERMAN ARMY showing most enthusiasm for sending camera crews to cover triumphal occupations and other set pieces.

Already very big business in the UNITED STATES, civilian cinema enjoyed a wartime boom in Europe, especially in GREAT BRITAIN, and became a staple entertainment for troops serving abroad, enthusiastically received by field marshals and conscripts alike. Both still and cinema photography were widely employed as PROPAGANDA tools. Stills released by all sides to illustrate war conditions were routinely doctored to ensure the appropriate message, with 'casualties' and 'advances' staged using captured uniforms and equipment. British propaganda chief Max AITKEN began producing official newsreels to accompany cinema features in 1918, a practice quickly adopted by his US opposite number, George CREEL, who was already using FOUR-MINUTE MEN to make speeches during intermissions.

War understandably interested film makers in the 1920s, but was never the dominant theme that it became during and after the Second World War, reflecting technical challenges not overcome until the 1930s and the relatively slight impact of the 1914–18 conflict on public consciousness in the overwhelmingly dominant US industry.

Finland A semi-autonomous Grand Duchy within the Russian Empire in 1914, Finland's response to the Russo-German war was essentially apathetic. Only a few thousand Finns volunteered for service in 1914, equally divided between the RUSSIAN and GERMAN ARMIES, and Finland was not directly affected by fighting on the EASTERN FRONT.

Finland's national assembly demanded virtual independence after the FEBRUARY REVOLUTION in 1917, but was dissolved by the Russian PROVISIONAL GOVERNMENT in July. New elections returned a pro-German, right-wing assembly, and its declaration of full independence in December was accepted by the Soviet regime in anticipation of an uprising by the left-wing Social Democrats.

An anti-Bolshevik militia (White Guard) had been formed during 1917 around Finns in German service, primarily to police Russian forces garrisoned in Finland, and socialist parties had formed a Red Guard, which staged a coup in Helsinki on 28 January 1918. The government fled to Vassy, where it appealed for German help while the White Guard gathered under former Russian General Mannerheim. Reinforced by the German Baltic Division (Rüdiger von der Goltz) from early April, Mannerheim defeated Red forces at the Battle of Viborg (28–29 April), ending any serious chance of a socialist uprising.

German attempts to establish military occupation of Finland ended with the ARMISTICE in November, and a new provisional government under Mannerheim took office when German forces withdrew in mid-December. A Defence Guard of 100,000 troops was assembled during 1919, but pressure from the Allied powers prevented its full-scale involvement in the RUSSIAN CIVIL WAR, and fighting was restricted to border incidents. Elections in July returned a moderate republican government under Professor Ståhlberg, and independence was confirmed by treaty with the Soviet government in October 1920.

Fisher, Admiral John, Baron (1841–1920) Principal architect of the wartime ROYAL NAVY, a dramatic figure whose single-minded energy and visionary enthusiasms shaped British prewar naval policy. On appointment as First Sea Lord in 1903 Fisher unleashed comprehensive reforms of training and operational procedures, ruthlessly retiring incompetent senior officers and making many enemies within a service unused to challenges.

Though he promoted the development of aircraft, SUBMARINES and light forces, Fisher's vision of future naval warfare – essentially that speed and big guns would be of paramount importance – was most completely embodied in the transformation of BATTLESHIP design. He triggered escalation of an international arms race by commissioning the revolutionary *DREADNOUGHT*, and fuelled it by ordering multiple successors. He also sponsored the evolution of BATTLECRUISERS. Brilliantly applied and internationally imitated, his theories proved largely irrelevant in a war dominated by smaller craft (see NAVAL WARFARE).

Ennobled and generally accepted as the greatest British admiral since Nelson, Fisher retired in 1910 but retained considerable influence in 1914. Following BATTENBERG's resignation in October 1914, he was recalled as First Sea Lord by naval minister CHURCHILL, arguably his equal in overbearing self-confidence. After a brief period of harmony, the two fell out over the DARDANELLES OPERATION. Fisher's initial qualified support turned to outraged fury at the depletion of the GRAND FLEET, and he resigned on 15 May 1915, a departure marked by well-publicized petulance. Ignoring pleas from Churchill and the press to change his mind, he completed his career as head of the Board of Inventions.

Fiume (Rijeka) See: ITALY; PARIS PEACE CONFERENCE; D'ANNUNZIO, G.

Flamanda, Battle of The ROMANIAN ARMY's attempt to preempt invasion from the south during its brief campaign of 1916. After an initial invasion of Transylvania to the north had stalled beyond the Carpathian mountains, and an attack by MACKENSEN's multinational Danube Army had penetrated the Dobrudja region in southeastern ROMANIA, the Crown Council changed its strategy. From 15 September General AVERESCU's Romanian Third Army on the Danube was reinforced by about 150,000 troops from the northern front, renamed the Southern Army Group (with a total strength of 15 infantry divisions) and instructed to attack across the river into BULGARIA.

The attack was launched on 29 September along an 80km front between Flamanda and Zimnicea, towards the western flank of Mackensen's forces in the Dobrudja, but Romanian superiority in infantry (80 per cent) and ARTILLERY (100 per cent) proved irrelevant as attempts to cross the Danube floundered. Bridges collapsed under the weight of artillery, ferries sank, and gunboats of the AUSTRO-HUNGARIAN NAVY's Danube Flotilla took a heavy toll. The only serious infantry combat was joined around Flamanda, at the northwest of the front, on the morning of 3 October, just before the offensive was abandoned. Failure, and the similar fate of a Russo-Romanian attack from the Dobrudja, left positions in the north vulnerable to counterattack from gathering Austro-German forces (see Battle of HERMANNSTADT). See also: ROMANIAN CAMPAIGN; MAP 14.

Flamethrowers One of many German innovations in the field of TRENCH WARFARE, based on portable and static flamethrower (*Flammenwerfer*) devices first tested in 1900 and deployed with three specialist battalions from 1911. Both types used pressurized air, carbon dioxide or nitrogen to force oil through a nozzle. Ignited by a spark or small charge, the oil became a fleeting jet of flame.

Used occasionally against French-held southeastern sectors of the WESTERN FRONT from October 1914, portable flamethrowers became a standard feature of limited German offensives on all fronts from mid-1915. Deployed in groups of six or more, each operated by two men, they were used to clear forward defenders at the start of an attack. Highly effective skirmishing weapons, their wider tactical value was limited by bulk, and they could only hit targets less than 25 metres away. Larger models, with an effective firing range of about 40 metres for some 40 seconds, were only suitable for defensive actions.

Experimental British flamethrowers, developed by 1917, were seldom used in action. Heavy models consumed prohibitive amounts of fuel and were never actively employed, and a more practical light design saw only fleeting combat in Flanders. The FRENCH ARMY made more widespread use of its one-man portable Schilt flamethrower. Slightly superior to the German counterparts in performance, it was similarly deployed for trench attacks in 1917–18.

Flanders, Battle for The final phase of the 'RACE TO THE SEA' on the WESTERN FRONT, six weeks of generalized fighting in October and November 1914 along a broad front stretching inland from the Flanders coast as far as Armentières (see MAP 2).

Engagement was preceded by a mutual build-up of forces in the region. After the failure of French attempts to outflank German lines around ARRAS, the BEF was transferred from positions on the AISNE to attempt the same manoeuvre further north. Units reached Flanders during the first ten days of October, linking up with two divisions of reinforcements originally sent to relieve ANTWERP, which fell on 10 October. The BELGIAN ARMY, retreating west along the coast, retired from Ostend on 12 October and began redeploying north of the British along the Yser Canal. Two corps of the new French Eighth Army gradually filled the gap between them.

Crown Prince RUPPRECHT's German Sixth Army was already deployed to meet the anticipated British advance, and Duke ALBRECHT's Fourth Army was transferred from the Champagne sector and heavily reinforced to attack on a broad front along the coast. Both sides had been trying to outflank the other since late September, but control of the Channel ports now became the major issue at stake.

An Anglo-French advance between La Bassée Canal (about 80km inland) and Armentières opened on 12 October but was outnumbered and repulsed. Attacks and counterattacks raged around La Bassée as Belgian positions on the YSER came under pressure from 18 October. The full-scale German offensive opened along the entire sector two days later, preempting a planned attack by the BEF from its SALIENT around Ypres. While German armies threatened Arras and Lille, fighting focused on the Yser between Ypres and the coast, and on the town itself.

Outnumbered Belgian forces opened the canal sluices on 26 October, flooding the northern sector of the front behind them as they withdrew to the Dixmunde–Nieuport RAILWAY. Dixmunde eventually fell to the German Fourth Army on 10 November, but Franco-Belgian forces held Nieuport. Ypres and its surrounds were under attack from 15 October and became the main target of German operations from 29 October (see First Battle of YPRES). German forces took the Messines Ridge south of the town, and broke through British positions to the east on 31 October. Reinforced by two French corps in the first days of November, the defenders held the town despite heavy losses.

Allied forces all along the sector remained under heavy pressure until 16 November, when rain ended the German attacks on the Yser and combat around Ypres began to die down. By the time a last German attack was repulsed five days later TRENCH WARFARE was developing all along the Western Front. Although Allied armies had lost some ground, the costly and inconclusive campaign in Flanders ended with both sides in possession of Channel port facilities, and with an unbroken line of opposing trenches extending from the Swiss border to the Channel coast around Nieuport.

Flers-Courcelette, Battle of Subsidiary British attack during the SOMME OFFENSIVE, an advance northeast along a 12km front from the Fourth Army's small salient on 15 September (see MAP 8). Employing 12 divisions under General RAWLINSON, it was most notable for the use of all 49 TANKS in British service, their first active operation anywhere. BEF commander HAIG's decision to deploy the tanks, rather than wait to use the new secret weapon en masse, was controversial at the time and not justified by events. They surprised and disrupted defences locally but were neither numerous nor reliable enough to achieve a major breakthrough. Bad weather and defensive reinforcements halted attempts to exploit initial gains of about 2km after three days, and German official reaction to the new weapon was that it could be defeated rather than imitated. On the British side, failure of the few surviving tanks to make any serious impression during a renewed attack on 25 September did not dim Haig's enthusiasm, and he asked for 1,000 to be built.

Florina, Battle of A limited attack by the CENTRAL POWERS in the SALONIKA theatre in August 1916, disrupting General SARRAIL's plans for a major Allied offensive deep into SERBIA. Preliminary Allied bombardments began on 10 August around Lake Doiran in the east, but minor advances by French troops in the sector were overshadowed by a mixed German and Bulgarian advance in the far west against the reconstituted SERBIAN ARMY around Florina.

Facing their first serious engagement since the 'GREAT RETREAT' of 1915, Serbian forces were driven back to the Lake Ostrovo region from 18 August, and were unable to retake the town with a counterattack next day. Fighting continued along a front east of Florina, centred on the Crno River, while Bulgarian forces in eastern Macedonia moved across the Greek border to take Seres on 25 August, meeting no opposition from GREEK ARMY units but surviving an ineffective bombardment by ROYAL NAVY warships as they approached the coastal fortress of Kavalla.

As ROMANIA's declaration of war on the Central Powers brought a halt to the latter's attacks at the end of the month, Bulgarian occupation of eastern Greece triggered a proclamation of rebellion in Salonika by ex-premier VENIZELOS. With civil war brewing behind the front, Sarrail postponed faltering Allied attacks in the Doiran sector, and relaunched a less ambitious operation in mid-September (see MONASTIR OFFENSIVE). See also: MAP 19.

'Flying Circus' Allied nickname for the first GERMAN ARMY AIR SERVICE *Jagdgeschwader* (fighter group), formed on the WESTERN FRONT in late June 1917. Commanded by von RICHTHOFEN, it comprised four elite FIGHTER squadrons of 12 aircraft each, and enjoyed immediate combat success against RFC and RNAS units during the Third Battle of YPRES. Single-seat units on all sides had previously been attached to local army commands, but Jagdgeschwader 1 was designed as a mobile tactical reserve controlled by headquarters and available for transfer wherever needed. Most of its equipment was partly packed for rapid RAILWAY transport along the front and this, along with the garish paintwork adopted by von Richthofen's pilots, gave rise to the circus comparisons. Three more fighter groups were formed in early 1918, all capable of inflicting heavy losses along a limited front, and their massed presence contributed to the rise of large-scale DOGFIGHTS. See also: AERIAL WARFARE.

Foch, Marshal Ferdinand (1851–1929) Aggressive French soldier whose unique influence on the course of the War stemmed from a long career as a military theorist. He established the concept of 'offensive spirit' as the dominant doctrine within the FRENCH ARMY and, although he maintained the need for tactical flexibility and strong ARTILLERY support of infantry, his ideas were extended by disciples into a creed of attack at all costs and under any circumstances.

Appointed in 1913 to command the elite XX Corps, part of DE CASTLENAU's Second Army facing the German frontier, Foch applied his theories in adversity during the failed invasion of LORRAINE in August 1914, conceiving and executing the counterattack at Trouée des Charmes that halted the German advance on Nancy. Promoted to command the new Ninth Army on 28 August, he again counterattacked when faced with a German breakthrough during the first MARNE battle.

Though costly and essentially defensive, his successes earned him further promotion in October to command the French Northern Army Group on the WESTERN FRONT, an appointment extended to include British and Belgian forces in the Flanders sector from January 1915. Foch's actual control over Allied forces was vested in his control of French reserves, and his unwillingness to commit them in numbers – especially at the Second Battle of YPRES–earned him a reputation among BEF commanders for wasting the lives of frontline troops.

Removed from the post when NIVELLE replaced JOFFRE as C-in-C in December 1916, Foch was recalled to favour the following May as chief of staff to PÉTAIN, and his reputation was fully restored by his success as coordinator of inter-Allied support to ITALY after the CAPORETTO disaster in autumn 1917.

From early 1918 Foch performed a similar role on the Western Front on behalf of the SUPREME WAR COUNCIL, struggling to co-ordinate Allied military actions without the power to give direct orders. The German SPRING OFFENSIVES in 1918 made a necessity of effective Allied cooperation and, with positive support from BEF C-in-C HAIG and British premier LLOYD GEORGE, he was promoted over Pétain and installed as Allied Supreme

Commander for the Western Front on 14 April 1918. His jurisdiction was extended to include the ITALIAN FRONT in June.

The position of generalissimo in 1918 bore little resemblance to the modern concept of supreme command. Foch operated with only a skeleton staff and his role remained essentially that of coordinator. Plans of attack were created at army or corps level, and Foch's ability to impose strategic coherence depended on force of personality.

His reorganization of Allied defences during the German attacks of the early summer was marked by cautious use of scant French reserves at the LYS and insistence on attack at the MARNE in July. Despite a clash with equally iron-willed AEF commander PERSHING over the employment of US forces, his undiminished willingness to attack was ideally suited to the situation once the German offensives had been halted. This willingness chimed with the plans of Haig, whose army was by then the strongest on the Allied side, and the two acted largely in concert during the successful offensives of the autumn.

Celebrated as the mastermind of eventual Allied victory, Foch headed ARMISTICE negotiations in November 1918, imposing terms that made German military recovery impossible. As senior Allied military advisor to the PARIS PEACE CONFERENCE he regarded CLEMENCEAU's hard-line nationalist approach to the VERSAILLES Treaty as insufficiently tough, but headed the inter-Allied committee charged with administering its terms in 1920. The experience was marred by factional squabbling within the French Army, as well as British doubts about his impartiality, and he refused subsequent offers of a political career.

Fokker D-I to D-IV Series of biplane FIGHTERS designed by the German Fokker company from late 1915, by which time its FOKKER E-TYPE monoplanes were obsolete. The original D-I and D-II models mounted a single, forward-firing MACHINE GUN, and were powered by 100hp and 120hp engines, respectively. Their indifferent performance was improved with the more powerful D-III, which had twin machine guns but suffered repeated engine trouble, a failing passed on to the slightly modified, but similarly mediocre D-IV. All these early versions were used in small numbers by the GERMAN ARMY AIR SERVICE, operating as escorts for reconnaissance craft and with early fighter units. They were never considered viable for the new combat groups (*Jagdstaffeln*) formed in autumn 1916, and were withdrawn once the superior ALBATROS D-I became available. A few also served with the AUSTRO-HUNGARIAN AIR SERVICE, some manufactured under licence in Budapest.

BRIEF DATA (D-III) Type: single-seat fighter; Engine: 160hp Oberursel; Max speed: 160kph; Ceiling: 4,700m; Armament: 2 × 7.92mm mg (forward).

Fokker D-VI German FIGHTER first flown in late 1917, a radical departure from earlier Fokker biplane designs, with a rounded fuselage similar to that of the FOKKER DR-I triplane. Better than anything available to the GERMAN ARMY AIR SERVICE at the time, it was ordered in only small numbers because the prototype FOKKER D-VII had already impressed in trials. Only 59 were built, most joining combat units on the WESTERN FRONT during the summer of 1918 but retiring to training duties once D-VIIs were available. The few machines used by Austro-Hungarian forces remained in action until the ARMISTICE.

BRIEF DATA Type: single-seat fighter; Engine: 110hp Oberursel; Max speed: 171kph; Ceiling: 4,000m; Armament: 2 × 7.92mm mg (forward).

Fokker D-VII The most successful German FIGHTER in 1918, a snub-nosed biplane ordered into production in January after the prototype won an official competition to find the best new combat design. To enable an initial order of 2,000 machines, the rival Albatros company was also instructed to build the type, which reached elite 'FLYING CIRCUS' pilots on the WESTERN FRONT in late April. First in action during the AISNE battle in May, it was not particularly fast but climbed quickly and possessed exceptional agility at high altitudes, giving a combat edge over all contemporary Allied types. Easy to fly and liked by pilots, D-VIIs were also produced with a 185hp BMW engine, pushing maxi-

mum speed close to 200kph. Most German fighter units in France were equipped with D-VIIs during the summer of 1918, and 760 machines had been delivered to the GERMAN ARMY AIR SERVICE at the ARMISTICE, when their success was reflected in a specific Allied demand for their surrender.
BRIEF DATA Type: single-seat fighter; Engine: 180hp Mercedes; Max speed: 187kph; Ceiling: 5,950m; Armament: 2 × 7.92mm mg (forward).

Fokker D-VIII One of the last German FIGHTER designs in service on the WESTERN FRONT, a high-winged monoplane developed after a FOKKER D-VII was found to be airworthy without its lower wing. After winning an official fighter trial in April 1918 it was ordered into production as a replacement for the D-VII, but three of the first six delivered suffered in-flight wing collapse. The problem was traced to spars joining the rear of the wing to the fuselage; these had been thickened to meet official biplane specifications and were unable to bend. It was reintroduced with its original spars, but only 85 of 400 ordered had reached combat status by the ARMISTICE.
BRIEF DATA Type: single-seat fighter; Engine: 140hp Oberursel; Max speed: 200kph; Ceiling: 6,350m; Armament: 2 × 7.92mm mg (forward).

Fokker Dr-1 German triplane FIGHTER, hastily designed in mid-1917 as a response to the British SOPWITH TRIPLANE and in action on the WESTERN FRONT from the end of August. The first production models were issued to Jagdgeschwader 1, better known as VON RICHTHOFEN's 'FLYING CIRCUS', and proved an immediate success. Although slow at combat altitudes, they climbed quickly and could match even the SOPWITH CAMEL's manoeuvrability.

Two Dr-1s broke up in mid-air during late October 1917, killing the pilots, and the type was speedily withdrawn. Returned to service at the end of the year with strengthened wings, it was tainted by official mistrust and equipped only a few combat units, although Richthofen himself continued to fly one. Production was halted once the original order for 320 machines had been fulfilled in May 1918, and it was withdrawn as obsolete during the summer.
BRIEF DATA Type: single-seat fighter; Engine: 110hp Oberursel or Le Rhône; Max speed: 184kph; Ceiling: 5,950m; Armament: 2 × 7.92mm mg (forward).

Fokker E-Type German monoplane generally regarded as the world's first genuine FIGHTER. In use on the WESTERN FRONT from mid-1915, it was the first military aircraft fitted with INTERRUPTER GEAR to enable use of a forward-firing MACHINE GUN. Commissioned in April 1915, the E-1 was a development of Dutchman Anthony Fokker's prewar D-type reconnaissance monoplanes, themselves near-copies of French MORANE-SAULNIER designs. The E-II reached the front the same autumn, strengthened but retaining an 80hp engine, and was rapidly replaced by the up-engined E-III, the most successful version (150 produced).

Not an otherwise exceptional aircraft, the E-Type's superior weaponry was first used purely for defensive escort of two-seater reconnaissance craft, but was most effective once new air-to-air combat techniques developed by German ACES were applied on missions dedicated to the destruction of enemy aircraft. About 40 E-Types were in action in France by December 1915, and a total of some 300 machines (including about 20 used by the AUSTRO-HUNGARIAN AIR SERVICE) brought down over 1,000 Allied craft, taking a particularly heavy toll of British BE-2 and VICKERS FB-5 two-seaters. The GERMAN ARMY AIR SERVICE retained effective control of the skies until new Allied types arrived in spring 1916, when an E-VI model with twin machine guns was produced in response. Its 160hp engine proved unreliable and it was quickly withdrawn. The few E-V machines were unrelated to the other Fokker E-Types. They were developed from the D-Type series in the spring of 1918, and were unsuccessful forerunners of the FOKKER D-VIII.
BRIEF DATA (E-III) Type: single-seat fighter/escort; Engine: 100hp Oberursel; Max speed: 140kph; Ceiling: 3,650m; Armament: 1 (sometimes 2) × 8mm mg.

Fonck, René (1894–1953) French airman who became a FIGHTER pilot with an elite CIGOGNES squadron in April 1917, having flown with a reconnaissance unit on the WESTERN FRONT since early 1915. Neither dashing nor daring, but a crack shot, he survived uninjured with 75 confirmed combat victories (once destroying 6 German aircraft in a single day), making him the most successful wartime Allied ACE.

Fortresses Powerful static defence points, armed with the heaviest ARTILLERY, were a standard feature of land warfare in the 19th century. They had evolved into sophisticated systems of mutually supporting strongholds surrounding a large central area, often a city. A substantial force garrisoning the centre could fill gaps between outlying forts, and represented a strategic weapon that could not be ignored in an age of relatively small armies. Schools of thought in all the continental European armies expected fortresses to be important in 1914. The RUSSIAN ARMY in particular devoted much of its prewar development to static defences, but they also formed a part of FRENCH and GERMAN ARMY planning.

Fortresses and their garrisons proved virtually useless in wars fought by massed armies. Modern siege artillery had reduced the best of them, at Belgian LIÈGE and NAMUR, to rubble by the end of August 1914, and heavy guns succeeded wherever they were deployed against fortresses. Other fortresses were left to 'wither on the vine', incapable of supporting strategically relevant forces for long. Most were stripped of their heavy artillery to provide reinforcements for field armies, and the only major land campaign focused exclusively on fortresses was the prolonged struggle for VERDUN, conducted as an exercise in attrition rather than possession. Though equally vulnerable to overland attack, coastal fortresses generally constituted a more effective defence against approach from the sea, putting warships at a positional disadvantage that was seldom challenged. See also: ANTWERP; DARDANELLES; KOVNO; NOVOGEORGIEVSK; PRZEMYSL.

Foscani, Battle of Indecisive action on the Romanian sector of the EASTERN FRONT. It began on 22 July 1917 as an attack from the River Sereth by General Zayonchkovski's Russo-Romanian forces in Moldavia, and was intended to support Russian forces retreating further north (see KERENSKI OFFENSIVE). Initial Allied successes in Moldavia were soon reversed by a counteroffensive from General MACKENSEN's multinational Danube Army. Launched on 6 August, the counteroffensive crossed the River Susitza north of Foscani to threaten the rear of Romanian forces in the eastern Carpathians by 9 August. General AVERESCU's drastically reorganized ROMANIAN ARMY defended well, delaying Mackensen before winning a minor victory at Okna (16 August). Although one Russian division at Foscani disintegrated of its own volition on 27–28 August, the line was held and fighting died down with the commencement of German operations around RIGA in the far north. See MAP 11.

Foudre The FRENCH NAVY's first AIRCRAFT CARRIER, originally completed in 1896 as an experimental TORPEDO BOAT depot ship, it was converted in turn into a repair ship, MINELAYER and seaplane depot ship (with a single aircraft hangar, in 1911) before hangar space was added in 1913. *Foudre* served in the MEDITERRANEAN, primarily as an adjunct to coastal seaplane stations, but also on ANTI-SUBMARINE patrols in the eastern Mediterranean and as a SUBMARINE tender.

Lacking the resources to emulate experiments in naval aviation pioneered by the RNAS, the French Navy used only four other converted seaplane carriers. The slow ex-liner *Campinas*, converted in 1915, was the only one used with fleet units, operating on the PALESTINE FRONT, and taking part in the 1916 operations at SALAMIS and ATHENS. Three cross-Channel ferries were also modified as seaplane carriers in 1916 (see *ENGADINE*). The faster *Rouen* was a CONVOY escort in the Mediterranean, while *Nord* and *Pas-de-Calais* operated with light forces at Dunkirk.

BRIEF DATA (*Foudre*, 1914) Displacement: 5,970 tons; Crew: 431; Dimensions: length 488.5ft (118.7m), beam 70.5ft (17.2m); Speed: 19.5k; Armament: 8 × 100mm gun, 4 × 60mm, 4 × 47mm, 4–8 × a/c.

Four-Minute Men Trained public speakers who became mainstays of government PROPAGANDA in the UNITED STATES after April 1917. Organized by CREEL's Committee on Public Information, they delivered four-minute speeches in churches and schools, at military camps, and during movie intermissions, promoting War Bonds, food conservation, and federal policy on any current issue. An estimated 75,000 Four-Minute Men, professionals and volunteers, made an average of more than a thousand wartime speeches each, reaching a total audience of almost 315 million. In a nation with a strong tradition of declamatory oratory they were a highly effective medium, and the best speakers, like French VERDUN veteran and priest Captain Périgard, became national celebrities.

Fourteen Points A programme for peace presented as a declaration of UNITED STATES war aims by President WILSON to Congress on 8 January 1918. Compiled with the help of his personal advisor, Colonel HOUSE, and a team of political experts headed by Sydney Mezes and Walter LIPPMANN, it amounted to fourteen paragraphs in its original sketchy form.

The first five dealt with general principles: Point 1 renounced secret treaties, demanding 'open covenants openly arrived at'; Point 2 required absolute freedom of the seas outside territorial waters, rendering BLOCKADE tactics illegal; Point 3 called for the removal of worldwide trade barriers wherever possible; Point 4 for arms reductions; and Point 5 for impartial arbitration of all colonial disputes.

Points 6 to 13 were concerned with specific territorial problems: Point 6, a gesture to the new Bolshevik government, called for the evacuation of all former Russian territory by the CENTRAL POWERS; Point 7 dealt with the complete restoration of BELGIUM; French claims to the provinces of Alsace and Lorraine were conceded in Point 8; Point 9 gave limited recognition to the territorial claims of ITALY. Point 10 conceded only 'autonomous development' to separatist nationalities inside AUSTRIA-HUNGARY; Point 11 dealt with the Balkans, calling for the immediate evacuation of occupied ROMANIA, MONTENEGRO and SERBIA, with the latter having access to the Adriatic coast; TURKEY was guaranteed sovereignty over its heartlands in Point 12, but its subject peoples were to be autonomous and the DARDANELLES open to international traffic; Point 13 recognized the existence of an independent POLAND, and its right to ocean access. Point 14 recommended the formation of a 'general association of nations' to guarantee the peaceful development of all states.

Containing basic similarities with the Bolshevik peace programme proposed by LENIN, the Fourteen Points were much more effectively publicized, attracting global popular enthusiasm (see CREEL, G.). Wilson was lionized as a visionary across six continents, even in countries where his programme ran contrary to ingrained national aspirations.

The other Allied governments made no formal response, but objected to the programme's failure to recognize Italian territorial ambitions (guaranteed by the secret Treaty of LONDON), its challenge to British naval domination, and its complete silence on the subject of REPARATIONS. The Central Powers viewed the programme as inimical to the continued existence of the Ottoman and Austro-Hungarian Empires, and it was scathingly received by governments, but its mildness relative to Anglo-French attitudes became more acceptable with the military crises of autumn 1918.

Approached for peace by the Central Powers in late September, Wilson insisted that the Points serve as the basis for ARMISTICE discussions, prompting urgent inter-Allied clarification of what were little more than outline proposals. Wilson modified Point 10 to demand full independence for Austro-Hungarian subject peoples, and Point 1 was interpreted to allow secret negotiations at the PARIS PEACE CONFERENCE, but the programme still left much room for ambiguity in the form in which it was accepted by the Allies on 4 November.

Franc-Tireurs French term for the civilian SNIPERS engaged in resistance to German occupation in 1870. The GERMAN ARMY of 1914 invaded BELGIUM and FRANCE in the belief that franc-tireurs had been trained in every town and village. Though a few genuine snipers were caught, the threat was officially exaggerated as justification for savage reprisals aimed at securing civilian cooperation by intimidation. See also: LOUVAIN; DINANT.

France The French Third Republic was created following the defeat of France by Prussia and the fall of Napoleon III in 1870, when the eastern provinces of Alsace and Lorraine became part of the newly united GERMANY. The Republic's president was elected every seven years by both houses of the National Assembly in joint session. He nominated the prime minister, who selected a cabinet and occupied one of its 12 ministries.

The Assembly comprised an indirectly elected Senate and a lower Chamber of Deputies, directly elected by most of the adult male population. The prewar Chamber was a turbulent hotbed of sectional and regional interests dominated by a broad spectrum of centre-left parties, and a cabinet's life was generally measured in months rather than years.

Regular threats of a royalist revival were reflected in chronic mistrust between republican politicians, especially the strong socialist movement, and the predominantly right-wing FRENCH ARMY. French socialists were at the moderate heart of the prewar SECOND INTERNATIONAL, but the French industrial working class was smaller and less volatile than its German counterpart.

Although prewar France possessed a well-established RAILWAY and canal network, and was among the world's leading trading nations, it was still an overwhelmingly agricultural country. Self-sufficient in foodstuffs, it was industrially sluggish relative to Germany or even GREAT BRITAIN. Concentrated in the north and east of the country, heavy industries were inefficient and most manufacturing was at workshop level in 1914.

Based on the introduction of mass conscription, military and socioeconomic preparation for recovery of the lost provinces ('*revanche*') was hampered by a relatively small population of about 40 million (1911). Attempts to compensate for Germany's larger manpower base by extending the terms of conscription provoked bitter political opposition from the left before the Three Year Law was passed in 1913, a prospect that encouraged Berlin to make war sooner rather than later.

The assumption that France and Germany would fight each other in any future general war was central to diplomacy before August 1914, but trading and imperial interests called for the security of MEDITERRANEAN communications with colonies in Indo-China and AFRICA. French control of northwest Africa had been sealed after diplomatic confrontations with ITALY over Tunisia (1881) and with Germany over Morocco (1911), and by 1914 French ambitions in the Middle East, especially in Christian Syria (i.e. the Lebanon), were straining previously good relations with TURKEY.

France had limited ambitions in the Balkans, but close ties with SERBIA were complemented by France's alliance with RUSSIA, concluded in 1892 as a balance to the TRIPLE ALLIANCE. Germany's allies, AUSTRIA-HUNGARY and ITALY, represented growing naval threats in the Mediterranean, where the FRENCH NAVY was concentrated after informal military arrangements with Britain released it from protection of northern waters in 1912. Anglo-Russian agreements in 1907 created a 'TRIPLE ENTENTE', but London refused to contemplate a full alliance.

Though ready to fight and assured of quick victory by the military (see PLAN 17), the French government was guided by Britain's uncertain attitude during the JULY CRISIS of 1914. President POINCARÉ and inexperienced prime minister VIVIANI were in Russia until 24 July and reached Paris five days later. Resisting Army demands for immediate mobilization, they sought to ensure British sympathy by withdrawing troops all along the eastern frontier on 30 July.

The assassination of socialist leader Jaurès on 31 July prompted fears of popular dissent, but mobilization the next day was greeted with a surge of belligerent patriotism. The planned arrest of dissidents listed on CARNET B was deemed unnecessary and the Assembly voted for an immediate political truce (*Union Sacrée*).

Conscription permitted very few exemptions and almost 2.5 million men were called up within a few weeks, bringing manpower crises to industry and agriculture. Military requisition of transport systems and the creation of a 'Zone of the Armies', placing most of eastern France under martial law, added to short-term economic paralysis. Disruption multiplied with military defeat in the Battles of the FRONTIERS and the German advance into northeastern France, which threatened Paris until victory on the MARNE in early September.

Once the WESTERN FRONT had stabilized, it passed through the industrial heart of France. German occupation covered 6 per cent of the country, including 10 per cent of the population, 14 per cent of the industrial workforce, about two-thirds of iron and steel capacity, and 40 per cent of coal mines. To compensate, old mines were reopened, installations near the front were given maximum possible protection, and hydroelectric capacity had been doubled by 1918, but France remained dependent on imports for some 40 per cent of its iron and coal until 1919.

The threat to Paris, and its incorporation into the Zone of the Armies, drove the government to Bordeaux in early September 1914. It remained there until mid-December, and martial law continued in Paris until spring 1915, allowing C-in-C JOFFRE and a large general staff (GQG) uninterrupted control over wartime strategy. Rigid press censorship reduced war news to a few bland military communiqués. Ministers and journalists were equally unwelcome at the front.

Massive expenditure of war materials during the apparently decisive early battles brought a SHELL CRISIS by late September 1914, predating similar problems in other countries. With ammunition output running at about 100,000 shells per week against military demands for 700,000, efforts were made from October 1914 to mobilize the private sector in a field dominated by government arsenals.

Initial priority was given to increased production regardless of cost, and all firms remotely capable of the task were given over to munitions work. Resources were concentrated on the larger, more efficient firms from spring 1915, but small companies were kept active by a specialization policy, producing individual parts or components for assembly elsewhere. New armaments factories were built only from 1917, when all hope of quick victory had gone.

Under the direction of junior war minister Albert THOMAS, manpower shortages were addressed by encouraging employment of WOMEN and teenagers (and later prisoners of war), utilizing refugees from Belgium and the northeast (who numbered more than a million), and establishing national agencies to redirect labour from areas of high unemployment. A central labour exchange was set up in Paris from November 1914, and similar organizations were created in 1915 to recruit on behalf of the war and agriculture ministries.

Employers remained primarily concerned with the recovery of skilled labour from the military. About 500,000 conscripts had returned to industry under military jurisdiction by the end of 1915, prompting arguments about their wage levels. Better training of replacements proved a more effective long-term solution, and the armaments workforce tripled between January 1915 and April 1916.

Total battle casualties had reached 1.4 million men by the end of 1915, out of 5.5 million called up, but popular morale and political unity held up reasonably well. Food prices had risen 40 per cent in 18 months by spring 1916, but this was compensated for by wage rises. Civilian commodities remained fairly plentiful and there were few general shortages, but the slightly hysterical mood of the frontline cities and Paris, where small-scale ZEPPELIN raids began in March 1915, was unrepresentative of a dour atmosphere elsewhere.

Some opposition to war re-emerged, stimulated by the first international ZIMMERWALD conference in spring 1915, but was confined to small minority groups and underground publications. An unbroken stream of optimistic official PROPAGANDA had a more divisive effect, eroding faith in the military by promoting unrealistic expectations.

Evident failure to expel the invaders damaged the previously impregnable position of Joffre, but Viviani, a fledgling premier surrounded by more experienced figures, bore the brunt of criticism for failing to assert political authority over the Army. His resignation on 29 October 1915 brought a broad coalition to power under the moderate socialist BRIAND.

The monumental struggle for VERDUN occupied most of 1916 and was a watershed for the French war effort, quickly developing the characteristics of a national crusade. Vast expenditure of lives and materials in the cause suspended nascent popular war weariness and created a rich attendant mythology (embracing air ACES, the VOIE SACRÉE and commanders like PÉTAIN).

The initial inadequacy of Verdun's defences, blamed on Joffre, brought the question of political authority to a head. The government's standing was improved by subsequent recovery at Verdun and the British offensive on the SOMME, but France was more vulnerable in economic and morale terms from late 1916.

Despite a poor harvest and price rises, food queues still reflected distribution inequalities rather than real shortages. Some restrictions were placed on bread and sugar consumption, and official 'meatless days' were ordered from early 1917, but greater hardship was caused by serious coal and oil shortages during a very cold winter. A new Economic Council established in late 1916 introduced sharp restrictions on lighting and electricity use, and petrol was regulated in April 1917.

War weariness was expressed as resignation rather than pacifism, despite an upsurge of left-wing peace agitation in factories from November 1916, and the government refused to risk popular uprising by suppressing 'defeatist' publications and organizations such as the Committee of Syndicalist Defence. Outrage from the military and an equally independent pro-War press was directed particularly at interior minister MALVY.

Joffre's removal in December 1916 marked the end of military autonomy. His successor, NIVELLE, commanded only the Western Front but promised rapid victory with a massive spring offensive and temporarily restored popular enthusiasm. His plans attracted intense military and political opposition but were backed by the cabinet in mid-March, provoking the resignation of new war minister LYAUTEY and the government's collapse.

Total failure of the NIVELLE OFFENSIVE in April and May 1917 brought a major morale crisis. The widespread FRENCH ARMY MUTINY was concealed from the public but matched by a surge of protest marches, strikes and labour unrest on the home front, further stimulated by the FEBRUARY REVOLUTION in Russia. In 1916 there were only 98 strikes in France, but almost 300,000 men took part in 689 stoppages during 1917.

The vital area of shell production had been placed under a separate government artillery department from May 1915, and a ministry of munitions was established in December 1916. Led by Thomas until the following September, it allowed industrialists to determine production and distribution priorities by arrangement among themselves. Allocation of skilled workers from the forces, and of increasingly scarce imports, gave the government some control, but it was prepared to accept high prices and made no attempt to manage domestically produced resources until July 1918. All restrictions on private enterprise were lifted in November 1918 (see WAR SOCIALISM).

Industrial output was broadly satisfactory by early 1917 but the effects of German SUBMARINE WARFARE curtailed imports, starving non-essential industries of raw material and manpower. A critical shortage of agricultural labour forced the return of 300,000 farmers from the Army between April 1917 and the following January, along with 32,000 miners, 8,000 railwaymen and 5,000 teachers. They were not replaced by women, who were never employed as military auxiliaries.

Nivelle's replacement, Pétain, had restored calm to the Army by July 1917, but a new coalition under former finance minister RIBOT faced increasingly polarized political debate. Demands for immediate peace by socialists during a stormy June session of the Chamber brought accusations of treason from pro-War elements and rejection of a request to attend the international STOCKHOLM CONFERENCE.

Real or imagined enemy agents provided scapegoats for military failure and social tension, with Malvy forced to resign in July 1917 after implication in an espionage scandal that helped bring down Ribot in early September (see *Le BONNET ROUGE*). The shortlived PAINLEVÉ government contained familiar names and infuriated 'patriotic' critics by maintaining a conciliatory attitude to peacemongers. After its collapse on 13 November Poincaré recalled Georges CLEMENCEAU, an ardent champion of 'war to the end', from the political wilderness.

Clemenceau immediately rounded on dissidents. Socialists were again excluded from the cabinet and faced arrest, while some 1,700 suspected agitators or enemy agents were imprisoned by the end of the year (see CAILLAUX, J.). Unions were informed that acts of industrial sabotage – two took place in Paris during November – would be met by troops. With AEF concentration in France offering concrete hope of eventual victory, Clemenceau's hard line, and the distraction of major TREASON TRIALS, helped to preserve morale through a winter of tightening austerity.

Rationing of fuel and some foods was introduced in early 1918, again to smooth distribution and eliminate queues. Propaganda was centrally organized for the first time under a single government agency and concentrated largely on food conservation. Its anti-German 'hate' campaigns were hardly needed as raids on Paris by GOTHA bombers and direct shelling of the capital signalled a mood of national crisis during the German SPRING OFFENSIVES (see PARIS GUN).

About 500,000 evacuees left Paris in the first days of the German advance, and Clemenceau emerged as an icon of national resistance, exercising an unceremonious domination over cabinet, unions and military authorities. Continuing industrial disputes, including strikes by Paris munitions workers in May, were resolved by threats. Clemenceau also ignored arguments against the creation of a supreme Allied command under FOCH.

The approach of victory was overshadowed by the arrival of the global INFLUENZA epidemic in August. Clemenceau's view of public morale led to the censorship of all reference to the disease until mid-October, by which time it was killing 1,200 people per day in the capital alone.

Arguments about war had been replaced by a vigorous peace debate before the ARMISTICE in November. French losses in devastated territory, economic disruption and military casualties brought loud calls for revenge on Germany. As delegation leader at the PARIS PEACE CONFERENCE Clemenceau championed French imperial interests against the idealism of US president WILSON, but was criticized in France for failing to secure higher REPARATIONS or the occupation of the German Rhineland by the VERSAILLES Treaty.

Economic reconstruction was begun immediately, but the social tensions revealed in wartime France persisted into the 1920s and beyond. An atomized party structure produced more than 40 governments over the next 20 years, encouraging extraparliamentary extremists on both political wings and hastening the Third Republic's collapse in 1940.

Franchet d'Esperey, General Louis (1856–1942) Energetic and resourceful French officer. He led I Corps with General LANREZAC's Fifth Army at CHARLEROI in August 1914, successfully defending the right of the line, and took command of the Army just before the MARNE battle in September. Promoted after the victory to lead the Eastern Army Group on the WESTERN FRONT, he was considered as a replacement for JOFFRE in late 1916, but his strong Roman Catholicism made him unpopular with influential anticlerical circles within the FRENCH ARMY, and he instead commanded the Army Group in Champagne through 1917.

An ardent advocate of 'offensive' doctrine, his unwillingness to employ DEFENCE IN DEPTH contributed to early German successes during the Third Battle of the AISNE in May 1918, and in the command shake-up that followed he was removed from the Western Front to lead Allied forces in SALONIKA.

An early supporter of strong Allied commitment to the BALKAN FRONT, and well-informed on regional affairs, he brought a new aggression to the theatre, adopting a battle plan prepared by his predecessor (GUILLAUMAT) and launching the overwhelmingly successful VARDAR OFFENSIVE in September. Allied commander in the Balkans until 1920, he was promoted Marshal of France in 1922 and remained on active service into his late seventies.

François, General Hermann von (1856–1933) A corps commander with the German Eighth Army on the EASTERN FRONT in August 1914, his unwillingness to obey defensive orders was a significant feature of the opening campaign in EAST PRUSSIA. Although he briefly commanded the Eighth Army during October 1914, he was returned to corps command after defeat at the second MASURIAN LAKES battle. Understandably mistrusted by senior commanders, particularly LUDENDORFF, he was not given another important combat role. See also: Battles of STALLUPÖNEN, GUMBINNEN, TANNENBERG; First Battle of the MASURIAN LAKES.

Franz Ferdinand, Archduke (1863–1890) The heir presumptive to the throne of AUSTRIA-HUNGARY (i.e. never formally named as such) since 1889, Franz Ferdinand took his role as Emperor-in-waiting very seriously. A vigorous promoter of naval expansion and military modernization, but less anxious than his friend CONRAD for an early war with SERBIA, he surrounded himself with a personal cabinet of moderate conservative advisors (the 'Belvedere Circle'), regarded by contemporaries as a breeding ground for official imperial policy.

Franz Ferdinand and his wife, Duchess Sophie, were fully aware that a visit in June 1914 to Sarajevo in Austro-Hungarian Bosnia was dangerous, but accepted the risk as a matter of duty. Their assassination by the Serbian nationalist PRINCIP on 28 June triggered the subsequent JULY CRISIS throughout Europe. Regarded by some Austrian historians as an enlightened figure planning a gradual programme of social reform under the crown, Ferdinand is more conventionally seen as a reactionary committed to an alliance between a powerful monarchy and aristocratic landowners.

Franz Josef I, Kaiser (1830–1916) Habsburg Emperor since 1848, and ruler of AUSTRIA-HUNGARY since 1867, Franz Josef was a formidable opponent of nationalist, separatist elements, but a series of personal tragedies (including the premature deaths of his wife, son and brother) drove him into depressed isolation in the later decades of his reign. He accepted foreign minister BERCHTOLD's decision for war during the JULY CRISIS of 1914, and the military assumed effective control of wartime imperial policy-making. Content to operate primarily as a figurehead, and publicly confident, he was privately aware by 1916 that victory was impossible and the survival of the Empire unlikely. Old and tired, he remained a personal force for imperial unity, and his death on 21 November 1916 removed one of the few emotional ties binding his subjects. He was succeeded by his great-nephew KARL I.

Frauenlob One of 10 Gazelle Class 'protected' CRUISERS built for the GERMAN NAVY at the turn of the century, and one of the few retained in frontline service by August 1914. Particularly vulnerable to MINES or TORPEDOES, the Gazelles were generally regarded as expendable and suffered heavy losses. *Ariadne* was sunk at HELIGOLAND BIGHT in 1914, *Undine* was torpedoed in the BALTIC by a British SUBMARINE the following November, and *Frauenlob* was one of only two large German warships sunk at JUTLAND.

BRIEF DATA (*Frauenlob*) Displacement: 2,150 tons; Crew: 264; Dimensions: length 344.5ft (104.4m), beam 40ft (12.1m); Speed: 21.5k; Armament: 10 × 4.1in gun, 2 × 17.7in TT.

Frederick, Archduke (1856–1936) Like most royal commanders within the AUSTRO-HUNGARIAN ARMY, Frederick enjoyed high wartime rank but little real military influence. He performed a largely honorific role as

Army C-in-C from August 1914 while chief of staff CONRAD controlled strategy and dispositions. An orthodox political and military conservative, his main contribution was as a diplomatic counter to the overweening behaviour of German field commanders on the EASTERN FRONT, and he was promoted field marshal to ensure continued parity with HINDENBURG. Frederick was appointed military deputy to KARL I in November 1916, but dismissed when the new Emperor decided to do without strategic advice in December. He retired the following February.

Freikorps Private military formations recruited from among German soldiers returning home after the ARMISTICE in 1918 and deployed to suppress a feared left-wing revolution in GERMANY. Armed and financed by the right-wing industrial interests behind the wartime THIRD SUPREME COMMAND, the Freikorps ('Free Corps') were led by some of the GERMAN ARMY's best-known officers and comprised battle-hardened veterans from every theatre of war.

Offered to the new parliamentary government to put down popular protests against living conditions in Berlin and other large cities from early 1919, the Freikorps easily crushed the SPARTACUS LEAGUE in January and had largely completed a brutal purge of left-wing elements in workers' organizations throughout Germany by April. Much of the liberal outrage at their employment in protection of an avowedly socialist government was directed at the minister responsible for coordinating the arrangement, Gustav NOSKE. Freikorps units (and the army) made no attempt to prevent the right-wing 'Kapp Putsch' of 1920. See also: GERMAN REVOLUTIONS.

French, Field Marshal Sir John (1852–1925) British cavalry officer chosen to lead the BEF to BELGIUM in August 1914. His reputation for dash and vigour, established during colonial operations in Africa, may have influenced the cautious tone of his original instructions from British war minister KITCHENER, but he proved an uncertain and timid leader in practice.

Swinging from unrealistic optimism before his first engagement at MONS to utter pessimism during the subsequent Allied retreat on the WESTERN FRONT, he was acutely conscious that he commanded GREAT BRITAIN's only land defence force, and by late August his main aim was its escape home. After a visit from Kitchener in early September he was persuaded to commit the BEF, albeit cautiously, to the French counteroffensive on the MARNE, and his confidence returned for a time after the victory.

Never able to liaise effectively with French commanders, and often in conflict with his own field officers, his handling of the BEF during the more static operations of 1915 was epitomized by an inept performance during the ARTOIS–LOOS OFFENSIVE, and he was replaced by HAIG in December 1915. In command of British home forces until 1918, when he became lord lieutenant of Ireland, he retired in 1921 after producing a notoriously unreliable memoir of the 1914 campaigns. See also: SMITH-DORRIEN, H.; WILSON, H.

French Army Rebuilt in reaction to the disastrous Franco-Prussian War of 1870, the French Army of 1914 was primarily designed for war against GERMANY. Conscription laws were reformed in 1872 to provide a larger trained reserve, based on short-term mass service with a reduction in the number of exemptions. After 1905 the laws were modified to raise the number of men available for wartime mobilization to 3 million. Expansion of the French Army alarmed GERMAN ARMY planners, but barely kept pace with a much faster rate of population growth in Germany. Further refinements in 1913 came too late to influence manpower levels the following year.

Defeat in 1870 was generally ascribed to the adoption of a defensive attitude against an attack-minded enemy. Attacking doctrine (variously described as 'offensive spirit', '*élan*' or '*offensive à l'outrance*') completely dominated tactical developments to 1914, with the stress laid on the psychological effects on opponents of rapid CAVALRY charges and fearless infantry assaults.

Although the perceived need to attack or defend FORTRESSES prompted some development of MACHINE GUNS (the Army had less than 2,200 in September 1914), heavy ARTILLERY and the tools of TRENCH WARFARE, they were not considered important in the context of offensive field operations. Field artillery, based on the excellent medium 'SOIXANTE-QUINZE', was deployed in small mobile batteries intended for rapid accompaniment of attacking infantry rather than thorough reduction of hostile positions. Doomed with hindsight, faith in spirit over firepower had many important advocates in other European armies, and remained an important influence in French military thinking as late as 1917.

French military affairs were highly politicized, a legacy of the Napoleonic link between army and state (see SARRAIL, M.). The French president was titular C-in-C of the Army, but official control was vested in the war minister, heading a council of senior officers (*Conseil Supérieur de la Guerre*) with the field C-in-C as vice president.

In practice the field army's General Staff, or GQG (*Grand Quartier Général*), retained a jealous hold on all planning and administration, and field commander JOFFRE effectively banished politicians from the front until 1917. His successors had less complete authority over strategic decisions, but political control was not fully established until spring 1918, when CLEMENCEAU used the Allied SUPREME WAR COUNCIL to force PÉTAIN's subordination to the more aggressive FOCH.

The peacetime field army in August 1914 comprised a total of 47 divisions (777,000 French and 46,000 colonial troops) in 21 regional corps, most of two divisions with attached cavalry and field-artillery units. Apart from the single North African corps, including colonial units considered among the Army's elite, the corps were deployed inside France alongside 8 independent cavalry divisions, with strength concentrated in five armies along the eastern frontier (see PLAN 17). Separate overseas forces, generally comprising about 60 per cent native troops, were stationed in North Africa (about 75,000 men), Indo-China (32,000) and Madagascar (3,000).

A further 2.9 million men had been mobilized by mid-August 1914, and another 2.7 million by the following June, stretching resources to include men aged 45. Crippling losses during the opening campaigns on the WESTERN FRONT decimated the pool of experienced officers and NCOs, and recruitment steadied as training and supply struggled to match manpower expansion. By the ARMISTICE a total of 8,317,000 million men, including 475,000 colonial troops, had been called up.

Apart from transforming its size, conditions on the Western Front altered the structure and balance of the French Army. In common with other forces it subdivided to meet expanded commitments, with 12 armies in the field by 1918, and the proportion of artillery to infantry strength greatly increased. By 1918 about 40 per cent of all French troops on the Western Front were artillerymen, and infantry numbers had dropped to 850,000 from 1.5 million in June 1915. Increasing use of machine guns (66,000 were available in November 1918), ARMOURED CARS, TANKS and other technical services also drained basic infantry strength, as did the mushrooming aviation service (the AÉRONAUTIQUE MILITAIRE).

After halting the German invasion at the MARNE in September 1914, French forces on the Western Front were committed to a series of unproductive BREAKTHROUGH offensives in CHAMPAGNE and ARTOIS through 1915, and spent 1916 desperately defending the VERDUN sector. Close to exhaustion by late 1916, the Army collapsed in 1917 after the failure of the NIVELLE OFFENSIVE (see FRENCH ARMY MUTINY). Rescued by Pétain's recuperative policies, despite opposition to his defensive strategy from many field commanders, the Army managed one last major counterattack to end the German SPRING OFFENSIVES of 1918, but was never again committed to a mass offensive and played a largely supporting role to BEF and AEF forces during the climactic victories of 1918.

Defence of France was the overwhelming preoccupation of successive field commanders, but a substantial expeditionary force was deployed at SALONIKA (reflecting French public sympathy for SERBIA). A corps also fought at GALLIPOLI, four divisions served on the ITALIAN FRONT from late 1917, and smaller detachments saw action in PALESTINE and AFRICA.

France mobilized fewer troops in wartime than the British Empire, but suffered almost 50 per cent more casualties (about 4.2 million, including 1.3 million dead). Losses in proportion to men committed ran at three times the rate of later years in 1914, when the doctrine of 'offensive spirit' was applied in its fullest form.

Even in 1918 some French generals were reluctant to betray the concept by employing DEFENCE IN DEPTH techniques, but other symbols of *élan* were abandoned more quickly. Old-fashioned infantry uniforms (featuring highly visible red trousers) and white officers' gloves, such good targets in 1914, were gradually replaced by safer pale-grey garments during 1915, with steel 'Adrian' helmets replacing red and blue cloth 'kepis'.

French Army Air Service See: AÉRONAUTIQUE MILITAIRE.

French Army Mutiny Temporary collapse of the frontline FRENCH ARMY after the NIVELLE OFFENSIVE on the WESTERN FRONT in spring 1917. Beginning in the last two days of April, rebellion spread to parts of 54 divisions, and widespread disturbances lasted until about 10 June. The mutiny was never a coherent movement, but a series of reactions to the combination of repeated heavy casualties, disappointment at the 'decisive' offensive's total failure, very poor conditions, low pay and cancelled leave.

Some units deserted (French desertions reached a record 27,000 in 1917), others demanded peace, while yet others threatened direct action against the capital. However, the mutineers generally proved amenable to pacification by new French C-in-C PÉTAIN, who visited 90 divisions to hear grievances in person and introduced immediate increases in rations, leave allowances and medical facilities.

Some rebel units were repressed but executions were kept to a minimum, and the Army was quietly back in position by July. It was pronounced fit for action in August, but Pétain and other military leaders regarded its condition as unstable through the autumn, restricting attacks to a few limited operations for demonstration purposes.

A long stretch of the Western Front had been left virtually undefended for several weeks, but French authorities managed to keep the extent of disturbances almost completely secret. Almost no news of the mutinies reached the French public or Allied commands until they were substantially over.

Along with many French conservatives, the Army high command regarded the collapse as the work of PACIFIST or socialist agitators, a view stimulated by the Russian FEBRUARY REVOLUTION and a spate of simultaneous civilian demonstrations and strikes in FRANCE. It renewed its demands for government suppression of left-wing dissent, and the mutinies were used by the CLEMENCEAU government as the basis for charges laid against leading pacifists during the TREASON TRIALS of 1918. See also: CATTARO; KIEL MUTINY; SINGAPORE MUTINY.

French Navy The French Navy had suffered several decades of decline after 1870 as resources were concentrated on the build-up of land forces facing GERMANY. Large-scale reconstruction was begun in 1909 by marine minister BOUÉ DE LAPEYRÈRE and continued by his successors, so that naval expenditure almost doubled between 1910 and 1914. Fourteen new BATTLESHIPS were ordered from French shipyards, along with light CRUISERS and DESTROYERS previously neglected in favour of coastal-defence SUBMARINES and large cruisers for commerce raiding.

Diplomatic entente with GREAT BRITAIN from 1904 enabled concentration of forces against Italian and Austro-Hungarian naval expansion in the MEDITERRANEAN, which threatened trade routes to southern French ports and communications with North African colonies. Agreement with the ROYAL NAVY in 1912 effectively established a British sphere of influence in northern waters, where the French could not hope to compete with Anglo-German resources, and all major French warships were concentrated with the Mediterranean battlefleet ('Armée Navale') by August 1914.

Few of the newly ordered ships had been

completed on the outbreak of war, but the fleet included 19 battleships (but only 2 COURBET Class dreadnoughts), 32 old cruisers, 86 destroyers, 34 (mostly elderly) submarines and 115 coastal TORPEDO BOATS. Another new dreadnought (*Paris*) joined within a month, but the Navy suffered from a general shortage of fast, modern ships (see *DANTON*).

Armée Navale commander Boué de Lapeyrère initially concentrated the fleet to protect troop transports from Africa, attracting criticism for failing to attempt long-range pursuit of the German MITTELMEERDIVISION. With its escape and ITALY's declaration of neutrality, the main immediate threat to Allied shipping in the Mediterranean was the AUSTRO-HUNGARIAN NAVY, and from mid-August the French Navy's major units were based in Malta in order to patrol the southern Adriatic against any break-out. Their effectiveness was restricted by the vulnerability of large warships to submarines (see *LEON GAMBETTA*), shortage of fast light cruisers or destroyers, and a lack of nearby secure bases.

Offensive operations in the Adriatic were confined to the sporadic supply of Allied forces on the BALKAN FRONT, offshore bombardments of Austrian naval bases at CATTARO and Lissa, and unsuccessful attempts by submarines to penetrate the main Austrian base further north at Pola. After Italy joined the Allies in May 1915, a large portion of the French fleet remained on more distant watch from Corfu, and new dreadnoughts were protected from serious risk once they entered service.

Old battleships were less precious, and four were sent to join the DARDANELLES operation in early 1915, along with six destroyers, a few submarines and a handful of minesweepers. Heavy losses during the main attempt to force the Straits in March, including four submarines and the pre-dreadnought *BOUVET*, were replaced from stock, and participation was maintained until the end of the campaign.

French transports and ARMED MERCHANT CRUISERS helped to evacuate Serbian forces from the coast of ALBANIA to Corfu in early 1916 (see 'GREAT RETREAT'). Most Allied troops and supplies reached SALONIKA under French flags and protection, although U-BOATS sank three Navy transports and the cruiser *CHÂTEAURENAULT*. The French fleet dominated Allied demonstrations of strength off the Greek coast during 1916, culminating in the December ATHENS LANDING. This episode, which was followed by French seizure and commissioning of GREEK NAVY vessels, heightened political criticism of the Navy's performance in FRANCE and brought the replacement of DARTIGE, Lapeyrère's successor, by Admiral GAUCHET.

Growing numbers of German U-boats were a major threat to Allied shipping in the Mediterranean from 1915, exposing the inadequacy of French ANTI-SUBMARINE policy. In line with Allied 'offensive' methods, French ships patrolled most of the central Mediterranean area. The Navy eventually used 11 torpedo boats, some 200 pursuit ships and almost 750 armed trawlers, along with more than 1,100 armed merchant ships, against submarines. This force remained totally inadequate until the belated introduction of regular CONVOYS from late 1917, and more than 500 French ships (891,000 tons) were eventually lost to U-boats (see *HANDELSKRIEG*).

Subsidiary naval operations in the Mediterranean included a permanent blockade of the Syrian coast by a small force of cruisers, old battleships and light forces, which protected French economic and political interests in the region; this force also helped in the defence of SUEZ in 1915, and supported operations in PALESTINE during 1917.

The French commander in the Mediterranean was officially also Allied C-in-C for the theatre, but the title meant little in practice. Effective local command rested with whichever country had most ships involved in a region, and the C-in-C was only expected to take practical overall control in the unlikely event of a decisive general battle. Relations between French and other Allied commands, generally courteous, were primarily concerned with division of resources and anti-submarine patrol zones.

Outside the Mediterranean, several small ships were lost in pursuit of German commerce raiders, and two squadrons of cruisers took part in Atlantic-convoy escort duties from late 1916. Light forces based around Dunkirk were constantly embroiled with their German counterparts in the English Channel.

In August 1914, the French Navy possessed only 8 seaplanes, but by the ARMISTICE it operated 1,264 aircraft (almost all seaplanes) and 37 AIRSHIPS. Mostly operated from coastal stations as reconnaissance, light-bombing and anti-submarine craft, they played a marginal role and were never used for overland or AIRCRAFT CARRIER operations as pioneered by the British RNAS (see *FOUDRE*).

A brigade of 6,500 infantry-trained sailors (*fusiliers marins*) took part in the Battle of the YSER on the WESTERN FRONT in late 1914, and a battalion remained in the theatre into 1918. French Navy gunners also served on the Belgian canals, shelling German land positions from river barges, and were deployed on heights overlooking both the Dardanelles and Cattaro.

French naval shipyards, distracted by their additional role as suppliers of some 8,500 guns to the FRENCH ARMY, produced 45 anti-submarine sloops and gunboats and 132 patrol ships in wartime, but only 3 BRETAGNE Class battleships, 2 destroyers and 21 submarines. The French Navy's total losses in action (excluding other causes) were 4 battleships, 6 cruisers, 23 destroyers and torpedo boats, 14 submarines, 7 auxiliary cruisers, 46 various patrol craft, and 26 transports or other auxiliaries. See also: AUGAGNEUR, J.; LACAZE, M.

Frezenberg, Battle of See: Second Battle of YPRES.

Friedrichshafen FF-33 German floatplane produced from late 1914 and used by the GERMAN NAVY in several FIGHTER and reconnaissance versions. Early reconnaissance FF-33 and FF-33b models were often unarmed, but the main production FF-33e (188 built) was fitted with two-way RADIO and carried a small bomb load. Later reconnaissance versions included the FF-33j, with improved instruments and radio, and all three types served with German coastal stations in Europe. An FF-33e attached to the commerce raider *WOLF* in the Indian and Pacific Oceans became famous from 1916, assisting its parent ship in the destruction or capture of 28 Allied vessels. The FF-33f fighter, armed with rear and forward MACHINE GUNS, entered service from October 1915. Along with modified FF-33h and FF-331 designs, the latter the main production fighter (135 built), it flew patrol, reconnaissance and escort missions over the North Sea and English Channel. Reconnaissance FF-33s were gradually replaced from mid-1917, but fighters remained in service until the ARMISTICE, by which time just under 500 of all versions had been built, making it the most common aircraft in use with the wartime German Navy.

BRIEF DATA (FF-33e) Type: two-seater reconnaissance floatplane; Engine: 150hp Benz; Max speed: 120kph; Armament: observer's small arms, light bombs (hand thrown).

Friedrichshafen FF-49 Armed floatplane that began to replace the FRIEDRICHSHAFEN FF-33 series as a standard GERMAN NAVY reconnaissance craft from May 1917. Larger and stronger than its predecessor, it was better able to survive harsh conditions in the North Sea, where it served until the ARMISTICE. Some later models were additionally fitted with a forward-firing MACHINE GUN, and a total of 218 FF-49s were built, including 25 FF-49b versions with the guns removed in favour of a small bomb load.

BRIEF DATA (FF-49) Type: two-seater armed reconnaissance floatplane; Engine: 200hp Benz; Max speed: 150kph; Armament: 1 × 7.92mm mg.

Friedrichshafen G-Types Twin-engined biplane bomber in action with GERMAN ARMY AIR SERVICE units on the WESTERN FRONT from late 1916. The original G-II model, driven by 220hp engines, could lift a bomb load of only 150kg and was quickly superseded by the larger G-III. Along with GOTHA G-TYPES, which it resembled, the G-III was a mainstay of the German STRATEGIC BOMBING force from early 1917. Produced in large (but uncertain) numbers, it was in service until the ARMISTICE, taking part in regular night attacks against Belgian and French targets but rarely, if ever, joining long-range raids on England. A G-IIIa version, with biplane tail design but otherwise similar, also went into full production and was used alongside the G-III, but G-IV and G-V developments were rejected for military use in 1918.

BRIEF DATA (G-III) Type: medium/heavy bomber; Crew: 2–3; Engine: 2 × 260hp Mercedes; Max speed: 134kph; Armament: 2–4 × 7.92mm mg, max bomb load 1,400kg.

Frontiers, Battles of the Collective term for the collision of French and German invasion plans on or close to the eastern French frontiers in August 1914. The confrontation comprised four distinct and almost simultaneous battles – in LORRAINE, in the ARDENNES forests, at CHARLEROI and at MONS – each affecting the ultimate course of the others and amounting to a general Allied defeat all along the WESTERN FRONT.

French C-in-C JOFFRE followed the prewar PLAN 17 in launching invasions of Germany through Lorraine (14 August) and the Ardennes (20 August), both repulsed by tactically superior German forces in their line of advance. Although the French Lorraine armies held at a line in front of Nancy, the southern flank of the Ardennes force was exposed, encouraging its full retreat by 23 August. A gap thus appeared to the right of the FRENCH ARMY's northern wing, which had been turned to face the German invasion of BELGIUM, and the GERMAN ARMY's main strike force (see SCHLIEFFEN PLAN). The enforced retirement of the northern wing from Charleroi the same night left another gap to the right of the British Expeditionary Force (BEF), which withdrew from Mons shortly afterwards, and by 24 August Allied armies were retreating or on the defensive all along the front. The French Army in particular had suffered enormous casualties among its best troops, but remained sufficiently coherent to regroup at the MARNE in defence of Paris. See MAP 4.

Fuller, Colonel John (1878–1966) An important influence on the development of armoured warfare, Fuller was the senior figure in a group of officers guiding the new British TANK service. As chief of staff to the Tank Corps from June 1917, he argued strongly for mass deployment of tanks on suitable ground, but saw their chief function as long-range strategic penetration beyond enemy lines. Tank officers, like pilots, were generally regarded as eccentrics by senior BEF commanders, and Fuller gained approval to try his methods only in late 1917, when his absolute insistence on holding back reserves was ignored at CAMBRAI. The mistake prompted Fuller to produce his famous 'Plan 1919' for victory by long-range tank attacks with strong air, motorized and ARTILLERY support, ignored in Britain but studied in GERMANY as a blueprint for later blitzkrieg tactics.

Furious Unique British warship, planned as a 'light battlecruiser' but eventually in wartime service as the ROYAL NAVY's largest AIRCRAFT CARRIER. The ultimate expression of Admiral FISHER's influential preference for big guns and high speed over protection, light BATTLECRUISERS were enormous ships with very thin armour, but wartime experience with MINES and TORPEDOES had exposed their lack of hull protection as a major liability.

Planned with four massive 18-inch guns, the biggest ever mounted on a British warship, the redundant *Furious* had its forward turret removed while under construction and replaced by a 70-metre take-off deck, with hanger space for three SHORT 184 seaplanes and five SOPWITH PUP landplanes. It entered service in July 1917, but the weight of its remaining turret proved too much for efficient operation and the deck unsuitable for landings. After some debate, *Furious* was sent for further conversion in late 1917, returning to service the following March with anti-torpedo bulges built onto the hull, a second flight deck in place of the rear turret (which was later fitted to a MONITOR) and much more hangar space.

Landings at sea still proved virtually impossible because of turbulence from the central superstructure and funnels, so that *Furious* was no more a genuine carrier than the smaller conversions already available. Joining the GRAND FLEET in the North Sea, it took part in the TONDERN RAID of July 1918, but pilots were still required to ditch in the water. Given a flush deck in the 1920s, *Furious* remained in service until the Second World War (see *ARGUS*).

BRIEF DATA (*Furious*, 1918) Displacement: 22,000 tons; Crew: 737; Dimensions: length 786.5ft (238.3m), beam 88ft (26.7m); Speed: 32.5k; Armament: 10 × 5.5in gun, 5 × 3in AA, 24 × a/c.

G

Galicia, Campaign in (1914) The opening campaign of the war between RUSSIA and AUSTRIA-HUNGARY on the EASTERN FRONT, conducted simultaneously with the Russo-German campaign in EAST PRUSSIA. The Austro-Hungarian province of Galicia was a natural point of conflict for the two empires, and both planned offensives in the region for August 1914 (see MAP 11).

The prewar PLAN 19 committed 47 RUSSIAN ARMY divisions to an invasion of Galicia. To resolve arguments between STAVKA (Russian central command) and army group commander IVANOV the planned offensive was split into two. The strongest force, comprising the Third (RUZSKI) and Eighth (BRUSILOV) Armies, was to attack towards Lvov from the eastern frontier, where the main Austro-Hungarian attack was expected. The Fourth (Salza) and Fifth (PLEHVE) Armies were deployed to the northwest, detailed to attack the northern frontier and with potential support from a new Ninth Army forming around Warsaw. Thirty-five Russian infantry divisions were in position by 18 August, rising to 45 by the end of the month.

Austro-Hungarian chief of staff CONRAD's plans suffered delay and confusion. Having promised his German allies an attack into Russian Poland, Conrad wavered until the last moment between concentrating most of his 48 divisions in Galicia and sending a substantial force to the BALKAN FRONT. Contradictory orders fuelled chaos on the RAILWAYS and only 31 infantry divisions had reached the Galician region by 28 August, most of them detrained far to the rear of their intended positions.

Despite these setbacks, Conrad went ahead with plans for an offensive. The First (DANKL) and Fourth (AUFFENBERG) Armies were committed to a northward attack into Poland. The Third Army (Brudemann), still awaiting formation of the Second Army in its rear, advanced east from Lvov to forestall Russian attacks.

Delays meant that the first battles in the northern sector, where each side fielded about 350,000 men, opened inside Austria-Hungary. Ignoring indications that Austro-Hungarian strength was greatest in the sector, the Russian Fourth Army crossed the frontier on 18 August and blundered into the Austrian First Army five days later.

Forced back to prepared positions around KRASNIK, and then north towards Lublin, Russian forces called up reinforcements and halted Austrian pursuit at the end of the month, by which time fighting had spread along the front as both sides received support from neighbouring armies.

Plehve's Russian Fifth Army, turning laboriously southwest to the Fourth Army's aid, collided with Auffenberg's Austrian Fourth Army marching north. Narrowly escaping encirclement around KOMAROW (26–31 August), Plehve retreated north of Cholm from 1 September. On the same day, Conrad issued orders for Auffenberg to relieve Austro-Hungarian forces on the eastern frontier, where the Third Army had run into the larger Russian Third and Eighth Armies.

Mistaking its dense concentration on a narrow front for lack of numbers, Brudemann attacked the Russian Third Army on the ZLOTA LIPA river (26–28 August). Outnumbered Austro-Hungarian divisions were heavily defeated, but Ruzski's failure to pursue enabled retreat to the Gnila Lipa. Reinforced from the Balkans, and with General BÖHM-

ERMOLLI's Second Army now occupying the southern end of the front, Conrad ignored Brudemann's new and accurate reports of Russian numerical superiority and ordered another attack at the GNILA LIPA on 29–30 August.

The failure of this attack convinced Conrad to sanction a full-scale retreat west of Lvov to good defensive positions on the River Wereszyca, and he ordered Auffenberg's Fourth Army to turn southeast against the flank of the advancing Russians. Ruzski inched after the retreat, entering Lvov on 3 September before wheeling northwest in belated response to demands from both Ivanov and Stavka that he help Plehve.

The following day Ruzski met the Austrian Fourth Army coming the other way near Rava Ruska. With both forces tired and short of supplies, a week of fighting ended in deadlock west of Lvov.

Russian counterattacks in the northwest eroded the Austro-Hungarian position during early September. The reinforced Russian Fourth Army (now under EVERT) drove the Austrians back from Lublin along the east bank of the Vistula, and Plehve's revived Fifth Army moved against Auffenberg's rear at Rava Ruska. By 9 September the Austrian Third and Fourth Armies were threatened with encirclement, and after an unsuccessful appeal for German reinforcements, Conrad ordered a general withdrawal on 11 September.

Plans to make a stand on the River San were abandoned when the position of Evert's Russian forces became clear, and the disorganized Austro-Hungarian armies reached positions beyond the Carpathian mountains east of Kraków in mid-September. Leaving only the fortress of PRZEMYSL to resist Russian advances, they paused to recover from an estimated 400,000 losses since mid-August.

The Russians had suffered about 250,000 casualties, and pursuit by the Fourth, Fifth and Ninth Armies was slow. Wet weather, continuing supply crisis, command uncertainty, the distraction of besieging Przemysl and sheer exhaustion meant that no attempt was made to cross the Carpathians. From 24 September Ivanov began pulling troops away from the front to meet the threat of a new German Ninth Army forming around Kraków, and the focus of operations on the Eastern Front switched to the POLISH CAMPAIGNS.

Galliéni, General Joseph (1849–1916) Distinguished French colonial warrior, who retired from the FRENCH ARMY in 1914 but was recalled as C-in-C JOFFRE's deputy in August. As Joffre's only rival in military stature, Galliéni was kept away from staff headquarters and given the thankless task of organizing the defence of Paris from late August. He immediately shocked a poorly informed government by announcing that German forces would be in the capital by early September, and mobilized his limited resources with immense vigour.

Although Joffre was publicly credited with the subsequent victory on the MARNE, some commentators regard Galliéni as its architect. Among the first to spot an attacking opportunity when the German First Army turned east in early September, he sent the Sixth Army to strike its flank from Paris on his own authority, and subsequently blocked German counterattacks by rushing reserves to the front.

Galliéni was appointed war minister in October 1915, with a brief to establish political control over Joffre's virtually autonomous high command, but the C-in-C's popular reputation in FRANCE proved unassailable and he resigned in March 1916 after a dispute over the handling of operations around VERDUN. The strain of office broke his failing health and he died three months later.

Gallipoli Front The Allied invasion of western TURKEY (1915–16), begun as a purely naval attempt to break through the Dardanelles Straits in February 1915 but dominated by land battles after the landing of British, British imperial and FRENCH ARMY troops on the Gallipoli Peninsula in late April (see MAP 20).

The strategic importance of the Turkish Dardanelles Straits was widely recognized in 1914. They linked the MEDITERRANEAN with the Sea of Marmora, giving access to Constantinople, much of the Ottoman Empire's industrial base and the BLACK SEA (through the even narrower Bosporus Channel). Any penetration of the Sea of Marmora by hostile navies could open a vital supply route between western Europe and RUSSIA, knock Turkey out of action, and possibly secure the support of GREECE and BULGARIA.

The Dardanelles were a difficult tactical proposition, guarded by the Gallipoli Peninsula to the north and the shore of Ottoman Asia Minor to the south, with clifftop fortresses overlooking restricted shipping lanes. Worldwide professional opinion in 1914 regarded a purely naval attack on the Straits as inadvisable, and all early Allied plans for an offensive assumed the need for land operations to capture at least one shoreline.

The unlikely decision to mount a purely naval operation, the brainchild of unorthodox British naval minister CHURCHILL, was reached in a haphazard and opaque fashion over several months, while Anglo-French diplomats and politicians ignored evidence of virtual German control in Turkey, maintaining improbable efforts to woo Constantinople.

Britain's naval specialist on Turkish affairs (Admiral Limpus) was transferred to Malta, and foreign secretary GREY's opposition helped to ensure a noncommittal British response to a Greek government offer of 60,000 troops for a joint invasion of Turkey (20 August 1914). The fall of the VENIZELOS government meant that by the time Turkey was at war in October the offer was conditional on Bulgarian participation.

Battles on the WESTERN FRONT dominated Anglo-French attention through the autumn, but the idea of using Mediterranean naval supremacy to open an alternative front gained ground with influential 'EASTERNERS' in GREAT BRITAIN. Churchill ordered a demonstration bombardment of the outer fortress defences by Admiral Carden's patrolling naval squadron on 2 November, and from late November he held naval transports ready in EGYPT. Turkish authorities were meanwhile given time to reorganize and re-equip scant regional defences.

In early January 1915 the western Allies received a plea from RUSSIAN ARMY C-in-C Grand Duke NIKOLAI for action to divert pressure from the CAUCASIAN FRONT (see SARIKAMISH). British First Sea Lord FISHER and War Council secretary Colonel Hankey responded by recommending a full-scale invasion of the Dardanelles region by British, Indian, Greek and Bulgarian troops, with naval support from old BATTLESHIPS. Diplomatically optimistic and never likely to receive practical support from BEF commanders or war minister KITCHENER, the plan was used by Churchill as an opportunity to pursue his own aggressive agenda.

In a loaded telegram to Carden, Churchill demanded and received a blueprint for naval penetration of the Straits, though not a professional endorsement of the idea. Eloquently presented as a plan of action to a depressed War Cabinet on 13 January, it won Churchill broad approval for action of some sort. The vagueness of cabinet conclusions allowed some members, like Fisher, to imagine they were supporting their own operational agenda, but Churchill interpreted the meeting as giving him authority to activate Carden's scheme for a gradual reduction of the Dardanelles defences by old, expendable battleships.

Timed for 19 February, the operation was formally authorized at the next Council meeting on 28 January. Absence of any plan to exploit a breakthrough was noted by opponents in both Britain and FRANCE, where naval minister AUGAGNEUR ignored professional advice before committing a FRENCH NAVY squadron to the operation. Political enthusiasm and confidence remained high, and both governments believed a purely naval operation could be broken off if damage to prestige was threatened.

Belated opposition from Fisher and other military experts was barely investigated in a British cabinet dominated by Kitchener, and on 16 February he ordered the only available British infantry division to stand by for the Dardanelles, along with AUSTRALIAN and NEW ZEALAND FORCES stationed in Egypt. The French government, unwilling to cede political influence in the region, announced it was sending a corps of its own two days later, but

Churchill refused to wait for them.

A large fleet of (mostly superannuated) British and French battleships began attacks on the outer forts on 19 February, but failed against an improved defensive system and halted pending army support after an abortive attempt to burst through the Straits on 18 March (see DARDANELLES OPERATION).

The need for ground forces had already been recognized by both Allies, and the French corps of 18,000 colonial troops had sailed for the theatre on 10 March. Two days later Kitchener appointed General HAMILTON to command a British Mediterranean Expeditionary Force of 75,000 men, dominated by almost untried ANZAC troops. A surprised Hamilton had little idea of his exact mission, but after discussion with naval commander DE ROBECK he agreed on 27 March to an invasion of the Gallipoli Peninsula.

Allied preparations were marked by vagueness, confusion, delay and over-confidence, allowing more time for reinforcement of Turkish land defences around the Straits. Turkish Fifth Army commander LIMAN VON SANDERS, who took over regional defence in late March, distributed six divisions (84,000 men) at strategic points on Gallipoli and the Asian shore, but Hamilton's eventual decision to attack the southern peninsula with multiple landings struck at the least defended part of the system.

Though ineptly commanded, poorly equipped and thrown back with heavy casualties wherever serious resistance was met, the GALLIPOLI LANDINGS of 25 April established two beachheads: at HELLES on the southern tip of Gallipoli, and up the Aegean coast near Gaba Tepe, a location subsequently known as ANZAC COVE.

The ANZAC position was a dour redoubt from the start, perched on a tiny warren of clifftop ridges, and Hamilton's first attempts to expand the beachheads came in the south, where General Hunter-Weston launched a series of clumsy attacks towards KRITHIA. Failure, and belated appreciation of Turkish defensive capability, prompted a reappraisal of the campaign in London, where the Dardanelles Committee met for the first time on 7 June to plan its future.

Despite bitter opposition from commanders in France, Hamilton's timid requests for reinforcement and more ammunition had been partly answered in May (see SHELL SCANDAL), but Turkish strength had grown more quickly as troops were diverted from the PALESTINE and CAUCASIAN FRONTS. Kitchener, hitherto content to maintain limited pressure on Gallipoli, accepted Churchill's argument that a rapid decision was needed and committed three new BRITISH ARMY divisions to the theatre for a major offensive.

Hamilton planned an ambitious three-pronged operation – a feint at Helles, a breakout north from the Anzac Cove beachhead, and a major landing at Suvla Bay by his new divisions under General Stopford, which would then link up with the Anzac attack and sweep across the peninsula to the Dardanelles. Meanwhile he allowed Hunter-Weston to mount further costly and unsuccessful attacks towards ACHI BABA in Helles.

Although it achieved initial surprise, and Stopford's landings were almost unopposed, the SUVLA BAY OFFENSIVE stalled in all three sectors as Hamilton again failed to impose his intentions on manifestly inadequate field commanders. Launched late on 6 August, the entire offensive had largely ground to a halt by 10 August, although sporadic fighting continued everywhere for several days (see SARI BAIR).

Deadlocked at three beachheads, each hemmed in by apparently impregnable positions on higher ground, Hamilton's only remaining option was to push south from Suvla Bay towards Anzac Cove, barely 5km away. The corps at Suvla was given more reinforcements and a completely new set of experienced commanders, but KEMAL's defenders held off further attacks against SCIMITAR HILL and HILL 60 during late August, after which fighting subsided into a muted form of Gallipoli's peculiarly claustrophobic TRENCH WARFARE.

An increasingly desperate Hamilton, having lost 40,000 men to battle and disease in August, asked for 95,000 replacements but was offered 25,000. Against a tide of Anglo-French disillusionment, Churchill still lobbied for greater commitment to the theatre and

Kitchener appeared fully to agree for the first time. He supported a proposal by French General SARRAIL for a joint invasion of the Asian coast, but the idea was blocked by French C-in-C JOFFRE as resources were concentrated in France for the ARTOIS–LOOS OFFENSIVE.

The critical situation in SERBIA relegated Gallipoli to the background of French planning in late autumn. Sarrail's plan was shelved for the foreseeable future, and Kitchener was pressured into releasing 75,000 men for an Allied landing at SALONIKA, a commitment later doubled against his wishes by the British government.

Troops for Salonika could only come from Gallipoli, where Hamilton's credibility was faltering. Criticism of his management reached London in September from the dismissed Stopford, from his own staff officers, and from the press via journalist Keith MURDOCH. The possibility of evacuation, considered by the British government since May, was relayed to Hamilton on 11 October in a wire from Kitchener. Asked to provide estimates of evacuation casualties Hamilton gave a figure of 50 per cent, reflecting his outrage at the idea and sealing his removal at the next meeting of the Dardanelles Committee on 14 October.

His replacement, General Monro, toured all three fronts within a day of his arrival on 28 October and recommended withdrawal. Kitchener, belatedly determined to maintain the expedition, was sent to Gallipoli to make a final decision on 3 November, and travelled intending to sanction a renewed naval attack on the Dardanelles.

After seeing Gallipoli for the first time, he rejected the idea and on 15 November recommended evacuation of the Suvla and Anzac positions. The Admiralty blocked efforts by KEYES and WEMYSS to revive the naval plan, before the government finally ordered evacuation of all three beachheads on 7 December. Meanwhile blizzard conditions on Gallipoli during November called the operation's viability into question and added exposure to a long list of medical crises facing ground forces.

Subsequently represented by Allied PROPAGANDA as a triumph in adversity, the evacuation of almost 105,000 men, 5,000 animals and 300 guns from Anzac Cove and Suvla Bay was an efficient combined operation carried out in difficult conditions. Thousands of casualties were expected and gradual withdrawal, begun on 10 December, was covered by elaborate attempts to disguise nocturnal removals from at least 100,000 watching Turkish troops. The last 20,000 men were taken from the beaches on the night of 19–20 December, and the entire operation was completely undisturbed.

The first of 35,000 Allied troops and 3,700 animals were evacuated from Helles in late December and the task was completed in rough seas on the night of 8–9 January 1916. The entire withdrawal was registered as causing three Allied casualties, but mountains of supplies and munitions were left behind.

About 480,000 Allied troops had taken part in the Gallipoli campaign, including substantial British, French, Senegalese, Australian, New Zealand and INDIAN ARMY forces, as well as contingents from Newfoundland, Russia and the Syrian Jewish community. Total British and imperial casualties of 205,000 included 43,000 dead, 90,000 evacuated sick, and more than 33,600 ANZAC losses (one-third killed). French and French colonial losses of about 47,000 included some 5,000 dead. Turkish casualties are estimated at 250,000, with perhaps 65,000 killed, although some Allied sources presume much higher figures.

The TURKISH ARMY's greatest wartime success, the campaign is generally regarded as an example of British strategic 'drift' and tactical ineptitude. The major role played by ANZAC forces in the land campaign, which became a byword for futile self-sacrifice by ill-led troops, provoked a combination of intense pride and outrage in AUSTRALIA and NEW ZEALAND, feelings since viewed as vital stimuli to independent national awareness.

Gallipoli Landings Second phase of the Allied offensive on the GALLIPOLI FRONT, the landing of British, British imperial and French troops on the southern Gallipoli Peninsula on 25 April 1915, planned after naval forces failed to break through the DARDANELLES Straits in February and March (see MAP 20).

The British and French governments had begun sending troops to the Aegean in mid-March, without clearly defining their function except as support for naval operations. Some 18,000 French colonials under General d'Amade left Bizerte on 10 March. General HAMILTON, surprise appointment to command 75,000 BRITISH ARMY, INDIAN ARMY, AUSTRALIAN and NEW ZEALAND FORCES (ANZAC) and ROYAL NAVY troops, sailed for the forward Allied base at MUDROS (on the Aegean Island of Lemnos) four days later.

Units arrived in the eastern Mediterranean apparently at random, and those reaching Mudros found it ill-equipped for large-scale habitation. After the naval defeat of 18 March Hamilton spent two weeks hastily reorganizing at Alexandria in Egypt, making no attempt to disguise his intentions. The only element of surprise, the precise location of the proposed landings, was preserved by poor liaison between Hamilton and Dardanelles naval commander DE ROBECK, each assuming the other was planning an attack.

Hamilton's army left Egypt equipped with wholly inappropriate ARMOURED CARS, but without medical and administrative staff, GRENADES or other TRENCH WARFARE prerequisites. It knew little about the terrain on Gallipoli, and reconnaissance was impossible because British war minister KITCHENER had refused the expedition RFC support.

Allied delays helped LIMAN VON SANDERS, in command of the new Turkish Fifth Army from 25 March, to bring up large-scale reinforcements. In mid-March only some 20,000 troops were scattered around almost 200km of coastline either side of the Straits, but a month later six divisions (about 84,000 men) were ready in new positions.

Linian von Sanders deployed two divisions at the narrow neck of the Gallipoli Peninsula around Bulair and the Gulf of Saros, considered the most likely and strategically valuable target. Two more were stationed on the Asian coast around Besika Bay, geographically difficult to defend and within range of the main Allied battlefleet. A fifth division, Colonel KEMAL's 9th, covered the southern tip of Gallipoli, and another was in the centre of the Peninsula as a general reserve.

Hamilton's eventual plan of attack was guided by his stated priority, rendering the Straits safe for the fleet. He elected to divide his main strength between landings on the southern tip of Gallipoli (the HELLES area), directly threatening Straits defences, and at the narrow point about 15km up the Aegean coast, north of Gaba Tepe.

Feigned landings by the Royal Naval Division at Bulair and by French forces at Besika Bay opened the attack. The main attacks followed at Gaba Tepe (Z Beach) by ANZAC, and at five points on the southern toe (Y, X, W, V and S Beaches). The Y and S attacks, against beaches slightly further up each coast of the peninsula, were smaller operations by separate units added at the last moment, but all were under the overall command of General Hunter-Weston. Part of the French corps landed on the Asian shore around the fortress of Kum Kale, at the mouth of the Straits.

Inadvertently striking at the least defended sectors, the attack was flawed by poor planning. Hamilton deliberately gave his field commanders a free hand in planning their operations, but his general orders stressed the importance of successful landings rather than rapid advance to secure the southern peninsula. He did not insist on coordinated timing of attacks, and much was left to the initiative of Hunter-Weston.

At Z Beach, afterwards known as ANZAC COVE, some 8,000 troops were ashore by 08.00, but landed too far north and were forced to scale steep cliffs to establish a beachhead. Resistance, though generally light, caused heavy casualties to a detachment landed even further north at Ari Burmu.

Nearly 3,000 men at Y Beach reached land unopposed by 06.00, and the slightly smaller force at S Beach made a similarly easy landing, but was ordered to dig in by Hunter-Weston. D'Amade's landing force of 3,000 men took Kum Kale unopposed, but was not fully ashore until 17.30 that evening.

The main Helles invasion by the enlarged 29th Division at X, W and V Beaches was directly opposed by only about 1,000 Turkish troops, thinned by the preceding naval bombardment. Attackers were safely ashore at X Beach and had occupied surrounding cliffs by 06.30; about 90 surviving Turks at W Beach, protected by underwater barbed wire and a few MACHINE GUNS, inflicted 533 casualties on the 950-strong landing party before withdrawing, leaving the operation in chaos.

The landing on V Beach was led by the hastily armoured troopship *River Clyde*, which took 2,000 men right into the shore under the fortress of Sedd-el-Bahr, while another 1,000 approached in ships' boats. Holding their fire until the last moment, defenders caused such carnage that only about 50 men had reached shore cover when Hunter-Weston ordered the main force to land at 08.30.

Less than 2km away off W beach, but uninformed of the situation on V Beach or elsewhere, Hunter-Weston refused Hamilton's offer to redirect the main assault to Y Beach, where troops were vainly awaiting orders to advance. Hamilton, aboard the battleship *QUEEN ELIZABETH*, enjoyed a better overview of the situation than Hunter-Weston (a privilege shared by the press) but failed to intervene.

By afternoon Allied forces were still struggling to establish themselves at Anzac Cove, where Kemal sacrificed 2,000 men in a series of counterattacks by most of his division. Informed that rapid evacuation was technically impossible, ANZAC field commanders Godley and Bridges dug into their tiny beachhead by nightfall, establishing a front that remained essentially unaltered throughout the summer.

At V and W Beaches the small beachhead was consolidated throughout the day, and accurate reports that defenders at Helles still numbered less than 2,000 in the afternoon were not believed. Allied forces at other points on Helles remained passive or awaiting orders.

Beginning with the appearance of transports off Bulair at dawn on 25 April, Liman von Sanders was bewildered by the proliferation of landings but not pressurized anywhere to divert major reserves before evening, by which time Allied confusion had narrowed the field. Turkish reserves drove outnumbered Allied troops from Y Beach during the night, and a Turkish counterattack at Kum Kale (defeated with 1,700 casualties) was enough to persuade French forces to end what they regarded as a demonstration.

Turkish forces at Helles retired to a new line across the peninsula south of Krithia at dawn on 26 April, uninterrupted by confused British units. Hunter-Weston had gathered his strength for an attack on the line by 28 April, by which time it had been reinforced to match attacking numbers diminished by some 6,000 casualties (see Battles of KRITHIA).

Gallwitz, General Max von (1852–1937) Competent and experienced Prussian artillery officer. He commanded an 'army group' detached for the investment of NAMUR on the WESTERN FRONT in August 1914, but was transferred to the EASTERN FRONT to join HINDENBURG's Ninth Army at the end of the month. His corps was merged into a new Army Group Gallwitz (later redesignated the Twelfth Army) in central Poland for the following summer's TRIPLE OFFENSIVE, and he moved to the BALKAN FRONT to lead the Eleventh Army for the autumn invasion of SERBIA. Returning to the Western Front in March 1916, he served at VERDUN before taking command of German defences at the SOMME in mid-July. Reassigned to the Fifth Army in August by the new THIRD SUPREME COMMAND, Gallwitz played a minor part in the YPRES campaign of 1917 before returning to the Verdun sector, where Army Group Gallwitz ended the War facing the strong US–French ST MIHIEL and MEUSE–ARGONNE OFFENSIVES. He resigned from the GERMAN ARMY in December 1918 and served as a conservative Reichstag deputy during the early 1920s.

Gangut The four Gangut Class BATTLESHIPS (*Gangut*, *Petropavlovsk*, *Poltava* and *Sevastopol*) were the RUSSIAN NAVY's first dreadnoughts, ordered in 1909 and finally completed in September 1914. All four were in the BALTIC by early 1915, but were seldom used outside the safe waters of the Gulf of Finland, acting as a deterrent to any German seaborne attack towards Petrograd (St Petersburg). Their design, which incorporated ice-breaking bows, was criticized by officers, and they were notoriously uncomfortable for crews. All survived without taking part in any major surface actions and were later renamed for Soviet service, but *Petropavlovsk* was damaged by a TORPEDO from a British patrol boat at Kronstadt during the RUSSIAN CIVIL WAR.

BRIEF DATA (*Gangut*, 1914) Displacement: 23,370 tons; Crew: 1,125; Dimensions: length 594ft (180m), beam 87ft (26.4m); Speed: 23k; Armament: 12 × 12in (305mm) gun, 16 × 130mm, 2 × 65mm AA, 4 × 18in TT.

Garros, Roland (1882–1918) Eminent prewar French pilot, who served with the AÉRONAUTIQUE MILITAIRE on the WESTERN FRONT from August 1914. In March 1915, his MORANE-SAULNIER L monoplane was the first combat aircraft fitted with DEFLECTOR GEAR, but Garros was captured when it was shot down in April 1915. He later escaped and returned to service as a FIGHTER pilot, but was killed in action around Vouziers on 5 October 1918. See also: INTERRUPTER GEAR.

Gas Military use of airborne poisonous chemicals had been anticipated before 1914, but until TRENCH WARFARE produced a mutual need for new attacking ideas it was generally dismissed as an uncivilized weapon. The GERMAN ARMY was the first to attempt its use, and to take on the difficulties of judging air density, wind conditions and concentration. The Germans' initial experiment with small irritant gas canisters inside shrapnel shells, near Neuve Chapelle on the WESTERN FRONT in October 1914, was not noticed by French troops, and a more concerted gas attack in January 1915, at BOLIMOV on the EASTERN FRONT, failed because xylyl bromide (tear gas) froze in cold weather.

Lethal chlorine gas was first released from cylinders and carried by the wind to French colonial troops as the opening salvo of the second YPRES battle in April 1915. Destroying the respiratory organs of its victims in a matter of seconds, it spread total panic, but surprised and nervous German troops failed to exploit the sudden gap created in Allied lines. Immediately infamous, the attack ended divisions among senior German officers over the use of gas, but damaged fragile relations with neutral countries, especially the UNITED STATES.

Use of gas canisters required ideal conditions and could be very risky. The first British retaliatory attack on the Western Front, during the ARTOIS–LOOS OFFENSIVE on 25 September 1915, blew back into attackers' faces, and all three main armies suffered comparable disasters during 1915. From 1916 gas shells for use with ARTILLERY became the norm, increasing both range of attack and the variety of gases that could be used.

The only chemical to inflict more overall casualties than chlorine was mustard gas, or Yperite, an almost odourless substance introduced to German operations at RIGA in September 1917. Its delayed-action symptoms – internal and external blistering accompanied by vomiting and often death – hampered detection and protection. Its strength enabled tiny quantities to be added to high explosive shells, providing further heavy disguise, but its persistence in soil, remaining active for several weeks in affected areas, was a mixed blessing.

Other respiratory gases delivered in shells included bromine (introduced by German defenders at the SOMME), phosgene and chloropicrin. A nerve gas obtained from prussic acid was used occasionally by the FRENCH ARMY.

Gas was never the decisive weapon anticipated by its early proponents, and countermeasures were in operation within days of its introduction at Ypres. The primitive masks issued to Allied troops in mid-1915 – cotton pads dipped in bicarbonate of soda and held over the face – were steadily improved, and by 1918 infantry on both sides were equipped with filter respirators using charcoal or antidote chemicals to neutralize gases.

In a limited tactical context, surprise use of gas remained an effective terror weapon for clearing enemy forward positions on most fronts, and both sides on the Western Front planned to fill between a third and half of their shells with poisonous chemicals in 1919.

The German Army was the most prolific wartime user of gas, taking delivery of more than 68,000 tons, followed by the French (about 36,000 tons) and British (about 25,000 tons). Although only 3 per cent of gas casualties were fatal in the short term, hundreds of thousands of injured victims lived truncated, disabled lives into the postwar era, contributing to the banning of all chemical weapons in 1925, a prohibition still nominally in force.

Gauchet, Admiral Dominique-Marie (1853–1931) Volatile French naval officer who replaced Admiral DARTIGE in command of FRENCH NAVY units at the DARDANELLES in October 1915, a command characterized by disputes over Allied priorities in the Aegean. On 14 December 1916, in the aftermath of the ATHENS LANDING fiasco, he succeeded Dartige as C-in-C of the French battlefleet ('Armée Navale') and nominal Allied commander in the MEDITERRANEAN. He concerned himself primarily with the dignities of office and the role of his BATTLESHIPS stationed at Corfu. Apart from bemoaning the lack of DESTROYERS available for an improbable confrontation with the AUSTRO-HUNGARIAN NAVY, he displayed little interest in the formation of effective ANTI-SUBMARINE tactics and exercised no real influence over their development. Particularly unpopular with other Allied naval commanders, he retained his post until his retirement in 1919.

Gaza, First Battle of Turkish victory on the PALESTINE FRONT in March 1917, and the first major British offensive of the campaign. After occupying EL ARISH in Sinai in December 1916, the ANZAC Mounted Division (see AUSTRALIAN FORCES) led British forces up to the Palestine border, clearing isolated Turkish forward outposts at Magheba (22 December) and Rafa (7 January) before demands for reinforcements on other fronts forced theatre C-in-C MURRAY to postpone further advance. British water pipes and light RAILWAYS from the Nile Delta reached El Arish by early February, as Murray concentrated his best troops with the 'Eastern Force' in Palestine, now reduced to three infantry and the equivalent of four CAVALRY divisions.

Turkish Expeditionary Force commander KRESSENSTEIN occupied a new defence line in early March, from the coastal fortress town of Gaza to Beersheba, some 40km southeast (see MAP 22). Blocking the only feasible path into Palestine, and potential British links with the ARAB REVOLT, the line was reinforced by two depleted divisions, bringing combat strength in mid-March to 18,000 men. It included small German MACHINE GUN, ARTILLERY and air detachments, the latter's modern RUMPLER C-TYPES and HALBERSTADT D-TYPES establishing combat superiority over more numerous RFC machines.

Though outnumbered 2 to 1, Kressenstein was under orders from Fourth Army commander DJEMAL PASHA to hold the position. Murray and Eastern Force commander General Dobell were equally determined to attack at the first opportunity, in anticipation of a further Turkish retreat, and received permission from London for an operation against Gaza itself.

Dobell massed the main bulk of Eastern Force near the coast behind the Wadi Ghazi, about 8km short of the town, by the evening of 25 March. It crossed the wadi early next morning, undetected in a dense sea fog, and cavalry penetrated between defenders east and southeast of Gaza to cut off the town's rear. The main infantry attack that morning, by a division against the southeast approaches to Gaza, failed in difficult terrain, but intervention by the encircling cavalry enabled infantry to take most of the ridge east of Gaza by dusk.

Both sides lapsed into confusion once darkness fell. Kressenstein, believing the battle lost, cancelled a call for reserves. A pessimistic Dobell recalled the cavalry from behind Gaza, leaving two infantry divisions on the ridge exposed to a Turkish counterattack, which (along with water shortages) forced a general British retreat the next day. Dobell's force had lost 4,000 men, against about 2,400 Turkish and German casualties, but Murray's report to London tripled estimated Turkish losses and represented the battle as a victory, prompting enthusiastic support for a renewed offensive. See: Second Battle of GAZA.

Gaza, Second Battle of Second attempt by British forces in PALESTINE to breach the Turkish defensive line between Gaza and Beersheba (see MAP 22), ordered from London in response to General MURRAY's misleading reports of the first battle. A company of eight Mark 1 heavy TANKS and 4,000 GAS shells were sent to Palestine for a renewed assault on the town, and further reinforcements were promised for a subsequent advance on Jerusalem, reflecting the theatre's new status as Britain's most promising 'SIDESHOW'.

Small-scale reinforcements brought defending forces back up to a strength of some 18,000 men, supported by 68 guns. Fully aware of British preparations, Turkish commander von KRESSENSTEIN concentrated most of his troops along the east of the line, leaving the area around Beersheba only lightly protected. His gamble that British forces, with twice the manpower and ARTILLERY strength, would attack in the same place was backed by intensive development of fortifications around Gaza.

With no hope of surprise, and without sufficient water to attempt encirclement via Beersheba, British Eastern Force commander General Dobell attempted to take Gaza by a frontal assault on 19 April, preceded by artillery bombardment with support from warships off the coast. His infantry advance became bogged down in complex Turkish defensive systems, and by nightfall had made only trivial gains at a cost of almost 6,500 casualties (against about 2,000 Turkish losses). Although army commander DJEMAL PASHA vetoed Kressenstein's plan for a counterattack, water shortages forced Dobell to withdraw next day.

In the aftermath of defeat, shocked British authorities replaced Dobell with General Chetwode, and General ALLENBY took over from Murray in June. The frontline settled into desultory, heat-impaired TRENCH WARFARE while both sides consolidated for an anticipated resumption in the autumn. See BEERSHEBA–GAZA LINE.

Geddes, Sir Eric (1875–1937) Energetic and pragmatic British administrator. A civil RAILWAY manager in August 1914, he won the admiration of munitions minister LLOYD GEORGE as his deputy director of supply in 1915. Appointed to head the BEF transport section, and then as BRITISH ARMY Inspector General of Transport, Geddes exchanged an honorary rank of major general for one of vice admiral, becoming administrative controller of the ROYAL NAVY from May 1917. Two months later he was appointed navy minister, and a seat in parliament was arranged at the next available by-election. Resented as a bureaucrat by many senior naval professionals, his good initial relations with First Sea Lord JELLICOE foundered on the issue of CONVOYS, of which Geddes was an important advocate, and worsened over proposed administrative reforms. Instrumental in Jellicoe's dismissal in December, Geddes left the Admiralty early in 1918 but continued to serve in the Imperial War Cabinet until the end of the year.

Gemmerich Belgian border post about 50km from LIÈGE, and site of the first hostile German crossing into BELGIUM just after 08.00 on 4 August 1914. Despite German belief that the BELGIAN ARMY would offer at most token defence of their neutrality, frontier guards at Gemmerich immediately opened fire on the six brigades of the 'Army of the Meuse' under General Emmich. The northern location of the crossing also shattered Belgian hopes that Germany planned a more direct attack on France through the Ardennes forests, merely skirting the southern tip of Belgium on the way. See also: SCHLIEFFEN PLAN; MAP 4.

George V, King (1863–1936) King of GREAT BRITAIN and IRELAND, Emperor of INDIA and ruler of the dominions of the British Empire since the death of his father, Edward VII, in 1910. Though bound by well-established political restraints, he initially played a more active part in internal politics than his father, intervening in several of the ASQUITH government's prewar constitutional disputes. However, he readily accepted a largely symbolic role in wartime. Mostly resident in London, he restricted himself to uncontroversial PROPAGANDA work, prohibiting use of ALCOHOL in the royal household from 1915 and following voluntary government guidelines on restricted food consumption from 1917. He corresponded regularly with BEF commander HAIG, but made little attempt to influence foreign policy beyond occasionally querying support for republican movements, notably in GREECE. George renounced all German titles in June 1917 and simultaneously ordered the alteration of royal family names (Hanover became Windsor, BATTENBERG translated to Mountbatten), a gesture that helped the British monarchy survive four years of war with an enhanced popular reputation.

Georgette, Operation See: LYS OFFENSIVE.

Georgia See: TRANSCAUCASIA.

Gerard, James (1867–1951) New York judge who had vigorously supported the WILSON presidential campaign of 1912 and was rewarded with appointment as US ambassador to Spain in early 1913. Transferred to Berlin later that year, despite complete lack of diplomatic experience or German language, he was generally regarded by Wilson as a straightforward conduit for German government PROPAGANDA. During 1916 his reports of probable hostile action in MEXICO and South America as revenge for US arms sales to the Allies were taken seriously by Colonel HOUSE but largely ignored by the president. He retired from international diplomacy after his mission ended in war the following spring.

German Army Recognized as the most efficient land force in the world, the Imperial German Army of 1914 incorporated the ground and air forces of all the German states, although the kingdom of Bavaria maintained an autonomous military administration. Developed out of the Prussian Army, its structure reflected the Prussian concept of a nation in arms, expressed as universal mass conscription for short-term military service followed by a longer period in reserve. A blueprint for conscript armies all over the world, the Prussian system placed great value on the quality of training, maintaining a large corps of long-service officers and NCOs for the purpose.

The militaristic culture associated with Prussia contributed a caste of senior officers – headed by Kaiser WILHELM II as C-in-C – that was steeped in the aristocratic, political and economic life of the state. Despite the appearance of democratic institutions in GERMANY, the Army's direct connections with the monarchy and powerful industrial interests gave it an important voice in foreign policy.

Planning and operational control were conducted by the General Staff (OHL) under the Army chief of staff, who was effective C-in-C of the field armies but dependent on approval from the crown for all major decisions. No army was more efficiently mobilized, effectively manoeuvred or meticulously prepared for every tactical and supply eventuality.

The peacetime German Army comprised 25 corps (700,000 men) in August 1914, each of 2 divisions with attached CAVALRY regiments and other support forces. Each corps, of which 3 were Bavarian, was responsible for a particular German region, and each was shadowed by reserve formations designed to mobilize simultaneously. Within a week of mobilization some 3.8 million men were under arms.

At the opening of hostilities formations were grouped into 8 Army commands, 7 in the west and 1 in EAST PRUSSIA. A further 10 were created to meet wartime needs (Ninth to Nineteenth Armies – there was no Thirteenth); four were dissolved and subsequently reformed. They were often linked as Army Groups for overall command purposes, usually named after their commander. Army Groups were controlled either directly from OHL or through their front command, which might embrace the armies or command systems of local allies.

Various composite or special forces were also wholly or partly formed from German units, including the 'Bugarmee' and 'Südarmee' on the EASTERN FRONT, the 'Danube Army' in the ROMANIAN CAMPAIGN, YILDERIM FORCE in PALESTINE, and many detachments for particular missions, again usually given their commander's name. Individual

German units, especially of technical troops, erved on every front, and reinforcement of he TURKISH, BULGARIAN and AUSTRO-HUNGARIAN armies on their respective battlefronts was gradually transformed into virtual German control by 1918. Most small colonial rmies (*Schutztruppe*) in AFRICA were quickly neutralized by Allied invasions in 1914–15, as was the far eastern garrison at TSINGTAO; the urviving (largely native) army in EAST AFRICA was never reinforced.

German Army equipment was generally uperior to that of its opponents in 1914. Because OHL planned a preemptive strike on French and Belgian FORTRESSES, heavy ARTILLERY, GRENADES, MORTARS, FLAMETHROWERS, engineering tools and other siege quipment later applicable to TRENCH WARFARE had been carefully developed, along with fficient modern RIFLES and MACHINE GUNS. Only 24 of the latter were initially provided or each division, but the figure compared avourably with ratios in other armies and rew to more than 350 per division by 1918. n the field of AERIAL WARFARE the GERMAN ARMY AIR SERVICE established combat superiority everywhere during 1915.

By 1916 German design ingenuity and roduction efficiency were being outweighed y Allied economic capacity. As output uffered under the stress of over-extension and BLOCKADE, the German Army could not fford to experiment with new weapons after 1917, and the TANK was anyway dismissed by German strategists as unnecessary and defeatble (see TANK FORTS).

The Army's all-round tactical edge over all pponents – first demonstrated at the Battles f the FRONTIERS and in EAST PRUSSIA during August 1914 – was only lost during the final Allied offensives on the WESTERN FRONT of 1918, but strategic leadership was less successul. Custodian of the SCHLIEFFEN PLAN for war n 1914, chief of staff MOLTKE weakened its mpact with a secondary offensive in LORRAINE and transfers to the east. He was eplaced by FALKENHAYN after the invasion of BELGIUM and FRANCE failed at the MARNE.

Falkenhayn presided over tactical success in he east and a crushing invasion of SERBIA in 1915, but returned to the Western Front in 1916, committing the Army to a disastrous campaign of attrition at VERDUN. Along with the BEF's summer SOMME OFFENSIVE, Verdun inflicted fatal damage on German manpower resources. About 2.85 million men were in service on the Western Front and 1.7 million in the east at the end of August 1916, but the Army was never again able to mount an offensive on one front without dangerously weakening the other.

Recognition of weakness relative to growing Allied strength prompted the adoption of a defensive stance by the command team of HINDENBURG and LUDENDORFF (the THIRD SUPREME COMMAND), which replaced Falkenhayn in late August 1916. Offensives in the east were suspended in the hope that RUSSIA would self-destruct, and frontline troops in France were withdrawn to strongly fortified HINDENBURG LINE positions from spring 1917. Resources were built up under the HINDENBURG PROGRAMME for a decisive strike before the UNITED STATES became a significant military factor. Apart from a demonstration attack on RIGA and a small-scale (but highly successful) commitment to the ITALIAN FRONT at CAPORETTO, the Army remained on the defensive through 1917, repelling the Allied NIVELLE and YPRES Offensives in France.

The failure of SUBMARINE WARFARE to bring quick victory, and the speed of US military build-up, compelled the Third Supreme Command to launch an all-or-nothing offensive on the Western Front in spring 1918. Despite the introduction of new INFILTRATION TACTICS, the ultimate failure of the SPRING OFFENSIVES in France took place against a background of economic and political collapse triggered by the Hindenburg Programme, leaving the Army incapable of surviving the well-equipped Allied offensives in the autumn.

By November 1918 the German Army had suffered an estimated 5 million casualties, including 1.75 million dead. The GERMAN REVOLUTIONS prevented full, ordered demobilization, and returning formations mostly just disintegrated, although some served as border guards on the eastern frontier, and others reformed as irregular FREIKORPS units.

Almost a million troops had been left in eastern Europe to supervise schemes for economic exploitation, and many of these formed irregular units, some taking part in the RUSSIAN CIVIL WAR and many resorting to brigandage (see e.g. POLAND; LATVIA). The Treaty of VERSAILLES restricted the German Army's size to 100,000 men and effectively prohibited use of modern mechanized weapons. See also: BREAKTHROUGH TACTICS; DEFENCE IN DEPTH; TRENCHES.

German Army Air Service The aviation section of the GERMAN ARMY, responsible for aircraft, AIRSHIP, BALLOON and ANTI-AIRCRAFT operations. Powered flight in Germany began with the first ZEPPELIN in 1900, and the Army's initial interest in aviation concentrated on lighter-than-air craft. As late as March 1911, the Army employed only 2 planes (lent by civilians), but funding enabled 37 to be purchased by the end of the year.

Partly in response to the rapid growth of the French AÉRONAUTIQUE MILITAIRE, plans were accepted in 1912 for a force of 2 or 3 aviation units (*Feldflieger Abteilung*) to be attached to each field army. Although not uniformly equipped, 33 air units (including 3 Bavarian) were active in August 1914, one each for the eight field armies and 25 corps headquarters, and 10 assigned to FORTRESSES. Each field unit had six aircraft, made up of various unarmed types intended solely for ARTILLERY observation or reconnaissance. With airships detailed for long-range reconnaissance, these planes were originally deployed on solo patrols.

Most early German machines were inferior to or copies of French designs. The most common type, the TAUBE, provided vital reconnaissance information before the Battle of TANNENBERG, but was soon regarded as unsuitable for frontline operations. No system existed for central correlation of aerial reconnaissance, and the Army High Command (OHL) had no overall picture of Allied troop movements on the WESTERN FRONT until the eve of the first MARNE battle.

German airmen on the Western Front adopted a generally defensive posture after the expansion of AERIAL WARFARE in 1915. Development of armed, specialized FIGHTERS wit INTERRUPTER GEAR, along with prevailin west winds and persistent Allied 'offensiv patrols', gave German pilots a distinct shor range combat edge from autumn 1915 (se FOKKER E-TYPES). Eroded during 1916, bu emphatically reasserted by ALBATROS an HALBERSTADT D-TYPE fighters from the au tumn, German combat domination encou aged concentration on fighter strength.

Combat aircraft were being grouped *Kommandos* for special operations from la 1915, and specialist fighter units (*Jagdstaffel* were formed in autumn 1916. Establishme of the first permanent *Jagdgeschwader* (fight group) the following April, when Germa domination was at its peak, created a mobil reserve of elite combat pilots, capable massing quickly at vital points along the fro (see FLYING CIRCUS, BLOODY APRIL). Th Service generally compensated with technic quality for a growing shortfall in productio capacity relative to the Allies on the Wester Front, but from early 1918 the best Germa combat aircraft (like the later FOKKER TYPES) were both outclassed and outnum bered in France.

German two-seater armed-reconnaissanc light-bombing and general-utility aircra were similarly superior to their Allied cou terparts until late 1917. Along with specia ized artillery-cooperation units (first forme in autumn 1915), they were attached to fiel armies throughout the War, although central air staff came into being from Marc 1915 with the appointment of Major Thom sen as Chief of Field Aviation (*Feldflugchef* Thomsen instituted rapid infrastructur growth, reorganizing home-defence and ant aircraft units, but his plans for a central controlled air arm were rejected unnecessary.

Central control was applied to specialize bombing units, also using small two-seate until 1917. The first, codenamed the 'Carrie Pigeon Unit, Ostend', was established October 1914 for mass raids on England an France, but a few day operations demonstrate the unsuitability of its unarmed AVIATIK TYPE aircraft, and it switched to night attack from January 1915.

The unit achieved little in France, but proved highly effective as a tactical reconnaissance and bombing reserve when moved to the EASTERN FRONT in April. By early 1916 there were five bombing groups, each with 36 machines (in six *Staffeln*). Redesignated High Command Battle Groups (*Kagohl*), they were controlled directly by OHL and partly housed in RAILWAY wagons for rapid transfer wherever needed.

Deployed, along with most other available resources, in support of ground operations at VERDUN and the SOMME in 1916, the *Kagohl* were forced to concentrate on direct support of troops on the battlefield rather than in their planned short-range bombing role. Direct ground-support operations became the most important form of short-range aerial warfare from 1917, prompting the redeployment of *Kagohl* C-Types as ground-support units (*Schusta*) for battlefield and escort work.

Faster, stronger ground-support craft (such as the HALBERSTADT CL-TYPE) were introduced from 1917, but although GERMANY developed heavily armed and (ultimately) armoured aircraft for 'trench fighting', production capacity was not capable of matching Allied output or experimental variety after 1917 and *Schusta* losses were always heavy (see JUNKERS J-I).

By August 1916, just before the formation of the *Jagdstaffeln*, the Air Service as a whole comprised 7 *Kagohl* (over 200 C-type machines), 81 army field units, and 45 artillery units, but Army aviation was completely reorganized and a massive expansion scheme adopted under the HINDENBURG PROGRAMME from October 1916.

A General of the Air Service (*Kogenluft*) – General von Hoeppner, with Thomsen as his chief of staff – was made directly responsible to the THIRD SUPREME COMMAND for all branches of aerial warfare. Field units were placed under Army rather than corps command, increasing the scope and size of units available for single operations, and fighter strength was expanded to 58 *Jagdstaffeln* by spring 1917. Three *Kagohl* units were returned to their original STRATEGIC BOMBING role, equipped with multi-engined GOTHA G-TYPES and (later) REISENFLUGZEUG heavy bombers, and from October 1917 bombers were organized as seven groups (*Bogohl*) with a total of 144 aircraft.

Another ambitious expansion plan, known as the 'America Programme', was introduced from spring 1917. A response to the entry of the UNITED STATES into the War, the programme planned an extra 40 fighter units and 17 'A' category units by March 1918, when US involvement was expected to become materially significant. Although its targets were never approached in practice, the Service was able to field 3,668 machines on the Western Front when the KAISERSCHLACHT battle began on 21 March.

Losses were high throughout the SPRING OFFENSIVES, although 60 per cent were accidents unconnected with enemy action, and by mid-1918 an estimated 350 new airmen per month were needed to maintain a strength of more than 2,500 pilots on the Western Front. Although Allied aircraft losses were heavier (487 aircraft against 150 German in June) they had much greater reserves to draw on.

German aircraft production, supposedly at 2,000 per month from December 1917, in fact averaged under 1,100 for the first six months of 1918, and a further expansion plan accepted by LUDENDORFF in June was rendered meaningless by critical shortages of materials and lack of trained aircrew. From August 1918 the role of the Air Service in France was entirely defensive, concentrating on reconnaissance and ground support as German armies retreated and Allied numerical, supply and personnel advantages multiplied.

Although always concentrated primarily on the Western Front, German aircraft enjoyed clear superiority over the RUSSIAN AIR SERVICE on the Eastern Front, where few of the best designs or pilots were deployed. They were also active from autumn 1915 on the BALKAN FRONT. The first Middle East unit had been formed in February 1916 for operations in PALESTINE, and five field units were sent to TURKEY with YILDERIM FORCE the following spring. German air activity on the ITALIAN FRONT began during the build-up to the CAPORETTO OFFENSIVE of autumn 1917, and for a while Gotha bombers were used in the theatre. Operations in all other theatres were scaled down in the new year, but by spring 1918 there were still 307 German aircraft serving in Macedonia, Italy and the Middle East.

When fighting ceased in November 1918 the German Army Air Service possessed a total of 2,709 frontline aircraft (in 284 units of one sort or another), 56 airships, 186 balloon detachments and about 4,500 flying personnel. Its battle losses to November 1918 were 6,840 killed, 7,350 wounded and 1,372 missing, along with 3,128 aircraft destroyed. As part of the ARMISTICE agreement all fighter and bomber aircraft, including those still in the factories, were surrendered to the Allies, and all senior staff officers were forced to resign.

Demobilization of forces in most theatres took place in early 1919, but many fighter pilots from France joined units still active on Germany's eastern borders. Equipped with the latest production aircraft they flew in support of irregular forces fighting in ESTONIA and LATVIA. Home-defence units remained in being until June 1919, largely because their demobilization procedures collapsed, and a few aircraft were operated for internal policing, but remnants were disbanded from June 1919 in accordance with the Treaty of VERSAILLES, and the German Army Air Service officially ceased to exist on 8 May 1920. See also: ACES.

German Navy Until the 1890s German naval strength consisted of a few small coastal-defence vessels, and the country's military energies were concentrated almost exclusively on the powerful GERMAN ARMY. Mounting enthusiasm for sea power was expressed in the theories of Admiral TIRPITZ, who advocated the construction of a large modern navy with the dual function of protecting GERMANY's growing overseas empire and securing its northern coastline from any conceivable attack. Strongly supported by Kaiser WILHELM II, who appointed Tirpitz minister of marine in 1897, massive expansion was authorized by a succession of Navy Laws beginning in 1898.

Protection of the northern coastline was always paramount and called for security against the biggest regional sea power, the ROYAL NAVY. Tirpitz modelled his new HIGH SEAS FLEET on the British GRAND FLEET, building it around squadrons of battleships, and rapid growth was achieved in terms of production and technical advance.

The Royal Navy responded by withdrawing strength from other theatres and mobilizing its larger shipbuilding capacity. British introduction of dreadnought BATTLESHIPS and BATTLECRUISERS raised the stakes in a high-profile arms race that seriously damaged prewar Anglo-German relations. Though Tirpitz attempted to keep pace, German yards fell behind schedule, and spiralling expenditure threatened to provoke political upheaval.

Once sure that the Royal Navy could not be outbuilt, Tirpitz assumed it would attempt a close wartime BLOCKADE of German ports, and planned short-range attacks on British patrol squadrons. New warships were designed accordingly. Battleships were heavily protected and highly seaworthy, with less speed or range than their British counterparts. Fast, light CRUISERS were built as fleet scouts, along with TORPEDO BOATS and DESTROYERS for hit-and-run attacks, but development of SUBMARINES was relatively slow and primarily concerned with coastal protection. Fast surface ships were earmarked for long-range commerce raiding and trade protection.

By August 1914 the German Navy was the second largest in the world and at least the equal of any other in technical proficiency. Its main strength comprised 17 dreadnoughts, 5 battlecruisers and 20 PRE-DREADNOUGHTS, 7 modern light cruisers and 18 older cruisers. Only 10 of its 28 submarines were of any real military value (see *U-19*). Three more battlecruisers and 2 dreadnoughts were completed in wartime, along with another 6 light cruisers, but shipbuilding after 1916 concentrated largely on U-BOATS.

Major units were overwhelmingly concentrated with the High Seas Fleet. Its main bases at Wilhelmshaven (North Sea) and Kiel (Baltic) were linked by canal, and subsidiary bases included Heligoland, CUXHAVEN and Sonderburg. Military gains provided wartime bases for light forces in Belgium (principally

Ostend and ZEEBRUGGE) and the Baltic states (e.g. Libau). The only major overseas formations were the MITTELMEERDIVISION in the MEDITERRANEAN and Admiral SPEE's East Asiatic Squadron in the Pacific. Individual cruisers, ARMED MERCHANT CRUISERS and AUXILIARY COMMERCE RAIDERS were dotted around world trade routes.

Britain's decision to impose a long-range blockade of the North Sea deprived the High Seas Fleet of its principle function. Still too small to attempt a direct confrontation with the Grand Fleet, it was forced to undertake dangerous long-range raids on the British coast (see SCARBOROUGH RAID). Although it kept larger numbers of British (and ultimately US NAVY) warships tied to the theatre by its very existence, the fleet's inactivity under successive commanders Ingenohl and Pohl called into question its value to the German war effort.

Tirpitz gradually lost influence with Wilhelm, who forbade risk-taking in the North Sea after losses at the DOGGER BANK and JUTLAND (the latter under the more aggressive command of SCHEER), after which German dreadnoughts offered no further active threat to British warships.

Opportunities for offensive action in the eastern BALTIC were also limited. The RUSSIAN NAVY avoided any possibility of a major surface action, and apart from occasional operations in support of ground forces on the EASTERN FRONT (see ALBION), German battleships had little role to play in the mine-infested theatre.

Inactivity, spartan conditions and supply shortages contributed to poor morale from 1917, and the fleet had disintegrated into revolutionary mutiny by autumn 1918 (see GERMAN REVOLUTIONS; KIEL MUTINY). Surrendered after the ARMISTICE, it could barely muster the fuel to steam to Scotland, where its most modern units scuttled themselves in June 1919.

Light forces – torpedo craft, seaplanes and coastal-defence ships – were far more active, fighting intense miniature wars with similar Allied units along the northern fringes of the WESTERN and Eastern fronts (see IRBEN STRAITS). Naval use of aircraft was largely confined to coastal seaplane stations – only one home-based cruiser (*Stuttgart*) carried an aircraft – and most Fleet aerial reconnaissance was performed by Navy ZEPPELINS, which also undertook STRATEGIC BOMBING of English targets.

Long-range activities by surface ships were shortlived. Admiral SOUCHON's Mediterranean ships were part of the TURKISH NAVY from August 1914, and the East Asiatic Squadron was destroyed at the FALKLAND ISLANDS in December. Remaining surface raiders had been interned or destroyed by spring 1915, leaving only U-boats to continue large-scale operations against Allied commerce, and by late 1916 the Navy's resources were almost entirely concentrated on SUBMARINE WARFARE (see *HANDELSKRIEG*).

Three divisions of naval infantry took part in the fighting on the Western Front, two of them created during the War and all three strengthened with army recruits from 1917 (see SCHRÖDER, L.).

Control of strategy, hitherto exercised through the Kaiser and the imperial naval minister, was completely reorganized from mid-1918, reflecting an overall dictatorship established by the THIRD SUPREME COMMAND in Germany. A new Naval Supreme Command was created under Scheer in August, purging senior ranks of liberal or pessimistic elements, and plans were laid for a massive increase in U-boat construction as part of the HINDENBURG PROGRAMME. Overrun by political, economic and military reality, its half-built submarines were dismantled after the ARMISTICE.

The expensive surface fleet as designed by Tirpitz was never more than an adjunct to military operations, and the entire Navy was disbanded under the terms of the VERSAILLES Treaty. See also: CAPELLE, E.; HIPPER, F.; HOLTZENDORFF, H.; MULLER, H.; TROTHA, A.; Battles of CORONEL, HELIGOLAND BIGHT.

German Revolutions The disintegration of imperial GERMANY from autumn 1918 embraced a generalized breakdown of established authority all over the country. Many of its immediate political effects were regionalized. The kings of Bavaria, Saxony and Württemberg had abdicated by mid-November, and royal regimes were generally replaced by constitutional governments in the German states, although a left-wing workers' revolutionary government under Kurt Eisner held power in Bavaria until mid-1919. In national terms, two distinct revolutions took place in late 1918, and a third appeared imminent.

The first phase was engineered by the military and industrial leadership of the THIRD SUPREME COMMAND. Faced with defeat and the collapse of civil order, it transferred power to elected representatives of the Reichstag. In line with a High Command decision authorized by LUDENDORFF on 26 September, the moderate Prince MAX VON BADEN replaced HERTLING as imperial chancellor on 3 October, and formed a cross-party government dominated by moderate socialists of the Social Democratic Party (SDP).

In granting the constitutional demands of parliamentarians at a stroke, the old regime planned to defuse popular unrest. The transfer of power also enabled it to await the opportunity for a countercoup while the new government took responsibility for making peace. Socialist Reichstag deputies, mostly committed to gradual reform, accepted the poisoned chalice as an opportunity for a peaceful transition to democracy.

Despite Ludendorff's dismissal on 26 October, escalating food riots, strikes and peace protests forced a second act of revolution on Reichstag socialists in an attempt to retain control (see KIEL MUTINY). Bereft of any real authority, Prince Max met an SDP deadline by resigning in the Reichstag during the morning of 9 November, making an unauthorized announcement of WILHELM II's abdication and handing power formally, though with no legal authority, to SDP leader EBERT. Against Ebert's wishes, vice chancellor SCHEIDEMANN then proclaimed a German Republic from the Reichstag balcony. Wilhelm fled to the Netherlands, leaving Ebert head of a provisional government pending new Reichstag elections.

From early November Germany experienced the widespread formation of workers' and soldiers' councils, which bore a structural resemblance to Russian SOVIETS. Like the mass protests and strikes of the period, they were primarily concerned with securing peace, representation and basic commodities, but government suspicion increased as their less committed members returned to normal life, emphasizing the efforts of vociferous left-wing agitators.

The prospect of a left-wing coup haunted both the provisional government and the far right, and the cabinet accepted General GRÖNER's offer of army support for the new regime. Coordinated by Gröner and cabinet member Gustav NOSKE, the remnants of the GERMAN ARMY and the newly formed irregular FREIKORPS were recruited to maintain order and suppress the supposed threat of Bolshevism. A disorganized revolt by the SPARTACUS LEAGUE was easily crushed in January 1919, and over the next three months Freikorps units systematically repressed all signs of militant activity in councils throughout Germany.

German Southwest Africa See: Conquest of SOUTHWEST AFRICA.

Germany A federation of 22 central European kingdoms or principalities and three independent Hanseatic cities (Hamburg, Bremen and Lübeck), Germany's components varied in size from the tiny principality of Schaumberg-Lippe (340 square kilometres) to Prussia, more than a thousand times larger and comprising 64 per cent of the continental empire's land area.

Unification in 1871 had been a by-product of Prussian military success, and the Empire was dominated by its largest state in 1914. The King of Prussia, WILHELM II, was also German Emperor (Kaiser), controlling ministerial appointments, imperial foreign policy and the armed forces, though large states like Bavaria, Saxony and Württemberg retained military autonomy in peacetime.

Based on the mineral wealth of the Ruhr region, Germany's industrial development was the fastest in the world. Between 1880 and 1913 coal production had risen 400 per cent, steel output had multiplied tenfold, and large secondary industries – chemicals, engineering and armaments, for instance – had become fully established. The volume of international trade had also quadrupled.

Population had boomed from 41 million to 65.3 million in 40 years, with 40 per cent of the growing labour force employed in industry. The agricultural sector accounted for a reduced 35 per cent but still kept peacetime Germany virtually self-sufficient in basic foodstuffs. Development was hastened by a modern infrastructure of excellent roads and RAILWAYS, which in turn encouraged population movements towards the industrial cities, but a sustained production boom also needed expanding export markets on a colonial scale.

The political situation inside prewar Germany was no less volatile. Rapid growth of an industrial working class and a technocratic middle class (*Mittelstand*) was not reflected in the constitution, which concentrated power in the monarchy and its allies among the landed aristocracy, the military and industrial magnates.

The Kaiser's legislative power at imperial level was theoretically qualified by two constitutional bodies. The upper house (*Bundesrat*) comprised representatives of the states and cities. Conservative in character, its block vote system (based on size) gave Prussia an absolute veto over any decision. Deputies in the lower house (*Reichstag*) were elected by universal manhood suffrage, but its powers were limited to ratification of legislation by the imperial cabinet, which was led by the crown's appointed chancellor.

Much internal administration remained in the hands of state governments. The Prussian cabinet (nominated by the King and in direct control of most of the GERMAN ARMY) exerted a powerful influence on imperial policy and was barely restrained by constitutional fetters, with elections to the lower *Landtag* strongly biased in favour of the wealthy. Similar partial suffrage systems, effectively guaranteeing support for the status quo, dominated the constitutions of most other states.

The wide spectrum of parties in the Reichstag reflected some of the stresses and tensions at work in 1914. Regional and religious differences were still important political factors, displayed in a profusion of small sectional groupings and in the strength of the the Centre Party (*Zentrum*), which spoke for Germany's large Catholic minority (see ERZBERGER, M.).

National parties defined along socioeconomic lines included the agrarian conservative *Deutsch-Konservative Partei* (DKP) and the smaller *Reichspartei* (RP), both of which gave qualified support to government internal policies (see WESTKARP, K.). Middle-class interests were guarded by, among others, the National Liberal Party (NLP), also inclined to compromise with the chancellor (see STRESEMANN, G.). The centre-left Progressive People's Party (FVP) was a coalition of small parties formed in 1910 to press for constitutional reform.

The socialist Social Democratic Party (SDP), led by Hugo HAASE and Friedrich EBERT, supported a relatively moderate programme of gradual reform. To the right of the socialist spectrum at street level, it was regarded as a pack of rabid revolutionaries by all shades of conservative opinion. It won 110 seats in the 1912 elections, becoming the largest party in the Reichstag for the first time. Its strength effectively ended all hope of regular pro-government majorities in the Reichstag, and by 1914 a major constitutional conflict seemed inevitable.

Extraparliamentary political activity was even more polarized. Although unions were recognized by few German employers, strikes were a serious problem before 1914, with calls for an eight-hour working day forming the core of workers' demands. Socialist community organizations had sprung up in all walks of working-class life and, in an atmosphere generally free from media censorship or cultural repression, printed criticism of the regime was rife.

A conservative campaign – spearheaded by powerful and influential 'patriotic' organizations such as the Pan-German, Navy and Defence Leagues – was financed by wealthy conservatives, and lobbied above all for an aggressive foreign policy backed by maximum military expansion. Every radical organization had its right-wing counterpart – even the prewar movement for WOMEN's rights was opposed by a German Women's League

(BDF) of patriotic conservatives.

The ruling elites expected revolution at any time throughout the early 20th century, and prewar foreign policies were partly designed to provide outlets for social pressure without the need for reform. Wilhelm had personally guided the policy of *Weltpolitik*, which sought to make Germany a world rather than just a European power. Embracing pan-Germanism, the need for colonial markets, domination of continental Europe, and an arms build-up for a short, decisive war, the policy had failed by 1914.

Germany gained few overseas possessions, but FRANCE, RUSSIA and GREAT BRITAIN were provoked into an arms race that threatened to surround Germany with superior forces by 1916. Tax battles fought by imperial chancellor BETHMANN HOLLWEG to pay for military (especially naval) expansion had exacerbated social tensions and Reichstag hostility, and the Army was on permanent standby against civilian uprising. Fear of external and internal threats led to a siege mentality, which in turn dictated that the Army's SCHLIEFFEN PLAN for quick military victory should be tried sooner rather than later. Modern historians generally agree that the main impetus for turning the JULY CRISIS of 1914 into a general war came from Berlin.

The immediate social effect of war, presented to the German people and politicians as a defensive struggle against Russian and French attack, was complete national unity. Spontaneous popular enthusiasm, matched by Reichstag support and the declaration of a political truce (*Burgfrieden*), delighted Wilhelm but amazed conservative leaders and the Army, which immediately took over much civil administration under the Prussian Siege Law, a 19th-century measure giving the military enormous powers in time of national crisis.

Like all other belligerents in 1914, Germany was in no way prepared to fight a prolonged war embracing every aspect of national life. The government envisaged a maximum duration of nine months, but unforeseen military stagnation produced unimagined demands for war materials, money to pay for them, and manpower.

Arms production was rapidly outstripped by expenditure at the fronts, and the Army was dependent on current output for reinforcement by October 1914. Massive orders to existing arms firms inflated the prices of raw materials without solving the problem, which worsened as the Allied BLOCKADE tightened. Strong criticism from heavy-industrial interests prompted extension of the Prussian War Ministry's KRA (War Materials Department) to control distribution of goods throughout Germany.

The KRA improved output, but its stranglehold on supplies and concern with manufacturers' profits unbalanced the rest of the economy. Smaller industries were alienated and only ever given a token share of war business. The government became increasingly dependent on large established firms, giving their leaders a disproportionate share in policy-making. In addition, the extortionate prices charged by arms manufacturers multiplied financial problems and encouraged inflation.

German wartime financial policy mostly consisted of raising new taxes to meet rising routine expenditure, and of borrowing money to pay for military expenses by issuing war bonds. The government's enormous debt to subscribers could only be paid in the event of victory, a factor influencing its consistent refusal to contemplate a genuine compromise peace.

Until 1916 the KRA system was superficially effective – the military enjoyed material superiority over its enemies, and industrial profits were mushrooming – but battles at VERDUN, JUTLAND and the SOMME in 1916 revealed the extent of Allied industrial mobilization and called for a drastic reappraisal of requirements.

At the same time civilian shortages of food and manufactured goods were exacerbated by a manpower crisis in agriculture and a succession of bad harvests. Strikes in Berlin and the Ruhr, along with renewed demands for constitutional reform from the Reichstag, evidenced war weariness and the breakdown of the political truce.

The regime's response to these convergent crises was a sharp lurch to the right. Until

1916 government had operated in partnership with heavy industry and the Army, with the Emperor as arbiter. Bethmann Hollweg's civilian administration, embracing the most moderate elements of the ruling clique, had sought to maintain social cohesion through persuasion and compromise with the Reichstag, conceding a few minor constitutional points in return for general cooperation. The replacement of FALKENHAYN as Army chief of staff by HINDENBURG in August signalled an alliance of extremist military and industrial forces, with the Kaiser under their almost exclusive influence.

Effectively led by Hindenburg's deputy, LUDENDORFF, the new THIRD SUPREME COMMAND sought absolute military victory and sweeping territorial annexations. The HINDENBURG PROGRAMME, a blueprint for massive military expansion enabled by broad interpretation of the Siege Law, was imposed in autumn 1916 and established a virtual military dictatorship over the entire economy. Plans were laid to reorganize the Army and the GERMAN NAVY along more centralized lines, and moderate military or political opponents were manoeuvred out of office with the Kaiser's acquiescence.

Planned on the false assumption that 'unpatriotic' slack remained to be economically exploited, and spearheaded by conscription of labour under the Patriotic Service Law, the Hindenburg Programme could never hope to match production expectations and had serious socioeconomic repercussions.

The cold winter of 1916–17 brought a major nutrition crisis to German cities, and starvation faced those unable to compete in a booming black market. Infant mortality mushroomed, and some estimates put civilian deaths from malnutrition by 1918 at over 700,000. Calls for immediate peace during the mass strikes of April 1917 were echoed in a major public debate about war aims.

Public discussion of what constituted acceptable peace terms had been taking place since 1915, drawing on PROPAGANDA from right-wing expansionists and internationalist proponents of peace on the left. Much of the parliamentary spectrum was united in opposition to the Supreme Command's extreme prerequisites for peace, and the debate about war aims became embroiled with more general demands for constitutional reform.

With the military pressing Wilhelm to adopt unrestricted SUBMARINE WARFARE (see *HANDELSKRIEG*), Bethmann Hollweg attempted to prevent war with the UNITED STATES by a PEACE OFFER in December 1916, but its final form and diplomatic failure only reflected the divergent ambitions of the Supreme Command and parliament. Bethmann Hollweg wrung a last token concession to compromise with the Reichstag in the spring, Wilhelm's promise of postwar constitutional reform in Prussia, but it was too little too late.

The main parties combined to demolish *Burgfrieden* with the PEACE RESOLUTION in July 1917, and dissatisfaction on both sides brought down Bethmann Hollweg in its aftermath. His successors, Supreme Command appointees MICHAELIS and HERTLING, possessed little authority with either side, and Reichstag opinion was virtually ignored from autumn 1917 (see FATHERLAND PARTY).

The unrestricted submarine campaign from February 1917 was a miscalculated gamble on total military victory, representing the regime's only hope for long-term survival. The expenditure of men and materials to carry out politico-economic subordination of eastern Europe after the collapse of Russia was a desperate attempt to maintain the German economy pending a last great SPRING OFFENSIVE on the WESTERN FRONT (see Treaties of BREST-LITOVSK, BUCHAREST). The failure of the offensive in June and July 1918, followed by the first Allied counteroffensive at AMIENS in August, convinced the Supreme Command that US participation had made Allied victory inevitable.

German internal propaganda, private and official, had been extremely effective in shielding both public and politicians from the gravity of the military situation. Reichstag leaders were not officially informed of impending defeat until late September, and the shock to middle-class opinion completed the home front's collapse into revolution.

Almost a million workers had struck in January alone, prompting a rash of repression and the arrest of SDP leader Ebert. Bread queues and food riots, everyday occurrences by the spring, brought only a search for public scapegoats among socialists and the Jewish community. Industrial production and the Army in France collapsed simultaneously, but the first phase of the GERMAN REVOLUTIONS was engineered from above.

Ludendorff and the Supreme Command transferred executive power to the Reichstag on 3 October 1918, intending to wait in the wings while those they considered responsible were forced to make peace. Aware of the opprobrium they risked, Reichstag leaders accepted the offer of government under Prince MAX VON BADEN, partly because they were afraid of more radical revolution from below. ARMISTICE negotiations were opened the following day.

Popular uprising seemed very likely in early November. Poor conditions and long-term inactivity in the HIGH SEAS FLEET erupted in the KIEL MUTINY after senior naval officers attempted to launch an unauthorized suicide attack on the British. The revolt quickly threatened to develop into a full-scale proletarian uprising, with soldiers' and workers' councils (similar in structure to Russian SOVIETS) springing up in cities all over Germany during the first week of November.

Unable to muster a semblance of control, Prince Max resigned on 9 November and announced the Kaiser's abdication. Socialist vice chancellor SCHEIDEMANN subsequently proclaimed the formation of a republic from the balcony of the Reichstag. The Kaiser was told of his abdication afterwards and fled to exile in the Netherlands the next day.

Many contemporaries regarded the relatively moderate council movement, which never seriously threatened to set up an alternative administration, as the work of Bolshevik agitators. Haunted by the spectre of the OCTOBER REVOLUTION, the new regime reached rapid agreement with the military, ultimately led by General GRÖNER. With hordes of unemployed troops to call on, right-wing elements were quick to offer practical assistance in the form of FREIKORPS, paramilitary units that put down a minor uprising by the left-wing SPARTACUS LEAGUE in early 1919 before embarking on bloody destruction of the council movement.

Reichstag elections held in January 1919 returned an increased SDP majority (with some 38 per cent of the national vote) but left the chamber in its usual splintered condition. Right-wing forces generally gave their temporary support to the moderate regime that emerged, but carefully fostered myths of an unbeaten army let down by traitors at home. The harsh VERSAILLES peace settlement imposed by the Allies contributed to a period of chronic political and economic instability in the early 1920s, provoking deep popular resentments that were exploited by left- and right-wing extremists.

Gheluvelt See: First Battle of YPRES.

Giant Aircraft See: RIESENFLUGZEUG.

Giolitti, Giovanni (1842–1928) The most powerful politician in ITALY during the early years of the 20th century, Giolitti was prime minister four times between 1892 and 1914. A skilled political manager with few ideological scruples, his resignation as premier during a general strike in March 1914 was widely interpreted as a temporary means of escaping economic backlash from the Italo-Turkish War (1911–12). A powerful force for neutrality during the JULY CRISIS, he was the foremost opponent of Italian military intervention over the succeeding months, arguing for acceptance of Austro-Hungarian concessions in early 1915 and maintaining close contacts with German and Austro-Hungarian diplomats. Though his large body of parliamentary supporters was able to force the SALANDRA government's resignation on the eve of war, Giolitti refused the chance to form a new administration in an atmosphere of fervent popular interventionism. He retired to his native Piedmont when war was declared, returning to head the government for a fifth time in June 1920.

Gneisenau See: *SCHARNHORST*; Battles of CORONEL, the FALKLAND ISLANDS.

Gnila Lipa, Battle of the The second major Austro-Hungarian attack on the Russian armies invading eastern GALICIA in 1914. After its defeat on the ZLOTA LIPA River (26–28 August) the Austro-Hungarian Third Army withdrew west to the Gnila Lipa River, covering approaches to the fortress city of Lvov from the southeast and east. Unmolested by the Russian Third Army (RUZSKI), Austrian strength at the Gnila Lipa reached 14 infantry divisions by 30 August, with the newly formed Austro-Hungarian Second Army (BÖHM-ERMOLLI) taking up position along the southern part of the line. Unconvinced by reports revealing Russian numerical superiority (22 divisions), chief of staff CONRAD ordered the Second Army to halt the Russian advance with a frontal attack. Launched on 29 August, it was a complete failure, and was abandoned on 1 September. Conrad withdrew his eastern forces behind Lvov and diverted strength south from his offensive around KOMAROW to attack Ruzski's flank. Though Russian forces captured 20,000 men and 70 guns at the Gnila Lipa, retreating divisions were not pursued. See MAP 10.

Goeben German BATTLECRUISER completed in April 1912. Faster and with a more efficient turret arrangement than the preceding *VON DER TANN*, it was sent straight from sea trials to the MEDITERRANEAN as the flagship of the GERMAN NAVY's only force in the theatre. A major potential threat to Anglo-French trade and troop movements in the event of war, *Goeben* suffered repeated boiler trouble and was due to be replaced in summer 1914, but instead underwent emergency repairs at the Austrian port of Pola in July before fleeing to the DARDANELLES, which it reached on 10 August (see MITTELMEERDIVISION).

Along with its companion ship *BRESLAU*, *Goeben* was transferred to the TURKISH NAVY and was its greatest asset during the war in the BLACK SEA, operating as a raider against Russian trade routes and coastal installations. Twice damaged by MINES in 1915, and subsequently under repair for several months, *Goeben*'s sorties became steadily less effective as the RUSSIAN NAVY took a firm grip on the theatre.

The end of hostilities with RUSSIA freed *Goeben* for a return to the Mediterranean in January 1918. It destroyed two British MONITORS off Imbros en route to raid the Allied base at MUDROS, but was again mined and ran aground in a vain effort to pull the stricken *Breslau* to safety. The British SUBMARINE *E-14* was destroyed trying to finish it off, and *Goeben* was towed back to Constantinople, but was laid up in dock until the ARMISTICE. Renamed *Yuraz*, it survived to remain in Turkish service until 1960. See also: SOUCHON, W.

BRIEF DATA (1914) Displacement: 22,640 tons; Crew: 1,053; Dimensions: length 610ft (184.9m), beam 96.75ft (29.3m); Speed: 29k; Armament: 10 × 11in gun, 12 × 5.9in, 12 × 3.4in, 4 × 19.7in TT.

Goltz, Field Marshal Colmar, Baron von der (1843–1916) Prussian officer who left the GERMAN ARMY as a major in 1883 to take up a training post with the TURKISH ARMY, returning home 13 years later as a lieutenant general and reaching field marshal's rank in 1911 after another spell in TURKEY. No admirer of the SCHLIEFFEN PLAN, Goltz was given only a background role as military governor of occupied BELGIUM in August 1914, but Turkey's alliance with the CENTRAL POWERS prompted his transfer to Constantinople in December. An ill-defined role as the Sultan's 'adjutant general' created friction with LIMAN VON SANDERS, until Goltz replaced Liman with the First (Bosporus) Army in March 1915. Regarded as an encumbrance by war minister ENVER PASHA, his schemes for a major attack on the British in EGYPT or INDIA were met with indifference, but he accepted nominal command of the Sixth Army on the MESOPOTAMIAN FRONT in October. He supervised the defence of CTESIPHON in November and the subsequent siege of KUT, but died days before the garrison's surrender in April 1916. Persistent rumours that he was poisoned by Turkish officers were never confirmed.

Gompers, Samuel (1850–1924) Veteran trade unionist, born in Britain but a US citizen since the Civil War, who was head of the American Federation of Labor (AFL) from

1886 until his death. Under his leadership the AFL became a moderate promoter of cooperation between business and labour, its membership (2.37 million in 1917) and ambitions largely restricted to white male workers in skilled trades. Though prominent in the prewar struggle for US union rights against the growing power of big commercial 'trusts' or corporations, Gompers was simultaneously engaged in a broad contest for leadership of US labour against left-wing groups such as the Socialist Party of America and Industrial Workers of the World (IWW).

He quickly recognized the advantages for his membership of participation in a war boom after 1914, and was publicly supporting PREPAREDNESS by 1916. Appointed as advisor to the Council of National Defense in October, he worked consistently to mobilize working-class opinion and productivity for war, but his position was compromised after April 1917 by a sharp swing to the right in government and popular attitudes. Despite attempts to separate workers' rights and socialism in the public mind, and close cooperation with PROPAGANDA chief CREEL, a nationwide 'Reds' scare after the OCTOBER REVOLUTION helped business interests to brand labour disputes in general as 'unpatriotic', and by 1919 left-wing elements in the UNITED STATES had been effectively routed.

Goremykin, Ivan (1839–1917) Russian lawyer and bureaucrat whose ultra-conservative political views and general subservience to the wishes of the crown fitted the requirements of Tsar NICHOLAS II in early 1914, when Goremykin returned from semi-retirement in the Council of State to become prime minister.

Goremykin played little part in foreign policy and no significant role in the JULY CRISIS, concerning himself almost exclusively with wartime resistance to constitutional reform. Mutually hostile relations with the Duma and a complete disregard for popular opinion earned crown support but brought heavy political criticism after military defeats on the EASTERN FRONT exposed the government's inert socioeconomic performance.

He was alone among civilian ministers in supporting the Tsar's assumption of direct military command in September 1915, but his position weakened at a court subsequently dominated by the Tsarina ALEXANDRA. Renewed liberal demands for his removal, coupled with Alexandra's desire for a more vigorous defence of crown privileges, brought his dismissal and retirement in February 1916. After the FEBRUARY REVOLUTION in 1917 Goremykin fled to the Caucasus, where he was killed at Christmas, probably by a revolutionary mob.

Göring, Hermann (1893–1946) Commander of the late von RICHTHOFEN's *Jadgstaffel* on the WESTERN FRONT from July 1918, Göring ended the War as an ACE with 22 combat victories. After working in Scandinavia, he returned to GERMANY in 1923 to become a high-profile member of the Nazi Party.

Gorizia (Gorz) Town on the River ISONZO some 15km inland from the Adriatic coast. It was the focus of attacks by Italian forces until its capture during the sixth offensive in the area of August 1916 (sometimes known as the Battle of Gorizia). Subsequent offensives on the ITALIAN FRONT were conducted immediately east of Gorizia, including the eleventh Isonzo attack in August and September 1917. See MAP 21.

Gorlice–Tarnow Offensive Austro-German attack on the EASTERN FRONT, launched from positions south of Kraków on 2 May 1915 and maintained until late June. Though German chief of staff FALKENHAYN preferred to concentrate forces in the west, and hoped that continued weakness would persuade Vienna to concede territorial demands to ITALY, the AUSTRO-HUNGARIAN ARMY's poor condition after the CARPATHIAN offensives persuaded him to begin preparations for an eastern operation in mid-April.

Eight German divisions were transferred from France, and two from the central Carpathians, to lead an attack from the Gorlice–Tarnow sector as the new Eleventh Army (MACKENSEN). A total of 120,000 men were equipped to WESTERN FRONT standards, with plentiful heavy ARTILLERY support,

MORTARS and ammunition. Eight divisions of the Austro-Hungarian Fourth Army (JOSEF FERDINAND) were to advance alongside the Germans to the north. Though Mackensen was answerable to the Austro-Hungarian high command at Teschen, the German high command moved east to supervise from Pless.

Russian plans to attack in the Bukovina region to the southeast and in the Carpathian passes south of the Gorlice–Tarnow area had left only the northwestern wing of Radko-Dimitriev's Third Russian Army (56,000 men supported by 141 light guns) facing Mackensen's armies. Crammed in shallow forward TRENCHES, they suffered shortages of provisions, shovels, modern RIFLES, training, ammunition and reserves. Though informed of German plans by deserters and a strongly pro-Russian local population, Radko-Dimitriev considered his defences adequate.

The Austro-German attack opened on 2 May with a four-hour PRELIMINARY BOMBARDMENT, massive by eastern standards, and heavy mortar fire, which scared away most of those not killed. The remains of two Russian corps fled some 25km in two days, sacrificing local reserves in haphazard minor counter-attacks.

The arrival of the nearest Russian reserve corps on 4 May, a setback at Biecz and inevitable supply difficulties all prevented Mackensen from cutting off the rest of the Russian Third Army, most of which had retreated to the River Wisloka (80km west of the River San) by 6 May. Strung along a 100km front, outflanked by German forces to the north and the Austro-German Südarmee to the south, the Third Army had been reduced to about quarter strength, and had virtually exhausted its shell supplies.

Few reinforcements reached the Third Army. ALEXEEV's northwestern command was distracted by German operations in KURLAND, and Russian RAILWAY systems were incapable of supplying reserves or ammunition quickly. A feeble counterattack by the Third Army near the Dukla Pass on 7–8 May failed completely, and Austro-German attacks on the north of the line forced a further retreat. Despite regional commander IVANOV's urgent appeals to STAVKA (Russian central command), the Third Army was not permitted full withdrawal to the San until 10 May, by which time its losses had exceeded 200,000 men (140,000 as prisoners).

German attacks on the San opened successfully on 16 May, and had established a defensible bridgehead north of the Russian-held fortress town of PRZEMYSL by 19 May, but attempts to push south to the fortress were held. The Austro-Hungarian Fourth Army's advance was also slowed, and Radko-Dimitriev launched fresh reserves against it on 19 May. Ten Russian divisions had arrived from the CAUCASIAN FRONT and the northwestern command by 20 May, but the Russian attack's early success lost impetus when it was extended to German positions further south, and it was finally halted with heavy losses on 25 May.

The Russian Ninth Army attacked with greater success around the River Dneister in the far southeast, its 120,000 troops forcing 80,000 Austro-Hungarians out of the Bukovina by mid-May. But Przemysl fell on 4 June and, reserves exhausted, the Russian Third Army was compelled to retreat east towards Lvov, dragging back both the Eighth Army to its south and the victorious Ninth.

Both sides were further reinforced before mid-June, when Mackensen began a series of successful attacks on the flanks of widely separated retreating Russian armies. Ivanov ordered the complete evacuation of Galicia from 20 June, and Austro-German forces entered Lvov two days later. Over the next few days the Südarmee recrossed the Dneister, after which the advance halted to enable Austro-German planners to consider their options. The offensive had taken quarter of a million prisoners and captured 224 guns for the loss of 90,000 men. See MAP 10; TRIPLE OFFENSIVE.

Gotha G-Types Large, twin-engined GERMAN ARMY AIR SERVICE biplane designed for long-range bombing operations and in production as the G-I from 1915. A structural curiosity, it had a pencil-shaped fuselage suspended from the upper wing, 160hp 'PUSHER' engines fixed to the lower, and a twin-finned tailplane. It was also manufactured in a G-WU floatplane version. Both versions were seriously underpowered, and were replaced in 1916 by the three-seater G-II, with 220hp engines, two MACHINE GUNS, and a more conventional structure. The G-II served for a time on the BALKAN FRONT, but was withdrawn when the new engines proved dangerously unreliable. Its replacement, the G-III, had a third gun and 260hp engines, but was vulnerable to attack from a blind spot beneath the tail, and the first version to be produced in numbers (230 machines) was the G-IV.

Essentially the same as its predecessor but with rear-gunner access to the underside of the fuselage, G-IVs were operative from early 1917 and grouped on the Channel coast with *Bombengeschwader 3* for a resumption of daylight STRATEGIC BOMBING raids over England, no longer viable for ZEPPELINS. The G-V, in action from August 1917, was the first of several later minor structural variations used for the same purpose.

The attacks on England, begun by about 30 machines on 13 June 1917, caused relatively little damage but had a considerable effect on British public opinion. The aircraft itself was easily distinguished by its giant wingspan (almost 24 metres), and 'Gotha' became an Allied generic term for any German bomber. British FIGHTERS, withdrawn from the WESTERN FRONT to calm popular outrage, climbed too slowly to be effective.

Fragile and clumsy, but well-armed, Gothas were eventually forced into night raids from September 1917, after superior British SE-5 interceptors, aided by an improved early-warning system, had begun to inflict combat casualties. Steadily mounting losses, almost all due to accidents or ANTI-AIRCRAFT fire, brought abandonment of raids the following May, by which time 61 machines had been destroyed. Gothas were then used exclusively over the Western Front.

BRIEF DATA (G-IV) Type: medium/heavy bomber; Crew: 3; Engine: 2 × 260hp Mercedes DIV; Max speed: 141kph; Ceiling: Range: 480km; Armament: 3 × 7.92mm mg, max bomb load 500kg (on external racks).

Gotha WD-XIV Purpose-designed biplane torpedo bomber, the only one of several twin-engined seaplanes built by the Gotha company to enter full production. Operating from GERMAN NAVY coastal bases in 1917–18, the twin-finned WD-XIV was not a success in its intended role despite intensive training of pilots and crew. Its power plants were barely sufficient to carry a single TORPEDO at launching speed, and it presented a slow, stable target for defensive gunfire. German aerial torpedo operations were finally abandoned amid mounting losses in 1918. After unsuccessful attempts to use WD-XIVs as MINE-LAYERS, survivors of the 69 machines produced were adapted for long-range reconnaissance work.

BRIEF DATA Type: two-seater naval torpedo bomber; Engine: 2 × 220hp Benz; Max speed: 134kph; Armament: 2 × 7.92mm mg, 1 × torpedo.

Gough, General Sir Hubert (1870–1963) British cavalry officer who led a division of the BEF on the WESTERN FRONT during 1914–15, became a corps commander early in 1916, and took command of the British reserve (later Fifth) Army on the eve of the SOMME OFFENSIVE. Failure of his attacks around Bullecourt during the ARRAS offensive in spring 1917, and collapse of his initial advance during the late-summer YPRES campaign, cemented a reputation for poor staff work and over-confident offensive enthusiasm. Not a man to suspend offensive action on grounds of changed or unfavourable circumstances, 'Thruster' Gough's faith in CAVALRY attacks defied contemporary experience, and an unfortunate arrogance of bearing added to his general unpopularity. Though C-in-C HAIG regarded him as the most dashing of his army commanders, Gough was blamed for the Fifth Army's collapse at the start of the German KAISERSCHLACHT Offensive in March 1918. Replaced by General BIRDWOOD, he remained unemployed until 1919 and retired in 1922.

Gouraud, General Henri (1867–1946) Promoted general shortly before the outbreak of war in 1914, Gouraud commanded a division of the French Fourth Army on the WESTERN

FRONT and led French forces at GALLIPOLI from March 1915. Invalided out of the theatre after being wounded on 30 June, he returned to action in December at the head of the Fourth Army in Champagne. Though transferred to govern Morocco when General LYAUTEY became war minister in December 1916, he rejoined the Fourth Army in early 1918. The Fourth Army played important roles in the MATZ and MARNE engagements but, close to exhaustion, his troops struggled to match the pace of AEF forces during the MEUSE–ARGONNE OFFENSIVE.

Grand Fleet The main strike force of the British ROYAL NAVY, a concentration of 35–40 modern BATTLESHIPS and BATTLECRUISERS supported by a vast armada of CRUISERS, DESTROYERS, SUBMARINES and other smaller craft (later including AIRCRAFT CARRIERS). Intended to enforce the Navy's prime directives at any given time, it was deployed in the North Sea throughout the War, based at Scapa Flow in the Orkney Islands (see MAP 16). Its principal roles were to protect Britain against possible invasion and to secure the naval BLOCKADE of GERMANY. Both tasks required numerical superiority over the German HIGH SEAS FLEET pending its presumed destruction in the decisive battle for which the Grand Fleet had been designed. Because the German fleet successfully avoided defeat at sea, and the realities of NAVAL WARFARE precluded an attack on German bases, the Grand Fleet functioned as a giant deterrent, handled with great caution by its wartime commanders, Admirals JELLICOE and BEATTY. See also: Battle of JUTLAND.

Graves, General William (1865–1940) Experienced US ARMY staff officer. He was assistant chief of staff until June 1918, when he was promoted major general and briefly commanded the 8th Division in California. In August he was given command of an American Expeditionary Force to Siberia, where RED ARMY units were fighting Admiral KOLCHAK's anti-Bolshevik forces and an independent CZECH LEGION was fighting for itself. JAPANESE NAVY warships had arrived at Vladivostok, ostensibly to aid the Czechs, prompting Anglo-French commitment of ground forces. Under pressure from his European allies to internationalize the operation, US President WILSON reluctantly agreed to send a contingent, but his orders to Graves were deliberately ambiguous and noninterventionist. Restricted to protection of Allied property in Vladivostok, rescue of the Czechs and vague assistance to the democratic liberty of 'the Russian people', Graves resolutely resisted Allied pressure to commit his 9,000 troops to combat with Red Army forces. He remained a strictly uncontroversial presence in Russia until recalled in April 1920, when Kolchak had been defeated and the Czechs evacuated.

Great Britain The superpower of the 19th-century world, the British Empire in 1914 included the 'white' dominions of CANADA, AUSTRALIA, NEW ZEALAND and SOUTH AFRICA, large parts of the rest of AFRICA, INDIA, many islands in the WEST INDIES and a number of protectorates or colonies in South America and the Pacific.

Guarded by the enormous ROYAL NAVY and transported by a merchant marine of more than 9,000 vessels (over 18 million tons), British trade was the main dynamic of an economy otherwise in decline. Britain's shipbuilding industry remained the world's largest and most efficient, but productivity in the coal and iron industries was relatively poor by north European standards. Chemical and light engineering capacity was backward compared to GERMANY, which supplied most of Britain's dyes, drugs and ball bearings, all vital to war production. A comprehensive transport system, including some 38,000km of RAILWAYS, had become second class in terms of operational efficiency.

Agriculture still occupied more workers than any other economic sector, but the relatively small amount of land available to feed a population of some 45 million (including Ireland) meant that imports from imperial sources made up more than half Britain's nutritional intake.

Political authority under a long-established constitutional monarchy, headed by King-Emperor GEORGE V from 1910, resided in a cabinet formed by the majority party of the lower House of Commons, elected by some 8 million registered voters. The aristocratic House of Lords possessed only a partial veto over legislation. The governing Liberal Party, in power since 1906 and under ASQUITH since 1908, depended on parliamentary support from 84 Irish Nationalists and Ramsay MACDONALD's 42 socialists to push through social reform, constitutional changes and Irish legislation against strong opposition from Bonar LAW's Conservative Party.

Home affairs dominated government thinking in mid-1914. Strikes had reached unprecedented levels in 1913, alongside a fervent campaign for WOMEN's suffrage, and controversy over commitment to Irish Home Rule threatened regional civil war in 1914. A politically inspired mutiny against Home Rule by BRITISH ARMY officers in IRELAND dominated headlines in early July.

Broadly dedicated to preserving a highly advantageous status quo, British foreign policy was conducted on a global basis, embracing alliance with JAPAN from 1902. Clashes of imperial interest with FRANCE and RUSSIA had been resolved by loose agreements (1904 and 1907) that fell short of full alliance but drew Britain into strictly European power struggles. In addition, the rapid expansion of the GERMAN NAVY triggered a costly naval arms race alongside mounting mutual suspicion. Britain had no fundamental quarrel with GERMANY, or its alliance partners ITALY and AUSTRIA-HUNGARY, but was bound by treaty to uphold the neutrality of BELGIUM.

The JULY CRISIS in 1914 forced Britain to decide for or against supporting France in a war, but Asquith presided over a cabinet split between interventionists (including navy minister CHURCHILL and foreign secretary GREY) and anti-War 'radicals'. The position of pivotal finance minister LLOYD GEORGE was uncertain, and public enthusiasm for involvement was muted. Asquith resisted pressure from Conservatives and the French government until the German invasion of Belgium was confirmed on 4 August. Berlin's failure to respond to an immediate ultimatum brought a British declaration of war on Germany at 23.00 that night. Opposition from some socialists and the resignation of two ministers barely detracted from an appearance of national unity.

Like all belligerents in 1914, Britain had made plans for a short war. Unlike other powers it expected to fight a primarily naval war, based on a comprehensive BLOCKADE of enemy trade routes, and possessed neither a mass army nor conscription. Mobilization of land forces, including volunteer reserves, initially affected only some 750,000 men, and Britain suffered less immediate economic disruption than other states. Otherwise London witnessed the spontaneous outbursts of popular patriotism, optimism, enthusiasm, xenophobia and 'spy fever' common to other belligerent capitals.

The government immediately took wide emergency powers through the DEFENCE OF THE REALM ACT (DORA), passed rapidly through parliament on 8 August. Initial government reluctance to make use of DORA beyond necessary control of railways and scarce sugar supplies emphasized a spectatorial attitude encapsulated in the slogan 'business as usual'. With the war expected to end in a few weeks, no invaders at the gates and no great conquests afoot, the British public underwent more emotional than practical disruption in 1914, being exposed to a welter of jingoistic private and official PROPAGANDA (see AMIENS DISPATCH).

Public optimism was not shared by the new war minister, Lord KITCHENER, whose face was adorning recruitment posters by 6 August. In effective control of the early British war effort, he was one of the few important Europeans expecting a long and costly conflict. His campaign to create a mass volunteer army was an immediate success in numerical terms, attracting some 2.6 million recruits by the end of 1915, but the campaign inflicted enormous random losses on skilled workforces just as the war ministry was bombarding munitions firms with orders.

By late 1914 this system of war management, or lack of one, was manifestly failing. Ammunition production, facing a spectacular rise in demand, had provided only about 5 per cent of 10 million shells ordered by the end of the year. All other weapons output was behind schedule, and orders from allies, especially RUSSIA, often went completely unfulfilled. Attempts to 'dilute' depleted workforces with unskilled labour, particularly women, met with resistance from unions.

The Shells and Fuses Agreement of March 1915 between unions and employers accepted dilution for the duration of hostilities, and an effective industrial truce was confirmed by the 'Treasury Agreement' at the end of the month. Unofficial strikes continued to take place, often in protest against price rises or unauthorized dilution, but stoppages remained well below immediate prewar levels until 1918, when more than a million man-hours were lost.

The British public had suffered relatively little discomfort by spring 1915. Unemployment had almost disappeared and higher wages generally matched sharp price rises, but heavy battle casualties and the prospect of a long war had instilled a general sense of government mismanagement, heightened by a German naval raid on SCARBOROUGH in December 1914. It found focus in the 'SHELL SCANDAL' of May 1915, when complaints by BEF field commanders exposed the extent of munitions supply failure.

Asquith was forced to include eight Conservatives and one Labour representative in a new coalition cabinet from 25 May, in which arms administration was transferred from Kitchener to a new munitions ministry under Lloyd George. Staffed by experienced industrialists, the ministry quickly became the vital instrument of British economic mobilization.

Dealing directly with military authorities to formulate greatly increased estimates of requirements, the ministry had co-opted and converted some 2,000 small concerns to war work by the end of 1915. Although never able to gain control of big private concerns, it spread contracts and profits around a far wider field, breeding streamlined production techniques, pushing down prices, and imposing some limitations on profits. Government-run munitions production was also expanded from a handful of arsenals in 1914 to some 70 establishments by late 1915 and more than 200 by 1918.

Armaments capacity had expanded to produce an entire year's shell output at 1914 levels within a matter of days by mid-1916. Six times as many heavy ARTILLERY pieces were being produced, and 14 times as many MACHINE GUNS, with comparable increases in the production of aircraft and all other ground weapons. British forces henceforth enjoyed growing superiority over opponents in both quality and quantity of equipment.

Industrial and military expansion required increased central control over manpower resources from mid-1915. From July the Munitions of War Act enabled the government to declare any business a vital 'controlled establishment', in which voluntary labour restrictions became legally binding and workers were banned from seeking jobs elsewhere. Doubts that dwindling voluntary recruitment could match the Army's manpower requirements prompted calls for conscription, introduced for the first time with the MILITARY SERVICE ACT of January 1916. Conscription did not always proceed smoothly, but was reluctantly accepted as necessary by unions and socialists.

Distribution of raw materials and resources was taken into partial government control during 1915. Coal supplies, shipping space, railways, agricultural produce, munitions, wool, iron and most foodstuffs were all subject to at least some official sanction by the end of the year. The popular diet remained dull, and although the supply situation was not desperate, consumption of ALCOHOL was restricted as a social measure.

Episodes like the death of Edith CAVELL, the *LUSITANIA* sinking and occasional STRATEGIC BOMBING raids on southeast England by ZEPPELINS (which killed 38 people in attacks on central London in early September 1915) heightened a public mood more overtly aggressive than that of the military. A steady reduction in public optimism during 1916 was accompanied by a gradual tightening of government food controls in the face of mounting losses to SUBMARINE WARFARE.

Military failures at GALLIPOLI, on the MESOPOTAMIAN FRONT and at JUTLAND, along with high-level strategic arguments (see 'EASTERNERS') and fallout from the EASTER

RISING in Ireland, all contributed to a steady weakening of Asquith's position. The death of Kitchener in June 1916, heavily mourned by the public, removed a major obstacle to cabinet coordination but focused criticism on the premier. The ultimate tactical failure of the SOMME OFFENSIVE brought the coalition's collapse on 5 December, sparked by the resignation of Kitchener's successor, Lloyd George, who became prime minister of a new coalition on 7 December 1916.

By the end of 1916 mounting popular war weariness was being exacerbated by renewed pressure to reinforce the BEF, and the effects of submarine attacks were forcing redirection of economic priorities towards food supply. In response, new ministries controlling food, local government, trade, shipping and national service were put in the hands of experienced businessmen (see WAR SOCIALISM).

Propaganda was used to mobilize volunteer 'land armies' for work in agriculture, and 3 million additional acres of land were put under cultivation by late 1918, but renewed calls for female and teenage workers had little effect on overall manpower shortages. The integration of colonial leaders into the policy-making process, begun at the Imperial Conference of March 1917, sustained a valuable source of troops and labour battalions, whereas raids on packed public entertainments by military police in search of 'slackers' for war service were cosmetic sops to press sensationalism.

Popular morale was lifted by the arrival of the first US 'DOUGHBOYS' in August 1917, but was dented in the autumn by renewed GOTHA bombing raids and the gruesome failure of the YPRES offensive. War weariness did not imply pacifism, and peace initiatives by Pope BENEDICT XV and US President WILSON met with solid public hostility. A small knot of anti-War British socialists, led by MacDonald, gained no significant union support, and Wilson's FOURTEEN POINTS of January 1918 met with only qualified popular and political approval.

Britain had gone to war with no specific territorial ambitions, but by 1917 public support was overwhelmingly behind the permanent destruction of German military potential. Wartime diplomacy had meanwhile bound the government to partition of the German colonial, Ottoman and Austro-Hungarian Empires among the Allies. By early 1918 the OCTOBER REVOLUTION had removed obligations to Russia, but the Treaty of LONDON and the SYKES–PICOT AGREEMENT remained incompatible with anything less than total victory.

Unrestricted submarine warfare brought Britain to within a few weeks of starvation in spring 1917, but this was largely kept from the public (see *HANDELSKRIEG*). Beer and confectionery supplies were cut in June 1917, price limits imposed on basic goods in August, and coal rationing introduced in November, but the government relied on appeals to reduce consumption until February 1918, when meat and fats were rationed in London. The system was extended to the whole country in April, and full ration books for all meat and dairy produce issued in July.

The dramatic early success of the German KAISERSCHLACHT Offensive on the Western Front in spring 1918 provoked an unprecedented sense of national crisis in Britain, transforming a public mood of disgruntled resignation into energetically revived unity. Conscription was dramatically stepped up, affecting men up to 50 from May, and unions accepted further dilution for frontline reinforcement. Women penetrated the workforce to a greater extent than ever before, and were rewarded with a promise of suffrage in April.

Weariness returned during the second half of the year, exacerbated from mid-June by the arrival of the INFLUENZA pandemic (which killed 200,000 people in Britain). This drop in morale was expressed in a wave of industrial stoppages from August, including a unique police strike in London. The autumn collapse of the CENTRAL POWERS suspended unrest, and popular attention focused on ensuring the draconian treatment of defeated belligerents at the PARIS PEACE CONFERENCE, where the British delegation was led by a re-elected Lloyd George.

Few of the political institutions established in wartime Britain survived into the 1920s, and – despite the limited introduction of female suffrage in 1918 – no sweeping postwar constitutional changes took place, but cultural values and social structures were permanently altered by the needs of total war. After a short postwar boom, Britain lapsed into accelerated economic decline accompanied by political crisis in Ireland and serious industrial unrest.

Great Powers Contemporary term describing those nations and empires, mostly European, that were held capable of shared responsibility for international relations by virtue of their global military and economic influence. No precise criterion defined a Great Power, but pretensions to global influence were generally confirmed by participation (as 'interested powers') in international conferences to settle conflicts involving third parties.

Undisputed Great Powers in 1914 included GREAT BRITAIN, FRANCE, GERMANY, RUSSIA and the UNITED STATES, although the USA self-consciously avoided entanglement in European, Middle Eastern or African affairs. AUSTRIA-HUNGARY's Great Power status was manifestly in doubt by the early 20th century, and Ottoman TURKEY was generally regarded as a Great Power only in name. Despite its economic and political fragility, the exuberant young state of ITALY wanted to be considered a Great Power, and had achieved nominal recognition as such before 1914, but the interests of JAPAN were only just developing a global dimension.

'Great Programme' Plan for the expansion and reform of the RUSSIAN ARMY that became law in June 1914. Following the 'little programme' of 1908 and a further reorganization in 1910, it raised the government's annual expenditure on the army, authorizing an immediate increase in peacetime recruitment to 585,000 men per annum, the modernization of ARTILLERY, and the expansion of military RAILWAYS. Planned by war minister SUKHOMLINOV, the programme reflected rapid economic growth in RUSSIA, and in theory elevated the Army to superpower status, but was neither efficiently applied nor matched by reform in other areas. Artillery resources were wasted on FORTRESSES; tactical emphasis on CAVALRY meant that transport was dominated by the needs of horses; and the Army's PLAN 19 for war precluded efficient concentration of forces. These weaknesses were not apparent to planners elsewhere, and the Great Programme was instrumental in persuading GERMANY into military action before it took effect.

'Great Retreat' (Russian) The RUSSIAN ARMY's withdrawal from Poland in the summer of 1915. 'Great' in the sense that it transferred the front line some 350km east of Warsaw (see MAP 11), the retreat was barely controlled by a high command (STAVKA) that had repeatedly refused appeals for a general withdrawal earlier in the year. Begun on 22 July, under pressure from the TRIPLE OFFENSIVE in Galicia, northwest Poland and Lithuania, the retreat was an improvised affair until mid-September, when Stavka ordered withdrawal from POLAND in order to transfer forces north to the active front around VILNIUS. Regarded as a shambles by contemporary Russian critics, its international reputation as a success derived from the failure of pursuing German forces to catch the seven escaping armies. Frustrated German commanders later ascribed the effects of rough terrain, poor communications and lengthening supply lines on their pursuit to Russian brilliance. Stavka's 'scorched earth' policy was also credited with great success, but was selectively applied, with most major Polish landowners using highly placed contacts on both sides to secure exemption.

'Great Retreat' (Serbian) The evacuation of SERBIA by its Army and government from late November 1915, after a two-pronged invasion by the CENTRAL POWERS in early October had driven Serbian and Montenegrin forces into the plateau lands of Kosovo (see MAP 19; BALKAN FRONT). Heavy snow slowed operations by both sides from 17 November, but roads out of Kosovo were gradually closed by Austro-German forces to the north and west and by Bulgarians to the east. Attempts by French forces at SALONIKA to interfere with Bulgarian operations made little progress, and SERBIAN ARMY chief of staff PUTNIK ordered his troops into the hills on 23 November.

Separating into four groups, they used the only escape route still available, through the mountains into MONTENEGRO and ALBANIA. Accompanied by King PETER, Crown Prince ALEXANDER and premier PAŠIĆ (one of many septuagenarians in the Serbian force), the retreat took place in blizzard conditions, was short of provisions, and suffered harassment by local tribesmen. Although the Montenegrins remained in their homeland, uncounted numbers of civilian refugees joined the flight, along with 20,000 prisoners of war, and estimates of the numbers who died on the journey vary up to about 200,000.

Survivors began reaching the Albanian coast in the first week of December, and a joint rescue operation was mounted by Allied MEDITERRANEAN naval forces to evacuate them from the Albanian ports of Valona (Vlora or Vlorë) and Durazzo (Durrës). Valona was held by the ITALIAN NAVY, and Durazzo was temporarily occupied against the threat of interference from the nearby AUSTRO-HUNGARIAN NAVY base at CATTARO. Although delayed by Italian reluctance to risk escort warships, the evacuation eventually proceeded almost uninterrupted through late December and early January. An estimated 155,000 Serbs, most in poor physical condition, were shipped to the Greek island of Corfu, occupied by the FRENCH NAVY in early January, and most military personnel were redeployed at Salonika in the autumn.

Greece Constitutional monarchy established in 1829, after a popular uprising had freed the country from Ottoman control. A revolution in 1862 had deposed King Otto I (a Bavarian prince elected to the throne in 1832), and his Danish successor, George I, oversaw steady territorial expansion, culminating in the annexation of Crete and Lemnos, along with parts of Turkish Macedonia and Thrace, in the Balkan Wars of 1912–13. George was assassinated in Macedonian Salonika on 18 March 1913, and succeeded by his strongly pro-German son CONSTANTINE I, whose relations with equally pro-Allied prime minister VENIZELOS deteriorated after 1914.

The constitution enabled both Constantine and the elected legislature to act as representatives of neutral Greece after August 1914, but both factions soon accepted the need for neutrality as long as TURKEY and BULGARIA remained in threatening positions of armed uncertainty. Constantine, supported by Colonel METAXAS and the pro-German majority of GREEK ARMY officers, turned down a German offer of alliance on 4 August, and discussions between the Venizelos cabinet and Entente governments faltered amid Anglo-French unwillingness to compromise Turkish, Russian and Bulgarian negotiations.

Military and socioeconomic circumstances also argued for peace. The armed forces, especially the GREEK NAVY, were being built up to counter anticipated Turkish aggression, but reorganization was still in progress in 1914. The majority of a primarily rural, largely Christian population of some 4.8 million was engaged in unmechanized agriculture, with less than 50,000 men, mostly shipbuilders, employed in heavy industry. The mercantile marine (some 300 steamers in 1913) was the most important transport system in a country with less than 2,000km of RAILWAYS in operation by 1914.

Uneasy political consensus collapsed in 1915 as the Allied DARDANELLES operation and the CENTRAL POWERS' invasion of SERBIA brought war closer to Greece. Venizelos resigned in March after his proposal to aid the Allies had been vetoed by Constantine, who subsequently opened treaty negotiations with Berlin. A landslide victory for Venizelos in the June elections undermined the King's position, and he was unable to prevent mobilization to defend Serbia or the premier's invitation to open SALONIKA to Allied forces.

Royal non-cooperation forced Veizelos to resign in early October 1915, and his supporters boycotted subsequent elections, enabling Constantine to establish a virtual autocracy with the assent of a largely pro-German legislature. But with armed opposition gathering around Venizelos, crisis came in autumn 1916.

The Army's acceptance of Bulgarian incursions into northern Macedonia prompted Venizelos to proclaim an alternative government in Crete in September. He went on to establish a Committee of National Defence at

Salonika in October, and began recruiting volunteers for an Army of National Defence to fight with the Allies. Allied distrust of the royalist regime was expressed in a naval BLOCKADE, seizure of Greek warships and weapons, and coercive operations at SALAMIS and ATHENS, the latter a minor battle for which the King was largely blamed.

The fall of French premier BRIAND had removed the last important objector to Allied interference in Greek affairs. The Athens government was presented with an ultimatum demanding Constantine's removal on 11 June 1917, and he left the country next day, the crown passing to his second son, Alexander. Venizelos returned to Athens to form a government, which declared war against the Central Powers on 29 June.

Venizelos had been restrained from using his Army of National Defence in a march on Athens, but its 60,000 troops (four divisions) now formed the basis of a national army mobilized for action on the BALKAN FRONT. Nine divisions (about 250,000 men) joined Allied forces in Macedonia from July 1918, taking part in the autumn VARDAR OFFENSIVE, and ships commandeered by the Allies were returned to participate in the Mediterranean ANTI-SUBMARINE campaign.

Venizelos pursued his expansionist claims on parts of Turkish Asia Minor at the PARIS PEACE CONFERENCE, and ordered the military occupation of SMYRNA in 1919. Greek forces met strong Turkish resistance, organized by Mustapha KEMAL, and lack of popular support for war was reflected in Venizelos's defeat at the 1920 elections. The sudden death of Alexander in October 1920 brought Constantine back to the throne until 1922, when the final defeat of Greek forces in Asia Minor prompted a period of uneasy republican peace.

Greek Army The peacetime strength of the Greek Army before 1912 was about 32,000 officers and men, organized into three divisions and raised through limited conscription of adult males. By the end of the Balkan Wars in late 1913 some 210,000 men were in service, about half of them with the four infantry divisions (and one CAVALRY division) in active frontline service. Reorganization from early 1914 provided for a wartime army of five corps, each containing cavalry, field ARTILLERY and three infantry divisions.

The peacetime regular army was strongly royalist, and most senior officers supported the pro-German stance of King CONSTANTINE I. The King resisted moves by prime minister VENIZELOS to mobilize reserves in support of the Allies until September 1915, when about 150,000 men were called up in fulfilment of defensive treaty obligations with SERBIA (see BALKAN FRONT). With Venizelos out of office, forces in northern Macedonia cooperated with Bulgarian advances in 1916, prompting the ex-premier to form his own volunteer Army of National Defence at SALONIKA.

Four volunteer divisions were ready by June, when Venizelos returned to office and declared war on the CENTRAL POWERS, and were used as the basis of a second mobilization for war. Although most royalist officers were exiled (see METAXAS, J.), mobilization was slow. Many units had recently been demobilized at Allied insistence and a few pro-German or anti-War mutinies were suppressed with executions of their leaders. Plans to raise five corps proved over-ambitious, and nine divisions in three corps (about 250,000 men) eventually took the field. Joining the successful 1918 VARDAR OFFENSIVE from Macedonia, they eventually suffered about 100,000 losses, including 15,000 dead.

Greek equipment in 1914 was distinctly second class. Some modern RIFLES had been introduced, but many units still used single-shot weapons, and the army's heavy artillery amounted to a few old fortress guns. From September 1916 Allied forces at Salonika equipped the Army of National Defence, which used a wide variety of (predominantly French) surplus weapons and uniforms. Official forces with the Allies in Macedonia were similarly equipped, and supported by a small air service in 1918, comprising Greek pilots flying a handful of Allied machines, including SOPWITH CAMELS.

Greek Navy Greek naval interests were confined to the Aegean Sea, and the conscript Greek Navy's prewar development was primarily directed against incursions by the

TURKISH NAVY. GREECE lacked major shipyards and had not managed to purchase any dreadnoughts by 1914. Its three old French BATTLESHIPS, built in the early 1890s, were of only limited coastal-defence value, and the most important ships were the US-built PRE-DREADNOUGHTS *Kilkis* and *Lemnos*, transferred to Greece in 1914. In addition, the Navy possessed 1 powerful armoured CRUISER, 1 old light cruiser, 14 DESTROYERS (of which 4 were valuable modern boats), 13 coastal TORPEDO BOATS and 2 SUBMARINES.

Powerful Allied naval forces were in the Aegean from August 1914, effectively dictating the wartime activities of the Greek Navy. Its attitude to the Allies reflected the ambivalent position of the Greek government in the wake of the 1915 SALONIKA landings. The Greek general staff discussed joint operations with the GERMAN NAVY in autumn 1915, and U-BOATS in the MEDITERRANEAN were instructed to spare Greek shipping. Allied forces treated all Greek ships with great suspicion and, lacking a genuinely secure base, warships were virtually interned in the Gulf of Athens.

The SALAMIS crisis of November 1916 brought the Greek Navy's effective seizure by the FRENCH NAVY, which commandeered its light craft, disarmed bigger units and occupied coastal ARTILLERY batteries. After Greece joined the Allies in June 1917, seized vessels were gradually returned to Greek command as crews became available. Torpedo boats and destroyers joined Allied ANTI-SUBMARINE patrols in the Aegean, and the best destroyers were employed in the Allied blockade in the DARDANELLES in 1918. Relations with French forces remained strained, but Greek ships worked in close cooperation with the ROYAL NAVY Aegean Squadron until the ARMISTICE.

Grenades Small bombs thrown by hand or fired from a rifle. Used since the 15th century, but regarded as suitable only for siege operations by Napoleonic times, their potential value in the similar conditions of TRENCH WARFARE was noted by many observers of the Russo-Japanese War in 1904–05. The GERMAN ARMY in particular pursued development and production, and by August 1914 had large numbers available. The FRENCH and RUSSIAN ARMIES had expected to besiege German FORTRESSES, and therefore possessed a nucleus of practical designs, but the BRITISH ARMY was almost completely lacking in grenades until spring 1915, and remained deficient everywhere except the WESTERN FRONT well into 1916.

Though usually dangerous to the user on open ground – particularly so in the case of 'fragmentation' varieties with weakened casings doubling as shrapnel – grenades became increasingly important in all theatres where trenches were attacked. They appeared in numerous types and shapes, but all relied on either impact (percussion) or timed fuses for detonation. Sophisticated impact devices were developed with fuses on every facet, but timed grenades became the norm, relying on delayed throwing to avoid their swift return.

The concept of the 'pin', igniting a delayed fuse when pulled, was common in later grenades, including British MILLS BOMBS. This device generally superseded 'stick' grenades, which ignited the fuse on leaving their handle. The ubiquitous 'cricket ball' grenade, named from its appearance and size, employed the more traditional method of striking the fuse like a match before throwing.

British troops at GALLIPOLI had no grenades, stimulating a major industry in improvised weapons, particularly the precisely named 'jam-tin bomb'. Small numbers of home-made grenades, a hobby of trench fighters everywhere, appeared on all static fronts and they were a standard weapon of irregular forces, notably during the ARAB REVOLT and the RUSSIAN CIVIL WAR.

Formal deployment of hand grenades in trench fighting was concentrated in grenadier or 'bombing' parties, sent in to clear enemy positions with massed attacks. By 1918, these had grown sufficiently in number to form a major component of any infantry attack on the Western Front, except by the relatively under-equipped AEF forces.

Rifle grenades were attached to a rod and dropped down the barrel, or placed in a cup attached to the barrel, before being launched by the blast from a (usually) blank cartridge. Rod grenades were inaccurate and never used in large numbers, but had a slightly greater range than cup grenades, which could seldom be projected more than about 180 metres. Cup launchers were pioneered by the British and French, who had developed an improved version using finned grenades, with a range of about 400 metres, by the time German forces adopted the type in 1918.

Grey, Sir Edward (1862–1933) British foreign minister from 1905 until 1916. He was the main architect of imperial foreign policy up to 1914, a subject virtually exempt from British public criticism. He sought peaceful growth as a means of trade expansion, encouraging friendship with FRANCE and RUSSIA as a way of ending imperial differences, but attempted to stand aside from continental rivalries by stopping short of full alliance and seeking international arbitration of Great Power disputes.

Never actively hostile to GERMANY, he nevertheless regarded the prospect of German hegemony over northern Europe as dangerous to GREAT BRITAIN. His diplomacy, cautious to the point of opacity, contributed to international uncertainty in 1914. Grey argued for the defence of France in British interest during the JULY CRISIS of 1914, and his key speech to the House of Commons on 2 August successfully united political opinion in defence of BELGIUM.

Grey's gloomy and celebrated view of the coming conflict ('The lights are going out all over Europe . . .') was reflected in an uncertain wartime performance. He misjudged the political moods of TURKEY and BULGARIA, greatly complicating relations with GREECE and ROMANIA, and the failure of his Balkan diplomacy contributed to a steady erosion of prestige at home. Excluded from ASQUITH's Inner War Cabinet in November 1915, he was ennobled in July 1916 before being replaced by BALFOUR in the LLOYD GEORGE government of December. Grey's only subsequent official role was as head of a diplomatic mission to Washington in September 1919, which failed to influence US rejection of the VERSAILLES Treaty.

Grigorovich, Admiral Ivan (1853–1930) Able and flexible RUSSIAN NAVY officer, famous as the commander of besieged Port Arthur during the Russo-Japanese War of 1904–05, who became navy minister in 1911. Grigorovich guided plans for large-scale naval reconstruction through the Duma before 1914, and overcame conservative opposition to ensure organizational reform. His policy of concentrating strength in the BALTIC SEA presumed only a temporary defensive posture, and he planned offensive actions in the BLACK SEA, but wartime control by STAVKA (Russian central command) forced caution on both fleets.

Grigorovich enjoyed good relations with naval interests in the Duma, and was generally regarded as having liberal tendencies. He also retained the confidence of Tsar NICHOLAS II and conservative courtiers, but his warnings about naval unrest in late 1916 were ignored. Ousted by the FEBRUARY REVOLUTION of 1917, he retired but remained in RUSSIA through the OCTOBER REVOLUTION and RUSSIAN CIVIL WAR before receiving permission to emigrate to France in 1923.

Gröner, General Wilhelm (1867–1939) Accomplished German staff officer, who played a vital role during GERMAN ARMY mobilization in August 1914 as colonel in charge of field RAILWAYS, and was promoted major general the following June. Appointed head of a new food-supplies office in May 1916, he remained in charge of railways until the late autumn, when he became head of the Supreme War Bureau, charged with implementing the vast production targets demanded by the HINDENBURG PROGRAMME.

A committed right-winger and a frequent critic of FALKENHAYN's policies, Gröner was the THIRD SUPREME COMMAND's most trusted administrator, but alienated military and industrial leaders by recognizing the practical need for social cooperation. In July 1917 he proposed worker participation in management and price restraints against excessive industrial profits. He went to the WESTERN FRONT as a divisional commander in August.

He was transferred east in February 1918, becoming chief of staff to Army Group EICHHORN in late March and administering economic exploitation of the UKRAINE, but was recalled to Berlin as deputy Army chief of staff after LUDENDORFF's dismissal on 29 October. Authorizing immediate withdrawals of German forces in France, he informed the government of MAX VON BADEN of the need for an immediate ARMISTICE on 6 November, and told Kaiser WILHELM II that abdication was unavoidable on 9 November.

Later that day he reached agreement with Social Democratic Party leader EBERT, offering to support the republican government in return for a promise not to impose drastic reforms on the officer corps, a pact that effectively guaranteed the military a substantial role in postwar GERMANY. Remaining at his post to supervise the Army's demobilization, he retired from active service in September 1919 to pursue a political career, occupying several postwar cabinet posts.

Großer Kurfürst German KÖNIG Class BATTLESHIP, completed in 1914 and one of the busiest GERMAN NAVY dreadnoughts. Stationed with the HIGH SEAS FLEET and present at JUTLAND, *Großer Kurfürst* also suffered MINE damage, a TORPEDO hit and a collision with its sister ship *Kronprinz Wilhelm* before being surrendered to the Allies after the ARMISTICE. BRIEF DATA See *KÖNIG*.

Guard Army Elite RUSSIAN ARMY force, comprising two infantry and one cavalry corps (60,000 men) in peak physical condition, and given specialized training throughout the first half of 1916. Intended as the main strike force for that year's summer offensives, it was trained in obsolete methods by superannuated instructors, and led by the elderly and incompetent General Bezobrazov, whose main qualification was personal influence with Tsar NICHOLAS II. When the Guard Army was ready for action in August it was sent to the front around KOVEL, where it was sacrificed in a series of fruitless BREAKTHROUGH attempts. Bezobrazov was dismissed in the autumn, and General GURKO appointed to rebuild the Army, but it never again fought as a complete unit.

Guatemala Republic in southern Central America, with a population approaching 2 million in 1914. It was typically influenced by US economic interests, but also accommodated German and other European settlements. German agents were active from 1914 in attempting to keep the country neutral, but President Cabrera – a virtual dictator in power since 1898 in the face of almost permanent rebellion – followed the UNITED STATES into hostilities with GERMANY, breaking off relations on 27 April 1917. War was never formally declared, but Guatemala confiscated German possessions and opened facilities to US forces as a precaution against attack by their common neighbour, MEXICO.

Guchkov, Aleksandr (1862–1936) A leading member of the moderate reformist Octobrist group at the centre of the Russian party-political spectrum, Guchkov moved towards its left wing in response to the increasingly conservative behaviour of government ministers before 1914. The major Duma parties voted for a political truce in August 1914, and Guchkov became a useful bridge between liberal opinion and industrial interests, being appointed to head the government's new War Industries Committee in June 1915. Responsible for coordinating an emergency increase in arms production, he was inhibited by the regime's refusal to contemplate social or fiscal reforms, and a short-term boom proved unsustainable.

A committed monarchist, Guchkov was contemplating the deposition of NICHOLAS II to save the crown by early 1916. His plans possibly gained qualified support from General ALEXEEV and other senior RUSSIAN ARMY officers, but were postponed by two heart attacks that year. The FEBRUARY REVOLUTION erupted soon after his return to health, and his contacts remained useful to the shaky new regime.

As war minister in the liberal PROVISIONAL GOVERNMENT from March 1917 he was viewed as a radical by the high command and as a representative of the old regime by the Petrograd SOVIET. His attempts to restrain socialist restructuring of the armed forces ended with his resignation in mid-May after foreign minister MILIUKOV's affirmation of support for Allied war aims brought mass anti-government protests in Petrograd (St Petersburg). He fled to Paris after the OCTOBER REVOLUTION and never visited the Soviet Union. See also: RUSSIA; ORDER NUMBER ONE.

Guillaumat, General Marie (1863–1940) Experienced FRENCH ARMY officer. He led a division on the WESTERN FRONT in August 1914, rising to replace NIVELLE in command of the Second Army around VERDUN in December 1916. He attacked north of the fortress the following August, in the first significant French action after the NIVELLE OFFENSIVE. In command at SALONIKA from December 1917, he planned the offensive later carried out by General FRANCHET D'ESPEREY and soothed inter-Allied relations strained by his predecessor, General SARRAIL. He was recalled to Paris as military governor (and a handy replacement should PÉTAIN fail as C-in-C) in June 1918. Appointed to the SUPREME WAR COUNCIL after the second MARNE battle had secured French positions on the Western Front, he returned to frontline action in command of the Fifth Army, advancing through the Ardennes, as the War ended.

Guise, Battle of Counterattack by the French Fifth Army during its retreat after the Battle of CHARLEROI, fought along the River Oise southeast of Guise on 29 August 1914, and also known as the Battle of Guise–St Quentin (see MAP 2).

General LANREZAC's weakened Fifth Army was facing north towards the pursuing German Second Army on 27 August, with a gap to its right and the BEF retreating on its left. Lanrezac, whose relations with C-in-C JOFFRE were worsening, at first refused to accept an order to advance northwest between Guise and St Quentin, intended to gain time for a new French Sixth Army to assemble at the northern end of the WESTERN FRONT, but a visit from Joffre changed his mind. An offer of help from General HAIG's nearby British corps was vetoed by BEF commander FRENCH, and after spending 28 August wheeling his troops into position, Lanrezac began his advance early next morning.

French plans had fallen into German hands, and Lanrezac's advance was met by the full weight of von BÜLOW's Second Army. In the west around St Quentin the French left wing was forced back across the Oise and withdrawn to support the right at Guise, where a German flank attack threatened. The French rallied and launched a full assault on the town early that evening, ending the day in occupation but in a dangerously exposed position.

Abandoning plans to form a counteroffensive line along the River Aisne, Joffre gave the order to retreat that night. Although the order did not reach Lanrezac until the next morning, von Bülow launched no further attacks and the Fifth Army withdrew, destroying the Oise bridges behind it.

Unaware of its details, the French public viewed the battle as a defeat, and fears for the safety of Paris intensified, but by delaying von Bülow's advance (and convincing him that the FRENCH ARMY was not beaten) the action gained vital time for Joffre to plug gaps in his overall line. See also: Battle of LE CATEAU; First Battle of the MARNE.

Gumbinnen, Battle of The first major engagement of the 1914 campaign in EAST PRUSSIA, a frontal attack on 20 August by the German Eighth Army (PRITTWITZ) against the invading Russian First Army (RENNENKAMPF). The Eighth Army had been pulled forward from prepared positions on the Angerapp Line by an unauthorized advance to attack Russian forces just inside the eastern border at STALLUPÖNEN on 17 August. Needing to disable the Russian First Army before turning to meet the Russian Second Army invading from the south, Prittwitz chose to confront the slow Russian advance at the first opportunity. Leaving a corps to guard his rear, he ordered three corps (and an additional division) into a line stretching south from Gumbinnen, some 40km inside the frontier (see MAP 12).

Delayed by roads clogged with East Prussian refugees, concentration was still in progress when the northern German corps attacked at 04.00 on 20 August. The other two German corps – MACKENSEN's in the centre and BELOW's in the south – did not reach the front for another four and eight hours, respectively, and the extra division missed the battle altogether.

The Russian right fought hard until its shell supply ran out during the afternoon, when it collapsed, but forewarned ARTILLERY routed the later German advance in the centre, forcing Mackensen into a disorderly retreat and persuading Below to join it. Convinced of an imminent Russian breakthrough, Prittwitz ordered the whole Eighth Army back to positions on the Vistula, effectively conceding East Prussia.

Widely viewed as a panic measure, the order was never carried out by field commanders, and Prittwitz was immediately replaced by HINDENBURG. Rennenkampf chose not to exploit his partial victory, pausing to rationalize supply and organizational problems. Confident that German forces were in full retreat, the Russian First Army remained where it was, while revised orders transferred the German Eighth Army south (see Battle of TANNENBERG).

Gurko, General Vasili (1864–1937) Russian officer, politically connected with GUCHKOV and other moderate liberals in the Duma. He commanded a division under General RENNENKAMPF in EAST PRUSSIA and during the Battle of ŁÓDŹ in November 1914. Given command of VI Corps, a swollen offshoot of the Russian Second Army (Smirnov), he led the Russian counterattack at the Battle of BOLIMOV in January 1915 and replaced General Bezobrazov in command of the GUARD ARMY in autumn 1916, charged with restoring its fighting strength after heavy losses at KOVEL. During ALEXEEV's illness he became temporary chief of staff at STAVKA (Russian central command) from December 1916 until the following February, and was given control of the Western Army Group after the FEBRUARY REVOLUTION, but disputes with the PROVISIONAL GOVERNMENT over preparations for the KERENSKI OFFENSIVE led to his dismissal in June 1917, after which he retired from military life. Arrested for monarchist sympathies in August, he was allowed to leave Russia for exile in Italy.

H

Haase, Hugo (1863–1919) The leading left-wing figure in the German Social Democratic Party (SDP) when he became its co-chairman (with EBERT) in 1913, Haase personally opposed the SDP commitment to war in August 1914, but voted for war credits in accordance with party discipline. Publicly opposed to annexationist war aims, Haase formed a splinter group (the Social Democratic Working Union) to vote against credits in March 1916, and finally left to head the pacifist Independent Social Democratic Party (USPD) in April 1917.

In November 1918 he rejected workers' revolution and joined the SDP in the Council of People's Commissars, again as co-chairman with Ebert. He resigned in late December as a protest against government use of army units to suppress unrest in Berlin, but gave USPD support to the SDP government after the elections in early 1919. He was assassinated by a lone right-wing gunman on 7 November. See also: GERMANY; GERMAN REVOLUTIONS.

Haelen, Battle of The first CAVALRY engagement of the War, fought on 12 August 1914 at a river crossing some 30km northeast of LOUVAIN, the initial line of the BELGIAN ARMY's main defence (see MAP 4). Little more than a skirmish by later standards, it was one of the few setbacks suffered by the Germans during their invasion of BELGIUM. Advance squadrons of the German cavalry corps (MARWITZ) found the sole Belgian cavalry division guarding the bridge at Haelen early in the morning, and spent the entire day charging it with lances and sabres. Belgian commander de Witte dismounted his troops and greeted the charges with massed RIFLE fire, holding the bridge and inflicting heavy casualties. Some Belgian observers interpreted the victory as fatal to German plans, but its main significance lay in exposing mounted cavalry's obsolescence as an offensive weapon.

Haig, Field Marshal Sir Douglas (1861–1928) British cavalry officer who commanded the BEF from December 1915. An orthodox and urbane figure, Haig was married to a former maid of honour with the royal family, enjoyed good relations with King GEORGE V, and was comfortable in political circles, serving as advisor to war minister HALDANE (1906–08) and director of military operations before taking command of BEF I Corps in August 1914. He handled his forces competently during the early engagements on the WESTERN FRONT, particularly the first YPRES battle, and led the First Army from December 1914. A year later he was a predictable choice as successor to C-in-C FRENCH.

Not a particularly innovative commander, he shared the illusion of imminent BREAKTHROUGH with other Allied generals, and his loyalty to failed field officers, reflected in continuity of command within the BEF, is generally regarded as a weakness. The SOMME and YPRES campaigns of 1916–17 established Haig's name as synonymous with attrition in GREAT BRITAIN, but attacks were sometimes forced on him by Allied requirements, most notably before the NIVELLE OFFENSIVE of 1917, when the BEF was temporarily placed under French command.

Completely committed to concentrating Allied resources on the Western Front, Haig made a long-term enemy of leading 'EASTERNER' and eventual prime minister LLOYD GEORGE, but with dogged support from imperial chief of staff ROBERTSON and in the absence of any obvious successor he held on to his job through repeated disappointments. His position was weakest in spring 1918, when Robertson's removal was followed by the German KAISERSCHLACHT and LYS Offensives, but he retained vital support from field commanders and developed a generally constructive relationship with new Allied supremo FOCH.

The coordination of successful British advances in autumn 1918, beginning at AMIENS in early August, reflected Haig's efficient staff work and preparation, and his insistence that victory could be achieved quickly eventually dissuaded the government from holding back resources for the following year.

Haig took command of British home forces in 1919 and retired in 1921, receiving a peerage and £100,000 from the government. Always popularly identified with casualties rather than victories, he remains one of the most controversial figures in British military history, regarded by some authorities as the architect of Allied success in 1918 and by others as the epitome of unimaginative generalship.

Haireddin Barberosse One of two old BATTLESHIPS purchased by the TURKISH NAVY from GERMANY in 1910, *Haireddin Barberosse* was 20 years old by 1914 and suitable only for coastal defence in home waters. Its loss – it was torpedoed in the Sea of Marmora by the British submarine *E-11* on 8 August 1915 – was a serious blow to morale but barely affected Turkish strength in the BLACK SEA. BRIEF DATA (*Haireddin Barberosse*, 1914) Displacement: 10,050 tons; Crew: 568; Dimensions: length 380.5ft (115.3m), beam 64ft (19.4m); Speed: 17k; Main armament: 6 × 11in gun, 8 × 4.1in, 8 × 15.5pdr, 2 × 18in TT.

Haiti Caribbean republic, independent from France since 1804, occupying the western side of the island of Hispaniola, which it shares with the Dominican Republic. During the period 1908–16 frequent border clashes and prevailing internal anarchy in both republics prompted the establishment of American protectorates to safeguard US industrial and agricultural interests.

US Marines were landed in the Dominican Republic in June 1914, and military occupation formally proclaimed in November 1916. In Haiti – ruled by six different presidents in three years – the economy collapsed completely before US Marines occupied the country in late 1915. Under martial law, the national congress appointed a new president, Sudre Dartiguenave, in April 1916, and control of all internal economic and military institutions by the UNITED STATES was announced the following month. Although Haiti declared war against GERMANY on 12 July 1918, the republic made no positive contribution to the Allied cause, and serious riots against US control took place during 1918–19. US military occupation remained in force in the Dominican Republic until 1924, and for a further 10 years in Haiti. See also: CUBA.

Halberstadt C-Types German biplanes produced for armed reconnaissance work, but initially used in only small numbers. The C-III saw some service in 1917, but the most important version was the C-V, which operated (along with the RUMPLER C-VII) in a specialist PHOTO-RECONNAISSANCE role from summer 1918. Usually fitted with RADIO equipment, excellent high-altitude performance enabled it to function despite overwhelming Allied aerial superiority over the WESTERN FRONT, and it was built in quantity by at least four German contractors.

BRIEF DATA (C-V) Type: two-seater photo-reconnaissance; Engine: 220hp Benz; Max speed: 165kph; Ceiling: 7,500m; Armament: 2 × 7.92mm mg.

Halberstadt CL-Types German biplanes designed from early 1917 to meet official specifications for a new CL category of armed reconnaissance aircraft, lighter and more agile than C-type machines. The first production version in action was the CL-II, introduced in late 1917 and used for direct support of infantry, or 'trench fighting', on the WESTERN FRONT. During and after the Battle of CAMBRAI in November they were generally deployed in mass attacks on hostile positions, a dangerous but effective tactic used increasingly by the GERMAN ARMY AIR SERVICE in 1918 (see AERIAL WARFARE). A CL-IIa version – with a 185hp BMW engine and a more streamlined nose – was produced simultaneously, and an aerodynamically improved CL-IV model was in service from spring 1918. From autumn 1918 they were employed more defensively, operating as interceptors and escorts.

BRIEF DATA (CL-II) Type: two-seat ground-attack/reconnaissance; Engine: 160hp Mercedes; Max speed: 168kph; Ceiling: 4,100m; Armament: 2 or 3 × 7.92mm mg, optional grenades, light bombs (on wing racks).

Halberstadt D-Types A series of biplane FIGHTERS produced from 1915 by the German Halberstadt company, a prewar subsidiary of the British Bristol concern that had previously built licensed Fokker designs along with its own B-Type trainers. Its first single-seater, the 100hp D-I with a synchronized forward MACHINE GUN, performed escort duties for the GERMAN ARMY AIR SERVICE on the WESTERN FRONT from early 1916. A modified, 120hp D-Ia version, with staggered wings and an Argus engine, also reached squadrons before large-scale production began in early 1916 with the Mercedes-powered D-II, otherwise essentially the same as the D-Ia. The D-II was rapidly followed by the D-III, again with only minor design changes, and about 110 of these main production models were built (some by other companies under licence). Small numbers of the 150hp D-IV and slightly streamlined D-V versions joined them in service during 1916.

In the autumn of 1916, Halberstadt Ds were attached to new fighter squadrons (*Jagdstaffeln*), their structural strength and manoeuvrability complementing the superior performance and armament of ALBATROS D-TYPES in establishing German air superiority during early 1917. Although some later models were fitted with a second machine gun, Halberstadts had become obsolete by late 1917. They were gradually withdrawn in the latter part of the year, survivors serving for a few months around SALONIKA and in the Middle East.

BRIEF DATA (D-II) Type: single-seat fighter/escort; Engine: 120hp Mercedes; Max speed: 144kph; Ceiling: 4,000m; Armament: 1 or 2 × 7.92mm mg.

Haldane, Richard, Lord (1856–1928) British Liberal politician, educated in Germany, who was a highly effective war minister for seven years to 1912, instituting much-needed eforms and creating the BEF as a continental uropean task force. In early 1912 he led a nission to Berlin in an unsuccessful attempt to alt Anglo-German naval rivalry, and he emained in the cabinet as lord chancellor in ugust 1914. His abilities were widely ppreciated across the British political spec-rum, but his known German sympathies rovoked a major press campaign for his emoval from office in 1915. His complete vithdrawal from public life provoked wide-pread criticism of the NORTHCLIFFE news-apers that hounded him, particularly the ensationalist *Daily Mail*. See also: BATTEN-ERG, L.

Iamilton, General Sir Ian (1853–1947) ucid, literate (and thus widely unpopular) British officer who counted war minister ITCHENER among several important friends. Given command of home forces in August 914, he was Kitchener's surprise choice on 12 March 1915 to lead 75,000 troops to the ALLIPOLI FRONT as the Mediterranean Expe-itionary Force. Opinions of his role in the ALLIPOLI LANDINGS differ, but most com-nentators regard the operation as an opportu-ity lost through inept field command, epicting Hamilton as passive and over-onfident. In directing subsequent operations t KRITHIA, ANZAC COVE and SUVLA BAY he isplayed limited imagination and excessive ptimism, earning eternal infamy among NZAC troops; but he was never reinforced in me to impose numerical superiority in ifficult terrain. His replacement in October 915, after he had forlornly recommended vacuation of the Gallipoli peninsula to itchener (a course of action immediately dvocated by his replacement, General Monro), marked the end of Hamilton's active areer.

Iandelskrieg German term meaning 'trade varfare', and used to describe the GERMAN IAVY's campaigns against non-military ship-ing. Prewar plans had assigned the role of ttacking Allied trade and troop transport etworks to fast surface warships and dis-uised AUXILIARY COMMERCE RAIDERS, but espite initial successes they were soon neu-tralized by the ROYAL NAVY (see MAP 15; NAVAL WARFARE). Unable to disturb GREAT BRITAIN's long-range economic BLOCKADE with its surface fleet, the German Navy diverted its SUBMARINES to *Handelskrieg* as a form of counterblockade.

Attacks by submerged submarines on merchant shipping had hardly been consi-dered before 1914, and a large body of opinion on all sides regarded the idea as barbaric. All attacks on non-military shipping were governed by international laws ('prize rules'): commanders were required to halt the victim, search it, give fair warning of seizure or sinking, and endeavour to protect the lives of occupants.

These restrictions – which would require an attacking submarine to surface – were effectively crippling for submarines in crowd-ed areas, and German naval thinking regarded 'unrestricted' attacks on commercial vessels as a necessary step by autumn 1914. Prolonged arguments at high-command level in GER-MANY centred on efforts to persuade Kaiser WILHELM II that the benefits outweighed the dangers.

Attacks without warning on unarmed ships were generally considered war crimes, and some neutral shipping was almost certain to be destroyed. Serious damage to sensitive rela-tions with ITALY and the UNITED STATES was only justifiable if success was guaranteed. Supporters of unrestricted attacks, including Navy chief of staff Pohl and naval minister TIRPITZ, exaggerated the prospect of swift results, sparking clamorous public demand for them to be given the chance. Opponents, headed by chancellor BETHMANN HOLLWEG, produced figures suggesting that more than 200 submarines would be needed to enforce an effective counterblockade of Britain (against about 20 then available).

Damage to the HIGH SEAS FLEET at the DOGGER BANK in January 1915 probably influenced Wilhelm's early acceptance of the military view. On 4 February Germany declared the waters around Britain and Ireland a 'war zone' in which all Allied merchant shipping would be sunk without warning. Danger to neutral shipping was considered inevitable.

Immediate protests from the US and Italian governments briefly delayed the campaign, but it opened on 22 February with only marginal restrictions. Concentrated against shipping in the south Irish Sea, in the English Channel and off the northeast English coast, a total of 16 patrolling U-boats (never more than 6 at once) sank 85,000 tons of Allied shipping in March. Development of the DOVER BARRAGE forced U-boats from the North Sea to avoid the English Channel from mid-April, and with four U-boats already lost, sinkings for the month fell to 50,000 tons.

The re-opening of bases on the Belgian coast, closed after the CUXHAVEN RAID in late 1914, helped sinkings top 100,000 tons per month in May, June and July 1915, for the loss of three U-boats. However, the campaign's economic effects were negligible, and diplomatic problems with the US reached crisis point after the destruction of *LUSITANIA* in early May and *ARABIC* in August, reopening controversy within the German command.

On 27 August the Kaiser issued new orders restricting attacks on passenger ships, prompting BACHMANN's resignation as chief of naval staff and his replacement by HOLTZENDORFF. Pohl, by now High Seas Fleet commander, called off his U-boats, and Flanders submarines were restricted to coastal defence. Between February and the end of September 1915 U-boats sank almost 750,000 tons of (mostly British) shipping, less than 4 per cent of British merchant carrying capacity. Despite the deployment of more than 2,100 British armed auxiliaries in ANTI-SUBMARINE activities, the Germans lost only 12 long-range boats, suggesting that more submarines might achieve decisive results.

The focus of *Handelskrieg* shifted to the MEDITERRANEAN. Five U-boats were stationed at CATTARO in the Adriatic by late 1915, and a few dismantled UB-BOATS and UC-BOATS were sent by RAILWAY to join the small Austro-Hungarian flotilla at Pola. Originally targeted against military shipping, particularly Allied forces at the DARDANELLES, they were concentrated on supply traffic in the eastern Mediterranean after Allied landings at SALONIKA in October. U-boats had sunk 58 ships by late November and enjoyed almost unbroken success in the theatre, which contained few US ships. Five U-boats sent to the BLACK SEA were far less successful, and the flotilla was never seriously reinforced.

German submarine strength almost doubled in the year from February 1915. During the spring, Holtzendorff and new High Seas Fleet C-in-C SCHEER led renewed military pressure for an unrestricted campaign, still opposed by Bethmann Hollweg, but a war council in early March agreed to only a limited campaign against Britain, with unrestricted warfare to follow two weeks later if the British failed to relax their blockade.

The limited campaign began on 15 March 1916, and reflected uncertain instructions to U-boat commanders, with some observing regulations and others attacking without warning, but the unrestricted campaign was brief, sinking some 250,000 tons of Allied shipping before the loss of *SUSSEX* brought angry US protests and another suspension on 20 April. All U-boat commanders (except those operating in the Aegean 'war zone') were subsequently ordered to obey prize rules, and activity in British waters was restricted to MINELAYING.

U-boats destroyed 662,131 tons of registered shipping (256 ships) in the Mediterranean during the second half of 1916, losing only two small boats in the process. Meanwhile Scheer, commanding half of all active boats, refused to operate around Britain under prize rules.

The political struggle over *Handelskrieg* in Germany reached crisis point after the THIRD SUPREME COMMAND gained control of the Army in autumn 1916. The Navy was permitted to conduct a restricted campaign against Britain from September and instructed to begin preparations for unrestricted warfare, which included ordering 86 new submarines. Bethmann Hollweg meanwhile sought some alternative to war with the USA, but was unable to gain international backing for his tentative peace overtures.

High Seas Fleet submarines were officially committed to a restricted campaign in British waters from October, sinking about 300,000 tons of Allied shipping per month to January 1917 in a target area extended to include the

Bay of Biscay. By late December 1916 85 submarines were active in the campaign – 38 with the High Seas Fleet, 25 on the Belgian coast and 22 based in the Adriatic. Three boats also performed successfully in the ARCTIC theatre during late 1916.

The effects of the 1916 campaign, though kept from the public, were already causing serious concern in Britain, fuelling a long controversy over the potential value of CONVOYS. In Germany the well-publicized prospect of defeating Britain within six months had united press, public opinion and much of the Reichstag behind the Navy's view. Allied rejection of the GERMAN PEACE OFFER at the turn of the year finally wrecked Bethmann Hollweg's resistance, and the Kaiser ordered unrestricted submarine warfare on 7 January 1917, to be prosecuted 'with the utmost energy' from 1 February.

Germany possessed 111 U-boats at the time – including 18 in the Mediterranean, 53 in home bases and 33 in Flanders – and about 40 could be operative at any one time. The large boats were now capable of patrolling for up to a month, the small boats for up to a fortnight, and another 80 boats were due into service that year.

Sinkings in February 1917 leapt to 230 ships (464,599 tons), 50 of them in the Mediterranean. Losses included 70 neutral ships, and more than 300 other neutral vessels refused to sail. As the weather improved and more boats came into service, March figures reached 507,001 tons and topped 400,000 tons in the first two weeks of April, bringing Britain close to supply crisis and forcing the issue of convoys to a conclusion.

The large-scale use of convoys was first authorized on 27 April, on the same day that Allied naval leaders agreed to divert all Far East traffic away from Suez and round the Cape of Good Hope, entailing great delay and expense. The USA entered the War in April, but overall figures for the month – 834,549 tons sunk, 354 ships lost and only two U-boats destroyed – suggested that the submarine could prove decisive before US involvement became important.

May figures showed a reduction to 549,987 tons, and 7 submarines were lost, but sinkings rose again to 631,895 tons (272 ships) in June, two-thirds lost in the southwestern approaches to Britain. Only 2 U-boats were lost and 150 were in service by the end of the month, prompting British plans to suspend all unescorted sailings and reducing imports to levels sustainable for less than two months.

The slowly expanding convoy system (in which the British Admiralty still had little faith) was having only limited effect, and July sinkings totalled 492,320 tons. More convoys came into operation in August, but the shortage of escort craft was exacerbated by continued Allied preference for 'offensive' anti-submarine methods and by the successes of long-range U-cruisers (see *U-155*). Sinkings for the month were almost unchanged at 489,806 tons. Britain nevertheless showed no outward sign of collapse, and German plans were laid for a longer campaign than originally envisaged, with orders for 95 new boats.

Public disappointment and accelerating political polarization enabled the Third Supreme Command to secure Bethmann Hollweg's replacement by the more pliable MICHAELIS, but losses fell to 315,907 tons in September, and only two ships were sunk while actually with convoys. U-boats were being forced to attack inshore, where they could be sure of finding convoys but where anti-submarine forces were strongest, and 11 were lost. Sinkings rose again to 429,147 tons (5 submarines lost) in October, but slow application of systemized convoying in the Mediterranean was a major factor.

The battle remained deadlocked at this level until late spring 1918, although British imports were further curtailed by the use of shipping to bring the AEF to Europe. U-boat losses averaged about 7 per month to spring 1918, and were more than made up by new commissions. Ambitious building programmes meant that 273 new boats were on order by the ARMISTICE.

Allied anti-submarine capacity was also improving. More escorts, particularly aircraft, were becoming available, and reorganization of the Dover Barrage again forced High Seas Fleet U-boats to avoid the English Channel. The NORTHERN BARRAGE restricted alternative routes to the British western approaches, and a growing proportion of losses were concentrated in the Mediterranean. A new tactic – the 'wolfpack' – was tried in May at the western approaches, where nine U-boats were grouped to attack frequent convoys. Poorly coordinated, they sank only three ships in two weeks.

The tide turned in May 1918, when 14 U-boats were sunk, including 4 in the Mediterranean, which had at last been organized into 18 convoy routes. Allied losses in the Mediterranean were halved in June, and overall losses for the month were down to 240,426 tons (mostly to TORPEDOES and submarine-laid MINES). Another factor in diminishing returns was the waning efficiency of German submariners. By July 1918 over 150 U-boats had been lost, and less experienced crews were being asked to face greater difficulties.

By September 1918, with losses down to 187,800 tons, U-boats had been checked rather than defeated. New building still outstripped losses, but the German military and political situation was crumbling. The Flanders flotilla was withdrawn to Germany in September, because security of the ports could no longer be guaranteed, but the German Navy's new Supreme Command continued to act as if victory in 1919 was a possibility, placing orders for many more U-boats and discussing expansion plans with German shipbuilders as late as 1 October.

Morale and discipline in the submarine service remained good, with sinkings continuing into October, but High Seas Fleet submarines were recalled from *Handelskrieg* on 21 October to join surface ships in a last mission against the British Grand Fleet. The subsequent KIEL MUTINY did not involve U-boat crews, which generally remained loyal but lacked supplies or bases to provide significant opposition.

U-boats in the Mediterranean remained active until 4 November, when Austria-Hungary signed an armistice with the Allies and the 15 ocean-ready boats were forced to evacuate Cattaro. Most returned to bewildered inactivity in Germany, and *U-34* (responsible for sinking some 170,000 tons of Allied shipping since 1914) was the last wartime loss, sunk in the Straits of Gibraltar on 9 November.

Handley Page 0/100 The first successful twin-engined British bomber. Development began in late 1914 in response to ROYAL NAVY specifications for a long-range patrol craft. Privately increased by naval air chief Sueter, who asked Handley Page designers to produce a genuine long-range bomber, specifications were met by late 1915, and production 0/100s were in service with the RNAS at Calais from November 1916. After losses were sustained during initial daylight raids on the Belgian coast, they were switched to night-bombing operations against German SUBMARINE bases, airfields and RAILWAY centres behind the WESTERN FRONT. Although only 46 were built before the improved HANDLEY PAGE 0/400 took over production, the 0/100s remained on night duties until the ARMISTICE, and two machines took part in the PALESTINE campaign.

BRIEF DATA Type: bomber; Crew: 4; Engine: 2 × 266hp Rolls Royce; Span: 100ft (30.5m); Max speed: 85mph (136kph); Ceiling: 2,100m; Armament: 3–5 × 0.303in mg, max 16 × 112lb bomb.

Handley Page 0/400 An improved version of the HANDLEY PAGE 0/100 twin-engined bomber, physically almost identical to its predecessor and similar in performance. Originally ordered in small quantities for RNAS use, the 0/400 was put into mass production from late 1917 as a response to attacks on England by German GOTHA G-TYPES. In active service from spring 1918, it became the RAF's standard bomber, equipping seven squadrons with the INDEPENDENT AIR FORCE for STRATEGIC BOMBING raids against German industrial and military targets. Capable of carrying the largest available bombs, groups of up to forty 0/400s could deliver the major long-range attacks planned by bombing theorists but were accident-prone and vulnerable to ANTI-AIRCRAFT fire, so that results never matched expectations. About 550 British 0/400s were produced in wartime, and 107 built under licence in the US, many remaining in both military and civil service for some years.

ɜRIEF DATA As for Handley Page 0/100, except: ːngine: 2 × 275hp Sunbeam or 375hp Rolls ƙoyce; Max speed: 98mph (157kph); Armament: -5 × 0.303in mg, max bomb load 1,800lb or × 1,650lb bomb.

Iandley Page V/1500 The largest wartime ɜritish aircraft, intended for long-range STRA-EGIC BOMBING raids into the heart of ɟermany. First flown in May 1918, it was too ate to see active service, although 3 of an nitial order for 250 machines reached the RAF n early November 1918.

ɜRIEF DATA Type: heavy bomber; Crew: 4; pan: 126ft (38.2m); Engine: 4 × 375hp Rolls ʻoyce; Max speed: 97mph (155kph); Ceiling: ,950m; Armament: 4–5 × 0.303in mg, max omb load 5,000lbs (2,273kg).

Ianna, Battle of The second of three failed ɩnglo-Indian attempts to break through to esieged KUT on the MESOPOTAMIAN FRONT see MAP 23). After suffering heavy losses at HEIKH SA'AD, about 10,000 men under ɟeneral Aylmer were available for the peration. Many were close to exhaustion, nd the rainy season made overland advance ery difficult, but C-in-C NIXON (too sick to ːave BASRA) remained confident – reinforce-nents were en route to the front, and a ʻussian force in western PERSIA was reported ɔ be approaching the area.

Retreat from Sheikh Sa'ad had been re-ersed by new Turkish commander KHALIL ASHA. His forces were deployed in trenches ehind a riverlet off the east bank of the ʻigris, with reserves concentrated about 5km priver at the Hanna defile, a 1km-wide strip f land between water and marshes. Aylmer's ttempt to cut inland and outflank the ositions on 13 January was spoiled by poor econnaissance, and Turkish forces inflicted ,600 casualties before retiring to strong renches across the mouth of the defile.

Nixon vetoed a proposal for the Kut arrison to abandon the town and attack from he rear, and several subsequent attempts at rontal assault failed in heavy rain, which revented river crossings and delayed re-nforcements. In a final effort on 21 January, n attack by some 4,000 troops of 7th Division suffered all the disadvantages associated with BREAKTHROUGH TACTICS on other fronts. Preceded by an ineffectual 20-minute ARTIL-LERY bombardment, which served only to alert defenders, the infantry suffered 60 per cent casualties at the hands of well-sited Turkish MACHINE GUN positions, gaining nothing.

The wounded underwent even worse privations than those at CTESIPHON and Sheikh Sa'ad, and Aylmer called off a planned resumption when he witnessed the condition of his force the following day. With reserves trapped by transport bottlenecks, an estimated 10,000 Turkish troops facing him, and at least another 25,000 between Hanna and Baghdad, he regarded immediate relief of Kut as impossible, but was ordered to try again by new C-in-C General Lake (see Battle of DUJAILA).

Hannover CL-Types Small German bi-plane designed in mid-1917 to meet official specifications for a light, agile machine to perform both reconnaissance and ground-attack duties. Nimble at high altitude and easy to fly, it was an immediate success as the CL-II on the WESTERN FRONT from January 1918. Its distinctive biplane tail, narrower than usual, reduced the blind spot beneath the aircraft, and the rear gunner/observer was almost hidden under the wing, both advan-tages in combat.

Hannovers were used in large numbers throughout the last phases of the war in France, operating as escorts for larger machines as well as in their anticipated roles, but were reduced to entirely defensive duties during the autumn. A total of 439 CL-IIs were built, and several modified versions were produced, including the streamlined 160hp CL-III (80 built) and 180hp CL-IIIa (537 built). A number of CL-IIa (a Roland-built CL-III), 190hp CL-IIIb and big-winged CL-IIIc versions also served with field units, but no production records exist.

BRIEF DATA (CL-II) Type: two-seater reconnais-sance/ground attack; Engine: 180hp Argus; Max speed: 165kph; Ceiling: 7,500m; Armament: 2 × 7.92mm mg (1 forward).

Hanriot HD-1 Designed and built in France during 1916, but hardly used by the French AÉRONAUTIQUE MILITAIRE (which preferred the SPAD S-VII), the HD-1 was an important addition to Italian and Belgian FIGHTER strength. Similar in appearance to British Sopwith designs, it was agile and rugged, but somewhat underarmed by contemporary standards. Attempts to double its firepower created an unacceptable drop in performance, and it proved impossible to fit a larger engine, but the Hanriot was very popular with Italian pilots. From autumn 1917 it replaced the NIEUPORT 11 as the ITALIAN AIR FORCE's standard fighter, equipping 16 of its 18 combat squadrons at the ARMISTICE. In total, 831 HD-1s were built for Italian use, many under licence in Italy, and another 125 equipped Belgian fighter units on the WESTERN FRONT. A few (including one or two HD-2 floatplane conversions) were also employed by the FRENCH NAVY and the US NAVY in defence of coastal stations in France.

BRIEF DATA (HD-1) Type: single-seat fighter; Engine: 110hp Le Rhône; Max speed: 175kph; Ceiling: 6,350m; Armament: 1 × 0.303in mg.

Hansa-Brandenburg C-I German-designed biplane that was a mainstay of the AUSTRO-HUNGARIAN AIR SERVICE from 1916, reflecting the Hansa-Brandenburg company's close Viennese connections. Built in Austria under licence (and fitted with a variety of 160–230hp engines), it was reliable, easy to fly and readily adaptable to improvised airstrips, performing adequately in reconnaissance, ARTILLERY-spotting and light-bombing roles. Though partly replaced by improved PHÖNIX C-1 and UFAG C-1 designs from early 1918, it remained active with many units until the ARMISTICE.

BRIEF DATA Type: two-seater armed reconnaissance; Engine: 160hp Austro-Daimler; Max speed: 139kph; Ceiling: 5,750m; Armament: 1 or 2 × 8mm mg, light bombs.

Hansa-Brandenburg CC Small 'PUSHER' flying boat fighter designed by Ernst Heinkel and ordered by the GERMAN NAVY in May 1916. Production CCs, powered by a 150hp Benz engine, entered service the following February and satisfied operational requirements, but the German Navy had little interest in flying boats and took only 3 machines. No record exists of their operational careers. The type was much more widely used by the AUSTRO-HUNGARIAN NAVY, and from late 1916 until the ARMISTICE a further 135 machines operated against Italian raids on Adriatic and Aegean ports. Up-engined and produced under licence as the CC-A by the Phönix company of Vienna, it was faster than the NIEUPORT 11 fighter mainstay of the ITALIAN AIR FORCE, and remained effective until the sheer weight of opposing numbers brought heavy losses in late 1918.

BRIEF DATA (CC-A) Type: single-seat fighter flying boat; Engine: 185hp Austro-Daimler; Max speed: 175kph; Armament: 1 or 2 × 7.92mm mg (forward).

Hansa-Brandenburg D-I Biplane FIGHTER designed in Germany during 1916, but built only by the Austro-Hungarian Phönix and Ufag companies. Nicknamed the 'Spider' ('*Spinne*') after its unique, asterisk-shaped strut design, it was the standard fighter of the AUSTRO-HUNGARIAN AIR SERVICE from autumn 1916. Never more than an adequate weapon, its tendency to lurch suddenly in flight caused many fatal accidents. Its MACHINE GUN was positioned on the wing above the pilot, where it spoiled aerodynamic performance and was inaccessible if jammed. Lacking the power to compete in combat by early 1917, it could not be adapted to take larger engines and was withdrawn during the summer.

BRIEF DATA (Phönix) Type: single-seat fighter; Engine: 160hp Austro-Daimler; Max speed: 186kph; Armament: 1 × 8mm mg.

Hansa-Brandenburg KDW Floatplane version of the HANSA-BRANDENBURG D-I, one of a series of naval FIGHTERS that served with the GERMAN NAVY from September 1916. Attached in small numbers to seaplane stations on the Channel coast, and believed to have served with German units in the Adriatic, it was rendered obsolete by the success of the two-seater HANSA-BRANDENBURG W-12 and was withdrawn from early 1918. Fifty-eight KDWs were built, some powered by 160hp engines, along with one or two 200hp versions, designated the Hansa-Brandenburg W-11.

BRIEF DATA (KDW) Type: single-seat floatplane fighter; Engine: 150hp Benz; Max speed: 171kph; Armament: 2 × 7.92mm mg (forward).

Hansa-Brandenburg W-12 German floatplane in production from February 1917 that operated as a reconnaissance and patrol craft from seaplane stations at ZEEBRUGGE and Ostend. Its tailplane design – with the fin pointing downwards – gave the observer an excellent field of fire, and W-12s inflicted heavy losses on RNAS seaplanes over the English Channel, prompting the formation of a British FIGHTER unit specifically for their defence in July 1917. Although production was halted in March 1918, after 145 had been built, W-12s remained in frontline service until the ARMISTICE.

BRIEF DATA Type: two-seater armed reconnaissance floatplane; Engine: 160hp Mercedes or 150hp Benz; Max speed: 160kph; Armament: 2 or 3 × 7.92mm mg (1 or 2 forward).

Hansa-Brandenburg W-29 Successful German floatplane designed in late 1917, a low-winged monoplane that retained the fuselage and tail design of the HANSA-BRANDENBURG W-12. Added to GERMAN NAVY seaplane strength on the Flanders and North German coasts from April 1918, it was a fast, manoeuvrable machine, able to compete with the best RNAS seaplanes in combat. It was used as an escort for small warships and deployed in swarms for attacks on ROYAL NAVY vessels. Summoned by RADIO, W-29s sank several TORPEDO BOATS and crippled one British SUBMARINE (*C-25*) with MACHINE GUN fire alone. Seventy were built in 1918, along with at least 30 of an enlarged W-33, a 260hp version entering service at the ARMISTICE. The design was much imitated by postwar manufacturers.

BRIEF DATA (W-29) Type: two-seater floatplane escort/naval attack; Engine: 185hp Benz; Max speed: 165kph; Armament: 2 × 7.92mm mg (forward).

Harbord, General James (1866–1947) Efficient US ARMY staff officer and longtime associate of General PERSHING. He was appointed AEF chief of staff in May 1917. Rewarded for his role in the organization of Pershing's army with command of a marine brigade in May 1918, he was promoted to lead the AEF's 2nd Division on the WESTERN FRONT in July. Harbord's shortlived command included combat with the French Tenth Army at the Second Battle of the MARNE, where his naive willingness to launch infantry attacks without strong ARTILLERY support attracted unfavourable comment. On 28 July he became head of the AEF's important supply section, acting as Pershing's second in disputes with Army chief of staff MARCH over increased estimates. Harbord's handling of transatlantic logistic challenges was impeccable.

Harmsworth, Alfred See: Lord NORTHCLIFFE.

Haus, Admiral Anton (1851–1917) Operations commander of the AUSTRO-HUNGARIAN NAVY and head of the war ministry's naval section from February 1913 until his death from pneumonia four years later. Generally considered one of Europe's shrewdest naval strategists, Haus recognized that the real value of his battlefleet lay in its continued existence as a deterrent to Allied fleets in the MEDITERRANEAN. He consistently refused to risk major warships in sorties beyond the Adriatic or in support of ground forces on the ITALIAN FRONT, arguing that the danger of major losses outweighed any possible strategic gains. Though one of the few Austro-Hungarian leaders in favour of unrestricted SUBMARINE WARFARE, Haus attracted regular criticism from Germany, but his defensive approach enjoyed the steady support of his own high command and was maintained by Admiral NJEGOVAN, his successor in both posts.

Havrincourt, Battle of Relatively minor engagement fought on the WESTERN FRONT during a lull in the great Allied offensives of 1918. Three divisions of the British Third Army (BYNG) captured the village of Havrincourt from four German divisions on 12 September 1918, a feat that emphasized the GERMAN ARMY's rapidly declining fighting strength (see MAP 2). Along with simultaneous AEF success at ST MIHIEL, and a victory next day at EPÉHY, the action encouraged British C-in-C HAIG to hasten preliminary operations against the HINDENBURG LINE.

Heavy Tanks General term used to describe the earliest Allied TANKS, and the official designation for the five rhomboid-shaped models (Mark I to Mark V) used by the BEF on the WESTERN FRONT. All British 'heavies' were modifications of the original Mark I design, in active service from September 1916, with 'male' (artillery-armed) machines weighing slightly more than 'female' models, which had MACHINE GUNS only. Guide-wheels attached to the rear of early models were quickly abandoned as unnecessary.

The Mark IV and several slightly different Mark V versions, available from mid-1917, had a slightly faster top speed (7.5kph), carried 14mm armour and mounted an extra machine gun on female models. Main armament was carried in side turrets (sponsons).

Cumbersome, vulnerable to ARTILLERY attack, prone to frequent breakdowns, and captured in large numbers whenever British forces were compelled to retreat, combat 'heavies' were eventually used exclusively as a shock weapon at the start of major attacks, with subsequent exploitation left to the slightly more mobile 'WHIPPET' medium tanks. Dozens of heavy tanks were also built without armament for use as supply vehicles.
BRIEF DATA (Mark I) Weight: male 28 tons, female 27 tons; Max Speed: c 6kph; Crew: 8; Max armour: 12mm; Armament: male 2 × 6pdr, 4 × mg, female 5 × mg.

Heinrich, Prince of Prussia (1862–1929) Younger brother of Kaiser WILHELM II and a naval officer from 1877, Heinrich was a respected professional seaman and a major figure in the prewar GERMAN NAVY. He commanded the HIGH SEAS FLEET from 1906 until dismissed in 1909 for opposing the policies of naval minister TIRPITZ. Royal dismissal took the form of promotion to grand admiral and appointment as inspector general to the Navy, but in July 1914 he was given a deliberately marginal role commanding forces in the BALTIC SEA. Frustrated in his efforts to secure a more active role for his forces (he favoured the annexation of Denmark for the purpose of establishing new North Sea bases) Heinrich withdrew to his estates when his command was dissolved on 1 February 1918. Forced to flee in disguise from revolutionary sailors at KIEL in November, he was allowed to remain in postwar GERMANY, and lived in luxurious retirement until his death.

Helgoland The second batch of dreadnoughts built for the GERMAN NAVY, *Helgoland*, *Thüringen*, *Ostfriesland* and *Oldenburg* were completed in 1911–12 with bigger main armament than the previous WESTFALEN Class, but retained a clumsy turret arrangement. All four served with the HIGH SEAS FLEET, playing a minor part in the Battle of JUTLAND but otherwise avoiding conflict with the British GRAND FLEET, and all four were scrapped in 1919.
BRIEF DATA (1914) Displacement: 22,800 tons; Crew: 1,113; Dimensions: length 546ft (165.4m), beam 93.5ft (28.3m); Speed: 21k; Armament: 12 × 12in gun, 14 × 5.9in, 14 × 3.4in, 6 × 19.7in TT.

Heligoland Bight, Battle of The first major naval engagement of the war in the North Sea, initiated in late August 1914 by British light forces as a raid on German DESTROYER patrols off the German naval base on the island of Heligoland. Commodores Tyrwhitt and KEYES, respective commanders of Harwich cruisers and SUBMARINES, planned to attack the destroyers with two light CRUISERS (*FEARLESS* and *ARETHUSA*), 25 destroyers and three submarines. Substantial German forces were to be lured towards another group of submarines supported by the battlecruisers *NEW ZEALAND* and *INVINCIBLE*, then stationed in the Thames Estuary. The Admiralty agreed to the scheme on 24 August, and (without informing Tyrwhitt) gave permission for Admiral BEATTY to bring out his three LION Class battlecruisers from their base at Rosyth.

The raid took place on 28 August, but German naval intelligence was aware of the plan and Tyrwhitt's forces were themselves led to where a strong cruiser force was waiting. The arrival of Beatty's high-speed warships in response to Tyrwhitt's call for help turned the fight, and in the ensuing gun battle they sank the German light cruisers *Köln*, *Mainz* and *Ariadne*, seriously damaged three more and sank a destroyer. On the British side *Arethusa* was badly damaged but was towed safely home.

A minor British victory, secured through Beatty's willingness to risk his BATTLE-CRUISERS in the mine-infested Heligoland Bight, the action revealed deficiencies in ROYAL NAVY operating techniques and staff organization, with units often unaware of each other's presence and mistakenly firing on their own side. See MAP 16.

Helles Area covering the southernmost tip of the Gallipoli Peninsula, invaded by Allied ground forces during the GALLIPOLI LANDINGS of 25 April 1915 (see MAP 20). By the following morning a Turkish defensive line had formed some 5km inside Helles, stretching across the peninsula from the Aegean to the DARDANELLES (about 7km), and this narrow front was the focus of fierce and costly fighting throughout the campaign on the GALLIPOLI FRONT. Though not included in the original British evacuation plan for Gallipoli, Helles was finally abandoned in early January 1916. See KRITHIA; ACHI BABA; SUVLA BAY OFFENSIVE.

Henderson, Arthur (1863–1935) British socialist politician, a veteran trade unionist who entered parliament in 1903 and played a leading role in the organization of the Labour Party as a national political force. A supporter of GREAT BRITAIN's commitment to war against the CENTRAL POWERS, Henderson replaced MACDONALD as Party leader in August 1914 and became the first Labour member of a British cabinet as head of the education board in the ASQUITH coalition from May 1915. In practice he operated as the government's industrial-relations trouble-shooter, working to encourage union cooperation in the expansion of munitions production and soothing disputes over the 'dilution' of skilled workforces with unskilled labour. Although a key member of the LLOYD GEORGE administration from December 1916, and part of the prime minister's inner war cabinet, Henderson remained personally committed to the ideals of internationalism, and was treated with suspicion by right-wing political forces. After visiting RUSSIA in the aftermath of the FEBRUARY REVOLUTION in 1917, he came out strongly in favour of British participation in the STOCKHOLM CONFERENCE of international socialists, prompting scorn in the popular press and his dismissal from the cabinet. He maintained his position as a leading moderate in the British labour movement, returning to office as home secretary in the minority Labour government of 1924, and as foreign secretary from 1929 to 1931. He was awarded the Nobel Peace Prize in 1934 for his work towards international disarmament.

Hentsch, Colonel Richard (1969–1918) See First Battle of the MARNE.

Hermannstadt, Battle of Opening attack of the Austro-German counteroffensive against the ROMANIAN ARMY in Transylvania during the ROMANIAN CAMPAIGN of autumn 1916. The right wing of the Romanian First Army (Curcel), at the centre of the 300km front, had halted its invasion of Transylvania just beyond the Carpathian mountains in mid-September, when its strength was reduced to two infantry divisions by the transfer of forces to the southern border. Isolated and strung out along a difficult supply route, they were attacked either side of Hermannstadt by two corps of FALKENHAYN's German Ninth Army on 27 September. Surprised, unable to call on reserves and unfamiliar with modern weapons, they were driven back into the mountains over the next two days. Further east, another German attack drove part of the Romanian Second Army back into the Predeal Pass, and ARZ VON STRAUSSENBERG's Austro-Hungarian First Army in the north-east pushed the remaining Romanian invaders back into Moldavia by early October. See MAP 14.

Hertling, Georg von (1843–1919) Veteran German Catholic politician and academic philosopher who became minister president of the Bavarian constituent assembly in 1912. A firm opponent of constitutional reform and all types of socialism, he was one of the few major political figures to defend imperial chancellor BETHMANN HOLLWEG's position in July 1917, and was considered a candidate for the succession. Personally anxious to remain in Bavaria, Hertling reluctantly accepted the chancellorship after the resignation of MICHAELIS, taking office on 1 November 1917. He proved unwilling to cooperate with reformists in the Reichstag, and was unable to influence the THIRD SUPREME COMMAND. He resigned gratefully at the generals' behest on 3 October 1918 and retired to his estate in Bavaria.

Highflyer Typical of the 26 old 'heavy protected' CRUISERS (over 5,000 tons) still in ROYAL NAVY service in August 1914, *Highflyer* was at Gibraltar in 1914, crippling the German ARMED MERCHANT CRUISER *Kaiser Wilhelm der Große* on 27 August. It later served as British flagship in the West Indies, and a sister ship, *Hyacinth*, was stationed in EAST AFRICA throughout the War. The other Highflyer Class vessel, *Hermes*, was converted as an AIRCRAFT CARRIER in 1913.

BRIEF DATA (*Highflyer*, 1914) Displacement: 5,600 tons; Crew: 450; Dimensions: length 370ft (112.1m), beam 54ft (16.4m); Speed: 20k; Armament: 11 × 6in gun, 9 × 12pdr, 2 × 18in TT.

High Seas Fleet The main battle formation of the GERMAN NAVY, a powerful force of 27 modern BATTLESHIPS and BATTLECRUISERS, a mixture of old and new CRUISERS, and supporting smaller craft. Developed as a direct challenge to the ROYAL NAVY's anticipated close BLOCKADE of GERMANY, it was not regarded as capable of defeating the whole British GRAND FLEET in 1914 and its main wartime strategy was to whittle down British strength before any large-scale confrontation was attempted.

This limited aggression was abandoned after the fleet suffered heavy damage at JUTLAND in May 1916. Kaiser WILHELM II personally forbade the taking of further risks, German investment in surface warships declined, and North Sea operations were subsequently restricted to occasional limited sweeps against Allied CONVOY escorts.

Although the geographical position of its bases enabled the Fleet to operate periodically in the eastern BALTIC, its major warships were of limited value in a theatre dominated by MINES and light forces (see Operation ALBION). Idle and neglected, spartan and uncomfortable, the warships became fertile breeding grounds for revolutionary socialism, and were subject to frequent outbreaks of indiscipline from mid-1917.

In late October 1918 the Fleet was ordered to undertake a suicidal mass attack on the British Grand Fleet, but was paralysed by the large-scale KIEL MUTINY and remained in a state of revolutionary chaos at the ARMISTICE. Sufficient order was restored for the Fleet to steam to Scotland by 21 November, and it was formally surrendered in the Firth of Forth that day. Most old or small ships were scrapped or converted for postwar minesweeping, but modern units were taken to Scapa Flow where, still manned by German skeleton crews, they conspired to scuttle themselves on 21 June 1919. See also: NAVAL WARFARE.

Hill 60, Battle for A final British attempt to break out of ANZAC COVE on the GALLIPOLI FRONT. Taking the form of a northeasterly attack on the important Turkish position of Hill 60, it was conceived in support of General de Lisle's attack on SCIMITAR HILL of 21 August 1915. Named after its height in metres (like many frontline landmarks), Hill 60 was the only substantial rise in an otherwise flat area separating the Anzac and SUVLA positions. Battle losses, sickness and exhaustion meant that Anzac Cove commander BIRDWOOD could only mount a limited attack, using a composite force of about 3,000 reasonably fit troops under General Cox.

Detailed reconnaissance was impossible under heavy fire and in thick scrubland, but it was assumed that the ring of Turkish trenches on Hill 60 commanded its summit. Attacks against the hill's western slopes from the evening of 21 August captured only preliminary trenches and suffered heavy losses to flanking fire until 27 August, when Cox launched another full-scale assault. The Turkish ring fell after 36 hours of intense trench fighting, but was overlooked from the east by a second, equally formidable Turkish line. Birdwood abandoned further offensive operations with the loss of 2,500 men. See MAP 20.

Hindenburg, Field Marshal Paul von Beneckendorf und von (1847–1934) German infantry officer, retired in 1911 after a solid but unspectacular career but recalled to replace General von PRITTWITZ in EAST PRUSSIA on 22 August 1914. He arrived at the front 24 hours later, meeting new chief of staff LUDENDORFF for the first time en route.

He played little active part in the immediate victory at TANNENBERG, planned in advance by Colonel HOFFMANN's Eighth Army staff and executed under Ludendorff's control, but was hailed as its hero in GERMANY, an impression multiplied by PROPAGANDA after the less conclusive MASURIAN LAKES battle. In November 1914 the 'saviour of East Prussia' was promoted field marshal and given command over all German forces on the EASTERN FRONT.

Hindenburg's greatest military attributes were stately appearance and imperturbable calm under pressure, interpreted as vacuity by some commentators. Though well known in military circles, his dependence on Ludendorff for major decisions was not popularly recognized. Ludendorff's energetic campaign to present limited offensive successes in the east as great victories, denied decisive reinforcement by Army chief of staff FALKENHAYN, served to cement his chief's reputation as the greatest living German.

Hindenburg became GERMAN ARMY chief of staff from 29 August 1916, a move prepared in advance by right-wing interests as military failures made Falkenhayn's position untenable. With Ludendorff at his side as quartermaster general, Hindenburg was the symbol behind which the THIRD SUPREME COMMAND established a militarist dictatorship. Central control of socioeconomic resources by the Army and heavy industry was carried out under the HINDENBURG PROGRAMME, and he occasionally used the threat of resignation to override bureaucratic or royal opposition. Though he approved the Supreme Command's annexationist war aims, and was in favour of unrestricted SUBMARINE WARFARE, he made little effort to instigate policy.

A paragon of stoicism, he remained at his post despite Ludendorff's resignation in late October 1918, and proved equally amenable to the instructions of his successor, General GRÖNER. He retired from active service, still generally revered, in June 1919 and subsequently cooperated with Ludendorff in the mythologizing of recent German history. Elected president of the German republic in 1925, he played a characteristically passive role in the appointment of Adolf Hitler as chancellor in 1933.

Hindenburg Line System of German defensive fortifications built behind northern and central sectors of the WESTERN FRONT from September 1916 and still under construction when it was overrun by Allied forces in autumn 1918. One of the first actions taken by the new German command team of HINDENBURG and LUDENDORFF, the decision to build the defences was a major turning point in German military thinking, which had hitherto rested on the assumption of further advances in France.

The term 'Line' was a British misnomer for a system of linked fortified areas stretching behind the Western Front from the northern coast to Verdun, and extending to a depth of up to 15km. Each area or 'position' (*Stellung*) had its own intricate system of mutually supporting strongpoints festooned with barbed wire, trenchworks and firepower.

The Wotan Stellung covered the Front from the coast to Cambrai; Siegfried Stellung, the oldest and most complex section of the system, stretched south about 65km to the St Quentin area; Alberich Stellung covered the next sector about as far south as Laon; Brunhilde protected the Front in Champagne; and the last and least developed segment,

Kriemhilde Stellung, stood behind the Argonne Forest and extended to Metz (see MAP 2).

German withdrawal to the central sector of the Line disrupted Allied offensive plans in 1917 (see NIVELLE OFFENSIVE; Operation ALBERICH), and the German SPRING OFFENSIVES of 1918 temporarily advanced the front far beyond some sectors, but the Allied offensives of autumn 1918 brought them up to its outposts all along the front.

The British First Army (HORNE) had taken the Wotan position as early as 2 September. Victories at AMIENS and ALBERT by HAIG's army group had culminated in the capture of forward positions in front of Siegfried around EPÉHY on 18 September. By late September these forces were ready to assault the main Siegfried position, and the US-French MEUSE-ARGONNE OFFENSIVE was poised to attack the Kriemhilde position to the southeast.

Allied commanders were aware that they faced a major obstacle and foresaw heavy casualties, with equally unpleasant political repercussions in the event of failure. Informed German opinion recognized that the Line represented the only realistic hope of halting the Allied advance on foreign soil, and that the GERMAN ARMY was close to disintegration.

Overall planning by Allied supreme commander FOCH was largely a matter of improvising around plans formulated at army or corps level. The Argonne offensive got underway on 26 September, targeted at the railway junction town of Mézières, but attacks by Haig's four armies (three British and one French) against the crucial Siegfried Stellung came to individual fruition over the next few days.

The Argonne Offensive soon became bogged down in difficult terrain, but the British First Army won a costly victory at the CANAL DU NORD on 27 September. King ALBERT's predominantly Anglo-Belgian Flanders Group launched its own successful COURTRAI OFFENSIVE in the north the following day, and the British Fourth Army (RAWLINSON) stormed the strongest section of Siegfried at the ST QUENTIN CANAL on 29 September, effectively breaching the Line beyond repair.

Although it took a concentration of four British armies (Fourth, Third, First and Fifth) and the French First Army until 5 October to finally clear the Hindenburg Line, Siegfried's collapse sealed the German THIRD SUPREME COMMAND's final acceptance of the need for an ARMISTICE (see GERMANY). With no remotely comparable fortifications to fall back on, retreat became the only military option available to the GERMAN ARMY. See CAMBRAI OFFENSIVE.

Hindenburg Programme The constitutional means by which the THIRD SUPREME COMMAND in GERMANY imposed a virtual dictatorship over Germany from autumn 1916. The basis of the programme was total subordination of German socioeconomic life to a massive increase in military production, prompted by the growth in Allied arms output revealed during the VERDUN and SOMME battles on the WESTERN FRONT.

First put before the Prussian war ministry on 31 August 1916, two days after HINDENBURG's appointment as GERMAN ARMY chief of staff, it was enacted by an acquiescent Kaiser WILHELM II using the far-reaching Prussian Siege Law for emergency national defence. The Programme demanded tripled MACHINE GUN production, doubled output of ammunition, and similarly huge increases in the production of MORTARS, ARTILLERY, aircraft, and the materials for TRENCH WARFARE.

All suitable factories were turned over to war work. Unsuitable or inefficient firms were starved of labour and materials before being closed down by an 'Integration of Factories' committee. The Patriotic Service Law (December 1916) conscripted all able-bodied males not already fighting to work in designated vital industries, and attempted the systematic recruitment of WOMEN for the first time. This had little effect on a labour resource already stretched to the limit, and the policy of deporting workers from BELGIUM and POLAND proved both impractical and diplomatically damaging (see MERCIER, J.).

Distribution of all raw materials was controlled centrally by the Supreme War Bureau, led by General GRÖNER and effectively an organ of the Supreme Command. It took over the functions of both the KRA and the arms procurement bureau, pouring resources unreservedly into the development of heavy industry. Lavish plans were laid for new factories, roads and other developments without regard for feasibility.

The German economy buckled almost immediately under the strain. Failure to find untapped labour resources forced the Army to release more than 1.2 million skilled workers from service in September, and almost 2 million more the following July. The virtual seizing up of the RAILWAY system, exacerbated by the demands of the ROMANIAN CAMPAIGN, was delaying vital coal deliveries by October, after which a cold winter brought urban starvation and political opposition. By spring 1917 few major production increases had been achieved.

Short-term output improved with the decision, in February 1917, to cut back expenditure on investment programmes, and some targets had been reached by autumn 1917, notably those for machine guns and light artillery. The effort was clearly unsustainable, but the Supreme Command preferred a gamble on total military victory to the certainty of revolution without it. Gröner's pragmatic attempt to curtail manufacturers' profits in mid-1917 secured only his dismissal, and industrial interests blocked Ludendorff's similar move the following July. Desperate faith in final victory kept the Programme going long after its aims had become fantasies, culminating in a massive SUBMARINE construction scheme authorized in September 1918.

Hipper, Admiral Franz von (1863–1932) Commander of BATTLECRUISERS with the German HIGH SEAS FLEET in August 1914. As the Fleet's forward strike force, his ships were deployed on coastal raids against eastern England, notably at SCARBOROUGH in December 1914, earning notoriety in the Allied press as 'Hipper's babykillers'. Strenuous British efforts to intercept Hipper almost succeeded at the DOGGER BANK in January 1915, and his battlecruisers were at the heart of fighting at JUTLAND in 1916. In August 1918 he took over the High Seas Fleet from SCHEER, who became head of a new GERMAN NAVY Supreme Command (see THIRD SUPREME COMMAND). In October Hipper planned a last sortie of the entire Fleet against the British GRAND FLEET, a suicide mission that triggered the KIEL MUTINY. After failing to rally sailors against Prince MAX VON BADEN's government, he presided over the Fleet's surrender before retiring from active service in December 1918.

Hoffmann, General Maximilian (1869–1927) Pragmatic and confident German staff officer who performed a crucial planning role throughout the war on the EASTERN FRONT. As colonel in charge of military operations with the Eighth Army (PRITTWITZ), he had already formulated the battleplan used at TANNENBERG by the time the new command team of HINDENBURG and LUDENDORFF arrived on 23 August 1914. He remained as Ludendorff's deputy for the next two years, planning a series of tactical successes in 1915 that established the popular reputations of his immediate superiors.

Hoffmann became Prince LEOPOLD's chief of staff for the whole theatre when Hindenburg was given supreme command of German forces in August 1916. He effectively controlled strategy during the latter stages of the war with RUSSIA, indirectly sponsoring the OCTOBER REVOLUTION by arranging the return to Petrograd (St Petersburg) of exiled socialist leaders (including LENIN), and by suspending attacks after success at RIGA in September 1917 threatened to revive patriotic Russian unity. He negotiated the BREST-LITOVSK Treaty signed in March 1918, with the Bolshevik government, and remained to oversee its implementation until the ARMISTICE in November.

Holtzendorff, Admiral Henning von (1853–1919) Commander of the German HIGH SEAS FLEET from 1909, with SCHEER as his chief of staff, Holtzendorff opposed the GERMAN NAVY's rapid prewar expansion by TIRPITZ and argued against concentration of strength against the British GRAND FLEET in the North Sea. Manoeuvred into resignation in 1913, he was in retirement until recalled as head of the naval General Staff (*Admiralstab*) in spring 1915. An important convert to unrestricted SUBMARINE WARFARE during the year, he was guilty of exaggerating its potential effects on GREAT BRITAIN's capacity to wage war, and of ignoring evidence to the contrary. In December 1916 he was responsible for the influential memorandum suggesting a full campaign would bring victory in six months, and the relative failure of the subsequent unrestricted campaign undermined his position. After arguments with the THIRD SUPREME COMMAND over war aims and production priorities, he was superseded by Scheer's new Naval Supreme Command in August 1918 and effectively retired.

Home Fronts Contemporary term reflecting the extension of warfare to civilian life from 1914. See: Introduction; AUSTRIA-HUNGARY; GREAT BRITAIN; FRANCE; GERMANY; ITALY; RUSSIA; TURKEY; UNITED STATES; and entries for other belligerent states.

Honduras Central American republic, ravaged by internal turmoil throughout the early 20th century, and policed by US Marines from 1912. Economically dependent on US trade and investment, the right-wing government of Francisco Bertrand obediently joined the UNITED STATES in war, breaking off diplomatic relations with GERMANY on 17 May 1917. War was formally declared the following July, but the country's 500 troops were fully occupied at home and its only active contribution was confiscation of German assets.

Hood, Admiral Horace (1870–1916) One of the youngest admirals in the ROYAL NAVY, and generally considered one of its best, Hood succeeded Admiral BEATTY as naval secretary to Winston CHURCHILL in 1913 and accompanied his chief to ANTWERP in October 1914. Later that month he took command of the light forces at Dover, then actively engaged in defence of FLANDERS, before transferring to the GRAND FLEET the following summer as commander of the Third Battlecruiser Squadron. The Squadron formed Admiral JELLICOE's heavy scouting force during the Battle of JUTLAND, and Hood was the most senior casualty of the action, killed when his flagship, *INVINCIBLE*, exploded and sank under fire from German BATTLECRUISERS.

Horthy de Nagybánya, Admiral Miklós (1868–1957) Hungarian naval officer who became captain of the new fast cruiser *NOVARA* in late 1914, taking part in several surface actions that confirmed his reputation as one of the AUSTRO-HUNGARIAN NAVY's most aggressive leaders. Horthy probably planned the raid that sparked the OTRANTO STRAITS action in May 1917, from which he emerged with great credit. In March 1918, following mutiny at CATTARO and the resignation of Admiral NJEGOVAN, Horthy was promoted rear admiral and appointed C-in-C of the battlefleet over the heads of many more senior officers.

Chosen to revitalize a service generally regarded as war weary, he maintained his predecessors' concern to protect the fleet as a deterrent, but was anxious to improve morale by responding to raids by Italian light forces. His only major offensive operation, against the OTRANTO BARRAGE in June 1918, was abandoned after loss of the dreadnought *SZENT ISTVÁN*, but Horthy preserved the loyalty of his fleet until the disintegration of AUSTRO-HUNGARY. On 31 October 1918, on orders from KARL I, he handed over the fleet to the South Slav (Yugoslav) National Council. Returning to Hungary, he organized and led the anti-Communist uprising at Szeged against the new government of Béla Kun, entering Budapest in November 1919 and becoming regent in March 1920, a post he held until 1944.

Hotchkiss Gun The FRENCH ARMY's standard wartime heavy MACHINE GUN, although by no means the only type used (see ST ÉTIENNE GUN). A reliable 8mm weapon, weighing 40–50kg, it was available in several marks, starting in 1900 and culminating in the air-cooled 1914 model. Its greatest weakness, a metal strip magazine holding only 24–30 cartridges, was replaced by a 249-shot metal belt after 1915. The weapon was also used by the AEF on the WESTERN FRONT and by Allied Balkan armies.

Only about 2,200 heavy machine guns were in French Army service at the start of the War, and despite their growing importance in TRENCH WARFARE conditions on the Western Front no more than 19,000 were in service at the ARMISTICE, reflecting concentration on light weapons such as the 1915 CHAUCHAT.

A lighter (12kg) version of the Hotchkiss, available since 1909, was designed as an infantry assault weapon but proved too bulky for portable use in 1914. It was later restricted to second-line defensive positions, but stripped-down models were regularly fitted to Allied aircraft and TANKS.

House, 'Colonel' Edward (1858–1938) Texas Democrat politician and former plantation owner (the military title was a nickname) who became Woodrow WILSON's most intimate political advisor after supporting his successful bid for the US presidency in 1912. His self-confident enthusiasm for international affairs focused first on Latin America, but he acted as Wilson's principal intermediary at home and in Europe after August 1914.

An early advocate of the 'limited preparedness' adopted by the president in late 1915, he was central to Wilson's recruitment of support from moderate reformers like Walter LIPPMANN. House visited European capitals as Wilson's emissary in 1915 and 1916, reaching agreement with British foreign secretary GREY in February 1916 to call GERMANY to a peace conference on pain of US military intervention. The arrangement was quickly vetoed by the British government, and House was unable to elicit positive responses to Wilson's PEACE NOTE in December.

Along with Wilson and Lippmann, House was responsible for drafting the FOURTEEN POINTS peace programme unveiled in January 1918, and he helped modify it for provisional acceptance by the Allies before the ARMISTICE agreement. His diplomatic shortcomings were exposed at the PARIS PEACE CONFERENCE, and he could only urge compromise with Anglo-French national interests. Unable to persuade the president to bend before powerful US opposition to ratification of the peace treaties, he broke relations with Wilson permanently from June 1919 after a private dispute that was never explained.

Hughes, William (1864–1952) Welsh barrister who emigrated to AUSTRALIA in 1884 and entered the New South Wales state parliament a decade later. He joined the first commonwealth parliament in 1901 and became Attorney General in 1910, before assuming leadership of the Labour Party and becoming prime minister on the resignation of Andrew FISHER in October 1915. A firm advocate of increased self-representation for the white dominions of the British Empire, but a committed supporter of wartime imperial policy, he was regarded as a major international figure in London but as a powerful political bully in Australia, suspected of ignoring national sentiment to retain favour with the British. Splitting and then quitting the Labour Party over the conscription issue in 1916, he remained in office at the head of two consecutive coalition governments until 1923. His forceful claims for Australian MANDATES in the Pacific, and a white supremacist attitude to international relations, caused considerable resentment at the PARIS PEACE CONFERENCE.

Huj, Battle of See: BEERSHEBA–GAZA LINE.

Human Torpedoes The idea of attaching a motor and a crew to a TORPEDO, enabling it to be guided until it was very close to its target, had been tried with some success during the American Civil War (1861–65), and was considered by all the major combatant navies after 1914. The ITALIAN NAVY, which invested most of its attacking energies in operations by light forces, pioneered the practical wartime use of human torpedoes in 1918, carrying out several attacks on major Austro-Hungarian naval bases. Essentially floating warheads, piloted by a two-man crew sitting astride the weapon, human torpedoes were towed as close as possible to the shore by DESTROYERS or SUBMARINES, and delivered their attacks at night. Although most attacks were spotted by defenders or snared in protective booms, human torpedoes scored one major success, sinking the Austro-Hungarian dreadnought *VIRIBUS UNITIS* in Pola (Pula) harbour on the night of 31 October 1918. Despite the fact that it was carried out against almost undefended installations, the raid helped cement the high reputation enjoyed by Italian light forces, and encouraged widespread development of human torpedoes (and midget submarines) in Italy and elsewhere during the arms build-up before the Second World War.

Hungary See: AUSTRIA-HUNGARY.

Hussarek von Heinlein, Max, Baron (1865–1935) Law professor who served as Austrian education minister under successive governments from 1911 until his appointment to succeed CLAM-MARTINIC as prime minister in July 1917. His attempt to find a peaceful constitutional means of reconciling separatist nationalities within AUSTRIA-HUNGARY, endorsed by Emperor KARL I in the OCTOBER MANIFESTO of 1918, met with opposition from Hungarian premier WEKERLE and representatives of nationalist groups. The defeat of the Manifesto brought Hussarek's resignation on 27 October, and he returned to an academic career in Vienna.

Hussein Ibn Ali, Sherif (1854–1931) Wily tribal ruler of the southern Hejaz region, on the Red Sea coast of central Arabia, and politico-religious figurehead of the independence movement that culminated in the ARAB REVOLT. The acknowledged senior Islamic Sherif (direct descendant of Mohammed's daughter), he was one of few genuine rivals to the Sultan of TURKEY as the faith's spiritual leader, and his domain included the holy cities of Mecca and MEDINA.

After 18 years of 'protective' custody in Constantinople, Hussein and his sons were released by the YOUNG TURK regime in 1908. Relations with the new government soon cooled and by 1914 he was working towards independence for the Hejaz. During 1914–15, Hussein used his sons to establish contact with British forces in EGYPT, and with secret Arab nationalist elements in Damascus. Once the Revolt began Hussein remained in his heartland, collecting tributes as the self-styled 'King of the Hejaz', while his sons Ali, FEISAL, ABDULLAH and Zeid served as field commanders. King Hussein received an annual British subsidy until forced to abdicate in favour of Ali in 1924, and was exiled to Cyprus after Ibn SAUD's successful coup in 1931.

Hutier, General Oskar von (1857–1934) Prussian officer who led XXI Corps on the EASTERN FRONT from April 1915 and two years later took over the Eighth Army around RIGA. Attacking on 1 September 1917, at the start of the final German northern offensive against Russia, von Hutier surprised defenders and took the city by employing new INFILTRATION TACTICS, subsequently known as 'Hutier tactics' within the GERMAN ARMY and widely adopted on other fronts. Transferred to the WESTERN FRONT with the new Eighteenth Army in October, von Hutier repeated his tactics to great initial effect during the KAISERSCHLACHT Offensive of March 1918, and succeeded temporarily at the MATZ in June before his army was thrown onto the defensive.

Hydrophones See: ANTI-SUBMARINE WEAPONS.

Hymans, Paul (1865–1941) Belgian Liberal Party politician who led a diplomatic mission to the UNITED STATES on behalf of a coalition cabinet in August 1914. His success in securing political support and humanitarian aid from Washington brought appointment as ambassador to GREAT BRITAIN in February 1915, where he worked to counter King ALBERT I's refusal of full alliance with the Entente powers and coordinated the alternative Declaration of SAINTE-ADDRESSE (February 1916).

Hymans was recalled to join the cabinet at Le Havre as finance minister in October 1917, reflecting hardening political opposition to royal hopes of a separate peace with GERMANY, and he replaced de BROQUEVILLE as foreign secretary the following January. Strongly associated with Belgian nationalist hopes of expansion into LUXEMBOURG and the

Netherlands, his support for close cooperation with the Allies dominated foreign policy through 1918.

Hymans led the Belgian delegation seeking REPARATIONS at the PARIS PEACE CONFERENCE, where his efforts to gain greater representation for small nations at the LEAGUE OF NATIONS were largely ignored but influenced his appointment as its first president in 1919.

I

Ibn Saud, Abdul Aziz (1880–1953) Arab head of the conservative, puritanical Wahabi sect, and ruler of the isolated central-Arabian Sultanate of Najd, based on Riyadh. Exiled by the Turks as a child but restored by a Bedouin revolt in 1902, he expanded his territory in 1913 by conquering the Gulf province of Al Hasa. Hostile to both British and Ottoman imperialism, the Wahabis regarded other tribal powers in Arabia as heretics, particularly the Sherifians of HUSSEIN IBN ALI and the Shammar tribes of southern Syria. Though Saud remained outside the ARAB REVOLT from 1916 he recognized the need to support the winning side, accepting British assistance and undertaking minor raids against Turkish forces, but his main wartime activity was an attack against the pro-Turkish Shammar Confederacy. Saud became the most powerful postwar figure in Arabia, ousting Hussein Ibn Ali from the Hejaz region in 1931, and renaming his expanded kingdom Saudi Arabia in 1932.

Immelmann, Max (1890–1916) German FIGHTER pilot, an ACE with 15 victories when he was killed on 18 June 1916. A friend and rival of Oswald BOELCKE, he was best known for the invention of the 'Immelmann turn', a simultaneous loop and roll that became a standard DOGFIGHT manoeuvre.

Imperatrica Maria The first modern BATTLESHIP to operate in the BLACK SEA, and the first of three ordered for the RUSSIAN NAVY in 1911, *Imperatrica Maria* finally reached active service in July 1915 and began offensive patrols in October. Used less sparingly than the newer battleships of other navies, it screened minelayers, bombarded coastal installations and covered troop landings. From Christmas 1915 it was joined by the second ship, *Imperatrica Ekatarina II.*

Well-protected aginainst MINES and capable of outgunning any other ship in the theatre, they were withdrawn whenever SUBMARINES threatened and lacked the speed to pin down their main surface quarry, *GOEBEN*. Though never damaged in action, *Imperatrica Maria* sank in Sevastopol harbour after its magazines exploded on 20 October 1916, probably a result of inadequate protection against 'flash' fires (see *VANGUARD*). After the FEBRUARY REVOLUTION in 1917, *Imperatrica Ekatarina II* continued operations as the *Svobodnaia Rossia*, and was sunk by a Russian destroyer in June 1918 to prevent it falling into German hands. The third ship (*Imperator Aleksandr III*, later the *Volya*) reached the Black Sea in 1918. Taken over by the GERMAN NAVY in October, it saw no active wartime service.

BRIEF DATA (*Imperatrica Maria*, 1915) Displacement: 22,600 tons; Crew: 1,252; Dimensions: length 167m, beam 27.1m; Speed: 21.5k; Main armament: 12 × 12in gun, 20 × 130mm, 4 × 75mm AA, 4 × 18in TT.

Indefatigable Name ship of a class of three British BATTLECRUISERS completed in early 1911 (see *AUSTRALIA; NEW ZEALAND*). Deployed in the MEDITERRANEAN in August 1914, *Indefatigable* took part in the DARDANELLES operation before joining the GRAND FLEET in home waters, and was sunk when 11-inch gunfire from the German battlecruiser *VON DER TANN* caused a magazine explosion at JUTLAND. More than 1,000 of its swollen battle complement were killed.

BRIEF DATA (1914) Displacement: 18,750 tons; Crew: 800; Dimensions: length 590ft (178.8m), beam 80ft (24.2m); Speed: 27k; Armament: 8 × 12in gun, 16 × 4in, 3 × 21in TT.

Independent Air Force The STRATEGIC BOMBING arm of the RAF, formed in June 1918 to carry out mass raids on industrial and military targets deep inside Germany, and independent of ground commanders' immediate tactical needs. Led by Major General TRENCHARD, Britain's most strident advocate of strategic bombing, it comprised four squadrons of day bombers and five of night bombers by August and was expanded throughout over the next four months.

Stationed at various airfields in eastern France, the Force dropped some 350,000 tons of bombs in 162 raids, and was used in conjunction with other large Allied formations as an independent command during major ground offensives on the WESTERN FRONT. Long-range raids faced vastly improved ANTI-AIRCRAFT defences in 1918, and the Force suffered heavy losses, with 153 pilots and 194 other aircrew killed or missing. Plans to add Italian, US and Belgian units to Trenchard's strength were halted by the ARMISTICE.

India British administration of imperial India, generally regarded as the Empire's most important outpost, was a bureaucratic superstructure overlaying hundreds of ethnically, religiously and linguistically divided states, kingdoms and principalities of every size. India's 320 million population was in no sense one nation, and its Hindu majority was further divided along strict caste lines. British dominion, or Raj, operated as a superimposed dominant caste working in alliance with existing administrative classes to maintain order and providing developmental benefits in return for economic exploitation.

British King GEORGE V was Emperor of India, ruling through an appointed viceroy who liaised with GREAT BRITAIN via the cabinet minister for India. The viceroy, resident in New Delhi and Simla, appointed his own cabinet from about 6,500 British officials, and native bureaucrats filled the vast majority of minor posts. Almost two-thirds of the subcontinent's 4.5 million square kilometres was directly controlled by the viceregal regime, divided into 13 major provinces. The remainder comprised about 700 autonomous states, some of them very small, ruled by hereditary princes giving direct allegiance to the King-Emperor.

British rule was generally accepted with enthusiasm by the Hindu upper castes, but emergence of an educated native political class brought increasing pressure for Indian participation in decision making. The establishment of purely advisory elected institutions from 1909 provided a platform for a more concerted campaign by the Indian National Congress (founded in 1885), which was not inherently anti-British in 1914 and generally treated war in Europe as an opportunity to prove its fitness for responsible self-government.

Large Muslim communities in northeast and northwest India posed a greater direct threat to British control and public order. Violent clashes with neighbouring Hindu communities were commonplace in Bengal, and Muslim political leaders veered between support for the limited aims of Congress and demands for full independence.

Local violence was endemic to the subcontinent, and the British-led INDIAN ARMY (supplemented by 'Imperial Service' troops from the autonomous princedoms) was regularly called upon to quell minor uprisings. The warlike Muslim peoples of the northwest frontier region dominated native recruitment to the peacetime army (along with 'martial' Sikhs), but also caused the most serious and frequent trouble, especially near the northwestern borders with AFGHANISTAN and PERSIA.

Prewar colonial administrators, led by viceroy Lord Hardinge (1910–16), tended to overestimate the revolutionary potential of Congress and assumed that war in Europe would encourage concerted Muslim uprisings, especially if TURKEY was among the opponents. In the event the northwest frontier experienced fewer uprisings than usual, and sporadic German attempts to supply Muslim revolutionary cells in Bengal achieved nothing.

After giving itself wider powers of arrest and law enforcement with the Defence of India Act (1915), Hardinge's administration only gradually accepted a sense of relative security. Its initial reluctance to part with men and equipment for expeditions to EAST AFRICA and the MESOPOTAMIAN FRONT – which were under Indian government control until 1916 – contributed to defeats in both theatres, but later British criticism tended to overlook cutbacks forced on the Indian Army by the rapid prewar reform of the BRITISH ARMY.

Some extra wartime demand for Indian exports, particularly in JAPAN, was balanced by loss of trade with GERMANY, but a rise in British demand for cotton and jute (and ultimately for manufactured sandbags) created a minor boom in both of India's main industries. The small iron and steel industry also experienced unlimited demand for shells and RAILWAY materials (India had 56,000km of lines in 1914), but the overall effect was minimal on an economy almost wholly diffused into village units.

The support given to Britain by more than half a million Indian troops and the native bureaucracy as a whole was partially rewarded by the introduction of provincial Indian assemblies in 1919, but their strictly limited powers, viewed by Indian political elites as a poor reward for demonstrated loyalty, stimulated more militant nationalism in the 1920s.

Indian Army Like the bureaucratic administration of INDIA itself, the Indian Army was a largely native force drawn from volunteers throughout the subcontinent but officered and controlled by the British. Primarily dedicated to internal policing and the defence of India's troublesome northwest frontier with AFGHANISTAN, it had been organized along regional lines until the late 19th century, but reforms instigated by C-in-C KITCHENER (1902–09) had produced a national field army of 10 divisions (155,000 men) backed by an internal security force of some 80,000 troops.

About a quarter of infantry and CAVALRY troops, and almost all ARTILLERY personnel, were British, ensuring loyalty and encouraging European standards in native units. Indian Army officers, though British, were generally specialists in colonial warfare and multi-ethnic man-management, but were less familiar with the latest European technology and techniques. Most serving Indians came from the subcontinent's traditionally warlike cultures: Punjabi troops comprised about half of all native strength, and Nepalese Gurkha units were considered the Army's fighting elite. Prewar estimates allowed for two divisions and a cavalry brigade to fight overseas, but the Army as a whole was designed for colonial skirmishes. Starved of funds by British concentration on home forces, it was poorly equipped by European standards.

The Army remained ultimately under British strategic control, and Indian administration fears for frontier security were overruled to provide troops on the WESTERN, MESOPOTAMIAN, GALLIPOLI and PALESTINE FRONTS, as well as in EAST AFRICA and EGYPT. The Indian Army as a whole contained 573,000 men by November 1918, and more than 1.3 million men served during wartime, of whom about 72,000 were killed. The relative tranquillity of internal affairs enabled home forces, largely comprising British reservists, to be reduced to 15,000–20,000 troops for much of the War.

Indian troops displayed a consistently high degree of loyalty to the British Empire, despite the prejudiced views of some British officers, occasional skirmishes between hostile units, and doubts about the willingness of Muslims to fight Turkish forces in the Middle East. Militarily, their least successful operations were on the Western Front, where the Indian Corps (two divisions and a cavalry brigade) served from September 1914 and suffered enormous casualties before the infantry were withdrawn to other theatres in late 1915. Loss of British Indian Army officers, and a shortage of sympathetic replacements, contributed to a collapse of morale on the Western Front not repeated under appalling conditions in Mesopotamia and at Gallipoli.

Indian Army forces remained under Indian government authority until they entered a

British theatre of war, when they came under the command of the senior British officer. The exceptions were Mesopotamia and East Africa, where operations under purely Indian control (until 1916) suffered from poor logistic and technical support. Although it operated primarily in 'SIDESHOWS', the Indian Army was a valuable manpower asset to the Allies, and its contribution added weight to postwar claims for native political representation in India. See also: SINGAPORE MUTINY.

Indicator Nets The only proven means of detecting a submerged SUBMARINE in August 1914. Adapted from the light steel nets used by Japanese whalers, they were originally strung around major naval bases but were adapted from early 1915 to augment ANTI-SUBMARINE measures in narrow seaways, most notably the Allied barrages at DOVER and OTRANTO. Dropped from drifters (small fishing boats), which remained on watch and in RADIO contact with patrolling warships, indicator nets for barrages were up to 100 metres long, set at various depths and weighted or moored to the seabed. An entangled submarine would either be forced to surface or drag attached marker buoys wherever it went. Small numbers of MINES were also fixed to most nets. U-boats could avoid indicator nets by passing them on the surface in darkness, or diving through gaps caused by a shortage of drifters or poor station-keeping. Skilled submariners could normally disentangle boats from nets without serious damage, and when a boat was indicated there was at first no way of attacking it underwater (see DEPTH CHARGES).

Infantry Tactics The many and varied functions of prewar foot soldiers included defence of static positions and occupation of other areas under military control, but the universal assumption that a future war would be won by a successful opening offensive meant that their most important role in 1914 was as an army's basic assault weapon.

Small professional forces, such as the prewar BRITISH ARMY and US ARMY, were able to concentrate training on precise uniformity of manoeuvre, a high standard of RIFLE competence and other detailed aspects of infantry advance, but leaders of the mass conscript armies in continental Europe were required to focus on more basic problems of propelling vast numbers of relatively untrained troops forward as quickly and effectively as possible.

French and German doctrine dominated European infantry tactics before 1914, and was copied or adapted by all the other continental armies. The FRENCH ARMY's theory of *élan* (or *offensive à l'outrance*) placed great emphasis on the psychological effect of massed BAYONET charges supported by CAVALRY and mobile 'SOIXANTE-QUINZE' field ARTILLERY. Infantry was to be sent into action without equipment for entrenchment or other defensive manoeuvres, on the grounds that repeated waves of massed assault were irresistible if delivered with sufficient speed and aggression. The GERMAN ARMY, which expected to attack well-protected FORTRESSES in Belgium, France and Russia, planned its infantry advances more cautiously, providing field armies with heavier artillery support, MORTARS, and other equipment for breaking down established defences.

All prewar infantry tactics had failed to anticipate the enormous advantages bestowed on well-fortified defenders by MACHINE GUNS and static artillery support, but the lesson was quickly driven home during the opening engagements on the WESTERN FRONT. German troops were cut to pieces when they attempted to storm the fortresses at LIÈGE in August 1914, and terrible losses suffered by French infantry charges during the Battles of the FRONTIERS were multiplied by defensive naivety. By the end of 1914 both sides on the WESTERN and EASTERN FRONTS had discovered that TRENCHES provided highly effective defence against direct infantry attack, and the tactical struggle over the next four years revolved around the problem of overcoming them.

The search for a means by which infantry could perform its planned assault role was led by field commanders on the congested Western Front. Attacks involving mass conscript armies in confined areas could hardly be planned in detail beyond their opening exchanges, and the conditions of TRENCH

WARFARE meant that any advance into hostile territory was subject to almost inevitable communications breakdown, so that commanders were encouraged to keep offensive tactics very simple.

Their first response was BREAKTHROUGH TACTICS, the concentration of greater numbers of men and maximum available artillery along a narrow front in the hope of completely overwhelming its defences and reaching unprotected areas behind the lines. The infantry's role was simply to emerge from its trenches and advance towards planned targets, but improved trench systems and new DEFENCE IN DEPTH tactics ensured that troops could only reach and occupy initial targets at great cost. Exploitation of any limited success was virtually impossible before superior defensive communications brought reinforcements to the threatened sector. Despite increasingly powerful PRELIMINARY BOMBARDMENTS (and the development of shock weapons such as GAS, GRENADES and FLAMETHROWERS), breakthrough tactics failed completely on the Western Front, and although MACKENSEN's Austro-German forces smashed great holes in Russian lines on the Eastern Front during 1915, the need for concentration before every infantry attack precluded rapid long-range advance.

German chief of staff FALKENHAYN's plan to 'bleed the French Army white' at VERDUN from February 1916 ushered in a new phase of the tactical struggle in France: war of attrition. A conscious attempt to seek victory by exhausting enemy manpower resources, attrition was also a stated aim of the Allied SOMME OFFENSIVE later that year, but had little impact on the attacking tasks expected of infantry. The scale of attacks continued to increase, but mushrooming artillery support, the development of sophisticated CREEPING BARRAGE techniques and direct assistance from combat aircraft (see AERIAL WARFARE) were still adjuncts to operations that generally culminated in concentrated infantry charges.

The first large-scale demonstration of an alternative to breakthrough concentration took place in the east, where the Russian BRUSILOV OFFENSIVE of summer 1916 used surprise and the disruptive effects of multiple attacks along a broad front to devastate Austro-Hungarian positions in Galicia. Russian tactical success could not be exploited, and the lesson went unheeded in Allied armies, which remained committed to ponderous and unsuccessful extensions of breakthrough and attrition doctrine throughout 1917.

The German high command absorbed many of BRUSILOV's methods in perfecting INFILTRATION TACTICS, devised by General von HUTIER and first employed at RIGA in September 1917. Infiltration methods employed specially trained and equipped units of 'stormtroopers' to penetrate enemy lines quickly and knock out support services in rear areas before the main infantry assault took place. Hutier's methods brought great tactical victories at CAPORETTO on the ITALIAN FRONT in late 1917, and during the 1918 SPRING OFFENSIVES in France, but could not transform infantry into a weapon capable of sustaining long-range offensive operations, and the problem of strategic exploitation was eventually circumvented rather than solved by the Allies on the Western Front.

Foreshadowed by the meticulous Japanese capture of TSINGTAO in 1914, and later by General PLUMER's limited success at MESSINES, Allied PEACEFUL PENETRATION techniques were developed by AUSTRALIAN FORCES on the Western Front (under General MONASH) from spring 1918. In a conscious attempt to achieve secure gains without unsustainable casualties, infantry advance was reduced to a secondary operation intended to occupy a strictly limited area already devastated by precisely coordinated attacks from heavy artillery, aircraft, machine guns, TANKS and every other available support weapon.

Peaceful penetration was the basis of successful Allied offensives in France and Belgium during the second half of 1918, but was a painstaking means to overall victory. Rapid strategic thrusts were still impossible at the ARMISTICE, and the postwar development of fast, armoured assault vehicles and aircraft confirmed the long-term reduction of infantry's role in major offensive operations to that of an occupying force. See also: LEAPFROG.

Infiltration Tactics Important development in offensive TRENCH WARFARE tactics, first postulated in print by a French infantry captain in 1915 but pioneered in practice by the GERMAN ARMY from autumn 1917. The first use of fully developed infiltration tactics is credited to General von HUTIER, in the German Eighth Army's successful attack on RIGA of 1 September 1917, and they were generally known in German circles as 'Hutier tactics'.

Infiltration tactics were a radical departure from orthodox BREAKTHROUGH assaults against entrenched positions, which became more sophisticated during the War but remained a matter of securing the flanks of every advance before further progress was attempted (see LEAPFROG) and were completely ineffective against DEFENCE IN DEPTH.

Instead of following a long PRELIMINARY BOMBARDMENT with a massed infantry rush at wrecked forward trenches, small forces of 'stormtroopers' (initially companies, later battalions) were slipped between enemy strongpoints after a short 'hurricane' barrage. Heavily armed with light MACHINE GUNS, MORTARS, FLAMETHROWERS (and sometimes light ARTILLERY), their job was to surprise rear areas and artillery positions. Heavily defended positions would be bypassed and dealt with by the main infantry attack, following up to storm frontline trenches, and forward units would be given priority in the use of aircraft support and reinforcements.

In pursuing maximum penetration wherever it was most possible, infiltration tactics revived the possibility of sudden, large-scale territorial gains as defenders were forced to fall back beyond prepared second- and third-line TRENCHES. They did not solve the supply and transport difficulties that prevented long-distance exploitation, which proved impossible when they were used at the CAPORETTO, CAMBRAI and KAISERSCHLACHT battles. When Allied armies on the Western Front finally adopted a form of infiltration tactics, during the relatively open warfare of autumn 1918, their use was restricted to limited, predetermined infantry advances. See also: PEACEFUL PENETRATION.

Influenza Pandemic Viral infection, known colloquially as 'Spanish Flu', that killed an estimated 70 million people worldwide in 1918–19. Reaching the Middle Eastern battle zones in spring 1918 it spread north and west, striking western Europe in the summer and crossing the Atlantic in the autumn. In that it reached Turkish, Austro-Hungarian and German lines some weeks before seriously affecting their Allied counterparts (a geographical accident) the disease had some military effects, unquantifiable in the context of Allied victory that year, but its most profound impact was on home fronts less inured to sudden death. Often fatal after a brief fever, its virulence was linked by contemporaries with deprivation among European populations, but Europe was not particularly hard hit in a global context. No such conditions existed in the UNITED STATES, where the disease took at least 400,000 lives, most of them otherwise healthy people aged 20 to 40. The pandemic died away in mid-1919, unexplained and untreated. See also: GREAT BRITAIN; FRANCE.

Interrupter Gear A mechanism, also known as synchronizing gear, that enabled the pilot of an aircraft to fire a MACHINE GUN through the propeller, which was linked by a shaft to the trigger to block fire whenever they were in line. Interrupter systems had been developed before 1914 in France, Germany, Russia and Britain, but military authorities did not envisage armed aircraft and they were ignored.

Allied authorities treated the idea with suspicion even after the need for FIGHTER aircraft became clear, probably because low-quality ammunition and lack of a suitable machine gun rendered the system dangerous. Other forward armament systems were tried with limited success, and the DEFLECTOR GEAR of French pilot Roland GARROS fell into German hands in April 1915, prompting an official German request for a similar system. The Fokker company came up instead with its own version of interrupter gear, which was fitted to FOKKER E-TYPE monoplanes and used on the WESTERN FRONT from autumn 1915. Its immediate success convinced other air arms of the need for synchronized armament, and from mid-1916 various mechanisms, including hydraulic and twin-gunned variations, were standard equipment for armed aircraft on all sides.

Invincible The world's first BATTLECRUISER, an international sensation when completed for the ROYAL NAVY in 1908, and name ship of a class including the *Indomitable* and *Inflexible*. *Invincible*'s wartime career displayed both the strengths and weaknesses of battlecruisers: its speed and firepower were demonstrated at HELIGOLAND BIGHT and the FALKLAND ISLANDS, but its defensive weakness was shown up at JUTLAND in 1916, when the ship exploded and sank after one of many hits from German battlecruisers caused a cordite 'flash' to the magazine.

Its sister ships *Indomitable* and *Inflexible* served in the MEDITERRANEAN for a time in 1914 (see MITTELMEERDIVISION). *Inflexible* took part in the Falklands action and the DARDANELLES operation, where it was damaged by a MINE. *Indomitable* was present at the DOGGER BANK engagement, and both were at Jutland, surviving with the GRAND FLEET until relegated to reserve duties in 1919.

BRIEF DATA (*Invincible*, 1914) Displacement: 17,250 tons; Crew: 750; Dimensions: length 567ft (171.9m), beam 79ft (23.9m); Speed: 26k; Armament: 8 × 12in gun, 16 × 4in, 3 × 21in TT.

Irben Straits A narrow channel (less than 30km across in places) between the island of Ösel (Saaremaa) and the Russian mainland. The Straits, which form a modern frontier between Estonia and Latvia, are the main entrance to the semi-enclosed Bay of Riga, scene of the most intense wartime naval activity in the BALTIC SEA (see MAP 16). Russian light craft and coastal-defence ships had occupied the Bay in strength from autumn 1914, using an even narrower northern entrance guarded by the heavily fortified island of Moon (Muhu). They began mining the Straits from spring 1915, and the GERMAN NAVY made two attempts to force them during August as support for ground forces in KURLAND.

The first attempt was abandoned after two minesweepers were lost to patrolling Russian DESTROYERS. The second, begun on 16 August, was supported by capital units of the HIGH SEAS FLEET. After skirmishes in which the Russian battleship *SLAVA* was damaged and a new German destroyer sunk, German minesweepers cleared a safe passage through the Straits on 18 August. By the time German forces advanced along the coast of Ösel the following morning further fields had been laid in their path, and they were compelled to retreat. German ships resumed their advance on 20 August but turned back on sighting a periscope and withdrew completely that afternoon. Four Allied SUBMARINES were active in the area, and the British *E-1* damaged the BATTLECRUISER *Moltke*.

Russian destroyers laid hundreds more MINES in the aftermath of the action, and ARTILLERY defences on Moon were increased. The German Navy laid mines of its own and used light forces, backed by increasing numbers of aircraft and AIRSHIPS, in a campaign of harassment that continued until the fall of RIGA in early September 1917. With Russian forces restricted to bases on Ösel and the coast north of Riga, but still committed to defending the Straits, the struggle for the Bay climaxed with Operation ALBION, an ambitious combined German military and naval attack that captured Ösel and Moon but allowed RUSSIAN NAVY forces to escape. Although the contest for the Straits ended at that point, mines continued to claim shipping in the area for many weeks.

Ireland Under English domination since the Middle Ages, Ireland had been subject to complete union with GREAT BRITAIN from 1801. Its population of just under 4.5 million (1911) was predominantly rural and Catholic, with industrial development concentrated in the northern region of Ulster. Irish nationalism underwent a resurgence in the 19th century, and from the 1880s the movement for autonomy ('Home Rule') won support from the British Liberal government. The concept aroused controversy in London, where Home Rule Bills were defeated in 1886 and 1893, and was strongly opposed by the Protestant, 'Unionist' majority in Ulster.

The ASQUITH government, supported by

84 southern Irish members of parliament, passed a third Home Rule Bill through the House of Commons in May 1914, pushing Ulster close to civil war. Dispute between the main British parties erupted into crisis when it appeared that BRITISH ARMY troops in Ireland would refuse to fire on Ulster Unionists if called upon to enforce Home Rule. In the wake of the 'Curragh Mutiny', regional commander General GOUGH, all his officers, Army chief of staff FRENCH and war minister Seeley all resigned, leaving the latter post vacant when the JULY CRISIS brought a sudden end to controversy.

The outbreak of war suspended plans to introduce Home Rule and quietened Protestant agitation for the duration. Although Ireland was considered too sensitive for the imposition of conscription through the MILITARY SERVICE ACTS from 1916, northern and southern Irishmen volunteered in large numbers for British military service.

Inside Ireland the Sinn Fein movement for full independence gathered strength for a rebellion in the hope of German aid, and the EASTER RISING in Dublin of April 1916 was put down at enormous cost to British prestige in the south. By 1919 Home Rule had become redundant in the face of southern determination for immediate independence, and partition of north and south followed three years of sporadic civil war. An Irish Free State was created in the south as a dominion of the Empire in 1922, and Ulster became a semi-autonomous British province.

Iringa, Battle of Main engagement on the secondary southern front of the Allied 1916 offensive in German EAST AFRICA that also included advances on TABORA and MOROGORO. The southwestern corner of the colony was invaded by RHODESIAN FORCES, mostly volunteer units, under General Northey, which took Bismarckburg (Mbala) at the southern end of Lake Tanganyika in June (see NAVAL AFRICA EXPEDITION) and advanced northeast. About 2,000 German and ASKARI troops of Major Kraut's Southwestern Group withdrew skilfully until late October, by which time Northey had reached the town of Iringa, about 400km southwest of Dar-es-Salaam.

Anxious to prevent a Rhodesian advance blocking communications with General Wahle's forces who were retreating from Tabora, Kraut changed his tactics to launch a major attack on Iringa, cutting rear supply lines and ambushing reserves while Wahle's forward columns advanced against the town itself. Although the attack failed in confused jungle fighting, and several hundred of Wahle's men surrendered after getting lost, defenders suffered comparable casualties and the two German armies successfully joined forces across the Rufugi River to the southeast. Poised to reach General LETTOW-VORBECK's main army about 300km east (near the British base of Kilwa), they were subsequently pursued by General SMUTS from the north. The Rhodesians concentrated on clearing pockets of German resistance further west. See MAP 18.

Iron Duke The Iron Dukes were the last class of ROYAL NAVY 'super-dreadnoughts' with 13.5-inch guns (see *ORION*), and *Iron Duke* itself, completed in spring 1914, was the first British capital ship designed with ANTI-AIRCRAFT guns. The most modern major unit with the GRAND FLEET in August 1914, it served as Admiral JELLICOE's flagship until late 1916 and was at JUTLAND along with its sisters *Marlborough*, *Benbow* and *Emperor of India*. Though *Marlborough* was torpedoed it limped home under its own steam and the rest of the class survived undamaged.

BRIEF DATA (*Iron Duke*, 1914) Displacement: 26,400 tons; Crew: 995; Dimensions: length 620ft (187.9m), beam 89.5ft (27.2m); Speed: 22k; Armament: 10 × 13.5in gun, 12 × 6in, 2 × 3in AA, 4 × 21in TT.

Isolationism Total disinterest in international affairs, particularly those of Europe, the traditional, popular and liberal foreign policy of the UNITED STATES in the 19th century. Challenged before 1914 by business and industrial interests seeking active diplomatic support for economic expansion into Latin America, the Pacific and CANADA, isolationism was subsequently attacked by their representatives in the PREPAREDNESS

MOVEMENT and formally abandoned by President WILSON in April 1917. Wilson's defeat in 1920, and rejection of the VERSAILLES Treaty by Congress, signalled a partial withdrawal from international politics, reflected in postwar disarmament and refusal to join the LEAGUE OF NATIONS, a stance weakened by US involvement in global naval and trading agreements during the 1920s.

Isonzo Offensives A prolonged series of Italian attacks against Austro-Hungarian positions along the Isonzo River sector of the ITALIAN FRONT (see MAP 21). Variously counted as 10 or 11 offensives (with some authorities including the subsequent CAPORETTO OFFENSIVE as a twelfth), they were almost uniformly futile and tactically bankrupt, made more costly by difficult geographical conditions.

When ITALY declared war in May 1915, chief of staff CADORNA was committed to some kind of immediate attack by the Treaty of LONDON. Fourteen of the 25 AUSTRO-HUNGARIAN ARMY divisions in the theatre (commanded by Archduke EUGEN) were massed along the Isonzo, but the sector offered the best chance of significant territorial conquest. Any attack that failed to neutralize at least one of the line's main defensive strongpoints – Monte Nero at the northern end of the line and the Carso plateau along the southern littoral – would be exposed to envelopment from the flanks, and the first offensive was focused on the Carso from 23 June.

A good organizer, Cadorna had quickly assembled a numerically superior force, but attempted an imperfect imitation of WESTERN FRONT tactics. Seeking a BREAKTHROUGH by massed infantry assault without waiting for his ARTILLERY to concentrate, he dissipated limited resources by simultaneous subsidiary attacks in the Trentino and in the central Isonzo around Gorizia (Gorz). Two divisions of Austro-Hungarian infantry were quickly sent to reinforce sector commander BOROEVIC, whose forces prevented any river crossings before Cadorna suspended operations on 8 July.

After a pause to bring up artillery, during which TRENCH WARFARE conditions were established all along the Isonzo, the Italian Second and Third Armies repeated their attacks in the same areas, making trivial gains in the Carso after two days of heavy fighting from 18 July but again failing to hold new forward positions around Gorizia. After losing 60,000 men in two weeks (against 45,000 Austro-Hungarian casualties), Cadorna halted attacks on 2 August.

The third offensive, launched in worsening weather conditions during early October, used a total of 1,200 field guns and switched the main point of attack to Gorizia. Officially ended on 3 November, and completely unsuccessful, it merged almost imperceptibly with the fourth offensive, which began on 10 November and ended in early December, when winter prevented further activity until March 1916.

Without substantially altering the front line, the attrition of 1915 damaged both Armies. Despite the transfer of 12 divisions to the theatre since June, Austro-Hungarian commanders were sufficiently worried by the loss of another 72,000 men since October to appeal for German military assistance late in the year. The Italian Army's additional 115,000 casualties had hurt its offensive capability, and it was barely fit to carry out the fifth offensive, promised to Allied leaders in 1916 as a means of relieving pressure on VERDUN.

Italian artillery opened the offensive along the central Isonzo on 12 March, but its main focus was again Gorizia. It barely got underway before bad weather forced a halt, and no resumption was possible before Cadorna's single-minded campaign was interrupted by the Austrian TRENTINO OFFENSIVE in May.

Again demonstrating his administrative gifts, and making effective use of a superior RAILWAY system, Cadorna responded to political and popular pressure in Italy by returning immediately to the attack after the Trentino sector had stabilized. Nine Austrian divisions faced 22 Italian divisions on the Isonzo when the sixth offensive opened on 6 August 1916, and the main attack got across the river to take Gorizia on 9 August. Gradually reinforced, defenders stopped further advances after 12 August, and Italian forces had gained about 5km along a 20km front by the time fighting died down on 17 August.

The biggest Italian land victory up to that date, Gorizia prompted a change of tactical approach by Cadorna, who launched three more major attacks east of the town (in September, October and early November) without the usual diversionary operations, but greater concentration had no effect and further substantial gains proved impossible.

Reinforced to a total strength of 38 divisions, against only 14 Austro-Hungarian, Cadorna again agreed to cooperate with Allied offensives elsewhere by launching an attack of his own in spring 1917. Returning to the Carso, he launched infantry along a 40km front from the coast on 14 May after a two-day PRELIMINARY BOMBARDMENT, and had pushed to within 15km of Trieste by the end of the month. Subsidiary attacks in the usual places failed, and a major Austrian counter-attack from 3 June recovered lost ground by mid-month. Casualties were heavy: more than 150,000 Italian and about half as many Austro-Hungarian.

Cadorna could muster one more giant reinforcement from Italian manpower resources, and by August he had assembled 51 divisions for a repeat attack on the Carso and Gorizia sectors in August and September. Opened in the coastal zone on 19 August, it was most successful further north, where CAPELLO's Second Army advanced almost 10km. Stretched all along the Italian Front and anticipating collapse, authorities in Vienna stepped up their pleas for aid from Berlin, and the effective end of hostilities on the EASTERN FRONT brought GERMAN ARMY forces to the theatre for the first time during September.

Aware of preparations for a joint offensive by the CENTRAL POWERS, Cadorna halted the eleventh offensive on 12 September and ordered forward units to withdraw to more defensible positions. He was ignored by Capello, who remained east of the river and exposed to the attack at Caporetto that transformed the pattern of operations in the theatre from late October.

Istanbulat, Battle of See: SAMARRAH OFFENSIVE.

Italian Air Force Established as an independent military arm on 7 January 1915, the Italian air service was the only wartime force apart from the British RAF to achieve that status. The ITALIAN ARMY had created an Aeronautical Section for balloon operations in 1884, and received its first aeroplanes, purchased from France and Germany, in 1910. Nine machines sent to Tripoli as the 'Air Army' during the Italo-Turkish War of 1911–12 (see ITALY) were the first aircraft anywhere in the world to perform military operations, carrying out inaugural reconnaissance, bombing and ARTILLERY cooperation missions. Their effectiveness was a major factor in convincing European military opinion of the value of air power.

Despite a flourishing school of air theorists and great popular enthusiasm for aircraft, conviction was not matched by rapid technical development in Italy. Comprising separate balloon and aircraft commands under the overall directorship of Colonel Moris, the new *Corpo Aeronautico Militare* (CAM) had few pilots or aircraft at the time of its formation. The first operational squadrons (*squadriglia*) were formed for artillery observation in March 1915, and Italian flying schools were operational immediately before the outbreak of war with AUSTRIA-HUNGARY. With an aero industry capable of producing only 12 engines and 30–50 aeroplanes per year, the CAM depended on French-built machines and had a frontline strength of only 58 aircraft, 91 (French-trained) pilots and 20 officer observers.

Along with orthodox army cooperation work (see AERIAL WARFARE), the CAM pursued a consistent interest in STRATEGIC BOMBING by aeroplanes and army AIRSHIPS. The only Italian-designed aircraft fit for frontline combat in 1915 was the CAPRONI CA heavy bomber, and an emphasis on long-range operations was encouraged by conditions on the ITALIAN FRONT. Dangerously mountainous, it offered only limited scope for tactical bombing, but plentiful long-range targets could be reached in Austria and the Balkans.

During 1915 the AUSTRO-HUNGARIAN AIR SERVICE enjoyed a distinct operational advantage on the Italian Front, but Allied aid and a concerted expansion of the Italian aero industry (which produced 279 machines in the year to May 1916) enabled an improvement in strength and facilities during the enforced winter lull in operations. By March 1916 the CAM fielded 7 squadrons of Capronis, 10 reconnaissance squadrons (8 with FARMAN F-40s and 2 with VOISINS), 7 artillery-spotting units (5 with CAUDRON G-IVs and 2 with Farmans), 5 FIGHTER units equipped with NIEUPORT 11s, and 1 seaplane squadron.

New PHOTO-RECONNAISSANCE and artillery techniques were perfected during the winter of 1915–16, and a series of emergency alpine airstrips reduced the torrent of fatal accidents. Fighter units became more important, although they were not equipped with interrupter gear until early 1917, and the scale of Caproni operations was stepped up as more bombers became available, beginning with a 30-aircraft raid against Pergine airfield in July.

Following another lengthy winter break, tactical bombing was resumed in force during the ISONZO OFFENSIVES of May and August 1917, but lack of experience in daylight work was reflected in a very poor success rate. In all, the CAM fielded 145 aircraft at the height of the May battle and an average of 225 throughout the latter part of August. Losses suffered during the defeat at CAPORETTO in November, when German units were moved south to join the battle, were quickly made good by British and French reinforcements, along with high-quality new Italian machines (such as the ANSALDO SVA-5) and the attachment of Italian-trained US aircrew to CAM units.

Further expansion took place once German units had departed in the new year. At the decisive PIAVE battle in mid-1918 the CAM fielded 221 fighters, 56 bombers and 276 other frontline aircraft, supported by 54 RAF fighters and 46 Allied reconnaissance craft. Allied fighters shot down 107 enemy aircraft and 7 balloons in the 10 days from 15 June 1918, emphasizing the extent of Italian qualitative superiority and of the material crisis facing the Austro-Hungarian Air Service.

Italian Army Developed out of the Piedmont Army that fought for national unification from the mid-19th century, the Italian Army was little more than an internal police force until the introduction of universal conscription in 1907. Subsequent expansion was hindered by the country's poverty, so that only about 25 per cent of those eligible for conscription received training, and a truncated programme virtually closed the Army down in winter.

Further reforms were interrupted by ITALY's war with TURKEY in 1911, which had severely depleted military resources when it ended the following year. The Army's theoretical peacetime strength in 1912 of just under 300,000 men bore little relation to reality, with some units down to 10 per cent of establishment, few experienced NCOs, and a shortage of trained officers. The economic crisis after the Italo-Turkish War slowed reconstruction, so that the officer corps was still almost 15,000 men below requirements by mid-1914, with the ARTILLERY arm particularly short of commanders and equipment.

The general staff (*Comando Supremo*) and its new chief, General CADORNA, understandably supported ITALY's declaration of neutrality in early August 1914, but recognized the likelihood of eventual involvement in the War. Artillery strength was quietly built up during late 1914, a clumsy mobilization procedure was streamlined, and Cadorna concentrated troops along the northeastern borders with AUSTRIA-HUNGARY. Government plans for the Army to help expand ITALIAN NAVY influence in ALBANIA were rejected, the first of several refusals to support political ambitions in the Balkans at the expense of frontier defences.

The Army was able to field 25 infantry and 4 CAVALRY divisions (about 550,000 men) in May 1915, grouped into four field armies, but they still had only about 120 heavy or medium artillery pieces – a potpourri of obsolete siege or fortress guns – and some 700 MACHINE GUNS. The Treaty of LONDON with the Allies, and popular pressure to recapture the 'lost' provinces of the Trentino and the Venetian Plains, nonetheless obliged Cadorna to adopt an offensive policy on the ITALIAN FRONT.

He chose the most direct route into the heart of Austrian territory, launching an unsuccessful series of mass attacks on the ISONZO River in 1915 that cost some 300,000 men and 3,000 precious field guns. Seven more 'BREAKTHROUGH' attempts on the Isonzo to autumn 1917 produced only one substantial victory (at GORIZIA in 1916), more than matched by the Austro-Hungarian success in the TRENTINO during May 1916.

Despite heavy losses throughout, and clear signs of weakening morale – especially among troops from industrial cities or the rural south – the Army grew rapidly, and at its peak in October 1917 it comprised 65 infantry divisions. More than 12,000 machine guns were in service, including Anglo-French weapons supplied as aid, an efficient Italian-made Peroni model, and the double-barrelled VILLAR PEROSA light aircraft gun, converted for use by specialist *Alpini* mountain troops. Most frontline infantry carried modern, magazine-loaded Mannlicher RIFLES, although reserves were still using a variety of older small arms, and specialist TRENCH WARFARE weapons had been introduced in numbers, including several thousand MORTARS.

Though criticized for lack of strategic and tactical imagination, the Comando Supremo ignored the press and hardly consulted the government on policy issues throughout Cadorna's regime, supported by nominal C-in-C King VICTOR EMMANUEL III, and generally unwilling to disturb overwhelming concentration of strength with the nine armies on the Isonzo and Trentino, Cadorna released one double-sized division to fight on the BALKAN FRONT from autumn 1915. Substantial forces also took part in the suppression of the SENUSSI uprising in Libya, and small detachments were sent to the WESTERN FRONT, GALLIPOLI and PALESTINE.

The Austro-German CAPORETTO OFFENSIVE in October 1917 effectively finished the Italian Army as an attacking force. Another 300,000 men and vast amounts of materiel were lost, including most trench artillery and almost all the bulky old heavy guns. The cautious General DIAZ took over from Cadorna in early November, managing to stabilize the front at the PIAVE RIVER and repulsing a renewed Austro-Hungarian attack at the PIAVE, but citing food and clothing shortages, along with low morale and disciplinary problems, among his reasons for refusing the SUPREME WAR COUNCIL's plea for him to undertake an offensive of his own.

Military policy under the ORLANDO government was formulated through a joint council, and Diaz was more open to political influence than his predecessor. Cabinet pressure to ensure Italy's bargaining position at the postwar conference table eventually forced him into action in September 1918. Reinforced by the Allies, and able to field more than 1,100 heavy guns, the VITTORIO VENETO OFFENSIVE routed an even more debilitated AUSTRO-HUNGARIAN ARMY and advanced almost 100km before the ARMISTICE.

Easily the biggest success of an otherwise disappointing campaign, the final battle brought the Italian Army's total wartime casualties to 462,000 killed and almost 955,000 wounded, out of about 5.2 million men in all branches of active service.

Italian Front A theatre that rivalled the GALLIPOLI FRONT for claustrophobic lack of strategic movement, the Italian Front was the main area of conflict in the land war between ITALY and AUSTRIA-HUNGARY, covering long-disputed frontiers that were at the heart of deteriorating prewar relations between the two powers. Stretching east from the Swiss frontier along the foothills of the Alps, the Front offered strictly limited options for large-scale military operations, which were possible only around the Trentino Valley which jutted into northern Italy as an Austrian-held SALIENT. Manoeuvre was also feasible to the east, where the line cut south across plateau lands around the Isonzo River on Italy's modern border with Slovenia and formed the gateway to territories long coveted by Italian nationalists. See MAP 21.

The Treaty of LONDON of spring 1915 contracted Italy to an attack on Austria-Hungary, an action entirely in tune with popular feeling and foreign-policy priorities but less so with military realities. The ITALIAN ARMY, still recovering from an exhausting war with TURKEY (1911–12) and already suffering from BLOCKADE-induced wartime supply shortages, was desperately short of modern equipment, especially ARTILLERY and aircraft (see ITALIAN AIR FORCE).

The smaller AUSTRO-HUNGARIAN ARMY contingent in the theatre, though depleted by the demands of the BALKAN and EASTERN FRONT campaigns, occupied a series of connected mountain positions established long in advance for ease of defence. The Trentino positions, defended by only 11 divisions, offered Italian chief of staff CADORNA the best apparent chance of success, but 'lost' Italian provinces in Venezia and the important Adriatic port of Trieste lay beyond the Isonzo line. Assembling his forces hastily but efficiently, Cadorna chose the more ambitious option and launched the first of eleven offensives on the ISONZO in June 1915.

Generally costly, tactically naive and territorially unproductive, the sequence of Italian attacks at either end of the Isonzo sector lasted until autumn 1917, connected by periods of TRENCH WARFARE all along the river and interrupted only by the Austro-Hungarian TRENTINO OFFENSIVE of May and June 1916. Cadorna rushed troops belatedly to the defence of his rear lines at Asiago in early June, and counterattacks were already wearing down Austrian forces when the Russian BRUSILOV OFFENSIVE forced Austro-Hungarian commander CONRAD to postpone further attacks in Italy.

Under pressure as a potential scapegoat for a shocked Italian public Cadorna responded characteristically by demonstrating his talent for rapid concentration (and the quality of north Italian RAILWAYS) to launch a sixth Isonzo offensive in August. The most successful of his attacks, it took Gorizia at the northern edge of the Carso plateau and encouraged a further series of BREAKTHROUGH attempts until winter ended operations for the year.

Conditions on the Italian Front were similar to those in French or Flanders trenches, but weather conditions were more extreme, the few main battle zones were generally even more crowded, and troops were less well provided with clothing, food and medical supplies. Both armies survived on lower rations than their counterparts on the Western Front, and the economic effort of maintaining a large-scale static front brought both sides close to collapse.

Austria-Hungary's internal condition was the more serious, exacerbated by accelerating political collapse. Although Cadorna's resumption of Isonzo offensives in 1917 damaged Italian morale and gained virtually no ground, it put a critical stress on Austro-Hungarian manpower resources. In the autumn, with the eleventh Isonzo battle threatening to make major gains around Gorizia, Vienna's repeated requests for German military assistance were answered.

Intended only as a limited offensive to prevent further Italian attacks, the CAPORETTO OFFENSIVE of late October was spearheaded by only six divisions of German reinforcements, along with ARTILLERY, technical units and a GERMAN ARMY AIR SERVICE detachment (including heavy GOTHA machines in a theatre characterized by STRATEGIC BOMBING operations). Cadorna's lacklustre defensive planning, and overconfidence by local commander CAPELLO, assisted a far greater victory than German or Austrian planners had anticipated.

Short of reserves in difficult country, Austro-German attacks stalled at the Piave River from mid-November and the front had stabilized there by late December. Italian defeat had prompted an immediate change of government, ORLANDO replacing BOSELLI as prime minister, and brought DIAZ to command in place of Cadorna. Defeatism and PACIFISM, rife in Italian armies and newspapers during 1917, disappeared as the Army was reconstructed with Allied help agreed at the RAPALLO CONFERENCE (6–9 November).

British and French forces from the Western Front (a total of 11 divisions, plus a token AEF regiment) were fighting in Italy from early December, and the theatre was briefly accorded genuinely international status. As modern Allied guns and aircraft were transferred to the front, German units began pulling out in the new year to redeploy for the

SPRING OFFENSIVES in France.

While Diaz cautiously rebuilt morale and strength by restricting operations to occasional raids, the Austro-Hungarian Army was allowed to decay in peace until it passed formally under German strategic control in May 1918. Almost without reference to the Austrian high command or chief of staff ARZ VON STRAUSSENBERG, front commanders Conrad and BOROEVIC were then reinforced for a double attack at the PIAVE in June.

Poorly conceived and executed by demoralized forces, it was an abject failure and triggered the Army's final collapse, but Diaz was strongly criticized for not pursuing his beaten enemies beyond the river. He remained under Allied and government pressure to launch an offensive throughout the summer, and was eventually threatened with dismissal by expansionist foreign minister SONNINO. His reluctant attack towards VITTORIO VENETO, backed by 7,700 guns and a large Allied air force, swept aside the remnants of Austro-Hungarian forces during the last week of October, and had advanced to the Tagliamento and Trento by the armistice with Austria-Hungary on 3 November. See also: Treaty of ST GERMAIN.

Italian Navy Rapid expansion of the Italian Navy (*Regia Marina*), fully underway from 1909, was a major complication facing prewar naval strategists in the MEDITERRANEAN. Italy was an ally of GERMANY and AUSTRIA-HUNGARY, but also the latter's rival for control of the Adriatic, and Italy's naval growth was inspired by competition with the AUSTRO-HUNGARIAN NAVY as well as the prospect of a united challenge to overall Anglo-French control of the theatre.

The Navy mobilized for war against the Allies in July 1914, but its eventual neutrality indirectly aided the German MITTELMEER-DIVISION's escape to TURKEY and enabled expansion to continue uninterrupted into 1915. Better-funded than the ITALIAN ARMY, the Regia Marina grew into a compact but impressive force, based around five dreadnoughts completed since 1912 (a sixth was completed in 1916) and 8 fairly useful PRE-DREADNOUGHTS.

Smaller warships included 18 old 'armoured' or 'protected' CRUISERS, but only 3 modern light cruisers. Despite chief of staff REVEL's preference for development of light forces, most of the 49 DESTROYERS were old, small and fragile. None of the 85 TORPEDO BOATS and 25 SUBMARINES was suitable for long-range operations.

The main battlefleet, commanded by Admiral ABRUZZI until his replacement by Revel in early 1917, was based at Taranto throughout the War. Important secondary bases were maintained close to the ITALIAN FRONT at Venice, and on either side of the Otranto Straits at Brindisi and the southern Albanian port of Valona (Vlöre), occupied and fortified in 1915.

The battlefleet's main wartime activity was a constant watch over the Austro-Hungarian fleet at Pola (Pula). It was considered too precious to risk in secondary operations, and a surface attack on the main Austrian fleet at Pola was never seriously considered. Warships were of limited support value to ground forces on the ISONZO; and several plans to seize operational bases on the Dalmatian coast were rejected for lack of military support. Projected inter-Allied fleet operations foundered on the Navy's unwillingness to accept Allied command over Italian ships in the Adriatic, or to use the battlefleet anywhere else. Apparent inactivity, combined with regular Austro-Hungarian 'hit-and-run' raids on the eastern Italian coast, fuelled heavy press criticism of the fleet's performance from an early stage centred on the contention that its modern BATTLESHIPS were a waste of money.

Italian cruisers and destroyers in the Adriatic were more active. Operations from Venice were strictly curtailed after the early loss of the *AMALFI*, but a mutual raiding campaign developed in the southern Adriatic focused on Allied communications with the BALKAN FRONT and maintenance of the OTRANTO BARRAGE.

The Treaty of LONDON in 1915 had promised Anglo-French naval aid, particularly in the form of modern destroyers and other ANTI-SUBMARINE vessels, but Allied shortages elsewhere left the Italian Navy with insufficient resources to defend its coastline from submarine attacks, and vital supply lines suffered delay and disruption. Coal shortages not only restricted the movements of warships, but curtailed use of RAILWAYS in Italy, so that by 1917 much internal supply traffic travelled in vulnerable coastal sailing ships. By 1918, the situation had been partly remedied by British, French, Japanese and US destroyers, and by widespread adoption of CONVOYS.

Italian submarines achieved almost no wartime successes, and the Navy's only really effective offensive operations were carried out by a variety of small TORPEDO craft. Innovative designs daringly handled, they scored a number of startling successes in 1918, including the destruction of two Austro-Hungarian dreadnoughts (see MAS BOATS; HUMAN TORPEDOES; BARCHINI SALTATORI).

Though it emerged from the War essentially intact, and helped prevent the Austro-Hungarian fleet from being a major factor in the Mediterranean, the Navy was otherwise able to offer little help to its increasingly exasperated Allies. The only modern capital ship lost was *Leonardo da Vinci*, sabotaged at anchor in 1916 (see *CONTI DI CAVOUR*), and relatively quiet performance was reflected in total wartime casualty figures of 3,169 dead and 5,252 wounded. See also: *REGINA ELENA; BENEDETTO BRIN;* Battle of the OTRANTO STRAITS.

Italy The Kingdom of Italy, ruled by the House of Savoy, emerged from a long nationalist struggle for unification of its many city-states, kingdoms and principalities beginning with a revolution in 1848. The southern kingdom of 'Sardinia and the Two Sicilies' was united with the northern Lombard/Venetian regions in 1866, after Austria had been forced to renounce control, and French troops evacuated the independent papal states in 1870. By 1914 only the Vatican and San Marino retained independence within Italy, but large Italian populations remained within AUSTRIA-HUNGARY beyond the northern frontier in the Trentino (South Tyrol) and Trieste regions.

Italy's population of 34.7 million (1911), most dense in the industrial north and overcrowded Naples, was almost entirely dependent on imports for industrial raw materials, and peacetime coal shortages reduced the effectiveness of RAILWAYS (about 17,000km). Though primarily an agricultural economy, Italy also relied on imports of some foods, notably grain from RUSSIA and GERMANY.

The constitutional monarch, VICTOR EMMANUEL III since 1900, exercised power through a cabinet drawn from a two-tier national assembly, the lower house elected by universal adult male suffrage. Although political groupings were mostly formed along regional lines, reflecting the preoccupations of most Italians, national parties were gathering strength in the lower house: 79 socialists and 70 radicals held seats after the 1913 elections, in which Liberal premier Giovanni GIOLITTI retained office with a greatly reduced majority.

Recovery of the 'lost' northern provinces ('Irredentism') was the predominant national issue in Italian politics up to 1914, and the prime objective of a foreign policy that also sought MEDITERRANEAN security and economic growth through colonial expansion. AUSTRIA-HUNGARY, menacing Italy's long Adriatic coastline and blocking colonial ambitions in the Balkans (especially in ALBANIA), was the main obstruction on all counts, but Russia's Balkan interests and Anglo-French naval cooperation after 1904 also threatened Italian interests.

Competition with TURKEY for colonial influence culminated in a war for control of the Libyan provinces of Tripoli and Benghazi from September 1911. After fighting in Libya itself had proved inconclusive, and done little for Italy's military reputation, Italian naval bombardment of the DARDANELLES in autumn 1912 was followed by the outbreak of war between Turkey and the independent Balkan states in October (see INTRODUCTION; BALKAN FRONT). Constantinople immediately made peace with Italy, ceding Libya, Rhodes and the Dodecanese islands, but the victory exhausted Italian military resources and destabilized the economy into 1914.

No major clash of interests affected relations with Germany, and Italy's membership of the TRIPLE ALLIANCE (1882) had been accompanied by an upsurge in German economic penetration of the rapidly industrializing north. Seen by successive governments (and business interests) as essential protection for expansionist policies, the Alliance was formally renewed as late as 1912, but association with Austria-Hungary remained anathema to an irredentist public, and Italy's adherence in the event of war was always open to doubt.

Giolitti's successor in spring 1914, the relatively inexperienced SALANDRA, still faced shortages of civilian and military supplies, along with civil unrest in Ancona and a widespread rail strike. Living standards were very low, particularly in the south and among the urban working classes, and the country was ill-equipped for mobilization. The JULY CRISIS brought loud demands for neutrality from socialists, pacifists and republicans, the latter denouncing Austrian ambitions in SERBIA as anti-Italian. Lack of consultation by the CENTRAL POWERS during the crisis left the government free to respond to popular pressure and its declaration of neutrality on 2 August was widely anticipated.

Political and popular opinion in Italy remained polarized between intervention and neutrality, but the government moved slowly towards the Allies during the autumn and winter. Italian troops were removed from the French to the Austrian border, and a steady build-up of military strength got underway, hampered by the effects of Allied BLOCKADE. Fears of Austrian expansion from the Balkan Front prompted occupation of the Albanian port of Valona (Vlöre), begun in late October (with agreement from Germany) and complete by Christmas.

Salandra, briefly operating as foreign minister after the death of SAN GIULIANO, contributed to public debate in October by defining Italy's apparently mysterious foreign policy as based on '*sacro egoismo*', meaning 'self-interest'. Well received inside Italy as a pledge to pursue irredentist ambitions, the phrase made a lasting and damaging impression on overseas opinion, interpreted as an expression of greed in an era of crusading rhetoric.

Popular opinion was also swinging towards the ENTENTE. Volunteer units fighting for France were treated as popular heroes, while demonstrations in Rome forced the Army to guard both the Austro-Hungarian embassy and the (neutralist) Vatican. A government reshuffle in November 1914, especially the appointment of SONNINO as foreign minister, strengthened the interventionist lobby within the cabinet. By 3 December Salandra was referring to differences with the Central Powers' war aims in parliament, and Austria-Hungary's renewed invasion of Serbia provoked strong protest on 9 December.

A powerful German diplomatic mission under ex-chancellor von Bülow reached Italy in mid-December, establishing immediate contact with Giolitti and other non-interventionist politicians. Backed by a sympathetic press campaign against Allied blockade measures, von Bülow and Austrian ambassador Macchi spent early 1915 in talks with Sonnino aimed at satisfying Italian territorial demands in return for a free hand in the Balkans.

Despite German pressure on Vienna to offer first Albania and later (1 April) the Trentino, Sonnino followed hardening irredentist opinion in Italy by insisting on recovery of both the Trentino and Trieste, far more than Austria-Hungary was prepared to give. Rejection of his demands, finally stated publicly on 8 April, left a clear path for ongoing Allied talks with Sonnino. Allied diplomats had no difficulty conceding Austro-Hungarian territory, and the Treaty of LONDON between Italy and the Allies, signed on 26 April, granted virtually every Italian ambition in Europe and north Africa, along with substantial Allied military and economic aid, in return for an Italian declaration of war against Austria-Hungary.

The approach to war was accompanied by a period of dramatic political agitation inside Italy. A passionate interventionist speech by nationalist poet D'ANNUNZIO on 5 May ignited a furore of anti-German demonstrations in Milan and Turin, well orchestrated by expansionist business interests and political agitators. D'Annunzio took his message on tour, speaking in Rome on 14 May after a week of popular war fever boosted by the *LUSITANIA* sinking.

Salandra's parliamentary opponents on all sides gathered around a neutralist position, prompting the cabinet's resignation on 13 May. Its reinstatement by the King three days later, effectively a royal mandate for war, was followed by the granting of full emergency powers from both houses of parliament on 20 May, opposed by 74 left-wing deputies in the lower house. The ITALIAN ARMY was mobilized and war declared against Austria-Hungary on 23 May.

Opposition to the war continued in Italy after May 1915, gathered around Pope BENEDICT XV and a small but vociferous bloc of parliamentary 'Peace Socialists'. Fostered by continuing German PROPAGANDA, pacifism at home was regarded as a serious problem by the Army, and chief of staff CADORNA withheld 'sensitive' information from political authorities whenever possible, including casualty figures for his early ISONZO OFFENSIVES. The King left Rome on 25 May and remained near the ITALIAN FRONT without ever seriously interfering with the Army General Staff (*Comando Supremo*).

Italy's first year at war was militarily disappointing: the Italian Front lapsed quickly into evident stalemate, with operations almost impossible during the Alpine winter; the expensive ITALIAN NAVY appeared powerless to take offensive action in the Adriatic; Allied offensives on GALLIPOLI and the WESTERN FRONT were costly failures; and the Central Powers made sweeping conquests on the BALKAN and EASTERN FRONTS before Germany turned to attack VERDUN. Revolt of the SENUSSI in north Africa brought war with Turkey from 20 August 1915, and BULGARIA's alliance with Austria-Hungary meant war from 10 October.

Uncertain national commitment to war was exacerbated by loud press and political criticism of military leaders, and by further economic disruption. The collapse of grain imports from August 1914 had been partly offset by imports from the UNITED STATES and CANADA, while home agricultural production remained at about 90 per cent of 1914 levels until 1917. Low prewar living standards, especially in the south, left little room for even these cutbacks, and although the Army existed on smaller rations than its Anglo-French counterparts, the main brunt of shortages fell on civilians.

Rural communities were generally able to subsist quite comfortably at first, although recruitment of manpower and the bad harvest of 1916 eventually brought widespread hardship. Urban food crises struck earlier and harder, exacerbating resentment of the increased rations, military exemption and high wages enjoyed by war workers.

The government attempted to control black markets in scarce materials and food by imposing price limits, at first restricted to military requisitions but extended to various basic civilian necessities from March 1916. Ration cards were issued for bread in 1917, and extended to other foods later in the year, remaining in use until 1921. No real attempt was made by the government to reorganize the distribution of other resources until late 1917.

The Austro-Hungarian invasion of Italy in the TRENTINO OFFENSIVE of May 1916 triggered a national sense of crisis and demonstrations of unity comparable with those witnessed elsewhere in August 1914. Salandra's (justifiable) attempt to blame Cadorna for the defeat could not assuage the wrath of his opponents, and his government resigned on 12 June. A new coalition under veteran political 'fixer' Paolo BOSELLI included the leaders of the pro-War socialists (BISSOLATI) and of the clerical party (Meda), along with the bellicose ORLANDO as interior minister.

Italy eventually declared war against Germany on 28 August 1916, risking German military involvement on the Italian Front in a move timed to coincide with ROMANIA's declaration of war against the Central Powers. The declaration reflected a need for improved relations with the Allies, beset by mutual suspicion since 1915. Italian leaders were unwilling to concede Allied command in the Adriatic, and Anglo-French authorities complained at Italian reluctance to commit forces to actions elsewhere. Italians responded to accusations of unbridled *sacro egoismo* by citing shortfalls in aid promised under the London pact.

By mid-1916 food and coal imports were

running at a fraction of national requirements, and were being further eroded by a successful German SUBMARINE WARFARE campaign in the Mediterranean. By early 1917 only 25 per cent of trains could be fuelled, and bread queues filled the streets of all major cities. A wave of renewed pacifist sentiment followed peace initiatives by the Pope and US President WILSON, further stimulated by the Russian FEBRUARY REVOLUTION. Strikes in northern Italy erupted into a workers' revolt in Turin during August, and the enforced conscription of ringleaders after its military suppression spread disaffection to the Army.

Military defeat at CAPORETTO in autumn 1917 again rescued national unity from apparent disintegration. As refugees poured south into central Italy, Boselli lost a vote of confidence and his government resigned on 25 October. Orlando took over as premier, and his new cabinet, in which Sonnino retained his post, dismissed suggestions of a separate peace with the Central Powers and secured substantial Allied military support at the RAPALLO CONFERENCE on 5 November. He replaced Cadorna with the more defensively minded DIAZ, and established a joint War Council to coordinate relations between military and political authorities.

Once the front stabilized in December, pacifist attacks on the government were resumed with the revelation of the London pact's secret clauses, and another poor harvest signalled a rapid return to economic reality. Serious famine struck cities far from the front in early 1918, especially Naples, Messina and Palermo, and the bulk of assistance from the USA (which was not at war with Austria-Hungary) went to France and Britain.

Accelerating inflation brought a government attempt to mobilize resources through a national Exchange Commission, given control over exports as well as powers to requisition and redistribute all war supplies (see DALLOLIO, A.; NITTI, F.). Little remained to be mobilized and manpower resources were similarly close to exhaustion, with males born in 1900 already committed to action by mid-1918. The Navy was virtually paralysed by lack of fuel, and ground positions were considered sustainable only as long as German forces remained distracted in France.

The US FOURTEEN POINTS peace programme of January 1918 was better received by peasants in Italy than by politicians, whose colonial ambitions it broadly forbade, and the possibility of imminent Austro-Hungarian collapse kept pacifists at bay as the year progressed. The encouragement of separatist nationalism within Austria-Hungary became a major function of Italian propaganda, and was accompanied by limited political support for exiles after the unofficial 'ROME CONGRESS of Oppressed Nationalities' in April.

The AUSTRO-HUNGARIAN ARMY launched a final, failed offensive at the PIAVE RIVER in June before collapsing under socialist and nationalist influences. Still technically outnumbered and desperately short of supplies for exhausted troops, Diaz resisted Allied demands to counterattack but eventually bowed to political demands for a decisive victory, mopping up the Austro-Hungarian Army's remains at VITTORO VENETO in September, after which Italy was again united by the prospect of rich rewards.

Recovery from economic disarray was hampered by continued Allied sanctions against Germany in 1919, at which Italian delegates to the PARIS PEACE CONFERENCE (headed by Orlando and Sonnino) protested in vain. Balkan territories promised by the Pact of London were given to independent YUGOSLAVIA, and the Orlando government fell after signing the VERSAILLES Treaty in June 1919. Led by D'Annunzio, outraged nationalists occupied Fiume in September, and wartime demagogue Benito MUSSOLINI emerged as the leader of expansionist, right-wing political forces that held power under the monarchy for two decades after 1922.

Ivangorod, Battle of The opening engagement of the Russian invasion of Silesia on the EASTERN FRONT in October 1914 (see POLISH CAMPAIGN), taking the form of an advance west across the Vistula by the Russian Fourth (EVERT), Ninth (Lechitski) and Fifth (PLEHVE) Armies. Russian forces began massing for the invasion in late September, but were delayed by command indecision, bad weather and supply problems. Only advance units were in position by 11 October, when they were ordered to cross the river at Ivangorod and Novo-Alexandriya, the only suitable sites along their 90km front. Pinned down by Austro-German ARTILLERY and short of bridging equipment, the attack was called off as futile five days later.

With German forces still returning from Warsaw, eight divisions were defending the river when ten Russian divisions repeated the crossing attempt on 22 October. Three more Russian divisions arrived over the next four days, and CONRAD's plan to launch a flank attack by the Austro-Hungarian First Army (DANKL) failed against weight of numbers. The Austrians retreated to the southwest on 26 October, having lost 40,000 men, and LUDENDORFF ordered a German withdrawal from Russian Poland next day. See also: MAP 10; Battle of ŁÓDŹ.

Ivanov, General Nikolai (1851–1919) Veteran RUSSIAN ARMY officer appointed in 1914 to command the southwestern group of armies in the Galician theatre. A supporter of war minister SUKHOMLINOV, Ivanov was deeply embroiled in the Army's factional disputes and consistently frustrated efforts to transfer resources from GALICIA to meet crises elsewhere. Inveterately cautious, he made no effort to exploit tactical successes over Austro-Hungarian forces in the Galician, POLISH and CARPATHIAN campaigns of 1914–15, and was dismissed after the GORLICE-TARNOW OFFENSIVE drove his armies out of Galicia in the spring. His career was revived by well-placed factional allies, and he reappeared later that year as Tsar NICHOLAS II's military advisor at STAVKA (Russian central command). Largely ignored by chief of staff ALEXEEV, but given the hopeless task of pacifying Petrograd during the FEBRUARY REVOLUTION of 1917, he was officially retired after the OCTOBER REVOLUTION and was killed commanding a White army in the RUSSIAN CIVIL WAR.

Izzet Pasha, Ahmed (1864–1937) Experienced TURKISH ARMY officer who was a qualified supporter of the YOUNG TURK regime, and war minister until his replacement by ENVER PASHA in January 1914. Izzet's role was restricted to unofficial criticism of the government's military policies until April 1916, when he was given command of the Second Army for the summer offensive on the CAUCASIAN FRONT. Its comprehensive failure ended his military career, but he served as military representative during the BREST-LITOVSK negotiations in early 1918. A recognized moderate acceptable to the military, Izzet was appointed grand vizier in October 1918, and his non-partisan cabinet signed an armistice with the Allies at MUDROS on 30 October. His cabinet fell on 11 November, amid accusations of assisting the wartime government's escape to exile, but Izzet filled several postwar cabinet posts before retiring in 1922.

J

Jackson, Admiral Sir Henry (1855–1929) Unspectacular British naval officer, a pioneer of applied RADIO technology, who became head of the ROYAL NAVY's infant war staff in 1913. On FISHER's resignation as First Sea Lord in May 1915, Jackson was a surprise appointment as his replacement. Quickly enmeshed in administrative trivia, he was responsible for ineffectual attempts to extend the DOVER BARRAGE but otherwise made little mark, and his partnership with naval minister BALFOUR was generally viewed as uninspired. Replaced by JELLICOE in late 1916, he saw out hostilities as aide-de-camp to King GEORGE V.

Jadar River, Battle of the The opening engagement of the war on the BALKAN FRONT in August 1914, and a decisive defeat for the first invasion of SERBIA by the AUSTRO-HUNGARIAN ARMY's southern forces. Delayed by inefficient mobilization and denied overall numerical superiority by manpower demands on the EASTERN FRONT, some 450,000 Austro-Hungarian troops were deployed on the Serbian border under the command of General POTIOREK, who launched an attack as soon as they were assembled on 12 August. Its immediate target was the large SALIENT of Serbian territory jutting into Austro-Hungarian Bosnia west of Belgrade, bordered by the Drina River to the southwest and the Save to the immediate northwest of the capital.

The main Austro-Hungarian attack, by the Fifth Army and part of the Sixth, was across the Drina by 13 August, and a secondary advance led by half the Second Army (held en route for Galicia) crossed the Save. The Fifth Army advanced some 10km to take the border town of Loznica on 14 August, and the Second took Sabac two days later, bringing them up against some 360,000 SERBIAN ARMY troops under Field Marshal PUTNIK (and about 40,000 men of the MONTENEGRO citizen army) established along a shortened 50km line between the two towns, on high ground southeast of the Jadar River. Serbian forces counterattacked on 17 and 18 August, and had driven the tactically naive Austrians back to the frontier by 20 August. A final attack two days later pushed them back across the Drina, and the invasion was officially abandoned, with 40,000 admitted losses, on 25 August. See also: Battle of the DRINA RIVER; MAP 19.

Japan The island empire of Japan experienced rapid economic development from the late 19th century, and by 1914 possessed thriving iron, steel, shipbuilding and textile industries. Though self-sufficient in armaments, it was not yet a significant factor in the global economy. Traditional agricultural and silk-weaving activities remained strong at village level, but an expanding population (about 55 million in 1915) created a large labour surplus. Good internal communications, with about 8,500km of RAILWAYS complete by 1914, encouraged the flow of labour to industrial centres.

Emperor Yoshihito became head of state in 1912, inaugurating the Taisho Era (of which 1914 was Year 3) and occupying the throne until 1926, although his son Hirohito held power as regent from 1921. The Emperor governed through an appointed executive prime minister and 10-man cabinet responsible to a parliament elected by limited male suffrage. Political leaders were drawn from an appointed upper house of dignitaries, and the Emperor was also advised by a privy council (*genro*). In contrast to an atmosphere of complete religious tolerance, all political activity by WOMEN was prohibited.

Prewar foreign policy was committed to expansion into mainland Asia at the expense of CHINA and RUSSIA. War with China in the 1890s brought the annexation of Korea, Taiwan, various Pacific islands and part of southern Manchuria; Russian eastward expansion was halted by Japanese victory in the Russo-Japanese War of 1904–05. This success emphasized Japan's growing international standing (it was the first non-white nation to contract a full alliance with GREAT BRITAIN in 1902); it also fuelled popular nationalism, and promoted military influence in public life.

Army influence suffered a backlash during the shortlived Katuro administration (1913–14), but recaptured control of military ministries under the Okuma regime from April 1914. Okuma's resignation in October 1916, engineered by a hostile *genro*, brought aggressively expansionist General Terauchi Masatake to power as prime minister.

Japan used the terms of the alliance with Britain to declare war on GERMANY on 23 August 1914, and secured its immediate war aims by occupying German-held Pacific islands and concessions on mainland China (see TSINGTAO). Japanese control of Manchuria was steadily extended, and an attempt was made in 1918 to secure a military foothold in Siberia (see RUSSIAN CIVIL WAR). Wartime operations were otherwise largely limited to the powerful JAPANESE NAVY.

High transportation costs reduced European trade but new markets opened, especially for textiles and other manufactured goods in INDIA and AUSTRALIA. Trade with the UNITED STATES and China multiplied. Diversification of output increased the factory labour force from 1.2 million in 1914 to 2 million in 1918, but the chief beneficiaries were the owners, who used surplus labour to keep wages relatively low. Agricultural wages climbed even more slowly, and an overall 400 per cent wartime rise in rice prices provoked rural food riots from July 1918.

The most serious public disturbances in Japan for more than a decade, they spread to affect more than 30 provinces and brought down the Matasake cabinet in September. Hara Kei, head of a new non-party cabinet, ruthlessly suppressed civil disobedience and nascent labour movements, authorizing more than 10,000 arrests and a number of executions.

Most of Japan's large wartime trade surpluses were held as cash by the postwar government, and evaporated during a depression in the early 1920s, but heavy capital investment did take place in China, where indigenous coal, iron and steel industries came completely under Japanese control by 1918 (see TWENTY-ONE DEMANDS). Postwar control was effectively assured by broad international acceptance of Japan's dominant role in China at the PARIS PEACE CONFERENCE, where both powers were among the delegates (see LANSING–ISHII AGREEMENT).

Japanese Navy The emergence of the Imperial Japanese Navy as a world power, confirmed by its defeat of the RUSSIAN NAVY in 1905, was a by-product of rapid prewar industrialization and JAPAN's growing territorial ambitions. The fleet of 1905 had been built around BATTLESHIPS purchased from GREAT BRITAIN, six of which were in service in August 1914, along with eight captured Russian battleships (see *PERESVIET*) and two 1910 PRE-DREADNOUGHTS built in Japan. Two new dreadnoughts and four BATTLECRUISERS, all but one built in Japan, were in service by mid-1914.

Designed in imitation of the British GRAND FLEET, the fleet was also equipped with 14 modern light CRUISERS, 6 older cruisers, 55 DESTROYERS, 56 TORPEDO BOATS and 17 small coastal SUBMARINES. Experiments in naval aviation, begun in 1917, were not seriously pursued until the 1920s.

Two more battlecruisers and four dreadnoughts were completed in wartime, along with large numbers of smaller warships, and by 1919 Japan had the third most powerful navy in the world (after Britain and the USA). Japanese shipyards also provided a dozen new destroyers for the FRENCH NAVY (completed in less than a year from November 1916) and more than 80 ANTI-SUBMARINE trawlers for FRANCE and ITALY.

Relative to its size, the Japanese Navy played a small wartime role. Major warships took part in the occupation of German concessions in CHINA (see TSINGTAO) and the Allied hunt for German surface raiders in the Pacific (see Battle of CORONEL), and Japanese units also provided protection for Allied CONVOYS in the far east.

Eight modern Japanese destroyers, commanded by Admiral Sato in the light cruiser *Akashi*, joined British escort forces in the MEDITERRANEAN from mid-1917, based at Malta and primarily responsible for escorting troopships. Another four destroyers arrived in August, when the armoured cruiser *Idzumo* relieved *Akashi*, and two more were taken over from the ROYAL NAVY and manned by Japanese crews. Allied requests for more destroyers were refused in early 1918, on the grounds that they were needed to deal with instability in China and Siberia, where Japanese ships occupied Vladivostok during the RUSSIAN CIVIL WAR.

Although never in action, the Japanese battlefleet suffered two major wartime losses, both caused by accidents. The battlecruiser *Tsukuba* exploded at Yokosuka on 14 January 1917, and Japan's first dreadnought, *Kawachi*, suffered a similar disaster in Tokuyuma Bay on 12 July 1918. Most of Japan's major warships were discarded in the early 1920s, in accordance with international restrictions on naval strength.

Jaslowiec, Battle of See: SHCHERBACHEV, D.; BRUSILOV OFFENSIVE.

Jean Bart See: *COURBET*; OTRANTO BARRAGE.

Jebel Hamrin, Battle of Failed Anglo-Russian attempt to encircle 15,000 Turkish troops under Ali Ishan Bey, retreating from operations against Russian forces in PERSIA during March 1917. Ishan was attempting to make contact with Turkish forces defending the area north of BAGHDAD, and a composite Anglo-Indian force of about 8,000 men (General Keary) was sent from Baghdad to the probable Turkish rendezvous point at Baquba on 14 March. The Turkish garrison of Baquba withdrew northwest towards Ishan's approaching army three days later.

Unaware that the Russian advance from PERSIA had been halted by news of the FEBRUARY REVOLUTION, and expecting to crush Ishan between two armies, Keary moved up to new Turkish positions in the foothills of the Jebel Hamrin mountains, where 4,500 troops were dug into high ground beyond two canals. British canal crossings took time and revealed preparations for an attack on 25 March. Without the benefit of surprise it failed, suffering 1,200 casualties and giving Ishan time to escape southwest towards Turkish forces on the Tigris. Keary continued northwest when he found the road clear and eventually met up with Russian units in the mountains on 4 April. Discovering no Turks and only 3,000 turbulent Russians, Keary rejoined the main British advance on SAMARRAH. See MAP 23.

Jellicoe, Admiral Sir John (1859–1935) Britain's best-known admiral in August 1914. A gunnery expert who was Admiral FISHER's longstanding choice to lead the GRAND FLEET in wartime, Jellicoe was duly appointed its commander on 4 August 1914. Contemporary public opinion anticipated a major naval battle in the North Sea, and expected the Navy to prevent any attacks by German ships on mainland Britain (see SCARBOROUGH RAID). Disappointment on both counts was eventually blamed on Jellicoe's inherently defensive attitude, popularly contrasted with the more aggressive posture of his eventual successor, Admiral BEATTY.

An inflexible and detailed series of operational instructions imposed caution on more adventurous officers, and he was not without critics within the Navy, but the Royal Navy's primary task was to maintain its economic BLOCKADE of GERMANY, and Jellicoe's unwillingness to lose ships guaranteed its continue strategic dominance of the German HIGH SEA FLEET.

His performance at JUTLAND in 1916 wa viewed by many as halfhearted, particularl his precautionary turn away from an antici pated TORPEDO attack at the height of th action, and he was under some pressure t resign before his appointment as First Se Lord, effectively naval chief of staff, in lat 1916. He performed the job uneasily and wit little understanding of its political dimensio opposing the introduction of CONVOYS fo merchant ships but working energetically t increase other ANTI-SUBMARINE resource Abruptly removed from office by LLOY GEORGE on 24 December 1917, he retire from active service, but accepted the post o governor general of NEW ZEALAND after th War.

Jerusalem, Fall of Climax of the Britis autumn offensive on the PALESTINE FRONT i 1917. Victories at the BEERSHEBA–GAZA LIN and MUGHAR RIDGE had forced KRESSEN STEIN's Turkish Eighth Army north beyon Jaffa to positions behind the River Auja British C-in-C ALLENBY barely paused befor switching his main attack inland agains Fehvzi Pasha's Seventh Army, some 15,00 men guarding approaches to Jerusalem at th end of fragile supply lines. Both Allenby an German C-in-C FALKENHAYN were unde orders to avoid any fighting in or near th holy city itself.

An attack on Turkish Seventh Arm positions west of Jerusalem and a diversionar advance against the Auja were launched on 1 November. Slowed by rains but meeting onl limited resistance, the main force turned nort short of Jerusalem on 21 November, aimin to cut the road to Falkenhayn's HQ at Nablu and surround the city, but was halted b strong Turkish positions on the Zeitun Ridg and the mound of Nabi Samweil. Both side suffered about 50 per cent losses in two days o inconclusive fighting. The secondary coasta attack kept two Turkish divisions occupie but could not cross the Auja.

Falkenhayn, with much of his YILDERI FORCE still en route for the theatre, launched major counterattack against the thin CAVALRY screen guarding British supply lines east of Nabi Samweil early on 27 November, but a breakthrough was prevented by British reserves. Further west, an attack by two Turkish divisions made little progress against the lightly held area inland from the coast. Both degenerated into static warfare over the next few days, giving Allenby time to bring up plentiful reinforcements.

A renewed British offensive began in pouring rain on the night of 7/8 December. Infantry wheeled east towards the Jerusalem suburbs, using the main road to bring up artillery support, and two fresh divisions, attacking without a PRELIMINARY BOMBARDMENT, had pushed surprised defenders back some 7km by dawn. They had been halted south and east of Nabi Samweil by evening, when operations were suspended to allow a convergent advance to come up from the south via Bethlehem.

The pause gave outnumbered and demoralized Turkish forces an opportunity to escape, and by morning the entire force just north of Jerusalem was in retreat towards Nablus and Jericho. The city formally surrendered that day and Allenby made his official entry (on foot) on 11 December. British forces near the coast advanced across the Auja after a surprise attack on 20 December, and the RFC flew constant light bombing raids against the Seventh Army's retiring columns, but heavy rain and thick mud delayed ground pursuit north of Jerusalem.

Yilderim units still reaching the frontline brought Seventh Army strength up to about 20,000 combat troops by Christmas, and Falkenhayn launched a night counterattack against the Khadase Ridge just north of Jerusalem on 26/27 December. Against 33,000 defenders in the sector the attack was reversed into a British advance from 28 December, both sides suffering about 1,500 casualties before the Seventh Army fell back on Jericho. Exhaustion and rain then halted operations for the winter season.

The loss of Jerusalem was a huge blow to Ottoman imperial prestige in the Middle East and finally wrecked the offensive potential of Yilderim Force. For the Allies, Allenby's success offset bad news from RUSSIA, CAPORETTO and CAMBRAI, and British campaigns on the MESOPOTAMIAN FRONT were put on hold in preparation for a decisive offensive in Palestine. See MAP 22; Battle of MEGIDDO; TRANSJORDAN.

Joffre, Marshal Joseph (1852–1931) French officer of engineers who made his fairly modest prewar fighting reputation in colonial expeditions. Untainted by political or religious connections, he was a consensus choice for chief of general staff in 1911, a position that carried de facto command of the FRENCH ARMY in time of war. A magisterial and autocratic figure, Joffre purged the Army of 'defensively minded' commanders, lobbied for increased military budgets, and adopted the PLAN 17 blueprint for invasion of GERMANY.

His rigid adherence to the Plan and tardy recognition of German numerical superiority exacerbated defeats at the Battles of the FRONTIERS in late August, but his belated decision to place the Fifth Army in the path of the German invasion at CHARLEROI and his last-minute creation of a Sixth Army to plug gaps in the subsequent retreat helped frustrate the SCHLIEFFEN PLAN.

Although others, particularly GALLIÉNI, claimed the credit for spotting the chance to attack the German flank on the MARNE in early September, Joffre's calm readiness to exploit the opportunity and his efficient orchestration of the subsequent victory earned him an almost unassailable position as the saviour of FRANCE.

Joffre's wartime command was marked by almost complete subordination of state authority to the military. From August 1914 he ruled a large 'Zone of the Armies' as virtual dictator, and information was withheld from both government and public whenever possible. The BRIAND administration endeavoured to impose a degree of political control from autumn 1915, but the decline of Joffre's reputation followed only gradually from the repeated failure of BREAKTHROUGH attempts on the WESTERN FRONT by massed infantry assaults in CHAMPAGNE and ARTOIS.

The manifestly inadequate condition of defences at VERDUN in February 1916, and the weariness induced by the subsequent ten months of fighting for the fortresses, finally brought his removal from power in December. Still too popular to be dismissed, he was promoted Marshal of France and reduced to ceremonial duties, heading the French military mission to the UNITED STATES in 1917 and serving as a figurehead president of the SUPREME WAR COUNCIL in 1918.

Josef, Archduke (1872–1962) One of the younger and more active royal generals in the AUSTRO-HUNGARIAN ARMY, he commanded an infantry division with the Second Army during the GALICIA campaign of August 1914, and led VII Corps during subsequent CARPATHIAN operations. From July 1915 his corps fought on the ITALIAN FRONT, where he remained until after the ninth ISONZO OFFENSIVE in autumn 1916, when he was promoted to command Austro-Hungarian forces in the ROMANIAN CAMPAIGN. His growing professional reputation suffered a major setback in January 1918, when he was the only senior officer to vote in favour of the Army's division into regional forces, and his last senior appointment was as CONRAD's replacement in command on the Italian Trentino sector. Josef's estates lay in Hungary and he led a royalist counterrevolution in Communist-controlled Budapest during 1919. Briefly regent in the autumn, he was replaced by Admiral HORTHY in September at Allied insistence.

Josef Ferdinand, Archduke (1872–1942) Godson of Austro-Hungarian Emperor FRANZ JOSEF, he led the Fourth Army on the EASTERN FRONT in August 1914. Lionized by PROPAGANDA after initial success in GALICIA but regarded as a frivolous aristocrat by professional soldiers, he escaped blame for the disastrous 'BLACK-YELLOW' OFFENSIVE of September 1915 but was finally removed from command when the BRUSILOV OFFENSIVE virtually destroyed his army in June 1916. See also: Battle of LUTSK.

July Crisis, 1914 The period between the assassination of Archduke FRANZ FERDINAND on 28 June 1914 and the outbreak of general war in early August. It was the holiday season in Europe, with senior diplomats and politicians away from their desks, and public attention in most countries remained focused on local issues until the last days of July.

The murder excited an active war party within AUSTRIA-HUNGARY into demands for a punitive attack on SERBIA, but the imperial Crown Council decided against an immediate invasion pending guarantees of support from its alliance partner, GERMANY. Enquiries about Germany's attitude were rewarded on 5 July with an open promise from Kaiser WILHELM II and chancellor BETHMANN HOLLWEG to back any action Vienna chose to take. Modern opinion is agreed that this represented a provisional decision for general war by the German government.

The path to a general conflict was clear to diplomats. Serbia's security had been guaranteed by RUSSIA, and the Austro-German alliance stipulated common cause if either were at war with Russia. Treaty obligations required FRANCE to join Russia in any European war, and GREAT BRITAIN was practically, if not technically, bound to the defence of France by a series of informal military agreements. Other powers, notably ITALY and TURKEY, were bound by public or secret alliance to one side or the other, but appeared unwilling or unable to fight.

Vienna still hoped to fight Serbia without toppling the dominoes. An ultimatum to the Serbian government was delayed to allow a cooling-off period until 23 July, just after French prime minister VIVIANI and president POINCARÉ had put to sea from St Petersburg, where they had confirmed their willingness to back Russia in defence of Serbia. A conciliatory Serbian reply, accepting most demands but not allowing Austro-Hungarian armies into Serbia in search of the Archduke's killers, was rejected by Vienna on 26 July. Austria-Hungary declared war on Serbia two days later and the Serbian Capital of Belgrade was bombarded on 29 July, bringing the international diplomatic crisis to a head.

Popular opinion everywhere was suddenly alerted to the likelihood of general war. Viviani and Poincaré reached Paris on 29 July to popular demonstrations of militant nationalism, and Russia, determined to protect its last Balkan ally, mobilized its armies facing Austria-Hungary on the same day.

Both Austria-Hungary and Russia ordered general mobilization on 30 July, and the FRENCH ARMY was withdrawn 10km all along the German border to avoid any danger of starting hostilities and alienating British support. On 31 July, a Friday, Germany demanded Russian demobilization within 12 hours, and guarantees of neutrality from France within 18 hours, by way of pleading self-defence. As German forces were ordered to *Kriegsgefahr* (a preliminary stage of mobilization) panic closed stock exchanges worldwide.

The German ultimatum to Russia expired without compliance at noon on 1 August, and an announcement from Paris shortly afterwards declared that France would 'act in accordance with her own interests'. Both Germany and France ordered mobilization that afternoon, triggering their armies' respective SCHLIEFFEN PLAN and PLAN 17 offensives. With the Russian PLAN 19 getting underway, the AUSTRO-HUNGARIAN ARMY marching to the attack, and Italy expected to declare neutrality, Britain's position apparently remained in the balance.

The ASQUITH cabinet, in which GREY and CHURCHILL were the leading interventionists, needed a *casus belli* to convince public opinion – and a strong pacifist section of the governing Liberal Party – to support France, so that British intentions hinged on the issue of Belgian neutrality, about to be violated by the GERMAN ARMY.

Germany declared war on Russia in the evening of 1 August, but on the same day Wilhelm twice attempted to stop the invasion of BELGIUM and France. Initially informed by Army chief of staff MOLTKE that logistic arrangements could not be changed, he later sent personal telegrams cancelling the invasion in the west, but they arrived too late to stop German units entering LUXEMBOURG, and were countermanded when his hopes of British neutrality faded.

With street crowds waiting for news in every major European capital, a German ultimatum to Belgium was delivered on the evening of 2 August, demanding the right to occupy the country and repel alleged French incursions from the west. On 3 August Grey finally made it clear in parliament that Britain would fight for Belgian neutrality, and that German conquest of northwestern Europe was against Britain's national interests. Later that day Belgian King ALBERT I announced Belgium's decision to fight if invaded, and Germany declared war on France. When Germany invaded Belgium (at GEMMERICH) the next day, a British ultimatum to Germany required a 'satisfactory' explanation by midnight (23.00 British time). Its failure to arrive placed Britain at war with Germany and completed the opening of the conflagration. See also: BALKAN, WESTERN, EASTERN FRONTS.

July Days Uprising against the Russian PROVISIONAL GOVERNMENT begun on 16 July 1917 by a regiment of MACHINE GUN troops in Petrograd (St Petersburg) as an armed protest against the failed KERENSKI OFFENSIVE. The anti-War Bolsheviks, still a relatively small force and unsure of the revolt's depth, decided to join the uprising next day, when the movement spread to sailors in Kronstadt and civilians in major towns all over RUSSIA. The government retained sufficient military support to restore order within a few days, and the Bolsheviks were temporarily suppressed, with several leading agitators imprisoned and LENIN forced to flee to Finland. The episode improved Bolshevik standing with an increasingly pacifist popular constituency, undermining the credibility of both the government and the moderate socialists controlling the Petrograd SOVIET. See also: OCTOBER REVOLUTION.

July Offensive See: KERENSKI OFFENSIVE.

Junkers CL-I German reconnaissance biplane, an all-metal enlargement of the JUNKERS D-I produced from March 1918. Its innovative, internally braced airframe was light enough to fulfil CL (armed light reconnaissance) category specifications, and it was the best all-round performer of its type to reach German units on the WESTERN FRONT. It was also much more difficult to construct than wooden types, and only 47 had reached active service by the end of the War. Like the D-I, it was later in action with German irregulars against Bolshevik forces in FINLAND, ESTONIA and LITHUANIA.

BRIEF DATA Type: two-seater reconnaissance; Engine: 160hp Mercedes; Max speed: 168kph; Armament: 3 × 7.92mm mg (2 forward).

Junkers D-I The first all-metal aircraft in active military service, a monoplane FIGHTER developed from prototypes first flown in 1915 but not in production until March 1918. It was a successful design – fast, agile and very strong – and greatly influenced future developments, but it could not be built quickly. Only 41 were issued to GERMAN ARMY AIR SERVICE fighter units on the WESTERN FRONT, although several fought with German anti-Bolshevik forces in the RUSSIAN CIVIL WAR.

BRIEF DATA Type: single-seat fighter; Engine: 180hp Mercedes; Max speed: 185kph; Ceiling: 6,000m; Armament: 2 × 7.92mm mg (forward).

Junkers J-1 German two-seater biplane, developed by Hugo Junkers and Anthony Fokker as an armoured ground-attack craft, and modified from Junkers' earlier all-metal prototypes so that its rear fuselage was wooden. The first J-1s joined infantry support units on the WESTERN FRONT from late 1917. Equipped with RADIO for fast-response trench-fighting and infantry-supply duties, early models performed effectively during the 1918 SPRING OFFENSIVE, although their weight made use of improvised airstrips difficult. Popular with pilots, the J-1 was more complex to build than conventional designs, and only 227 were produced before the ARMISTICE.

BRIEF DATA Type: two-seater ground support; Engine: 200hp Benz; Max speed: 155kph; Armament: 3 × 7.92mm mg (2 synchro).

Jutland, Battle of The only wartime confrontation, on 31 May 1916, between the British GRAND FLEET and the German HIGH SEAS FLEET. Something of an anti-climax despite the involvement of 274 warships and some 70,000 seamen, the battle was a minor tactical victory for the GERMAN NAVY but left the ROYAL NAVY's strategic control of the North Sea unbroken.

The world's great battlefleets had been designed to contest maritime supremacy in huge, decisive duels, but the circumstances of modern NAVAL WARFARE forced all navies to protect their deterrent value. By spring 1916 neither the Royal Navy's attempts to draw the smaller German fleet into the North Sea nor the German campaign of nuisance raids on the English east coast had engineered the major battle sought by the British (see HELIGOLAND BIGHT; DOGGER BANK; SCARBOROUGH RAID; CUXHAVEN RAID).

The appointment of Admiral SCHEER as High Seas Fleet C-in-C in February 1916 brought a positive response to criticism of the Fleet's inactivity. Once aerial reconnaissance had established that the main British fleet was not at sea, Scheer planned a raid on the English port of Sunderland by Admiral HIPPER's BATTLECRUISERS. British battlecruisers at Rosyth were expected to come out in pursuit and be led onto the main German fleet, shadowing close behind. Thirteen U-BOATS were stationed off British North Sea bases (with orders to remain in position until 1 June) to take advantage of hasty departures by would-be rescuers.

Poor visibility and high winds prevented the use of ZEPPELINS for aerial reconnaissance through late May. Scheer abandoned the proposed attack on Sunderland, settling for a less ambitious sweep along the Danish coast, again led by battlecruisers as bait. Anxious to use his SUBMARINE trap, Scheer sailed the High Seas Fleet from the Jade River at 01.00 on 31 May.

Grand Fleet C-in-C JELLICOE had put to sea two hours earlier. Given advance warning of Scheer's intent to sail (but not his destination) by the ROOM 40 codebreaking unit on 30 May, Jellicoe unwittingly placed the two fleets on a collision course by heading for the scene of his own planned operation, a sweep down the Danish coast set for 2 June.

The Grand Fleet boasted 37 modern capital ships, the High Seas Fleet 27. Most of the British ships had bigger main armament than their counterparts but less useful secondary guns, important only for countering DESTROYERS. British DIRECTOR-CONTROL gunnery systems were inferior in poor visibility, and German disadvantage in firepower was compensated by a roughly equivalent superiority in armour protection. The British force included eight less useful 'armoured' CRUISERS, and six vulnerable PRE-DREADNOUGHTS accompanied the High Seas Fleet.

Both fleets possessed excellent light cruisers for scouting purposes, but the British, with 26 at sea, enjoyed a 2-to-1 numerical advantage. British destroyers were generally intended as a defence against their smaller, more offensively deployed, German counterparts. Submarines, though present on the peripheries of the battle, played no significant active part, and AERIAL WARFARE was represented by a single seaplane from the carrier *ENGADINE* (see *CAMPANIA*).

Operational planning embraced most technical disparities, but could not legislate for the vulnerability of big British ships to internal explosion, the Royal Navy's frequent signalling lapses, or the unexpected inferiority of British heavy shells, which frequently disintegrated harmlessly on contact.

Once at sea, in the absence of aircraft, fleet movements were largely governed by sharp lookouts and guesswork. Vanguards converging throughout the morning of 31 May had no idea of each other's whereabouts until mid-afternoon, when scouting cruisers with both battlecruiser forces made contact as they investigated a stationary Danish merchant ship. After a brief gunfire exchange both groups concentrated on guiding the battlecruisers into what each believed was a trap for the other.

Unaware of the approaching Grand Fleet, Hipper allowed Admiral BEATTY's six battlecruisers to manoeuvre to his south and into Scheer's path before swinging his five big ships to meet them. Hipper did not know that Beatty's strength was augmented by four new QUEEN ELIZABETH Class battleships, temporarily left behind and out of sight (through poor British signalling) when the battlecruiser forces opened fire at 15.45, just under 13km apart and closing fast.

Beatty immediately turned south to increase the range for his biggest guns and cut off what he assumed was a German retreat. Hipper followed suit and the lines of battlecruisers exchanged broadsides along parallel courses for the next hour.

The action went badly for the British. In hazy visibility made worse by gunsmoke the position of the sun helped German gunners, and three British ships (*LION*, which lost a turret, *TIGER* and *Princess Royal*) were damaged before *INDEFATIGABLE* received the last of five hits in quick succession and blew up at 16.03. At 16.25 a full broadside from *DERFFLINGER* straddled *Queen Mary* and it too exploded, disappearing completely within ninety seconds.

At about the same time 15 German and 12 British destroyers, with a light cruiser per side, began a close-range gun and TORPEDO battle in between the battlecruisers. A torpedo hit on *SEYDLITZ* caused only slight damage, and each side lost two destroyers. The four Queen Elizabeths came within extreme range with their 15-inch guns at around 16.30 and were soon scoring hits from a distance of more than 17km. With *NEW ZEALAND* completely unharmed and three other battlecruisers still essentially operative, the odds swung back to the British.

Ten minutes later Beatty's advance scouting force (four TOWN CRUISERS) reported the entire High Seas Fleet within range. Beatty, informed by the Admiralty that afternoon that Scheer was still in port, immediately turned round and sped north towards Jellicoe, Hipper following suit to prevent his 'escape'.

The Queen Elizabeths missed the turn in worsening light and, again hampered by poor signalling, were forced to execute a difficult reversal under Hipper's (and some of Scheer's) big guns. *Barham* and *Malaya* suffered damage in the process, but the battleships scored hits in return, slightly damaging two of Scheer's dreadnoughts and causing serious flooding in *Seydlitz*.

British battlecruisers and battleships quickly pulled beyond the main German fleet, dragging Hipper's battered units with them. The dipping sun became more of an obstacle than an advantage to German gunnery, and *VON DER TANN* had no main armament left at all. At 17.25 Beatty turned his ships east, moving towards a prearranged rendezvous with Jellicoe and crossing Hipper's path to prevent him reporting the trap.

Hipper launched a destroyer and cruiser attack as a delaying tactic, but three more British battlecruisers under Admiral HOOD came within range from the east, severely damaging three German light cruisers and launching an attack by their own screening destroyers. With only *Moltke* still undamaged, Hipper assumed that Hood's force was the Grand Fleet in full strength.

Jellicoe, aboard *IRON DUKE*, thought he was 20km northwest of Beatty until just after 18.00, when his scouts sighted *Lion* in combat with opponents beyond visual range. The Grand Fleet was not in battle formation and, with action obviously imminent but no exact information about his opponent's position, Jellicoe ordered the fleet to form a line to port (turning east) at 18.15. Smoothly executed, the manoeuvre was complete by 18.30, just in time to put the Grand Fleet in perfect position, 'crossing the T' of the High Seas Fleet.

Scheer was compelled to turn east as hostile warships appeared to his north and northwest. With the main fleets about to engage, *Warspite*, one of the Queen Elizabeths joining the battle line's tail, jammed its rudder and was forced to make two full circles within range of German battleships, surviving 13 hits in the process. Also at the rear of the line, a squadron of British cruisers ran into the German battlefleet. *Defence* was blown to bits immediately, and the severely damaged *WARRIOR* sank later.

The British battlecruiser squadrons had linked up and were steaming to the front of the line, when a sudden improvement in visibility illuminated Hood's flagship, *INVINCIBLE*, long enough for it to attract concentrated fire. It became the third British battlecruiser to explode after a shell penetrated a turret at 18.33.

The Grand Fleet opened fire immediately afterwards and Scheer, recognizing his dangerous position, ordered a 'battle turn-away' (*Gefechtskehrtwendung*) at 18.35. Essentially an about-turn by every ship at once, it was brilliantly executed and the Grand Fleet had only a glimpse of its foe before it disappeared west into the murk. The British believed they had sunk several ships during the few minutes of contact, but the only German loss was the cruiser *Wiesbaden*. Jellicoe would not follow into a possible submarine trap or minefield, and ordered his ships to turn southeast and then south, hoping to intercept Scheer's homeward journey before dark.

The High Seas Fleet turned north and then back upon itself, intending to get around the rear of the British line, but Scheer overestimated Jellicoe's speed and steamed back into the Grand Fleet's broadsides, which opened up at about 19.10. Scheer later portrayed this as a deliberate attacking move, but most historians agree that he blundered into a very dangerous position.

Scheer ordered Hipper's weakened ships to charge the Grand Fleet, sent in his destroyer flotillas and ordered another 'battle turn-away' as Jellicoe pulled briefly away from the danger of torpedo attack. A German destroyer was sunk and Hipper's ships took a further pounding before turning away, but the German fleet was again disappearing to the west within a few minutes and firing had ceased by 19.30.

Still confident that Scheer could not get home, Jellicoe turned his fleet southwest to intercept its presumed route. Beatty's battlecruisers, about 10km ahead, sighted Hipper's force heading south at 20.15, just before sunset, and opened fire a few minutes later. The attack finished off *Lützow*, which ground to a halt and later sank, and knocked out the last heavy guns of *Seydlitz* and *Derfflinger* before Scheer sent his six vulnerable predreadnoughts into a holding attack at 20.30. They occupied Beatty's guns for a few minutes before following the rest of the fleet in escaping to the west.

By 21.00 Scheer had again turned south and night had fallen. At that point the fleets were less than 10km apart and converging, but they never again met. Scouting forces of both sides continued the battle through the night, engaging in several confused and costly actions.

The German cruiser *FRAUENLOB* was sunk by the British *Southampton*, itself seriously damaged; six destroyers were lost in a dash at the main German fleet in the hour either side of midnight, but they damaged the battleship *Nassau* and sank two light cruisers; a flotilla attack on the six pre-dreadnoughts sank *Pommern* with all hands; the British armoured cruiser *Black Prince* was blown to bits by battleships when it joined the wrong fleet in the dark. The final contact with German battleships came at 02.30, when a British light cruiser and four destroyers again found the pre-dreadnoughts, but sank only a single destroyer.

Partly because of effective RADIO jamming by German destroyers, no reports of these actions reached Jellicoe. Anxious not to have a night battle against opponents with superior searchlights, and having received a signal from the Admiralty suggesting that Scheer was behind him, Jellicoe continued to steam south. The High Seas Fleet, including its pre-dreadnoughts and crippled battlecruisers, escaped round the rear of the British line and reached the comparative safety of Horn's Reef at around 03.00. Jellicoe turned for home half an hour later. The last casualty of the action was the German dreadnought *Ostfriesland*, badly damaged by a British MINE in the Jade River approaches at 05.30, but submarines missed both fleets on their return to home ports.

The German Navy's immediate claim to victory was backed up by the 'score' in sinkings, and its ships had displayed enormous resilience. The performance of the Royal Navy, riddled with missed opportunities and operational deficiencies, provoked disappointment in GREAT BRITAIN. Controversy, centred on Jellicoe's alleged over-caution, has surrounded the action ever since, but a majority of modern commentators regard caution as having been justified by the battle's long-term effects.

Jellicoe was able to pronounce the Grand Fleet again ready for sea by 2 June, but the High Seas Fleet was crippled for many months, its surviving battlecruisers and several battleships in need of extensive reconstruction. It was never again risked in a major North Sea expedition, or allotted the resources for efficient operation by the German High Command. See MAP 16.

K

K-1 First of the very large, fast British SUBMARINES built in 1917–18 for operations with the GRAND FLEET. K-types never had the chance to prove themselves in fleet action, but *K-1* was one of three lost to collisions in the North Sea, reinforcing the most obvious argument against their deployment in crowded battle zones.

BRIEF DATA (1917) Displacement: 1,883 tons; Crew: 50–60; Dimensions: length 338ft (102.5m), beam 26.5ft (8m); Speed: 25k (surface), 9k (submerged); Armament: 1 × 4in gun, 1 × 3in AA, 8 × 18in TT.

'Kadaver' Rumour A story spread by Anglo-French PROPAGANDA in April 1917 that the GERMAN ARMY was boiling down dead troops for their fats. It was based on a mistranslation of the word Kadaver, meaning 'animal corpse', in a German newspaper report on the use of dead horses. Released on the heels of widespread outrage at the German 'scorched earth' policy employed during Operation ALBERICH, the story retained widespread credibility in Allied countries throughout the period.

Kaiser The five Kaiser Class BATTLESHIPS (*Kaiser*, *Friedrich der Große*, *Kaiserin*, *Prinz Regent Luitpold* and *König Albert*) were the most modern in service with the GERMAN NAVY in August 1914, but never took part part in any serious fighting, though all but *König Albert* were at JUTLAND. Interned at Scapa Flow after the ARMISTICE, they were scuttled by their German crews in June 1919.

BRIEF DATA (*Kaiser,* 1914) Displacement: 24,380 tons; Crew: 1,088; Dimensions: length 564ft (170.9m), beam 95.25ft (28.9m); Speed: 23k; Armament: 10 × 12in gun, 14 × 5.9in, 8 × 3.4in, 4 × 3.4in AA, 5 × 19.7in TT.

Kaiserschlacht German name ('Kaiser's Battle') for the opening attack of the SPRING OFFENSIVES on the WESTERN FRONT in 1918. Begun on 21 March, it is also known as the Michael Offensive (after its operational codename) or the Second Battle of the Somme.

The end of the war on the EASTERN FRONT in late 1917 gradually freed GERMAN ARMY strength for offensive operations elsewhere. Aware that internal stresses and war with the UNITED STATES condemned GERMANY to defeat in a prolonged war, and that all-out *HANDELSKRIEG* ('trade warfare') had failed to knock out GREAT BRITAIN, the German THIRD SUPREME COMMAND planned a decisive victory in France before large-scale US reinforcements could arrive. The BEF was seen as the main obstacle to victory, and LUDENDORFF planned the Somme operation, striking where British and FRENCH ARMY defensive zones met, as a means of separating the two forces.

On the Allied side, costly and unsuccessful offensives in 1917 had left commanders little option but to remain on the defensive while efforts were made to rebuild manpower and establish command unification (see SUPREME WAR COUNCIL). Though the mass transfer of German forces to France in early 1918 was noted, and an attack expected, it was generally believed that Germany could not field sufficient strength to achieve the breakthrough that had eluded the Allies.

German strength on the Western Front increased by 30 per cent between November 1917 and March 1918, by which time Allied manpower levels had dropped by a quarter since the summer. A total of 63 German divisions of the Seventeenth (BELOW), Second (MARWITZ) and Eighteenth (HUTIER) Armies were assembled for the attack along a 90km front stretching from Arras to La Fère. They faced 14 divisions of the British Third Army (BYNG) in the north, backed by the majority of British reserves, and 12 divisions of General GOUGH's Fifth Army stretched along the southern two-thirds of the sector.

Careful maintenance of secrecy, ARTILLERY support from more than 6,000 guns (firing an unusually large proportion of GAS shells), efficient INFILTRATION TACTICS and a thick morning mist all helped the offensive achieve early success. Protected by aircraft and a CREEPING BARRAGE, German infantry made spectacular progress against thin, poorly organized defences in the south and were held only in the far north around Arras.

With losses in the south threatening to leave his flank exposed, Gough began retreating to half-prepared new defensive lines on 22 March, but failed to destroy vital bridges and causeways, allowing the German Eighteenth Army to pursue at speed and force a further retirement. By 25 March the whole British Fifth Army front had retired some 40km west, dragging the right wing of the Third Army back, and Hutier's forward units reached Montdidier two days later, some 65km beyond their start point.

Most attacking strength had been concentrated around Arras in the north, but Ludendorff now instructed Marwitz to push between the British armies towards Amiens, and allocated all nine divisions of German reserves to the operation. The Eighteenth Army was ordered to pause pending a turn towards Paris, but Below's unsuccessful attacks on Arras were continued until 28 March. On 26 March the German Second Army's advance on Amiens was halted by exhaustion, supply difficulties and the British Third Army around Villers-Bretonneux, some 20km short of the city.

French C-in-C PÉTAIN delayed transfer of reinforcements to the front, prompting BEF commander HAIG to support the appointment of FOCH as overall 'Allied Coordinator' of reserves, but French reinforcements under General FAYOLLE had arrived to halt a renewed advance on 30 March, and 15 German divisions, most of them utterly exhausted, failed in a final attempt to reach Amiens on 4 April. Recognizing that the opportunity for strategic gain had passed, Ludendorff halted the operation on 5 April and switched the theatre of battle to Flanders, where the LYS OFFENSIVE opened on 9 April.

Though a huge tactical success, the Kaiserschlacht offensive failed to break Allied lines and cost the German Army 250,000 casualties it could not afford. Allied losses were slightly lower. The crisis meanwhile prompted reform of the Allied command system, promoted radical reassessments of material requirements in the United States, and temporarily dispelled mounting civilian war weariness in FRANCE and Britain. See MAP 9.

Kamerun See: CAMEROON.

Karl I, Kaiser (1887–1922) A CAVALRY officer in the AUSTRO-HUNGARIAN ARMY until the assassination of his uncle, Archduke FRANZ FERDINAND, in 1914 left him heir to the throne of AUSTRIA-HUNGARY. He was a liaison officer during the opening campaign in GALICIA, was promoted and recalled to court in summer 1915, but returned to action in May 1916, commanding a corps on the ITALIAN FRONT before returning to Galicia in the wake of the BRUSILOV OFFENSIVE.

His fighting career ended by the death of FRANZ JOSEF, Karl became Austrian Emperor (Kaiser) on 21 November 1916 and King of Hungary on 30 December. A humanitarian man with liberal tendencies, and greatly influenced by his pro-Allied wife, Princess Zita of Bourbon-Parma, the new Kaiser attracted support from moderate politicians in both his kingdoms, but was regarded as weak-willed and volatile by both political extremes.

The appointment of liberal, reformist prime ministers, beginning with CLAM-MARTINIC in Austria, failed to quell minority separatism or left-wing republicanism, especially after a royal amnesty had released the Empire's most committed political opponents from prison. The replacement of CONRAD as Army chief of staff by ARZ VON STRAUSSENBERG increased royal influence over the military, and Karl introduced a series of reforms – banning duels, ending flogging, halting STRATEGIC BOMBING and restricting the use of poison GAS – that outraged senior commanders.

Karl recognized but deplored Austria-Hungary's military dependence on GERMANY and was committed to seeking a compromise peace with the Allies. A clumsy personal approach to the French government through Prince SIXTUS of Bourbon in March 1917 achieved nothing at the time, but provided good PROPAGANDA for the Allies a year later and ended all hope of influencing German policy. German control over the Austro-Hungarian war effort culminated in effective economic and military union a few weeks later, reluctantly accepted by Karl during a visit to WILHELM II at Spa on 11 May 1918.

Peace offers made to the Allies later in the year were all rejected as too little too late, and Karl's attempt to establish a federation of autonomous states in Austria – the OCTOBER MANIFESTO – met the same fate. The Emperor accepted the disintegration of Austria-Hungary with some grace, permitting imperial soldiers to join national armies on 31 October and renouncing his constitutional powers on 11 November. He subsequently changed his mind, refusing to abdicate his thrones formally and belatedly endeavouring to rally royalist support. He fled to Switzerland in March 1919 with British help, and two attempts to return to Hungary in 1921 were blocked by the HORTHY government.

Károlyi von Nagykároly, Mihály, Count (1875–1955) Liberal Magyar aristocrat who left ANDRÁSSY's opposition Independence Party in mid-1916 to form his own radical group in the Hungarian assembly, demanding full national autonomy, land reform and universal suffrage. In a belated attempt to contain popular revolt, Emperor KARL I named Károlyi to replace prime minister WEKERLE on 31 October 1918, by which time Hungarian independence was a virtual fait accompli. Károlyi requested and received release from his imperial oath the next day and proclaimed a republic on 11 November, serving as its head of state until Béla Kun's Communist uprising drove him into exile in March 1919.

Kazakov, Alexander (1891–1919) Generally accepted as the most successful wartime Russian FIGHTER pilot, Kazakov won his 17 confirmed victories on the EASTERN FRONT, where AERIAL WARFARE remained relatively primitive. His first victims were brought down by the simple but drastic method of ramming in mid-air, and he may have destroyed large numbers of hostile aircraft in remote areas with no witnesses. Despite his expertise in forced landings, Kazakov was eventually killed serving with anti-Bolskevik forces during the RUSSIAN CIVIL WAR. See also: ACES.

Kemal Pasha, Mustapha (1881–1938) The most successful TURKISH ARMY commander of the period. Though primarily interested in military affairs he was involved in revolutionary activities from his earliest commission as a junior officer in Damascus, but was overshadowed by more politically inclined officers during the YOUNG TURK revolution of 1908. He was considered a potential rival by war minister ENVER PASHA in 1914, and remained military attaché to BULGARIA until late in the year, when he took command of the 19th Division at GALLIPOLI.

Kemal's leadership during the GALLIPOLI LANDINGS of April 1915, and the SUVLA BAY OFFENSIVE in August, was characterized by fanatical determination to halt Allied advances regardless of cost and made him a popular hero in TURKEY. Promoted general and transferred to the CAUCASIAN FRONT in 1916, he emerged from a disastrous summer offensive with more credit than other commanders. In 1917 he took command of the Seventh Army at Aleppo as part of the German-led YILDERIM FORCE. He resigned in October, a protest at Enver's attempt to exploit collapse of the RUSSIAN ARMY in the Caucasus, but returned to command the following August, leading the Seventh Army through a prolonged retreat after defeat at MEGIDDO, and becoming overall commander of Turkish armies north of ALEPPO just before the ARMISTICE.

In the political vacuum following the collapse of the Young Turk regime, Kemal organized nationalist forces in Anatolia against Allied partition of Turkey (see Treaty of SÈVRES), proclaiming a revolutionary government in May 1919 and leading a successful guerrilla war against GREEK ARMY forces attempting to occupy SMYRNA. First president of the Turkish Republic from 1924, he led the progressive westernization of Turkish culture, adopting the additional name 'Atatürk' ('Father of the People') in 1934.

Kerenski, Aleksandr (1881–1970) Russian socialist lawyer, a representative of the small Trudovik party in the Duma and the chamber's best-known radical spokesman in 1914. Kerenski and nine other Trudoviks joined a few Menshevik and Bolshevik socialists in opposing the Duma's otherwise unanimous endorsement of war in August 1914, and he remained a vociferous critic of the regime until illness forced his temporary retirement in late 1915.

Returning to Petrograd (St Petersburg) in mid-1916, his attacks on the crown became more extreme before the FEBRUARY REVOLUTION of 1917, earning him a dual role as vice chairman of the new Petrograd SOVIET and justice minister in the PROVISIONAL GOVERNMENT. As the token socialist in the first Provisional coalition, he recognized the growing distance between the government and mass opinion, using his left-of-centre credentials to gain authority within a shaky liberal cabinet.

A firm supporter of war against German 'militarism', Kerenski took over the war ministry in mid-May 1917 and planned a military offensive on the EASTERN FRONT to evict German forces from Revolutionary soil. Carried through despite strong popular protests, the KERENSKI OFFENSIVE finally broke the cohesion of the RUSSIAN ARMY.

Kerenski replaced Prince LVOV as premier at the height of the offensive in July. Isolated amidst right-wing threats of counterrevolution, radical urban masses, rural anarchy and the threat of imminent conquest, he veered between repression and conciliation. Bolsheviks and other radicals were imprisoned after the JULY DAYS demonstrations, forcing LENIN to flee to Finland, and elections for a constituent assembly were postponed until November. He brought more socialists into a second coalition in early August, but the fall of RIGA in early September persuaded him to authorize Army C-in-C KORNILOV to restore order in the capital.

Rumours that Kornilov planned a dictatorship briefly united socialists against the prospect of counterrevolution, prompting a temporary swing to the left by Kerenski. He officially proclaimed a socialist republic on 14 September, released radical leaders from prison, and gave moderate socialists a majority in a new coalition from 8 October.

His attempt on 5 November to arrest leaders of the Bolshevik revolutionary command (MRC) triggered their successful uprising. He fled Petrograd during the OCTOBER REVOLUTION (which took place in November by the western calendar), joining hastily assembled loyal troops for a march on the capital that petered out when confronted by revolutionary forces on 12 November. Then only 36 years old, Kerenski spent the rest of his life in exile.

Kerenski Offensive The RUSSIAN ARMY's final attack on the EASTERN FRONT in 1917, also known as the Second Brusilov or July Offensive. In an atmosphere of political and economic turmoil following the FEBRUARY REVOLUTION, and with the Army rapidly disintegrating under the influence of military SOVIETS, the PROVISIONAL GOVERNMENT sought to unite popular sentiment and Allied credit by mounting a 'Liberty Offensive' to defend the Revolution against the 'imperialist' CENTRAL POWERS.

Planned by war minister KERENSKI and C-in-C BRUSILOV, it was a repeat of the 1916 BRUSILOV OFFENSIVE along the whole Galician sector, except that lack of reliable forces restricted it to two main thrusts. Brusilov himself took command of the combined Seventh and Eleventh Armies (31 divisions known as the 'Red Army') for an attack against the Austro-German Südarmee (BOTHMER) along a 65km front around Brody. Launched on 1 July, it took 10,000 prisoners on the first day and forced the Südarmee back towards Lvov, but low morale, poor supply lines and the rapid arrival of German reserves (including 6 divisions from the WESTERN FRONT) slowed the advance to a crawl within a few days, and offensive operations were called off from 16 July.

Further southwest, in the Bukovina region, the Russian Eighth Army (KORNILOV) attacked along a 100km front south of the Dneister on 6 July, and broke through Austrian lines west of Stanislau on 8 July. By 12 July the Eighth Army had advanced some 30km, and was approaching the Drohobicz oilfields, but the mood of the troops and their lack of supplies prevented sustained progress.

By 19 July, when Bothmer's reinforced Südarmee counterattacked, Russian forces were static or withdrawing all along the Galician front. Aimed at Brody, the main attack was preceded by a seven-hour PRELIMINARY BOMBARDMENT, enough to cause the disintegration of Brusilov's right wing. Bothmer advanced 15km on the first day, after which Brusilov's remaining units evaporated as most troops gave up and went home. By the time the front stabilized during the first week of August, Austro-German forces had recrossed the Galician frontier either side of the Dneister, recapturing Stanislau and Tarnopol on 24 July and reaching Czernowitz on 3 August.

A supporting offensive by Russo-Romanian forces in Moldavia met a similar fate when MACKENSEN's Danube Army counterattacked around FOSCANI from 6 August. Apart from the experimental German offensive around RIGA in September, no more serious fighting took place on the Eastern Front. The Russian Army (commanded by Kornilov from 1 August) virtually ceased to exist, and German leaders recognized that RUSSIA could be left to self-destruct. See MAP 10.

Keyes, Admiral Sir Roger (1872–1945) Admired by contemporaries as dashingly inventive or dismissed as recklessly aggressive, Keyes was the ROYAL NAVY's best-known wartime firebrand, an apparently ideal choice as captain (with the honorary title of commodore) in command of the British SUBMARINE service in 1912. From August 1914 he sought ways to make a major impact on the German HIGH SEAS FLEET in the North Sea but was let down by technical weaknesses, especially in TORPEDOES. His submarines failed to match U-BOAT successes against warships, and after criticizing the GRAND FLEET's apparent passivity he was transferred to the DARDANELLES, where aggression was thought more appropriate, in February 1915. As chief of staff to successive commanders Carden and DE ROBECK, he lobbied consistently for a renewed attack after the failure of 18 March, and was given strong support by Admiral WEMYSS, but was frustrated by entrenched high-command caution. Keyes returned to home waters as captain of a BATTLESHIP in June 1916, and was promoted rear admiral in command of the Fourth Battle Squadron a year later. In October 1917 he became Admiralty planning director, organizing and leading the ZEEBRUGGE RAID the following April. See also: DOVER BARRAGE.

Khadairi Bend, Battle of the First of a series of cautious but effective operations against Turkish defences around the town itself during the Second Battle of KUT in early 1917, and a good example of British commander MAUDE's characteristic caution. A loop in the Tigris immediately north of Kut, surrounding a strongly fortified SALIENT of high ground, Khadairi Bend was defended by two concentric lines of deep trenches. British troops began SAPPING towards trenches after taking Turkish outposts on 22 December, and were within 200 metres of the eastern lines, nearest to Kut, by 7 January. Diversionary attacks were launched all along the Tigris front over the next two days, and the main action on 9 January was preceded by the most effective ARTILLERY bombardment of the campaign to date. Though they mounted two strong counterattacks, the outnumbered defenders were gradually overwhelmed by British artillery and pushed towards the river. The Khadairi position was in British hands by 29 January, leaving Maude overlooking the main Turkish strongpoints on the opposite bank.

Khadase Ridge, Battle of the See: JERUSALEM.

Khalil Pasha (1864–1923) Wartime commander of the Turkish Sixth Army on the MESOPOTAMIAN FRONT and military governor of the Baghdad region, with responsibility for all Ottoman territory southwest of ALEPPO. Khalil conducted a varied campaign, initially allowing field commanders to retreat from large-scale attacks, and counterattacking effectively after the Anglo-Indian failure at CTESIPHON. The successful siege of KUT persuaded him to a more aggressive policy, but a proposed sweep into PERSIA was halted by a renewed British offensive in late 1916, and his persistent commitment of forces to costly defensive actions after the fall of BAGHDAD hastened the eventual collapse of his army.

Khanaqin, Battle of Main engagement of a prolonged campaign fought on the Mesopotamian border with western PERSIA in 1916–17. General Baratov's RUSSIAN ARMY division (about 15,000 infantry and 7,500 cavalry) pushed slowly west of Tehran from late 1915, driving a combined force of renegade Persian troops and Arab irregulars steadily towards the border. Despite the arrival of Turkish reinforcements in mid-January 1916, Baratov broke through to take Kermanshah on 26 February and reached Kharind, 200km from Baghdad, in mid-March. British hopes that he could assist the defence of KUT on the MESOPOTAMIAN FRONT proved illusory. Baratov remained at Kharind until June, when he unsuccessfully attacked Turkish positions across the border at Khanaqin on the River Diyala (see MAP 23).

The TURKISH ARMY XIII Corps (Ali Ishan Bey) was sent to Khanaqin as part of Baghdad commander KHALIL's plan to attack British rear areas via Persia (see Second Battle of KUT), and slowly advanced on the Russians over the following months. Operations by both sides suffered from heat and the unbiased hostility of local Arabs, but Baratov fell back steadily until XIII Corps was recalled to join the defence of BAGHDAD in February 1917. By the time withdrawal was fully underway, in mid-March, Baghdad had fallen but Baratov's force had been brought to a standstill by the FEBRUARY REVOLUTION. Ishan became a thorn in the side of the subsequent British advances on SAMARRAH (see Battle of JEBEL HAMLIN) as Baratov's army merely occupied the Khanaqin area, ruthlessly stripping it of supplies and being steadily eroded by desertions until its remnant withdrew to Kermanshah in June. It saw no further action, retiring north to the Caspian coast by the end of the year.

Kiel Mutiny Rebellion by German sailors of the HIGH SEAS FLEET following an attempt by senior officers to launch a final suicide sortie against the British GRAND FLEET at the end of October 1918. Planned verbally by Admiral SCHEER and senior naval staff officers as a means of salvaging the GERMAN NAVY's battered reputation, the operation was mounted in secret without authority from the government of Prince MAX VON BADEN.

Rumours reached crews at the main Navy bases of Kiel and Wilhelmshaven, and Fleet commander Admiral HIPPER faced widespread failure of his crews to return from shore leave and refusal to work when he ordered his battle squadrons to sea on 30 October. He abandoned the mission and dispersed his ships. The Third Battle Squadron was sent to Kiel, where its crews went ashore to organize protests against the admirals' action, making contact with industrial workers in the port.

Mutiny overwhelmed the naval station at Kiel, forcing base commander Crown Prince HEINRICH to flee in disguise. Workers and sailors organized themselves into mass councils, forming ad hoc committees to formulate demands, which escalated to include immediate peace and constitutional reform. The council movement spread south to factories and barracks throughout Germany over the following week, raising the spectre of Russian-style revolution in Berlin (see SOVIETS).

Naval leaders immediately sought scapegoats for a mutiny at least partly attributable to prolonged inactivity and harsh conditions, and incoming naval cabinet chief TROTHA spoke for general opinion in viewing it as the work of Bolshevik infiltrators. The government's representative in Kiel, moderate socialist Gustav NOSKE, had reported the situation out of control on 6 November, and a march on Kiel by naval ground forces under Admiral SCHRÖDER was halted by the cabinet on the grounds that it would provoke rebellion. Convinced that a workers' revolution had begun, parliamentary socialists took power and proclaimed a republic on 9 November. See also: GERMAN REVOLUTIONS.

Kiggell, General Sir Launcelot (1862–1954) Orthodox BRITISH ARMY staff officer occupying a relatively junior position at the war ministry until November 1915, when he was appointed deputy chief of the Imperial General Staff (CIGS) before moving to the WESTERN FRONT in December as chief of staff to new BEF commander HAIG. The two were friends, both considered 'safe' rather than spectacular, but Kiggell went to extraordinary lengths to reinforce Haig's natural optimism, including the suppression of intelligence to support the latter's arguments. A strong advocate of BREAKTHROUGH TACTICS, his influence upset other BEF commanders and there were calls for his removal before he collapsed from 'nervous exhaustion' in late 1917, becoming commander of forces on the Channel Islands on his recovery in early 1918.

King Edward VII British PRE-DREADNOUGHT completed in 1905 as lead ship of a class of eight, including *Hibernia* and *Africa*, both of which took part in early AIRCRAFT CARRIER experiments. Designed with additional 'intermediate' armament of four 9.2-inch guns, the King Edwards were the only obsolete capital ships employed with the GRAND FLEET in August 1914, forming the Third Battle Squadron (informally known as the 'Wobbly Eight') until withdrawn in April 1915. *Hibernia* subsequently served in the DARDANELLES and *Zealandia* in the MEDITERRANEAN. The remainder were transferred to the Thames Estuary as a deterrent against German BATTLECRUISER raids on the English east coast. Most survived in secondary duties or as depot ships, but *King Edward VII* was sunk by a MINE off Cape Wrath on 6 January 1916 and *Britannia* was torpedoed by a U-BOAT off Cape Trafalgar on 9 November 1918, the last battleship casualty of the War. The surviving ships were scrapped within two years of the ARMISTICE.

BRIEF DATA (*King Edward VII*, 1914) Displacement: 17,500 tons; Crew: 777; Dimensions: length 454ft (137.6m), beam 78ft (23.6m); Speed: 19k; Armament: 4 x 12in gun, 4 × 9in, 10 × 6in, 12 × 12pdr, 5 × 18in TT.

King George V Name ship of a class of four British 'super-dreadnought' battleships completed in 1912–13 (see *ORION*). Slightly larger than earlier classes, *King George V*, *Centurion* and *Ajax* served in the GRAND FLEET throughout the War, but *AUDACIOUS* was sunk by a MINE in October 1914. The DIRECTOR-CONTROL system for secondary guns and searchlights fitted to *Centurion* became standard wartime equipment on large British warships. *Centurion* was the only one of the class to survive beyond the mid-1920s, serving as a floating ANTI-AIRCRAFT battery and harbour blockship during the Second World War.
BRIEF DATA (*King George V*, 1916) Displacement: 23,000 tons; Crew: 812; Dimensions: length 598ft (181.2m), beam 89ft (27m); Speed: 22k; Armament: 10 × 13.5in gun, 16 × 4in, 2 × 4in AA, 2 × 21in TT.

Kitchener, Field Marshal Horatio, Earl (1850–1916) Britain's most distinguished soldier in 1914. After a long and uniquely successful colonial career, he was effective military governor of EGYPT from 1911 until August 1914, when he happened to be in London and was appointed war minister to the ASQUITH government on 3 August.

A towering figure within the BRITISH ARMY, and popularly regarded as infallible, Kitchener was an ideal symbol for patriotic enthusiasm in GREAT BRITAIN. His mandarin air was magnified by a stern, enigmatic personality, ill at ease with debate or politicians. Other ministers generally regarded his control over military strategy as inevitable, but submitted to his monosyllabic judgements with increasing unease.

Almost alone among senior European strategists, and without saying why, Kitchener expected a long war, predicting millions of casualties over at least three years. His response was the immediate creation – with the aid of perhaps the world's most celebrated recruitment poster – of a mass volunteer army. The consequent flood of volunteers disrupted British labour distribution and caused serious military supply problems, for which Kitchener took some of the blame (see SHELL SCANDAL), but provided the BEF on the WESTERN FRONT with vital mass reinforcements in 1915.

Kitchener the strategist was arbitrary, contradictory and prone to certainty without the benefit of information. He generally recognized the need for concentration of strength on the Western Front, loyally supporting the tactical policies of FRENCH and HAIG, but he gave wavering approval for operations at GALLIPOLI, and made no provision for their organization or adequate reinforcement. His political reputation suffered badly from the Gallipoli campaign, and he was unable to prevent large-scale commitment to the SALONIKA expedition in autumn 1915.

An offer of resignation in early 1916 was refused, but his official visit to Tsar NICHOLAS II in June was a relief to most of the cabinet. Kitchener was killed on 5 June when his transport, the CRUISER *Hampshire*, struck a MINE and sank off the Orkney Islands. Always protected from public criticism in Britain, and mourned with full imperial ceremony, he had become a major obstacle to efficient communications between army and cabinet.

Kluck, General Alexander von (1846–1934) Experienced German field commander who led the First Army in the opening campaigns on the WESTERN FRONT from August 1914. A middle-class Prussian (with few political connections and no staff experience), his reputation for boldness and aggression matched the leading role assigned to his Army by the SCHLIEFFEN PLAN.

The First Army duly swept through BELGIUM, but a costly frontal engagement with the BEF at MONS highlighted a difference in temperament between von Kluck and cautious Second Army commander BÜLOW. Kluck sought to outflank defending forces, intending (in accordance with the Schlieffen Plan) to pass west of Paris, but Bülow held him close to the slower-moving centre, unwilling to let a gap appear in the German front. This tactical problem, allied to von Kluck's overconfident assumption that Anglo-French forces were beaten, contributed to the First Army's disastrous turn east of the French capital just before the pivotal MARNE battle in early September. He remained in command of the First Army on the Western Front until March 1915, when a severe leg wound forced his retirement from active service. See also: Battle of LE CATEAU.

Kolchak, Admiral Aleksandr (1874–1920) Able and aggressive RUSSIAN NAVY officer who was a captain with the Baltic Fleet in 1914, receiving rapid promotion under Admiral von ESSEN until appointed commander of BLACK SEA forces in July 1916. Kolchak used his fleet's growing strength to establish convincing superiority over the TURKISH NAVY in the theatre, using MINES to virtually blockade hostile shipping in the Sea of Marmora. He retained control of the fleet after the FEBRUARY REVOLUTION of 1917, but was eventually deposed by a sailors' SOVIET in June and sent to Washington as naval attaché by the PROVISIONAL GOVERNMENT. Returning via Japan at the time of the OCTOBER REVOLUTION, he crossed into Siberia to take command of anti-Bolshevik White forces in the region, seizing control of part of the trans-Siberian railway and establishing a regional government at Omsk from February 1919. After RED ARMY forces retook most of Siberia a year later, Kolchak was captured and shot at Omsk (see RUSSIAN CIVIL WAR).

Kolubara River, Battle of the Decisive engagement ending the third invasion of SERBIA by the AUSTRO-HUNGARIAN ARMY in 1914. After failures at the JADAR and DRINA RIVERS in August and September, the forces of Austro-Hungarian BALKAN FRONT commander POTIOREK were again brought up to a strength of over 400,000 men and he was allowed to plan a new attack. Launched on 8 November it was a more sophisticated operation than its predecessors, advancing southeast in three columns against Belgrade in the east, Valyevo in the centre and Sabac to the west. Stretched to defend an 80km attacking front, the SERBIAN ARMY withdrew steadily – allowing the capture of Valyevo on 15 November – and the attackers had taken up positions on the Kolubara River, 80km beyond the Drina, by the end of the month. At the northern end of the front, Belgrade was evacuated and in Austrian hands by 2 December, a relatively easy operation hailed as a great victory in Vienna.

Having waited until his enemy was tired, with its lines of communication and supply extended, Serbian commander PUTNIK launched a counterattack across the Kolubara on 3 December. Austrian forces were driven from the Rudnik heights west of the river after two days of exceptionally heavy combat, and were tumbling back towards the frontier by 6 December. Valyevo was retaken on 9 December, and the Austrian armies recrossed the Drina three days later. Protected by gunfire from naval MONITORS, they were not followed by almost equally exhausted Serbian troops, but Putnik's victory was completed by the recapture of Belgrade, which was abandoned on 15 December by the occupying Austrian troops prior to their retreat across the Save River.

Potiorek had lost over 225,000 men in the operation and was replaced a week later by Archduke EUGEN, who spent almost a year rebuilding strength. Serbian losses of about 170,000 troops could not be replaced, and though victory was loudly celebrated by Allied leaders, they were unwilling to divert substantial reinforcements from other theatres. See also: MAP 19; Conquest of SERBIA; SALONIKA.

Komarów, Battle of Major engagement fought between Russian and Austro-Hungarian forces in GALICIA during the last week of August 1914. After the initial Austro-Hungarian success at KRASNIK, General PLEHVE's Russian Fifth Army was diverted southwest to assist retreating Russian forces. It collided with the Austro-Hungarian Fourth Army (AUFFENBERG) advancing slowly north in similar strength along an 80km front. The first meeting came at the western end of the front on 26 August, when Plehve's right-hand corps exposed its flank to Austro-Hungarian ARTILLERY fire and was routed, enabling Auffenberg's left to reach Zamosc, between the Russian Fifth and Fourth Armies. Further east, two Russian corps attacked the Austrian centre on 27 August, virtually wiping out an infantry division before the front stabilized into heavy infantry combat around the town of Komarów. Auffenberg persuaded chief of staff CONRAD to send an additional corps from eastern Galicia to attack an isolated Russian corps in the far east, and it broke through disorganized defences by 30 August.

Although the Austro-Hungarian Fourth Army had taken 20,000 prisoners and 100 guns since 26 August, no serious attempt was made to turn its flank victories into encirclement. Only vaguely aware of Russian dispositions, the Austrian left wing pulled back from Zamosc on 30 August, and the right withdrew the following day. On 1 September, as Plehve retreated north to safety beyond Cholm, the Austrian Fourth Army was diverted south to assist the Third and Second Armies around Lvov (see Battle of the GNILA LIPA).

König Class Class of four German BATTLESHIPS completed in 1914 as slightly larger and better armoured versions of the earlier KAISER Class. *König*, *Markgraf*, *GROßER KURFÜRST* and *Kronprinz Wilhelm* joined the HIGH SEAS FLEET from late 1914. They participated fleetingly in the Battle of JUTLAND, surrendered at the ARMISTICE, and were scuttled in Scapa Flow the following June.

BRIEF DATA (*König*, 1914) Displacement: 25,390 tons; Crew: 1,136; Dimensions: length 580ft (175.8m), beam 97ft (29.4m); Speed: 23k; Armament: 10 × 12in gun, 14 × 5.9in, 6 × 3.4in, 4 × 3.4in AA, 5 × 19.7in TT.

Königsberg German light CRUISER, built in 1907 and very similar to the earlier BREMEN Class ships. Detached fron Admiral von SPEE's East Asiatic Squadron in August 1914, it was sent to patrol the coast of EAST AFRICA, where it sunk the old British cruiser *PEGASUS* in September but was trapped and eventually destroyed by British warships in the RUFUGI DELTA.

BRIEF DATA (1914) Displacement: 3,400 tons; Crew: 350; Dimensions: length 378ft (114.5m), beam 43.5ft (13.2m); Speed: 23.5k; Armament: 10 × 105mm, 2 × 17.7in TT.

Körber, Ernst von (1850–1919) Austrian prime minister on his retirement in 1904, he returned to politics in February 1915 as imperial administrative controller of Bosnia-Herzegovina. Regarded as a moderate constitutional reformer, but with a history of opposition to Hungarian self-assertion, he was appointed Austrian prime minister after the assassination of STÜRGKH in October 1916. Körber immediately fell into dispute over renewal of the imperial *Ausgleich* ('Compromise') with Hungary, taking a strong line against demands for division of the Army into national components. Poor relations with KARL I, who favoured acceptance of Hungarian terms, hastened his resignation on 14 December, and he became a leading unofficial critic of imperial policies.

Kornilov, General Lavrenti (1870–1918) A divisional commander in 1914 with BRUSILOV's Russian Eighth Army in GALICIA, Kornilov was transferred to the Third Army in 1915 but captured with most his troops in May after his division was caught in the Carpathian foothills by the GORLICE-TARNOW OFFENSIVE. His escape the following summer ensured rapid promotion, and he took over the Eighth Army from General Kaledin in late 1916.

After the FEBRUARY REVOLUTION, his known liberal sympathies brought his appointment to command the Petrograd (St Petersburg) military district, but he resigned in May 1917 and assumed command of the Ninth Army in the Bukovina region, where he achieved a fleeting success at the start of July's KERENSKI OFFENSIVE. On 1 August he replaced Brusilov as C-in-C of the RUSSIAN ARMY, leading his few remaining loyal troops in the retreat from RIGA in September before disputes with the PROVISIONAL GOVERNMENT brought his dismissal on 8 September.

He marched on Petrograd, reaching the suburbs five days later, but was blocked by massed railway workers and persuaded to surrender on 14 September by temporary C-in-C General ALEXEEV. The prospect of right-wing insurrection helped trigger the OCTOBER REVOLUTION and Kornilov escaped death or imprisonment by fleeing to Cossack settlements on the Don, where he and Kaledin organized an abortive anti-Bolshevik rising in December. He remained the most prominent White military leader during the RUSSIAN CIVIL WAR until killed in action by Bolshevik forces. See also: RUSSIA.

Kovel Offensive A series of Russian attacks from the River Stokhod towards the important RAILWAY junction of Kovel between July and October 1916 (see MAP 13). Conceived as an attempt to extend the BRUSILOV OFFENSIVE north beyond the line of the Pripet Marshes, the drive on Kovel signalled resumption of the BREAKTHROUGH TACTICS that had failed at Lake NAROCH. Without time to prepare more subtle tactics, BRUSILOV massed the Eighth Army, Third Army and new GUARD ARMY (a total of some 250,000 men, including virtually all available reinforcements) against a narrow front held by German forces under General von der MARWITZ.

Russian forces possessed a 2-to-1 manpower advantage in the sector, even greater superiority in ARTILLERY (with more than 100 heavy guns), and sufficient aircraft to compensate for their technical inferiority. The attack opened across almost impassable marshland on 28 July, and the Guard Army forced a small gap in the German line at a cost of 60,000 men before it was called off in early August.

General EVERT took over the Kovel front from Brusilov and ordered 17 more attacks on the narrow wedge forced in German lines, pouring reinforcements into the battle until the offensive was finally halted in early October. The attacks became literally bogged down either side of the Stokhod and suffered accordingly, extending a broad similarity with the simultaneous SOMME OFFENSIVE in France. Their main immediate consequence was the destruction of the Guard Army. In a wider context, concentration of resources against Kovel weakened Russian attacking potential in the opening phases of the ROMANIAN CAMPAIGN.

Kövess von Kövesshàza, Field Marshal Hermann, Baron (1854–1924) Hungarian infantry general, due for retirement in 1914 at the end of an unspectacular career in imperial service, but retained in command of XII Corps during the early campaigns on the EASTERN FRONT. Kövess took part in the battles for GALICIA and the CARPATHIANS, as well as the GORLICE-TARNOW OFFENSIVE of mid-1915, before assuming command of the Austro-Hungarian Third Army, which fought on the BALKAN FRONT as part of Army Group MACKENSEN and entered Belgrade on 9 October 1915. Advancing into MONTENEGRO and ALBANIA by the following February, the Third Army moved to the ITALIAN FRONT for the TRENTINO OFFENSIVE of May 1916, but Kövess was transferred back to Galicia in the wake of the Russian BRUSILOV OFFENSIVE, leading the Seventh Army in the Bukovina region from October. The following summer's abortive Russian KERENSKI OFFENSIVE made little impact on Seventh Army positions at the southern end of the front, and Kövess led a virtually unopposed counteradvance to take Czernowitz in early August 1917. Immediately promoted field marshal and ennobled, he was given overall command of the Third and Seventh Armies in January 1918 but joined the growing list of unemployed Austro-Hungarian generals in April, following signature of the BREST-LITOVSK Treaty. Ongoing collapse of the home front in AUSTRIA-HUNGARY left him without a command until 3 November, when he was named supreme commander of the AUSTRO-HUNGARIAN ARMY by Emperor KARL I. By that time most of the Army had disintegrated into national forces, and Kövess proceeded almost directly from his meaningless appointment into retirement.

Kovno (Kuanas) Imposing Russian fortress system on the River Niemen (Nemunas), about 120km west of VILNIUS (see MAP 10). Designed for conditions in the 1880s, it was nevertheless equipped with more than 1,300 guns, reflecting the RUSSIAN ARMY's commitment to FORTRESSES, and was regarded as the defensive anchor of the Russian position along the northernmost stretch of the EASTERN

FRONT. When Kovno was threatened by the German KURLAND OFFENSIVES in July 1915, STAVKA (Russian central command) ordered it held and sent the Tenth Army (Sievers) to protect its approaches, but fortress commander Grigoriev made no effort to organize the outer forts against infantry attack, and the German Tenth Army (EICHHORN) was able to bring up its heavy ARTILLERY at leisure. Attacks on Kovno began on 8 August, and an infantry assault was repelled the following day, but after Russian artillery had inadvertently wiped out some of the outer defences the garrison surrendered the main fortress on 17 August, along with all its guns and ammunition. See also: NOVOGEORGIEVSK.

KRA The main wartime instrument of government economic control in GERMANY until autumn 1916. Formed within the Prussian war ministry in August 1914 and the brainchild of heavy industrial interests, led by Walter RATHENAU of the electrical firm AEG, the KRA was charged with purchasing, allocating and reselling goods vital to arms production, as well as vetting industrial requisitions and promotion of ERSATZ production. Its jurisdiction was quickly extended to include the entire German Empire (with the consent of other German states) and by 1916 it covered every aspect of the economic war effort through 25 departments, each responsible for distribution of a particular commodity.

Unprecedented munitions consumption and the Allied BLOCKADE provided initial impetus for centralized control, but the KRA emerged as the fiefdom of a few big industrialists. Its commercial transactions were run by the industries themselves, ensuring low purchase rates, high selling prices, large-scale investment in new plant, and enormous manufacturing profits. Armaments requirements were formulated by the War Committee for German Industry, with big business strongly represented. When the failure of German industry to match Allied economic mobilization became clear during the VERDUN and SOMME battles of 1916, military subordination of German economic life was extended in the HINDENBURG PROGRAMME.

Kramàr, Karel (1860–1937) Relatively moderate Czech member of the Austrian upper house who was arrested in May 1915 and charged with inciting desertion by Czech units in the AUSTRO-HUNGARIAN ARMY. After a celebrated trial lasting until November 1916, which served as a rallying cause for Czech separatists, Kramàr was sentenced to 15 years hard labour. Released from prison in July 1917, under Emperor KARL I's general amnesty for political prisoners, he worked for the establishment of an independent Czech state. After representing Czechoslovakia at the PARIS PEACE CONFERENCE, he resigned from the BENEŠ administration over its refusal to aid anti-Communist forces in the RUSSIAN CIVIL WAR.

Krasnik, Battle of The opening engagement of the war on the EASTERN FRONT between RUSSIA and AUSTRIA-HUNGARY, fought in northwest GALICIA from 23 September 1914. As part of the RUSSIAN ARMY's prewar PLAN 19, the Russian Fourth Army (Salza) crossed the frontier from Poland on 18 August. Because of delays in Austro-Hungarian mobilization, it met no resistance until 23 August, when two divisions under General Voyshin ran into five divisions of the Austro-Hungarian First Army (DANKL), itself advancing slowly towards the border south of Krasnik. Both sides were taken by surprise, but outnumbered Russian forces were stretched along a 30km line of advance and retreated to Krasnik under attacks from both flanks over the next three days. Salza was replaced by EVERT, who was forced to retreat towards Lublin by a further series of Austro-Hungarian flanking manoeuvres, but was steadily reinforced from the new Ninth Army (Lechitski) forming around Warsaw. Austrian pursuit lost impetus as supply lines became stretched, and by 1 September the Austro-Hungarian First Army had halted, heavily outnumbered. Both sides then called for support from neighbouring forces to the east (see Battle of KOMARÓW). See MAP 10.

Krasnostav, Battle of See: BUG OFFENSIVE.

Kressenstein, General Friedrich, Kress von (1870–1948) Bavarian-born German artillery officer posted to LIMAN VON SANDERS' military mission in TURKEY from early 1914 and attached to DJEMAL PASHA's Fourth Army in the autumn. Kressenstein conceived and promoted the attack on the SUEZ CANAL that opened hostilities on the PALESTINE FRONT in early 1915, and was a resourceful commander of the 'Desert Force' in Sinai during British advances to ROMANI and EL ARISH in 1916. He led the successful double defence of GAZA, but is best remembered by Turkish historians for his failure to anticipate ALLENBY's tactics when the BEERSHEBA–GAZA LINE fell in early November 1917. Superseded by FALKENHAYN on 5 November, he remained in command of the Turkish Eighth Army, defending the coastal sector of the front, until transferred to the CAUCASIAN FRONT in mid-1918 to head a German column sent to occupy Tbilisi (see DUNSTERFORCE).

Kriegsmarine See: GERMAN NAVY.

Krithia, Battles of The opening land offensive on the GALLIPOLI FRONT, a clumsy Allied attempt to break through Turkish positions across the southern tip of the peninsula, occupied and reinforced immediately after the GALLIPOLI LANDINGS of 25 April 1915 (see MAP 20).

Losses had reduced field commander Hunter-Weston's fighting strength in the HELLES sector to about 14,000 men (including about 5,000 French troops) and Turkish defenders had been reinforced to similar strength. British C-in-C HAMILTON ordered the capture of the village of Krithia and the commanding 200-metre hill of Achi Baba, about 2km beyond, as the first stage of his plan to steamroller Turkish defences overlooking the DARDANELLES, and Hunter-Weston launched an ill-organized frontal attack at 08.00 on 28 April.

Attacks at either end of the 7km line were held by defenders occupying ravines in the west, and by ARTILLERY from across the Straits in the east. A ragged advance in the centre was successfully counterattacked by only 200 Turkish infantry, and Hunter-Weston called off the battle that night having lost 3,000 men. Under orders from war minister ENVER PASHA, Turkish Fifth Army commander LIMAN VON SANDERS launched major counterattacks on the nights of 1 and 3 May, both repelled with heavy casualties after fighting dominated by French SOIXANTE-QUINZE field batteries.

Hunter-Weston's exhausted troops were reinforced from other sectors to bring strength up to 25,000 men for a renewed offensive on 6 May. Artillery lacked ammunition, commanders were barely briefed and the simple frontal advance gained only a few yards in a day of largely uncoordinated fighting. The attack was repeated with similar results on 7 May, and again the next morning. A final charge on Krithia itself later on 8 May, using every available shell for a PRELIMINARY BOMBARDMENT, gained and held about a kilometre of Turkish territory, bringing losses up to about 6,000.

Hamilton issued relatively strident demands to London for four more divisions and 25,000 shells, reducing his stated ambition to the capture of Achi Baba in advance of a renewed naval operation. Kitchener, whose attempt to wrest shells for Gallipoli from BEF commander FRENCH triggered a British SHELL SCANDAL in mid-May, promised only one division.

The Helles front subsided into TRENCH WARFARE, punctuated by small-scale Allied attacks, until Hunter-Weston's third and final operation against Krithia and Achi Baba on 4 June. Planned with new French commander GOURAUD, it enjoyed initial success despite an ineffective bombardment by EIGHTEEN-POUNDERS firing shrapnel. Turkish counterattacks retook trenches on the French right that afternoon before driving out attackers all along the line, and Hunter-Weston abandoned the effort that night for the loss of another 6,000 men. A shocked Kitchener agreed to send much larger reinforcements, and Hamilton switched his main offensive effort to the ANZAC COVE sector further north.

Krivoshein, Aleksandr (1858–1921) Russian minister of agriculture from 1908 until 1915, he was one of several moderate ministers who restrained MAKLAKOV's bid to reduce the Duma to consultative status. After supporting mild parliamentary reform proposals in summer 1915, and opposing Tsar NICHOLAS II's assumption of direct military command in September, he was the first of several leading moderates dismissed. He held no other wartime office, but joined General Wrangel's White regime in the Crimea during the RUSSIAN CIVIL WAR and emigrated to France after its defeat.

Krobatin, Field Marshal Alexander, Baron von (1849–1933) A close associate of AUSTRO-HUNGARIAN ARMY chief of staff CONRAD and Archduke FRANZ FERDINAND, Krobatin was appointed imperial war minister in 1912, and fully endorsed military calls for an immediate attack on SERBIA during the JULY CRISIS of 1914. After struggling for more than two years to obtain supplies without ever threatening to harness the economy efficiently, Krobatin was isolated in the Crown Council after the dismissal of Conrad in March 1917, and was transferred to a field command in April.

Krobatin led the Tenth Army on the ITALIAN FRONT and was promoted field marshal (5 November) for his part in the victory at CAPORETTO. Moved to the Tyrol as part of Archduke JOSEF's Army Group, he played a secondary role in the failed PIAVE Offensive of June 1918, but took command of the sector when mutinies forced the Archduke's flight on 26 October. His offer of armistice to the Italians was turned down on 31 October, and the incoherent remnants of his armies were overrun a few days later at VITTORIO VENETO. He retired immediately after the War.

Kühlmann, Richard von (1873–1948) German diplomat who became foreign secretary to the MICHAELIS government in August 1917 after wartime postings as ambassador to the Netherlands and TURKEY. His strong industrial connections were reflected in a firm commitment to German economic and political expansion, especially in central and northern Europe, but he regarded the extreme annexationist policies of the THIRD SUPREME COMMAND as unrealistic. The partial adoption of General BESELER's scheme for Polish autonomy (November 1917) was a victory for Kühlmann over LUDENDORFF's preference for outright annexation, secured by direct appeal to the crown, but his argument that harsh treatment of RUSSIA might rekindle war in the east failed to moderate the BREST-LITOVSK Treaty. Despite Kühlmann's simultaneous imposition of the severe BUCHAREST settlement on ROMANIA, right-wing interests were already working to secure his downfall. His speech at the Reichstag on 14 June 1918, in which he publicly doubted outright victory in the west, united conservative opinion against his perceived 'defeatism'. He was dismissed by Kaiser WILHELM II on 8 July and replaced by the less troublesome Admiral Hintze.

Kun, Béla (1885–1938) See: AUSTRIA-HUNGARY.

Kurland Offensives Extension of German operations to LATVIA, on the northern edge of the EASTERN FRONT, began in April 1915 as a diversion from the imminent GORLICE-TARNOW OFFENSIVE. The desolate coastal region of Kurland, thinly populated and lightly defended, had until then been virtually ignored by both sides. The front line stood 150km east of Riga, the nearest strategically valuable prize, and Russian planners regarded the fortress of KOVNO (Kuanas), far to the south, as a sufficient deterrent to attack (see MAP 10).

An independent German force of 7 CAVALRY and 5 infantry divisions under General von Lauenstein, later named the 'Niemen Army', advanced rapidly through Kurland towards Riga from 26 April. Under pressure from STAVKA (Russian central command) and the RUSSIAN NAVY's Baltic Fleet (which attempted to occupy the coastal fortress of Libau, but was outpaced by the German advance), northern regional commander ALEXEEV committed 18 divisions to the area's defence, slowing the German advance by early June. A Russian counterattack at Szawli, south of Riga, on 9 June only achieved deadlock, and Alexeev was forced to pour more troops into the area to hold a line stretching to positions just above Kovno.

German leaders included a further Kurland operation in plans for the summer TRIPLE OFFENSIVE. Begun on 13 July, it quickly pierced the Russian Fifth Army's ragged defences and swept towards Riga. The Russian 'GREAT RETREAT' from Poland, begun on 22 July, released a new Russian Twelfth Army to protect Riga, and the Russian Tenth Army was reinforced around Kovno, but overall numerical superiority (20 divisions to 13 German) was wasted. Each defending army remained close to its supply base and the Niemen Army advanced into a gap between them. Stavka still feared a major attack on the BALTIC coast, and although Alexeev regarded Kurland as strategically insignificant, he was compelled to send more reinforcements in late July.

A separate Russian command under General RUZSKI was established for the area on 17 August, by which time Russian strength in Kurland had reached 28 divisions. Accumulation came too late to prevent the fall of Kovno, and the Tenth Army gave ground east towards Vilnius while the Fifth fell back on Riga. Ruzski grouped his reinforcements near the coast, leaving an 80km gap which Alexeev, promoted to overall chief of staff in early September, refused to fill by further weakening the new lines in the centre.

Still convinced that a great strategic victory could be won in the north, Ludendorff concentrated a new force for a major offensive in the south of the sector during early September (see VILNIUS OFFENSIVE). See also: Battles of RIGA and the AA.

Kuropatkin, General Alexei (1848–1925) Veteran Russian officer, removed from senior command in the aftermath of the Russo-Japanese War (1904–05). Recalled to active service as a corps commander in late 1915, he was given command of the northern army group the following February, with responsibility for the whole front north of Poland (see MAP 10). Kuropatkin shared the faults of his predecessor, RUZSKI, in almost every respect. Cautious to the point of inertia, irrevocably committed to redundant BREAKTHROUGH TACTICS and unwilling to release resources for operations elsewhere, he was dismissed in July. Ruzski was reinstated, and Kuropatkin dispatched to the governorship of Turkestan. Briefly arrested after the FEBRUARY REVOLUTION in 1917, he was subsequently permitted to retire in peace. See also: Battle of Lake NAROCH.

Kut, First Battle of Final British attempt to relieve the siege of KUT in April 1916, a series of increasingly desperate frontal attacks against deep Turkish defences in front of the town. After the battles of HANNA and DUJAILA the Anglo-Indian Tigris Corps was reinforced by General MAUDE's British 13th Division, and Turkish C-in-C KHALIL PASHA brought up reserves from Baghdad, so that both forces comprised around 30,000 men. British forces had about 25 per cent ARTILLERY superiority (130 field guns) but little hope of assistance from about 9,000 weak and hungry troops in Kut itself.

Tigris Corps commander Gorringe reopened operations by attacking the Hanna position, now backed by two lines of deep trenches at Fallahiyeh and Sannaiyat. Maude's GALLIPOLI veterans were sent against the first line at dawn on 5 April, but found it deserted and regrouped for a frontal attack on the Fallahiyeh position in the evening. The position was taken after a costly advance across flat, mud-soaked terrain, and reserves were brought up for an attack on Sannaiyat the following morning. A secondary advance on the other bank made easier progress against relatively weak opposition, but Gorringe had lost 2,000 by the end of the day.

Strong defences, the poor condition of reserves and delays over unfamiliar ground combined to frustrate the attack on Sannaiyat, which collapsed after two hours with 1,200 casualties. The failure was repeated on the evening of 7 April, and again at dawn on 9 April, before Gorringe transferred his main force against the Bait Aisa position on the other bank, where seasonal floods had cut the overland route to Kut.

Despite heavy rain and further delays, forward outposts were stormed on 15 April and the main position fell two days later with only light casualties. Using superior river crossing facilities, Khalil concentrated 10,000 men for counterattacks during the night. Indian troops held, inflicting an estimated 4,000 casualties, but their 1,600 losses ended any hope of further advance.

With 5,000 Anglo-Indian reserves still delayed on the way from BASRA, Gorringe made a final effort against Sannaiyat on 22 April, led by a single brigade and preceded by a conventional bombardment. Turkish defenders evacuated their first two lines of trenches before counterattacking in force and inflicting another 1,300 casualties, bringing total battle losses for the Tigris Corps to about 23,000 since January. Apart from a quixotic attempt to send the armoured supply ship *Julnar* through Turkish lines, the relief of Kut was abandoned and the garrison surrendered on 30 April. See MAP 23.

Kut, Second Battle of Both sides on the MESOPOTAMIAN FRONT reorganized their positions on the Tigris after the fall of KUT in April 1916. Turkish C-in-C KHALIL PASHA shortened his lines some 15km upriver (at the junction of the Tigris and Shatt-al-Hai) in mid-May to release troops for a proposed sweep towards the Gulf through PERSIA. Reinforced Anglo-Indian units followed, but the 5 Anglo-Indian divisions deployed on the Tigris from early summer had lost 30,000 men to sickness alone by the time overdue reform of supply systems took effect in August. Direct control over the campaign passed from India to London, with the relatively junior General MAUDE promoted to frontline command in July and given the entire theatre in August.

Under instructions to minimize losses, Maude had about 150,000 troops (half at the front) by October and planned a limited offensive against Kut before the winter rains. Local Turkish corps commander Karabekir Bey, outnumbered 3 to 1 and aware of the impending attack, had been strengthening trench systems but received no reinforcements.

The British bombardment opened on both sides of the river during the night of 13/14 December, and operations began at dawn with a secondary attack against the Sannaiyat positions on Maude's right. Karabekir Bey committed most of his reserves against this, and the main advance on the other bank met relatively light resistance as it moved towards Kut. Led by an unusually effective CAVALRY screen, it was in position to cross the Tigris and get behind Sannaiyat by 15 December, having suffered under 300 casualties.

Maude consolidated, making only one half hearted attempt to ford the river on 20 December, but news of the battle brought a relaxation of restraints from London, and he drove up the left bank to take the fortified KHADAIRI BEND in late January 1917. From 25 January he employed the same tactics – ARTILLERY concentration followed by limited advance and consolidation – to take the main Turkish strongpoint south of Kut, along the only fordable stretch of the Shatt-al-Hai, by the time flooding prevented further operations around Kut on 16 February.

Maude attacked again over drier ground at Sannaiyat on 17 February, gaining nothing but persuading Khalil to abandon his Persian plans. With about 10,000 troops left to hold Kut, and only another 3,000 men deployed around Baghdad, Khalil recalled a corps fighting against Russian forces in western Persia. Meanwhile Maude was making meticulous preparations to cross the river behind Kut to cut off any Turkish retreat.

Turkish reserves were drawn to dummy preparations elsewhere on the river, and the RFC frustrated Turkish aerial reconnaissance, so that an Anglo-Indian pontoon crossing just before dawn on 23 February achieved initial surprise, but an advance on the Kut garrison was halted the following morning by a strong Turkish rearguard, which covered and then followed a skilfully executed retreat.

Pursuing Anglo-Indian cavalry was unable to get past MACHINE GUNS on the road to Baghdad, although slower ARMOURED CARS had greater success on their Mesopotamian debut. The Turkish retreat was disrupted by MARSH ARAB ambushes and British naval action at NAHR-AL-KALEK, but British land pursuit petered out on 27 February at Aziziyeh, 100km beyond Kut. See MAP 23. See also: BAGHDAD.

Kut, Siege of The small Mesopotamian town of Kut was abandoned by Turkish forces after the Battle of ES SINN in October 1915. After occupying the town and advancing further north, General TOWNSHEND's 6th Indian Division made a stand at Kut after being pursued back down the Tigris from CTESIPHON in November. Exhausted Anglo-Indian troops began fortifying the town on 4 December, but it was difficult to defend or relieve, with good field positions for Turkish troops in the surrounding floodplains. Further withdrawal would have been possible before Colonel Nur-Ud-Din's forces surrounded the town on 7 December, but as it was well stocked with supplies and, as his troops were in very poor condition, Townshend decided to stay.

Behind a perimeter of shallow trenches and mud walls, with outposts on the far side of the river, the town contained about 10,000 troops (75 per cent infantry), along with 2,000 sick or wounded, about 3,500 non-combat personnel and 6,000 local civilians, some held as hostages against subversion. The divisional CAVALRY, useless in a siege but a drain on supplies, was ordered back to BASRA on 6 December to join a relief force gathering under General Aylmer. Townshend felt he could hold out for two months, and MESOPOTAMIAN FRONT C-in-C General NIXON was confident of retaking Kut within that time.

The siege began with Turkish attacks on the perimeter from 9 December until Christmas Eve, when Nur-Ud-Din launched a major offensive against the northeast rim. British MACHINE GUN fire from secondary trenches was the decisive factor in repelling the attack and inflicting more than 900 Turkish casualties, against 315 defenders killed or wounded. Leaving Kut blockaded by a holding force supported by a ring of ARTILLERY, Nur-Ud-Din redirected his main effort to blocking relief attempts at SHEIKH SA'AD and HANNA in January. Hampered by logistic disarray, further British attacks at DUJAILA in March and against the entire Turkish position on the Tigris in April (see First Battle of KUT) failed to achieve decisive breakthrough. The attacks incurred heavy losses, and attempts at relief were abandoned after 22 April.

Townshend's initial estimate of food stocks, which had encouraged over-hasty relief attempts, were calculated with his troops on full rations. A reassessment in late January, taking local produce and army livestock into account, concluded that Kut could hold out until mid-April, but sickness and hunger had rendered troops incapable of supporting relief efforts or harassing besieging forces by late March. Townshend apart, morale was poor, though light bombing raids by German aircraft stiffened resistance by hitting the overcrowded hospital.

British aircraft dropped supplies in Kut during April, but were unable to carry significant quantities of food, and a failed attempt on 24 April to bring supplies upriver aboard the improvised blockade runner *Julnar* represented the last realistic hope of prolonged resistance. With his troops close to starvation, Townshend opened negotiations with the new Turkish commander KHALIL PASHA two days later. British attempts to buy parole for the garrison were rejected by the Turkish government, and Townshend surrendered unconditionally on 30 April.

Though marginal to Britain's strategic priorities in Europe, the loss of Kut was more significant in an imperial context, and some commentators have argued that British influence in the Middle East never fully recovered from the blow to its prestige. More directly, it persuaded the British government to assume direct responsibility for operations in Mesopotamia, hitherto under the control of the Indian government. See also: MAP 23; Second Battle of KUT.

Kutno, Battle of See: Battle of ŁÓDŹ.

L

La Bassée Canal See: Battle for FLANDERS.

Lacaze, Admiral Marie-Jean-Lucien (1860–1955) French officer, a former assistant to prewar navy minister DELCASSÉ, who commanded a BATTLESHIP squadron until relieved in March 1915 after a dispute with C-in-C BOUÉ DE LAPEYRÈRE. He returned to politics in October, replacing AUGAGNEUR as naval minister in the BRIAND government, but had no more success in overcoming inter-Allied jealousies and strategic differences than other naval authorities in the MEDITERRANEAN. He faced constant criticism in the Chamber of Deputies, which took a lively and active interest in naval affairs throughout the conflict, and eventually succumbed to determined hostility from socialist deputies. He resigned on 2 August 1917, shortly before the fall of the RIBOT government, to become prefect of the Toulon naval base.

Lafayette, Escadrille French FIGHTER unit formed in 1916 from US volunteers flying with the AÉRONAUTIQUE MILITAIRE on the WESTERN FRONT. A number of Americans had served with French forces since 1914, avoiding loss of UNITED STATES citizenship by volunteering through the French Foreign Legion, and several sons of wealthy and influential families had become aircrew. Their consistent lobbying for an American Squadron, backed by the PREPAREDNESS MOVEMENT in the USA, bore fruit with the establishment of an *Escadrille Américaine* in April 1916, containing seven US pilots under French commanders. After complaints from US Secretary of State LANSING that its high public profile compromised US neutrality, the name was changed to *Escadrille Lafayette* in December.

The squadron, number 124, was operational from May 1916, scoring 13 victories in combat around Verdun equipped with NIEUPORT 11 fighters before re-arming with SPAD S-VIIs. A total of 38 US pilots, of whom 9 were killed in action, served with the squadron, scoring 38 confirmed victories before the transfer of American personnel to the USAAS in February 1918, after which the unit continued in French service as the *1ère Escadrille de Chasse Américaine.*

Lammasch, Heinrich (1853–1920) Austrian lawyer and conservative politician, a well-known pacifist and monarchist, who was threatened with imprisonment in August 1914. Personal intervention by Emperor FRANZ JOSEF I left him free to make appeals for 'peace without victory' and to denounce GERMANY, attitudes corresponding closely to those of the new Emperor KARL I from late 1916. Lammasch was twice offered the post of Austrian minister-president before accepting the role on 25 October 1918. Quickly appreciating that Allied war aims precluded an idealistic peace, he resigned on 11 November. After representing the new Austrian Republic as signatory to the Treaty of ST GERMAIN, Lammasch spent his last months campaigning for its future neutrality.

Langemarck, Battle of See: Third Battle of YPRES.

Lanrezac, General Charles (1852–1925) The FRENCH ARMY's most respected prewar strategist, and regarded as the epitome of 'offensive spirit', Lanrezac led the Fifth Army in August 1914. On the northern wing of the invasion of Germany proposed by PLAN 17, he was better placed than most to appreciate the dangers of a massive German invasion through BELGIUM, and quickly lost faith in the idea of attacking to the east.

Though the Fifth Army was eventually withdrawn from the invasion of the ARDENNES and deployed to face any German threat from the north, Lanrezac's attitude was considered unnecessarily alarmist. Denied reinforcements and let down by the late arrival of the BEF, he was ordered to attack an army twice the size of his own at CHARLEROI. His subsequent retreat, though strategically justifiable, demolished the remains of his reputation.

Blamed for the collapse of the Allied position in Belgium by both the British and French high commands, his relations with C-in-C JOFFRE deteriorated to crisis point during the Battle of GUISE. Generally perceived as a spent force, he was retired just before the French counterattack at the MARNE and replaced by the more reliably aggressive FRANCHET D'ESPEREY.

Lansing, Robert (1864–1928) American lawyer whose career in intergovernmental litigation led to his appointment as legal advisor to the federal State Department (foreign ministry) in April 1914. He succeeded Bryan as secretary of state in June 1915, after the latter's resignation in protest at President WILSON's response to the *LUSITANIA* disaster.

Though Wilson controlled diplomatic responses to German SUBMARINE WARFARE, Lansing was responsible for protests to Britain over Allied BLOCKADE tactics. Their harsh tone masked a conviction that the UNITED STATES would eventually declare war on GERMANY: he pressured a dubious Wilson into tacit acceptance of substantial US bank loans to the Allies from October 1915, and recommended recognition of the Carrenza regime in MEXICO as preparation for war in March 1917.

Lansing retained a long perspective on wartime foreign policy. In December 1917 he endorsed the pivotal LANSING–ISHII AGREEMENT with JAPAN, and he instructed the secret 'Inquiry' think tank to concentrate on Latin American affairs as early as April 1918 (see LIPPMANN, W.). His wartime European diplomacy was overshadowed by Wilson's personal contribution, and he viewed the FOURTEEN POINTS, especially plans for collective security through a LEAGUE OF NATIONS, as insufficiently precise or pragmatic to generate a working peace.

Lansing's willingness to compromise with Allied demands, especially over application of 'war guilt' to the CENTRAL POWERS, damaged his relations with Wilson during the PARIS PEACE CONFERENCE, and his criticisms of the resultant VERSAILLES Treaty provided ammunition for its many opponents in the USA. He was dismissed on 7 February 1920, ostensibly for calling cabinet meetings on his own initiative.

Lansing–Ishii Agreement Exchange of notes between Japanese special envoy Ishii Kikujiro and US secretary of state LANSING in November 1917. They accepted JAPAN's position of special influence in CHINA but also confirmed Chinese territorial integrity and the 'Open Door' policy of equal international opportunity in trade and commerce. Though seen on both sides as a welcome palliative to growing economic rivalry in the Pacific, the Agreement was interpreted by Japan as sanctioning political as well as economic interference in China and provoked serious resentment in the USA before its abandonment in 1923.

Latvia Baltic homeland of the Lettish people, which under the Russian Empire was divided into the imperial provinces of Livonia and KURLAND. It consisted mostly of large estates owned by Germans in the Tsar's service, and was an important source of food for RUSSIA's major cities.

From April 1915, when the GERMAN ARMY launched its first offensive in Kurland, the EASTERN FRONT divided the region in half. Western and central parts suffered heavy loss of agricultural, industrial and RAILWAY resources to a combination of German exploitation and war damage. The population of RIGA, close to the line on the Russian side, fell by more than half between 1913 and 1917. About 750,000 Letts had fled into Russia by late 1916, and a three-division Lettish corps was fighting with the RUSSIAN ARMY.

The Russian PROVISIONAL GOVERNMENT granted autonomy to the Letts in July 1917, but full independence was declared by a Latvian National Council after the OCTOBER REVOLUTION. A RED ARMY force invaded in late 1918, capturing Riga on 3 January 1919 and proclaiming a soviet republic. The National Council was evacuated by ROYAL NAVY forces policing the BALTIC, but restored in May when a multinational militia (*Landwehr*) retook Riga.

Dominated and trained by a large contingent of German irregulars, commanded by former general Rüdiger von der Goltz, the *Landwehr* staged a military coup in June, but was defeated by a combined Lettish-Estonian army (supplied by the western Allies) and Goltz was forced to leave the country in July. The Council government resumed its quest for independence, refusing to allow General YUDENICH to cross Latvian territory with a White army and expelling the last Red Army elements from the country by early 1920. The Soviet government accepted the fact of Latvian independence with the conclusion of the Treaty of Riga in August 1920. See also: MAP 25; RUSSIAN CIVIL WAR.

Law, Andrew Bonar (1858–1923) Canadian-born leader of a strong Conservative and Unionist opposition in the British parliament from 1911, he agreed a political truce with the ASQUITH government from August 1914. An unspectacular and conscientious figure, he restrained his party's criticism of cabinet war management, focusing attacks on navy minister CHURCHILL (a former Conservative) until the 'SHELL SCANDAL' of May 1915 brought him into a coalition government as colonial minister. Though not included in the five-man War Council established from November, Law was central to the maintenance of political unity. A committed 'EASTERNER', he moved steadily closer to LLOYD GEORGE through 1916, conspiring with CARSON, AITKEN and others to install him as prime minister in December. Becoming chancellor of the exchequer (finance minister) in the new cabinet, he supervised credit agreements with the UNITED STATES but devoted most of his energy to parliamentary management. Unable to prevent the appointment of Churchill as munitions minister in July 1917, he otherwise gave solid wartime support to Lloyd George and joined him on a coalition platform at the December 1918 elections. In the less demanding role of Lord Privy Seal, he was a signatory of the VERSAILLES Treaty in June 1919 and retired in 1921, returning briefly to office as prime minister in 1922.

Lawrence, Lieutenant Colonel T(homas) E(dward) (1888–1935) Welsh-born scholar of Arab affairs, celebrated as 'Lawrence of Arabia' for his leading military and political role in the ARAB REVOLT from 1916. An archaeological student in the Middle East for several years after 1909, he was commissioned after BRITISH ARMY height restrictions had been lowered in 1915 and worked as a junior officer in the Cairo department monitoring Arab nationalist activities, the Arab Bureau.

On a factfinding mission to the Arab-held port of Jiddah in October 1916, Lawrence travelled inland to evaluate the leaders of the Arab Revolt. Reporting that only FEISAL IBN HUSSEIN (his 'Armed Prophet') was likely to lead an Arab victory, he was sent back into Arabia to direct liaison and joined Feisal in early November at the key defence of YENBO. Their immediate bonding opened up a fertile channel of Anglo-Arab communication that was to become an effective military alliance in PALESTINE by 1918.

Legend and history merge in Lawrence's Arabian campaigns, reflecting not only their geographical remoteness but also his own understanding of the hero-figure's psychological impact on contemporary Arab culture. His sympathy with Arab motives and deliberate cultivation of his own legend were highly effective political weapons, and his extraordinary position among the Revolt's senior commanders was never questioned by Arabs.

Unsullied by formal military training, he made innovative tactical use of ARMOURED CARS, air support and other mobile forces, particularly in attacks on Turkish RAILWAYS. His responsibility for Arab strategy, embracing long-range penetration into northern Arab areas and the deliberate slow bleeding of Turkish strength (see MEDINA), has been questioned by some commentators.

Ideologically committed to Arab nationalism and loyal to Feisal, Lawrence married Arab priorities with the conflicting demands of British interests, establishing mutual trust where many other European officers failed. Probably aware of Anglo-French protectorate plans embodied in the SYKES–PICOT AGREEMENT, he vigorously promoted Arab regimes in DERA and other captured towns, against opposition from British authorities on the spot.

Physically and emotionally battered by the campaign (and sexually abused while in Turkish captivity), he made several attempts to resign before finally being allowed to leave Arabia after the fall of DAMASCUS in October 1918. He later acted as Feisal's advisor at the PARIS PEACE CONFERENCE and served with the British Colonial Office until 1922, but changed his name to rejoin both the Army and the RAF as an enlisted man during the later 1920s. His posthumously published *Seven Pillars of Wisdom*, an expanded version of an earlier account of the Arab campaign, is an acknowledged literary masterpiece. See also: Battles of AQABA, PETRA, TAFILA.

League Of Nations The international organization envisaged by the FOURTEEN POINTS peace programme of 1918 and established at the PARIS PEACE CONFERENCE in April 1919. US president WILSON's vision of a congress of democracies, mutually disarmed to ensure collective security, was challenged in Paris by French premier CLEMENCEAU, who sought an armed alliance against German recovery. A compromise was arranged by Wilson and British Empire delegates (SMUTS and Lord Chelmsford), but clauses giving individual members more freedom of action and building the League Covenant into the VERSAILLES Treaty were later added at Wilson's insistence. Wilson weakened his bargaining position on other issues to win these concessions, which were intended to silence opposition inside the UNITED STATES, but the League was ultimately rejected by the US Congress. None of the CENTRAL POWERS were permitted to join the original League, and it was boycotted by the Soviet Union, but survived until 1940 as a largely impotent forum for international debate.

'Leapfrog' Because of the time taken to secure the flanks of a newly occupied trench line, attackers on the WESTERN FRONT from late 1914 were unable to advance quickly beyond their first targets. 'Leapfrogging' simply involved deploying back-up formations directly behind attacking units, ready to overtake as soon as first objectives were reached. The tactic was standard practice for all sides once the widespread adoption of DEFENCE IN DEPTH had rendered the capture of first-line TRENCHES meaningless. See also: INFANTRY TACTICS.

Le Cateau, Battle of British rearguard action during the Allied retreat along the WESTERN FRONT after the Battles of the FRONTIERS in late August 1914. Though celebrated in Britain, the action was similar in scale and purpose to dozens fought by the FRENCH ARMY during the course of the retreat.

The BEF's II Corps was caught by the pursuing German First Army near Le Cateau, about 50km southwest of MONS, during the night of 25 August (see MAP 2). Unable to retreat without being attacked in the process, corps commander SMITH-DORRIEN made the unavoidable decision to fight the following morning.

His three divisions, augmented by the small CAVALRY Corps, were unable to make contact with General HAIG's I Corps, retreating down the opposite side of the River Oise, but only three German divisions, backed by the ARTILLERY of two more, were in position for the fight. German First Army commander von KLUCK's eastern corps was too far out of position to take part, and two western corps were engaged in an attempt to outflank the BEF (ultimately frustrated by General MAUNOURY's new French Sixth Army).

German artillery opened fire at dawn on 26 August. Fighting with RIFLES from shallow TRENCHES, British troops restricted German infantry to a slow advance, and were able to begin a fairly orderly retreat in the early evening. Casualties were high on both sides, particularly among British units that failed to receive the withdrawal order, but at a cost of some 8,000 men the BEF delayed von Kluck's pursuit sufficiently to enable them to make a relatively unmolested retreat. See also: First Battle of the MARNE.

Le Hamel, Battle of Small but significant Allied victory on the WESTERN FRONT during the relatively quiet phase between the second MARNE battle in July 1918 and the Allied AMIENS offensive in August. It was the most spectacular of a number of local victories by Allied forces at a time when the GERMAN ARMY's offensive capability had waned and the first wave of INFLUENZA was sweeping its trenches.

Launched on 4 July, it was conceived as an attempt to straighten a small westerly bulge in the line opposite the British Fourth Army (RAWLINSON) east of Amiens, an important preliminary to any major offensive employing massed ARTILLERY support, which would otherwise be exposed to flanking fire. It was planned by new Australian Corps commander MONASH and executed by its 4th Division, supported by all available MACHINE GUN units and 60 HEAVY TANKS. Four companies of US troops, attached to the Corps for training, also took part.

The attack was an unqualified success, sweeping the surprised and lightly entrenched defenders of the German Second Army (MARWITZ) out of the SALIENT. Its objectives, the village of Le Hamel and the woods to either side, were secured within an hour and a half, and nearly 1,500 prisoners were taken for the loss of about 1,000 men. Apart from re-emphasizing the value of precise planning and absolute secrecy, the victory demonstrated the effectiveness of the PEACEFUL PENETRATION tactics pioneered by AUSTRALIAN FORCES. See MAP 2.

Lemberg German name for the eastern Galician city of Lvov, now part of Ukraine but the capital of Austro-Hungarian Galicia in 1914. The city was the main focus of the opening Austro-Russian campaigns in GALICIA, sometimes known as the Battles of Lemberg. See also: EASTERN FRONT.

Lenin, Vladimir Ilyich (1870–1924) Left-wing revolutionary politician and ideologue, an early leader of the Bolshevik Party who remained an influential figure in RUSSIA despite a long exile after the 1905 revolution. An astute political analyst and tactician, his simplistic, repetitive oratory reflected strategic clarity. His unwillingness to compromise with fellow travellers was well-known before 1914 within both the SECOND INTERNATIONAL and the broad church of Russian socialism.

Briefly interned in the Austro-Hungarian part of POLAND when war broke out, he subsequently moved to Switzerland, where his Marxist analysis of the 'imperialist' War was expressed through theses and speeches to the international socialist ZIMMERWALD MOVEMENT. Anticipating the spread of revolutionary PACIFISM in Russia, he recommended national military defeat as the first step to revolution, but had few firm supporters anywhere before mid-1917.

Lenin was the most important of many exiled revolutionaries helped by German agents seeking to destabilize the Russian war effort in 1917. Willing to use any means available to reach Russia after the FEBRUARY REVOLUTION, he accepted (along with 31 other Russian exiles) German transportation to Petrograd (St Petersburg) in a technically neutral 'sealed' train via Germany and Sweden. Recognizing the danger to his political credibility, Lenin was careful to distance himself from all contact with German authorities, but the journey was sensationalized by Allied PROPAGANDA and suggestions that he was a German agent cast an occasional shadow over his subsequent career.

Paraded triumphantly through Petrograd when he arrived on 16 April, he delivered his 'April Thesis' to the Petrograd Soviet next day. Demanding immediate transfer of power to the SOVIETS and comprehensive redistribution of wealth, along with immediate peace, the programme won support from TROTSKI but was viewed as fanatical by the more moderate majority.

Lenin went back to exile in Finland after the JULY DAYS protest provoked an outburst of repression by the PROVISIONAL GOVERNMENT, but popular opinion swung towards his doctrinaire pacifism during the autumn. Lenin returned from Finland on 23 October to begin organizing armed uprising with Trotski, and the OCTOBER REVOLUTION brought him to power from 8 November

(October by the old Russian calendar) as chairman of a Bolshevik executive appointed by the soviets.

The new regime proclaimed common ownership of land, banks, industries and other property, disbanded the Army, released details of Russia's secret treaties with the Allies, and instigated peace negotiations with the CENTRAL POWERS (see Treaty of BREST-LITOVSK). Barely in control of the capital amid economic anarchy and a wide-ranging RUSSIAN CIVIL WAR, Lenin was preoccupied with internal affairs into the 1920s, and played no part in the Allied peacemaking process.

Peacetime reconstruction in Russia got fully underway from 1921, when Lenin introduced a more market-orientated New Economic Policy, but his health never fully recovered from wounds caused by an assassination attempt in August 1918, and he was a diminished force after the first of several heart attacks in early 1922.

Leon Gambetta French 'armoured' CRUISER, completed in 1903 and typical of the designs built for the FRENCH NAVY before 1911. Generally large, slow and poorly armed, French cruisers reflected contemporary concern with coastal defence and trade protection, and were unsuited to fleet operations. Ten light cruisers ordered for 1915 were never built, and 22 armoured cruisers were still in French service when hostilities opened.

The seven newest armoured cruisers, including *Leon Gambetta*, operated with the main French battlefleet in the MEDITERRANEAN, and older ships performed trade-protection duties, although a few saw service with the Syrian BLOCKADE squadron. One of four lost in action, *Leon Gambetta* went down with most of its crew on the night of 24 April 1915, torpedoed by the Austro-Hungarian *U-5* while patrolling in the Gulf of Otranto.

BRIEF DATA (*Leon Gambetta,* 1914) Displacement: 12,250 tons; Crew: 734; Dimensions: length 488.5ft (148m), beam 70.5ft (21.4m); Speed: 22k; Armament: 4 × 194mm gun, 16 × 164.7mm, 1 × 4in, 22 × 47mm, 4 × 450mm TT.

Leopold, Prince of Bavaria (1846–1930) Competent but unexceptional GERMAN ARMY commander, recalled from retirement to lead the Ninth Army on the EASTERN FRONT in April 1915. His army took Warsaw on 4 August, during the Central Powers' TRIPLE OFFENSIVE, and he was immediately given overall control of Austro-German armies along the central sector of the front (Army Group Leopold), a move designed by chief of staff FALKENHAYN to curb the influence of HINDENBURG and LUDENDORFF. After Falkenhayn's fall the following August, Leopold replaced Hindenburg as supreme commander on the Eastern Front. Overshadowed by chief of staff HOFFMANN, he retired again after the conclusion of the BREST-LITOVSK Treaty in March 1918.

Le Prieur Rockets A form of rocket armament for aircraft, invented by French naval airman Lieutenant Le Prieur and used from 1916 to ignite ZEPPELINS and other German AIRSHIPS. Four simple rockets were fitted to the interwing struts on either side of a biplane FIGHTER, and fired simultaneously by an electric switch. The device was widely used by the AÉRONAUTIQUE MILITAIRE on NIEUPORT 17S, and less commonly on SOPWITH PUPS or SOPWITH CAMELS. The rockets scored several successes, but were withdrawn in 1918 once incendiary bullets had become a standard component of airborne MACHINE GUN ammunition.

Le Quesnoy Ancient walled town in western Belgium that was successfully stormed by NEW ZEALAND troops during the British Third Army's attack on the SAMBRE of 4 November 1918. The action at Le Quesnoy demonstrated the determination and ability of some German units to fight on despite the collapse of resistance elsewhere. In keeping with the medieval setting, but covered by modern massed ARTILLERY, the attackers scaled the outer ramparts of the town, parleyed with its commandant and stormed the inner walls when he refused to capitulate. The defenders finally gave up when fighting reached the town streets, surrendering more than 2,400 prisoners and 100 guns.

Lettow-Vorbeck, General Paul von (1870–1964) Experienced German colonial soldier, veteran of tribal campaigns in SOUTH-WEST AFRICA, who commanded forces in EAST AFRICA from January 1914. Inspiring exemplary discipline, loyalty, endurance and tactical skill in both German and ASKARI troops, he led the colonial army (*Schutztruppe*) through an undefeated defensive campaign against much larger British imperial forces.

Retreating after an initial victory at TANGA to draw enemy resources into deep pursuit, he outwitted a succession of British commanders, improvising to overcome mounting supply problems and launching a succession of 'hit-and-run' counterattacks. Although a total of 350,000 Allied troops and auxiliaries captured most of East Africa, Lettow-Vorbeck's tactical victory at MAHIWA in October 1917 and his subsequent escape across MOZAMBIQUE with less than 3,000 troops, mostly well-trained Askaris, cemented his international fame.

Promoted general in the field and twice wounded, he shared conditions of extreme hardship with his troops, and the broadly chivalrous, if ruthless, nature of his campaign was appreciated by Europeans all over the world. The *Schutztruppe* finally surrendered on 25 November 1918 at Abercorn in Northern Rhodesia (modern Zambia), having heard of the ARMISTICE two days late. Lettow-Vorbeck was honoured as a hero by all sides, subsequently enjoying a reputation for guerrilla warfare rivalled only by British Arab leader LAWRENCE. On returning to GERMANY in March 1919, he put himself at the head of a FREIKORPS brigade fighting SPARTACIST forces in Berlin (see GERMAN REVOLUTIONS), but was forced to retire from the GERMAN ARMY after declaring support for the right-wing Kapp Putsch in 1920. See also: AFRICA.

Lewis Gun An early light MACHINE GUN design that originated in the UNITED STATES (1911) but was first manufactured in BELGIUM and GREAT BRITAIN. Easier to produce and far lighter than the standard British VICKERS GUN, the air-cooled Lewis was still too heavy (12kg) for efficient portable use but became the standard support weapon with British and Belgian infantry on the WESTERN FRONT from 1915. Its distinctive disc magazine held 47 or 97 rounds of 0.303-inch ammunition, and it was a generally reliable weapon, adapted for widespread use on ARMOURED CARS, TANKS and aircraft. The spade-handled aircraft version could not be adapted for use with INTERRUPTER GEAR, but was otherwise the best of its type in Allied service. A US (0.30-inch) version went into production in 1917, and was used in limited numbers by both the AEF and the USAAS.

LFG Aircraft See: ROLAND C-II and D-TYPES.

Liberia Small west African republic, slightly larger than Portugal, founded by liberated Afro-American slaves and independent since 1847 (see MAP 17). Inhabited by about 10,000 descendants of the original settlers and some 2 million natives, Liberia was an important staging post for German trade with South America. German transatlantic commerce collapsed completely on the outbreak of war (see NAVAL WARFARE), but a telegraph station at the capital, Monrovia, remained in German hands until 1917. The pro-Allied government's US-led police force and its single customs ship were too busy dealing with tribal unrest to attempt its capture until 1917, after which President Daniel Howard declared war on GERMANY (4 August 1917) and the German garrison was deported. The following April a U-BOAT reached Monrovia, where it bombarded the cable station and sank the customs ship, providing military justification for Liberia's place at the PARIS PEACE CONFERENCE.

Liebknecht, Karl (1871–1919) See: SPARTACUS LEAGUE.

Liège, Siege of The first major action of the war on the WESTERN FRONT. Liège guarded the best natural entrance into BELGIUM along the frontier with GERMANY, blocking a narrow gap between the Ardennes forests to the south and the Dutch border to the north. Built on high ground and virtually surrounded by the River Meuse (almost 200 metres wide at that point) it was circled by FORTRESSES to create a defensive area widely regarded as impregnable.

The 12 main forts had been built in the 1880s to hold the line of the Meuse against invasion from any direction. Constructed on high ground 6–10km from the city, with 3–5km between each, they were almost completely buried underground with only the main gun cupolas visible. Armed with a total of 400 retractable guns, the largest of them 210mm howitzers, they were further protected by infantry garrisons, searchlights, MACHINE GUN posts and deep dry moats.

Hardly updated by 1914, they were only lightly garrisoned in August. The BELGIAN ARMY, which was intended to fill gaps between the forts, was dispersed around the country and the only infantry unit at Liège was General Leman's 3rd Division in the city itself. Belgium's neutrality also delayed active preparations for their defence, which only began on 2 August (see JULY CRISIS).

The city was the first target of the German SCHLIEFFEN PLAN, and a force of six brigades (about 60,000 men, against some 25,000 defenders) was sent northwest from General von BÜLOW's Second Army to occupy the forts as a preliminary to the main invasion of Belgium. Designated the 'Army of the Meuse' and commanded by General von Emmich, it approached the city on 4 August to find the main bridges over the Meuse destroyed. Attempts to cross the river on pontoons met with unexpected fire from Belgian infantry, and two brigades attacking from the south were held off. To the north of the city, German forces managed to cross the river near Visé, and in the centre the fort line stood east of the river, so that Emmich was able to launch an attack on the forts themselves the following morning.

Repeated infantry assaults into the night of 5 August achieved nothing except heavy German casualties, but a brigade led by Emmich's deputy chief of staff, LUDENDORFF, broke through the line between two of the forts at the centre of the attack and had gained heights above the city by the next afternoon. The breakthrough persuaded Leman to evacuate the Belgian 3rd Division, saving it from possible encirclement, but he rejected German attempts to secure surrender of the forts by parley, by ZEPPELIN attack and by ARTILLERY bombardment of the city, which was occupied on 7 August. German infantry attacked the eastern forts until 9 August, after which the attack paused to await the arrival of giant siege guns.

Two 'BIG BERTHAS' and nine Austrian SCHLANKE EMMA 305mm howitzers reduced all 12 forts to rubble within four days of their arrival on 12 August. Leman surrendered from the last fort when it fell on 16 August, and the following day the German Second and Third Armies began their massed advance on NAMUR. Despite loud praise from Allied PROPAGANDA, the defence had delayed tight German schedules by only two days. See MAP 4.

Liggett, General Hunter (1857–1935) US infantry commander stationed in the PHILIPPINES until 1917 and appointed the AEF's first corps commander in January 1918. Arriving in France in March, he assumed tactical control of I Corps during operations around Soissons on the WESTERN FRONT in July. He was retained in France despite AEF commander PERSHING's well-known aversion to overweight officers, and his tactical acumen and cautious realism were well-suited to operational conditions. His troops played a major part in the inaugural US victory at ST MIHIEL in September, and he adapted quickly to overcome both organizational problems and well-established German defences during the subsequent MEUSE–ARGONNE OFFENSIVE. Promoted to command the First Army when US forces were reorganized in October, he planned the attack on the southern section of the HINDENBURG LINE that brought US forces to the German border by November. Remaining in Europe until mid-1919, he returned to command a corps in the US until his retirement in 1921.

Liman von Sanders, General Otto (1855–1929) Prussian cavalry officer who served in staff and divisional commands before becoming head of the German military mission to TURKEY in late 1913 and, despite Russian protests, inspector general of the TURKISH ARMY the following January. Uncomfortable in the dual role of diplomat and soldier, he resented direct military control exercised by the YOUNG TURK administration and argued over jurisdiction with German ambassador von Wangenheim, but accepted command of the Turkish First Army in the Bosporus in August 1914.

Always primarily concerned with German interests, Liman von Sanders lobbied the government for military alliance with the CENTRAL POWERS while working to improve training and reorganization, a process already begun by a cadre of relatively youthful Turkish officers. Given command of the Fifth Army at GALLIPOLI in March 1915, he was credited with masterminding the Allied failure, but celebrity made little difference to his status in Turkey. He was unable to halt the ARMENIAN MASSACRES or to prevent war minister ENVER PASHA's renewal of offensives on the CAUCASIAN FRONT in 1916.

In February 1918 he took command of YILDERIM FORCE, but was overwhelmed by General ALLENBY's much larger army on the PALESTINE FRONT. Returning to Constantinople to oversee repatriation of German troops after the ARMISTICE, he was arrested by the British as a suspected war criminal in February 1919. He retired shortly after his release in August.

Linsingen, General Alexander von (1850–1935) Conventional GERMAN ARMY officer whose career progressed rapidly with the rise to power of his mentor, FALKENHAYN. Sent to the EASTERN FRONT in December 1914 as a corps commander with EICHHORN's new Tenth Army, he was given command of the Austro-German Südarmee, formed in the central CARPATHIANS for attack on PRZEMYSL, in mid-January 1915. He replaced MACKENSEN in control of the BUG OFFENSIVE in July, and was given command of Army Group Linsingen, covering the southern Polish sector of the line, after the Russian 'GREAT RETREAT'. His group's Austro-Hungarian southern wing was shattered by the BRUSILOV OFFENSIVE in summer 1916, but German forces prevented significant Russian gains further north and held off the subsequent offensive towards KOVEL. Linsingen remained in the post until the BREST-LITOVSK Treaty was signed in March 1918, when he returned to GERMANY as regional military commander of the Brandenburg area.

Lion Class Class of British BATTLECRUISERS popularly known as the 'Big Cats', that comprised *Lion*, *Princess Royal*, and the slightly larger *Queen Mary*. The biggest ship in the ROYAL NAVY on completion in 1912 and the first battlecruiser to mount 13.5-inch guns, *Lion* was the flagship of the GRAND FLEET's battlecruiser force in the North Sea and all three took part in the HELIGOLAND BIGHT battle. *Queen Mary* missed the DOGGER BANK action, where *Lion* suffered heavy damage, and all three were at JUTLAND in 1916. *Princess Royal* came through the battle virtually undamaged, but *Lion* was again seriously battered by gunfire and *Queen Mary* exploded, sinking with the loss of almost 1,300 lives. Fitted with additional ANTI-AIRCRAFT guns from late 1916, *Lion* and *Princess Royal* remained in service until the mid-1920s.

BRIEF DATA (*Lion*, 1914) Displacement: 29,700 tons; Crew: 1,061; Dimensions: length 700ft (212.1m), beam 88.5ft (26.8m); Speed: 29k; Armament: 8 × 13.5in gun, 16 × 4in, 2 × 21in TT.

Lippmann, Walter (1889–1974) Respected American liberal journalist who co-founded the influential *New Republic* magazine in 1914, guiding political criticism in the UNITED STATES out of its sensationalist 'muckraking' phase. Lippmann was among several leading pacifist liberals persuaded (initially by presidential advisor HOUSE) to support President WILSON's programme of 'limited preparedness' for war in 1916. Able to see the war as a crusade for liberal values, he approved of the government's increasing involvement in wartime social and economic management, and had great personal faith in Wilson's ability to impose a liberal peace on Europe.

As secretary to the wartime 'Inquiry', a secret investigation into world affairs conducted by about 125 researchers and experts, Lippmann coordinated its work into a programme for peace. The resulting document

'The War Aims and Peace Terms It Suggests', was presented to House on 22 December 1917 and formed the basis for the territorial sections of the FOURTEEN POINTS in January 1918. Disenchanted by the Treaty of VERSAILLES, Lippmann withdrew his support for Wilson from mid-1919 and his influence declined with the subsequent collapse of 'Progressive' politics in the USA (see ROOSEVELT, T.)

Lithuania Russian Baltic province occupied by German forces on the EASTERN FRONT from summer 1915. From late 1917 an attempt was made to set up a puppet state under German control by establishing a Lithuanian Council (*Taryba*), which proclaimed a kingdom and offered the crown to Prince Wilhelm of Urach, a member of the Württemberg royal family. He became King Mindove II in July 1918, but was formally deposed in November and an independent republic announced under President Smetona. The withdrawal of German forces was followed by a limited RED ARMY invasion, and by January 1919 a SOVIET government in the capital, Vilnius, was competing with Smetona's *Taryba* administration at Kovno. The Russians were expelled by a newly constituted Lithuanian Army, backed by a Polish contingent sent against the common enemy at Vilnius. Independence was sealed in July 1920, when the peace of Tartu ended Bolshevik aggression, but a German administration controlled the southwestern Memel region until 1923, and the final recovery of Vilnius from Polish forces took until 1927. See MAPS 10, 25.

Lloyd C-Types Austro-Hungarian reconnaissance biplanes, produced in 1915–16 as the C-II, C-III and C-V, each with a larger engine than its predecessor. Early models were unarmed, but a rear-firing MACHINE GUN was fitted to the shared cockpit on later versions. Good performers at high altitude, Lloyds saw action on the ITALIAN FRONT and during the ROMANIAN CAMPAIGN, but were gradually replaced by HALBERSTADT or PHÖNIX C-TYPES during 1917.

BRIEF DATA (C-II) Type: two-seater reconnaissance; Engine: 145hp Hiero; Max speed: 120kph; Armament: observer's small arms, light bombs (hand thrown).

Lloyd George, David (1863–1945) Welsh politician, a charismatic orator and vigorous social reformer who was chancellor of the exchequer and a leading figure on the Radical, reformist wing of the Liberal Party in 1914. The pivotal figure in a cabinet divided by the JULY CRISIS, his eventual commitment to war in defence of BELGIUM ensured broad government unity in early August.

As wartime finance minister Lloyd George introduced tax increases and measures against ALCOHOL consumption, but quickly became a critic of what he viewed as lethargic, unimaginative war management by the ASQUITH government. By early 1915 he was openly attacking war minister KITCHENER's haphazard organization of the munitions industry, and he was the cabinet's most influential 'EASTERNER'.

At the head of a new munitions ministry from May 1915, he led a rapid reorganization of GREAT BRITAIN's economic war effort, extending production to hundreds of small firms and multiplying output of shells and weapons over the next year. Kitchener's death in June 1916 gave Lloyd George the war ministry, and his relations with BEF commanders, always marked by mutual suspicion, worsened as he lobbied for greater concentration at SALONIKA.

Asquith's inability to impose the necessary socioeconomic strictures at home, or to dictate policy to imperial chief of staff ROBERTSON, brought Lloyd George together with Conservatives and the press to bring down the cabinet in late 1916, and he became prime minister of a new coalition on 7 December.

Appointing a streamlined war cabinet to make major strategic decisions, he extended government controls over the economy through a set of new ministries headed by leading businessmen. Careful to cultivate press and public popularity for a broad policy of 'war to the finish' (he brought press baron Lord NORTHCLIFFE into the government from February 1918), he was less successful in winning military support for his strategic preferences.

He eventually persuaded the ROYAL NAVY to introduce CONVOYS as the main defence against SUBMARINE WARFARE, but his relations with HAIG and Robertson were marked by prolonged disputes over the NIVELLE OFFENSIVE and the YPRES attack in 1917. Lloyd George sought to bypass Army chiefs by promoting a unified Allied command through the SUPREME WAR COUNCIL in November 1917, replacing Robertson with the more pliable WILSON in February 1918, and Haig's objections were eventually silenced by the crisis of the German KAISERSCHLACHT Offensive in March.

Lloyd George's coalition won an overwhelming victory in the December 1918 elections, which were dominated by popular demands for revenge on GERMANY. In his own 1917 statement of war aims, Lloyd George had stressed the independent aspirations of small nations, but as chief British delegate at the PARIS PEACE CONFERENCE he was forced to play a pragmatic role, weaving a middle course between CLEMENCEAU's aggressive French nationalism and the liberal ideals of US president WILSON, while also taking account of home opinion. The coalition ended in October 1922, and Lloyd George never again held office, although he remained a brooding political presence in interwar Britain.

Lodge, Henry Cabot (1850–1924) Long-time advocate of US economic expansion overseas and a Republican ally of Theodore ROOSEVELT until the split of 1912, after which he led the Party's majority conservative wing. Among the most tenacious opponents of social reform in the prewar era, and a leading advocate of PREPAREDNESS after 1914, Lodge recognized the political opportunities afforded by the crisis of 1917, using it both to attack president WILSON and to weaken the non-interventionist 'Progressive' faction in his own party.

Support for Roosevelt's plan to lead a volunteer regiment in April 1917 was the first of many attempts to embarrass the government; Lodge went on to criticize the administration for slow mobilization, shortage of RAILWAY equipment, failure to prevent strikes, and delays in aircraft production.

Lodge was able to obstruct Wilson's policies more effectively after the mid-term elections in November 1918 returned a Republican Congress. As chairman of the Senate Committee on Foreign Relations, he led the campaign against ratification of the VERSAILLES Treaty from July 1919, delaying the Committee's initial recommendation in order to allow a build-up of popular hostility, and to give him time to formulate amendments (the 'Lodge Reservations') that were at the heart of the subsequent rejection of the Treaty by Congress.

Łódź, Battle of Attack by the German Ninth Army (MACKENSEN) on Russian forces gathering for an offensive through Silesia in November 1914 (see POLISH CAMPAIGNS). After victory at IVANGOROD in late October, the four Russian invasion armies had been delayed while shell-damaged RAILWAYS were repaired and attempts made to alleviate supply shortages. German commander LUDENDORFF used the respite, and a superior rail system, to transport most of the Ninth Army north to Torúnin, in position to strike the Russian Second Army (Scheidemann) on the northern wing of the Russian invasion force.

Russian forces were ill-prepared for the attack. The Russian First Army (RENNENKAMPF) had been moved south from East Prussia to protect the flank of the Second, but was holding a very long front. Attacking southeast on 11 November, four German corps struck the isolated corps on the left wing of the Russian First Army; the Russian corps collapsed two days later, losing two-thirds of its infantry and fleeing back to the Vistula. Accepting Northern Army Group commander RUZSKI's view that the German attack was a feint by a small force, STAVKA (Russian central command) proceeded with the invasion of Silesia, allowing the German Ninth Army to inflict serious damage on the corps on the right wing of the Russian Second Army at Kutno (14–15 November).

The rest of the Second Army then wheeled round to protect its supply centre at Łódź, and on 16 November its southern neighbour, PLEHVE's Fifth Army, was ordered to support it, effectively cancelling the Silesian invasion. Marching nonstop, with some units covering more than 100km in two days, both Russian armies had reached Łódź by the time German forces arrived on 18 November. Relief attacks from the east by parts of the Russian First Army were too disorganized to penetrate German screens and Ludendorff, expecting a Russian retreat beyond the Vistula, ordered an immediate assault on the town.

With more guns than the Ninth Army, almost twice as many men and plentiful supplies, the Russian defenders held off attacks for a week. German units began to run short of ammunition from 23 November, and the battle was suspended two days later. One German corps did establish itself in the east of the town and was almost surrounded, but escaped to rejoin the Ninth Army by 26 November.

Claiming a great strategic victory and determined to take Łódź, overall German front commander HINDENBURG demanded reinforcements from the west, and four corps arrived to resume attacks in early December. Though costly and unsuccessful, they persuaded Ruzski to order Russian withdrawal from Łódź on 6 December, by which time their supplies were low and casualties high (100,000 men since 18 November).

German forces pursued the Russian Fifth and Second Armies to a line on the Bzura and Rawka Rivers, west of Warsaw, and launched repeated frontal attacks against their new positions. With ammunition very low and Ninth Army losses also approaching 100,000, German attacks slackened after 13 December. Although the offensive had halted Russian invasion plans it achieved no decisive strategic breakthrough, and the year ended in entrenched stalemate west of Warsaw. See also: MAP 10; Second Battle of the MASURIAN LAKES.

Löhner C-I Last of a series of Austro-Hungarian biplanes, dating back to the prewar B-I, used in small numbers for reconnaissance and light bombing by the AUSTRO-HUNGARIAN AIR SERVICE until 1917. Like its predecessors, the C-I (which entered service in 1916) was rendered vulnerable to attack by a low operational ceiling.

BRIEF DATA Type: two-seater reconnaissance; Engine: 160hp Austro-Daimler; Max speed: 140kph; Ceiling: 2,500m; 1 × 8mm mg, light bombs (hand thrown).

Löhner L Sturdy and particularly seaworthy 'PUSHER' flying boat used in large numbers by the AUSTRO-HUNGARIAN NAVY for reconnaissance, patrol, night-bombing and ANTI-SUBMARINE work from 1915 to 1918. Successfully employed over the Adriatic and against Italian coastal targets (often in squadron strength), Löhners sunk a French SUBMARINE, *Foucault*, on 15 September 1916, and were manoeuvrable enough to win a series of combat victories for leading Austrian ACE Gottfried Banfield. Of more than 200 built, including 36 PHOTO-RECONNAISSANCE versions, only 30 were lost in action, and a captured example was copied by the Italians for their MACCHI M-TYPE design. Löhners were sometimes fitted with alternative (usually 140hp) engines, and anti-submarine models usually carried DEPTH CHARGES in place of bombs.

BRIEF DATA (L) Type: two-seater flying boat; Engine: 160hp Austro-Daimler; Max speed: 104kph; Armament: 1 × 7.92mm mg, max bomb load 200kg.

London, Treaty of The agreement that committed ITALY to war on the side of the Allies, signed on 26 April 1915. Along with substantial military and economic aid to Italy (including an immediate £50 million loan from GREAT BRITAIN), the London pact promised postwar REPARATIONS and granted almost every Italian territorial ambition. In addition to the Trentino (South Tyrol) and Trieste regions to the north (then ruled by Austria-Hungary), Italy was to control the Dalmatian and Adriatic coastlines, although the city of Fiume (Rijeka) was withheld as a gesture to Russian pan-Slav interests. The Dodecanese archipelago (annexed in 1912 but claimed by GREECE) was to become formally Italian, along with an expanded domain in Libya, and Italian claims to the Adalia region in Turkish Asia Minor were accepted (see MAP 1).

The Treaty quickly became a source of diplomatic controversy. What to Italian statesmen appeared a justified expression of national aspirations was viewed by some Allied authorities as a form of international blackmail. Aid provisions also caused arguments as Allied supplies of food, fuel and MEDITERRANEAN naval firepower fell short of Italian expectations.

Allied secret treaties were made public by the Bolshevik government after the OCTOBER REVOLUTION in RUSSIA, and their contents appeared in the western press from late December 1917. News of the London Treaty provoked understandable anger in SERBIA and Greece, but also caused controversy in Italy, where the government was embarrassed by a clause prohibiting Allied response to peace proposals by Pope BENEDICT XV. Italian fears that the Treaty's territorial clauses would be superseded by Allied support for Balkan independence movements ultimately proved justified, and Italy received few of its promised rewards at the PARIS PEACE CONFERENCE. See also: ST JEAN DE MAURIENNE CONFERENCE; YUGOSLAVIA: D'ANNUNZIO, G.; SONNINO, S.

Lone Pine, Battle of Attack of 6 August 1915 by the 1st Australian Division (4,600 men) against the Turkish-held 'Lone Pine' position, about 100 metres southeast of the front at ANZAC COVE (see MAP 20). Planned by ANZAC commander BIRDWOOD as a diversion to draw Turkish reserves away from his main attack on SARI BAIR Ridge, itself part of General HAMILTON's wider SUVLA BAY OFFENSIVE on the GALLIPOLI FRONT, the Lone Pine action opened at 17.30 on 6 August and developed into a ferocious two-day trench fight.

Turkish TRENCHES were found to have solid roof structures through which defenders could fire at will, forcing Australian infantry to enter shellholes and fight along the passages in virtual darkness. Although Australian troops eventually secured the position late on 8 August – a limited tactical success and the most tangible gain of the Sari Bair battle – Turkish commanders never regarded the attack as more than a diversion. Of about 7,000 Turkish and 3,000 Australian casualties, 90 per cent were killed, and the action remains infamous as one of the most brutal of a gruesome campaign.

Loos, Battle of See: ARTOIS–LOOS OFFENSIVE.

Lorraine, Invasion of A major component of the FRENCH ARMY's planned multiple invasion of Germany in August 1914, one the Battles of the FRONTIERS. As envisaged by the French PLAN 17, and anticipated by the German SCHLIEFFEN PLAN, the French First and Second Armies marched into German-occupied Lorraine on 14 August, despite the initial failure of preliminary operations in Alsace (see Battle of MULHOUSE). As they advanced east from a line in front of the Moselle, General Pau's reinforced 'Army of Alsace' resumed its southern offensive.

South of the Grand Couronné, the hilly region east of Nancy, General DUBAIL's First Army approached the strongly defended town of Sarrebourg. General DE CASTLENAU's Second Army, which had lost one corps transferred to the Fifth Army near CHARLEROI, faced the similarly daunting target of Morhange. The German Sixth and Seventh Armies, under the overall command of Crown Prince RUPPRECHT, were intended to defend the Sarrebourg–Morhange line, retreating to draw French forces into a 'sack' for their ultimate encirclement by armies sweeping down from the north.

The French armies advanced against thickening German rearguards, their rapid infantry charges no match for entrenched troops backed by MACHINE GUNS and heavy ARTILLERY. Rupprecht, impatient for action, convinced chief of staff MOLTKE to alter his plans to permit a major counteroffensive, aimed at driving the French back beyond the Moselle and Nancy. It was launched on 20 August, catching the French Second Army, spearheaded by General FOCH's XX Corps, as it renewed attacks on Morhange. Without TRENCHES of their own to fall back on, de Castlenau's army retreated back to the fortified high ground of the Grand Couronné.

Chased into France by the German Sixth

Army, the retreat forced the French First Army to pull back from Sarrebourg. With gaps appearing between French armies all along the WESTERN FRONT, C-in-C JOFFRE also withdrew the Army of Alsace, even though it had retaken Mulhouse and the surrounding area against greatly reduced opposition. By 22 August both Lorraine armies were back to the fortress zones of Belfort, Epinal and Toul.

In defiance of the Schlieffen Plan, Rupprecht was reinforced for a full-scale attempt to break through the Trouée des Charmes, a natural gap between the heights of Epinal and Toul. Making efficient use of reconnaissance aircraft, French forces in well-established defensive positions were warned of the attack, which came on 24 August, and German gains were restricted to a small SALIENT, greatly reduced by counterattacks on both its flanks next morning.

The French line held despite heavy casualties over the next three days and a subsequent erosion of strength to meet crises further north. Rupprecht's 26 divisions in the sector, reinforced by artillery from Metz, were badly missed by the Germans at the MARNE, and battered away until the end of the month without breaking through, beginning a stalemate in the sector that remained essentially unbroken until 1918. See MAP 4.

Louvain (Leuven) Belgian city on the road between LIÈGE and Brussels, famed for its high Gothic architecture, university and unique library of ancient manuscripts (see MAP 4). The city was occupied on 19 August 1914 by the advancing German First Army during the invasion of BELGIUM, and remained fairly peaceful for several days as the mass of the First Army passed through en route for the capital. Some hostages were taken and shot – standard practice during the invasion – but troops generally behaved well until 25 August, when rearguards were raided by units of the BELGIAN ARMY from Antwerp.

The German rearguards fell back on Louvain, causing chaos during which shots were fired and general violence erupted. Belgian witnesses later claimed that confused troops shot each other in the dark, but German authorities believed themselves victims of concerted Belgian resistance and retaliated by systematically sacking, looting and burning the city over the next five days. The library, the university and many public buildings were completely gutted. Clergymen, women, and children were among the victims of mass shootings.

Though terror was perceived by the GERMAN ARMY as a legitimate extension of warfare intended to induce rapid civilian submission, this view was not shared by neutral diplomats or the international press, which began reporting the events in Louvain in terms of German 'barbarism' on 29 August. The mayhem ceased the following day, with the German government still insisting that 'entire responsibility' rested with the Belgians. The German actions had made an indelible mark on world opinion, especially in the UNITED STATES, and more than any other single event the sack of Louvain turned the War on the WESTERN FRONT into a crusade for Belgian liberation. It was the subject of several official postwar investigations, with a view to punishing those responsible, but no WAR CRIMES were ever proved. See also: DINANT.

Louvemont, Battle of See: Battle of VERDUN.

Ludendorff, General Erich (1865–1937) Energetic and self-confident GERMAN ARMY officer, a specialist in mobilization logistics, who was appointed deputy chief of staff (quartermaster) to BÜLOW's Second Army in early August 1914. Within a week he had become a popular celebrity, leading a brigade into LIÈGE on 6 August to threaten its ring of FORTRESSES from within.

Transfer to the EASTERN FRONT on 22 August as chief of staff to new Eighth Army commander HINDENBURG, and subsequent victories at TANNENBERG and the MASURIAN LAKES, cemented Ludendorff's status. Public adulation was focused on the largely inert Hindenburg, but Ludendorff's enthusiasm for self-publicity ensured that he received credit in military circles.

The command team took over the entire eastern theatre in November, enabling Ludendorff to display his gifts for rapid concentration and mobilization of forces. He reacted quickly to overtrump Russian invasion plans during the POLISH CAMPAIGN of late 1914, and the following year's well-coordinated GORLICE-TARNOW and TRIPLE OFFENSIVES made sweeping territorial gains.

Orthodox contemporary opinion accepted Ludendorff's view that Army chief of staff FALKENHAYN's failure to accept more ambitious plans denied him decisive success. More recent studies recognize the important contribution made by other commanders (notably MACKENSEN) and doubt the likelihood of a purely military victory over RUSSIA in 1915.

Ludendorff bitterly opposed Falkenhayn's diversion of resources to the BALKAN and WESTERN FRONTS from autumn 1915. Using the eastern command team's unblemished reputation to mobilize support from right-wing contacts inside GERMANY, he helped engineer Falkenhayn's demotion once military setbacks had weakened the latter's position in 1916. Promoted full general, Ludendorff became German Army quartermaster to Hindenburg as chief of staff on 29 August.

Under Hindenburg's name and Ludendorff's direction, their THIRD SUPREME COMMAND sought radical militarization of German socioeconomic life through the HINDENBURG PROGRAMME, bypassing parliamentary restraints in alliance with the major war industries. Ludendorff led military demands for total victory, massive postwar annexations and crippling REPARATIONS. He threw the Army behind the adoption of unrestricted SUBMARINE WARFARE, and used mounting influence over an enfeebled WILHELM II to engineer the dismissal of relative moderates inside and outside the armed forces.

The resignation of chancellor BETHMANN HOLLWEG in July 1917, and the subsequent dismissal of GRÖNER as head of the Supreme War Bureau, left Ludendorff as 'silent dictator' in effective political, military and economic control of Germany. Supported by a compliant Hindenburg, he operated in concert with the industrial magnates on whom the war effort depended, ignoring demands for price (and profit) controls during 1917 in pursuit of military victory before decisive US intervention or internal revolution made it impossible.

Russian collapse after the OCTOBER REVOLUTION triggered a full-scale annexation programme in eastern Europe, and Ludendorff was the moving force behind the extortionate BREST-LITOVSK and BUCHAREST Treaties, showing little regard for Germany's inability to enforce their conditions.

Ludendorff withdrew German forces in France to secure defensive positions in anticipation of major Allied attacks in 1917 (see HINDENBURG LINE), and resources were concentrated for an all-out effort to break through on the Western Front with the SPRING OFFENSIVES of 1918. Their failure was followed by successful Allied counterattacks, and Ludendorff was apparently convinced of ultimate failure from 8 August, the highly successful first day of the Allied AMIENS OFFENSIVE. Modern commentators place his recognition of inevitable defeat several weeks earlier.

His demand for immediate peace on 29 September and his transfer of power to Prince MAX VON BADEN's moderate reformist government were calculated to suspend internal disorder while parliamentary parties took responsibility for surrender. The Supreme Command's plans were upset by the depth of civilian unrest during the GERMAN REVOLUTIONS, and socialist ministers were able to force Ludendorff's resignation on 26 October.

He left Germany for temporary exile in Sweden, where he began a politically motivated campaign to mythologize German defeat. Ludendorff's postwar writings made an important contribution to the legend of an unbeaten army 'stabbed in the back' by traitorous enemies on the home front. He later led the National Socialists in the Reichstag (1924–28) before breaking with the party to concentrate on an eccentric personal campaign against Jesuits, Jews and Freemasons.

Luger Pistol The GERMAN ARMY's standard wartime PISTOL, a Swiss design (1900) first produced in Germany in 1904 and in service from 1908 as the Parabellum Pistole 08. The Luger fired a 7-round clip of 9mm ammunition, loaded into the butt, and was generally regarded as an excellent weapon, highly prized by Allied looters. Although more than

1.5 million Lugers are thought to have been produced in wartime GERMANY, supply was never able to match demand, and other pistols were in regular use from 1914, particularly the Beholla 7.65mm automatic. A 30-round Luger modification with an extended butt (the M17) was also used as a light automatic RIFLE on the WESTERN FRONT in 1918.

Lusitania Gigantic and opulent Cunard liner, at 32,000 tons the largest passenger vessel in wartime transatlantic service when it was torpedoed by the German *U-20* on 7 May 1915. En route for Britain from New York with more than 1,900 passengers and crew on board, it was within sight of the western Irish coast at Kinsale and manoeuvring to confuse U-BOATS reported in the area. Though easily able to outrun any stalking SUBMARINE, it turned directly into the path of *U-20*, which holed it to starboard with a TORPEDO. After a second, larger explosion, *Lusitania* rolled to starboard and sank in about twenty minutes. The roll prevented the launch of more than half the lifeboats and 1,198 people died, including 124 US citizens.

Coming after the German declaration of intensified SUBMARINE WARFARE around Britain, the sinking had far-reaching repercussions. Greeted initially as a success by the German press, but as an outrage by Allied and neutral observers, it had a powerful effect on public and political opinion in the UNITED STATES, already upset by previous attacks on passenger ships. German apologies and renewal of restrictions on U-boat commanders had little positive effect, and the incident was a major PROPAGANDA defeat for the CENTRAL POWERS.

In a heated propaganda campaign of their own, British authorities repeatedly accused *U-20* of attacking *Lusitania* with two torpedoes, citing the second explosion as evidence of intent to cause maximum casualties. Consistent German denials attributed the second explosion to a secret cargo of heavy munitions. The ship may have carried Allied small arms and ammunition, a regular practice that complicated attempts to immunize passenger and hospital ships from enemy attack, but evidence from the wreck refutes both claims and suggests that the second explosion was caused by coal dust igniting in *Lusitania*'s almost empty bunkers.

Lutsk, Battle of Pivotal engagement during the first phase of the Russian BRUSILOV OFFENSIVE on the EASTERN FRONT in June 1916. The town of Lutsk had been the focus of heavy fighting in 1915 during the abortive Austro-Hungarian 'BLACK-YELLOW' OFFENSIVE, and was heavily fortified as a reserve position by the Austro-Hungarian Fourth Army (JOSEF FERDINAND). General Kaledin's Russian Eighth Army broke through Austro-Hungarian lines on 5 June and drove defenders from the hills overlooking Lutsk from the south next day. The inhabitants fled in panic when Russian ARTILLERY began shelling the town, but barbed wire surrounding fortified positions stopped the defenders from escaping and most of the garrison was captured. The collapse of Lutsk ended the Fourth Army's effective resistance after it had lost almost 130,000 men in two days. See MAP 13.

Luxembourg Small, autonomous Grand Duchy under the constitutional leadership of the Grand Duchess Marie Adelaide in 1914 (see MAP 1). The economic life of the largely French-speaking population (about 250,000) was dominated by a customs union with GERMANY, which also ran the RAILWAYS. Though Luxembourg's neutrality was guaranteed by all the major European powers, German troops occupied the Duchy on 1–2 August 1914, as a preliminary to the SCHLIEFFEN PLAN, and remained until November 1918.

They were met with formal protest, but the state's 300 troops did not attempt military resistance, and the government retained control of internal affairs. The Luxembourgeois were left largely alone by the occupation, but a few were conscripted into the GERMAN ARMY, communications with the outside world were strictly controlled, and economic exploitation brought considerable hardship from 1917.

Popular dissatisfaction with the allegedly pro-German government erupted into republican unrest after the capital was occupied by the AEF from 22 November 1918, culminating in Marie-Adelaide's abdication in favour of her sister, Charlotte Adelgonde. Postwar economic links tied the state increasingly to FRANCE.

Luxemburg, Rosa (1870–1919) See: SPARTACUS LEAGUE.

LVG B-Types Unarmed German biplanes, the design basis for a successful line of LVG C-TYPE armed two-seaters, but useful and very stable craft in their own right. A few B-Is were operational with the GERMAN ARMY AIR SERVICE in August 1914 and flew reconnaissance over the WESTERN FRONT until withdrawn to training duties late in the year. In 1915 a smaller, faster B-II version, with a 120hp engine, was introduced to frontline squadrons and remained in widespread use into 1916. A purpose-built B-III trainer appeared in 1917.

BRIEF DATA (B-I, 1914) Type: two-seater reconnaissance/trainer; Engine: 100hp Mercedes; Max speed: 110kph; Armament: small arms.

LVG C-Type Successful series of reconnaissance biplanes, developed from the unarmed LVG B-TYPES and in German service as the C-I from 1915. An up-engined version of the prewar B-I, the C-I was the first operational two-seater to be armed by the GERMAN ARMY AIR FORCE, carrying a single MACHINE GUN. The faster C-II, structurally almost identical to the B-II but with a 160hp engine, also appeared in 1915 and took over production until withdrawn in early 1917. It flew reconnaissance and light-bombing missions on various fronts, including the first aircraft attack on London on 28 November 1916, when a C-II bombed Victoria Station. Some 250 C-I and C-II machines were produced, later models carrying the additional forward-firing machine gun incorporated into a radically improved C-V, which reached frontline service in mid-1917. Structurally redesigned for streamlining and stability, and similar in appearance to the contemporary DFW C-V, the C-V was one of the most effective multi-purpose aircraft of the period, performing reconnaissance, ARTILLERY-spotting, light-bombing and ground-support duties on the WESTERN and PALESTINE FRONTS. It usually needed FIGHTER escort and was handicapped by poor forward vision, but remained in frontline service until the ARMISTICE, along with a lighter C-VI version that took over production in early 1918. An estimated 1,000 C-V and C-VI models were eventually built.

BRIEF DATA (C-V) Type: two-seater reconnaissance/light bomber; Engine: 200hp Benz; Max speed: 166kph; Ceiling: 5,000m; Armament: 2 × 7.92mm mg, max bomb load 113kg (on wing racks).

Lvov See: LEMBERG; Campaign in GALICIA.

Lvov, Georgii, Prince (1861–1925) A leading prewar spokesman for rural landed interests at the imperial Russian court, Lvov served as interior minister for seven years from 1886, and became a member of the first imperial parliament (Duma) after the revolution of 1905. His commitment to enhancing the constitutional status of *zemstvos* (elected rural assemblies dominated by local landowners) earned him a reputation as a moderate reformer before 1914.

As head of the All-Russian Union of Zemstvos, Lvov supervised voluntary relief work during the first months of the War, but by 1915 he was voicing complaints from provincial nobles about the government's economic dependence on the heavy industrial giants of Moscow and Petrograd (St Petersburg). In June 1915 he was appointed chairman of Zemgor, a new umbrella organization for both the Union of Zemstvos and the All-Russian Union of Town Councils (representing the smaller urban communities). Established to coordinate greater provincial involvement in war production, Zemgor played an important part in improving medical and supply services to the RUSSIAN ARMY by 1916, but was always regarded with suspicion by the government, and accounted for only an estimated 5 per cent of imperial RUSSIA's overall war production.

Lvov was named prime minister of the new PROVISIONAL GOVERNMENT after the FEBRUARY REVOLUTION in 1917, in an attempt by

Duma politicians to unite urban and landed interests behind a liberal regime. He never exercised genuine authority over an increasingly radical political situation in Petrograd, and direction of cabinet policy passed quickly to justice minister KERENSKI, the only socialist in the government. Lvov remained nominal prime minister after a cabinet reshuffle in May 1917, but was in practice subordinate to the Petrograd SOVIET and Kerenski. Lvov played no further active part in Russian internal affairs after Kerenski became premier in July 1917, and emigrated to France after the OCTOBER REVOLUTION, subsequently heading a delegation of Russian parliamentary exiles at the PARIS PEACE CONFERENCE.

Lyautey, General Hubert (1854–1934) Unrepentantly royalist French officer, an expert colonial administrator and former protégé of General GALLIÉNI. Lyautey's prewar military career climaxed with his appointment as governor general of colonial Morocco in 1911. Highly successful in the role, he expected a senior field command in August 1914. Possibly because his stature might rival JOFFRE's, he remained in Morocco until December 1916, when he was called to Paris as war minister in the reshuffled BRIAND cabinet. Visits to the WESTERN FRONT quickly convinced him that the proposed NIVELLE OFFENSIVE was a mistake, but his power to stop it was almost immediately restricted by the removal of military transportation and arms supply from ministry control. He resigned after the Offensive received a final cabinet vote of confidence on 14 March – precipitating the government's fall two days later – and returned to the business of pacifying interior tribes in Morocco.

Lys Offensive The second phase of the German SPRING OFFENSIVES on the WESTERN FRONT in 1918, launched in Flanders after attacks in Picardy had petered out in early April (see KAISERSCHLACHT).

Only fear of bad weather in mud-drenched terrain had prevented the German THIRD SUPREME COMMAND from directing its first assault (codenamed 'George') against the British First and Second Armies in Flanders, and plans for a secondary attack in the region were already in place when the first offensive faltered east of Amiens.

The Flanders plan was quickly extended to become an alternative offensive (codenamed 'Georgette'), intended to capture the commanding heights of Mont Kemmel, Cassel and Mont des Cats, force Allied evacuation of the YPRES salient, and drive on to the Channel coast at Dunkirk (see MAP 9).

With the advantages of firm ground and a thick morning mist, the attack began on 9 April along a narrow front east of the River Lys between Béthune and Armentières. Supported by a vast concentration of ARTILLERY, it met with immediate success, striking hardest against a weak PORTUGUESE corps around Laventie and breaking through almost at once. British units on either side, tired and under strength after transfer from the Somme defence, were pushed back with heavy casualties, retreating more than 5km on the first day.

The offensive lasted for another 19 days, but German gains were never again so spectacular. The battlefront was extended gradually northwards into the Ypres area from the original breakthrough point as German forces pushed towards the coast, bringing the relatively fresh BELGIAN ARMY into the fight alongside the British Second Army (PLUMER). Myriad local engagements brought victories and defeats for both sides as the German line inched forward.

Commanders on both sides recognized the pivotal nature of the struggle. German leaders HINDENBURG and LUDENDORFF felt the key to overall victory lay in cutting off British supply lines in Flanders, but agreed with northern regional commander Crown Prince RUPPRECHT that local victories in Flanders were meaningless unless an Allied strategic withdrawal could be forced.

On the Allied side, British C-in-C HAIG faced defeat for the second time in a month. Exhorting his armies to hold out at all costs, he appealed desperately for reserves to new Allied Supreme Commander FOCH, who at first refused to release them from the sectors further south, where FRENCH ARMY C-in-C PÉTAIN expected a new German attack at any moment. Considerable French forces were eventually sent to Flanders in time for the last week of a battle that had disintegrated into a tangle of subsidiary engagements.

The German advance reached a point 8km short of the vital RAILWAY junction at Hazebrouck, some 18km beyond its start point and 35km from Dunkirk. The important prize of Mont Kemmel was taken from French forces on 25 April, but no further progress was made against disciplined defenders. With both sides close to utter exhaustion, major strategic movement ceased to be a practical possibility, and Ludendorff officially suspended the offensive on 29 April.

Both sides suffered about 110,000 casualties in the 20 days of combat, but the GERMAN ARMY was less able to withstand the losses than its opponents. Allied planning was bolstered by the gathering strength of the AEF in France, but the same prospect offered Ludendorff little choice but to try for an immediate victory elsewhere (see Third Battle of the AISNE).

M

Maan, Siege of The Arabian RAILWAY town of Maan, about 100km northeast of AQABA, was an important Turkish base for operations against Arab raids from early 1917, when the capture of WEJH by ARAB REVOLT forces threatened communications north of besieged MEDINA (see MAP 22). After British failure at AMMAN halted northward progress to the Dead Sea and TRANSJORDAN in spring 1918, Arab Northern Army commander FEISAL accepted demands from his chieftains for an attack on Maan, as a matter of prestige and to secure future advances against threats from the rear. Arab Army regulars under Jafaar Pasha attacked the town from the north, south and west on 17 April, with support from British ARMOURED CARS and camel units (with Muslim personnel). Despite numerical superiority over the 3,000 defenders, operations were postponed when Jafaar's small French ARTILLERY detachment (two mountain guns) ran out of shells. Surrender negotiations were opened, but 3,000 Turkish troops arrived from Amman before agreement could be reached. After cutting all supply links to Medina, Jafaar maintained the siege until September, when the defenders evacuated Maan and marched north. Harassed by mounted tribesmen, 4,500 survivors surrendered to British forces in Transjordan on 28 September.

McAdoo, William (1863–1941) Energetic and forceful US treasury secretary (finance minister), in office since 1913 and president WILSON's son-in-law. Influential enough to be known as the 'Crown Prince', McAdoo was generally willing to compromise his liberal principles for the sake of economic pragmatism.

Along with secretary of state LANSING, he argued in favour of low-interest loans to the Allies during the period of US neutrality, hoping that financial assistance would render US military involvement unnecessary. In mid-1917 he temporarily halted loans to Britain pending assurances that they were not being reinvested elsewhere, but after Lansing blocked the move he made no further attempt to attach political conditions and concentrated on financing the war effort.

McAdoo originally hoped to raise the cost of US involvement in the War by a combination of 'Liberty Bond' sales to the public and increased taxation on high incomes. Conservative resistance to tax rises, inflation (which more than halved the dollar's domestic purchasing power in wartime) and spiralling estimates of government spending persuaded him to concentrate on bond sales after a long struggle in Congress over new taxes on profits. Although federal tax income rose from $788 million in 1916 to over $5 billion in 1919, four oversubscribed issues of Liberty Bonds, all backed by national PROPA-

GANDA campaigns, had raised $21 billion by the ARMISTICE.

McAdoo doubled as director general of the federally controlled RAILWAY system from late December 1917, holding both posts and several committee chairs until exhaustion led to his resignation in January 1919. His postwar bid for high office ended with his failure to achieve the Democratic presidential nomination in 1924.

Macchi M-5 Italian biplane flying boat, a FIGHTER developed in response to the Austro-Hungarian HANSA-BRANDENBURG CC, and using a similar 'PUSHER' design. In action for the ITALIAN NAVY over the Adriatic from early 1918, it was a manoeuvrable, competitive combat machine, primarily employed as an escort for coastal bombing raids. It could outperform the PHÖNIX D-TYPE fighters used by the AUSTRO-HUNGARIAN NAVY, and 344 were built, remaining in service until the ARMISTICE and eventually equipping five full squadrons.

BRIEF DATA Type: single-seat fighter flying boat; Engine: 160hp Isotta-Fraschini; Max speed: 189kph; Ceiling: 4,550m; Armament: 1 × 0.303in mg.

MacDonald, J(ames) Ramsay (1866–1937) Scottish socialist politician, instrumental in the formation of the British Labour Party and its chairman until August 1914, when his Independent Labour Party (ILP) group opposed Britain's declaration of war and he resigned his positions. Trade union representative Arthur HENDERSON became Labour Party leader, subsequently serving in the ASQUITH and LLOYD GEORGE coalitions.

Along with fellow ILP leaders Keir Hardie and Philip Snowden, MacDonald maintained an anti-War stance, suffering harsh treatment from the press and winning little popular support in a general atmosphere of wartime industrial truce. In August 1917, British seamen preempted government prohibition by refusing to transport MacDonald and other socialist leaders to the STOCKHOLM CONFERENCE, and he lost his seat in the election of December 1918. Always regarded with suspicion by right-wing elements in Britain, he returned as leader of the Labour opposition in 1922.

Macedonian Front See: SALONIKA.

Machine Guns All machine guns in use by the armies of 1914 were heavy models, weighing between 40kg and 60kg, even without carriages, mountings, heavy ammunition supplies and (sometimes) armoured shields. Standard 1914 weapons required an operational crew of three to six men and were generally positioned on a flat trajectory tripod. They could fire 400–600 rounds of small-calibre ammunition per minute, fed on a fabric belt (usually about 250 rounds) or a metal strip (up to 30 rounds).

Intense heat in the gun's barrel required cooling, either by air vents or by using a water bag, to prevent buckling and jamming. Guns still jammed frequently, especially with inexperienced crews or in hot conditions, and required constant changes of ammunition pack or water, which on some models evaporated in less than two minutes.

Because of this, machine guns were usually grouped in sections of three or more for defensive purposes. Each was estimated by contemporaries as the firepower equivalent of between 60 and 100 RIFLES, although their aimed range was shorter than a massed volley of rifle fire. Established in fixed strongpoints, sited to cover likely attack routes, they made direct infantry assault against prepared positions costly wherever they were used.

Widely recognized by contemporaries and historians as the dominant defensive infantry weapon of the age, the machine gun's offensive limitations are often overlooked. Even when transported on wheeled carriages or broken down for haulage by pack animals they could not keep up with fast-moving infantry, and ARTILLERY was far more important to most attacks in most places. Along roads or on flat surfaces the problem was solved by the development of machine-gun-carrying ARMOURED CARS, and heavy machine guns were eventually also carried by TANKS for use over broken ground on the WESTERN FRONT (which engaged the greatest concentration of machine guns).

Light, portable machine guns existed in 1914 – a few Danish Masden guns were in Russian service by August – but they were largely a wartime development. Weighing only 9–14kg, and mostly firing at a rate comparable with heavy models, they could be carried by one man and were integrated in much larger numbers into attacking infantry units in all theatres by 1918. Ammunition (carried on belts, magazines or drums) remained a bulky problem, but, with the development of more sophisticated INFILTRATION and PEACEFUL PENETRATION tactics on the Western Front, aircraft were increasingly used to drop supplies to forward machine guns. Automatic rifles and sub-machine guns, even lighter but often carrying only a 10- or 20-shot magazine, were also developed in small numbers.

Light machine guns could also be mounted on aircraft, and from 1915 (particularly after the German development of INTERRUPTER GEAR) they played an important role in AERIAL WARFARE. Aerial weapons eventually used chain link to replace fabric in ammunition belts, as the fabric often trailed and became entangled with the aircraft's controls. The development of air-to-ground attack methods prompted the deployment of high-trajectory heavy machine guns as ANTI-AIRCRAFT weapons in France and Italy, sometimes mounted on lorries; and as naval aviation progressed heavy machine guns were added to warship armament for the same purpose. Machine guns were also a useful addition to the armament of naval transports (see e.g. GALLIPOLI LANDINGS), and were the principal weapons of the earliest surface-armed SUBMARINES. See also: BERGMANN, BROWNING, CHAUCHAT, FIAT-REVELLI, HOTCHKISS, LEWIS, MARLIN, MAXIM, ST ÉTIENNE, SCHWARZLOSE, VICKERS and VILLAR PEROSA GUNS; MASCHINENGEWEHR.

Mackensen, Field Marshal August von (1849–1944) A corps commander with the German Eighth Army (PRITTWITZ) on the EASTERN FRONT in August 1914, Mackensen played a major part in the opening EAST PRUSSIA campaign. Transferred to the Ninth Army for the POLISH CAMPAIGN in late September 1914, he led the force sent to besiege Warsaw and the attack on ŁÓDŹ, by which time he had replaced HINDENBURG as Ninth Army commander. The following April he took over the Eleventh Army, and was in overall field command during the GORLICE–TARNOW OFFENSIVE in May.

Promoted field marshal as a reward for its success in June 1915, Mackensen went on to drive up the River BUG during the summer's TRIPLE OFFENSIVE, securing his position as the acknowledged master of BREAKTHROUGH TACTICS, based on painstaking concentration of overwhelming force to batter a narrow stretch of enemy front regardless of speed or surprise.

Mackensen's methods were equally effective elsewhere. From September 1915 he controlled the invasion of SERBIA on the BALKAN FRONT, and he commanded the multi-national Danube Army during the ROMANIAN CAMPAIGN the following autumn. From early 1917 until the ARMISTICE he headed occupying forces in ROMANIA, a post more concerned with economic exploitation than fighting. He was briefly interned in France before returning home to retirement in 1919. See also: SEECKT, H.

Mahiwa, Battle of The bloodiest battle of the war in German EAST AFRICA and its last major engagement, fought in the virtually uncharted southeastern corner of the colony on 17–18 October 1917 (see MAP 18). General van Deventer's British imperial forces had begun an offensive from the coast in mid-September, and German commander LETTOW-VORBECK stationed 1,500 men (and his last two field guns) in strong positions on a ridge about 80km inland. South African General Beves sent his tired Anglo-Nigerian brigade (4,900 troops) up the ridge in a simple frontal attack on both mornings, losing 2,700 men before the attempt was finally called off. Lettow-Vorbeck, whose victory received heavy publicity in GERMANY, lost just over 500 troops. Unable to afford even slight battle losses, he withdrew south towards the border with MOZAMBIQUE.

Maistre, General Paul (1858–1922) Chief of staff to the French Fourth Army in August 1914, he benefited from C-in-C JOFFRE's wholesale purge of senior officers and was promoted directly to corps command after the first Battle of the MARNE. His XXI Corps held the sector of the WESTERN FRONT around Armentières for most of 1915, and was at both VERDUN and the SOMME the following year, but was held in reserve during the NIVELLE OFFENSIVE in spring 1917. After the Offensive's failure Maistre took over the Sixth Army from MANGIN, charged with its recovery from the mutiny of early summer. Transferred to command the Tenth Army on the ITALIAN FRONT after the CAPORETTO OFFENSIVE in November, he returned to France to command the Centre Army Group after the German SPRING OFFENSIVES of 1918, advancing it slowly on the right flank of AEF forces during the final MEUSE-ARGONNE OFFENSIVE in the autumn.

Maklakov, Nikolai (1871–1918) Ardent monarchist selected as a conservative strongman for the important Russian interior ministry in early 1913. Closely identified with prewar moves to curtail the role of the Duma (parliament), he was the most powerful cabinet voice against concessions to reformers after 1914. A strong influence over elderly premier GOREMYKIN, he opposed all suggestions of partnership with liberal representatives, and prevented foreign minister SAZONOV from promising reforms to POLAND. A favourite target of government critics, Maklakov and three other right-wing ministers were sacrificed by Tsar NICHOLAS II in June 1915, a gesture of appeasement to the Duma, whose support for the administration had been shaken by defeats on the EASTERN FRONT. Relegated to relatively junior administrative tasks and unemployed after the FEBRUARY REVOLUTION, Maklakov was shot by the Bolsheviks in 1918.

Malazgirt, Battle of Russian counterattack on the CAUCASIAN FRONT in early August 1915 that ended a limited offensive by the Turkish Second Army, ordered by war minister ENVER PASHA to drive Russian forces out of Turkish Armenia. Despite continuing supply problems, Armenian rebel activity, serious losses during December's SARIKAMISH battle and diversion of strength to meet the Allied invasion at GALLIPOLI, the Turkish advance from 10 July forced Russian units west of Lake Van into retreat north and east. Mus was taken on 27 July, and its ARMENIAN population badly treated, but Turkish supply lines became desperately weak.

Russian Caucasus Army commander YUDENICH drew the Turkish advance forward as he gathered limited reserves for a counterattack. The counterattack struck the Turkish northern flank at the Plain of Malazgirt on 5 August, and was followed by secondary attacks all along the line, forcing headlong and costly Turkish retreat and ending Enver's offensive ambitions in the region for a year. By late August the front had stabilized on a broken and sparse line east of RIZE (on the BLACK SEA coast), ERZURUM and Bitlis, but Yudenich was losing troops steadily to the simultaneous emergency on the EASTERN FRONT and attempted no exploitation of his success until 1916. See MAP 24.

Malinov, Alexander (1867–1938) Moderate liberal former prime minister (1908–11) of BULGARIA, who was the leading political supporter of alliance with RUSSIA, and by extension the ENTENTE. He opposed the drift towards economic dependence on Germany and Austria-Hungary after the Balkan Wars of 1912–13, and urged neutrality up to and after Bulgaria's alliance with the CENTRAL POWERS in September 1915. His reputation for compromise brought his appointment as premier in June 1918, but immediate peace overtures were rejected by the Allies and failed in their ulterior object of persuading GERMANY to resume large-scale aid to Bulgaria. Further appeals to Germany for military aid on the BALKAN FRONT were ignored in August, and Malinov, ignoring Tsar FERDINAND I's instructions to fight to the death, asked the Allies for an armistice in September. He remained in office until 28 November, when he resigned in protest at Romanian occupation of the disputed Dobrudja region.

Malvy, Louis (1875–1949) French commerce minister in 1913 and interior minister from March 1914, Malvy was a close prewar ally of Joseph CAILLAUX and regarded by right-wing observers as his virtual puppet. Solidly supported by parliamentary Radicals, he maintained a conciliatory attitude towards wartime dissent, arguing successfully against mass precautionary arrests in August 1914 (see CARNET B). Malvy had enough parliamentary support to hold his post in successive coalitions, but came under heavy personal attack from CLEMENCEAU during 1916. Suspicion of clandestine 'defeatism' – a contemporary euphemism for aiding the enemy – mounted in 1917 as he consistently refused to suppress pacifist agitators or literature and supported French participation in the STOCKHOLM CONFERENCE. Implication in the *Le BONNET ROUGE* espionage scandal eventually forced his resignation on 31 August, and he was arrested in late November as part of Clemenceau's clampdown on dissident opinion. Although acquitted of treason in August 1918, he was convicted of criminal negligence and sentenced to five years exile (see TREASON TRIALS).

Mandates A form of colonial administration designed to circumvent anti-imperialist sentiment at the PARIS PEACE CONFERENCE. Former Turkish territories and German colonies were ceded to 'mandated' powers for administration on behalf of the LEAGUE OF NATIONS. Three classes of mandate were established in 1919. Class-C territories were those deemed 'backward', and these became an integral part of the controlling state. Class-B territories were those offering more developed investment prospects, and the mandated rulers were required to maintain an 'open door' to economic interests from other countries. Class-A territories were considered capable of functioning as sovereign states after a period of 'guidance'.

GREAT BRITAIN and FRANCE were the main beneficiaries of the system. Britain took control of the new Middle Eastern States of Iraq, Palestine and Transjordan, while France administered Syria and the Lebanon. All five, previously part of the Ottoman Empire, were Class-A Mandates. Of the German colonies in AFRICA, EAST AFRICA became a British Class-B Mandate, TOGOLAND and CAMEROON were partitioned under Anglo-French control as Class-C Mandates, and SOUTHWEST AFRICA (also Class C) was given to SOUTH AFRICA. The German Pacific colonies all became Class-C Mandates: German New Guinea and the Bismarck Islands were mandated to AUSTRALIA; German Samoa was given to NEW ZEALAND; the Mariana, Caroline and Marshall Islands passed to JAPAN; and the island of Nauru was controlled by Britain. Plans to create UNITED STATES mandates in northwestern TURKEY (around Constantinople) and in Armenia were dropped when Congress rejected the VERSAILLES Treaty.

Mangin, General Charles (1866–1925) The most consistently aggressive French general on the WESTERN FRONT, his commitment to offensive tactics merited the nickname 'Butcher' but won several famous victories. He came to prominence at the Battle of CHARLEROI in August 1914, commanding the brigade that stopped and then successfully counterattacked a dangerous German advance across the Meuse. At VERDUN in 1916 he rose from a divisional command in the Fort Douaumont sector to lead the Third Army during successful counterattacks in October and December.

One of the few senior French officers who fully supported the NIVELLE OFFENSIVE, Mangin commanded the Sixth Army during its disastrous main attack at the AISNE, and was quickly relieved of his post in the aftermath. He remained in the wilderness until mid-1918, when the similarly aggressive FOCH recalled him to command the Tenth Army, part of his inter-Allied reserve on the WESTERN FRONT. Mangin's vital counterattack at the second MARNE battle restored his reputation (though his troops still hated him), and he retained the command throughout 1918, attacking towards Metz as part of General DE CASTLENAU's Army Group East at the ARMISTICE.

Mannock, Edward (1887–1918) The highest scoring air ACE with British forces, he shot down 73 hostile aircraft (mostly flying an SE-5A) in 14 months before his death, caused by ground fire, on 26 July 1918. British FIGHTER pilots were not accorded the official celebrity or freedom of action granted to their French or German counterparts, and Mannock was well-known only within the armed services.

March, General Peyton (1864–1955) Forcefully efficient US ARMY officer, colonel of a field regiment in April 1917 but transferred to Europe in command of an ARTILLERY brigade and promoted head of all AEF artillery in August 1917. He was recalled as assistant US Army chief of staff the following March and became chief of staff proper in May, appointed by secretary for war BAKER to revitalize the Army's administrative performance. March greatly increased the importance of his office over the next six months, supervising rapid growth of the AEF and streamlining organization regardless of military opposition. He abolished distinctions between the Regular Army, National Guard and National Army for the duration (see SELECTIVE SERVICE SYSTEM), and established distinct commands for special services, including GAS warfare, TANKS, and the USAAS. Strongly supported by Baker, he also sought to restrain the independence of AEF commander PERSHING, disputing control of promotions in Europe and proposing the attachment of staff officers to Pershing's headquarters.

Marl Plain, Battle of the See: SAMARRAH OFFENSIVE.

Marlin Gun A lighter version, modified for aircraft use, of the American Colt-Browning 0.30-inch MACHINE GUN (which saw only limited use with AEF ground forces). Air-cooled and using a 250-round belt feed, the Marlin was adaptable for use with INTERRUPTER GEAR and saw widespread service on USAAS aircraft in 1918. A few were also fitted to RENAULT LIGHT TANKS in AEF service.

Marne, First Battle of the The first vital turning point in the war on the WESTERN FRONT, marking the failure of the German SCHLIEFFEN PLAN and effectively saving FRANCE from rapid conquest after defeats at the Battles of the FRONTIERS in August 1914.

At the end of August the three armies of the German invasion's northern wing were sweeping south towards Paris and points east. In front of them, the French Fifth and Sixth Armies, along with the BEF, were retreating in apparent disorder. Four German armies in eastern France seemed likely to break dwindling French defences in LORRAINE, and Kaiser WILHELM II was preparing a triumphal entry into Nancy.

His confidence was shared by General von KLUCK, in command of the First Army on the far right of the German advance and detailed to encircle Paris from the east. On 31 August, believing his opponents beaten, von Kluck decided to pass to the west of Paris and get behind the slowest of the retreating French armies, General LANREZAC's Fifth. Closing a potentially dangerous gap between the German First and Second Armies, the move was approved by Second Army commander von BÜLOW and GERMAN ARMY chief of staff MOLTKE.

Von Bülow's certainty of French weakness had been undermined by a tactical defeat at GUISE. Planned reinforcements had been diverted to a major offensive from Lorraine, and Moltke had detached two corps from the northern invasion to the EASTERN FRONT, causing gaps to appear between all three of his northern armies.

The withdrawal of two French corps from Lorraine suggested to both men that von Kluck's turn, though closing a gap, could expose his flank to counterattack from the west. At the same time it improved the chances of capturing Nancy and enveloping French forces in Lorraine. Fearing catastrophe, Moltke wavered, ordering von Kluck to advance more slowly on 2 September.

Considering himself in pursuit of escaping victims, von Kluck ignored the order, and his forward units had reached the River Marne, about 50km east of Paris, by 3 September. An order to halt and face any threat from Paris arrived on 5 September, and von Kluck reluctantly began withdrawing his tired troops to a position level with the Second Army.

The French discovery of von Kluck's eastward turn – revealed by papers from a dead German officer on 2 September and confirmed next day by reconnaissance aircraft – came amid desperate attempts to prepare the defence of Paris. Under General GALLIÉNI's military command from 28 August, Paris was garrisoned by a single brigade of naval infantry until 1 September, when French C-in-C JOFFRE ordered General MAUNOURY's retreating Sixth Army to fall back on the capital. An Algerian division from the south coast completed the 'Army of Paris' under Galliéni's overall command.

With the city barely fortified and attack expected within 48 hours, the French government departed for Bordeaux on the night of 2/3 September, an example followed by perhaps 500,000 civilians.

Joffre viewed the fate of Paris as part of a wider picture, and his main concern was to group French forces into the best position for a counteroffensive. Leaving the 'Army of Paris' to threaten the German flank, he ordered a provisional retreat on 2 September to a line along the Rivers Seine and Aube, southeast of Paris and over 60km south of the Marne.

By the following afternoon both the French Fifth Army and the BEF were across the Marne, just ahead of their pursuers. Joffre expected to give battle about a week later and began his preparations by replacing Lanrezac with the more aggressive FRANCHET D'ESPEREY. As details of the German First Army's new direction became clear, Joffre remained cautious about an immediate strike on von Kluck's flank, but Galliéni in Paris took unilateral action, ordering the Sixth Army to advance east on the morning of 4 September.

Joffre accepted the fait accompli in the afternoon, suspending further retreat and ordering an attack at the Marne for 7 September. In the evening, when Galliéni had made it clear that the Sixth Army could not be delayed, the attack was brought forward a day. The BEF, holding a crucial point in the line between the Sixth and Fifth Armies, was not under Joffre's command and C-in-C Sir John FRENCH was only persuaded to join the attack after his forces had retreated for another day, so that they arrived at the battle several hours late.

Most of the French Sixth Army attacked the corps protecting the German First Army's flank on the morning of 6 September, achieving complete surprise. Von Kluck wheeled his entire force to meet it, reopening a 50km gap between himself and von Bülow into which the Fifth Army advanced, followed by the British. The rest of the French line was relied upon to hold: the Ninth and Fourth Armies by attacking the German Third and Fourth in a line further east of Paris; the Third Army by protecting the sector around VERDUN; and the depleted First and Second Armies by holding off two German armies in Lorraine.

The main battle continued for three days along a 150km front from Compiègne, 65km northeast of Paris, to Verdun, while the essentially separate battle in Lorraine reached its climax. German breakthrough was prevented all along the line, although the Ninth Army barely held its ground and the Sixth only avoided collapse after 600 Paris taxis were used to rush 6,000 reserves to the front. The Fifth Army's attacks forced a 'hole' into which the BEF advanced virtually unopposed. Unaware that open space lay ahead, it failed to exploit the opportunity fully before the German high command (OHL) ended hopes of a decisive breakthrough by ordering a general retreat.

A shocked Moltke, beset by poor communications over conquered territories and unable to gain a clear picture from field commanders, expected the German line east of Paris to give at any moment. On 8 September he called off Prince RUPPRECHT's prolonged offensive on Nancy and sent a staff officer, Colonel Hentsch, to decide on the situation at the Marne. It was Hentsch, in the absence of a decision from any other quarter, who ordered a general retreat of the First and Second Armies on 9 September, but von Kluck's southernmost units were already being withdrawn north to avoid the BEF, virtually compelling von Bülow to fall back. Followed slowly by exhausted Allied armies, the entire south-facing German line pulled back some 65km to the River Aisne, establishing a new line on the heights beyond the river by 13 September.

The battle cost both sides about 25 per cent casualties, and Joffre received most contemporary credit for a famous victory, but the German Army was not beaten and its successful retreat effectively ended all hope of a short war (see First Battle of the AISNE). See MAP 5.

Marne, Second Battle of the Crucial battle fought east of Paris in July 1918. It marked the final collapse of the German SPRING OFFENSIVES, and ushered in a series of decisive Allied counteroffensives on the WESTERN FRONT.

The military situation east of Paris in June 1918 was superficially similar to that in September 1914 (see First Battle of the MARNE). The German advance over the AISNE in late May reached the Marne around Château-Thierry by 5 June, leaving the capital apparently exposed. Although a French counterattack at the MATZ restricted German gains just to the north, the FRENCH ARMY was close to exhaustion, and C-in-C PÉTAIN doubted its ability to fight another major action. Further north the main bulk of the BEF was still recovering from the German KAISERSCHLACHT and LYS OFFENSIVES, and was expecting further attacks. Both GREAT BRITAIN and FRANCE faced imminent manpower crises, and the influx of AEF troops was not yet being felt on the battlefield.

The GERMAN ARMY was not the force it had been four years earlier. Successive offensives had cost around a million casualties since late March, and failed to break Allied resistance decisively. Shortages of men and supplies were harming morale, but economic breakdown in GERMANY and US intervention meant that renewed offensives offered the only chance of ultimate victory.

Strategic controller LUDENDORFF prepared a two-pronged advance from the Marne towards Reims prior to a major assault from Flanders, but Allied commanders were using a relatively quiet period in mid-June to plan attacks of their own, and Allied supremo FOCH bypassed Pétain to plan a counteroffensive against the western flank of the German SALIENT with Tenth Army commander MANGIN.

The German attack at the Marne came first, in the small hours of 15 July. Twenty-five divisions of the German First and Third Armies, supported by almost 5,000 guns, attacked the French Fourth Army east of Reims, while a further 17 divisions of the Seventh Army advanced against the French Fifth (and the left wing of the Sixth) to the west.

Each side was well-informed of the other's plans by prisoners and deserters, and the French were expecting an attack. The Fourth Army had been withdrawn from forward positions before the bombardment began, and DEFENCE IN DEPTH lured German forces into empty space before a counterattack pinned them down.

West of Reims, the German Seventh Army enjoyed a more successful first day, making steady progress along a widening front and establishing a bridgehead over the Marne. French forces – including two US divisions – were less effectively deployed than their eastern counterparts, and the situation appeared critical by early afternoon. Pétain decided to requisition US reserves intended for the planned counterattack, effectively postponing it, but the order was countermanded by Foch, who also persuaded HAIG to loan Mangin four British divisions.

The German position around Reims worsened steadily. A day's fighting on 16 July produced no gains at all west of the city, and small losses around the bridgehead to the east. The pattern was repeated the next day, and the German high command suspended attacks during the night. Before the order was delivered, the main French counterattack hit the German right flank at dawn on 18 June.

It was executed by 16 divisions of the French Tenth Army and 8 divisions of the Sixth, supported by a total of 2,033 guns, 513 tanks and 1,143 aircraft (including the AÉRONAUTIQUE MILITAIRE's new Air Division, along with RAF and USAAS units). Although primarily a French operation, it was spearheaded by two strong divisions of the AEF and included both British and ITALIAN ARMY infantry.

Surprised defenders took heavy losses and

fell back almost 10km in two days of heavy fighting. Mangin pressed forward the attack despite Pétain's refusal to release reserves from the Marne bridgehead, and German forces began an orderly withdrawal late on 20 July. It continued until 3 August, leaving the German armies east of the Rivers Aisne and Vesle, where they had been before the offensives of May and June. Allied losses were high – more than 95,000 French, 13,000 British and 12,000 US casualties – but the German Army suffered an estimated 168,000 casualties in the battle.

The victory shifted the initiative to the Allies on the Western Front. Ludendorff's plan to attack Flanders again was postponed and never revived, freeing British forces further north to prepare their own counter-offensives, and growing confidence inspired Allied commanders towards strategic cooperation. See also: MAP 9; AMIENS OFFENSIVE.

Marsh Arabs Native tribespeople of Ottoman Mesopotamia, inhabiting the inhospitable floodplains around its rivers. Much of their limited local resource base was wrecked or requisitioned by Turkish and Anglo-Indian forces during the four-year campaign on the MESOPOTAMIAN FRONT, and their impartial hostility towards both sides was a constant element in military operations. Not directly involved in the ARAB REVOLT, scores of sabre-armed Marsh Arabs mounted on small, nimble ponies formed an independent third party on the fringes of most actions in the theatre, and shadowed the movements of occupying armies. Though occasionally enlisted as allies by Turkish commanders (see Battle of SHAIBA), they proved extremely unreliable and tended to harass any weakened forces. Expert at concealment and evasion, they also took a steady toll in loot from the warring armies. Their influence in the theatre declined with the multiplication of British strength in Mesopotamia after 1916, but they remained an ubiquitous nuisance, and suppression of Marsh Arab activities was cited as a secondary objective of Anglo-Indian offensives following the capture of BAGHDAD in March 1917.

Martinsyde G-100 British biplane, designed as a long-range escort FIGHTER, that was attached to RFC bombing and reconnaissance units on the WESTERN FRONT from early 1916. Too bulky and cumbersome for effective combat work, its relatively powerful engine gave good lifting power and it was redeployed as a bomber from mid-1916. Introduced from late 1916, the 160hp G-102 could carry thirteen 20lb bombs, earning the nickname 'Elephant' (eventually applied to both types). A total of 270 Elephants were built, performing adequately in France until replaced by the AIRCO DH-4 during 1917. The last was withdrawn in November, but a few served as fighters and bombers on the MESOPOTAMIAN and PALESTINE FRONTS until the ARMISTICE, and two were with DUNSTERFORCE at Baku in 1918.

BRIEF DATA (G-100) Type: single-seat escort fighter/bomber; Engine: 120hp Beardsmore; Max speed: 95mph (152kph); Ceiling: 4,250m; Armament: 2 × 0.303in mg, 10 × 20lb bomb.

Martinsyde S-1 British biplane developed from a sporting design in 1914 and in RFC service at the start of the War. Similar to the SOPWITH TABLOID and BRISTOL SCOUT, but inferior in performance, a few S-1s were attached to squadrons as scouts on the WESTERN FRONT. About 60 are believed to have been built, but they had disappeared from France by mid-1915, and four machines used during the initial occupation of KUT proved unsuited to desert conditions.

BRIEF DATA Type: single-seat scout; Engine: 80hp Gnôme Monosoupape; Max speed: 87mph (139kph); Ceiling: 4,850m; Armament: 1 × 0.303in mg.

Marwitz, General Georg von der (1856–1929) German commander whose CAVALRY corps screened the German invasion of BELGIUM in August 1914, covered the First Army's flank during the First Battle of the MARNE, and took part in the battle for FLANDERS. With TRENCH WARFARE established on the WESTERN FRONT, the corps was dissolved at the end of 1914 and Marwitz took an infantry corps to the EASTERN FRONT. He led a specially formed ski corps during the

CARPATHIAN CAMPAIGN of spring 1915, and was given a special army group to counter-attack north of the BRUSILOV OFFENSIVE in summer 1916. Returning to France as commander of the Second Army in December 1916, he achieved his greatest success in overall command of German counterattacks at the Battle of CAMBRAI in late 1917, and played a central role in the KAISERSCHLACHT Offensive of March 1918, just failing to break through British lines. His exhausted troops cracked under the Allied AMIENS OFFENSIVE in August, and Marwitz was moved to the Fifth Army around the Meuse, ending the War in retreat from the US–French MEUSE–ARGONNE OFFENSIVE. He retired in December 1918.

Masaryk, Tomáš (1850–1937) A leading prewar campaigner for Czech independence, Masaryk represented the radical Young Czech Party and later the moderate Realist Party in the Austrian parliament (*Reichsrat*) before 1914. Avoiding arrest in August 1914 he left Vienna for Geneva in December and worked energetically to rally Allied support for Czech national aspirations. Moving to London in March 1915, he co-founded the Czechoslovak National Council, based in Paris, but functioned primarily in an ambassadorial role while BENEŠ coordinated political direction. Masaryk's opportunistic negotiations with the Bolshevik government in RUSSIA enabled the formation of the CZECH LEGION from late 1917, and a successful visit to the UNITED STATES in 1918 was rewarded in May with the 'LANSING Declaration', supporting the principle of an independent CZECHOSLOVAKIA. The collapse of AUSTRIA-HUNGARY and unanimous support from the western Allies enabled the establishment of an independent Czechoslovak republic in mid-November, and Masaryk was named head of state by the National Assembly, a post he held until his death.

Mas Boats General designation given to TORPEDO BOATS in service with the ITALIAN NAVY. Italy led the world in the design of fast, modern motor boats in 1914, producing craft that could both outpace and outlast their counterparts with other navies. Operative primarily in Adriatic waters, the Mas boat service earned a wartime reputation for enterprise and daring in marked contrast to the lethargy attributed to the main battlefleet, carrying out regular raids on Austro-Hungarian coastal targets and scoring numerous successes against MINELAYERS and other light forces. Several boat designs were used by the service, most notably the very durable Schichau Type, two of which took part in the most celebrated torpedo-boat action of the War, sinking the Austro-Hungarian dreadnought *SZENT ISTVÁN* on the open sea in June 1918. See also: BARCHINI SALTATORI.

Maschinengewehr The GERMAN ARMY's standard heavy MACHINE GUN in 1914, manufactured at a variety of government arsenals, was designated Maschinengewehr 08 after the year of its adoption. An almost unaltered copy of the MAXIM GUN, it was a solid and reliable weapon, water-cooled and firing 7.92mm ammunition from a 250-round fabric belt. More than 12,000 were deployed with frontline units in August 1914, and the design remained in service throughout the War (see SPANDAU GUN).

A less bulky version for mobile use, designated the Maschinengewehr 08/15, was given a pistol butt and generally stripped down, but was no more successful as an assault weapon than comparable Allied light machine guns. It proved more effective as an aircraft weapon, and was used by the GERMAN ARMY AIR SERVICE to supplement the PARABELLUM GUN. The 08/15 was most widely employed for defensive purposes on the WESTERN FRONT during autumn 1918, by which time a more genuinely portable, air-cooled Maschinengewehr 08/18 was just coming into service.

Masurian Lakes, First Battle of the The first German offensive on the EASTERN FRONT, an attack by the German Eighth Army in EAST PRUSSIA against the invading Russian First Army, launched on 7 September 1914. After its victory at GUMBINNEN on 20 August, General RENNENKAMPF's Russian First Army had remained passive during the Russian

Second Army's defeat at TANNENBERG. By the end of August Rennenkampf had advanced most of his troops west towards Königsberg (modern Kaliningrad), but his southern corps had moved southwest into difficult country among the Masurian Lakes in a belated effort to aid the Second Army. Turning northeast after Tannenberg, Eighth Army commanders HINDENBURG and LUDENDORFF planned to encircle Rennenkampf by breaking through this relatively weak flank.

Reinforced by two infantry corps and a cavalry division from the WESTERN FRONT, the Eighth Army comprised 18 infantry and 3 cavalry divisions. With Rennenkampf's army replenished from reserves, and a new Russian Tenth Army (Pflug) forming to the southeast, Russian forces retained overall numerical superiority, but were concentrated in the north. Expecting an attack from the Königsberg area, Rennenkampf and army group commander ZHILINSKI relied on the arrival of Tenth Army units to secure the left and withdrew the rest of the First Army a few kilometres east beyond the River Alle (Lava).

Efficient redeployment enabled Ludendorff's strengthened southern corps (FRANÇOIS) to attack either side of the southern Lakes on 7 September. Outnumbered 3 to 1, and refused large-scale assistance by the incomplete Tenth Army, the Russian defenders quickly scattered, and François swung north towards Lötzen (Giżycko) to cut off Rennenkampf's retreat. Frontal attacks by five more German corps all along the line stretching northwest were less successful, making only limited gains, and Rennenkampf was able to begin a fairly orderly withdrawal on 9 September.

With German infantry suffering from exhaustion and mounting supply problems, tactical initiative passed to gathering Russian forces once both armies were east of the Prussian border after 13 September. Reorganizing behind the River Niemen (Nemunas), the Russian First and Tenth Armies inflicted a series of local defeats on pursuing German troops from 20 September, and launched a joint counteroffensive from 25 to 28 September (Battle of the Niemen), compelling the German Eighth Army to abandon its advance and return to the frontier.

Russian forces had lost 125,000 men, but the battle was not the strategic triumph claimed by German Eighth Army commanders. Their own casualties, 100,000 men since mid-August, could not easily be replaced, and the growing RUSSIAN ARMY remained an active threat beyond the border. See also: POLISH CAMPAIGN; MAP 12.

Masurian Lakes, Second Battle of the German attack in the East Prussian sector of the EASTERN FRONT, the northern half of a two-pronged Austro-German offensive in early 1915 (see CARPATHIAN OFFENSIVES). Also known as the Winter Battle, it was intended to outflank and expose Russian positions in central Poland and force a general Russian retreat beyond the Vistula (see MAP 10).

German chief of staff FALKENHAYN had been reluctant to sanction offensives in the east, but the need to impress potential Balkan allies persuaded him to accept LUDENDORFF's plans for an attack on the Russian Tenth Army (Sievers) from EAST PRUSSIA. Eight divisions of the newly formed German Tenth Army (EICHHORN) were sent east to join the Eighth Army (BELOW) in an advance north and south of the fortified Angerapp Line, running through the Masurian Lakes (see MAP 12).

By early February about 150,000 German troops faced a similar number in the Russian Tenth Army. Although the Germans enjoyed a slight superiority in ARTILLERY, their greatest advantage derived from STAVKA's (Russian central command) preoccupation with plans for a Russian offensive across East Prussia's southwestern border. While the majority of Russian forces in the region were being formed as a new Twelfth Army (PLEHVE) for the invasion, the Tenth was stretched along a broad front, far from any support.

The whole of the German Eighth Army struck Sievers' southern wing on 7 February, and its three divisions were driven back more than 100km in a week. In the north, Eichhorn's attack hit the overstretched Russian right on 9 February, and it disintegrated over the next two days, some units retiring on the supply centre of KOVNO (Kuanas) while others fled in disorder.

The central three corps of the Russian Tenth Army were threatened with encirclement, but with communications cut senior commanders had little idea what was happening. Army Group commander RUZSKI ordered Sievers to hold his position while the Twelfth Army prepared to counterattack from the southwest, but trapped Russian forces began a retreat on 14 February. Though large parts of two corps escaped by the roads north and south, the whole of XX Corps (Bulgakov) was surrounded in the Forest of Augustovo and its last 12,000 men surrendered on 21 February, bringing total Tenth Army losses to 56,000.

Some German Tenth Army units moved west and engaged elements of the growing Russian Twelfth with mixed success, while the German Eighth Army moved south against Osowiec. It had failed to take the well-defended fortress by early March, when German forces retired back to the frontier in the face of mounting Russian strength. As Stavka's attention turned south to the Carpathians, Ruzski was ordered to hold defensive positions in the north, and the campaign ended with both sides close to their original positions. Ludendorff, who claimed 100,000 prisoners at Augustovo, subsequently represented the battle as a great strategic victory.

Mata Hari (1876–1917) The stage name of Dutch dancer and prostitute Margaretha Geertruida Zelle, who worked in Paris from 1905, and who was accused of being one of hundreds of paid agents peddling military or economic information across the lines on the WESTERN FRONT. Arrested and executed by the French in 1917, she denied espionage charges but appears to have been operating for both sides. The nature of her profession rather than of her offence attracted unusually strong publicity in FRANCE, where an increasingly hysterical pro-War press was exposing supposed spies and traitors on a daily basis by late 1917. See also: *Le BONNET ROUGE.*

Matz, Battle of the Attack by the German Eighteenth Army (HUTIER) on French lines north of the new positions established on the WESTERN FRONT by the German advance from the AISNE in early June 1918. Also known as the Battle of Noyon or Noyon-Montdidier, its immediate purposes were to broaden the new German front around Château-Thierry, and to draw Allied forces south from Flanders, still the main focus of LUDENDORFF's strategic planning.

Deserters, numerous on both sides, had informed French commanders of the coming assault before ARTILLERY fire from both sides opened the battle at midnight on 8/9 June, but failure to employ DEFENCE IN DEPTH again enabled attacking German infantry to advance almost 10km on the first day, taking more than 8,000 prisoners. Efficient French regrouping slowed German progress the next day, and no important positions were taken.

At 11.30 on 11 June, by which time the attack had become completely bogged down, a new French Tenth Army (MANGIN) launched a surprise counterattack. Hastily formed from reserves by Army Group commander General FAYOLLE, with strong support from ground-attack aircraft and TANKS, the Tenth Army regained a little ground and maintained the initiative until the battle ended indecisively on 13 June.

Although hardly an Allied victory, and a German defeat only in an overall strategic context, the Matz marked a watershed in the year's French campaigns. In the lull that followed on the Western Front, Allied armies began to take the offensive in various small actions along the line (see Battle of LE HAMEL). Two divisions of the AEF had led Mangin's attack on 11 June, and US strength in France was growing at a rate of 250,000 men a month. Although Ludendorff intended further attacks in Champagne and Flanders, Allied commanders were developing their own plans for a major counteroffensive. See also: MAP 9; Second Battle of the MARNE.

Maude, General Sir F. Stanley (1864–1917) The most successful commander on either side of the MESOPOTAMIAN FRONT. Maude led a brigade on the WESTERN FRONT from October 1914, but was seriously wounded. He was promoted on recovery to command the 13th Division at GALLIPOLI, which suffered more than 50 per cent losses before its transfer to Mesopotamia in March 1916. As a BRITISH ARMY officer Maude benefited from London's decision to take over direct control of the theatre from the Indian government after the failure to relieve KUT in April. Maude replaced INDIAN ARMY officer General Gorringe as commander of the frontline Tigris Corps in July, and assumed command of the entire front in August. At the same time Anglo-Indian forces in Mesopotamia were reorganized, reinforced and equipped for the first time on a scale to match their logistic requirements.

Maude proceeded to lead a series of cautious but effective offensives up the Tigris, beginning with the Second Battle of KUT and climaxing with the capture of BAGHDAD in March 1917. Maude's careful preparations, unbroken success and growing reputation in the Muslim world inhibited British attempts to scale down commitment in Mesopotamia, and operations were expanded to preempt threats from Turkish forces on the Rivers Euphrates, Diyala and Tigris.

After taking SAMARRAH in April and reopening operations after the hot season with attacks on RAMADI and TIKRIT, Maude died suddenly of cholera in Baghdad on 18 November 1917. Rumours that he was poisoned are not supported by the available evidence, and he probably contracted the disease from contaminated milk. Though a major blow to frontline morale, his death enabled chief of imperial staff ROBERTSON to restrict operations under his successor, General Marshall.

Maunoury, General Michel (1847–1923) Veteran French artillery officer recalled from retirement to lead the hastily assembled 'Army of Lorraine' in August 1914. Its seven divisions began to organize on 21 August, and briefly joined the First and Second Armies retreating in LORRAINE before being transferred northwest to form the core of a new Sixth Army at the far north of the WESTERN FRONT. Barely redeployed in time to meet the oncoming German First Army, Maunoury's Sixth Army helped to prevent the encirclement of the neighbouring BEF around LE CATEAU, but was ordered to fall back on Paris and placed under the direct command of General GALLIÉNI on 1 September. Maunoury helped to plan the Sixth Army's attack on the flank of the German First Army that opened the MARNE battle on 6 September, and his forces held off a full-scale counterattack over the next two days. Severe wounds ended his active career early in 1915.

Maxim Gun The world's first automatic MACHINE GUN, invented in the UNITED STATES by Hiram Maxim in 1884. Water-cooled and belt-fed, it was gradually adopted by European armies and was the blueprint for most heavy machine gun design in the early 20th century. The GERMAN ARMY's standard MASCHINENGEWEHR and the British VICKERS GUN were both derivatives of the Maxim, as was the RUSSIAN ARMY's standard 7.62mm Pulemyot Maxima (1910) model, a reliable and rugged 250-round adaptation that was still in service during the Second World War. Russian troops also used an older, Vickers-made version of the original Maxim, imported from Britain to supplement inadequate home production, and veteran Maxims remained in widespread use with minor European armies throughout the War.

Max von Baden, Prince (1867–1929) Heir to the German principality of Baden, his early wartime role was confined to welfare work for prisoners of war, but he became something of a rallying point for moderate conservative opinion following his public opposition to the introduction of unrestricted SUBMARINE WARFARE in early 1917. His appointment as chancellor of GERMANY on 3 October 1918 represented a compromise between the THIRD SUPREME COMMAND and the Reichstag, each with different motives for seeking a moderate reformist government to supervise the conclusion of peace with the Allies (see GERMAN REVOLUTIONS). Caught between socialist demands for Kaiser WILHELM II's abdication (backed by mounting popular unrest) and right-wing refusal to countenance the move, Max was forced out of office when the KIEL

MUTINY threatened imminent workers' revolution in early November. He met a socialist deadline by announcing Wilhelm's abdication and his own retirement in the Reichstag on 9 November, before handing power to Social Democratic Party leader EBERT, earning the vociferous contempt of right-wing elements in postwar German society.

Mayo, Admiral Henry (1856–1937) Former aide to US navy secretary DANIELS whose subsequent appointment as commander of a division of the US NAVY Atlantic fleet was enlivened by the 'Tampico Incident' with MEXICO, which culminated in temporary US occupation of the Mexican port of Veracruz in April 1914. Promoted vice admiral in 1915, he became admiral in command of the Atlantic fleet in June 1916 and was sent to London to discuss Allied naval cooperation in August 1917. He endorsed CONVOYS as the most effective ANTI-SUBMARINE tactic and strongly supported plans for the Anglo-American NORTHERN BARRAGE, arguing for concentration on small warship construction after his return to the USA. An able administrator, he presided over a steady wartime improvement in the Atlantic fleet's operational efficiency, and was commander of a new 'US Fleet' from January 1919 until his retirement in the summer.

Medina, Siege of Medina, in the Hejaz region of Arabia, is a Muslim holy city, second in importance only to Mecca, and was similarly forbidden to unbelievers on pain of death (see MAP 22). The ARAB REVOLT opened outside Medina in June 1916, but two initial attacks on the Turkish-held city by some 30,000 poorly armed Arabs failed completely against well-sited ARTILLERY and MACHINE GUNS within the fortifications. The rebels withdrew to guard the road to Mecca, and garrison commander Fakhri Din repaired the RAILWAY to Damascus, enabling 16,000 Turkish troops to assemble in the city by November, supported by a flight of German aircraft. Although plans for a breakout failed, and Arab penetration north of Medina threatened to cut its rail lifeline permanently, Fakhri Din felt strong enough to ignore C-in-C ENVER PASHA's instruction to evacuate the city in early 1917 (see YENBO; WEJH).

Some British and Arab strategists, including LAWRENCE, recognized that a campaign of limited harassment against the city diverted resources from the PALESTINE and MESOPOTAMIAN FRONTS without threatening rebel operations elsewhere. These tactics eventually kept 25,000 Turkish troops employed in the northern Hejaz region, and the 'siege' was generally a long-range operation involving little direct fighting. Although supply difficulties became critical by 1918, Medina held out until starving troops mutinied and surrendered to Arab forces in January 1919.

Mediterranean Sea At the heart of global maritime communications and commerce, the Mediterranean theatre embraced a complex web of international interests (see MAP 16). Much of GREAT BRITAIN's prewar commercial traffic, including 75 per cent of its oil, depended on passage through the SUEZ CANAL and the Straits of Gibraltar, and both were regarded as imperial strategic priorities. Security of its southern ports was economically vital to FRANCE, enabling communications with its north African empire and planned expansion into the Middle East.

A long Mediterranean coastline and dependence on industrial imports made free passage even more vital to ITALY, which also had its own recently conquered colony in Libya to protect. The narrow Otranto Straits, at the southern end of the Adriatic, represented AUSTRIA-HUNGARY's only maritime link with the wider oceans. Both countries regarded control of the Adriatic as crucial to security from the other and to the fulfilment of competing ambitions in the Balkans.

Regional decline had restricted TURKEY's Mediterranean interests before 1914, but its control of the Dardanelles link with the BLACK SEA blocked RUSSIA's westerly ambitions. Constantinople was also preparing for local confrontation with GREECE for dominance of the busy Aegean.

Strategists on all sides assumed that wartime control over Mediterranean sea-lanes would be decided by major battlefleet confrontations, and the prewar period was characterized by a naval arms race. Although the ROYAL NAVY restricted its Mediterranean commitment in order to concentrate on the North Sea, agreement with the FRENCH NAVY from 1912 enabled the latter (modernized since 1909) to focus exclusively on the theatre. The ITALIAN and AUSTRO-HUNGARIAN NAVIES built fleets of modern BATTLESHIPS, either for combined use against France or deployment against the other.

Though GERMANY had no substantial territorial claims in the region, its diplomatic and commercial ambitions were well known, and the small but powerful MITTELMEERDIVISION of the GERMAN NAVY was a factor in the equation. Both the TURKISH and GREEK NAVIES invested public funds in attempting to purchase big capital ships of their own. Even the RUSSIAN NAVY, virtually destroyed in 1905, was engaged in a construction programme that envisaged eventual possession of the Dardanelles.

Italy's failure to go to war with its TRIPLE ALLIANCE partners in August 1914, along with the prompt escape of the Mittelmeerdivision, upset the balance of power intrinsic to all battlefleet calculations, and the expected confrontation never came. The outnumbered Austro-Hungarian fleet stayed in the Adriatic and, once troops from North Africa had been safely ferried to Europe, the French and (from May 1915) Italian fleets were permanently stationed on watch in case it broke out. Both sides recognized that the consequences of defeat outweighed any possible strategic gain from offensive action (see NAVAL WARFARE).

Smaller or older warships, not regarded as relevant to battlefleet strength, were more active all over the theatre. Italian and Austro-Hungarian light forces fought a continuous but indecisive battle of raid and ambush in the Adriatic, neither side contributing significant support to ground forces on the ITALIAN FRONT. The contest remained fairly even, with both sides suffering occasional losses and crippling coal shortages, until the collapse of Austria-Hungary in autumn 1918. Operations in the southern Adriatic focused initially on Allied attempts to supply the BALKAN FRONT and to evacuate the SERBIAN ARMY, but were later centred on the inter-Allied OTRANTO BARRAGE.

Apart from occupying undefended new bases (the Italians took Valona in southern ALBANIA, the British occupied Turkish Cyprus, and France 'borrowed' Corfu from neutral Greece), Allied navies in the Mediterranean undertook only one major offensive, an unsuccessful attempt to force the Dardanelles Straits (see DARDANELLES OPERATION) that quickly evolved into an army-support operation for the GALLIPOLI FRONT.

Allied landings at SALONIKA from autumn 1915 turned the Aegean into another major army-support zone, and the French led large-scale attempts to coerce support from the Greek government in 1916 (see SALAMIS OPERATION; ATHENS LANDING). A long-term blockade of the Dardanelles remained under British control, while the French Navy maintained a squadron off Syria, and both countries sent naval detachments to assist land operations in PALESTINE.

Overall command of Allied forces was nominally invested in successive commanders of the French battlefleet, but control over individual operations was in practice exercised by the country with the most ships involved. The Italian Navy jealously guarded command in the Adriatic, the British accepted no other authority over their principal spheres of interest, and lack of inter-Allied cohesion was reflected in arguments over strategic and supply priorities, most evident in the joint conduct of defensive warfare against German SUBMARINES.

First deployed to menace Dardanelles operations in spring 1915, long-range U-BOATS entered the theatre via the Gibraltar Straits and were based on CATTARO in the southern Adriatic. Initially concentrated against plentiful military targets, they were committed primarily to commerce warfare from late 1915, but also carried out occasional supply missions to SENUSSI forces in North Africa. The Mediterranean's calm, shallow waters were ideal for submarine operations, and they enjoyed great success on busy trade routes protected by inadequate numbers of ineffectually employed Allied ANTI-SUBMARINE craft.

Allied defence against Mediterranean submarines was divided into national zones of responsibility corresponding roughly to prewar strategic interests. Each country operated an independent system of patrols and submarine hunts, although a few particularly large, fast or important cargoes were always given close warship escort. The system left an abundance of easy prey, and its failure threatened to paralyse Italy altogether until the belated introduction of regular CONVOYS to the theatre in spring 1918. Bolstered by Greek, US NAVY and JAPANESE NAVY forces, the Allies were subsequently able to curtail but not defeat the submarine threat. See *HANDELSKRIEG*.

Collapse of the CENTRAL POWERS in autumn 1918 forced U-boats to quit the theatre, and broke up the Austro-Hungarian Navy, leaving the battered Turkish fleet as the only hostile force facing the Allies at the ARMISTICE. Allied battleships steamed ceremonially up the Dardanelles and anchored at Constantinople. A strong French battleship contingent subsequently aided anti-Bolshevik forces fighting on the Crimean Black Sea coast (see *POTEMKIN*; *DANTON*), and smaller Allied craft were kept busy throughout 1919 removing MINES from the Mediterranean and Black Seas.

Medshidiye One of two old protected CRUISERS that were the main offensive weapons of the TURKISH NAVY before it took control of the German MITTELMEERDIVISION in August 1914. Completed in 1904, *Medshidiye* was no match for RUSSIAN NAVY cruisers in the BLACK SEA, and was sunk off Odessa by a MINE in April 1915 during the only major Turkish raid on Russian ports that year. Raised by the Russians in June, it was refurbished and put into service in October. After serving as the minelayer escort *Prut* until the end of hostilities in November 1917, the ship was returned to TURKEY by the Bolshevik government in 1918.

BRIEF DATA (*Prut*, 1916) Displacement: 3,200 tons; Speed: 22k; Armament: 10 × 130mm gun, 4 × 75mm AA, 2 × 17in TT.

Megiddo, Battle of Opening stage of the final British offensive on the PALESTINE FRONT, also known as the Battle of Armageddon. Intended to knock TURKEY out of the War, it was Britain's major military operation outside the WESTERN FRONT in 1918. British commander ALLENBY's plans for a late spring attack were postponed by the German SPRING OFFENSIVES in France, which depleted infantry strength and compelled a period of reorganization, but he promised the British government a comprehensive victory in the autumn.

Allenby faced a 100km Turkish line north of JERUSALEM, running roughly east from the coast above Jaffa but turning south at the River Jordan to bar British access to TRANSJORDAN (see MAP 22). Allenby's 57,000 infantry, 12,000 cavalry and 540 guns, with another 30,000 troops in immediate reserve, enjoyed mounting technical and qualitative superiority over Turkish troops, whose morale was reflected in 1,100 desertions in the month from mid-August. Of 100,000 Turkish and German combat troops south of Damascus, the frontline YILDERIM FORCE totalled only about 29,000 infantry and 3,000 CAVALRY, supported by 400 ARTILLERY pieces. Another 6,000 besieged troops at MAAN were theoretically within striking distance, but Yilderim commander LIMAN VON SANDERS was denied major reinforcement by renewed Turkish commitment to the CAUCASIAN FRONT.

Allenby had always intended to attack the Turkish Eighth Army in the west, where flat coastal plains were ideal for cavalry operations, and Turkish forces occupied the north bank of the Nahr el Auja river. Timing for any lengthy action was predetermined – after the summer heat and well before the late autumn rainy season – but any cavalry success depended on surprise.

The RAF's Palestine Brigade, comprising 105 aircraft by September, played an important reconnaissance, ground-support and bombing role before and during the autumn offensive. Its superior British SE-5 and BRISTOL FIGHTER units had gradually overwhelmed the GERMAN ARMY AIR SERVICE contingent in Palestine, which had shrunk from 56 aircraft in October 1917 to 5 by early September 1918. German reconnaissance weakness aided an elaborate British disinformation campaign, backed by threatening operations towards AMMAN and DERA in Transjordan. Allenby's deceptions persuaded Liman von Sanders to concentrate about a third of his strength against the eastern end of the front.

The main offensive opened at dawn on 19 September, after a short PRELIMINARY BOMBARDMENT and raids by AIRCO DH-9 bombers on communications links all along the front. Four infantry divisions under General Bulfin, including a token French colonial force, stormed Turkish lines stretching along the river from the coast. Effective air and artillery cover, including offshore naval support from two British DESTROYERS, helped the Allied force to overrun two lines of TRENCHES almost immediately. Two cavalry divisions charged into the gap created and across the coastal plains of Sharon and Armageddon. By late afternoon Turkish Eighth Army headquarters at Tel Karm, 25km behind the lines, had been captured, along with 7,000 men and 100 guns.

Two divisions under General Chetwode launched a secondary attack north of Jerusalem at noon, gradually forcing KEMAL PASHA's Turkish Seventh Army back on its base at Nablus with heavy casualties, until by the following dawn it was in line with the remnants of the Turkish Eighth Army. Confusion among Turkish commanders was sealed by events in the east, where two cavalry divisions raided into Transjordan and the Turkish Fourth Army's main base at Dera was surrounded by 5,000 Arab troops under LAWRENCE (see ARAB REVOLT).

British infantry pressure forced defenders away from the coast as Allenby's cavalry, accompanied by light ARMOURED CARS, sped ahead to occupy the only escape routes for the main Turkish armies. Apart from a brief action near Tel Megiddo (10km west of El Affule), the British met little resistance and held the RAILWAY stations at El Affule and Beisan, about 70km and 100km beyond the original lines, by the afternoon of 20 September. A raid on Liman von Sanders' GHQ at Nazareth caused its evacuation, and a British brigade blocked infantry retreat lines through the Dothan Pass, capturing a further 6,000 prisoners.

Next day a mostly German force of some 2,000 troops fought its way east towards the Jordan, but otherwise most of the Turkish front was driven into a net of British cavalry. Nablus fell at noon, Nazareth shortly after, and bombing raids against the passes and river fords leading east into Transjordan inflicted heavy casualties. Cavalry brigades sent up the coast on 22 September took the supply ports of Acre and Haifa before the Acre brigade sped to the Jordan to block the only eastward route not occupied by British ground forces, a 40km gap between Beisan and British divisions in Transjordan. By evening on 24 September all escape routes had been blocked and almost 40,000 prisoners captured.

Denied reinforcements from Damascus, Liman von Sanders attempted to hold a new line along the Jordan south of the Sea of Galilee, but AUSTRALIAN cavalry swept aside the few hundred troops holding the position on 25 September. A stand at Dera by the remnants of the Turkish Seventh Army and the Fourth Army from Amman, ordered there on 22 September, was quickly broken by Arab forces, and by 26 September Allenby's cavalry was in pursuit of a general Turkish retreat towards DAMASCUS.

Menin Road The main road leading east from the Flanders town of Ypres. Scene of some the heaviest fighting by BEF forces on the WESTERN FRONT, particularly during the First and Third Battles of YPRES, it became a powerful and enduring popular symbol for national sacrifice in GREAT BRITAIN, famously depicted in the stark canvases of British war artist Paul Nash. See MAP 6.

Menin Road Bridge, Battle of the See: Third Battle of YPRES.

Mercier, Cardinal Désiré (1851–1926) Former professor of theology at the University of LOUVAIN and Roman Catholic primate of BELGIUM in 1914, he was the most outstanding resident protester at the conditions of German wartime occupation. Required to travel to Rome in late August 1914 for the election of Pope BENEDICT XV, he returned only after most of the country had been conquered. In the King's absence he assumed the role of spokesman for Belgian nationalism through a series of open letters to his flock, widely publicized in the Allied and neutral press.

Occupying authorities in Belgium typically deported (or executed) dissident clerics, broadly viewed as dangerous potential resistance leaders. Though arrested briefly in January 1915, Mercier was generally protected by his high rank, his celebrity in neutral countries, and his reputation among German Catholics. His appeals to the Pope and neutral governments helped to pressurize the German government into abandoning the deportation of Belgian labourers from mid-1917, and he was also a strident voice against Germany's encouragement of Flemish separatism.

Mesopotamian Front The war in what is now Iraq, begun in November 1914 as a limited demonstration of strength by British imperial forces in the Persian Gulf and gradually expanded into a full-scale British invasion of Turkish Mesopotamia (see MAP 23).

As war with TURKEY approached in autumn 1914, the British took steps to protect oil supplies from Abadan, situated on the Persian bank of the Shatt-al-Arab (the confluence of the Rivers Tigris and Euphrates) and within easy reach of Turkish forces on the other bank at BASRA. By the time war was formally declared on 5 November, the first 5,000 troops of an INDIAN ARMY expeditionary force (Force 'D' under General Barrett) were already in position at the mouth of the Shatt-al-Arab, supported by the ROYAL NAVY's Gulf Division.

Barrett's orders from the Indian government, drafted while Turkey was still neutral, made provision for an attack on Basra as a form of 'forward defence'. The port was taken on 23 November, becoming the main base for Anglo-Indian operations in the region. Forward defence prompted a further Anglo-Indian advance to take QURNA, upriver at the junction of the Tigris and Euphrates, in early December.

Turkish forces, supported by Arab irregulars, gathered to retaliate in early 1915. Raids against Qurna and the Persian oil pipeline at AHWAZ preceded a major offensive in April, which was defeated at SHAIBA. Though far from conclusive, Shaiba encouraged both the Indian government and new Mesopotamian commander NIXON to attack and take Turkish bases at AMARA on the Tigris and NASIRIYEH on the Euphrates, leaving the whole of southern Mesopotamia under Anglo-Indian control by late July 1915.

At this stage Anglo-Indian operations remained under the control of the Indian government, which liaised with London through successive ministers for India (Lord Crewe and Austen Chamberlain). The relative ease of early victories, and Turkish willingness to retreat when seriously attacked, fostered a belief (expressed in Nixon's original orders) that the capture of Baghdad, 400km to the north, could be achieved with minimal loss and expenditure.

Despite doubts in London, where Mesopotamia was seen as a strategic backwater, Nixon's proposals for further advances, ostensibly to neutralize forward Turkish bases, were authorized by Indian Army C-in-C Beauchamp-Duff and viceroy Lord Hardinge. The British government was unwilling to divert troops from the WESTERN FRONT, EGYPT or GALLIPOLI, but made no serious attempt to prevent escalation in Mesopotamia, accepting assurances that Nixon was adequately equipped for the task.

He wasn't. The scale and quality of equipment available to the expeditionary force reflected prewar economies in the Indian Army. Advancing from Basra, the expeditionary force faced Turkish defences, searing heat, floods, mirages, disease and hostile MARSH ARABS at the end of lengthening supply lines. Supply depended on imports to Basra, which had no large-scale docking facilities, and on river transport along the Tigris and Euphrates in the absence of roads or RAILWAYS through the hinterland.

An acute shortage of boats and failure to institute logistic reforms characterized the first 18 months of the Anglo-Indian campaign, along with repeated underestimation of requirements by Nixon (who remained at Basra most of the time) and the Indian administration. Frontline forces, depleted to guard the lengthening bottleneck from Basra, were left short of arms, ammunition, mule transport, medical facilities and engineering equipment. They also lacked an efficient line of retreat.

General TOWNSHEND, opposed to further advance but overruled by Nixon, led the 6th Indian Division up the Tigris in late September 1915. Outwitted by Townshend at ES SINN, Turkish forces retreated upriver. Townshend followed but failed to dislodge more determined Turkish resistance at CTESIPHON, only 40km from Baghdad, in late November. Seriously weakened and heavily outnumbered, he retreated to Kut and was surrounded by four Turkish divisions from 7 December.

The defeat galvanized the British and Indian governments into reinforcing the theatre. Two divisions promised for the occupation of Baghdad were hurried to Basra, and a third transferred from Gallipoli. Nixon, still confident of easy victories, sent the first of them up the Tigris for an immediate attempt to relieve Kut. Because supply and transport arrangements from Basra remained in chaos, Turkish commander Nur-Ud-Din had time to establish good positions south of Kut, and attacks by the slowly expanding Tigris Corps at SHEIKH SA'AD, HANNA and DUJAILA were halted with heavy losses in early 1916.

General Nixon was invalided home in January and replaced by General Lake, who belatedly concentrated larger forces for a final attempt to relieve Kut in April 1916. Its failure, and Townshend's subsequent surrender to Turkish Mesopotamian C-in-C KHALIL PASHA (30 April), were massive blows to British prestige in the Middle East and a watershed in the campaign (see First Battle of KUT; Siege of KUT).

Along with associated scandals over medical shortages, the defeats prompted the British government to assume control of the campaign during the summer, when temperatures approaching 50 °C precluded offensive operations by either side. Most of the Indian Army officers involved in the campaign up to that date were replaced, with General MAUDE rising from a divisional command to become front C-in-C in August. Further reinforcements brought total Anglo-Indian strength in the theatre up to 150,000 by the autumn, and British Army officers were appointed to institute a reform of supply and logistic systems.

Founded on the expansion of port facilities at Basra, reforms transformed conditions for frontline forces by the end of 1916. Purpose-built supply ships were deployed, a light railway was constructed from Basra to rear areas at Sheikh Sa'ad (and later Baghdad), the number of motor vehicles in the theatre was raised from 300 in July 1916 to over 7,000 by 1918, and a metalled road was built towards the front. In July 1916 about 300 tons of supplies were reaching Sheikh Sa'ad daily, but a year later 2,000 tons per day were reaching Baghdad, twice as far from the coast.

Logistic changes were reflected in mounting Anglo-Indian tactical superiority. The RFC had brought 24 modern BE-2C fighters to Mesopotamia by the end of 1916, some equipped for PHOTO-RECONNAISSANCE, and the supply of MACHINE GUNS, field ARTILLERY, ARMOURED CARS, trench-fighting equipment and medical facilities was greatly increased. Manpower reinforcements outnumbered losses to sickness for the first time in the autumn, and British commitment to Mesopotamia expanded steadily until late 1917, when some 250,000 men were deployed in the theatre (about half of them at the fronts) against at most about 50,000 ill-equipped Turkish troops.

The strategic value of further advance in Mesopotamia was dubious. Against increasingly desperate manpower shortages in France, the presence of Russian forces in PERSIA offered some prospect of cutting off Khalil's entire army, and pressure in Mesopotamia was of indirect value to Allied forces in PALESTINE and on the CAUCASIAN FRONT, but defence of oil supplies and recovery of prestige remained the most tangible gains on offer.

Maude was allowed to undertake a limited offensive towards Kut in December 1916, which swept British forces to Aziziyeh, only 70km from Baghdad, by late February 1917 (see Second Battle of KUT). Khalil abandoned plans for an offensive through Persia to attack British supply lines and fell back on BAGH-

DAD, which was taken by British forces on 11 March. The majority of Khalil's force again retreated safely, and awaited reinforcement by Ali Ishan Bey's corps from western Persia.

Maude was impelled to undertake further offensive operations aimed at securing and administering his gains. By late the following spring his front line had extended up the Tigris to SAMARRAH, up the Euphrates as far as FALLUJA, and east towards Persia to stop Ali Ishan's troops coming though the JEBEL HAMRIN mountains. Despite London's preoccupation with operations in Palestine, another limited offensive opened in the autumn with attacks on all three fronts, prompted by reports of the new, German-led YILDERIM FORCE forming for an advance down the Euphrates, combined with a general expectation that Turkish forces would retreat when attacked and lingering hopes that Russian forces would join the campaign (see KHANAQIN).

Shorter supply routes and internal lines of communication permitted Khalil's main force, about 50km north of Samarrah at Tikrit, to join with forces in the mountains or on the Euphrates for a possible counterattack down any of the rivers. An Anglo-Indian advance up the Euphrates to RAMADI in late September produced a rare Turkish surrender, but an ambitious attempt to capture Hit revealed the limitations of long-range motorized operations, and Maude returned to deal with Ali Ishan's Turkish XIII Corps in the mountains to the east.

Two divisions under General Marshall were sent up the Diyala from mid-October, but Ali Ishan again escaped into the hills. At the same time Maude sent General Cobbe's two divisions up the Tigris against new Turkish advanced positions north of Samarrah. When both Turkish forces retreated Marshall was ordered not to follow Ali Ishan, but Cobbe pursued Khalil's troops towards TIKRIT, which fell after a concentrated attack on 5 November. The Turkish garrison again escaped, along with most of its supplies and equipment.

Offensives on all three fronts had failed to destroy Turkish counterattack capability when Maude died of cholera in mid-November, signalling a reduction of British commitment. Maude's successor, Marshall, was instructed to reduce manpower levels and, after a further advance up the Diyala failed to trap Ali Ishan, large-scale offensive operations ceased while Marshall reorganized his forces.

Fighting resumed on a smaller scale in March 1918 with a renewed Anglo-Indian advance up the Euphrates. Signs of faltering Turkish morale were amplified in early March, when the 5,000 troops at Hit retreated upriver without being attacked, but Khalil responded characteristically by replacing their commander (Subri Bey) and instructing his successor (Nazmi Bey) to defend a new position at Khan Baghdadi, which was surrounded, attacked and taken in late March.

Marshall spent the hot season organizing his command for a final offensive on the Tigris, distracted by preparations for the independent 'DUNSTERFORCE' expedition to TRANSCAUCASIA. General collapse of the CENTRAL POWERS obviated the need for further action in Mesopotamia by the autumn, but the British advance to ALEPPO from Palestine cut across any Turkish retreat and, although final preparations were disrupted by an outbreak of INFLUENZA, Marshall attacked the last defensive line at Fathah Gorge on 18 October. Demoralized Turkish troops fell back slowly until 29 October, when 12,000 troops and 50 guns surrendered. Marshall sent a column under General Fanshawe to capture Mosul, 120km north of Tikrit and held by Ali Ishan's remaining troops. An Allied armistice with Turkey was agreed on 30 October and became effective at noon on 1 November, enabling Fanshawe to occupy Mosul the following afternoon.

The campaign had cost 97,579 Anglo-Indian CASUALTIES (including 31,109 dead), and overall Turkish losses are unknown but presumed higher. A British commission of enquiry into the campaign – begun in August 1916 – reinforced the generally accepted view that it had been a gigantic mistake, although the Commission's politically inspired condemnation of Indian administrators and commanders was later discredited.

Messines, Battle of Limited but successful British attack on the WESTERN FRONT, carried out by the Second Army (PLUMER) on 7 June 1917. Its target was the Messines Ridge, a natural strongpoint just southeast of YPRES that had been a small SALIENT in German hands since late 1914 (see MAP 6). In a wider context, the attack signalled British C-in-C HAIG's decision to transfer Allied attacks north to Flanders after the failure of the NIVELLE OFFENSIVE had left the FRENCH ARMY incapable of further offensive action.

Plumer had been planning to take Messines since mid-1916, but in a limited operation with no attempt at a conventional BREAKTHROUGH. His tactics involved maximum use of ARTILLERY, TANKS and GAS to minimize infantry casualties during the capture, foreshadowing British operations in late 1918 (see PEACEFUL PENETRATION), but his plans were centred on 20 MINES under German lines. Beginning in January 1917, more than 8,000 metres of tunnel were dug in the face of active German 'countermining', and although one mine was discovered and exploded the other 19 were filled with 600 tons of explosive.

Bombardment of German forward positions began on 21 May, and was intensified a week later, more than 2,300 guns and 300 heavy MORTARS taking part. Loss of surprise was offset by the simultaneous explosion of the mines to devastating effect at 03.10 on 7 June. Clearly audible in London, the blast killed an estimated 10,000 men, and nine divisions of infantry advanced in its wake under a CREEPING BARRAGE, taking all their preliminary objectives within three hours. Allied reserves from the British Fifth Army (GOUGH) and French First Army (ANTHOINE) had reached their final objectives by mid-afternoon.

German counterattacks the following day failed completely, losing more ground as they were repelled, but the counterattacks continued in diminishing force until 14 June, by which time the entire Messines salient had been occupied by the British. A much-needed boost to morale in GREAT BRITAIN and FRANCE, the battle was the first on the Western Front since 1914 in which defensive casualties (25,000) exceeded attacking losses (17,000). See also: Third Battle of YPRES.

Metaxas, Colonel Joannis (1871–1941) Deputy chief of staff of the GREEK ARMY in 1914, and the most influential military figure at the wartime court of King CONSTANTINE I. Metaxas steered GREECE towards alliance with the CENTRAL POWERS after the fall of prime minister VENIZELOS in September 1915, acting as liaison in direct discussions until Allied pressure forced the demobilization of the Greek Army and his own transfer to a minor training post in 1916. Already forming royalist paramilitary groups in Macedonia, he was credited with organizing military resistance to the Allied ATHENS LANDINGS in December but could not subsequently persuade Constantine to take personal command of pro-German units in the north. He was exiled to Corsica along with other senior royalist officers after the King's abdication in June 1917, and played no further active wartime role, but was the most important right-wing figure in postwar Greek politics.

Meuse–Argonne Offensive Joint AEF and FRENCH ARMY advance on the WESTERN FRONT in autumn 1918. Begun in late September in front of the Argonne Forest east of Verdun, it drove north up the west bank of the River Meuse and was at the Belgian border by the ARMISTICE (see MAP 2).

The AMIENS and ALBERT Offensives had been the focus of Allied advances in France since early August 1918, but Allied supreme commander FOCH was planning a switch of emphasis to the French–US sector further south by the end of the month.

An attack north towards vital RAILWAY junctions at Mézières, 50km from the front, offered the prospect of cutting off the entire German Second Army to the northwest, but Allied forces faced dense forests on high ground hemmed in by the Rivers Aisne, Aire and Meuse. Attackers could only advance through two valleys guarded by four separate lines of defence, of which the third and strongest, Kriemhilde Stellung, formed the southernmost block of the HINDENBURG LINE.

With French forces displaying clear signs of battle weariness, fresh and fit AEF troops were given the main attacking role, and Foch informed US commander PERSHING on 30 August that the Argonne operation would take precedence over the long-planned ST MIHIEL attack. Pershing's decision to accept the logistic and physical challenge of both attacks has been criticized as naive, but was made under protest.

Two-thirds of the 600,000 US and French troops employed for the Offensive, scheduled to begin at dawn on 26 September, were engaged at St Mihiel until 16 September. The considerable logistic challenge of bringing them rapidly into the battle zone while another 220,000 French and Italian troops were moved out fell to Colonel George C. Marshall (who was to become US ARMY chief of staff in the Second World War, and subsequently US secretary of state). Marshall's success made his reputation and enabled the attack to begin on time.

The US First Army (LIGGETT) was grouped to the east of the front, supported by 189 French RENAULT light tanks, and French forces on the left used more than 300 tanks (including 29 heavies). Total ARTILLERY support of almost 5,000 guns was backed by General MITCHELL's 500 aircraft, but the AEF's various battle arms were relatively unpractised, and this proved a major disadvantage in an operation heavily dependent on efficient support for otherwise exposed infantry.

With General GOURAUD's French Fourth Army displaying symptoms of fatigue, and German MINES further slowing progress, Allied forces advanced at most 3km along a 64km front on the first day, and new logistic problems emerged as the offensive inched into more heavily defended territory. Impatient at the failure of inexperienced advance units to sweep aside well-entrenched defenders, Pershing and his commanders threw reserves into the narrow, congested battlefronts. Frontline confusion was matched in rear areas as the three roads into the battle zone became irrevocably jammed, and the front had advanced only some 16km, at far greater cost than anticipated, when attacks ground to a halt on 30 September.

The offensive was resumed on 4 October, but the pattern of fighting remained the same for the rest of the month. Despite rapid erosion of their position to the north, and the ravages of INFLUENZA, the German defenders clung tenaciously to excellent positions, counterattacking whenever possible. As late as 1 November, by which time the collapse of German resistance was clearly imminent, a major Allied push met with only mixed success.

A rapid advance of 8km by US Army V Corps pulled other US and French forces forward in its wake, but defenders were able to regroup and hold a line until 4 November, when the bulk of defending forces went into full retreat. Exhausted troops of the French Fourth Army were unable to make rapid progress, but two fresher US corps had advanced a further 32km to the heights overlooking Sedan by 9 November. They were still there when the ARMISTICE was declared, by which time French units had reached the approaches to Mézières.

Mexico The federal republic of Mexico was a huge and disorderly country of some 2 million square kilometres containing about 15 million people in 1910. Coherent independent development began with the presidency of General Porfirio Díaz, who governed the country for all but four years between 1876 and 1911. His overthrow by Francisco Madero signalled a period of instability that drew increasing levels of military intervention from the neighbouring UNITED STATES, Mexico's partner for 75 per cent of all trade and the main market for its gold, lead, silver and copper exports.

President Huerta, who seized power in February 1913 after the murder of Madero, was forced to resign in July 1914 after he interned US NAVY personnel at Tampico and Admiral MAYO's marines occupied Veracruz. Francisco ('Pancho') Villa proclaimed a rebel government in the north before US client Venustiano Carranza established a shaky regime in mid-1915, recognized by Washington in October.

Allied PROPAGANDA and the PREPAREDNESS MOVEMENT exploited Mexican upheavals to influence US public opinion from 1914, suggesting that Huerta and Villa were in

German employ. Villa helped their cause by repeatedly avoiding capture by Carranza's forces and inflicting casualties on US citizens in a notorious cross-border raid against Columbus, New Mexico, in March 1916. A US ARMY detachment, some 10,000 men under General PERSHING, crossed into Mexico in pursuit of Villa on 15 March.

Pershing's troops failed to corner Villa, despite occasional actions with his rearguards, and fought small engagements with Mexican regulars once Carranza's initial permission for the expedition turned to hostility. By late summer war seemed probable, with 150,000 US National Guardsmen mobilized along the Mexican border, but after Carranza agreed to adopt a more liberal constitution Pershing extricated his army in early February 1917.

Carranza's simultaneous proposal for a suspension of neutral Latin American trade in food and war materials to belligerents was generally interpreted as a pro-German gesture, and revelation of the ZIMMERMANN NOTE on 1 March appeared to confirm collusion with the CENTRAL POWERS. Mexican denials were popularly disbelieved in the USA, where the incident promoted public support for war with Germany, but trade relations were not seriously interrupted. The owners of neutral Mexico's mining and emerging oil industries enjoyed a temporary war boom on the back of increased US demand, and Carranza survived until his murder opened another three-year civil war in 1920.

Michael, Operation See: KAISERSCHLACHT.

Michaelis, Georg (1857–1936) German civil servant, head of the grain section with the KRA from August 1914 and in charge of national food distribution with the Supreme War Bureau from February 1917 (see HINDENBURG PROGRAMME). Michaelis was the THIRD SUPREME COMMAND's eventual choice as chancellor BETHMANN HOLLWEG's successor in mid-July 1917, appointed after Kaiser WILHELM II refused to accept either former chancellor Bernhard von Bülow or erstwhile naval minister TIRPITZ. Without parliamentary support of his own, Michaelis had little choice but to follow the dictates of LUDENDORFF and the Supreme Command until clumsy attempts to blame the Social Democratic Party (SDP) for naval unrest in the autumn irredeemably wrecked his Reichstag position. He resigned on 31 October to be replaced by the equally obscure HERTLING. See also: GERMANY.

Micheler, General Alfred (1861–1931) Commander of the French Tenth Army at the SOMME in 1916 and of the Reserve Army Group during the NIVELLE OFFENSIVE of April 1917, his opposition to the latter matured into open dispute with NIVELLE in its aftermath. Micheler returned to command of the Fifth Army, holding the position until May 1918, when he was dismissed after ignoring PÉTAIN's advice to prepare DEFENCE IN DEPTH before the German SPRING OFFENSIVES.

Military Service Acts, 1916 The first conscription laws ever passed in GREAT BRITAIN, a response to the twin problems of supplying manpower to the mushrooming BRITISH ARMY and maintaining rapid growth in the munitions industry. The first Bill was presented on 5 January and became law the following month, calling up single men and childless widowers aged 18 to 41, starting with those who had already 'attested' willingness to serve under Lord DERBY's voluntary registration scheme. Clergymen, vital war workers and conscientious objectors were exempt, but 'absolutist' objectors who refused alternative non-combatant service were rarely granted exemption by local tribunals.

Unfamiliarity with the conscription process soon showed. Married attestees began to receive call-up papers during March, before many unattested bachelors, prompting protests and a revised second Act in May. Never applied to IRELAND, British conscription radically expanded during the crisis on the WESTERN FRONT of spring 1918. A new Act passed in April of that year extended compulsory service to 51-year-olds, all males born in 1898–99 were called up regardless of occupation in May, and more than 100,000 conscripts were 'combed out' of war industries in the first half of the year. Most exemptions had been reinstated by December, when the last c more than 2.3 million British conscripts entered service.

Miliukov, Paul (1859–1943) Russian historian and a founder member of the centre-left Kadet Party. A supporter of gradual constitutional reform, he joined the majority of Duma deputies in giving full support to the national war effort after August 1914, greatly encouraged by alliance with the western democracies.

A major figure in the Duma's 'Progressive Bloc' from mid-1915, he was pushed closer to dissent by royal rejection of its moderate reform programme and the subsequent reactionary behaviour of the GOREMYKIN and STÜRMER cabinets. By November 1916, when his angry criticisms of the Empress ALEXANDRA contributed to the temporary appointment of the more moderate Trepov as premier, he regarded the regime as being more interested in the maintenance of autocracy than in military victory.

An acknowledged authority on international affairs, Miliukov became foreign minister in the PROVISIONAL GOVERNMENT after the FEBRUARY REVOLUTION in 1917. To the right of most ministers, he was viewed with suspicion by the SOVIETS and justified their doubts by pursuing a policy of diplomatic continuity. Seeking cooperation with the Allies and maintenance of Russia's expansionist claims on the DARDANELLES, he reaffirmed his commitment to prior agreements in a postscript to the Petrograd Soviet's definition of Russian war aims as 'peace without annexations or indemnities' (18 April). Soviet-inspired popular outrage compelled his resignation over the issue in mid-May, and he joined anti-Bolshevik forces on the Don after the OCTOBER REVOLUTION, emigrating permanently to France in 1919.

Millerand, Alexandre (1859–1943) French moderate socialist who moved to the right as war minister under POINCARÉ in 1912 and supported the introduction of three-year conscription in 1913. Brought into the VIVIANI government as war minister in August 1914, he made little attempt to interfere with JOFFRE's military autocracy, supporting the high command's suggestion that the cabinet leave Paris in early September and subsequently acting as a buffer for political criticism of the Army. From May 1915 his power over economic war management was curtailed by the formation of separate departments to administer ARTILLERY and ammunition supply, and he excited strong parliamentary opposition by supporting Joffre's dismissal of SARRAIL in July 1915. Still backing Joffre's refusal to reinforce Sarrail in SALONIKA, he was replaced by GALLIÉNI when the Viviani coalition fell in October and was not recalled to wartime office. Briefly premier in 1920, he defeated CLEMENCEAU to become president of FRANCE later that year.

Mills Bomb Because the BRITISH ARMY had almost no GRENADES in 1914 it was eventually able to standardize on the Mills Bomb, which became the most recognizable weapon of its type. Introduced in spring 1915, it was an egg-shaped, time-fused bomb with a cast-iron case structurally weakened to break up as shrapnel. Though supply to the BEF was initially slow, and other British armies were forced to rely on improvised grenades well into 1916, more than 33 million Mills bombs were eventually issued to British and AEF units.

Milne, General George (1866–1948) British ARTILLERY officer, who was a colonel with the BEF during the early battles on the WESTERN FRONT in 1914. He was a major general and chief of staff to the British Second Army in autumn 1915, when he was transferred to the BALKAN FRONT in command of the 27th Division. Sent to SALONIKA as a strong-willed foil to domineering French C-in-C SARRAIL, Milne was given little opportunity to display his military abilities before 1918. His forces had grown to corps size by January 1916, and by the end of the year he led an army, but limited Allied commitment to the theatre and crippling environmental conditions restricted its offensive potential. His limited attacks at Lake Doiran in spring 1917 failed with heavy losses (see Battle of Lake PRESPA), but collapse of the BULGARIAN ARMY in autumn 1918 turned the final VARDAR OFFENSIVE into a rout. While

SERBIAN ARMY forces moved into AUSTRIA-HUNGARY, Milne led British troops east to TURKEY and remained in Constantinople until 1920.

Milner, Alfred, Lord (1854–1925) British colonial administrator of Anglo-German descent, a committed imperialist credited with organizing rapid economic reconstruction in SOUTH AFRICA after the Boer War. He was co-opted from private business activities in 1914 to serve on government committees organizing food and coal production, and brought into the LLOYD GEORGE coalition in December 1916. As a member of the five-man War Council, but otherwise without portfolio, he was one of several imperial advisors to the prime minister, playing a leading role in the creation of the Allied SUPREME WAR COUNCIL and the appointment of FOCH as Allied overall commander. On 19 April 1918 he replaced Lord DERBY as war minister, advocating intervention in the RUSSIAN CIVIL WAR, and he became colonial minister after elections in December.

Minelayers Ships needed very little specialist equipment for laying MINES, which could simply be dropped overboard to stern, and the main requirements for a minelayer were speed and stealth. The converted fishing craft or colliers intended for the task by prewar navies were found unsuitable in wartime, and fast DESTROYERS were the most common type of ship used, a number being adapted with mine racks and extra carrying capacity by British, Russian and German forces. SUBMARINES were also a highly effective method of delivering small numbers of mines to precise locations, a tactic pioneered by German UC-BOATS and imitated in a small number of Allied boats. Converted passenger ships or ferries were often used for their speed, but every type of fast vessel, from small motor launches to the battlecruiser *GOEBEN* in the BLACK SEA, could be used for minelaying, and naval aircraft were employed from about 1916. Defensive minefields remained the province of slower auxiliaries.

Minenwerfer One of the GERMAN ARMY's most valuable infantry-support weapons, a series of short-range, high-trajectory bomb throwers (or MORTARS) that used a charge to project high-explosive, GAS or incendiary shells. In contrast to early improvisations forced on the Allies, they were small-scale precision ARTILLERY pieces, mostly with barrels rifled for accuracy. About 150 were available in August 1914, designed for use against eastern French FORTRESSES, and production was stepped up with the stabilization of European fronts late that year. Used in light (76mm), medium (170mm) and heavy (245mm) versions, all with a maximum range of about 1,000 metres, they were grouped in specialist engineering companies for both local and general operations, making an important contribution to early German superiority in TRENCH WARFARE.

Mines, Land The modern concept of the land mine as a compact, hidden anti-personnel explosive was relatively new in 1914. Primitive explosive devices were used, buried and triggered by some kind of spike protruding above ground, but many Europeans considered them unacceptably barbaric. Early use of land mines in German SOUTHWEST AFRICA brought protests from South African leaders, but they were not strictly speaking illegal and were hardly effective, relying on the force of their explosion alone to cause casualties.

Improvised mines, rendered much more dangerous by the addition of shrapnel (anything from stones or metal fragments to bullets), were standard weapons of the ARAB REVOLT, RUSSIAN CIVIL WAR and other guerrilla campaigns. They eventually became a standard defensive weapon on the WESTERN FRONT, where German forces buried fields of MORTAR bombs for defence against TANK attacks in 1918.

Conventional mines in 1914 were tunnels dug beneath enemy positions in frontline areas, an extension of TRENCH WARFARE commonplace since the 16th century. Generally either used for secret deployment of infantry or filled with explosives and blown up beneath enemy positions, mines in busy sectors of the WESTERN FRONT became an almost private subterranean battlefront (see VIMY RIDGE; Battles of ARRAS, CAMBRAI).

Specialist miners, usually drawn from coal-producing regions, worked under constant threat of discovery, often by opposing mines only yards away. Secrecy depended on silence over a long period, and mining battalions included listening parties employed to monitor the progress of enemy mines. Discovered mines generally had their 'cover blown' (i.e. were blown up), either by hostile 'counterminers' or preemptive self-destruction, and sudden underground explosions were an everyday occurrence near long-contested hills and ridges. See also: SAPPING; Battle of MESSINES.

Mines, Naval Waterproof floating bombs, a principal naval weapon of the period and responsible for more warship sinkings than any other. The vast majority were 'contact mines', attached to the seabed by a chain and detonated when a ship struck their protruding antennae. Some offshore installations were protected by 'controlled mines', activated by a nearby observer, and the British developed a magnetic mine in 1918, detonated by the field of a passing hull but not used in large numbers until the Second World War. An American magnetic mine, used for the NORTHERN BARRAGE in 1918, proved effective but dangerously unstable.

Mines were used by the thousand in all busy theatres, defensively to protect harbours and coastal installations from surface attack, and offensively to disrupt trade routes or catch hostile warships close to their home bases.

Laying minefields was a skilled enterprise. Success in sinking or banishing hostile shipping depended on the avoidance of detection, and on the location of mines in threatening yet unexpected places. This often meant laying fields immediately after an area had been swept, a dangerous enterprise that resulted in many MINELAYERS being destroyed by their own earlier efforts.

A poorly laid field, or loss of a loaded minelayer close to home waters, could cause enormous problems for friendly shipping, especially in the BLACK SEA and BALTIC theatres, where contested waters became virtual no-go areas for both sides. The quality of mines varied considerably, with the ROYAL NAVY in particular suffering from a lack of prewar interest in their potential, and genuinely effective British mines were not widely available until late 1917. See also: DARDANELLES; *AUDACIOUS*; SUBMARINE WARFARE; NAVAL WARFARE.

Mišić, Field Marshal Zivojin (1855–1921) Aggressive SERBIAN ARMY officer, a former deputy to chief of staff PUTNIK, who was recalled to the post in July 1914. He led the First Army during the third Austro-Hungarian offensive on the BALKAN FRONT in November, winning a famous victory (and promotion to field marshal) at the KOLUBARA in early December. Mišić suffered severe exposure during the 'GREAT RETREAT' of late 1915, which he had opposed in favour of a last stand, and was unable to return to his post until September 1916. After taking part in the advance on MONASTIR and holding off a Bulgarian counterattack, Mišić became a firm advocate of a major offensive from SALONIKA. His case weakened by the fragile condition of his troops, he had to wait until September 1918 before the VARDAR OFFENSIVE confirmed his belief that the BULGARIAN ARMY was ready to collapse. As chief of staff from July 1918, and effective Serbian C-in-C, he led the Army deep into former AUSTRIA-HUNGARY before hostilities ended, greatly facilitating the almost immediate creation of YUGOSLAVIA.

Mitchell, General William (1848–1936) Pioneer commander of the USAAS who briefly commanded the US ARMY's signals aircraft before transferring to Spain as a military attaché in 1917. When the UNITED STATES declared war in April he moved to Paris and toured the WESTERN FRONT, learning modern AERIAL WARFARE techniques from RFC commander TRENCHARD. On General PERSHING's arrival in June, Mitchell (still a major) presented his ideas for a massive AEF air arm and was given responsibility for training and organization of the first pilots. He led the first US squadrons in active service from March 1918 and eventually commanded several hundred frontline USAAS aircraft. An international Air Brigade of almost 850 machines under Mitchell's command supported the ST MIHIEL offensive in September, and he led a 500-strong air fleet against ground targets during the subsequent MEUSE–ARGONNE OFFENSIVE, but the ARMISTICE ended ambitious plans for massive STRATEGIC BOMBING attacks on GERMANY. Mitchell's postwar career was dominated by a vain struggle to persuade military authorities to invest heavily in aviation technology.

Mittelmeerdivision, Escape of the The opening action of the naval campaign in the MEDITERRANEAN, a confused Allied attempt to eliminate the only substantial GERMAN NAVY force in the theatre, comprising the battlecruiser *GOEBEN* and the light cruiser *BRESLAU*. In the Mediterranean since 1912, Admiral SOUCHON's Mittelmeerdivision ('Mediterranean Division') left the Austro-Hungarian port of Pola (Pula) at the end of the JULY CRISIS to disrupt transportation of French colonial troops to Europe from North Africa.

At Messina for coal on 2 August, when ITALY's neutrality was announced, they sailed for North Africa that night and arrived off the Algerian coast early on 4 August, receiving news of war with France en route. *Breslau* bombarded Bône (Annaba), and *Goeben* exchanged fire with shore batteries at Philippeville (Skikda), but Souchon received an inaccurate signal that afternoon announcing German alliance with TURKEY, and was ordered to make for Constantinople.

Returning to Messina for coal, the Mittelmeerdivision passed close by two British BATTLECRUISERS (*INDEFATIGABLE* and *Indomitable*). Since Germany was not yet at war with Britain, *Goeben* accelerated away to avoid pursuit and to mask problems with its boilers, but Souchon's position at Messina appeared critical. Allowed only the statutory 24 hours in a neutral port, and unable to refuel fully, he learned of the AUSTRO-HUNGARIAN NAVY's unwillingness to come to his assistance from the Adriatic and that alliance with Turkey was less than certain.

Faced with vastly superior Anglo-French forces in the theatre, and the choice of running to Pola or Constantinople, he decided to chance Turkish benevolence and put to sea on 6 August. He headed east after a feint towards the Atlantic, shadowed by the British TOWN CRUISER *Gloucester*, on watch at the entrance to the Adriatic.

After a brief skirmish with *Breslau*, lack of fuel forced *Gloucester* to break off on the afternoon of 7 August, but four larger ROYAL NAVY cruisers (see *WARRIOR*) were patrolling south of Corfu, in position to intercept the German ships. Squadron commander Admiral Troubridge made to intercept but changed his mind and withdrew. Imprecise RADIO orders from London had mentioned avoiding action against a 'superior force', which the Admiralty intended to mean the Austro-Hungarian fleet but Troubridge interpreted as referring to *Goeben*.

Other Allied opportunities to intercept were missed. Three British battlecruisers were in position to catch *Goeben* in Messina, but commander Admiral Milne chose to obey earlier orders and avoid Italian territorial waters. On 8 August he received a signal (sent in error) to open hostilities against the Austro-Hungarian fleet, and turned north to rendezvous with Troubridge at the entrance to the Adriatic. The FRENCH NAVY's Mediterranean fleet commander, Admiral BOUÉ DE LAPEYRÈRE, was primarily concerned with protection of troopships from North Africa, and chose to employ his BATTLESHIPS on an unauthorized CONVOY system.

Souchon's ships proceeded unmolested to the Aegean, where they refuelled and entered the DARDANELLES with Turkish permission on 10 August. Allied diplomatic protests at neutral Turkey's behaviour were sidestepped by the adoption of both vessels, complete with their German crews, into the TURKISH NAVY, a move justified by the seizure of two Turkish battleships under construction in Britain.

Though the cautious performance of the Austro-Hungarian Navy attracted criticism in GERMANY, the escape was a military and diplomatic success for the CENTRAL POWERS. The Mittelmeerdivision was a threat to Allied shipping in both the Mediterranean and the BLACK SEA, and the episode improved German relations with Turkey.

Inept high command coordination, the complications of Italian neutrality and British delays in declaring war all played a part in the Allied failure, as did diplomatic inability to anticipate Turkish collusion. Played down at first by Allied sources, the escape provoked controversy once its consequences became clear. All three Allied admirals involved were criticized for lack of initiative, and Troubridge was court-martialled (but acquitted) on charges of negligence. See MAP 16.

Moltke, Field Marshal Helmuth von (1848–1916) Nephew and namesake of the Prussian field marshal famed for victories in the wars of 1866 and 1870, the younger von Moltke succeeded Schlieffen as GERMAN ARMY chief of staff in 1906. Though maintaining his predecessor's war plan, he progressively compromised its massive northern bias in response to French military build up along the frontier further south.

Troubled by the prospect of war, he played a largely inert role in the JULY CRISIS of 1914, apart from insisting to a wavering WILHELM II that, once ordered, the SCHLIEFFEN PLAN could not be reversed. Beset by communications breakdowns during the campaigns of August, he was unable to resist either the fear of Russian attack on the EASTERN FRONT or the opportunity of an unplanned victory against French forces in LORRAINE, and distracted troops from the main German invasion of northern France.

As the invasion approached Paris in early September he failed to issue decisive instructions to field commanders before or during the vital MARNE battle, allowing subordinates on the spot to order a general retreat. On 14 September, in the process of planning a resumption of attacks in northern France, Moltke was retired and replaced by war minister FALKENHAYN.

Monarch Class The oldest PRE-DREADNOUGHTS in frontline service with the wartime AUSTRO-HUNGARIAN NAVY, the Monarchs (*Monarch*, *Budapest* and *Wien*) were completed in 1896–97 and stationed at CATTARO in 1914, part of a coastal-protection force (V Division) that also included old armoured CRUISERS. They helped defend the base against French and Montenegrin troops in October 1914, and *Budapest* played a marginal role in attacks on Allied supply lines to the SERBIAN ARMY in late 1915. The Division also provided coastal support for the Austro-Hungarian offensive against MONTENEGRO on the BALKAN FRONT in January 1916. On 9 October 1917, shortly after *Wien* and *Budapest* had been transferred to support operations on the ITALIAN FRONT, *Wien* was torpedoed and sunk in a raid on the harbour by Italian MAS BOATS.

After the Cattaro mutiny in February 1918, the surviving Monarchs were disarmed and taken out of service, primarily to release crews for other duties. Their larger Habsburg Class successors, used as coastal-defence ships in the northern Adriatic, had been retired in late 1917, while three slightly faster Erzherzog Class vessels took over the defence of Cattaro. All Austro-Hungarian pre-dreadnoughts were scrapped in 1919.

BRIEF DATA (*Monarch*, 1914) Displacement: 5,600 tons; Crew: 400; Dimensions: length 323ft (97.9m), beam 56ft (17m); Speed: 17k; Main armament: 4 × 9.4in gun, 6 × 5.9in, 12 × 3pdr, 2 × 17.7in TT.

Monash, General John (1865–1931) Australian territorial militiaman not commissioned to join the Australian Imperial Force (AIF) until early September 1914, when a fourth Australian Brigade was formed under his command. Monash led his brigade at GALLIPOLI in 1915 before taking command of the 3rd Australian Division, which he trained and took to France. A reputation for careful, efficient organization, earned as part of General PLUMER's British Second Army at MESSINES and the third YPRES battle, was cemented from May 1918, when he succeeded BIRDWOOD in command of the Australian Corps. As the shock troops of General RAWLINSON's British Fourth Army, his corps won a series of efficient victories at LE HAMEL, the AMIENS OFFENSIVE, and the climactic assault on the HINDENBURG LINE. A pioneer of the PEACEFUL PENETRATION tactics employed by AUSTRALIAN FORCES from spring 1918, he recognized the dependence of infantry on efficient close support from ARTILLERY, TANKS, MACHINE GUNS and aircraft. Generally regarded as one of the most successful generals on either side on the WESTERN FRONT, he returned to postwar civilian public service as Australia's most famous soldier.

Monastir Offensive Ambitious but ultimately limited Allied offensive in the SALONIKA theatre of autumn 1916. Allied forces had been freed for offensive action by completion of the fortified zone around the Greek port in April. Commanding general SARRAIL had moved his forces up to the Serbian frontier northwest of Salonika in the early summer, meeting no opposition from the GREEK ARMY (which was demobilized in July). He planned an offensive all along the 200km line stretching from Lake Doiran to Kavalla, on the Aegean coast east of Salonika, with the main drive to the west into Serbia towards Skopje. In a wider context the offensive was intended to prevent any Bulgarian attack on the Dobrudja region as part of the agreement that brought ROMANIA into the war in late August.

Although Sarrail commanded half a million troops in the area, sickness had reduced frontline strength to less than 100,000 men, including British units under General MILNE (whose cooperation depended on confirmation from London) and the reconstituted SERBIAN ARMY, in position to the west of the line since July but of uncertain combat value. Italian and Russian detachments also arrived during the summer, but cooperation with Italian forces in ALBANIA was politically difficult.

Aware of Sarrail's plans, German front commander von BELOW and his Bulgarian counterpart ZHEKOV cooperated in a limited spoiling operation around FLORINA to the west, combined with an advance across the Greek frontier in the east, shortening the front and forcing Sarrail to postpone operations until mid-September.

The renewed offensive was more limited in scope, intended to recover Florina and push into southern Serbia, but dependent for further progress on the success of subsidiary advances elswhere. Serbian units, reinforced by French and Russian detachments, advanced towards Florina from 13 September, and the British attempted to make progress up the Struma River the next day. Bulgarian units in the far east occupied the major coastal fortress of Kavalla on 14 September, unopposed by Greek garrison troops.

Although Franco-Russian forces entered Florina on 18 September, and moved on Monastir (Bitola) alongside Serbian units advancing through hills either side of the Crno River, strong Bulgarian resistance forced them to inch their way north while British operations on the Struma subsided into deadlock. Little progress was made by early October, with the British still well short of Seres, their primary objective, but Bulgarian counterattacks all along the line on 14 October were similarly unsuccessful.

Operations were increasingly hampered by rain and fog from 21 October, and although Serbian troops established contact with Italian forces west of Lake Prespa in southern Albania, German reinforcements held up the Crno advance until mid-November, while British operations degenerated into TRENCH WARFARE on the Struma and around Lake Doiran.

By 12 November Serbian and French troops were still 25km from Monastir, but exhaustion prompted a general Bulgarian retreat from 14 November. Monastir was evacuated on 18 November and occupied by Allied forces next day. Minor Allied advances in the west during late November, scaled down as unrest inside Greece provoked fears for the base at Salonika (see ATHENS LANDING), ended with the front stablilizing north and east of Monastir by mid-December, after which bad weather halted action for the winter. See MAP 19.

Monchy-le-Preux See: Battle of ARRAS; VIMY RIDGE; SCARPE OFFENSIVE.

Monitors Light, shallow-draught warships designed for river work or coastal defence. Extensively used by colonial powers during the 19th century, and an important weapon in the American Civil War, monitors had since been replaced in major navies by faster craft with lighter armament. However, they were still used by the AUSTRO-HUNGARIAN NAVY for its DRINA and Danube flotillas along the Serbian border, guarding the Austrian retreat from the KOLUBARA RIVER in December 1914, and were rediscovered by the wartime ROYAL NAVY.

Three light monitors under construction for the BRAZILIAN NAVY were requisitioned by the British in autumn 1914, and 35 new monitors were completed before production was stopped in 1916. Two conversions of Norwegian coastal-defence ships were also completed in 1918. With no need for speed or thick armour, monitors were cheap and easy to build. Their main armament was usually a single two-gun turret culled from redundant or captured warships. Light monitors with 9.2-inch or smaller main armament were numbered M-15 to M-33, and the 16 heavy monitors carried surplus BATTLESHIP guns (12- to 15-inch). Three Lord Clive Class ships received 18-inch turrets in 1918 (see *FURIOUS*).

British monitors were used to bombard German coastal positions on the WESTERN FRONT, to protect home ports, at the DARDANELLES in 1915, in the eastern MEDITERRANEAN, and during the prolonged RUFUGI DELTA battle in EAST AFRICA. Five were sunk by enemy action and another by accident in Dover harbour.

BRIEF DATA (*Erebus*, 1916) Displacement: 8,000 tons; Crew: 223; Dimensions: length 405ft (122.7m), beam 88ft (26.7m); Speed: 12k; Armament: 2 × 15in gun, 8 × 4in, 2 × 12pdr.

Mons, Battle of The first engagement between British and German ground forces on the WESTERN FRONT, fought on 23 August 1914, and one of the Battles of the FRONTIERS (see MAP 4). After a cautious advance from the Belgian coast, the British Expeditionary Force (BEF) was well behind schedule for a planned meeting with French forces on the Sambre near CHARLEROI when it met German First Army patrols near the town of Soignies on 22 August. British commander Sir John FRENCH was unaware of German victories in LORRAINE and the ARDENNES, or of the GERMAN ARMY's overwhelming numerical strength in BELGIUM, and expected to meet a force smaller than his own five divisions. Dismissing intelligence reports suggesting otherwise, he prepared to attack from the nearby Mons Canal, but changed his mind during the night and ordered defensive formations.

General von KLUCK's German First Army, northern spearhead of an invasion force totalling 38 divisions, had no idea where the British were until he found them blocking his path. Forbidden by the high command to risk loss of contact with General von BÜLOW's Second Army by outflanking the BEF, he launched a frontal attack on its positions the following morning.

The two British infantry corps, under Generals SMITH-DORRIEN and HAIG, were deployed east and west of Mons on a 40km front, the eastern wing reaching towards General LANREZAC's French Fifth Army to the south, with ALLENBY's cavalry division in reserve. In total, about 70,000 British troops with 300 guns faced some 160,000 Germans with 600, but von Kluck's main attack against Smith-Dorrien's corps suffered terrible losses to expert RIFLE fire and had made no progress by mid-afternoon.

Von Kluck brought in reserves from the flanks as British forces began a slow process of withdrawal to their second lines of defence. By late in the evening, when the extra German corps had gathered for a full-scale assault, British commanders had realized the approximate size of their enemy and the order was given to retreat. Haig's corps was able to withdraw virtually unmolested, but communications inefficiency delayed Smith-Dorrien's retirement until the German attack was underway. Von Kluck made little attempt at pursuit, preferring to tend his heavy casualties.

Having lost about 1,600 men in a minor action relative to the battles being fought further south, the BEF began a long retreat. Despite the preference of French and his chief advisor WILSON for an immediate withdrawal to the coast, British war minister KITCHENER ordered the BEF to remain in contact with FRENCH ARMY forces retreating to the MARNE.

The Battle of Mons was celebrated in GREAT BRITAIN as a triumph diluted by the French failure at Charleroi, giving rise to an enduring popular myth that a slightly larger

British force would have driven back the German Army. See Battle of LE CATEAU.

Montenegro Tiny Balkan state, less than 15,000 square kilometres of mountainous country with a population of about half a million in 1914, that had been more or less successfully claiming independence from the Ottoman Empire for some six centuries since its liberation from the medieval Serbian empire (see MAP 19). Although in theory a constitutional monarchy, the country had been ruled since 1860 by the autocratic Nicholas I (self-proclaimed king since 1910). Montenegro was economically and ethnically close to SERBIA, its ally against TURKEY in the Balkan Wars (1912–13), and political union was discussed in both countries.

Montenegro mobilized its entire adult male population (except Muslims, who were taxed in lieu of service) against AUSTRIA-HUNGARY in August 1914, under the King's direct command but with a Serbian chief of staff. Seasoned guerrilla fighters with a tradition of self-defence, largely equipped with obsolete Russian weapons, 40,000 Montenegrins shared the Serbian victories on the BALKAN FRONT in 1914, and undertook small raids of their own into Habsburg Bosnia. Late in the year they made ineffectual attempts to support FRENCH NAVY attacks on the AUSTRO-HUNGARIAN NAVY's fortified Montenegrin enclave at CATTARO.

Nicholas refused to join the 'GREAT RETREAT' into Albania after the invasion of SERBIA by the CENTRAL POWERS in autumn 1915, and his forces surrendered when Montenegro was overrun in January 1916. With an underdeveloped agricultural economy, no large towns, few roads and only a single RAILWAY line, Montenegro was not a strategically valuable capture.

Nicholas fled to Italy and then France in early 1916, sending his second son to Vienna as a form of diplomatic insurance against victory by the CENTRAL POWERS. With no army, he was powerless to prevent Serbian moves to absorb Montenegro as part of a postwar settlement. The Corfu Declaration of July 1917, agreeing to autonomous status for Montenegro within a Serb-led future YUGOSLAVIA, was signed by a Serb-sponsored Montenegrin national committee based in Switzerland.

Montenegro's recapture by Serbian forces in 1918 made unification a virtual certainty, and the Montenegrin national assembly voted to depose Nicholas in November. Montenegro duly became part of postwar Yugoslavia, and a few minor incursions by monarchists, supplied from Italy, faded after the King's death in 1921.

Morane-Saulnier A-1 French monoplane FIGHTER, in full production for the AÉRONAUTIQUE MILITAIRE from late 1917 and in service the following January. Although some 1,200 were built, including versions with 160hp engines and twin guns, it was withdrawn from frontline service in March 1918 as superior new types became available. A number were purchased as advanced trainers by the USAAS and the BELGIAN AIR SERVICE in 1918.

BRIEF DATA Type: single-seat fighter; Engine: 120hp Le Rhône; Max speed: 197kph; Ceiling: 5,600m; Armament: 1 × 0.303in mg.

Morane-Saulnier BB Handsome but mediocre French two-seat reconnaissance biplane, a close relative of the MORANE-SAULNIER N monoplane. It was used in small numbers by the AÉRONAUTIQUE MILITAIRE, the RFC and the RNAS between November 1915 and early 1917.

BRIEF DATA (BB, RFC) Type: two-seater reconnaissance/escort; Engine: 110hp Le Rhône; Max speed: 144kph; Armament: 1 or 2 × 0.303in mg.

Morane-Saulnier L 'Parasol' French high-wing tractor monoplane, best known of a series of basically similar two-seaters designed by the Morane company between 1912 and late 1915. An attempt to combine the speed and visibility of monoplane design with the strength and stability of biplanes, the Parasol entered French service in late 1913. Hundreds served with the AÉRONAUTIQUE MILITAIRE on the WESTERN FRONT during 1914–15, and it was also used in smaller numbers by the RFC, the RNAS and the RUSSIAN ARMY AIR SERVICE. A structurally improved LA version, introduced in 1915, was employed in small numbers by British and French forces.

A successful reconnaissance plane and light bomber, as well as the standard choice for agent-dropping operations, the Parasol was faster and more mobile than contemporary German two-seaters, and downed several in early RIFLE duels. A Parasol's 20lb bombs were responsible for the first air-to-air destruction of a ZEPPELIN in February 1915, and DEFLECTOR GEAR was first fitted to the type in March of that year. About 600 Parasols were built in France, most of which had been withdrawn from frontline service by late 1915. Copies produced by several German companies served with the GERMAN ARMY AIR SERVICE, mostly as the Pfalz A-1.

BRIEF DATA (Type L) Type: two-seat reconnaissance/light bomber; Engine: 80hp Gnôme or Le Rhône; Max speed: 115kph; Ceiling: 4,000m; Armament: 6 × 20lb bomb (hand-thrown), observer's small arms or 1 × 8mm mg.

Morane-Saulnier N 'Scout' French mid-wing monoplane, in service with the AÉRONAUTIQUE MILITAIRE from late 1914 and one of the first purpose-designed FIGHTERS to appear on the WESTERN FRONT after DEFLECTOR GEAR was fitted as standard the following spring. From 1916 it was fitted with superior INTERRUPTER GEAR. A few Type N fighters also served with the RFC from March 1916 (their British nickname, 'Bullet', reflecting appearance rather than speed), and they equipped a single Russian squadron on the EASTERN FRONT. Though popular with pilots in 1915, and better able to defend themselves than other contemporary Allied aircraft, they lacked range and were never more than the equal of German FOKKER E-TYPES. Only about 40 were built as Allied production efforts concentrated on the superior NIEUPORT 11 fighter.

BRIEF DATA (1917 model) Type: single seat fighter/escort; Engine: 80 or 110hp Le Rhône; Max speed: 164kph; Ceiling: 4,000m; Armament: 1 × 8mm mg.

Morhange, Battle of See: Battle of LORRAINE.

Morogoro Offensive The major British offensive of 1916 in GERMAN EAST AFRICA, launched in early March by new theatre commander General SMUTS. With 23,000 combat troops at his disposal, Smuts attacked almost as soon as he took command, taking the small northern towns in the Kilimanjaro region and the RAILWAY terminus at Moshi by 13 March, but failing to catch retreating German forces. Rain and disease halted the advance in late March, and Smuts used the pause to reorganize his troops and prepare a new multiple offensive.

Secondary advances from Northern Rhodesia (modern Zambia), the Belgian Congo (modern Zaïre) and Portuguese Mozambique (PORTUGAL declared war on Germany in March) acted as diversions from major attacks south to the colony's Central Railway by General van Deventer's column and east along the Usambara line by a larger force under Smuts.

After struggling for a month through heavy rains, and losing half his 4,000 troops to sickness, van Deventer was just over halfway when German attacks on 9–10 May, followed by another swift retreat, forced him to rest at Kondoa Irangi until late June. Smuts marched east from 22 May and took the European settlement at Amani, 50km inland from Tanga, before turning south towards Morogoro, 185km west of Dar-es-Salaam on the Central Railway. His exhausted men paused in late June, and 500 Indian troops took Tanga without opposition on 3 July.

Both groups reached the Central Railway in late August. German forces again retreated south and Morogoro was occupied on 26 August, followed by Dar-es-Salaam on 3 September. Smuts attempted to continue the pursuit, but sick and hungry troops came to a standstill at Kisaki, an evacuated German base about 200km further south.

Smuts finally gave up in late September, returning to consolidate in Dar-es-Salaam. German commander LETTOW-VORBECK's army remained at large, retaining the capacity to hurt, disrupt and evade British forces, but British public and political opinion considered the battle for East Africa won with the capture of the railway, and the simultaneous success of the Anglo-Belgian advance on TABORA. See also: MAP 18.

Mortars Portable high-trajectory ARTILLERY for close-range attacks on fortifications had been a feature of siege warfare in the 18th century, after which their use dwindled until the outbreak of static TRENCH WARFARE on the WESTERN FRONT in late 1914. Mortars were designed to lob the heaviest possible projectile over a short distance, and needed sufficient mobility to get close to hostile positions and keep up with infantry operations.

Distinguished by a broad, stubby barrel, into which the projectile was dropped to be fired by a pre-loaded explosive charge, wartime models were eventually capable of throwing heavy howitzer shells up to about 2km, but the biggest needed large crews to carry them into broken battlefield terrain. For greater accuracy some had rifled barrels (as used in contemporary field and heavy artillery), but most wartime mortars (especially in Allied service) were smooth-bored for ease of manufacture.

The potential value of mortars was demonstrated by the Japanese during their war with Russia of 1904–05, but impressed only the GERMAN ARMY, which produced a series of rifled MINENWERFER designs never matched by contemporary rivals in terms of quality. Other armies of the CENTRAL POWERS were largely dependent on German weapons throughout.

No trench artillery was available to the BRITISH ARMY in 1914, and the FRENCH ARMY was forced to rely on antiquated early 19th-century mortars. Both armies were required to improvise at first, and a bizarre variety of catapults, spring mechanisms and other crude projectors were used on the Western Front and at GALLIPOLI, where only a handful of Japanese mortars were available to British troops. Never able to reach targets more than about 250 metres away, and only vaguely accurate, they were replaced by conventional mortars from late 1915.

The most successful Allied weapon was probably the British STOKES MORTAR, widely available from 1916 and standard equipment in 3-inch, 4-inch and 6-inch (Stokes-Newton) versions by 1918, but a full spectrum of French and Belgian light (75mm), light-medium (150mm) and heavy (240mm) projectors was available by 1917. Other Allied armies were almost invariably supplied with modern mortars from Anglo-French stock.

Morval, Battle of See: SOMME OFFENSIVE.

Möwe The most successful German AUXILIARY COMMERCE RAIDER, it left Hamburg for the South Atlantic under an illegal Swedish flag in December 1915, laying MINES en route, and returned three months later having sunk 14 Allied merchant ships. Its mines claimed, among others, the British *KING EDWARD VII*. On a second cruise to the South Atlantic it sank 20 merchantmen between November 1916 and its return to Germany in March 1917.

BRIEF DATA (1916) Displacement: 4,800 tons; Crew: 235; Speed: 14k; Armament: 5 × 5.9in (150mm) gun, 1 × 105mm, 4 × 19.7in (500mm) TT, c 300 mines.

Mozambique, Invasion of The Portuguese colony of Mozambique was invaded in November 1917 by about 2,200 German troops escaping from larger British forces in German EAST AFRICA to the north (see MAP 18). Northern Mozambique was a fertile plantation area dotted with well-supplied and ill-defended Portuguese outposts, but colonial relations with native peoples were very poor and the Germans were generally welcomed as liberators. General LETTOW-VORBECK's army entered the country on 25 November, brushing aside a ragged force of about 1,000 Portuguese-led ASKARIS. Deployed in small raiding parties, the German force rapidly replenished critical food, medical, transport, small-arms and ammunition supplies from colonial depots. British authorities in East Africa eventually secured Portuguese permission to enter Mozambique and landed two columns (some 8,000 men) on the coast at Porto Amelia in spring 1918.

For three months British forces pursued Lettow-Vorbeck south as he attacked small Portuguese concentrations en route. German troops had covered another 550km by 3 July, when they captured the railway town of Nhamacurra and its plentiful supplies. As British forces were rushed to his next presumed objective, the port of Quelimane, Lettow-Vorbeck swung back to the north, skirmishing with delayed British units on the way. Despite an outbreak of INFLUENZA, the German army marched all the way back to the northern frontier, crossing the Rovuma River into East Africa on 28 September 1918.

Mudros Small port on the Greek Aegean island of Lemnos, some 50km off the Dardanelles Straits, that was commandeered by the British ROYAL NAVY in early 1915. Possessing a wide natural harbour suitable for large warships, but otherwise completely without facilities for military installations, Mudros was placed under the supervision of Admiral WEMYSS and turned into a primitive base in time for the DARDANELLES OPERATION in the early spring. The base was unable to support massed troop arrivals from late March, forcing preparations for the GALLIPOLI LANDINGS to be transferred to EGYPT. Subsequently the base struggled to cope with casualties, troop transports, naval dockyard requirements and heavy supply traffic during the campaign on the GALLIPOLI FRONT. Mudros remained in use by Allied naval forces blockading the Dardanelles throughout the War, and the armistice between Turkey and the Allies was signed in the harbour on 30 October 1918.

Mughar Ridge, Battle of Second stage of General ALLENBY's late 1917 offensive on the PALESTINE FRONT. After overwhelming the BEERSHEBA–GAZA LINE in early November, Allenby paused briefly to evaluate the danger to his inland flank from the Turkish Seventh Army (Fevsi Pasha). YILDERIM FORCE C-in-C General FALKENHAYN had sent its three divisions on a wide sweep though the desert against the advice of staff officers, and Allenby shared their view of its prospects. Leaving only the Australian Mounted Division to guard the flank, he ordered the rest of his mounted force to support a renewed assault on coastal positions held by the Turkish Eighth Army (von KRESSENSTEIN).

Infantry divisions attacked a ridge just northwest of Junction Station, where the RAILWAY to Beersheba joined the Haifa–Jerusalem line, on 13 November. The attack became bogged down in rocky terrain obstructed by thick cactus bushes at El Mughar, the highest village on the ridge, until 800 CAVALRY (with ARTILLERY and MACHINE GUN support) stormed the village from the north. By evening the whole ridge had been cleared by infantry and at least 1,400 Turkish troops killed or captured, against 616 British casualties. British ARMOURED CARS entered Junction Station the following morning, severing communications between the two outnumbered Turkish armies and driving von Kressenstein's forces back beyond Jaffa.

The Seventh Army, exhausted by its long desert march, could only push the Australians back a few kilometres and achieved no breakthrough, eventually withdrawing to bar approaches to Jerusalem itself. Warned by London not to risk over-extension and expecting a major Yilderim counterattack, Allenby paused again before a final advance on JERUSALEM. See MAP 22.

Mulhouse, Battle of The opening attack by the FRENCH ARMY in August 1914, an intrinsic element of its PLAN 17 and a prelude to the Battles of the FRONTIERS. An attack on Alsace (in German hands since 1870) was intended to guard the flank of major invasions further north, and a special detachment of the French First Army, one CAVALRY and two infantry divisions under General Bonneau, was assigned the task. The towns of Mulhouse and Colmar were its initial objectives, and it faced part of the German Seventh Army (von Heeringen).

The French crossed the frontier at 05.00 on 7 August, taking the border town of Altkirch after a BAYONET charge. Bonneau, afraid that light German defences were drawing him into a trap, advanced no further that day. Ordered to move on to the Rhine as quickly as possible next day, French troops entered Mulhouse shortly after German forces had withdrawn north. The French were greeted as liberators by the majority of the population, but

German reserves coming south from Strasbourg counterattacked the French left around Cernay on the morning of 9 August. Unable to concentrate his forces quickly and with no reserves, Bonneau fell back gradually. A reserve division sent to the front by C-in-C JOFFRE that afternoon was too little too late, and the following morning Bonneau withdrew to escape encirclement, leaving the inhabitants of Mulhouse open to reprisals.

The capture of Mulhouse had been greeted with unrestrained joy in FRANCE, where public and politicians knew little or nothing about movements at the front, and Bonneau was immediately dismissed. Four divisions were added to a reformed 'Army of Alsace', which advanced and retreated alongside the main LORRAINE invasion later in the month. See MAP 4.

Müller, Admiral Georg von (1854–1940) Former adjutant to both Prince HEINRICH and WILHELM II, appointed chief of the Kaiser's naval cabinet from 1908. All naval business went through Müller before reaching Wilhelm, enabling the former to regulate policy. Strongly against any major confrontation between the German HIGH SEAS FLEET and the ROYAL NAVY, Müller was also a powerful influence against the extension of SUBMARINE WARFARE, earning the deep distrust of TIRPITZ and other like-minded admirals but retaining the ear of the Kaiser. When Wilhelm authorized unrestricted submarine attacks in January 1917, Müller changed his mind and set about persuading chancellor BETHMANN HOLLWEG to do the same. Few naval colleagues were convinced by the volte-face, and Müller was increasingly marginalized under the THIRD SUPREME COMMAND. He was retired when the GERMAN NAVY was reorganized under SCHEER's Supreme Naval Command in August 1918, but his replacement by TROTHA had not become effective when the command system disintegrated under revolutionary pressure in late October (see KIEL MUTINY).

Murdoch, Keith (1885–1952) Australian journalist given permission to visit ANZAC COVE on the GALLIPOLI FRONT in August 1915. Allied press coverage of the campaign had been strictly limited, and criticisms of its management by the few correspondents on the peninsula were rigidly censored. On his arrival, Murdoch was briefed by Ellis Ashmead-Bartlett, one of only two British reporters at Gallipoli. Ashmead-Bartlett filled Murdoch in on the facts behind persistent rumours of discontent and gave him a letter for British prime minister ASQUITH, but was overheard by the other British reporter, Henry Nevinson, who arranged for its seizure by French police at Marseilles. An outraged Murdoch wrote his own letter to Australian premier Fisher, a passionate rendering of Ashmead-Bartlett's views that reached Asquith and the British cabinet. Ashmead-Bartlett was recalled to London, and both he and Murdoch received powerful support from newspaper magnate Lord NORTHCLIFFE in a press campaign that helped bring about Gallipoli C-in-C HAMILTON's dismissal and the eventual Allied evacuation of the theatre.

Murray, General Sir Archibald (1860–1945) British staff officer who relinquished a divisional command in August 1914 to become chief of staff to BEF commander Sir John FRENCH. Regarded as a strictly conventional soldier, Murray proved a nervous assistant to an irresolute commander, suffering a stress-related breakdown and being replaced by ROBERTSON in early 1915. Rising from deputy to chief of the Imperial General Staff (CIGS) in September, Murray was again replaced by Robertson in December and given command of frontline imperial forces in PALESTINE, becoming British C-in-C in the Middle East from March 1916. He advanced slowly east of Sinai until halted in two attempts to take GAZA during early 1917. Relieved by ALLENBY in June, he was retained in home commands until his retirement in 1922.

Mussolini, Benito (1883–1945) Italian political agitator and journalist who resigned from the Socialist Party in 1915 over its opposition to war with AUSTRIA-HUNGARY. Joining the Italian Army, he was wounded at the ISONZO before returning to edit the Milan newspaper *Il Popolo d'Italia*. One of a number of extreme nationalist demagogues demanding Italian territorial expansion and suppression of anti-War elements, his wartime influence never rivalled that of Gabriele D'ANNUNZIO, the main inspiration behind the formation of the Fascist movement in March 1919. Mussolini's wartime activities were highly mythologized during and after his ascent to dictatorship over ITALY in the 1920s, and many histories written before 1940 share an exaggerated view of their importance.

Mutinies Most wartime armies and navies experienced some form of mutinous reaction as war weariness eroded the fighting enthusiasm displayed by belligerent populations when they joined the War, but the nature, scale and timing of such outbursts depended on a combination of social and military circumstances. Most cases of disobedience, mass desertion or refusal to fight were primarily attributable to simple discontent within conscript armies that were ill-led, ill-supplied, required to serve in appalling physical conditions and exposed to long periods of boredom punctuated by costly actions; but several comprehensive mutinies among ground forces took place against a backdrop of socioeconomic collapse at home.

The disintegration of the imperial RUSSIAN ARMY in 1917 was fuelled by terrible physical conditions, military failure and a chronic shortage of competent NCOs and officers, but also by the flow of PACIFIST and anti-monarchist PROPAGANDA from turbulent Russian cities. Events that took place in remote EASTERN or CAUCASIAN FRONT locations amid generalized communications chaos defy detailed reporting, but literally hundreds of formations killed or dismissed their officers after the FEBRUARY REVOLUTION. Many continued in service under the joint control of elected officers and soldiers' SOVIETS, but morale evaporated during the failed KERENSKI OFFENSIVE of July 1917 and the Army had effectively collapsed before the OCTOBER REVOLUTION.

Non-German-speaking units within the multiracial AUSTRO-HUNGARIAN ARMY, especially Polish, Czech and South Slav troops, were never considered entirely reliable by many of its officers, most of whom were Austrian Germans. Despite occasional well-publicized episodes, such as the defection of the entire 29th (Prague) Infantry in April 1915, the Army's integrity held up better than expected until the BRUSILOV OFFENSIVE of summer 1916, when mass desertions among Czech and Ruthene formations contributed to catastrophic Austro-Hungarian defeats. Nationalist agitation on the home front and frontline war weariness combined to erode further the loyalty of minority populations through 1917 and 1918, so that few reliable units remained in imperial service by the end of the War.

The TURKISH ARMY collapsed in similar circumstances. The ARAB REVOLT in the southern Ottoman Empire had prompted the defection of many Arab officers and entire CAVALRY units in 1916, but military defeat and the breakdown of supply systems produced a more general (and largely apolitical) reaction from late 1917. Weary, disillusioned, ill-fed and with no hope of victory, Turkish forces in PALESTINE and elsewhere voted for peace with their feet in 1918, and an estimated half a million troops had deserted by the time it came in October.

Large-scale mutinies also broke out in the FRENCH and ITALIAN ARMIES during 1917. More than fifty French divisions on the WESTERN FRONT took part in unauthorized demonstrations of varying intensity after the failed NIVELLE OFFENSIVE of the spring, most simply refusing to go back into the line (see FRENCH ARMY MUTINY), and parts of the Italian Second Army surrendered without a fight at CAPORETTO later that year. Although Allied authorities tended to blame pacifist (and specifically Bolshevik) propaganda for promoting rebellion, mutinous troops in both armies were primarily concerned with immediate matters of personnel safety and comfort, and morale recovered when conditions improved and victory again appeared possible.

The GERMAN ARMY was virtually immune from mutiny of any sort until the Allied counteroffensives in France of August 1918, after which some units refused to fight or deserted during the long retreat east. That much of the Army remained loyal and disciplined until the end, despite desperate supply shortages, rampant INFLUENZA and political disintegration in GERMANY, reflected the unsurpassed quality of its training and organizational methods, as well as a deep reserve of self-belief in a force accustomed to victory wherever it was committed in strength.

Small-scale outbursts of misbehaviour and riotous disturbance were rife within the wartime BRITISH ARMY, especially among AUSTRALIAN and NEW ZEALAND FORCES, but most chronicled episodes were euphemistically described by authorities as 'loyal indiscipline'. The only incident around the main battlefronts to be officially categorized as mutiny was an outbreak of generalized rioting at Étaples during September 1917. Triggered by poor conditions at a local training camp, it lasted for four days and resulted in one execution. Strenuous attempts by German and Turkish propaganda agencies to incite rebellion among Muslim troops in British service were responsible for the short-lived SINGAPORE MUTINY in 1915, but were otherwise conspicuously unsuccessful. The absence of any more serious British mutiny is difficult to explain fully, but the fact that imperial troops were all deployed overseas acted as a major disincentive to desertion and diluted the effects of pacifist agitation, while belief in the possibility of ultimate victory was again an important stimulus to sustained loyalty.

Wretched conditions and the expectation of defeat were primarily responsible for the mass desertions and surrenders suffered by the ROMANIAN ARMY in late 1916, and the BULGARIAN ARMY in 1918, but morale within the SERBIAN and BELGIAN ARMIES was bolstered by a sense of acute national crisis. Belgian forces were additionally protected from the worst effects of war weariness by King ALBERT I's refusal to take part in costly Allied offensives on the Western Front. The American Expeditionary Force (AEF) was still relatively fresh (and flushed with a series of hard-earned victories) when the War ended.

The combined pressures of long-term inactivity, spartan conditions, rigidly applied discipline and political events at home brought unrest to the GERMAN, AUSTRO-HUNGARIAN and RUSSIAN NAVIES during the War's latter stages. The neglected warships of the German HIGH SEAS FLEET were fertile ground for discontent after their withdrawal from North Sea operations in 1916, and the first major disturbances among crews broke out at Wilhelmshaven on 31 July 1917. Triggered by the cancellation of stokers' leave aboard the KAISER Class dreadnought *Prinz Regent Luitpold*, it was quickly suppressed, but prompted sufficient improvement in conditions to prevent further trouble until October 1918, when the much more serious KIEL MUTINY erupted in response to the High Command's attempt to send the fleet on a last suicide mission.

Events at Kiel played a major role in the escalation of GERMAN REVOLUTIONS in November 1918, but the CATTARO MUTINY by Czech nationalist sailors in February 1918 was relatively marginal to the wider picture of Austro-Hungarian collapse, while the Russian BALTIC and BLACK SEA fleets generally retained loyalty and discipline for longer than the Army. Although the crews of Russian Navy warships formed soviets and refused to serve under unpopular officers in 1917, they remained a disciplined operational force until after the October Revolution. Despite subsequent desertions, and an armed uprising by sailors protesting about poor conditions at Sevastopol in 1918, the imperial Navy's disintegration was a side effect of the RUSSIAN CIVIL WAR rather than a series of mutinies, with most ships and their crews opting to fight for one side or the other.

N

Nahr-Al-Kalek, Battle of The effective destruction of Turkish river forces on the Tigris by the ROYAL NAVY gunboats *Tarantula, Mantis* and *Moth*, which accidentally outran British ground forces on 26 February 1917, after the Second Battle of KUT. About 30km beyond the town they were attacked by four Turkish ships, including the captured British MONITOR *Firefly*, at Nahr-Al-Kalek. They sank three in a gunnery duel, recovered *Firefly* intact, and captured several hundred infantry on the shore, but ground troops were too far behind to capitalize on the delays caused to the Turkish retreat. See also: MESOPOTAMIAN FRONT.

Namur Fortress city at the junction of the Rivers Sambre and Meuse in southeast Belgium (see MAP 4). Like LIÈGE to the northeast, it had been surrounded in the 1880s by a ring of elaborate forts, designed to combine with infantry to hold the rivers against invasion from any direction. After Liège fell on 16 August, the German Second and Third Armies advanced on Namur. Despite a garrison low on morale and ammunition, the forts were expected to hold out at least until the French Fifth Army, stationed across the Sambre to the southwest, could make contact with the Belgian 4th Division inside the city itself.

General von BÜLOW's Second Army arrived first, and its ARTILLERY began firing on the forts on 21 August. A special force under General von GALLWITZ was detailed to invest the city while the bulk of the Army attacked the French around CHARLEROI, and only one regiment of French troops reached Namur, bringing its total defensive strength up to about 37,000, against never less than 107,000 attackers. Massive German BIG BERTHA and SCHLANKE EMMA siege guns repeated their destruction of the forts at Liège, and by 23 August the Namur forts were close to collapse. Belgian forces evacuated the city that morning, and German troops entered the city the same night, encouraging a French retreat from the Sambre. See also: Invasion of BELGIUM.

Narev, Battle of the Attack into northeast Poland from East Prussia by the German Army Group GALLWITZ, part of the TRIPLE OFFENSIVE on the EASTERN FRONT in summer 1915. After a precise four-hour PRELIMINARY BOMBARDMENT by more than 1,000 guns on 13 July, 20 German divisions (about 200,000 men) attacked southeast towards the River Narev, about 40km north of Warsaw. The main German advance in the centre, by 11 divisions concentrated along a 40km front, struck at 7 weak Russian divisions with less than 200 guns, holding shallow TRENCHES at the join between the First (Litvinov) and Twelfth (Churin) Armies.

Scattered by the bombardment, poorly coordinated by the two generals and with no reserves, the Russian defenders fled, losing 70,000 men in two days and allowing Gallwitz to advance some 10km into a gap between the two armies. Regional commander ALEXEEV withdrew Russian forces to the Narev, where belated reinforcements from the central Polish front held the German advance, restricting it to a bridgehead at the north of the line and counterattacking elsewhere.

Under pressure from the simultaneous BUG and KURLAND OFFENSIVES, STAVKA (Russian central command) ordered a general withdrawal from forward positions in Poland on 22 July. Alexeev pulled the Narev armies further east, leaving Warsaw undefended and only the fortress of NOVOGEORGIEVSK as an obstacle to pursuit. The 'GREAT RETREAT' eventually brought the Narev armies into Russia itself, along a line north of the Pripet Marshes. See MAP 10.

Naroch, Battle of Lake Major Russian attack from positions east of VILNIUS, on the northern sector of the EASTERN FRONT, in March 1916. Virtually forced on RUSSIAN ARMY chief of staff ALEXEEV by the CHANTILLY agreement to support any threatened ally indirectly, it was triggered by a French appeal for help at the start of the VERDUN offensive on the WESTERN FRONT.

Withdrawals to other fronts had left just over 1 million German and Austro-Hungarian troops facing 1.5 million Russians on the Eastern Front by early 1916, and Alexeev chose to attack in the north where the disparity was greatest. General KUROPATKIN's Northern Army Group was detailed to drive from the northeast towards Vilnius, but the main attack was planned from the line east of the city, where General Smirnov's Second Army (part of EVERT's Western Army Group) was built up to a strength of 350,000 men and almost 1,000 guns, against the 75,000 men and 400 guns of the German Tenth Army (EICHHORN).

Evert's staff planned a BREAKTHROUGH operation, massing men and ARTILLERY along a 2km stretch to the north of the Second Army's front for a concentrated blow by 100,000 men under General Pleshkov. An imitation of German tactics in 1915, made possible by the rapid increase in RUSSIA's munitions output, the attack was particularly ill-prepared, lacking detailed reconnaissance, effective supply systems or provision for rapid deployment of reserves. Smirnov was replaced at the last moment, and General Ragoza held overall control when the offensive began with a notoriously inaccurate PRELIMINARY BOMBARDMENT on 18 March.

Infantry attacks began later that day, but closely bunched Russian troops made excellent targets for forewarned German artillery and Pleshkov lost 15,000 men in the first few hours. Weight of numbers enabled the Russians to overrun forward German TRENCHES, but attackers were vulnerable on either side of their small SALIENT and driven back before support could arrive. Further attacks on 19 and 21 March suffered similarly in a thaw-induced mudbath.

Elsewhere, the planned advance from Kuropatkin's front around Riga, begun on 21 March, was halted within a day with 10,000 losses, and the Second Army's central group failed to attack at all. The only small success came in the south of the Second Army's front, where three corps under General Baluyev advanced a few kilometres along the shores of Lake Naroch in thick fog.

Baluyev and Pleshkov repeated their attacks to no effect for a few more days, and artillery duelling continued until late April, when German counterattacks retook what little ground had been lost. The battle cost the Russian Army more than 110,000 men, and failed to divert German strength from the Western Front. German losses were about 20,000. See also: BRUSILOV OFFENSIVE; MAP 10.

Nasiriyeh, Battle of The second part of General NIXON's summer offensive on the MESOPOTAMIAN FRONT in 1915 (see AMARA), an attack up the inundated banks of the Euphrates towards the main Turkish supply base of Nasiriyeh (see MAP 23). The operation, conducted in floods and searing heat, began with the capture of forward Turkish positions by an British brigade on 5 July. Commander General Gorringe awaited reinforcement from another brigade before attacking a second line on 13 July, when infantry advancing along the narrow sandbars of the east bank were ambushed by local tribesmen and forced to withdraw. With more than half his troops sick, Gorringe called up further reserves of infantry and ARTILLERY before launching an attack up the other bank on 24 July. Active strength on each side was about 5,000 men, but superior artillery strength and reconnaissance from a single British aircraft helped Indian troops storm Turkish trenches by late afternoon. Both sides suffered about 500 casualties, but the British captured over 1,000 prisoners and 15 guns as the remaining defenders fled. Turkish forces immediately abandoned Nasiriyeh, retiring to KUT and leaving the whole of southern Mesopotamia under Anglo-Indian control.

Naval Africa Expedition Bizarre British operation designed to ensure naval control over AFRICA's second largest lake, Lake Tanganyika. The Belgian Congo and German EAST AFRICA faced each other across the Lake, 675km from north to south but only 15–50km wide. A small portion of its southwestern shore was inside British Northern Rhodesia (see MAP 18).

Two small armed steamers ensured German control on the outbreak of European war, sinking the only Belgian ship large enough to carry armament on 22 August 1914. This provoked Belgium into abandoning its policy of neutrality in Africa (see BERLIN ACT), and prompted Belgian fears of an uprising by pro-German tribes in the Congo coastal region.

Acting on a proposal by local British prospector John Lee, the ROYAL NAVY (which possessed no charts for the area) authorized the Naval Africa Expedition to capture the Lake in April 1915. Two 12-metre launches were adapted to take 3-pounder guns and sent to Cape Town on a civilian liner. The boats reached Elizabethville (modern Lubumbashi), capital of the Belgian Congo's Katanga province, by RAILWAY on 26 July, still some 650km from their destination. Hauled overland, they reached Lukuga (halfway up the Lake's western coast) in late October, but were hidden from alerted German patrols until 26 December, when they damaged and captured the smaller German gunboat.

Expedition commander Spicer-Simson's habits of wearing a European woman's skirt and displaying his tattoos to awestruck natives brought him great local fame, and regional tribes abandoned pro-German sympathies in his favour. His strictly military strength was augmented in early 1916 by a few SHORT 827 seaplanes, sent in crates, and three old Belgian ships were also armed. This fleet combined to destroy the larger German steamer on 9 February, but a third German ship, armed with a 105mm gun rescued from the RUFUGI DELTA, had been launched on the Lake in June 1915.

Ignoring it, Spicer-Simson sailed his flotilla to the southwestern end of the Lake in May to assist RHODESIAN FORCES attacking Bismarckburg, which fell on 8 June 1916. After failing to intervene or prevent the garrison's escape, an emotional Spicer-Simson suddenly invalided himself home. Naval activity on Lake Tanganyika subsided with his departure, and Spicer-Simson created heroic legends about the Expedition that were subsequently accepted by popular British accounts. The Royal Navy heard testimony from other Expedition members (all 28 returned alive) and Spicer-Simson never received another active command.

Naval Warfare Naval power exerted a multilayered influence on the conduct and outcome of the First World War. In its most broadly strategic application, it offered control of maritime communications in any given theatre, enabling free movement of supply and military strength but denying the same to any hostile power. In 1914 this capacity to enforce and evade BLOCKADE was considered of primary importance, but was perceived as dependent on the possession of unchallenged superiority in major warships.

Apart from ships specifically dedicated to the long-range protection or destruction of non-military maritime traffic (CRUISERS), warship superiority was expressed in battlefleets, based around squadrons of heavily armed modern BATTLESHIPS, themselves protected at sea by flotillas of DESTROYERS and light cruisers. The battlefleet's primary task was to destroy, or at least neutralize, hostile battlefleets, with control of sea traffic in any theatre passing to whoever won the presumed decisive confrontation between fleets.

The battlefleet had been developed by the ROYAL NAVY, by far the world's largest and effectively the index of contemporary naval power. Charged with protecting the massive maritime communication network of the British Empire, and with effectively blockading any potential enemies, it maintained battlefleet capability greater than the next two largest forces combined, as well as secondary fleets at imperial bases all over the world.

Unchallenged since the Napoleonic era, Britain's battleship dominance was threatened on two fronts by the turn of the century. New, cheap weapons – torpedoes carried by fast TORPEDO BOATS or invisible SUBMARINES, and MINES laid by auxiliaries – could sink the biggest contemporary warships. At the same time the GERMAN NAVY began a rapid expansion that could only be directed against British domination of the North Sea. The British response, led by Admiral FISHER, was to embark on a massive upgrading of the battlefleet. The British *DREADNOUGHT*, completed in late 1906, was an entirely new type of battleship, and the first of more than 30 built for the Royal Navy over the next decade.

Fast, powerful and hugely expensive, dreadnoughts (including BATTLECRUISERS) were the prime naval currency in 1914. Germany built as many as possible but was outpaced by Britain; the AUSTRO-HUNGARIAN, ITALIAN and FRENCH NAVIES conducted a local race of their own in the MEDITERRANEAN, which ended in an approximate draw in 1915; the US and JAPANESE NAVIES expressed nascent Pacific rivalry in dreadnoughts; after defeat by the Japanese in 1904, the RUSSIAN NAVY built them for its European fleets; the BRAZILIAN NAVY ensured regional dominance by purchasing two dreadnoughts from British yards; and two more British-built dreadnoughts ordered by the TURKISH NAVY were almost complete in mid-1914.

Giant battleships proved to be the great military white elephants of the age. Held in mutually deterrent stand-off in all theatres by fear of smaller weapons, they fought only one (indecisive) major battle, at JUTLAND in 1916. The real naval battles were fought by light forces, mining or supporting coastal ground forces, by submarines against Allied commerce, and by obsolete fleet vessels in the DARDANELLES or on trade routes all over the world.

Most technical developments reflected this trend, with ANTI-SUBMARINE techniques making spectacular progress, along with submarine design and the development of naval aviation, pioneered almost exclusively by the wartime RNAS. The most ingenious technical work was carried out by Italian light forces, whose BARCHINI SALTATORI were the most extraordinary military craft of the period. Perhaps the most bizarre wartime naval operation was the British NAVAL AFRICA EXPEDITION's occupation of remote Lake Tanganyika in 1915. See: MEDITERRANEAN, BALTIC and BLACK SEAS; *HANDELSKRIEG*; SUBMARINE WARFARE; ARCTIC THEATRE; AIRCRAFT CARRIERS.

Nek, Battle of the See: Battle of SARI BAIR.

Neuilly, Treaty of Peace signed between the Allied powers and BULGARIA on 27 November 1919, which gave western Thrace to GREECE, the Dobrudja region to ROMANIA, and adjusted the new frontier with YUGOSLAVIA. The relatively mild territorial penalties reflected Anglo-French desire to maintain stability in the Balkans, but Bulgaria was required to pay REPARATIONS and limit its army to 20,000 men. See PARIS PEACE CONFERENCE; MAP 25.

Neuve Chapelle, Battle of British attack on the WESTERN FRONT, north of La Bassée and west of Lille, intended as part of a major Allied offensive in the Artois region in March 1915 (see MAP 2). French C-in-C JOFFRE's plan to repeat his first long offensive in CHAMPAGNE with an Anglo-French attack was postponed when British reinforcements intended to relieve two French corps around YPRES were delayed by plans for a landing on GALLIPOLI. As a demonstration of British offensive capabilities, BEF commander Sir John FRENCH elected to go ahead with his part of the scheme.

Targeted initially at the village of Neuve Chapelle, the aim of the attack was to capture the heights of Aubers Ridge and to threaten German-held Lille. Four divisions of General HAIG's First Army advanced along a 3km front on the morning of 10 March. Well-coordinated attacks quickly broke through a line held by a single division of the German Sixth Army and captured the village.

Once breakthrough had been achieved, the British experienced the coordination and supply problems that plagued attackers on both sides of the Western Front until 1918. As the BEF became bogged down, Crown Prince RUPPRECHT rushed reserves to the front and counterattacked. Though the British held the ground they had gained, attempts at further advance towards Aubers were abandoned on 13 March. At a cost of about 13,000 casualties (and 15 per cent of all its ammunition) the BEF had gained 2 square kilometres of land

and inflicted similar losses on the German Sixth Army. See also: Second Battle of YPRES; ARTOIS OFFENSIVE.

New York Commissioned into the US NAVY in 1913 and completed the following year, *New York* and her sister ship *Texas* were well-armoured BATTLESHIPS and the first US vessels equipped with 14-inch main guns. Their crowded secondary armament proved difficult to handle in rough weather, and both had five of their 5-inch guns removed during 1918. As flagship of the 4th Dreadnought Squadron, *New York* became part of the British GRAND FLEET's 6th Battle Squadron from December 1917, and *Texas* joined the same unit early in 1918. Both ships were present at the surrender of the German HIGH SEAS FLEET in November. Extensively refitted in the 1920s, they remained in frontline service until the end of the Second World War.

BRIEF DATA (*New York*, 1917) Displacement: 27,000 tons; Speed: 21k; Crew: 865; Armament: 10 × 14in gun, 21 × 5in, 4 × 3pdr, 2 × 1pdr, 4 × 21in TT.

New Zealand New Zealand and outlying dependent islands were governed in 1914 as an autonomous Dominion of the British Empire. A national assembly was elected by universal adult suffrage, although WOMEN were not allowed to hold seats, and the majority party's representatives formed a cabinet technically appointed by the governor on behalf of the British crown.

A total population of just over 1.1 million (1916) – including about 50,000 Maoris and some 250,000 British-born citizens – shared the enthusiasm of the main Liberal and Reform Parties in supporting the British war effort. Reform leader William Massey was re-elected as premier with a tiny majority in December 1914, after a campaign fought on issues of war management rather than participation, and in August 1915 he formed a coalition National Government with Sir Joseph Ward's Liberals.

Boycotted by the small socialist party and never particularly popular, the National Government remained in power through uncontested 1917 elections. Both Massey and Ward were in London with the Imperial War Cabinet from 1916, and internal management devolved largely upon defence minister Allen. Basic manpower shortages had slowed volunteer recruitment to NEW ZEALAND FORCES by mid-1916, and Allen introduced conscription from August. Generally accepted without protest, it was cited as a grievance in the miners' strike of April 1917, but no other serious political disturbance occurred until the Liberals left the coalition in August 1919. A Reform government was confirmed at subsequent elections.

Increased demand for New Zealand's main exports, wool and refrigerated meat, was offset by shrinking shipping space, prompting European customers to favour shorter transatlantic supply routes. Release of merchant shipping from emergency duties in 1919 brought a massive export boom, but wartime exports generally remained steady around the levels achieved in 1913, when New Zealand had the highest per capita trade volume in the world.

Conspicuous commitment to British interests, proportionally greater than the more celebrated contribution made by AUSTRALIA, earned New Zealand a share in the wider national recognition granted postwar white British dominions (see BORDEN, R.), and wartime occupation of German (Western) Samoa was formalized as a MANDATE.

New Zealand An INDEFATIGABLE Class BATTLECRUISER built in GREAT BRITAIN for the ROYAL NAVY but paid for by the government of NEW ZEALAND. Completed in January 1912 it remained in Europe and served with the GRAND FLEET, coming through the battles of HELIGOLAND BIGHT, the DOGGER BANK and JUTLAND without serious damage. *New Zealand* undertook a tour of British overseas dominions before retiring in 1921.

BRIEF DATA (1917) As for *Indefatigable* except – Armament: 8 × 12in gun, 10 × 4in, 1 × 4in AA; 2 × 21in TT.

New Zealand Forces All able-bodied New Zealand males received some military training from age 12 in peacetime. Since 1911 adults under 25 had formed a part-time national militia, the Territorial Army, organized by a permanent strength of about 600 men, and some 25,000 Territorials became the nucleus of new volunteer regiments established for imperial service overseas from August 1914. The first New Zealand troops left the country almost immediately, occupying the German Pacific islands of Western Samoa without meeting resistance.

The New Zealand Expeditionary Force (NZEF) for imperial service in Europe, commanded throughout the War by General Godley, left with AUSTRALIAN FORCES in October, and subsequent departures were coordinated with Australian arrangements. More than 124,000 New Zealanders eventually joined the Army, of whom over 100,000 served overseas, almost 10 per cent of the population. As well as infantry, ARTILLERY and CAVALRY (manned by expert rural horsemen), NZEF units included a MACHINE GUN corps, a cyclist battalion and a Maori Contingent, the latter formed in 1914 and subsequently in action as the New Zealand (Maori) Pioneer Battalion. Equipment and uniforms (details apart) were essentially the same as those of the BRITISH ARMY.

Mixed with Australian troops in the ANZAC during initial operations in EGYPT and on the GALLIPOLI FRONT, NZEF units were reorganized as the New Zealand Division in February 1916 but still fought alongside Australians and were indistinguishable from them in terms of combat record on the WESTERN FRONT and in PALESTINE. Only the tendency of most opponents to mistake them for Australians prevented NZEF troops from gaining a comparable international reputation. The intensity of fighting endured by the NZEF was reflected in total casualties of almost 58,000, including 17,000 dead.

The New Zealand Navy had been formally established as an independent force in 1913, on condition of its immediate release to imperial control (as the New Zealand Division) in time of war. In 1914 its strength amounted to three old 'protected' CRUISERS and a few TORPEDO BOATS, which remained in the southern oceans for regional defence. The Navy's main weapon was a BATTLECRUISER, for which the government had paid Britain £1.5 million. Lent to the GRAND FLEET as soon as it was completed in 1912, *NEW ZEALAND* served in European waters throughout the War.

Newfoundland Modern Canadian province that was a separate British colony until 1949, ruled by an appointed governor with an elected representative assembly. Newfoundland declared war alongside GREAT BRITAIN in August 1914, without opposition from the population (about 250,000) or assembly, and 500 Newfoundlanders sailed with CANADIAN FORCES to Europe. Some 6,500 men served in the wartime Newfoundland Regiment, which saw action at GALLIPOLI and on the WESTERN FRONT, suffering just over 2,000 fatalities. About 2,000 Newfoundlanders also served in the ROYAL NAVY through the Newfoundland Naval Service, and a further 500 transported their professional skills to Scotland as a forestry battalion.

Nicaragua Typical of contemporary Central American republics, Nicaragua was economically dependent on the UNITED STATES and suffered from chronic internal disorder. A virtual client-state since the landing of US Marines in 1912, it declared war against GERMANY on 8 May 1917, but the 400-man Nicaraguan Army played no active role.

Nicholas II, Tsar (1868–1918) Ruler of the Russian Empire since 1894 and an autocrat until the revolution of 1905, Nicholas subsequently governed through a fragile parliamentary system. Narrowly educated and denied political responsibility until the sudden death of his father, Nicholas was stubborn, gullible, prone to long periods of apathy, and unconcerned with constitutional or social reform. Increasingly dominated by the Empress ALEXANDRA, but frequently swayed by attentive courtiers, his main interests were dynastic and his policies, such as they were, aimed at passing an undamaged inheritance to his only son.

Persuaded that earlier social upheavals, particularly the revolution of 1905, had been the superficial work of fanatics, the Tsar retreated from liberal concessions into a period of political repression before 1914, oblivious to a renewal of urban tensions accompanying rapid industrial growth. His technically absolute control over foreign policy was in practice minimal, and his attempts at personal diplomacy invariably clumsy. Appalled but impotent during the JULY CRISIS in 1914, he followed the advice of foreign minister SAZONOV and military authorities in committing RUSSIA to war.

Nicholas enjoyed united support from the political establishment after August 1914, but the crown's position was steadily eroded as economic ineptitude and political insensitivity were matched by major military defeats from 1915. The Tsar's brief flirtation with liberal politicians during the summer of 1915 ultimately worsened relations with the Duma (the elected assembly) when he reversed into reaction in September, and his decision earlier that month to take direct command of the RUSSIAN ARMY at STAVKA (central command) linked him personally to its continued failures. His absence from the capital, Petrograd (St Petersburg), allowed his wife and her equally unpopular right-wing entourage to dominate court affairs and exercise a strong influence on appointments.

By late 1916 royalist elements in the Duma were warning Nicholas of imminent revolution from below, but he refused to contemplate constitutional reform. During the 1917 FEBRUARY REVOLUTION, which he misinterpreted from Stavka as a minor rising, his routine suppression orders to the Petrograd garrison on 10 March sparked its mutiny. Nicholas only abandoned plans to return to the capital when the Army high command recommended abdication on 13 March, and he renounced the throne two days later. The monarchy ended when the throne was declined next day by his brother, Grand Duke Michael.

The Tsar and his immediate family were arrested, but negotiations to secure a place of overseas exile were slowed by the PROVISIONAL GOVERNMENT's reluctance to allow Nicholas to become a focus for overseas opposition, and ended by the reluctance of Britain and France to accept them. The family was moved to the remote Siberian city of Ekaterinburg (Yekaterinburg) just before the OCTOBER REVOLUTION, and was executed by Bolsheviks in July 1918.

Niemen, Battle of the See: First Battle of the MASURIAN LAKES.

Nieuport 10 The first of many French Nieuport biplanes to enter wartime production. Sporting the distinctive V-shaped wing struts common to most Nieuports, it entered service with the AÉRONAUTIQUE MILITAIRE on the WESTERN FRONT in summer 1915, and also flew for the RNAS in the MEDITERRANEAN. Originally unarmed, it was built in two reconnaissance versions – the pilot occupying the back seat in the AR and the front in the AV – but later models were fitted with a fixed, upward-firing MACHINE GUN so that they could be used as improvised single-seat FIGHTERS, reflecting an Allied shortage of air combat machines. A few were built under licence in Italy and used by the ITALIAN AIR FORCE in 1915, but the type was replaced everywhere once purpose-designed fighters were available.

BRIEF DATA (10) Type: two-seat reconnaissance; Engine: 80hp Gnôme or Le Rhône; Max speed: 140kph; Ceiling: 4,000m; Armament: 1 × 0.303in mg.

Nieuport 11 Successful French fighter, an agile machine developed from a racing design and in Allied service from summer 1915. First in action with the RNAS at the DARDANELLES and on the WESTERN FRONT, it joined French AÉRONAUTIQUE MILITAIRE squadrons from the early autumn. In partnership with the British AIRCO DH-4, and despite lacking INTERRUPTER GEAR for its forward MACHINE GUN, it gained combat superiority over German FOKKER E-TYPES during 1916, most notably in the air battles around VERDUN. Its greatest failing was a structural weakness of the lower wing struts, which occasionally broke in mid-air with fatal consequences. Built in large (but indefinite) numbers by French concerns, Nieuport 11s were withdrawn from the Western Front as obsolete in early 1917, but 836 machines were built under licence in Italy and remained the standard fighters of the ITALIAN AIR FORCE until replaced by HANRIOT HD-1s in the autumn. The type was also operated by the BELGIAN and RUSSIAN AIR SERVICES.

BRIEF DATA (Italian model) Type: single-seat fighter; Engine: 80hp Le Rhône; Max speed: 155kph; Ceiling: 5,450m; Armament: 1 × 0.303in mg.

Nieuport 12 French reconnaissance biplane, an enlarged version of the earlier NIEUPORT 10, with a rear-firing MACHINE GUN fitted as standard and another added for the pilot once INTERRUPTER GEAR became available. In WESTERN FRONT service from mid-1915 with the French AÉRONAUTIQUE MILITAIRE and both British air arms, it was often used as an emergency single-seat FIGHTER and performed occasional light-bombing missions. British RNAS models also operated as fighters off GALLIPOLI. Although later examples mounted a 130hp engine, they were outperformed by new types introduced from early 1916 and were withdrawn from the Western Front that year, although a few served elsewhere with the RFC into 1917.

BRIEF DATA (12) Type: two-seat armed reconnaissance/fighter; Engine: 110hp Clerget; Max speed: 157kph; Ceiling: 3,400m; Armament: 1 or 2 × 0.303in mg.

Nieuport 16 A more powerful version of the NIEUPORT 11, with a synchronized MACHINE GUN that tended to cause nosedive if the engine cut out. Operating in small numbers on the WESTERN FRONT with both the AÉRONAUTIQUE MILITAIRE and the RFC during 1916, it was also used for reconnaissance work, and a few were fitted with LE PRIEUR ROCKETS.

BRIEF DATA Type: single-seat fighter; Engine: 110hp Le Rhône; Max speed: 166kph; Armament: 1 × 0.303in mg.

Nieuport 17 French biplane FIGHTER, a larger and more powerful development of the NIEUPORT 11, that was one of the most successful and enduring warplanes of the period. First flown in early 1916, and in action on the WESTERN FRONT from March, it proved too nimble and climbed too quickly for contemporary German HALBERSTADT D-TYPES. Important to the Allied air operation over the SOMME from late June, it was matched with the arrival of the first ALBATROS D-TYPES in September but remained standard equipment with AÉRONAUTIQUE MILITAIRE squadrons until the late summer of 1917. Nieuport 17s were also employed by the BELGIAN AIR SERVICE, and adopted in numbers by the RFC and RNAS once it became clear in autumn 1916 that no new British designs were imminent. Apart from unknown numbers produced in France, they were built under licence in ITALY and RUSSIA, seeing widespread service with both air arms.

Early machines had only a high-firing forward MACHINE GUN, soon replaced or supplemented by a synchronized weapon, and LE PRIEUR ROCKETS could be fitted for attacks on BALLOONS. Some later models, designated 17bis, were given a 130hp Clerget engine, and a two-seat trainer version (the Nieuport 21) was used in France, in Russia and by the USAAS, which purchased 200 (along with 75 single-seaters for advanced training). See also: ACES.

BRIEF DATA (17) Type: single-seat fighter; Engine: 110hp Le Rhône; Max speed: 171kph; Ceiling: 5,250m; Armament: 1 or 2 × 0.303in mg.

Nieuport 24 Biplane FIGHTER, a more powerful and streamlined development of the successful NIEUPORT 17 design, that was almost obsolete when it entered French service on the WESTERN FRONT in mid-1917. Most French models were withdrawn to training duties during the summer (although some were retained as a matter of pilot preference), and the USAAS purchased 261 surplus machines as trainers in November 1917. The British RFC and RNAS made greater use of the machine, keeping it in service on the Western, PALESTINE and MESOPOTAMIAN FRONTS well into 1918. The 50 machines built under licence in Britain generally mounted a second (high-firing) MACHINE GUN.

BRIEF DATA (French) Type: single-seat fighter; Engine: 130hp Le Rhône; Max speed: 186kph; Ceiling: 5,500m; Armament: 1 or 2 × 0.303in mg.

Nieuport 27 The limitations of the basic Nieuport 'V-strutter' FIGHTER design were emphasized in its final incarnation, the Nieuport 27. Supplied to French, British and Italian forces during the second half of 1917 and early 1918, it failed to out-perform the NIEUPORT 24 and was outclassed by modern fighters on both sides. Never employed in large numbers on active service, it was used most extensively by the USAAS, which purchased 287 machines as trainers.

BRIEF DATA Type: single-seat fighter; Engine: 120hp Le Rhône; Max speed: 186kph; Ceiling: 5,500m; Armament: 1 or 2 × 0.303in mg.

Nieuport 28 A radical departure from previous Nieuport designs, with rounded wings, a conventional strutting system and a more slender fuselage, the 28 was used in very small numbers by the French AÉRONAUTIQUE MILITAIRE, which had better FIGHTERS available, but the USAAS purchased 297 machines from March 1918. They equipped the first US squadrons active on the WESTERN FRONT but were far from popular with pilots, suffering from a dangerous tendency to lose wing fabric in steep dives. The fault had been corrected by July, but US squadrons were already receiving superior SPAD S-XIII fighters.

BRIEF DATA Type: single-seat fighter; Engine: 160hp Gnôme Monosoupape; Max speed: 205kph; Ceiling: 6,050m; Armament: 2 × 0.303in mg (forward).

Nikolai, Grand Duke (1856–1929) Uncle of Tsar NICHOLAS II and the leading opponent of war minister SUKHOMLINOV's reform programme before 1914. An impressive physical figure and RUSSIA's best-known soldier, he was mistrusted as a rival for popular affection by the Empress ALEXANDRA, and his appointment as C-in-C of Russian forces in August 1914 reflected the job's drawbacks as much as the need for a suitably inspiring figurehead.

Once the high command (STAVKA) had supervised mobilization it exercised little authority over distant regional commanders, and Nikolai's active role was restricted to occasional grave edicts, usually forbidding retreat, while day-to-day administration was handled by DANILOV. Despite opposition from most of his cabinet, the Tsar responded to military disasters on the EASTERN FRONT in 1915 by taking personal command at Stavka in early September, and transferred his uncle to the CAUCASIAN FRONT.

Based in Tiblisi, Nikolai lent largely passive support to the successful offensives planned by General YUDENICH during 1916, and was occasionally consulted by liberal monarchists. His recommendations of constitutional reform were ignored by Nicholas, and he joined other field commanders in urging abdication during the FEBRUARY REVOLUTION. Dismissed by the PROVISIONAL GOVERNMENT, he remained in the Crimea until March 1919, when he left for exile in Italy and France.

Nitti, Francesco (1868–1953) Italian Radical deputy who ended a long political association with former prime minister GIOLITTI over the issue of neutrality in late 1914, favouring cooperation with the Allies to ensure their postwar economic support. After visiting the UNITED STATES in summer 1917 to plead for economic aid, he joined the ORLANDO cabinet as treasury minister in October, and used his office to establish central control over raw materials and manufactured goods through a government Exchange Commission. His influential cabinet position ensured the dismissal of munitions minister (and rival supremo) DALLOLIO, but concentration of meagre resources only emphasized the need for aid, and Nitti was active in obtaining Anglo-American financial credits, food and coal for ITALY during 1918. Opposed to colonial expansion, he resigned in January 1919, but returned to office as prime minister in June. His cabinet survived only a year, and he was driven into exile by the MUSSOLINI government in 1924.

Nivelle, General Robert (1856–1924) A competent tactician as a regimental colonel in 1914, Nivelle benefited from French C-in-C JOFFRE's regular purges of failed generals, rising to corps command by late 1915 and leading the Second Army from April 1916. He made his wider reputation in the defence of VERDUN, which he commanded in its final phases, and became a national hero after a series of successful counteroffensives east of the Meuse in October and December 1916.

Praised for his innovative CREEPING BARRAGE tactics, he announced that by extending them in a massive offensive he could effectively end the war on the WESTERN FRONT 'in 48 hours'. The idea galvanized increasingly pessimistic public opinion in FRANCE, and he replaced Joffre as C-in-C in December 1916.

Nivelle's plans were not well received by his own senior officers, especially PÉTAIN, or by BEF commanders, but he received political backing from the BRIAND cabinet (though denied Joffre's autocratic control over strategic decisions) and won significant support from the British government. New premier LLOYD GEORGE was particularly impressed by his confidence, and placed the BEF under temporary French control to ensure its cooperation in February 1917.

Launched in April 1917, the NIVELLE OFFENSIVE was an almost complete failure. Nivelle continued with the operation in the face of tactical disadvantages and loss of surprise, repeating his unsuccessful tactics until French forces were exhausted. His flair for self-publicity, which contributed to German foreknowledge of the offensive, also raised expectations of total victory and magnified the shock of defeat. Nivelle was removed from power at the first opportunity, Pétain taking his place on 15 May, and spent the rest of his career in minor North African commands.

Nivelle Offensive The Allied spring offensive on the WESTERN FRONT in 1917. General NIVELLE's elevation as FRENCH ARMY C-in-C above senior colleagues in December 1916 met a popular and political demand in FRANCE for renewed military vigour. His plan for a massive offensive, mobilizing all available resources for one concentrated BREAKTHROUGH, contained little innovation, but his claim that it would effectively end the War 'in 48 hours' energized an increasingly weary French population.

Nivelle's basic strategy was the same as JOFFRE's in 1915 – attacking the flanks of German-held France in ARTOIS and CHAMPAGNE. Though still convalescing from the trauma of VERDUN, the French Army was to take the lead role. Despite the availability of light TANKS, Nivelle's tactics differed from Joffre's mainly in scale, and involved launching more than a million men on a broad front between Roye and positions east of Reims. Further north, the BEF was detailed to undertake a secondary assault around ARRAS (see MAP 2).

Preparations for the offensive were delayed by a series of squabbles with BEF commander HAIG, and by disputes within the French Army, where a considerable body of opinion led by General PÉTAIN opposed the whole operation. In March 1917, German forces along the front from Arras to Soissons were withdrawn to the HINDENBURG LINE system of fortifications, disrupting planned British and French attacks in the sector (see Operation ALBERICH).

Popular expectations in France remained high throughout early 1917, but by mid-March the BRIAND government was expressing doubts about the offensive. Met by Nivelle's threat to resign, they subsided into a final vote of confidence in the plan on 14 March, prompting the immediate resignation of war minister LYAUTEY and the collapse of the government two days later. Despite obvious signs that Nivelle's stated priority of surprise had not been achieved, the offensive went ahead in April.

British operations around Arras from 9 April made limited if costly gains, but the French assault further south, beginning a week later, was an almost complete failure. Both attacks were repeated regularly throughout April and into May, but had little effect except to raise Allied casualties for the campaign to close to 350,000. Although the British operation was viewed as a limited victory, the French Army had suffered a clear defeat (see Second Battle of the AISNE).

A massive blow to French popular and military morale, Nivelle's failure brought his dismissal on 15 May, and was a factor in the downfall of the RIBOT government in September. Its immediate military effect was to cripple the French Army, which collapsed into mutiny from mid-May (see FRENCH ARMY MUTINY), and it forced the BEF to assume the main Allied offensive role in France for the rest of the War.

Nixon, General Sir John (1857–1921) Conventional INDIAN ARMY officer appointed to command British forces on the MESOPOTAMIAN FRONT in April 1915. His predecessor, General Barrett, had been ordered only to defend the BASRA region, but Nixon was instructed by the Indian government to aim for capture of BAGHDAD, a fact not known by the British government until late May, by which time advances on AMARA and NASIRIYEH had already been authorized. Nixon's confidence and his low opinion of Turkish defences were important factors in the fatal extension of British supply lines to CTESIPHON in November and the subsequent failure to relieve KUT. Based in Basra, far from the front line, and prevented from leaving by worsening health, Nixon overruled the doubts of field commanders TOWNSHEND and Aylmer, ordering advances without pressing the Indian government for vital transport, engineering, TRENCH WARFARE and medical equipment. Nixon's health gave way in early 1916 and he was invalided back to India on 18 January. Replaced by General Lake, he held no further active command. The British Mesopotamia Commission, established to investigate the campaign in 1917, specifically condemned Nixon's attempts to conceal the lack of facilities for wounded combatants.

Njegovan, Admiral Maximilian (1858–1930) Commander of the AUSTRO-HUNGARIAN NAVY's First Battleship Squadron in August 1914, he took over the main fleet at Pola (Pula) following the death of Admiral HAUS in February 1917. Promoted full admiral in command of the entire service later in the year, he was also made head of the War Ministry Naval Section, but failed to ease racial tensions within individual warships and desperate shortages of fuel and supplies. The CATTARO mutiny of February 1918 emphasized the need for a more vigorous command system, and Njegovan was dismissed into retirement on 1 March, his fleet command going to the much younger Admiral HORTHY and his political post to Admiral Huber. A new role as Emperor KARL I's personal advisor was filled by Admiral Keil.

No Man's Land British term that was the accepted description of ground between opposing TRENCHES by 1914. On the WESTERN FRONT in particular, No Man's Land was a permanent, if fluctuating, geographical feature for more than three years. Typically reduced to cratered wasteland, littered with corpses and other battle detritus, its width along the Western Front could vary between about twenty metres and almost a kilometre. Inevitably the focus of major engagements, it was often very quiet during daylight hours between actions, but was a scene of intense activity at night. See TRENCH WARFARE.

Norman Thompson NT Series British flying boats used in small numbers by the RNAS from 1915 to 1918. The single-engined NT-2B, an ungainly biplane deserving the nickname 'Ruptured Duck', was a basic trainer in use from 1917, and about 150 were built. The twin-engined NT-4 and the more powerful NT-4A equipped several ANTI-SUBMARINE patrol units in Britain from 1915 and were later used as trainers.

BRIEF DATA (NT-4A) Type: patrol flying boat; Crew: 2–4; Engine: 2 × 200hp Hispano-Suiza; Max speed: 95mph (152kph); Armament: 1 × 0.303in mg, light bombs.

Northcliffe, Alfred, Lord (1865–1922) Anglo-Irish newspaper mogul, born Alfred Harmsworth, who owned several British national dailies in the early 20th century, most notably the semi-official *Times* and the hugely popular *Daily Mail*. Often credited with the invention of modern tabloid journalism, he was one of the most influential private citizens in GREAT BRITAIN, using mass communication to lobby for a more forceful foreign policy and military expansion. He adopted a high public profile in wartime, and his newspapers consistently demanded strong central control of labour and resources. Northcliffe was never afraid to use (uncensored) editorials for savage expression of his own views, and the *Mail* in particular encouraged jingoistic xenophobia, attracting criticism for hysterical campaigns against 'pro-Germans' such as HALDANE and BATTENBERG (see 'SHELL SCANDAL'). Northcliffe's energies were channelled into government service by LLOYD GEORGE. After turning down an offer of the air ministry, he became director of PROPAGANDA against enemy countries in February 1918. Disappointed at his exclusion from the PARIS PEACE CONFERENCE, he led popular calls for a punitive settlement with GERMANY, and subsequently toured the British Empire as a self-appointed imperial ambassador.

Northern Barrage Ambitious Allied attempt to bar the northern exits of the North Sea to U-BOATS with minefields from the Orkneys to the Norwegian coast. It was also the most important single operation carried out by the wartime US NAVY. Intended to complement the DOVER BARRAGE in the English Channel, the barrage became feasible from July 1917 with the availability of new American magnetic MINES, triggered by proximity to a SUBMARINE and more suitable for covering large areas. Lobbied by US Admiral MAYO, the British Admiralty approved the scheme in August (too late for that year's good weather), and mines were shipped to Scotland during the winter. From June to October 1918 a fleet of small vessels laid some 69,000 mines across the northern exits. More than 80 per cent were US-laid, including all those in the critical central zone of the barrage.

Despite elaborate attempts at disguise (hindered by several thousand premature explosions) the GERMAN NAVY was well aware of the process, and its commanders were able to find safe routes through the barrage. The mines were inefficient, with little support from patrolling warships, and Allied claims that the North Sea was 'sealed' had little substance. U-boat transits through the barrage area actually increased to over 40 per month during late 1918, and the barrage claimed only three confirmed victims. See also: ANTI-SUBMARINE WEAPONS; *HANDELSKRIEG*; MAP 16.

Noske, Gustav (1868–1946) A leading member of the moderate, or 'gradualist', school that dominated prewar parliamentary socialism in GERMANY, and a specialist in military affairs, Noske was an ardent supporter of political truce and commitment to war in August 1914. Disillusioned with government aims and management by 1917, he supported the Reichstag PEACE RESOLUTION in July.

After a brief spell as local governor during the KIEL MUTINY, he was recalled to Berlin on 27 December to join EBERT's provisional cabinet and given control of military affairs at a time of extreme turbulence in the capital. He presided over the recruitment of FREIKORPS volunteers to put down SPARTACIST rebels and became defence minister in the SCHEIDEMANN government from February 1919, resigning in March 1920 after failing to secure military support against the right-wing 'Kapp Putsch'.

Novara Class Class of three light CRUISERS that were the most effective weapons of the wartime AUSTRO-HUNGARIAN NAVY. *Helgoland* and *Saida* were in service by August 1914, and *Novara* joined them at CATTARO in early 1915. Generally able to outrun any better-armed warship in the theatre, the Novaras spearheaded all the Navy's significant surface operations in the southern Adriatic, where they were regarded as the Allies' most dangerous opponents. *Novara* itself, commanded by Captain HORTHY until March 1918, was lucky to survive the Battle of the OTRANTO STRAITS in May 1917, but all three remained in service to the ARMISTICE.

BRIEF DATA (*Novara*, 1915) Displacement: 3,440 tons; Crew: 320; Dimensions: length 411ft (124.5mm), beam 42ft (12.7m); Speed: 30k; Main armament: 8 × 3.9in gun, 2 × 18in TT.

Novogeorgievsk Important Russian fortress on the River Vistula, 35km northwest of Warsaw (see MAP 10). Built for the military conditions of the 1880s and obsolete by 1914, Novogeorgievsk remained the greatest military symbol of Russian rule in POLAND, and was the only fortress defended when the RUSSIAN ARMY withdrew from the TRIPLE OFFENSIVE in late July 1915. Garrisoned by only three depleted divisions, but armed with 1,600 guns and almost a million shells, it was generally expected to hold out for months.

Its fate demonstrated the intrinsic weakness of FORTRESSES. Outer forts no longer protected the main structure from modern long-range ARTILLERY, and the construction of a new perimeter remained unfinished. Unlike the Austro-Hungarian fortress at PRZEMYSL, it enjoyed no protection from the surrounding terrain, and a good local network enabled attack by RAILWAY ARTILLERY. Surrounded by the German Tenth Army (EICHHORN) in early August, Novogeorgievsk was pulverized into submission six days after heavy artillery reached the area on 13 August.

Noyon-Montdidier, Battle of See: Second Battle of the MARNE.

O

Oberndorf Raid Failed Anglo-French experiment in daylight STRATEGIC BOMBING of GERMANY, carried out against the Mauser RIFLE works at Oberndorf on 16 October 1916. The raid was conducted by 12 FARMAN F-40s and 6 BREGUET 4s of the AÉRONAUTIQUE MILITAIRE's *Groupe de Bombardement 4*, with 13 SOPWITH STRUTTERS and 6 Breguets (all crewed by Canadians) of RNAS No.3 Wing. Fighter escort was provided by 19 Strutters, along with four NIEUPORT 17s of the Escadrille LAFAYETTE.

Facing a round trip of some three hours and heavy ANTI-AIRCRAFT concentration en route, 18 of the bombers found Oberndorf, but only 12 dropped their bombs in the target area, killing five civilians and causing enough structural damage to partially disrupt the rifle works for two days. Nine bombers and one Nieuport were destroyed by anti-aircraft fire or German fighters, which caught all but the first squadron in the air.

Allied authorities considered the raid a failure, and that they lacked suitable aircraft for daylight operations. French bombers were switched to night raids over the following weeks, but were returned to army cooperation work by the end of the year. The RNAS carried out a few smaller coastal raids before No.3 Wing was broken up to provide RFC reinforcements in early 1917.

October Manifesto Royal declaration issued by Emperor KARL I of AUSTRIA-HUNGARY on 16 October 1918 that sought to transform the Austrian and Bosnian parts of the Empire into a federation of semi-autonomous states, each with its own representative parliament. Formulated by Austrian premier HUSSAREK, it was never likely to satisfy South Slav, Polish or Czech elements bent on full independence. The inclusion of a guarantee to leave the political status of Hungary unaltered failed to dissuade Hungarian prime minister WEKERLE from denouncing the Manifesto, and further ensured the opposition of the Empire's Romanian, Croat, Slovak, Serbian and Ruthene minorities. The rapid rejection of the Manifesto signalled the effective collapse of the Empire.

October Revolution Coup in Russia by the radical socialist Bolshevik Party, led by LENIN and TROTSKI, that seized power in Petrograd (St Petersburg) over three days from 5 November 1917 (24 October by the Julian calendar then used in Russia). Lenin returned to Russia from temporary exile in Finland on 23 October, demanding seizure of power by the SOVIETS, arrest of the PROVISIONAL GOVERNMENT and immediate peace. Agreed by the Bolshevik Central Committee, the policy was gradually implemented as the party gained influence in the Petrograd Soviet at the expense of Menshevik and Social Revolutionary (SR) delegates tainted by collaboration with the government.

On 29 October the Petrograd Soviet created a Military Revolutionary Committee (MRC). Effectively run by Trotski as a revolutionary command centre, it quickly gained control over disaffected garrison troops and workers' militias (RED GUARDS). Trotski's plan for an insurrection on 7 November, to coincide with the second National Congress of Soviets in Petrograd, was brought forward by pressure of events to 5 November after the garrison at the central barracks declared support for the MRC, along with the crew of the CRUISER *Aurora* on the Neva.

Premier KERENSKI authorized the arrest of leading Bolsheviks and summoned loyal troops from the suburbs on the same day, but revolutionary soldiers, sailors and Red Guards began occupying telegraph offices, telephone exchanges, railway stations and other strategic points. At 10.00 on 7 November the MRC proclaimed power in the hands of the Petrograd Soviet, and the cabinet's attempt to barricade themselves in the Tsar's Winter Palace ended in their arrest after the Palace was stormed early the following morning. A majority of Bolsheviks and their supporters at the Congress, which had opened the previous night, endorsed Lenin's government on 8 November, after a walk-out by dissenting Mensheviks and more moderate SRs. Government was entrusted to a Soviet of People's Commissars, a purely Bolshevik cabinet with Lenin as chairman and Trotski in charge of foreign affairs.

The Revolution remained weak and unstable through its first years of economic collapse and civil war, but had enormous global impact. By agreeing an armistice with the CENTRAL POWERS in December and signing the BREST-LITOVSK Treaty in March 1918 the government ended the war on the EASTERN FRONT. Collapse of Russian control over the Empire's 'nationalities' unleashed political anarchy across eastern Europe and TRANSCAUCASIA. The Bolshevik government's decision to publicise its predecessors' secret wartime treaties immediately after the Revolution caused acute political embarrassment among the Allies, especially the revelation of the Treaty of LONDON (see PARIS PEACE CONFERENCE).

Although Lenin and Trotski were disappointed in their hope for the rapid westward spread of revolution, their success stimulated worker uprisings in GERMANY, and to a lesser extent elsewhere. Forcing the parameters of international socialism to the left (see ZIMMERWALD MOVEMENT), the Revolution frightened democratic governments into military support for anti-Bolshevik forces in the RUSSIAN CIVIL WAR. Anti-Bolshevik PROPAGANDA, as expressed in a virulent 'Red Scare' that gripped the USA until 1920, became a permanent feature of democratic societies until the late 1980s. See also: FEBRUARY REVOLUTION.

Order Number One Notorious decree issued by the Petrograd SOVIET on 15 March 1917, three days after its formation during the FEBRUARY REVOLUTION. Adopted at the instigation of local garrison troops, it ordered all soldiers and sailors in the Petrograd (St Petersburg) military district to form representative committees and place firearms in their charge. It was intended to prevent the use of weapons against the Revolution, but was interpreted by troops throughout the RUSSIAN ARMY as an instruction to overthrow unpopular officers. With full-scale mutiny apparently imminent, a second order was hastily issued to stress the need for discipline, and the formation of committees was eventually renounced after C-in-C ALEXEEV and war minister GUCHKOV threatened to resign. The Order paradoxically slowed the Army's disintegration, by hastening the removal of dangerously unpopular commanders and enabling the Soviet to exert a degree of popular authority over troops.

Orion Class British class of BATTLESHIPS ordered in 1910 as the first warships equipped with 13.5-inch guns, and popularly known as 'super-dreadnoughts'. The four Orions were designed to outgun the GERMAN NAVY's biggest units (given 12-inch guns from 1909) in the battleship confrontation that was central to ROYAL NAVY war plans.

Expensive DREADNOUGHTS with big guns dominated prewar British naval shipbuilding, and super-dreadnoughts were viewed by press and public, along with many politicians and naval strategists, as the main index of naval power. Eight more were ordered and completed before the end of 1914 (see *KING GEORGE V*, *IRON DUKE*, *ERIN*), but this attracted criticism from opponents of First Sea Lord FISHER for restricting the development of fast, modern CRUISERS.

Along with its sisters, *Monarch*, *Thunderer* and *Conqueror*, *Orion* formed the Second Battle Squadron of the GRAND FLEET in 1914. Although present at JUTLAND in 1916, they were never engaged in the decisive action for which they were designed, but their existence helped to prevent a serious challenge to Britain's long-range naval BLOCKADE of GERMANY. Wartime modifications included the addition of ANTI-AIRCRAFT guns and searchlights, along with additional protection against cordite explosion, and most were given anti-torpedo bulges in their hulls.

BRIEF DATA (*Orion*, 1916) Displacement: 22,500 tons; Crew: 800; Dimensions: length 584ft (177m), beam 85ft (25.75m); Speed: 22k; Armament: 10 × 13.5in gun, 16 × 4in, 1 × 4in AA, 1 × 3in AA, 2 × 21in TT.

Orlando, Vittorio (1860–1952) Italian lawyer and politician, a prewar minister under Giovanni GIOLITTI, who became minister of justice in the SALANDRA reshuffle of November 1914 and used his oratorical skills to argue for war against AUSTRIA-HUNGARY. Promoted to interior minister in the BOSELLI government in June 1916, he maintained a policy of conciliation with an active popular anti-War movement. Heavily criticized by the military, but supported by a majority in the chamber of deputies, he eventually switched to suppression in August 1917 after Turin suffered serious strikes and riots.

Appointed prime minister on 30 October, Orlando's first priority was ITALY's survival after the Army's disaster at CAPORETTO. His reassurances of continued commitment to war secured large-scale Allied aid at the RAPALLO CONFERENCE (5 November), and he replaced chief of staff CADORNA with the more politically responsive DIAZ. On the home front he presided over a radical extension of government economic powers by treasury minister NITTI, and reacted to renewed pacifist agitation in the new year by arresting leading anti-War socialists.

Generally prepared to subordinate foreign minister SONNINO's plans for territorial gain to cooperation with the Allies, Orlando upset nationalist opinion by meeting informally with Slav delegates at the ROME CONGRESS in April 1918, and by accepting FOCH's appointment as Allied strategic supremo on the ITALIAN FRONT in June.

His position as head of the Italian delegation at the PARIS PEACE CONFERENCE was dominated by a widening gap between Allied priorities and Italian territorial demands, while chaotic demobilization and economic paralysis fostered internal unrest. Orlando walked out of the Conference on 24 April 1919 in protest at plans to give the eastern Adriatic coast to YUGOSLAVIA, but after returning to the conference for signature of the VERSAILLES Treaty he was held responsible for its alleged mistreatment of Italy. Forced to resign on 19 June, he remained in parliamentary opposition until the mid-1920s.

Osowiec See: Second Battle of the MASURIAN LAKES.

Otranto Barrage Longstanding Allied naval operation designed to block the passage of SUBMARINES from the Adriatic to the MEDITERRANEAN through the Straits of Otranto. The Barrage was established from autumn 1915 as a standing 'line' of ANTI-SUBMARINE trawlers stretching southeast from the Italian port of Brindisi, equipped with INDICATOR NETS and protected by patrols of Allied aircraft and warships stationed at either end of the line.

Pressure on Allied anti-submarine resources in the Mediterranean meant that the Barrage was never fully equipped. The initial 60 trawlers sent from Britain were too few to maintain more than a notional guard along a line of approximately 100km. Only about 20 could be on station at any given time, and although numbers were steadily increased there were always gaps for submarines to use.

Allied strategists consistently overestimated the effectiveness of the Barrage, assuming it to be responsible for the loss of U-BOATS without trace, but it had no actual effect on the passage of submarines. By May 1917, when losses to Austrian raids forced trawlers to abandon night work altogether (see Battle of the OTRANTO STRAITS), the Austrian *U-6* was its only confirmed victim. Even when US NAVY forces brought warship patrols up to strength in 1918 the Barrage was always more of an inconvenience than a threat to U-boats, but remained central to Allied anti-submarine policy in the Mediterranean until the ARMISTICE. See also: DOVER BARRAGE.

Otranto Straits, Battle of the The biggest surface action of the naval war in the MEDITERRANEAN, a raid on 15 May 1917 by modern Austro-Hungarian light CRUISERS and DESTROYERS against the ANTI-SUBMARINE trawlers of the Allied OTRANTO BARRAGE. With few other attacking options available to its surface fleet, the AUSTRO-HUNGARIAN NAVY habitually sent destroyers to attack the British trawlers whenever a U-BOAT went missing without known cause. In an enlarged attack, apparently planned by Captain HORTHY as a purely tactical demonstration of strength, the cruisers *NOVARA*, *Helgoland* and *Saida* sailed from CATTARO at nightfall on 14 May, disguised as destroyers to prevent the early mobilization of heavy Allied warships. Two destroyers sailed separately to make a diversionary attack on the Barrage, and a large supporting force was held at readiness in Cattaro. SUBMARINES were stationed off the Italian bases at Valona and Brindisi, the latter some 65km closer to the trawlers than Cattaro (see MAP 16).

The cruisers separated at the Barrage and sank 14 ships in about two hours from 03.30. The destroyer squadron sank a munitions ship and its escorting destroyer. Carried out with considerable care for the crews of hopelessly outgunned trawlers, who were usually given time to escape, the cruiser attack was over by sunrise, by which time Allied warships were steaming to block its withdrawal.

Four destroyers on patrol to the northeast made contact with the cruisers at 07.00, shadowing them at a safe distance. Two British TOWN CRUISERS (*Dartmouth* and *Bristol*), four Italian destroyers and their fast flotilla leader *Aquila* ran into the two Austrian destroyers at about 07.45. Shots were exchanged, and *Aquila* disabled, before the Austrian ships escaped into well-protected waters around Durazzo. Leaving two destroyers to guard *Aquila* against submarine attack, the squadron eventually intercepted Horthy's force at around 09.00.

Allied numerical superiority was lost during the ensuing high-speed chase. Two Allied destroyers broke down, two were left with them as guards, and *Bristol* was unable to keep up, leaving *Dartmouth* (escorted by two destroyers) to engage the Austrians at long range with its 6-inch main guns. Gunfire damage forced *Novara* to a stop, and the whole squadron halted while it was taken tow by *Saida*, but the distant smoke of Austrian reinforcements (led by the old BATTLESHIP *Sankt Georg*) prompted an Allied withdrawal. Despite the presence of a French submarine on its route home, the Austrian force escaped intact, but *Dartmouth* was torpedoed and badly damaged on the way home by the German *UC-25*, and an assisting destroyer was sunk by one of its MINES, completing a fortunate tactical victory for the Austro-Hungarians that persuaded the Allies to abandon night operation of the Barrage.

Ottoman Empire See: TURKEY.

Owen, Wilfred (1893–1918) British poet who served with the BEF on the WESTERN FRONT. His bleak reflections of life in the trenches were neglected by patriotic publishers until after his death in action, but have since been recognized as among the most powerful anti-War statements in the English language.

P

Pacifism In the years immediately before 1914, the term 'pacifist' described both those who abhorred all war on ideological grounds, and those who rejected war between states as the conventional tool of international diplomacy – a broader definition than that generally recognized today.

The former category included 'conscientious objectors', who refused combat roles in wars on religious or moral grounds, and 'absolute conscientious objectors', who rejected any involvement at all in national or imperial struggles. Objectors were routinely given non-combatant military positions in conscript forces, usually as medical orderlies, cooks or labourers, but absolute objectors were not recognized at all in most belligerent countries, and were generally imprisoned if they persisted in refusing service. Although a few thousand absolute objectors in GREAT BRITAIN and the UNITED STATES passed stern official examinations to secure exemption from new conscription laws – often through longstanding membership of a well-established non-violent religious sect, such as the Society of Friends – they frequently found themselves ostracized in their local communities, particularly in Britain (see MILITARY SERVICE ACTS; SELECTIVE SERVICE ACT; WHITE FEATHERS; YORK, A.).

The body of pacifist opinion opposed to the militarism and aggressive nationalism of prewar conservative European culture was numerically and politically more significant. At a time when the competing ambitions of GREAT POWERS were widely expected to produce a giant military conflict, pacifism denied the right of states to use war as a means to achieve their geopolitical aims. The revolutionary wing of the socialist SECOND INTERNATIONAL could accurately describe itself as pacifist, in that it rejected war between workers as a capitalist imposition, and liberal ISOLATIONIST opinion in the USA was pacifist in deploring any military extension of aggressive statecraft.

Pacifism developed a third meaning in wartime, denoting a simple preference for peace over 'war to the end'. A broad spectrum of anti-War elements were thus able to describe themselves as pacifists (or be so labelled by pro-War 'patriots'). These included Pope BENEDICT XV, who sought to end the War on the grounds that it was senseless carnage, politicians and agitators for a compromise settlement in all the belligerent countries, and revolutionary socialists (such as the German SPARTACUS LEAGUE), who preached national 'defeatism' as a means to hasten the collapse of established regimes. The most important example of wartime revolutionary pacifism, and a good illustration of its transitory nature, was the Bolshevik Party in RUSSIA. Although it steadfastly rejected all participation in 'capitalist war' from 1914, and supported LENIN's uncompromising commitment to an immediate ceasefire after the OCTOBER REVOLUTION, the Party was by no means opposed to violence (including state aggression) in principle, as was comprehensively demonstrated during the RUSSIAN CIVIL WAR.

Painlevé, Paul (1863–1933) Leader of the small Republican-Socialist group in the French parliament from 1910, Painlevé emerged as one of General SARRAIL's strongest supporters in summer 1915, and achieved cabinet status for the first time in October as education minister in the BRIAND government. Attracted by General PÉTAIN's defensive approach during the VERDUN battle in 1916, Painlevé lobbied for his appointment as C-in-C in December and refused the war ministry in protest at NIVELLE's entirely offensive strategy. He took the post in the RIBOT coalition of March 1917, but was unable to persuade the cabinet to cancel the

NIVELLE OFFENSIVE. Quick to respond to its failure by installing Pétain as chief of staff on 29 April, and C-in-C on 15 May, he recognized the FRENCH ARMY's need for recuperation and influenced the exercise of moderation in punishing the widespread FRENCH ARMY MUTINY. Painlevé became the last and least experienced of four compromise wartime premiers on Ribot's fall in early September. Relying on a largely unchanged coalition structure, his administration was effectively paralysed by rampant political polarization, and opposition from left and right forced his resignation on 13 November 1917. Not called upon by CLEMENCEAU, he remained out of office until the mid-1920s.

Palestine Front Campaign fought between British and Turkish forces for control of the southwestern Ottoman Empire from 1915 until the Armistice (see MAP 22). Much of the actual fighting was performed by British imperial troops from India, Australia and New Zealand, while the multi-ethnic TURKISH ARMY was bolstered by German units and staff officers.

The campaign's genesis lay in the strategic position of EGYPT and the SUEZ CANAL in 1914. Nominally an Ottoman province, Egypt was under effective British military occupation as a means of securing the Canal, but Turkish authorities expected its largely Muslim population to rebel in support of any serious challenge to the British presence. The governor of Turkish Syria, DJEMAL PASHA, encouraged by German advisors, led his Fourth Army in a long-prepared attack on the Canal in February 1915, but a brief operation curtailed by desert conditions failed to inspire uprising or dislodge 30,000 INDIAN ARMY and ANZAC troops deployed on its banks, supported by an Anglo-French naval detachment.

The Canal was not seriously threatened after February 1915, but raiding activities by Colonel von KRESSENSTEIN's small 'Desert Force' on the Egypt–Palestine border caused continued alarm in London and Cairo. British strength in Egypt was depleted to feed the WESTERN FRONT and GALLIPOLI in 1915, but evident Turkish preparations for a second attack prompted a major reorganization of the Suez defence system from early 1916.

The Mediterranean Expeditionary Force was shipped from Gallipoli to Egypt, where General MURRAY took command of Canal protection. A new forward defence scheme, already planned by Egyptian C-in-C General Maxwell, was begun with the construction of trench lines 10km east of the Canal together with a major expansion of road, RAILWAY and water links to the front (see EGYPTIAN FORCES). Murray took overall command of the theatre in March, but was informed by imperial chief of staff ROBERTSON that his 14 infantry divisions constituted a strategic reserve for transfer to France as required.

By mid-1916 only four infantry divisions remained to defend Suez, nine having departed to France and another to the MESOPOTAMIAN FRONT, but British supply facilities were being pushed into the Sinai Desert. New railway links from Port Said and Qantara converged by mid-May on the coastal town of ROMANI, 30km east of the Canal, where a second Turkish attempt on Suez failed in August. Murray then received permission to establish a forward base at El Arish, over 100km along the coast and menacing Turkish positions in Palestine.

Heavily dependent on CAVALRY for forward operations, Murray's only effective reconnaissance tool in desert conditions was the RFC's 5th Wing, based at Ismailia on the Canal from early 1916 and largely equipped with all-purpose BE-2 two-seaters. Primarily engaged in short-range reconnaissance and mapping work, the RFC received valuable support from RNAS seaplanes aboard the carriers *BEN-MY-CHREE*, *Anne*, *Raven* and *Empress*, which carried out ground-attack and reconnaissance work from Palestinian coastal waters throughout 1916–17.

By early 1917, a supply route had been established right across the Sinai peninsula including 350km of new roads, 575km of railway, and some 500km of water pipes from reservoirs in Egypt. Kressenstein retreated into Palestine before General Chetwode' 'Desert Column' could attack EL ARISH in December, and British advance units reached water supplies on the border just before Christmas.

Murray's overall strength exceeded 150,000 men by the end of the year, about half available for operations in Palestine. After cavalry had cleared forward Turkish outposts, he prepared an attack on the Turkish defence line between Gaza and Beersheba, guarding access to Palestine and blocking any contact between Murray's right flank and the growing ARAB REVOLT. Two attempts to take GAZA, in March and April 1917, ended in costly defeats. The second failure, a frontal assault accurately predicted by newly arrived modern German aircraft, ended campaigning on the front for the summer and prompted a radical expansion of British commitment to Palestine under General ALLENBY, who took over from Murray in late June.

During a summer of sporadic TRENCH WARFARE, British troops and supplies were massed at the front for an autumn offensive. Turkish defences were steadily improved in anticipation of a complete reorganization under General von FALKENHAYN's new YILDERIM FORCE, but the 33,000 troops at the line, mostly infantry, faced 95,000 attackers, with comparable superiority in supporting ARTILLERY and ammunition. The RFC regained control of the air with the arrival of modern BRISTOL FIGHTERS in the early autumn, and German reconnaissance problems helped Allenby achieve surprise with his inland attack on the BEERSHEBA–GAZA LINE at the end of October.

Falkenhayn's elite units were only just arriving at the front, and his first task on taking command at Jerusalem (5 November) was to order a general withdrawal from the Beersheba–Gaza Line. Despite pursuit and heavy losses, some 15,000 Turkish troops escaped to form a new line about 30km southwest of Jerusalem by 10 November. Falkenhayn's immediate counterattack failed to break through the single cavalry division holding Allenby's right flank, and British infantry drove Kressenstein's Eighth Army from coastal positions along the MUGHAR RIDGE, breaking through to cut the railway link between the two Turkish armies at Junction Station on 14 November.

The British paused for the winter rains on the threshold of JERUSALEM, and Palestine appeared to offer the best prospects for decisive Allied success in 1918. In January the Allied SUPREME WAR COUNCIL's Joint Note 12 accepted that no decisive result was likely on the Western Front before 1919, strengthening the longstanding arguments of 'EASTERNERS' in Britain. The British War Cabinet decided to scale down operations in Mesopotamia, and General SMUTS visited Allenby in February to order a 'decisive' offensive against TURKEY.

Allenby's total fighting strength in February was about 112,000 men. Despite opposition from 'Westerners' HAIG and Robertson, who feared a mass influx of German troops to the Western Front from the inactive EASTERN FRONT, three infantry divisions were sent from Mesopotamia and a cavalry division from France. There were only some 39,000 Germano-Turkish combat troops in Palestine, with perhaps another 80,000 Turks available for emergency concentration in the theatre and 10,000–15,000 besieged in MEDINA.

Allenby reorganized his command, establishing a separate military administration for Egypt, extending supply facilities and appointing authorities to newly captured territories. Establishments of livestock, lorries, artillery and ammunition were expanded. Operations in 1918 opened with a limited offensive east into TRANSJORDAN, supported by Arab Revolt forces moving up the eastern Dead Sea coast (see Battle of TAFILA). Probing advances elsewhere along the front convinced Allenby to launch his major offensive on the flat coastal plains to the west. As in the autumn, and again with the help of complete air superiority, Allenby took care to convince Falkenhayn that his offensive would come on the other flank, towards the vital rail and communications centre of DERA.

General LIMAN VON SANDERS took command of Yilderim Force along the main 100km frontline from the coast to the River Jordan on 1 March. His understanding of Turkish methods stimulated improved tactical coordination, and he made strenuous efforts to strengthen his front by combing overstaffed rear units, but the Second Army guarding his rear at Aleppo and much of the Fourth Army in Arabia (including three divisions still protecting Yemen and Aden) remained under independent leadership. Efficient control was further disrupted by Turkish leader ENVER PASHA's decision to send a further 50,000 men to the CAUCASIAN FRONT in 1918, including some of Yilderim's German battalions.

The condition of Turkish troops in Palestine was deteriorating. Regional Ottoman administration had virtually broken down, with government contracts unpaid from 1917, railway communications in crisis and most economic activity being diverted to British needs by Arab smugglers. Shortages of coal, wood, clothing, food and ammunition damaged morale, along with resentment of German influence and mounting Arab hostility both inside the Army and throughout the native populations. Cancellation of summer leave in the overstretched Yilderim Armies helped British PROPAGANGA (mostly from air-dropped leaflets), and desertions were running at more than 1,000 per month by September.

Allied crisis on the Weston Front forced Allenby to send 60,000 of his best infantry to France between late March and August 1918. Although Indian reinforcements arrived during the summer and his important cavalry arm remained largely undiminished, plans for a major offensive were delayed until the autumn. A large British cavalry contingent was left in Transjordan, persuading Liman von Sanders to concentrate a third of his forces in that sector by late August, but Allenby planned his main attack along the western plains.

The MEGIDDO (or Armageddon) offensive, rapidly followed by British and Arab advances on DAMASCUS, broke Turkish resistance in the theatre. Virtually the whole of Palestine was in Arab nationalist revolt by mid-October, and only a few thousand troops escaped to join the defence of central Turkey. The rapid spread of malaria and INFLUENZA among Allenby's troops had little military impact, and ALEPPO fell to relatively small forces just before Turkey ceased hostilities on 31 October.

Total Turkish and German casualties in the theatre are unknown, but the final offensive from mid-September 1918 – one of the quickest opposed advances in modern warfare – took 75,000 prisoners (including 3,400 Germans and Austrians), along with 360 artillery pieces and a huge stock of other materiel. British and imperial forces suffered less than 6,000 losses over the same period, and 51,451 battle casualties throughout the campaign from January 1915.

Allied victory triggered immediate diplomatic problems, never satisfactorily resolved. The SYKES–PICOT AGREEMENT and the BALFOUR DECLARATION both intrinsically restricted Arab independence, effectively promised to the leaders of the Arab Revolt by LAWRENCE and other local British authorities. Arab grievances were only partially satisfied at the PARIS PEACE CONFERENCE, and Anglo-French administrations presided over a period of widespread unrest in the new MANDATES of Palestine, Syria, Lebanon, Iraq and Transjordan (with wartime Arab leaders FEISAL and ABDULLAH prominent throughout) as well as a nationalist uprising in Egypt.

Pals' Battalions Popular term used to describe BRITISH ARMY units composed of volunteers who shared close civilian ties. Battalions of 'pals' or 'chums' – connected through schools, villages, sports clubs or places of work – enlisted together from all classes of British society, even after the MILITARY SERVICE ACTS introduced conscription to GREAT BRITAIN in 1916. Pals' Battalions were often encouraged to join up en masse by guarantees of postwar employment and economic aid from employers or unions.

Panama Central American republic, a province of Colombia until a revolt of 1903, sponsored by the UNITED STATES as a means of securing control over territory either side of the then incomplete Panama Canal (opened 1914). Economically and politically dominated by the USA, and with a vested interest in ending SUBMARINE WARFARE, Panama was at war with GERMANY from 8 April 1917 and put its four lightly armed gunboats on full local alert.

Parabellum Gun A modified version of the GERMAN ARMY's 7.92mm MASCHINENGEWEHR that was adopted by the GERMAN ARMY AIR SERVICE in late 1914 as the standard weapon for its first armed aircraft. Fitted with a lighter recoil casing, and with its ammunition belt enclosed in a circular metal drum to avoid wind interference, the Parabellum proved unsuitable for use with INTERRUPTER GEAR, but was used throughout the War by observers in two-seater craft, usually being mounted on a metal ring for all-round field of fire. See also: SPANDAU GUN.

Parachutes The parachute was well known in 1914 and was standard wartime equipment for BALLOON and AIRSHIP crews. The types employed by contemporary air services were strapped to the outside of the vessel and attached to the user by a long cord, which automatically opened the 'chute when he jumped. Though pilots on all sides made regular requests for their issue, these early parachutes were generally regarded as too fragile for use on aircraft. Little effort was made by air authorities to pursue alternative designs that could be worn by the jumper, partly because they were costly but primarily on the grounds that the crew of an armed aircraft had no right to such protection. Although a few German pilots were given wearable models in 1918 (when the shortage of trained aircrew had become acute), and both sides used them for dropping agents behind enemy lines, no Allied aircrew were ever issued with parachutes, and the RFC in particular considered requests for their use tantamount to cowardice.

Paravane A wartime British invention, widely used to protect large Allied ships from MINES. Shaped like a small torpedo, it was towed either side of a ship's bows and carried an explosive charge to detonate mines or cut their cables. The British regarded paravanes as a success and credited them with saving at least 50 vessels from serious damage.

Paris Gun A German 380mm Max E Railway Gun adapted by the Krupp company to bombard Paris from extreme distance, the Paris Gun was the ultimate expression of contemporary RAILWAY ARTILLERY design. A lengthened barrel was reduced to 210mm calibre by lining, making it possible to shoot a 120kg shell into the stratosphere, where reduced wind resistance enabled greatly increased range. The system posed unique operational problems. Firing caused such erosion of the lining that each shell needed to be wider than the last, and each propellant charge slightly different. Barrels reached about 240mm calibre before replacement, after about 20 shots.

Inevitably far from accurate, and lacking the weight of projectile to cause serious damage, the gun was first used in March 1918. Striking Paris from the unprecedented range of 130km it caused an international sensation and some initial panic in the French capital. A total of 367 shots (or 320 according to French sources) were fired at Paris before German forces on the WESTERN FRONT retreated in August, but material damage was slight and the attacks had no discernible long-term effect on French public morale. Planned and crewed by the GERMAN NAVY, which had little other use for its heavy artillery, the Paris Gun was a useless expense in strictly military terms but a great PROPAGANDA success in GERMANY.

Paris Peace Conference The assembly of Allied leaders called to formulate a peace settlement after the ARMISTICE. Opened on 12 January 1919, it continued at various locations in and around Paris until 20 January 1920. Leaders of 32 Allied and Associated states (with their expert retinues) attended, representing about 75 per cent of the global population, but negotiations were dominated by the five 'powers with general interests' – the UNITED STATES, GREAT BRITAIN, FRANCE, ITALY and JAPAN.

Twenty-three other states qualified as 'powers with special interests', including all other independent Allied belligerents, the major dominions of the British Empire, CZECHOSLOVAKIA and the Arab 'Hejaz' (see ARAB REVOLT). Four South American republics – Bolivia, Ecuador, Peru and Uruguay – took part in sessions affecting their economic interests. No representatives of the CENTRAL

POWERS were invited, and the Soviet government refused to attend.

Two representatives from each of the 'Big Five' met from the start as the Council of Ten to deal with immediate military and humanitarian aid problems. It quickly became the forum for most significant discussion of territorial questions, and a summit Council of Four was established from March, enabling the French, British, US and Italian leaders to wrangle in private. Its deliberations came to be seen as a confrontation between liberal US president WILSON and nationalist French premier CLEMENCEAU, with British prime minister LLOYD GEORGE contriving mediation and Italian premier ORLANDO interested only in Italian affairs. Their disputes were underpinned by the threat of a US retreat into ISOLATIONISM.

The USA was anxious to re-establish GERMANY as a business partner, but British, Italian and (especially) French delegations faced intense press and public pressure for a punitive peace settlement. Contradictory wartime diplomacy – the LONDON Treaty, the ST JEAN DE MAURIENNE arrangement, the SYKES–PICOT AGREEMENT, the BALFOUR DECLARATION and the LANSING–ISHII AGREEMENT, for instance – made satisfaction of all Allied claims impossible. Volatility within the power vacuum created in eastern and southeastern Europe made revision of the annulled BUCHAREST and BREST-LITOVSK treaties both urgent and impossibly complex.

The compromises eventually forced on delegates reflected the erosion of Wilson's apparently dominant position. He gave ground elsewhere in return for modifications to his LEAGUE OF NATIONS project, and the territorial arrangements formulated in Paris bore little relation to his FOURTEEN POINTS.

The system of MANDATES allowed colonial administration by another name, satisfying the claims of AUSTRALIA and SOUTH AFRICA and endeavouring to give everybody a share of the former Ottoman Empire. Recognition of Italian interests in TURKEY caused arguments with GREECE, which eventually seized SMYRNA. Orlando, furious at the donation of eastern Adriatic territories to the new YUGOSLAVIA (and at Wilson's attempt to appeal over his head to Italian public opinion), walked out of the Conference in April, and D'ANNUNZIO's maverick force of Italian irregulars occupied the port of Fiume (modern Rijeka) from September. Japan was permitted to keep the conquered province of Shantung, prompting Allied CHINA to reject all the Paris decisions.

The treaties with the defeated powers that emerged from the Conference – named after the Paris suburbs of VERSAILLES (Germany), ST GERMAIN (Austria), TRIANON (Hungary), NEUILLY (Bulgaria) and SÈVRES (Turkey) – imposed territorial losses, financial liabilities (REPARATIONS) and military restrictions on all the Central Powers. Insufficiently severe to appease European public opinion, they were vicious enough to create deep and lasting resentments in the defeated countries, above all in Germany.

The US Congress refused to ratify the Versailles Treaty in November 1919, emphasizing the dissatisfaction felt even by supposed beneficiaries, and the Conference closed in an atmosphere of failure. Pessimism was justified by the subsequent collapse of a peace never fully adopted, adhered to or enforced by its makers. See MAP 25.

Pašić, Nikola (1845–1926) The dominant political figure in SERBIA throughout the early 20th century, Pašić was a member of the National Assembly (*Skuptshina*) from 1878 and formed the first of 22 cabinets in 1892. Imprisoned and discredited in 1899 after clashes between his republican Radical Party and the crown, he returned to power in 1904 under the new dynasty of King PETER and, apart from a brief fall from grace in 1908, remained in office until 1918.

His most serious internal difficulties were with the military, which had overthrown the old dynasty in 1903 and expected support for an aggressive, expansionist foreign policy aimed at the establishment of 'Greater Serbia'. Although he supported military reform and participation in the Balkan Wars (1912–13), Pašić was unwilling to provoke AUSTRIA-HUNGARY into war over extremist demands for the unification of the southern Slavs under a single state (see BLACK HAND). Tension between military and civil authorities over the administration of conquered territories in Macedonia provoked a constitutional crisis in June 1914, when Crown Prince ALEXANDER took executive authority from the King and Pašić was obliged to call an election.

A contemporary reputation for deviousness contributed to a general, but probably inaccurate, assumption that Pašić was implicated in the assassination of Archduke FRANZ FERDINAND on 28 June. Pašić was aware that the JULY CRISIS almost certainly meant war, and hastened to confirm promised Russian support before replying to the Austrian ultimatum of 23 July in terms that established Serbia's innocence without preventing conflagration.

The outbreak of war suspended internal disputes, enabling Pašić to concentrate on securing Allied military aid on the BALKAN FRONT and diplomatic support for an enlarged postwar South Slav state. Neither had been achieved before General MACKENSEN's invasion of SERBIA by the CENTRAL POWERS drove the government and Army out of the country. Pašić took part in the 'GREAT RETREAT' of late 1915, and re-established his government in Corfu at the start of 1916.

Balancing Serbian ambitions simply to acquire part of the Austro-Hungarian Empire and the determination of exiled Croats and Slovenes to create a federal YUGOSLAVIA, Pašić reached a compromise agreement, the CORFU DECLARATION, with the 'Yugoslav Committee' of Anton TRUMBIĆ in July 1917. Despite the earlier repression of Black Hand leaders, Pašić sought to circumvent the Corfu Declaration by trying to prevent Allied recognition of the Committee as a government-in-exile and seeking to ensure Serbian control of any postwar state.

By late 1918, when the collapse of Austro-Hungarian authority forced both sides to a decision, Pašić was losing his grip over Serbian politics to Prince Alexander, who emerged to dominate pan-Slav discussions in Belgrade during November. Deprived of the premiership in the new 'Kingdom of Serbs, Croats and Slovenes' (later renamed Yugoslavia), he was its Serbian representative at the PARIS PEACE CONFERENCE, and won considerable territorial gains for the new state through the Treaties of NEUILLY and ST GERMAIN. Despite its name, the postwar kingdom was effectively dominated by Serbian interests, which returned Pašić to power briefly in 1921, and again for two years before his death.

Passchendaele Popular name for the Third Battle of YPRES, a contemporary byword for useless slaughter derived from the name of the ridge that was the last objective taken by the offensive on 6 November 1917.

Peaceful Penetration Term coined by AUSTRALIAN FORCES forces with the BEF to describe their innovative offensive tactics on the WESTERN FRONT. Perfected in a series of highly successful raids across NO MAN'S LAND during early summer 1918, and demonstrated on a larger scale at LE HAMEL in July, 'peaceful penetration' developed from the assumption that infantry's role was to occupy territory, rather than to expend itself attempting to reach it. In practical terms, it meant placing maximum possible reliance on mechanized weapons – MACHINE GUN units, TANKS, AERIAL support and ARTILLERY – to devastate a limited quadrant of enemy territory. Infantry would then occupy and secure the area, usually supplied from the air, while other mechanized forces were concentrated to prevent counterattacks. In that it sought no dramatic BREAKTHROUGH into undefended territory beyond the front lines, peaceful penetration was a radical departure from orthodox Allied tactics in France. Its success depended on meticulously planned close cooperation between the various battle arms, a speciality of Australian commander MONASH, and it was imitated with varying degrees of efficiency by other Allied commanders during the offensives of autumn 1918. See also: INFILTRATION TACTICS; INFANTRY TACTICS.

Peace Note, US A note to all belligerent nations issued on 18 December 1916 by President WILSON of the neutral UNITED STATES, requesting clear statements of their war aims as a prelude to any ceasefire discussions. An attempt to mediate before SUBMARINE WARFARE forced the USA into war with the CENTRAL POWERS, but delayed by presidential elections in November, the Note came only six days after a widely condemned German PEACE OFFER, spreading diplomatic confusion to largely unconstructive effect. The Central Powers replied on 26 December by virtually repeating their earlier offer, and the German leadership adopted an unrestricted submarine campaign on 9 January 1917. The Allies condemned the first German offer in a note to the USA on 30 December, but waited until 10 January before answering Wilson. Alongside demands for restitution of French and Belgian territory, their vague references to the liberation of national groups from foreign domination alarmed prospective peacemakers in AUSTRIA-HUNGARY but formed a working basis for Wilson's FOURTEEN POINTS programme of early 1918.

Peace Offer, German A call for peace by the CENTRAL POWERS, issued by German chancellor BETHMANN HOLLWEG in the Reichstag on 12 December 1916. Moves for peace reflected a pessimistic view of military, social and economic prospects among politicians in both GERMANY and AUSTRIA-HUNGARY, and were hastened by Bethmann Hollweg's search for an alternative strategy to intensified SUBMARINE WARFARE. He had hoped that the UNITED STATES would initiate peace proposals before military influence over Kaiser WILHELM II became irresistible. Informed by ambassador BERNSTORFF in early October that no action could be expected until after the November US elections, Bethmann Hollweg sought approval to make an offer of his own. The THIRD SUPREME COMMAND's agreement, from a position of strength after the ROMANIAN CAMPAIGN, was qualified by strict conditions, including acceptance of unrestricted submarine warfare if the offer failed.

Repeating that Germany had been forced into war to exercise freedom of national development, the offer stressed that German forces were secure in occupied territory and called for the Allies to open talks on the grounds that continued fighting was futile. It made no mention of peace terms, or of REPARATIONS and guarantees already stipulated by the Allies. Allied reactions were predictably negative, and the US administration was infuriated by German statements linking the offer with anticipated efforts by President WILSON. Wilson issued his own PEACE NOTE on 18 December without reference to the German offer, effectively discrediting it, and the Kaiser's decision to adopt unrestricted submarine warfare had been taken by the time Berlin replied to Wilson on 10 January.

Peace Resolution Joint declaration by the socialist and centre parties in the German parliament (Reichstag) demanding peace without annexations or indemnities. Tabled by Matthias ERZBERGER on 7 July 1917, and carried five days later by 212 votes to 126, it directly opposed the ambitious expansion plans of the THIRD SUPREME COMMAND and conservative Reichstag groups, marking the formal end of *Burgfrieden* ('political truce') in Germany and the climax of a heated national debate about war aims. Chancellor BETHMANN HOLLWEG, unable to support the resolution or its right-wing opponents, was forced from office almost immediately, and the semblance of political consensus was not recovered in wartime GERMANY.

Pegasus The first wartime Pegasus was an obsolete British CRUISER sunk by the German light cruiser *KÖNIGSBERG* at Zanzibar in September 1914 (see RUFUGI DELTA). The second was a former passenger liner bought by the ROYAL NAVY and converted as an AIRCRAFT CARRIER. In service from 1917, *Pegasus* and the similar *Nairana* were operative in the North Sea and the ARCTIC THEATRE before transferring to the MEDITERRANEAN in 1918, by which time they were equipped with wheeled FIGHTERS.

BRIEF DATA (1917) Displacement: 2,070 tons; Crew: 275; Dimensions: length 332ft (100.6m), beam 43ft (13m); Speed: 21k; Armament: 2 × 12pdr gun, 2 × 12pdr AA, 7 × a/c.

Peresviet One of eight old Russian BATTLESHIPS captured by the JAPANESE NAVY in 1905 and still active in August 1914. Completed in 1902, *Peresviet* (*Sagami* in Japanese service) was one of the more modern captured ships, but was known for its unreliability at high speeds. Sold back to Russia under its original name in 1915, *Peresviet* relieved the cruiser *ASKOLD* in the MEDITERRANEAN, taking part in Allied naval demonstrations off GREECE in 1916 (see ATHENS LANDING) before being sunk by MINES at Port Said on 4 January 1917. The even older battleship *Tango* (ex-*Poltava*) was returned to Russian service in 1916. Renamed *Tchesma*, it served in the ARCTIC until the end of the RUSSIAN CIVIL WAR.

BRIEF DATA (*Sagami*, 1914) Displacement: 13,500 tons; Crew: 732; Dimensions: length 435ft (131.8m), beam 71.5ft (21.7m); Speed: 19k; Armament: 4 × 10in gun, 10 × 6in, 16 × 12pdr, 2 × 18in TT.

Pershing, General John J. (1860–1948) The US ARMY's most experienced combat officer, Pershing's varied career had embraced fighting in the Indian Wars, CUBA and the PHILIPPINES (and service as US observer in the Russo-Japanese War) before he led the punitive raid against Pancho Villa in MEXICO in early 1917. His appointment to command the AEF in May 1917 was no surprise, and he arrived in France the following month, becoming a full general in October.

Pershing's absolute determination to use the AEF as a national fighting unit, emphasizing the formal position of the UNITED STATES as an 'associated power' unencumbered by alliances, was rooted in mistrust of Allied tactics and strategy. He believed his fit, fresh troops could break the deadlock of TRENCH WARFARE, but rejected piecemeal expenditure of men and materials in costly offensives carried out with exhausted allies.

After a long struggle to resist Anglo-French demands for emergency reinforcement, the German KAISERSCHLACHT Offensive in late March 1918 softened Pershing's attitude, though never to the complete satisfaction of British and French commanders aware that they were providing the vast bulk of AEF equipment (see Battles of LE HAMEL, CANAL DU NORD, CANTIGNY, CHÂTEAU-THIERRY, BELLEAU WOOD).

Pershing's carefully planned victory at ST MIHIEL in September won Allied applause, but his immediate commitment of tired troops for the opening phase of the MEUSE-ARGONNE OFFENSIVE was less successful. The decision was effectively forced on him by Allied strategic requirements, but criticisms of his logistic organization and tactical performance in the Argonne were more justified. Rapid reorganization during October 1918, aided by a readiness to dispense with inefficient officers, bore fruit as the final US drive beyond the HINDENBURG LINE to Sedan vindicated his maintenance of AEF integrity.

Pershing argued for complete military victory over Germany before the ARMISTICE. Strongly committed to the imposition of punitive ceasefire terms, he was kept away from the PARIS PEACE CONFERENCE and spoke out against the Treaty of VERSAILLES. On his return to the USA in September 1919 he became the first US 'General of the Armies'. See also: Generals MARCH, LIGGETT, HARBORD.

Persia Economically undeveloped and internally unstable, Persia (modern Iran) formed an independent buffer between the Russian Empire and British INDIA. The Anglo-Russian Convention of 1907 arbitrarily divided the country into spheres of interest, giving GREAT BRITAIN economic control of the south and RUSSIA of the north; the neutral zone in the centre (including Tehran) became an arena of intense prewar competition between British, Russian and German agents.

Shah Mahommed Ali was deposed in favour of his 13-year-old son Ahmed Mirza in 1909, prompting tighter British control over increasingly important oil supplies from the southwest of the country, maintained by a network of financial and military support to provincial authorities. Russia effectively controlled the only significant military forces in the country (the Cossack Brigade and the Gendarmerie, about 15,000 men in total) and used its own troops to maintain order in the north.

The outbreak of war helped German efforts to supplant Anglo-Russian influence. Anglo-Indian forces on the MESOPOTAMIAN FRONT occupied the Persian coastal communications centre at Bushire in October 1914, and the inland pumping station of AHWAZ the following spring, providing ammunition for an intensive German PROPAGANDA campaign led by ambassador Prince Heinrich of Reuss. Backed by lavish expenditure on arms and pensions, the campaign had reduced British influence in southern Persia to a few garrisoned enclaves by late 1915, at which point GERMANY controlled 10 of the 17 Persian banks.

Persia came closest to alliance with the CENTRAL POWERS when the Swedish-officered Gendarmerie accepted German control in November 1915, prompting the dispatch to Tehran of a Russian division from the CAUCASIAN FRONT under General Baratov. The Shah, whose personal relations with the Allies remained fairly good, declined to leave Tehran to join German agent Wassmuss with the Gendarmerie, which began independent destabilizing operations.

Baratov slowly forced Wassmuss and his irregulars west, but was held short of the Mesopotamian border until March 1916, when he reached Karind, some 200km from Baghdad. Despite British hopes that he could materially assist the relief of KUT, Baratov made no further move until June, when his attempted advance was pushed back into Persia (see KHANAQIN). The British SOUTH PERSIA RIFLES had eliminated German influence and restored some order to southern and central regions by the end of the year.

With the decline of direct German influence, internal unrest subsided until Russian control of the north slackened in 1917. A rebellion in the northwest by pro-German tribesmen under Kuchik Khan was halted by the British 'DUNSTERFORCE', and an uprising by the Kahsgai people ended when its chief was deposed. British policing operations strained Anglo-Persian relations, and the South Persia Rifles were expelled in spring 1918, but an agreement in 1919 secured peaceful British supervision of oil supplies. A successful rebellion led by Reza Khan Pahlavi (commander of the Cossack Brigade and Shah from 1925) followed incursions by RED ARMY forces in 1920.

Perthes, Battles of See: First CHAMPAGNE OFFENSIVE.

Pétain, General Henri-Philippe (1856–1951) Cautious but successful FRENCH ARMY commander, a respected prewar theoretician who opposed the prevailing doctrine of 'offensive spirit' and stressed the importance of ARTILLERY support. His heretical tendencies restricted his promotions, and he was still a regimental colonel with General LANREZAC's Fifth Army in August 1914, but he subsequently enjoyed rapid elevation: to divisional command during the First Battle of the MARNE, and to corps command by October. From July 1915 he led the French Second Army, holding the front south of Verdun.

The initial success of the German attack on VERDUN in 1916 prompted C-in-C JOFFRE to appoint Pétain in direct command of the defence on 26 February. Ordered, however unwisely, to hold the sector at all costs, Pétain made good his famous promise – *'Ils ne passeront pas!'* ('They shall not pass!') – earning popular acclaim for a policy of artillery-based defensive operations backed by expert organization of supplies and manpower resources (see VOIE SACRÉE).

Promoted in May 1916 to command Army Group Centre, which covered the Verdun sector, his recommendation of withdrawal from the position was overruled by Joffre. His successor in direct command of Verdun, NIVELLE, took the credit for counterattacks that regained much of the ground lost during the year, and was elevated above Pétain to replace Joffre in December, but the failure of the NIVELLE OFFENSIVE in spring 1917 finally discredited the doctrine of attack at all costs and left the French Army in crisis. With widespread mutiny threatening front line units (see FRENCH ARMY MUTINY), Pétain became C-in-C on 15 May.

By improving the living conditions of soldiers at the front and restricting himself to defensive operations, Pétain gradually restored the fighting capacity of the French Army. His tactical ideas remained fundamentally alien to many French commanders, and their failure to practice DEFENCE IN DEPTH was a major factor in the collapse of French positions during the AISNE Offensive of May 1918. Though Pétain retained his post he was officially subordinated to Allied Supreme

Commander FOCH, and played a relatively minor role in planning the successful Allied offensives of the autumn.

Promoted field marshal two weeks after the ARMISTICE, he remained active in French military affairs, serving briefly as war minister in 1934 and becoming ambassador to Spain in 1936. In 1940, aged 83, he returned to head the Vichy government in unoccupied France and was condemned to death for treason after the Second World War. The sentence was commuted by Charles de Gaulle, who had been a junior officer in Pétain's regiment at CHARLEROI in August 1914.

Peter I, King (1844–1921) Born Prince Peter Karadjordjevic, into one of the two dynasties struggling for control of 19th-century SERBIA, he was exiled when his father was deposed as ruler of the semi-autonomous Ottoman state in 1859. Returned to power in 1903, after a military coup had overthrown the Obrenovic dynasty, he was unable to impose a settlement of persistent conflicts between military and civil authorities. Success in the Balkan Wars brought demands from both to administer Macedonia after 1912, and the ensuing crisis forced Peter to pass executive power to his second son, ALEXANDER, in June 1914. His retirement was seriously interrupted by war. He joined the Army on the BALKAN FRONT in December 1914, leading its parade through Belgrade after the victory at KOLUBARA, and again providing symbolic leadership during the full-scale invasion of SERBIA in October 1915. After surviving the GREAT RETREAT, carried all the way, he withdrew finally to Greece, emerging only to accept nominal sovereignty of the new YUGOSLAVIA in December 1918.

Petra, Battle of Small action that confirmed the establishment of ARAB REVOLT forces in northern Arabia during late 1917. After the occupation of AQABA over the summer, and its development as a supply port, FEISAL's Northern Arab Army expected an attack from several thousand Turkish troops based about 100km northeast at MAAN (see MAP 22). Feisal's chief tactician, LAWRENCE, launched a series of train-wrecking raids designed to provoke a retaliatory Turkish raid against Aqaba's formidable inland defences. They achieved their objective when four reduced infantry battalions, with small-scale CAVALRY, ARTILLERY and air support, attacked the Arab outpost at Petra on 27 October. Forced to march through a narrow pass to reach the ancient city, the attackers were ambushed from the cliffs and massacred by about 550 Arab Army and Bedouin irregular troops, ending TURKISH ARMY offensive ambitions in the region.

Petragge Raid The RUSSIAN NAVY's pioneering amphibious warfare techniques in the BALTIC SEA were first employed on 22 October 1915, when 2 gunboats, supported by 2 PRE-DREADNOUGHTS (*Orlica* and *SLAVA*) and 15 DESTROYERS, landed 536 troops near Petragge, west of the Bay of Riga and just behind German lines on the EASTERN FRONT (see MAP 11). German troops withdrew from the area at once, but the landing force was re-embarked later that day in the absence of support from other RUSSIAN ARMY units. The raid had a considerable effect on German thinking, prompting deployment of a CAVALRY division for coastal defence in the area, and encouraging similar operations by the GERMAN NAVY (see Operation ALBION).

Pfalz D-III Streamlined biplane FIGHTER, delivered to GERMAN ARMY AIR SERVICE combat units (*Jagdstaffeln*) on the WESTERN FRONT from September 1917. The Pfalz shared combat duties with a variety of other designs, but proved inferior to both the FOKKER DR-1 and ALBATROS D-V. Strong in the dive but otherwise less sprightly than it looked, it was avoided by experienced pilots and generally used by beginners or for attacks on observation BALLOONS.

A modified D-IIIa version, with a 180hp engine and rounded wing tips, brought little improvement, but production was stepped up from early 1918, reflecting an acute lack of high-performance alternatives and the mushrooming demand for fighters at the front. Some 600 were built in total, and about half were still in action, although quite obsolete, in early autumn 1918.

BRIEF DATA Type: single-seat fighter; Engine: 160hp Mercedes; Max speed: 165kph; Ceiling: 4,500m; Armament: 2 × 7.92mm mg (forward).

Pfalz D-XII The second original Pfalz FIGHTER design to enter full production, after a succession of prototypes had been rejected. Ordered after heavy lobbying on its behalf by the Bavarian government, the D-XII joined German units on the WESTERN FRONT from September 1918 to augment limited supplies of the superior FOKKER D-VII. Though able to compete with modern Allied types, it was less agile than the Fokker and its complex strutting system hindered field maintenance. About 180 had reached the front by the ARMISTICE.
BRIEF DATA Type: single-seat fighter; Engine: 180hp Mercedes; Max speed: 184kph; Ceiling: 5,600m; Armament: 2 × 7.92mm mg (forward).

Pfalz E-Types The Bavarian government's active desire to control supply of its semi-autonomous military forces worked consistently in favour of the Bavarian Pfalz company. The unarmed Pfalz A-I (80hp) and A-II (100hp) monoplanes, direct copies of the French MORANE-SAULNIER L, were in service from late 1914, and a series of E-Type FIGHTERS was ordered in 1915. The E-I and the 100hp E-II were mid-wing monoplanes based on another Morane-Saulnier design, the prewar Type H sports model, and fitted with INTERRUPTER GEAR. About 100 examples flew as escorts, singly or in pairs, for reconnaissance units on both the WESTERN and EASTERN FRONTS. The later E-III (an armed conversion of the two-seater A-II), 160hp E-IV and Mercedes-powered E-V were only used in small numbers. Outclassed by new Allied NIEUPORT 11 and AIRCO DH-2 fighters from early 1916, Pfalz E-Types had disappeared from frontline units by the summer.
BRIEF DATA (E-I) Type: single-seat fighter; Engine: 80hp Oberursel; Max speed: 144kph; Ceiling: 3,050m; Armament: 1 × 7.92mm mg.

Pflanzer-Baltin, General Karl von (1855–1925) Austro-Hungarian commander whose flexible responses to the problems of TRENCH and alpine warfare, and concern for discipline and morale, were untypical of the AUSTRO-HUNGARIAN ARMY. Brought out of retirement in late 1914 to command the Seventh Army (which was created to occupy the southern sector of the EASTERN FRONT after the opening campaign in GALICIA), he was given Army Group Pflanzer-Baltin for the CARPATHIAN OFFENSIVE of early 1915, winning its only success by taking Czernowitz on 17 February.

The Seventh Army halted the Russian BESSARABIAN OFFENSIVE in late 1915, but was broken up by the BRUSILOV OFFENSIVE the following June. Pflanzer-Baltin remained in field command of the army group reformed with German reinforcements in July, but was effectively controlled by the GERMAN ARMY through chief of staff SEECKT. From July 1918 Pflanzer-Baltin took command of Austro-Hungarian forces in ALBANIA, where news of the ARMISTICE was slow to arrive, and his surrender on 18 November was the last act of the Austro-Hungarian Army.

Phalanx Tactics See: BREAKTHROUGH TACTICS.

Philippines The Philippine Islands had been a formal UNITED STATES dependency since 1908, but a US civil government had been in control since the defeat of the Spanish regime in 1901. An increasing number of Filipinos joined the government as the islands were coached towards full independence through a period of rapid trade expansion with the USA. The right to eventual independence was conceded by the USA in 1916, but the archipelago's increased strategic importance in the context of postwar Pacific rivalries delayed full self-government until 1946. Automatically at war alongside the USA from April 1917, Filipino authorities seized German vessels in Manila harbour, and several thousand Filipinos joined the US forces, including many of the mixed US/Filipino police force.

Phönix C-I Austrian development of the German-designed HANSA-BRANDENBURG C-I, that joined AUSTRO-HUNGARIAN AIR SERVICE units on the ITALIAN FRONT from early 1918.

More effective at high altitude than the UFAG C-I (another modification of the Brandenburg in service at around the same time), it was used principally for PHOTO-RECONNAISSANCE work, and 110 were delivered in wartime.

BRIEF DATA Type: two-seater armed reconnaissance; Engine: 230hp Hiero; Max speed: 176kph; Ceiling: 6,800m; Armament: 2 × 8mm mg, light bombs (external racks).

Phönix D-Types Austrian FIGHTER, designed in early 1917 as a replacement for the HANSA-BRANDENBURG D-I. The new biplane used essentially the same fuselage as its predecessor, but had a more conventional wing design, synchronized armament, and room for a bigger engine. Reasonably fast, but initially prone to structural faults and never particularly agile, it was a standard AUSTRO-HUNGARIAN AIR SERVICE weapon from the start of 1918, appearing in virtually identical D-I and D-II versions and remaining active until the ARMISTICE. A few also served with land-based AUSTRO-HUNGARIAN NAVY units, and a 230hp D-III reached naval formations in autumn 1918.

BRIEF DATA (D-II) Type: single-seat fighter; Engine: 200hp Hiero; Max speed: 180kph; Armament: 2 × 8mm mg.

Photo-Reconnaissance Aerial photography for army reconnaissance purposes was generally carried out at corps level for the benefit of local commanders, who could build exact 'photo-maps' of enemy positions by piecing together the pictures obtained by aircrew. Long-range 'strategic' reconnaissance was almost always visual rather than photographic, and involved gathering intelligence about RAILWAY movements, troop build-ups or industrial installations for use at army or general staff level.

Short-range photo-reconnaissance was perfectly suited to the static conditions of TRENCH WARFARE, and took place almost constantly, but it was always highly dangerous work. Camera equipment was heavy and cumbersome in 1914, weighing down aircraft that were anyway required to fly straight and steady beneath the clouds along enemy lines. Easy targets for ANTI-AIRCRAFT fire, two-seater camera craft were tempting prey for armed FIGHTERS, and the majority of aircraft shot down on all fronts were reconnaissance types.

Development of cameras on both sides proceeded rapidly after 1915. Observers, who at first struggled with hand-held cameras in freezing conditions, were equipped with a series of improved fixed instruments, usually viewing through a hole in the fuselage floor. Cameras also became lighter and capable of focused shots from greater heights, and, as aircraft performance improved, specialist photo-reconnaissance types emerged, high-performance machines stripped of extraneous armament and other equipment for maximum altitude (see RUMPLER C-TYPES). See also: AERIAL WARFARE.

Piave River, Battle of the The last major Austro-Hungarian attack on the ITALIAN FRONT, in June 1918, an attempt to exploit gains made during the CAPORETTO OFFENSIVE in late 1917. The AUSTRO-HUNGARIAN ARMY's condition deteriorated badly during the first half of 1918: German support was withdrawn to take part in the SPRING OFFENSIVES on the WESTERN FRONT; equipment and supplies were low; and numerical superiority in divisions masked the shrunken condition of many units. The ITALIAN ARMY had meanwhile been re-equipped from a growing Allied arms surplus, and was deployed in good defensive positions by commander DIAZ.

The front line nevertheless stood on the Piave only a few kilometres from the Italian cities of Venice, Padua and Verona, and German demands for a supporting offensive across the river were backed by front commanders CONRAD and BOROEVIC. Confronted by demands from both for the necessary reinforcement, chief of staff ARZ VON STRAUSSENBERG divided his available strength, intending to catch defenders in a pincer by opening with a direct assault on the river by Boroevic and following up with an attack by Conrad in the Trentino (see MAP 21).

Boroevic, commanding the Fifth and Sixth Armies, opened the offensive on 10 June, crossing the Piave along the coast and advancing a few kilometres before Italian counterattacks forced him into retreat from 19 June. Difficulties recrossing the rapid river exposed Austro-Hungarian forces to strong flank attacks, and they eventually got across with 150,000 losses on 22 June. Conrad attacked Allied lines from the Trentino on 15 June, but made no lasting gains and lost 40,000 men in a week. The defeat accelerated Austro-Hungarian decline, and the Army virtually ceased to exist as a coherent force, but Diaz chose not to test its defences until the autumn (see VITTORIO VENETO OFFENSIVE).

Pickelhaube The distinctive spiked helmet worn by GERMAN ARMY infantry, originally an elaborate design including imperial or state crests. An enduring image of the period, the leather *Pickelhaube* was being produced in a plain economy version, with spike removed, by August 1914, and was abolished in favour of the simple 'coal scuttle' steel helmet in 1916.

Piłsudski, Józef (1867–1935) Polish nationalist agitator, born in Russian POLAND but exiled in 1908 after serving five years hard labour for anti-Tsarist activities. Encouraged by Austro-Hungarian authorities in Galicia, he began assembling a private military force that became part of the AUSTRO-HUNGARIAN ARMY in August 1914, eventually joining the Polish Legions that fought on the EASTERN FRONT in 1916 (see POLISH FORCES).

Piłsudski commanded a brigade in the Polish Legions until October 1916, when German rejection of demands for more Polish officers provoked his resignation. On 5 November 1916, when the occupying CENTRAL POWERS established Poland as a semi-autonomous client state, Piłsudski was given command of its armed forces, the 'Polish Auxiliary Corps'. His disputes with German authorities came to a head in March 1917, when he refused the oath of allegiance on behalf of his troops, and he was arrested on 30 July (see BESELER, H.).

Released from imprisonment in GERMANY at the ARMISTICE, he took command of the small independent Polish Army on his return. Filling a power vacuum as the German puppet administration disintegrated, he formed a provisional government in December and was named head of state by the new coalition government of January 1919. Remaining in Poland to command the army while prime minister Paderewski headed the national delegation at the PARIS PEACE CONFERENCE, Piłsudski led the defeat of RED ARMY forces in the RUSSO-POLISH WAR of 1920.

Pistols Pistols were the standard armament for officers in all combatant armies during the First World War. They were also carried by agents, military police, aircrew and the operating personnel of TANKS, ARMOURED CARS and other military vehicles. There were three types of modern pistol in 1914: revolvers, clip-loaded automatics or 'blow-back' types (in which the expanding gases of the propellant reloaded the gun by forcing the bolt back during firing). All the major armed forces possessed more or less efficient standard designs, but pistols, like most other weapons, were in short supply throughout the War, and many alternative models were pressed into service.

The most famous wartime pistol was probably the GERMAN ARMY's standard LUGER, but it was never available in sufficient numbers, and other German models were in use from 1914. The Beholla 7.65mm automatic was being issued from 1914, and the extremely powerful Mauser Automatic, used by the ITALIAN NAVY in its original 1894 model (which could hold up to 20 7.63mm rounds), was ordered into mass production as a 9mm weapon in 1915.

Both the AUSTRO-HUNGARIAN and ROMANIAN ARMIES relied principally on the sturdy 1912 Steyer Automatic, which fired an 8-round clip of 9mm bullets, but Hungarian home army forces used the reliable 7.65mm Fegyvergyar design. The TURKISH and BULGARIAN ARMIES depended almost exclusively on German supplies (or military captures) for small arms, and their best-equipped units used Mausers or Behollas.

The FRENCH ARMY was well served by its 6-round, 8mm Lebel Revolver (1892), an accurate weapon that was still in service at the end of the Second World War, and the BRITISH ARMY employed more than 300,000 of its Webley Mk.IV (1915) 0.455-inch revolvers, developed from an 1887 design. The Webley Self-Loading automatic (1913) was rejected by the British Army as too complex, but saw service with the ROYAL NAVY.

The US ARMY and US NAVY were issued with their standard 0.45-inch Colt Automatics in 1911, and the type was also used (in 0.455-inch calibre) by the British Royal Navy, RNAS and RFC. US forces also employed about 150,000 Colt Revolvers (another type sold to the British) and a similar number of Smith and Wesson Revolvers (both 0.45-inch).

The ITALIAN ARMY's standard Glisenti 9mm automatic (1910) was similar to the Luger but less durable and never available in remotely sufficient numbers. Its main alternative, the Beretta 7.65mm automatic (1915) was a relatively inaccurate old design updated for mass issue, and the even older 0.45-inch Bodeo Revolver (1891) was also used in large numbers.

The BELGIAN ARMY was supplied with licence-produced versions of the American Browning. The 7.6mm blowback Model 1900 (the weapon used to assassinate Archduke FRANZ FERDINAND in June 1914) was most common, but the 9mm Model 1903 was also produced in large numbers. Hard-pressed RUSSIAN ARMY officers were theoretically issued with old Mauser Automatics or French-designed Nagant Revolvers, but in practice used a bewildering variety of imported or obsolete weapons, and the SERBIAN ARMY relied on French surplus stock in wartime.

Plan 17 Strategic plan for the wartime deployment of the FRENCH ARMY, originally the brainchild of General FOCH and adopted without consultation by C-in-C JOFFRE in 1913. A blueprint for the invasion of GERMANY, in response to a presumed German attack on FRANCE, it was quite flexible, setting out several possible lines of attack without imposing the precise targets and timetables that characterized the German SCHLIEFFEN PLAN. The invasion's southern wing would attack into LORRAINE, after a preliminary operation in Alsace to bring its flank to the Rhine. Depending on German movements, a northern attack would either aim at Germany through the southern ARDENNES forests or swing northeast into LUXEMBOURG and BELGIUM.

Plan 17 was a radical departure from the more defensive strategy of Joffre's predecessor Michel, who had intended to focus French forces on the Belgian frontier to meet the attack indicated by intelligence reports. In an army dogmatically committed to offensive warfare a majority of officers believed with Joffre that manpower limitations and fear of British involvement would persuade Germany to attack further south. Evidence of German build-up on the Belgian frontier was welcomed in summer 1914 as weakening defences in Alsace and Lorraine, but the possibility of the GERMAN ARMY using reserves to make good its defensive deficiencies was not considered.

Distributed to commanders of the five French home armies in February 1914 (although each saw only relevant segments), Plan 17 went relentlessly into action in August. French armies marched east while the main German attack swept through Belgium, but Joffre and the general staff (GQG) adhered rigidly to their offensive scheme until 24 August, when calamitous Allied defeats in the multi-faceted Battles of the FRONTIERS revealed the imminent threat of encirclement on the WESTERN FRONT.

Plan 19 The RUSSIAN ARMY's current plan for war in August 1914. As written in 1910 by General DANILOV, with the support of war minister SUKHOMLINOV, the Plan concentrated four armies (19 out of 28 corps) for an immediate invasion of German EAST PRUSSIA in the event of war, assuming that GERMANY would attack FRANCE and leave only a small garrison in the east. Alternative attacks against Austro-Hungarian GALICIA, and towards central Germany through Silesia, were considered, respectively, less important and less practicable. Danilov also proposed to dismantle Russia's chain of FORTRESSES.

The Plan aroused immediate opposition from Sukhomlinov's many enemies within the army, headed by Grand Duke NIKOLAI, and from ARTILLERY theorists committed to fortress defence. Their principal argument, that AUSTRIA-HUNGARY represented a greater threat to RUSSIA than Germany, gained credence during a series of political crises in the Balkans, and Plan 19 was substantially altered in May 1912.

The invasion of East Prussia was retained, its strength reduced to two armies, and 47 divisions were committed to Galicia. Fortresses were to be maintained. The revised plan diluted Russian numerical superiority over the CENTRAL POWERS in 1914, and this was further dissipated when an attack through Silesia by two armies was added on 7 August 1914. See also: EASTERN FRONT; SCHLIEFFEN PLAN; PLAN 17.

Plehve, General Wenzel von (1850–1916) One of several Germans owing allegiance directly to Tsar NICHOLAS II and occupying senior positions in the RUSSIAN ARMY, Plehve was one of its most efficient generals. In command of the Fifth Army for the proposed invasion of GALICIA in August 1914, he escaped encirclement with a prompt retreat after the Battle of KOMAROW and recovered quickly to threaten Austro-Hungarian forces north of Lvov. Transferred rapidly north to take part in the POLISH CAMPAIGN, the Fifth Army played a vital role in the defence of ŁÓDŹ in November 1914. Plehve was given the new Twelfth Army in early 1915 (see Second Battle of the MASURIAN LAKES), and subsequently returned to the Fifth Army. Although he briefly commanded the northern sector of the EASTERN FRONT during the following winter, his health was poor and he was invalided out of the Army in February 1916.

Pless Convention Military agreement between BULGARIA and the CENTRAL POWERS signed at German supreme command headquarters in Pless on 6 September 1915. A mutual defence treaty was signed the same day in Sofia. The two documents contracted Bulgaria to join a German-led invasion of SERBIA on the BALKAN FRONT within 35 days and to fight either GREECE or ROMANIA if they joined the Allies. In return Germany promised Bulgaria postwar control of the Macedonian coast, part of the Romanian Dobrudja region and Greek Thrace, the latter secured with the reluctant agreement of TURKEY. The Convention also provided for financial and military aid from Germany in return for priority claims on Bulgarian food exports, beginning a cycle of economic exploitation that eventually helped undermine Bulgarian popular commitment to the alliance.

Plumer, General Sir Herbert (1857–1932) One of the most efficient British commanders on the WESTERN FRONT, he replaced General SMITH-DORRIEN in charge of II Corps when the BEF was reorganized in late 1914, and replaced him again in May 1915 as commander of the Second Army, in which capacity he was responsible for the sector around YPRES until autumn 1917.

Plumer was one of the few Allied generals in France who quickly understood the importance of careful planning and technical precision, and he achieved a major success with a series of limited set-piece advances at MESSINES in June 1917. Similar tactics in September enabled the Second Army to salvage some gains from the wreckage of General GOUGH's offensive at Ypres.

Sent to the ITALIAN FRONT at the head of an Anglo-French army after the disaster at CAPORETTO in November 1917, he was recalled to Flanders in time to conduct the Second Army's defence at the LYS the following April, and played a relatively minor role in the final COURTRAI OFFENSIVE by King ALBERT's Flanders Army Group.

Poelcappe, Battle of See: Third Battle of YPRES.

Poincaré, Raymond (1860–1934) The one constant at the centre of wartime French politics, Poincaré had been a moderate conservative deputy for 25 years when he succeeded CAILLAUX as prime minister in January 1912. Primarily interested in foreign affairs, he expected European war sooner rather than later, and consistently advocated military expansion. After successfully campaigning for the French presidency in late 1912, a rare active bid for a largely ceremonial position, he took office the following February intending to exert real authority.

Using his right of nomination to install docile prime ministers, Poincaré gave strong support to the extension of conscription into the FRENCH ARMY, and remained closely involved with foreign policy. He was the guiding figure behind French government actions during the JULY CRISIS of 1914, and some historians regard his guarantees of support to RUSSIA as a major contribution to the breakdown of peace.

A powerful mediating influence over the VIVIANI coalition, formed in August, he was nevertheless unable to assert convincing authority over the Army high command or C-in-C JOFFRE, who treated the president like any other politician and ignored him. After replacing Viviani with BRIAND in autumn 1915, Poincaré expected a stronger stand against the military from an old ally, but their relationship had deteriorated badly by the time Joffre was finally removed in December 1916.

Poincaré chose a less independent successor in RIBOT to carry through the NIVELLE OFFENSIVE, which had the president's full support. Its failure, together with mounting social tension, the rapid fall of Ribot and the even faster demise of his inexperienced successor, PAINLEVÉ, forced Poincaré to abandon the principle of national coalition in November 1917 and choose between supporters of total war and a growing PACIFIST minority. Aware that either choice called for a strong premier, he was forced to accept subordination to the aggressively pro-War prime minister CLEMENCEAU throughout 1918. After failing in a bid for leadership of the French mission at the PARIS PEACE CONFERENCE on the extreme nationalist platform proposed by Marshal FOCH, Poincaré returned to the Senate at the end of his term in 1920 and was twice prime minister before his retirement in 1929.

Poland The independent kingdom of Poland had ceased to exist in the late 18th century. In 1914 most of the region was a province of imperial RUSSIA, but AUSTRIA-HUNGARY administered GALICIA, and GERMANY had taken part of Silesia to the west (see MAP 1). Polish nationalism had survived partition, but its leadership was divided in August 1914. National Democratic Party leader Roman Dmowski, based in Habsburg Galicia, supported the Allies as most likely to encourage a unified Poland by stripping the CENTRAL POWERS of their territories. Józef PIŁSUDSKI, building a private army in Galicia, was the best-known nationalist seeking liberation from Russian control.

About a million Poles, mostly conscripted, served in the armies of both sides on the EASTERN FRONT (see POLISH FORCES), much of which was fought in greater Poland. Some of Poland's heavy industry (engineering, textiles and mining) was dismantled and taken east by Russian imperial authorities in late 1914, and the POLISH CAMPAIGNS devastated large tracts of the country, while the economy collapsed into hyperinflation (see GREAT RETREAT).

In the absence of firm Russian promises of unification and autonomy (see SAZONOV, S.) the German occupation of Russian Poland (from autumn 1915) temporarily weakened Dmowski's position. Exiled to London and Geneva, the National Democrats were reduced to a long-range PROPAGANDA campaign.

The Central Powers established a semi-autonomous 'Congress Poland' in November 1916, ruled by a puppet Council of State, but delayed any concessions to real independence until after the War. Germany meanwhile began deporting workers under the HINDENBURG PROGRAMME and extracting economic resources for the home front.

Piłsudski's refusal (March 1917) to have his new Polish Auxiliary Corps swear allegiance to the Central Powers provoked his arrest in July, and a new 'Regency Council' was formed in August under the supervision of German and Austro-Hungarian governors (see BESELER, H. VON). Vienna's influence over joint strategy had already evaporated, and the Regency Council signalled the end of experiments in mediation with Polish nationalists by the German THIRD SUPREME COMMAND. Polish interests were not represented at BREST-LITOVSK, and the collapse of Germany in

November 1918 offered the first real opportunity for Polish independence.

With tens of thousands of irregular Russian and German troops roaming the country, the Regency Council resigned almost immediately. Piłsudski returned from imprisonment in Germany and took command of three Polish corps formed for Allied service by the Russian PROVISIONAL GOVERNMENT in late 1917 and since returned to Poland under German control. As commander of the only real authority in the country, Piłsudski formed a new, broadly socialist, government in the absence of a credible alternative.

Dmowski's relatively conservative National Democrats were included in a new coalition government formed in January 1919, with Piłsudski as head of state and the pianist Paderewski as prime minister. Paderewski and Dmowski led the Polish delegation at the PARIS PEACE CONFERENCE, while Piłsudski prepared the army against the threat of Bolshevik aggression, eventually manifested in a Russo-Polish war in 1920. An enlarged Poland, complete with a 'corridor' of former German territory to the Baltic, was among the most controversial creations of the VERSAILLES Treaty (see MAP 25).

Polish Campaigns, 1914 The second phase of the war on the EASTERN FRONT, a complicated and indecisive series of offensives that followed from the campaigns of manoeuvre in EAST PRUSSIA and GALICIA. With the northern and southern sectors of the front deadlocked by bad weather, supply problems and mutual exhaustion, the massive central SALIENT of Russian Poland became the focus of contention from autumn 1914 (see MAP 11).

Of the contending forces, the AUSTRO-HUNGARIAN ARMY was already in poor condition and short of reserves after suffering heavy losses. The RUSSIAN ARMY had also suffered enormous casualties, but was only just approaching full mobilized strength and (marginal) overall manpower superiority. The victorious German Eighth Army, reinforced from the WESTERN FRONT at the end of August, remained relatively efficient, and its effective commander, LUDENDORFF, was the first to launch an offensive.

Ordered by FALKENHAYN to aid his allies, Ludendorff visited Austro-Hungarian chief of staff CONRAD on 18 September to propose an attack south from East Prussia against the flank of Russian armies advancing towards Kraków. Good RAILWAY links enabled advance units of a new German Ninth Army – comprising four corps and a CAVALRY division subtracted from the Eighth Army – to arrive north of Kraków by 22 September.

General IVANOV, commanding Russian forces in the Galician sector, was already considering withdrawal from the Carpathians, partly in response to pessimistic forecasts by the new overall commander in East Prussia, General RUZSKI. On hearing news of the German concentration Ivanov turned his forces north to meet the threat on 24 September. The move was sanctioned by STAVKA (Russian central command) as a preparation for its own invasion of Germany by the shortest route through western Poland, as envisaged in the Army's prewar PLAN 19 and recommended by RUSSIA's allies.

Ivanov was ordered to bring three armies – the Fourth (EVERT), Fifth (PLEHVE) and Ninth (Lechitski) – back beyond the San River and up the east bank of the Vistula, and Ruzski was told to leave the re-forming Second Army (SCHEIDEMANN) in position west of Warsaw. In theory able to call on twice the combined Austro-German strength in the central sector, the Russian invasion was inefficiently prepared and hampered by command confusion, with Ivanov and Ruzski ultimately sharing overall control. While the Second Army, assembling in Warsaw, pillaged the city for food, a few elements of the three southern armies had occupied a 90km front along the east bank of the Vistula by 8 October.

Austro-German forces could meanwhile manoeuvre at will in Poland and north-western Galicia. Under HINDENBURG's direct command, the German Ninth Army launched its attack on 28 September, but its intended victims had gone. Five German divisions under General MACKENSEN then marched on Warsaw, where Russian forces (about nine divisions) retreated into the city. While the rest of the German Ninth Army took up positions on the Vistula, Mackensen advanced to within 10km of the city by 12 October, where he was ordered to dig in pending reinforcement.

Austro-Hungarian forces followed the Russian withdrawal from the Carpathians as far as the San, relieving the siege of PRZEMYSL on 9 October, but repeated attempts to cross the river failed completely against the Russian Third and Eighth Armies. German and Austro-Hungarian PROPAGANDA, endorsed by field commanders, claimed both advances as great victories, but they involved no lasting gains or major combat.

The first Russian attempt to cross the Vistula opened on 11 October at IVANGOROD, one of only two fords along the invasion front (the other was at Novo-Alexandriya), but the operation collapsed within a few days. German ability to read Russian signals had alerted Ludendorff to the danger on the Vistula: Mackensen's Warsaw force was pulled back from 20 October, and Conrad agreed to transfer his First Army (DANKL) from the San to join the defence.

Ten divisions (out of a total invasion force of 30) took part in a successful Russian crossing from 22 to 26 October, forcing Dankl to withdraw southwest. Ludendorff ordered a general withdrawal from Russian Poland on 27 October, and German forces retreated to a line northwest of Kraków. Conrad's operations on the San were exposed by the retreat, forcing him to abandon 120,000 men inside Przemysl and to return to positions west of the Carpathians.

By early November the Russian invasion had stalled beyond the Vistula, again disrupted by dissent between its northern and southern commands. Torn between attacking beyond the San and defending against possible German attack from East Prussia, Stavka allowed the Russian invading armies to be pulled towards their respective flanks (and supply bases) by Ivanov and Ruzski, and the operation was postponed amid logistic chaos.

Made aware of Russian delays by intercepted signals, Ludendorff transferred most of the Ninth Army (now under Mackensen, with Hindenburg as overall C-in-C in the east) north by rail to attack the northern flank of the advanced Russian Second Army. Launched on 11 November, the German attack drove the Russian Second and Fifth Armies back on their supply base of ŁÓDŹ, then west of Warsaw after the city was abandoned on 6 December.

Further south, Ivanov had been pursuing the Austro-Hungarians into the Carpathians, forcing them to retreat to Kraków. Ivanov launched the Russian Fourth and Ninth Armies into a frontal attack against the city on 25 November, with the Third Army advancing simultaneously from the east. The siege was still in progress, drawing Russian reserves from the Carpathians, when Łódź fell to the Germans and Ivanov withdrew towards the San. Slow Austrian pursuit brought both sides back to their earlier autumn positions, and the year ended with the widespread establishment of TRENCH WARFARE on Poland's flanks. See also: CARPATHIAN OFFENSIVES; Second Battle of the MASURIAN LAKES.

Polish Forces Although wartime POLAND was not an independent state, a number of distinctively Polish land forces fought on both sides. The AUSTRO-HUNGARIAN ARMY's Polish Legion, drawn mostly from Polish GALICIA, comprised two infantry and two CAVALRY brigades and remained in being throughout the War. A Polish Legion was formed in the RUSSIAN ARMY in December 1914 for campaigns in its home sector of the EASTERN FRONT, but was dispersed into Russian units the following February, reflecting opposition to nationalist self-expression in RUSSIA. After the FEBRUARY REVOLUTION in 1917, the PROVISIONAL GOVERNMENT formed a 'Polish Army' of three corps, which was still in the process of completion when it surrendered to German forces in February 1918 and was returned to Poland.

The most independent military expression of Polish nationalism was the creation of a separate Polish Army within the FRENCH ARMY, authorized on 4 June 1917. Commanded by General Josef Haller, it was recruited from émigrés serving with the French, Poles within the Russian Expeditionary Force to the WESTERN FRONT, and Germano-Polish prisoners of war. Polish citizens living in North America had been given training facilities in

Canada in January 1917, and large numbers of these also joined Haller, who commanded more than 80,000 troops when his force returned to Polish service in April 1919. See also: RUSSO-POLISH WAR; PIŁSUDSKI, J.

Polivanov, General Alexei (1855–1920) Russian aristocrat and staff officer, deputy minister of war from 1906, who supervised SUKHOMLINOV's military reform programme until he was dismissed in 1912 for supporting the retention of FORTRESSES. Out of office in 1914, he replaced his former chief in June 1915, and used his contacts with influential liberals such as GUCHKOV to promote collaborative organization of war production through War Industries Committees (see RUSSIA).

Polivanov's loyalty oath as a serving officer prevented him from signing the cabinet's petition against Tsar NICHOLAS II's assumption of military command at STAVKA (Russian central command), and he was spared by the subsequent purge of liberals in the government, but he and foreign minister SAZONOV were increasingly isolated in a conservative cabinet from autumn 1915. He fell victim to the the Empress ALEXANDRA's machinations in March 1916, when he was dismissed after a contrived quarrel with RASPUTIN. Not recalled to office until after the FEBRUARY REVOLUTION, he headed an ultimately futile commission on military regulations for the PROVISIONAL GOVERNMENT, and joined the RED ARMY as a technical advisor shortly before his death from typhus.

Polygon Wood See: Third Battle of YPRES.

Pomilio P-Types Useful Italian biplanes introduced to ITALIAN AIR FORCE reconnaissance units as the P-C from March 1917. Though fast enough to operate without an escort, and reasonably well armed, it suffered extreme in-flight stability problems. After a series of fatal crashes an underside fin was added to a new C-D model, and a more radically altered 300hp C-E version, with a new tailfin design, entered service from February 1918. Faster, more stable and fitted with synchronized forward armament, it became the standard Italian reconnaissance and ARTILLERY-spotting aircraft by late 1918. At least 1,600 P-Types served on the ITALIAN FRONT, equipping 30 squadrons, more than any other wartime Italian design.

BRIEF DATA (P-C) Type: two-seater armed reconnaissance; Engine: 260hp Fiat; Max speed: 179kph; Armament: 2 × 8mm mg.

Portugal A turbulent republic since the revolution of 1910, Portugal was governed by President de Arriaga until his term of office ended in 1915, when he resigned after surviving royalist risings, military plots and a rapid succession of prime ministers. Dr Bernadino Marchada took power in August 1915, and retained a shaky hold on the office until December 1917, when a military uprising in Lisbon led by Major Sidonio Paes forced him into exile.

Royalist agitation and military unrest, climaxing in a naval mutiny at Lisbon in January 1918, continued under Paes, but foreign policy was more straightforward. Linked with GREAT BRITAIN by alliance since the Middle Ages, and in competition with German colonial and trading interests in Africa, Portugal declared its support for the Allies on 7 August 1914.

Though internal tensions rendered parliament's assent to military involvement (23 November) meaningless, Portuguese troops were already skirmishing with German troops on the frontier between MOZAMBIQUE (Portuguese East Africa) and German EAST AFRICA. African operations expanded steadily, especially after German agents incited tribal uprising in Angola, but did not provoke a full-scale declaration of war, partly because the British government regarded Portugal as a military liability in 1914.

German ships in Portuguese harbours were seized at the request of the British in February 1916, and ex-King Manoel, exiled in Britain, called for a suspension of royalist activities pending defeat of the CENTRAL POWERS. This prompted GERMANY to declare war against Portugal on 9 March, and war with AUSTRIA-HUNGARY followed a week later.

About 100,000 Portuguese eventually fought in AFRICA and on the WESTERN FRONT, and despite British financial assistance (loan facilities agreed in August 1916 provided some £23 million) the combined effort wrecked Portugal's fragile economy. Popular discontent was fuelled by a resumption of militant royalism after the ARMISTICE, and the assassination of Paes in December 1918 sparked a year of civil war. See also: PORTUGUESE FORCES.

Portuguese Forces The peacetime Portuguese Army was conscripted, but widespread exemptions kept numbers down to a relatively affordable 33,000 men in 1914. Steadily expanded from September 1914 for colonial operations, its size mushroomed after PORTUGAL entered the War in March 1916, and the wartime Army eventually employed about 183,000 men and 335 guns. Training of a Portuguese division began at once, under the supervision of Allied military missions, and a Portuguese Expeditionary Force was formed under General de Alorn in January 1917. After further training in England, 40,000 Portuguese troops (two divisions) reached the WESTERN FRONT by mid-1917, occupying part of the sector held by the BEF until spring 1918, when they were withdrawn after the defeat at the LYS. Almost 100,000 Portuguese eventually saw service in Flanders or colonial MOZAMBIQUE, of whom 21,000 were listed as casualties, including over 7,000 dead.

Plans to expand the conscript Portuguese Navy had not come to fruition by August 1914, when it included one small old BATTLESHIP (*Vasco da Gama*), four CRUISERS, nine DESTROYERS and a single SUBMARINE. With naval forces consistently implicated in anti-government rebellions throughout the period they played little active part in the wider conflict after 1916. The Army Air Service was tiny, consisting in 1914 of three obsolete aircraft purchased by public subscription. A few surplus Allied machines were purchased over the next two years, and Allied pilot instructors were sent to PORTUGAL, but no Portuguese aircraft saw active service.

Potemkin The old Russian BATTLESHIP *Potemkin* was completed in 1903 but was extensively refitted and renamed *Pantelimon* after taking part in a revolutionary mutiny during 1905. Along with its sisters *Hevstafi* and *Ioann Zlatoust* (both belatedly finished in 1910), it was the most modern of 7 PRE-DREADNOUGHTS in wartime service with the BLACK SEA fleet, operating primarily as a coastal-defence vessel. Its original name was restored after the FEBRUARY REVOLUTION, but was again altered to *Boretz za Svobodu* in 1918. It was destroyed in April 1919, along with five other pre-dreadnoughts, by anti-Bolshevik naval forces supported by Anglo-French warships (see RUSSIAN CIVIL WAR).
BRIEF DATA (*Pantelimon*, 1914) Displacement: 12,800 tons; Crew: 731; Dimensions: length 386ft (116.9m), beam 74ft (22.4m); Speed: 16k; Main armament: 4 × 12in gun, 16 × 6in, 14 × 12pdr, 4 × 18in TT.

Potiorek, Field Marshal Oskar (1853–1933) One of CONRAD's rivals for the post of AUSTRO-HUNGARIAN ARMY chief of staff in 1906, and its inspector general from 1911, Potiorek doubled as military governor of Bosnia after 1912 and was directly responsible for security during Archduke FRANZ FERDINAND's fatal visit to Sarajevo in June 1914. When AUSTRIA-HUNGARY declared war on SERBIA in late July, Potiorek was given overall command of the Fifth and Sixth Armies on the BALKAN FRONT, and used excellent court connections to overrule Conrad and retain four divisions of the Second Army (diverted at the last moment for operations in GALICIA) for successive invasions of Serbia. Three defeats – at the JADAR, DRINA and KOLUBARA RIVERS – reduced the front to long-term inactivity by December 1914 and cost Potiorek his command. He was replaced by Archduke EUGEN on 22 December and retired from the Army in the new year.

Pre-Dreadnoughts Contemporary term describing BATTLESHIPS designed before the British *DREADNOUGHT* set new standards for heavy armament, speed and protection in 1906. Sometimes subdivided into 'intermediate' battleships, rendered prematurely obsolete by *Dreadnought*, and 'old' battleships, 19th-century designs that would anyway be out of date, they were generally regarded as unfit for modern fleet actions.

The ROYAL NAVY possessed 29 operational pre-dreadnoughts (with another 20 in reserve) in August 1914. Most were stationed in minor theatres all over the world or used as BLOCKADE guardships, although the 8 KING EDWARD VII Class vessels served with the GRAND FLEET for a time, and two ships, *Venerable* and *Revenge* (renamed *Redoubtable* in early 1915), were used to bombard coastal German positions on the WESTERN FRONT from late 1914, the latter remaining in position until its replacement by MONITORS in October 1915 (see *CANOPUS*).

Six of the GERMAN NAVY's 20 pre-dreadnoughts were with the HIGH SEAS FLEET at JUTLAND, and others were active in the BALTIC SEA. The FRENCH NAVY had 17 pre-dreadnoughts in the MEDITERRANEAN in 1914, the AUSTRO-HUNGARIAN NAVY 12 and the ITALIAN NAVY 8. The RUSSIAN NAVY used 9 pre-dreadnoughts, the TURKISH and GREEK NAVIES two each. The world's main non-European naval powers, the USA and Japan, possessed 23 and 16, respectively, in 1914.

Particularly active in the Mediterranean, pre-dreadnoughts were used more freely than precious modern units, carrying out regular coastal bombardments and escort operations (see DARDANELLES; SUEZ CANAL; ATHENS LANDING; PALESTINE FRONT). Casualties were high, mostly to MINES or TORPEDOES, and the British eventually lost 11 pre-dreadnoughts, the French and Russian Navies 4 each, the Turkish and Italian Navies 2 each, and the Austro-Hungarian Navy 1. The JAPANESE NAVY's sole casualty exploded in harbour, and the only German pre-dreadnought loss, *Pommern*, was sunk at JUTLAND.

Preliminary Bombardment The simplest and most common wartime ARTILLERY tactic, an attack by all available guns on the target of an imminent infantry advance. The idea that defenders and fortifications could be wiped out or reduced to docility by bombardment was tested to extremes on the WESTERN FRONT – culminating in a massive three-week barrage before the SOMME OFFENSIVE in 1916 – and was imitated in miniature on other fronts. It stimulated a rapid expansion of heavy artillery capacity that continued until the ARMISTICE, but preliminary bombardments failed repeatedly. Acting as an unmissable warning signal to defenders, they gave plenty of time to bring up reinforcements. In addition, they were unable to destroy sophisticated TRENCHES or kill their occupants, and left attackers to struggle through devastated terrain. Lack of any clear alternative and evident room for technical improvement delayed serious deviation from the tactic for major offensives in Europe until after the unproductive carnage of 1916, when a sense of stalemate encouraged use of short 'hurricane' bombardments or sophisticated CREEPING BARRAGE techniques. See also: BREAKTHROUGH TACTICS.

Preparedness Movement General description applied to the multi-faceted campaign of 1915–20 to secure the permanent, large-scale enlargement of US national military forces. Dominated and sponsored by expansionist US business, political, military and intellectual interests, and strongest in the urban northeast of the country, its most prominent spokesmen were ex-President Theodore ROOSEVELT and former US Army chief of staff General WOOD. The campaign focused on demands for universal military training and service (UMT&S), and played a vital role in establishing mass recruitment on the US political agenda (see SELECTIVE SERVICE ACT).

Generally envisaged as a limited version of peacetime conscription on the contemporary European model, UMT&S was promoted as necessary for the efficient protection of US global economic interests, and as a democratic means of revitalizing popular commitment to the nation at a time of nascent social unrest. Pressure groups like the National Security League, founded in December 1914, preached UMT&S to political and commercial elites, and the Military Camps Training Association (called 'Plattsburgers' after their first camp) was the best known of several unofficial groups concerned with preparing future officers for a mass army.

Though 'conscriptionists' were increasingly influential in political circles during 1915–16, their policies and long-term aims excited widespread opposition across a broad socio-political spectrum. Agrarian, union, immigrant, Afro-American, liberal, pacifist, feminist and socialist interests were among those suspicious of the movement's challenge to traditional American principles of anti-militarism and local self-defence (see AMERICAN UNION AGAINST MILITARISM).

Despite a massive publicity effort during 1916, the movement never achieved sufficient popular support to exert a decisive influence on government policy, and the WILSON administration's eventual adoption of the SELECTIVE SERVICE SYSTEM reflected the movement's influence only in that it appeared acceptably moderate by comparison. The strictly temporary introduction of conscription represented effective defeat for the wider cause, and the movement was diffused into the business of direct war management after 1917, though it remained the resort of elite conservative interests until the election of right-wing Republican Warren Harding to the White House in 1920.

Prespa, Battle of Lake The main action on the BALKAN FRONT in 1917, an otherwise quiet year in the theatre north of SALONIKA. After the relative failure of his MONASTIR OFFENSIVE the previous autumn, Allied C-in-C SARRAIL had received strong political support for a spring resumption to divert German strength from the NIVELLE OFFENSIVE on the WESTERN FRONT. Given formal operational control over Allied armies at Salonika in January 1917, he planned a carefully coordinated repeat of the previous autumn's drive into SERBIA.

Sarrail's manpower strength had increased to over 600,000 men by early 1917, but many of his basic problems remained unsolved. Sickness, and the need to protect Salonika as civil strife engulfed GREECE reduced frontline strength to a little over 100,000 men, and a larger number of German and Bulgarian troops were still holding excellent high ground all along the front. Operational coordination between national units was by no means complete, and the SERBIAN ARMY in particular was showing signs of mutinous war weariness.

Operations all along the front began on 11 March with attempts by Franco-Serbian forces to advance north on a line between Monastir and Lake Prespa to the west. General MILNE's British contingent began a subsidiary attack next day around the Lake Doiran sector at the opposite end of the front, but other planned attacks in the centre failed to start at the right time.

Spotted in advance by GERMAN ARMY AIR SERVICE units, the attacks were met by rapid reinforcement and halted within a week, gaining only a few hundred metres at a cost of some 14,000 losses to battle and sickness. By 19 March German counterattacks had forced the western flank back onto Monastir itself, compelling Sarrail to abandon actions elsewhere. Fighting died down after 22 March with Allied troops still in occupation of Monastir, but the town remained in range of German ARTILLERY.

British attacks in the Doiran sector were resumed in late April, without threatening the long-term stalemate in the area, and fighting flared up again in the first half of May, focused on Lake Doiran and an advance in the west by French and rebel Greek forces. Mutiny in RUSSIAN ARMY units, spreading rapidly to French formations, forced Sarrail to halt all offensive operations after mid-May, and the Salonika front remained quiet until autumn 1918. See VARDAR OFFENSIVE; MAP 19.

Prezan, General Constantine (1861–1943) Competent ROMANIAN ARMY commander who led the Fourth Army in the invasion of Transylvania at the start of the ROMANIAN CAMPAIGN in August 1916 (see MAP 14). A reinforced Austro-Hungarian First Army (ARZ VON STRAUSSENBERG) drove his forces back into the Carpathians by early October, but he withdrew in good order and his military reputation suffered no damage. Appointed chief of staff in November, he became C-in-C when King FERDINAND I resigned the position a year later, on the eve of an armistice with the CENTRAL POWERS. He retained command of the remnant in arms after the conclusion of the BUCHAREST Treaty in May 1918, and held the post until his retirement in 1920.

Princip, Gavrilo (1894–1918) Bosnian-born Slav nationalist, resident in SERBIA and armed (along with two accomplices) by the BLACK HAND organization for an assassination attempt on Austro-Hungarian heir presumptive FRANZ FERDINAND during his state visit to Sarajevo in June 1914. Their first attempt, a bungled bomb throwing, alerted the royal party and prompted a change of itinerary, but Princip shot the Archduke and his wife when poor security organization gave him a second opportunity shortly afterwards. The assassination sparked the JULY CRISIS and is generally credited with triggering the First World War, but Austrian claims that Princip was working on behalf of the Serbian government were groundless. Tried for his crime and found guilty on 28 October, he was spared the death sentence because of his youth and got 20 years hard labour, but died of tuberculosis in prison on 28 April 1918.

Prittwitz, General Maximilian von (1848–1929) Silesian-born officer who commanded the German Eighth Army defending EAST PRUSSIA in August 1914. Regarded as hesitant by some of his officers, notably operations expert HOFFMANN, Prittwitz misread the result of his first major battle, at GUMBINNEN on 20 August, and immediately ordered a full-scale retreat west to the Vistula. Although he changed his mind the following morning after consulting field commanders, Prittwitz had already confirmed his pessimistic view of the situation over the telephone to Berlin, and a shocked MOLTKE ordered his dismissal. General HINDENBURG was hastily summoned as a replacement, and Prittwitz was retired.

Prohibition (US) Political agitation for federal laws banning the manufacture and sale of ALCOHOL had been a major sociopolitical issue in the UNITED STATES since the mid-1890s, dividing politicians into 'wets' and 'drys' regardless of party affiliation. Increasing support for the anti-alcohol 'drys' had been insufficient to win passage of a Prohibition Bill in 1914 (although secretary DANIELS imposed it on the US NAVY that year).

The defeat was partly attributable to an alliance between the brewing industry and its best customers, the German-American community. Once the USA was at war in 1917, the connection stimulated a 'dry' campaign to associate alcohol with the enemy, and the industry came under more cogent attack as wasteful at a time of national economic mobilization. Persuaded by Food Board chief Herbert Hoover, President WILSON curbed production in 1917 by forbidding the use of foods for alcohol manufacture, and full prohibition was established by the 18th Amendment to the US constitution of 3 December 1918. Scheduled to come into effect from July 1919, but postponed until January 1920, it made the sale and manufacture (but not possession) of alcohol a federal offence, and remained in effect until repealed in 1933.

Propaganda The publication or broadcast of information designed to influence wartime popular opinion towards a particular cause or viewpoint was not new in 1914. Books, newspapers, periodicals, leaflets, posters, poems, paintings, photographs, monumental sculpture and oratory were already familiar tools of imperial propaganda, and burgeoning mass literacy in western and central Europe had been heavily exploited by both governments and private interests during the immediate prewar years, primarily to generate support for national rearmament or expansion programmes. All the main belligerent governments, especially those in the most economically developed states, launched ambitious public-information programmes immediately on the outbreak of war, using every medium available to contemporary culture and technology, and the four-year struggle was accompanied by a chorus of propaganda on an unprecedented scale.

The British, French and German governments set a wartime pattern in 1914 by recruiting eminent cultural figures to produce propaganda material. British campaigns were spearheaded by the most celebrated artists of the age – including world-famous writers such as Wells and Kipling – and other Allied governments followed suit, so that the War was a fertile period for many branches of the arts, especially the fields of poster art and illustration. The German administration also made use of artists, but preferred to place university professors in charge of propaganda output, investing its messages with an air of academic veracity.

Official wartime propaganda fell into three broad categories, aimed at home, enemy and neutral audiences. Although they worked with essentially the same material and sought to encourage similar views, each was generally handled by separate departments in 1914, administered through the interior, war and foreign ministries, respectively, of the main belligerent governments. By 1918, state propaganda in GREAT BRITAIN, FRANCE, GERMANY and the UNITED STATES had been organized into centralized administrations, typified by the US Committee on Public Information (CPI) under George CREEL, or AITKEN's Ministry of Information in Britain.

Broadly speaking, government propaganda for home consumption concentrated first on establishment of national unity behind a just cause, and on recruitment – the latter a particularly important issue in Britain (and its dominions), which had no conscript army. Backed by a wave of spontaneous popular nationalist enthusiasm, a flood of articles, speeches and posters (of which the most celebrated depicts Lord KITCHENER exhorting the British to national service) pushed home the need for military recruits, and by early 1915 parallel campaigns in France, Britain and Germany were exhorting civilians to work in munitions industries.

Although manpower crises on the military and industrial fronts prompted regular recruitment drives everywhere, with later campaigns often focusing on those WOMEN and teenagers not yet involved in war industries, the increasing need for resource conservation and production efficiency came to dominate home-front propaganda from 1916. Campaigns for the preservation of food and fuel supplies through reduced consumption, beginning with the introduction of voluntary meatless days in most countries, were backed by drives for increased food production through additional labour in the fields or conversion of land to agricultural use. Governments also attempted to regulate the behaviour of civilians by campaigning against ALCOHOL abuse, sexual indulgence, and any other form of activity considered to have a negative effect on overall war efforts.

National security, fundraising and public morale were the other main concerns of official home-front propaganda. The first was a matter of encouraging public circumspection by maintaining an atmosphere of constant vigilance against espionage, and fundraising efforts were dominated by campaigns for the sale of war bonds, but the field of public morale was more complex and controversial, embracing xenophobic propaganda and the large-scale promotion of military disinformation by every warring state.

Whipping up hatred of the enemy was hardly necessary in most countries. Contemporary populations were largely ignorant of overseas cultures, and the spontaneous public xenophobia displayed all over Europe during the 1914 JULY CRISIS never really subsided, but governments on both sides fuelled race hatred by promoting grotesque images of enemy behaviour. Atrocities committed by the GERMAN ARMY during the invasion of BELGIUM gave the Allies an early opportunity to present German troops as monsters, and this was the theme of most hate propaganda by both sides. As war weariness became more of a problem for belligerent governments, greater emphasis was placed on this type of material, culminating in fantastic distortions such as the Allied 'KADAVER' story of 1917.

Manipulation of war-related information for home consumption was universal. Although western democratic governments made self-conscious efforts to produce 'propaganda of truth', this in effect meant little more than formal avoidance of known untruths in a conflict characterized by the uncertainty of most data and the lack of access to opposition sources. Autocratic regimes were less scrupulous, pragmatically reporting the course of the War in whatever terms seemed most likely to preserve popular support.

The overall result was mostly nonsense. Official reports of military operations on all sides required audiences to accept unlikely levels of success with improbable regularity.

Defeats were generally reported as small-scale 'tactical retirements' or not admitted at all. Various Italian naval disasters, the loss of the British dreadnought *AUDACIOUS* and the British defeat at TANGA were among many Allied military setbacks covered up for the sake of popular morale – usually with the effect of maximizing their impact when they finally became known – while defeat was virtually unknown to official German, Habsburg, Ottoman and Russian chroniclers.

Learned sources were simultaneously used by all powers to provide 'scientific' arguments suggesting that victory was imminent or inevitable. German arguments in favour of unrestricted SUBMARINE WARFARE, and numerous British works proving that naval BLOCKADE was crippling the CENTRAL POWERS were among the most important of such campaigns. Both backfired, generating popular disappointment when rapid victory failed to materialize.

The commissioning of official war artists to produce images of frontline life was also counterproductive in morale terms, despite restrictions on subject matter (British war artists, for instance, were only allowed to depict corpses in positions of peaceful repose). Though eyewitness works were invariably bleak, their impact was less immediate or widespread than that of a far larger body of work by home-based artists and illustrators committed to providing romantic views of martial glory.

Photographs were in great demand for use by a welter of war-related books and periodicals (official or privately sponsored) in all the more developed wartime societies. Although genuine frontline snapshots were increasingly available as new portable cameras were taken to battle zones by troops, widespread use was made of prewar archive pictures or staged photographs taken away from the front line. Routinely doctored or given misleading captions to provide the appropriate message, the photographs printed for public edification (including a small number of colour plates) exploited the relative naivety of target audiences for whom the new medium of FILM conveyed an inherent sense of legitimacy.

Moving pictures were also available for popular audiences in a propaganda context. German field units on the WESTERN FRONT were frequently accompanied by movie cameras when the conquest of an important or well-known landmark was in prospect, and official newsreels were shown in British and American cinemas from 1917. Propaganda film was always sanitized for public display, and the most famous example of wartime cine-documentary, a British sequence showing the opening phases of the SOMME OFFENSIVE in 1916, was compiled by mixing staged footage with genuine battle sequences.

Newspapers remained the primary means of mass communication in developed countries throughout the War, and press censorship was an important element of government propaganda policy everywhere. Blanket censorship was practised by the autocratic regimes of Turkey and Russia, where publication of opinion and military information was equally restricted, and criticism of official policy frequently resulted in the suppression of complete editions or enforced closure. The relaxation of censorship in both empires, forced by revolutions in Russia and permitted by a desperate YOUNG TURK regime from spring 1918, unlocked an uncontrollable flood of criticism that hastened imperial collapse.

Editorial opinion was not in theory restricted in the western Allied states or in Germany, but could generally be controlled when necessary under emergency wartime powers, and was in practice restrained by severe limits on the amount of data available to editors. French, British and Italian military authorities allowed few war correspondents to join frontline units, and their output was subject to close scrutiny by field commanders, so that newspapers were forced to rely on daily official communiqués for war information.

Although newspaper readers were inevitably subject to a diet of sanitized misinformation most of the time, criticisms and revelations of military difficulties did find their way into Allied newspapers, often with powerful effects on popular opinion (see MURDOCH, K.). Fragile French and Italian coalition cabinets were plagued by unruly fourth estates, which indulged in loud criticism of incumbent regimes and debated fundamental issues of war and peace. The British government faced no such challenge on fundamentals, and apparently independent criticisms of its war management were usually inspired by official sources, reflecting policy disputes at high command or cabinet level (see AMIENS DISPATCH; SHELL SCANDAL).

Editorial freedom in Germany was hampered by an almost complete ignorance of military realities imposed by the high command, and press opinion again reflected policy arguments at the highest level, focusing on the pros and cons of SUBMARINE WARFARE and taking part in a triumphalist national debate over war aims. In the United States, where freedom of opinion was constitutionally guaranteed, wartime federal control of the mails effectively prevented the widespread circulation of any printed matter deemed unsuitable.

In an age before broadcast RADIO and television, personal appeal was an important propaganda weapon everywhere: the impassioned rabble-rousing of demagogues such as D'ANNUNZIO in Italy or Horatio Bottomley in Britain was used to whip up popular enthusiasm for war; and fighting heroes (especially air ACES in Germany, Italy and France) were paraded for popular acclaim and often required to sell war bonds in the process. More than any other major wartime power, the USA maintained a tradition of public oratory as a news medium, and Creel's WIB made an industry of declamatory speechifying, hiring 75,000 FOUR-MINUTE MEN to deliver brief propaganda messages all over the country.

Government propaganda aimed at neutral audiences overseas used essentially the same approach as that designed for home markets: basically a combination of triumphalism and defamation of the enemy. Competition took place between the main belligerents for the favours of all neutral countries, but the failure of a high-profile German campaign in Italy from late 1914 reflected the marginal impact of propaganda on European populations preoccupied with nationalist ambitions. German long-range propaganda, transmitted via radio stations to well-funded agents, was more successful in the Middle East, causing serious destabilization in PERSIA, and damaging relations between the Allies and ARAB REVOLT leaders.

The neutral United States, which contained at least 10 million German-speakers, was easily the most important area of propaganda competition between the main powers from 1914. The eventual triumph of Allied opinion owed much to the advantage of shared (official) language, to German persistence in submarine warfare, and to the support of influential east-coast business interests, but perhaps the greatest single blow in the propaganda war was struck by the ROYAL NAVY in August 1914, when it cut transatlantic cable links between Germany and the United States.

Official propaganda aimed at enemy populations was restricted by obvious difficulties in reaching the interior of hostile territories. Although the German government's logistic and financial support for PACIFIST or revolutionary cells in hostile countries was a form of propaganda, and although aircraft were used by the western Allies to drop leaflets deep inside Germany from late 1917, most effort was concentrated on undermining the morale of opponents at the fronts.

Contemporary mythology, especially in Britain, maintained that leaflet propaganda contributed to the collapse of the German Army in France during autumn 1918, but modern commentators recognize that such campaigns were only rarely effective. The success attributed to British propaganda in PALESTINE from autumn 1917, when desertions from the Turkish Army reached unprecedented levels, reflected conditions in which starving troops could expect a far better lifestyle as prisoners of war.

Although governments were responsible for the most comprehensive wartime propaganda campaigns, unofficial sources contributed an enormous amount of material for home audiences. Alongside spontaneous outbursts of jingoism from artists and writers, material sponsored by powerful extraparliamentary interests was used to encourage popular support for specific policy agendas. The FATHERLAND PARTY in Germany, funded by industrialists and the Army, followed a tradition set by the great 'patriotic leagues' in the prewar period, pouring resources into a massive campaign in support of the radical THIRD SUPREME COMMAND dictatorship from 1917. The PREPAREDNESS MOVEMENT represented right-wing political, military and business interests in the USA, and backed its demands for national armament in 1916 with a publicity programme worthy of any government.

Rebel or pacifist propaganda inevitably had less access to distribution networks, mass publication techniques or popular celebrities, but nevertheless managed considerable impact on most European home fronts. Given access to a printing press, and often funded by enemy agencies, small groups of committed individuals could reach large, potentially volatile audiences in congested industrial cities and frontline zones. Though hardly a problem in Britain and the USA (a virulent American 'reds scare' notwithstanding), seditious agitation undoubtedly helped fuel the mass of strikes and demonstrations that accompanied mounting war weariness in Russia, Germany, France, Italy and Austria-Hungary.

Official propaganda generally held underground agitation responsible for industrial discontent, nationalist uprising and MUTINY wherever they occurred. The suppression of small publications (such as the French *LE BONNET ROUGE*) was eventually treated as a major national security issue in all the continental empires, but their importance was exaggerated as a means of maintaining popular vigilance and deflecting criticism from established executives.

Religious authorities played a major propaganda role, usually in support of government policies. The established churches of Protestant regions, the Orthodox Church in Russia and a host of Catholic prelates throughout central and western Europe gave unstinting moral and practical support to the propaganda arguments of their respective national regimes. In print and in sermons (from the pulpit or the frontline chapel) Christian populations at war were universally reassured that God was on their particular side.

In the Ottoman Empire, where religious and parliamentary authorities competed for political ascendancy under the dual jurisdiction of the Sultan, Muslim leaders declared a holy war (*Jihad*) against the Allies in 1914. Despite loud support from Kaiser WILHELM II – the self-styled 'friend of Islam' whose proclaimed conversion to the faith was well received in many remote regions – hopes of inciting large-scale Muslim rebellion within the British Empire proved optimistic (see SUEZ CANAL; SINGAPORE MUTINY). On the home front, many Ottoman religious leaders considered the Young Turk regime dangerously secular, and their propaganda efforts were concentrated on a battle to maintain ritual observances and traditional restrictions on the behaviour of women.

It is difficult to be precise about the overall effect of propaganda on wartime audiences. Distinguished by its scale, which set new and enduring standards for public-information control, rather than its content, which was often simplistic by modern standards, it quickly provoked scepticism in some quarters, particularly among sophisticated urban communities. But despite a rich canon of contemporary cartoons and other forms of satire, there is evidence that what the experienced soldier recognized as rubbish was believed by at least some civilians. The German population was undeniably shocked by official revelations of military weakness in autumn 1918, and reports in soldiers' memoirs revealing incomprehension of the War's realities among home communities everywhere are too frequent to be ignored.

Although modern historians question the contemporary view of propaganda as the vital element in the formation of wartime public opinion, its long-term effects are not disputed. The promotion of an unrealistic view of fighting conditions to home audiences contributed to a breakdown in communications between soldiers and civilians that was felt long after the ARMISTICE. Official perpetration of myths about the actual course of the War furnished postwar political opportunities for MUSSOLINI in Italy, helped right-wing elements to destabilize the Weimar Republic in Germany, and provided a focus for popular discontent everywhere else during the decades that followed.

Protopopov, Aleksandr (1866–1918) Russian textile manufacturer, a moderate Octobrist deputy in the Duma and its vice chairman from 1914 (see RUSSIA). In charge of the War Industries Committee on metals from mid-1915 he was a relatively minor political figure when appointed interior minister in September 1916. His acceptance of the post in a highly unpopular cabinet was considered an act of political treachery by many deputies, and his reputation was further clouded by rumours of treason, arising from an earlier (and probably innocent) meeting with a German banker in Stockholm.

Chosen on the advice of Empress ALEXANDRA, who perceived in Protopopov a strong figure to bolster the faltering STÜRMER cabinet, he was perhaps the least sympathetic Tsarist minister of the period. Vain, bullying and anxious to increase the powers of his office, he suffered from advanced syphilis, which rendered him physically weak and mentally unstable. Retained after Stürmer's fall in November, his dominant presence in the short-lived cabinets of premiers Trepov and Golitsyn outraged an increasingly militant opposition. Arrested by the PROVISIONAL GOVERNMENT, he was still in prison during the OCTOBER REVOLUTION and was executed by the Bolshevik regime on New Year's Day.

Provisional Government (Russia) Liberal administration in nominal control of Russia after the 1917 FEBRUARY REVOLUTION. Formed on 15 March by politicians from the recently dissolved parliament (Duma), and led by the independent liberal Prince LVOV, it contained one self-proclaimed socialist in justice minister KERENSKI. Continuity with the old regime's supporters was maintained by the inclusion of former industry minister GUCHKOV along with industrialists Konovalov and Tereshchenko. All three, and MILIUKOV at the foreign ministry, were regarded with suspicion by the Petrograd (St Petersburg) Soviet, which refused official participation in the government.

Although Lvov's cabinet abolished many tsarist institutions, and promised sweeping social reforms after the election of a Constituent Assembly, it never had sufficient mass or military support to establish control over urban radicalism or rural anarchy, and the government's personnel bias was steadily adjusted to the left under pressure from the socialist SOVIETS. A new coalition from 18 May included four relatively moderate socialists, including Social Revolutionary (SR) leader Chernov, but a minority of radicals, including the Bolsheviks, again refused participation.

Kerenski became premier in July, imprisoning leading radicals after the JULY DAYS disorders and restoring capital punishment in the RUSSIAN ARMY. He included seven socialists and an equal number of liberals in a new cabinet from early August, but was effectively powerless to combat urban radicalism or peasant anarchy by the autumn. Facing a sharp rise in revolutionary temperature after General KORNILOV's ineffectual rising in September, Kerenski sought to recover the government's socialist credentials with a third coalition from 8 October. Its brief, impotent life served only to discredit moderate socialists after it was overthrown by the OCTOBER REVOLUTION. See RUSSIA.

Przemysl Austro-Hungarian fortress on the River San, an imposing symbol of Habsburg rule defended as an isolated obstacle to Russian forces during the retreat from northeast GALICIA in September 1914 (see MAP 10). Relieved for a few weeks in early October, when Russian forces withdrew north for the POLISH CAMPAIGNS, the fortress was again besieged after the Russian victory at IVANGOROD forced another Austro-Hungarian withdrawal. Invested by the Russian Eleventh Army (Selivanov), its defence became a major public issue in AUSTRIA-HUNGARY, and relief of its 120,000-strong garrison was the main aim of CONRAD's abortive CARPATHIAN OFFENSIVE in early 1915.

The RUSSIAN ARMY's shortage of modern heavy ARTILLERY, and its inability to transport antiquated big guns across poor roads and thick mud enabled the defenders to hold out until 22 March, when supply shortages forced them to surrender. The Austro-German GORLICE–TARNOW OFFENSIVE retook the fortress on 4 June, and it was never again threatened.

Despite the importance attached to Przemysl by both sides, its fate never affected the strategic position on the EASTERN FRONT, and the main side effect of its long resistance was to encourage the subsequent Russian defence of the fortress at NOVOGEORGIEVSK.

'Pusher' Aircraft Any aircraft in which the power plant and propeller were situated behind the crew, as opposed to 'tractor' machines with the engine in front. Popular with designers, particularly in Britain, during the early years of the War, the arrangement offered the advantages of stable flight for reconnaissance and a clear field of forward fire, but development of air-to-air combat and INTERRUPTER GEAR made speed tactically essential, and the faster tractor types dominated AERIAL WARFARE after 1916.

Putnik, Field Marshal Radomir (1847–1917) Although a veteran of SERBIA's Balkan conflicts in the 1870s and 1880s, Putnik's liberal political connections appeared to have ended his career when he was pushed into early retirement in 1895. Recalled to active service after the coup that brought King PETER to power in 1903, he became chief of the SERBIAN ARMY's general staff the following year and remained in the post until his death. Three spells as war minister before 1914 aided a programme of military modernization that bore fruit in the two Balkan Wars (1912–13).

He was on holiday in Austria at the start of the JULY CRISIS in 1914, but was allowed to return home. Nominally under C-in-C Prince ALEXANDER, he took effective field command of Serbian forces on the BALKAN FRONT, frustrating ill-planned Austro-Hungarian invasions at the DRINA in August and at the SAVE in September before advancing across the border to threaten Austrian positions in Bosnia. His veteran forces, used to mountain warfare, retreated deep into the hills before a third invasion in November, extending Austro-Hungarian supply lines before successfully counterattacking at KOLUBARA in early December.

Denied Allied reinforcements until it was too late (see SALONIKA), and prevented from launching a preemptive summer attack on BULGARIA by the Anglo-French desire to appease Sofia, Putnik recognized that he could not hope to defeat the major invasion launched by the CENTRAL POWERS in October 1915. Outnumbered, short of artillery and riddled with typhus, his army was driven back into the plateau lands of Kosovo and began its 'GREAT RETREAT' across the mountains to the Adriatic on 23 November. The elderly and ailing Putnik was carried by sedan chair through bitter mountain blizzards, and was seriously ill by the time he reached the Albanian port of Scutari (Shkodër) on 7 December. Passing command to Field Marshal MIŠIĆ, he was evacuated to France, where he died in May 1917.

Q

Qingdao See: TSINGTAO.

Queen Elizabeth Class The first BATTLESHIPS completed with 15-inch main guns, the five ships of the Queen Elizabeth Class joined the ROYAL NAVY in 1915–16. Their new guns proved particularly efficient, and oil-fired turbines gave them sufficient speed to operate with BATTLECRUISERS, a role performed by *Queen Elizabeth's* sister ships (*Warspite*, *Barham*, *Valiant* and *Malaya*) at JUTLAND.

Completed in January 1915, *Queen Elizabeth* itself was being refitted at the time of Jutland after operations at the DARDANELLES. Its deployment away from home waters had caused controversy at a time when British numerical superiority over the German HIGH SEAS FLEET seemed marginal, and was terminated at the first sign of U-BOATS in May 1915. From late 1916, *Queen Elizabeth* served as

GRAND FLEET C-in-C BEATTY's flagship, and all five ships survived, heavily modified, to serve in the Second World War.

BRIEF DATA (*Queen Elizabeth*, 1915) Displacement: 31,000 tons; Crew: 955; Dimensions: length 640ft (193.9m), beam 90.5ft (27.4m); Speed: 25k; Armament: 8 × 15in gun, 12 × 6in, 2 × 3in AA, 4 × 21in TT.

Queen Mary See: *LION*; Battle of JUTLAND.

Qurna, Battle of Successful attempt by Anglo-Indian forces on the MESOPOTAMIAN FRONT to consolidate their capture of BASRA in November 1914. The TURKISH ARMY's 38th Division (about 2,000 troops under Colonel Subhi Bey) retreated some 80km upriver from Basra to the town of Qurna, at the junction of the Rivers Tigris and Euphrates and flanked by both. British commander General Barrett sent a small force against the position on 4 December. Involving two Indian infantry battalions supported by a small fleet of gunboats, the attack drove Turkish batteries from the east bank of the Tigris opposite Qurna, but was unable to cross the river under fire from the town. Reinforcements were sent from Basra, bringing British strength up to about 2,100 troops and 16 field guns, but a second attempt on 6 December again faltered at the river. On 8 December troops crossed the Tigris several kilometres beyond the town, approaching it in the rear while gunboat fire distracted the defenders, but the garrison surrendered before the planned dawn attack. Turkish casualties are unknown, but the British took over 1,000 prisoners and lost 29 men killed. The battle established a stable front line in Mesopotamia until the following April, and encouraged Indian imperial authorities to favour further offensive action. See MAP 23.

Q-Ships Decoy vessels employed by Allied navies as an ANTI-SUBMARINE weapon. Also known as Special Service Ships, they sailed disguised as unarmed merchantmen but carried concealed naval armament. Too small to merit attack with precious TORPEDOES, they were standard targets for surfaced SUBMARINES, which at first generally gave warning and allowed time for evacuation before sinkings (see SUBMARINE WARFARE). Q-ships would open fire with up to four guns when some of the crew had taken to boats and the attacker had closed for inspection or easy shooting.

The first British and French Q-ships entered service in November 1914, and they eventually sank 11 U-BOATS, but they were not produced in large numbers until 1917, by which time German commanders had learned to expect decoys, and torpedo rather than surface attacks had become general practice. The ROYAL NAVY eventually employed an estimated 366 Q-ships, everything from small sailing vessels to 4,000-ton steamers; 61 were lost in action, and 2 of the FRENCH NAVY's 15 decoys were also sunk. Q-ships were also employed in small numbers by the ITALIAN and RUSSIAN NAVIES.

The Royal Navy used a few trawlers to tow old submarines, submerged but in contact by wire telephone and ready to surface against any attacker. The method claimed at least one victim, sinking *U-40* off Aberdeen in June 1915. See also: AUXILIARY COMMERCE RAIDERS.

R

'Race to the Sea' Phrase commonly used to describe the last mobile phases of the war on the WESTERN FRONT in autumn 1914. After Allied attempts to force a German retreat from the AISNE were defeated by well-entrenched defenders, both sides transferred forces north from late September, not in a race to the coast but in a mutual attempt at outflanking in the only direction not already occupied.

Allied attacks at ALBERT and ARRAS were checked by German forces before both sides converged on FLANDERS from early October. With Belgian forces retreating west from ANTWERP, occupation of the coast became a genuine strategic priority for the first time. Though it opened with Allied attacks in the southern part of the sector, the battle for Flanders developed into a large-scale German offensive from the coast to Armentières. In six weeks of fighting, heaviest around the YSER Canal near the coast and the town of YPRES inland, Allied forces barely prevented a German breakthrough, but when fighting subsided in late November the 'race' had ended in a draw. The Western Front stood unbroken to the coast around Nieuport and both sides controlled some Channel ports. See MAP 2.

Radetsky Class The three Radetsky Class BATTLESHIPS (*Radetsky*, *Erzherzog Franz Ferdinand* and *Zrinyi*) were the most modern PRE-DREADNOUGHTS with the wartime AUSTRO-HUNGARIAN NAVY. Completed in 1910–11, they were generally counted as 'semi-dreadnoughts' equivalent to the French DANTON Class. They formed part of the battlefleet at Pola from August 1914, but *Radetsky* was sent to support older Monarch Class pre-dreadnoughts at CATTARO after French forces had occupied hills overlooking its forts. With the FRENCH NAVY unwilling to risk its own battleships in the area, *Radetsky*'s big guns forced French troops to retire. Apart from this action, the class remained a largely theoretical influence on operations in the MEDITERRANEAN, and survived to be scrapped in Italy in 1919.

BRIEF DATA (*Radetsky*, 1915) Displacement: 14,500 tons; Crew: 880; Dimensions: length 456ft (138.2m), beam 82ft (24.8m); Speed: 20k; Main armament: 4 × 12in gun, 12 × 5.9in, 18 × 12pdr, 2 × 12pdr AA, 3 × 17.7in TT.

Radio Though speech radio was not a popular broadcast medium by 1918, wireless telegraphy (W/T) was standard military/diplomatic equipment with the major belligerent powers by 1914, and was widely employed by wartime ground, air and naval forces. Static TRENCH WARFARE conditions enabled the use of more secure field telephone cables for most ground communications, but once troops moved beyond prepared lines wireless became a vital tool for overseeing operations.

In this context radio played an important role in equipping ARTILLERY-spotter and reconnaissance aircraft once they had sufficient power to carry wireless sets weighing about 50kg. Radios were also fitted to STRATEGIC BOMBING aircraft in the latter stages of the war, and regularly equipped BALLOONS, AIRSHIPS, flying boats and patrol seaplanes.

Large naval vessels were almost all fitted with radio, which had revolutionized the degree of central supervision exercised by naval staff organizations since the turn of the century. This was by no means an unmixed blessing: orders from afar were often inappropriate to the situation at sea or unclear in their meaning (see e.g. MITTELMEERDIVISION).

The consistent ability of Britain's ROOM 40 intelligence unit to translate the GERMAN NAVY's codes, and to pinpoint SUBMARINE positions by their broadcasts illustrated the military risk involved in radio operation. All sides possessed more wireless sets than trained operators in 1914, and early campaigns were riddled with uncoded transmissions, most notably on the EASTERN FRONT, where the RUSSIAN ARMY's few radio sets consistently provided German forces with detailed information of Russian dispositions and plans.

Radoslavov, Vasil (1854–1929) Bulgarian Liberal politician, and a trusted henchman of Tsar FERDINAND I. Radoslavov's first premiership (1899–1901) had earned him notoriety for corruption beyond even that of his predecessors. His preference for close international relations with GERMANY and AUSTRIA-HUNGARY over BULGARIA's traditional ties with RUSSIA coincided with the Tsar's views in 1913 and brought his reinstatement as premier. Sharing direction of foreign policy with Ferdinand, he forced ratification of a large Austro-German loan through a hostile parliament during the 1914 JULY CRISIS, and played a leading role in subsequent negotiations with both sides, managing to persuade

Allied diplomats of his seriousness until September 1915.

German exploitation of Bulgarian resources, shortages on the home front and Radoslavov's agreement to deploy BULGARIAN ARMY forces in the ROMANIAN CAMPAIGN fuelled rising parliamentary and popular dissent, but he retained the support of a sufficient number of deputies to ensure the cabinet's survival at the Tsar's pleasure. Ferdinand lost patience after the Treaty of BUCHAREST confirmed German control of ROMANIA, and in June 1918 he appointed a new government under MALINOV as a sop to popular anti-War sentiments. Radoslavov remained at the head of a powerful group of pro-War deputies until his flight to Berlin in early October. Sentenced to death in absentia by the STAMBOLISKI regime, he was formally pardoned in 1929.

RAF (Royal Air Force) The independent British air force, formed on 1 April 1918 and uniting the military RFC with the naval RNAS under the direct control of an air ministry. Administrative rather than operational motives impelled the change, which absorbed the ROYAL NAVY's separate procurement systems and gave hard-pressed military authorities access to its surplus of high-quality aircraft. Unification also eased the creation of a massed STRATEGIC BOMBING formation, the INDEPENDENT AIR FORCE under General TRENCHARD, but had no practical effect on the operations of most units in either branch of the service. By December 1918 the RAF possessed more than 22,000 aircraft, a doubling of overall British air strength since January, and 291,000 personnel, making it comfortably the world's largest air force. Total British air force casualties (1914–18) included just over 3,000 aircraft and 16,623 personnel, of whom 6,166 aircrew were killed.

Railway Artillery The first recorded use of ARTILLERY on railcars was during the American Civil War of 1861–65, but rail guns first came into widespread use on the wartime WESTERN FRONT, where the proliferation of RAILWAY links to a static battle zone provided ideal circumstances for their use as a mobile reserve.

The FRENCH ARMY put dozens of reserve, COASTAL and fortress guns, all without mountings, on railway trucks from late 1914. They had to be removed from the carriage for firing and wore out quickly, but provided useful reinforcement at a crucial time and were soon followed by purpose-built designs.

Smaller French weapons were generally mounted directly onto rolling stock, and later onto turntables, but heavy pieces required more sophisticated sliding, hydraulic or spring systems to handle recoil from various directions. The heaviest types were usually lifted off the rails on shock-absorbing jacks before operation; among these types was the 520mm Schneider howitzer, which fired a 1,420kg shell, the biggest used anywhere in wartime.

The British began using surplus naval guns on sliding mounts in 1915, and modified versions remained the most common type. Bigger howitzers were also employed, but an ambitious scheme to mount Britain's coastal-defence batteries on a railway system was abandoned on cost grounds. A similar idea was proposed in the UNITED STATES, where enthusiasm for rail mountings had always been strong, and at least one US NAVY rail gun served in France.

A number of very heavy German rail guns saw action on the Western Front, including the 380mm Max E Railway Gun, used at VERDUN in 1916 and also for long-range bombardment of Allied positions from northern Belgium, where it avoided detection by withdrawing into a tunnel after every shot. In general the heaviest railway guns could reach targets 20–30km away, but the GERMAN NAVY's infamous 'PARIS GUN' bombarded the French capital from a record 130km.

Railways The most important contemporary means of overland mass transport and haulage, railways were vital to the deployment and supply of military forces and to the wartime mobilization of economic resources. Their importance was widely recognized, and the extent of a state's internal railway network was regarded as a prime indicator of economic development and military potential.

The UNITED STATES, with about 400,000km of railway by 1914, was in a class of its own, but the much smaller area of GERMANY contained an impressive 61,500km of track, most of it state-run. Some 38,000km of British railways were complemented by a worldwide colonial network, including 56,000km in INDIA alone. Of the other major European powers, FRANCE had some 40,000km of track, AUSTRIA-HUNGARY about 45,000km, RUSSIA about 74,000km (more than two-thirds state-owned) and ITALY 17,000km.

With about 9,000km of lines, BELGIUM was fairly typical of the intense development in smaller north European states. The vast Ottoman Empire's 6,750km of track was mostly foreign-owned. ROMANIA had 3,750km of track, BULGARIA 2,250km and SERBIA only about 900km, less than thriving colonial trading posts like EGYPT, which had 2,400km of railway in 1913.

The most developed networks were sufficient for all basic needs in all parts of a country, but less advanced states were often dependent on individual lines to remote areas. Such lines were constructed for economic purposes or as an adjunct to long-range central control – like the sole Turkish-owned line into the Arabian Hejaz region – and also as strategic links with contested frontier zones.

Expensive to build and usually requiring at least technical assistance from elsewhere, most of the railways in less developed countries were built and owned by European or North American concerns. Designed primarily to aid economic exploitation, they generally ran direct to the industrial heartlands of continental Europe, like the controversial German Berlin–Baghdad Railway, or from the hinterland of more remote territories to coastal trading centres, like most lines in AFRICA and all those in CHINA.

Not all railways were of equal practical value. Broad gauge and narrow (light) railways were very different in cost, durability and capacity terms. Unreliable, single-track connections on varying gauges, typical of most railways within the Ottoman Empire, were of far less strategic value than the multi-track, sophisticated systems of western Europe, designed to avoid bottlenecks and built to universal specifications within the country concerned.

Efficient management was as important as possession, and was handled in wartime by military authorities in most European countries. Their first challenge, expected by many to be their last, was the rapid mobilization and immediate supply of mass armies. Railway mobilization in Britain, France and (especially) Germany was reasonably efficient, but Russia and Austria-Hungary experienced some chaos, and chaotic mobilization in TURKEY paralysed the system on a semi-permanent basis.

Turkish trains virtually stopped running after the RUSSIAN NAVY successfully blockaded BLACK SEA coal ports in 1916, and the Italian railway system was running only 25 per cent of trains by 1917, most of them burning wood, because of the country's dependence on MEDITERRANEAN coal imports. Wear and tear from extraordinary levels of use, and the unprecedented level of ongoing military demand contributed to shortages of rolling stock and locomotives for civilian supplies in many European states.

Most armies in Europe were attacking towards reasonably developed rail systems that gave defenders the advantage of excellent internal communications. Attackers were invariably cut off from supply and reinforcement railheads as soon as they made any significant advance. The general habit of building railways to a gauge incompatible with that of cross-border rivals further hindered the progress of advancing armies, notably in EAST PRUSSIA.

Some further development of major strategic railways took place in wartime, notably the completion of the Berlin–Baghdad line, but most new connections were hastily constructed light railways leading to frontline zones. Light railways already in use for local or industrial purposes all over the world were torn up and transferred to military sites, and existing railways on both sides of the Western Front became host to dozens of tributary spurs; some, like the single light track leading to VERDUN, became lifelines for besieged forces. British forces on the PALESTINE and

MESOPOTAMIAN FRONTS were dependent on new light railways to haul men and supplies to otherwise inaccessible fronts.

A great deal of fighting took place on or around railways. Tracks and embankments provided natural lines of retreat or defence for troops on all fronts, and railways were the axis of much ground fighting in the more mobile campaigns. Use of RAILWAY ARTILLERY on the Western Front turned trains into direct weapons of war, and attacks on hostile railway systems were standard military practice everywhere, from raids by the ROYAL NAVY to cut Turkish lines around SMYRNA, through the train-wrecking activities of ARAB REVOLT forces, to the destruction of trains as a standard component of offensive AERIAL WARFARE.

Ramadi, Battle of Untypically decisive Turkish defeat on the MESOPOTAMIAN FRONT in September 1917, and the opening engagement of a general British offensive in the theatre. On the Euphrates 30km west of FALLUJA, the town of Ramadi was the nearest concentration of Turkish strength to Baghdad; it was also an important local irrigation control point and the centre for illegal food traffic to Turkish forces further north. An attack by a motorized column in July, the only Anglo-Indian advance attempted during the high summer of 1917, was halted after one day in the face of determined resistance from about 1,000 defenders and searing heat, which caused two-thirds of 566 casualties. Further losses were inflicted by hostile Arab tribesmen during the withdrawal.

The operation was repeated in greater strength when temperatures dropped slightly. Supported by ARMOURED CARS, a division attacked up the east bank of the Euphrates on 28 September. Turkish positions, now manned by some 4,000 men, were sited to repel an attack close to the river bank, but the benefit of motorized transport enabled Brooking to surprise the Turkish flank. British CAVALRY circled round Ramadi to cut the road to Hit, deploying as infantry on arrival, and the defenders were surrounded once British infantry had stormed ridges overlooking the town. Attempts to break out at night were caught by cavalry, and the garrison surrendered next morning.

In an immediate attempt to capture Hit, guarding the road between Turkish forces on the Tigris and the Euphrates, an entirely motorized force of 400 infantry in lorries, with armoured cars and motor ambulances, set out on 1 October. The broken road proved too much for fragile vehicles and the attack was abandoned 10km short of its target next morning, after which C-in-C MAUDE switched his main effort to the other sectors (see TIKRIT). See MAP 23.

Rapallo Conference Emergency meeting of Allied leaders ORLANDO, LLOYD GEORGE and PAINLEVÉ on 5 November 1917 to coordinate responses to the crisis on the ITALIAN FRONT. Held in the northwest Italian port of Rapallo, at the height of the Austro-German CAPORETTO OFFENSIVE, it reversed the withdrawal of Anglo-French ARTILLERY units lent for the eleventh ISONZO OFFENSIVE in September, and promised substantial ground and air reinforcement to maintain the ITALIAN ARMY's line at the PIAVE RIVER. The new Italian government also received guarantees of increased economic aid in return for a definite commitment to the Allied cause, and General CADORNA's suggestion that peace might be forced on his battered ITALIAN ARMY brought his dismissal on 7 November. The most far-reaching action taken by politicians at Rapallo, reflecting British and Italian determination to curb the independence of senior field commanders, was the creation of a permanent Allied committee for coordination of strategy, later called the SUPREME WAR COUNCIL. The Council eventually matured into a unified military command under General FOCH, one of its original military representatives along with Cadorna and the British General WILSON.

Rasputin, Grigor (c 1871–1916) Infamous Russian 'holy man' and political intriguer, who gained access to the royal family around 1905 and secured a close relationship with the Empress ALEXANDRA through his apparently inexplicable ability to heal the heir to the throne's haemophiliac attacks. Rasputin was publicly recognized as a major influence on court affairs from about 1910, and his notoriously debauched lifestyle and reputed influence over appointments made him a regular source of press scandal, including suggestions that he was in German pay. Rasputin's precise role in shaping government policy remains obscure, but he certainly supported Alexandra's extreme conservative inclinations and shared her patronage of docile ministers. His assassination on the night of 29–30 December 1916, though generally applauded, had little lasting effect on political processes in RUSSIA other than removing a buffer for criticism of the monarchy.

Rathenau, Walter (1867–1922) German industrialist, whose father was head of the electrical giant AEG, and who was first chief of the KRA, controlling economic management of the war effort from autumn 1914. One of the few influential figures in GERMANY to anticipate a prolonged war, he adapted an AEG employee's plan for centralized distribution of vital raw materials and took it to Prussian war minister FALKENHAYN on 9 August 1914. The original scheme envisaged distribution to a broad spectrum of large and small manufacturers capable of munitions work, but Rathenau's version placed regulation in the hands of big businesses for their own benefit.

Although an earnest admirer of traditional Prussian values and a monarchist committed to national expansion, Rathenau resigned in April 1915, largely owing to entrenched anti-Semitic attitudes among his peers. He became chairman of AEG after his father's death in June 1915, and from 1916 helped engineer the politico-military primacy of the THIRD SUPREME COMMAND, but opposed them on a number of vital issues, notably the declaration of unrestricted SUBMARINE WARFARE and annexation of eastern Europe. He nevertheless recognized that only victory could prevent social upheaval inside Germany, and was urging mass civilian resistance to the Allies when the War ended.

Rathenau re-entered politics as a member of the German Democratic Party immediately after the ARMISTICE, attending the PARIS PEACE CONFERENCE as an economic expert and subsequently holding office as minister for reconstruction (1919–21) and foreign minister (1922). After signing the controversial Rapallo treaty with the Soviet Union in April 1922, he was assassinated in June by right-wing extremists in Berlin.

Rava Ruska See: Campaign in GALICIA.

Rawlinson, General Sir Henry (1864–1925) Experienced British soldier who led the detachment sent to aid the defence of ANTWERP in October 1914. He took command of a corps around YPRES once the Antwerp force had been absorbed into the main BEF, and remained on the WESTERN FRONT for the rest of the War, being promoted to command the Fourth Army in late 1915. At the SOMME in 1916 his proposal for a strictly limited infantry attack, equipped to hold small gains, was mixed disastrously with C-in-C HAIG's more ambitious plans. Apart from brief spells in command of the Second and Fifth Armies, and as British representative on the SUPREME WAR COUNCIL from February 1918, Rawlinson remained with the Fourth Army until after the ARMISTICE, leading it through the AMIENS OFFENSIVE and the attack on the HINDENBURG LINE during the decisive Allied advances of 1918.

RE-7 Ponderous British biplane, purpose-designed as a day bomber in 1915, that joined RFC units on the WESTERN FRONT from the end of the year. Inadequately armed and powered, its limitations were quickly apparent and it was soon withdrawn from reconnaissance and escort duties. Used as heavily escorted short-range bombers during the SOMME OFFENSIVE in mid-1916, RE-7s were completely withdrawn from frontline service once new BE-12s became available later in the year. Although they only equipped one complete squadron, small numbers were attached to many other units, and the RFC used a total of 224 RE-7s.

BRIEF DATA Type: two-seater day bomber; Engine: 150hp Royal Aircraft Factory; Max speed: 85mph (136kph); Ceiling: 3,100m; Armament: 1 × 0.303in mg, max bomb load 336lbs (152kg).

RE-8 British biplane developed at the Royal Aircraft Factory in 1916 as a multi-purpose replacement for the obsolete BE-2 series. Armed with forward and rear MACHINE GUNS, it joined RFC units late in the year, but a tendency to spin out of control and ignite on crash landing, along with initial engine problems, made it immediately unpopular with aircrew. Successfully modified by spring 1917, the RE-8 became the most widely used British two-seater, though it was always vulnerable to FIGHTER attack, and losses mounted in 1918. More than 4,000 were eventually built, flying bombing, ARTILLERY-spotting, reconnaissance and ground-attack operations on the WESTERN FRONT until the ARMISTICE. RE-8s also served with the RFC on the ITALIAN and BALKAN FRONTS, with the BELGIAN AIR SERVICE, and with White forces in the RUSSIAN CIVIL WAR.

BRIEF DATA Type: single-seat multipurpose; Engine: 150hp Royal Aircraft Factory; Max speed: 98mph (157kph); Ceiling: 4,000m; Armament: 2 or 3 × 0.303in mg, max bomb load 260lbs.

Red Army The army of the Russian Bolshevik regime and subsequently of the Soviet Union, but originally the name given to the main strike forces used in the PROVISIONAL GOVERNMENT's summer KERENSKI OFFENSIVE in 1917. The more permanent Red Army was created by the Bolshevik government after the BREST-LITOVSK Treaty had ended the war on the EASTERN FRONT in March 1918. Formed from former RUSSIAN ARMY units reconstituted as military SOVIETS and from the RED GUARD revolutionary militia in Petrograd (St Petersburg) and Moscow, it was generally commanded by political appointees with 'advisors' recruited from the more liberal elements of the imperial senior command.

Between 1918 and 1921 small Red Army forces campaigned all over the former empire, either in defence against White forces during the RUSSIAN CIVIL WAR or in small-scale support of Bolshevik uprisings in newly independent frontier provinces, including POLAND, FINLAND and the Baltic states. Units also briefly penetrated PERSIA and Japanese-held northern CHINA.

Its ultimate victory in the Civil War owed much to the dispersal of White resources among independent commands and to the organizational gifts of Commissar for War TROTSKI, but was also helped by possession of the Russian Army's heavy ARTILLERY and an ammunition store of some 18 million shells.

Red Guards Workers' militia organizations established by SOVIETS in RUSSIA during 1917. Until the ineffectual KORNILOV coup of early September, Red Guards remained an occasional and largely unguided force that protected workers' institutions and popular protests in Moscow, Petrograd (St Petersburg) and Kiev. Armed by the Petrograd Soviet to meet imminent counterrevolution, they came under Bolshevik control from late October, following formation of the party's Military Revolutionary Committee to coordinate armed revolt. Combining with disaffected garrison troops in Petrograd, the Guards played an important policing role during the subsequent OCTOBER REVOLUTION, and were generally absorbed in the RED ARMY during the RUSSIAN CIVIL WAR.

Regia Marina See: ITALIAN NAVY.

Regina Elena Class A class of four small Italian BATTLESHIPS completed in 1907–08. Given light main armament but thick armour protection, they were faster than most PRE-DREADNOUGHTS and regarded by some authorities as large CRUISERS. All four were deployed with the main ITALIAN NAVY battlefleet at Taranto in May 1915, but were transferred to more forward bases from July. They remained at Brindisi or Valona, either side of the OTRANTO BARRAGE, until spring 1918, when three were returned to Taranto. Two of the class, *Roma* and *Vittorio Emanuele*, joined Allied forces in the Aegean during late 1918, primarily to represent ITALY's territorial ambitions in the eastern MEDITERRANEAN.

BRIEF DATA (*Regina Elena*, 1915) Displacement: 12,625 tons; Crew: 1,000; Dimensions: length 475ft (143.9m), beam 73.5ft (22.3m); Speed: 21k; Main armament: 2 × 12in gun, 12 × 8in, 24 × 14pdr, 2 × 18in TT.

Renault Light Tank The most effective French TANK of the period, developed in 1917 as an infantry-support weapon. In contrast to heavy French designs, which mounted SOIXANTE-QUINZE field guns and were regarded as mobile ARTILLERY batteries, the Renault was a good cross-country machine and its armoured, revolving turret gave excellent field of fire without compromising crew protection. Though inferior to the British 'WHIPPET' machines, Renaults took over French tank production from October 1917 and served on the WESTERN FRONT with both FRENCH ARMY and AEF units. Involved in all the major Allied attacks on the southern sectors of the Front during 1918 (about 380 took part in the MEUSE–ARGONNE OFFENSIVE), they suffered very heavy losses, and their effectiveness was limited by lack of back-up armament and the frequency of MACHINE GUN failure.

BRIEF DATA Weight: 6.5 tons; Max speed: c 9kph; Crew: 2; Max armour: 16mm; Armament: 1 × mg or 1 × 37mm gun.

Rennenkampf, General Paul von (1853–1918) German-born RUSSIAN ARMY officer whose leadership of the First Army during the failed invasion of EAST PRUSSIA in August 1914 led to allegations of corruption and even treason. Sector commander ZHILINSKI tried to have him removed, but Rennenkampf's cavalry connections saved his job until after the Battle of ŁÓDŹ in November 1914, when failure to cut off the rear of German forces trapped in the town sealed his dismissal. He retired to the Black Sea coast, where he was shot for refusing to join Bolshevik forces after the OCTOBER REVOLUTION.

Reparations Payments in compensation for costs and damages incurred in war. Both the CENTRAL POWERS and the European Allies planned to exact reparations in the event of victory, but the UNITED STATES placed a different interpretation on the concept of 'compensation' mentioned by the ARMISTICE agreement in November 1918, regarding payments as applying only to illegal wartime actions like the occupation of BELGIUM. Allied authorities argued that assignment of 'war guilt' to the Central Powers in the Armistice agreement implied that the whole conflict was illegal.

Fuelled by aggressive popular demands in GREAT BRITAIN, FRANCE and ITALY for full reparations, the debate was not resolved during the PARIS PEACE CONFERENCE, and the treaties that emerged assigned an unspecified debt to each defeated state, with a commission appointed to affix amounts and proportions. As the only nation capable of significant payment, GERMANY was required to make large-scale contributions in kind before the commission set a charge of £6.6 billion plus interest in May 1921. Only about 12 per cent of the bill was ever paid, and all the defeated states received compensatory loans, but the imposition provoked great bitterness (especially in Germany) before reparations were abandoned during the financial collapse of the early 1930s.

Respirators See: GAS.

Revel, Admiral Paolo, Count Thaon di (1859–1948) Energetic ITALIAN NAVY chief of staff, appointed in April 1913, who promoted construction of SUBMARINES and coastal warships rather than expensive DREADNOUGHTS. Though he took part in talks with his Austrian counterpart, HAUS, Revel never favoured Italian support for the CENTRAL POWERS against superior Allied forces in the MEDITERRANEAN. Once ITALY was at war, he regarded a decisive confrontation with the AUSTRO-HUNGARIAN NAVY as desirable but, recognizing the battlefleet's vulnerability, he established the 'no-risk' policy that subsequently characterized Italian fleet operations. Apparent inaction attracted political criticism at home, and he was transferred to command naval forces at Venice in October 1915, the post of chief of staff being taken by new naval minister Corsi. Revel returned to the post in February 1917, simultaneously replacing ABRUZZI in direct command of the battlefleet, and his consistently defensive posture exasperated Allied leaders, with whom relations were never good. Revel remained active after the ARMISTICE, serving as navy minister in the MUSSOLINI government for two years from 1922.

RFC (Royal Flying Corps) The air arm of the BRITISH ARMY from 1912 until 1918. The ROYAL NAVY administered its own air arm before 1912 and, after a brief period under combined command, between January 1914 and April 1918. Military aviation in Britain began in 1878, when a BALLOON unit had been formed within the Royal Engineers, and the first powered (non-rigid) Army AIRSHIP flew in 1907. Private aircraft flights took place in Britain for the first time in the following year, and an Air Battalion was formed in 1911, its twin aircraft and airship sections reflecting official division of priorities. Progress was relatively slow, and the Army had only 11 qualified pilots by January 1912, compared with 8 in the Navy and 263 in the French AÉRONAUTIQUE MILITAIRE.

Military aviation was organized as a single Royal Flying Corps, with military, naval and training wings, from May 1912. In August the home-produced BE-2 was ordered as standard equipment, and by the end of the year the RFC comprised one squadron of airships and three of aircraft, each with a nominal strength of 12 machines. The naval wing, never more than nominally under Army administration, was formally reconstituted as the Royal Naval Air Service (RNAS) in January 1914, taking control of all airships in the process, and RFC strength in August 1914 was four operational squadrons (63 machines), with three more forming in Britain.

Reaching the WESTERN FRONT from mid-August, the squadrons were a heterogeneous mixture of BE-2, BE-8, FARMAN MF-7 and various sports models. Quickly caught up in the retreat of the BEF, they carried out reconnaissance and light bombing missions under army orders and gradually expanded alongside the ground forces they served. In November field units were reorganized as 'wings' of two squadrons each, one wing for each army of the BEF, and with three more squadrons attached to RFC headquarters at St Omer.

Stagnation on the Western Front from early 1915 greatly extended the RFC's range of activities, but without aircraft suitable for the task, RFC bombing and offensive reconnaissance was a makeshift business throughout 1915. The vast majority of operations were carried out by the much better-equipped Aéronautique Militaire, which fielded some 1,150 frontline aircraft to the RFC's 166 in May.

Field commander Henderson was recalled to GREAT BRITAIN as head of the air staff in August 1915, and the aggressive TRENCHARD took his place. Insisting on offensive patrols over enemy lines at all times, but unable to call on new designs to counter German combat superiority, he relied on numbers, throwing aircrew into action after minimal training and pressing for increased production of existing types which had been modified but were essentially obsolete.

As a result the RFC was saddled with hundreds of unsuitable machines long after competitive FIGHTERS like the AIRCO DH-2 and NIEUPORT 11 became available in 1916, and many remained in service well into 1917. Growing resentment of apparently useless sacrifice among field officers was heightened by strong public and political criticism in Britain, where the 'Fokker Scourge' was regarded as a national disgrace.

Attempts to stem losses by deploying aircraft in larger formations simply increased the number of obsolete targets without providing effective protection, and homogeneously equipped combat units, armed with purpose-designed DH-2 and FE-2 fighters, were not an important factor until late spring 1916. Casualties remained high throughout the first half of the year, with an average of two aircrew losses per day, but increased aircraft production and the slight respite provided by German preoccupation with VERDUN enabled constant numerical expansion.

Like other air arms on the Western Front, the size and character of the RFC was redefined by the great battles of 1916. At the opening of the SOMME OFFENSIVE in July the RFC fielded 185 aircraft in the area of the offensive, supported by more than 200 Aéronautique Militaire machines. By November, though offensive reconnaissance and tactical bombing missions still dominated, battlefield aircraft were increasingly being used for ground-support and command-liaison operations.

The need for first-class fighters to protect all other working aircraft was also growing, as emphasized from September 1916 by a second phase of German combat superiority on the Western Front, which ended the RFC's brief period of relative freedom to cross enemy lines on army business. By the end of the year the only British fighter capable of matching the latest German types was the SOPWITH PUP, which the RFC was required to exchange or borrow in small numbers from the RNAS.

Specialist types were also required for infantry-contact and day-bombing operations, both highly vulnerable to ever more organized ground fire, while Trenchard's belief (shared by the RNAS) that the best way to defeat enemy fighters was by attacking their factories and depots encouraged development of larger aircraft for STRATEGIC BOMBING purposes.

Little had changed by spring 1917, except that German fighters had become even better and the scale of combat had increased. The RFC fielded 365 aircraft (25 squadrons) in support of the ARRAS attack in April, out of its total strength of 764 aircraft (41 squadrons) operational on the Western Front. The following weeks, infamous as 'BLOODY APRIL', saw aircraft losses touching 50 per week as German fighters tore into the obsolete relics sent trundling over the lines.

The arrival of BRISTOL FIGHTER and SE-5 machines from mid-May signalled a gradual reduction of losses, and from late 1917 new designs like the SOPWITH CAMEL, SOPWITH TRIPLANE, AIRCO DH-4 and HANDLEY PAGE 0/400 established technical superiority over German forces in almost every department of AERIAL WARFARE, an advantage that was never relinquished.

The formal merger of British military and naval flying services under a single air ministry was planned from late 1917. With mushrooming air fleets operating in ever larger formations, the general aim was to concentrate forces more efficiently, and in particular to mount a large-scale strategic bombing offensive against GERMANY, believed to be building a 4,000-strong bomber fleet of its own.

At the start of 1918, the RFC operated almost 4,000 combat aircraft, the vast majority on the Western Front, and employed 114,000 personnel. Trenchard was promoted from the field in January, being replaced at the front by Salmond, and the RFC officially ceased to exist with the establishment of the RAF on 1 April. Although resources were committed to the strategic-bombing experiment of the INDEPENDENT AIR FORCE, reorganization had little effect on operational procedures.

Primarily concerned with the Western Front, RFC units also flew in support of army operations on all other British battlefronts, except GALLIPOLI, playing a particularly important part in victories on the PALESTINE FRONT but suffering from tropical conditions in AFRICA and poor facilities on the MESOPOTAMIAN FRONT. A substantial force (initially six squadrons) was sent to the ITALIAN FRONT after the CAPORETTO battle in autumn 1917, and the RAF fielded 26 reconnaissance and 56 fighter aircraft at the decisive battle at the PIAVE in June 1918. See RAF. See also: ACES.

Rhodesian Forces The African colony of Rhodesia, divided into Northern and Southern administrations (modern Zambia and Zimbabwe, respectively) by the Zambesi River, contributed a higher percentage of its white male population to wartime service than any other territory of the British Empire. About 2,700 men of the volunteer Northern Rhodesia Rifles, formed in 1914 by local game hunter Major Boyd Cunningham and including a single native battalion, fought on the southern frontiers of German EAST AFRICA. They were supported by some of the 1,800 Southern Rhodesia Volunteers and the smaller Rhodesian police force, which also occupied parts of German SOUTHWEST AFRICA in September 1914 and performed reserve duties in SOUTH AFRICA during the BOER REVOLT. Cunningham's force was disbanded in late 1915, but volunteer formations continued in service throughout the campaign in East Africa (see Battle of IRINGA), which eventually ended on Rhodesian soil in 1918. Including individuals who travelled to join British forces on the WESTERN FRONT, a total of 6,831 Rhodesians (from some 12,000 adult male Europeans) saw military service and 732 were killed.

Ribot, Alexandre (1842–1923) Seasoned French politician, an inveterate centrist and former prime minister who was recalled to office as finance minister in VIVIANI's August 1914 coalition, remaining in office during BRIAND's premiership. He gambled on a short war with a policy of loans rather than tax increases, and made vain efforts to interest the British in fuller Allied economic cooperation (see ALLIED MARITIME TRANSPORT COUNCIL).

Selected by President POINCARÉ as Briand's successor (and foreign minister) in March 1917, Ribot accepted the appointment despite poor health and failing energy. After authorizing the controversial NIVELLE OFFENSIVE in early April, he followed the recommendation of new C-in-C PÉTAIN and war minister PAINLEVÉ for military recuperation in its aftermath.

His main contribution to foreign policy was the reversal of Briand's sympathetic attitude towards the Greek king, CONSTANTINE I, who was forced into exile by the Allies in June 1917. At home he resisted demands on the right for suppression of PACIFISTS, alienated the left by refusing permission for socialists to attend the international STOCKHOLM CONFERENCE, and lost the support of a large parliamentary Radical bloc with the dismissal of interior minister MALVY in late August.

Completely isolated, he resigned on 7 September 1917, remaining in the Painlevé cabinet as foreign minister and a political liability until October. Never again in office, he approached peace from a familiar central position, arguing for the highest possible REPARATIONS but against French control of the Rhineland.

Richthofen, Manfred von (1892–1918) The most celebrated air ACE of the period, Richthofen was originally a Prussian CAVALRY officer, but transferred to the GERMAN ARMY AIR SERVICE in May 1915. After operating as an observer on the EASTERN FRONT and with bomber units in Belgium, he flew reconnaissance two-seaters at VERDUN in early 1916 and became a FIGHTER pilot on the WESTERN FRONT in August, joining BOELCKE's new *Jagdstaffel 2*.

In command of the unit from January 1917, by which time he had shot down 15 aircraft, he became GERMANY's most famous pilot after the deaths of Boelcke and IMMELMANN, his reputation enhanced by a rapid series of victories in the spring that took his 'score' to 52 by the end of 'BLOODY APRIL'.

From June he commanded *Jagdgeschwader 1*, first of the new mobile 'FLYING CIRCUSES'. Subsequently treated as a valuable PROPAGANDA asset, he was deliberately protected by other pilots, who sometimes softened up targets for him to finish off. Richthofen's appetite for ruthless killings was exaggerated by Allied propaganda and he became a figure of popular hatred in FRANCE and GREAT BRITAIN. He eventually shot down 80 Allied aircraft, the highest score of any pilot on either side, before his death to ground fire while flying his FOKKER DR-1 in combat against SOPWITH CAMELS on 21 April 1918.

Rickenbacker, Edward (1890–1973) The most successful and celebrated USAAS flying ACE, with 26 confirmed victories, including 4 BALLOONS. A famous racing driver, Rickenbacker was in Britain as a test driver in April 1917, becoming an officer of engineers before his transfer to the newly formed 94th Squadron in March 1918. Rickenbacker took part in the first USAAS patrol over the WESTERN FRONT, by three NIEUPORT 28S around Toul on 19 March, and became an official ace with his fifth victory on 30 May.

Riesenflugzeug German term, meaning 'giant aircraft', that became an official designation from late 1915, when the GERMAN ARMY AIR SERVICE issued specifications for a long-range, multi-engined design intended solely for STRATEGIC BOMBING attacks on Allied industrial and population centres. Military interest in Riesenflugzeug (R-Type) aircraft had been stimulated by the inadequacy of ZEPPELINS for the task, and by the successes of four-engined Russian SIKORSKI IM bombers on the EASTERN FRONT in 1914. As co-proprietor of the Zeppelin-Staaken company, Graf Zeppelin had sponsored development of the first R-Type from September 1914, and prototypes were tested on the Eastern Front from February 1916. By the end of the year, the first two R-Type units (each with six aircraft) had been formed, and they joined GOTHA G-TYPES in raids on southern England from September 1917.

Several companies built giants but only ZEPPELIN-STAAKEN R-TYPES were used operationally in any quantity, although others were used as trainers, and four prototype Siemens-Schuckert machines were used operationally on the Eastern Front in 1917. Most machines were structural 'one-offs', and many different engine configurations were employed, although 18 standard Zeppelin-Staaken R-VIs and were produced.

All R-Types were built to technologically advanced specifications, with the latest navigational equipment, two-way RADIO, oxygen gear, PARACHUTES, walk-through fuselage, and engines capable of in-flight repair. They were generally reliable, defensively well-armed and capable of carrying a significant bomb load, especially on the short-range, tactical missions for which they were increasingly employed.

Rifles Because MACHINE GUNS and MORTARS were cumbersome, and GRENADES a one-shot weapon, concerted rifle fire remained fundamental to all wartime infantry fighting, especially fired in volleys against attacking troops. The rifle had been subject to intense development in Europe during the late 19th century, and from the 1890s most major armies introduced small-bore, bolt-action weapons firing multiple (usually five) rounds from a spring-loaded clip inserted into the magazine.

This basic design remained unchanged throughout the 1914–18 period, and was used by most major armies and better-equipped units of smaller forces, but the GERMAN ARMY's standard 7.92mm Mauser (1898) used a superior system incorporating clip and magazine into a single detachable mechanism. It was rivalled by the BRITISH ARMY's 10-shot box magazine developed for the 0.303-inch Lee-Enfield (1907), and also used in late-War US ARMY and CANADIAN models. The FRENCH ARMY's old 8mm Lebel rifle (1886) was standard issue in 1914, but was replaced from 1916 by the 5-shot Berthier.

Older, single-shot weapons with bigger bores remained in common wartime use – as standard equipment in minor armies or by reserve and colonial units of the major powers. The strain on resources experienced by all European belligerents meant that every available rifle of whatever age was generally pressed into use somewhere.

The performance of all reasonably modern rifles was roughly similar: they could be aimed accurately over about 600 metres and at a general area up to about 1,400 metres, half the average maximum range. Although magazine technology could affect firing rate, the prime determining factor in attaining rapid, accurate fire was the rifleman's skill. The small, highly trained BEF of August 1914 was able to fire an estimated 15 rounds per minute during its action at MONS, but such virtuosity in large formations was rare in later mass armies.

Individual expert riflemen generally made their mark through SNIPING, which proliferated in TRENCH WARFARE conditions but could also have a powerful effect in more mobile actions (see YORK, A.). Backwoods familiarity with rifles contributed to the particularly high reputation enjoyed by some British dominion and AEF units.

Apart from a general preference for short-barrelled 'carbines' at the expense of more cumbersome long-barrelled weapons, wartime development of rifle technology was minimal, with the accent on mass production rather than experimentation. Long-barrelled rifles were among the first weapons regularly used aboard aircraft, but were discarded as soon as suitable machine guns became available (see AERIAL WARFARE). Periscopes were fitted for trench fighting, and a one-shot, tripod-mounted 13mm German Mauser was developed for use against Allied TANKS in 1918, proving effective against the original light machines. See also: BAYONETS.

Riga, Battle of The final Russo-German engagement of the War on the EASTERN

FRONT, an attack by General von HUTIER's German Eighth Army on Russian positions around Riga, at the extreme north of the line (see MAP 11). Launched on 1 September 1917, it was intended to clear the potentially troublesome Russian coastal SALIENT west of the port (see Battle of the AA), and to encourage collapse of the Russian war effort by suggesting a threat towards Petrograd (St Petersburg). It also offered Hutier a chance to test his new INFILTRATION TACTICS in a major operation.

The area was defended by the Russian Twelfth Army, commanded by C-in-C KORNILOV and virtually the last coherent force at his disposal. Forewarned by the arrival of German reinforcements from Galicia, the Twelfth Army began preparations for retreat even before the attack opened along a 5km front on the River Dvina south of Riga.

Hutier's tactics were a complete success. His carefully prepared divisions established a bridgehead over the river on the first day, and the Russian Twelfth Army fled immediately. Riga was evacuated on 2 September, and the German Eighth Army pursued stragglers along the Dvina for three weeks. Its proposed northwesterly advance towards Petrograd was abandoned as unnecessary almost at the outset, as breakdown of government and the OCTOBER REVOLUTION effectively ended Russian military operations. See RUSSIA.

Rize Landing The first major amphibious operation carried out by Russian forces in the BLACK SEA, a landing of 7 April 1916 by 16,000 troops on the Turkish coast at Rize, in direct support of operations around TRABZON on the CAUCASIAN FRONT (see MAP 24). Preparations (including the construction of special flat-bottomed landing craft) had been underway for some weeks, and a small-scale rehearsal had taken place in early March, when 2,100 troops landed at Atina and to the west of Rize. Troop transports were supported by a strong RUSSIAN NAVY force, including the new dreadnought *IMPERATRICA MARIA*, three CRUISERS, and three improvised AIRCRAFT CARRIERS. The bay at Rize was protected against SUBMARINES by a cordon of INDICATOR NETS. The major Russian warships departed early after sighting a U-BOAT, but the operation was successfully completed within nine hours, and half the troops involved were in action at the front the following day. The landing contributed significantly to the Russian capture of Trabzon on 19 April, and its success prompted rapid expansion of the Navy's coastal support role.

RNAS (Royal Naval Air Service) The air arm of the British ROYAL NAVY, by far the largest and most successful maritime air force of the period. Before 1912 British naval aviation merely kept pace with slow developments elsewhere, concentrating on BALLOONS and AIRSHIPS for reconnaissance. The Navy's first rigid airship, *Mayfly*, collapsed on launch in 1911, encouraging the Navy's airship commander, Captain Sueter, and naval minister CHURCHILL to pursue their support for aircraft. The formation of the RFC in May 1912 established a strength of 12 aircraft for its naval wing (which also took over army airships), but the Navy never relinquished effective control of its aircraft to the RFC, ordering equipment through its own suppliers and presiding over accelerated development at its own bases.

The first flight from a moving ship was achieved in May 1912, and the first seaplane carrier, *Hermes*, was commissioned a year later. By the end of 1913, as the Navy began building a chain of coastal air stations, its pilots had carried small bomb loads and equally heavy RADIO equipment.

Independence from the RFC was re-established on 1 January 1914, with the formation of the Royal Naval Air Service, comprising 217 pilots and 95 aircraft (55 of them seaplanes). Some 80 aircraft and 8 airships were operational in August 1914, making the RNAS larger than the army's RFC. Its stated operational roles – fleet reconnaissance, patrolling coasts for enemy ships and SUBMARINES, attacking enemy coastal territory and aircraft (especially airships), and defending home installations – remained essentially unaltered to 1918.

The generally poor performance of seaplanes (which could only be used in very clear, calm conditions) hampered strictly maritime operations during 1914–15. The sinking of *Hermes* delayed plans for fleet cooperation, and the prolonged RUFUGI DELTA battle demonstrated the shortcomings of naval aviation in tropical/colonial conditions. Although AIRCRAFT CARRIER development was soon resumed with the *ARK ROYAL*, early maritime activity was largely confined to coastal patrols.

Land-based defensive operations were focused on the threat of ZEPPELINS both as long-range land bombers and as reconnaissance craft for the German HIGH SEAS FLEET. Though responsible for defence of all British airspace until February 1916, the RNAS had no aircraft capable of intercepting Zeppelins at night or at sea, and suffered public criticism for its inability to prevent mounting civilian casualties during the STRATEGIC BOMBING raids of 1915.

Offensive operations concentrated on the destruction of airships in their bases. No.1 Naval Wing, sent to support initial ground operations on the WESTERN FRONT, carried out light bombing raids on German targets in the process of retreating to Dunkirk, and a single SOPWITH TABLOID destroyed Zeppelin Z-9 in its sheds at Düsseldorf in October 1914. A raid on Friedrichshafen by three AVRO 504S based at Belfort caused considerable damage in late November, and on Christmas Day seven aircraft took part in the world's first carrier strike during the CUXHAVEN RAID.

Naval aircraft played a small but portentous role in the DARDANELLES operation of 1915–16. The *Ark Royal* took part in the initial phase, but was seldom able to get its machines airborne, and a squadron from the growing landplane force (No.3 Naval Wing) carried out PHOTO-RECONNAISSANCE for the GALLIPOLI LANDINGS. The faster seaplane tender *BEN-MY-CHREE* reached the theatre in the summer, and its new SHORT 184S sank two Turkish vessels in the only successful airborne TORPEDO attacks of the War.

By 1916 the RNAS possessed plentiful seaplanes and flying boats, equipping 50 coastal stations, but its 50 BRISTOL SCOUTS remained the only naval design capable of intercepting Zeppelins. Two light but powerful designs, the SOPWITH STRUTTER and the smaller SOPWITH PUP, enabled the RNAS to tackle enemy aircraft in conjunction with fleet units from late 1916, equipping coastal stations, seaplane carriers and individual warships.

Superior to any contemporary Allied design, Strutters and Pups also helped extend RNAS activity on the Western Front, equipping combat units at coastal bases and at the SOMME, where No.8 Naval Wing fought on temporary attachment to the hard-pressed RFC between October 1916 and the following spring. Naval FIGHTER squadrons remained in action on the Western Front until the ARMISTICE, flying first-class SOPWITH TRIPLANES and SOPWITH CAMELS during 1917–18 (see BLACK FLIGHT).

Despite the lack of a suitable heavy bomber, the Navy's early interest in strategic bombing was maintained in 1916. RNAS No.3 Wing, equipped with a variety of British and French two-seaters, was put under French command at Luxeuil and carried out a number of daylight attacks on German industrial and military targets, culminating in a failed Anglo-French raid on OBERNDORF in October. The need to use every available machine in support of ground operations in France prompted suspension of long-range bombing operations from early 1917, but they were eventually resumed under the aegis of the RAF in 1918.

From early 1917, excellent long-range CURTISS H-12 and FELIXSTOWE flying boats were available for coastal patrol work, which became more important after the extension of German SUBMARINE WARFARE in February. Equipped with DEPTH CHARGES and radio, and ultimately organized in the effective 'SPIDER'S WEB' patrol system, seaplanes, flying boats and airships provided effective protection for CONVOYS and sank several U-BOATS.

Although development of true aircraft carriers was not completed in wartime, the provision of high-performance landplanes for shipborne operations became commonplace during 1917, and by March 1918 about 55 Strutters and Pups were at sea with GRAND FLEET units.

In contrast to the shortages suffered by the RFC, the Navy's private supply system always provided the RNAS with plenty of modern aircraft, and the need to make use of its considerable surplus stock was an argument for its loss of independence. At the time of its absorption into the RAF on 1 April 1918, the RNAS comprised 67,000 officers and men (including many Canadians and other Empire citizens), operating 2,949 aircraft, 103 airships and 126 coastal air stations. See RAF. See also: TONDERN RAID.

Robertson, General Sir William (1860–1933) The only man in the history of the BRITISH ARMY to rise from private to field marshal, Robertson began the War as quartermaster general to the BEF and succeeded MURRAY as chief of staff to Sir John FRENCH early in 1915. He was HAIG's only real rival for the succession when French was replaced a year later, but was instead brought home as chief of the Imperial General Staff (CIGS), effectively the liaison between Army and cabinet. A blunt, efficient administrator who never forgot to drop his aitches, Robertson was a confirmed 'WESTERNER' throughout, supporting Haig against all pressure – especially from prime minister LLOYD GEORGE – to divert resources away from the WESTERN FRONT. Creation of the inter-Allied SUPREME WAR COUNCIL in November 1917, and the appointment of General WILSON as its British representative undermined Robertson's influence over strategic decision-making, and he was removed from office in February 1918 (see Lord DERBY). Reduced to a minor home command, he replaced French as C-in-C of internal forces in June, and the political nature of his dismissal was recognized when he was promoted field marshal in 1920.

Roland C-II Influential German two-seater design, a fast biplane developed by the LFG company (which used the name Roland to avoid confusion with the LVG company) and first produced in October 1915. Its sleek, piscine appearance, giving rise to the nickname '*Walfisch*' ('Whale'), was created by attaching the top wing directly to a deep fuselage, offering the crew unrestricted upward vision and field of fire. Although designated a C-type (armed-reconnaissance) machine, the Whale's speed enabled its use as a FIGHTER escort over France, but its performance was hampered by slow rate of climb and poor manoeuvrability. A C-IIa version, introduced from August 1916, addressed the problems by strengthening the wings, enlarging the tail and adding a forward MACHINE GUN, but combat performance continued to suffer from a blind spot below and forward. Although no match for the best fighters by 1917, the Whale had a long active career, and a few remained on the quiet sectors of the WESTERN FRONT until autumn of that year, by which time about 300 had been produced.

BRIEF DATA (C-IIa) Type: two-seater reconnaissance/escort; Engine: 160hp Mercedes; Max speed: 165kph; Ceiling: 4,000m; Armament: 2 × 7.92mm mg.

Roland D-Type German series of FIGHTER aircraft, derived from the innovative ROLAND C-II two-seater and produced by the same LFG company. Limited numbers of the twin-gunned, 160hp D-I '*Haifisch*' ('Shark') saw action from late 1916, but shared the C-II's poor manoeuvrability and downward vision. A slightly raised top wing was the most important of several modifications to the D-II, which reached units in early 1917, and a 180hp D-IIa quickly followed. About 300 of these early models were built, along with 175 D-III versions, also introduced in 1917, which had new struts and a longer tailfin. Contemporary with the superior ALBATROS D-TYPES, they were used on the EASTERN and MESOPOTAMIAN FRONTS, and over quiet parts of the WESTERN FRONT, although most D-IIIs were restricted to training duties.

The D-IV was an experimental triplane, featuring a fuselage made of wooden boards warped across a framework to give a boat-like appearance. Like the failed D-V biplane it never entered production, but the system was retained for the Roland D-VI biplanes, manufactured in small numbers during 1918. Ordered as a precaution against shortages of the FOKKER D-VII, the D-VIa (180hp) and faster D-VIb (200hp) saw limited service in France late in 1918 and were used by the GERMAN NAVY to defend seaplane bases.

BRIEF DATA (D-II) Type: single-seat fighter; Engine: 160hp Mercedes; Max speed: 168kph; Ceiling: 4,000m; Armament: 2 × 7.92mm mg.

Romani, Battle of The second attempt by Turkish forces on the PALESTINE FRONT to disrupt British control of the SUEZ CANAL, launched in summer 1916. After the failure of February 1915, preoccupation with the GALLIPOLI FRONT restricted Turkish offensive operations from Palestine to raids into the Sinai peninsula by the 3,600 strong 'Desert Force' under German Colonel von KRESSENSTEIN. British forces meanwhile edged east from the Canal along newly constructed coastal roads, RAILWAYS and water pipelines (see MAP 22).

Kressenstein developed plans for a renewed assault on Suez in early 1916, intending to block traffic by occupying its east bank. Scheduled for the autumn, it was brought forward because the collapse of SERBIA on the BALKAN FRONT speeded up overland transport of large-scale German reinforcements to Turkey. About 16,000 Turkish and Arab troops had assembled on the Sinai–Palestine border by June, awaiting support from German MACHINE GUN, ANTI-AIRCRAFT, heavy ARTILLERY and other technical detachments, including a GERMAN ARMY AIR SERVICE unit equipped with 12 modern FOKKER E-TYPE, AVIATIK C-TYPE and ALBATROS C-TYPE machines.

The Turkish line of advance in early July was dictated by British destruction of watering depots in all but the northern coastal parts of the Sinai Desert, where the main British force (two and a half infantry divisions, with strong CAVALRY support) was deployed about 30km east of the Canal in fortified positions south and west of the town of Romani. Kressenstein's slightly outnumbered force was in front of Romani by mid-July, but paused for two weeks because heavy artillery was still expected.

The bemused British were considering an attack of their own when Turkish troops outwitted cavalry patrols to launch a surprise attack on lines south of the town in the small hours of 4 August, gaining part possession shortly afterwards but failing to make further progress during the day. Counterattacks had overrun forward Turkish positions by the following morning, when water shortages forced the Turks to withdraw. Kressenstein retreated over 100km to EL ARISH, and British cavalry held in reserve was unable to cut him off in a sandstorm.

Though proclaimed as a victory by Turkish PROPAGANDA, the battle marked the end of any direct military threat to the Suez Canal. Kressenstein's expedition suffered an estimated 4,000 casualties and lost 4,000 more men as prisoners, against 1,100 British losses (mostly from the ANZAC Mounted Division).

Romania Formed from the former Ottoman Empire provinces of Wallachia and Moldavia, Romania was recognized as an independent state in 1878. It was a constitutional monarchy in 1914, ruled by King CAROL I (a relative of Kaiser WILHELM II), but the indirectly elected National Assembly had little control over a Crown Council of appointed ministers. Participation in the Second Balkan War of 1913 had increased the country's size to almost 140,000 square kilometres, with the addition of the Bulgarian Dobrudja region, and raised the population to over 7.5 million (see MAP 1).

Romania's economy, though primarily based on agriculture in the fertile Wallachian plains, was also benefiting from its Ploesti oilfields, the output from which was becoming of increasing importance to industrial and military processes. Romania depended heavily on GERMANY and AUSTRIA-HUNGARY, which shared domination of trade, commerce and capital investment. Germany was considered friendly, and had financed the construction of the state-owned RAILWAYS (about 5,000km by 1914), but Austria-Hungary, accused of maltreating 3 million Romanians in Transylvania, was the *bête noire* of prewar popular opinion.

Although linked to both Germanic states by a secret treaty of 1883, King Carol cited the Transylvanian issue as preventing fulfilment of its obligations, and declared Romanian neutrality on 3 August 1914. Romania's pivotal geographical position, combined with an inflated military reputation since 1913, brought diplomatic offers from both belligerent blocs of military and economic aid. Only the ALLIES could offer Transylvania, and King Carol's obvious support for the CENTRAL POWERS damaged his personal popularity.

Carol's death in October 1914 cemented the growing political influence of liberal, francophile prime minister BRATIANU, and new king FERDINAND I's Austro-German connections were balanced by a British wife. Bratianu was allowed to develop a vaguely pro-Allied policy aimed at maximum territorial gain.

By mid-1916, stimulated by the successful Russian BRUSILOV OFFENSIVE, Bratianu and Ferdinand were sufficiently persuaded of eventual Allied victory to intervene against the Central Powers, and Romania declared war on 27 August 1916. Heralded by the Allies as decisive, the ROMANIAN ARMY's contribution was extremely limited. The Central Powers invaded Wallachia and the Dobrudja, and had conquered both by early December, gaining control of most of the country's natural resources, including its oil (despite large-scale sabotage by British agents). King and government retired northeast to Jassy, where they supervised the defence of Moldavia by the remnant of the Army with Russian reinforcements (see ROMANIAN CAMPAIGN).

Promises of land and electoral reform enabled the regime to retain sufficient support for the Army to be partially rebuilt (with French assistance) and for an offensive to be launched from Moldavia in July 1917, but Russian collapse after the fruitless KERENSKI OFFENSIVE left Romanian forces in an impossible position. Facing large-scale (potentially revolutionary) brigandage from Russian irregulars as well as strong enemy forces, Ferdinand resigned command of the Army to General PREZAN in December, avoiding direct association with an inevitable armistice.

Bratianu agreed a ceasefire with Germany on 9 December before himself resigning, but formal peace negotiations dragged deep into 1918 as the Central Powers squabbled among themselves and new premier AVERESCU refused harsh German terms. Bratianu, still the country's guiding political force, organized Averescu's replacement in March by the pro-German leader of the conservative faction, Marghiloman, and the Treaty of BUCHAREST was concluded in May. Never signed by Ferdinand, it formalized Romania's status as a virtual economic colony of the Central Powers.

With most economic resources under German military administration, the country was ruthlessly stripped of food and raw materials from early 1917. Romania had already provided the Central Powers with 850,000 tons of grain in the two years to August 1916, and a further 2.2 million tons of foodstuffs were removed before the ARMISTICE, most going to Germany and Austria. Financial and gold reserves were confiscated, and Germany took over all transport systems. Invasion, occupation and starvation had caused an estimated 500,000 civilian deaths by late 1918.

Lack of royal confirmation enabled Bratianu to renounce the Bucharest Treaty just before its annulment at the ARMISTICE, and Romania again declared war on 10 November 1918. Bratianu returned to office from December until the following September to press Romania's territorial claims at the PARIS PEACE CONFERENCE, and the size of 'Greater Romania' was almost doubled by the Treaties of NEUILLY and TRIANON (see MAP 25).

Romanian Army Under legislation regularly refined up to 1913, ROMANIA's peacetime army was manned by limited conscription, and all adult males spent time in the territorial reserve. The regular strength of just under 100,000 men was almost quadrupled with mobilization of the reserve for the Second Balkan War in 1913, and full mobilization in 1916 provided an army of 860,000 trained troops. A total of 23 infantry and 2 CAVALRY divisions were deployed as four armies at the start of the ROMANIAN CAMPAIGN.

Though numerically well-equipped, the Army was overstretched by rapid expansion, lacking modern equipment and competent leadership. Almost half of some 1,300 ARTILLERY weapons, most concentrated in FORTRESSES, were obsolete. The infantry possessed few MACHINE GUNS and a poor standard RIFLE in the 1893 Mannlicher. Some infantry units went to war with more than 40 per cent shortages in rifles, and most wore brightly coloured, 19th-century uniforms. Lack of experienced officers to conduct training left most troops with little grasp of tactics or manoeuvre.

Though some overseas observers noted the Army's unsuitability for modern warfare before 1916, it enjoyed an inflated European reputation after easy victories over the BULGARIAN ARMY in 1913. Most Allied authorities expected great things when it joined hostilities with an invasion of Hungarian Transylvania in August 1916, but the CENTRAL POWERS crushed Romanian forces and occupied most of the country by mid-December 1916, reducing the Army to a remnant of some 70,000 men in the north-eastern province of Moldavia.

Kept together by King FERDINAND and General PREZAN (the King's eventual successor as C-in-C), the Army was radically reorganized by a French military mission under General BERTHELOT and performed with greater efficiency in support of the Russian KERENSKI OFFENSIVE. It could not hope to challenge German-controlled forces in Moldavia seriously after the RUSSIAN ARMY collapsed in late 1917, and was drastically reduced to perform local policing tasks after the Treaty of BUCHAREST in May 1918. See also: AVERESCU, I.

Romanian Campaign The brief war of movement on the EASTERN FRONT that followed ROMANIA's declaration of war against the CENTRAL POWERS on 27 August 1916. The decision to join the Allies had been made while the Russian BRUSILOV OFFENSIVE was driving Austro-German forces west through Galicia, and was seen by some strategists on both sides as a military turning point.

The 650,000-strong ROMANIAN ARMY was expected to make a significant regional impact, distracting BULGARIAN ARMY forces away from SALONIKA and threatening AUSTRIA-HUNGARY through Transylvania, but Allied optimism overlooked the difficulties of defending Romania (much of which formed a SALIENT between two hostile powers, Austria-Hungary and Bulgaria) and the decayed condition of the Army. By late summer, defeats had forced the Central Powers to reorganize under German control, increasing the likelihood of an invasion from two frontiers.

Advised by the British to attack south towards SALONIKA, the Romanian high command instead chose to send its First (Curcel), Second (Crainiceanu) and Fourth (PREZAN) armies north through the difficult Carpathian passes into Hungarian Transylvania, leaving only the Third Army (Toshov) to guard the Bulgarian border.

Some 400,000 Romanians advanced across the frontier from 28 August, along a 300km front defended only by 35,000 men of the Austro-Hungarian First Army (ARZ VON STRAUSSENBERG). They occupied the south-eastern corner of Transylvania unopposed, but the advance was halted within a fortnight by a combination of crippling supply problems and command inertia, giving time for Austro-German reinforcements to arrive as the German Ninth Army, commanded by the newly demoted FALKENHAYN.

After initial hesitation, BULGARIA had declared war on Romania in early September, and a combined Bulgarian, Turkish, Austro-Hungarian and German force (MACKENSEN's Danube Army) was assembled for an attack into the southeast Romanian Dobrudja region, an ethnically Bulgarian province including Romania's entire Black Sea coastline. Operations began on 2 September with a successful diversionary attack on the Danube fortress of Tatrakan, which fell on 6 September after a one-day siege. Further east, Silistria fell on 8 September, freeing Mackensen's forces to enter the Dobrudja.

A promised Allied offensive to support Romania from Salonika made no progress at all (see Battle of FLORINA) and the only source of direct military aid, RUSSIA, was preoccupied with its own faltering KOVEL OFFENSIVE. Russian chief of staff ALEXEEV would send only a token force of some 50,000 troops (General ZAYONCHKOVSKI's Dobrudja Army) to reinforce six and a half Romanian divisions in the Dobrudja.

Forced to abandon attacking plans in Transylvania, half Romania's northern forces were transferred from 15 September to form a 15-division 'Army Group South' under AVERESCU for an offensive across the Danube. Launched between Zimnicea and FLAMANDA at the end of September, it failed to get across the river and was abandoned as a failure on 3 October, as was a subsidiary Russo-Romanian attack in the Dobrudja.

The 10 Romanian divisions left in Transylvania – strung out along fragile supply lines and deployed as mutually isolated corps – were now outnumbered by the Austrian First and German Ninth Armies, which comprised more than 200,000 men by the time Falkenhayn began a counteroffensive on 18 September.

After a decisive victory against isolated Romanian units in the centre of the front around HERMANNSTADT (27–29 September), Austro-German forces drove the weakened Romanian divisions back across the Carpathians, and Transylvania was almost completely reoccupied by 6 October. As Falkenhayn advanced into the passes further west, aiming to link up with Mackensen's armies, Averescu's reinforcements were returned north and fought a series of delaying actions from mountain positions.

Freed from the threat of another attack across the Danube, Mackensen renewed his own offensive into the Dobrudja on 21 October, using Bulgarian and Turkish units equipped with heavy ARTILLERY, GAS and MORTARS, none of which Romanian troops near the coast had experienced. The Romanians quickly withdrew without informing Russian units in the centre, and led the mass retreat that followed. Constanta, Romania's main port, was taken intact on 23 October as the attack drove towards the Danube delta and the Russian frontier, threatening to cut links between Bucharest and the coast.

With operations elsewhere on the Eastern Front dying down, large-scale Russian reinforcements were at last allocated to Romania from late October. A total of 36 infantry and 11 CAVALRY divisions were eventually sent, based around a new 'Army of the Danube' (Sakharov), but poor RAILWAYS prevented most from arriving before December. Although Russian forces were able to stabilize the line in the Dobrudja, protecting Moldavia and their own frontier, they hardly contributed to the defence of the main Wallachian lowlands.

Falkenhayn's forces broke through the passes into western Wallachia in early November, and reached the central plains to threaten Bucharest in mid-month. Transferring five divisions west from the Dobrudja, Mackensen crossed the Danube around Sistova on 23 November. Brushing aside depleted Romanian forces, he too turned east towards the capital. Gathering his remaining forces west of Bucharest, new Romanian C-in-C Averescu attempted a counteroffensive on the River ARGES (1–4 December), but it barely slowed the invasion before collapsing, and the remnant of the Romanian Army (about 70,000 men) withdrew north.

Bucharest fell on 6 December, and the vital oilfields of Ploesti were taken, but not before British agents had fired many of the wells. Worsening weather and gathering Russian strength (boosted by withdrawal from the Dobrudja after 17 December) checked Mackensen's pursuit of the retreat at Urziceni and Rimnicu-Sarat in late December.

The front stabilized along the River Sereth (Siret) on the border of Moldavia, where German attacks failed to establish viable bridgeheads across the river and ceased after 20 January. With both sides suffering acute supply problems, and the Central Powers arguing over division of captured territory, fighting virtually ceased in Romania until the KERENSKI OFFENSIVE of July 1917.

Along with three-quarters of its territory Romania lost most of its army, and could make no further contribution to the Allied war effort. The country's natural resources, mostly abandoned intact in Wallachia and Dobrudja, came under effective control of GERMANY, with benefits outweighing the 60,000 casualties suffered by the conquerors. See MAP 14.

Romanian Navy Consisting of the old CRUISER *Elizabetha* (with four 6-inch guns as main armament), four MONITORS, four small DESTROYERS and three TORPEDO BOATS, the Romanian Navy was divided into flotillas based at the BLACK SEA port of Constanta and the naval arsenal at Galatz, on the Danube. It saw no significant action apart from occasional skirmishes with light craft of the AUSTRO-HUNGARIAN NAVY.

Rome Congress of Oppressed Nationalities Meeting in April 1918 between exiled leaders of national groups within AUSTRIA-HUNGARY, unofficially sponsored by the Italian government after discussions with exiles in London. The Congress was primarily concerned to formally announce the nationalist aspirations of the Czech and South Slav (Yugoslav) delegations, but also achieved considerable PROPAGANDA impact inside Austria-Hungary and some practical progress towards independence. Although unwilling to compromise its own territorial ambitions by lending direct support to Yugoslav nationalism, the Italian government formally recognized the Czechoslovak Committee as a government-in-exile (21 April) and authorized the formation of a Czech Corps from its prisoners of war (see CZECH FORCES). See also: CZECHOSLOVAKIA; YUGOSLAVIA.

Room 40 Secret ROYAL NAVY intelligence department, operative from December 1914, that worked to decipher intercepted German RADIO messages, passing information direct to the Navy's Operations Department (OD). Established to exploit the Russian capture of GERMAN NAVY cipher codes from a cruiser wrecked in the BALTIC, along with charts and dispositions taken from a destroyer in the North Sea, its information was treated with circumspection by the OD, but Room 40's wartime chiefs, Sir Alfred Ewing and Commander James, established close links with the Navy's intelligence section, which set up a chain of radio listening posts in southern England.

Staffed by some of Britain's best mathematical minds, Room 40 was able to keep abreast of frequent changes to keys or codes, aided by regular captures of completely new signal books. Equally skilful German codebreakers were simultaneously at work interpreting British signals, but the Royal Navy made relatively sparing use of radio. Heavy German wireless traffic was curtailed after 1916, but the need to instruct numerous U-BOATS by radio continued to provide Room 40 with a steady flow of information.

Publicly ascribed to luck and espionage, the work of Room 40 was a great tactical asset but was not always used effectively. It predicted German movements before the Battle of JUTLAND, but poor liaison with OD led to the transmission of inaccurate information to the GRAND FLEET, and routine predictions of U-boat movements were consistently devalued by the impotence of British ANTI-SUBMARINE measures. See also: SCARBOROUGH RAID; Battle of the DOGGER BANK.

Roosevelt, Theodore (1858–1919) The central figure in US politics during the early 20th century. Roosevelt's 'Progressive' policies of economic expansion abroad and internal legislation against monopolistic corporations had split the Republican Party during his presidency (1901–09), and he had effectively assured Democratic victory in the 1912 presidential elections by running on an independent ticket, but in 1914 he remained a flamboyant, unorthodox and powerful political figure.

A close friend of General WOOD, Roosevelt was the most vigorous spokesman for the PREPAREDNESS MOVEMENT after 1914, and responded to the US declaration of war in April 1917 by offering to lead a corps of 25,000 volunteers into immediate action on the WESTERN FRONT. The offer reflected his romantic vision of war, but also embraced party-political motives. Unwilling to risk the (unlikely) prospect of the ailing Roosevelt becoming a war hero, and facing a Republican amendment attaching Roosevelt's offer to the SELECTIVE SERVICE ACT, President WILSON eventually banned all volunteers from the new conscript army.

Roosevelt subsequently played an important role in Republican reunification, collaborating with former rival LODGE to plan victory in the November 1918 congressional elections. His health collapsed after his son was killed serving as a USAAS pilot in France, and he died less than two months after the ARMISTICE.

Royal Aircraft Factory See: BE-, FE-, RE- and SE- Series aircraft.

Royal Flying Corps See: RFC.

Royal Naval Air Service See: RNAS.

Royal Navy The naval arm of the British Empire and the most tangible expression of GREAT BRITAIN's global power. Much bigger and more expensive than the prewar BRITISH ARMY, it was by far the most powerful navy in the world, a position unchallenged since the early 19th century.

The Royal Navy's basic responsibilities included policing colonies and trade routes, defending long British coastlines and imposing BLOCKADE on hostile powers. Ability to carry out these tasks depended on comprehensive battle superiority over all possible challengers, and the British calculated that this required possession of a battlefleet bigger than the world's two next largest put together, or any other likely combination of opponents.

Squadrons of BATTLESHIPS with an array of smaller supporting warships formed the basis of the battlefleet, and long-range trade protection required scores of reasonably fast CRUISERS. Nineteenth-century naval inventions – MINES, TORPEDOES and SUBMARINES – were regarded as threats rather than opportunities for offensive innovation, and prewar tactical development was concentrated on defence against them.

A degree of complacency was also reflected in falling naval budgets by the turn of the century, when the sudden challenge of German naval expansion sparked radical reorganization and modernization under Admiral FISHER, effective C-in-C (First Sea Lord) from 1903. After purging superannuated ships, admirals and techniques, Fisher ordered the revolutionary *DREADNOUGHT* and its successors to apply his theories of offensive fleet warfare. In an atmosphere of mounting competition with the GERMAN NAVY he presided over a massive increase in spending.

Reform was continued by naval minister (First Lord of the Admiralty) CHURCHILL, who founded a naval staff organization in 1912. The navy's headquarters (the Admiralty) in London had hitherto provided only administrative leadership, but development of RADIO enabled central control of long-range strategy. Barely established by 1914, the Naval Staff's wartime performance was generally poor, and its existence may have discouraged field initiative.

By early 1914 the Royal Navy included 18 modern dreadnoughts, with another 6 in service by the end of the year, along with 10 BATTLECRUISERS. The first fast light CRUISERS were in fleet service (see *ARETHUSA*), as well as 35 fairly modern TOWN and SCOUT CRUISERS. Older vessels included 29 PRE-DREADNOUGHTS and more than 150 cruisers built before 1907. A quarter of around 200 DESTROYERS were fast modern ships, but reform had generally left Britain little better-equipped than other major belligerents in TORPEDO BOATS and submarines.

Development of naval aviation was favoured by both Churchill and Fisher, though never at the expense of battlefleet investment, and largely with a view to fleet cooperation. After characteristically lagging behind other navies until the immediate prewar years, plentiful resources enabled the rapid and well-organized growth of a multi-purpose air arm, the RNAS.

The growing likelihood of war with GERMANY, and diplomatic understandings with FRANCE and RUSSIA, prompted a concentration of major warships with the GRAND FLEET in the North Sea, to face the new German HIGH SEAS FLEET. Strength in other theatres, notably the MEDITERRANEAN (where the FRENCH NAVY took over much of the British role), was reduced, and all but two of Britain's modern capital ships, along with most modern smaller ships, were stationed in home waters.

Other than destruction of the High Seas Fleet, the Grand Fleet's main strategic aim was enforcement of the blockade against Germany. Threats from torpedo craft and mines, and pessimism about the Grand Fleet's (considerable) margin of numerical superiority, prompted the adoption of a long-range blockade strategy. Most of the Grand Fleet's big ships were stationed at Scapa Flow in the Orkneys or Rosyth in Scotland, menacing any large-scale breakout attempt by the Germans; cruisers, destroyers, submarines and light forces were clustered around the British coast – most densely at the southeastern bases of Dover and Harwich (see MAP 16).

Elsewhere, a squadron of two battlecruisers and eight cruisers formed the bulk of the Mediterranean fleet, with its main bases at Gibraltar, Malta and Alexandria. Squadrons of pre-dreadnoughts and older cruisers operated from other overseas bases, covering every navigable sea not considered home waters by another major navy. Semi-autonomous naval forces for regional or imperial defence were provided by the dominions of Canada, Australia and New Zealand, all of which raised money for warships built in Britain and worked in conjunction with strictly British units, usually in their home oceans.

The Grand Fleet was on manoeuvres and still fully mobilized when war was declared (see BATTENBERG, L.), but failure to provide adequate anti-submarine protection for its main bases forced new C-in-C JELLICOE to withdraw his battleships to the northern Irish coast until mid-1915.

The fleet was cautiously handled after early losses (see *CRESSY*; *AUDACIOUS*), making frequent but unadventurous sweeps of the North Sea, and relying on provocative raids by light forces to bring German ships out for battle. Its greatest tactical asset, the ROOM 40 codebreaking unit, was able to provide accurate information about German movements from late 1914, and gave Admiral BEATTY's battlecruiser squadrons several opportunities to ambush similar German forces.

While raids by German battlecruisers on British coastal towns brought heavy criticism on the home front, battle opportunities were spoiled by a combination of bad luck, poor communications and worse staffwork. The one chance given to Jellicoe or Beatty (his successor from late 1916) to catch the whole High Seas Fleet was lost in similar circumstances at JUTLAND, raising additional questions about the quality of British ships, shells and gunnery (see CUXHAVEN RAID; SCARBOROUGH RAID; Battles of HELIGOLAND BIGHT and the DOGGER BANK).

Navy leaders felt compelled to retain maximum strength in the North Sea, but the possibility of offensive action elsewhere was a constant planning theme. A breakthrough into the BALTIC was discussed, but the only major strategic offensive undertaken, the DARDANELLES OPERATION in 1915–16, was a prolonged and costly failure. Offensive campaigns carried out by British submarines in the Baltic and the Dardanelles were more effective, but were restricted by the perceived need to keep most submarines with the Fleet or for coastal defence.

Rapid German military gains on the WESTERN FRONT in 1914 sparked a continuous battle for control of the French and Belgian Channel ports, requiring deployment of large coastal and seaplane forces based at Dover – including MONITORS for army-support bombardment. As German SUBMARINE WARFARE intensified, more light craft were required to patrol the western approaches to British home waters, to maintain the DOVER BARRAGE, and to escort supplies to Russia via the ARCTIC.

Aside from the GALLIPOLI FRONT, and the bungled attempt to trap the German MITTELMEERDIVISION in August 1914, British Mediterranean forces took part in Allied operations to protect SUEZ, to rescue the SERBIAN ARMY, and to supply SALONIKA, but their main preoccupation was the battle against U-BOATS. The war against submarines in the Mediterranean and home waters was critical to the British war effort, and its outcome was uncertain until the introduction of regular CONVOYS and US NAVY assistance from autumn 1917. See *HANDELSKRIEG*; ANTI-SUBMARINE WEAPONS.

The Royal Navy's long-range performance was more certain. The threat of German surface raiders had been eliminated by mid-1915, though not without alarms and embarrassments (see Battles of CORONEL, the FALKLAND ISLANDS, the RUFUGI DELTA). Transportation of troops and supplies from the British Empire to Europe was never again seriously threatened at source.

A division of naval infantry was formed in August 1914, comprising mobilized reservists for whom there was no ship. The Naval Division (renamed the 63rd Division in 1916) took part in land operations on the Western nt and at Gallipoli, functioning under tish Army command (see ANTWERP). ritish wartime shipbuilding concentrated easingly on destroyers and other anti- marine craft, although 6 more dread- ghts and 2 battlecruisers entered service n 1915, several AIRCRAFT CARRIERS were duced, and 35 modern light cruisers had n commissioned by the ARMISTICE. Losses December 1918 included 2 dreadnoughts, attlecruisers, 11 pre-dreadnoughts, 25 ous cruisers, 54 submarines, 64 destroyers, onitors and 10 torpedo boats. Total naval alties were 34,642 dead and 4,510 wound- See also: ARMED MERCHANT CRUISERS; FOUR, A.; GEDDES, E.; NAVAL AFRICA EXPE- ON; *ORION*, Q-SHIPS; WEMYSS, R.

yal Sovereign Class Class of five BATTLE- S, slower than the preceding QUEEN ABETHS but with thicker turret armour, entered service with the British GRAND T from 1916. Only the *Revenge* and the *al Oak* were present at JUTLAND, but *al Sovereign* and *Resolution* joined the Fleet tly afterwards. The fifth ship, *Ramilles*, damaged during launch and its comple- delayed until late 1917, when it briefly eared in experimental pink camouflage re conforming to the normal dazzle- ting pattern. All five remained in service ing the Second World War.

EF DATA (*Revenge*, 1916) Displacement: 50 tons; Crew: 937; Dimensions: length 624ft .1m), beam 88.5ft (26.8m); Speed: 23k; ament: 8 × 15in gun, 14 × 6in, 2 × 3in AA, 21in TT.

fugi Delta, Battle of the Protracted and sual naval action between 27 British ships and the German light CRUISER *IGSBERG*. Patrolling the coast of EAST CA to attack merchant shipping and guard man colonial interests, *Königsberg* sur- ed and sank the old British cruiser Pegasus Zanzibar on 29 September 1914. The dern British TOWN CLASS cruiser *Chatham* sent to track down the raider, which ed into the delta of the Rufugi River, a e of riverlets, mangrove swamps and ds surrounded by impenetrable jungle (see MAP 18). Unable to follow into the shallow, uncharted waterways of the delta or effectively patrol its many exits, *Chatham* sank two colliers to block the main exits and awaited reinforcement.

The old cruiser *Fox* and two armed tugs joined *Chatham* on patrol throughout the autumn while attempts were made to establish *Königsberg*'s position. A fragile CURTISS H-4 flying boat, with civilian pilot, was shipped to the delta from SOUTH AFRICA and spotted the *Königsberg* some 20km upriver on 24 November. The plane crashed on 10 December, by which time the German ship had moved. Two seaplanes shipped out by the RNAS reached the area in late February 1915, but were incapacitated by the heat and replaced by three SHORT 827s, which eventually located *Königsberg* on 25 April, almost seven months after its arrival.

Although *Chatham* was sent to the DARDANELLES in May, the ROYAL NAVY sent the similar *Weymouth*, two river MONITORS (*Severn* and *Mersey*) with powerful 150mm armament, three older cruisers, an ARMED MERCHANT CRUISER, the armed liner *Laurentic*, and small craft to watch the Delta exits. Two FARMAN HF-20 and two CAUDRON G-III biplanes were also shipped in as gunnery spotters and light bombers, although half the aircraft broke down immediately.

The two monitors moved upriver on the morning of 5 July 1915, running the gauntlet of *Königsberg*'s shore-mounted secondary guns before engaging the ship itself at about 10km range (13km according to German sources). A day-long gunnery duel left all three ships only slightly damaged, and bad weather delayed resumption until 11 July, when the monitors launched separate, successive attacks, silencing *Königsberg*'s guns by the early afternoon. Both remaining aircraft had crashed, and the monitors retired on the strength of earlier reports that *Königsberg* was on fire and settling in the mud.

Aerial reconnaissance in early August confirmed the cruiser's effective destruction but also revealed the extent of German salvage operations. German East African commander LETTOW-VORBECK rescued *Königsberg*'s ten 105mm guns (the most powerful ARTILLERY in the theatre), ammunition, small arms, supplies and crew for his ongoing guerrilla campaign.

Rumania See: ROMANIA.

Rumpler 6B German floatplane FIGHTER, a modification of the successful RUMPLER C-TYPE reconnaissance landplane, designed in response to the GERMAN NAVY's increasing (if temporary) interest in seaplanes and in service as the 6B-1 from July 1916. Bigger and clumsier than the ALBATROS W-4 or HANSA-BRANDENBURG KDW, it had a higher operational ceiling than either, performing reliably in the battle with RNAS forces in the English Channel and shooting down several RUSSIAN NAVY aircraft over the BLACK SEA. A 6B-2 version, structurally improved but with slightly inferior performance, was introduced from October 1917, and 88 of the two types were built before production stopped in January 1918.

BRIEF DATA (6B-1) Type: single-seat floatplane fighter; Engine: 160hp Mercedes; Max speed: 152kph; Ceiling: 4,950m; Armament: 1 × 7.92mm mg.

Rumpler C-Types Successful German series of reconnaissance biplanes developed from the unarmed, 100hp Rumpler B-I, one of the most common types in German service in August 1914. Some 200 B-Is were built before the armed Rumpler C-I began to appear in early 1915. Its top speed of 150kph, small bomb load and one or two MACHINE GUNS made the C-I a versatile reconnaissance and light-bombing weapon, used on the WESTERN FRONT until some 250 machines were withdrawn as obsolete in late 1916. Retained until early 1918 with GERMAN ARMY AIR SERVICE units in PALESTINE, they remained active as trainers until the ARMISTICE.

A C-III design was rejected after combat trials in France, but the streamlined, up-engined C-IV performed successfully on the Western, Palestine and ITALIAN FRONTS from early 1917. Excellent high-altitude performance (produced by Rumpler's distinctive swept-back wing design) protected it from all but the best Allied FIGHTERS, and it specialized in long-range reconnaissance work.

An improved, 240hp C-VII, produced from late 1917, could operate efficiently at 7,000 metres while carrying RADIO equipment, and a specialist PHOTO-RECONNAISSANCE (C-VIIR) version was stripped of all extraneous equipment for an even higher ceiling. Both types remained operationally viable in late 1918.

BRIEF DATA (C-IV) Type: two-seater armed reconnaissance; Engine: 260hp Mercedes; Max speed: 170kph; Ceiling: 6,350m; Armament: 2 × 7.92mm mg, max bomb load 100kg.

Rupprecht, Crown Prince (1869–1955) Heir to the throne of Bavaria and the most competent of several royal commanders in the GERMAN ARMY, Rupprecht led the Sixth Army in August 1914 and held overall command of German forces in LORRAINE. He achieved initial success against a French invasion and persuaded chief of staff MOLTKE to sanction a major counteroffensive in late August (partly to satisfy the regional amour propre of his predominantly Bavarian forces), but he failed to break through French defences east of the Moselle, contributing to the failure of the SCHLIEFFEN PLAN. Remaining on the WESTERN FRONT until the ARMISTICE, he was promoted field marshal in July 1916 and transferred in August to command the northern group of German armies ('Army Group Rupprecht'). Generally regarded as an efficient, careful leader, his disapproval of central strategic policies was reflected in poor relations with both FALKENHAYN and the THIRD SUPREME COMMAND, but his private criticism never developed into outright opposition. He was one of the first German field commanders to recognize imminent defeat in 1918 and retreated from the Allied COURTRAI OFFENSIVE in October despite orders to hold his positions. Deprived of his inheritance by the GERMAN REVOLUTIONS, he retired into private life after the armistice.

Russia The Russian Empire in 1914 incorporated European Russia (the 'Fifty Provinces'), POLAND, semi-autonomous FINLAND, Central Asia, large parts of TRANSCAUCASIA, and Siberia, the last-named covering over half an overall land area of about 22 million square kilometres (see MAP 1).

Its 166 million population (1910) was concentrated in Europe and most were Orthodox Slavs, but at least 5 million Jews, 13 million ethnic Turks and literally dozens of other nationalities lived under imperial rule. Demands for regional autonomy were a perennial source of unrest and political debate, and the Empire's coherence was limited by poor internal communications, with few roads, fewer telegraphs and some 74,000km of ill-managed, second-class RAILWAYS.

Until 1906 all political power was vested in the crown, which governed through appointed civil servants, but defeat by JAPAN in the war of 1904–05 was followed by a revolution in the capital, St Petersburg, and Tsar NICHOLAS II was persuaded to accept a form of constitutional government.

Elected on a narrow franchise, the Russian parliament (Duma) was largely representative of business and landed interests. The upper Council of State was half appointed by the Tsar and half elected by church, aristocratic, business or academic groups. Both representative bodies were restricted to ratification of certain government measures, and could be dismissed by the monarch at any time.

Revolutionary pressure subsided for a number of years after 1906, as socialist parties retreated into introspection and industrial unrest dropped to relatively low levels. Political opposition focused on the Duma, which was splintered into small parties with little common ground against a repressive regime under premier Stolypin. The liberal Kadet and Progressive Parties generally opposed government measures, while the right-wing Nationalist and Moderate Rightist Parties supported them, and the Octobrist group wavered in the centre. The left-wing Menshevik, Social Revolutionary (SR) and Trudovik parties were hardly represented.

At court, where the Empress ALEXANDRA emerged as a powerful force for reaction, complacency inhibited long-term alliances with Duma parties or genuine concessions to reform. The Duma was hardly consulted by ministers after the assassination of Stolypin in 1911. His successor, Kokovstov, faced a return to industrial strife as limited rights won since 1905 were circumnavigated by employers.

From 1912, when hundreds of striking miners were massacred at the Lena goldfields, dire predictions of revolution from the Duma's centre-left were backed by a return to revolutionary levels of industrial unrest. Strikes during the first half of 1914 involved almost half the total industrial workforce, and a huge St Petersburg dispute ended just before the outbreak of war. Soviet historians subsequently argued that imminent revolution was interrupted only by the War.

The poor conditions and volatility of urban labour reflected very rapid industrialization, with activity overwhelmingly concentrated around Moscow and St Petersburg. The industrial workforce rose by a third in three years from 1910, stimulated by lavish government rearmament orders, and overcrowded St Petersburg was Europe's unhealthiest capital by 1914. Whether Russia was entering a sustained phase of modern economic development, and whether uninterrupted development could have prevented later upheavals, remain controversial questions.

Booming industries employed no more than 3 million people by 1914, compared to at least 27 million agricultural workers in European Russia alone. Overwhelmingly rural, Russia was the world's largest food exporter before 1914. Peasant land reforms since 1905 had begun to break up the inefficient system of communes, but the process of transferring land to smallholders (*kulaks*) had barely begun by 1914 and most peasants remained politically apathetic. The most efficient farmers, providing surpluses to feed mushrooming city populations and armies, were the great landowners concentrated near the western frontiers.

The landed classes and other interests in the Duma fostered an illusion of stability by endorsing the government's rearmament and foreign-policy realignment after 1905. Economic ambition and emotional sympathy for fellow Slavs combined to produce political consensus behind a bid to control the DARDANELLES, along with support for independent BULGARIA and SERBIA against the ambitions of TURKEY and AUSTRIA-HUNGARY.

Entente with GREAT BRITAIN in 1907, ending long disputes over PERSIA and AFGHANISTAN, had freed Russian diplomacy for action over the Dardanelles Straits, but foreign ministers Isvolski and SAZONOV were aware that Russia was militarily weak, and preferred Turkish control to that of a stronger power. Russian action before 1914 was limited to suppression of Turkish elements in the Russian Caucasus, encouragement of ARMENIAN revolt inside Turkey, and diplomatic protests at any sign of British or German predominance in Constantinople.

The 1907 understanding with Britain completed a TRIPLE ENTENTE with FRANCE, Russia's ally and financial benefactor since 1892. French alliance ruled out the understanding with GERMANY preferred by conservative elements, especially the western landowners, but provided security against an increasingly hostile Austria-Hungary. Russian relations with Bulgaria cooled during the Second Balkan War (1913), and passive support for Serbia had been little help in the latter's escalating disputes with Vienna since 1903. Russia's foreign policies hinged on retaining the faltering faith of Serbia by 1914, prompting soldiers and diplomats to agree on mobilization against the possible destruction of Serbia by Austro-Hungary in the JULY CRISIS.

Enthusiasm for war gripped almost the whole established political spectrum once war was declared, fuelled by government insistence on its 'defensive' nature and general anticipation of a short conflict. The name of the capital was russified to Petrograd, and only the Duma's 21 socialist deputies opposed (or abstained from) suspending attacks on the government and granting war credits. Peasants and urban workers greeted mobilization with acquiescence: strikes virtually ceased for the first year of war and most revolutionaries withdrew into exile.

Despite the loss of about a million men, the opening campaigns on the EASTERN FRONT did not seriously dent RUSSIAN ARMY morale or political support from the educated classes. Resources were stretched by commitment against TURKEY on the CAUCASIAN FRONT from November, but the campaign offered huge potential rewards, secretly confirmed after Allied governments offered Constantinople and the Dardanelles in return for Russian acceptance of the Treaty of LONDON. Political consensus crumbled with military disasters on the Eastern Front in 1915, which cost the Army almost 2 million men. Russia lost KURLAND, LITHUANIA and much of Belorussia, along with Polish coalmines and heavy industries, although some plant was saved by being transported east.

Russia was unprepared for wastage of men and materials on such a vast scale, and was less equipped to adapt for total war than the western belligerents. Until spring 1915 the Tsar's government was simply a customer of industrialists concerned primarily with profit. Corruption and overpricing were given free rein, with government dependence exaggerated by the failure of Allied or US firms to meet lavish Russian orders.

A central War Industries Committee (WIC) was formed under the liberal GUCHKOV from June 1915 to coordinate the supply of materials and orders to big companies. Local committees were formed in all major industrial areas, and smaller firms in the provinces eventually received about 10 per cent of government orders. Special councils for defence, food, fuel and transport, established in August 1915, included representatives of government, industry, Duma, and Council of State.

Although the new commissions had no control over allocation of labour or raw materials, rapid production increases were stimulated by huge guaranteed profits for big companies. Output of weapons and ammunition rose from 43,000 tons in 1913 to almost 400,000 tons in 1916, and the Army was relatively well equipped for the successful summer BRUSILOV OFFENSIVE.

Funded from coal and iron reserves and maintained by cutbacks in civilian requirements, expansion could not be sustained. Heavy industrial output began to drop in late 1916, and Allied imports were never able to reach Russia in sufficient quantities to alter the overall picture (see ARCTIC THEATRE). Many skilled workers were drafted before exemptions were introduced in 1915, and expansion was further limited by lack of surplus labour from a shrunken non-military sector.

Agricultural-machinery production halved in 1915, fertilizers became scarce, and the Army commandeered any horses it could find. Shortages mostly hurt the rich western landowners, who used modern techniques to produce surpluses for town markets. Rural peasants facing transport failure and shortage of consumer goods in towns sold less of their harvests every year between 1914 and 1917. Cities swollen by 6 million arrivals in two years were desperate for grain by late 1916.

Food shortages wrecked the fragile social truce in urban districts. From late 1915 there were conscription riots in several cities, and civilian disillusion spread to largely peasant armies as the draft was widened. Jobs were plentiful but unrest was stirred by low wages, abandonment of labour reform, spiralling prices, high rents, long queues for food or fuel, and serious overcrowding. Strikes returned close to prewar levels from 1916.

Government attempts at price control were ineffective against apathy or hostility from rural peasants and business interests. A state project for centralized control of coal supplies was vetoed by an alliance of mine owners and other industrialists. Sporadic food rationing from autumn 1916, starting with the introduction of sugar cards in Moscow, only inflated prices on a thriving black market. Moscow's food supply was 60 per cent below requirements by January 1917, and Petrograd was down to a few days' grain supply when bread riots broke out in early March.

Government financial policy encouraged inflation. The socially motivated step of banning production and sale of vodka from August 1914 instantly eradicated a third of the state's tax revenue, and income from railway traffic and customs duties plummeted. Attempts were made to raise extra revenue by indirect taxation of consumer goods, a shrinking drop in the ocean by 1916, and the war effort was ultimately financed by negotiating loans and printing money. Income and excess-profit taxes were introduced from 1916, but were kept hopelessly low to avoid depressing industrial growth or alienating conservatives.

The military disasters of 1915 brought a few gestures by the monarchy to forestall concerted opposition. The Duma was recalled on 1 August and four unpopular ministers dismissed, including interior minister MAKLAKOV. Equally afraid of repression from above and revolution from below, the Duma's right and centre parties joined a group from the Council of State to form a Progressive Bloc, which presented a mild programme for liberal reform in late August.

Premier GOREMYKIN, a committed enemy of liberalism since his appointment in 1914, easily convinced Tsar Nicholas to reject the programme. Nicholas suspended the Duma on 16 September and dismissed several moderate ministers, most of whom had opposed his assumption of direct military command earlier in the month. Supported only by Goremykin and his favourite generals, Nicholas replaced Grand Duke NIKOLAI as C-in-C despite warnings that the monarchy would be held directly responsible for military failure.

The Duma accepted its suspension meekly, afraid that serious criticism would unlock mass rebellion. In January 1916 Goremykin was replaced by STÜRMER, a protégé of Alexandra and RASPUTIN with a (false) reputation as a German agent. His appointment fuelled gathering political resentment of the Tsarina, whose machinations with ultra-conservatives secured the dismissal of war minister POLIVANOV in March 1916 and of Sazonov in July.

In November 1916 Kadet leader MILIUKOV appealed in the Duma (recalled to vote new war credits) for a more competent and moderate cabinet, a change of mood that persuaded the Tsar to replace Stürmer with the relatively moderate Trepov. The universally loathed PROTOPOPOV retained most influence as interior minister, and Trepov was dismissed once he had clinched the Duma's peaceful adjournment on 30 December. Prince Golitsyn, a political nonentity without experience or ambition, took his place as the Tsar's last premier.

Neither the murder of Rasputin on the night of 29–30 December nor the return of the Duma in January 1917 had much effect on wider events. After agreeing the budget in advance and professing support for the war effort – with the moderate socialist KERENSKI one of only two opponents – the chamber went into voluntary recess after three days.

By the end of 1916 police had infiltrated or suppressed most unions and radical political organizations, and Workers' Groups on local WICs were the only legal channel for mass political expression. Grudgingly permitted from autumn 1915 to encourage urgent productivity increases, they were dominated by pragmatic Mensheviks and SRs. Until late 1916 the important Petrograd group sought to collaborate with other classes in achieving gradual revolution, but rising competition from militant radicals forced it to become more activist, joining socialist parties in calling for massive strikes in the capital in early 1917.

From 8 March (24 February by the old Russian calendar) the strike movement in Petrograd developed into an unplanned uprising, joined by troops from 10 March. Nicholas abdicated on 15 March and the monarchy ended with his brother's refusal to accept the throne next day. The Army high command acquiesced in the revolution, hoping it would appease the dangerous mood of frontline troops. See FEBRUARY REVOLUTION.

A liberal PROVISIONAL GOVERNMENT, led by the independent Prince LVOV, was formed on 15 March to occupy the political vacuum. From a very early stage its power was limited by the emergence of socialist SOVIETS all over Russia, most notably the volatile Petrograd Soviet, which refused to join the cabinet but was able to mobilize mass protest as a veto over government policy.

Dominated by Mensheviks and Social Revolutionaries, the Petrograd Soviet reached a working agreement with industrialists on 10 March and spread chaos in the Army by ordering the formation of soldiers' committees (see ORDER NUMBER ONE). It demanded 'peace without annexations or indemnities' (14 March) before giving qualified support to the regime's policy of remaining at war as a defence against German invasion.

The government moved steadily to the left during 1917 in search of popular or soviet approval, Kerenski becoming its leading figure after the formation of a coalition with socialists from 18 May. The ministers most associated with the old regime, Miliukov and Guchkov, were replaced, but a minority of the Soviet Executive Committee, including LENIN's 11 radical PACIFIST Bolsheviks, rejected participation and dismissed hopes of imminent peace through the STOCKHOLM CONFERENCE.

Political exiles streamed back into Russia but Lenin's April Thesis demanding 'all power to the soviets' was still regarded as fantastic by most delegates to the Petrograd Soviet, and he was tainted by his German connections. Veteran 1905 campaigner TROTSKI was one of the few senior socialists to offer unqualified support to Lenin, but the Bolsheviks benefited from their obvious separateness as the regime slid into economic and military crisis.

Increased taxes on profits, formation of a central Economic Council and state monopolies for grain and coal were all ineffective, and printing money to pay for war materials doubled prices in six months to August 1917. Amid worsening shortages, shutdowns closed 261 firms in Moscow alone during August and September. Continuation of war while theoretically propounding peace was the government's principal weakness. The KERENSKI OFFENSIVE in July was a focus for Bolshevik-inspired mass protest, and the failure of the Offensive broke the fragile peace within the Army, already fertile ground for pacifist agitation.

The JULY DAYS 'armed protest' movement in Petrograd, begun on 16 July, pushed the government into open repression. Kerenski took the premiership on 21 July, restored the death penalty at the front (overruling soviet opposition), and appointed KORNILOV as the new Army C-in-C. Another coalition was formed from 4 August, with seven socialists and seven liberals, but initiated no substantial policy changes. Elections for a Constituent Assembly were postponed until November, and radical leaders, including Trotski, were briefly imprisoned. Lenin went into temporary exile in Finland.

Urban unrest was matched in the countryside. Troops were being used to put down disorders by April 1917, but the regime was too weak to restrain spontaneous land seizures by peasants and too poor to buy crops for the towns. Peasant soviets demanded full local political control for their land committees in May, and SR leader Chernov quit the cabinet on 3 August over its refusal to comply. When partial land reform was introduced in late October it made little impact on generalized anarchy. Peasant troops were often unwilling to fire on rural communities, and deserted in numbers to join the land share-out.

German resumption of offensive warfare on the Eastern Front, suspended since March in the hope that Russia would sue for peace, brought the fall of RIGA on 3 September and convinced Kerenski that national security required urgent restoration of urban order. Kornilov was authorized to march on the capital, but his halfhearted cavalry advance ended with his arrest on 14 September amid fears that he planned a dictatorship.

The 'Kornilov Revolt' destroyed the remnants of officer control over the Army and restored Bolshevik credibility among socialists alerted to possible counterrevolution. Kerenski made a bid to recover his socialist credentials by forming a new coalition on 8 October, dominated by Mensheviks and SRs but still including liberals. It exercised no real authority and was ignored by the Bolsheviks, who won a majority in the Moscow Soviet on 7 October. Trotski was elected chairman of the Petrograd Soviet next day and Lenin demanded immediate revolution when he returned from exile on 23 October.

The Petrograd Soviet still sought a mandate from the masses through either the Constituent Assembly or the Second All-Russian Congress of Soviets (both due in November), but Bolshevik plans for a coup to coincide with the Congress were brought forward two days to take advantage of popular unrest. It met little serious resistance from 5 November (24 October by the old Russian calendar). The Petrograd Soviet's new Military Revolutionary Committee (MRC) claimed power on the morning of 7 November; well-organized RED GUARDS stormed the Tsar's Winter Palace, where the cabinet was besieged, early the next morning. A large minority of Mensheviks and many SRs spared Lenin the dangers of power-sharing by walking out of the Congress, which had opened the previous night.

Lenin's manifesto, accepted overwhelmingly by Congress on 8 November, pledged land to peasant committees, democracy in the army, worker control of industry, bread for the towns, consumer goods for the country, self-determination for national minorities, and an immediate proposal of armistice with the CENTRAL POWERS. A purely Bolshevik government was announced in the form of the Soviet of People's Commissars (with Lenin as chairman) before the Congress adjourned itself.

The Bolshevik government fulfilled its uncompromising peace programme almost immediately, relying on the outbreak of revolution in Germany and elsewhere to rescue Russia from a punitive settlement. Armistice in December was followed by a long period of delay while foreign minister Trotski played for time, but the BREST-LITOVSK Treaty of March 1918 reflected Russia's impotence under the threat of German invasion.

The OCTOBER REVOLUTION's global impact fell short of inspiring successful workers' uprising in Germany or elsewhere, and the regime was preoccupied with establishing internal control throughout the next three years. The Army had broken up, a new RED ARMY was still in the process of formation, and the first engagements of a sprawling RUSSIAN CIVIL WAR were being fought against a backdrop of continued peasant anarchy.

The November 1918 Constituent Assembly elections gave only 25 per cent of the popular vote to the Bolsheviks, with 58 per cent going to the SRs, but Lenin governed in the name of the soviets, in which he led the most popular and best-organized party. The threat of tsarist restoration was forestalled by the royal family's impromptu execution in Siberia.

Faced with continued peasant uprising, famine and civil war, the revolutionary government refused to play any part in the PARIS PEACE CONFERENCE or subsequent treaties, remaining on an economic war footing until 1921 and in diplomatic isolation until 1922, when it signed the Rapallo Treaty with

Germany. See also: CENTRAL ASIAN REVOLT; SUKHOMLINOV, V.

Russian Army In terms of sheer size, the armies of imperial RUSSIA were regarded as a potentially unbeatable force in 1914. The Empire's estimated manpower resource included more than 25 million men of combat age by 1912, and war minister SUKHOMLINOV's policy of military expansion after 1908, culminating in the 1914 GREAT PROGRAMME, persuaded both AUSTRIA-HUNGARY and GERMANY that the Russian 'steamroller' would be irresistible by 1916. Until then, its main area of vulnerability was thought to be slow mobilization capacity (see SCHLIEFFEN PLAN).

The Army's annual intake and training programmes were limited by a conscription system riddled with exemptions and anomalies, bureaucratic inability to penetrate the Empire's outer reaches, and prewar budget restrictions. Modernization was hampered by a determined clique gathered around C-in-C Grand Duke NIKOLAI, ensuring concentration of resources on isolated FORTRESSES and a bloated CAVALRY arm.

A number of discredited generals had been removed after defeat by JAPAN in 1905, but shortage of competent officers available from a narrow elite caste remained a serious problem, as did the lack of NCOs willing to perform long service under often brutal conditions. With vast operational areas to cover, the Army was served by poor roads and RAILWAYS that were barely capable of fulfilling peacetime requirements. Under the Army's ambitious PLAN 19, they were expected to supply simultaneous invasions of EAST PRUSSIA and GALICIA, reflecting the factional nature of the command system dividing the Empire's western frontier defences.

The standard infantry weapon in 1914 was the Mosin-Nagant RIFLE (1891), usually used with fixed BAYONET, and most MACHINE GUN units were equipped with modern Maxims manufactured in Russia, but by 1915 troops were being issued with anything that could shoot and a wide variety of imported small arms saw limited use. Artillery relied on obsolete, clumsy fortress weapons for most of its heavy ordnance, but some 1910-pattern light howitzers were produced under licence from FRANCE. Medium and field ARTILLERY units were generally equipped with old Krupp 90mm guns, but the more modern 76.2mm model was also used. Russian forces were seldom equipped with the specialized weapons and tools of TRENCH WARFARE (which depended on limited imports), and mechanized forces were restricted to a few motor vehicles and detachments of Allied ARMOURED CARS.

As mobilized in August 1914 the Army comprised 37 corps (each initially of one cavalry and two infantry divisions), along with 11 'armies' of mounted COSSACKS. Organized into 12 military districts, with most units concentrated in the western provinces, the corps were formed and ready for action in EAST PRUSSIA and GALICIA more quickly than anybody expected.

The Army's war effort up to 1917 was concentrated primarily on the EASTERN FRONT, but 22 divisions were committed to the CAUCASIAN FRONT from November 1914, and small detachments also served on the BALKAN and WESTERN FRONTS. The Army suffered appalling losses everywhere and, though reasonably successful against Turkish and Austro-Hungarian forces, was regularly defeated by the GERMAN ARMY.

Exorbitant levels of manpower and material wastage had not been anticipated by the planners, nor had the duration of the conflict, and Russia was given little help from Allied imports. Russian industry did not to respond to increased demand for weapons and munitions until mid-1915, by which time the Army had lost almost 3 million men. Although casualties could eventually be replaced, infrastructural weakness continued to make conscription difficult (see CENTRAL ASIAN REVOLT).

Even when rapid expansion produced sufficient supplies in 1916, the effects of a crumbling transport system were compounded by militant rivalry between regional commanders, who conspired to disrupt each other's operations by hoarding resources. The central military command (STAVKA) was reduced to impotence by poor lines of communication with front or rear authorities, and by the inert leadership of Grand Duke Nikolai and General YANUSHKEVICH, a situation only slightly improved after Tsar NICHOLAS II and General ALEXEEV took over in autumn 1915.

The mediocrity of the high command reflected a desperate shortage of young, vigorous or factionally untainted generals. With the exceptions of BRUSILOV in Galicia and YUDENICH in the Caucasus, steady rotation of senior commands among veteran monarchists produced unambitious or incompetent leaders, and their imperfect adherence to attritional BREAKTHROUGH TACTICS contributed to repeated offensive failures. Most experienced junior officers and NCOs were wiped out in the early campaigns.

The Army remained a coherent force after crushing defeats in 1915, but PACIFISM and revolution spread from the home front during 1916. Improvements in medical and equipment supply made little difference to war-weary peasant soldiers, except to convince them that the fight would continue. The idea was reinforced by the strictly temporary success of the BRUSILOV OFFENSIVE in summer 1916, when the Army was at its peak frontline strength of some 2.6 million men. A cut in infantry bread rations from late 1916 suggested worse privation to come.

Garrison troops in Petrograd (St Petersburg), Moscow and other cities were the most susceptible to revolutionary ideas. From late 1915 there were conscription riots in several cities, and soldiers in Petrograd refused to fire on strikers for the first time in October 1916. The following month 5,000 troops demonstrated with strikers in the UKRAINE, and the Army played a pivotal role in the FEBRUARY REVOLUTION.

Army leaders had hoped to maintain the monarchy by removing the monarch, and most accepted the PROVISIONAL GOVERNMENT with varying degrees of suspicion. Despite a flurry of revolutionary activity after the Petrograd Soviet issued its ORDER NUMBER ONE, and a marked reduction in the Army's anyway limited offensive potential, troops generally maintained discipline in the Revolution's first months.

Worsening physical conditions, increasing radicalism on the home front, and the new regime's commitment to continued war contributed to a steady decline in discipline and numbers during 1917. Collapse was finally triggered by the doomed effort of the KERENSKI OFFENSIVE in the summer, defeat at RIGA in early September, and General KORNILOV's threatened right-wing counterrevolution a few days later.

After the OCTOBER REVOLUTION the Army was officially disbanded, though it had already disintegrated in practice. Troops returned to the fields or enlisted with national forces gathering in their provincial homelands. Some officers fled to exile, others were executed or imprisoned by the new regime, but many of the Army's commanders took part in the RUSSIAN CIVIL WAR with anti-Bolshevik White forces or with the new RED ARMY, which attracted many of the best former imperial officers.

Almost 15 million men served in the wartime Russian Army. Casualties totalled an estimated 1.8 million killed, 2.8 million sick or wounded, and 2.4 million taken prisoner. Civilian deaths in invaded territories, victims of rural or urban unrest, and casualties during the Civil War can only be guessed at, but probably contributed at least another 2 million fatalities.

Russian Army Air Service Aircraft development was taken up at an early stage in RUSSIA, but development of a military service was haphazard. The RUSSIAN ARMY established an air arm in 1912 and secured generous funding to buy large numbers of machines. By August 1914 it possessed 360 aircraft (along with 16 airships), the largest air force in the world at the time, but they were mostly obsolete craft with little military value and less standardization.

The wide variety of aircraft operated by air battalions at Petrograd (St Petersburg), Warsaw and Vladivostok in 1914 reflected an enduring problem facing the splintered Russian aero industry, which was never given a sufficient share of limited industrial resources to enable large-scale expansion or conglomeration. Fewer than 1,000 aircraft were in service by summer 1917, and most were provided by FRANCE, including NIEUPORT 11s, SOPWITH STRUTTERs, SPAD VIIs and CAUDRON G-IIIs. Russian-built machines like the Anatra and Lebed reconnaissance two-seaters were inferior copies of foreign designs and never mass-produced.

On the outbreak of war, available aircraft and pilots were attached to field armies on the EASTERN FRONT for deployment as field commanders saw fit. Most served as all-purpose army-liaison and reconnaissance craft, and tactical development was very slow. Air units were only grouped into working types – combat, reconnaissance and bombing craft – from spring 1916, after efficiently organized German air support had caused havoc with mixed formations during the GORLICE–TARNOW and TRIPLE OFFENSIVES.

The poorly trained Russian service, chronically short of spares for imported machines, remained at a disadvantage even when GERMAN ARMY AIR SERVICE strength in the theatre was reduced again to its customary smattering of second-class aircraft and pilots from 1916. By the end of the year production, transport and fuel-supply breakdowns had reduced Russian air power to marginal status, and it was not a significant factor in the upheavals of 1917.

The one important Russian contribution to AERIAL WARFARE was the excellent, advanced and virtually invincible SIKORSKI IM series of heavy bombers, which carried out long-range attacks from early 1915, influencing the development of German RIESENFLUGZEUG long-range bombers and providing a the link between pioneering early designs and a mushrooming postwar industry. Sikorskis, along with isolated clusters of smaller Army machines, fought on both sides in the RUSSIAN CIVIL WAR, but none were organized as a coherent service. See also: KAZAKOV, A.

Russian Civil War Multi-faceted uprising by anti-Bolshevik forces during the three years after the OCTOBER REVOLUTION of 1917, a period marked by political confusion, regional anarchy and intermittent fighting. Various counterrevolutionary forces (collectively known as the 'White Army' and including small forces from many other countries) were gradually defeated by the Bolshevik RED ARMY.

Opposition from right-wing (and particularly military) elements throughout the former Empire, and from separatist movements in its outlying provinces, was already a serious problem when the Bolsheviks seized power, and the new regime faced military uprising as early as December 1917. A Japanese force landed at Vladivostok in the far east to aid a White Army under Admiral KOLCHAK in an attack into Siberia (see GRAVES, W.), where a CZECH LEGION of former prisoners of war was also active, and the Don Cossacks of southern Russia and the Caucasus marched north under General KORNILOV. Kornilov was killed in action in March 1918, but the Cossacks advanced deep into Russia under General Denikin, and Kolchak had established a Siberian White Government at Omsk by early 1919.

Largely to protect their own interests in the ARCTIC THEATRE, a small Anglo-French force landed at Murmansk in June 1918, took Archangel (Arkhangelsk) the following month, and established a regional puppet government. Elements of the Red Army intervened to support socialist rebellions in the Baltic states of FINLAND, LATVIA, ESTONIA and LITHUANIA, and joined anarchy in the UKRAINE once the departure of German forces in November sparked the collapse of a puppet government under General Skoropadski.

A summer offensive by Denikin occupied the Ukraine during the second half of 1919, and the Red Army's attempts to concentrate against him were complicated by the invasion of a Polish army under General PIŁSUDSKI, which took Kiev in May 1920. A White Army under General YUDENICH attacked Petrograd (St Petersburg) from Russia's BALTIC coast in autumn 1919, and was fighting in the suburbs of the capital by October.

Lacking coherent overall command or strategy, White forces began to collapse from late 1919. The Anglo-French expedition abandoned operations in the north from October, and Yudenich was forced back by superior Red Army ARTILLERY, subsequently concentrated against Denikin, who retired from the Ukraine in December.

Piłsudski quickly withdrew from Kiev, giving the Bolsheviks effective military control of the Ukraine by late 1919, and Denikin's army was pursued to the BLACK SEA coast, where it was shipped into exile by Allied navies. A remnant under General Wrangel attempted a final offensive from the Crimea, but was driven back and itself evacuated in November. Although the Japanese retained possession of Vladivostok until 1922, the Red Army had retaken most of Siberia by early 1920, capturing and executing Kolchak in February.

Recognition of independence for the Baltic states, formally completed by peace with Finland in October 1920, ended organized military resistance to the Bolshevik regime, although rural food shortages provoked widespread peasant unrest throughout Soviet Russia during 1920, and a naval mutiny at Kronstadt was put down by the Red Army the following spring. See also: TRANSCAUCASIA.

Russian Navy Crushing defeat by the JAPANESE NAVY in the Russo-Japanese War of 1904–05, followed by mutinies in its Baltic and Black Sea fleets, had reduced the Russian Navy to disarray by 1906, and despite subsequent large-scale reconstruction its reputation remained very poor in 1914. Because it fought in relatively obscure theatres, and received little official publicity, its performance as one of the more aggressive and tactically advanced wartime navies was underestimated by contemporaries.

Successive prewar reconstruction programmes were hampered by bureaucratic reluctance to provide funds, as well as the inefficiency and import-dependence of shipyards in RUSSIA. Of 5 BATTLESHIPS, 4 BATTLECRUISERS, 58 DESTROYERS, 10 light CRUISERS and 28 SUBMARINES ordered before August 1914, only the large destroyer *Novik* was in active service when war broke out, and many vessels failed to arrive before 1917.

On the positive side, the Navy was well supplied with fuel, weapons and ammunition by 1914, suffering no serious shortages prior to 1917, and a new generation of officers, epitomized by Admiral von ESSEN, was propelled to senior rank by the disasters of 1904–05.

Naval strategy refocused on the west after 1905. The BALTIC SEA was regarded as the main theatre of operations, and the Navy's primary task was to protect coastlines from potential invasion, with interruption of German trade as a secondary aim. Modifications to the RUSSIAN ARMY's war plans (see PLAN 19) had committed Essen's Baltic Fleet to an almost entirely defensive role before 1914, with the Bay of Riga and the coast of KURLAND virtually ignored and no plans for offensive operations by surface ships.

The Baltic Fleet in 1914 comprised 4 battleships, 10 old cruisers, 21 destroyers, 50 TORPEDO BOATS and 11 submarines. New GANGUT Class battleships were in service from late 1914, and its strength in small ships (especially mine craft) grew rapidly up to 1917. Naval aviation was steadily expanded, and by autumn 1917 about 60 seaplanes, flying boats and FIGHTERS were available.

Stronger than GERMAN NAVY forces deployed in the theatre, the fleet engaged in successful offensive mining operations, supported coastal forces (see PETRAGGE RAID) and held off German attacks on the IRBEN STRAITS until the end of the war on the EASTERN FRONT.

In its other important sphere of action, the BLACK SEA, the Navy originally planned to occupy the Bosporus and DARDANELLES Straits in the event of war with TURKEY, and to support military operations on the anticipated CAUCASIAN FRONT, but expansion of the TURKISH NAVY prompted a more defensive BLOCKADE policy after 1912.

In early November 1914 the Black Sea Fleet comprised 5 pre-dreadnoughts, 2 light cruisers, 8 destroyers and 4 submarines, along with 8 minelayers, 17 torpedo boats, 7 coastal gunboats and sundry auxiliary craft. Two modern battleships were in service by the end of 1915 (see *IMPERATRICA MARIA*), and the fleet received large numbers of destroyers, mine craft and submarines before supplies became disorganized in 1917.

The Turkish Navy provided steadily dwindling opposition. Russian MINES, submarines and surface raiders took a heavy toll of Turkish supply traffic, blockaded the vital coal port of Zonguldak, and provided effective support for Army operations (see RIZE LANDING). The fleet's largest warships, while careful to avoid tangling with the German battlecruiser *GOEBEN* on unfavourable terms, played a full part in all operations.

A weak Siberian Flotilla of cruisers and TORPEDO BOATS was retained in the far east to protect coastal waters around Vladivostok, but apart from an early loss to the German commerce raider *EMDEN* the port remained quiet until its occupation by Japanese forces during the RUSSIAN CIVIL WAR. A flotilla of minesweepers, ANTI-SUBMARINE craft, icebreakers and old warships was also sent to protect merchant traffic in the ARCTIC THEATRE from 1915, and a single Russian warship was attached to Allied forces in the eastern MEDITERRANEAN (see *ASKOLD*; *PERESVIET*).

The Navy survived the FEBRUARY REVOLUTION in 1917 without losing cohesion or willingness to fight, although a number of unpopular commanders were voted out of office by sailors' SOVIETS, and ships with imperial names were rechristened. After the OCTOBER REVOLUTION, and the end of hostilities on all fronts in November 1917, most personnel responded enthusiastically to the establishment of the Red Navy, which officially replaced the Imperial Russian Navy on 11 February 1918.

Russian warships became valuable prizes for both sides in the Civil War, and several Black Sea units were sunk or scuttled to prevent them falling into revolutionary hands. Others were seized (but never used) by the CENTRAL POWERS after the BREST-LITOVSK Treaty, and a few ANTI-SUBMARINE craft were commandeered by Allied forces in the Arctic during 1918. See also: Admirals EBERHARDT, GRIGOROVICH, KOLCHAK; *SLAVA*; *POTEMKIN*.

Ruzski, General Nikolai (1854–1918) A strong supporter of war minister SUKHOMLINOV until 1915, Ruzski led the Russian Third Army in GALICIA during the opening campaigns on the EASTERN FRONT before taking over the northwestern army group around EAST PRUSSIA in September 1914. Military caution personified, and generally regarded as one of the RUSSIAN ARMY's least effective commanders, Ruzski gained some credit for halting the German offensive around ŁÓDŹ in November 1914, but with Sukhomlinov's political position weakening he resigned the following March. Like many Russian generals, he could rely on factional interests to ensure re-employment, and he was twice more appointed to lead northern army groups on the Eastern Front. In August 1915 he was given a new far northern group on the Baltic coast (see VILNIUS). Replaced by KUROPATKIN in February 1916, he was reinstated by Tsar NICHOLAS II in July, and played a major role in persuading the monarch (stranded at northern group HQ) to abdicate during the FEBRUARY REVOLUTION. Finally dismissed in its aftermath, Ruzski travelled south to join other Tsarist generals in the Caucasus, where he was arrested and executed after the OCTOBER REVOLUTION.

S

Sablatnig SF-Types Series of German floatplanes, of which the SF-II, SF-V and SF-VIII were put into production for the GERMAN NAVY. Most of the 26 SF-IIs built were used as trainers in 1916–17, but a few SF-Vs (out of 91 built) suffered heavy losses on active service from northern coastal stations during 1917. The SF-VIII was a purpose-designed, unarmed training version produced from spring 1918.

BRIEF DATA (SF-V) Type: two-seater reconnaissance floatplane; Engine: 150hp Benz; Max speed: 136kph; Armament: 1 × 7.92mm mg.

Saint-Addresse, Declaration of Set of guarantees given to BELGIUM by the ENTENTE

POWERS in February 1916, promising to restore the country's postwar independence and back Belgian claims to REPARATIONS from GERMANY. The Declaration represented a compromise with King ALBERT I's refusal to enter into full alliance with the Entente and a victory for the pro-Allied majority in the Belgian cabinet. Careful phrasing freed the Allies from any obligation to satisfy Belgian nationalist ambitions for postwar expansion into Luxembourg and the Netherlands (see HYMANS, P.).

St Étienne Gun One of two MACHINE GUN designs developed at the French government's St Étienne arsenal as potential improvements on the FRENCH ARMY's standard HOTCHKISS GUN. The first effort, the 1905 Puteaux machine gun, was rejected by the military, and the St Étienne was hardly more successful. Poorly manufactured using cheap materials, it suffered chronic overheating problems and was only used from 1914 because Hotchkiss production was incapable of matching demand. Despite replacement of its 30-shot metal-strip magazine by a belt, and wartime improvements in production standards, the gun was withdrawn completely in 1916.

St Germain, Treaty of The final peace settlement between the Allies and the new Austrian Republic. Signed on 10 September 1919 it confirmed the disintegration of AUSTRIA-HUNGARY into independent national elements, giving Galicia to POLAND, Slovenia and Bosnia-Herzegovina to YUGOSLAVIA, and Moravia to CZECHOSLOVAKIA. Allied territorial ambitions were partially satisfied, with ITALY receiving the disputed zones on the ITALIAN FRONT (see MAP 21), and ROMANIA taking the Bukovina region on the EASTERN FRONT. Despite a small territorial gain from Hungary by the Treaty of TRIANON, the former Austrian Empire lost more than 70 per cent of its prewar population. Permitted only a small postwar army (30,000 men) and required to pay REPARATIONS, the Republic was also expressly banned from political union with GERMANY. See MAP 25.

St Jean de Maurienne Conference Inter-Allied meeting of 19 April 1917, at a small town in the French Alps, that was attended by British prime minister LLOYD GEORGE, French premier RIBOT and Italian foreign minister SONNINO. The main purpose of the meeting was to examine the prospects for a separate peace with AUSTRIA-HUNGARY (see SIXTUS AFFAIR). The conference agreed to recognize an Italian sphere of influence in postwar TURKEY, offering Sonnino the provinces of SMYRNA and Adalia in return for leeway to discuss a Balkan settlement with Vienna (and acceptance of French ambitions in the eastern Mediterranean). The need to consult RUSSIA, promised control over Turkish Asia Minor in 1915, was mentioned, but Russia's interests were largely ignored by the western Allies after the FEBRUARY REVOLUTION. The promise of Italian expansion into Turkey caused serious arguments at the PARIS PEACE CONFERENCE in 1919, with GREECE in particular disputing claims to Smyrna.

St Mihiel, Battle of The first major attack planned and carried out by the AEF on the WESTERN FRONT. Despite its distance from any embarkation points, the German-held St Mihiel SALIENT in the front south of VERDUN was selected for the first US offensive when staff officers reached Europe in mid-1917. By the time sufficient forces were ready to attack in summer 1918, the strategic importance of the Salient had declined in the context of major Allied offensives further north (see AMIENS OFFENSIVE).

US commander PERSHING faced Allied pressure to abandon the operation, scheduled for mid-September. Overall Allied commander FOCH informed him in late August that the AEF would form a major element of the planned MEUSE–ARGONNE OFFENSIVE, due to begin in late September, but Pershing chose to continue with a limited attack at St Mihiel. Widely perceived by Allied commanders as a naive gesture of faith in his troops, the decision also reflected the operation's importance to US morale.

The US First Army, incorporating a French colonial corps, took up station on a 65km stretch of the front around St Mihiel on 30

August. Aware that the attack was coming, and that defences could not be effectively reinforced, the German supreme command authorized a partial withdrawal from the salient.

The German withdrawal was still in progress when almost 300,000 US troops of I Corps (LIGGETT) and IV Corps (Dickman) attacked the southern face of the salient at 05.00 on 12 September, after a four-hour bombardment by (predominantly French) ARTILLERY. A secondary assault on its north-western edge by V Corps (Cameron), supported by 110,000 French troops, opened three hours later. Infantry support included 267 French light TANKS, 154 of them US-manned, and almost 1,500 Allied aircraft under US General MITCHELL.

Months of meticulous planning, and efficient work by inexperienced US troops, contributed to a successful first day. The main attack from the south had advanced 9km to reach Thiancourt by 11.30, the secondary force captured the village of Dommartin, and by 16 September the entire salient had been 'pinched out'. The offensive was then halted to enable mass transfer of forces to the Argonne sector, and attacks in the area were eventually resumed on 10 November, when the AEF's Second Army began a limited offensive towards Metz (see MAP 2).

The St Mihiel victory vindicated Pershing's consistent refusal to break up his army, but also suggested future logistic difficulties. The AEF's shortage of experienced staff officers was reflected in jams of men and materiel blocking rear areas during the battle, and similar scenes offered easy targets for German aircraft and artillery in the better-defended Argonne.

St Quentin Canal, Battle of the The most important action in the battle for the HINDENBURG LINE on the WESTERN FRONT in autumn 1918. Crammed with traps and barbed wire, the Canal's sheer sides dropped 50–80 metres into several metres of water or mud. It formed an integral part of the Hindenburg Line at its most complex and defensible point between the towns of St Quentin and Vendhuille (see MAP 2). The British Fourth Army (RAWLINSON) and the French First Army (Debeney reached the position in mid-September, an the main task of forcing an initial crossing fel to the Fourth Army's Australian Corp (MONASH) and its US reinforcements.

A large-scale attack could only be attempted at one place – a strip of fairly firm ground just over 5km wide, where the canal ra through a tunnel in front of Bellicourt. Thre German strongholds still occupied the strip and behind them lay a mass of well-prepare defences. Meticulous planning was upset b supply and communications problems affecting the whole of the Allied advance, and preliminary operation by an AEF regiment t clear the strongholds failed on 27 September two days before the scheduled attack.

The US regiment had apparently disappeared by the following morning, leaving th outposts intact, but Monash was refused postponement by Rawlinson and the attack over the tunnel at Bellicourt opened in dens fog at dawn on 29 September. Advancing infantry was supported by 1,000 guns and 141 TANKS, but inexperienced US troops leading the attack became badly confused, and the day ended with Allied forces well short of the Lin itself.

Aware of heavy casualties (5,400 US an 2,400 AUSTRALIAN) and the loss of 75 tank (see TANK FORTS), Rawlinson believed th battle lost, but a subsidiary attack succeede further south, where elements of IX Corp (Braithwaite) had been detailed to cross th canal at Bellenglise. This subsidiary attack used a variety of ramshackle engineering improvisations to get two divisions across th canal in the morning. Rapidly reinforced by forces from Bellicourt they had advance 6km into the strongest section of the Hindenburg Line by nightfall, taking 5,400 prisoner and effectively destroying the Line's integrity

Salamis Operation Planned landing in Jun 1916 of some 8,000 Allied troops at the Bay o Salamis in GREECE, proposed after virtuall unopposed advances by BULGARIAN ARMY units into Greek eastern Macedonia ha exacerbated unrest in Athens. Six French BATTLESHIPS, two CRUISERS and some 5 smaller craft were assembled for the oper ation, but it was cancelled at the last minute when the Greek government acceded to demands for demobilization, the immobilization of shipping, the dissolution of the government, and expulsion of German agents.

The naval force was reassembled after the Allied defeat at FLORINA in August 1916 rekindled doubts about Greek reliability. Led by MEDITERRANEAN C-in-C Admiral DARTIGE, it was augmented by Allied forces including light cruisers, the old Russian battleship *PERESVIET*, a British AIRCRAFT CARRIER, and large numbers of ANTI-SUBMARINE craft. A new set of Allied demands, including the surrender of 13 interned German and Austro-Hungarian ships, was accepted on 3 September, but Admiral Dartige chose to neutralize the GREEK NAVY. An ultimatum of 10 September demanded the disarming of its coastal-defence battleships, seizure of its smaller vessels, and occupation of coastal batteries. The Greek government again bowed to pressure, and Greek light forces officially joined the FRENCH NAVY on 7 November. The Allied fleet remained in the Bay, ready to exert further influence on a persistently unstable situation. See ATHENS LANDING.

Salandra, Antonio (1853–1931) An experienced minister but not considered among the great political figures of the day, Salandra was regarded as a caretaker when he became prime minister of ITALY after GIOLITTI's resignation in March 1914. Salandra faced immediate shortages created by the Turkish war of 1911–12, together with a wave of strikes culminating in widespread rioting during June, but the international JULY CRISIS diverted any threat to his government's survival.

Salandra spoke for most Italian opinion in declaring neutrality on 2 August, but subsequent diplomacy was conducted against a backdrop of sharp internal divisions. Salandra's own commitment to *sacro egoismo* (pursuit of Italy's national interests), and the interventionist SONNINO's appointment as foreign minister in November, worked against accommodation with AUSTRIA-HUNGARY. Rising popular support for intervention on the side of the Allies was matched by parliamentary opposition, which forced the cabinet's resignation on 13 May, but Salandra was reinstated three days later once it became clear that no neutralist administration could survive.

Salandra's tenure as wartime premier is generally viewed as inert. He avoided hostilities with GERMANY and made some attempt at systematic economic mobilization (see DALLOLIO, A.), but military policy passed almost exclusively under the control of chief of staff CADORNA, who brushed off Salandra's sporadic attempts to assert political authority. Lack of military success, crowned by the TRENTINO defeat of May 1916, forced the government's resignation on 10 June. Salandra held no office in the subsequent BOSELLI and ORLANDO administrations, although he was a member of the Italian delegation at the PARIS PEACE CONFERENCE and later represented Italy at the LEAGUE OF NATIONS.

Salient Any bulge of any size in a line between opposing armed forces. Forces occupying a salient face the obvious disadvantage of having to defend on three sides, often prompting attacks aimed at expanding the position on one side and 'pinching off' the bulge on the other. In the static conditions of the Western Front, some salients became longstanding features. The small salients around ST MIHIEL and YPRES were the focus of large-scale attacks by both sides, and the entire German position in northern France from 1914–18 formed a large salient, dictating the pattern of repeated Allied offensives from 1915. See MAP 3.

Salmson 2 French biplane in service with AÉRONAUTIQUE MILITAIRE units on the WESTERN FRONT from early 1918. Sturdy, well-armed and reasonably fast, it became the standard French reconnaissance, light-bombing and ground-attack craft on the front, but also equipped two French escadrilles on the ITALIAN FRONT and the USAAS, which purchased 705 machines in April 1918. The design's main weakness was a poor cockpit layout, which prevented in-flight communication between pilot and observer, but the type was well liked by crews and a total of 3,200 were built in wartime.

BRIEF DATA Type: two-seater armed reconnaissance; Engine: 260hp Canton-Unné; Max speed: 184kph; Ceiling: 5,000m; Armament: 3 × 0.303in mg, light bombs.

Salonika (Thessaloniki) Strategically important Greek port on the Aegean coast of Macedonia, part of the Ottoman Empire until the First Balkan War of 1912 and still the subject of Bulgarian and Austro-Hungarian ambitions in 1914–15 (see BALKAN FRONT). Despite relatively primitive harbour facilities, a direct RAILWAY link with Belgrade made Salonika the most efficient potential route for Allied aid to SERBIA on the Balkan Front. After much deliberation, mobilization of the BULGARIAN ARMY in September 1915 prompted Allied acceptance of an invitation from Greek prime minister VENIZELOS to land troops at Salonika.

With GREECE mobilizing and expected to join the Allies, the first Anglo-French troops (but almost no equipment) arrived at Salonika on 5 October 1915. Venizelos resigned the same day under pressure from pro-German King CONSTANTINE, and an invasion of Serbia by the CENTRAL POWERS opened on 6 October. Five Allied divisions (four French and one British) assembled at Salonika in an atmosphere of mounting local distrust, but by the time substantial forces had been sent north to aid the SERBIAN ARMY the latter had been driven into ALBANIA (see GREAT RETREAT; Conquest of SERBIA)

By late November French commander SARRAIL was withdrawing his men back into Greece, alongside a small British advance contingent. With Bulgarian and German forces gathered on the frontier, and potential Greek hostility threatening his base, Sarrail turned Salonika and its surrounds into an entrenched defensive zone, which by April 1916 was comparable with fieldworks on the WESTERN FRONT. Despite political opposition from Anglo-French 'WESTERNERS' to expansion of the Salonika force (see CALAIS CONFERENCE), British reinforcements under General MILNE had swollen its strength to more than 160,000 troops by late January 1916, with naval support from PRE-DREADNOUGHTS, CRUISERS and a MONITOR.

Given overall Allied command of the fortified area, Sarrail deported enemy nationals, cut the rail link east to Constantinople, and forced the surrender of Greek ARTILLERY overlooking the approaches to Salonika harbour. Ignoring Greek protests he gradually assumed full administrative control over the fortified area, proclaiming an official state of siege in June 1916 and beginning an embroilment in Greek politics that made Salonika the headquarters of revolutionary pro-Allied activity.

Military action against the Central Powers was less energetic. Plans for an autumn 1916 offensive all along the 110km line were preempted by a Bulgarian attack on FLORINA in August, and the limited Allied advance that eventually took place struggled across the Serbian border to take MONASTIR in November. Bulgarian occupation of Greek Kavalla put pressure on the British sector of the line to the west, and offensive operations were abandoned until the following spring.

By early 1917 some 600,000 French, British and Serbian troops, along with a small RUSSIAN ARMY contingent, were based on Salonika as the 'Army of the East', and were in contact with Italian forces in ALBANIA, but the unhealthy, humid environment of the overcrowded town and its marshy surrounds took a huge of toll of disease victims, leaving fewer than 100,000 men available for combat.

Sarrail launched a new offensive all along the line in spring 1917, but poor coordination forced its abandonment after an isolated British operation failed at Lake PRESPA in May. The 'armed camp' lived up to its popular reputation as 'Germany's biggest internment camp' for the rest of 1917, prompting increased pressure from Allied Westerners for its abandonment, and the universally unpopular Sarrail was removed at the end of the year.

Apart from local actions in spring 1918, new C-in-C GUILLAUMAT remained passive as German units on the front were withdrawn to the SPRING OFFENSIVES in France. Recalled to the Western Front in July, he was replaced by the more aggressive FRANCHET D'ESPEREY, who was reinforced by 250,000 GREEK ARMY troops before the major VARDAR OFFENSIVE of September. Though less affected by disease in the cleaner atmosphere of the hills, the 200,000 Bulgarian troops still defending the line were ill-equipped and weary, and Franchet d'Esperey's well-organized attacks triggered their total collapse.

A rapid advance to the Danube through BULGARIA gave an appearance of victory to operations on the Balkan Front by the ARMISTICE, but the Salonika expedition is generally regarded as a major waste of Allied resources. Although Allied troops suffered fewer than 20,000 battle casualties throughout the campaigns from Salonika, almost 450,000 men had been invalided out of the theatre with malaria alone by late 1918. Those invalids returned to action tended to fall sick again, and a total Allied commitment of just over 1 million men after October 1915 produced 1.3 million hospital cases. See MAP 19.

Samaria, Battle of See: MEGIDDO OFFENSIVE.

Samarrah Offensive A series of actions on the MESOPOTAMIAN FRONT following the Anglo-Indian capture of BAGHDAD in March 1917. Some 10,000 Turkish troops to the north threatened the city's security, particularly if they linked up with Ali Ishan Bey's 15,000 men retreating from PERSIA or flooded the plains from one of several points further up the Rivers Tigris and Euphrates. British manpower requirements on the WESTERN FRONT could only be relieved from Mesopotamia after this threat had been removed.

A major offensive from Baghdad, to drive the Turks towards 21,000 Russian troops under General Baratov in western Persia and 50,000 more snowed in on the CAUCASIAN FRONT, was deemed impossible without control of the railhead at Samarrah, 130km to the north. British C-in-C MAUDE, with about 45,000 frontline troops at his disposal, elected to launch limited attacks up the Tigris along with holding operations in the west, to prevent flooding of the Euphrates, and in the northeast to block Ali Ishan.

Regional Turkish commander KHALIL PASHA's decision to contest every defensible point up the Tigris to Samarrah set the pattern for the battles that followed. A raid on Turkish positions just north of Baghdad on 13 March forced a 35km withdrawal to the junction of the Tigris and Adhaim rivers. On 19 March a brigade occupied FALLUJA, a key flood-control point on the Euphrates, but a force sent to intercept Ali Ishan suffered a sharp defeat at JEBEL HAMRIN on 25 March.

Ali Ishan was able to move west towards 5,000 Turkish troops sent back down the Tigris to met him at Dogameh. Maude sent most of his CAVALRY to prevent the meeting and focused infantry attacks on the Dogameh trenches, which fell after a costly frontal attack across the Marl Plain on 31 March. The defenders retreated back to the Adhaim junction. Delayed by a call to help the cavalry at SHIALA, General Marshall's corps attacked at the Adhaim on 18 April, and Turkish forces withdrew another 35km upriver to Istanbulat, crossing the Tigris to defend strong fortifications (and the railway to Samarrah) between the river and the Al Jali Canal.

British forces on that bank cleared the main defences close to the river with a series of attacks at staggered intervals on 21 April, an intense fight during which some positions changed hands three times. Early the following morning Turkish troops retreated again to hold a ridge less than 10km from Samarrah station against repeated attacks, but British reserves moving up from the Adhaim convinced local commander Shefket to abandon Samarrah, and he retreated north early on 23 April.

Operations around Istanbulat cost some 2,000 British casualties, slightly more than estimated Turkish losses, and Maude's forces throughout Mesopotamia had suffered about 18,000 battle casualties since mid-March. More than twice as many fell to sickness in the same period, making a pause necessary and large-scale withdrawals to other theatres impossible. See Battles of the BOOT, RAMADI; MAP 23.

Sambre Offensive Last major attack of the climactic Allied offensives on the WESTERN FRONT in 1918, a largely processional march into occupied BELGIUM. Launched on 4

November, immediately after the VALENCIENNES advance had brought HAIG's Army Group across the Belgian border, it employed all four of the Group's armies (British First, Third and Fourth, and French First) and confirmed the collapse of Prince RUPPRECHT's Army Group North. At the centre of the front, the British Third and Fourth Armies took almost 10,000 prisoners in one day, and although some German units continued to offer more than token resistance (see LE QUESNOY) many others proved unable or unwilling to fight. Along with the continuing US–French MEUSE–ARGONNE OFFENSIVE from the south, the attack convinced the German THIRD SUPREME COMMAND to seek an immediate ARMISTICE. See MAP 3.

SAML Italian reconnaissance biplane developed during 1916 from the German AVIATIK B-1 design, built under licence in prewar ITALY. Both the SAML-1 and a modified SAML-2, with an extra wing-mounted MACHINE GUN, were in service from early 1917, performing reconnaissance, ARTILLERY-spotting, PHOTO-RECONNAISSANCE and occasional light-bombing duties. A total of 637 were produced by late 1918, and they eventually equipped 16 ITALIAN AIR FORCE squadrons, serving in ALBANIA as well as on the ITALIAN and BALKAN FRONTS.

BRIEF DATA Type: two-seater armed reconnaissance; Engine: 260hp Fiat; Max speed: 170kph; Armament: 1 × 6.5mm mg, light bombs.

Samsonov, General Alexander (1859–1914) Russian CAVALRY officer and former governor of Turkestan who was given command of the Second Army for the invasion of EAST PRUSSIA in August 1914, although he was openly pessimistic about the offensive's chances. Hampered by poor communications, short of supplies, misdirected by the high command and inadequately supported by the First Army, his forces were surrounded and destroyed at TANNENBERG (26–30 August). Stranded in wooded country with a few other officers, Samsonov shot himself on the night of 29/30 August.

San Giuliano, Antonio, Marquis di (1852–1914) Sicilian nobleman, a former Italian ambassador to London and foreign minister since March 1910, whose cultivation of German friendship and watchful obstruction of Austro-Hungarian expansion into the Balkans set a pattern for prewar diplomacy within the TRIPLE ALLIANCE. Still in office during the JULY CRISIS of 1914, he guided the SALANDRA government to neutrality in early August and sought to keep both belligerent groups friendly towards ITALY until a probable victor emerged, a policy slowly eroded after his death in office (see SONNINO, G.).

Sannaiyat, Battles of See: First and Second Battles of KUT.

Sapping Standard TRENCH WARFARE technique for approaching a hostile position without exposure to fire. Short trenches ('saps') were dug across NO MAN'S LAND directly towards the hostile position and joined at their far ends, to create a new, unbroken frontline trench, which was completed and fortified before the process was repeated. Involving thousands of yards of excavation for small territorial gains, sapping was slow and gruelling work (especially in tropical theatres), but was reliable and entailed relatively light casualties. See also: MINES.

Sarajevo See: Archduke FRANZ FERDINAND; PRINCIP, G.; JULY CRISIS.

Sari Bair, Battle of Allied attempt to break out of ANZAC COVE on 6 August 1915, forming the secondary pincer of the SUVLA BAY OFFENSIVE on the GALLIPOLI FRONT. Extension of the cramped Anzac sector north into difficult hill country had been considered by C-in-C HAMILTON since May, but had been prevented by Turkish reinforcement. British war minister KITCHENER's June decision to send three extra divisions to Gallipoli revived the plan in conjunction with a major landing further north at Suvla and a diversionary attack at HELLES (see MAP 20).

Two brigades were to move north up the coast from Anzac Cove, flanked by supporting columns, before swinging inland against the west flank and rear of Sari Bair Ridge, just northeast of the Anzac frontline. Command of the Ridge would prevent the Turkish Fifth Army from reinforcing Suvla and provide a commanding platform for future offensives.

ANZAC commander BIRDWOOD's strength was brought up to more than 45,000 men before the main columns moved north in the small hours of 6 August. Detailed reconnaissance had been impossible in conditions ideal for SNIPING, and the carefully planned operation quickly fell foul of the terrain. Exhausted in intense heat by a maze of steep climbs and sharp ravines, attackers ended the day well short of their preliminary targets – the heights of Chunuk Bair at the western end of the Ridge, and 'Hill Q' in its centre.

A strong diversionary attack southeast of Anzac Cove against the 'LONE PINE' position opened on the evening of 6 August and continued through the next day, eventually taking Turkish trenches on 8 August, but another supporting attack southwest of Chunuk Bair (at 'the Nek') failed in repeated charges against impenetrable gunfire. Birdwood waited in vain for support from the Suvla sector before the main drive towards Sari Bair was resumed on 8 August.

A New Zealand brigade quickly took the crest of Chunuk Bair as the defenders withdrew, but the New Zealanders were exposed to Turkish ARTILLERY and forced back to their original positions. Gurkhas approached Hill Q from the west and were established 100 metres from the summit by evening. Reinforcements got lost on the way, and the next morning a single battalion charged up the hill on its own, forcing defenders off the crest before being accidentally bombarded by Allied artillery (probably from a British offshore MONITOR).

Reserves rushed to Suvla and Anzac enabled Mustapha KEMAL, just given overall command of the two sectors, to launch a major counterattack in two waves from Chunuk Bair early on 10 August. The New Zealand position was just held, but few Gurkhas survived a ferocious defensive action at 'The Farm', a plateau near Hill Q that was abandoned when mutual exhaustion ended fighting that evening.

Neither side was capable of coordinated attacks for some time after 10 August. Birdwood's offensive took none of its objectives, cost 12,000 Allied casualties (against Turkish losses approaching 20,000) and extended the Anzac position by a few hundred square metres. Failure effectively ended hope of a breakout from the Cove, and Allied efforts subsequently focused on attempts to break in from Suvla as the Anzac sector reverted to high-pressure TRENCH WARFARE (see Battle of SCIMITAR HILL).

Sarikamish, Battle of The first major engagement on the CAUCASIAN FRONT, the climax of an offensive launched against Russian frontier positions by the Turkish Third and Second Armies (the 'Eastern Army') under the direct command of war minister ENVER PASHA. Enver's main strategic operation at the outbreak of war in October 1914, the offensive was slow to get underway, delayed by generalized transport breakdown in TURKEY and the disruptive activities of ARMENIAN and Kurdish tribesmen.

Aware that RUSSIAN ARMY forces in the region, about 100,000 men of the Caucasus Army (General Mishlaevski), were divided between headquarters at Tbilisi and the frontier bases of Kars and Ardahan, Enver split his 150,000 troops in an ambitious two-pronged attack on both forward outposts. Though still short of supplies and ammunition, most of which was carried to field units by peasant WOMEN, he began to advance from Erzurum on 18 November, prompting an immediate withdrawal of forward Russian units.

In worsening weather and across mountainous terrain, their routes predetermined by the few broad valleys, both groups of Turkish forces made slow progress. The smaller Second Army's march east on Ardahan ground to a virtual halt, giving Mishlaevski time to concentrate 60,000 men under General YUDENICH at Kars, some 200km northeast of Erzurum. Despite orders to retreat, Yudenich advanced to meet Enver's Third Army east of the town of Sarikamish, occupied by Turkish units on 25 December.

Russian attacks forced a Turkish withdrawal from the town on 28 December, and Enver's troops were in retreat by 4 January having suffered some 30,000 casualties. Yudenich caught the retreat at Kara Urgan three days later, surrounding two Turkish divisions during the course of a week's fighting, and exhausted Turkish Second Army troops retreated west after their first attack at Ardahan was repulsed by the Russian garrison on 4 January. Both Turkish armies were back in the fortified base of Erzurum by 20 January, their total strength reduced to 18,000 men.

The victory earned Yudenich promotion to command the Caucasus Army in January, but urgent concentration on the EASTERN FRONT left him without modern equipment or experienced troops, let alone reinforcements. He restricted operations in early 1915 to cautious exploitations of Turkish retreats forced by Armenian rebels around Lake Van in the south, and Enver was forced to abandon plans for a new spring offensive in response to the Allied DARDANELLES attack (see Battle of MALAZGIRT). See also: MAP 24.

Sarrail, General Maurice (1856–1929) Rare in the FRENCH ARMY but much more prevalent among the politicians in FRANCE, Sarrail's well-known socialist views ensured him a position of importance unconnected with his undoubted organizational skills, and he was given a crucial strike role in the invasion of the ARDENNES in August 1914. His troops fought well in the latter stages of the failed offensive, and he was promoted to command the Third Army at the end of the month. A rallying point for criticism of C-in-C JOFFRE, he was removed from command in 1915, a move that provoked a political outcry in France until he was given command of the French 'Army of the Orient', intended for GALLIPOLI but ultimately deployed at SALONIKA in the autumn.

Poor inter-Allied communications and difficult conditions worked to frustrate his only major offensive in the theatre, which took MONASTIR in November 1916, and his tenure was otherwise distinguished by political intrigue. Though he was given overall command of the Allied forces in the theatre in January 1917, embroilment in the internal affairs of GREECE aroused Allied suspicion of French motives in the region and did little to increase the efficiency of his growing army. He was dismissed in December 1917 by new prime minister CLEMENCEAU and retired from public life, returning in 1924 to a brief, unhappy spell as French High Commissioner in Syria.

Sarrebourg, Battle of See: Battle of LORRAINE.

Sassoon, Siegfried (1886–1967) British poet, novelist and soldier whose collection of anti-War poems, *Counterattack*, was released to critical and popular acclaim in 1918. In marked contrast to the lyrical optimism of Rupert BROOKE, who wrote about the prospect of battle, Sassoon's work displayed the bitterness and contempt for military leadership typical of artists on all sides who had been exposed to prolonged TRENCH WARFARE. His success signalled a long period of postwar literary reaction, as memoirs, novels and verses by frontline veterans all over western and central Europe reinforced a popular sense of revulsion to war.

Sazonov, Sergei (1860–1927) A competent international analyst and diplomat, generally independent of cabinet factions, Sazonov replaced Isvolski as Russian foreign minister in 1910. Military weakness convinced him to avoid any immediate conflict with TURKEY and prevented any direct involvement in the Balkan Wars (see BALKAN FRONT), but Sazonov felt compelled to make at least a gesture in SERBIA's defence during the 1914 JULY CRISIS. His wartime diplomacy brought immediate conflict with interior minister MAKLAKOV, who prevented Tsar NICHOLAS II from endorsing Sazonov's pledge to create a unified, independent POLAND after the War. Other long-term territorial arrangements were made with ROMANIA, which was promised Hungarian Transylvania in return for its benevolent neutrality in October 1914, and with the western Allies, who accepted future Russian control of the DARDANELLES in March 1915. A target for conservative elements gathered around the Empress ALEXANDRA, he was dismissed in July 1916 and became ambassador to London. He stayed in London after the FEBRUARY REVOLUTION, taking part in the PARIS PEACE CONFERENCE as a representative of anti-Bolshevik forces in the RUSSIAN CIVIL WAR.

Scarborough Raid Bombardment of the English North Sea coast towns of Scarborough, Hartlepool and Whitby by Admiral HIPPER's First HIGH SEAS FLEET Scouting Group (five BATTLECRUISERS with supporting light CRUISERS and DESTROYERS). The German attack began at 09.00 on 16 December 1914, killing 18 civilians in Scarborough.

Public and political outrage greeted the attack in GREAT BRITAIN, and the ROYAL NAVY was criticized for failing to prevent the raid, but in fact a powerful force commanded by Admiral Warrender had been sent to intercept Hipper after the ROOM 40 intelligence unit had provided fairly accurate advance warning.

Warrender's force consisted of six modern BATTLESHIPS, four fast battlecruisers, four heavy cruisers, six fast light cruisers and eight SUBMARINES, but Admiral JELLICOE's request to bring the rest of the GRAND FLEET into the action was turned down by the Admiralty, who were unaware that the whole German High Seas Fleet was following in support of Hipper.

Warrender made contact with the main German fleet and pursued what he thought were light forces in the early morning of 16 December. German C-in-C Ingenohl believed he had met the whole Grand Fleet and turned rapidly for home, ordering Hipper to carry on alone but making no mention of British activity.

Warrender was saved from the potential disaster of successful pursuit by RADIO reports of Hipper's bombardments, much further north than expected. The British ships reversed course, and a squadron of eight PRE-DREADNOUGHTS left Rosyth in Scotland to cut off any German retreat to the northeast. The rest of the Grand Fleet belatedly put to sea from Scapa Flow in the Orkney Islands.

Unaware that he was effectively surrounded, Hipper turned for home in fine weather at about 09.30, and was spotted about two hours later by British light cruisers, operating just ahead of Admiral BEATTY's four battlecruisers. After a brief exchange of fire, poor signalling inadvertently recalled the British cruisers, and contact with Hipper's roughly equal forces was permanently lost. See also: Battle of the DOGGER BANK; MAP 16.

Scarpe Offensive A supporting operation by General HORNE's British First Army to the north of the Allied advance on ALBERT in late August 1918. Horne's offensive opened on 26 August, five days after the main battle started. By WESTERN FRONT standards it made very rapid progress, capturing the heavily defended strongpoint of Monchy-le-Preux on the first day and linking up with the main attack at Bapaume from 29 August. All three British Armies then drove east towards Péronne (see MAP 2).

Scharnhorst Class The two Scharnhorst Class armoured CRUISERS, *Scharnhorst* and *Gneisenau*, were completed in 1907, and were promptly rendered obsolete for German HIGH SEAS FLEET operations by the development of BATTLECRUISERS. Used instead as wartime commerce raiders they were the most powerful components of Admiral SPEE's East Asiatic Squadron in the Pacific in 1914. Accompanied by light cruisers, *Scharnhorst* and *Gneisenau* left the Caroline Islands on 6 August and, hunted by dozens of British and Japanese warships, steamed slowly east to threaten Allied trade routes along the coast of South America. After bombarding French installations at Tahiti on 30 September, they were located by the ROYAL NAVY in October and defeated Admiral Cradock's under-equipped South America Squadron at CORONEL. Both were sunk by gunfire when Spee stumbled across a far superior British force at the FALKLAND ISLANDS on 8 December 1914.

BRIEF DATA (*Scharnhorst*, 1914) Displacement: 11,600 tons; Crew: 765; Dimensions: length 474.5ft (143.8m), beam 71ft (21.5m); Speed: 22.5k; Armament: 8 × 8.2in gun, 6 × 5.9in, 20 × 3.4in, 4 × 17.7in TT.

Scheer, Admiral Reinhardt (1863–1928) An early specialist in TORPEDOES during the 1890s, Scheer was vice admiral in command of the German HIGH SEAS FLEET's Second Battleship Squadron in August 1914. Transferred to lead the Third Squadron in late December, Scheer acquired a reputation for aggression amid public criticism of the Navy's apparent inactivity, and this reputation influenced his appointment to succeed Pohl as Fleet C-in-C in January 1916. A relatively bold foray into the North Sea led to the Battle of JUTLAND from 31 May, a lucky escape that he was able to present as a victory. His own subsequent recognition that surface ships were redundant in the North Sea and the BALTIC was expressed in complete support for the declaration of unrestricted SUBMARINE WARFARE (see *HANDELSKRIEG*), and he refused to commit large Fleet U-BOATS to long-range missions under restricted conditions in 1916. The virtual military dictatorship established by LUDENDORFF and HINDENBURG in 1917–18 was paralleled by the imposition of a new Naval Supreme Command, with Scheer at its head, on a reluctant WILHELM II in August 1918 (see THIRD SUPREME COMMAND). Scheer planned a final 'heroic' attack on the British GRAND FLEET in conjunction with HIPPER and TROTHA, but it was stifled by the KIEL MUTINY on 30 October. Dismissed by the Kaiser ten days later, Scheer was retired by the new German Republic in December 1918.

Scheidemann, Philipp (1865–1939) German socialist politician, an effective anti-monarchist orator who became one of the most enthusiastic socialist supporters of a 'defensive' war in 1914. Though generally concerned to demonstrate that democracy and patriotism were compatible in GERMANY, he was a focus for opposition to the THIRD SUPREME COMMAND's annexation plans during the war-aims debates of 1916–17 and led Social Democratic Party opposition to the BREST-LITOVSK Treaty in spring 1918. In October he joined MAX VON BADEN's cabinet as minister without portfolio, and he announced a German Republic from the Reichstag balcony following the resignation of the government on 9 November. Scheidemann was the Republic's first chancellor, from February 1919 until association with the draconian VERSAILLES Treaty forced his resignation in June, and he remained a Reichstag deputy until right-wing threats forced him to leave Germany in 1933. See also: GERMAN REVOLUTIONS.

'Schlanke Emma' ('Skinny Emma') Giant 305mm field howitzer designed and built for the AUSTRO-HUNGARIAN ARMY at the Skoda works but loaned to the GERMAN ARMY for the invasion of BELGIUM in August 1914. Although Allied agents had reported the design's existence some time before the first five appeared at LIÈGE in mid-August, their rapid destruction (alongside the German 'BIG BERTHA' guns) of reputedly the best FORTRESSES in Europe transformed international attitudes towards the use of heavy ARTILLERY for field operations. Smaller than the 420mm Big Bertha, they could lob 385kg shells at a rate of up to 10 per hour to a range of about 13km.

Schlieffen Plan The GERMAN ARMY's plan for war against FRANCE and RUSSIA. Conceived by Count Alfred von Schlieffen, German chief of staff for 15 years until his retirement in 1906, it was a direct response to the alliance between France and Russia of 1892, which was thought likely to compel GERMANY to fight both her powerful neighbours in any future war.

The first version of the Plan, approved by Kaiser WILHELM II in 1899, laid down the blueprint for a preemptive strike against France if and when war broke out with Russia. According to the calculations of the general staff, France and Germany would both be ready to fight a decisive battle on the 15th day of a war, but Russia would not be ready for six weeks, by which time France would have to be beaten.

In an age of mass armies, and with FORTRESSES lining the Franco-German borders, a direct attack was unlikely to achieve quick victory. It was necessary to get round the French positions and strike their rear, but mass manoeuvre was virtually impossible in the hilly woodlands along the frontier. To the south, neutral Switzerland was geographically invasion-proof, but the wide, flat plains of Flanders offered the chance of rapid passage through neutral BELGIUM (see MAP 4).

Reasoning that both sides in a war were bound to violate international guarantees of Belgian neutrality at some stage, and that the acquiescence of Belgian King Leopold (who died in 1909) could be purchased, Schlieffen planned to open any war with a massive invasion of Belgium. If the small BELGIAN ARMY fought it would be swept aside, and the battle would be over before potential aid from GREAT BRITAIN could cross the Channel to influence events.

Between 1899 and its final version in 1906, the Plan crystallized into a precise and inflexible schedule of operations. Thirty-four divisions, supported by heavy ARTILLERY, would invade Belgium, advancing rapidly to attack France in a broad band from the northern Ardennes to the industrial city of Lille. A much smaller force would hold the Franco-German frontier against an expected French attack, withdrawing steadily to pull the FRENCH ARMY forward while the main invasion came round behind them. Once in the 'sack', the French could be surrounded and destroyed. The main effort would then be transferred to the east, where Schlieffen nominated only eight divisions for the initial defence of EAST PRUSSIA.

Aware that this was too large a task for the regular German Army, Schlieffen took the revolutionary step of assigning an immediate frontline role to reserve units, a device that deceived the French into a disastrous underestimate of German manpower. In recognition of the economic effort involved in mass warfare, he also stipulated the immediate extraction of indemnities, raw materials and labour from Belgium and other conquered areas. His successor as chief of staff, MOLTKE, maintained the Plan but gradually subtracted from the strength of the northern wing to counter the prewar build-up of French military strength along the whole frontier.

With every movement timetabled down to the last detail, the revised Schlieffen Plan was activated with the occupation of Luxembourg on 2 August 1914, but accidents and miscalculations combined to engineer its frustration. The unexpected resistance of Belgium, Britain's immediate entry into the land war at MONS, tactical failures by field commanders and the speed of Russian offensive action in East Prussia all played a part, but Moltke's failure to maintain Schlieffen's concentration of forces in the north was crucial.

Fear of Russian attacks in East Prussia distracted two corps to the EASTERN FRONT at a vital time (see Battle of TANNENBERG), and powerful forces were tied to the southern wing of the French frontier for an opportunistic offensive from LORRAINE. Along with the successful French withdrawal from a position of potential encirclement after the Battles of the FRONTIERS, this dilution was primarily responsible for the Plan's ultimate failure at the MARNE in early September.

Schröder, Admiral Ludwig von (1854–1933) Veteran naval officer, recalled from retirement in August 1914 to command GERMAN NAVY forces along the Belgian coast. His division of marines was in action in northern Flanders from September, and took part in the capture of ANTWERP in October. Expanded to corps strength (three divisions), its advance was halted at the YSER in December, and Schröder spent the next four years guarding captured naval bases at Zeebrugge, Bruges and Ostende (see SUBMARINE WARFARE). Eulogized by German PROPAGANDA after the British ZEEBRUGGE RAID had failed in March 1918, the 'Lion of Flanders' was driven east with the Fourth Army during the Allied COURTRAI OFFENSIVE in October. He retired in November after orders to march his troops against the KIEL MUTINY had been countermanded by the government.

Schütte-Lanz Airship German rigid airship, a prewar competitor of the ZEPPELIN designs, that was used in small numbers for reconnaissance and bombing work by both the GERMAN ARMY AIR SERVICE and GERMAN NAVY. Although Schütte-Lanz (SL) airships incorporated several minor technical innovations later copied by Zeppelin designers, their operational efficiency was hampered by a wooden structure that absorbed considerable moisture in flight, and their fragility was such that they were openly detested by aircrew. The Army used its two SL airships on the EASTERN FRONT, with little success in difficult weather conditions, and the Navy's eight SLs were mostly employed on North Sea reconnaissance work.

Schwarzlose Gun Reliable but slow-firing 8mm MACHINE GUN that was the standard weapon of the AUSTRO-HUNGARIAN ARMY throughout the War, field units gradually equipping with the latest (1912) model. Simple to construct, it fired a 250-round magazine from a fabric belt, and its short barrel was usually fitted with a flash eliminator. Captured guns and ammunition were also used in large numbers by the ITALIAN and RUSSIAN ARMIES, and a stripped-down, air-cooled version was standard equipment with the AUSTRO-HUNGARIAN AIR SERVICE. Inferior to the LEWIS and VICKERS GUNS used on Allied warplanes, it could not be adapted to INTERRUPTER GEAR until 1917, and was never an entirely satisfactory weapon.

Scimitar Hill, Battle of The last major Allied offensive on the GALLIPOLI FRONT. After the debacle of the SUVLA BAY OFFENSIVE in early August, British C-in-C HAMILTON brought the veteran 29th Division from HELLES to lead a renewed offensive planned for 21 August, with a fresh division of (dismounted) CAVALRY deployed as reserve.

Hills north and east of Suvla Bay were to be stormed, but the main thrust was south against Turkish positions known as the 'W Hills' and Scimitar Hill. Its aim was a breakthrough to the central Allied beachhead at ANZAC COVE, and ANZAC commander General BIRDWOOD agreed to mount a limited attack of his own against HILL 60 at the southwestern edge of the Turkish position.

A simple frontal attack uphill against well-prepared defenders, launched in the intense heat and thick mist of early afternoon, the operation was a predictable failure. Subsidiary advances had been halted by mid-afternoon, and a division failed to reach the W Hills after losing its way. The 29th Division appeared to take Scimitar Hill but was thrown back by Turkish positions hidden on the far slopes. Sector commander De Lisle sent his reserves to Scimitar, but they suffered heavy losses in another frontal charge up the hill. The day's fighting gained nothing and cost 5,000 Allied casualties, many burned after shrapnel from supporting ARTILLERY set fire to dry brush.

Birdwood's operation at Hill 60 made only insignificant gains, and an increasingly desperate Hamilton asked for 95,000 reinforcements, against 40,000 losses in action or from sickness since early August. He was offered 25,000, effectively ending any immediate prospect of further large-scale attacks.

Scorched Earth Tactics See: Operation ALBERICH; GREAT RETREAT (Russian).

Scout Cruisers Generic name given to 15 light CRUISERS built for the ROYAL NAVY between 1904 and 1913. Designed for speed with little or no armour protection, they were intended as guards and leaders of DESTROYER flotillas, a role they performed in British home waters from 1914, although several were transferred to secondary theatres or SUBMARINE flotillas once new light cruisers became available in numbers (see *ARETHUSA*). See also: *FEARLESS*.

SE-5 British biplane fighter, designed by the Royal Aircraft Factory in late 1916 and in RFC service from April 1917. Built round a 150hp engine and armed with both synchronized and high-firing forward guns (see INTERRUPTER GEAR), it was an excellent all-round combat machine – fast, rugged, manoeuvrable at high altitude and easy to fly – remaining among the most successful warplanes on the WESTERN FRONT until the ARMISTICE. The more powerful SE-5a was in service by June 1917, but mass production was delayed by engine development problems and it only reached the RFC in numbers during early 1918. Used by several leading British ACES, they enjoyed combat superiority over all German types until the early summer, when they were matched but not outclassed by the new FOKKER D-VII. Some 2,700 SE-5/5a machines were delivered to the wartime RFC or RAF, and efficient factories produced another 2,500 in 1919.

BRIEF DATA (SE-5a) Type: single-seat fighter; Engine: 200hp Wolseley Viper; Max speed: 138mph (220kph); Ceiling: 6,650m; Armament: 2 × 0.303in mg, max bomb load 100lb.

Sea Scouts Small British observation AIRSHIPS, the original 'blimps', in RNAS service from May 1915. Non-rigid craft with the fuselage of a BE-2C aircraft attached as a cockpit, they were cheap and easy to build. Used on ANTI-SUBMARINE patrols in the English Channel and the Irish Sea, they had sufficient speed and endurance to operate as inshore CONVOY escorts. Three versions remained in use until the ARMISTICE, of which the SSZ (70 produced) was the most common. See also: COASTAL CLASS AIRSHIPS.

Seaplane Carriers See: AIRCRAFT CARRIERS.

Second International Organization established in 1889 to coordinate world socialist solidarity. Dominated by western European union leaders and parliamentarians, it was broadly divided between revolutionaries and 'gradualists', the latter seeking peaceful reform of capitalist systems. The two factions were led by strong French and German parties, respectively, before 1914, but were united around a policy of international workers' solidarity against war.

The International had issued a manifesto (1912) calling on all workers to resist war, and European governments remained uncertain of proletarian attitudes throughout pacifist demonstrations organized during the 1914 JULY CRISIS. The assassination of French socialist Jean Jaurès on 31 July deprived international PACIFISM of its most respected spokesman, and the Second International effectively ceased to exist as socialist leaders and unions accepted government definitions of a 'defensive' war in August. Wartime international socialism was coordinated through the 'ZIMMERWALD MOVEMENT', and postwar revolutionary socialism was dominated by the Third International (the 'Comintern'), founded by the Bolshevik government in March 1919 (see OCTOBER REVOLUTION).

Seeckt, General Hans von (1866–1936) German officer who served on the WESTERN FRONT as a corps chief of staff with von KLUCK's First Army in August 1914. Transferred to the EASTERN FRONT as von MACKENSEN's chief of staff with the Eleventh Army, he was credited with planning its successful BREAKTHROUGH TACTICS, used in the GORLICE–TARNOW OFFENSIVE, the TRIPLE OFFENSIVES and the conquest of SERBIA (on the BALKAN FRONT). After the collapse of the AUSTRO-HUNGARIAN ARMY during the Russian BRUSILOV OFFENSIVE in 1916, Seeckt held a succession of virtually independent commands as 'controlling staff officer' with various Austro-Hungarian armies, before a posting to Constantinople in December 1917 to perform a similar role with the TURKISH ARMY. When he returned to GERMANY in 1919, Seeckt took over another crumbling force, replacing HINDENBURG as GERMAN ARMY chief of staff in the summer and supervising the Army's secret reconstruction in the early 1920s (see Treaty of VERSAILLES).

Selective Service Act The UNITED STATES had no experience of conscription before 1917, but 'universal military training' (UMT) was at the heart of the debate between the PREPAREDNESS MOVEMENT and liberal pacifists after 1914. President WILSON's apparent opposition to the concept was publicly reaffirmed as late as February 1917, but war secretary BAKER had composed provisional conscription laws the previous autumn. Motivated primarily by a desire to control loss of skilled workers to the services, Wilson announced his intention to raise troops by conscription when he asked Congress for permission to declare war on 2 April 1917.

Opposed by many of his southern and western supporters in Congress, Wilson initially considered trying an experimental volunteer system, but rallied Democrat support after ROOSEVELT's plan to lead his own volunteer unit to France made the draft a party-political issue. As passed on 18 May 1917, the Act prohibited all volunteers from joining the new 'National Army', although they were allowed in the separate National Guard militia and the regular US ARMY.

Service in the US NAVY remained exclusively voluntary.

All male US citizens aged 21 to 30 were required to register for the draft by 5 June, but government officials at all levels, clergymen, aliens, convicted criminals and munitions workers were exempt. Intake was later widened to include men aged 18 to 45, and exemptions were extended to cover shipyard workers, pacifist sects and conscientious objectors, of whom fewer than 4,000 were excused combat service. About 36 per cent of all registered Afro-American males were deemed eligible for service, but only about 25 per cent of whites, a differential largely accounted for by discrimination in local draft boards. A total of 6,373,414 men were conscripted into the wartime army. See also: 'DOUGHBOYS'; YORK, A.

Selle Offensive Official title given to the steady advance of HAIG's Allied Army Group beyond CAMBRAI on the WESTERN FRONT in late October 1918. Begun on 17 October, when the First Army (HORNE) took Douai in support of the COURTRAI Offensive in Flanders, the advance involved 26 Allied divisions and culminated in heavy fighting by General RAWLINSON's Fourth Army on 23–24 October. Unexpectedly strong resistance from 31 depleted GERMAN ARMY divisions in the sector convinced Allied commanders that GERMANY was not ready for unconditional peace, and they prepared to launch a further attack towards VALENCIENNES. See MAP 2.

Senussi North African tribal movement, loyal to descendants of the 19th-century Islamic reformist Sheikh es Senussi and based in Cyrenaica, the region of modern Libya centred on Benghazi. Sponsored and trained by TURKISH ARMY officers during the Italo-Turkish War of 1910–11, which gave ITALY colonial control of Libya, the Senussi temporarily expanded into neighbouring Tripolitania, but their influence had receded into Cyrenaica by the time TURKEY joined the War in November 1914. While ITALY remained neutral, Senussi leader Sidi Ahmad es Sherif accepted Turkish and German aid for operations against British EGYPT and French Saharan colonies.

Led by Ottoman General Jaafar Pasha, under the overall direction of ENVER PASHA's half-brother Nuri Pasha, seven Senussi battalions invaded western Egypt in mid-December 1915. Equipped with light ARTILLERY and MACHINE GUNS, and attracting support from border tribes, they were opposed by the British Western Frontier Force (General Dobell), a small contingent of second-line British imperial troops, EGYPTIAN FORCES and supporting CAVALRY squadrons. Turkish agitation meanwhile triggered a sympathetic tribal uprising in the Darfur province of the SUDAN.

Depleted by transfers to the PALESTINE FRONT, the Western Frontier Force was barely able to hold the Senussi at first, but German attempts to supply Sidi Ahmad by SUBMARINE proved inefficient, while Dobell was reinforced by ARMOURED CARS. Senussi forces lost ground from early 1916 and were decisively defeated at Aqqaqia (26 February), where an attack by SOUTH AFRICAN infantry was followed by a successful cavalry charge. Jaafar Pasha, wounded and taken prisoner during the battle, joined the ARAB REVOLT later in the year and became field commander of FEISAL's Northern Arab Army.

Pursued by British armoured cars and infantry, the Senussi fell back on a guerrilla campaign from Cyrenaica, raiding into Tripolitania and deep into French territory to the southwest, where they were supported by local Tuareg tribesmen. During the summer, despite the opening of tentative peace discussions with the Senussi, an Anglo-Italian cooperation agreement concerted the efforts of 60,000 Italian personnel in Tripolitania with the Western Frontier Force, eventually 35,000 strong. Air support from RFC reconnaissance units and Italian CAPRONI bombers helped push Sidi Ahmad's relatively tiny army back into his stronghold at the Siwa Oasis by the end of 1916.

A British column attacked Siwa in February 1917, taking the oasis but failing to trap Ahmad, and a French campaign recovered several outposts before defeating the Tuareg in April. Hostilities with Britain and Italy were suspended later that month, when Ahmad's pro-Allied cousin, Sidi Mohammed el Idris, became official head of the Senussi and accepted Italian aid to suppress rebel tribesmen. Sidi Ahmad mounted occasional guerrilla raids into French territories until early 1918, but was starved of Turkish supplies and escaped to Constantinople aboard a German submarine in August 1918. The fragile Senussi alliance with Italy collapsed in 1919 and Italian forces finally dispersed the movement in 1922.

Serbia A part of the Ottoman Empire from the 14th century until granted independence in 1878. Twentieth-century Serbia was shaped by a military coup in 1903, in which King Alexander was assassinated and the rival Karadjordjevic dynasty elected to power in the person of King PETER. He governed through an appointed cabinet (usually led by Nikola PAŠIĆ) that was responsible to a National Assembly (*Skuptshina*), elected by all civilian male taxpayers and dominated by moderate liberals.

Peter's regime, over which the military held considerable influence, contrasted a relatively liberal attitude in home affairs with a foreign policy based on territorial expansionism and pan-Slav aspirations. With diplomatic support from RUSSIA, Serbia sought access to the Adriatic through ALBANIA, and either federation with or absorption of Slav peoples in MONTENEGRO, TURKEY and AUSTRIA-HUNGARY.

The Balkan Wars of 1912 and 1913 (see Introduction) almost doubled the country's size to about 86,000 square kilometres, drove Turkey out of the region, and raised Serbia's mostly Slav population to an estimated 4.5 million, but made a dangerous local enemy of BULGARIA. Russian guarantees to both countries precluded practical intervention, and a qualified Serbian defence treaty with GREECE was intended to provide security against any alliance between Bulgaria and Austria-Hungary.

Serbian encouragement (not always officially inspired) of Slav separatist movements in Bosnia-Herzegovina and Croatia had soured relations with Austria-Hungary after 1903. Russian backing against Austrian aggression, unequivocal but temporarily impotent after 1905, was unable to prevent the Austro-Hungarian seizure of Bosnia in 1908, an event that outraged popular feeling in Serbia and turned the province into a dangerous bone of contention.

Serbia could hardly hope to win a war with an industrial power. An overwhelmingly rural society, it had few mineral or other industrial resources and fewer than 10,000 people employed in manufacture, almost all in Belgrade. The economy relied largely on exports of food and hides to GERMANY, Turkey and Austria-Hungary, while fuel, armaments and other military requirements had to be imported overland. Internal communications across mountainous terrain had to rely on poor roads and just two RAILWAY lines, which ran from Belgrade (on the navigable Danube) to Sofia and Constantinople.

Conflict between civil and military authorities came to a head immediately before the 1914 JULY CRISIS. A dispute over the administration of recently conquered Macedonian territories, promoted by the extreme nationalist BLACK HAND society, forced the aging King to relinquish executive authority to his second son, ALEXANDER, who became Prince Regent on 24 June 1914. An election campaign, called two years ahead of schedule to legitimize the change, was underway when Gavrilo PRINCIP's assassination of Austrian Archduke FRANZ FERDINAND provided an opportunity for Vienna to end Slav agitation.

The murder was planned by the Black Hand, but the Serbian government was almost certainly not implicated. Its reply to Vienna's ultimatum of 23 July was sufficiently accommodating to convince world opinion (and Kaiser WILHELM II) of a genuine desire to avoid conflict, but the Serbian government refused a demand to allow the AUSTRO-HUNGARIAN ARMY into Serbia in search of terrorists. Popular opinion in Serbia, as elsewhere, rallied to the call for a defensive war (made with greater justification than similar claims in Vienna, Berlin and St Petersburg), and only two socialist deputies opposed parliament's enthusiastic grant of war credits.

The SERBIAN ARMY could call on 350,000 men after full mobilization, many of them over-age and under-equipped. Its successful defence against three invasions by Austria-Hungary on the BALKAN FRONT in 1914 reflected both the skill of General PUTNIK's veteran troops in familiar mountain territory and the ineptitude of their opponents, but the effort left troops in a state of exhaustion, exacerbated as supply shortages aided the spread of typhus during the winter.

Serbia received some financial assistance from Britain to enable purchase of weapons, but the government's regular appeals for direct Allied military aid were denied by Anglo-French preoccupation with the WESTERN FRONT and GALLIPOLI. Concern to woo ITALY into the Allied camp with territorial concessions in the Balkans also prevented aid from Allied diplomats, who initially refused to fuel separatist dissent within the Austro-Hungarian Empire by committing themselves to postwar Slav unity.

Military assistance was finally sent via Greek SALONIKA in October 1915, but was too late to oppose a combined Austro-German and Bulgarian invasion. The Serbian Army, King, Regent and government, along with thousands of civilian refugees, were driven back into the Montenegrin hills by mid-November and eventually chose to take the only available escape route, retreating en masse across the Albanian hills in blizzard conditions from 23 November. Up to 200,000 died of exposure on the journey, but about 155,000 (including 85,000 troops) were evacuated by Allied MEDITERRANEAN forces at the turn of the year (see Conquest of SERBIA; 'GREAT RETREAT').

The government was re-established in exile on Corfu from early 1916, where Pašić supervised the Army's hasty redeployment at Salonika and instigated the elimination of the Black Hand leaders in December. Forced to cooperate with exiled Croats and Slovenes to achieve Allied recognition of a pan-Slav state, the Serbian government also reached agreement with the London-based Yugoslav Committee in July 1917, but distanced itself from the Committee's federalist concept of the state's future (see CORFU DECLARATION).

Most of Serbia remained under hostile occupation until late 1918, although a tiny enclave around MONASTIR (Bitola) was recaptured in late 1916. The country was divided for exploitation (principally of agricultural resources) between Bulgaria and Austria-Hungary, and their administration was harsh enough to provoke widespread popular rioting throughout. Total wartime civilian deaths in Serbia are estimated at about 650,000, almost 15 per cent of the population.

The Serbian Army played a major part in the successful Balkan Front offensives of autumn 1918, and Serbia's liberation was immediately followed by Austro-Hungarian collapse. By mid-November the government was back in Belgrade, meeting TRUMBIĆ and other nationalists to determine the region's political future. Both the Serbian nationalist and pan-Slav federalist extremes were overruled by Prince Alexander, who secured a compromise by which all parties in a new 'Kingdom of Serbs, Croats and Slovenes' accepted equal status under the crown. Proclaimed on 1 December 1918, and represented at the PARIS PEACE CONFERENCE, the new state was effectively dominated by Serbia throughout the 1920s, culminating in Alexander's suspension of parliamentary systems in 1929. See YUGOSLAVIA.

Serbia, Conquest of (1915–16) The successive failures of Austro-Hungarian forces to defeat SERBIA in 1914 had exhausted both sides, and most of 1915 passed quietly as Serbian leaders sought Allied military support to replace crippling losses, while the CENTRAL POWERS prepared a much bigger invasion for the autumn.

Austria-Hungary was anxious to reverse the disastrous defeat at the KOLUBARA RIVER, and German chief of staff FALKENHAYN wanted to open overland communications with TURKEY and Germany's latest ally, BULGARIA. Once the latter had signed the PLESS CONVENTION in early September, contracting to support an Austro-German offensive with an invasion into southeast Serbia, Falkenhayn overruled opposition from EASTERN FRONT commander LUDENDORFF and transferred forces to the Balkans.

Serbian leaders recognized the danger of an attack on two fronts by early summer, but were persuaded against a preemptive attack on Bulgaria by the Allies, who still regarded Bulgaria as a friendly power. Serbian pleas for military reinforcement were not refused but were delayed beyond usefulness by Anglo-French arguments and continued commitment to the GALLIPOLI FRONT. The first few French troops reached Greek SALONIKA (more than 450km from the front around Belgrade) on 5 October, one day before the Austro-German invasion opened in the north.

Some 200,000 typhus-ridden Serbian troops, lacking ARTILLERY and short of ammunition, faced more than 300,000 well-concentrated troops backed by heavy artillery under the overall command of General MACKENSEN. The Austro-Hungarian Third Army (General KOVESS) crossed the Save River to take Belgrade on 8 October, and the Eleventh Army (GALLWITZ) attacked across the Danube at Semendria (Smederevo) the next day. Two Bulgarian armies under General ZHEKHOV invaded from the east three days later, and were at Vranja, between Serbian and Allied forces, by 15 October.

The SERBIAN ARMY was driven back everywhere and the government fled south to the vital RAILWAY town of Niš, where it hoped to make contact with Allied reinforcements that never came. Mackensen came close to surrounding and annihilating Serbian forces at Kragujevac, and Niš fell to Bulgarian forces on 5 November, while French attempts to interfere with Bulgarian operations made little progress for another week. Delayed by the simultaneous mobilization of the GREEK ARMY, almost 45,000 French troops advanced into southern Serbia from Salonika, and attacked the Bulgarian Second Army about 15km inside the frontier from 11 November, but three days of fighting ended inconclusively when the Bulgarians broke off to pursue a full Serbian retreat.

By mid-November Serbian forces (along with the King, Crown Prince ALEXANDER and the PAŠIĆ government) had retreated into the plateau lands of Kosovo, the only direction open to them. Heavy snow slowed operations by both sides from 17 November, but Mackensen gradually sealed roads out of Kosovo, and Serbian commander PUTNIK ordered a final retreat into the Albanian mountains on 23 November.

The 'GREAT RETREAT' took place in blizzard conditions and cost thousands of lives, but ensured the survival of Serbia as a military entity. The conquest of the country was complete by early December. After a pause for bad weather Kovess led his army into MONTENEGRO in January 1916, accepting its military surrender on 25 January and pushing into northern ALBANIA. With railway links to Turkey open, the Balkan Front became less important to the Central Powers, and they never attempted a major attack on the growing Allied enclave at Salonika. See MAP 19.

Serbian Army A genuinely national force, built on a law of 1901 that rendered all male Serbians aged between 21 and 46, with very few exemptions, liable for compulsory military service. Recruits spent ten years either in uniform or on the active reserve list, and another 8 in the territorial militia. The system provided an Army of about 260,000, almost 10 per cent of the population, ready for mobilization at the start of the First Balkan War in 1912 (see Introduction).

Victory increased the country's population, and the Army was expanded accordingly. Although reorganization was only just underway when war broke out with AUSTRIA-HUNGARY in July 1914, the Army was able to mobilize some 360,000 men, including four field armies. The First and Second Armies were at full strength (about 64,000 men each), but the Third Army and the Army of the West, the latter defending the whole Bulgarian frontier, remained at about half strength. A single CAVALRY division reflected the mounted arm's virtual redundancy in mountainous conditions.

Expansion had not been matched by full rearmament, and reserve units were often barely armed and poorly clothed, but front-line troops were reasonably well-equipped. Infantry units used modern 7.65mm Mauser RIFLES, although reserves still used breech-loaders, and most field ARTILLERY batteries were armed with a variety of good quality 'quick-firing' weapons, including Schneider guns captured from BULGARIA in the Second Balkan War (1913), Krupp guns bought from GREECE or taken from TURKEY, and the first French SOIXANTE-QUINZES of a large order. Heavy artillery batteries employed efficient 120mm and 150mm howitzers.

Mobilization for war proceeded smoothly, a tribute to the organizational skills of chief of staff PUTNIK in a country beset by transport difficulties. Poor roads, sparse RAILWAYS and a shortage of modern vehicles meant that much supply traffic was drawn on primitive ox carts. Combat experience had provided a hard core of veteran officers and technical troops, and the Army lived up to its contemporary reputation for flexibility and boldness during the opening campaigns on the BALKAN FRONT.

The effort of resisting three successive Austro-Hungarian offensives in 1914 virtually exhausted the Army's manpower resources, so that men in their fifties were already being called up and many men in their seventies had emulated King PETER by joining the fight. Dependent on imports to replace heavy equipment losses, the Army was virtually without heavy artillery after a rapid retreat during November, and desperately short of ammunition after the KOLUBARA victory of early December. Supply failures condemned frontline forces to a cold and hungry winter in advanced positions inside Bosnia-Herzegovina as a typhus epidemic ripped through the trenches, and by autumn 1915 the First and Second Armies were down to about half strength.

Overwhelmed by the joint Austro-German and Bulgarian invasion in October 1915, the Army lost almost all its equipment and many more men during the 'GREAT RETREAT' of November and December, when it abandoned Serbia for the Albanian coast. Only about half of about 155,000 survivors evacuated to Corfu by late January were military personnel considered fit for service, and most of those were suffering from exposure and malnutrition.

After recuperation, some 80,000 troops were eventually redeployed at SALONIKA. The first units reached the port in March 1916, still emaciated and in rags but intended as symbols of continued Serbian resistance to conquest. Trained and completely re-equipped with FRENCH ARMY weapons, the new First and Second Armies joined Allied lines against Bulgarian forces from September. Serbian commanders, notably First Army commander MIŠIĆ, were among the most aggressive Allied leaders on the front over the next two years, and although Serbian troops displayed notably less enthusiasm for limited offensives under French command (see MONASTIR), they eventually swept to victory over war-weary BULGARIAN ARMY forces in the vanguard of the overwhelmingly strong Allied VARDAR OFFENSIVE from September 1918.

The Army's last wartime act was a surge into the Slav provinces of the crumbling Austro-Hungarian Empire, a political move designed to ease the creation of a new unified YUGOSLAVIA. On 1 December 1918 the Serbian Army became the dominant military force in a new 'Kingdom of Serbs, Croats and Slovenes', by which time it had suffered an estimated total of about 125,000 deaths since July 1914, 65 per cent due to sickness.

Sereth River Also known as the Siret River. See: ROMANIAN CAMPAIGN.

Sèvres, Treaty of The peace settlement between TURKEY and the Allies. It placed the DARDANELLES and the Bosporus under international control, ceded control of SMYRNA to Greece, and confirmed the independent status of former Ottoman provinces in the Middle East. Concluded in the latter stages of the PARIS PEACE CONFERENCE, it was signed by the strongly pro-Allied Sultan Mehmed VI on 10 August 1920, but was rejected by KEMAL PASHA's republican movement and substantially revised by the Treaty of Lausanne in 1923.

Seydlitz German BATTLECRUISER completed in May 1913. Similar to its immediate predecessors, *Moltke* and *GOEBEN*, *Seydlitz* served as flagship with Admiral HIPPER's Scouting Group, by far the most active component of the German HIGH SEAS FLEET. It took part in the SCARBOROUGH RAID of December 1914 and later survived heavy gunfire damage at the DOGGER BANK and JUTLAND. Surrendered to the Allies at the ARMISTICE, *Seydlitz* was scuttled at Scapa Flow in June 1919 and raised for scrap in 1930.

BRIEF DATA (1917) Displacement: 24,610 tons; Crew: 1,068; Dimensions: length 656ft (198.8m), beam 93.5ft (28.3m); Speed: 30k; Armament: 10 × 11in gun, 12 × 5.9in, 4 × 3.4in AA, 4 × 19.7in TT.

Shaiba, Battle of Main action of the first Turkish offensive on the MESOPOTAMIAN FRONT. After the defeat at QURNA, a new Turkish line of defence was established some 13km up the Tigris at Ruta, and a raid by some 3,000 Anglo-Indian infantry, supported by gunboats, was repelled on 21 January 1915. Another Turkish force crossed the Tigris into neutral (but pro-British) Persia, making for the oil-pumping station at AHWAZ. To the west, on the Euphrates, the main 'Right Wing Command' – some 6,000 men of the elite Constantinople Fire Brigade and a fluctuating number of Arab tribesmen (estimated at 10,000–20,000) – gathered at Nasiriyeh for an overland attack on the main British base at BASRA.

Steady reinforcement from India had raised British strength in Basra to almost 30,000 troops, but their fighting value in Mesopotamian conditions was limited by shortages of medical supplies, ARTILLERY, engineering equipment and river transport. Base commander Barrett's main defence was an entrenched position at Shaiba, 15km southwest of the port, manned by about 7,000 seasoned troops but virtually cut off by flooding from reserves at Basra.

The main Turkish offensive began with daylong bombardments of Shaiba and Qurna on 11 April. Shelling at Qurna continued almost uninterrupted for three days, punctuated by occasional attempts to infiltrate the town, but never threatened to dislodge the garrison. Operations at Shaiba followed a similar pattern until the morning of 13 April, when Turkish troops tried to outflank the position across the floods while Arab CAVALRY gathered for a frontal attack. The dispersal of the cavalry by two battalions of infantry prompted a general Turkish withdrawal into nearby woods, which were cleared by Anglo-Indian troops the following evening after a daylong infantry battle. Involving about 5,000 troops on each side, it cost some 1,200 British and 2,400 Turkish casualties (including their commander, who shot himself). General NIXON, who had arrived to take command of expanded Anglo-Indian forces on 9 April, used the victory at Shaiba as a springboard for subsequent attacks towards AMARA and NASIRIYEH. See MAP 23.

Shcherbachev, General Dmitri (1857–1932) The most enthusiastic proponent of French military methods in the RUSSIAN ARMY, Shcherbachev commanded IX Infantry Corps in GALICIA at the start of the war on the EASTERN FRONT, and led the Seventh Army's failed attack along the River Strypa during the BESSARABIAN OFFENSIVE of early 1915. Concentrating his forces along a very narrow front in imitation of BREAKTHROUGH TACTICS, he allowed defenders to strike at the flanks of his advance, which was quickly thrown back. At the start of the BRUSILOV OFFENSIVE in June 1916 he attempted similar tactics in defiance of instructions. His main assault along the Strypa again failed, losing 20,000 men, but a relatively small subsidiary attack near Jaslowiec on 4 June (forced upon him by BRUSILOV) broke through and destroyed the southern wing of the Austro-German Südarmee (BOTHMER). His reputation swollen by this fortunate success, he was given command of Russian forces in ROMANIA from April 1917, retaining the post until the end of the war in the east, and subsequently joining White forces on the Don during the RUSSIAN CIVIL WAR.

Sheikh Sa'ad, Battle of Opening battle of the Anglo-Indian attempt to relieve KUT in early 1916. After defeat at CTESIPHON an extra three Indian infantry divisions had been diverted to the MESOPOTAMIAN FRONT in December 1915, and front commander NIXON rushed the first of them (under General Aylmer) to the forward base at Ali Gharbi, 200km upriver from headquarters at BASRA (see MAP 23). Prompted by underestimates of Turkish strength and General TOWNSHEND's stated need for relief by early February, British haste was frustrated by continuing shortages of river and road transport.

Supplies were still in transit when Aylmer's 19,000 troops, supported by 46 guns, three MONITORS, assorted gunboats and two aircraft, began their advance up both banks of the Tigris on 4 January. Turkish commander Nur-Ud-Din had blocked the way to Kut with some 22,500 troops and 72 field guns entrenched either side of the Tigris at Sheikh Sa'ad, only about 15km upriver from Ali Gharbi, and they repelled a preliminary attack against both banks on 6 January.

The attempt was repeated when the main bulk of the British force arrived next day, but an advance up the east bank was outflanked by a counterattack and a smaller British attack on the other bank took only a single line of TRENCHES. Aylmer planned to repeat the operation on the night of 8/9 January, but the defenders withdrew before it could be launched. Exhausted Anglo-Indian troops occupied deserted trenches the following morning.

British medical facilities, which had been designed to treat only 250 casualties, were completely overwhelmed by more than 4,000. About 1,000 British and Indian wounded were still lying on the banks without medicines, doctors or field kitchens by 20 January. See also: Battle of HANNA.

Shell Crises The sheer scale of the War in Europe took all the main belligerents by surprise in 1914, and those with armaments industries experienced a startling disparity between prewar plans for munitions production and the demands of the armed forces. The area of quickest turnover was ammunition, and the biggest gap between planning and reality was in the supply of ARTILLERY shells.

The GERMAN ARMY used more shells at the MARNE in September 1914 than during the whole of the Franco-Prussian war of 1870–71, and the RUSSIAN ARMY was running out of shells on the EASTERN FRONT before the end of August. The need for economic reorganization was quickly recognized in FRANCE, GERMANY and AUSTRIA-HUNGARY, and up to a point addressed in RUSSIA. The shock of realizing the scale of requirements created a 'shell crisis' in each country, along with some (mostly ineffectual) parliamentary unrest. A similar situation faced ITALY in 1915, but the relatively small size of its armaments industry meant that most complaints on the home front were directed against Allied failure to supply aid. Only GREAT BRITAIN suffered a full-scale 'SHELL SCANDAL', the product of gradual induction into mass warfare, government laxity, and a relatively uncensored press.

'Shell Scandal' The furore following press exposure of BRITISH ARMY munitions shortages in May 1915. Unlike other European belligerents in 1914, GREAT BRITAIN was only gradually entangled in mass ground warfare, and economic reorganization to equip huge armies was slow to get underway. Popular pressure for a coalition to replace the ASQUITH government reached new peaks when a report in *The Times* of 14 May 1915 claimed that the BEF's initial failure in the ARTOIS OFFENSIVE was caused by a serious shortage of high-explosive ARTILLERY shells.

Written by influential correspondent Colonel Repington, in a semi-official newspaper and passed by the censor, the allegation carried great authority and sparked intense public debate. As intended by *The Times* owner Lord NORTHCLIFFE, his political allies and senior WESTERN FRONT commanders, the scandal fatally damaged the Liberal government, which was replaced by a coalition on 25 May, but it failed in its ultimate aim of discrediting war minister KITCHENER. Another Northcliffe newspaper, the populist *Daily Mail*, launched a direct attack on Kitchener over the following days, but he retained his popularity and his post, although munitions production was placed under a new ministry led by LLOYD GEORGE.

Shell Shock Psychological trauma inflicted by prolonged exposure to the stress of contemporary warfare. Most commonly suffered by troops serving in the claustrophobic conditions of the WESTERN, ITALIAN and GALLIPOLI FRONTS – but also experienced to some degree in every theatre – shell shock could manifest itself in myriad forms of abnormal behaviour or distress. Victims typically suffered extreme panic attacks in relatively mild cases – often leading to sudden flight from the battlefield – but many victims were reduced to a catatonic state, which could persist or recur for years afterwards. Shell shock was well known to trench fighters everywhere, but military authorities knew little about the new science of psychology, and records give no indication of the number of wartime victims. Mild cases were often not recognized as such and treated as deserters, while severely traumatized or long-term victims received little or no active treatment.

Shiala, Battle of Subsidiary action on the MESOPOTAMIAN FRONT in April 1917, when part of Ali Ishan Bey's Turkish XIII Corps, advancing southwest towards British positions on the Tigris, met two British infantry brigades diverted from the SAMARRAH OFFENSIVE to assist outnumbered CAVALRY in holding the Turkish advance. The relief force collided with a flank attack by part of the Turkish 2nd Division on the morning of 11 April at Shiala, on the Diyala River some 30km west of the Tigris. Both sides were surprised, but British troops got to the only high ground in the area first, followed by their supporting EIGHTEEN-POUNDERS, and drove off repeated attacks by Turkish infantry. Ali Ishan's troops eventually fled, eluding pursuit by CAVALRY to make a fighting but temporary retreat into the Jebel Hamlin mountains (see MAP 23). See also: Battle of the BOOT.

Short 184 British seaplane in RNAS service from early 1915, the world's first operational torpedo bomber. A biplane with folding wings, it was designed on the initiative of British naval air chief Sueter, after a TORPEDO had been successfully launched from an earlier Short model in July 1914. During operations off GALLIPOLI, on 12 August 1915, a 184 became the first aircraft to sink a ship with a torpedo. They destroyed two more Turkish ships during the campaign, but launching the weapon remained a difficult, dangerous operation and the practice was gradually phased out.

Subsequently operating as standard patrol aircraft, 184s flew ANTI-SUBMARINE, reconnaissance and bombing missions from coastal bases in Britain and the MEDITERRANEAN. They were sometimes used aboard AIRCRAFT CARRIERS, and a 184 aboard the *ENGADINE* provided the only aerial reconnaissance at the Battle of JUTLAND. More than 650 were used by the RNAS, and various minor modifications or engine changes were made to later models, including the single-seat 184-D version, which carried an extra 265kg of bombs in place of an observer.

BRIEF DATA (184) Type: two-seater floatplane torpedo bomber; Engine: 225hp Sunbeam; Max speed: 84mph (134kph); Armament: 1 × 0.303in mg, max load 1 × 14in torpedo or 400lbs (181kg) bombs.

Short 320 British seaplane designed specifically for operations with large TORPEDOES and active with RNAS units from September 1917. After the failure of initial torpedo attacks on Austro-Hungarian SUBMARINES in the Adriatic they were re-armed as conventional ANTI-SUBMARINE patrol craft, operating from British and MEDITERRANEAN coastal stations. Of 127 machines produced, 50 remained in service at the ARMISTICE.

BRIEF DATA Type: two-seater floatplane torpedo bomber; Engine: 310hp Sunbeam; Max speed: 79mph (126kph); Armament: 1 × 0.303in mg, max load 1 × 18in torpedo or 460lbs (209kg) bombs.

Short 827 Small, versatile seaplane, a biplane used by the British RNAS for reconnaissance and light-bombing operations from 1915 until the end of the War. About 120 were built, including a few 140hp Short 830 versions. They served with British coastal stations on ANTI-SUBMARINE and AIRSHIP patrols, aboard seaplane carriers, with individual ships in home waters, on the MESOPOTAMIAN FRONT and in EAST AFRICA (see NAVAL AFRICA EXPEDITION).

BRIEF DATA (827) Type: two-seater reconnaissance floatplane; Engine: 150hp Sunbeam; Max speed: 61mph (98kph); Armament: 1 × 0.303in mg, light bombs (external racks).

Short Bomber British conversion of the successful SHORT 184 seaplane, and one of the first aircraft designed primarily for STRATEGIC BOMBING operations. Ordered by the RNAS in late 1915 for use by No.3 Wing, its new long-range bombing unit, it became operational early the following year. A total of 73 machines were eventually built for RNAS raids on German-held coastal positions, of which 15 were transferred to the RFC for preliminary attacks on the SOMME in June 1916. Though very large for single-engined machines, their bomb-carrying capacity was small, and replacement by HANDLEY-PAGE 0/100 heavy bombers, begun in autumn 1916, was completed by the following April.
BRIEF DATA Type: two-seater bomber; Engine: 225hp Sunbeam or 250hp Rolls Royce; Max speed: 77mph (123kph); Ceiling: 2,900m; Armament: 1 × 0.303in mg, 4 × 230lb or 8 × 112lb bomb (on wing racks).

SIA-9B In production from February 1918, the SIA-9B reconnaissance biplane eventually equipped three ITALIAN NAVY squadrons. Developed from the SIA-7 two-seater (produced in large numbers from 1917 but hardly used because of persistent wing failure), the SIA-9B was powered by the biggest engine used by any air wartime air force. Though fast and agile, it suffered the same structural weakness as its predecessor and was rejected by the ITALIAN AIR FORCE. An improved Fiat R-2 version (SIA took the name Fiat in 1918) was accepted, but was barely in service at the ARMISTICE.
BRIEF DATA Type: two-seater armed reconnaissance; Engine: 700hp Fiat; Max speed: 200kph; Armament: 2 × 6.5mm mg.

Siam Now called Thailand, Siam was an absolute monarchy in the early 20th century, ruled by the anglophile King Rama IV (as Crown Prince from 1910 to 1917). Siam declared war against the CENTRAL POWERS on 22 July 1917, but its army was only about 25,000 strong and its practical contribution was limited to confiscation of German property. A military mission was sent to the WESTERN FRONT in 1918, followed by medical and aviation personnel, but they were still in training at the ARMISTICE, after which Siam was given permanent possession of former German assets in the country at the PARIS PEACE CONFERENCE.

'Sideshows' Contemporary British term describing theatres of war outside the main European fronts, coined pejoratively by 'WESTERNERS' seeking to concentrate military effort in France. British land campaigns on the PALESTINE, BALKAN, GALLIPOLI and MESOPOTAMIAN FRONTS all qualified as sideshows, along with operations in AFRICA.

Sidi Ahmad es Sherif See: SENUSSI.

Siemens-Schuckert D-I The combat superiority of French NIEUPORT 17s over the WESTERN FRONT in mid-1916 prompted German authorities to commission copies. Siemens-Schuckert (SSW) was one of several companies given captured 17s, and its imitation D-I was ordered into production in November. Greatly superior ALBATROS D-TYPES were soon available, and most SSWs served units on the EASTERN FRONT, where they faced few modern adversaries. Less than a hundred had been built when production was halted in July 1917.
BRIEF DATA Type: single-seat fighter; Engine: 110hp Siemens Halske; Max speed: 171kph; Ceiling: 5,250m; Armament: 1 × 7.92mm mg.

Siemens-Schuckert D-IV A development of the failed Siemens-Schuckert D-III, the D-IV joined German FIGHTER units from autumn 1918. Although it lacked speed by contemporary standards, its exceptional agility made the D-IV one of the best dogfighters on the WESTERN FRONT, but a complex construction procedure meant that only 119 were delivered.
BRIEF DATA Type: single-seat fighter; Engine: 200hp Siemens Halske; Max speed: 189kph; Ceiling: 6,400m; Armament: 2 × 7.92mm mg.

Siemens-Schuckert R-Types See: RIESENFLUGZEUG.

Sikorski IM (Ilya Mourometz) Russian heavy bomber first flown in January 1914, it was a direct descendant of designer Igor Sikorski's 1913 'Le Grand', the world's first four-engined aircraft. A large biplane with a spacious enclosed cabin and twin tailfins, the Ilya Mourometz was in civilian service as a passenger aircraft from February 1914, and was ordered by the RUSSIAN AIR SERVICE in August.

The first 'Squadron of Flying Ships' was formed on the EASTERN FRONT in December 1914, based near Warsaw, beginning raids against German positions in eastern Poland on 15 February 1915. More than 400 attacks were carried out by IMs during the war, including regular long-range raids on targets in GERMANY and AUSTRIA-HUNGARY. Modifications of the original IM-G1 type carried more powerful engines (up to 255hp) and bomb loads of well over 700kg. The IM-C model introduced a turret behind the tail for the rear MACHINE GUNS.

Reliable and with good all-round armament, the Sikorski fleet proved almost invulnerable: of 73 machines delivered by the time of the OCTOBER REVOLUTION in 1917, only one was shot down by enemy FIGHTERS, and only another two were lost to mechanical failure. The surviving IMs fought on both sides during the RUSSIAN CIVIL WAR. See also: STRATEGIC BOMBING; REISENFLUGZEUG.

BRIEF DATA (IM-G1) Type: heavy bomber; Crew: 6; Engine: 2 × 200hp, 2 × 135hp Canton-Unné; Max speed: 100kph; Armament: 2 × 7.62mm mg, 535kg bomb load.

Sims, Admiral William (1858–1936) Infamous within the US NAVY for unofficially promising military support for Britain in 1910, Sims was transferred to Europe in April 1917 to liaise with Allied navies. His conviction that SUBMARINE WARFARE represented the greatest danger to the Allies brought immediate conflict with chief of naval operations BENSON, who resisted demands for release of ANTI-SUBMARINE forces from US coastal duties until the request was backed by Atlantic commander MAYO.

As commander of US naval forces in Europe from June 1917, Sims encouraged operational integration with the ROYAL NAVY, in contrast to the attitude of AEF commander PERSHING. He opposed the NORTHERN BARRAGE project as a distraction from the main task of CONVOY protection, and cemented an anglophile reputation with ceaseless requests for greater US commitment in the eastern Atlantic and the MEDITERRANEAN. Promoted full admiral in December 1918, Sims charged Benson and navy secretary DANIELS with obstructive inefficiency during a subsequent congressional hearing on naval affairs, provoking a controversy that overshadowed his retirement in 1922.

Singapore Mutiny The only major wartime mutiny by British or British imperial forces. The far eastern island base of Singapore was an important naval fortress guarding British trade routes between the Indian Ocean and the Far East. It was garrisoned in early 1915 by the 5th Light Infantry regiment of the INDIAN ARMY, and on 15 February garrison troops revolted against their British officers, killing some and driving survivors to barricade themselves in the commander's residence. The mutiny, by an entirely Muslim regiment, was the only success among many attempts by religious agitators to use German PROPAGANDA against Indian troops.

The rebels were prevented from entering Singapore itself by local police, and their attempt to free Turkish and German internees was rejected by the internees themselves. Sailors from British and French ships in the area joined a small Russian party, 200 deputized Japanese civilians, 150 troops under the Sultan of Johor and a multi-racial group of volunteer residents to force most of the disorganized mutineers to surrender. Others fled to the jungle and were captured once regular British forces arrived with trackers from Borneo. Subsequent court martials convicted 201 soldiers of mutiny, imposed 47 death sentences and imprisoned 64 men for life.

Sixtus Affair A clumsy attempt by Austro-Hungarian Emperor KARL I to promote an early peace with the Allies. Karl had promised to seek a settlement at his coronation in late 1916, and made direct overtures to the western Allies in spring 1917 through his wife's brothers, Princes Sixtus and Xavier of Bourbon-Parma, both officers in the BELGIAN ARMY. They held preliminary meetings with French government representatives in late March, apparently sanctioned by Austro-Hungarian foreign minister CZERNIN, but received no official encouragement, and hopes of a compromise peace faded. French premier CLEMENCEAU revealed records of the affair a year later in a successful bid to disrupt Austro-German relations. The German THIRD SUPREME COMMAND reacted by forcing Czernin's resignation and imposing formal military-economic union with GERMANY on AUSTRIA-HUNGARY in May.

Slava Russian PRE-DREADNOUGHT, completed in 1905, that performed valuable service as a wartime coastal-defence ship in the BALTIC SEA. Stationed in and around the Bay of Riga, *Slava* provided ARTILLERY support for ground forces fighting in KURLAND from 1915, and played a major part in the battle for the IRBEN STRAITS in 1916–17. It survived with only minor damage until the ALBION operation of October 1917, when it was crippled by gunfire from modern German BATTLESHIPS and scuttled to obstruct the entrance to Moon Sound.

BRIEF DATA (1914) Displacement: 15,000 tons; Crew: 750; Dimensions: length 397ft (120.3m), beam 76ft (23m); Speed: 18k; Main Armament: 4 × 12in gun, 12 × 6in (152mm), 20 × 12pdr, 4 × 18in TT.

Smith-Dorrien, General Sir Horace (1858–1930) Given command of the BEF's II Corps on the WESTERN FRONT in August 1914, following the sudden death of General Grierson, Smith-Dorrien handled his forces well against the main German attacks at MONS and LE CATEAU, but was never liked by volatile C-in-C FRENCH. His command was reorganized as the British Second Army in December 1914, but disputes with French reached a climax during the Second Battle of YPRES in May 1915. Repeatedly ordered into attacks he considered futile, Smith-Dorrien eventually proposed limited withdrawal and was dismissed on spurious grounds of failing health. Smith-Dorrien never held another major command after illness prevented a planned posting to EAST AFRICA.

Smuts, General Jan (1870–1950) South African soldier and statesman. Smuts was General BOTHA's political lieutenant in both the Transvaal and Union administrations after the Boer War (1899–1902), and as interior and defence minister in 1914 he became unpopular for using troops against striking miners. He returned to military command in spring 1915, joining Botha in the conquest of German SOUTHWEST AFRICA and taking field command of SOUTH AFRICAN FORCES after the campaign.

Promoted lieutenant general in the BRITISH ARMY to lead the multinational imperial force in GERMAN EAST AFRICA from early 1916, he was repeatedly outwitted by LETTOW-VORBECK's defensive tactics, but occupied a considerable amount of territory and gained a high reputation in GREAT BRITAIN. His appointment to the British War Cabinet in March 1917 reflected the admiration of prime minister LLOYD GEORGE, and he remained close to the heart of imperial war management for the duration. Smuts supported HAIG's plan to attack at YPRES in mid-1917, and argued for a major offensive on the PALESTINE FRONT in 1918, although he refused an offer to command British forces there. In June 1918 his own offer to Lloyd George of experienced leadership for the AEF on the WESTERN FRONT was not transmitted to US authorities.

He played an influential but ambiguous role at the PARIS PEACE CONFERENCE. Although anxious to counter the growing global dominance of the UNITED STATES, he was also President WILSON's most prominent ally in creating the LEAGUE OF NATIONS. In favour of REPARATIONS, and responsible for the MANDATE system of governing former German and Turkish Colonies, he nevertheless had reservations about the severity of the VERSAILLES treaty, and only signed it under protest. Prime minister of SOUTH AFRICA from August 1919 until 1924, and again from 1939 to 1948, Smuts played an active and senior role in the Second World War, and was the only man to sign treaties at the end of both global conflicts.

Smyrna Provincial department of the Ottoman Empire, centred on the eastern Aegean port of Smyrna (modern Turkish Izmir). Smyrna was an extreme example of local bureaucratic independence within a belligerent state, its experienced regional governor, Rahmi Bey, using the wartime collapse of internal communications in TURKEY to establish virtual home rule. Only those central government regulations that he personally approved were enacted in Smyrna, TURKISH ARMY requisitions were regularly refused and enemy nationals were neither interned nor deported. Although the garrison rebuffed an Allied naval attempt to take the port in spring 1915 (a subsidiary to the DARDANELLES operation), earlier ROYAL NAVY raids against the Smyrnan coast met full cooperation from Turkish troops, who even assisted in the destruction of RAILWAY links. Rahmi's administration could not prevent the breakdown of law and order general to the Empire in 1918, and the GREEK ARMY justified its postwar occupation of Smyrna (1919–22) as a 'civilizing mission', a claim rejected by an independent international commission but accepted by the Allies. The subsequent nationalist struggle to evict the Greeks provided the focus for Mustapha KEMAL's successful Turkish republican movement.

Snipers Marksmen concealed in good vantage points to pick off targets as the opportunity offered itself had performed a peripheral role in warfare for hundreds of years. Used by all armies in all theatres from 1914, snipers developed a specialized role in the context of static TRENCH WARFARE. They worked day and night on both sides of the lines on the GALLIPOLI, ITALIAN and WESTERN FRONTS, killing anybody careless enough to show themselves above frontline parapets. As a means of sapping enemy morale, and of maintaining an aggressive posture between battles, sniping took place in even the quietest sectors of a front and played a major part in the everyday lives of entrenched soldiers.

Snipers generally worked in two-man teams, one observer and one marksman. Observers were sometimes equipped with periscopes to avoid exposure to enemy fire, and marksmen invariably used RIFLES, occasionally also mounted with periscopes (or 'sniperscopes'). Sniping was dangerous – good camouflage and absolute stillness were vital to survival – and the marksmen themselves were required to function as assassins, often striking targets engaged in peaceful activities. Unofficial sniping nevertheless took place regularly on all sides, and many official snipers kept tallies of their 'scores', which frequently reached three figures. See also: FRANC-TIREURS.

'Soixante-Quinze' Universally understood shorthand (meaning 'Seventy-Five') for the world's best-known ARTILLERY weapon in 1914, the FRENCH ARMY's 75mm medium field gun. Relatively light and mobile, it had a maximum range of about 9,000 metres and was capable of a phenomenal 30 rounds per minute for short periods. Grouped in small batteries for immediate support of advancing infantry, Soixante-Quinzes formed the basis of French offensive tactics in 1914, and justified their very high reputation whenever they were given the chance to function in open, mobile conditions. The requirements of TRENCH WARFARE – long range, high trajectory and weight of shell – called for different types of weapon, and Soixante-Quinzes were overshadowed by heavier weapons on the WESTERN FRONT.

Somaliland East African region divided into French, British and Italian colonies, covering a total of about half a million square miles and with an estimated population of about 900,000 in 1914 (see MAP 17). None of the colonies was involved in fighting between Europeans, and the Somali camel trade benefited from a temporary regional war boom brought about by the presence of large Allied forces in EGYPT. In the British sector, however, local tribal leader Mullah Mahommed bin Abdullah had been in rebellion since the turn of the century, and had driven colonists from the interior by 1910. Garrison troops began operations against the 'Mad Mullah' in November 1914 and won an apparently decisive victory the following spring, but faced sporadic raiding until a further British offensive finally destroyed the rebel army in February 1920.

Somme Offensive The main Allied attack on the WESTERN FRONT in 1916. Launched on 1 July along a 30km front running roughly north of the River Somme between Amiens and Péronne, it eventually ended on 18 November (see MAP 2).

Planned in late 1915 as a joint Franco-British operation, the offensive was the brainchild of French C-in-C JOFFRE, and was accepted by new BEF commander HAIG despite his own preference for the relatively open ground of Flanders. Though concerned with territorial gain, it explicitly aimed to destroy German manpower reserves.

French troops were expected to bear the main burden of the operation, but the GERMAN ARMY's mass assault on VERDUN in 1916 turned the Somme operation into a large-scale British diversionary attack. Planning passed to Haig, who made slow and meticulous preparations, eventually settling on a scheme that combined his own ideas uneasily with those of General RAWLINSON, whose Fourth Army was to spearhead the attack.

After an eight-day PRELIMINARY BOMBARDMENT, which was expected to completely destroy German forward defences, Rawlinson's southern wing, at the centre of the attack line, was instructed to consolidate after a limited advance, and went into battle heavily laden with supplies for that purpose. To the north, the rest of the Fourth Army and one corps of ALLENBY's Third Army were ordered to attempt a complete BREAKTHROUGH, with CAVALRY standing by to exploit the gap created. Further south, a subsidiary advance by the French Sixth Army (FAYOLLE) was to begin at the same time.

In total, the attack deployed almost 750,000 men (27 divisions), seven-eighths of them from the BEF, against 16 front line divisions of the German Second Army (BELOW), but the medium ARTILLERY of the BEF – hampered by poor-quality ammunition – failed to destroy either barbed wire or the protective concrete bunkers beneath German TRENCHES, enabling the defenders to take full advantage of excellent positions on higher ground when British infantry attacked at 07.30 on 1 July.

French forces, with more heavy artillery, achieved surprise by delaying their attack at the last moment and made some progress on the first day, but the BEF made only tiny gains, consolidated rather than exploited, at the southern end of its front. Forced back to its trenches everywhere else along the line, it suffered more casualties (58,000 men, a third of them killed) than on any other day in the history of the BRITISH ARMY.

Haig renewed major attacks on Rawlinson's front in a series of limited and costly advances, securing the first line of German trenches by 11 July. A night operation on 13–14 July did achieve a limited and temporary breakthrough, but supporting attacks made insignificant progress and German reinforcements arrived in sufficient numbers to close the gap.

German artillery began transferring from Verdun on 11 July, and defending German forces in the British sector were more than doubled in the first 18 days of the battle. From 19 July, German forces were reorganized, the southern wing becoming a new First Army under von GALLWITZ, who also took overall command of the defence.

With both sides heavily committed, as at Verdun, the battle developed an extra-strategic momentum of its own, fuelled by a common belief that the other side was on the point of exhaustion. British commanders in particular glimpsed real success behind every encouraging sign, but a few small victories, like the capture of Pozières by two AUSTRALIAN divisions on 23 July, could not be followed up.

The front remained substantially unaltered throughout August, but the line of assault was widened in early September. The French Tenth Army (MICHELER) joined the battle on a 20km front to the south, and a renewed British attack, known as the Battle of FLERS-COURCELETTE, was launched northeast from the Fourth Army's small SALIENT on 15 September. Employing 12 divisions and using TANKS for the first time, it gained only a couple of kilometres.

Haig renewed attacks east of the salient on 25–27 September (the Battles of Morval and

Thiepval Ridge), and the pattern of limited Allied advances continued whenever weather allowed in October. British offensives beyond the Flers-Courcelette line, distinguished as the Battles of Transloy Ridges (1–20 October) and the Ancre Heights (1–11 October), were matched by French attacks in the south around Chaulnes and in the centre east of Morval.

Urged to continue the fight by Joffre, whose forces were now on the offensive around Verdun, the BEF made one last effort on the far east of the salient from 13 November, the Battle of the Ancre (or Beaumont Hamel), capturing the field fortress of Beaumont Hamel before snow caused a final suspension of operations.

Allied forces gained a crescent of shattered battlescape, 12km across at its deepest points, suffering 420,000 British and almost 200,000 French casualties. The battle wrecked the BEF's new volunteer mass army and added to the enormous strain imposed on the FRENCH ARMY at Verdun. Estimates of German casualties vary, averaging around 500,000, and the GERMAN ARMY never recovered from losses among junior officers and experienced NCOs on the Western Front in 1916.

Haig's inflexible repetition of flawed tactics at the Somme remains a source of controversy in GREAT BRITAIN, where failure brought the first signs of war weariness. Though unimaginative, his approach was partly dictated by French demands for continuous action on the Somme, and reflected his own unwillingness to attempt innovative manoeuvres with untried troops. See MAP 8. See also: KAISERSCHLACHT.

Sonnino, Giorgio Sidney, Baron (1847–1922) Italian conservative politician, a committed proponent of Italian colonial expansion but overshadowed by GIOLITTI before 1914. Convinced that prolonged neutrality would wreck hopes of postwar expansion, he was strongly in favour of joining the CENTRAL POWERS during the JULY CRISIS of 1914, but reacted to German setbacks on the WESTERN FRONT by modifying his views to support war on whichever side appeared likely to win.

As foreign minister (and a powerful presence in the cabinet) after a reshuffle of the SALANDRA government in November 1914, Sonnino presided over negotiations with both sides during the winter and spring, making territorial demands on AUSTRIA-HUNGARY that could never be met. The Treaty of LONDON (26 April 1915) with the Allies was an accurate reflection of his war aims, and he clung rigidly to its territorial provisions. He refused to modify territorial claims in the Balkans in aid of Allied negotiations with BULGARIA, and later expanded Italian claims to include parts of TURKEY (see ST JEAN DE MAURIENNE CONFERENCE).

Despite public association with an increasingly unpopular war, Sonnino retained office under BOSELLI from June 1916 and continued in virtually unchallenged control of foreign policy, but faced more serious challenges to his authority as part of the ORLANDO government from October. Publication of the London Treaty's secret clauses in December damaged his international reputation, and Orlando ignored his opposition in giving limited support to plans for an independent YUGOSLAVIA.

Sonnino's vision of Italy as a major force in an essentially unchanged European order was undermined by principles popularized in the FOURTEEN POINTS, and by summer 1918 he was urging chief of staff DIAZ to encourage postwar Allied generosity with a final offensive on the ITALIAN FRONT. His hopes for Balkan expansion were wrecked at the PARIS PEACE CONFERENCE, and the resultant treaties were greeted as a national defeat in Italy. Sonnino planned to force their revision by sending Italian troops to Turkish SMYRNA, but retired when the government fell in June.

Sopwith Baby British floatplane, an up-engined version of the SOPWITH SCHNEIDER biplane, that served with the RNAS from early 1916. Originally given a 110hp engine, later versions were often structurally modified to increase lift as the equipment used on naval missions expanded to include bombs, anti-AIRSHIP darts, an anchor, CARRIER PIGEONS and drinking water. The Baby was used in all RNAS theatres and 286 were built.

BRIEF DATA Type: single-seat patrol floatplane; Engine: 130hp Clerget; Max speed: 100mph (160kph); Armament: 1 × 0.303in mg (synchro, forward) or 48 darts, 2 × 65lb bomb.

Sopwith (F-1) Camel Celebrated and successful British biplane FIGHTER developed from the SOPWITH PUP and in full service with the RFC on the WESTERN FRONT from July 1917. Designed in late 1916 to cope with twin-gunned German ALBATROS D-TYPES, it was the first British fighter equipped with two synchronized forward MACHINE GUNS, and its name was derived from their hump-like casing. A difficult machine to fly, tending to spin out of control during the tight turns that were its speciality, the Camel was never popular with inexperienced pilots and caused many training deaths. In skilled hands, its exceptional agility and good rate of climb combined to make it a formidable weapon, and it was used by many Allied ACES. Standard equipment with British squadrons in France until the ARMISTICE, Camels eventually shot down 1,294 hostile aircraft.

Apart from air-combat duties, Camels armed with light bombs were used for ground-attack operations. Unarmoured, they suffered heavy losses to ground fire, and an armoured TF-1 version was abandoned at the prototype stage. A modified F-1 Camel was produced for night operations, with the pilot's seat repositioned to prevent temporary blindness from gun flashes. A 2F-1 model, with repositioned guns and shorter wings, was built for naval use, 129 being produced in all; these usually operated from AIRCRAFT CARRIERS, warship gun turrets or towed lighters. By November 1918 some 2,500 Camels were with the RAF in France and Belgium, and the type saw action on most other British fronts, as well as with Greek forces, the BELGIAN AIR SERVICE and the USAAS. A total of 5,140 Camels were built, and although quickly withdrawn from postwar British service they remained active with several smaller forces for many years.

BRIEF DATA (F-1, 1918) Type: single-seat fighter; Engine: 150hp Bentley Rotary; Max speed: 115mph (184kph); Ceiling: 6,650m; Armament: 2 × 0.303in mg (synchro), 4 × 25lb bomb.

Sopwith (5F-1) Dolphin Distinctively squat British biplane FIGHTER first flown in May 1917. Fast, agile and easy to fly, but plagued by engine trouble throughout its career, it reached RFC units on the WESTERN FRONT in January 1918. Its greatest weaknesses were the positioning of the top wing behind the pilot, designed for maximum forward visibility but often fatal in crash landings, and a slow starting engine that restricted its interception capacity. Though it was armed with two synchronized and two high-firing MACHINE GUNS, the latter were awkward to operate and often removed as unnecessary. Two squadrons of Dolphins took part in fierce air fighting over the German KAISERSCHLACHT offensive in late March, and they equipped two more squadrons from April, performing adequately as escort and ground-attack craft. A few were also used for home defence. More than 1,500 were built in wartime, and a 300hp Mark II was being developed in France at the ARMISTICE.

BRIEF DATA Type: single-seat fighter/ground attack; Engine: 200hp Hispano-Suiza; Max speed: 131mph (210kph); Ceiling: 6,350m; Armament: 4 × 0.303in mg.

Sopwith 'Pup' British biplane FIGHTER, known officially as the Sopwith Scout (by the RFC) or the Sopwith Type 9901 (RNAS), but named by pilots as a miniature of the contemporary SOPWITH STRUTTER. Both were hasty refinements of the SOPWITH TABLOID, designed in response to German combat superiority in late 1915. Light, compact and particularly easy to control, the Pup first flew in February 1916, undertook combat trials on the WESTERN FRONT from May, and was in full service with both British air arms by the year's end.

Though lightly armed and underpowered, its spectacular manoeuvrability at high altitudes gave the Pup an edge in combat with the hitherto untouchable ALBATROS D-III, although its impact on overall German air superiority was restricted by lack of numbers in 1916. Pups eventually equipped three army and two naval squadrons, operating successfully as frontline fighters until autumn 1917.

The RFC used then for home-defence (often with a 100hp engine) and training purposes until the end of the War, eventually commissioning about 1,600 of the type. The RNAS used 170 Pups, including several versions purpose-designed for AIRCRAFT CARRIER work. The Type 9901a, produced in 1918, had skids for deck landings, and 55 W-III models with folding wings and retractable undercarriage were built by the Beardsmore company.

BRIEF DATA (naval 9901) Type: single-seat fighter; Engine: 80hp Le Rhône (sometimes Gnôme or Clerget); Max speed: 111mph (178kph); Ceiling: 5,300m; Armament: 1 × 0.303in mg (synchro, forward) or 8 × rockets.

Sopwith (TF-2) Salamander Armoured biplane that was the first British production aircraft designed specifically for ground-attack missions. The increasingly important task of direct infantry cooperation had previously been undertaken by conventional, unarmoured machines, but a standard 30 per cent loss rate was deemed unacceptable. A development of the SOPWITH SNIPE, the TF-2 Salamander (TF for 'Trench Fighter') was first built in April 1918 after attempts to devise an armoured SOPWITH CAMEL had failed. Ordered into mass production the following month, it was just joining RAF units on the WESTERN FRONT at the ARMISTICE.

BRIEF DATA Type: single-seat ground attack; Engine: 230hp Bentley Rotary; Max speed: 125mph (200kph); Ceiling: 4,000m; Armament: 2 × 0.303in mg (forward).

Sopwith Schneider Small British naval biplane, a version of the SOPWITH TABLOID fast reconnaissance scout that won the 1914 Schneider Trophy. It was used by the RNAS for ANTI-SUBMARINE and ZEPPELIN patrols from early 1915. Operating around the British coast, in the MEDITERRANEAN and off EAST AFRICA, it was also used for early experiments with AIRCRAFT CARRIERS, but was gradually supplanted by the more powerful SOPWITH BABY from early 1916. A total of 136 were produced.

BRIEF DATA Type: single-seat patrol floatplane; Engine: 100hp Gnôme Monosoupape; Max speed: 92mph (148kph); Ceiling: 3,000m; Armament: 1 × 0.303in mg.

Sopwith (7F-1) Snipe British biplane FIGHTER, developed in late 1917 around a new 230hp Bentley engine but delayed by a series of minor pre-production modifications. It eventually equipped only three squadrons on the WESTERN FRONT in autumn 1918. Strong, manoeuvrable and fast-climbing, it was regarded as the best Allied fighter in service at the ARMISTICE. Almost 500 Snipes were built in 1918, and it was a mainstay of the postwar RAF, remaining in service until 1927.

BRIEF DATA Type: single-seat fighter; Engine: 230hp Bentley Rotary; Max speed: 121mph (194kph); Ceiling: 6,050m; Armament: 2 × 0.303in mg (forward).

Sopwith '1½ Strutter' Versatile British biplane, officially the Sopwith Two-Seater but named after its short central wing struts. It joined the RNAS in April 1916, and the RFC in May, as the first British machine to enter service fitted with INTERRUPTER GEAR. Both arms threw their 'Strutters' straight into combat as FIGHTERS on the WESTERN FRONT, where the British faced a desperate shortage of quality aircraft. Its strong armament compensated for lack of manoeuvrability against single-seat machines, and its original 110hp engine was replaced in later models, but it was outclassed by German ALBATROS D-TYPES from late September and phased out of fighter units during 1917.

Strutters remained active on other duties until the ARMISTICE. Naval models served on early AIRCRAFT CARRIERS, as bomber escorts and in a single-seat modification as bombers. Another single-seat version, with twin forward guns, was used in RFC home-defence squadrons, and a total of 1,513 British Strutters were eventually built. Three times as many were produced in France, used by the French AÉRONAUTIQUE MILITAIRE in reconnaissance (1A-2), single-seat bomber (B-1) and two-seat bomber (1B-2) versions. The type was also employed by the BELGIAN, RUSSIAN and ROMANIAN AIR SERVICES, and the USAAS purchased 514 French models for use on the Western Front in 1918.

BRIEF DATA Type: two-seat fighter; Engine: 130hp Clerget; Max speed: 106mph (170kph); Ceiling: 4,700m; Armament: 2 × 0.303in mg.

Sopwith Tabloid Small British light bomber and scout, based on a two-seat sports biplane of 1913. It was the fastest and most manoeuvrable aircraft in use by any army in August 1914, but only a few were available to the RFC on the WESTERN FRONT and for RNAS operations over the English Channel. A maximum bomb load of 20lbs restricted its offensive value, although a light bomb from a Tabloid was credited with the destruction of ZEPELLIN sheds at Düsseldorf in October 1914. Despite the addition of a side- or high-mounted MACHINE GUN it was rendered obsolete by the development of specialist FIGHTERS, and only 39 had been built when production was suspended in June 1915. The RNAS also used its few Tabloids into 1915, notably during the DARDANELLES OPERATION.

BRIEF DATA Type: single-seat scout; Engine: 100hp Gnôme Monosoupape; Max speed: 92mph (148kph); Ceiling: 3,000m; Armament: pilot's small arms or 1 × 0.303 mg.

Sopwith Triplane Innovative and outstandingly successful British FIGHTER, a development of Sopwith's standard box-like airframe given three small wings to improve climb rate and manoeuvrability. Prototypes underwent combat testing from June 1916, and the design was immediately ordered by both British air forces, but the RFC's urgent need for aircraft prompted it to exchange its quota for 60 naval SPAD S-VII fighters in February 1917, and Triplanes were eventually used only by the RNAS.

Entering full service with naval squadrons on the WESTERN FRONT in April 1917, the Triplane outpaced, outmanoeuvred and outclimbed the best contemporary German fighters, and its pilots scored heavily before it was matched by a new generation of designs in the autumn (see BLACK FLIGHT). By then the even better SOPWITH CAMEL was becoming available in numbers, and the last Triplane was withdrawn from France in November 1917. Elsewhere, a single 'Tripehound' served on the BALKAN FRONT and another operated (with skis) on the EASTERN FRONT. A few Triplanes were fitted with twin guns, and a few others given bigger engines, but less than 150 were built and their career was brief. Their disproportionate impact on the course of aerial combat was reflected in a rash of German triplane designs during 1917–18, most notably the FOKKER DR-I.

BRIEF DATA Type: single-seat fighter; Engine: 130hp Clerget; Max speed: 117mph (187kph); Ceiling: 6,200m; Armament: 1 × 0.303in mg (synchro, forward).

Souchon, Admiral Wilhelm (1864–1946) Commander of the the German MITTELMEERDIVISION from October 1913, Souchon was officially named C-in-C of the Turkish battlefleet after his ships, *GOEBEN* and *BRESLAU*, were transferred to the TURKISH NAVY in August 1914. Like his military counterpart, LIMAN VON SANDERS, Souchon was expected to pursue German strategic aims by Berlin but remained directly responsible to the YOUNG TURK government, specifically marine minister DJEMAL PASHA. Souchon enjoyed greater freedom of action than Liman von Sanders, but all strategic decisions were made by the Turkish government and his early commencement of offensive operations in the BLACK SEA was sanctioned by war minister ENVER PASHA. His repeated pleas for SUBMARINE support were never answered in strength, and he complained bitterly at the poor quality of Turkish ships, crews and repair facilities. Never happy with his role, he finally returned to Germany in September 1917, taking command of the Fourth Battleship Squadron with the HIGH SEAS FLEET, and leaving his German successor, Admiral Rebeur-Paschwitz, to preside over the Mittelmeerdivision's last operations.

South Africa Of the four 19th-century white South African colonies, Transvaal and Orange Free State (later Orange River Colony) were governed by European populations of predominantly Dutch and Huguenot origin, known as Afrikaners or Boers, while Natal and Cape Colony were ruled by British settlers. Guided by Boer politicians intent on reconciliation and economic development after the Boer War (1899–1902), the colonies had united in 1910 to form the Union of South Africa as a self-governing dominion within the British Empire.

An appointed British governor general was nominal head of state, but power rested with an Executive Committee, drawn from an elected national legislature and headed by General Louis BOTHA from 1910 until his death in 1919. As in most British colonial regimes, native peoples and WOMEN were barred from public office.

On the outbreak of European war Botha's immediate offer to send SOUTH AFRICAN FORCES overseas on imperial service was accepted for an invasion of German SOUTHWEST AFRICA, interrupted when Afrikaner opposition to pro-British commitment crystallized into a major BOER REVOLT in late 1914.

The military suppression of the Revolt enabled resumption of offensive operation, and the German colony fell in mid-1915, but Boer resentment – though subdued by the government's conciliatory attitude towards the defeated rebels – remained a potent factor in wartime politics. Botha's commitment to war enjoyed uncomplicated support from British South Africans, ensuring a steady flow of recruits for service in EAST AFRICA, and had the broad approval of moderate Afrikaner opinion, but more radical Boer opposition gathered around General Herzog's new Nationalist Party.

Fighting the 1915 election on a platform of neutrality and gradual progress towards full independence, the Nationalists almost defeated Botha's South African National Party, which remained in power only with the support of the anglophile Unionist Party. Dissent remained non-violent and was confined to a minority, but Botha was required to defend his political position at home, passing overseas command and diplomatic responsibilities to General SMUTS.

Industrialization was barely underway in South Africa by 1914, and it benefited less from wartime economic opportunities than more developed non-European countries. The most developed region, Cape Colony, was a major shipping centre, and the Union as a whole possessed a respectable 13,000km RAILWAY system, but agriculture and mining remained the principal industries and almost all manufactured goods were imported.

The main export was gold, which suffered a sharp relative price drop as one of the few metals not vital to modern warfare, and shrinking shipping capacity encouraged Europeans to buy agricultural goods from closer North American producers. Peace brought a short-term export boom in 1919, but South Africa's share in world trade dropped slightly over the decade from 1913.

Postwar South Africa, its economic potential increased by annexation of Southwest Africa as a Class-C MANDATE, was able to begin a process of genuine industrial investment, but remained in a state of political uncertainty until 1924, when Herzog's Nationalists became part of the longstanding coalition that began a systematic sociopolitical exclusion of native peoples.

South African Forces Defence of SOUTH AFRICA was organized on a national basis for the first time in 1912, when five regular mounted regiments and a small ARTILLERY section were formed from the police forces of the four Union states. Conscription was introduced at the same time, with half of European males aged 16 to 25 drafted by lots into the Active Citizen Force (ACF), a part-time national guard that incorporated volunteer state militias. Operative from mid-1913, it used surplus British equipment (gradually updated after 1914) and a wide variety of personally owned weapons.

Regulars and ACF units from the Transvaal were used to defeat the BOER REVOLT, and the ACF as a whole (50,000 men) was available for the purely South African campaign in German SOUTHWEST AFRICA. An infantry brigade (four regiments), heavy artillery units and technical troops were detached in late 1915 for imperial service in EGYPT and on the WESTERN FRONT, and the remainder of the ACF was expanded for service in EAST AFRICA.

Volunteer mounted forces dominated the Southwest Africa campaign and were at the heart of operations in East Africa. Originally organized as 'commandos' of up to 2,000 mounted 'burghers', they comprised white males of all ages from a particular neighbourhood. Hardy, aggressive and notoriously informal, a lifetime's mobility had taught them little about static military occupation, and their general disregard for logistic organization and in-camp sanitation often damaged relations with BRITISH and INDIAN ARMY personnel. The East African campaign was an unhappy experience for Union troops, and white South Africans were phased out of frontline operations whenever possible after late 1916 in favour of black African troops more accustomed to local conditions.

A total of 146,000 whites served in wartime South African units, including 30,000 deployed in Europe and 43,000 in East Africa. An estimated 10,000 more South Africans joined British military units, with more than 3,000 in the RAF by late 1918. Total casualties of 18,600 included 6,600 dead. Non-whites were prohibited from combat service, and tribal offers of active assistance were turned down by the government, but South Africa's black population contributed 85,000 men to labour battalions and other support services, including the South African Native Labour Contingent on the Western Front.

South Carolina Class The first of 14 modern BATTLESHIPS in service with the US NAVY by 1917, *South Carolina* and its sister *Michigan* were ordered in 1905, influencing the ROYAL NAVY's decision to rush-build the similar *DREADNOUGHT*. Not completed until 1909, they were regarded as robust, stable, reliable and capable of exceeding their published speeds, but were never tested against their contemporaries. Along with the two 1910 Delaware Class ships (with an additional main gun turret), two much larger ARIZONA Class ships and all 17 of the Navy's serving PRE-DREADNOUGHTS, the South Carolinas remained in American waters throughout the War. Two Idaho Class 'super-dreadnoughts' completed in wartime, *Mississippi* and *New Mexico*, were also retained in home waters (see *ORION*; *NEW YORK*).

BRIEF DATA (*South Carolina*, 1917) Displacement: 16,000 tons; Crew: 869; Dimensions: length 453.75ft (137.2m), beam 80.25ft (24.3m); Speed: 18.5k; Main armament: 8 × 12in gun, 16 × 3in, 2 × 21in TT.

South Persia Rifles Ostensibly native Persian militia formed and equipped by the British, with the Shah's permission, in March 1916. Designed to restore order in southern PERSIA and purge the region of German political and economic influence, the militia was commanded by British General Sir Percy Sykes, trained by Anglo-Indian NCOs and based on a battalion of Indian infantry. Targeting German interests, the Rifles had marched more than 1,500km by the end of the year, recruiting several hundred troops from the semi-independent Cossack Brigade and Swedish Gendarmerie in the process of effectively restoring British regional pre-eminence. The unit remained active until the Shah declared it a foreign force in spring 1918, when it was withdrawn and disbanded by the British, although some elements deserted to join a short-lived tribal rebellion in the north (see DUNSTERFORCE).

Southwest Africa, Conquest of Invasion of the German colony (modern Namibia) by SOUTH AFRICAN FORCES in 1915. More than 800,000 square kilometres of dry plateau land bordered by the coastal strip of the Namib Desert, the country contained some 15,000 Europeans and an estimated 100,000 Africans in 1914. The German colonial army in Southwest Africa had no black troops, reflecting poor relations with the native tribes, and relied on 3,000 first-class German soldiers organized for internal policing. Bordered by British territories to the east and south, and Portuguese Angola to the north, the colony's geographical position was complicated by a British coastal enclave around Walvis (or Walfish) Bay, including the only harbour suitable for warships. (see MAP 17).

Over 50,000 European troops were available to SOUTH AFRICA in 1914, and prime minister BOTHA's offer of imperial service in August brought a British request to seize Southwest Africa's two largest German harbours (Swakopmund and Lüderitzbucht), along with all the colony's RADIO facilities. During September the ROYAL NAVY Cape Division took the harbour at Swakopmund, 1,800 South Africans were landed at Lüderitzbucht, and a panhandle of territory in the northeast (the Caprivi Strip) was occupied independently by RHODESIAN troops. Another 2,500 South Africans were sent over the Orange River frontier, suffering a minor defeat at Sandfontein on 26 September before offensive operations were interrupted by the BOER REVOLT.

German support sustained the Revolt in the border region until January 1915, but by early February the advance had resumed in the south. Botha assembled a mixed South African and imperial 'Northern Force' at Swakopmund, including a battery of Royal Navy ARMOURED CARS. Another 6,000 South African volunteers were concentrated at Walvis Bay. The Northern Force crossed the desert towards the colonial capital of Windhoek, 280km east, harassed by retreating German units (see MINES, Land), which enjoyed plentiful supplies, ARTILLERY support and use of the colony's central north–south RAILWAY. The Lüderitzbucht and Orange River columns were joined in mid-April by a third force of 2,000 men from the southeastern border. Under the overall command of General SMUTS, the three groups (Southern Force) advanced north along the railway towards Windhoek from 14 April. German forces on both fronts retired another 200km north up the railway to Omaruru, and the capital was taken unopposed on 13 May.

German Governor Seitz rejected Botha's surrender demand on 20 May, and the South African advance resumed after a pause for resupply. Omaruru was occupied on 20 June by Botha's mounted troops, who continued to pursue German forces another 200km north until they surrendered on 9 July. Total South African losses for the campaign were slight – 266 killed (153 by disease or accident), against 1,331 German fatalities. Botha's decision to send German civilian reservists home was criticized in GREAT BRITAIN, where the campaign was otherwise viewed with unrestrained admiration, but an enthusiastic response from Botha's Anglo-African constituents was not echoed by Afrikaner elements.

Soviets Democratic councils formed by workers and troops during the revolution of 1905 in RUSSIA, which reappeared at the start of the FEBRUARY REVOLUTION of 1917 and played a central political role for the next seven decades. Socialist agitators had been able to infiltrate the Workers' Groups legally attached to government War Industries Committees from 1915, and the Petrograd (St Petersburg) Group formed the basis for a Petrograd Soviet of Workers' (and later Soldiers') Deputies established in the capital on 11 March 1917.

A creation of socialist intellectuals and politicians, and dominated by pragmatic Mensheviks and Social Revolutionaries (SRs), the Petrograd Soviet elected KERENSKI among its first officials and established itself as a watchdog against counterrevolution, rejecting direct participation in the PROVISIONAL GOVERNMENT but giving it limited, qualified support.

Able to call on mass protest in opposition to government policies, its decrees carried the weight and inherent weaknesses of government policy statements. The Soviet's international appeal of 14 March for workers to unite in a 'peace without annexations or indemnities' became a globally understood indictment of the war aims of both sides, and of the settlement eventually reached by the PARIS PEACE CONFERENCE. As a call for peace it was undermined in the short term by the behaviour of Provisional foreign minister MILIUKOV and by the Soviet's subsequent support for continuation of 'defensive' war against the CENTRAL POWERS.

Hundreds of worker, peasant and military councils sprung up in response to the Petrograd Soviet's exhortations during March and April 1917, generally taking over local administration from new government-appointed 'commissars'. A national conference of soviets took place in late March, and a First Congress of Russian Soviets in June.

The cabinet eventually included several Soviet deputies, but they represented only factions, and the Petrograd assembly as a whole moved to the left, lurching to support the Bolsheviks when TROTSKI became chairman of its Executive Committee in early October. Trotski timed the OCTOBER REVOLUTION to coincide with a second national congress called for November (October by the old Russian calendar), and this body endorsed the new PACIFIST regime on 8 November before dissolving itself.

LENIN's failure to win a majority in subsequent Constituent Assembly elections prompted him to establish soviets as the basis of government legitimacy in the revolutionary constitution of July 1918. Soviets were also a feature of the GERMAN REVOLUTIONS in 1918–19, and of uprisings in BULGARIA around the time of the ARMISTICE, but in neither case were they able to survive as long-term political institutions.

Spad A-2 Armed reconnaissance biplane in service with the French AÉRONAUTIQUE MILITAIRE from late 1915. Reflecting official doubts about the safety of INTERRUPTER GEAR, the design achieved forward armament by placing observer and MACHINE GUN inside a wooden 'pulpit' in front of the propeller. At a time when nose-first crashes were a regular occurrence this was dangerous and uncomfortable for the observer, and only 42 machines were delivered before production was halted. Another 57 were sent to RUSSIA for operations on the EASTERN FRONT, where they remained in action for longer in the absence of replacement types. A more powerful A-4 version was produced in 1916, but only the 10 machines sent to Russia were used operationally.

BRIEF DATA (A-2) Type: two-seater fighter/reconnaissance; Engine: 80hp Le Rhône; Max speed: 160kph; Armament: 1 × 0.303in mg.

Spad S-VII Small French biplane FIGHTER, designed in late 1915 and in service with AÉRONAUTIQUE MILITAIRE squadrons on the WESTERN FRONT from autumn 1916. Originally fitted with a 150hp engine, but given larger power plants (up to 200hp) as they became available, it lacked the agility of the contemporary NIEUPORT 17 but was stronger and faster. Favoured by French ACES, it remained standard equipment with frontline units until its gradual replacement by the SPAD S-XIII was completed in early 1918. The type equipped two RFC squadrons on the Western Front from late 1916, reflecting an acute lack of modern British fighter designs, and a few served on the MESOPOTAMIAN FRONT. More than half of the 220 manufactured under licence in Britain were ordered for the RNAS but transferred to the RFC in exchange for SOPWITH TRIPLANES. Two escadrilles of the BELGIAN AIR SERVICE used the type, as did the RUSSIAN AIR SERVICE and the crack 'Squadron of Aces' of the ITALIAN AIR FORCE. In total more than 5,500 S-VIIs were built, and the last air force to invest in the design was the USAAS, which bought 189 machines in December 1917.

BRIEF DATA Type: single-seat fighter; Engine: 180hp Hispano-Suiza; Max speed: 191kph; Ceiling: 5,500m; Armament: 1 × 0.303in mg.

Spad S-XIII Highly successful French biplane FIGHTER, a larger and more powerful development of the SPAD S-VII, which it gradually replaced on the WESTERN FRONT from the late summer of 1917. Fast, sturdy and well armed, it was the AÉRONAUTIQUE MILITAIRE's standard fighter by early 1918, also equipping eleven squadrons the ITALIAN AIR FORCE and an escadrille of the BELGIAN AIR SERVICE. Few S-XIIIs were used by the British, but the type replaced the NIEUPORT 28 as the main fighter with the USAAS, which bought 893 in March 1918 and ordered another 6,000. In service from July, they were eventually employed by 16 American squadrons, but the mass order was cancelled after the ARMISTICE.

Almost 8,500 S-XIIIs were built by nine French companies, later models housing a 235hp engine, and the type was in French service until 1923. A 220hp S-XII, armed with a cannon firing through the propeller shaft and one MACHINE GUN, was also put into production during 1917 and field tested by French ACES, but the cannon's volcanic recoil spoiled combat performance and few of the 300 built were used. In 1918 the cannon-armed version was produced as the S-XIV floatplane for the FRENCH NAVY, and 40 were built by the end of the year.

BRIEF DATA (S-XIII) Type: single-seat fighter; Engine: 200hp Hispano-Suiza; Max speed: 208kph; Ceiling: 6,750m; Armament: 2 × 0.303in mg (forward).

Spad S-XVII Last of the successful Spad series of wartime FIGHTERS, a heavy biplane with the emphasis on durability and agility rather than speed. Only 20 were produced and most were issued to the ACES of the French 'CIGOGNES' group in autumn 1918.
BRIEF DATA Type: single-seat fighter; Engine: 300hp Hispano-Suiza; Max speed: 200kph; Ceiling: 6,750m; Armament: 2 × 0.303in mg (forward).

'Spandau' Gun Conventional Allied misnomer for a modified version of the 7.92mm MASCHINENGEWEHR that became standard forward-firing armament on GERMAN ARMY AIR SERVICE warplanes from late 1915. The 'Spandau' replaced the lighter PARABELLUM, which was unsuitable for use with INTERRUPTER GEAR but continued to be used by observers. Like the Parabellum it was fitted with an enclosed ammunition belt to counter slipstream. Many of the guns were produced under licence by the Spandau arsenal near Berlin, and its trademark was mistaken for an official designation by the Allies.

Spanish Flu See: INFLUENZA PANDEMIC.

Spartacus League Revolutionary political organization formed in 1915 by a handful of left-wing Social Democratic Party (SDP) members in GERMANY. Its leaders, Reichstag deputy Karl Liebknecht and ideologue Rosa Luxemburg, were firmly against the prosecution of war in August 1914, and Liebknecht registered parliament's only vote against a second round of war credits in December of that year. Luxemburg's arguments against war and capitalism began appearing in the anonymous 'Spartacus Letters' from mid-1915, and the Spartacus League was formed later that year as a splinter group within the far more moderate SDP.

Liebknecht was imprisoned by the THIRD SUPREME COMMAND in 1917, but was released in October 1918 and reclaimed leadership of the group during the GERMAN REVOLUTIONS. Spartacists and other left-wingers united as the German Communist Party (KPD) on 1 January 1919, and what is known as the Spartacist Revolt was a period of uncoordinated mass unrest in Berlin during the first two weeks of January, culminating in brutal repression by GERMAN ARMY and FREIKORPS units rushed to the capital. Liebknecht and Luxemburg were summarily shot by the Army on the night of 15 January, and all the leaders of the KPD had been arrested by mid-January. The enduring myth of an organized Bolshevik coup was a creation of right-wing PROPAGANDA.

Spee, Admiral Maximilian Graf von (1861–1914) Danish-born officer whose entire adult life was spent in the GERMAN NAVY. A rear admiral from 1910, he commanded the East Asiatic Squadron in the Pacific in 1914, and spread panic through Allied trade routes all over the southern hemisphere by detaching light CRUISERS for individual long-range raiding as soon as war was declared. Tracked to the west coast of South America, he destroyed the ROYAL NAVY's relatively weak regional squadron at CORONEL on 1 November 1914, but was himself caught and outgunned by a British fleet at the FALKLAND ISLANDS in December. Spee, who had visited the Falklands against the advice of his captains, was among 2,200 German sailors killed during the battle (as were his two sons), and was mourned as one of GERMANY's first wartime martyrs.

'Spider's Web' Highly successful system of ANTI-SUBMARINE flying-boat patrols used in the North Sea by the British RNAS from May 1917. An octagonal pattern of 60-mile (96km) patrol lines, centred on the North Hinder lightship, enabled four of the latest long-range CURTISS H-12 or FELIXSTOWE flying-boats to cover an area of over 10,000 square kilometres in five hours. The Web lay across the known routes of surfaced U-BOATS crossing the North Sea to bases in Wilhelmshaven and Kiel (see ROOM 40), and its first victim was UC36 on 20 May 1917. Several more kills were later claimed and, although most were unconfirmed, the system certainly contributed to the restriction of U-boat traffic in British home waters, and remained in operation until the ARMISTICE.

Spring Offensives Collective description often applied to the GERMAN ARMY's three major attacks on the WESTERN FRONT of spring 1918. Planned using forces withdrawn from the inactive EASTERN FRONT (see Treaty of BREST-LITOVSK), the campaign was a gamble by the German THIRD SUPREME COMMAND, which hoped to end the war in France before US ARMY build-up made overall victory impossible. All three phases of the campaign – the KAISERSCHLACHT Offensive near Arras in late March, the Flanders attack on the LYS in April, and the third AISNE battle in May – made sweeping early gains and appeared likely to achieve a decisive breakthrough, but petered out as troops became exhausted and supply lines lengthened. The final advance, turned back at the MARNE in mid-June, left German forces incapable of further offensive action, and Allied armies never again lost the initiative (see AMIENS OFFENSIVE). See MAP 9. See also: GERMANY; FRANCE; GREAT BRITAIN.

Springfield Rifle The standard wartime RIFLE of the US ARMY, a reliable weapon produced in a short-barrelled version for all arms of the AEF in Europe and one of the few items of equipment they brought with them from the UNITED STATES. Also available in a Mk1 automatic rifle version, it was comparable in performance with the British Short LEE-ENFIELD and variants remained in US service until the Korean War.

Stallupönen, Battle of Opening engagement of the campaign in EAST PRUSSIA in August 1914. The Russian First Army (RENNENKAMPF) crossed the eastern border between the Masurian Lakes and the fortified zone around Königsberg on 15 August, and its southern flank was attacked two days later by a German corps under General von FRANÇOIS near the village of Stallupönen, less than 10km from the frontier. François had been specifically ordered to wait at prepared positions some 30km west, and ignored instructions to withdraw until after a Russian division had been forced to retreat, giving up 3,000 prisoners. The rest of the Russian First Army was unaffected by the attack but paused until 19 August, partly for reorganization but also because Russian invasion plans required it to delay. See also: PLAN 19; Battle of GUMBINNEN; MAP 12.

Stamboliski, Alexander (1879–1923) The leading anti-monarchist in prewar BULGARIA, parliamentary leader of the small national peasant party (BANU), and a fierce personal critic of Tsar FERDINAND I. In favour of republican status, arms reduction and international arbitration to settle territorial disputes, Stamboliski warned Ferdinand and prime minister RADOSLAVOV to expect revolution after alliance with the CENTRAL POWERS in September 1915, and was imprisoned for life when he made his sentiments public.

Released by the Tsar on 25 September 1918, after three years denouncing war from prison, he demanded an immediate armistice in return for calming revolutionary troop disorders on the BALKAN FRONT. On arrival at the garrison town of Radomir he was placed at the head of a revolutionary government, but its march on Sofia was defeated by German and loyal Bulgarian troops, and Stamboliski rejoined constitutional politics as a cabinet member from early 1919. Appointed prime minister by Tsar Boris III in October, his government signed the Treaty of NEUILLY with the Allies in November and embarked on a radical programme of tax reforms designed to benefit only the peasantry. He was murdered during a right-wing coup in 1923.

Standard Aircraft The Standard Aircraft Corporation of New Jersey underwent enormous expansion after the UNITED STATES entered the War, delivering its first three H-2 reconnaissance biplanes to the US ARMY in 1917 and becoming the nation's second largest manufacturer by the end of 1918. A few Standard H-3 reconnaissance models saw active service in MEXICO during early 1917, and the company's third design, the mass-produced SJ-1 Trainer, was second in importance only to the CURTISS 'JENNY' in providing instruction for the rapidly expanding USAAS. Standard's wartime resources were largely devoted to licensed construction of Allied designs – including the AIRCO DH-4, CAPRONI CA and HANDLEY PAGE 0/400 bombers. Its most successful wartime design, the E-1, was obsolete for its intended role as a home-defence FIGHTER, but was accepted by the USAAS as an advanced trainer in 1918.

BRIEF DATA (E-1) Type: single-seat trainer; Engine: 80hp le Rhône or 100hp Gnôme; Max speed: 168kph; Ceiling: 4,480m; Armament: none (provision for 1 × mg)

Stanley, Edward See: Lord DERBY.

Stavka The RUSSIAN ARMY's wartime central command. Headed before 1914 by a succession of nonentities chosen for their docility by war minister SUKHOMLINOV, it was expanded during the 1914 JULY CRISIS and given nominal overall control of Army operations. As long as mobilization was in progress, Stavka retained some influence over regional commands by controlling allocation of resources, but once it was complete the regional commands behaved with almost total disregard for central authority.

C-in-C Grand Duke NIKOLAI spent the first year of war in a converted train midway between the two main theatres of the EASTERN FRONT, with few staff, unreliable frontline communications and no consistent strategy. His chief of staff, YANUSHKEVICH, was one of Sukhomlinov's nonentities, and the impossible task of coordinating the war effort devolved on quartermaster general DANILOV.

Though often unaware of developments at the front until they were announced in the press, Stavka was blamed for the defeats of 1915, and Nikolai was replaced on 1 September, when NICHOLAS II took personal control, with ALEXEEV as chief of staff. Backed by the Tsar's personal authority Stavka became the genuine centre of Russian military policy, but still lacked bureaucratic facilities and a coherent strategy. Stavka headquarters at Mohiglev became a refuge for loyalist senior officers after the OCTOBER REVOLUTION until it was stormed by RED GUARDS on 3 December 1918, by which time the Russian Army had ceased to exist.

Stockholm Conference International conference of socialists held in the Swedish capital in July and August 1917, seeking to bring the minority anti-War ZIMMERWALD MOVEMENT together with the majority of 'patriot-socialists' working in alliance with belligerent governments. Arguments between Allied and German majority socialists had hitherto prevented any meeting, and had not been resolved when invitations to Stockholm were issued by the Russian Congress of Soviets in June 1917, effectively dooming the conference to failure. French, US and Italian socialists were anyway refused passports by their governments, and public opinion persuaded the British to rescind permission. Russian and neutral delegates met alongside the third meeting of Zimmerwald pacifists, but discussions were overshadowed by increasing turbulence inside RUSSIA, and basic differences between revolutionaries and patriots were not resolved.

Stokhod Offensive See: BRUSILOV OFFENSIVE.

Stöger-Steiner von Steinstätten, General Rudolf (1861–1921) Austrian soldier with good royal connections who led an infantry division in GALICIA from August 1914, and was a corps commander on the ISONZO from the following May. His appointment to succeed KROBATIN as imperial war minister in April 1917 represented a compromise between Austrian and Hungarian influences at court. Faced with the impossible (and connected) tasks of supplying the field armies and maintaining internal order, Stöger-Steiner regarded military victory as impossible by early 1918, when he recalled seven frontline divisions to quell urban unrest (see AUSTRIA-HUNGARY). Though bereft of real authority by late 1918, he remained at his post until November, vainly attempting to organize an orderly demobilization before retreating into private life.

Stormtroopers See: INFILTRATION TACTICS.

Strategic Bombing The potential of aircraft to launch long-range attacks deep inside hostile territory and to disrupt an enemy's vital socioeconomic processes had been recognized by the first prewar military aviation authorities. The idea that they could be a decisive weapon in any war between economically developed states, pioneered by Italian theorist Douhet, was well known throughout Europe but remained well ahead of technological progress in 1914.

Fleets of aircraft were assembled to carry out massed raids on hostile cities, factories and military installations at a very early stage, but units formed in 1914 by the GERMAN ARMY AIR SERVICE, AÉRONAUTIQUE MILITAIRE and RNAS were not equipped with machines remotely capable of the task in terms of lifting ability or endurance. German ZEPPELIN airships could reach targets, but existed in only small numbers and were prohibitively vulnerable.

The few Russian SIKORSKI IM heavy bombers were the only genuine strategic aircraft in operation, but their technically successful long-range raids (begun in spring 1915) were relative 'pinpricks' conducted by a handful of machines using primitive bombs. The rather smaller Italian CAPRONI CA bombers also entered the conflict in 1915, used in larger numbers against Austro-Hungarian targets, and the two designs stimulated development of viable types elsewhere.

By 1917 the German aero industry had produced aircraft capable of testing heavy-bomber theory. Its GOTHA G-TYPES began long-range operations against GREAT BRITAIN and FRANCE in mid-1917, and were ultimately accompanied by huge, technically advanced REISENFLUGZEUG machines. British HANDLEY PAGE designs were also capable of hauling significant loads over long distances, and the later Caproni marks performed efficiently on the ITALIAN FRONT.

Fleets of these and less suitable designs carried out long campaigns intended to vindicate the arguments of strategic bombing enthusiasts on all sides, loudest among them British air chief TRENCHARD, whose INDEPENDENT AIR FORCE in 1918 represented the biggest wartime experiment in the field. Broadly speaking these campaigns were costly and consistently disappointing. Improving ANTI-AIRCRAFT techniques and FIGHTER designs made even the best and most complex bombers unsafe for daylight operations, and they were usually unable to find, let alone hit, specific long-range targets at night. Compelled to carry out general 'area' attacks, their increased bomb loads remained insufficient to do significant damage to particular targets or to inflict widespread economic paralysis.

The pace of wartime aviation development nevertheless encouraged Trenchard and others to believe that bigger machines, better bombs, improved techniques and new sighting instruments were just around the corner at the ARMISTICE. Apart from direct support for ground forces (as perfected by the later Luftwaffe), strategic bombing was the only recognized option for future offensive use of aircraft in 1919. The postwar RAF was designed for strategic bombing, and by 1939 the unproven theory that massed air raids could win wars virtually overnight was widely accepted. See also: OBERNDORF RAID; AERIAL WARFARE.

Stresemann, Gustav (1878–1929) A National Liberal Party deputy in the German Reichstag from 1907, Stresemann was an advocate of constitutional reform, but this was balanced by his strong industrial connections, convinced monarchism, and commitment to colonial expansionism. On the right of his party, and a particularly strong supporter of prewar naval expansion, he was National Liberal leader Ernst Bassermann's closest advisor in 1914 and his successor in 1917. He gave personal support to the annexationist policies of the THIRD SUPREME COMMAND, but his calls for permanent control of BELGIUM and overseas expansion (rather than exploitation of eastern Europe) were ignored. The National Liberals broke with the socialist parties in January 1918 over the latter's support for munitions strikes in Berlin, and were swept out of existence in the atmosphere of political polarization surrounding the

GERMAN REVOLUTIONS. Stresemann returned to the Reichstag at the 1919 elections as head of his own German People's Party, briefly holding office as coalition chancellor in 1923, and more significantly as foreign minister (1923–29), in which role he negotiated the Locarno Pact with Russia (1925) and Germany's admittance to the League of Nations (1926).

Strypa, Battle of the See: BESSARABIAN OFFENSIVE.

Sturdee, Admiral Sir Frederick (1859–1925) An opponent of Admiral FISHER's prewar ROYAL NAVY reforms, Sturdee was appointed chief of the naval staff in August 1914 but showed little aptitude for staffwork. Doggedly maintaining CRUISER patrols in the North Sea (see *CRESSY*), he allowed naval minister CHURCHILL to dominate policy making and was dismissed on Fisher's return to office in October. Given command of the south Atlantic task force in November, he achieved a somewhat fortunate victory at the FALKLAND ISLANDS, which brought him national acclaim.

Sturdee took command of the Fourth Battle Squadron with the GRAND FLEET in February 1915 (see *DREADNOUGHT*). He led it at JUTLAND, and was among the strongest subsequent critics of fleet commander JELLICOE's performance. He was King GEORGE V's nominee to succeed Jellicoe in December 1916, but was passed over in favour of BEATTY and received no further wartime advancement.

Stürgkh, Karl, Count von (1859–1916) A trenchant conservative dedicated to the maintenance of imperial AUSTRIA-HUNGARY under Germanic domination, Stürgkh was appointed minister-president of Austria in 1911. He reacted to persistent opposition from socialist and Czech nationalist groups by suspending the Austrian parliament in March 1914 and governing by royal decree until his death. Stürgkh's 'absolutism' drove political tensions into extraconstitutional expression, and his wartime policies encouraged open revolt. Imposing strict press censorship and restricting the right of popular assembly, he allowed the military to infiltrate both bureaucratic appointments and civil policing in Austria. Regarded as too moderate by extreme militarists, Stürgkh was assassinated on 21 October 1916 by the son of socialist leader Viktor ADLER.

Stürmer, Boris (1848–1917) Retired Russian bureaucrat who remained active at court in 1914, establishing contacts with RASPUTIN and other conservative figures, and was a surprise appointment to replace the even older GOREMYKIN as prime minister in February 1916. Regarded by the crown as a fresh but politically reliable face, Stürmer's workload was limited by poor health. Popular with the Empress ALEXANDRA, he sought stability by excluding dissent, was detested by many cabinet colleagues and was a confirmed enemy of the Duma. From March 1916 he was also interior minister, but exchanged the portfolio to replace SAZONOV at the foreign office in July, leading the Empress to suspect him of personal ambition. Under attack for incompetence from all sides, and discredited by rumours of his complicity with the CENTRAL POWERS, Stürmer was finally sacrificed in November 1916. Arrested after the FEBRUARY REVOLUTION, he died in prison on 2 September 1917. See also: RUSSIA.

Submarines Serious worldwide naval interest in ships that could travel underwater began in the mid-1880s, aroused by the development of self-propelling TORPEDOES. At first France led the world in the design and construction of steam-powered underwater boats, which fell into two broad categories: true submarines, cigar-shaped with a conning tower, were single-hulled vessels intended to travel only underwater and restricted to very short-range operations; boat-hulled 'submersibles' were longer-range surface craft that could dive underwater for a few minutes at a time.

The distinction was blurred in the work of independent US designer J. P. Holland, whose small *Holland X* (1901) was enclosed in two hulls, using air pumped between them to control buoyancy and underwater trim. The design set the standard for European navies, and by 1914 both GREAT BRITAIN and GERMANY were producing relatively large, diesel-powered boats capable of long-range offensive patrol work.

Though slow, fragile, uncomfortable and able to dive for only a few hours at a time, the submarine was a potential threat to battlefleet orthodoxy, guaranteeing opposition from conservative naval leaders worldwide (see NAVAL WARFARE). Professional and public opinion also shared doubts about the moral acceptability of 'underwater torpedo boats'. Every major navy had its enthusiasts for greatly expanded submarine forces, and all were interested in long-range 'offensive' boats, but none regarded their development as a major priority before 1914.

The FRENCH NAVY possessed the world's largest submarine fleet in August 1914, but few of its 123 boats were fit for military operations, and the service suffered from constant prewar experimentation, which precluded standardization and created severe maintenance difficulties. Failure to develop a reliable diesel engine meant that most long-range boats were steam-powered and dangerously slow to dive. Mechanical unreliability, poor periscopes, ill-positioned hydroplanes (for underwater stability) and restrictions on diving depth imposed by externally mounted torpedo tubes also hampered wartime performance.

French shipyards completed only 28 new boats in wartime (against 15 losses and dozens of retirements), and most Allied submarine development was carried out by the British, who engaged in series production of ever larger and more powerful craft. Britain had produced the first diesel-powered offensive patrol boats from 1909, and had 17 D- and E-Type vessels in service by August 1914, along with 40 older B- and C-Types for coastal operations.

The E-Type design, regularly improved and enlarged, was the mainstay of British wartime operations (see *E-11*). Another 46 were built up to 1917 (including 6 minelayers), and overall production included a further 88 boats of various experimental types, culminating in giant 'fleet' submarines (see *K-1*). With 137 serving boats at the ARMISTICE and 78 more under construction, the ROYAL NAVY possessed the largest and most successful Allied fleet, although it suffered 54 wartime losses, including 7 boats scuttled in the BALTIC when German forces overran FINLAND in 1918.

The RUSSIAN NAVY possessed 41 coastal submarines in August 1914, and some two dozen new boats were in service by late 1917, but their weapons and other equipment were generally inferior and they had little success, sinking only a handful of steamers and sailing craft in the Baltic and the BLACK SEA.

The ITALIAN NAVY had only 25 coastal boats by 1915, and material shortages meant that very little wartime construction was possible. Targeted against warships in the Adriatic and around the country's long coastline, they shared the surface fleet's logistic difficulties and scored no significant successes, against 7 boats lost.

Although the US NAVY possessed 51 boats in 1914, none were suitable for long-range operations and most were obsolete. Expansion from 1915 produced a few long-range (L Class) boats over the next two years, and they served without loss or significant success on wartime ANTI-SUBMARINE patrols.

The AUSTRO-HUNGARIAN NAVY possessed seven small coastal boats in August 1914, but only five were suitable for active service. No wartime production was possible, and six boats under construction were taken over by GERMANY in November 1914, but a few small German boats were sent in pieces to the Adriatic base of Pola and assembled for use by Austro-Hungarian crews. German submarines operating from Adriatic bases often flew the Austro-Hungarian flag to enable attacks on Italian shipping before Italy declared war on Germany, but Austrian successes were few.

The GERMAN NAVY ultimately possessed the largest, most technically advanced and ambitiously deployed contemporary submarine service, but had no boats before 1906. Long-range diesel-powered boats were in service from 1913 (see *U-19*), but only 10 were available the following August, intended to operate against warships in the North Sea, while 18 older boats covered coastal defence and training.

The German Navy opted for series production of relatively few designs, with consequent benefits to maintenance, training standards and operational experience. Its best 1914 submarines had reliable engines, excellent periscopes, relatively efficient torpedoes and an operational range of up to 6,500km. A further 134 U-BOATS were operational in wartime, along with 132 small UB-BOATS and 79 minelaying UC-BOATS. All three types became steadily larger and more seaworthy, with a general slight increase in surface and submerged speeds, quicker diving times, better torpedoes, and bigger surface armament. Variations on basic designs included *U-71* to *U-80*, built as long-range minelayers or supply ships, and massive 'U-cruisers' (see *U-155*).

Deployed against commerce and skilfully handled, German submarines came close to achieving decisive results in 1917, but the number of boats at sea (never more than 61) was insufficient to paralyse Allied maritime communications completely. Wartime losses were very high, with 192 boats sunk or interned before the Armistice and more than 5,400 crew killed. See SUBMARINE WARFARE; *HANDELSKRIEG*.

Submarine Warfare Prewar naval strategists divided operational use of SUBMARINES into offensive and defensive categories. Defensive warfare involved coastal boats lying in wait against attacks on home ports or attacking warships engaged in close BLOCKADE. Most of the small submarines designed in the previous decade were capable of these short-range operations in 1914. Offensive submarine warfare – defined in 1914 as attacking warships further afield, ideally in or near their bases – was regarded by some naval leaders as intrinsically unethical, and by most as a major threat to battlefleet safety.

Except as a deterrent to surface attack, defensive coastal boats proved less important than expected in wartime. Close blockades were not generally attempted using warships, and coastal raids by surface ships were usually too fleeting to be caught by slow submarines.

Long-range offensive boats, sometimes towed to distant targets, were in their infancy, but the few suitable German and British submarines made an immediate wartime impression with their patrols in the North Sea and the Heligoland Bight, respectively, persuading the British GRAND FLEET into temporary retreat on the northern Irish coast, and obliging the German HIGH SEAS FLEET to use the Kiel Canal for access to the western Baltic. An early rash of warship sinkings contributed to a generalized outbreak of 'periscopitis' (the sighting of imagined submarines or their imaginary secret bases) that affected belligerent fleet commanders everywhere (see e.g. *CRESSY*; *AMALFI*).

Wartime technical development was dominated by the British and German services, and both quickly recognized serious weaknesses in their performance against warships. Hostile fleets proved hard to find once at sea, and the reconnaissance value of submarines was further limited by lack of reliable long-range RADIO (the British were frequently required to use CARRIER PIGEONS). Warships could generally avoid submarine attack by zigzagging at high speed, and most early sinkings were made possible by failure to adopt rehearsed anti-submarine manoeuvres.

Submarines were also too slow for opportunistic action against fleets and had no surface guns in 1914, so that sighting by even small warships (unsuitable for torpedo attack) forced them to dive. Slow diving times, just over a minute for the best British boats but three to four minutes for U-BOATS, made any kind of contact with enemy fleet DESTROYERS highly dangerous. The complex new technology of submarines was ill-suited to regular wartime operation, so that breakdowns and damage routinely reduced all sides to about a third of their nominal strength.

Submarine successes against warships never entirely dried up – the old British PRE-DREADNOUGHT *Britannia* was sunk off Cape Trafalgar on 10 November 1918 – but became far less frequent as fleets were handled with increasing caution. The ROYAL NAVY nevertheless maintained most of its best submarines with the Grand Fleet, and developed faster 'fleet' boats for the purpose (see *K-1*). The GERMAN NAVY generally kept only a few defensive submarines with the High Seas Fleet itself, but occasionally recalled large numbers to take part in fleet actions, usually stationing them off British bases to little effect (see Battles of JUTLAND, the DOGGER BANK).

The submarine's reputation as a potentially decisive weapon was most amply fulfilled in its role as a commerce raider. Large-scale operations against supply and transport shipping became feasible once wartime experience demonstrated the long-range potential of modern boats. The British sent a few submarines into the BALTIC and the DARDANELLES with considerable success, and RUSSIAN NAVY submarines sank one or two steamers, but from late 1914 the German Navy diverted its main submarine effort to Allied trade routes. Early German sinkings, and most Allied, were conducted under 'prize rules' – requiring a submarine to surface, search and warn any non-military target – but these rules were gradually abandoned as part of GERMANY's all-out commerce campaign from early 1915. See HANDELSKRIEG.

The requirements of commerce warfare dictated the design and development of U-boats from 1915. Increased range and surface speed, faster diving times and better TORPEDOES were obvious requirements, but alternative weapons were needed to deal with smaller ships while conserving limited torpedo supplies. Surface guns steadily increased in size up to 150mm, but shells were bulky cargo and commanders preferred to scuttle small ships or sink them with explosive charges whenever possible.

German UC-boats were developed as MINELAYERS, sinking more than a million tons of Allied merchant shipping, and small numbers of boats were adapted for the role by Allied navies. British (and French) boats were also regularly employed as ANTI-SUBMARINE craft – particularly in surface ambushes at destinations located by ROOM 40 intercepts – and were responsible for destroying 17 U-boats with torpedoes. The German Navy occasionally used MEDITERRANEAN U-boats to supply SENUSSI forces in North Africa, and submarines on all sides dropped or rescued agents behind enemy lines. See also: NAVAL WARFARE; *U-155*; ARCTIC THEATRE.

Sudan African territory jointly administered by Britain and EGYPT since their suppression of large-scale tribal unrest in the late 19th century. Endemic lawlessness and Turkish agitation among the largely Muslim population required the wartime presence of some 14,000 Egyptian Army troops in the Sudan (see EGYPTIAN FORCES), along with a battalion of British infantry (and ARTILLERY support) at the capital, Khartoum. The Sudanese economy, moribund and confused in 1914, enjoyed a wartime boom generated by the supply requirements of British forces in Egypt and EAST AFRICA, and Turkish attempts at political destabilization met with little success. Ottoman emissary Elmaz Bey was arrested when he tried to incite rebellion among Egyptian troops at Port Sudan in 1915, and a Turkish-inspired rebellion in the autonomous western province of Darfur ended in 1916 with the annexation of the territory by Arab irregulars in Anglo-Egyptian service. Independent tribal disobedience, mostly expressed as brigandage or religious fervour, was generally on a very small scale, although risings in the Nuba mountains, on the Eritrean border and just inside Uganda required more serious military responses in 1917–18. See MAP 17.

Suez Canal Vital trade artery linking Suez on the Red Sea with Port Said in the MEDITERRANEAN, running for about 150km on the edge of the Sinai peninsula (see MAP 22). The Canal's integrity was considered vital to British strategic interests, and British troops had occupied its host nation, EGYPT, since the establishment of an informal protectorate in the 1890s.

An attack across Sinai was feared if TURKEY joined the CENTRAL POWERS, and reports of roads being built across Ottoman Palestine seemed to confirm this expectation, but British concern with the WESTERN FRONT outweighed worries about the potential danger to Suez in 1914. Though INDIAN ARMY troops were stationed in Egypt en route for France, serious preparation for Canal defence was only begun once Turkey's intentions became clear.

Troops were then held in Egypt, and by

January 1915 about 70,000 troops from India, Britain, Australia and New Zealand were gathered under General Maxwell, 30,000 of them available for Canal defence. Weakness in ARTILLERY was compensated by the presence of an Anglo-French naval squadron, headed by the British PRE-DREADNOUGHTS *Swiftsure* and *Ocean*, and a small air reconnaissance force operated from primitive converted AIRCRAFT CARRIERS. The railway junction (and river influx point) at Ismailia, in the centre of the Canal, was the most obvious and heavily defended target, but smaller forces were concentrated all along the Canal, broadly divided into northern, central and southern zones.

Turkish preparations for a strike on Suez had been underway since August 1914. The Turkish Fourth Army, based in Damascus, was responsible for Ottoman Syria and Palestine, and commander DJEMAL PASHA planned a popular Muslim uprising in Egypt to back a major invasion.

Operations were restricted by lack of roads and RAILWAYS. Suez could only be reached by a march across 300km of desert from the forward base at Beersheba, itself 100km beyond a much-interrupted series of rail links from the north. A chain of supply and water stations was established across Sinai, but the desert march was only feasible during the brief rainy season.

Djemal's Suez Expeditionary Force, about 25,000 troops in two main 'echelons', left Beersheba on 14 January 1915 with only two months to complete its mission, and just four days at the Canal between withdrawals for water supplies. Once the columns had concentrated in early February, he planned to storm Ismailia in force after feints all along the canal had confused defenders. Surprise was vital to success, but aircraft warned British authorities of the general attack area on 1 February.

A dawn advance by the main Turkish force against east bank defences near Ismailia was held by Indian infantry on 3 February, and fighting had died down by mid-morning. Feints elsewhere had proved too small to distract the defenders seriously, and Ismailia was soon reinforced by AUSTRALIAN infantry. The Turkish Expeditionary Force retired in good order that night, returning to Beersheba by mid-February. The action cost about 150 British casualties, and the TURKISH ARMY admitted to losing 1,400 men.

Defeat was a serious blow to Djemal's military reputation, and to the morale of Turkish forces promised lavish prizes from the new Egypt. Both sides were subsequently distracted by the requirements of the GALLIPOLI and MESOPOTAMIAN FRONTS, and Turkish plans for a further offensive were delayed until early 1916. See: Battle of RAMADI; PALESTINE FRONT.

Sukhomlinov, General Vladimir (1848–1926) A trusted military advisor to Tsar NICHOLAS II, appointed war minister in 1909, Sukhomlinov sought to reform the RUSSIAN ARMY's antiquated tactical doctrines, reducing the predominant role of CAVALRY in offensive operations and of FORTRESSES in defensive warfare. He secured finance for massive military expansion with cooperation from liberal nationalist politicians in the Duma, but was restricted by entrenched opposition from the Army's prestigious cavalry and ARTILLERY arms, which had the backing of Grand Duke NIKOLAI and other senior aristocratic figures (see GREAT PROGRAMME; PLAN 19).

Expecting a short war, Sukhomlinov argued successfully for full mobilization against both AUSTRIA-HUNGARY and GERMANY during the latter stages of the 1914 JULY CRISIS. Aware that the central Army command (STAVKA) had little actual control over individual fronts, he evaded the Tsar's efforts to install him as wartime C-in-C.

Partly because he upset vested interests, and partly because he was a corrupt official with a notoriously debauched lifestyle, Sukhomlinov was one of the most controversial figures in contemporary Russian society. Some of his many enemies, including former deputy minister POLIVANOV, conspired to damage his reputation fatally in spring 1915, when one of Sukhomlinov's agents in the Army, Colonel Miasoedov, was arrested and executed on flimsy treason charges. Held responsible for subsequent military defeats on the EASTERN FRONT, Sukhomlinov was dismissed by the Tsar in June and placed under house arrest in early 1916. Released during the FEBRUARY REVOLUTION but re-arrested in September 1917, he was finally freed to German exile in May 1918.

Super-Dreadnoughts See: *ORION.*

Supreme War Council The organ of combined Allied command over military operations in western Europe, formed on 9 November 1917 at the RAPALLO CONFERENCE. Originally no more than a consultative committee established to coordinate support for the ITALIAN FRONT in the wake of the CAPORETTO defeat, its first military representatives were Generals FOCH (France), WILSON (Britain), BLISS (USA) and CADORNA (Italy). Italian involvement was largely honorary, since ITALY was dependent on Allied military and economic aid, and subsequent US participation was largely apolitical, but the Council represented a means for the governments of GREAT BRITAIN and FRANCE to increase their strategic authority over military commanders.

British premier LLOYD GEORGE promoted the appointment of Foch to command a strategic reserve of Allied troops on the WESTERN FRONT, directly responsible to the Council, as a means of curtailing HAIG's independence, and CLEMENCEAU later worked directly with Foch to overrule the defensive plans of French C-in-C PÉTAIN. The crisis of the German SPRING OFFENSIVES led to Foch's promotion (with Haig's support) as Allied supreme commander on the Western Front in April and for the Italian Front in June. The Council subsequently functioned as a forum for preliminary Allied debates over ARMISTICE and peace terms.

Sussex French cross-Channel ferry torpedoed without warning by the German SUBMARINE *UB-24* on 24 March 1916, a week before the second unrestricted campaign against British shipping was due to begin. Fifty civilians were killed, including a number of US citizens, prompting an ultimatum from the WILSON government, announced to Congress on 19 April, demanding an immediate halt to unrestricted attacks. Germany immediately complied, ordering all U-boats in British and MEDITERRANEAN waters (except the Aegean) to adhere to 'prize rules', sparing passenger ships and searching all merchantmen before sinkings. See also: *LUSITANIA*; *ARABIC*; *HANDELSKRIEG.*

Suvla Bay Offensive The main Allied summer offensive on the GALLIPOLI FRONT in 1915. Allied C-in-C HAMILTON had failed in repeated efforts to break through Turkish lines at HELLES in the south, and plans to extend the besieged ANZAC COVE beachhead had been postponed for lack of reinforcements against growing Turkish forces. The Anzac Cove plans were revived in expanded form when British war minister KITCHENER promised Hamilton three more divisions in June.

Aware that he was expected to win a decisive victory, Hamilton planned an ambitious triple offensive for early August. Exhausted Anglo-French forces at Helles, under the temporary command of General Street, were to carry out a holding attack, and General BIRDWOOD's longstanding plan was adopted for an advance north of Anzac Cove against Sari Bair Ridge. The plan's main novelty was a major landing further north on the Aegean coast at Suvla Bay.

With Turkish forces occupied elsewhere, Suvla was expected to be lightly defended, and Hamilton intended most of three divisions under General Stopford to advance rapidly inland over relatively easy ground and make contact with Anzac Cove. From a greatly enlarged northern front, 60,000 troops would then cut off the southern peninsula and secure the DARDANELLES (see MAP 20).

Stopford and his division commanders were completely new to modern warfare, a weakness compounded by Hamilton's characteristic failure to coordinate overall operational planning. Street and Birdwood were not fully aware of their primary role as cover for Stopford's invasion, and Stopford was allowed to proceed with a cautious agenda based on consolidation of a beachhead at Suvla.

The offensive opened on 6 August and immediately lost cohesion. Street exceeded his brief in Helles and attempted a full-scale attack, which broke down completely by 10

August. The SARI BAIR operation suffered delay and confusion, and the attack across exhausting terrain was driven back with heavy losses the same day, although a subsidiary attack captured LONE PINE further south.

Turkish regional C-in-C LIMAN VON SANDERS, aware of the British build-up for an attack, had spread his forces to meet most eventualities, but only 1,500 men and five field guns (the 'Anafarta Detachment') were stationed at Suvla when the first of 20,000 British troops landed at about 22.00 on 6 August, meeting no concerted opposition but subject to steady SNIPING. Poor reconnaissance confused the landings, but assembly on the beaches was completed by the following morning.

Stopford made no serious attempt to advance his inexperienced troops until evening, when positions in the hills immediately inland were occupied at a cost of 1,700 casualties. Liman von Sanders heard about the landing at about the same time and ordered five divisions to the sector, expecting them to arrive too late to save the Anafarta force.

Satisfied that his mission was accomplished, Stopford ignored vague orders from Hamilton to advance and rested his men throughout 8 August. Hamilton arrived at Suvla by late afternoon, but only increased confusion with attempts to organize an immediate occupation of the commanding Tekke Tepe ridge to the east.

Liman von Sanders was less tolerant of delays to Turkish reinforcements from Bulair, which had halted for rest northeast of Tekke Tepe, dismissing their commander (Feizi Bey) and placing the entire sector under KEMAL PASHA. By next morning Kemal's troops had occupied the crest of the Ridge and the heights of the Anafarta Spur to the south, repelling uncoordinated British advances over the next few days and steadily reinforcing to surround the beachhead.

Having conjured defensive stalemate from a position of enormous advantage, Stopford was replaced by General de Lisle on 15 August. Divisional commands were given to experienced WESTERN FRONT generals MAUDE, BYNG and Fanshawe, but they inherited a tactical position similar to that at Anzac Cove. The fronts at Suvla and Anzac Cove were little more than 5km apart, and subsequent British operations were concerned with connecting them (see Battle of SCIMITAR HILL). Compound failure of the northern offensives cost about 18,000 Allied casualties, as well as several thousand new cases of dysentery at Suvla. Turkish losses exceeded 18,000 in the Anzac sector alone, along with casualties at Suvla variously estimated at between 9,000 and 20,000 men.

Sydney Class Class of three CRUISERS, typical of TOWN CRUISER designs, in wartime use with AUSTRALIAN FORCES. The British-built *Sydney* and *Melbourne* were completed in 1913, and the Australian-built *Brisbane* (which served exclusively in the Pacific) was completed in 1915. *Sydney* and *Melbourne* were the main warships of the ROYAL NAVY's Australian squadron in August 1914. They took part in the Allied search for German surface raiders in the southern oceans (see CORONEL), and *Sydney* sank the German light cruiser *EMDEN* at the Cocos Islands on 9 November. Both ships subsequently transferred to the West Indies and joined the GRAND FLEET in the North Sea after JUTLAND. They were returned to Australia in 1919.

BRIEF DATA (*Sydney*, 1914) Displacement: 5,400 tons; Crew: 475; Dimensions: length 458ft (138.8m), beam 49ft (14.8m); Speed: 25.5k; Armament: 8 × 6in gun, 1 × 3in AA, 2 × 21in TT.

Sykes–Picot Agreement Secret agreement to partition the Ottoman Empire among the Allies, arranged by British politician Sir Mark Sykes and French diplomat Georges Picot in early 1916. After TURKEY entered the War in November 1914, Allied assumptions of ultimate victory promoted the need to define territorial interests in the region, a situation complicated by the Anglo-French concession of Constantinople to RUSSIA in 1915. Appointed in November 1915, the two negotiators had achieved a broad understanding by February 1916, accepted in principle by Allied ministers in the second half of May.

The Agreement, which ignored promises made to ARAB REVOLT leaders by British authorities, gave Russia control of the ARMENIAN and Kurdish lands in the northeast Ottoman Empire; FRANCE was given effective control over Syria, the Lebanon and Turkish Cilicia (on the southeast coast of Asia Minor); Britain was to take over Mesopotamia as far inland as BAGHDAD, and exercise economic domination over much of PALESTINE and TRANSJORDAN. An unspecified international administration was to govern JERUSALEM and surrounding areas, but remaining parts of Arabia were to be independent. Among the secret treaties made public after the OCTOBER REVOLUTION in Russia, the arrangement polluted relations between Arab and Allied authorities into and far beyond the PARIS PEACE CONFERENCE. See also LAWRENCE, T.; FEISAL IBN HUSSEIN.

Synchronizing Gear See: INTERRUPTER GEAR.

Syria See: ARAB REVOLT; PALESTINE FRONT; TURKEY.

Szent István The last VIRIBUS UNITIS Class dreadnought, completed in November 1915 and the most valuable unit lost in action by the AUSTRO-HUNGARIAN NAVY. During one of its very few offensive operations, a dawn raid of 10 June 1918 against Allied ships of the OTRANTO BARRAGE, *Szent István* was sunk by fast Italian MAS BOATS. The sinking, which prompted abandonment of the raid, was captured on FILM and can still be seen.
BRIEF DATA See *VIRIBUS UNITIS*.

T

Tabora Offensive Anglo-Belgian attack into German EAST AFRICA of summer 1916, illustrative of the peculiar political and military conditions influencing operations in colonial AFRICA. Since its decision to abandon African neutrality in late August 1914 (see BERLIN ACT), the Belgian government had been seeking British aid for an invasion of northwestern East Africa from the Congo (see MAP 18). Governor Belfield of British East Africa blocked cooperation until early 1916, when General SMUTS proposed a joint advance to support his MOROGORO OFFENSIVE further east.

Agreement was reached in March to attack the German headquarters settlement of Tabora, on the colony's main RAILWAY, and two brigades of General Tombeur's Belgian colonial 'Force Publique' (10,000 ASKARIS, mostly Scandinavian officers, and 12 field guns) crossed into East Africa in June. A smaller British imperial force under General Crewe reached the southern shores of Lake Victoria at about the same time. Belgian colonial authorities were suspicious of British designs on the mineral-rich Katanga region, and the Allied armies ignored plans for mutual cooperation, embarking instead on a race south to the railway.

Both were frustrated by sharp German counterattacks and equally brisk retreats, but the Belgians won the race, taking the western railhead at Kigoma on 28 July and marching down the line to reach the forward defences of Tabora on 9 September. After a fierce rearguard action, some 5,000 German troops, accompanied by colonial administrators, escaped south just before the town was occupied on 19 September, and headed towards General LETTOW-VORBECK's main force. Having suffered almost 1,300 casualties, Tombeur declined further pursuit, and General Crewe's exhausted troops halted when they arrived at Tabora six days later.

Tafila, Battle of An attempt by Turkish forces to prevent the expansion of ARAB REVOLT operations north up the Dead Sea coast in early 1918, and one the most famous victories ascribed to LAWRENCE. At the request of British PALESTINE FRONT commander ALLENBY, elements of the Arab

Northern Army (FEISAL IBN HUSSEIN) pushed north from AQABA to disrupt Turkish grain and wood supplies from central Arabia. Without halting raids against the Turkish garrisons of MAAN and MEDINA, Feisal detached warbands commanded by his brother Zeid and sent them to the Dead Sea in mid-January. Though hampered by food shortages and coordination problems, the advance began well, taking Shobek and Tafila with little difficulty by mid-January.

The threat to Dead Sea trade routes brought 1,000 Turkish troops south on 23 January, and they overwhelmed Arab forward positions at Tafila the next day. Lawrence took command of the defence, concentrating about 500 troops on a 5km front where ridges either side converged into a road. After a delay while they removed MACHINE GUN posts manned by townspeople, Turkish troops established apparent tactical superiority by occupying the ridges. Unable to dig trenches in the rocks, and pinned down by accurate fire from the defensive line in the centre, they were outflanked on both sides by small Arab parties, and collapsed under the pressure of coordinated charges, losing 300 dead and a further 250 prisoners against only 65 Arab casualties. Arab forces pushed on to the Dead Sea port of El Mezra, where seven small warships of the Germano-Turkish Dead Sea flotilla surrendered on 28 January. See MAP 22.

Talaat Pasha, Mehmed (1874–1921) A minor post-office official until the YOUNG TURK revolution of 1908, and subsequently Ottoman interior minister, Talaat began his second term in office in early 1914. He guided TURKEY towards alliance with GERMANY in close association with war minister ENVER PASHA, but his precise role in relation to other leaders remains obscure. He and Enver were probably the only men fully informed about the secret alliance with Germany in July 1914, but he seems not to have shared Enver's optimism. Viewing war as a gamble by an Empire close to collapse, he apparently worked to maintain neutrality into October before giving Enver full support.

Talaat's wartime ministry supervised the subordination of society to the needs of the military, with maintenance of order and distribution of food supplies among his primary concerns. Despite later denials, his office was held responsible for the ARMENIAN MASSACRES and for widespread famine throughout the Empire, the latter exacerbated by profit-motivated mismanagement. Protected from personal criticism by strict censorship, Talaat remained at the heart of government into 1918, frequently handling negotiations with Berlin and becoming grand vizier when Said Halim Pasha resigned as nominal head of government in February 1916.

His opposition could not prevent Enver's renewal of operations on the CAUCASIAN FRONT from late 1917, and his political position collapsed with the fortunes of the military. From mid-1918 the relaxation of press censorship exposed him to virulent public attack, and he was widely regarded as a public enemy by the time he and the cabinet resigned on 14 October. His flight aboard a German ship on 2 November averted certain arrest, and he remained in exile in Berlin, where he was assassinated in an Armenian act of revenge.

Tampico Incident See: MEXICO; MAYO, H.

Tanga, Battle of First major engagement of the war in German EAST AFRICA, an amphibious attack in November 1914 by INDIAN ARMY forces on the colony's busiest port. Situated on a high plateau above its almost enclosed harbour, Tanga was only about 80km from the border with British East Africa, and was the coastal terminus of the strategically important Usambara RAILWAY (see MAP 18). It had been visited by a British warship on 17 August but was spared bombardment in return for a promise of local non-aggression, an agreement not regarded as binding by British imperial authorities.

The attack was planned by General Aitken, who had been ordered to conquer the entire colony with 8,000 poorly trained Indian reserves (Indian Expeditionary Force 'B'). Arriving at Mombasa on 31 October, Aitken made no attempt to conceal his intentions or reconnoitre Tanga in detail before attacking, and German East African commander Colonel LETTOW-VORBECK used advance warning to bring up reinforcements for the single company guarding Tanga. British delays were compounded after the CRUISER *Fox* arrived ahead of the invasion on 2 November to renounce officially the August agreement, and was allowed to believe that MINES had been laid in the harbour. The entire British force was eventually ashore about 3km south of Tanga by the evening of 3 November, and advanced on the town early next morning.

Attacking troops were allowed to bunch near the coast, and no forward patrols were sent to examine the town. German reserves arriving from the hinterland easily broke up two parties advancing on Tanga, and the attack had degenerated into confused jungle skirmishing by the afternoon. Fighting was interrupted by swarms of angry bees, which forced both sides to flee. The engagement is often called the 'Battle of the Bees', but they were a regular hazard of East African bush fighting.

With about 1,000 troops at his disposal, Lettow-Vorbeck counterattacked in the evening, driving British troops from poorly prepared positions and forcing a confused withdrawal that took all day on 5 November and left Force B's supplies on the beaches. The attack had cost 847 British casualties (360 dead), and German losses of 148 (67 dead) were eased by the capture of 16 machine guns, several hundred RIFLES and 600,000 rounds of ammunition. Lettow-Vorbeck's victory made him famous at home, prompting the GERMAN NAVY to prepare supply operations. Aitken was replaced, but the defeat at Tanga was not made public in GREAT BRITAIN for several months.

Tank Forts One of several successful methods devised by the GERMAN ARMY for dealing with the threat of TANKS on the WESTERN FRONT in 1918. Each 'fort' consisted of one or two field guns grouped in forward positions with several MACHINE GUNS, anti-tank RIFLES and an escort of infantry. Each field division was equipped with at least six such groupings. As a means of delivering the ARTILLERY needed to destroy armoured vehicles at close quarters, they were an effective response to Allied use of HEAVY TANKS in close support of infantry during the second half of the year.

Tanks Armoured, tracked vehicles mounting MACHINE GUNS or light ARTILLERY were developed from a blend of ideas and influences (mostly British but with French input), in response to the need for a mobile weapon to support infantry attacks in TRENCH WARFARE conditions on the WESTERN FRONT.

Discussed by BEF field officers from autumn 1914, the idea of an armoured motor vehicle, using the caterpillar tracks already in use for some agricultural machinery, was first officially mentioned by Colonel Hankey, secretary to the British Committee for Imperial Defence, in a memorandum of 26 December 1914 on 'special devices'.

The ROYAL NAVY, already using ARMOURED CARS in Flanders, was working along similar lines and considering projects varying from 'shields on wheels' to 'landships' with light CRUISER armament. Ideas germinated within the RNAS were passed to naval minister CHURCHILL, who read Hankey's memo and secured the formation of a technical Landships Committee in February 1915.

The committee produced its first technical specifications in June, demanding a minimum land speed of 4mph (6.4kph), rapid all-round manoeuvrability, and a range of at least 20 miles (32km). The US-built Holt caterpillar tractor was eventually selected as the basis for the chassis. The first prototype proved dangerously top-heavy, but a wooden mock-up of a second sufficiently impressed BEF observers in September for C-in-C HAIG to order 40 in advance.

Amid hopes that the new machines could break through German lines within a day, British munitions minister LLOYD GEORGE approved the project in February 1916, and full production of the Mark I HEAVY TANK began in April. Ultimately named after their coded transit designation as 'water tanks', the first Mark Is entered service with the Heavy Section of the Machine Gun Corps, renamed the Tank Corps, in June 1916.

Originally formed into companies of 24

machines, they were reorganized into battalions of 75 machines from October 1916 and into two-battalion brigades from early 1917. Early tactical doctrine stressed their infantry-support value, and cooperation from artillery and aircraft to knock out enemy batteries was considered important, although the RFC had not yet developed efficient ground-attack techniques.

Senior BEF commanders were willing to use tanks for other tasks – including small-scale attacks on particular objectives, mobile light-artillery operations, and transport or haulage duties – and their debut during the SOMME OFFENSIVE was an anti-climax. Against the advice of relatively junior officers in field command of tank units, Haig ordered Fourth Army commander RAWLINSON to mass all 49 serviceable Mark Is in an attack on a limited objective during the Battle of FLERS-COURCELETTE on 15 September 1916.

The Tanks were only made available for this action at the expense of under-trained crews and under-tested vehicles, but their relative failure hardly dimmed the enthusiasm of Haig or the British press, although it encouraged a body of opposition among conservative field commanders. The immediate terror they inspired in German infantry was not shared by the THIRD SUPREME COMMAND, which quickly resolved to concentrate on defeating tanks rather than disrupt urgent production schedules by imitation (see A7V).

The British had 60 Mark I and Mark II 'heavies' in service by spring 1917, but the improved Mark IV was delayed until after the attack at ARRAS in April, when piecemeal deployment and the ground-churning effects of PRELIMINARY BOMBARDMENT again undermined effectiveness. Mark IVs, strong enough to resist new German anti-tank RIFLES, were used in a minor role at MESSINES in June 1917, but most were ditched in marshy ground without reaching their targets.

Every available tank was deployed for the summer YPRES offensive. Spread out along the offensive line, with forward, secondary and reserve units attached to each sector, they were again bogged down in heavily bombarded mud, but tank commanders were allowed a massed attack on firm ground at CAMBRAI in November. Their stunning effect on the first day at Cambrai was spoiled by failure to withhold reserves for exploitation (again contrary to Tank Corps advice), but decided their role in future British offensives.

From late 1917 a lighter, more manoeuvrable design – the Medium or 'WHIPPET' Tank – was introduced to the Western Front, becoming the mainstay of British tank operations in 1918. Still very slow, prone to breakdown, and vulnerable to organized German artillery defence in 1918 (see TANK FORTS), they were almost useless in retreat, and half of the 370 British machines had to be abandoned during withdrawal from the German KAISERSCHLACHT Offensive in late March.

Other basic weaknesses included poor visibility, with communications consisting of messages tapped on the hull by infantrymen, and appalling operating conditions, characterized by noxious fumes, searing heat and the prospect of sudden incineration.

Stimulated by British progress, French research into *chars d'assaut* got underway in late 1915, with the Schneider-Creusot factory conducting experimental work under the supervision by Colonel Estienne, field commander of FRENCH ARMY tanks. Practical development began in February 1916, when the first orders for an armoured vehicle on a Holt tractor base were placed with the Schneider-Creusot and St Chalmond companies.

The two resulting designs both carried 75mm field guns as main armament, and were deployed as mobile artillery. Used for the first time at the start of the NIVELLE OFFENSIVE in April 1917, they were too narrow for effective cross-country manoeuvring, and production was switched to the RENAULT LIGHT TANK in October 1917. Surviving 'heavies' remained in service, operating in groups of four, and the far more numerous Renaults were deployed in battalions of 75 machines as close-support infantry weapons. Used by French and AEF forces during the later campaigns in France, they were never as effective or reliable as the comparable Whippets, which also equipped some US forces in 1918.

The opening assault of the Allied AMIENS OFFENSIVE was led by all 414 available British tanks massed on a narrow front. Their breakthrough on the first day was of great tactical value, but only 145 were fit for action on the second day, and dwindling numbers reduced their importance in subsequent actions. Specialist tactics designed for tanks had never been fully applied at the ARMISTICE, and their subsequent reputation as a war-winning weapon, especially strong in Britain, was partly created by postwar writers attempting to counter the entrenched conservative preference for CAVALRY (see FULLER, J.).

Tannenberg, Battle of Spectacular victory by the German Eighth Army over the Russian Second Army in late August 1914, effectively ending the Russian invasion of EAST PRUSSIA. General SAMSONOV's Second Army had been advancing slowly into the southwestern corner of the province since 20 August, intending to link up with the Russian First Army (RENNENKAMPF) advancing from the northeast. Rennenkampf's task was to preoccupy the Eighth Army while Samsonov brought his larger force into position in its rear, but he halted to recuperate after an inconclusive victory at GUMBINNEN on 20 August, expecting a German retreat to the Vistula.

German Eighth Army commander PRITTWITZ was dismissed for ordering just such a retreat. His replacements, HINDENBURG and LUDENDORFF, reached the front on 23 August and adopted a more aggressive plan, already proposed and detailed by deputy operations chief HOFFMANN. A screen of CAVALRY was left to delay and confuse Rennenkampf, while I Corps (FRANÇOIS) was rushed by RAILWAY to threaten Samsonov's left wing in the far southwest. The Eighth Army's other two corps at Gumbinnen were marched south to attack Samsonov's right, and a fourth corps stayed where it was, at prepared positions in the Second Army's path.

Advancing slowly into East Prussia, hampered by chaotic supply and communications lines, Samsonov was unaware of Rennenkampf's inertia or of German manoeuvres to surround him. Assured by overall commander ZHILINSKI, acting on Rennenkampf's assumptions, that his job was to cut off retreating German forces, Samsonov pushed his three central corps (12 divisions) to the west, leaving his weak northern corps holding a 60km front far to the northeast, where it was expected to meet up with the First Army. Most of his southern corps remained over the border around Mława until 27 August.

Samsonov's central group reached German lines on 22 August, and fought its way slowly forward over the next six days. Weight of numbers (and a series of effective flanking manoeuvres) brought a few local Russian successes, and the central group continued advancing into a trap long after German attacks had turned its flanks.

German delays and luck contributed to Samsonov's prolonged confusion. In the southwest, François was ordered to attack the Russian left wing on 25 August, but refused to advance until his ARTILLERY was in position on the morning of 27 August. When the attack came, two divisions broke through thinly held Russian lines and cut communications with the centre by taking the frontier town of Soldau, pinning most of the Russian left to the frontier. François ignored Ludendorff's initial order to move north towards Scholz and pushed east to cut off retreat from the centre.

In the northeast, Ludendorff delayed the final order to transfer from Gumbinnen until 25 August, aware that Rennenkampf might yet advance. Marching southwest on 26 August, corps commanders MACKENSEN and BELOW met and attacked Samsonov's left wing at Bischofsberg. Taken by surprise, and with its two divisions separated, it retreated for the border with heavy casualties.

Unconfirmed reports of large German forces moving south were believed only by STAVKA (Russian central command), but Zhilinski ignored instructions to speed the First Army towards Samsonov and issued orders for its cautious move west to Königsberg on 26 August. Informed of the move by intercepted RADIO messages, Ludendorff ordered Below to join the German centre and sent Mackensen to meet up with François.

Mackensen's and François's forces met on 29 August in Willenberg, and Samsonov was surrounded.

During 28 August, his communications in disarray and troops critically short of supplies, Samsonov became aware of the danger. One central corps had been routed and the main strength of his remaining forces was in cavalry, dispersed and virtually useless on the fringes of the battle. With artillery fire closing in from all sides, he cut remaining communications with headquarters and ordered a general retreat that night.

Disorganized Russian units manoeuvred blindly inside the German cordon, unable to locate its many weak spots, and were slaughtered or captured. Feeble relieving attacks from the frontier were halted without penetrating the ring, and only 10,000 of an estimated 150,000 men escaped. General Samsonov, lost in the forests, shot himself on 29 August. Almost 100,000 prisoners and 400 guns were taken by the Eighth Army, which lost less than 20,000 men.

The victory spawned an enduring myth in GERMANY that Hindenburg and Ludendorff were infallible, and shocked Allied opinion into believing the RUSSIAN ARMY beaten, but its significance was overrated. An immense tactical success, Tannenberg had not exhausted Russian resources in East Prussia, and had been an essentially defensive victory. The problems of attacking in 1914 became clear when German forces went on to the offensive in September (see First Battle of the MASURIAN LAKES). See MAP 12.

Taube Early centre-wing monoplane, built around a slender, tubular fuselage and designed by Austrian engineer Igo Etrich in 1910. The Taube ('Dove') was manufactured by various German and Austrian companies after Etrich waived patent rights in 1914, and appeared in a bewildering variety of slightly different versions. At a time when speed, manoeuvrability and armament were considered unimportant, its stable flight performance offered excellent reconnaissance capacity and was useful for early experiments in aerial bombing (in 1911 a Taube in Libya was the first aircraft to drop a bomb).

The type gained great fame at the start of the War, to the extent that any German machine was usually called a 'Taube' by Allied soldiers in 1914. It played a much-praised reconnaissance role (alongside AIRSHIPS) at TANNENBERG in late August, and a single machine bombed Paris on the WESTERN FRONT every evening during early September. Another lone Taube took part in the defence of TSINGTAO until November. Altogether about 500 Taubes were active with the GERMAN ARMY AIR SERVICE before they were replaced by more modern biplanes during spring 1915. Also widely employed by the AUSTRO-HUNGARIAN AIR SERVICE and the ITALIAN AIR FORCE, they were retained as trainers by all three forces until early 1917.

BRIEF DATA (German Kondor Taube II, 1914) Type: two-seat reconnaissance; Engine: 100 or 120hp, generally Mercedes; Max speed: 115kph; Ceiling: 3,000m; Armament: observer's small arms or hand-thrown bombs.

Tel es Sheria, Battle of See: Battle of the BEERSHEBA–GAZA LINE.

Thiepval Ridge, Battle of See: SOMME OFFENSIVE.

Third Supreme Command The military-industrial dictatorship established from late August 1916 by the GERMAN ARMY High Command under Generals HINDENBURG and LUDENDORFF (the tenures of chiefs of staff MOLTKE and FALKENHAYN had been the first and second supreme commands, respectively). Engineered into office by an alliance of senior army officers and heavy industrial magnates – both of which interest groups were strongly represented in wartime government (see KRA) – the Command sought to mobilize every aspect of German life for the production of weapons and munitions, hastening the economic and social collapse of a system already stressed to breaking point by the war effort (see HINDENBURG PROGRAMME). The High Command's decision to hand constitutional power to elected parliamentary representatives, authorized by Ludendorff on 29 September 1918, marked the effective end of the dictatorship (see GERMAN REVOLUTIONS). See also: GERMANY.

Thomas, Albert (1878–1932) French socialist of the 'gradualist' school, advocating cooperation with liberal parties as an opportunity to achieve reform. He gave full support to the VIVIANI government's calls for national unity in August 1914, and was entrusted with a vital position as under-secretary for munitions at the war ministry in May 1915. This new post – created as a means to recover political control from the alliance of war minister MILLERAND and the FRENCH ARMY high command – was used by Thomas to reorganize arms production in FRANCE completely.

Recognizing labour shortage as the main obstacle to expansion, he secured large-scale exemptions and releases from military service, promoted the employment of WOMEN, and mobilized labour from among refugees, colonial communities and prisoners of war. Improved training schemes were introduced to ensure long-term development, and strikes discouraged by generous wage rises.

Promoted to full ministerial status in December 1916, Thomas was a special ambassador to Petrograd (St Petersburg) after the FEBRUARY REVOLUTION, charged with encouraging the socialist PROVISIONAL GOVERNMENT to remain at war. Though personally sympathetic to KERENSKI he could not influence the wider situation in RUSSIA or dissuade the SOVIETS from inviting German delegates to the international STOCKHOLM CONFERENCE.

French delegates were ultimately refused passports for the Conference, prompting socialist withdrawal from the French government, and forcing Thomas to resign his ministry on 12 September 1917, shortly after his return to France. Excluded from CLEMENCEAU's administration, he participated in the PARIS PEACE CONFERENCE as a labour-relations expert, and drafted the relevant sections of the VERSAILLES Treaty.

Tiger Designed as a LION Class BATTLECRUISER but modified to resemble the British-built, Japanese *Kongo*, *Tiger* was completed in October 1914 with increased size, weight, secondary armament and engine power, joining the ROYAL NAVY's First Battlecruiser Squadron in the North Sea before the end of the year. It took part in the DOGGER BANK battle the following January, and suffered 21 heavy shell hits at JUTLAND in 1916, but was repaired in less than a month and survived the War.

BRIEF DATA (1914) Displacement: 35,000 tons; Crew: 1,185; Dimensions: length 704ft (213.3m), beam 90.5ft (27.4m); Speed: 30k; Armament: 8 × 13.5in gun, 12 × 6in, 2 × 3in AA, 4 × 21in TT.

Tikrit, Capture of Climactic engagement of the Anglo-Indian offensive on the MESOPOTAMIAN FRONT in autumn 1917, typical of operations in the campaign's latter stages. Following the Turkish defeat on the Euphrates at RAMADI in September, British C-in-C MAUDE sent two divisions under General Cobbe up the Tigris against new Turkish advanced positions 13km north of SAMARRAH. In mid-October, as soon as he was aware of British preparations, local Turkish commander Ismail Hakki Bey withdrew back to his original line in front of the town of Tikrit. Reinforced by a CAVALRY division, but unable to cut off the retreat, Cobbe concentrated his forces and attacked the town on 5 November.

On the west bank of the Tigris, built on cliffs overlooking the river, Tikrit was defended by a ring of trenches on its landward side. A strong frontal attack took the first line of Turkish trenches after three hours of heavy fighting, but defenders at the second line inflicted heavy casualties on a reckless CAVALRY charge before executing a skilful retreat into hills upriver at Fathah Gorge. Though they occupied Tikrit on 6 November, British forces found no supplies or equipment in the town, and Maude broke off his attempt to destroy Turkish counterattack capability. See MAP 23.

Tirpitz, Admiral Alfred von (1849–1930) Main sponsor of the GERMAN NAVY's rapid growth in the early 20th century, and an early expert in the use of TORPEDOES, Tirpitz was Prussian naval minister from 1897. Beginning with the Navy Laws of 1898 and 1900, he worked to overcome preoccupation with land warfare in GERMANY, but relied heavily on strong support from Kaiser WILHELM II after the British *DREADNOUGHT* redefined the scale and expense of naval construction. By 1914 Tirpitz was losing the arms race against the ROYAL NAVY, and was pessimistic about his fleet's chances when war broke out in August.

The German HIGH SEAS FLEET was denied a positive wartime role, and Tirpitz increasingly favoured concentration on SUBMARINE construction. Though a committed supporter of unrestricted SUBMARINE WARFARE, his influence declined along with interest in (and funding for) the surface fleet. He resigned in protest against continued restrictions on U-boat activities in March 1916, and to his surprise was allowed to retire. A strong supporter of the THIRD SUPREME COMMAND from 1917, and nominal leader of the right-wing FATHERLAND PARTY, he returned to parliamentary politics as a Reichstag deputy for the National Party in the 1920s.

Tisza de Boros-Jĕno, Istvàn, Count (1861–1918) Son of a Hungarian prime minister, he himself became premier as head of the Liberal Party from 1903 to 1905. Appointed premier for a second time in 1913, he was a determined campaigner for Hungarian national status within AUSTRIA-HUNGARY, and strove to maintain a constitutional system that guaranteed regional power to the ethnic Hungarian landowners. Hungary's main external preoccupations concerned ROMANIA, and Tisza argued successfully against an immediate attack on SERBIA during the JULY CRISIS of 1914.

Once war had been declared, Tisza took part in diplomatic efforts to appease ITALY and enjoyed good relations with Austro-Hungarian foreign minister BURIAN, but continued to adopt a forceful regional stance on internal affairs. Immediate pressure on food supplies from Hungary's agricultural economy, and a bad harvest in 1914, persuaded him to halt free passage of foodstuffs into Austria from spring 1915. His policy of supplying home needs before releasing surpluses for imperial use contributed to social tensions in Vienna, where he was accused of attempting to blackmail the government into accepting changes to the imperial structure.

His position under Emperor KARL I was weakened by a (perhaps unjustified) popular reputation as a force for all-out war, and by increasing pressure for constitutional reform within Hungary. Dismissed in May 1917, Tisza briefly took a commission in the Hungarian home army. He was assassinated by Communists in Budapest on 31 October 1918.

Togoland German protectorate on the west African coast between the British colony of Gold Coast (now Ghana) and French Dahomey (Benin). Stretching some 600km inland from a 50km strip of coastline, and bigger than modern Togo, the German colony had been established in 1844 and its frontiers settled since the turn of the century (see MAP 17). Stable and fairly prosperous, it was the only financially self-supporting German colony in 1914.

Unlike Germany's other African possessions, Togoland possessed no coherent defence force, only a paramilitary internal security police of 560 African recruits, scattered around the country's villages and led by 8 Germans. The only military installation of any strategic importance was the powerful RADIO station 200km inland at Kamina, an immediate target of the British ROYAL NAVY in its operations against German commerce raiders (see Battle of CORONEL).

Ignoring an appeal for regional peace by Togoland's absent governor (see BERLIN ACT), a French-led force of 150 Senegalese infantry crossed the coastal border from Dahomey on 6 August. The main port and capital of Lomé, only 25km from the Gold Coast, was evacuated by the German colonists and occupied by about 600 (mostly African) troops of the British West African Frontier Force, shipped from Accra on 12 August. Patrols in pursuit upcountry made contact with German rearguards on or before 15 August, the first land action anywhere in the war between Britain and Germany.

Joined by the Senegalese on 18 August, the British force followed the German colonists north up the Chra River and the German-built light RAILWAY, suffering 73 casualties in a confused attempt to storm a temporary German position on 22 August before the colonists blew up the wireless station and surrendered on 26 August. Allied PROPAGANDA published unsubstantiated accounts of German brutality to natives, but the brief campaign had little other external impact, and Togoland's internal economy was running normally within a few weeks. See also: Wars in AFRICA.

Tondern Raid British bombing raid against a ZEPPELIN base on the German–Danish border at Tondern on 18 July 1918. The only wartime attack launched from the deck of an AIRCRAFT CARRIER, and the only major seaborne operation undertaken by the RAF, it was the third British attempt to bomb the base, two operations using seaplanes having failed in 1916. Escorted by a light CRUISER squadron and eight DESTROYERS, the carrier *FURIOUS* launched seven SOPWITH CAMELS at dawn, each specially fitted with wing racks for two 50lb bombs. One aircraft crashed in the sea with engine trouble (and was rescued by a destroyer), but the six others reached the target, protected by overcast conditions from detection by nearby German FIGHTERS. After scoring several hits on the base and destroying two Zeppelins (L54 and L60), two Camels force-landed in neutral Denmark and three ditched in the sea because the landing deck of *Furious* was inoperable. One aircraft and all five pilots were recovered, but the fate of the sixth machine was never known.

Torpedo Boats Fast, light surface craft were the first naval vessels used to carry TORPEDOES in the late 19th century. Almost any motor boat could be fitted with between one and four torpedo tubes, offering even small navies an effective means of destroying major warships, and torpedo boats remained the cheapest and most common means of deploying the relatively untried new weapon in 1914.

Faced with the prospect of swarms of torpedo boats attacking at high speed from any hostile shore, prewar battlefleets had been forced to undertake a major revision of tactics. Batteries of small surface guns had been added to the armament of BATTLESHIPS and CRUISERS, and fast DESTROYERS had been developed specifically to protect fleet units. Uncertainty about the effectiveness of these and other countermeasures, especially in case of night attack, encouraged the ROYAL NAVY to abandon plans for a close BLOCKADE of German ports and contributed to generalized caution in the deployment of wartime battlefleets.

Torpedo boats were used by every combatant navy, and an enormous variety of types saw service, but they fell into two broad categories. Most of the older boats were very small craft, lacking the range, strength and stability necessary for long-range operations. Generally used only to defend coastal installations, they were plagued by breakdowns and structural damage whenever pressed into regular action. Larger boats, in service with most of the major navies in 1914, were capable of performing a wide range of ANTI-SUBMARINE and general patrol duties, and their construction was a high priority for all active naval shipyards throughout the War. Equipped with searchlights and light surface armament (including MACHINE GUNS for ANTI-AIRCRAFT defence), they played an important role in the prolonged battles fought between light naval forces in the MEDITERRANEAN SEA, the BALTIC SEA, the BLACK SEA and the crowded waters around the southern British Isles.

Although torpedo boats scored numerous wartime successes against light forces, they were seldom given the chance to attack major warships. The sinking of the Austro-Hungarian dreadnought *SZENT ISTVÁN* by Italian MAS BOATS in the Adriatic was exceptional, and the question of their effectiveness in fleet actions remained an area of uncertainty for postwar naval planners. See also: NAVAL WARFARE.

Torpedoes Self-propelled underwater missiles launched from a tube located on the deck or inside the hull of a warship. Developed in the late 1860s, torpedoes offered a cheap way to sink a large vessel, and were soon fitted to small TORPEDO BOATS, which relied on speed and darkness to get within range. The potential of SUBMARINES for launching torpedoes had been generally recognized well before 1914, and torpedo-armed DESTROYERS had been developed for ocean-going operation. Tubes had also been fitted to larger warships, but were generally removed as superfluous after 1916.

Torpedoes in 1914 carried a contact-triggered explosive warhead, and were driven by compressed air. They had a maximum range of around 10,000 metres, but a general tendency to wander off course meant that ideal range was something under a kilometre. Duds were also a problem, particularly with French and Russian torpedoes, while British torpedoes regularly lost their set depth and ran harmlessly underneath targets. Torpedoes became larger, ran straighter, travelled further and kept better depth in later wartime versions, but failure to explode remained a common failing, although German types were generally superior.

The constant threat of torpedo attack helped to paralyse the world's battlefleets, but torpedoes destroyed relatively few warships (see NAVAL WARFARE; *CRESSY*). Their greatest impact – launched from submarines – was against seagoing trade and troop transport, but the relative bulk, unreliability and expense of torpedoes meant that most sinkings by submarines were carried out using surface armament or set explosive charges. Seaplanes were also employed as torpedo carriers, by the British RNAS from 1915 and later by the GERMAN NAVY, but both sides abandoned experiments pending the development of more powerful aero engines (see SHORT 184). See also: *HANDELSKRIEG*; SUBMARINE WARFARE.

Town Cruisers Group name for 20 four-funnelled British CRUISERS named after towns or cities and built between 1910 and 1916. As fast as the much smaller SCOUT CRUISERS, Towns were designed for long-range trade protection as well as operations with battlefleets, an idea copied from German designs (see *BRESLAU*). The first five ships carried two 6-inch and ten 4-inch guns, but secondary armament was replaced by more main guns for later classes, and the two ships of the final Birkenhead Class, originally ordered for the GREEK NAVY, carried ten 5.5-inch guns.

In keeping with their dual function, Towns were deployed on trade routes all over the world and with the GRAND FLEET in the North Sea, taking part in most of the ROYAL NAVY's major surface operations. Only two (*Falmouth* and *Nottingham*) were lost, both to TORPEDOES during late 1916, but several survived severe damage. See also: *SYDNEY*.

Townshend, General Sir Charles (1861–1924) Ambitious INDIAN ARMY officer, posted to the MESOPOTAMIAN FRONT in April 1915 to take command of the 6th Indian Division. A veteran of several prewar colonial campaigns, Townshend arrived with a reputation as a lucky soldier, immediately justified by the spectacular capture of AMARA and victory at ES SINN. He subsequently argued for consolidation, but was ordered up the Tigris towards Baghdad by C-in-C NIXON and was defeated at CTESIPHON. His division retreated to KUT in early December 1915, and was besieged by Turkish forces until the town's surrender 30 April 1916.

Townshend attracted professional criticism during the siege for failing to assess accurately or organize available food supplies, and for his early acceptance of a purely passive role during relief operations. Poor relations with the Indian majority of his 10,000 troops also contributed to the garrison's generally inert performance. He remained a prisoner in TURKEY until the armistice of 1918 (which he helped negotiate on Mudros), and was treated as an honoured guest while most of his troops were brutally maltreated elsewhere. Despite popular status as the 'Hero of Kut', Townshend was never given another command, a fate shared by other Indian Army officers responsible for the early Mesopotamian campaigns.

Trabzon, Fall of Second stage of the Russian campaign on the CAUCASIAN FRONT in 1916, an imaginative strike north from the main battle zones around ERZURUM and Mus. Within a week of capturing Erzurum on 16 February, Russian commander YUDENICH was marching a strong detachment north towards Trabzon, a useful BLACK SEA supply port, which would also provide protection for an otherwise exposed flank. While the general offensive was extended south to reoccupy Bitlis, rekindling Allied fantasies of a Russian advance on BAGHDAD, the RUSSIAN NAVY landed 2,100 troops west of Trabzon in early March, and another 16,000 at RIZE in early April. They joined the main column in ten days of heavy fighting around Trabzon before the bulk of Russian forces got across the Kare Dere river. The port surrendered on 17 April, after which Yudenich resumed his main advance beyond Erzurum, having distracted Turkish forces from the centre of the front and disrupted regional commander Abdul Kerim's plans for a counteroffensive. See MAP 24.

Tractor Aircraft Aircraft with engines positioned at the front of the machine, pulling it through the air (compare PUSHER AIRCRAFT). See: FIGHTERS.

Transcaucasia The strip of land south of the Caucasus Mountains between the Caspian Sea and the BLACK Sea that formed the only frontier between RUSSIA and TURKEY in 1914. It included the Russian provinces of Georgia and Azerbaijan, as well as the vaguely defined Armenian homelands stretching either side of the border.

Prewar Armenian nationalism had been fostered by the Russian government as a weapon against Ottoman integrity, and an unofficial Armenian assembly existed in 1914. Russian attitudes towards Georgian and Azerbaijani nationalists were entirely repressive, but all three organized representative assemblies after the 1917 FEBRUARY REVOLUTION. Meeting in Tbilisi during August, they agreed to merge for mutual protection as the Transcaucasian Republic from 17 September 1917.

Technically a federation, the republic was in practice dominated by Georgia and quickly disintegrated. Muslim Azerbaijan sought close relations with CENTRAL ASIANS to the northwest, Armenia wanted reconciliation with Turkey and Georgia was anxious to pursue economic development under German protection. All three faced possible incursions from RED ARMY forces after the BREST-LITOVSK Treaty enabled the Soviet government to concentrate on internal affairs. The Republic was officially broken up into its component states on 26 May 1918, when Armenia (Erivan) signed the separate Treaty of Batum with Turkey, and all three had become Soviet provinces by late 1920. See CAUCASIAN FRONT; MAP 24. See also: ARMENIAN MASSACRES.

Transjordan Campaign In early 1918 British offensive operations on the PALESTINE FRONT and the northern progress of the ARAB REVOLT converged on Transjordan, the Turkish-ruled Arab lands east of the River Jordan, in the modern state of Jordan (see MAP 22). After the conquest of JERUSALEM, British commander ALLENBY planned his main offensive along the coastal plains to the west, but extended his eastern flank into Transjordan as a diversionary threat to the vital RAILWAY link of DERA.

In advance of British operations against Jericho and the northern Dead Sea region, Allenby enlisted direct support from the Arab Revolt. Part of the Arab Northern Army (FEISAL) pushed north from its base at AQABA to the southeastern Dead Sea coast by late January, capturing TAFILA and disrupting Turkish grain and wood supplies to central Arabia.

Allenby's advance on Jericho, 20km east of Jerusalem, began on 19 February. Delayed by difficult terrain, it reached the city two days later, by which time Turkish forces had evacuated east beyond the river to Es Salt and Amman. A composite force under General Shea – infantry and CAVALRY divisions with strong ARTILLERY support – was detached for a further offensive into Transjordan, but rain delayed his advance until 21 March. Meanwhile Allenby launched consolidating attacks on his main fronts to the west from 9 March.

Most Arab forces were concentrated further south for the proposed siege of MAAN by late March, and Arab operations in the north were delayed by a second Turkish attack on Tafila, which forced the garrison's evacuation until 18 March. An Arab column under LAWRENCE eventually marched to rendezvous with Shea, but turned back on news of its defeat at AMMAN.

The defence of Amman was supervised by new YILDERIM FORCE commander General LIMAN VON SANDERS, who launched an unsuccessful surprise attack on the remaining British bridgeheads east of the Jordan on 11 April. At the same time a feint towards Dera by the ANZAC Mounted Division impressed him as an indication of British plans, despite a simultaneous limited attack on a Turkish salient near the coast.

The German SPRING OFFENSIVES on the WESTERN FRONT forced Allenby to postpone his main attack until autumn, but a second British invasion entered Transjordan on 30 April. General Chauvel led two divisions of cavalry, one of infantry and two Indian brigades against Turkish Fourth Army HQ at Es Salt and the nearby stronghold of Shunet Nimrin. Although cavalry took Es Salt, Liman von Sanders had reinforced the sector in preparation for a limited advance of his own, and the support promised for the British by local Arab tribes failed to materialize. Counterattacks had closed around Es Salt by the end of the next day, but Liman von Sanders spared his own troops by allowing British forces an avenue of retreat, and Chauvel had recrossed the Jordan by the evening of 4 May.

The British suffered 1,600 casualties, but Liman von Sanders lost 2,000 men and was persuaded to retain a third of all his troops in the Transjordan sector. Allenby's efforts to keep them there centred on the continued presence of the Desert Mounted Corps (four divisions) in the Jordan Valley, based at Bethlehem. In sweltering heat, Liman von Sanders made only one unsuccessful attempt to dislodge it, a night attack of 13/14 July by about 5,000 men, before half the Desert Mounted Corps moved west for the MEGIDDO Offensive in September, when 15,000 dummy horses helped conceal the transfer from German aerial observers.

Transylvania See: ROMANIA; AUSTRIA-HUNGARY; ROMANIAN CAMPAIGN.

Treason Trials (French) A series of sensational trials in FRANCE during the first half of 1918, following the mass arrests of PACIFISTS, dissidents and suspected German sympathizers by the CLEMENCEAU government in November 1917. Revealing a network of pacifist agitators in German pay, the trials encouraged national vigilance, provided an excuse for military setbacks, and generally distracted public attention at a time of crisis on the WESTERN FRONT. Spies like Paul Bolo-Pasha, Pierre Lenoir and the staff of *Le BONNET ROUGE* were duly executed, but more nebulous charges against senior political figures, including former interior minister MALVY, could not be substantiated. The most influential French spokesman for peace, ex-premier CAILLAUX, was kept from trial until 1920.

Trenchard, General Hugh (1873–1956) Bombastic BRITISH ARMY officer transferred to the RFC in 1913 and in command of the home training squadron in August 1914. He reached the WESTERN FRONT in November as commander of No.1 Wing and replaced Henderson as the the RFC's field commander in France from August 1915. Aware that Allied aircraft were inferior to GERMAN ARMY AIR SERVICE weapons, but determined to play an active role in the conduct of TRENCH WARFARE, Trenchard deployed his forces in line with the BEF's official aggressive posture. Sending out large numbers of obsolete aircraft on constant army-support missions across German lines, he accepted heavy losses of men and machines more cheerfully than many of his field commanders (see BLOODY APRIL).

His faith in the offensive potential of AERIAL WARFARE was primarily pinned on the development of efficient STRATEGIC BOMBING aircraft. He lobbied London for the creation of a mass bombing fleet, and his preliminary appointment as chief of staff to the RAF in January 1918 reflected the government's commitment to the concept. Unhappy as an administrator, he resigned in April and shortly afterwards took command of the INDEPENDENT AIR FORCE. Despite its lack of significant success in raids over GERMANY before the ARMISTICE, he remained convinced that technological progress would make bombers the decisive weapon in future wars, and guided development of the postwar RAF as a strategic force.

Trench Artillery See: MORTARS.

Trenches Digging holes in the ground was the generally accepted method of improvising defensive infantry fortifications in 1914. Earthworks were difficult to destroy from a distance, absorbing bullets and most contemporary ARTILLERY shells, and could be extended into passageways to allow maximum freedom of manoeuvre.

Early wartime trenches were little more than connected foxholes, not intended for long-term occupation and often dug by infantry without shovels or other requirements of 'position' warfare. On the EASTERN FRONT, where great offensives regularly rolled lines back hundreds of kilometres, trenches remained relatively ill-prepared, shallow and readily abandoned, but the static intensity of the WESTERN FRONT encouraged the development of highly sophisticated trench systems. These influenced trench systems elsewhere, especially on the ITALIAN FRONT, although German technical assistance was only partly responsible for the complex networks designed by the TURKISH ARMY at GALLIPOLI and in PALESTINE.

The idea of a trench 'line' is misleading. From spring 1915 trenches on the Western Front evolved into a series of lines extending back from NO MAN'S LAND at a variety of depths and angles. The basic design of all systems incorporated a frontline trench, usually zigzagged for maximum field of fire against attack, and deep enough to protect infantry from SNIPERS or most shrapnel explosions. Communications passages led back to a similar 'support' trench, and a 'reserve' trench was usually located still further in the rear.

The GERMAN ARMY pioneered the use of second-line trenches (in autumn 1915), and introduced concrete fortification for local strongpoints or deep underground bombardment shelters. Once the idea of DEFENCE IN DEPTH was adopted from 1916, German trench lines (usually better maintained than those of the Allies) were often separated by 2–3km and linked by chains of concrete MACHINE GUN posts (see HINDENBURG LINE).

Though initially geared exclusively to attack, French forces fighting on their own soil had access to plentiful supplies of entrenchment tools. By late 1914 their trenches were lined with timber, protected by sandbags and included habitable accommodation facilities. A bewildering number of variants on the basic trench system were subsequently used by the FRENCH ARMY, partly reflecting internal arguments over defensive tactics.

The BEF's rain-soaked Flanders trenches were unhealthy mudbaths in 1914, and troops were forced to sleep in improvised caves scraped out of the walls (see TRENCH FOOT). British trench systems were only equipped to Franco-German standards from mid-1916, but adhered to the general pattern apart from a predilection for isolated listening posts ('sap lines') jutting into No Man's Land.

Supply of trench systems on the Western Front was maintained by increased use of lorries and a proliferation of spur roads and RAILWAYS towards both sides of the frontline zone, a procedure made hazardous by devastated terrain and the proximity of hostile artillery and aircraft.

In the absence of efficient portable RADIO sets, local communications centred on labyrinthine field-telephone networks. Prone to breakdown and line-tapping, field telephones needed support from human or animal messengers, particularly during offensive operations, when both transport and communications tended to collapse as soon as an entrenched army moved forward. See also: MINES; SAPPING; TRENCH WARFARE.

Trench Fever Debilitating disease contracted by troops engaged in long-term TRENCH WARFARE, especially along the relatively warm sectors of the WESTERN and ITALIAN FRONTS. Victims displayed the symptoms of INFLUENZA or typhoid and, although most recovered, they were usually hospitalized for several weeks. The cause of 'trench fever' was identified in 1918 as excretions from lice, which permanently infested all TRENCHES, and is now known to be the micro-organism *Rickettsia quintana* (intermediate in structure between bacteria and viruses), transmitted by the bites of body lice.

Trench Foot A fungal infection of the feet caused by cold, wet and insanitary conditions, trench foot could turn gangrenous and result in amputation. The first cases developed in the soaking, ill-drained BEF trenches on the WESTERN FRONT during late 1914, causing 20,000 casualties in the BRITISH ARMY alone over the following winter. It became less common once living conditions improved from 1915, but still claimed a steady trickle of victims, especially in the damp northern lowlands of France. Generalized failure of preventive treatment (amounting to regular inspection of troops' feet and making them change their socks) persuaded many commanders on both sides that the condition, like bullet wounds to the hand, was an indicator of poor morale. See also: TRENCH WARFARE.

Trench Warfare When deadlock on the WESTERN FRONT produced massively defended systems of opposing TRENCHES with no vulnerable flanks, new weapons and tactics were needed to deal with a state of semi-permanent pitched battle along a very broad front. The Western Front was the usual test-bed for new techniques, but intense trench warfare took place on many other fronts and was sometimes, as at ANZAC COVE, gruesomely modified by geographical conditions.

Weaponry requirements, gradually fulfilled after an initial phase of desperate improvisation, were those of old-fashioned siege operations writ large. Heavy ARTILLERY, mostly howitzers, was ranged behind the lines to plunge shells onto earthworks and other defences, kill any troops in the open, and knock out enemy batteries. Short-range, mobile MORTARS and fixed heavy MACHINE GUNS were essential anti-personnel weapons, and GRENADES were an ideal small arm for use in confined spaces. Light, portable machine-guns and FLAMETHROWERS were increasingly used at platoon level for the same effect, but RIFLES (and to a lesser extent BAYONETS) remained the infantryman's basic trench-fighting tools.

Though TANKS, used exclusively in major battles, had little impact on everyday trench warfare, advances in the field of AERIAL WARFARE were very relevant, both indirectly through developments in PHOTO-RECONNAISSANCE, which forced greatly increased use of camouflage from 1916, and directly through the advent of ground-attack 'contact patrols'. The other main wartime innovation in weaponry, poison GAS, was directed specifically against trench systems, but, although universally employed as a shock weapon from 1915, it was largely neutralized by improved respirators.

An array of accessories refined the use of trench weapons. Barbed wire, originally laid in thin strands with tin cans attached as a warning system, was soon used in strength and depth, carefully positioned to force attackers into killing zones. Ammunition used by artillery was extended to include starshells for night illumination and smoke shells for tactical effect, as well as gas, high-explosive, shrapnel and incendiary shells (for use by frontline ANTI-AIRCRAFT batteries).

Major offensives were usually preceded by extensive refinement, repair and extension of both trenches and rear facilities in the immediate area, but the patterns of routine trench warfare were mostly established outside the campaigning season, which meant during the winter on the Western Front.

Logistic operations – construction and repair work, transportation and supply, running messages, laying cables or barbed wire – were conducted at night whenever possible, and comprised the main active business of trench troops. Other operations were conducted in a spirit of token aggression, as a means of theoretically remaining on the offensive.

Domination of NO MAN'S LAND was official BEF policy, expressed in the growth of MINE construction and SNIPING, and also in the practice of trench raiding. Trench raids – which were local night attacks aimed at capturing prisoners, gathering intelligence and generally causing disruption – were initiated by the BEF in November 1914, became standard procedure the following year, and were an everyday occurrence by spring 1916. Their frequency has prompted some commentators to regard them as a medium for competition among junior officers.

The GERMAN ARMY quickly took up trench raids, and tit-for-tat attacks became a matter of routine. Specialist German *Sturmtruppen* ('stormtroopers') were formed to incorporate them into offensive INFILTRATION TACTICS during the KAISERSCHLACHT Offensive in 1918. The FRENCH ARMY officially considered trench raiding a waste of lives until late 1917, when it was used to test offensive capability after the summer's mutiny.

The extent of immediate danger from attack varied considerably on different fronts and within the Western Front. On quiet sectors, like the southernmost stretches of the Franco-German lines, boredom, desertion and malingering were often major problems, especially among troops transferred from active zones.

Physical conditions also varied dramatically with geography or season, and were often appalling. From autumn 1914 British and Belgian trenches in Flanders were usually flooded and always damp, forcing construction of high barricades and triggering an epidemic of TRENCH FOOT. On the EASTERN FRONT, ill-equipped Russian and Austro-Hungarian units froze to death en masse during the winter CARPATHIAN OFFENSIVES of 1915, and the universally cold winter of 1916–17 increased sickness rates on all European fronts.

Most trenches in tropical conditions, especially the insanitary systems operated by the TURKISH ARMY, were palaces of disease. European casualties to sickness in AFRICA, in PALESTINE, at GALLIPOLI and on the MESOPOTAMIAN FRONT, serious at the best of times, were multiplied wherever trenches stood for long periods.

Even the best-kept frontline positions (usually German) were confined areas littered with dead bodies and crowded with tired, under-nourished troops, ideal conditions for the spread of infectious or transmitted disease, as ultimately demonstrated by the devastating impact of the 1918–19 INFLUENZA pandemic on trenches everywhere.

Occasional large-scale fraternization episodes, like the famous Anglo-German football match of Christmas 1914, were soon eliminated on the Western Front (and were one of the reasons why the British increased their trench raiding). Fraternization could never be stopped in theatres where troops shared language or culture with hostiles in nearby trenches, and multinational Russian, Turkish and Austro-Hungarian forces were particularly susceptible to 'arrangements' between opposing troops. See also: INFANTRY TACTICS.

Trentino Offensive The only offensive by the AUSTRO-HUNGARIAN ARMY on the ITALIAN FRONT before autumn 1917, and the only major action to take place away from the ISONZO sector. The attack, launched in May 1916 into the Trentino valley in the South Tyrol from the Alps to the west, is sometimes called the Asiago Offensive after the town at the centre of the heaviest action (see MAP 21). The Offensive was planned by Austro-Hungarian chief of staff CONRAD, and aimed at fulfilling his long-held ambition of cutting off Italian forces at the Isonzo.

Granted a respite from defending the Isonzo by the rapid failure of the ITALIAN ARMY's March offensive, secure on the BALKAN FRONT and apparently safe on the EASTERN FRONT, Conrad assembled 18 divisions of the Eleventh Army (DANKL) and the Third Army (KOVESS) in the Trentino sector by mid-May, under the nominal command of Archduke EUGEN. Despite FALKENHAYN's refusal to divert German support from VERDUN, Austrian forces enjoyed a significant superiority in ARTILLERY strength, with some 2,000 guns including giant SCHLANKE EMMA howitzers.

Italian chief of staff CADORNA was aware that the attack was coming, but remained in offensive positions around the Isonzo and allowed the Italian First Army (Brussati) to do the same in the Trentino. When the Austro-Hungarian PRELIMINARY BOMBARDMENT opened in the Trentino on 14 May, Brussati's 100,000 troops were outnumbered 4 to 1 in men and artillery.

Advancing along a 70km front, the attack

forced Italian lines back some 8km (beyond Posina) in the centre by 22 May, and a renewed attack two days later pushed Brussati's central divisions back another 10km beyond Asiago, which was evacuated on 29 May. The Italian line had bulged but not broken, and Cadorna used a good RAILWAY system to rush 400,000 troops into the sector by early June.

The attack was held in the plains south of Asiago, and Austro-Hungarian losses were mounting when the successful Russian BRUSILOV OFFENSIVE forced a rapid transfer of forces to the Eastern Front on 10 June. Facing strong Italian counterattacks on the flanks of his new SALIENT, Eugen was ordered to withdraw to a line less than 5km from his starting point.

The Austro-Hungarian Army had suffered about 150,000 casualties and was never again able to mount an offensive of its own on any front, relying on German command and reinforcement until the ARMISTICE. The Italian Army had lost 147,000 men in the action but was almost immediately thrown back onto the offensive, partly in response to the political crisis created by a sense of invasion in ITALY. The SALANDRA government fell on 12 June, amid calls for greater political control over military planning, but another rapid transfer of troops brought Cadorna a face-saving victory at Gorizia in the sixth Isonzo battle.

Trianon, Treaty of Punitive peace settlement imposed on Hungary by the Allies after the PARIS PEACE CONFERENCE. Signed on 4 June 1920, it stripped the former Hungarian Kingdom, part of AUSTRIA-HUNGARY until October 1918, of over 60 per cent of its prewar population and territory. Most went to ROMANIA, which took Transylvania and much of the Banat region. In addition, Slovakia and Ruthenia were confirmed as part of CZECHOSLOVAKIA, Croatia as part of YUGOSLAVIA, and smaller portions of territory were also lost to Austria, POLAND and ITALY. Hungary was permitted an army of only 35,000 men and required to pay REPARATIONS. Described by the Allies as a redistribution of authority along ethnic lines, the Treaty caused long-term resentment in Hungary, and the new republic's foreign policy was dominated by attempts to secure its revision. See MAP 25.

Triple Alliance One of the two great power blocs that dominated prewar European diplomacy, originally a Dual Alliance between GERMANY and AUSTRIA-HUNGARY (agreed in 1879) but expanded in 1882 to include ITALY. Relations between Rome and Vienna, founded on mutual friendship with Germany, deteriorated rapidly in the immediate prewar period, reflecting territorial disputes in the northern Adriatic and the Balkans, and Italy's failure to go to war with its partners in August 1914 was widely expected. See also: TRIPLE ENTENTE; JULY CRISIS.

Triple Offensive An attempt by the CENTRAL POWERS on the EASTERN FRONT to force RUSSIA into a separate peace by destroying its armies, rather than by territorial conquest. Conceived as a follow-up to the successful GORLICE-TARNOW OFFENSIVE in Galicia, it was planned in early July 1915 by GERMAN ARMY chief of staff FALKENHAYN. Resisting proposals for attacks deep into Russia from theatre commanders HINDENBURG and LUDENDORFF (and from Austrian chief of staff CONRAD), Falkenhayn planned to cut off Russian forces in the Polish SALIENT at the centre of the Front (see MAP 11).

General MACKENSEN's 'Bug Army' in northern Galicia, with Austro-Hungarian support to the east, had already begun an advance north towards Brest-Litovsk on 29 June. In northwest Poland, on the southern edge of East Prussia, a new Army Group GALLWITZ was assembled to attack southeast towards the River NAREV and Warsaw. To further confuse Russian deployment of reserves, Falkenhayn ordered the 'Niemen Army' in the far north to renew its attacks in KURLAND.

Massive casualties in the spring, logistic inefficiency and rivalry between regional commands had left RUSSIAN ARMY reserves thinly scattered. Poor TRENCHES and communications, lack of supplies, poor morale and the vulnerability of positions in Poland all argued for a large-scale general retreat, as did Polish-sector commander ALEXEEV. Committed to defending a series of FORTRESSES in Poland, STAVKA (Russian central command) forbade withdrawal.

The BUG OFFENSIVE from the Galician frontier quickly exposed Russian weakness, breaking through Russian lines around Krasnostav on 18 July. Russian reinforcements from central Poland stiffened defences on the Narev, but Stavka ordered a general retreat from Poland on 22 July, leaving only the fortress of NOVOGEORGIEVSK garrisoned.

Austro-German forces all along the Polish front (including the central army groups under WOYRSCH and Prince LEOPOLD) followed the Russian armies east, and the 'GREAT RETREAT' continued until the end of September. Cholm and Lublin, some 150km southeast of Warsaw, were taken by the Bug Army at the end of July; unprotected Warsaw fell on 4 August; Ivangorod, on the Vistula, was occupied by Austro-Hungarian forces the next day; Novogeorgievsk fell on 19 August after a three-week siege; in the east Brest-Litovsk fell on 25 August, and Osowiec in the north on 26 August. The remnants of seven Russian armies escaped encirclement to a line inside Russia itself, between Czernowitz in the south and Dunaberg in the north.

The renewed attack in Kurland, also begun on 13 July, quickly pierced the Russian Fifth Army's ragged defences and swept towards Riga and KOVNO, where Russian reinforcements released by the retreat in Poland were concentrated. Poor coordination between the Russian Fifth and Tenth Armies wasted a mounting manpower advantage, and the Russians were forced east to a line running southwest from Riga to the Lithuanian capital of Vilnius.

Preoccupied with preparations for an offensive on the BALKAN FRONT, Falkenhayn suspended attacks on the Eastern Front on 2 September. Hindenburg and Ludendorff ignored the order, instead concentrating 47 divisions for the VILNIUS OFFENSIVE from 7 September. Despite reinforcements, Vilnius was abandoned and taken on 19 September, but German attacks were unable to pierce new Russian lines to the east. In worsening weather conditions, Ludendorff called off the offensive on 26 September.

The equally ambitious Austro-Hungarian 'BLACK-YELLOW' OFFENSIVE in the south failed completely in September, and fighting along the Eastern Front, now an almost straight line from the Baltic coast to ROMANIA, petered out completely as winter set in. Despite the loss of perhaps 2 million men in 1915, Russia had not been decisively beaten or battered into making peace, but Falkenhayn was able to concentrate on subsequent operations in SERBIA secure from the threat of attack in the east.

Trotha, Admiral Adolf von (1868–1940) Commander of the dreadnought *KAISER* with the German HIGH SEAS FLEET in August 1914, Trotha was strongly in favour of a confrontation with the British GRAND FLEET and an advocate of unrestricted SUBMARINE WARFARE, attitudes that facilitated his appointment as chief of staff to new Fleet commander SCHEER in January 1916. A former protégé of TIRPITZ, and an unequivocal supporter of the dictatorial THIRD SUPREME COMMAND, Trotha organized naval support for the right-wing, extraparliamentary FATHERLAND PARTY from autumn 1917, and played a central part in the reorganization of the GERMAN NAVY under a centralized Supreme Command in August 1918. Designated to replace Admiral MÜLLER as head of the naval cabinet, he remained with the Fleet under HIPPER to smooth the latter's assumption of command, and the two were directly responsible for organizing its final, aborted suicide mission in late October (see KIEL MUTINY). Trotha remained with the shrunken postwar service, but resigned in October 1920 after being implicated in the failed 'Kapp Putsch'. Always a dedicated proponent of naval rearmament, he filled a number of political posts for naval affairs during the early years of the Hitler regime.

Trotski, Leon (1879–1940) Russian socialist revolutionary who spent most of his adult life before 1917 in Siberian or overseas exile. An early supporter of LENIN and an enthusiastic student of military affairs, he made a reputation of his own during the 1905 revolution, returning to St Petersburg to lead the SOVIET strike movement. Exiled again in the aftermath of the revolution, he spent the first years of the War in Zürich, Paris and New York, rejecting Lenin's policy of national 'defeatism' at the first ZIMMERWALD conference in 1915.

He returned from New York to Petrograd (St Petersburg) after the 1917 FEBRUARY REVOLUTION. Arriving in early May, he found his own theory of 'permanent revolution' in total agreement with Lenin's 'April Thesis' demands for the immediate overthrow of the PROVISIONAL GOVERNMENT. Head of the Petrograd Soviet from October 1917, Trotski became Lenin's chief political deputy, and was the principal active organizer of the OCTOBER REVOLUTION.

As people's commissar for foreign affairs from 8 November, Trotski prolonged peace negotiations with the CENTRAL POWERS in anticipation of workers' revolution in GERMANY, a course initially supported by Lenin. Eventually overruled by his more pragmatic leader, Trotski withdrew from the negotiations before the signature of the BREST-LITOVSK Treaty to become commissar for war. Willing to defy radical opinion and employ former Tsarist officers as 'advisors', Trotski organized the RED ARMY as a conventional military force and directed its ultimately successful defence of the Revolution in the RUSSIAN CIVIL WAR. Lenin's ill health from 1922 left Trotski isolated as Stalin disposed of potential rivals for the succession. Expelled from the Communist Party in 1927, he was exiled two years later and murdered in 1940 by a Soviet agent in Mexico City.

Trumbić, Ante (1864–1938) Croatian nationalist leader, born in Austro-Hungarian Dalmatia and a member of the Austrian lower house since 1897. A relatively moderate figure, he sought constitutional reform of Slav provinces within AUSTRIA-HUNGARY, and was not associated with separatist or pan-Slav movements sponsored from SERBIA. His position had hardened by 1914, and he fled to ITALY after the JULY CRISIS to seek international support for South Slav independence. Disappointed by Allied and Italian coolness, and forced to compete with an expansion programme put forward by the Serbian government, he formed the 'Yugoslav Committee' in May 1915. With Trumbić as chairman, and the Hungarian Croat Frano Supilo as roving ambassador, the Committee worked from London to establish the principle of liberation for 'oppressed' Habsburg Slavs as an Allied war aim, and to persuade the Serbian PAŠIĆ government to accept the idea of a federal postwar YUGOSLAVIA. Willing to compromise for the sake of Allied support, Trumbić got his chance after the 1917 FEBRUARY REVOLUTION in Russia removed Serbia's strongest diplomatic support, and a vague agreement was announced in the CORFU DECLARATION of July 1917. Pašić still worked to block federalist plans behind the scenes, as did the Italian government, which had territorial ambitions of its own in Croatia (see ROME CONGRESS), and negotiations with Serbian ruler Prince ALEXANDER in November 1918 produced another compromise in the new 'Kingdom of Serbs, Croats and Slovenes'. As foreign minister, Trumbić was preoccupied with Italian claims on the eastern Adriatic coast at the PARIS PEACE CONFERENCE, but once the dispute had been settled in 1920 he turned to protection of threatened minority rights in the new Kingdom, and was publicly regretting the dissolution of Austria-Hungary by the time Alexander's dictatorship was established in 1929.

Tsingtao (Qingdao) The main German military installation in the Far East, a fortified naval base in the leased concession of Kiaochow in northeast China. Garrisoned by 4,000 troops (and one aircraft) it was attacked by the Japanese Army's 18th Division (some 23,000 men) under the experienced General Kamio. Kamio was ordered to prepare the attack on 16 August 1914, some days before JAPAN declared war on GERMANY, and international suspicion of Japanese ambitions in CHINA prompted the attachment of 1,500 British troops to the operation. The garrison surrendered on 7 November after a methodical siege, during which Kamio's tactics – avoiding costly frontal assaults, attacking mostly at night, and making maximum use of ARTILLERY support – foreshadowed methods eventually employed on the WESTERN FRONT in

1918. Japan remained in occupation of Tsingtao until 1922.

Turkey Contemporary international references to 'Turkey' in 1914 described the Ottoman Empire, a great swathe of the Middle East ruled by the Sultan of Turkey in his capacity as Khalif of the orthodox (Sunnite and Shi'ite) Muslim world (see MAP 1). Executive control over the Empire rested with the Sultan's appointed grand vizier and cabinet, at the head of a mostly Turkish bureaucracy, although the governors of the Empire's four provinces (Anatolia, Syria/Mesopotamia, Kurdistan/Armenia and Arabia) enjoyed considerable autonomy.

Sultan Abdul Hamid II ('the Damned') reigned as an autocrat, bolstered by a strictly orthodox religious hierarchy, until the YOUNG TURK revolution forced him to accept a constitution and an elected representative assembly in 1908. The assembly deposed him after a failed countercoup in 1909 and installed the kindly but elderly Mohammed V.

A series of military defeats in the 19th century had compelled the grant of reparations and zones of influence ('the Capitulations') within the Empire to European powers. By 1914 GREAT BRITAIN was in effective control of EGYPT (which was technically an Ottoman province), and economically dominant in the Persian Gulf; France was cementing its influence over Syria and the Lebanon; RUSSIA sought expansion through Armenia towards the MEDITERRANEAN; and ITALY claimed similar privileged status in parts of the eastern Mediterranean. The recent territorial losses of Bosnia-Herzegovina to AUSTRIA-HUNGARY (1908), of Libya to Italy in the war of 1911–12, and of Macedonia to independent regional powers in the First Balkan War (1912) had practically eliminated Ottoman influence from Europe and north AFRICA.

The surviving Empire contained an estimated 25 million people in 1914, including about 14 million Turks as well as large Arab, Christian Syrian, Armenian, Kurdish, Greek and Circassian minorities. No official racial distinction existed under the Sultans, and tolerance had attracted many smaller linguistic and religious groups to the Empire.

Minority representatives took a substantial share of government appointments, but nationalist, separatist movements had mushroomed before 1914, especially in Syria, Arabia and Armenia. Often sponsored by European powers, nationalist organizations had been repressed under Abdul Hamid, and the Young Turk revolution's more liberal policies were abandoned after an extremist caucus within the ruling Union and Progress Party (UPP) seized effective control in Constantinople from January 1913.

Led by ENVER, TALAAT and DJEMAL, in alliance with a cabal of senior bureaucrats, the caucus embarked on a policy of rapid industrialization, military reorganization and cultural 'Turcification' under the guise of constitutional government. Its restrictive attitude towards minorities exacerbated tensions already fuelled by supply shortages, bureaucratic breakdowns and a flood of refugees from Libyan and Balkan wars (see Introduction).

Surrounded by hostile states and greedy empires, and with international tensions unlikely to allow a long period of reconstruction, Turkey could not afford diplomatic isolation in 1914, and the regime sought a protective alliance with one of the major European power blocs.

Anglo-French influence in Turkey, traditionally strong, was waning fast in relation to German activity in banking, development, trade and military affairs. Kaiser WILHELM II had visited Constantinople to claim friendship with Islam, and GERMANY was building the Berlin–Baghdad railway link, given final diplomatic clearance by Britain in a provisional agreement just before the 1914 JULY CRISIS. A German military mission under LIMAN VON SANDERS reached Constantinople in December 1913, and its growing influence on the TURKISH ARMY, controlled by Enver as war minister from January 1914, provoked concern but no diplomatic countermeasures from the ENTENTE POWERS. Germany could also offer the inducement of future gains against Russia, the enemy most immediately feared in Constantinople.

Enver and the ruling cabinet inner circle

constituted a war party in Turkey at a time when most of the government, the bureaucracy and political opinion were committed to neutrality and undecided on the direction of foreign policy. The motives of the war party were a complex mixture of pan-Turkish ideology, resentment of Entente predation, an opportunistic desire to join the winning side, and a genuine belief in the moral and social benefits of war.

Unknown to most of the cabinet, Enver and Talaat signed a defensive alliance with Germany in July 1914. The pact remained secret after August, enabling genuine negotiations with Allied diplomats to continue while Enver worked to create a political climate for joining the CENTRAL POWERS.

Allied clumsiness helped. Whatever its military merits, CHURCHILL's decision to commandeer two Turkish BATTLESHIPS under construction in Britain was a public-relations disaster in Turkey, which had paid for the ships by public subscription (see *ERIN*). The subsequent escape of the German MITTELMEERDIVISION to Constantinople, and the nominal purchase of its two modern warships by the TURKISH NAVY, was another PROPAGANDA defeat for the Allies and gave the GERMAN NAVY enormous influence over Turkish policy, not least because its guns covered the capital.

Allied diplomats continued to mistake sympathetic voices in Constantinople for powerful ones, and the British in particular went out of their way to avoid further provocation, despite Turkey's closure of the DARDANELLES in August and its repudiation of the Capitulations in September.

German naval commander SOUCHON, with the contrivance of Enver, put war beyond doubt on 29 October 1914 by launching a preemptive attack on RUSSIAN NAVY bases in the BLACK SEA, and hostilities with the Entente began two days later. Bemusement and disappointment in London were reflected in a delay before Britain formally declared war on 5 November.

Turkey was incapable of national mobilization for war in the manner of industrial European nations. Its largely rural, agricultural economy was primitive and regionalized, connected by few roads and less than 6,000km of fragmented, inefficient RAILWAYS, of which only the light Hejaz line into Arabia was Turkish-owned. Motorized road transport was almost non-existent, and rolling stock was in short supply, the majority of vehicles being drawn by oxen. Turkey had no RADIO communication, and the sparse telegraph system could barely handle peacetime traffic. Although Constantinople could talk to Berlin by telephone, the invention had not penetrated the rest of the Empire.

Ottoman heavy industry employed only about 15,000 workers in 1914, almost all in companies owned by foreign capital, and state munitions output was restricted to a couple of small factories near Constantinople, the Empire's only major magnet for goods and services. Fuel supplies were extremely vulnerable, coal from the Empire's Black Sea fields reaching Constantinople by sea. Turkey could not afford large-scale coal imports, and peacetime shortages were reflected in heavy deforestation. Manpower resources, already drained by two years of war, were dwindling under pressure from poor public health (especially in crowded, insanitary cities) and a chaotic conscription system that placed most of the burden of service on the Anatolian peasantry.

Turkey's disadvantages were multiplied in wartime by a combination of military circumstances and internal mismanagement. Mobilization was the signal for random seizure of the transport 'system' by local military authorities, and its immediate collapse was rendered irrevocable by the need to supply four separate battlefronts from early 1915 (see below). Rolling stock was always scarce (although VIP trains remained available throughout) and road-construction programmes were virtually abandoned (the vital military road to the PALESTINE FRONT was not completed until February 1916). Shortage of animals meant that peasant WOMEN played an important role as ammunition 'mules' for frontline troops.

Allied naval BLOCKADES of the Mediterranean and Black Seas brought acute fuel crisis, requiring the assignment of 30,000 troops to undertake overland coal transport, and completely halting supplies to the southern provinces. Food shortages in the capital, entirely dependent on imports in peacetime, followed immediately from the collapse of rural communications, worsening as the provinces grew used to subsistence. By 1915 the drain of men from the fields, an influx of refugees from the CAUCASIAN FRONT and a plague of locusts in Palestine had spread famine to the provinces, and in the absence of large-scale relief capability a sharp decline in public health was beyond government control.

Instant dependence on the Central Powers for military supplies and foodstuffs could not be met until the conquest of SERBIA and alliance with BULGARIA opened an overland link to Constantinople in early 1916. Government response to distribution crises in food and raw materials was limited to the appointment of officials with absolute powers over particular commodities, generally monopolists reaping enormous profits by arrangement with military requisitioning authorities. Arbitrary government price controls – an attempt to ease inflation – increased popular dependence on black markets. Financial measures to pay for war – printing Turkey's first paper money in 1915, and arranging large cash or gold loans from Berlin and Vienna – contributed to an overall tripling of prices in 1916 alone.

Under pressure from the Party Congress and German officials, the government made some efforts at closer regulation from 1916. A Food Board was set up in April 1916 under German supervision, but its attempts to regulate profits were watered down by private interests. German administrators also attempted to promote agricultural efficiency in the provinces from 1916, sponsoring planting and ploughing programmes through voluntary organizations.

Although Islamic authorities played an important PROPAGANDA role in the first two years of war, promoting the concept of a *Jihad* ('Holy War') against the Allies to limited worldwide effect (see SINGAPORE MUTINY), the period saw a general reduction of conservative religious influence in Ottoman life. Women took a greater part in war work and public life than ever before, with girls' schools springing up for the first time all over Constantinople. Women's rights were also promoted by a number of distinctly Turkish nationalist groups that fostered pan-Turkish and anti-clerical ideas.

Wartime pressures separated the Anatolian heartlands and Constantinople – successfully defended on the GALLIPOLI FRONT in 1915 – from the rest of the Empire. British advances on the MESOPOTAMIAN and PALESTINE FRONTS were compounded by a successful ARAB REVOLT, which alienated a growing portion of the southern Empire from mid-1916. Russian advances in the CAUCASIAN FRONT had been assisted by Armenian rebels since August 1914, and government attempts to deport the entire Armenian population from the region ended in mass slaughter (see ARMENIAN MASSACRES). Though it remained under nominal Ottoman control until 1918, Syria was ruled by Djemal as a virtually independent province, and strong local governments in SMYRNA and elsewhere were able to ignore central policies at will.

Political control at the centre remained with Enver and Talaat throughout, despite impotent dissent from within the UPP and the practical authority exerted by growing numbers of German officers and bureaucratic advisors. As war minister, Enver displayed consistent but often unrealistic ambition, and his response to the collapse of Russian forces in the Caucasus after the 1917 OCTOBER REVOLUTION was a policy of territorial expansion in the region, fatally weakening Turkish defences on other fronts.

Carried out despite opposition from senior figures in the Army, notably Mustapha KEMAL PASHA, and a serious clash of interests with German ambitions in TRANSCAUCASIA, the campaign damaged relations with Germany and hastened the Empire's ultimate socioeconomic collapse. By mid-1918 agricultural production was at a virtual standstill (only 10–15 per cent of rural conscripts ever returned to the fields), while the starving countryside was at the mercy of tribal brigands and more than half a million deserters by then at large.

With the southern fronts collapsing, Enver was forced to withdraw from the Caucasus by mid-1918, and the abolition of hitherto rigid press censorship in June, primarily to enable 'unofficial' criticism of the BUCHAREST Treaty, uncorked a stream of protest against the regime.

In an attempt to salvage the party's reputation, a moderate opposition group was formed inside the UPP and took several important cabinet posts, including the interior ministry in July. A general amnesty for political prisoners was declared the same month, and political exiles were allowed back into Turkey from August, opening another floodgate of dissent. By September, Enver was clinging to office by concealing disastrous military defeats from the rest of the cabinet, and on 7 October 1918 the entire UPP government resigned.

The UPP dissolved itself in disgrace, and a new cabinet under the moderate IZZET PASHA signed an armistice with the Allies at MUDROS on 30 October. The war leadership fled to revolutionary Russia in German ships, and rumours that the Izzet government had conspired in their flight prompted its resignation on 11 November. The rump of the Empire – those parts not absorbed by the Allied MANDATES of Palestine, Iraq, Syria, the Lebanon and Transjordan, and the new states of Arabia and the Transcaucasian Republic – came under Allied military occupation immediately afterwards.

Allied occupation took place with the cooperation of the new Sultan, Mehmed VI, who had succeeded Mohammed in July. Mehmed dissolved parliament and governed through the extreme conservative cabinet of Damad Ferid. The drastic reduction of Turkey's size imposed by the Treaty of SÈVRES, and Allied unwillingness to prevent Greek seizure of Smyrna in May 1919 stimulated an anti-government nationalist movement, led by Mustapha Kemal and represented by an alternative government in Sivas in eastern Turkey from September 1919 (see MAP 24).

The Sultan dismissed his cabinet and called new elections in October, but an overwhelming nationalist victory brought an Allied clampdown in March 1920, with Constantinople placed under martial law and parliament again dissolved. Joined by remaining military elements, Kemal's gradual military victory over the Greeks made him sufficiently strong to depose the Sultan, and he became head of a new Turkish Republic from 1922, subsequently securing a revision of the Sèvres Treaty in Turkey's favour by the Treaty of Lausanne in 1923.

Turkish Air Service See: TURKISH ARMY.

Turkish Army The conscript army of the Ottoman Empire included Arab, Armenian, Kurdish and Syrian units, but its most reliable troops were Anatolian Turks. Christians and Jews were restricted to labour battalions, and all but a quarter of some 250,000 liable males typically avoided peacetime conscription. Starved of resources in the late 19th century, the army's organizational and technical weakness was exposed during the Balkan Wars of 1912–13, but much-needed reform was begun by the new YOUNG TURK government of 1913 and developed by a German military mission under LIMAN VON SANDERS from December 1913.

Little progress had been made by August 1914, when 36 active divisions were available, organized into three armies. Each division theoretically comprised three battalions, a MACHINE GUN detachment and 36 field guns, but there was little uniformity in practice, except in shortages of trained officers and medical services. Thirty-four new divisions were mobilized in wartime, but desertions and defeats meant that full strength was never above 43 divisions, eventually deployed as nine armies and a separate force to combat the ARAB REVOLT. The Army took in almost 3.5 million men in the four years from November 1914, and official fighting strength reached 1.5 million in early 1916, but actual numbers probably never exceeded 1 million. Although each infantry division officially comprised 15,000–19,000 men, many were at less than quarter strength by 1917.

Some frontline infantry, notably at GALLIPOLI, were armed with modern RIFLES and a variety of German TRENCH WARFARE weapons, but by late 1917 most troops were suffering from shortages of equipment, food and clothing. Losses not replaced since the

Balkan Wars meant that ARTILLERY units were always undersized, with ammunition (some of it produced in Constantinople) both scarce and extremely unreliable. Very few heavy guns were available, and antiquated fortress artillery was often pressed into field service. Transport was in equally short supply, although camels proved very effective in desert conditions.

Turkish CAVALRY was largely ineffective, hampered by the unreliability of Kurdish and Arab reserve units, which made up more than half the total and tended to pursue their own tribal grievances (see ARMENIAN MASSACRES). Support and technical services were generally of a lower standard than those of European armies, although many signals and searchlight units were manned by German troops. The tiny air service was trained in Germany, commanded by German officers and eventually equipped with a few AEG C-TYPE reconnaissance machines.

Strategic control rested with war minister ENVER PASHA. He was careful to avoid forming too many purely German units (see YILDERIM FORCE), but GERMAN ARMY influence grew steadily during wartime. About 800 German officers controlled most staff positions – and also the RAILWAYS – by late 1917, but mutual relations were never good, and resentment of well-fed German troops during the final campaigns in PALESTINE contributed to a dramatic rise in desertions. Peasant troops abandoned combat en masse in autumn 1918, and the return of survivors to the fields is credited with rescuing the Turkish economy from complete collapse.

Until the disasters of 1918, Turkish troops earned their contemporary reputation for durability and reliability. Poor generalship was primarily responsible for offensive failures on the CAUCASIAN FRONT and against the SUEZ CANAL, and the eventual defeats in Palestine and on the MESOPOTAMIAN FRONT were preceded by years of stubborn defence. The Army's greatest success was the defence of Gallipoli in 1915, characterized by General KEMAL's sacrificial massed counterattacks. Turkish units also took part in operations with the CENTRAL POWERS on the BALKAN FRONT and in the ROMANIAN CAMPAIGN.

Bureaucratic incompetence in the crumbling Ottoman Empire made accurate assessment of wartime losses impossible, and published figures vary, but most list 470,000–530,000 battle deaths and about 770,000 wounded. Almost half a million more troops were invalided out of service, of whom about 20 per cent died, most suffering from malaria, dysentery, typhus or INFLUENZA in an Army that employed only 2,500 doctors (half of them reserves) throughout the War. See also: TURKEY.

Turkish Navy The prewar Turkish Navy was expanded in response to potential hostility from greatly superior Russian forces in the BLACK SEA and from the growing GREEK NAVY, its main regional competitor in the Aegean. Without the facilities to build major warships, TURKEY bought two old BATTLESHIPS and four DESTROYERS from GERMANY in 1910, and later ordered seven new gunboats from French yards, an Italian CRUISER, and two new dreadnoughts from GREAT BRITAIN.

The two dreadnoughts, *Sultan Osman I* and *Reshadieh*, were ready for delivery in August 1914 but were taken over by the ROYAL NAVY (see *ERIN*). The subsequent public outcry in Turkey encouraged closer relations with Germany, but ENVER PASHA had anyway offered to send both ships directly to a German port.

Material compensation reached Constantinople in mid-August when the German MITTELMEERDIVISION (*GOEBEN* and *BRESLAU*) was transferred to Turkish service. Its early sorties into the BLACK SEA under the Turkish flag technically put the Navy at war before the rest of the country, and hostilities were opened with a German-led attack on Russian Black Sea ports on 29 October 1914.

Wartime operations in the MEDITERRANEAN virtually ceased once the Allies instituted an effective blockade of the DARDANELLES in early 1915, and the Navy's role in the defence of the Straits themselves was limited to laying MINES and occasional raids by destroyers or TORPEDO BOATS. The few larger warships waited behind them to defend against any breakthrough. The only warship lost in the theatre was a coastal gunship sunk off Beirut in December 1914 by the Russian cruiser *ASKOLD*, and the Navy's greatest success was the sinking of the old British battleship *Goliath* by the destroyer *Muvanet* in April 1915.

During the second half of 1915, Turkish home waters were also threatened by British submarines, which sank numerous Turkish merchant craft and two of the Navy's three old battleships – the antiquated *Messudiyeh* in the Dardanelles and *HAIREDDIN BARBEROSSE* in the Sea of Marmora.

German ships and coastal-defence forces apart, the fleet was of generally poor quality. The old cruisers *MEDSHIDIYE* and *Hamidiye* were no match for their Russian counterparts in the Black Sea, and the 19 various torpedo boats and 7 patrol boats were only capable of short-range work. Turkish seamanship and gunnery were also relatively poor, and German officers were seconded to the larger Turkish ships as well as to training facilities and the best torpedo boats.

Turkish naval strategy in the Black Sea remained essentially defensive until late 1917. Although some offensive mining and coastal bombardment was carried out, operations were hampered by serious damage to *Goeben* and *Breslau*, which both struck mines and spent long periods in ill-equipped dockyards. The flotilla of U-BOATS active in the theatre from September 1915 also achieved less than its Mediterranean counterparts.

Permanently short of escort and minesweeping craft, and barely able to maintain access to the Bosporus through massed Russian minefields, the Navy lost *Medshidiye*, 13 gunboats, 4 torpedo boats and a destroyer, along with several minecraft and auxiliaries, before the Russian OCTOBER REVOLUTION in 1917 offered the prospect of strengthening the fleet with seized ships. The poor condition of Russian vessels, the prolonged nature of the peace negotiations (see BREST-LITOVSK) and Turkey's acute shortage of trained naval personnel were among the factors that prevented significant seizures until after the armistice of November 1918.

Twenty-One Demands Ultimatum presented to CHINA by the government of JAPAN on 18 January 1915, listing 21 grievances to be settled immediately under threat of war. Part of a consistent Japanese wartime policy of economic and political expansion, begun with the seizure of the German base at TSINGTAO in late 1914, the Demands required China to end the practice of leasing coastal territories to foreign powers, to grant virtual Japanese control over Manchuria and Shantung (Shandong), to allow Japanese part-ownership of its heavy industries, and to accept 'advisors' into every stratum of government activity. The Chinese government, beset by internal instability, had little choice but to concede, although Japan's closest European ally, GREAT BRITAIN, intervened to prevent the appointment of advisors. The incident stimulated intense anti-Japanese sentiment inside China, and heightened US suspicions of its main economic rival in the Pacific.

U

U-20 One of the early diesel-powered U-BOATS (U-19 Class) that were the basis for the GERMAN NAVY's wartime development of long-range 'offensive' SUBMARINES. Completed in 1913, and one of 10 in service by August 1914, it was stationed with the HIGH SEAS FLEET in the North Sea throughout its career. After a few months on offensive patrols against ROYAL NAVY warships it was transferred to commerce warfare (*HANDELSKRIEG*) from early 1915. Its commander (Schwieger) outraged neutral opinion by firing at a hospital ship in the English Channel on 1 February, and achieved lasting infamy in May by sinking the passenger liner *LUSITANIA*. Grounded off the west coast of Jutland in November 1916, *U-20* radioed for help and was answered by a salvage party with warship escort. The boat could not be moved and was blown up, but RADIO intercepts had alerted the British submarine *J-1*, which arrived to inflict TORPEDO damage on two escorting BATTLESHIPS.

BRIEF DATA (1916) Surface displacement: 650 tons; Crew: 32; Dimensions: length 210.5ft (63.8m), beam 20ft (6.1m); Speed: 15.5k (surface), 9.5k (submerged); Armament: 4 × 19.7in TT, 1 × 88mm gun.

U-155 One of seven giant German DEUTSCHLAND Class merchant SUBMARINES (*U-151* to *U-157*) converted as warships and known as U-cruisers. Intended primarily for surface attacks, their 150mm (6-inch) main armament could outrange most warships and armed merchantmen. Although clumsy and slow in the dive, a range of more than 20,000km (and untypically comfortable crew conditions) enabled them to reach shipping lanes far from Allied protection. The first to enter service, *U-155* accounted for 19 Allied merchant ships (53,000 tons) on its maiden cruise to the Azores from June to September 1917, and later undertook patrols off the US coast. Two U-cruisers were subsequently destroyed by British ANTI-SUBMARINE measures: *U-154* was torpedoed by the British submarine *E-35* on 11 May 1918 after RADIO intercepts revealed its position, and *U-156* was sunk by MINES in September 1918.

BRIEF DATA (*U-155*, 1917) Surface displacement: 1,510 tons; Crew: 76; Speed: 12.5k (surface), 5.5k (submerged); Armament: 2 × 19.7in TT, 2 × 150mm gun, 9–14 mines.

UB-Boats Small German submarines designed for ease of construction, and initially intended to release larger boats from coastal-protection duties. They entered service from spring 1915, and served mainly from the Belgian ports of ZEEBRUGGE and Ostend (along with minelaying UC-BOATS), in the BLACK SEA and in the Adriatic, seven being sent to the AUSTRO-HUNGARIAN NAVY by RAILWAY for final assembly in Pola.

Early UBs (*UB-1* to *UB-17*), though reliable and useful for short-range operations, were too small for the requirements of commerce raiding. The UB-II Class boats (*UB-18* to *UB-47*, ordered in 1915) were twice the size – with a surface speed of over 9 knots and much greater operational range – but retained their predecessors' ease of construction. By 1918 the type had evolved into the still larger UB-III Class (*UB-48* to *UB-132*), with a surface displacement of over 500 tons, five torpedo tubes and 4.1-inch (105mm) surface armament. The later models were rugged fighting craft, and faster underwater than the the larger U-BOATS. A total of 66 German UB-boats were lost, along with two Austro-Hungarian boats. See also: *HANDELSKRIEG*; SUBMARINE WARFARE.

BRIEF DATA (*UB-1*, 1915) Surface displacement: 127 tons; Crew: 14; Dimensions: length 92.25ft (63.8m), beam 9.75ft (6.1m); Speed: 6.5k (surface), 6k (submerged); Armament: 2 × 17.7in TT, 1 × mg.

U-Boat Derived from the German *Unterseeboot*, meaning 'submarine', the term was commonly used in Allied countries to denote all GERMAN NAVY submarines, although the 'U' prefix was properly applied only to large, long-range German craft, as opposed to the smaller UB-BOATS and UC-BOATS. All SUBMARINES serving with the AUSTRO-HUNGARIAN NAVY were also designated U-boats. See also: *U-20*; *U-155*; SUBMARINE WARFARE; *HANDELSKRIEG*.

UC-Boats Small, prefabricated German SUBMARINES, like UB-BOATS but designed as MINELAYERS. They were introduced to operations in the English Channel from June 1915. Their capacity to lay small pinpoint fields with little likelihood of detection made them a useful weapon, and they were also employed in the BALTIC, MEDITERRANEAN and BLACK SEAS. The 410-ton UC-II Class boats (*UC-16* to *UC-79*) were available from 1916; they could cruise for more than 11,000km, carried 18 MINES along with three TORPEDO tubes, and had 88mm surface armament. The bigger, better UC-III Class boats ordered in 1917 were never active, but mines were also carried by specialized long-range U-BOATS (*U-71* to *U-80*) and aboard large all-purpose

'U-cruisers' (see *U-155*). See also: SUBMARINE WARFARE.

BRIEF DATA (*UC-1*, 1915) Surface displacement: 168 tons; Crew: 14; Dimensions: length 111.25ft (33.7m), beam 10.3ft (3.1m); Speed: 6.5k (surface), 5k (submerged); Armament: 12 mines.

Udet, Ernst (1896–1941) The highest scoring German air ACE to survive the War, he scored most of his 62 victories in the crowded skies over the WESTERN FRONT after spring 1918. Like Hermann GÖRING, he used the popular acclaim accorded to FIGHTER pilots to launch a successful postwar career, playing a vital role in the development of the Luftwaffe in the 1930s.

Ufag C-I Austrian biplane developed from the HANSA-BRANDENBURG C-I design and in action on the ITALIAN FRONT from March 1918. The main differences between the Ufag and the PHÖNIX C-I, another contemporary derivative of the Hansa-Brandenburg, were in wing and tail design, giving it superior speed and agility but a lower operational ceiling. Both were accepted in service after competitive trials, and an estimated 100 Ufags were primarily employed for visual reconnaissance or ARTILLERY spotting.

BRIEF DATA Type: two-seater armed reconnaissance; Engine: 230hp Hiero; Max speed: 189kph; Armament: 2 × 8mm mg , light bombs (external racks).

Ukraine The area encompassed by the modern Ukrainian state formed part of the Kiev province within European RUSSIA in 1914, and stretched into the southern parts of Russian and Austro-Hungarian POLAND. Prewar Ukrainian nationalism within the Russian Empire was centred on Kiev, but was effectively suppressed in one of the most militarily active areas of imperial control until the FEBRUARY REVOLUTION in 1917.

The new PROVISIONAL GOVERNMENT in Petrograd (St Petersburg) contested political authority with the Central Rada, a nationalist assembly established in Kiev, and with socialists of the workers' and soldiers' SOVIETS that were springing up in urban areas all over the region. By autumn the Rada had established itself as the most coherent political force in the Ukraine, drawing on widespread support from the important peasant sector and cooperating with Soviets in the north.

The Russian OCTOBER REVOLUTION enabled the Rada to declare a Ukrainian People's Republic (UPR) in November 1917, but it was unable to reach a power-sharing agreement with regional Bolsheviks, who formed a rival administration at Kharkov in December. The creation of the UPR prompted military intervention by Bolsheviks disbanded from the RUSSIAN ARMY, who marched on Kiev in the new year. The Rada responded by accepting an invitation from the CENTRAL POWERS to join the peace conference at BREST-LITOVSK, declaring formal independence from Bolshevik Russia on 22 January 1918, and inviting German and Austro-Hungarian forces to occupy the Ukraine (see *BROTFRIEDEN*).

Ruthless economic exploitation followed under General EICHHORN's military command. The mass removal of grain to Austria caused immediate hardship, and attempts to force peasants to grow more contributed to an atmosphere of revolutionary unrest. Eichhorn was assassinated in late July 1918, and the collapse of GERMANY in November triggered three years of anarchy as 14 different governments claimed control of the Ukraine before Bolsheviks, backed by RED ARMY forces, established a reasonably secure government in 1921 (see RUSSIAN CIVIL WAR). The Bolshevik regime joined the Soviet Union but conceded some representation to nationalist and peasant leaders until the Stalinist repression of the early 1930s. See MAP 25.

Ukraine Offensive Name sometimes given to the second phase of the BRUSILOV OFFENSIVE on the EASTERN FRONT in July 1916.

United Kingdom See: GREAT BRITAIN.

United States of America The USA in 1914 comprised 48 autonomous states under an elected federal administration headed by the president and his nominated cabinet. Chosen every four years by indirect male suffrage through a college of states' electors, the president's executive powers were (and are) subject to assent from two directly elected chambers of Congress, the lower House of Representatives and the smaller upper house, the Senate.

The national political landscape was dominated by the composite Republican and Democratic Parties, but a reformist 'Progressive' faction had split from the Republicans and run its own candidate (former president Theodore ROOSEVELT) in the 1912 presidential elections, which turned into a landslide for Democrat reformer Woodrow WILSON. Politically inexperienced and less flamboyant than opponents like Roosevelt or LODGE, Wilson was an adept manipulator of idealist popular sentiment, an important factor in a constituency of small communities and local newspapers.

Concentration of economic power in the hands of a few large corporations (largely based in the northeast) encouraged expansion overseas and limitation of political controls over big business by the early 20th century. Anxious to develop economic influence in South America and the Pacific, corporate interests were broadly represented by conservative Republicans and opposed by a spectrum of liberal reformers seeking to increase public supervision and maintain ISOLATIONISM.

Debate was complicated by powerful regional antagonisms between the landed south, the industrial northeast, and the newer western and midwestern states. An increasingly militant industrial working class, locked in a hard struggle for union recognition and suffering high unemployment during a depression in 1913–14, was a growing threat to business profit, but exerted little or no revolutionary pressure.

The USA possessed plentiful natural resources and an expanding population of some 100 million, boosted by more than 12 million immigrants since 1900. Marshalled by a vigorous entrepreneurial class using new mass-production techniques, the US economy was the greatest threat to GREAT BRITAIN's global economic domination by 1914, and its growth was rivalled only by GERMANY. The world leader in coal and steel production, the USA was both a heavy industrial power and a major producer of raw materials, with wheat, cotton and oil accounting for more than a third of exports. Trade and industry were served by a transport system based on 400,000km of privately owned RAILWAYS and the nation's long, navigable rivers.

The USA had no overseas alliances and no intention of going to war in 1914. Wilson's declaration of strict neutrality (19 August) reflected both popular isolationism and the divisive potential of European conflict on 'hyphenated' groups. In a nation with strong Anglo-French ties, the sensibilities of more than 10 million first- or second-generation Germans, and of the Irish, Polish, Slav, Armenian and Czech populations (among others), could not easily be ignored.

After a brief hiatus in world trade, a major export boom gave eastern magnates an important stake in Allied victory: German and Austro-Hungarian merchant shipping disappeared from the oceans, and the Allies quickly exhausted their cash and saleable US investments with a flood of orders for armaments and raw materials.

Closer to Europe than AUSTRALIA or other alternative suppliers, the USA exported goods worth $825 million to Allied countries in 1914, and $3.2 billion in 1916. A $500 million Anglo-French loan was arranged by a consortium of east-coast banks in October 1915, and by April 1917 US banks had extended $2.6 billion of credit to help the Allies spend about $7 billion. The CENTRAL POWERS owed only $27 million. US businesses also gained from a sudden lack of European competition to confirm their economic domination in CANADA and Latin America.

Global economic status stimulated the internal PREPAREDNESS MOVEMENT, a broad alliance of campaigners for greater international political involvement and expansion of the armed forces. Well-funded by conservative businesses, with strong support in Washington and among a military circle led by General WOOD, the preparedness lobby used PROPAGANDA to whittle down opposition from liberal, pacifist, feminist, reformist and socialist elements, which had crystallized into pressure groups like the AMERICAN UNION AGAINST MILITARISM after 1914.

The USA was a propaganda battleground between the European belligerents throughout the neutrality years. The Allied cause was aided by sustained popular sympathy for BELGIUM, identification of the German monarchy with autocratic militarism, and suspicion of German interference in MEXICO and Latin America. Anti-German feeling was fuelled by German attempts at industrial sabotage (including a fire at a munitions factory that led to the expulsion of German military attachés in December 1915), but its most powerful stimulus was the gradual extension of SUBMARINE WARFARE, which caused genuine outrage even in the largely apathetic west.

German propaganda concentrated less successfully on the Allied naval BLOCKADE, which was irritating to US interests but involved no deaths and paid financial compensation for confiscations. 'Hyphenated' populations within the USA contributed support for both sides according to their origins, stimulated by episodes like the EASTER RISING and the ARMENIAN MASSACRES.

The German submarine campaigns were directly responsible for ending US neutrality. Wilson's stern note to Germany after the *LUSITANIA* sinking in May 1915 brought the resignation of secretary of state Bryan, the administration's senior pacifist spokesman, and his replacement by the pro-Allied LANSING. The *SUSSEX* sinking the following April brought a renewed warning that the USA would hold Germany 'strictly accountable' for further losses. Although this warning prompted a temporary cessation of U-BOAT attacks on neutral shipping, deflecting criticism by the preparedness lobby, the ultimatum effectively made the resumption of attacks a war issue.

Wilson announced support for 'limited preparedness' in September 1915, and the National Defense Act of December permitted limited expansion of the US ARMY, US NAVY and merchant marine, carried out by isolationist secretaries BAKER and DANIELS as a sop to liberal sensitivities. A Council of National Defense to coordinate government and business planning was established the following August. Opposition was appeased by the continued rejection of conscription and by new taxes on high incomes to pay for the expansion.

Wilson's 1916 election campaign was planned around home issues, but the slogan 'he kept us out of the war' (forced on him by party organizers) was largely responsible for a very narrow victory over Republican Charles Hughes. Once re-elected, Wilson pursued the only likely means of avoiding war, issuing a PEACE NOTE (18 December 1916) to all the belligerents requesting a statement of their war aims. Coming immediately after an unconvincing German PEACE OFFER, it helped seal Berlin's decision to commence unrestricted submarine warfare.

Wilson remained publicly against intervention in early 1917, speaking in favour of 'peace without victory' in the Senate on 22 January, and moved cautiously after German ambassador BERNSTORFF announced the new submarine offensive on 31 January. The USA broke diplomatic relations with Germany on 4 February, and popular hostility was intensified by publication of the ZIMMERMANN NOTE on 1 March. Wilson had already asked Congress for $100 million for the defensive arming of merchant ships, a grant delayed until 9 March by a minority of Senate pacifists.

On 2 April, against the backdrop of a railway strike, Wilson asked for permission to go to war, approved in the Senate on 4 April by 82 votes to 6, and in the House by 373 to 50 on 6 April. Still avoiding alliances, the USA joined the conflict as an 'Associated Power' by declaring war against the German government (rather than its subjects) on 6 April. War against AUSTRIA-HUNGARY was not declared until 7 December.

Public reaction was a limited version of the jingoism experienced in Europe. Outbursts of violent popular xenophobia threatened the lives and property of Germans, and a large number of German words in common US usage were outlawed. The FEBRUARY REVOLUTION in RUSSIA had freed many US liberals to support a national crusade against autocracy, and sections of most anti-interventionist organizations opted to take an active role in anticipated wartime political changes. Official union support for war (led by Samuel

GOMPERS) was based on the expectation of postwar labour reforms.

Opposition continued, but its repression was indicative of a wartime transformation in government methods. Although direct censorship of the press was politically impossible, foreign newspapers were censored under the Trading With The Enemy Act (October 1917), and emergency federal control over the mail system enabled suppression of undesirable publications.

The Espionage Act (June 1917) and Sedition Act (May 1918) allowed the federal administration to arrest dissenters for a wide range of 'disloyal' activities, and most of over 1,600 people imprisoned were charged with spoken offences. The Socialist Party of America, which remained resolutely pacifist throughout, suffered particular harassment, with leader Eugene Debs receiving a 20-year prison sentence for unpatriotic speeches after the OCTOBER REVOLUTION in Russia had sparked a nationwide 'Reds' scare.

The same legislation prohibited draft dodging, but the completely new experience of mass conscription under the SELECTIVE SERVICE ACT (18 May 1917) passed off fairly smoothly, eventually rendering about 24.5 million men liable for wartime conscription, of whom 6,373,414 were inducted. Facing a huge training and camp-construction programme, as well as urgent rearmament and the creation of an air force (see USAAS), neither the US Army nor the US Navy was ever in a position to threaten political control of economic mobilization.

The War Industries Board (WIB) was established in July 1917, along with Food, Labor, Trade and Finance Boards. Charged with coordination of all Allied arms requirements, and headed by trusted Wilson aide Bernard Baruch, the WIB brought together industrial leaders and military advisors, operating a system of priority designation for all war-related goods and materials. Though the system worked efficiently and fairly harmoniously, smaller manufacturers regarded links between WIB officials and some of its biggest customers with suspicion, but a bill to replace coopted tycoons with civil servants was defeated in early 1918.

Price rises, already evident during the neutrality boom, also brought accusations of profiteering against the relatively efficient big businesses. Emergency legislation in March 1917 taxed the profits of war industries at between 20 and 60 per cent, and in September the government intervened to fix the prices of freight and raw materials. The railways, suffering serious shortages of rolling stock, were under federal control from 27 December 1917 (see MCADOO, W.).

Unprecedented centralized control led to a massive increase in output, especially in the armaments sector. Apart from supplying its own forces, the wartime USA supplied Britain with almost a billion rounds of bullets, 31 million shells, 1.2 million RIFLES, more than half a million tons of explosives, 42,000 lorries, 3,400 aircraft engines, 866 aircraft, and 1,400 gun carriages. Russia was supplied, via Britain, with over 500 million bullets, almost a million rifles, and 24,500 MACHINE GUNS. Few heavy guns or US-designed aircraft (and no TANKS) reached Europe, but were planned for 1919 and beyond.

The most valuable direct contribution to the Allied war effort came from a radically enlarged shipbuilding industry. Priority allocation of materials and large-scale investment enabled construction of 341 new shipyards in 1917–18. In 1914 US yards were completing 17,000 tons of shipping per month; in 1916 the figure had risen to 42,000 tons; by 1918, standardization, with three-quarters of all new vessels built to 'Liberty Ship' patterns, had boosted production to 253,000 tons per month.

American food exports to Europe peaked in 1916, after which the use of shipping for military supply limited them to about twice 1913 quantities. Although the USA suffered no food shortages on the home front, Herbert Hoover's Food Board supervised voluntary campaigns to prevent waste and increase arable acreage. Bread production tripled between 1914 and 1918, while meat and dairy output rose by almost 400 per cent. Farmers almost doubled their profits in the same period, and industry as a whole experienced about a 120 per cent rise in profits, although the ALCOHOL trade suffered the ultimate sanction of PROHIBITION.

As the Allies' major supplier the USA also became their main banker, and total Allied imports from the USA of $10.3 billion were financed with over $7 billion in credits. Since the money was being spent in the USA, American businessmen rejected suggestions of close inter-Allied economic cooperation as interference. Anxious to invest their wealth in postwar European reconstruction, they also defeated Allied proposals to continue the blockade of Germany into the 1920s.

Industrial transformation brought social upheaval, though on a less dramatic scale than in Europe. High demand for labour bolstered a strong prewar female suffrage movement by introducing 40,000 more WOMEN into the industrial workforce by 1918. A demographic shift of black workers to northern factories had relocated some 350,000 Afro-Americans by 1920, bringing new racial tensions to the northeast and prompting some southern communities to pass laws banning the departure of cheap labour.

Wartime government propaganda was controlled by a Committee on Public Information (CPI), headed by publicist George CREEL, but a mass of private material emanated from the forces behind the Preparedness Movement. Creel doubled as the president's personal propagandist, ridiculing Lodge and other leading opponents at home, and promoting international recognition of Wilson's proposals for long-term peace.

Wilson was embarrassed by the Bolshevik government's revelation of Allied postwar territorial plans in December 1917 (see Treaty of LONDON; SYKES–PICOT AGREEMENT), and his own peace plan issued in January 1918, the FOURTEEN POINTS, was a comprehensive denunciation of imperialism in its prewar form. As a deliberate appeal to worldwide popular idealism it was a great success, but the Points were never fully endorsed by Allied governments, and – despite popular adulation during his two visits to Europe for the PARIS PEACE CONFERENCE – Wilson was unable to impose them on Allied leaders.

The compromise Treaty of VERSAILLES was generally viewed as a defeat for Wilson in the USA. Mid-term elections in 1918 had returned a strongly Republican Congress that refused to ratify the Treaty (thus rejecting US membership of the LEAGUE OF NATIONS) in November 1919 and again the following March. His popularity broken, Wilson suffered a major coronary in October 1919 and played no part in the 1920 presidential election, which returned Warren Harding as the candidate of a reunited Republican Party. Harding's slogan of 'return to normalcy' reflected popular disenchantment with foreign affairs.

The American Expeditionary Force (AEF) had begun fighting on the WESTERN FRONT in spring 1918, and had played an important part in the battles for final victory, but the US military experience was less all-pervasive than that of the European belligerents. Though illuminated by popular heroes like General PERSHING, Alvin YORK and Eddie RICKENBACKER, it was overshadowed by sociopolitical shifts at home, and peace brought only a brief period of celebration. Home affairs were dominated by increasingly hysterical fears of Bolshevik conspiracy – completing the wartime rout of left-wing political forces – and by the arrival of the INFLUENZA epidemic, which killed 400,000–500,000 Americans in the 36 affected states over nine months from autumn 1918.

Unrestricted Submarine Warfare See: *HANDELSKRIEG*; SUBMARINE WARFARE; NAVAL WARFARE.

USAAS (United States Army Air Service) The aeronautical arm of the US ARMY, part of which fought with the American Expeditionary Force (AEF) in 1918. Powered flight was pioneered in the UNITED STATES in 1903, but official military contact was not made with the Wright Brothers until 1907. Displaying less enthusiasm for the new arm than its European counterparts, the Army eventually provided funds to purchase aircraft in 1911, and instituted the Curtiss Aviation School at San Diego in 1913, the same year that the US NAVY opened its flying school in Pensacola. An act of Congress in July 1913 provided for an Aviation Section of 60 officers and 260 men, and it possessed 20 aircraft by August.

A squadron of Army aircraft took part in the 1917 expedition into MEXICO, but all crashed or were lost in action, providing graphic evidence of the need for better equipment, training and tactics. Congress promptly voted $13 million to develop the Aviation Section, and the renamed US Army Air Service possessed 1,185 serving personnel and some 260 planes by April 1917.

None of the aircraft were fit for combat in Europe, and the arrival of French and British aviation missions in the USA signalled a major effort to bring American air power up to date. Congress voted $640 million to build 22,000 planes to French designs, twice as many engines, and a full range of spare parts, and 263 operational squadrons were to be in France by June 1918. These targets were never approached in practice, but rapid industrial expansion and mushrooming training facilities did produce a phenomenal growth of US air power.

The 1st Squadron of the USAAS arrived in France on 3 September 1917, by which time training airfields were already being constructed in Europe, but shortages of equipment, lack of instructors, initial failure to exploit the skills of trained US pilots serving with other armies, and the AEF's general preoccupation with building up infantry forces all contributed to delays in getting US aircrew operational over the WESTERN FRONT.

Under the aggressive command of Colonel (later Brigadier General) MITCHELL, an efficient system of deployment gradually emerged, and the first FIGHTER patrols over German lines began in late March 1918, after which US air strength built up rapidly along the relatively quiet sector of the front between Verdun and Nancy (see MAP 2).

Daylight bombing raids began in June, and in the same month Mitchell established the 1st Air Brigade under his personal command around Château-Thierry and Belleau Wood. When the AEF launched its first major attack at ST MIHIEL in September, Mitchell commanded a supporting force of almost 1,500 aircraft (mostly squadrons from other Allied nations), and USAAS units played an important ground-support role throughout the subsequent MEUSE–ARGONNE OFFENSIVE.

American-designed and -built flying boats operated with the US Navy, but design of Army combat machines remained the province of European industry. US designers concentrated on answering the urgent need for training aircraft, producing thousands of their most successful type, the Curtiss JN series. Mass production of European combat designs was undertaken by the US automobile industry, led by Dayton-Wright and Fisher Auto in Ohio, which built small quantities of several European bombers and almost 5,000 of the British-designed AIRCO DH-4, although tooling-up problems delayed production until it was effectively obsolete.

Otherwise, the USA provided raw materials and engines for European aero industries and bought completed machines from the Allies. By late 1918 the USAAS had taken delivery of 4,881 French, 258 British and a few Italian aircraft, and virtually all its combat machines were drawn from these. They included small numbers of many Allied designs, but frontline fighter (or 'pursuit') pilots usually flew NIEUPORT 28S – which had been rejected by the AÉRONAUTIQUE MILITAIRE – or marginally superior SPAD S-VIIIS. The first genuinely competitive SPAD S-XIII fighters began reaching US squadrons in July 1918. Apart from DH-4s, bomber squadrons were mostly equipped with French BREGUET and SALMSON machines.

The USAAS mustered 45 squadrons (740 combat aircraft and 1,250 aircrew) in Europe at the ARMISTICE, and 202,000 personnel (11,400 aircrew) worldwide. Most machines were recognizably obsolete and, in what was known as the 'Billion Dollar Bonfire', large numbers were burned in Europe as scrap. The wartime US Balloon Service, technically part of the USAAS, grew almost as dramatically as the aircraft arm, expanding from a strength of 20 (borrowed) balloons in January 1918 to more than 600 in November. See also: ACES; AERIAL WARFARE; Escadrille LAFAYETTE.

US Army The ground forces of the UNITED STATES were relatively tiny in 1914. The professional regular Army comprised 98,000 men, of whom some 45,000 were stationed at overseas bases (such as the PHILIPPINES) and about 29,000 were needed for home defence. The remaining strike force of about 24,000 men – even if reinforced by the 27,000 troops of the state militia (National Guard) available for service outside their home states – was considered inadequate by expansionist interests in the USA, and the Army's size was a source of major controversy during the period of neutrality before 1917.

An enlarged 'continental' army staffed by conscription was seen by the PREPAREDNESS MOVEMENT as a means of protecting overseas economic assets, and as a solution to perceived social problems. Led by General WOOD, senior officers were understandably in favour, but the idea was denounced as militarism by liberal elements. President WILSON's acceptance of 'limited preparedness' in December 1915 increased the standing army to over 140,000 men and made provision for a volunteer trained reserve of 400,000 (absorbing the National Guard). Still tiny by European standards, this force was in the process of assembling when the regular 1st Division, led by General PERSHING, undertook its ultimately futile punitive raid into MEXICO in spring 1916.

When the USA declared war in April 1917 Wilson demanded and received a mandate to institute conscription for a new 'national army', separate from the regular force and the National Guard (mobilized in July) but deployed alongside them in Pershing's American Expeditionary Force (AEF) to Europe. Conscripts under the SELECTIVE SERVICE ACT were automatically drafted into the new force, and volunteers were accepted only by the established branches.

The 1st Division was sent to Europe immediately, but the AEF's role was largely symbolic until spring 1918. Pershing collected and organized his troops, exasperating Allied commanders by refusing to lend units to other armies. At the same time the rapid build-up of fit, well-fed 'DOUGHBOYS' (500,000 by May 1918, and 1 million by July) was a powerful stimulus to Allied morale, especially in FRANCE. The build-up of US forces also prompted the Germans to plan an all-out series of offensives on the WESTERN FRONT (the 1918 SPRING OFFENSIVES) to end the War before Allied manpower superiority became overwhelming.

Pershing moderated his attitude in response to the Spring Offensives of 1918, detaching troops to join the French defence during the AISNE offensive in May and the second MARNE battle in June (see Battle of CANTIGNY). US troops also took part in Anglo-French attacks at LE HAMEL and CANAL DU NORD (among others) before Pershing launched his own meticulously planned offensive at ST MIHIEL in September.

The efficient but limited success at St Mihiel silenced Pershing's critics in Europe and the USA, where his independence, frequent dismissals of field officers and inflationary assessments of requirements provoked disputes with Army chief of staff General MARCH in 1918. The last major US combat operation on the Western Front, the MEUSE-ARGONNE OFFENSIVE, was a less straightforward success, revealing the AEF's organizational inexperience and shortage of competent field officers, but also highlighting Pershing's adaptability.

The AEF arrived in Europe armed only with RIFLES, and relied mostly on French MACHINE GUNS for infantry support until the arrival of Browning guns from the USA in 1918. The home Army used its own 3-inch field guns and 6-inch howitzers, but the AEF employed Anglo-French ARTILLERY in Europe, mostly the French SOIXANTE-QUINZES and 155mm howitzers but also British howitzers and RAILWAY ARTILLERY. Manufacture of TANKS was underway in the USA by 1918, and a few US-built RENAULT machines crossed the Atlantic in wartime, but the US Tank Corps used only British and French machines in action from September 1918. The rapidly expanded USAAS was similarly dependent on European air forces for its equipment. Apart from a few liaison squadrons, the US CAVALRY was left at home.

Poised on the German border near Sedan when the War ended, the AEF eventually comprised three armies, each of three corps, with a total of 1.3 million combat troops. More than 2 million troops eventually reached Europe, many too late too see action, and the AEF suffered 264,000 casualties, including 50,000 killed in battle and half as many by disease. About 380,000 Afro-Americans served in the wartime US Army, and 200,000 were sent to Europe, but only 42,000 were classified as combat troops. Completely segregated, they fought in the 93rd Division (of 100 eventually formed) and as the 157th Division in the less racially sensitive FRENCH ARMY. The conscript armies were rapidly demobilized on their return to the USA in 1919, leaving a small regular force commanded by officers of reduced peacetime rank.

US Navy The UNITED STATES emerged as an international naval power in the 1890s, when a major construction programme created a battlefleet along European lines. The Spanish-American War of 1898, and the increasing influence of expansionist elements, promoted rapid naval growth in the early 20th century, as the USA sought to protect and extend flourishing trade routes in both the Pacific and the Atlantic.

The US Navy was the world's third largest by 1914, after the ROYAL NAVY and the GERMAN NAVY, comprising some 300 warships of all classes. Frontline forces included 17 PRE-DREADNOUGHTS and 10 modern BATTLESHIPS (see *SOUTH CAROLINA, NEW YORK, ARIZONA*), along with 32 old-style CRUISERS, 56 DESTROYERS of varying age and quality, 51 SUBMARINES, and 21 TORPEDO BOATS.

A major expansion programme begun in August 1915 focused US naval strategy on the Atlantic, and provided the basis for a massive shipbuilding boom over the next four years. Although US yards completed another six dreadnoughts by mid-1918, resources were concentrated on light craft and merchant ships. Output of merchantmen, destroyers and other ANTI-SUBMARINE craft exceeded 100 ships per month by mid-1918, when the US Navy possessed more than 1,000 warships.

The wartime US Navy's most high-profile operations – the attachment of nine modern battleships to the British GRAND FLEET from December 1917, and the creation of the NORTHERN BARRAGE – reflected its willing subordination to overall Allied command in Europe, and naval relations with the Allies were generally excellent, being only occasionally undermined by US national interests (see BRAZILIAN NAVY; Admirals SIMS, BENSON and MAYO).

US-built merchant ships made an enormous contribution to Allied carrying capacity, and warships played an important part in CONVOY and other anti-submarine work. US ships escorted almost two-thirds of the troops sent to Europe across the Atlantic, and joined desperately stretched Allied escort forces in the MEDITERRANEAN. The main bulk of naval forces, including all the submarines and hundreds of civilian craft temporarily commissioned for coastal patrol, nevertheless remained concentrated on the Atlantic seaboard of the USA. Many ships in US waters were crewed by volunteer reserves, because conscription was not applied to the US Navy, but forces sent to Europe were almost entirely drawn from regular strength, expanded to almost 140,000 men by late 1918. The Navy's most serious wartime losses were the cruiser *San Diego*, sunk by MINES from a U-boat off New York, and two destroyers lost on anti-submarine work in European waters.

Shipborne naval aviation was pioneered in the prewar USA, but the Navy was slow to develop the field and had no AIRCRAFT CARRIERS until the 1920s. Its limited number of operational flying boats was expanded after 1915, but most of the excellent US-built CURTISS H-12 flying boats were used by the far larger British RNAS. See also: DANIELS, J.

V

Valenciennes, Battle of Offensive by British forces in the northern sector of the WESTERN FRONT, launched on 1 November 1918 to follow up the advance of the Fourth Army at the SELLE. General BYNG's Third Army attacked towards the Franco-Belgian border city of Valenciennes, which was captured by CANADIAN units on 2 November, and the GERMAN ARMY's virtual disintegration was confirmed by a continuation of the action begun at the SAMBRE on 4 November. See MAP 2.

Vanguard One of nine British BATTLESHIPS built as near copies of the *DREADNOUGHT* design. Small differences in mast and turret design distinguished the three groups: *Bellerophon*, *Temeraire* and *Superb* (1909); *St Vincent*, *Vanguard* and *Collingwood* (1910); and *Neptune*, *Colossus* and *Hercules* (1911). A tenth ship, *Agincourt*, was built in Britain for Brazil, sold to TURKEY while under construction, and commandeered by the ROYAL NAVY in August 1914. Later British battleships all had larger main guns.

All ten ships were with the GRAND FLEET and were present (though inactive) at JUTLAND. *Temeraire* and *Superb* later served in the MEDITERRANEAN, but most remained quietly in the North Sea. The exception was *Vanguard*, which exploded while loading ammunition on 9 July 1917 and sank at anchor in Scapa Flow, one of only two modern British battleships lost. The surviving ships, all of which had been modified to include ANTI-AIRCRAFT guns, were retired in 1919.

BRIEF DATA (*Vanguard*, 1914) Displacement: 19,250 tons; Crew: 800; Dimensions: length 536ft (162.4m), beam 84ft (25.5m); Speed: 22k; Armament: 10 × 12in gun, 18 × 4in, 2 × 18in TT.

Vardar Offensive The final, successful offensive by Allied forces based in SALONIKA. It was launched in September 1918, and by the ARMISTICE had reached the Danube. The withdrawal of German forces to the WESTERN FRONT in early 1918 had left only 200,000 dispirited BULGARIAN ARMY troops to hold a line from the Aegean coast in the east to the border of ALBANIA in the west, reviving Allied hopes of an attack on AUSTRIA-HUNGARY through the Balkans.

New Allied Balkan C-in-C GUILLAUMAT, appointed in December 1917, postponed his intended attack when the German SPRING OFFENSIVES forced concentration of defences in France, and was himself transferred to command the defence of Paris in June 1918, but his successor, General FRANCHET D'ESPEREY, adopted his plans for attacks all along the line basically intact. Reinforcement by the GREEK ARMY from July gave him a combat strength roughly equal to opposing commander ZHEKHOV but vast superiority in ARTILLERY, ammunition and supplies.

The offensive opened on 15 September, with the SERBIAN ARMY under Marshal MIŠIĆ, flanked by French units, advancing up the Vardar River along a 25km front. It gained about 10km on the first day as disorganized Bulgarian forces fell back. An Anglo-Greek attack around Lake Doiran began on 18 September and achieved similarly unprecedented success, taking positions in a day that had held for almost for three years, and by 19 September Allied forces north of MONASTIR had crossed the Crno River to approach Prilep.

Retreat degenerated into rout after 25 September, when Franchet D'Esperey refused a ceasefire offer from Sofia. Veles fell to Serbian troops that day and the British crossed the Bulgarian border, General MILNE's western flank taking Strumica on 26 September. The French entered Skopje on 29 September as ARMISTICE talks began with the Bulgarian government. The AUSTRO-HUNGARIAN ARMY forces on the BALKAN

FRONT began withdrawing to protect the Empire's southern borders after BULGARIA surrendered on 30 September, by which time almost 90,000 Bulgarian troops had been captured.

The CENTRAL POWERS' position in the Balkans collapsed rapidly through October. While the British moved east towards Constantinople, and Italian troops concentrated on securing the occupation of ALBANIA, both Serbia and Bulgaria had been cleared of remaining German units by the end of the month. The Serbian Army reoccupied Belgrade on 1 November, and Allied armies were lined along the Danube when Austria-Hungary capitulated on 4 November. See MAP 19.

Vaux, Fort See: Battle of VERDUN.

Venizelos, Eleutherios (1864–1936) The leading figure in early 20th-century Greek politics. Venizelos played an important part in the Cretan independence movement, becoming the island's first independent prime minister in 1905. He moved to Athens at the invitation of royalist Army officers in 1909, and became prime minister of GREECE from 1910. His regime was marked by military reform, territorial acquisition and close co-operation with the crown, but relations with King CONSTANTINE I were soured by the approach of European war in 1914.

Regarding renewed war with TURKEY as inevitable, Venizelos pursued alliance with the ENTENTE POWERS, a stance grudgingly accepted by the pro-German Constantine and greeted with only a lukewarm Allied response. Strongly in favour of providing military aid for the DARDANELLES OPERATION, Venizelos resigned in March 1915 over Constantine's refusal to agree.

Re-elected by a landslide in June, eventually ratified by the King in August, Venizelos ordered mobilization of the GREEK ARMY and requested Allied assistance in defence of threatened SERBIA. Allied forces reached SALONIKA just as the King dismissed Venizelos (5 October), and he became a focus for anti-monarchist opposition during 1916, leaving Athens for Crete in September and forming a provisional revolutionary government in Salonika in October. Skirmishes between royalist and 'Venizelist' forces (equipped from Allied stock) began in November, and an Army of National Defence (four divisions) was almost ready to march on Athens when Constantine's deposition in June 1917 brought Venizelos peacefully back to power.

Venizelos guided the Greek war effort from late June until the ARMISTICE, and as Greek representative at the PARIS PEACE CONFERENCE he won substantial territorial gains at the expense of Bulgaria and Turkey in Thrace. Despite British sympathy he was not able to gain full international support for Greek administration of Turkish SMYRNA, and the Army was ordered to occupy the region in 1919. War weariness and the premier's long-term absence on diplomatic missions contributed to his defeat in the December 1920 elections.

Verdun, Battle of The longest battle of the First World War and the most costly in terms of battle casualties, fought from 21 February to 18 December 1916 around the fortified French garrison town of Verdun, on the River Meuse 200km east of Paris (see MAP 2). Verdun and its surrounding ring of forts had formed the heart of a French SALIENT on the WESTERN FRONT since 1914 (see Battle of the ARDENNES), but the battle of 1916 was fought for its own sake rather than for any territorial advantage.

German chief of staff FALKENHAYN had decided in December 1915 to attack Verdun. Reasoning that neither RUSSIA nor GREAT BRITAIN could be knocked out by a single blow, he sought to grind the French to defeat by attacking where they would feel compelled to defend. The stated intention of the operation was to 'bleed the FRENCH ARMY white' by inflicting unsustainable casualties over a long offensive.

The German Army used good RAILWAY facilities to concentrate unprecedented quantities of ARTILLERY and ammunition at the front in the new year, defended about 5km beyond Verdun's northern and eastern forts by the French Second Army. The fortress defences were being dismantled and reorganized, with only skeleton garrisons in position during the transition. Despite warnings from field commanders, French C-in-C JOFFRE (embroiled in planning the Allied SOMME OFFENSIVE) only began to take the threat to Verdun seriously in late January, drafting in a few reinforcements and replacing some of the guns previously stripped from the forts for frontline use.

When the attack began in late February, 1 million troops of Crown Prince WILHELM's German Fifth Army faced only about 200,000 defenders. A 21-hour PRELIMINARY BOMBARDMENT dropped over a million shells onto the area around the northern and eastern forts before infantry advanced along a 12km front northeast of the town in the late afternoon of 21 February. Despite unexpected resistance from surviving defenders, they drove French troops back to their second line of TRENCHES the next day.

On 24 February, the French Second Army retired along a wider front to a third line of defence within 8km of Verdun itself, abandoning the Woevre plain and exposing the poorly garrisoned fortress of Douaumont to capture. French reinforcements were already arriving around Verdun when Douaumont fell on 25 February, but the loss of the prestigious fortress triggered an eruption of national feeling in FRANCE that exceeded even Falkenhayn's expectations. French withdrawal at Verdun became a political and moral impossibility for the BRIAND government and the Army.

Second Army commander PÉTAIN, a committed fortress-stripper who regarded the system as anachronistic, was given control of the whole sector on 24 February. Joffre absolutely forbade withdrawal, so Pétain began a rapid reorganization of defences that saved a situation apparently beyond recall. Ordering every reserve gun to the front, he concentrated all available artillery against attacking infantry, bringing the German advance to a halt on 28 February.

Mutual shortage of ammunition forced a week's lull in the fighting, allowing Pétain to complete his reorganization. Attacked from the north and east, his salient relied for all supplies on one minor road, which was widened and kept open for a massive transport operation (see VOIE SACRÉE). Pétain also made best use of a constant stream of reinforcements, rotating units quickly in and out of the battle. Of the 330 infantry regiments of the French Army, 259 eventually fought at Verdun.

In an attempt to deal with Pétain's artillery positions, the German Fifth Army launched a new attack north and northwest of the town on 6 March. Ground was gained in heavy fighting along a 15km front, and German forces had advanced about 3km by early April, when they were stopped in front of heights around Mort Homme Hill. French and German losses in March were roughly equal, and the bloodletting damaged the German Army no less than the French.

New German infantry attacks all along the line from Avocourt in the northwest to the fortress of Vaux in the east were launched on 9 April and continued into early June. Mort Homme Hill was finally secured by German forces on 29 May, and Fort Vaux fell on 7 June after a protracted siege.

Another major attack towards forts west of Vaux began on 21 June and Pétain, by now promoted to command the regional Army Group, again sought permission to withdraw. It was refused, and credit for holding off the attack, which used phosgene GAS for the first time but petered out after 11 July, went to General NIVELLE, the aggressive new Second Army commander. At this stage heavy losses of men (315,000 French and 280,000 German casualties) and equipment, as well as ammunition shortages and the demands of Allied offensives elsewhere, forced a longer pause in the battle.

Inconclusive combat continued through the summer and early autumn, but the THIRD SUPREME COMMAND, in power from August in Germany, ruled out further major attacks at Verdun. While German forces were being drawn off to defend positions on the SOMME, the French were gathering for a counterattack, launched towards Douaumont and Vaux by General MANGIN's Third Army from 24 October.

Douaumont was retaken on the same day and Vaux on 2 November, before ammunition shortages again brought the attack to an end. From 15–18 December, Mangin's infantry resumed the attack northwest of the forts, and advanced about another 2km along a narrow front (the Battle of Louvemont), ending the struggle for Verdun.

Territorially, the German Army had advanced a few kilometres along about a 35km front, and a few villages had been obliterated. Strategically, the main effect of the battle was the irrevocable wounding of both armies. Estimates vary, but the French Army (the only Allied army that fought at Verdun) lost a probable total of about 550,000 men, and the German Army about 434,000. About half of all casualties were killed, and the survivors were said to be scarred for life by the experience. See MAP 7.

Versailles, Treaty of The peace agreement between GERMANY and the Allies, formulated at the PARIS PEACE CONFERENCE and signed by both sides on 28 June 1919 at the Palace of Versailles. The Treaty was completed by Allied delegates in late April, after three months of hard bargaining over its 440 clauses, and handed to German representatives on 7 May. Given three weeks to comment on the document, which it had not helped draft, the German government replied with a long list of complaints, reinforcing liberal criticisms of the Treaty's radical departure from the FOURTEEN POINTS, and pragmatic arguments by British leaders that the terms were too harsh. Most of the German complaints were ignored.

The final Treaty opened with the LEAGUE OF NATIONS covenant, and went on to deprive Germany of about 13.5 per cent of its 1914 territory, about 13 per cent of its economic resources, some 7 million people, and all its overseas possessions (which became MANDATES).

In the west, the disputed Alsace–Lorraine region was returned to FRANCE, and eastern BELGIUM was enlarged to include the border areas of Eupen and Malmédy. Intense French pressure for permanent occupation of the Rhineland and the Saar mining region was resisted by GREAT BRITAIN and the UNITED STATES, and the areas were instead placed under Allied occupation, to be gradually withdrawn over 15 years.

Part of East Prussia was given to LITHUANIA, the Sudetenland became part of CZECHOSLOVAKIA, and a plebiscite of the people of Schleswig was called to decide the Danish–German border. Along with Poznania and certain East Prussian provinces, the Treaty gave POLAND access to the sea via a strip of land (the 'Polish Corridor') to the former German port of Danzig (Gdansk), designated a 'free city' under League administration. Controversy over Silesia, originally given to Poland but granted a referendum after German objections were supported by LLOYD GEORGE, ended in its partition between Germany and Poland after an inconclusive poll in 1921.

Military clauses limited the GERMAN ARMY to 100,000 men, with a prohibition on conscription, heavy ARTILLERY, GAS, TANKS, aircraft and AIRSHIPS. The GERMAN NAVY was restricted to vessels under 10,000 tons, forbidden to employ SUBMARINES or aircraft, allowed only 1,500 officers, and required to open the Kiel Canal to international traffic. None of the military clauses set time limits, an omission later used as a justification for German rearmament.

The Treaty also assigned 'war guilt' to Germany, and on that basis enforced an immediate payment of REPARATIONS, pending a League of Nations decision on the full amount owed. Provision was made for the punishment of 'WAR CRIMES' committed by Kaiser WILHELM II and other leaders, and a proposed union between Germany and Austria was prohibited.

Criticized by liberal Allied opinion for being too harsh, and by the right as too lenient, the Treaty was rejected by Allied CHINA and by Congress in the USA, reflecting President WILSON's personal unpopularity as well as a retreat into prewar ISOLATIONISM. Ratified by the other Allies in January 1920, its subsequent enforcement became primarily an Anglo-French issue, with the British seeking modification and France demanding strict adherence to the terms. Though Germany was able to negotiate substantial revisions during the 1920s, the Treaty remained a burning source of popular resentment, exploited by right-wing elements and used as a vote-catcher by the National Socialists. See also: MAP 25.

Viborg, Battle of See: FINLAND.

Vickers FB-5 'Gunbus' British 'PUSHER' biplane and the first RFC aircraft specifically designed as a FIGHTER, with a free-mounted MACHINE GUN positioned on the nose. It reached squadrons on the WESTERN FRONT in July 1915, and was used for air-to-air combat and light bombing, but was quickly outmatched by faster German FOKKER E-TYPES. Production was suspended early in 1916, after more than 100 had been built, and surviving FB-5s were used exclusively as trainers from mid-1916. A streamlined, slightly faster FB-9 version (produced in small numbers from December 1915) was also withdrawn from frontline combat in July 1916, after suffering badly during the opening days of the SOMME battle.

BRIEF DATA (FB-5) Type: two-seat fighter/light bomber; Engine: 100hp Gnôme Monosoupape; Max speed: 70mph (112kph); Ceiling: 2,700m; Armament: 1 × 0.303in mg, optional rifle.

Vickers FB-12 British biplane FIGHTER first produced in June 1916, by which time its 'PUSHER' design was outmoded. A few were sent to the WESTERN FRONT in December for operational evaluation, but even fitted with 100hp engines they were considered no better than the obsolete FE-8 and AIRCO DH-2 types, which they physically resembled but were intended to replace. Vickers persisted with the pusher design into 1918, and a handful of later versions saw action with RFC home-defence units as the 110hp FB-12c or the 200hp FB-26 ('Vampire').

BRIEF DATA (FB-12) Type: single-seat fighter; Engine: 80hp Le Rhône; Max speed: 86mph (140kph); Ceiling: 4,400m; Armament: 1 × 0.303in mg.

Vickers FB-19 British single-seat FIGHTER biplane that was used in small numbers by the RFC from late 1916. Though Vickers abandoned its outdated 'PUSHER' design for the FB-19, combat trials revealed a dangerous blind spot, and the type was rejected for use on the WESTERN FRONT. Only 36 were built, but they travelled a long way in 1917, serving with home-defence forces, in PALESTINE, on the BALKAN FRONT and with a single RUSSIAN ARMY AIR SERVICE unit on the EASTERN FRONT.

BRIEF DATA (FB-19) Type: single-seat fighter; Engine: 100hp Gnôme Monosoupape; Max speed: 109mph (174kph); Ceiling: 4,850m; Armament: 1 × 0.303in mg.

Vickers Gun A modified version of the MAXIM GUN adopted by the BRITISH ARMY as its standard heavy MACHINE GUN in 1912. The water-cooled, 0.303-inch Vickers used a 250-round fabric-belt magazine and was a reliable weapon. Though lighter (19kg) than the Maxim, its weight and complexity of manufacture were disadvantages in the field, and it was generally superseded by the lighter LEWIS GUN on the WESTERN FRONT after 1915, remaining in service with British imperial forces elsewhere. Unlike the Lewis, the Vickers did prove adaptable to INTERRUPTER GEAR, and a stripped down, air-cooled version was the standard forward-firing armament on all British and French aircraft from 1916.

Villar Perosa Sub-machine Gun Introduced to ITALIAN ARMY infantry units in 1915, the Villar Perosa was the world's first genuine sub-machine gun. Also known as the Fiat or Revelli, depending on its place of manufacture, its distinctive twin barrels each fired a 25-round box magazine of 9mm PISTOL ammunition. Though quick-firing and portable, it was generally used as a static support MACHINE GUN before 1918, in which capacity its ammunition lacked hitting power. Most frontline Italian units had been re-equipped with a Beretta modification of the design by autumn 1918, when sub-machine guns were deployed in large numbers as infantry assault weapons.

Vilna See: VILNIUS OFFENSIVE.

Vilnius Offensive Final phase of the Central Powers' TRIPLE OFFENSIVE on the EASTERN FRONT, a German attack on the Lithuanian capital of Vilnius in September 1915. German chief of staff FALKENHAYN ordered a general halt to attacks on 2 September, but front commanders HINDENBURG and LUDENDORFF ignored him and concentrated 47 divisions for a great northern advance into the Russian heartland.

The 28 Russian divisions of General RUZSKI's army group in KURLAND were concentrated in the north around Riga and to the south around Vilnius. Using the same RAILWAYS that had frustrated rapid Russian manoeuvres earlier in the campaign, 33 divisions of the German Tenth Army (EICHHORN) were rapidly concentrated for an assault on Vilnius from the east.

The frontal attack opened on 7 September, and failed with the loss of more than 40,000 men, but a subsidiary advance by 6 divisions (including 3 of CAVALRY) swept through sparsely-held lines to cut the Vilnius–Riga railway to the north at Sventsiany on 12 September. Transfer of reserves from the central Polish fronts had brought Russian strength up to 40 divisions by 16 September, blocking Eichhorn's eastward advance.

With losses of 50,000 men in two weeks, Eichhorn turned his flanking force south towards Vilnius, which was abandoned and taken on 19 September. Russian reinforcements counterattacked from new positions northeast of Vilnius on the same day, preventing a planned advance by a new German infantry group (HUTIER), and further German attacks failed expensively in increasingly bad weather. Ludendorff halted the offensive on 26 September, ordering fortification of a line south from Riga. Many German units were subsequently transferred to the BALKAN FRONT, and the RUSSIAN ARMY was left to recover from the summer's defeats. See MAP 11.

Vimy Ridge Tactically important ridge running almost 12km just northeast of Arras and overlooking the town. It stood on or close to the WESTERN FRONT for almost four years after it was occupied by the Germans in September 1914, and was the focus of almost constant fighting until the Allied offensives of late 1918 moved the line permanently east (see MAP 2).

German engineers started digging under the chalk Ridge to improve defensive positions as soon as it was occupied, adding a network of artillery-proof TRENCHES and bunkers to a labyrinth of medieval caves and passages. Heavy ARTILLERY, protected from infantry attack by concrete MACHINE GUN posts, was installed to begin reducing Arras to rubble.

The French Tenth Army responded by digging its own system of trenches and MINES into the western slopes, a process continued and extended when the British Third Army took over the sector in March 1916. Repeated French attempts to take Vimy Ridge by frontal assault cost about 150,000 casualties between May and November 1915, but only emphasized the effectiveness of the German defences.

Anticipating a further attempt when the British arrived, the Germans themselves attacked in May 1916, capturing British forward trenches along a 2km front. After a failed counterattack, British offensive operations around Arras were suspended until the following spring, when a famous attack by four divisions of the Canadian Corps successfully stormed and captured the Ridge on 9 April 1917 (see Battle of ARRAS). Successfully defended during the KAISERSCHLACHT Offensive in spring 1918, it remained in Allied hands for the rest of the War. See also: Battle of ARTOIS.

Viribus Unitis Class Class of four dreadnoughts (*Viribus Unitis*, *Tegetthoff*, *Prinz Eugen* and *SZENT ISTVÁN*), which were the most valuable BATTLESHIPS with the AUSTRO-HUNGARIAN NAVY's main fleet at Pola (Pula), *Viribus Unitis* serving as its flagship throughout. *Viribus Unitis* was destroyed by Italian 'HUMAN TORPEDOES' in Pola early on 1 November 1918, when the harbour was barely guarded and the ship was flying the Croatian flag, the Austro-Hungarian Navy having effectively ceased to exist several hours earlier.

BRIEF DATA (*Viribus Unitis*, 1918) Displacement: 22,500 tons; Crew: 1,133; Dimensions: length 531.5ft (161m); Speed: 20k; Armament: 10 × 12in (305mm) gun, 12 × 5.9in (150mm), 18 × 70mm, 2 × 75mm AA, 4 × 533mm TT.

Vittorio Emanuele III, King (1869–1947) King of ITALY since the assassination of his father (Umberto I) in 1900, Vittorio Emanuele made little attempt to expand the monarchy's largely honorific role in Italian politics. As Italy moved close to war in spring 1915, his opinions and ultimate control of political appointments assumed greater importance. Kept fully informed about the negotiations and stipulations of the Treaty of LONDON, his support for war on the side of the Allies became clear in May 1915, when he reappointed the SALANDRA government three days after its parliamentary defeat.

Once at war the King moved to headquarters near the ITALIAN FRONT – leaving the Duke of Genoa to act as regent in Rome – but seldom exercised his powers as nominal C-in-C of the ITALIAN ARMY. He occasionally mediated in disputes between the government and the Army general staff, but his prime function was publicly to symbolize Italian unity and commitment to war, most notably through a series of pugnacious speeches after the defeat at CAPORETTO in late 1917.

Vittorio Veneto Offensive The last action of the campaign on the ITALIAN FRONT, launched on 23 October 1918 and continued until the armistice with AUSTRIA-HUNGARY on 3 November. By the autumn ITALIAN ARMY chief of staff Diaz was able to put 57 divisions into the field (including 2 British and 3 French), and some 7,700 guns gave him a comfortable superiority in ARTILLERY over 51 nominal AUSTRO-HUNGARIAN ARMY divisions in the theatre. Despite his doubts about the Italian Army's willingness or ability to fight, pressure from the SUPREME WAR COUNCIL and the ORLANDO government – the latter anxious to ensure possession of maximum territory in advance of peace negotiations – forced him to plan an offensive.

An attack northwest into the Monte Grappa sector (at the pivot of Austrian army groups under Archduke JOSEF and Field Marshal BOROEVIC) opened on 23 October, forcing the transfer of limited defensive reserves away from the main advance by four Italian armies across the Piave towards the town of Vittorio Veneto, about halfway to the River Tagliamento.

After initial difficulties crossing the river, the principal attack took Vittorio Veneto on 30 October, after which Austro-Hungarian resistance disintegrated completely. Allied forces had reached Trento in the west and the Tagliamento in the east when a ceasefire was called on 2 November, by which time the Italian Army had taken 300,000 prisoners in 10 days and suffered 38,000 casualties of its own. See MAP 21.

Viviani, René (1862–1925) An adaptable centrist as a cabinet minister under CLEMENCEAU and BRIAND in the early 20th century, Viviani was a skilled political speaker but lacked the prestige of his more experienced contemporaries in FRANCE. Nominated as prime minister by President POINCARÉ in June 1914, he gained sufficient parliamentary support to form a cabinet at the second attempt, and was barely secure in office when the JULY CRISIS broke.

Relying heavily on Poincaré both during and after the crisis, Viviani bowed to presidential pressure to form a national coalition government in late August, but it never succeeded in establishing political control over the military. By early 1915 the high command's refusal to allow government inspections of the WESTERN FRONT had become a major issue in parliament, and Viviani was never able to wrest sufficient resources from C-in-C JOFFRE to provide large-scale aid for SERBIA. Foreign minister DELCASSÉ's ultimate failure to prevent BULGARIA from joining the CENTRAL POWERS in September was the final blow to cabinet unity, and an exhausted Viviani resigned in October. He retained his cabinet post for a time but was never again close to the centre of power, accepting a marginal postwar role as French representative at the LEAGUE OF NATIONS.

Voie Sacrée Popular contemporary French name ('Sacred Way') for the minor road from the town of Bar-le-Duc to VERDUN, about 60km to the northeast. The road, along with one light RAILWAY, was the only open supply line to Verdun when General PÉTAIN took over defence of the fortress complex in late

March 1916. Pétain committed reserve divisions and labour battalions to urgent repair and reconstruction work, doubling the road's width to combat chronic congestion, and instituted a massive motorized supply operation. Under constant fire from German ARTILLERY, the road remained operational throughout the battle, carrying an average of 50,000 tons of ammunition and 90,000 men to the battle zone every week. The supply operation was heavily exploited in Allied PROPAGANDA, and the Voie Sacrée became part of the battle's rich popular mythology in FRANCE.

Voisin Bombers Famous series of French 'PUSHER' biplanes based on prewar Voisin 1 (70hp) and 2 (80hp) designs, both of which saw limited service as reconnaissance aircraft in 1914. Built in large numbers throughout the War, successively modified versions were the mainstay of AÉRONAUTIQUE MILITAIRE bombing operations on the WESTERN FRONT.

Most of the Voisins with French escadrilles in August 1914 were Voisin 3 two-seaters, the only aircraft in service anywhere with a MACHINE GUN as standard armament. With the same steel airframe and distinctive four-wheeled undercarriage as its predecessors, but up-engined to 120hp, it was slow, stable and sturdy.

Though able to lift only about 100kg of bombs, the type joined the first Aéronautique Militaire bombing units from late 1914, and was officially designated the standard French bomber early the following year. Mostly used for short-range tactical operations in support of ground forces, they also undertook STRATEGIC BOMBING missions, including a successful attack on poison GAS works at Ludwigshafen and Offau on 26 May. About 800 Voisin 3s were used by the Aéronautique Militaire on the Western Front, and they flew with all the Allied air forces, including the RUSSIAN AIR SERVICE on the EASTERN FRONT.

A Voisin 4 ground-support version was introduced in early 1915, fitted with a formidable 37mm cannon, but the latter's weight and recoil proved severe operational drawbacks. The 150hp Voisin 5 (350 built) and 155hp Voisin 6 models delivered later in the year represented attempts to update a design that was obsolescent but remained the best available. Forced to rely on numbers rather than quality of aircraft in the first half of 1916, the Aéronautique Militaire committed its Voisins en masse to the defence of VERDUN, where they suffered heavy casualties but made a valuable contribution to the maintenance of air parity over the front.

The next main production model, the Voisin 8 (1,100 built), entered service in autumn 1916. Though faster and capable of hauling a bigger load, it was never a viable day bomber and operated almost exclusively at night. From early 1918 most were replaced by the Voisin 10 version (900 built), which had reliable 300hp engines and carried a respectable 275kg load.

BRIEF DATA (Voisin 8) Type: two-seater night bomber; Engine: 3 × 230hp Peugeot; Max speed: 131kph; Armament: 1 × 8mm mg, max bomb load 180kg (400lbs).

Von der Tann The GERMAN NAVY's first large warship driven by modern turbine engines and its first BATTLECRUISER, completed in September 1910. Sturdier and slightly slower than its British counterparts, it operated with Admiral HIPPER's First Scouting Group in the North Sea from August 1914, taking part in the SCARBOROUGH RAID before suffering severe damage in a collision during the British CUXHAVEN RAID at Christmas. Back in action at JUTLAND, it suffered numerous hits from British battlecruisers and lost all its main armament, but remained afloat and sufficiently mobile to escape. Repaired very slowly, *Von der Tann* was surrendered after the ARMISTICE, scuttled in Scapa Flow in June 1919, and finally raised by the British for scrap in the early 1930s.

BRIEF DATA (1917) Displacement: 19,100 tons; Crew: 923; Dimensions: length 562ft (170.3m), beam 87ft (26.4m); Speed: 28k; Armament: 8 × 11in gun, 10 × 5.9in, 4 × 3.4in AA, 4 × 17.7in TT.

W

War Crimes Punishment of those responsible for barbaric wartime acts or held responsible for the War itself was a burning contemporary issue never satisfactorily resolved. At the PARIS PEACE CONFERENCE in 1919 argument centred on the fate of ex-Kaiser WILHELM II, subject to a vitriolic Anglo-French press campaign for his execution. Disputes between the Allies – the Japanese were particularly opposed to judicial sanction being applied to monarchs – were rendered irrelevant by the refusal of the Dutch authorities to hand over the exiled Kaiser for trial. Attempts to draw up a list of other war criminals foundered on Allied disagreements, and the few German commanders eventually charged were tried by a German military court. Although those found guilty received very light sentences, the trials established the legal concept of 'crimes against humanity'.

'War Socialism' Contemporary term used to describe intensified wartime interference by governments in national economic and social management. Driven first by the need to mobilize industry for unprecedented war production, and later by military disruption of industrial and agricultural manpower and production, the wartime governments of all the main belligerents attempted to establish centralized institutions for the distribution of raw materials, labour and foodstuffs. In general the means adopted bore little relation to socialist ideology, but involved alliance between governments and large private industries to fulfil lucrative military production orders. See GERMANY; GREAT BRITAIN; AUSTRIA-HUNGARY; FRANCE; ITALY; RUSSIA; TURKEY; UNITED STATES.

Warrior Class The four Warrior Class 'armoured' CRUISERS were completed in 1907, just before the first BATTLECRUISERS rendered them obsolete. Typical of later armoured cruisers, they sacrificed the thick deck armour of earlier classes in favour of greater firepower (see *CRESSY*). *Warrior* was in the MEDITERRANEAN in August 1914 as part of the First Cruiser Squadron, which missed the only real opportunity to intercept the German MITTELMEERDIVISION. Later transferred to the North Sea, *Warrior* was sunk by gunfire at JUTLAND. Its sisters served in the North Sea with the Second Cruiser Squadron, based at Cromarty. *Achilles* and *Cochrane* both played minor roles at HELIGOLAND BIGHT and Jutland, but *Natal* exploded while loading ammunition in 1915. Both survivors took up Atlantic CONVOY escort duties from autumn 1917, but *Cochrane* was wrecked by a storm in the Mersey on its recall in 1918.

BRIEF DATA (*Warrior*, 1914) Displacement: 13,550 tons; Crew: 700; Dimensions: length 505.5ft (153.2m), beam 73ft (22.1m); Speed: 23k; Armament: 6 × 9.2in gun, 4 × 7.5in, 3 × 18in TT.

Weizmann, Chaim (1874–1952) Jewish scientist and Zionist leader. He was born in Russian POLAND but became a naturalized British citizen in 1910. His pioneering work in the production of acetone from maize was of vital importance to the munitions industry in GREAT BRITAIN: acetone was used to gelatinize propellant charges for shells, and GERMANY had been Britain's only prewar supplier. Weizmann headed the ROYAL NAVY's research laboratories from 1916 until 1919, but devoted much of his time to lobbying for the Zionist cause once his production system was running smoothly, influencing the War Cabinet's BALFOUR DECLARATION of November 1917. Head of the World Zionist Organization from 1921, he was a scientific advisor to the British government in the Second World War before becoming the first president of independent Israel in 1946.

Wejh Arabian port on the Red Sea coast, taken in January 1917 by FEISAL IBN HUSSEIN's Northern Arab Army. After the successful defence of YENBO in December 1916 restored the ARAB REVOLT's flagging momentum, Feisal and his British advisor LAWRENCE conceived a bold raid against Turkish-held Wejh, almost 300km to the north. Feisal's force had grown rapidly in the latter part of December, and some 11,000 men (half of them mounted) advanced up the coast from 3 January, shadowed by a British troopship converted as a floating supply base. The operation, against only 1,200 garrison troops, was designed to demonstrate the breadth of the Revolt's appeal, with four major tribal forces represented on the march north. A ROYAL NAVY flotilla of five gunships and a seaplane carrier was to support a simultaneous amphibious landing north of Wejh by several hundred troops from two other tribal groups, and Feisal's brother Ali positioned his Southern Army north of MEDINA as security against large-scale Turkish intervention. The town fell almost immediately to the amphibious attack on 24 January, and the main body reached the town a few hours later. Wehj became Feisal's main HQ for the next six months, releasing rebel forces into northern Arabia for the first time and providing a base for raids against the Damascus RAILWAY (see MAP 23). See also: AQABA.

Wekerle, Alexander (1848–1921) Conservative opponent of constitutional reform who had been Hungarian prime minister twice before his recall to office in August 1917. Selected to appease the dominant Hungarian landowning class, Wekerle was pushed by Austro-Hungarian imperial requirements into an attempt at constitutional reform, rejected by the Hungarian parliament in late 1917. He retaliated against Vienna by forcing a major debate over Hungarian demands for control over half of the AUSTRO-HUNGARIAN ARMY, and by attempting to assume leadership of the increasingly militant popular republican movement from early 1918. He used the threat of an embargo on food exports to Austria to wreck Emperor KARL I's attempt at compromise through the OCTOBER MANIFESTO, and proclaimed an independent Hungary on 19 October. His creation remained technically ruled by the Emperor, as King of Hungary, and Wekerle was dismissed four days later. Replaced by Count KÁROLYI, he played no further part in Hungarian politics. See also: AUSTRIA-HUNGARY.

Wemyss, Admiral Rosslyn (1864–1933) British naval officer, an accomplished administrator who commanded a CRUISER squadron in 1914. In February 1915 he was sent to the eastern MEDITERRANEAN island of Lemnos, where he turned the primitive harbour of MUDROS into a main base for operations against the DARDANELLES. Wemyss passed up the chance to replace Carden in command of the operation in favour of the man on the spot, DE ROBECK, and instead commanded a battle squadron off the GALLIPOLI FRONT. From January 1916 he commanded the ROYAL NAVY's Egyptian Squadron, supporting operations on the PALESTINE FRONT and wrestling with the development of effective ANTI-SUBMARINE measures. A year later, as a vice admiral, he returned to London as deputy to naval minister GEDDES, and in December 1917 replaced JELLICOE as First Sea Lord. In favour of the NORTHERN BARRAGE and the ZEEBRUGGE RAID, he worked well with Geddes but was tainted by the manner of Jellicoe's dismissal. After representing the Navy at the PARIS PEACE CONFERENCE, he resigned in November 1919 amid calls for his replacement by BEATTY.

'Westerners' British term for those who regarded full military commitment to the WESTERN FRONT as the only means of defeating the CENTRAL POWERS. See 'EASTERNERS'.

Western Front The principal battle line in western Europe (see MAPS 2, 3), named from the German perspective. The Front opened with the German invasion of BELGIUM according to the SCHLIEFFEN PLAN on 2 August 1914. War triggered a French counterinvasion of GERMANY (see JULY CRISIS; PLAN 17), and the first actions on the Western Front were the mobile battles anticipated by planners.

German armies swept through Belgian defences at LIÈGE and NAMUR before clashing with the FRENCH ARMY and a token British Expeditionary Force (BEF) in the Battles of the FRONTIERS all along the eastern French border. By late August Allied armies were in full retreat in northern FRANCE, and fighting to hold eastern positions at the Moselle, but the main German invasion force, diluted by distractions to the EASTERN FRONT and the Moselle, was decisively halted at the MARNE – only 50km east of Paris – in early September (see MAPS 4, 5).

The three northern German armies retreated successfully to the AISNE River, northeast of Paris, and held off Allied attacks in mid-September. From the end of the month both sides tried to outflank the other in a series of small actions (the 'RACE TO THE SEA'), culminating in a major but inconclusive struggle for FLANDERS and the Channel ports.

Once fighting died down for the winter in mid-December the Front solidified into a 'line' of opposing TRENCHES stretching from Nieuport on the Channel coast to the Swiss frontier, turning sharply east in Champagne before turning south near the German border in Lorraine.

Both sides had suffered casualties and expended materials far beyond prewar expectations, and the winter of 1914–15 began a process of consolidation and concentration that saw the establishment of institutionalized TRENCH WARFARE and the continuous intensification of military activity in the theatre.

Contested exclusively by the GERMAN ARMY on one side, the Western Front was the main wartime preoccupation of the Allied French, BELGIAN and BRITISH ARMIES, as well as the associated American Expeditionary Force (AEF) from 1918. All suffered the majority of their battle CASUALTIES in the theatre. Large overseas contingents from the British and French Empires also fought in France, along with ITALIAN and RUSSIAN ARMY units, and PORTUGUESE, CZECH and POLISH FORCES.

Numbers of men active at the Front rose steadily to approach 10 million by 1917, and it was the main focus of wartime tactical and technological development in both ground and AERIAL WARFARE. Increasingly crowded with aircraft, ARTILLERY, TANKS, motor vehicles, animals, supplies and military infrastructure, the industrially developed area of northern France and Belgium that formed the front line was well suited to the maintenance of mass armies. Close to their bases, the main European armies were able to use efficient modern RAILWAYS for rapid transfer of goods or reserves along the front, enabling them to cover the rear of any sector as soon as it was threatened.

Once close to the front the situation was reversed. Increasingly heavy artillery and vast amounts of supply material had to be hauled across a wasteland torn up by bombardment from thousands of heavy guns and littered with military detritus. In the busy northern sectors mobility was often further hampered by rain and mud, and attacking forces of any size were effectively paralysed if they advanced beyond easy reach of established supply centres.

The combined effect of logistic factors was a pronounced tactical advantage for defenders, comprehensively demonstrated on the battlefield, where French C-in-C JOFFRE, commanding the vast majority of Allied forces and operating virtually without political restraints, was committed to driving occupying forces out of France at the first opportunity.

His tactics were simple and ineffective. A prolonged massed infantry assault all along the large SALIENT that was German-occupied France began in December 1914 and continued until March 1915, focused mainly on the southern edge in CHAMPAGNE. It was followed by essentially similar Anglo-French operations distinguished as the ARTOIS, second Champagne and ARTOIS-LOOS OFFENSIVES (see NEUVE CHAPELLE). All failed to achieve the anticipated BREAKTHROUGH into space beyond the trench lines, and well-established (though outnumbered) German defenders inflicted hundreds of thousands of casualties.

German Army attacking priorities were concentrated on the Eastern and BALKAN FRONTS in 1915, and its only major attack in the west was an experimental attempt to destroy the Allied salient around YPRES, using poison GAS in quantity for the first time (see

MAP 6). Like other weapons developed specifically to break the deadlock in France, gas proved of limited strategic value, and after early success the attack was held by rapidly expanding British forces.

All the major actions after 1914 were focused on the northern and central sectors of the Front, and activity on the 'quiet' sectors running south of Lorraine to the Swiss frontier was generally restricted to relatively desultory trench warfare.

The British Army's enormous growth during 1915, and the sheer breadth of French Army conscription, gave the western Allies a significant manpower advantage into 1916. At the same time, economic mobilization was starting to produce modern artillery, aircraft and trench weaponry in superior numbers (if not always quality). Joffre and new BEF commander HAIG (who replaced FRENCH in December 1915) were both confident that a major coordinated offensive in the spring would trigger a decisive victory, and lobbied for supporting actions on the Eastern and ITALIAN FRONTS.

Many military and political authorities in GREAT BRITAIN and France regarded the Western Front as the only decisive theatre of war, but dissent had been mounting since early 1915, especially in Britain, where an initial commitment of four infantry divisions to the theatre mushroomed by 1917 into a mass conscript army of 2 million. The 'EASTERNER' lobby had enough support to ensure that arguments continued into 1918, and that limited strength was diverted to 'SIDESHOWS' on the GALLIPOLI, SALONIKA, PALESTINE and MESOPOTAMIAN FRONTS. The only other substantial distraction came in autumn 1917, when Italian defeat at CAPORETTO prompted the temporary dispatch of British and French armies direct from France to the Italian Front.

Allied plans for a coordinated offensive were wrecked by a switch of German attacking strategy in 1916. German chief of staff FALKENHAYN launched an all-out attack on the French fortified zone of VERDUN in late February with the express intention of exhausting the French Army into collapse. A prolonged and gruesome battle of attrition that dragged into December, the offensive developed a momentum beyond the control of commanders on either side and inflicted irreparable damage on both armies (see MAP 7).

The main Allied attack of the year, led by the British at the SOMME in July, became in effect a diversionary counteroffensive and followed a similar pattern of bloody stalemate until November (see MAP 8). In total the two battles caused more than 2 million casualties, almost half of them to the German Army.

The new German THIRD SUPREME COMMAND team of LUDENDORFF and HINDENBURG abandoned offensive pretensions in France as soon as they took control in late August 1916, and made the immediate decision to withdraw to the new HINDENBURG LINE fortifications at the first opportunity. Efficiently prepared during the winter, the main bulk of the new Line was occupied in March 1917, initiating a defensive stance almost immediately undermined by war with the UNITED STATES (see Operation ALBERICH).

Anglo-French war weariness in late 1916, exacerbated by disappointments at JUTLAND, MONASTIR, KUT and Gallipoli, was assuaged by a change of government in Britain, where confirmed Easterner LLOYD GEORGE took power in December, and a change of command in France, where General NIVELLE was given a chance to make good his claim that CREEPING BARRAGE tactics used successfully at Verdun could win a rapid, decisive breakthrough.

Launched amid almost hysterical French popular euphoria and considerable Allied professional apprehension, the NIVELLE OFFENSIVE of spring 1917 was an unqualified disaster, although its British subsidiary at ARRAS achieved modest territorial gains. The French Army disintegrated into a large-scale MUTINY in its aftermath, well hidden from contemporary observers and quelled by July, but signalling exhaustion of the Army's offensive potential.

German forces were meanwhile stretched to support their faltering allies elsewhere, and were also required to administer conquered parts of ROMANIA, and to hold off Russian attacks in the east. Given the state of the

French Army, the attacking onus on the Western Front devolved on the BEF, now the largest army in the theatre. Like Joffre in 1915, Haig simply repeated tactics that had failed before. After a small, unrepeatable victory at MESSINES in June 1917, the main British attack struck from the YPRES salient at the end of July, and hammered away until early November without approaching a decisive breakthrough.

The year's fighting ended with another British 'one-off', an experimental massed TANK attack that won immediate success at CAMBRAI in November, but faltered because of all the usual exploitation difficulties and was quickly reversed by an early demonstration of German INFILTRATION TACTICS.

Although it had declared war in April 1917, the USA had not yet become a military factor on the Front, but could be expected to make an enormous impact during 1918 on Allied manpower and supply levels, which were already outstripping Germany's dwindling economic capacity. The military situation in early 1918 was superficially favourable to Germany, with the collapse of RUSSIA releasing forces for the west and ITALY at least temporarily neutralized, but (failing a reversal of trends in the SUBMARINE war) the high command was aware that only a quick decision in the west could avert ultimate defeat.

Allied public disenchantment with the stalemate was at its height in late 1917, but generals and politicians were expecting a major German attack in the spring and broadly agreed on continued concentration of resources on the Western Front. Few believed that Germany could muster sufficient strength for a successful offensive, and attention focused on the gradual coordination of British, French and AEF plans for renewed offensives to finally destroy the German Army.

An Allied SUPREME WAR COUNCIL had been created in November 1917, and French General FOCH was given command of a joint strategic reserve, but disputes among Haig, defensively minded French C-in-C PÉTAIN and the fiercely independent AEF commander PERSHING were not resolved until the 1918 German SPRING OFFENSIVES again threatened Paris.

Successive German assaults south of Arras (the KAISERSCHLACHT Offensive), on the LYS in Flanders and further south on the AISNE instilled a sense of Allied crisis that dispelled incipient PACIFISM on the home fronts and galvanized commanders into cooperation (see MAP 9). Foch was given overall command of Allied armies on the Western Front in April, using his authority to launch another successful counterattack on the MARNE in July, forcing the German Army back to its original positions.

Refinements of Allied INFANTRY TACTICS were accompanied by a massive influx of weapons and munitions in summer 1918, along with full-scale reinforcement from the AEF, which began operations in strength from late August and eventually fielded more than a million men. At the same time, German resistance on the battlefield – undermined by shortages of every kind and the first wave of INFLUENZA – at last began to crumble.

Foch, Haig and Pershing again drove at the flanks of the main German salient, beginning with an emphatic victory at AMIENS in the north in early August, and at ST MIHIEL in the south in mid-September, while Pétain's battered French forces played a supporting role and advanced more slowly in the centre. Subsequent offensives beyond the Hindenburg Line, in the MEUSE-ARGONNE sector and beyond COURTRAI in Flanders, drove German forces into orderly but rapid retreat as economic and political collapse forced the German authorities into seeking immediate peace (see GERMAN REVOLUTIONS).

Despite a minority school of military thought (most common among fresh US commanders) that recommended refusal of ceasefire terms and advocated a full-scale invasion of Germany, all fighting on the Western Front ceased with the ARMISTICE on 11 November. In the north, King ALBERT's Flanders Group was reoccupying Belgium unopposed, and US forces from the Argonne were at the German frontier overlooking Sedan. Haig's army group was across the eastern Belgian border, and French forces elsewhere had reclaimed all the ground lost in 1914.

Most of the familiar images still associated with the First World War in western Europe and the USA are derived from the experience of the Western Front. Though by no means the most statistically dangerous wartime theatre, it was a static killing field never matched for intensity and duration. Its traumatic, multi-faceted effects on participants and observers can be identified in most social, political and military developments up to and including the Second World War.

Westfalen Class The GERMAN NAVY's first response to the revolutionary British *DREADNOUGHT*, *Westfalen*, *Nassau*, *Posen* and *Rheinland* were completed in 1909–10. They were very similar to contemporary British designs, but four of the six 11-inch turrets were arranged either side of the superstructure, reducing the broadside potential. The Westfalens served with the HIGH SEAS FLEET, and all four were at JUTLAND, but they were never tested in combat with British BATTLESHIPS and were all scrapped after their surrender at the ARMISTICE.

BRIEF DATA (*Westfalen*, 1914) Displacement: 18,900 tons; Crew: 1,008; Dimensions: length 478ft (144.8m), beam 89ft (27m); Speed: 20k; Armament: 12 × 11in gun, 12 × 5.9in, 16 × 3.4in, 6 × 17.7in TT.

West Indies (British) Automatically committed to war alongside GREAT BRITAIN in 1914, the scattered British Caribbean colonies generally prospered during wartime, but surging world sugar and cotton prices benefited plantation owners rather than society as a whole, and some luxury industries, like the Dominica lime trade, suffered a decline. The colonies contributed about 15,000 troops for active service overseas, mostly on the WESTERN FRONT, in EGYPT and in EAST AFRICA. Two-thirds were Jamaicans, but contingents of 250–1,000 men were also sent from Trinidad and Tobago, Barbados, British Guiana (modern Guyana), British Honduras (modern Belize), Grenada, the Bahamas, St Lucia, St Vincent, and the Leeward Islands (Antigua, St Kitts-Nevis-Anguilla, Montserrat, and the British Virgin Islands). See also: CUBA; HAITI.

Westkarp, Kuno von (1865–1945) Wartime leader of the parliamentary Conservative Party (DKP) in GERMANY, Westkarp typified the views of extreme nationalist politicans, consistently promoting commitment to total military victory and demanding large-scale annexations in eastern and western Europe as the price of peace. In mid-1917 he helped engineer the fall of chancellor BETHMANN HOLLWEG, whom he considered a dangerous reformer, and a year later he played a leading role in the dismissal of 'defeatist' foreign minister KÜHLMANN. Publicly opposed to the Reichstag's PEACE RESOLUTION of July 1917, he regarded the Treaty of BREST-LITOVSK with Russia as too moderate, and was still anticipating the annexation of BELGIUM in September 1918. Like most senior right-wing politicians he retreated temporarily from public life during the GERMAN REVOLUTIONS of November, but he re-emerged after the 1919 Reichstag elections as a leading figure in the new German National People's Party (DNVP).

Weygand, General Maxime (1867–1965) French CAVALRY officer, a regimental colonel in August 1914, who was appointed chief of staff to the new Ninth Army under General FOCH later in the month and acted as his deputy and spokesman for the rest of the War. Promoted major general in 1916, he occupied his chief's place on the SUPREME WAR COUNCIL from December 1917 until the following April, becoming FRENCH ARMY chief of staff on Foch's appointment as Supreme Allied Commander and attending the ARMISTICE negotiations in that capacity. Remaining in active service until 1935, he was recalled to command in 1940.

'Whippet' Tank Officially the Mark A Medium TANK, introduced to British service in late 1917, the 'Whippet' was named for its speed relative to the lumbering HEAVY TANKS used since 1916. Though still desperately slow in battlefield terms, it was closer to the postwar concept of armoured warfare in purpose and design, intended as a CAVALRY-style exploitation weapon and armed with only anti-personnel MACHINE GUNS. Better-

suited than the 'heavies' to the comparatively mobile warfare on the WESTERN FRONT of 1918, it was faster and more durable than the lighter French RENAULT tank, also commonly described as a 'Whippet' by English-speakers.
BRIEF DATA (Mark A) Weight: 14 tons; Max Speed: 13.3kph; Crew: 3; Max armour: 14mm; Armament: 4 × mg.

White Armies See: RUSSIAN CIVIL WAR.

White Feathers By autumn 1915, huge losses on the WESTERN FRONT and a dwindling influx of volunteers for military service had combined to create a popular sense of manpower crisis in GREAT BRITAIN. Encouraged by government PROPAGANDA exhorting civilian 'slackers' to volunteer and sensationalist newspapers in search of scapegoats for a disappointing year on the battlefields, small groups of women began presenting any able-bodied young man out of uniform with a white feather, symbolizing their disgust at his apparent refusal to serve and announcing his status as a social outcast.

The practice spread to become a routine feature of British life, abating only after the German SPRING OFFENSIVES in 1918 had greatly reduced the stock of potential victims. Undertaken with bellicose enthusiasm by an active minority of zealots, the white-feather campaign aroused predictable resentment among frontline troops by afflicting (among others) soldiers on leave, convalescing invalids and those held in vital war industries. A largely British phenomenon, only occasionally imitated in FRANCE, ITALY and the UNITED STATES, the white feathers both reflected and widened the gulf between civilian and military perceptions of the War from 1915.

White Guard See: FINLAND.

'Whizz-Bang' Standard British slang for any light or field ARTILLERY shell, derived from the sounds of its passage through the air and subsequent explosion. Whizz-bangs were invariably high-velocity shells and, as the name suggests, gave personnel less time to take cover than the slower, heavier projectiles fired by howitzers.

Wight 'Converted' Seaplane British naval patrol aircraft, developed from a rejected prototype bomber design and used in small numbers by the RNAS as an ANTI-SUBMARINE craft from 1916. It served in most British naval theatres but never challenged the SHORT 184 as the standard RNAS patrol machine. Only 37 were built, but the type achieved fame for the then rare feat of sinking of a U-BOAT, in the English Channel on 18 August 1917.
BRIEF DATA Type: two-seater patrol floatplane; Engine: 275hp Rolls Royce Eagle; Max speed: 84.5mph (135kph); Ceiling: 2,900m; Armament: 1 × 0.303in mg, 4 × 112lb bomb.

Wilhelm, Crown Prince (1882–1951) Eldest of Kaiser WILHELM II's five sons. He was associated with the most aggressively militarist sections of prewar society in GERMANY, but had very little command experience when he led the Fifth Army in August 1914. Its initial successes in the ARDENNES made his military reputation, and he served as a field commander on the WESTERN FRONT throughout the War. In overall command of the German offensive against VERDUN from February 1916, he was promoted to lead 'Army Group Crown Prince' in September, in control of the three armies occupying the central section of the German line. His forces won a major victory at the AISNE in May 1918, but Wilhelm was quick to recognize the likelihood of defeat after the French counterattack at the MARNE and urged retreat on the THIRD SUPREME COMMAND. He resigned his commission at the ARMISTICE and followed his father into exile.

Wilhelm II, Kaiser (1859–1941) King of Prussia and Emperor of GERMANY, Wilhelm succeeded his father Frederick III (who ruled for only three months) in 1888. A mercurial figure, veering between flamboyant confidence and timid depression, Wilhelm was a convinced believer in autocratic monarchy, with an orthodox loathing of all things parliamentary or socialist. An enthusiast for rapid industrial development and military matters, especially the GERMAN NAVY, he pursued a global policy of his own (*Weltpolitik*) after the dismissal of chancellor Bismarck in 1890.

Surrounding himself with industrial magnates, military advisors and like-minded Prussian politicians, Wilhelm embarked on a programme of industrial and military expansion, combined with diplomatic attempts to extract territorial and economic concessions from other European powers. His weaknesses for high-profile personal diplomacy and incautious oratory hastened Germany's prewar diplomatic isolation and gained him a worldwide reputation as an arrogant militarist.

His ambitions for colonial expansion outside Europe were largely frustrated, and isolation abroad was matched by growing instability at home, fuelled by the crown's unblinking refusal to contemplate constitutional reform. By 1914 Wilhelm, together with the military and a broad spectrum of conservative supporters, was convinced that a short, victorious European war was the only solution to both internal and external problems.

Though he suffered a last-minute crisis of conscience during the JULY CRISIS, reflecting a strong sense of dynastic affinity with other European monarchies, Wilhelm's hopes for national unity through war were fully realized in August 1914, when he enjoyed the greatest popularity of his reign.

As head of state and C-in-C of the armed forces, he retained control of personnel appointments and steadfastly refused to risk the HIGH SEAS FLEET in a major battle, but was never able to maintain or impose a consistent wartime policy of his own. His vacillation on most major issues was echoed in German political strategies, as relatively moderate politicians like BETHMANN HOLLWEG competed for his ear with the right-wing military-industrial lobby.

Wilhelm spent most of his time at military headquarters after 1914, falling increasingly under the influence of right-wing militarists. The replacement of FALKENHAYN by HINDENBURG as Army chief of staff in August 1916 was engineered against his wishes, and the dictatorship subsequently imposed by the THIRD SUPREME COMMAND saw his retreat into blinkered acquiescence.

Endorsing the extreme annexationist policies of military and industrial leaders, but occasionally proposing a private peace between monarchs, Wilhelm authorized the HINDENBURG PROGRAMME in autumn 1916 and commitment to unrestricted SUBMARINE WARFARE in January 1917. Although personally enthused by the KAISERSCHLACHT Offensive on the WESTERN FRONT in March 1918, he played little part in the BREST-LITOVSK or BUCHAREST Treaties and was a figurehead during the transfer of executive power to parliament in early October (see GERMAN REVOLUTIONS).

Abdication was manifestly the only hope of saving the monarchy by late October, but Wilhelm was incapable of the decision and Prince MAX VON BADEN announced his abdication without official approval on 9 November. Wilhelm was immediately whisked by the Army to the Netherlands, where he renounced all claims to his thrones on 28 November. Despite a voluble popular campaign in western Europe, Queen Wilhelmina of the Netherlands refused his extradition for WAR CRIMES, and he remained in the Netherlands for the rest of his life.

Wilson, General Sir Henry (1864–1922) Francophile BRITISH ARMY officer, noted for his diplomatic rather than his military accomplishments. As commander of the British staff college he developed close contacts with his French counterpart, General FOCH, and as director of military operations at the war ministry from 1910 he worked to ensure Anglo-French cooperation, formulating plans for deploying the BEF with French forces in the event of war with GERMANY.

From August 1914 Wilson was BEF deputy chief of staff on the WESTERN FRONT, where his command of the language helped make him the most influential figure around C-in-C FRENCH. Operating as chief liaison with the FRENCH ARMY, he generally reinforced his commander's early pessimism. He remained the chief inter-Allied contact point in France until December 1915, when new C-in-C HAIG gave him command of IV Corps, but was returned to liaison duties from November 1916.

Poor relations with PÉTAIN brought his return to Britain in May 1917, but he quickly regained prominence as an ally of premier LLOYD GEORGE in his campaign to circumvent Haig's authority. An unofficial advisor at the RAPALLO CONFERENCE in early November 1917, Wilson was named British representative to the SUPREME WAR COUNCIL, and in March 1918 replaced Haig's main supporter, ROBERTSON, as imperial chief of staff (CIGS). He used his position to support the appointment of Foch as Allied supreme commander, and made no attempt to challenge political control of military policy in GREAT BRITAIN. Promoted field marshal and ennobled, Wilson retired from the army in 1922 to work for the Protestant cause in his native IRELAND, where he was assassinated by Catholic republicans in June 1922.

Wilson, Woodrow (1856–1924) Princeton professor of jurisprudence who made an immediate impression as a high-minded liberal reformer when he entered US politics as governor of New Jersey in November 1910. He gained the Democratic Party presidential nomination in 1912, and, after winning an easy victory over the divided Republicans, became president in 1913. He pursued a policy of cautious reform, balancing the needs of an expanding global economy and a powerful business class against the ISOLATIONISM and social concerns of liberal 'progressives'.

His foreign policy focused on peaceful development in US spheres of economic interest, and negotiations for a Pan-American Pact to guarantee stability in Latin America were interrupted by the outbreak of war in Europe. He placed great faith in direct appeal to popular opinion, making exhaustive public-speaking tours to explain controversial policy decisions.

Despite a personal preference for Anglo-French liberalism, Wilson's declaration of neutrality on 19 August 1914 included a plea for its unbiased application. His public stance remained strictly non-interventionist in the face of a loud right-wing PREPAREDNESS campaign, but the sporadic extension of German SUBMARINE WARFARE edged him towards war.

Stern warnings to Berlin followed the loss of the *LUSITANIA* in May 1915 and the *SUSSEX* the following April, but Wilson was aware that his threat to impose 'full accountability' in the event of a resumption by Germany of unrestricted submarine warfare amounted to an ultimatum. Though his narrow election victory in November 1916 was won on the catch phrase 'he kept us out of the War', Wilson knew the slogan was redundant and had opposed its use.

After re-election he attempted to render intervention unnecessary by promoting a negotiated settlement in Europe, but his PEACE NOTE of December 1916 only demonstrated the gulf between the belligerents and helped convince Berlin to adopt unrestricted submarine warfare.

The decision forced Wilson's hand. He readied political opinion for war with a request to arm US merchant ships on 26 February 1917, and with his release of the ZIMMERMANN NOTE to an increasingly anti-German public. A developing crisis with the troublesome government of MEXICO was abruptly settled, and on 2 April Wilson asked Congress for permission to declare war. He also sought its support to institute massive military expansion through conscription (see SELECTIVE SERVICE ACT), together with the imposition of necessary tax changes and the granting of substantial credits to the Allies.

Comprehensive wartime intrusion of government into US socioeconomic life was largely carried out by trusted executives like McADOO, BAKER and CREEL. Wilson and his close aide 'Colonel' HOUSE concentrated on planning a liberal 'peace without victories', in the belief that Allied financial dependence would enable the USA to dictate terms.

The FOURTEEN POINTS peace programme, presented to Congress on 8 January 1918, illustrated the difficulties of reconciling Wilson's aspirations with European ambitions, but his favoured tactic of appealing direct to public idealism gave it a peculiar political legitimacy.

Wilson's growing international reputation was at its peak when the ARMISTICE was signed. Approached for peace by the CENTRAL POWERS he compelled them to accept the Fourteen Points as the basis for negotiations and persuaded reluctant Allied governments to vaguely endorse a slightly modified version. On his visit to Europe in December 1918, and again in June 1919, he was hailed as a messianic peacemaker by adoring crowds everywhere.

He was less popular at home. Unsparing Republican accusations of administrative inefficiency, led by Senator LODGE, brought counterclaims of obstructionism from Wilson in October 1918, an outburst turned against him in subsequent mid-term elections, won by the reunited Republicans.

Irritating to European leaders, especially CLEMENCEAU, Wilson's self-conscious idealism was fatally undermined at the PARIS PEACE CONFERENCE. He eventually sacrificed his principles on ethnic self-determination and REPARATIONS to Anglo-French national interests in order to secure agreement for his most cherished project, collective world security through the LEAGUE OF NATIONS. Ignoring warnings from secretary of state LANSING, he took a flawed VERSAILLES Treaty and a damaged reputation back to a hostile Senate (not represented in Paris).

The latter stages of Wilson's presidency were a personal disaster. His rigid occupation of the moral high ground contributed to the general acrimony surrounding the peace, and precluded the compromise necessary to secure its passage through Congress. In October 1919 he was partially paralysed by a heart attack during a speaking tour and never fully regained his political grip. Congress refused to ratify the Versailles Treaty (which included the League of Nations covenant) in November 1919 and March 1920, and he saw out his term of office as a shrunken figure and political 'lame duck'. See also: UNITED STATES.

'Winter Battle', The See: Second Battle of the MASURIAN LAKES.

Wintgens–Naumann Expedition In February 1917 a small force of about 700 ASKARI troops (with a handful of Germans, several hundred bearers and three small field guns) broke away from German forces defending the southeastern corner of EAST AFRICA and marched north into British-held territory. The motives of its German officers, Captain Wintgens and Lieutenant Naumann, are obscure, but they had no authorization from C-in-C LETTOW-VORBECK. The column remained at large in hostile territory for eight months, eluding or defeating RHODESIAN FORCES from the southwest, Belgian colonial forces from TABORA and a special British brigade formed to deal with it. Nigerian infantry and South African CAVALRY had joined the chase by May, when Wintgens gave himself up to get treatment for typhoid, and more than 4,000 Allied troops were eventually committed to tracking down Naumann's remaining 500 Askaris. After a 3,000km pursuit, a miniature of the wider East African campaign, they were finally surrounded in the far north, near Mount Kilimanjaro, and the last 14 Europeans, 165 Askaris and 250 bearers surrendered on 2 October 1917. They had destroyed local supplies wherever they went, and fear of their reported atrocities (magnified or invented by the Allied press) had influenced military dispositions far from their sphere of action. In deference to their own PROPAGANDA the British arrested Naumann for murder after his capture, but he was never charged. See MAP 18.

Wolf German AUXILIARY COMMERCE RAIDER that reached the Indian Ocean in January 1917 and cruised undiscovered until the end of the year, sinking at least 12 Allied vessels and several more with its MINES before returning to Germany in February 1918. One of very few GERMAN NAVY ships to carry an aircraft, its FRIEDRICHSHAFEN F-33 seaplane (known as *Wölfchen*) proved a very useful reconnaissance and light-bombing weapon. Both *Wolf* and *Wölfchen* were well known in GERMANY, where their successes received heavy press coverage.

BRIEF DATA (1917) Displacement: 5,800 tons; Crew: 350; Speed: 10.5k; Armament: 2 × 5.9in (150mm) gun, 4 × 105mm, 4 × 19.7in (500mm) TT, 465 mines, 1 × a/c.

Women, Emancipation of Although NEW ZEALAND had become the first state to grant full voting rights to women in 1893 and Scandinavian women were the first to mount effective suffrage campaigns, the First World War is generally viewed as a watershed in the feminist struggle to win full civil rights, an impression created by the experiences of women in the industrialized regions of Allied democracies, particularly GREAT BRITAIN.

A country with a very limited democratic franchise and a large urban population, Britain was in the throes of a major campaign by the increasingly militant female 'Suffragist' movement in 1914. An informal truce from August 1914 did not long survive an influx of women into previously male-dominated munitions, public-transport and clerical work. The government issued an appeal for women to join a Register of Women for War Service in March 1915, and by August 1916 over 750,000 British women worked at jobs formerly held by men. Another 350,000 were in employment created by the war economy, and calls for female agricultural workers had attracted another 240,000 women into the Land Army by spring 1918.

The LLOYD GEORGE government regularly used PROPAGANDA to encourage reluctant employers to accept women, while socialist activists like Sylvia Pankhurst maintained pressure for an end to wage discrimination (women were paid on average 30 per cent less than men for the same jobs) and for improvements in poor working conditions, particularly dangerous in war factories using toxic substances. About 30,000 women demonstrated in London for the 'Right to Serve' in 1915, and women's non-combatant armed forces were formed from 1917.

Propertied women over 30 were allowed to vote from January 1918, and women over 21 became eligible to hold political office (but not vote) from November 1918. These lasting, if incomplete, gains were counterbalanced by the collapse of the female job market in 1919, but the constituency of politically and socially aware women in Britain had been permanently expanded.

Division between urban and peasant women was less significant in Britain than elsewhere. Most women in FRANCE were rural dwellers, whose war was spent replacing conscripts in the fields – hard labour with no political reward. The experience of women in industrial France was broadly similar to the British model, with a surge into hitherto male occupations encouraged by the government and marred by gross inequalities, but French women were never permitted to join the armed forces and had little tradition of constitutional activism, eventually receiving the right to vote in 1944.

Both ITALY and AUSTRIA-HUNGARY were sharply divided on regional lines. Women in the agrarian economies of southern Italy and Hungary, which provided most of the front-line troops, did not experience the employment opportunities accorded northern Italian and Austrian women.

Feminists had much to fight for in Muslim TURKEY, where the strain of total war enabled the YOUNG TURK government to disturb a tradition of absolute protection of women from employment or social contact. Liberal (male) intellectuals began attacking veiling and seclusion as a waste of resources from 1914, and women began working in offices, charities, street cleaning, hospitals and schools for the first time. A marked reduction of social restrictions in Constantinople – where lynching of 'fallen' women was practically abandoned and the number of girls' schools mushroomed – was not matched elsewhere in the Empire, where the vast majority of women worked the fields, although female ammunition bearers were a vital supply link to troops on the CAUCASIAN FRONT.

The TURKISH ARMY paid for a women's labour exchange to be set up in 1914, and the first female labour battalion was established in February 1918, but religious authorities maintained a constant campaign of reaction, and contact with women was widely blamed by conservatives for increased incidence of adultery and ALCOHOL abuse. Mustapha KEMAL's Turkish Republic introduced major reforms in the 1920s.

By contrast women in JAPAN made little wartime progress against a ban from all political activity finalized in 1900. Agitation for women's rights declined after socialists were suppressed in 1910 and was moribund until the foundation of a New Women's Movement in 1920, which won the right to hold political meetings in 1922.

In the UNITED STATES, where four states had permitted votes for women since the 1890s, a strong 'Suffragette' movement had produced the first female member of the House of Representatives in 1914. Employment in war industries added 30,000 women to the factory labour force in the industrial northeast but had little effect on the south, west or mid-west, and the granting of general female suffrage in 1920 was in response to decades of middle-class agitation rather than to a war-related crisis.

Polarization of political forces in GERMANY produced flourishing feminist and anti-feminist movements among women by 1914. The socialist SDP (Social Democratic Party) had 175,000 female members, but was matched by the conservative German Women's League, and feminism was attacked by the powerful nationalist interests behind the drives for rearmament and colonial expansion. Women flocked to work in wartime factories and public services, but were motivated by financial need on the part of middle-class families and war widows on fixed incomes. Official encouragement to female employment through the HINDENBURG PROGRAMME from late 1916 was hardly necessary, but constitutional agitation remained the preserve of a large but politically powerless radical left until the GERMAN REVOLUTIONS of 1918–19. A flourishing domestic-service sector, drastically reduced in most other European countries by 1920, signalled postwar conservative recovery.

Triumph of the radical left in RUSSIA provided the most complete wartime emancipation of women, theoretically affecting huge European and Asian populations. Under the autocratic Tsarist regime (which had authorized female suffrage in the semi-autonomous province of FINLAND in 1906), urban women were employed by wartime Russian factories in increasing numbers and under very bad conditions. Food and fuel shortages in Petrograd (St Petersburg) and Moscow helped radicalize working-class women, and they played a leading role in the FEBRUARY REVOLUTION of 1917. The OCTOBER REVOLUTION immediately announced full civil rights for women, along with equal pay and opportunities, promises kept within the context of a subsequent erosion of all human rights in the Soviet Union.

Wood, General Leonard (1860-1927) Chief of staff to the US ARMY until 1914, Wood's attempts to expand the Army during his term of office achieved little in the anti-militarist atmosphere of the day. A founder of the National Security League in 1914, Wood was the most influential military figure in the PREPAREDNESS MOVEMENT, working closely with former president Theodore ROOSEVELT, and was the political right's candidate for the AEF field command eventually given to General PERSHING. Wood was subsequently passed over for senior staff positions, fuelling Republican criticism of war secretary BAKER, and served out the War in training commands.

Woyrsch, Field Marshal Remus von (1847–1920) Veteran German infantry officer recalled from retirement in August 1914 to command a corps on the EASTERN FRONT. His forces were attached to the Austro-Hungarian First Army for a short time before becoming part of Army Section Woyrsch on the Silesian sector of the front in October. Woyrsch remained in POLAND until the end of the war on the Eastern Front, commanding Army Group Woyrsch, which covered the south of the country from August 1916 until its disbandment at the end of 1917. After the disbandment of his command, Woyrsch was promoted field marshal and returned to retirement.

Württemberg See: ALBRECHT, Duke of Württemberg; LITHUANIA; GERMANY.

Y

Yanushkevich, General Nikolai (1868–1918) Chief of staff to the RUSSIAN ARMY from early 1914 until September 1915, and second in command to C-in-C Grand Duke NIKOLAI at STAVKA (Russian central command) from August 1914, Yanushkevich exercised little real authority over frontline forces, leaving policy and administration to quartermaster general DANILOV. Yanushkevich was dismissed when Tsar NICHOLAS II took personal command at Stavka, and remained with the Grand Duke on the CAUCASIAN FRONT until the FEBRUARY REVOLUTION in 1917. He was killed there in unknown circumstances during the RUSSIAN CIVIL WAR.

Yenbo, Battle of Turkish attack on the rebel-held Arabian port of Yenbo, 230km west of Medina, in December 1916, a turning point in the fortunes of the ARAB REVOLT. The town was defended by about 8,000 well-armed but poorly trained men under FEISAL IBN HUSSEIN, stationed some distance inland. A column detached from Turkish forces occupying MEDINA outflanked forward defences in mid-November, leaving Feisal holding the line with about 5,000 troops while British advisor LAWRENCE supervised the improvement of the port's defences. A Turkish flanking manoeuvre scattered more than half Feisal's force in early December, and he was forced to retreat into the port, but the presence of a British MONITOR and four other ROYAL NAVY warships stationed just offshore – their guns trained on a brightly searchlit area in front of the town walls – persuaded the Turkish force to withdraw. The failure of the Turkish attack encouraged more Arab tribesmen to join Feisal in Yenbo, and the subsequent raid on WEJH confirmed the resurgence of the Revolt.

Yilderim Force Turkish–German army corps assembled at Aleppo (Halab) in Syria during summer 1917 for operations on the MESOPOTAMIAN FRONT. Based around two Turkish infantry divisions, it included three battalions of the German East Asiatic Corps with supporting MACHINE GUN, MORTAR and ARTILLERY units. Financed from Germany – where Turkish C-in-C ENVER PASHA's determination to recapture BAGHDAD chimed with LUDENDORFF's desire to stretch British resources in the Middle East – the Yilderim ('Thunderbolt') Force was largely German-officered, with former chief of staff FALKENHAYN in command.

Rapid deployment was impossible without the use of the unfinished RAILWAY link between Aleppo and Baghdad, but German engineers failed to meet a December deadline for its completion. British successes in PALESTINE meanwhile altered German strategic priorities in the Middle East and, after prolonged disputes between Enver and Falkenhayn, Yilderim Force was belatedly transferred there during the defence of JERUSALEM. Arriving as the Turkish front collapsed, it was never fully employed as an offensive force, instead becoming part of an increasingly disorganized withdrawal to DAMASCUS and beyond.

York, Sergeant Alvin C. (1887–1964). A semi-literate native of the Tennessee mountains, and lay deacon of a local pacifist sect, York was drafted into the AEF under the SELECTIVE SERVICE SYSTEM in October 1917 when his claim for exemption as a conscientious objector was rejected. Persuaded at his training camp that the Bible sanctioned active service, he reached the WESTERN FRONT with the 82nd Division in May 1918. On 8 October, during the MEUSE–ARGONNE OFFENSIVE, Acting Corporal York's platoon was caught by flanking German MACHINE GUN fire in a forward position east of the River Aire. An expert marksman, alone in thick brushwood overlooking German positions, he killed an estimated 25 German troops and induced the surrender of 132 more by SNIPING, subsequently receiving promotion, the Congressional Medal of Honor, immense PROPAGANDA coverage, and a generous citation from Allied Supreme Commander FOCH.

Young Turks Name by which the Ottoman Empire's Union and Progress Party (UPP) was popularly and internationally known. The party was formed out of the Committee for Union and Progress, a revolutionary group of young TURKISH ARMY officers and public officials that imposed a constitutional regime on Sultan Abdul Hamid II in 1908. Though the UPP won a majority in subsequent national assembly elections, it retained strong extraparliamentary roots in the military and the Ottoman bureaucracy. A military faction headed by ENVER PASHA forced the formation of a predominantly UPP government in January 1913, and control of public appointments had given it political supremacy by early 1914.

The General Council of the UPP became the centre of political decision in wartime TURKEY. A cabal of powerful party managers, headed by Enver and TALAAT PASHA, distributed patronage and war profits with sufficient skill to divide opposition, and was virtually able to ignore criticisms from the annual Party congress until 1918. Once defeat appeared certain in mid-1918, the General Council turned against its war leadership, filling vacant cabinet posts with moderate constitutionalists from the Party's long-subdued liberal wing in an attempt to secure a postwar political future. The UPP dissolved itself at a special convention on 20 October 1918, re-forming as the 'Modern Party' but never regaining popular support amid a welter of new parties.

Ypres, First Battle of The front line on the WESTERN FRONT solidified around the medieval Flemish town of Ypres in early October 1914, and stayed there for four years. After a brief German occupation from 3 October, the town was taken by the BEF, advancing into Flanders in the latter stages of the 'RACE TO THE SEA'. Constantly embattled, it remained in Allied hands for the rest of the War.

The first major German attempt to seize the town formed an integral part of a wider battle for FLANDERS. Duke ALBRECHT's German Fourth Army arrived in Flanders shortly after the BEF, and German attacks were launched all along the sector from mid-October, including attacks on the town itself from 15 October. Experienced BEF riflemen held their positions but suffered heavy losses, as did French forces guarding the north of the town. With Allied lines to the north and south pushed back, Ypres became the main focus of a renewed German offensive from 29 October.

The heaviest attacks came from the south and east. In the south, the Fourth Army had taken the Messines Ridge and the village of Wytschaete by 1 November. In front of Ypres it took Gheluvelt and broke through the British line along the MENIN ROAD on 31 October. With defeat apparently imminent, a British counterattack recovered Gheluvelt before the end of the day and, strengthened by the arrival of French reserves, held off further heavy attacks the next day.

The fate of Ypres remained in the balance for another 10 days. Kaiser WILHELM II arrived at the front to witness its conquest, but the defence was strengthened by another French corps from 4 November. With fighting in progress all along the northern sector of the Western Front, German attacks on the town again came close to forcing evacuation on 9 November, taking St Eloi the next day and peaking on 11–12 November with a ferocious attempt to retake Gheluvelt. Again suffering terrible losses, which effectively destroyed the BEF as a professional army, Allied forces held on and German attacks began to slacken the next day.

After another German set-piece attack had failed on 15 November – bringing total German casualties around the salient to about 135,000 (against about 75,000 Allied losses) – bad weather and exhaustion combined to reduce combat to localized skirmishing. By about 22 November the sector had solidified into static TRENCH WARFARE. See MAP 6.

Ypres, Second Battle of Attack by the German Fourth Army (Duke ALBRECHT) on Allied positions around Ypres during April and May 1915. The only major attack of the year by the GERMAN ARMY on the WESTERN FRONT, it marked the first large-scale use of poison GAS in the theatre.

German chief of staff FALKENHAYN's decision to concentrate attacking resources on the EASTERN FRONT in 1915 left little scope for operations in the west. Earlier Allied offensives in CHAMPAGNE and at NEUVE CHAPELLE indicated to Falkenhayn that limited operations offered the best chance of lasting success against entrenched defenders, and the attack was intended only to clear the SALIENT and to enable the German high command to test its volatile new weapon, chlorine gas.

After a brief PRELIMINARY BOMBARDMENT, gas was released against French and Algerian troops guarding the north of the salient on the morning of 22 April. Completely surprised, they fled in terror. Unnerved by the success of their own weapon, two German corps equipped with primitive respirators advanced cautiously into a 7km gap in the Allied line. The next day, some 3km beyond their start point, they halted after counterattacks by hastily deployed British reserves from the Second Army.

The loss of high ground to the north greatly weakened the Allied position. When a second gas attack gained ground against CANADIAN FORCES northeast of the town on 24 April, and fighting spread along the front as far as Hill 60 to the southeast, Second Army commander SMITH-DORRIEN proposed a general withdrawal to a line closer to Ypres. His C-in-C (FRENCH) reacted to the idea by sending Smith-Dorrien home, but accepted a similar recommendation by his replacement, General PLUMER. Withdrawal was delayed pending a French counteroffensive promised by General FOCH, in command of Allied reserves in the sector. Two French divisions attacked unsuccessfully on 29 April, and the BEF pulled back during the first three days of May.

Heavy fighting, and frequent gas attacks, continued around Ypres until 25 May. The Allied line held, although renewed German pressure took further high ground to the east in a battle lasting six days from 8 May, and a final major German assault forced a small Allied withdrawal on 24 May. Lacking the supplies or manpower to achieve a major victory, the Fourth Army then reverted to demolishing the town with heavy ARTILLERY, having reduced the Ypres salient to a third of its original size and inflicted almost 70,000 casualties for the loss of 35,000 men. See MAP 6.

Ypres, Third Battle of Major British offensive in Flanders, launched on 31 July 1917 and continued until November. Also known as 'Passchendaele', after the final objective gained in the campaign, it was the last great battle of attrition fought on the WESTERN FRONT.

British C-in-C HAIG's original plans for 1917 had envisaged an attack in Flanders, and he returned to the idea in May once the NIVELLE OFFENSIVE had failed. Its ultimate aim, at the height of the German *HANDELSKRIEG* campaign, was the destruction of SUBMARINE bases on the Belgian coast, but Haig's primary motive was his belief that the GERMAN ARMY was close to collapse, a view encouraged by the small success at MESSINES in June. Despite opposition from prime minister LLOYD GEORGE, Haig made meticulous preparations for a conventional mass BREAKTHROUGH attempt.

The opening attack was carried out by the British Fifth Army (GOUGH), with one corps of the Second Army (PLUMER) joining on its right and a corps of the French First Army (ANTHOINE) on the left, a total of 12 divisions. After a 10-day PRELIMINARY BOMBARDMENT by more than 3,000 guns (expending 4.25 million shells), the offensive opened at 03.50 on 31 July along an 18km front east of Ypres. Given time to prepare DEFENCE IN DEPTH, the German Fourth Army (Arnim) held off the main British advance around the MENIN ROAD, and restricted attackers to small gains on the left of the line around Pilcken Ridge. Further north, French infantry were quickly halted by the German Fifth Army (GALLWITZ).

Attempts to renew the offensive over the following days were hampered by pouring rain, turning the Flanders lowlands into a mud-churned swamp which rendered TANKS immobile and virtually paralysed the infantry. The weight of British bombardment had exacerbated the situation by destroying drainage systems, and no major attacks were possible until 16 August, when four days of fighting (the Battle of Langemarck) produced tiny gains for the British left and heavy casualties.

Haig effectively removed Gough from command of the operation by moving the Second Army's front north to the central Menin Road sector before attacks were resumed in September. Plumer planned a series of small-scale advances – never outrunning the range of supporting ARTILLERY – that began on 20 September with a carefully prepared attack along a narrow front either side of the road (Battle of the Menin Road Bridge).

Two further attacks, on 26 September and 4 October (Battles of Polygon Wood and Broodseinde), established British possession of the ridge east of Ypres. These costly gains persuaded some British commanders that the German defence was almost exhausted, and despite worsening rain Haig decided to continue attacks towards Passchendaele Ridge, some 10km east of Ypres.

Attacks on 9 October (Battle of Poelcappe) and 12 October (First Battle of Passchendaele) made little progress towards the Ridge as exhausted attackers floundered in the mud against an influx of German reserves well-supplied with mustard GAS. Haig persisted with three more assaults on the Ridge in late October, largely for reasons of national prestige, and the operation was called off after Passchendaele village was finally seized by British and CANADIAN infantry on 6 November.

The offensive cost the BEF about 310,000 casualties, and estimated German losses were slightly lower. The Ypres SALIENT had been widened by a few kilometres, but no Allied reserves were left for the year's final offensive at CAMBRAI. Haig was heavily criticized by contemporaries for continuing with the attacks long after they had lost any strategic value, a view shared by many modern commentators. See MAP 6.

Yser, Battle of the The BELGIAN ARMY's defence of the Yser Canal, running south from the Channel coast at Nieuport, northwestern Belgium, in late October 1914. Part of the wider battle for FLANDERS taking place simultaneously around YPRES and points south, the action was the climactic episode of the 'RACE TO THE SEA'.

Belgian forces retreating west from ANTWERP and Ostend were still deploying along the northern reaches of the Canal when the German Fourth Army (Duke ALBRECHT) began attacking their positions on 18 October. The Fourth Army launched a general offensive between Ypres and the coast on 20 October, preoccupying potential Allied reinforcements, and the Belgian position rapidly became critical.

At the centre of the Belgian front, a German division crossed the Canal near Tervaete on the night of 22 October, forcing defenders back to the Dixmunde–Nieuport railway on 24 October, where they were reinforced by a French division. At Dixmunde itself, 6,500 FRENCH NAVY troops under Admiral Ronarc'h suffered 50 per cent losses but held off attackers.

With a breakthrough towards Dunkirk and Calais apparently imminent, Belgian commander King ALBERT ordered the opening of the Canal locks at Nieuport on 25 October. It took three days to open the first gate, gradually letting in the sea to flood the low country between the Canal and the railway. After a last attack on 29 September, the Fourth Army was compelled to retreat from the rising waters. The main German effort in Flanders was then transferred to the Ypres SALIENT, and although Dixmunde was taken on 10 November, Belgian forces remained in control of Nieuport throughout the War. See MAP 2.

Yudenich, General Nikolai (1862–1933) The most consistently successful RUSSIAN ARMY general of the period, Yudenich served exclusively on the CAUCASIAN FRONT after becoming deputy chief of staff to the Caucasus Army in 1907. Chief of staff to General

Mishlaevski when war broke out with TURKEY in November 1914, his success at SARIKAMISH in December earned him popular celebrity and promotion to army command in January 1915, and he retained field control after Grand Duke NIKOLAI's transfer to the theatre in September.

After destroying a smaller Turkish offensive at MALAZGIRT in August 1915, Yudenich was reinforced for a series of limited but spectacular attacks in 1916, capturing ERZURUM in February, TRABZON in April and ERZINCAN in July. His safe distance from centres of political influence encouraged unbroken praise from Russian PROPAGANDA, but his options were restricted by diminishing supplies, faltering discipline and reorganized opponents from late 1916.

Briefly in command of the front after the FEBRUARY REVOLUTION, but with little actual control over his turbulent troops, he was retired by the PROVISIONAL GOVERNMENT and returned to Petrograd (St Petersburg) until the OCTOBER REVOLUTION, when he fled to FINLAND. In command of White forces formed to march on Petrograd, his advance to the suburbs in autumn 1919 was the crisis of the RUSSIAN CIVIL WAR, but he retired permanently to France after his outnumbered army was driven back into ESTONIA by better-equipped RED ARMY forces.

Yugoslavia The concept of a single state uniting Balkan Slavs dated back to the mid-19th century, but had developed two distinct strands by 1914. Broadly speaking, independent SERBIA sought a centralized state based on Belgrade, absorbing Slav populations in AUSTRIA-HUNGARY – which controlled ethnic Croats, Slovenes and Albanians – and in independent MONTENEGRO. Nationalist groups struggling for independence from Habsburg rule, and some Montenegrins, preferred a federation of autonomous states to a simple exchange of masters. Both strands regarded access to the Adriatic via ALBANIA or Bosnia-Herzegovina (annexed by the Habsburg Empire in 1908) as the key to future survival and prosperity as an independent power. See MAP 1.

The outbreak of general war offered an obvious opportunity to enlist international support for the removal of Habsburg domination in the Balkans, and nationalist leaders left the Empire for the capitals of its enemies during the 1914 JULY CRISIS. Suspicion of Serbian intentions kept most from Belgrade, and an influential party led by Dalmatian Croat Anton TRUMBIĆ travelled hopefully to neutral ITALY, where their reception was muted by Italian territorial ambitions on the eastern Adriatic coast.

Attempts to win support from the Allies for postwar Slav integrity were initially unsuccessful: RUSSIA preferred to promote the creation of independent but weak Balkan states under its protection; Anglo-French diplomats were primarily concerned with wooing Italian support; and Allied leaders were generally unready to envisage the break-up of Austria-Hungary. The PAŠIĆ government in Serbia meanwhile encountered the same obstacles to its own, less comprehensive territorial demands.

Though its details remained secret, Slav leaders could guess the gist of the LONDON Treaty between Italy and the Allies in April 1915, but mutual frustration only gradually brought Belgrade and the exiles closer together. A 'Yugoslav Committee', led by Trumbić and former Hungarian deputy Frano Supilo (also a Croat), was formed by exiles in May. Based in London, it cooperated with other exiled groups to lobby for the dismemberment of the Habsburg Empire, but split in 1916 over the issue of cooperation with the Serbian government, itself in exile on Corfu from late 1915.

Serbian refusal to endorse a federal future publicly prompted Supilo's departure to work for an an independent Croatia in mid-1916, but Trumbić maintained a dialogue with Pašić that culminated in the compromise CORFU DECLARATION of 27 July 1917.

Allied enthusiasm for nationalist movements was stimulated in 1917 by the failure of proposals for a separate peace with Austria-Hungary and a series of military setbacks, but South Slav delegates at the ROME CONGRESS of exiles in April 1918 were given less official encouragement than other groups. The Italian ORLANDO government offered Trumbić practical help in fomenting unrest among Croats within the AUSTRO-HUNGARIAN ARMY, but refused to discuss postwar territorial details.

Continued uncertainty, the relatively sudden collapse of Habsburg authority and astute manoeuvring by Prince ALEXANDER of Serbia all combined to force a compromise on federalists and 'Greater Serbians' in late 1918, and a new 'Kingdom of Serbs, Croats and Slovenes' was established under the Serbian monarchy on 1 December. Both Pašić and Trumbić represented the Kingdom at the PARIS PEACE CONFERENCE, where their frequent differences were subordinated to a struggle against Italian claims in Dalmatia.

Fuelled by Gabriele D'ANNUNZIO's seizure of Fiume (Rijeka) on Italy's behalf, the dispute was not formally ended until November 1920, and it temporarily masked the new state's inherent instability. Containing ten other linguistic groups apart from its three main ethnic components, it was divided on religious grounds into large Orthodox, Roman Catholic and Muslim populations. Chronic internal turmoil was eventually subdued by a royal dictatorship under Alexander from 1929, when the name Yugoslavia was officially adopted, but disputed borders with Albania, BULGARIA and Hungary continued to endanger stability into the 1930s (see Treaties of NEUILLY, TRIANON; MAP 25).

Z

Zamosc See: Battle of KOMARÓW.

Zayonchkovski, General Andrei (1862–1926) A protégé of General BRUSILOV, Zayonchkovski led the small Russian Dobrudja Army (three divisions) in the ROMANIAN CAMPAIGN from September 1916, and was in overall command of Russo-Romanian forces in the Dobrudja region throughout the campaign (see MAP 14). Several allied ROMANIAN ARMY units surrendered to his forces when they arrived, on the assumption that they were Bulgarians, and inter-army relations worsened from that point. Denied reinforcements by STAVKA (Russian central command), and let down by Romanian forces untrained in modern warfare, Zayonchkovski was driven from the Dobrudja by elements of MACKENSEN's Danube Army during October. Falling back into Moldavia, he remained on the defensive until replaced (at his own repeated request) by General SHCHERBACHEV in April 1917, after which he retired from the Army. He returned to serve in the RED ARMY in 1918, and fought against General Denikin's White forces in the UKRAINE during the RUSSIAN CIVIL WAR.

Zeebrugge Raid British attempt, on the night of 22/23 April 1918, to block the exits to Zeebrugge and Ostend harbours, the main bases for GERMAN NAVY light forces and SUBMARINES on the Belgian coast. In German hands since 1914, the ports were regarded by the ROYAL NAVY as a prime strategic target, but were heavily defended, easily reinforced overland, hemmed by minefields, and backed by warrens of navigable channels in which warships could hide.

First Sea Lord JELLICOE startled the government at the end of 1917 by claiming that GREAT BRITAIN's ability to wage war depended on the capture or neutralization of the ports as an ANTI-SUBMARINE measure, and a risky operation to block the harbours, planned by Dover commander KEYES, was accepted by the Admiralty in February 1918.

As a prelude to the main attack on Zeebrugge, the old CRUISER *Vindictive* was to land troops against shore batteries at the nearby entrance to the Bruges Canal, but offshore winds dispersed its smokescreen and it moored in the wrong place under heavy fire. Without support from its guns, landing parties failed to take the batteries, which helped prevent three old cruisers filled with concrete from scuttling in the allotted places. One of two old British SUBMARINES loaded with high explosives did reach its designated target and blew a gap in a RAILWAY viaduct, but the main attack suffered more than 500 casualties and resulted in only mild disruption of harbour traffic for a few days.

A smaller attack on Ostend, using two old cruisers as blockships, achieved nothing at all, yet the whole operation was presented as a major triumph by British PROPAGANDA. Keyes was ennobled, and the Raid received popular credit for the subsequent reduction of shipping losses to U-boats (see *HANDELSKRIEG*).

Zeppelin Rs-III A number of giant seaplanes were produced alongside the German REISENFLUGZEUG heavy-bomber fleet, but only the single Zeppelin Rs-III reached active service. A reliable, pilot-friendly machine designed by Professor Claudius Dornier, its unique design featured four engines (including two PUSHERS) lodged between a huge, low-wing monoplane, a fuselage manned by a single gunner, and a single hull containing the cockpits. The Rs-III first flew in November 1917 and was accepted into GERMAN NAVY service the following June. It operated as a long-range patrol craft over the North Sea until the ARMISTICE, when it was turned over to the Allies and used to clear MINES until 1921.

BRIEF DATA Type: long-range patrol seaplane; Crew: 6; Engine: 4 × 245hp Maybach; Cruising speed: 120kph; Armament: 3 × 7.92mm mg.

Zeppelins Rigid AIRSHIPS designed by German nobleman Graf (Count) Zeppelin and first flown in 1900. German military authorities initially saw more potential in development of non-rigid airships, but the LZ-3 was accepted into GERMAN ARMY service as the *Zeppelin Luftschiff 1* (Z-1) in March 1909. By August 1914 the Army was using seven military Zeppelins and three civilian models, all attached directly to the high command for strategic deployment, and one was in service with the GERMAN NAVY.

Apart from three Zeppelins in EAST PRUSSIA and two used for training, the Army fleet concentrated on the WESTERN FRONT in 1914. The time needed to set up operations made reconnaissance work impossible, but Zeppelins made an immediate impact as bombers, Z-6 successfully attacking LIÈGE on the night of 6/7 August, although it was withdrawn from service after a forced landing caused by ground fire.

This set the pattern for future operations: Zeppelins could deliver successful long-range bombing attacks, but were extremely vulnerable to attack and bad weather. Three more were lost to ground forces before the end of August, and another destroyed in its shed by a single British SOPWITH TABLOID on 8 October. By the following spring eight new Zeppelins had been commissioned, against a sixth loss on the EASTERN FRONT, and Army Zeppelins were redeployed in BELGIUM for STRATEGIC BOMBING attacks against England, Flanders and France. Paris suffered regular raids during March 1915, and London experienced its first attack on 31 May.

Larger Zeppelins, notably the P-Type with a bomb load of over 1,200kg, began entering service during 1915, and new extendible observation cars, which hung beneath the ship to direct bombing, enabled attacks from above clouds, but losses remained high. Despite reinforcements and restriction of operations to moonless nights, only six ships were operational by the start of 1916. The failure of four Army Zeppelins deployed against VERDUN in February 1916 (three were lost almost at once) ended their frontline career, but operations against the British and French coasts were continued on the grounds that their effect on enemy morale outweighed losses.

New models introduced in 1916 had a much higher ceiling, and initial raids in April (by five and four ships, respectively) were carried out without loss. The year saw the climax of long-range bombing by Zeppelins, with Britain alone suffering 22 of its wartime total of 53 Zeppelin raids, and the Army fleet on the Eastern Front grew to five ships, suffering only a single loss. Two Army ships were also sent to the BALKAN FRONT in 1916, but were destroyed and replaced by a third.

Reorganization of the GERMAN ARMY AIR

SERVICE, and greatly improved aircraft performance standards, contributed to the Army's loss of interest in Zeppelins from autumn 1916. Even the latest models were vulnerable to FIGHTER attack by 1917, and Army airship operations were discontinued altogether in June. Most surviving Army ships were scrapped, but three (and some crews) were transferred to the Navy, which continued to use airships of all types throughout the War.

Naval strength had been brought up to 12 Zeppelins by early 1915, mostly for observation work over the North and BALTIC seas. They also carried out a number of independent raids over Allied territory and were present (if ineffectual) at JUTLAND. Regular design improvements culminated in X-Type Zeppelins, with a 7,000m ceiling, one of which was shot down during the last raid against Britain on 5 August 1918.

A total of 115 Zeppelins saw military service, of which 77 were destroyed or damaged beyond repair, 7 captured, 22 scrapped and 9 handed to the Allies after the ARMISTICE. The most ambitious Zeppelin operation was the attempted supply of German forces in EAST AFRICA in late 1917 by naval ship L59, which reached the Sudan before being recalled by RADIO in the belief that the colony had fallen to the Allies.

Zeppelin-Staaken R-Types Largest and most successful of the German RIESENFLUGZEUG ('giant aircraft') heavy bombers. Beginning with the VGO-I, designed from November 1914 to test the viability of multi-engined STRATEGIC BOMBING aircraft, about 50 Zeppelin-Staakens were produced. Setting new standards in aircraft size and technical sophistication, they took a long time to build and each of the early models was an experimental prototype. Produced by four contractors, they were fitted with from three to six engines driving a variety of propeller configurations, and featured individual tail, wing and armament designs. Structurally advanced and generally very reliable, they shared enormous size, biplane tail wings and the capacity to carry up to 2,000kg of bombs.

Generally known by their production serial numbers, the first prototypes operated on the EASTERN FRONT from February 1916, and by the end of the year production had settled on the R-VI design, 12 of which joined GOTHA G-TYPES in long-range night attacks on England from September 1917. A total of 18 R-VI models were built (numbers R14 to R31), and were increasingly used for night raids behind the WESTERN FRONT, the shorter journeys enabling a full bomb load to be carried.

Several more versions appeared in 1917–18, again as prototypes built in ones and twos. They generally retained the unique engine arrangement of the R-VI – on which the engines were positioned in pairs driving one pusher and one tractor propeller – and travelled with a mechanic in each engine nacelle for in-flight repairs.

The Zeppelin-Staakens were easily Germany's best wartime strategic bombers, and only the R43 (one of three R-XIV types) was ever shot down, succumbing to British night FIGHTERS after being caught in searchlights over Abbeville on 10 August 1918.

BRIEF DATA (R-VI) Type: heavy bomber; Crew: 7; Span: 42m; Engine: 4 × 245hp Maybach; Max speed: 136kph; Ceiling: 4,250m; Armament: 5 × 7.92mm mg, max bomb load 2,000kg (4,400lbs).

Zhekov, General Nikola (1864–1949) A staff officer with the BULGARIAN ARMY during the Balkan Wars (1912–13), Zhekov was appointed war minister in the RADOSLAVOV government in August 1915, charged with preparations for the invasion of SERBIA in October. He left his cabinet post to assume direct command of the Army on the BALKAN FRONT from October 1915, but was unable to prevent effective German strategic control of Bulgarian formations during the invasion, or the subsequent flow of troops from the SALONIKA sector to join the ROMANIAN CAMPAIGN. His demands to be allowed a further invasion into Greek Macedonia were backed by Sofia but refused by the German high command, and he fell into dispute with his own government over the diversion of supplies away from his neglected battlefront. Although he helped nullify successive Allied offensives from Salonika in autumn 1916 and spring 1917 (see Battles of FLORINA and Lake PRESPA), Bulgarian historians criticize his defensive deployments after the departure of German units in early 1918. Low morale and supply shortages were nonetheless primarily responsible for the Bulgarian Army's collapse during the autumn VARDAR OFFENSIVE, which Zhekov missed through illness. He fled postwar BULGARIA, and was imprisoned for three years on his return in 1923.

Zhilinski, General Yakov (1853–1918) One of a rapid succession of ineffectual prewar chiefs of staff to the RUSSIAN ARMY, and subsequently head of the Warsaw military district, Zhilinski commanded the northwest sector on the EASTERN FRONT in August 1914 and was responsible for the invasion of EAST PRUSSIA. Conducting operations with the minimum of personal involvement, he blamed First Army commander RENNENKAMPF for defeats at TANNENBERG and the First Battle of the MASURIAN LAKES, but was himself accused of panic under pressure and dismissed in September. Like other veteran generals, Zhilinski benefited from factional upheavals, which helped to resurrect his career as Russia's representative with the French high command in late 1915. On chief of staff ALEXEEV's instructions, he worked to convince Allied authorities that Russia was ready to take part in a joint offensive programme (see Battle of Lake NAROCH). Retired after the FEBRUARY REVOLUTION in 1917, he was killed holding a White command in the RUSSIAN CIVIL WAR.

Zimmermann Note Telegram sent from German foreign minister Zimmermann, an experienced administrative functionary and a fervent supporter of unrestricted SUBMARINE WARFARE, to Ambassador BERNSTORFF in the UNITED STATES on 17 January 1917.

Informing Bernstorff of the decision to resume unrestricted U-BOAT attacks, via a Scandinavian transatlantic cable officially reserved for peace negotiations, Zimmermann added: 'Make Mexico a proposal of alliance on the following basis – make war together, make peace together, generous financial support, and an understanding on our part that Mexico is to reconquer the lost territory in Texas, New Mexico and Arizona.' The message also contained a suggestion that JAPAN could be induced to join an alliance.

Intercepted, along with several later messages, by both the US State Department and the ROYAL NAVY, the Note was shown to President WILSON on 24 February and released to the press on 1 March. Both Japan and MEXICO denied any collusion in the scheme, but Zimmermann admitted the Note's authenticity on 3 March. US public opinion – unimpressed by his complaints at Allied wiretapping, inflamed by several weeks of unrestricted submarine activity, and suspicious of Mexican intentions – swung conclusively behind war against GERMANY.

'Zimmerwald Movement' The wartime forum for international socialist and PACIFIST politics following the effective collapse of the SECOND INTERNATIONAL in August 1914. Its name derived from an inaugural conference of European pacifists invited by Swiss and Italian socialists to Zimmerwald, Switzerland, in September 1915. The Second International was formally abandoned, but the conference was divided along familiar lines between the revolutionaries of LENIN's left-wing minority and a more moderate reformist majority. A second conference at Kienthal in Switzerland failed to resolve differences the following April, and the Russian FEBRUARY REVOLUTION accentuated the split before a third meeting in July 1917, held as part of the general socialist conference at STOCKHOLM. The OCTOBER REVOLUTION shifted the focus of revolutionary socialism irrevocably to RUSSIA, and the Zimmerwald moderate wing returned to mainstream politics after the War.

Zlota Lipa, Battle of the The opening engagement of the Russian offensive into eastern GALICIA of August 1914, an attack by 8 divisions of General Brudemann's Austro-Hungarian Third Army against 22 divisions of General RUZSKI's Russian Third Army.

Despite instructions from army group commander IVANOV to hurry, and information that Austrian strength in the sector was less than anticipated, Ruzski had advanced east to the frontier at a rate of less than 10km per day, crossing around Brody on 20–21 August, and forcing BRUSILOV's Eighth Army to keep pace on his left. Convinced by their caution that he faced only isolated forward units, Brudemann was permitted to advance by Austro-Hungarian chief of staff CONRAD, and met four closely linked Russian corps along the Zlota Lipa river, east and southeast of Lvov, on 26 August.

Outnumbered more than two to one, and deprived of a corps sent to reinforce attacks around KOMAROW, Austro-Hungarian forces launched repeated frontal assaults across difficult terrain over the next two days, all repulsed with heavy casualties. Russian counterattacks forced them into a disorderly retreat from 28 August but Ruzski made no attempt at pursuit. Despite losses of over 50 per cent, the Austrians were able to establish new positions on the Gnila Lipa River, some 25km to the east. See MAP 10; Battle of the GNILA LIPA.

Select Chronology of the First World War

JUNE 1914 *Balkan troubles rekindled*

28 Assassination of Archduke Franz Ferdinand in Sarajevo

JULY 1914 *July Crisis interrupts European holiday season; Balkan Front opens*

6 German government confirms support for Austro-Hungarian reprisals against Serbia

23 Austrian ultimatum to Serbia • French leaders leave St Petersburg

24 Serbia appeals to Russia

28 Austria-Hungary declares war on Serbia

29 Belgrade bombarded

31 Russia mobilizes • Germany presents ultimata to Russia and France • secret German-Turkish pact

AUGUST 1914 *General European war; Western and Eastern Fronts open*

1 Germany declares war on Russia

2 German Army enters Luxembourg • Italy declares neutrality

3 Germany declares war on France

4 German troops enter Belgium at Gemmerich • Great Britain declares war on Germany

5 Austria-Hungary declares war on Russia

10 France declares war on Austria-Hungary • German Mittelmeerdivision allowed into Turkish waters

12 Britain declares war on Austria-Hungary • Battle of Haelen, Belgium • First Austro-Hungarian invasion of Serbia (to 25.8)

14 French invasion of Lorraine begins

15 Russian invasion of East Prussia begins

16 Fall of Liège

17 Battle of Stallupönen, East Prussia

18 Russian invasion of Austro-Hungarian Galicia begins

20 Battles of the Frontiers in France and Belgium (to 24.8) • Battle of Gumbinnen, East Prussia • Death of Pope Pius X

21 Serbian victory at the Jadar River

23 Japan declares war on Germany • BEF in action at Mons, Belgium • Battle of Krasnik, northern Galicia

25 Sack of Louvain, Belgium (to 30.8)

26 Battle of Tannenberg in East Prussia (to 30.8) • Komarów action in northern Galicia (to 30.8) • Battle of the Zlota Lipa in eastern Galicia (to 28.8) • Battle of Le Cateau, France • German surrender in Togoland

27 French *Union Sacrée* coalition cabinet formed under Viviani

28 North Sea Heligoland Bight action

29 Battle of Guise, France • Battle of the Gnila Lipa, eastern Galicia

SEPTEMBER 1914 *Invasions of France, East Prussia, Galicia, Serbia all fail; 'Race to the Sea' in France*

1 St Petersburg renamed Petrograd

2 French government leaves Paris

3 Election of Pope Benedict XV • Russian forces take Lvov, Galicia

5 Entente Powers renounce separate peace

6 First Battle of the Marne, France (to 10.9)

7 Second Austro-Hungarian invasion of Serbia (to 15.9) • First Battle of the Masurian Lakes, East Prussia (to 14.9)

11 Austro-Hungarian withdrawal from Galicia begins

14 German line in northern France holds at the Aisne (to 28.9) • Falkenhayn replaces Moltke as German chief of staff

15 Serbian victory at the Drina River

22 *U-9* sinks British cruiser *Cressy* and two others

24 Russians besiege Przemysl, Galicia
25 First Battle of Albert, France (to 29.9) • Hindenburg becomes Central Powers' C-in-C, Eastern Front
27 Allies take Douala, Cameroon
28 German offensive opens Polish campaigns

OCTOBER 1914 *Indecisive offensives in Poland; the Western Front reaches the Channel coast*

1 First Battle of Arras (to 4.10)
9 Maritz proclaims Boer Revolt, South Africa
10 Fall of Antwerp • Austro-Hungarian relief of Przemysl • Romanian King Carol I dies
12 Battles for Flanders underway (to c 16.11) • German forces besiege Warsaw
15 First Battle of Ypres, Flanders (to c 16.11)
16 First Canadian troops reach Britain • death of San Giuliano, Italy
18 Battle of the Yser, Flanders underway (to c 16.11)
20 German withdrawal from Warsaw
26 Russians cross Vistula River at Ivangorod, Poland
27 Central Powers begin withdrawal from Russian Poland • dreadnought *Audacious* sunk by mine
29 Turkey attacks Russian Black Sea bases and joins the Central Powers
30 German cruiser *Königsberg* trapped in the Rufugi Delta, East Africa

NOVEMBER 1914 *Western Front locks into trench warfare; renewed invasions of Poland and Serbia; Turkey at war; hostilities open in Mesopotamia and the Caucasus*

1 Battle of Coronel, Pacific Ocean
3 Bulgaria reaffirms neutrality • British attack on Tanga, East Africa (to 5.11)
5 Sonnino becomes Italian foreign minister
7 Anglo-Indian forces land in Turkish Mesopotamia • Tsingtao (Qingdao) falls to Japanese forces
8 Third Austro-Hungarian invasion of Serbia (to 15.12)
9 German raider *Emden* sunk by *Sydney*
11 German attack on Łódź, Poland (to 13.12)
16 Heavy rain in Flanders moderates fighting • Sultan of Turkey proclaims Islamic Holy War (*Jihad*) against the British Empire
18 Caucasian Front opens with Turkish advance from Erzurum
21 Anglo-Indian invasion of Mesopotania takes Basra
23 Portuguese parliament authorizes military commitment to the Allies
29 Renewed German offensive at Ypres (to 13.12)

DECEMBER 1914 *Western Front stagnant; Eastern Front subsides into trench warfare; Serbia again holds off invasion*

3 Serbian victory at Kolubara River (to 8.12)
6 Russian evacuation of Łódź
8 Spee's German naval squadron destroyed at the Falkland Islands • breakdown of Boer rebellion in South Africa • Anglo-Indian capture of Qurna, Mesopotamia
10 First French Champagne Offensive on the Western Front (to 17.3.15)
13 German attacks in Poland suspended • deadlock in the Carpathian Mountains
15 Austro-Hungarian withdrawal from Belgrade
16 German Navy bombards Scarborough and other English east-coast towns
17 Britain announces protectorate over Egypt
25 Italian Navy occupies Valona, Albania • Turkish Caucasian offensive defeated at Sarikamish (to 4.1.15) • British aircraft carriers raid Cuxhaven

JANUARY 1915 *Allied massed frontal assaults along the Western Front; both sides prepare offensives in Galicia*

3 Cardinal Mercier arrested in Belgium
13 Burian replaces Berchtold as Austro-Hungarian foreign minister
14 South African forces occupy Swakopmund, Southwest Africa
18 German victory at Jassin, East Africa • Japan presents 'Twenty-One Demands' to China
20 Opening Austro-Hungarian attacks in the Carpathians
24 Dogger Bank engagement, North Sea
31 First large-scale use of gas at Bolimov, northern Galicia (to 3.2)

FEBRUARY 1915 *Central Powers resume offensives along the Eastern Front; Palestine and Gallipoli Fronts open*

3 Turkish attacks fail to cross the Suez Canal
4 Germany announces submarine campaign in British waters (begins 18.2)
7 Second Battle of the Masurian Lakes, East Prussia (to 21.2)
17 Austro-Hungarian forces take Czernowitz, southern Galicia, and resume Carpathian Offensive
19 Initial Anglo-French bombardment of Dardanelles forts
25 Second bombardment of the Dardanelles

MARCH 1915 *Manpower build-up on the main fronts; Turkey holds the Dardanelles*

5 Allied naval bombardment of Smyrna (to 7.3)
6 Resignation of Greek Venizelos government
10 BEF attacks at Neuve Chapelle (to 13.3)
18 Failed Allied naval attack on the Dardanelles
19 British munitions unions agree war truce
22 Przemysl surrenders to Russian siege • First Zeppelin raid on Paris
25 Russian counteroffensive in the Carpathians (to 10.4)

APRIL 1915 *Gallipoli develops as Anglo-French second front; Italy joins the Allies*

8 Enforced deportations of Armenians begin in Turkey • Italy announces territorial demands to Austria-Hungary
11 Turkish offensive at Shaiba, Mesopotamia (to 14.4)
16 Vienna rejects Italian demands
20 Turkish forces besiege Armenians in Van
22 First successful gas attack opens limited German offensive at Ypres (to 24.5)
25 Allied landings at Helles and Anzac Cove, Gallipoli
26 Italy signs Treaty of London with the Allies • German advance into Kurland, north Russia
28 First Allied attack on Krithia, Gallipoli

MAY 1915 *Russian collapse in Poland; Allies held at Gallipoli; Italy at war*

2 Austro-German Gorlice–Tarnow Offensive begins in Poland (to 25.6)
6 Second Allied attack on Krithia (to 8.6)
7 Sinking of *Lusitania* off the Irish coast
9 Allied Artois Offensive, Western Front (to 19.6)
13 South Africans take Windhoek, Southwest Africa • Italian Salandra government resigns (reinstated 16.5)
14 British 'shell scandal' breaks
18 Unsuccessful Turkish assault on Anzac Cove, Gallipoli (to 24.5)
23 Italy declares war on Austria-Hungary
25 British Asquith coalition government formed
31 First Zeppelin raid on London

JUNE 1915 *Austro-German advance into Poland continues; Italian Front opens*

3 Central Powers retake Przemysl
4 Third British attack on Krithia • British capture Amara, Mesopotamia
8 US secretary of state Bryan resigns, Lansing succeeds
13 Venizelos wins Greek elections
22 Central Powers reoccupy Lvov, Galicia
23 First Italian Isonzo Offensive (to 8.7)
26 Polivanov replaces Sukhomlinov as Russian war minister
28 Failed Allied attack on Achi Baba, Gallipoli (to 5.7)
29 Austro-German Bug Offensive begins in Poland (to c 30.9)

JULY 1915 *Russia abandons Poland*

5 British attack on Nasiriyeh, Mesopotamia (to 24.7)
9 Surrender of German Southwest Africa
10 New Turkish offensive in the Caucasus
11 *Königsberg* disabled in the Rufugi Delta
12 Second Allied failure at Achi Baba (to 14.7)
13 German Narev Offensive begins in Poland (to c 30.9) • Kurland attacks resumed
18 Second Italian Isonzo Offensive (to 2.8)
22 Stavka (Russian central command) orders 'Great Retreat' from Poland

AUGUST 1915 *German submarine warfare restricted; Eastern Front redefined; unsuccessful Allied expansion of the Gallipoli Front*

4 German forces occupy Warsaw
5 Turkish Caucasian offensive defeated at Malazgirt
6 Suvla Bay Offensive on Gallipoli (to 10.8)

16 Battle for the Irben Straits, Baltic (to 20.8)
17 Fall of Kovno, Lithuania
19 Fall of Novogeorgievsk, Poland • Liner *Arabic* sunk by U-boat
20 Italy declares war on Turkey
21 Renewed British attacks fail at Scimitar Hill, Gallipoli
22 Venizelos confirmed as Greek premier
27 New German orders limit *Handelskrieg* by submarines • Austro-Hungarian 'Black-Yellow' Offensive in Galicia (to 25.9)

SEPTEMBER 1915 *Central Powers switch attacking emphasis to Serbia; Allies repeat breakthrough attempts in France*

2 Falkenhayn orders a halt to German eastern offensives
5 Tsar Nicholas II becomes Russian C-in-C • first Zimmerwald Conference of pacifists, Switzerland
6 Bulgaria signs Pless Convention with the Central Powers
7 German Vilnius Offensive in Lithuania (to 25.9)
19 Vilnius falls
25 Allied Champagne and Artois-Loos Offensives begin in France (to 6.11)
28 British take Es Sinn, Mesopotamia

OCTOBER 1915 *Two-pronged invasion breaks the Balkan Front despite Allied commitment to Salonika; Bulgaria at war; Allied pressure in France continues*

5 First Allied troops land at Salonika • resignation of Greek premier Venizelos
6 Austro-German invasion of Serbia
8 Belgrade taken
11 Bulgarian Army invades Serbia
12 Execution of Edith Cavell in Belgium
13 French foreign minister Delcassé resigns
14 Bulgaria declares war on Serbia • US Congress approves limited military expansion
21 Third Italian Isonzo Offensive (to 3.11)
26 Hughes becomes Australian prime minister
28 Briand government in France

NOVEMBER 1915 *Western Front static for the winter; Serbia collapses; British invasion of Mesopotamia checked*

5 German forces capture Niš, Serbia
10 Fourth Italian Isonzo Offensive (to 3.12) • Russian troops advance on Tehran, Persia
22 Battle of Ctesiphon, Mesopotamia (to 25.11)
23 Retreat and evacuation of Serbian Army (to 15.1.16)

DECEMBER 1915 *Allied attempts at strategic cooperation; Salonika expedition static*

3 German military attachés expelled from the USA
4 Anglo-French war summit at Calais, France
6 Allied Chantilly Conference
7 Anglo-Indian forces besieged in Kut, Mesopotamia
13 Senussi tribesmen attack western Egypt
19 Haig replaces French as BEF commander • Allies evacuate Suvla and Anzac Cove positions, Gallipoli
22 Bulgarian forces in position along the Greek frontier
26 British Naval Africa Expedition operative on Lake Tanganyika
27 Russian offensive in Bessarabia (to 10.1.16)

JANUARY 1916 *British stalled in Mesopotamia; Gallipoli Front closes; Russia takes the initiative in the Caucasus*

1 Allies take Yaounda, Cameroon
4 Battle of Sheikh Sa'ad, Mesopotamia (to 8.1)
5 Austro-Hungarian invasion of Montenegro
8 Allied evacuation of Helles, Gallipoli (completed 9.1)
10 Russian Erzurum Offensive begins in Caucasus (to c 5.9)
11 French forces occupy Greek Corfu
13 Battle of Hanna, Mesopotamia (to 21.1)
15 Scheer takes command of German High Seas Fleet
16 Sarrail takes Allied command at Salonika
24 British Military Service Act introduces conscription (in force from 9.2)
25 Montenegro surrenders
29 First 'tank' trial in Britain

FEBRUARY 1916 *Huge German offensive in France*

1 Stürmer replaces Goremykin as Russian prime minister
10 US war secretary Garrison resigns
16 Russian forces take Erzurum, Caucasus
18 German surrender in Cameroon

21 German Verdun offensive begins on the Western Front (to 18.12)
24 Pétain takes command of Verdun defences
25 German capture of Fort Douaumont, Verdun

MARCH 1916 *Verdun holds; Russian and Italian relieving offensives fail*
6 Baker becomes US war secretary
8 Battle of Dujaila, Mesopotamia
9 Germany declares war on Portugal
12 Fifth Italian Isonzo Offensive (to 29.3)
13 British Morogoro Offensive, East Africa (to 28.9)
15 Second unrestricted German submarine campaign begins
16 Tirpitz succeeded by Capelle as Prussian navy minister • Roques replaces Galliéni as French war minister
18 Russian offensive at Lake Naroch (to 20.4)
24 Liner *Sussex* torpedoed in the English Channel
29 Dismissal of Russian war minister Polivanov

APRIL 1916 *US pressure forces relaxation of submarine warfare; British fail to relieve Kut; Russian gains in the Caucasus*
5 First Battle of Kut (to 22.4)
7 Russian Black Sea fleet covers Rize landings
9 Renewed German offensive at Verdun
17 Russian Caucasus offensive takes Trabzon
20 Germany suspends unrestricted U-boat campaign
24 Easter Rising, Dublin (to 1.5)
30 Fall of Kut

MAY 1916 *Intense battle at Verdun; Italy invaded*
14 Austro-Hungarian Trentino Offensive, Italy (to 10.6)
29 German forces take Mort Homme Hill, Verdun
31 Battle of Jutland, North Sea (to 2.6)

JUNE 1916 (*Russian offensive in the east wrecks the Austro-Hungarian Army; Italy recovers*
3 State of siege proclaimed at Salonika • Russian advance through Persia halted at Khanaqin
4 Russian Brusilov Offensive in Galicia (to 7.7)
5 British war minister Kitchener killed at sea • Arab Revolt proclaimed near Medina
6 Russians take Lutsk, Galicia • Death of President Yuan Shih-kai, China
7 German capture of Fort Vaux, Verdun
8 Arab Revolt takes Mecca
10 New Zealand introduces conscription
12 Salandra government resigns in Italy
15 Boselli cabinet takes office, Italy
20 German reserves counterattack in northern Galicia (to 30.6)
21 US and Mexican forces clash at Carrizal

JULY 1916 *Allied Somme offensive refocuses the Western Front; Russian advance in Galicia stagnates*
1 Anglo-French Somme Offensive, France (to 18.11)
19 German Somme defences reorganized
23 Stürmer replaces Sazonov as Russian foreign minister • Australian troops capture Pozières, Somme
25 Russian Caucasian offensive takes Erzincan
28 Russian Kovel Offensive, Eastern Front (to 3.10) • Galician advance takes Brody

AUGUST 1916 *Attrition in France; Salonika and Palestine Fronts reactivated; Romania at war*
4 Turkish attack on Romani, Suez (to 5.8)
6 Sixth Italian Isonzo Offensive (to 17.8)
9 Italian offensive takes Gorizia
10 Battle of Florina, Salonika (to 27.8)
27 Romania declares war on the Central Powers, invades Transylvania • Wilhelm II reinstates restrictions on U-boat attacks
28 Italy declares war on Germany
29 Third Supreme Command (Hindenburg and Ludendorff) replaces Falkenhayn
31 Hindenburg Programme put before Prussian war ministry

SEPTEMBER 1916 *Allied advance from Salonika fails to protect Romania; deadlock in France, Galicia and Italy*
2 Central Powers attack southern Romania
3 British take Dar-es-Salaam, East Africa
10 Allied fleet at Salamis presents demands to Greek government

13 Allied Monastir Offensive from Salonika (to 15.12)
14 Seventh Italian Isonzo Offensive (to 27.9)
15 Romanian invasion of Transylvania curtailed • tanks used at Flers-Courcelette, Somme
19 Belgian forces take Tabora, East Africa
27 Battle of Hermannstadt, Romania (to 29.9)
29 Battle of Flamanda, Romania (to 3.10)
30 Venizelos forms rebel government in Crete

OCTOBER 1916 *Allies renew offensives in France*

1 Renewed British attacks on Ancre Heights and Transloy Ridges, Somme (to 20.10)
9 Matasake government in Japan
10 Eighth Italian Isonzo Offensive (to 13.10)
20 Russian dreadnought *Imperatrica Maria* explodes at Sevastopol
16 Major Allied air raid on Oberndorf, Germany
21 Assassination of Austrian premier Stürgkh
23 Central Powers take Constanta, Romania • German attack at Iringa, East Africa (to 31.10)
24 French counteroffensive retakes Fort Douaumont, Verdun
29 Körber becomes Austrian premier

NOVEMBER 1916 *Allied attacks lose momentum on all fronts; Central Powers threaten Bucharest*

1 Ninth Italian Isonzo Offensive (to 14.11)
2 French recapture Fort Vaux, Verdun
5 Central Powers announce creation of 'Congress Poland' • Lawrence joins Arab Army at Yenbo
7 Re-election of US president Wilson
13 Final British attacks on the Somme (to 18.11)
19 Allied forces take Monastir
21 Death of Austro-Hungarian Kaiser Franz Josef
29 Jellicoe becomes British First Sea Lord, Beatty C-in-C Grand Fleet

DECEMBER 1916 *Romania effectively beaten; signs of exhaustion throughout Europe*

1 Battle of the Arges, Romania (to 4.12) • Allied and Greek forces clash at Athens
4 German Patriotic Service Law passed under the Hindenburg Programme
6 Lloyd George replaces Asquith as British prime minister • Central Powers occupy Bucharest
8 Allied blockade of Greece
11 Lyautey becomes French war minister
12 Nivelle replaces Joffre as French Western Front C-in-C • German Peace Offer announced
13 British Kut offensive, Mesopotamia (to 27.2.17)
18 President Wilson's Peace Note issued
21 British forces occupy El Arish, Palestine
29 Murder of Rasputin in Petrograd

JANUARY 1917 *Peripheral fighting as peace initiatives fail*

7 Battle of the Aa, Lithuania (to 31.1)
9 British attack Khadairi Bend, Mesopotamia (to 29.1)
20 Romanian front stabilizes on Sereth River
22 Wilson's 'peace without victory' speech to US Congress
24 Arab Revolt takes Wehj

FEBRUARY 1917 *Germany gambles on rapid victory by submarines; unrest in Russia; Turkish retreat in Mesopotamia*

1 New German unrestricted submarine campaign begins
3 USA breaks diplomatic relations with Germany
4 Talaat Pasha becomes Turkish grand vizier
5 Senussi defeated at Siwa
21 German tactical withdrawal in France, Operation Alberich (to 31.3)
24 British retake Kut
26 Wilson asks US Congress for permission to arm merchant ships
27 Russian Duma convenes in Petrograd

MARCH 1917 *Russian Tsar overthrown; Germany faces diplomatic isolation; British success in Mesopotamia, failure in Palestine*

1 Austro-Hungarian Kaiser Karl I dismissses Conrad, Arz von Straussenberg becomes chief of staff • US disclosure of Zimmermann Note
8 February Revolution in Russia (to 15.3)

11 British take Baghdad, Mesopotamia • Allied Lake Prespa offensive from Salonika (to 22.3)
13 China breaks diplomatic relations with Germany
14 Lyautey resigns as French war minister
15 Tsar Nicholas II abdicates
16 Provisional Government formed in Russia, Alexeev becomes C-in-C
17 Briand government falls in France
19 French battleship *Danton* torpedoed
20 Ribot cabinet takes office, France
25 Battle of Jebel Hamrin, Mesopotamia
26 First Battle of Gaza, Palestine (to 27.3)
31 Karl I's peace initiative reaches the French government

APRIL 1917 *The USA at war; Allied Nivelle Offensive fails on the Western Front; temporary suspension of operations on the Eastern Front; record Allied air and shipping losses*

6 The United States declares war on Germany
7 Cuba declares war on Germany • Wilhelm II promises postwar reform of the Prussian constitution
9 Nivelle Offensive opens with British attack around Arras (to 17.5), where Canadian forces capture Vimy Ridge
16 Second Battle of the Aisne, Nivelle Offensive (to 20.4)
19 Second Battle of Gaza (to 20.4) • Allied St Jean de Maurienne Conference
23 British take Samarrah, Mesopotamia
24 Resumption of Allied Prespa attacks (to 15.5) • Costa heads new government in Portugal
27 Submarine attacks force Allies to divert shipping from Suez
28 US conscription approved through Selective Service System
29 Mutiny engulfs the French Army (to c 10.6)

MAY 1917 *French Army exhausted; Russian government moves to the left*

13 Resignation of Russian war minister Guchkov
14 Tenth Italian Isonzo Offensive (to 8.6)
15 Pétain replaces Nivelle as French C-in-C • Battle of the Otranto Straits, Adriatic
18 Kerenski becomes war minister in new Russian coalition
19 Pershing given command of the AEF
22 Resignation of Hungarian premier Tisza
24 Japanese destroyers enter Mediterranean service
30 First wartime meeting of Austrian Reichsrat • Lithuanian national council instituted

JUNE 1917 *BEF assumes attacking responsibilities on the Western Front; Greece at war*

4 Brusilov becomes Russian Army C-in-C
7 British attack at Messines, Flanders (to 14.6)
11 King Constantine of Greece abdicates
13 First Gotha raid on London
16 First All-Russian Congress of Soviets, Petrograd
25 Venizelos returns as Greek premier • first AEF troops reach France
29 Greece declares war on the Central Powers

JULY 1917 *Final Russian offensive fails on the Eastern Front; German political truce collapses*

1 Russian Kerenski Offensive in Galicia (to 19.7)
6 Arab Revolt takes Aqaba
7 Peace resolution tabled in the German Reichstag (passed 19.7) • Falkenhayn commands Yilderim Force in Turkey
9 British dreadnought *Vanguard* explodes at anchor
14 Resignation of German chancellor Bethmann Hollweg, replaced by Michaelis • Estonian national assembly meets
16 July Days demonstrations in Russia (to 20.7)
17 British King George V changes family name to Windsor
18 Feng Kuo-chang seizes power in China
19 Austro-German counteroffensive in Galicia (to 15.8)
21 Arrest of General Pilsudski in Poland
22 Battle of Foscani, Romania (to 28.8) • Kerenski heads new Russian provisional coalition • Siam (Thailand) declares war on the Central Powers
27 Corfu Declaration on future Yugoslavia
31 Major British offensive at Ypres, Flanders (to 6.11)

AUGUST 1917 *Attrition at Ypres; Italian Isonzo campaigns appear close to success; political upheaval in Paris*

1 Kornilov becomes Russian C-in-C
4 Liberia declares war on Germany
6 Kühlmann replaces Zimmermann as German foreign minister
14 China declares war on the Central Powers • papal plea for peace published
18 Eleventh Italian Isonzo Offensive (to 12.9)
20 Wekerle becomes Hungarian prime minister
31 Resignation of French interior minister Malvy

SEPTEMBER 1917 *Ypres attacks renewed; Russian Army disintegrates*

1 German offensive towards Riga, Eastern Front
3 Fall of Riga to infiltration tactics
7 Ribot cabinet falls in France
8 Dismissal of Kornilov, Alexeev again Russian C-in-C
12 Painlevé government takes office, France
14 Kornilov revolt collapses
17 Transcaucasian Republic established
20 Resignation of Alexeev • second phase of British Ypres Offensive begins
29 British take Ramadi, Mesopotamia

OCTOBER 1917 *Austro-German break-through in Italy; British breakthrough in Palestine distracts from continued failure at Ypres*

8 Final Provisional coalition formed in Russia
9 Sultan Hussein Kamel of Egypt dies
11 German Operation Albion takes Gulf of Riga (to 20.10)
12 First British attack on Passchendaele, Ypres
17 Battle of Mahiwa, East Africa (to 18.10)
20 Allies recognize exiled Polish National Committee
24 Austro-German Caporetto Offensive begins on the Isonzo (to c 30.12)
25 Fall of Boselli government in Italy
26 Brazil declares war on Germany
27 Turkish Army attacks Arabs at Petra
28 Orlando government takes office, Italy
31 Resignation of German chancellor Michaelis • British take Beersheba–Gaza Line, Palestine (to 8.11)

NOVEMBER 1917 *Third Supreme Command virtual dictators in Germany; Bolshevik revolution in Russia; Italian Army in retreat*

1 Hertling appointed German chancellor
2 Lansing-Ishii Agreement on Pacific interests between the USA and Japan
5 October Revolution, Russia (Lenin in power from 8.11) • British take Tikrit, Mesopotamia
6 Allied Rapallo summit (to 9.11) • British take Passchendaele
9 Allies create Supreme War Council • Diaz replaces Cadorna as Italian chief of staff
10 Italian retreat across the Piave complete
13 Resignation of Painlevé, France
15 Clemenceau becomes French premier
18 Death of General Maude, Mesopotamia
20 British massed tank attack at Cambrai, France (to 30.11)
25 German invasion of Mozambique from East Africa
28 Estonia declares independence
30 German counteroffensive at Cambrai (to 7.12)

DECEMBER 1917 *Fighting ends on the Eastern Front; civil war in Russia; Romania capitulates; Italian Front stabilizes; British success in Palestine*

1 Supreme War Council established at Versailles
2 Russian peace delegates reach Brest-Litovsk
3 Bolshevik forces overwhelm Stavka
6 Rebellion in Lisbon, Paes takes power
7 USA declares war on Austria-Hungary, followed by Panama (10.12) and Cuba (12.12)
8 Anglo-French troops join the Italian Front
9 British take Jerusalem, Palestine • Romania agrees armistice with the Central Powers • Bolsheviks announce White rebellion
13 Guillaumat replaces Sarrail at Salonika • White Cossacks take Rostov
16 Armistice on the Eastern Front
19 Conscription becomes effective in Canada
20 Central Powers' delegates reach Brest-Litovsk
26 Yilderim Force counterattacks north of Jerusalem (to 28.12)
31 US Navy battleships join the British Grand Fleet

JANUARY 1918 *German forces mass in France; Austro-Hungarian Empire tottering*

8 Wilson's Fourteen Points peace programme announced

10 Second Australian referendum rejects conscription

14 Ex-premier Caillaux arrested for treason, Paris

16 Strikes and riots in Vienna and Budapest (to 21.1)

20 Mittelmeerdivision wrecked in the Mediterranean

24 Arab victory at Tafila (to 26.1)

28 Bolshevik coup in Helsinki

FEBRUARY 1918 *German economic exploitation of eastern Europe underway; Turkey reoccupies the Caucasus*

1 Austro-Hungarian naval mutiny at Cattaro

6 Bratianu cabinet resigns, Romania

9 Averescu becomes Romanian prime minister • Central Powers sign 'Brotfrieden' peace with the Ukraine

10 Trotski announces Russian abstention from war

16 General Wilson replaces Robertson as British chief of staff

17 Operation Faustschlag, demonstration German offensive in Russia (to 19.2)

21 British take Jericho, Palestine

24 Turkish Caucasian reconquest takes Trabzon

25 Food rationing in London

MARCH 1918 *German Spring Offensives begin in France*

1 German forces occupy Kiev

3 Treaty of Brest-Litovsk signed

11 Turkish forces reoccupy Erzurum, Armenia

12 Japanese and Chinese troops fighting on Russian-Manchurian border

13 Central Powers occupy Odessa

21 German Kaiserschlacht Offensive on the Western Front south of Arras (to 5.4)

23 Long-range attacks by 'Paris Gun' begin (to 9.8) • British attack at Amman, Transjordan (to 30.3)

26 Debut of British 'Whippet' tanks in France

29 Foch appointed Allied 'coordinator' on the Western Front

APRIL 1918 *German successes in France provoke Allied civilian unity and military cooperation*

1 British air services united as the RAF

4 Final Kaiserschlacht attack towards Amiens

8 Rome Congress of Oppressed Nationalities (to 10.4)

9 German Lys Offensive opens on the Western Front • Clemenceau reveals Austro-Hungarian Kaiser Karl I's 1917 peace overtures

14 Foch becomes Allied C-in-C, Western Front

15 Resignation of Austro-Hungarian foreign minister Czernin, replaced by Burian • Turkish forces occupy Batum, Transcaucasia

17 Arab Army besieges Maan, Arabia (to 23.9)

21 Death in action of Richthofen

23 British Zeebrugge Raid • final North Sea sortie of German High Seas Fleet (to 25.4) • Guatemala declares war on Germany

28 Red Army defeated at Viborg, Finland (to 29.4)

29 Opening of *Le Bonnet Rouge* treason trials, France (to 15.5)

30 Second British attack in Transjordan (to 4.5)

MAY 1918 *US troops in action on the Western Front; Paris threatened by German attacks*

7 Peace of Bucharest between Romania and the Central Powers • Nicaragua declares war on Germany

11 Karl I of Austria-Hungary accepts military and economic union with Germany

25 Costa Rica declares war on Germany

26 Transcaucasian Republic dissolved, Armenia signs Treaty of Batum with Turkey

27 Third phase of the German Spring Offensives begins on the Aisne, France (to 6.6)

28 First AEF attack on the Western Front at Cantigny

29 Lansing declares US support for independent Czech and Southern Slav states

JUNE 1918 *German attacks halted; heavy air raids on Paris and Germany; Italian forces hold off Austro-Hungarian attacks*

3 Aisne offensive checked at Château-Thierry and Belleau Wood (to 12.6)

4 De Broqueville resigns as Belgian premier
6 Guillaumat transferred from Salonika to Paris
8 Franchet d'Esperay takes command at Salonika • First US mines laid in Northern Barrage • British Independent Air Force formed for strategic bombing
9 Battle of the Matz, France (to 13.6) • Austro-Hungarian dreadnought *Szent Istvan* torpedoed in the Adriatic
10 Austro-Hungarian Piave River offensive, Italy (to 22.6)
16 Malinov replaces Radoslavov as Bulgarian prime minister

JULY 1918 *Allies resume the initiative in France and intervene in Russia*

2 Wilson announces 1 million US troops sent to Europe
3 Death of Sultan Mohammed V of Turkey
4 Australian forces take Le Hamel, France
8 German foreign minister Kühlmann dismissed
12 Japanese dreadnought *Kawachi* explodes at anchor
13 Haiti declares war on Germany
15 Second Battle of the Marne, France (to 3.8)
16 Russian ex-Tsar and his family shot at Ekatarinburg, Siberia
19 Honduras declares war on Germany • British carrier strike at Tondern
20 German retreat at the Marne begins
24 Hussarek becomes Austrian premier
30 Assassination of German military dictator Eichhorn at Kiev, Ukraine
31 Anglo-French forces take Archangel (Arkhangelsk), Arctic theatre

AUGUST 1918 *Decisive Allied counter-offensives begin in France*

2 Scheer heads new German Navy supreme command, Hipper becomes C-in-C High Seas Fleet
3 British troops land at Vladivostok to aid the Czech Legion against Bolshevik forces
8 Allied Amiens Offensive opens on the Western Front (to 15.8), forcing collapse of German Second Army
11 Japanese Navy units reach Vladivostok
13 Britain recognizes Czechoslovak independence
17 US troops reach Vladivostok
21 Allied Albert offensive opens, Western Front (to 29.8)
25 British Dunsterforce assembled at Baku, Transcaucasia
26 Allied Scarpe Offensive begins, Western Front (to 29.8)
29 Lenin wounded by assassination attempt
30 Police strike in London (to 31.8)

SEPTEMBER 1918 *Successful Allied offensives in France, from Salonika and in Palestine; Bulgaria capitulates*

2 First Hindenburg Line positions breached by the BEF, France
3 USA recognizes Czechoslovakia
12 US St Mihiel Offensive, Western Front (to 16.9) • Battle of Havrincourt, France
14 British evacuate Baku
15 Allied Vardar Offensive from Salonika (to 4.11)
17 Arab forces surround Dera, Palestine
18 Battle of Epéhy, France
19 British Megiddo Offensive opens in Palestine (to 26.9)
24 Fall of Japanese Matasake cabinet
25 Italy recognizes Yugoslav independence • Franchet d'Esperay rejects Bulgarian armistice request
26 US–French Meuse–Argonne Offensive begins in France (to 11.11)
27 Allied attack on Canal du Nord, Hindenburg Line (to 1.10)
28 Lettow-Vorbeck re-enters German East Africa
29 Allies cross St Quentin Canal, Hindenburg Line
30 Allies sign armistice with Bulgaria • German chancellor Hertling resigns

OCTOBER 1918 *Austro-Hungarian Army driven back in Italy; Allied attacks elsewhere continue; first phase of German revolutions; Young Turk regime falls and Turkey surrenders*

1 British and Arab forces occupy Damascus, Palestine
3 Prince Max von Baden becomes German chancellor
4 Germany and Austria-Hungary ask US government for an armistice • Tsar Ferdinand of Bulgaria abdicates

5 Main Hindenburg Line positions cleared by Allied armies
6 Civil war formally declared in China
7 Turkish government resigns, Izzet Pasha becomes grand vizier
8 Allied attack on Cambrai, Western Front
10 Death of Russian White commander Alexeev
11 Hungarian premier Wekerle resigns
14 Allied Courtrai Offensive, Flanders (to 20.10) • provisional Czechoslovak government formed
16 Karl I publishes 'October Manifesto'
17 British Selle Offensive, France (to 24.10)
23 Italian Vittorio Veneto Offensive (to 4.11)
26 Ludendorff resigns • British occupy Turkish Aleppo (Halab) • Andrassy becomes Austro-Hungarian foreign minister
27 Gröner replaces Ludendorff as Hindenburg's deputy
28 Lammasch replaces Hussarek as Austrian premier
30 Turkey signs armistice with the Allies at Mudros • German High Seas Fleet mutiny begins
31 Count Károlyi becomes Hungarian premier

NOVEMBER 1918 *Collapse of the Central Powers; general armistice; overthrow of the German and Austro-Hungarian monarchies*

1 Serbian troops reoccupy Belgrade • British attack at Valenciennes, Belgium (to 2.11) • Austro-Hungarian dreadnought *Viribus Unitis* sunk at Pola
2 Allied Sambre Offensive, Western Front (to 11.11)
3 Austria-Hungary signs armistice with the Allies • German naval mutiny reaches Kiel
5 Allied Supreme War Council accepts German armistice terms • US Congress elections return Republican majority
7 King of Bavaria flees to exile
8 Foch receives German armistice delegates • socialist republic in Bavaria • King of Württemberg and Duke of Brunswick abdicate
9 Abdication and flight of Wilhelm II • revolution in Berlin, provisional socialist coalition formed
10 Romania re-opens hostilities with Germany
11 Armistice on all active fronts • Hungarian republic proclaimed • Karl I renounces imperial offices
13 Allied navies occupy Constantinople
14 Czechoslovak national assembly elects Masaryk president
21 German High Seas Fleet surrenders at Rosyth
22 Belgian King Albert re-enters Brussels
25 Last German forces in East Africa surrender
26 Last German troops leave Belgium

DECEMBER 1918

1 'Kingdom of Serbs, Croats and Slovenes' (Yugoslavia) founded, Belgrade
13 Armistice extended for one month
14 President Wilson arrives in Paris • British elections return Lloyd George coalition

JANUARY 1919

12 Paris Peace Conference opens
13 Arab Revolt takes Medina
15 Spartacus leaders Luxemburg and Liebknecht shot in Berlin
19 German Reichstag elections, Scheidemann becomes premier

FEBRUARY 1919

11 Ebert elected German president
14 Red Army invasion of Estonia
19 Attempted assassination of Clemenceau
20 Amir Habibulla Khan of Afghanistan murdered

MARCH 1919

17 Allies evacuate Odessa (to 8.4)

APRIL 1919

24 Italian delegates quit Versailles (to 6.5)

MAY 1919

13 Greek forces landed at Smyrna

JUNE 1919

20 Orlando government resigns, Italy • Scheidemann falls, Germany
21 German High Seas Fleet scuttles at Scapa Flow
28 Treaty of Versailles signed

JULY 1919

7 German government ratifies Versailles Treaty

AUGUST 1919

1 Overthrow of Communists in Budapest

SEPTEMBER 1919

10 Treaty of St Germain signed

12 D'Annunzio occupies Fiume (Rijeka)

27 Allied withdrawal from Archangel (Arkhangelsk)

OCTOBER 1919

12 Allied withdrawal from northern Russia complete

NOVEMBER 1919

19 US Congress rejects Versailles Treaty

27 Treaty of Neuilly signed

JANUARY 1920

20 Paris Peace Conference ends

JUNE 1920

4 Treaty of Trianon signed

AUGUST 1920

10 Treaty of Sèvres signed

MAPS

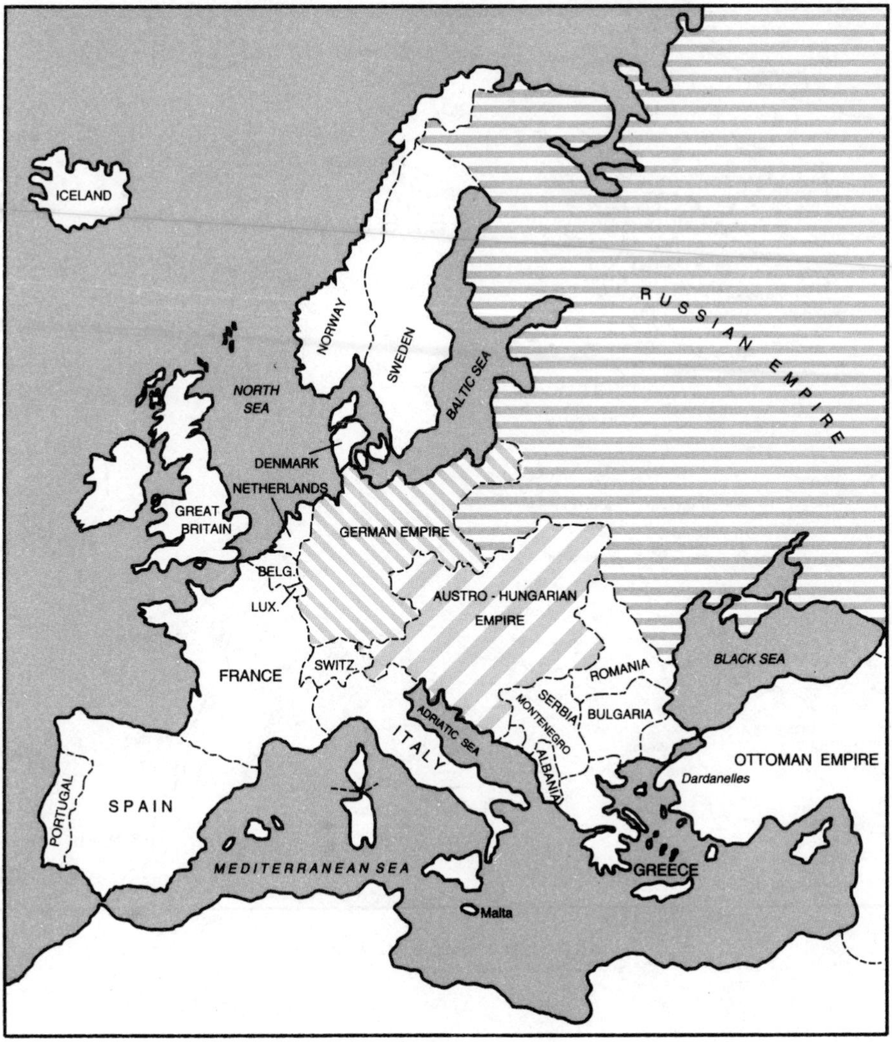

Map 1: Europe, July 1914

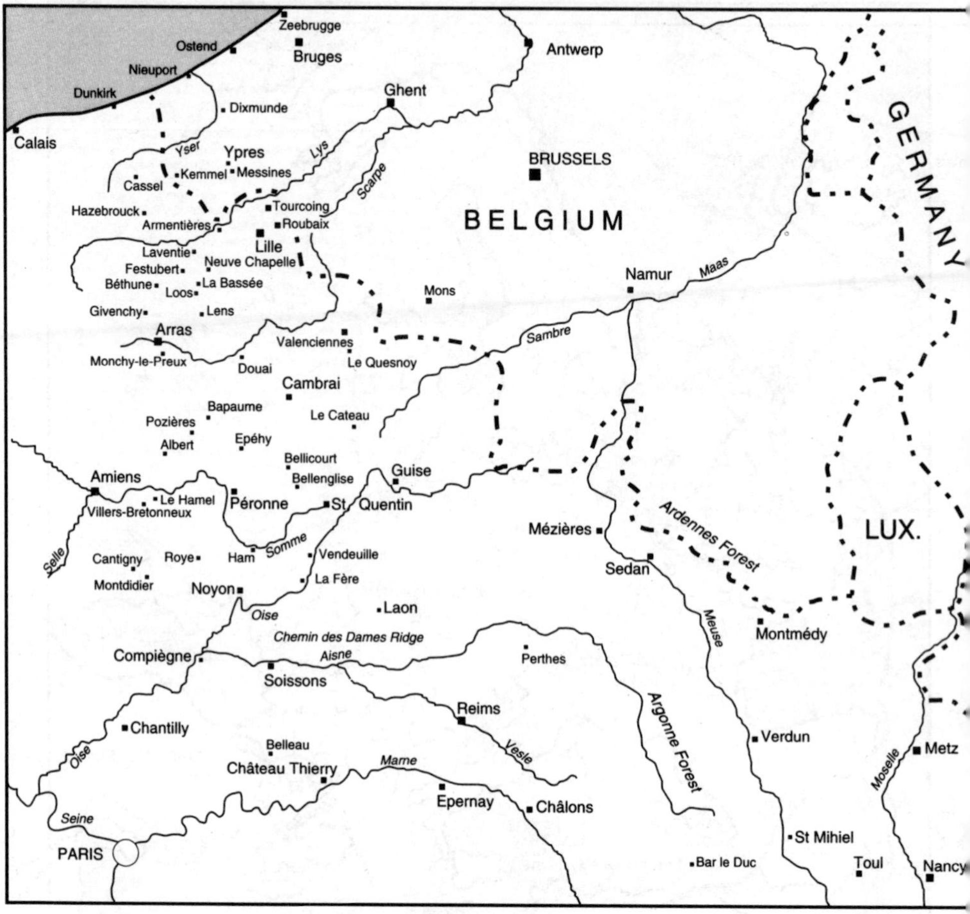

Map 2: Western Front, locations

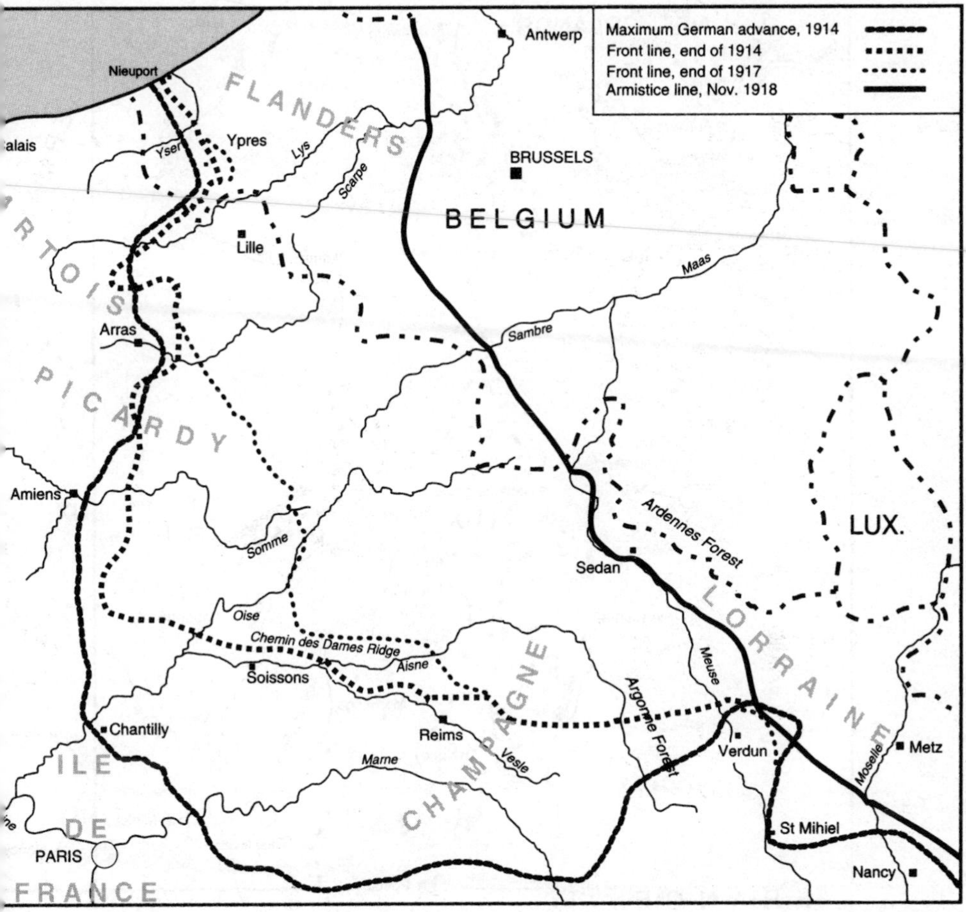

Map 3: Western Front, lines

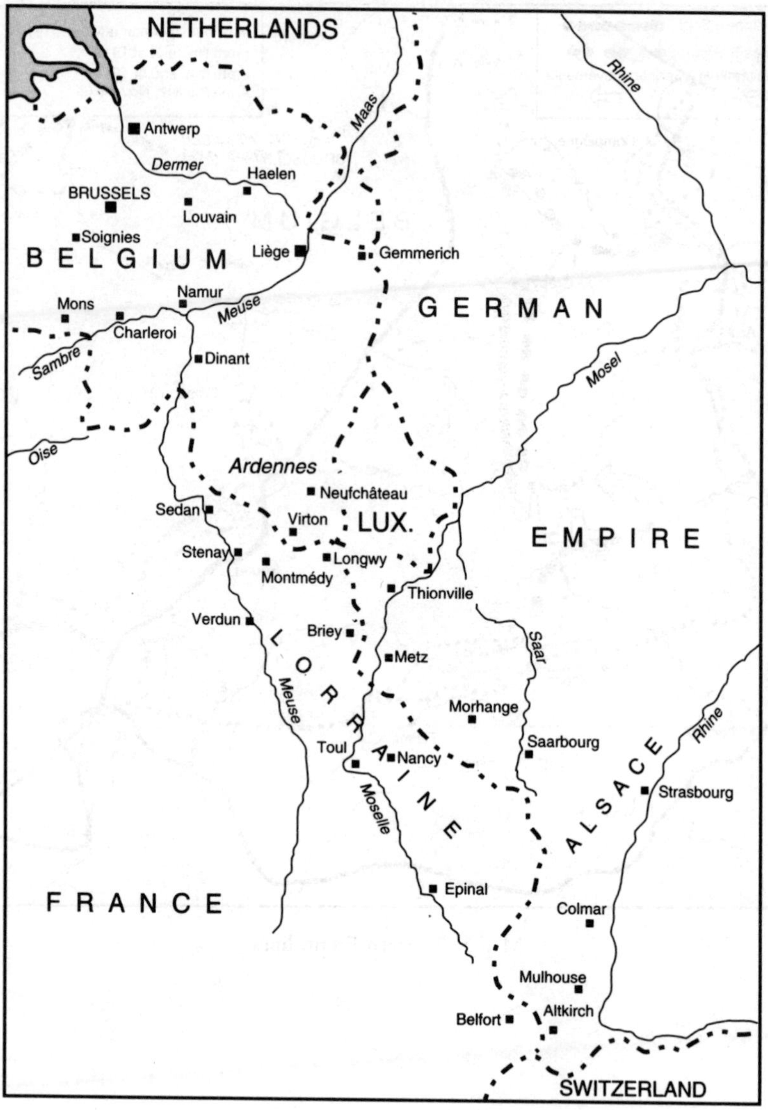

Map 4: Belgium and the Frontiers, 1914

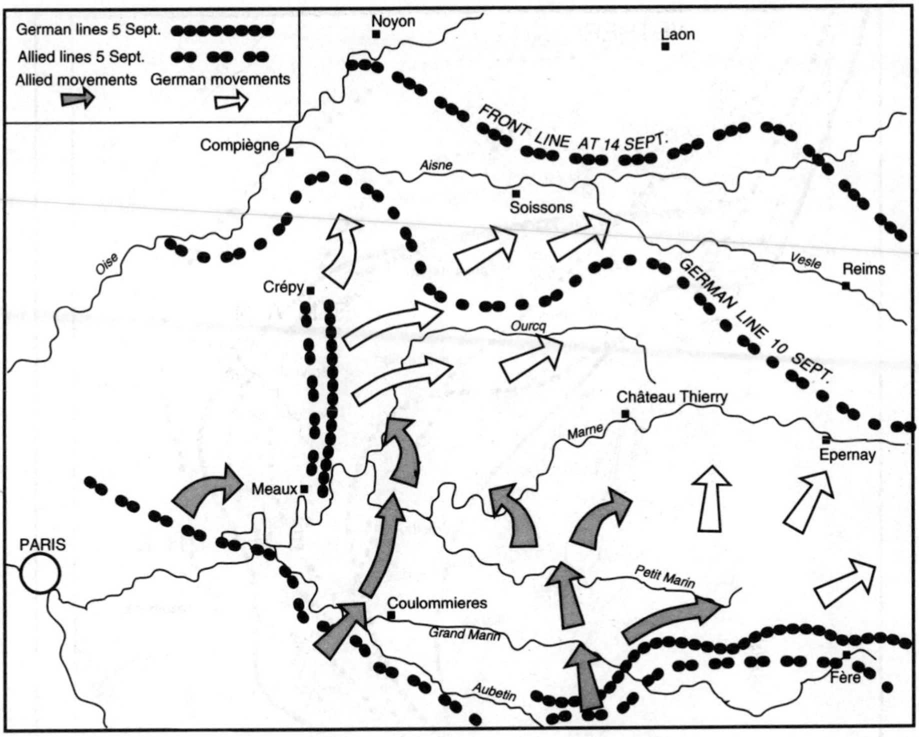

Map 5: The Marne, 6–14 September 1914

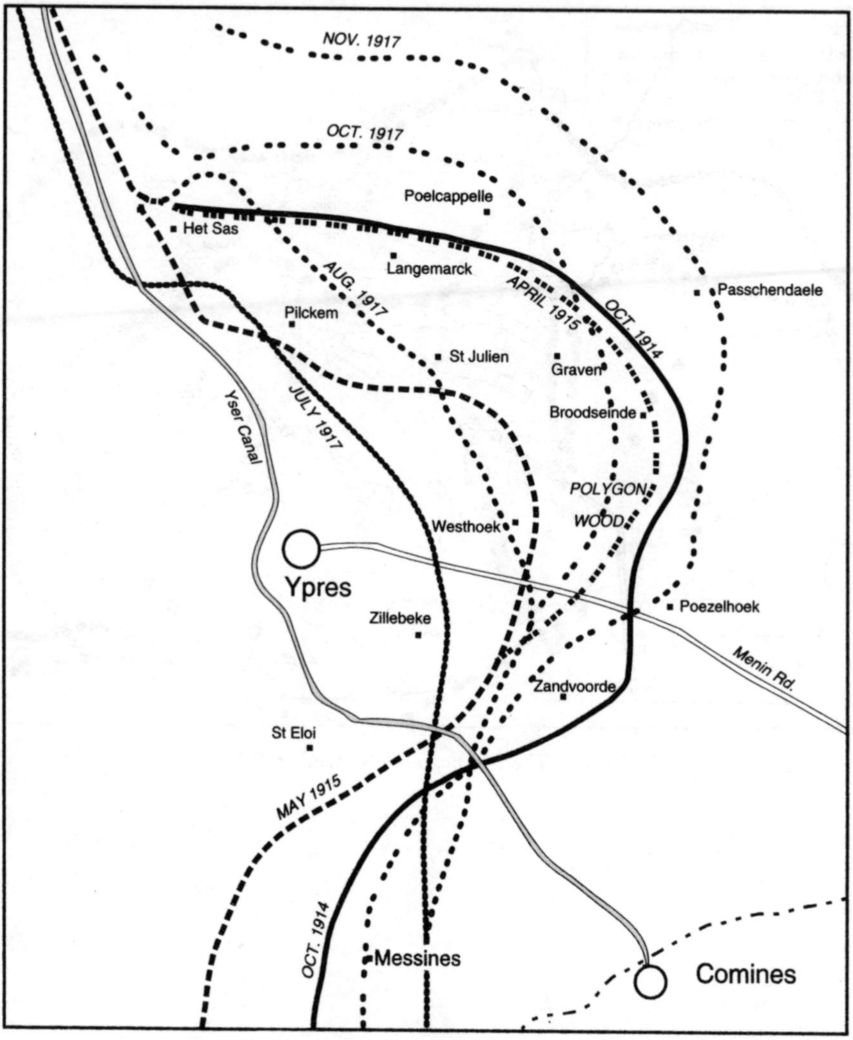

Map 6: Ypres Salient, 1914–17

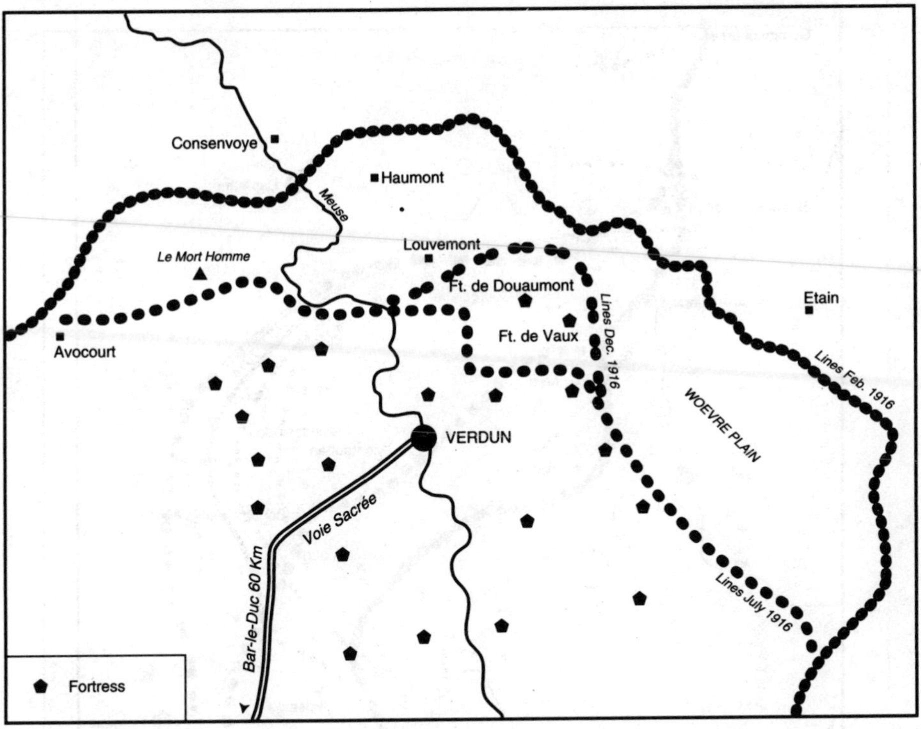

Map 7: Verdun, 1916

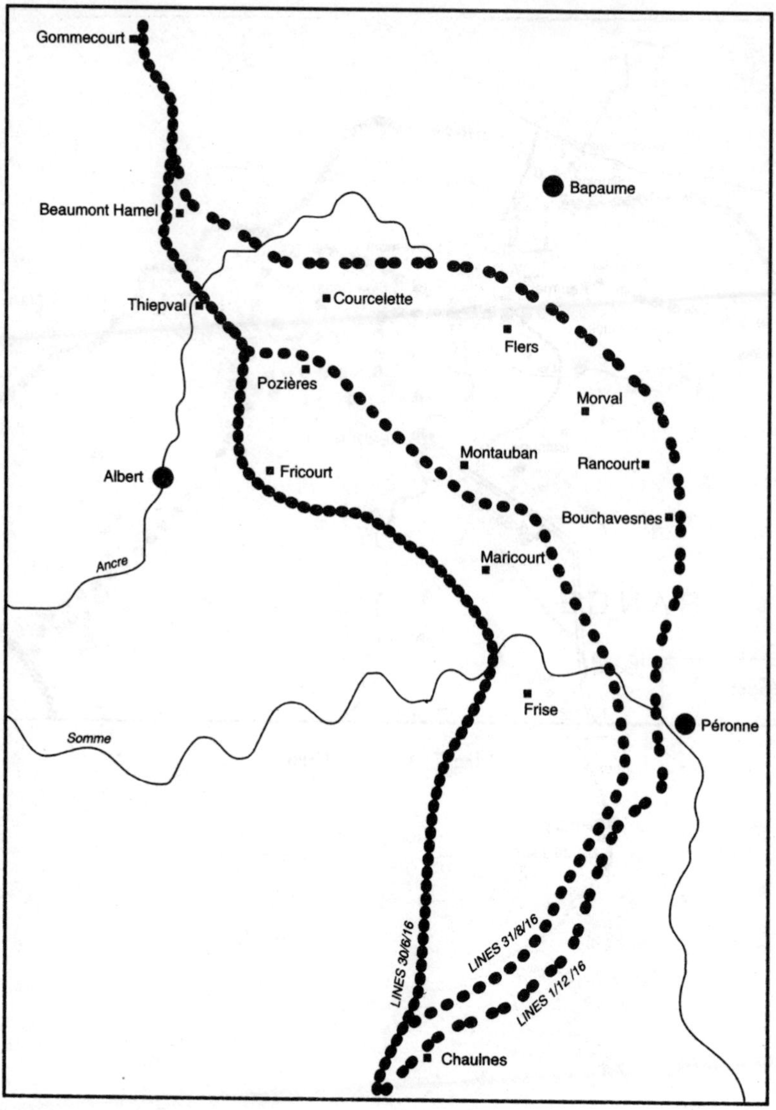

Map 8: Somme Offensive, 1916

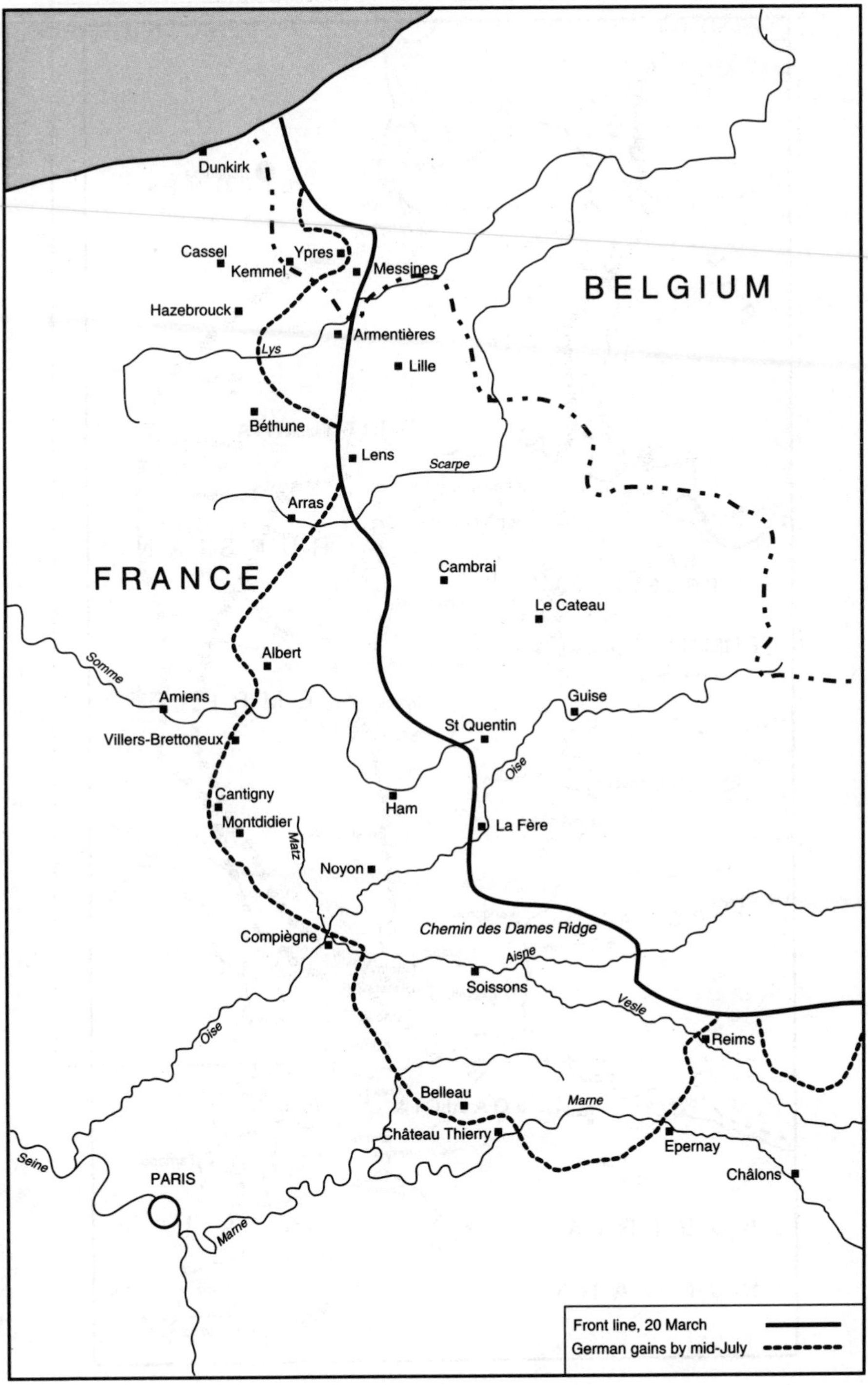

Map 9: German Spring Offensives, 1918

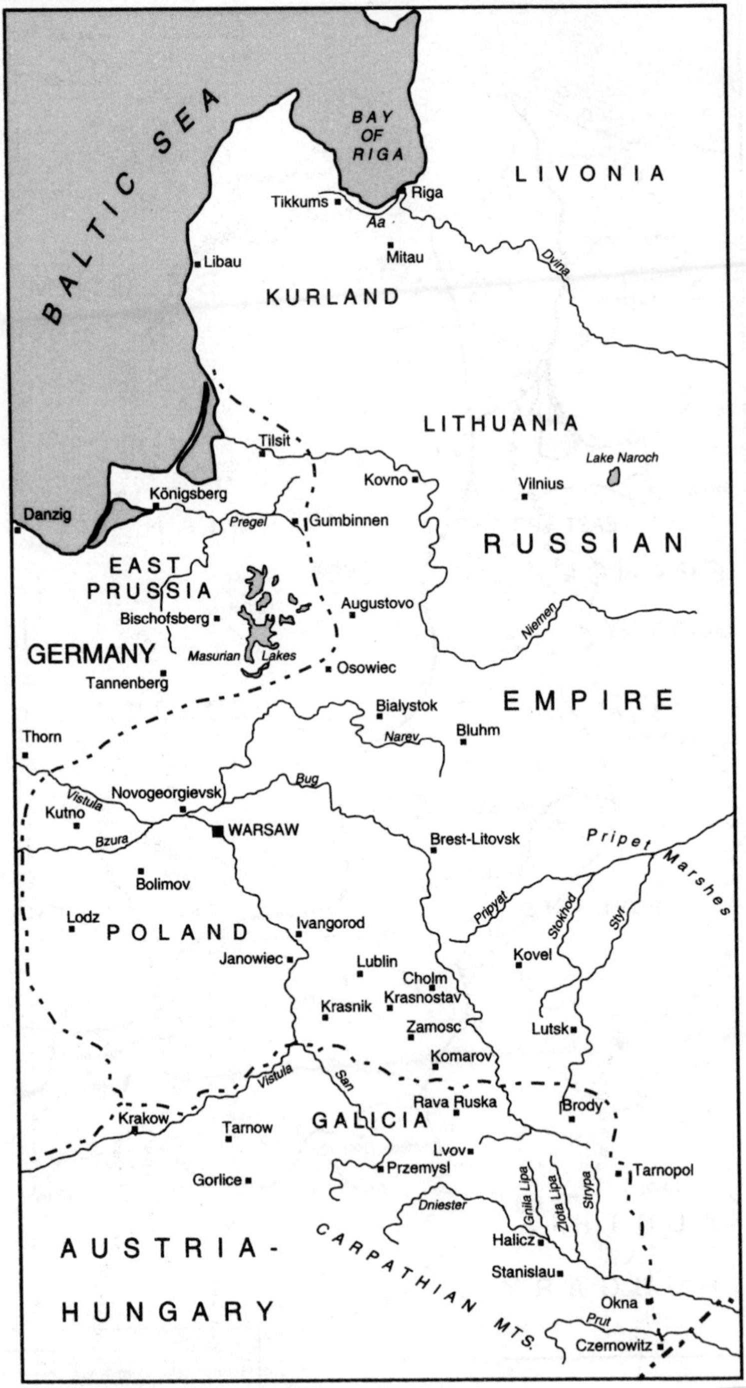

Map 10: Eastern Front, locations

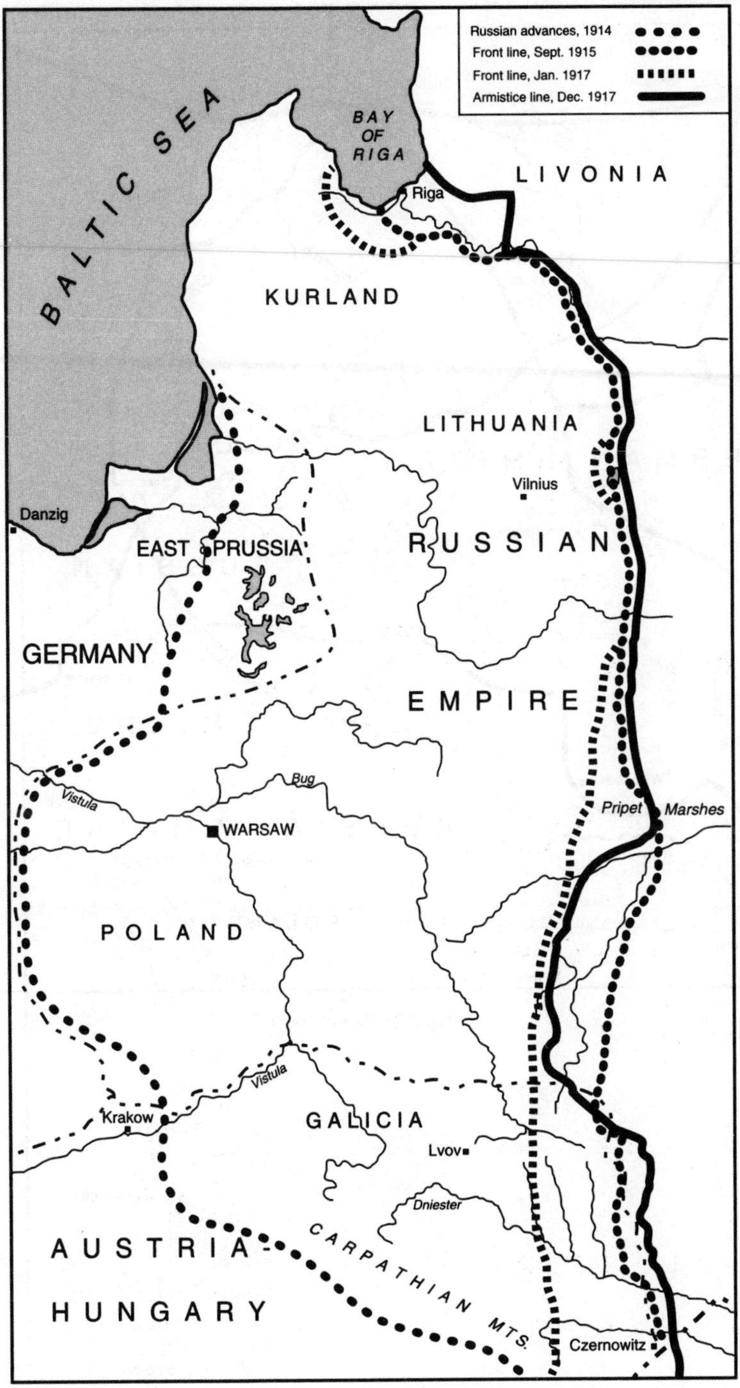

Map 11: Eastern Front, lines

Map 12: East Prussia

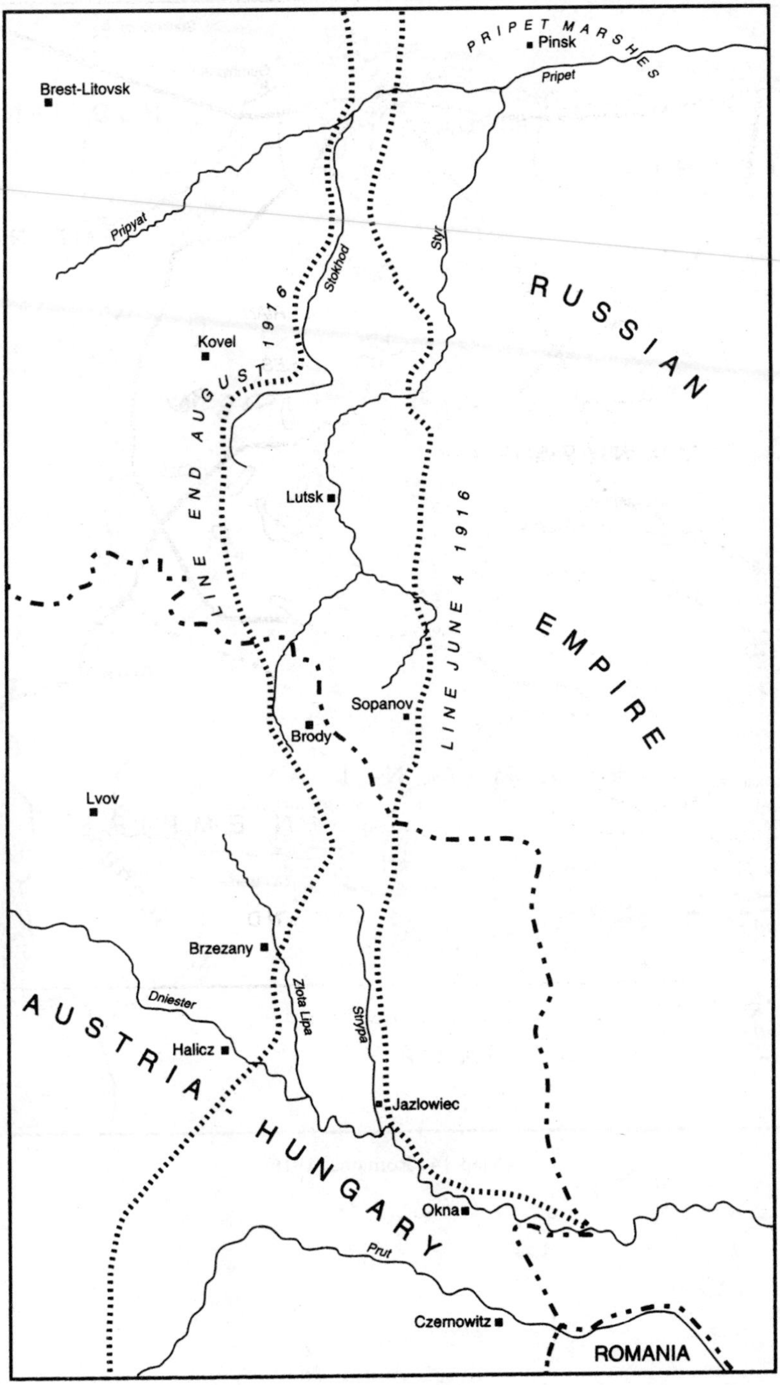

Map 13: Brusilov Offensive, 1916

Map 14: Romania, 1916

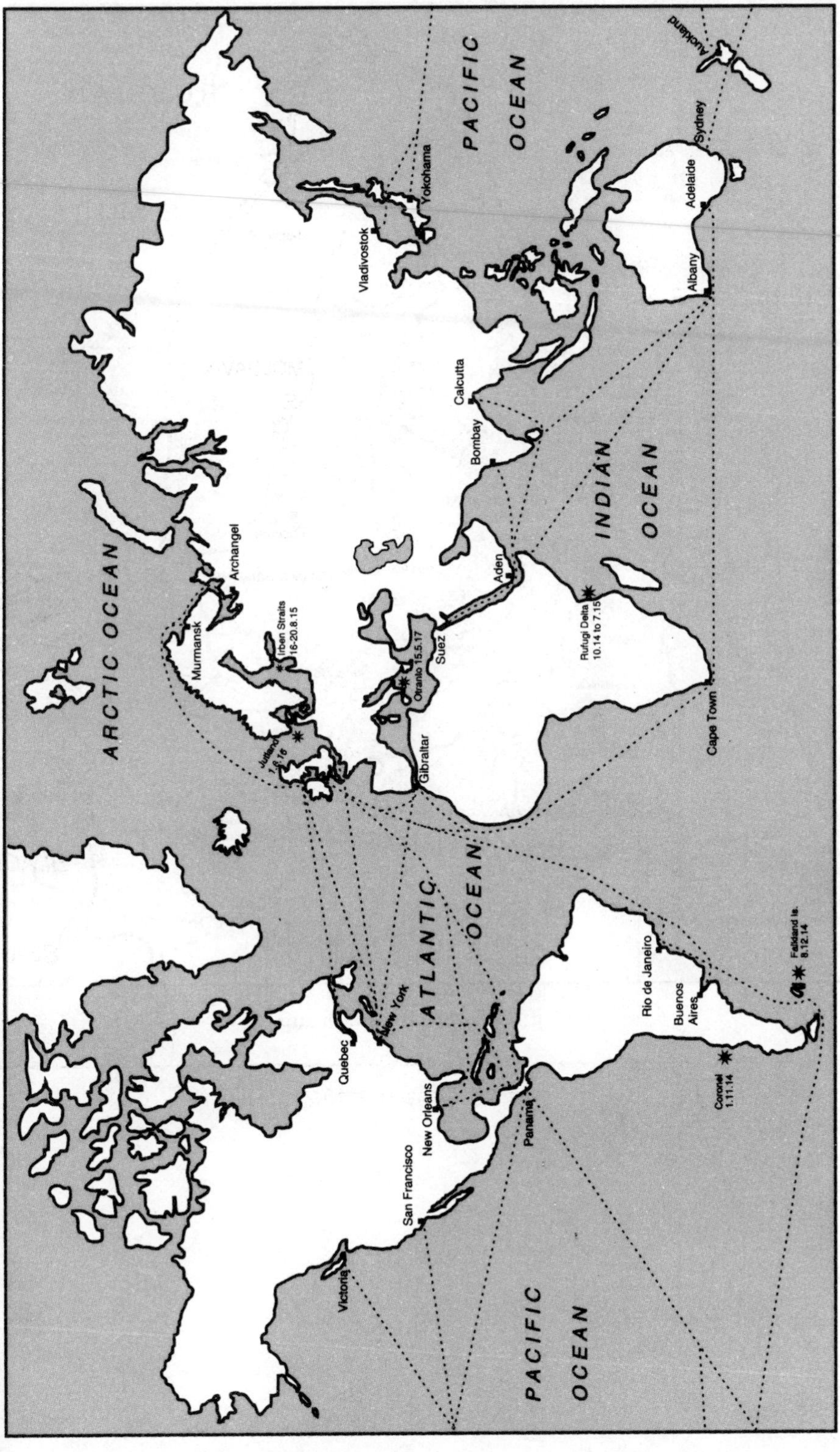

Map 15: Oceanic trade routes and conflicts

Map 16: European naval theatres

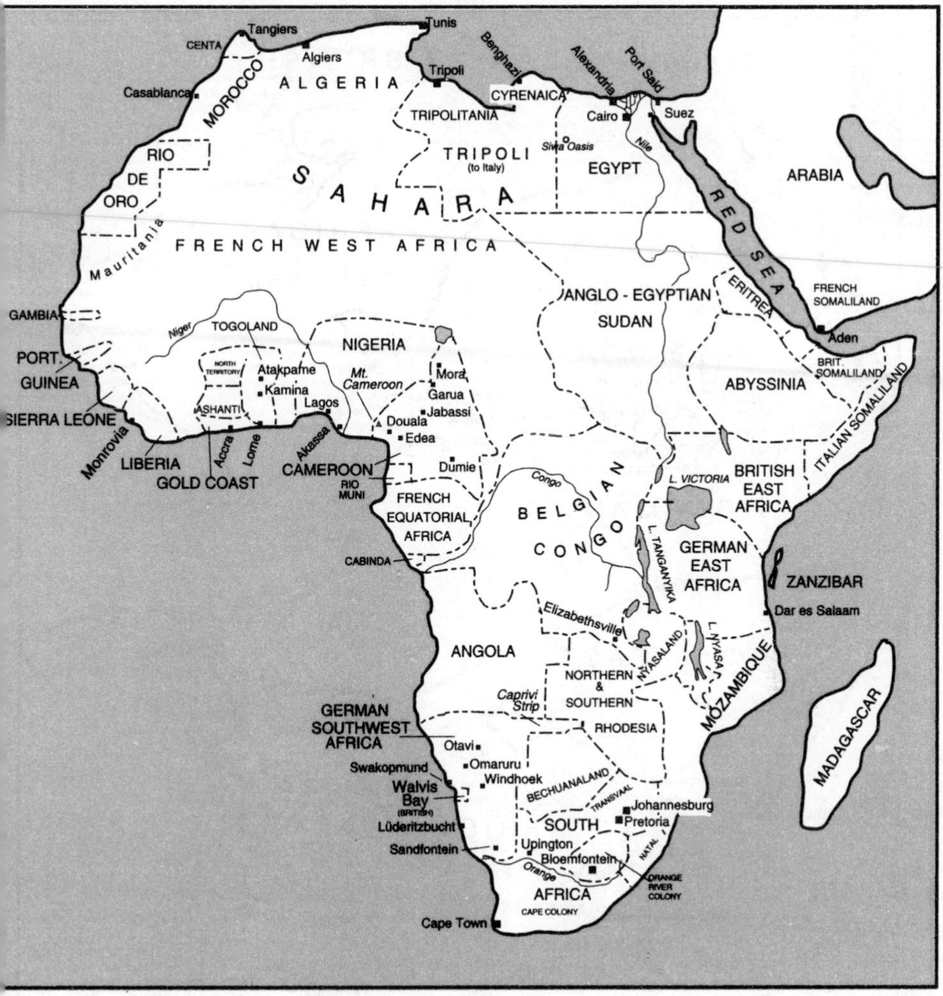

Map 17: Africa, 1914

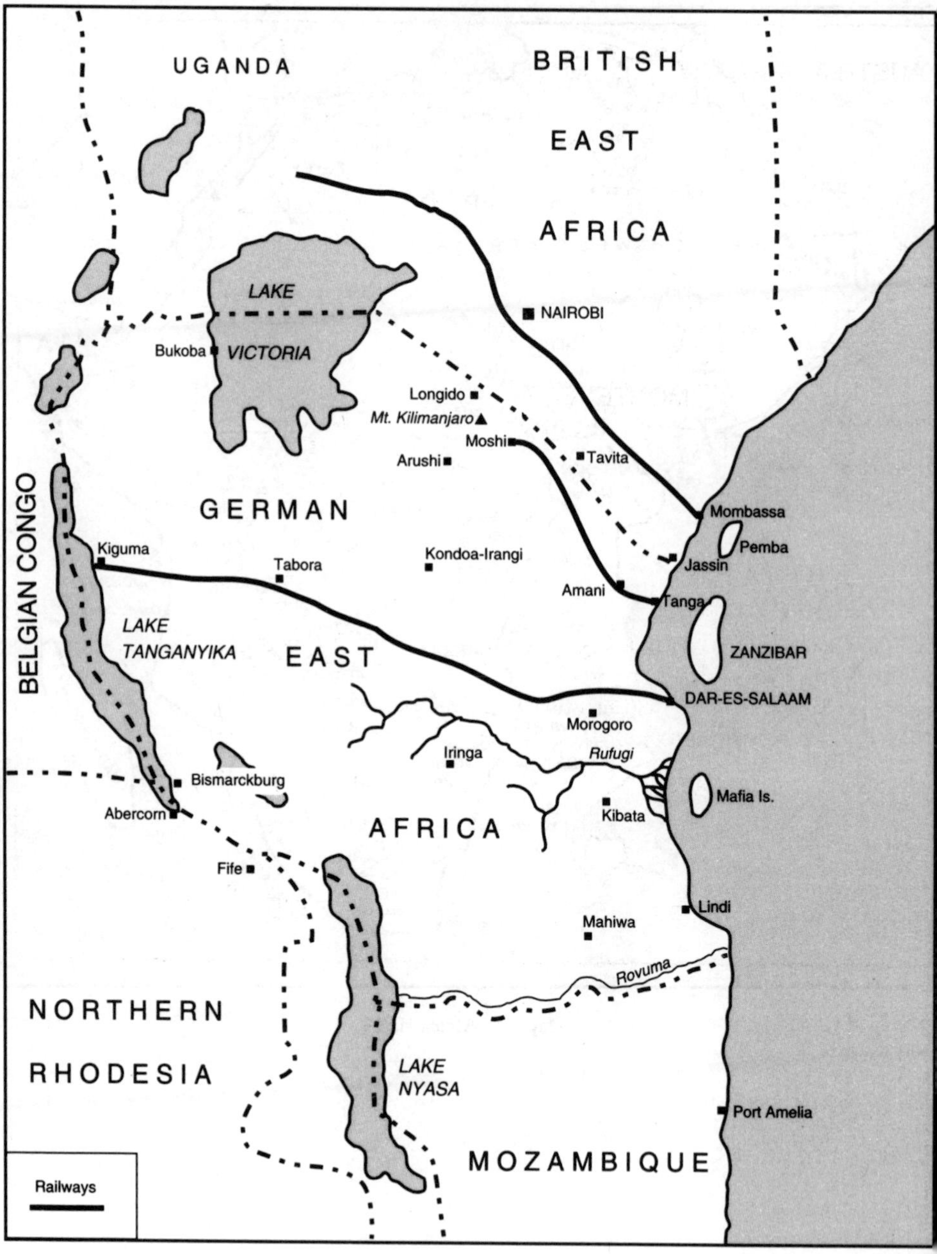

Map 18: East Africa

Map 19: Balkan Fronts

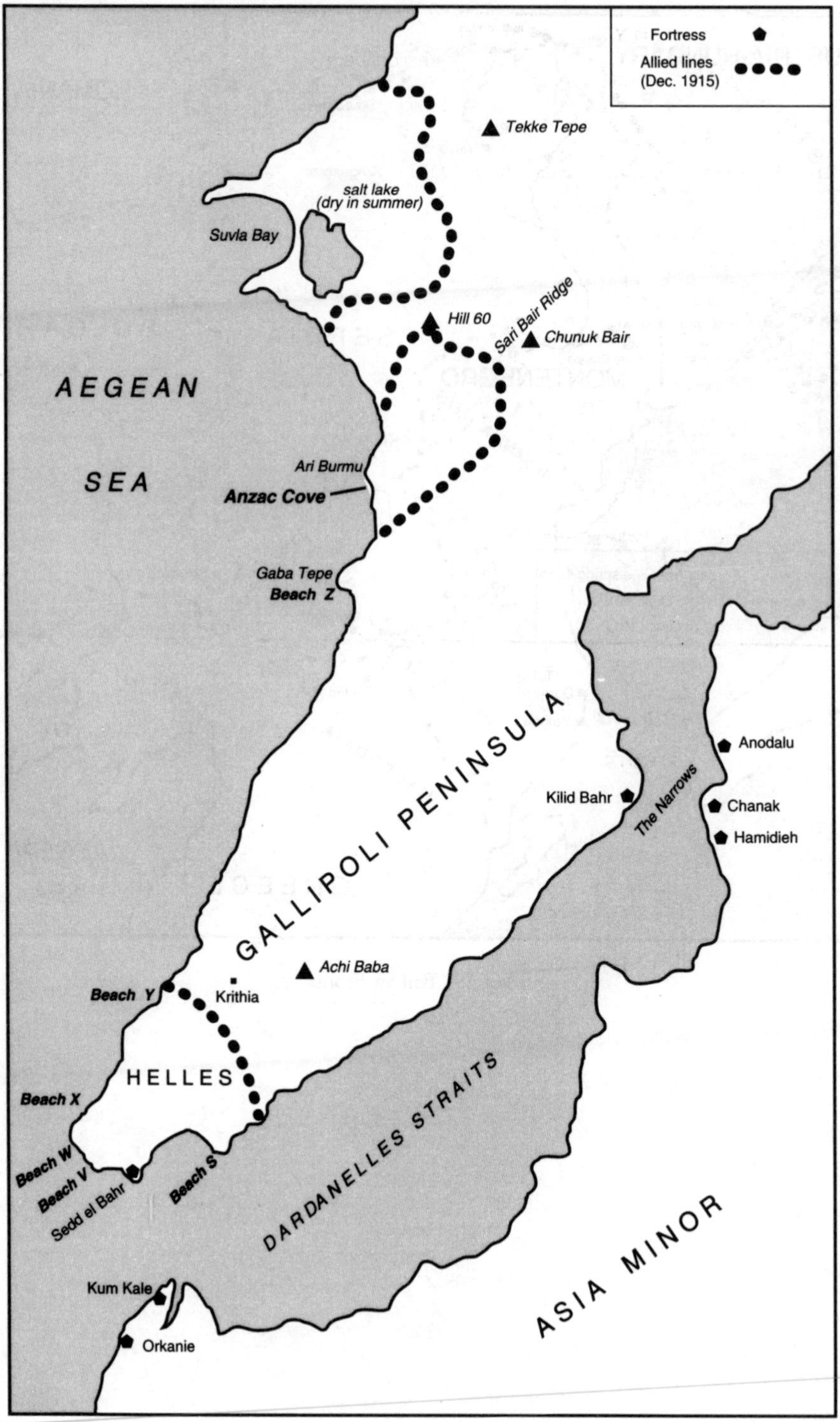

Map 20: Gallipoli Front

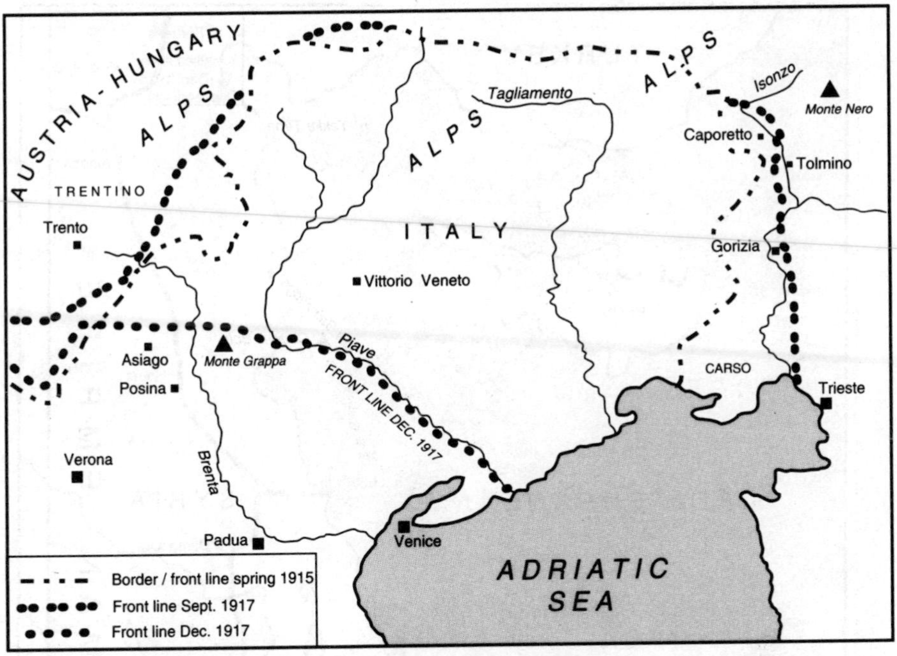

Map 21: Italian Front 1915–17

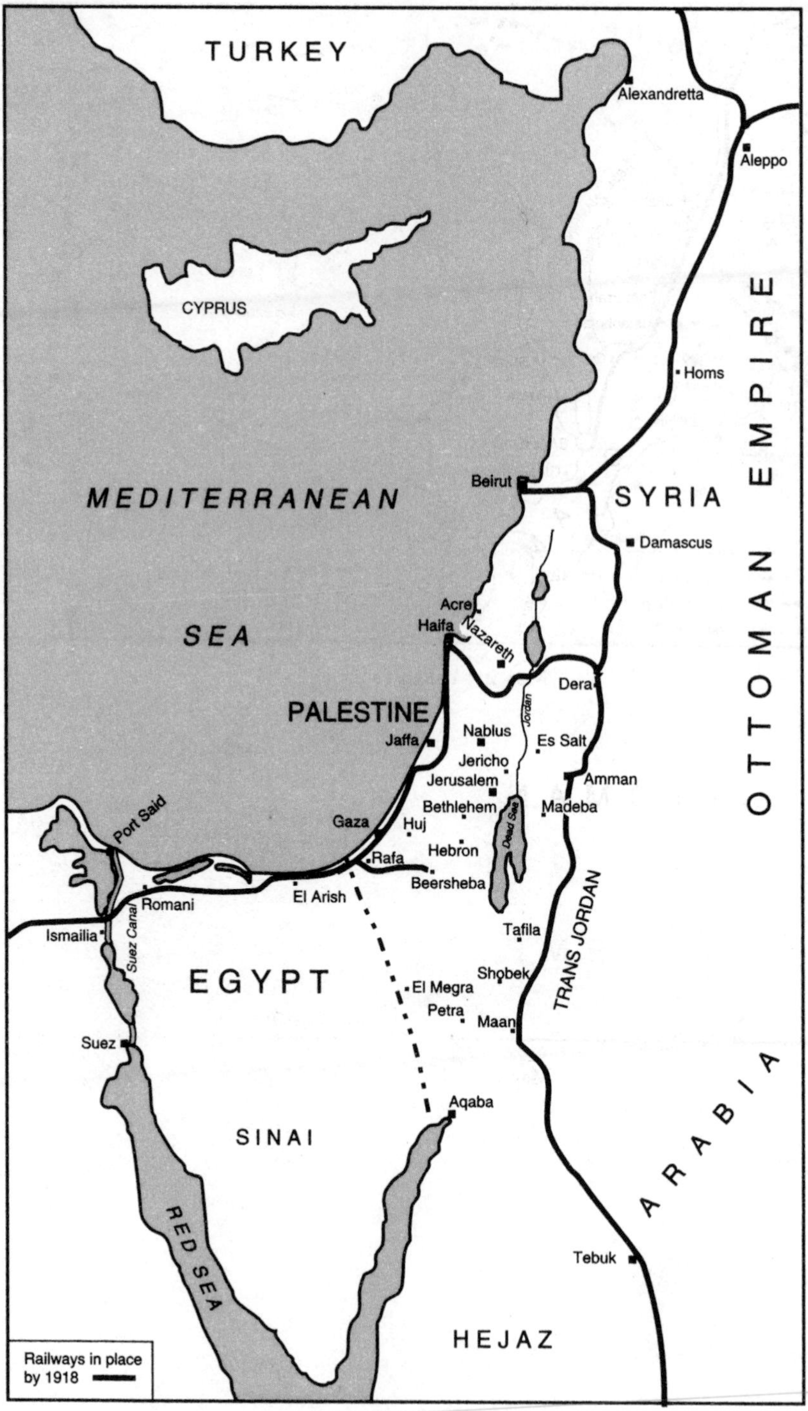

Map 22: Palestine Front

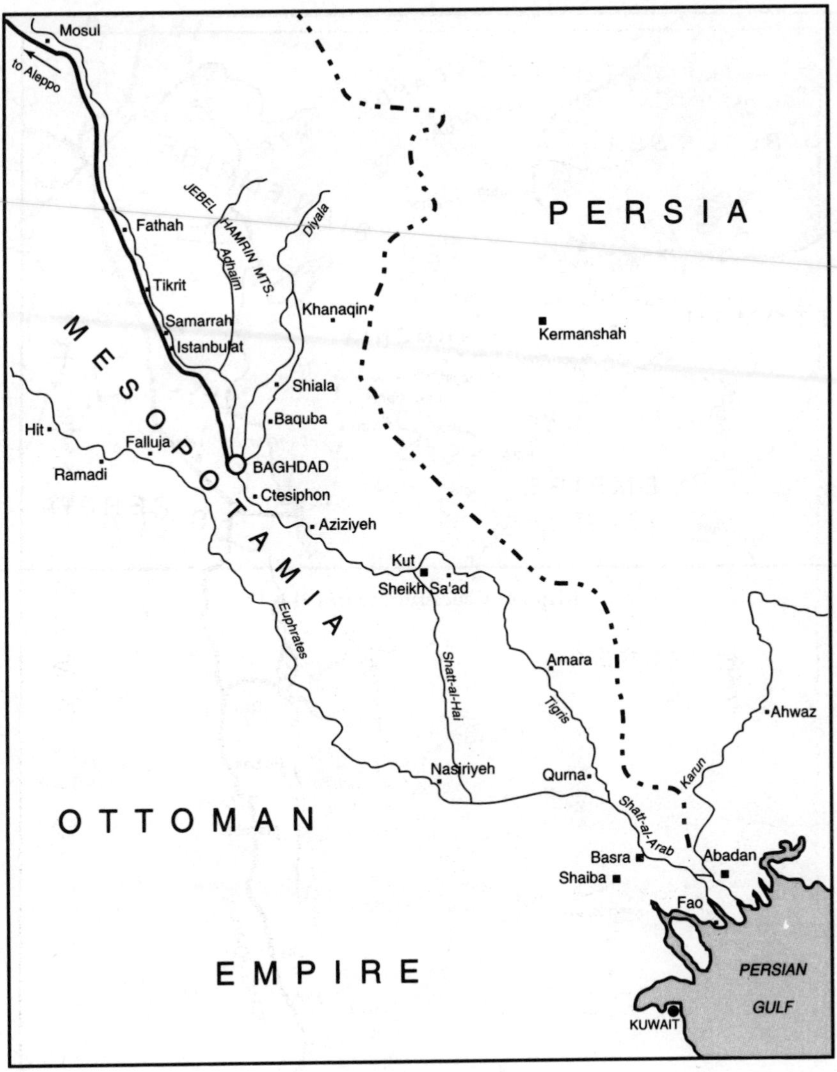

Map 23: Mesopotamian Front

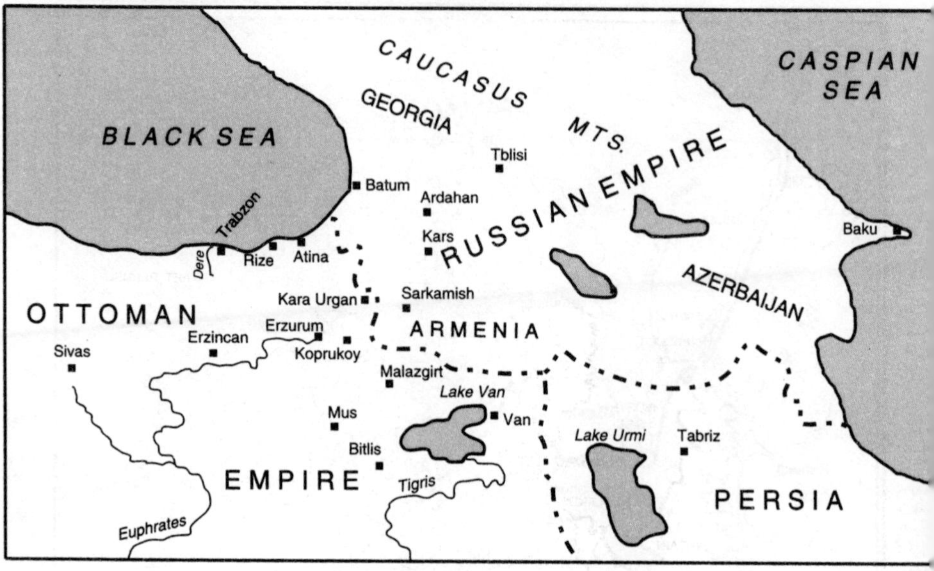

Map 24: Caucasian Front, 1914–17

Map 25: Europe, 1920